CHASE'S SPORTS

CALENDAR OF EVENTS

1998

Compiled by Steve Gietschier

CB

CONTEMPORARY BOOKS

☆ *Chase's 1998 SPORTS Calendar of Events* ☆

NTC/CONTEMPORARY PUBLISHING COMPANY
A TRIBUNE COMPANY
4255 W TOUHY AVE
LINCOLNWOOD, ILLINOIS 60646-1975
FAX: (847) 679-6388
PHONE: (847) 679-5500

Printed in USA

— NOTICE —

Events listed herein are not necessarily endorsed by the editors or publisher. Every effort has been made to assure the correctness of all entries, but neither the authors nor the publisher can warrant their accuracy. IT IS IMPERATIVE, IF FINANCIAL PLANS ARE TO BE MADE IN CONNECTION WITH DATES OR EVENTS LISTED HEREIN, THAT PRINCIPALS BE CONSULTED FOR FINAL INFORMATION.

GRAPHIC IMAGES

The interior illustrations were created for this book by Dan Krovatin. The photographs in the interior are the property of *The Sporting News* and are used with its permission. The photographs on the cover are used with permission and are from the following (clockwise from lower left): Patrick Roy—copyright © Jed Jacobsohn/Allsport; Martina Hingis—copyright © Shaun Botterill/Allsport; Picabo Street—copyright © Simon Bruty/Allsport; Grant Hill—copyright © Allsport USA; Tiger Woods—copyright © J. D. Cuban/Allsport; Mike Piazza—copyright © Jonathan Daniel/Allsport.

Gietschier, Steve
Chase's 1998 calendar of sports events,
Chicago, NTC/Contemporary Publishing Company   (c. 1997)

352 p., ill.
Includes index and tables.

ISSN: 1091-2959

ISBN: 0-8092-3015-1

The Library of Congress does not issue Cataloging in Publication information or a Library of Congress Number for publications classified as "Transitory."

TABLE OF CONTENTS

WELCOME TO *CHASE'S 1998 SPORTS CALENDAR OF EVENTS*

Welcome to the second edition of *Chase's Sports Calendar of Events*, a compilation of thousands of events from North America and around the world. The focus here is sports and recreational activities, covered in greater breadth and depth in this volume than in any other in print. *Chase's Sports Calendar of Events*, in fact, is the most thorough and detailed day-by-day record of notable events in the world of sports.

This second edition includes nearly 6,000 entries for events and observances occurring in 1998. They have been compiled in the tradition and style of the widely respected *Chase's Calendar of Events*, the standard reference source for information about events, observances, birthdays, historical anniversaries and much more. *Chase's Sports Calendar of Events* provides information that sports enthusiasts, recreation seekers and vacation planners need to know in order to plan their leisure-time activities. For librarians, public relations firms, schools, retailers, the media and the general public, *Chase's Sports Calendar of Events* is an essential planning tool. It is:

- *the* book that sports broadcasters, writers, reporters and talk show hosts will consult to find program ideas, background material, filler copy and information about forthcoming events;
- *the* source that sports fans will devour for interesting and amusing information about both legendary and lesser-known sports organizations, teams, stadiums and players;
- *the* guide that recreational athletes and nonathletes will consult for fun and challenging activities in which they can participate;
- *the* directory that the public will check to find sports and recreational organizations of all kinds, at all levels and in all parts of the US and Canada;
- and *the* reference work that public relations and promotions people will scan when looking for a sport or recreational event, team or organization for their clients or companies to sponsor.

Attempting to be inclusive, we have defined sports and recreation rather broadly, listing a wide variety of local happenings from all across the US and Canada as well as some events in other countries. The selection of these items reflects our editorial opinion about the important, interesting and unusual events in the world of sports and recreation coming up in the new year.

Sports Throughout the Year
Professional leagues in a variety of sports, some of whom had not begun their 1997 seasons when this book went to press, could not supply their 1998 schedules for inclusion here. To alleviate this problem, readers should consult not only the Directory of Sports Organizations beginning on page 308 for addresses and phone numbers but also the website addresses located throughout the book and in a special chart on the inside front cover.

New for 1998
Besides the types of events described below, the 1998 edition of *Chase's Sports Calendar of Events* includes three new features:

- Sportsquote of the Day: For Mondays in 1998, readers will find a quotation connected to a person or event commemorated on that date.
- Sportschaser of the Day: For Fridays in 1998, readers will find a sports trivia question, the answer to which is contained somewhere in that day's entries.
- Champions This Date: For certain events, like the Super Bowl or the World Series, that occur annually on or about the same date, readers will find past champions listed in special boxes on the appropriate dates.

1998 Spotlight
The sports spotlight in 1998 will shine on Nagano, Japan, site of the XVIIIth Winter Olympic Games. Through 1992, both the Winter Games and the Summer Games were held in the same year. Starting in 1994, the Winter Olympics moved to their own four-year cycle, two years removed from the Summer Games' cycle. Thus, the Summer Games were held in 1996 in Atlanta and will be held next in 2000 in Sydney, Australia. The Winter Games began their own rotation in 1994 in Lillehammer, Norway, and continue with the Nagano Games in 1998 and the Salt Lake City Games in 2002.

The Opening Ceremony of the Games will begin at 11 A.M. (local time) on Saturday, Feb 7, and the Closing Ceremony will commence at 7 P.M. on Sunday, Feb 22. Because of the time difference between Japan and the US—Japan is 14 hours ahead of Eastern Time in the US—the times of these ceremonies translate to 9 P.M., EST, Friday, Feb 7, and 5 A.M., EST, Sunday, Feb 22, respectively. Since Americans will view the Games on a tape-delayed basis on the CBS television network, events are listed in this book on the day they will happen in Japan.

Types of Events in *Chase's Sports Calendar of Events*
SPONSORED EVENTS: Sporting and recreational events sponsored by an individual or organization are listed with the name of the event, inclusive dates and places of observance (if local or regional), a brief description, the approximate attendance when provided and the sponsor's name and address—plus, if the sponsor agrees, phone number, fax number, Email address and website address.

HISTORIC ANNIVERSARIES, FOLKLORIC EVENTS AND BIRTHDAYS: Compiled from a wide variety of materials covering sporting and recreational events in virtually every part of the world, these entries are supported for accuracy whenever possible by two or more independent sources. Living persons are listed under "Birthdays Today."

HOLIDAYS AND SPECIAL OBSERVANCES: National holidays, traditional and religious observances and astronomical events, as well as special days, weeks and months related to the world of sports and recreation, are included.

Omissions/"Errors"
The omission of a sponsored event, particularly one listed in last year's edition, means that we did not receive notice in time or that the date of the event was set too late for inclusion. Discrepancies in dating are most often the result of tentative information that is later changed by the sponsoring individual or organization.

Errors in other listings, for which we apologize, are our responsibility. Please send corrections to us so that we can amend future editions.

We welcome the submission of new entries. Instructions for providing required information are on page 364. Final selection of events and observances included in *Chase's Sports Calendar of Events* is the decision of the editors.

Acknowledgments
Thanks to the many people who helped in a variety of ways to make this edition a reality: Martha Best, Beth Broadrup, Louise El, Gigi Grajdura, Pamela Juárez, Richard Spears, Susan Schwartz, Terry Stone, Kimberly Summers, Sandy Whiteley and James Meier. And, finally, to Donna, Katie and Sarah Gietschier.

And now we invite readers of this second edition to join with us in observing and celebrating sports and recreation in the coming year.

Steve Gietschier, Editor
August 1997

JANUARY 1 — THURSDAY
Day 1 — 364 Remaining

THURSDAY, JANUARY ONE, 1998. Jan 1. First day of the first month of the Gregorian calendar year, Anno Domini 1998, being second after Leap Year, and (until July 4th) 222nd year of American Independence. 1998 will be year 6711 of the Julian Period, a time frame consisting of 7,982 years, which began at noon, universal time, Jan 1, 4713 BC. Astronomers will note that Julian Day number 2,450,814 begins at noon, universal [Greenwich] time, Jan 1, 1998 (representing the number of days since Julian calendar date Jan 1, 4713 BC). New Year's Day is a public holiday in the US and in many other countries. Traditionally, it is a time for personal stocktaking, for making resolutions for the coming year, and sometimes for recovering from the festivities of New Year's Eve. Financial accounting begins anew for businesses and individuals whose fiscal year is the calendar year. Jan 1 has been observed as the beginning of the year in most English-speaking countries since the British Calendar Act of 1751, prior to which the New Year began on Mar 25 (approximating the vernal equinox). Earth begins another orbit of the sun, during which it, and we, will travel some 583,416,000 miles in 365.2422 days. New Year's Day has been called "Everyman's Birthday," and in some countries a year is added to everyone's age on Jan 1 rather than on the anniversary of each person's birth.

ALLEN, ETHAN: BIRTH ANNIVERSARY. Jan 1, 1904. Ethan Nathan Allen, baseball player and coach born at Cincinnati, OH. Allen played 13 seasons in the majors and had a career batting average of .300. He was the longtime coach at Yale, where George Bush played for him, and the inventor of a popular board game, All-Star Baseball. Died at Brookings, OR, Sept 15, 1993.

CLUB BASKETBALL OPENING GAMES: NEW JERSEY MASTERS AND SENIORS LEAGUES. Jan 1 (tentative). Statewide, NJ. Season began Dec 15, 1996 (tentative). Masters League for players age 40 and over, Seniors League for players 50 and over. For info: Bill Clancy, Club Basketball, USA, 215 North Ave W, Ste 205, Westfield, NJ 07090. Phone: (908) 756-4502. Fax: (908) 756-9698.

CompUSA FLORIDA CITRUS BOWL. Jan 1. Orlando, FL. Postseason college football game matching the second-place teams from the Big Ten and the Southeastern Conferences. Sponsors: CompUSA and the Florida Department of Citrus. Est attendance: 70,000. For info: Dylan Thomas, Assoc Exec Dir, Florida Citrus Sports Assn, Inc, One Citrus Bowl Place, Orlando, FL 32805-2451. Phone: (407) 423-2476.

COTTON BOWL: ANNIVERSARY. Jan 1, 1937. Texas Christian University beat Marquette, 16–6, in the first Cotton Bowl football game played at Fair Park Stadium, Dallas, TX. The game was moved to the Cotton Bowl in 1938.

DOG ARTISTS' REGISTRY AND EXHIBITION. Jan 1–10. The Dog Museum, St. Louis, MO. Want a painting of your champion hunting dog or obedience trials winner? The Dog Museum maintains a biographical listing of artists available by commission for dog portraits and dog-related art. Every other year the artists exhibit their work. Est attendance: 4,000. For info: Barbara Jedda, Curator, The Dog Museum, 1721 S Mason, St. Louis, MO 63131. Phone: (314) 821-3647. Fax: (314) 821-7381.

FIRST AMERICAN FOOTBALL LEAGUE CHAMPIONSHIP GAME: ANNIVERSARY. Jan 1, 1961. The Houston Oilers defeated the Los Angeles Chargers, 24–16, to win the first championship of the upstart American Football League. Houston quarterback George Blanda threw three touchdown passes, and Oilers receiver Billy Cannon was named the game's Most Valuable Player. The championship was played in Houston's Jeppesen Stadium before 32,183.

GREENBERG, HANK: BIRTH ANNIVERSARY. Jan 1, 1911. Henry Benjamin (Hank) Greenberg, Baseball Hall of Fame first baseman and outfielder born at New York, NY. One of the game's most prodigious sluggers, Greenberg hit 331 home runs and drove in 1,276 runs in only nine full seasons. Baseball's first Jewish superstar, Greenberg entered the army after playing just 19 games in 1941 and did not return to the Detroit Tigers until midway through the 1945 season. His grand slam on that season's last day won the pennant for the Tigers and propelled them toward a World Series triumph. Inducted into the Hall of Fame in 1956. Died at Beverly Hills, CA, Sept 4, 1986.

HANGOVER HANDICAP RUN. Jan 1. Veteran's Park, Klamath Falls, OR. Two-mile fun run at 9 AM on New Year's Day morning. The 1st place male and female finishers each take home a beer-can trophy. Est attendance: 60. For info: Hangover Handicap, 1800 Fairmont, Klamath Falls, OR 97601. Phone: (541) 882-6922. Fax: (541) 883-6481.

KEEFE, TIM: BIRTH ANNIVERSARY. Jan 1, 1857. Timothy John (Tim) Keefe, Baseball Hall of Fame pitcher born at Cambridge, MA. Keefe won 344 games in the 19th century. He pioneered the change of pace to complement his fastball and curve. Inducted into the Hall of Fame in 1964. Died at Cambridge, MA, Apr 23, 1933.

McKINNEY, BONES: BIRTH ANNIVERSARY. Jan 1, 1919. Horace Albert ("Bones") McKinney, broadcaster, basketball coach and player born at Lowland, NC. McKinney played at North Carolina State before World War II and North Carolina after the war. He was ordained a Baptist minister and then became basketball coach at Wake Forest, leading the Demon Deacons to a pair of ACC championships and a Final Four appearance in 1962. Died May 16, 1997.

NEWPORT YACHT CLUB FROSTBITE FLEET RACE. Jan 1. Newport Yacht Club, Long Wharf, Newport, RI. Annual New Year's Day race. Sponsor: Newport Yacht Club. Est attendance: 5,000. For info: Newport Yacht Club, PO Box 488, Newport, RI 02840. Phone: (800) 326-6030. Fax: (401) 849-9060.

NOKIA SUGAR BOWL. Jan 1. Louisiana Superdome, New Orleans, LA. Post-season college football game matching the No. 3 and the No. 5 teams in the Bowl Alliance. Sponsored by NOKIA Mobile Telephones. Est attendance: 72,000. For info: Nokia Sugar Bowl, 1500 Sugar Bowl Dr, New Orleans, LA 70112. Phone: (504) 525-8573. Fax: (504) 525-4867. WWW: http://www.nokiasugarbowl.com

ORANGE BOWL: ANNIVERSARY. Jan 1, 1935. Bucknell beat the University of Miami, 26–0, in the first Orange Bowl football game played at Miami Field Stadium. The game was moved to the Orange Bowl in 1938 and to Joe Robbie Stadium (now Pro Player Stadium) in 1996.

OUTBACK BOWL. Jan 1. Houlihan's Stadium, Tampa, FL. Post-season college football game matching the third-place teams from the Southeastern Conference and the Big Ten Conference. Sponsored by Outback Steakhouse. Est attendance: 74,000. For info: Tampa Bay Bowl Assn, Inc, 4511 N Himes Ave, Ste 260, Tampa, FL 33614. Phone: (813) 874-2695. Fax: (813) 873-1959.

PENGUIN PLUNGE. Jan 1. Mackeral Cove, Jamestown, RI. Annual plunge into the icy waters of Narragansett Bay to benefit Rhode Island Special Olympics. Annually, Jan 1. Est attendance: 2,000. For info: Rhode Island Special Olympics, 33 College Hill Rd, Bldg 31, Warwick, RI 02886. Phone: (401) 823-7411. Fax: (401) 823-7415.

POLAR BEAR SWIM. Jan 1. Sheboygan Armory, Sheboygan, WI. Each New Year's Day at 1 PM, more than 450 daring swimmers brave Lake Michigan's ice floes. Most are costumed, all are crazy. Refreshments and free live entertainment from 10–6. Sponsor: Sheboygan Polar Bear Club. Est attendance: 2,000. For info: Sheboygan Conv and Visitors Bureau, 712 Riverfront Dr, Ste 101, Sheboygan, WI 53081. Phone: (920) 467-8436.

POLO: CHALLENGE CUP. Dec 28, 1997–Jan 25. Wellington, FL. For info: Palm Beach Polo, Inc, 13420 South Shore Blvd, West Palm Beach, FL 33414. Phone: (561) 793-1440. Fax: (561) 790-3872.

ROSE BOWL. Jan 1. Rose Bowl, Pasadena, CA. Post-season college football game matching the champions of the Big Ten and the Pac-10 Conferences. Known familiarly as the "Grandaddy of Them All." Est attendance: 100,000. For info: Pasadena Tournament of Roses Assn, 391 S Orange Grove Blvd, Pasadena, CA 91184. Phone: (818) 449-4100. Fax: (818) 449-9066.

SNO'FLY: THE FIRST KITE FLY OF THE YEAR. Jan 1. Prairie View Park, Kalamazoo, MI. Keep the New Year's celebration in full flight at this high-flying alternative to (seemingly) endless football games. Sno'Fly takes off from the frozen lake at Prairie View Park. Est attendance: 500. For info: John Cosby, Mktg Coord, Kalamazoo County Parks Dept, 2900 Lake St, Kalamazoo, MI 49001. Phone: (616) 383-8778. Fax: (616) 383-8724. WWW: http://www.kalcounty.com

SOUTHWESTERN BELL COTTON BOWL CLASSIC. Jan 1. Cotton Bowl, Dallas, TX. Post-season college football game matching the second-place team from the Big 12 Conference and either the second-place team from the PAC-10 Conference or the champion of the WAC. Sponsored by Southwestern Bell. Est attendance: 68,000. For info: Cotton Bowl Athletic Assn, 1300 W Mockingbird, Ste 400, Dallas, TX 75247. Phone: (214) 634-7525. Fax: (214) 634-7764. Email: cotton@swbell.net. WWW: http://www.cottonbowl.com

SUGAR BOWL: ANNIVERSARY. Jan 1, 1935. Tulane University beat Temple University, 20–14, in the first Sugar Bowl football game played at Tulane Stadium, New Orleans. The game was moved to the Louisiana Superdome in 1975.

TOURNAMENT OF ROSES ASSOCIATION FOOTBALL GAME: ANNIVERSARY. Jan 1, 1902. Michigan defeated Stanford 49–0 in the first postseason football game. Called the Rose Bowl since 1923, it is preceded each year by the Tournament of Roses Parade in Pasadena, CA.

TOYOTA GATOR BOWL. Jan 1. Gator Bowl, Jacksonville, FL. Post-season college football game matching the second-place teams from the Atlantic Coast Conference and the Big East Conference. Sponsored by Toyota Motor Sales USA, Inc. Est attendance: 77,000. For info: Gator Bowl Assn, Inc., One Gator Bowl Blvd, Jacksonville, FL 32202. Phone: (904) 798-1700. Fax: (904) 632-2080.

BIRTHDAYS TODAY

Irvin Humphrey (Irv) Eatman, 37, football player, born Birmingham, AL, Jan 1, 1961.
Robert (Bobby) Holik, 27, hockey player, born Jihlava, Czechoslovakia, Jan 1, 1971.
Dewey LaMarr Hoyt, 43, former baseball player, born Columbia, SC, Jan 1, 1955.
Robert Dennis (Bob) Owchinko, 43, former baseball player, born Detroit, MI, Jan 1, 1955.
Derrick Vincent Thomas, 31, football player, born Miami, FL, Jan 1, 1967.
Ewell Doak Walker, Jr, 71, Heisman Trophy halfback, born Dallas, TX, Jan 1, 1927.

January 1998

S	M	T	W	T	F	S
				1	2	3
4	5	6	7	8	9	10
11	12	13	14	15	16	17
18	19	20	21	22	23	24
25	26	27	28	29	30	31

JANUARY 2 — FRIDAY
Day 2 — 363 Remaining

SPORTSCHASER OF THE DAY

When Joe Namath finished his college career at the University of Alabama, which American Football League team drafted him?

BOSSY SCORES 500th GOAL: ANNIVERSARY. Jan 2, 1986. Right wing Mike Bossy of the New York Islanders scored the 500th goal of his National Hockey League career in a 7–5 victory over the Boston Bruins. Bossy ended his career with 752 goals and was inducted into the Hockey Hall of Fame in 1991.

CHICK-FIL-A PEACH BOWL. Jan 2. Georgia Dome, Atlanta, GA. Post-season college football game matching the third-place team from the Atlantic Coast Conference and the fourth-place team from the Southeastern Conference. Sponsored by Chick-Fil-A. Est attendance: 71,000. For info: Peach Bowl, Inc, 235 Intl Blvd, Atlanta, GA 30303. Phone: (404) 586-8500. Fax: (404) 586-8508.

FEDEX ORANGE BOWL. Jan 2. Pro Player Stadium, Miami, FL. Post-season college football game matching the No. 1 and No. 2 teams from the Bowl Alliance. Sponsored by FedEx. Est attendance: 75,000. For info: Orange Bowl Committee, 601 Brickell Key Dr, Ste 206, Miami, FL 33131. Phone: (305) 371-4600. Fax: (305) 371-8565.

GRAND AMERICAN COON HUNT. Jan 2–3. County Fairgrounds, Orangeburg, SC. Coon hunters and sportsmen from all over the US and Canada bring their dogs to compete for Grand American Champion. An ACHA qualifying hunt. Est attendance: 30,000. For info: Carol P. Whisenhunt, Orangeburg County Chamber of Commerce, PO Box 328, Orangeburg, SC 29116-0328. Phone: (803) 534-6821. Fax: (803) 531-9435.

"GREATEST GAME OF THE DECADE" (1980s): ANNIVERSARY. Jan 2, 1982. San Diego's Rolf Benirschke kicked a field goal with 13:52 gone in overtime to give the Chargers a 41–38 victory over the Miami Dolphins in an AFC divisional playoff match-up, later named greatest game of the decade by the Pro Football Hall of Fame. The Dolphins overcame a 24–0 first quarter deficit, but San Diego scored the tying touchdown with 58 seconds remaining. One week later the Chargers lost the AFC championship game to Cincinnati, 27–7.

JOE NAMATH SIGNS CONTRACT: ANNIVERSARY. Jan 2, 1965. After finishing his college football career at the University of Alabama, quarterback Joe Namath signed a 3-year contract for an estimated $427,000 with the New York Jets of the American Football League. Namath was also drafted by the NFL's St. Louis Cardinals, but Jets owner Sonny Werblin won a bidding war for his services.

JUMP ROPE DAYS©. Jan 2 (the 2nd, 4th, 6th and 8th of each month). These days celebrate the underrated activity that is the art of jumping rope. Days derived from the childhood jingle, "2, 4, 6, 8, who do we appreciate?" For further info send $2 to cover cost of copying and postage to: Adrienne Sioux Koopersmith, 1437 W Rosemont, 1W, Chicago, IL 60660-1319. Phone: (773) 743-5341. Fax: (773) 743-5395. Email: kooper@interaccess.com.

KRESS, RED: BIRTH ANNIVERSARY. Jan 2, 1907. Ralph ("Red") Kress, baseball player and coach born at Columbia, CA. Kress played 14 years in the major leagues as an infielder, starting in 1927, and coached with the New York Mets in 1962. Died at Los Angeles, CA, Nov 29, 1962.

NASHVILLE FISHING EXPO. Jan 2–4. Annual event featuring the latest in fishing tackle, boats, boating equipment, guide services and other accessories. Top fishing pros will demonstrate their techniques. Tennessee State Fairgrounds, Nashville, TN. Est attendance: 10,000. For info: Daryl Hobby, Esau, Inc, PO Box 50096, Knoxville, TN 37950. Phone: (423) 588-1233 or (800) 588-ESAU. Fax: (423) 588-6938.

RICKARD, TEX: BIRTH ANNIVERSARY. Jan 2, 1871. George Lewis ("Tex") Rickard, sports promoter born at Leavenworth, KS. Rickard's promotion of boxing matches, especially involving Jack Dempsey, helped to make the sport a major attraction. Working with Madison Square Garden, he organized bicycle races and obtained an NHL team which he nicknamed Tex's Rangers. Died at Miami, FL, Jan 6, 1929.

WHITNEY, PINKY: BIRTH ANNIVERSARY. Jan 2, 1905. Arthur Carter ("Pinky") Whitney, baseball player born at San Antonio, TX. Whitney played 12 years in the major leagues and hit better than .300 in his first three seasons, 1928–1930. Died at Center, TX, Sept 1, 1987.

BIRTHDAYS TODAY

Royce Spencer Clayton, 28, baseball player, born Burbank, CA, Jan 2, 1970.

David Brian Cone, 35, baseball player, born Kansas City, MO, Jan 2, 1963.

Lake Dawson, 26, football player, born Boston, MA, Jan 2, 1972.

William (Bill) Madlock, Jr, 47, former baseball player, born Memphis, TN, Jan 2, 1951.

Gino Marchetti, 71, Pro Football Hall of Fame defensive end, born Smithers, WV, Jan 2, 1927.

Edgar Martinez, 35, baseball player, born New York, NY, Jan 2, 1963.

Forest Gregory (Greg) Swindell, 33, baseball player, born Fort Worth, TX, Jan 2, 1965.

Richard Stephen (Rick) Tabaracci, 29, hockey player, born Toronto, Ontario, Canada, Jan 2, 1969.

Pernell Whitaker, 34, boxer, born Norfolk, VA, Jan 2, 1964.

JANUARY 3 — SATURDAY
Day 3 — 362 Remaining

ARLETT, BUZZ: BIRTH ANNIVERSARY. Jan 3, 1899. Russell Loris ("Buzz") Arlett, baseball player born at Oakland, CA. Arlett started as a pitcher but a sore arm caused him to move to the outfield. He played only one year in the majors but had an outstanding minor league career, hitting 432 home runs. Died at Minneapolis, MN, May 16, 1964.

BROWNS' 2OT PLAYOFF WIN: ANNIVERSARY. Jan 3, 1987. Cleveland quarterback Bernie Kosar passed for 487 yards, an NFL playoff record, to lead the Browns to a double-overtime 23–20 victory over the New York Jets in an AFC divisional playoff game. The following week, Cleveland lost the AFC championship game, also in overtime, to the Denver Broncos by the identical score.

MELTON, CLIFF: BIRTH ANNIVERSARY. Jan 3, 1912. Clifford George (Cliff) Melton, baseball player born at Brevard, NC. Melton pitched eight seasons for the New York Giants (1937–1944) and lost two games in the 1937 World Series. Died at Baltimore, MD, July 28, 1986.

NEW YORK NATIONAL BOAT SHOW. Jan 3–11. Jacob Javits Convention Center, New York, NY. 88th annual show. The world's longest running marine exhibition offers a wide selection of boats from entry-level inflatable to luxurious cruiser. Informative boating and fishing seminars. For info: NMMA Boat Show, 600 Third Ave, 23rd Fl, New York, NY 10016. Phone: (212) 922-1212. Fax: (212) 922-9607.

RUTH SOLD TO YANKEES: ANNIVERSARY. Jan 3, 1920. Boston Red Sox owner and theatrical producer Harry Frazee sold pitcher–outfielder Babe Ruth to the New York Yankees for $125,000 and a $300,000 loan. Frazee used the loan several years later to produce *No, No, Nanette*, a hit musical.

STALLCUP, VIRGIL: BIRTH ANNIVERSARY. Jan 3, 1922. Thomas Virgil Stallcup, baseball player born at Ravensford, NC. Stallcup was the regular shortstop for the Cincinnati Reds from 1948 through 1951. In 1949, he walked only 9 times in 575 at-bats. Died at Greenville, SC, May 2, 1989.

STEINBRENNER BUYS YANKEES: 25th ANNIVERSARY. Jan 3, 1973. A group headed by shipping executive George M. Steinbrenner, III, bought the New York Yankees from CBS for $10 million.

BIRTHDAYS TODAY

Stanley George ("Frenchy") Bordagaray, 88, former baseball player, born Coalinga, CA, Jan 3, 1910.
Darren Arthur Daulton, 36, baseball player, born Arkansas City, KS, Jan 3, 1962.
James Samuel (Jim) Everett, III, 35, football player, born Emporia, KS, Jan 3, 1963.
Robert Marvin (Bobby) Hull, 59, Hockey Hall of Fame left wing, born Point Anne, Ontario, Canada, Jan 3, 1939.
Cheryl DeAnne Miller, 34, basketball coach, broadcaster and former basketball player, born Riverside, CA, Jan 3, 1964.
Luis Beltran Sojo, 32, baseball player, born Barquisimeto, Venezuela, Jan 3, 1966.

JANUARY 4 — SUNDAY
Day 4 — 361 Remaining

CELTICS RETIRE AUERBACH'S "NUMBER": ANNIVERSARY. Jan 4, 1985. To honor team president and former coach Arnold ("Red") Auerbach, the Boston Celtics retired uniform number 2 in a ceremony prior to a game against the New York Knicks. Auerbach began coaching the Celtics in 1950–51 and led them to 16 NBA championships as coach, general manager and president.

CORCORAN, TOMMY: BIRTH ANNIVERSARY. Jan 4, 1869. Thomas William (Tommy) Corcoran, baseball player born at New Haven, CT. Corcoran was an infielder who played around the turn of the century. He was a defensive specialist who later became a minor league umpire. Died at Plainfield, CT, June 25, 1960.

EARTH AT PERIHELION. Jan 4. At approximately 4 PM, EST, planet Earth will reach Perihelion, that point in its orbit when it is closest to the sun (about 91,400,000 miles). The Earth's mean distance from the sun (mean radius of its orbit) is reached early in the months of April and October. Note that Earth is closest to the sun during Northern Hemisphere winter. See also: "Earth at Aphelion" (July 3).

FIRST NFL EXPANSION CHAMP: ANNIVERSARY. Jan 4, 1970. The Minnesota Vikings became the first expansion team to win the NFL title when they defeated the Cleveland Browns, 27–7, in Minneapolis. The Vikings went on to lose Super Bowl IV to the Kansas City Chiefs.

January	S	M	T	W	T	F	S
1998					1	2	3
	4	5	6	7	8	9	10
	11	12	13	14	15	16	17
	18	19	20	21	22	23	24
	25	26	27	28	29	30	31

Red Auerbach

LAST AMERICAN FOOTBALL LEAGUE CHAMPIONSHIP GAME: ANNIVERSARY. Jan 4, 1970. The Kansas City Chiefs, aided by four interceptions, defeated the Oakland Raiders, 17–7, in the last American Football League championship game. The Chiefs went on to defeat the Minnesota Vikings in Super Bowl IV.

NEELY, JESS: 100th BIRTH ANNIVERSARY. Jan 4, 1898. Jess Claiborne Neely, football player, coach and administrator, born at Smyrna, TN. Neely played football at Vanderbilt and entered coaching after earning a law degree. He coached at Clemson and at Rice, winning six Southwest Conference titles. Died at Weslaco, TX, Apr 9, 1983.

NHL PUNCH LEADS TO INDICTMENT: ANNIVERSARY. Jan 4, 1975. In an NHL game between the Boston Bruins and the Minnesota North Stars, Bruins winger Dave Forbes punched Henry Boucha, fracturing his cheekbone and opening a cut that required 30 stitches to close. Forbes was indicted for using "excessive force," becoming the first professional athlete to be prosecuted for actions taken during a game. His trial that summer ended in a hung jury after which all charges were dropped.

ONLY PRO BOWL IN NEW YORK: ANNIVERSARY. Jan 4, 1942. The Chicago Bears, NFL champions by virtue of their 37–9 victory over the New York Giants, defeated the NFL All-Stars, 35–24, in the only Pro Bowl game ever played in New York. The small Polo Grounds crowd, 17,725, led the league to abandon the Pro Bowl one year later until a new format, matching one conference against the other, was introduced in 1951.

US FIGURE SKATING CHAMPIONSHIPS. Jan 4–11. Wissahickon Skating Club, Philadelphia, PA. More than 300 skaters will compete in five categories: men's, ladies, pairs, dance and figures divisions. The results determine the skaters' national ranking and funding, along with international assignments for the upcoming year. The event determines who gets to go to the World Championships. Est attendance: 100,000. For info: US Figure Skating Assn, 20 First St, Colorado Springs, CO 80906. Phone: (719) 635-5200. Fax: (719) 635-9548.

BIRTHDAYS TODAY

Rigoberto ("Tito") Fuentes, 54, former baseball player, born Havana, Cuba, Jan 4, 1944.

Gerald Garrison Hearst, 27, football player, born Lincolnton, GA, Jan 4, 1971.

Joseph William (Joe) Kleine, 36, basketball player, born Colorado Springs, CO, Jan 4, 1962.

Clifford Eugene (Cliff) Levingston, 37, former basketball player, born San Diego, CA, Jan 4, 1961.

Floyd Patterson, 63, former heavyweight champion boxer, born Waco, NC, Jan 4, 1935.

Donald Francis (Don) Shula, 68, former football coach and player, born Painesville, OH, Jan 4, 1930.

Michael (Mike) White, 62, former football coach, born Berkeley, CA, Jan 4, 1936.

☆   ☆   ☆

JANUARY 5 — MONDAY
Day 5 — 360 Remaining

CHASE'S SPORTSQUOTE OF THE DAY

"The objective of football is not to break men's bodies and spirits; it's to win football games." — Chuck Noll

BLOZIS, AL: BIRTH ANNIVERSARY. Jan 5, 1919. Albert C. (Al) Blozis, football player born at Garfield, NJ. Blozis competed in track and field and played football at Georgetown University where he earned a degree in chemistry in 1942. At 6'6" and 240 pounds, he was initially rejected for military service because of his size and played for the New York Giants in the NFL. Finally inducted into the army in late 1943, he went overseas in early 1945 and was killed in action when he ventured out in the snow to search for two missing soldiers in his command. Died in the Vosges Mountains, France, Jan 31, 1945.

FLETCHER, ART: BIRTH ANNIVERSARY. Jan 5, 1885. Arthur (Art) Fletcher, baseball player and coach born at Collinsville, IL. Fletcher played in the majors from 1909 to 1922, managed the Philadelphia Phillies from 1923 to 1926 and coached third base for the great New York Yankees teams of 1927 through 1945. Died at Los Angeles, CA, Feb 6, 1950.

GLOBETROTTERS LOSE: ANNIVERSARY. Jan 5, 1971. After posting victories in 2,495 straight games dating back to 1962, the Harlem Globetrotters suffered a rare defeat at the hands of their perennial opponents, the Washington Generals. In the closing seconds of a game in Martin, TN, a basket by Red Klotz gave the Generals a 100–99 win.

KAUFF, BENNY: BIRTH ANNIVERSARY. Jan 5, 1890. Benjamin Michael (Benny) Kauff, baseball player born at Pomeroy, OH. Kauff led the Federal League in batting in each of its two seasons, 1914 and 1915. He returned to the National League but a few years later was banned for life for alleged involvement in gambling. Died at Columbus, OH, Nov 17, 1961.

McKINLEY, CHUCK: BIRTH ANNIVERSARY. Jan 5, 1941. Charles Robert (Chuck) McKinley, tennis player born at St. Louis, MO. McKinley was nationally ranked in the early 1960s. He won Wimbledon in 1963 and combined with Dennis Ralston to win the US National Doubles title three times and the 1963 Davis Cup Challenge Round, 3–2, over Australia. Died at Dallas, TX, Aug 11, 1986.

MOON PHASE: FIRST QUARTER. Jan 5. Moon enters First Quarter phase at 9:18 AM, EST.

PICCARD, JEANNETTE RIDLON: BIRTH ANNIVERSARY. Jan 5, 1895. Jeannette Ridlon Piccard, balloonist born at Chicago, IL. Piccard became the first American woman to qualify as free balloon pilot in 1934 and one of first women to be ordained as Episcopal priest in 1976. She set the record for a balloon ascent into stratosphere (from Dearborn, MI) on Oct 23, 1934, at 57,579 ft with her husband, Jean Felix Piccard. She was an identical twin married to an identical twin. Died at Minneapolis, MN, May 17, 1981.

SEWELL, LUKE: BIRTH ANNIVERSARY. Jan 5, 1901. James Luther (Luke) Sewell, baseball player and manager born at Titus, AL. Sewell was a good defensive catcher who played with several teams. He managed the St. Louis Browns to their only American League pennant in 1944. Died at Akron, OH, May 14, 1987.

SHULA RETIRES: ANNIVERSARY. Jan 5, 1996. After 33 seasons as a head coach, Don Shula retired from the helm of the Miami Dolphins to become part-owner and vice-chairman of the team. Shula left the game as the winningest professional coach of all time with a record, counting regular season and playoff games, of 347–173–6. His teams made the playoffs 20 times and won two Super Bowls.

BIRTHDAYS TODAY

Earl Jesse Battey, 63, former baseball player, born Los Angeles, CA, Jan 5, 1935.

Warrick Dunn, 23, football player, born Baton Rouge, LA, Jan 5, 1975.

Robert Duvall, 67, actor (*The Natural*), born San Diego, CA, Jan 5, 1931.

Alexander (Alex) English, 44, former basketball player, born Columbia, SC, Jan 5, 1954.

Jeffrey Joseph (Jeff) Fassero, 35, baseball player, born Springfield, IL, Jan 5, 1963.

Charles Oliver (Charlie) Hough, 50, former baseball player, born Honolulu, HI, Jan 5, 1948.

Danny Lynn Jackson, 36, baseball player, born San Antonio, TX, Jan 5, 1962.

Joseph (Joe) Juneau, 30, hockey player, born Pont-Rouge, Quebec, Canada, Jan 5, 1968.

Ronald Dale (Ron) Kittle, 40, former baseball player, born Gary, IN, Jan 5, 1958.

Charles Henry (Chuck) Noll, 66, Pro Football Hall of Fame coach, born Cleveland, OH, Jan 5, 1932.

James Edwin (Jim) Otto, 60, Pro Football Hall of Fame center, born Wausau, WI, Jan 5, 1938.

Felton LaFrance Spencer, 30, basketball player, born Louisville, KY, Jan 5, 1968.

Samuel David (Sam) Wyche, 53, broadcaster and former football coach and player, born Atlanta, GA, Jan 5, 1945.

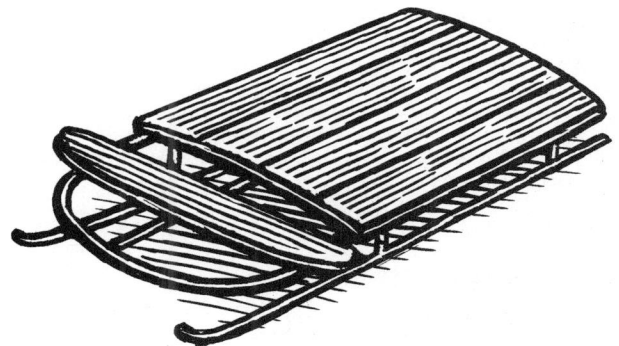

JANUARY 6 — TUESDAY
Day 6 — 359 Remaining

CARNIVAL SEASON. Jan 6–Feb 24. A secular festival preceding Lent. A time of merrymaking and feasting before the austere days of Lenten fasting and penitence (40 weekdays between Ash Wednesday and Easter Sunday). The word *carnival* probably is derived from the Latin *carnem levare*, meaning "to remove meat." Depending on local custom, the carnival season may start any time between Nov 11 and Shrove Tuesday. Conclusion of the season is much less variable, being the close of Shrove Tuesday in most places. Celebrations vary considerably, but the festival often includes many theatrical aspects (masks, costumes and songs) and has given its name (in the US) to traveling amusement shows that may be seen throughout the year. Observed traditionally in Roman Catholic countries from Epiphany through Shrove Tuesday.

CLUB BASKETBALL OPENING GAMES: NEW JERSEY LAWYERS LEAGUE. Jan 6 (tentative). Statewide, NJ. For info: Bill Clancy, Club Basketball, USA, 215 North Ave W, Ste 205, Westfield, NJ 07090. Phone: (908) 756-4502. Fax: (908) 756-9698.

CLUB BASKETBALL OPENING GAMES: NEW JERSEY CORPORATE SPORTS LEAGUE. Jan 6 (tentative date). Statewide, NJ. For info: Bill Clancy, Club Basketball, USA, 215 North Ave W, Ste 205, Westfield, NJ 07090. Phone: (908) 756-4502. Fax: (908) 756-9698.

FLYERS' RECORD STREAK: ANNIVERSARY. Jan 6, 1980. The Philadelphia Flyers used two 3rd-period goals to defeat the Buffalo Sabres, 4–2, and extend their NHL record for consecutive games without a loss to 35 (25–0–10). The streak came to an end on the following night when the Flyers lost to the Minnesota North Stars.

JOHNSON, BAN: 135th BIRTH ANNIVERSARY. Jan 6, 1863. Byron Bancroft (Ban) Johnson, Baseball Hall of Fame executive born at Cincinnati, OH. Johnson transformed the minor league Western League into the major league American League in 1901. He ruled as president with an iron hand and was eased out of power by the league's owners in 1927. Inducted into the Hall of Fame in 1937. Died at St. Louis, MO, Mar 28, 1931.

MASI, PHIL: BIRTH ANNIVERSARY. Jan 6, 1917. Philip Samuel (Phil) Masi, baseball player born at Chicago, IL. A catcher known for his defensive skills, Masi was involved in a famous pickoff play in the 1948 World Series. He was apparently picked off second by Cleveland Indians pitcher Bob Feller only to have the umpire call him safe. One batter later, he scored the game's only run. Died at Mount Prospect, IL, Mar 29, 1990.

NANCY KERRIGAN ASSAULTED: ANNIVERSARY. Jan 6, 1994. American figure skater Nancy Kerrigan was struck on the knee with an iron rod at Cobo Arena in Detroit where she had been practicing for the upcoming US Championships. The contest winner was Tonya Harding, who was later accused, along with her ex-husband, Jeff Gillooly, and three others, of planning and carrying out the attack. Kerrigan recovered in time to participate in the Winter Olympics at Lillehammer, Norway, in February, winning a silver medal. Harding came in 8th, suffering a broken lace and later a fall. In plea bargaining Gillooly admitted his role in the attack and testified that Harding had been involved in the planning. Her bodyguard and two others were later indicted, and Harding was put on two years' probation. Harding also was stripped of her US title and banned from the US Figure Skating Assn for life.

PLANTE GETS 300th VICTORY: 35th ANNIVERSARY. Jan 6, 1963. Jacques Plante of the Montreal Canadiens became the third goalie in National Hockey League history to win 300 games when the Canadiens defeated the New York Rangers, 6–0. Plante ended his career with 434 wins and was inducted into the Hockey Hall of Fame in 1978.

"PRO BOWLERS TOUR" TV PREMIERE: ANNIVERSARY. Jan 6, 1962. ABC's weekly coverage of professional bowling tournaments began with Chris Schenkel as the broadcast host. Over the years, he was assisted by Jack Buck (1962–64), Billy Welu (1964–74) and Nelson Burton, Jr (1974–97). The show made its last appearance on June 21, 1997.

WALLS, LEE: 65th BIRTH ANNIVERSARY. Jan 6, 1933. Ray Lee Walls, baseball player born at San Diego, CA. Walls played in the major leagues for ten years with five teams. In the ninth game played at the Los Angeles Coliseum, Walls, then a Dodger, hit three home runs over the 40-ft left field fence, 251 feet from home plate. Died at Los Angeles, CA, Oct 11, 1993.

BIRTHDAYS TODAY

Ruben Amaro, 62, former baseball player, born Veracruz, Mexico, Jan 6, 1936.

Paul William Azinger, 38, golfer, born Holyoke, MA, Jan 6, 1960.

Ralph Theodore Joseph Branca, 72, former baseball player, born Mt Vernon, NY, Jan 6, 1926.

Norman Wood (Norm) Charlton, III, 35, baseball player, born Fort Polk, LA, Jan 6, 1963.

James Alfred Farrior, 23, football player, born Ettrick, VA, Jan 6, 1975.

Charles Lewis Haley, 34, former football player, born Gladys, VA, Jan 6, 1964.

Louis Leo (Lou) Holtz, 61, former football coach, born Follansbee, WV, Jan 6, 1937.

Howard M. (Howie) Long, 38, broadcaster and former football player, born Somerville, MA, Jan 6, 1960.

Nancy Lopez, 41, LPGA Hall of Fame golfer, born Torrance, CA, Jan 6, 1957.

Early Wynn, 78, Baseball Hall of Fame pitcher, born Hartford, AL, Jan 6, 1920.

JANUARY 7 — WEDNESDAY
Day 7 — 358 Remaining

ATLANTA BOAT SHOW. Jan 7–11. Georgia World Congress Center, Atlanta, GA. 36th annual show. The region's premier nautical event offers the best selection of boats and marine accessories at the lowest prices. Informative boating and fishing seminars. NMMA Boat Shows, 400 Arthur Godfrey, Ste 310, Miami, FL 33140. Phone: (305) 531-8410. Fax: (305) 534-3139.

CONIGLIARO, TONY: BIRTH ANNIVERSARY. Jan 7, 1945. Anthony Richard (Tony) Conigliaro, baseball player born at Revere, MA. Conigliaro led the American League in home runs in 1965 and was one of the most beloved Boston Red Sox players of his generation. He was beaned by Jack Hamilton on Aug 18, 1967, and after missing all of 1968, made a comeback. Died at Boston, Feb 24, 1990.

	S	M	T	W	T	F	S
January					1	2	3
	4	5	6	7	8	9	10
1998	11	12	13	14	15	16	17
	18	19	20	21	22	23	24
	25	26	27	28	29	30	31

COWBOYS ADVANCE TO FIFTH SUPER BOWL: ANNIVERSARY. Jan 7, 1979. The Dallas Cowboys advanced to their fifth Super Bowl by defeating the Los Angeles Rams in the NFC championship game, 28–0. The Cowboys met the Pittsburgh Steelers in the first rematch of Super Bowl teams on Jan 21, but lost, 35–31.

FIRST BALLOON FLIGHT ACROSS ENGLISH CHANNEL: ANNIVERSARY. Jan 7, 1785. Dr. John Jeffries, a Boston physician, and Jean-Pierre Blanchard, French aeronaut, crossed the English Channel from Dover, England, to Calais, France, landing in a forest after being forced to throw overboard all ballast, equipment and even most of their clothing to avoid forced landing in the icy waters of the English Channel. Blanchard's trousers are said to have been the last article thrown overboard.

LAKERS SET VICTORY MARK: ANNIVERSARY. Jan 7, 1972. The Los Angeles Lakers defeated the Atlanta Hawks, 134–90, to win their 33rd game in a row, an NBA record.

MIZE, JOHNNY: 85th BIRTH ANNIVERSARY. Jan 7, 1913. John Robert (Johnny) Mize, Baseball Hall of Fame first baseman born at Demorest, GA. Known as the "Big Cat," Mize won the 1939 National League batting championship, four home run crowns and three RBI titles. He hit 51 homers in 1947, an NL record for lefthanded batters. After playing with the St. Louis Cardinals and the New York Giants, Mize was sold to the New York Yankees in 1949. He played part-time and pinch hit through 1953. Inducted into the Hall of Fame in 1981. Died at Demorest, June 2, 1993.

MONTGOLFIER, JACQUES: BIRTH ANNIVERSARY. Jan 7, 1745. Jacques Etienne Montgolfier, merchant and inventor born at Vidalon-lez Annonay, Ardèche, France. With his older brother, Joseph Michel, in Nov 1782, he conducted experiments with paper and fabric bags filled with smoke and hot air, which led to invention of the hot-air balloon and the first flight by a human. Died at Serrieres, France, Aug 2, 1799.

NHL'S LEADING SCORER: ANNIVERSARY. Jan 7, 1920. Joe Malone of the Quebec Bulldogs scored a pair of goals in a 4–3 victory over the Toronto Arenas to become the NHL's all-time scoring leader with 59 career goals.

SAN ANTONIO SPORT, BOAT AND RV SHOW. Jan 7–11. San Antonio Convention Center, San Antonio, TX. Boating, travel, hunting, fishing, camping, RVs and recreation show. 41st annual show. Sponsor: Boating Trades Assn of San Antonio, TX. For info: Mike Coffen, Double C Productions, Inc, PO Box 1678, Huntsville, TX 77342. Phone: (409) 295-9677. Fax: (409) 295-8859. Email: doublec@lcc.net. WWW: http://lcc.net/doublec

US TROTTING ASSOCIATION FOUNDING: ANNIVERSARY. Jan 7, 1939. The United States Trotting Association–the governing body for the sport of harness horse racing–was founded in Indianapolis, IN. The founding was actually a joining of several regional organizations, resulting in uniform rules and regulations. This unification spurred the growth of harness racing, now followed by nearly 25 million fans in North America each year.

BIRTHDAYS TODAY

Randy Burridge, 32, hockey player, born Fort Erie, Ontario, Canada, Jan 7, 1966.

Alvin Ralph Dark, 76, former baseball manager and player, born Comanche, OK, Jan 7, 1922.

Guy Andrew Hebert, 31, hockey player, born Troy, NY, Jan 7, 1967.

James Kenneth (Jim) Lefevbre, 56, former baseball manager and player, born Inglewood, CA, Jan 7, 1942.

Jeffrey Thomas (Jeff) Montgomery, 36, baseball player, born Wellston, OH, Jan 7, 1962.

Erric Demont Pegram, 29, football player, born Dallas, TX, Jan 7, 1969.

Craig Barry Shipley, 35, baseball player, born Sydney, Australia, Jan 7, 1963.

JANUARY 8 — THURSDAY
Day 8 — 357 Remaining

ALL-CANADA SHOW. Jan 8–11. Cervantes Center, St. Louis, MO. This consumer show allows individuals an opportunity to talk face-to-face with Canadian lodge representatives and outfitters to plan their hunting, fishing and adventure trips to Canada. For info: Rodney Schlafer, Show Dir, All-Canada Show, Bay-Lakes Mktg, Inc, 1889 Commerce Dr, Depere, WI 54115. Phone: (414) 983-9800 or (800) 325-6290. Fax: (414) 983-9985. WWW: http://www.allcanada.com

BUSBY, JIM: BIRTH ANNIVERSARY. Jan 8, 1927. James Franklin (Jim) Busby, baseball player born at Kenedy, TX. Busby played 13 seasons in the major leagues and hit .262 for six different teams. Died at Augusta, GA, July 8, 1996.

COOPER, WALKER: BIRTH ANNIVERSARY. Jan 8, 1915. William Walker Cooper, baseball player born at Atherton, MO. Cooper, a catcher, and his brother, pitcher Mort, formed a brother-brother battery for the St. Louis Cardinals. Cooper was a solid defensive catcher who hit well, too. He was traded from the Cards in 1946 and played for several other teams before finishing his career back in St. Louis. Died at Scottsdale, AZ, Apr 11, 1991.

FRESHMEN MADE ELIGIBLE: ANNIVERSARY. Jan 8, 1972. The NCAA announced that freshmen would be eligible to play varsity football and basketball starting in the fall of 1972.

KUCZYNSKI, BERT: BIRTH ANNIVERSARY. Jan 8, 1920. Bernard Carl (Bert) Kuczynski, baseball and football player born at Philadelphia, PA. Kuczynski was the first to play professional football and major league baseball in the same season. In 1943, he pitched for the Philadelphia Athletics and played football for the Detroit Lions. Died at Allentown, PA, Jan 19, 1997.

LES GRANDES DAMES SENIOR WOMEN'S TENNIS TOURNAMENT. Jan 8–12. Ballen Isles Country Club, Palm Beach Gardens, FL. Senior women's tennis (ages 40–80). Prize money. Est attendance: 3,000. For info: Mary Ann Plante, Pres, Les Grandes Dames, 915 Kentucky Ave, Winter Park, FL 32789. Phone: (407) 628-1682. Fax: (407) 628-1682.

MERCEDES CHAMPIONSHIPS. Jan 8–11. La Costa Resort & Spa, Carlsbad, CA. A PGA Tour tournament bringing together the tournament winners from the preceding calendar year. Formerly known as the Tournament of Champions. For info: PGA Tour, 112 TPC Blvd, Ponte Vedra Beach, FL 32082. Phone: (904) 285-3700.

NCAA EXPANDS FIELD TO 64: ANNIVERSARY. Jan 8, 1985. The NCAA Executive Council decided to expand the field for its Division I Men's basketball tournament to 64 teams, arranged in four 16-team regional brackets.

RICKERT, MARV: BIRTH ANNIVERSARY. Jan 8, 1921. Marvin August (Marv) Rickert, baseball player born at Longbranch, WA. Rickert and Chicago Cubs teammate Eddie Waitkus hit the first back-to-back inside-the-park home runs in major league history on June 23, 1946. Died at Oakville, WA, June 3, 1978.

SAN DIEGO BOAT SHOW. Jan 8–11. San Diego Convention Center and Marriott Marina, San Diego, CA. 10th annual show is largest one-stop nautical sports event on the West Coast. Features a wide selection of boats and accessories, plus informative boating and fishing seminars. For info: Jeff Hancock, NMMA, 4901 Morena Blvd, Ste 901, San Diego, CA 92117. Phone: (619) 274-9924. Fax: (619) 274-6760.

SEAHAWKS LOSE AFC TITLE GAME: ANNIVERSARY. Jan 8, 1984. The Seattle Seahawks reached the AFC title game for the first time in their history but were defeated by the Los Angeles Raiders, 30–14.

BIRTHDAYS TODAY

Garth Butcher, 35, hockey player, born Regina, Saskatchewan, Canada, Jan 8, 1963.
Dwight Edward Clark, 41, former football player, born Kinston, NC, Jan 8, 1957.
Charles Keith (Chuck) Cottier, 62, former baseball player and manager, born Delta, CO, Jan 8, 1936.
Eugene Lewis (Gene) Freese, 64, former baseball player, born Wheeling, WV, Jan 8, 1934.
Calvin Leon Natt, 1941, former basketball player, born Monroe, LA, Jan 8, 1957.
Randy Max Ready, 38, former baseball player, born San Mateo, CA, Jan 8, 1960.
Howard Bruce Sutter, 45, former baseball player, born Lancaster, PA, Jan 8, 1953.

JANUARY 9 — FRIDAY
Day 9 — 356 Remaining

SUPERBOWL CHAMPIONS THIS DATE
1977 Oakland Raiders

AVIATION IN AMERICA: ANNIVERSARY. Jan 9, 1793. A Frenchman, Jean Pierre Blanchard, made the first manned free-balloon flight in America's history at Philadelphia, PA. The event was watched by President George Washington and many other high government officials. The hydrogen-filled balloon rose to a height of about 5,800 feet, traveled some 15 miles and landed 46 minutes later. Reportedly Blanchard had one passenger on the flight, a little black dog.

BIRTH OF NEW YORK YANKEES: 95th ANNIVERSARY. Jan 9, 1903. Frank Farrell and Bill Devery bought the Baltimore franchise in the American League for $18,000 and moved the team to New York to compete with the New York Giants. The team became known as the Highlanders and later the Yankees.

January *1998*	S	M	T	W	T	F	S
					1	2	3
	4	5	6	7	8	9	10
	11	12	13	14	15	16	17
	18	19	20	21	22	23	24
	25	26	27	28	29	30	31

CHARLOTTE OBSERVER MARATHON, 10K AND EXPO. Jan 9–10. Charlotte, NC. 26.2-mile marathon, 10K race (Jan 10), and Runners Expo (Jan 9–10). For info: Observer Marathon, Box 30294, Charlotte, NC 28230. Phone: (704) 358-5425. Fax: (704) 358-5430.

FIRST 40-POINT BAA GAME: ANNIVERSARY. Jan 9, 1947. Don Martin of the Providence Steamrollers became the first player in the Basketball Association of America to score 40 points in a game, accomplishing the feat against the Cleveland Rebels. The BAA merged with the National Basketball League after the 1948–49 season to form the National Basketball Association.

GREAT HOUSTON GOLF SHOW. Jan 9–11. Houston, TX. A high-quality consumer trade show for the golf industry that showcases new products, purchasing opportunities, interactive entertainment and informative features. For info: David Shinykin, David Toushin & Assoc, 5775 Wayzata Blvd, Ste 859, Minneapolis, MN 55416. Phone: (612) 593-0353.

HIGH SCHOOL FREE THROW RECORD: ANNIVERSARY. Jan 9, 1979. New Orleans basketball player Daryl Moreau set a high school record by converting his 126th free throw in a row, a streak that lasted a year.

NC RV & CAMPING SHOW. Jan 9–11. Special Events Center, Greensboro Coliseum Complex, Greensboro, NC. A display of the latest in recreation vehicles and accessories by various dealers. Est attendance: 10,000. For info: Apple Rock Advertising & Promotion, 1200 Eastchester Dr, High Point, NC 27265. Phone: (910) 881-7100. Fax: (910) 883-7198.

RAIDERS WIN THEIR FIRST SUPER BOWL: ANNIVERSARY. Jan 9, 1977. The Oakland Raiders won Super Bowl XI, 32–14, over the Minnesota Vikings. Oakland's first Super Bowl triumph came in the Rose Bowl before a record crowd of 103,424. Raiders wide receiver Fred Biletnikoff was named the game's Most Valuable Player.

SAIL EXPO. Jan 9–17. The New Atlantic City Convention Center, Atlantic City, NJ. Largest indoor sailboat show in the nation with more than 200 fully-rigged sailboats available for inspection and boarding. Est attendance: 49,000. For info: Visitor Info, Atlantic City Conv & Visitors Authority, 2314 Pacific Ave, Atlantic City, NJ 08401. Phone: (609) 449-7130.

SPORTSCHASER OF THE DAY
What Frenchman made the first free-balloon flight in the US in 1793?

BIRTHDAYS TODAY

Tyrone Curtis ("Muggsy") Bogues, 33, basketball player, born Baltimore, MD, Jan 9, 1965.
Radek Bonk, 22, hockey player, born Kronov, Czechoslovakia, Jan 9, 1976.
Michael Leon (M. L.) Carr, 47, former basketball coach and former player, born Wallace, NC, Jan 9, 1951.
Richard Allen (Dick) Enberg, 63, sportscaster, born Mt Clemens, MI, Jan 9, 1935.
Mark Martin, 39, auto racer, born Batesville, AR, Jan 9, 1959.
Otis Junior Nixon, 39, baseball player, born Evergreen, NC, Jan 9, 1959.
Bryan Bartlett (Bart) Starr, 64, former football coach and Pro Football Hall of Fame quarterback, born Montgomery, AL, Jan 9, 1934.

JANUARY 10 — SATURDAY
Day 10 — 355 Remaining

GOALIE'S ONE-NIGHT STAND: ANNIVERSARY. Jan 10, 1980. The Boston Bruins gave goalie Jim Stewart his first and only start in the National Hockey League. Stewart surrendered three goals in the game's first four minutes and five in the first period. He was replaced and never played in the NHL again.

LAKERS' STREAK ENDS: ANNIVERSARY. Jan 10, 1972. The Milwaukee Bucks defeated the Los Angeles Lakers, 120–104, to snap the longest winning streak in major professional sports at 33 games. Milwaukee's Kareem Abdul-Jabbar, later to play for the Lakers, scored 39 points to hand Los Angeles its first loss since Oct 31, 1971.

NATIONAL WESTERN STOCK SHOW AND RODEO. Jan 10–25. Denver, CO. One of the nation's largest livestock shows with more than 30 breeds of animals, 25 rodeo performances, 10 horse shows, 2 Mexican shows and cutting-horse and sheep-shearing contests. 92nd annual. Est attendance: 625,000. For info: Natl Western Stock Show and Rodeo, 4655 Humboldt St, Denver, CO 80216. Phone: (303) 297-1166. Fax: (303) 292-1708.

NCAA CONVENTION. Jan 10–14. Atlanta Marriott Marquis and Hyatt Regency Atlanta Hotels, Atlanta, GA. For info: Sandy Linson, Publ Info, NCAA, 6201 College Blvd, Overland Park, KS 66211. Phone: (913) 339-1906. Fax: (913) 339-1950. WWW: http://www.ncaa.org

NORTHERN EXPOSURE/WOLF RIVER RENDEZVOUS IN SHAWANO. Jan 10–11 (tentative). Shawano, WI. Top sleddog racers from Europe, Canada and the US compete in 4-, 6- and 10-dog junior and amateur classes. The festival also features mutt sled dog races, skijoring (skiers pulled by dogs), snowshoe races, a buck-skinners encampment, candlelight ski, moonlight snowmobile ride, horse-drawn sleigh rides, cross-cut saw competition and chain saw carving. Est attendance: 6,000. For info: Promotions, Northern Exposure/Wolf River Rendezvous in Shawano, Shawano Area Chamber of Commerce, PO Box 38, Shawano, WI 54166. Phone: (715) 524-2139 or (800) 235-8528. Fax: (715) 524-3127.

PALMER DIAGNOSED WITH CANCER: ANNIVERSARY. Jan 10, 1997. Arnold Palmer, perhaps the most charismatic golfer of all time, was diagnosed with prostate cancer. Palmer underwent surgery at the Mayo Clinic on Jan 15, and on Mar 20 he returned to golf, carding an 81 in the first round of the Bay Hill Invitational. He also became a spokesman for the prevention of prostate cancer.

PRATT, DEL: 110th BIRTH ANNIVERSARY. Jan 10, 1888. Derrill Burnham (Del) Pratt, baseball player born at Walhalla, SC. Pratt was an outstanding second baseman who played 13 seasons in the majors (1912–1924). He hit .300 six times and was a defensive stalwart. Died at Texas City, TX, Sept 20, 1977.

SNOW SHOVEL RIDING CONTEST. Jan 10. Economy Park, Economy, PA. Contest begins at 1 PM. Participants ride snow shovels downhill, handles extended, instead of sleds. Best time is the winner. Est attendance: 80. For info: Beaver Co Tourist Promotion Agency, 215B Ninth St, Monaca, PA 15061-2028. Phone: (412) 728-0212. Fax: (412) 728-0456.

STAHL, CHICK: 125th BIRTH ANNIVERSARY. Jan 10, 1873. Charles Sylvester (Chick) Stahl, baseball player and manager born at Avila, IN. Stahl played with the Boston National League team in the late 1890s but jumped to the new American League in 1901. He became manager of the Boston Pilgrims during the 1906 season but committed suicide during the following spring training. Died at West Baden, IN, Mar 28, 1907.

"THE CATCH": ANNIVERSARY. Jan 10, 1982. San Francisco 49ers wide receiver Dwight Clark jumped high in the Candlestick Park end zone to snare a touchdown pass from Joe Montana as the 49ers defeated the Dallas Cowboys, 28–27, in the NFC championship game. "The Catch," as the play came to be called, propelled San Francisco to Super Bowl XVI, which they won, 26–21, over the Cincinnati Bengals.

WINTERFEST. Jan 10. Alpine Valley Ski Area, Chesterland, OH. A winter fun fest with volleyball in the snow, snowshoe obstacle race course, bikini slalom and a children's obstacle slalom. For info: Ohio Div of Travel & Tourism, 77 South High St, 29th Floor, Columbus, OH 43215-6108. Phone: (614) 466-8844. Fax: (614) 466-6744. WWW: http://www.travel.state.oh.us

WRIGHT, HARRY: BIRTH ANNIVERSARY. Jan 10, 1835. William Henry ("Harry") Wright, Baseball Hall of Fame player and manager born at Sheffield, England. Wright and his brother George were two of baseball's earliest pioneers. In 1869, he transformed the Red Stockings into the first openly professional club. He managed other teams and, after an eye disorder ended his career, he was named honorary Chief of Umpires in the National League. Inducted into the Hall of Fame in 1953. Died at Atlantic City, NJ, Oct 3, 1895.

BIRTHDAYS TODAY

Richard Elliott Dotson, 39, former baseball player, born Cincinnati, OH, Jan 10, 1959.
Frank William Mahovlich, 60, Hockey Hall of Fame left wing, born Timmons, Ontario, Canada, Jan 10, 1938.
Willie Lee McCovey, 60, Baseball Hall of Fame first baseman, born Mobile, AL, Jan 10, 1938.
James Jerome (Jim) O'Toole, 61, former baseball player, born Chicago, IL, Jan 10, 1937.
Glenn Allen Robinson, Jr, 25, basketball player, born Gary, IN, Jan 10, 1973.
William Anthony (Bill) Toomey, 59, Olympic gold medal decathlete, born Philadelphia, PA, Jan 10, 1939.

JANUARY 11 — SUNDAY
Day 11 — 354 Remaining

SUPERBOWL CHAMPIONS THIS DATE
1970   Kansas City Chiefs

BEARGREASE SLED DOG MARATHON. Jan 11–16. Duluth, MN. To commemorate John Beargrease, a Chippewa sled-dog mail carrier along the North Shore of Lake Superior from 1887–1900. A 500-mile endurance race with mushers and dogs from the US and Canada. Sponsor: Grand Portage Chippewa. Est attendance: 10,000. For info: Beargrease, Box 500, Duluth, MN 55801. Phone: (218) 722-7631.

CAREY, MAX: BIRTH ANNIVERSARY. Jan 11, 1890. Max George Carey, Baseball Hall of Fame outfielder born Maximilian Carnarius at Terre Haute, IN. Carey left the seminary to play baseball where he was best known as a base stealer. He played 20 years with the Pittsburgh Pirates and the Brooklyn Dodgers. Inducted into the Hall of Fame in 1961. Died at Miami Beach, FL, May 30, 1976.

DESIGNATED HITTER ADOPTED: 25th ANNIVERSARY. Jan 11, 1973. The American League changed its playing rules to allow for the use of a designated hitter, one player to bat for the pitcher throughout the game without being required to play in the field. The rule was intended to boost offensive production and to allow better starting pitchers to remain in the game longer. (See also Apr 6.)

DRISCOLL, PADDY: BIRTH ANNIVERSARY. Jan 11, 1895. John Leo ("Paddy") Driscoll, Pro Football Hall of Fame player and coach, born at Evanston, IL. Driscoll played at Northwestern, served in the Navy and then turned pro, playing with the Chicago Cardinals and the Chicago Bears. He coached high school and college football and then joined George Halas's Bears staff, taking over for Halas during a brief retirement in 1956 and losing the NFL title game. Inducted into the Hall of Fame in 1965. Died at Chicago, IL, June 29, 1968.

FLICK, ELMER: BIRTH ANNIVERSARY. Jan 11, 1876. Elmer Harrison Flick, Baseball Hall of Fame outfielder born at Bedford, OH. Flick played 13 years in the major leagues and hit .315. After the 1907 season, the Detroit Tigers offered to trade Ty Cobb to the Cleveland Indians for Flick, but Cleveland refused. Inducted into the Hall of Fame in 1963. Died at Bedford, Jan 9, 1971.

KANSAS CITY WINS SUPER BOWL IV: ANNIVERSARY. Jan 11, 1970. The Kansas City Chiefs defeated the Minnesota Vikings, 23–7, to win Super Bowl IV. The Chiefs, 14-point underdogs, evened the AFL's Super Bowl record at 2–2 with their triumph. Kansas City was led by quarterback Len Dawson, named the game's Most Valuable Player.

NBA SILVER ANNIVERSARY TEAM: ANNIVERSARY. Jan 11, 1971. The National Basketball Association announced its Silver Anniversary team. Ten players were selected: Paul Arizin, Bob Cousy, Bob Davies, Joe Fulks, Sam Jones, George Mikan, Bob Pettit, Bill Russell, Dolph Schayes and Bill Sharman. The coach was Red Auerbach.

ROWE, SCHOOLBOY: BIRTH ANNIVERSARY. Jan 11, 1910. Lynwood Thomas ("Schoolboy") Rowe, baseball player and manager born at Waco, TX. Rowe won 24 games for the 1934 Detroit Tigers, winners of the American League pennant, and 16 when the Tigers won the pennant in 1940. An exciting pitcher and a good hitter with a childhood nickname that stuck, his career was shortened by a sore arm. Died at El Dorado, AR, Jan 8, 1961.

BIRTHDAYS TODAY

Tracy Caulkins, 35, Olympic gold medal swimmer, born Winona, MN, Jan 11, 1963.
Ben Daniel Crenshaw, 46, golfer, born Austin, TX, Jan 11, 1952.
Darryl Dawkins, 41, former basketball player, born Orlando, FL, Jan 11, 1957.
Christopher Joseph (Chris) Ford, 49, basketball coach and former player, born Atlantic City, NJ, Jan 11, 1949.
James Clement (Jim) McAndrew, 54, former baseball player, born Lost Nation, IA, Jan 11, 1944.
Wonderful Terrific (Wonder) Monds, III, 25, baseball player, born Fort Pierce, FL, Jan 11, 1973.

January 1998	S	M	T	W	T	F	S
					1	2	3
	4	5	6	7	8	9	10
	11	12	13	14	15	16	17
	18	19	20	21	22	23	24
	25	26	27	28	29	30	31

Donald Louis (Don) Mossi, 69, former baseball player, born St. Helena, CA, Jan 11, 1929.
Freddie Solomon, 45, former football player, born Sumter, SC, Jan 11, 1953.

JANUARY 12 — MONDAY
Day 12 — 353 Remaining

SUPERBOWL CHAMPIONS THIS DATE	
1969	New York Jets
1975	Pittsburgh Steelers

ALL-CANADA SHOW. Jan 12–14. State Fair Grounds, Indianapolis, IN. This consumer show allows individuals an opportunity to talk face-to-face with Canadian lodge representatives and outfitters to plan their hunting, fishing and adventure trips to Canada. For info: Rodney Schlafer, Show Dir, All-Canada Show, Bay-Lakes Mktg, Inc, 1889 Commerce Dr, De Pere, WI 54115. Phone: (414) 983-9800 or (800) 325-6290. Fax: (414) 983-9985. WWW: http://www.allcanada.com

CLEVELAND RAMS MOVE TO LA: ANNIVERSARY. Jan 12, 1946. Less than a month after the Cleveland Rams won their first NFL title, the league gave owner Dan Reeves permission to move the team to Los Angeles. In approving this franchise shift, the NFL became the first major professional sports league to put a team on the West Coast. Fans in Cleveland quickly embraced the Browns, a team in the new All-American Football Conference until the two leagues merged in 1950.

CRISLER, FRITZ: BIRTH ANNIVERSARY. Jan 12, 1899. Herbert Orrin ("Fritz") Crisler, college football coach and administrator born at Earlsville, IL. Crisler played several sports at the University of Chicago and then coached three sports after graduating. He moved to Minnesota, Princeton and Michigan in 1938. His teams won 71 games and one national championship in ten years as Crisler became known as an innovative coach and a tireless athletic director. Died at Ann Arbor, MI, Aug 19, 1982.

HARROUN, RAY: BIRTH ANNIVERSARY. Jan 12, 1879. Raymond (Ray) Harroun, auto racer, born at Spartansburg, PA. Harroun began racing cars in 1905 and capped his career by winning the first Indianapolis 500 in 1911. His average speed was 74.59 mph. Instead of driving with a mechanic on board, he used his invention, the rear view mirror, to help him see his opponents. Harroun also invented the automobile bumper. Died at Anderson, IN, Jan 19, 1968.

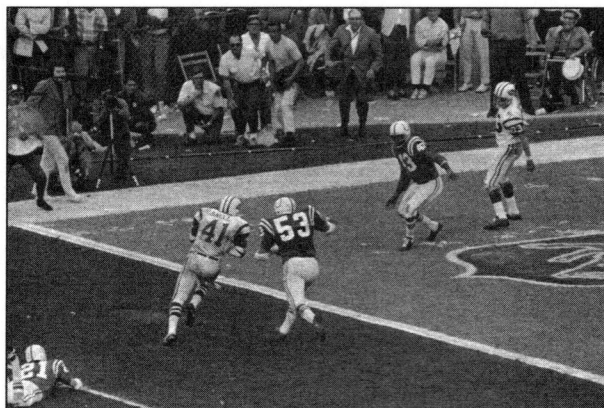

JETS WIN SUPER BOWL III: ANNIVERSARY. Jan 12, 1969. Overcoming their status as 17-point underdogs and

living up to quarterback Joe Namath's bold prediction, the New York Jets upset the Baltimore Colts, 16–7 in Super Bowl III. The Jets got a touchdown from fullback Matt Snell and three field goals from Jim Turner to become the first American Football League team to snatch a championship from an NFL team.

MAN WATCHERS WEEK. Jan 12–17. A week of appreciation for men who are well worth watching. List of activities available. Est attendance: 600. For info: Suzy Mallery, Suzy Mallery's Man Watchers Inc, 12308 Darlington Ave, Los Angeles, CA 90049. Phone: (310) 826-9101. Fax: (310) 820-3539.

MOON PHASE: FULL MOON. Jan 12. Moon enters Full Moon phase at 12:24 PM, EST.

PITTSBURGH WINS SUPER BOWL IX: ANNIVERSARY. Jan 12, 1975. The Pittsburgh Steelers defeated the Minnesota Vikings, 16–6, in Super Bowl IX. Led by their famed "Steel Curtain" defense, Pittsburgh held the Vikings to only 17 yards rushing. For the Steelers, it was their first Super Bowl victory and the first of four they would win over a six-year period.

SCHAYES SCORES 15,000 POINTS: ANNIVERSARY. Jan 12, 1960. Two years to the day after he became the NBA's leading career scorer, Dolph Schayes of the Syracuse Nationals became the first NBA player to score 15,000 points. He finished his career in 1963–64 with 19,249 points.

TWO-POINT CONVERSION: 40th ANNIVERSARY. Jan 12, 1958. The NCAA football rules committee made the first change in scoring rules since 1912 by introducing the optional two-point conversion. Under the rule, teams could kick for one point or run or pass for two points after touchdown.

CHASE'S SPORTSQUOTE OF THE DAY

"We're going to win Sunday. I guarantee it." — Joe Namath, three days before Super Bowl III

BIRTHDAYS TODAY

Scott David Burrell, 27, basketball player and former minor league baseball player, born New Haven, CT, Jan 12, 1971.

Casey Todd Candaele, 37, former baseball player, born Lompoc, CA, Jan 12, 1961.

Ulf Dahlen, 31, hockey player, born Ostersund, Sweden, Jan 12, 1967.

Joe Frazier, 54, former heavyweight champion boxer, born Beaufort, SC, Jan 12, 1944.

Michael Allen (Mike) Marshall, 38, former baseball player, born Libertyville, IL, Jan 12, 1960.

Michael Campanella (Campy) Russell, 46, former basketball player, born Jackson, TN, Jan 12, 1952.

Jocelyn Thibault, 23, hockey player, born Montreal, Quebec, Canada, Jan 12, 1975.

Jacques Dominique Wilkins, 38, basketball player, born Paris, France, Jan 12, 1960.

JANUARY 13 — TUESDAY
Day 13 — 352 Remaining

SUPERBOWL CHAMPIONS THIS DATE
1974   Miami Dolphins

CHAMBERLAIN SCORES 73 POINTS: ANNIVERSARY. Jan 13, 1962. Center Wilt Chamberlain of the Philadelphia Warriors set an NBA regular season record by scoring 73 points in a game against Chicago. Chamberlain had scored 78 points the previous December, but that game had gone into three overtime periods.

NCAA ADOPTS PROP 48: ANNIVERSARY. Jan 13, 1986. NCAA member schools voted overwhelmingly in convention to adopt Proposition 48, a controversial attempt to raise the academic performance of student-athletes. Prop 48 required incoming freshmen to score 700 or more on the Scholastic Aptitude Test (SAT) or 15 on the American College Testing (ACT) exam or graduate from high school with a 2.0 grade point average in order to be eligible for athletics during freshman year.

OLDEST GOLFER TO GET HOLE-IN-ONE: ANNIVERSARY. Jan 13, 1985. Otto Bucher of Switzerland became the oldest golfer to record a hole-in-one when he aced the 12th hole at a golf course in Spain. Bucher was 99 years old.

SCHULTE, FRED: BIRTH ANNIVERSARY. Jan 13, 1901. Fred William Schulte, baseball player born Fred William Schult at Belvidere, IL. Schulte was a dependable outfielder from 1927 through 1937. He hit .333 in the 1933 World Series for the New York Giants. Died at Belvidere, May 20, 1983.

BIRTHDAYS TODAY

Robert Herbert (Bob) Forsch, 48, former baseball player, born Sacramento, CA, Jan 13, 1950.

Thomas Joseph (Tom) Gola, 65, Basketball Hall of Fame forward, born Philadelphia, PA, Jan 13, 1933.

Kelly Stephen Hrudey, 37, hockey player, born Edmonton, Alberta, Canada, Jan 13, 1961.

James Kent Hull, 37, former football player, born Pontotoc, MS, Jan 13, 1961.

Nikolai Khabibulin, 25, hockey player, born Sverdlovsk, USSR, Jan 13, 1973.

Kevin Darnell Mitchell, 36, baseball player, born San Diego, CA, Jan 13, 1962.

Gwen Verdon, 72, actress (*Damn Yankees*), born Los Angeles, CA, Jan 13, 1926.

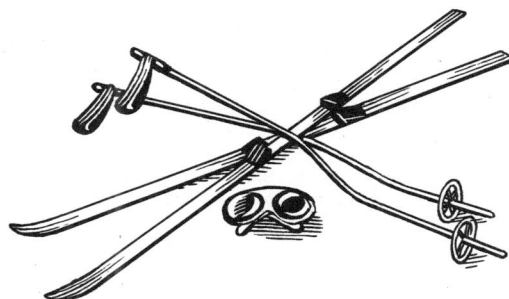

JANUARY 14 — WEDNESDAY
Day 14 — 351 Remaining

SUPERBOWL CHAMPIONS THIS DATE
1968   Green Bay Packers
1973   Miami Dolphins

ASPEN/SNOWMASS WINTERSKOL. Jan 14–18. Snowmass Village, CO. A winter carnival–celebrating winter and having winter fun. Ski and snowshoe races, Mad Hatter's Ball, ski splash, sculpture contest and torchlight parade. Est attendance: 5,000. For info: Randi Fox, PR, Snowmass Resort Assn, Box 5566, Snowmass Village, CO 81615. Phone: (800) SNOW-MASS. WWW: http://www.snowmassvillage.com

BOB HOPE CHRYSLER CLASSIC. Jan 14–18. Palm Springs, CA. A PGA Tour tournament played at 90 holes over four courses. Est attendance: 100,000. For info: Pat Bennett, PR and Production, Bob Hope Chrysler Classic, 39000 Bob Hope Dr, Rancho Mirage, CA 92270. Phone: (619) 346-8184 or (888) MRB-HOPE. Fax: (619) 346-6329. Email: info@bhcc.com. WWW: http://www.bhcc.com

BREWER, CHET: BIRTH ANNIVERSARY. Jan 14, 1907. Chester Arthur (Chet) Brewer, baseball player and manager born at Leavenworth, KS. Brewer pitched in the Negro Leagues, playing 14 seasons with the Kansas City Monarchs and five with the Cleveland Buckeyes. After retiring, he scouted for the Pittsburgh Pirates. Died at Los Angeles, CA, Mar 26, 1990.

GREEN BAY WINS SECOND STRAIGHT SUPER BOWL: 30th ANNIVERSARY. Jan 14, 1968. The Green Bay Packers won their second straight Super Bowl, defeating the Oakland Raiders, 33–14. Packers quarterback Bart Starr completed 13 of 24 passes for 202 yards and one touchdown and was named the game's Most Valuable Player.

JOLLEY, SMEAD: BIRTH ANNIVERSARY. Jan 14, 1902. Smead Jolley, baseball player born at Wesson, AR. Jolley played only four years in the majors, but in the minors he hit 334 home runs and twice drove in more than 180 runs. Died at Alameda, CA, Nov 17, 1991.

MIAMI COMPLETES UNDEFEATED SEASON: 25th ANNIVERSARY. Jan 14, 1973. The Miami Dolphins became the only team in NFL history to complete a season undefeated and untied by beating the Washington Redskins, 14–7, in Super Bowl VII. Miami finished the season 17–0.

NASHVILLE BOAT AND SPORTS SHOW. Jan 14–18. Nashville Convention Center, Nashville, TN. 12th annual show. The mid-South's largest selection of boats, accessories and fishing gear as well as numerous resort and travel exhibits. Informative boating and fishing seminars. For info: NMMA Boat Shows, 600 Third Ave, 23rd Fl, New York, NY 10016. Phone: (314) 567-0020. Fax: (314) 567-1810.

PHILADELPHIA BOAT SHOW. Jan 14–18. Civic Center, Philadelphia, PA. 62nd annual show features more than 600 power boats, engines and accessories from all major manufacturers, plus informative boating and fishing seminars. Est attendance: 65,000. For info: Jim Ranieri, Natl Marine Mfrs Assn, 514 Harriet Lane, Havertown, PA 19083. Phone: (610) 449-9910. Fax: (610) 449-1143.

SHIBE, BEN: DEATH ANNIVERSARY. Jan 14, 1922. Benjamin Franklin (Ben) Shibe, baseball executive born at Philadelphia, PA, 1838. Shibe built the Reach Sporting Goods Company, inventing the two-piece baseball cover and the cork-center baseball. He joined Connie Mack to found the Philadelphia Athletics in 1901. Died at Philadelphia.

STONEHAM BUYS GIANTS: ANNIVERSARY. Jan 14, 1919. Charles Stoneham, John McGraw and Francis X. McQuade bought the New York Giants from Charles Hempstead. The Stoneham family controlled the Giants for the next 56 years and moved them to San Francisco after the 1957 season.

January	S	M	T	W	T	F	S
1998					1	2	3
	4	5	6	7	8	9	10
	11	12	13	14	15	16	17
	18	19	20	21	22	23	24
	25	26	27	28	29	30	31

BIRTHDAYS TODAY

David Wilson (Dave) Campbell, 56, broadcaster and former baseball player, born Manistee, MI, Jan 14, 1942.
Terry Jay Forster, 46, former baseball player, born Sioux Falls, SD, Jan 14, 1952.
Swen Erick Nater, 48, former basketball player, born Denhelder, Netherlands, Jan 14, 1950.
Sergei Nemchinov, 34, hockey player, born Moscow, USSR, Jan 14, 1964.
Carlos Perez, 27, baseball player, born Nigua, Dominican Republic, Jan 14, 1971.
Wilfred Charles ("Sonny") Siebert, 61, former baseball player, born St. Marys, MO, Jan 14, 1937.
Gene Alden Washington, 51, former football player, born Tuscaloosa, AL, Jan 14, 1947.

JANUARY 15 — THURSDAY
Day 15 — 350 Remaining

SUPERBOWL CHAMPIONS THIS DATE	
1967	Green Bay Packers
1978	Dallas Cowboys

ALL-CANADA SHOW. Jan 15–18. Pheasant Run Mega Center, St. Charles, IL. This consumer show allows individuals an opportunity to talk face-to-face with Canadian lodge representatives and outfitters to plan their hunting, fishing and adventure trips to Canada. For info: Rodney Schlafer, Show Dir, All-Canada Show, Bay-Lakes Mktg, Inc, 1889 Commerce Dr, De Pere, WI 54115. Phone: (414) 983-9800 or (800) 325-6290. Fax: (414) 983-9985. WWW: http://www.allcanada.com

BAKER, HOBEY: BIRTH ANNIVERSARY. Jan 15, 1892. Hobart Amory Hare (Hobey) Baker, football and hockey player born at Wissahickon, PA. Baker attended Princeton University and was proclaimed one of the greatest athletes of his time. He captained the hockey team for two years, playing the rover position, and the football team for one season. After graduation in 1914, he played amateur hockey until enlisting in the army in 1917. Died in an airplane crash at Toul, France, Dec 21, 1918. The DeCathalon Athletic Club of Bloomington, MN, annually presents the Hobey Baker Award to the country's top college hockey player.

CHAMPIONSHIP SNOWMOBILE DERBY. Jan 15–18. Eagle River, WI. This annual professional snowmobile race is one of the largest gatherings of "sledders" in the world. Fans from all over the globe watch as more than 300 racers compete. 35th annual. For info phone: (715) 479-4424.

CHAPMAN, RAY: BIRTH ANNIVERSARY. Jan 15, 1891. Raymond Johnson (Ray) Chapman, baseball player born at Beaver Dam, KY. The first major league baseball fatality, Chapman was beaned by New York Yankees pitcher Carl Mays on Aug 16, 1920, and died at New York, Aug 17, 1920.

DAVIES, BOB: BIRTH ANNIVERSARY. Jan 15, 1920. Robert Edris (Bob) Davies, Basketball Hall of Fame guard born at Harrisburg, PA. Davies was an outstanding player in the 1940s and early 1950s. He won the MVP award in the National Basketball League in 1946–47. Inducted into the Hall of Fame in 1969. Died at Hilton Head, SC, Apr 22, 1990.

GENEWICH, JOE: BIRTH ANNIVERSARY. Jan 15, 1897. Joseph Edward (Joe) Genewich, baseball player born at Elmira, NY. Genewich pitched nine seasons in the major leagues after playing neither in college nor the minor leagues. Died at Lockport, NY, Dec 21, 1985.

INTERNATIONAL FINALS RODEO. Jan 15–17. State Fair Arena, Oklahoma City, OK. The top 15 money-winning IPRA cowboys and cowgirls compete for world championships in seven events. Prize money more than $250,000. Trade show, dances, bucking stock sale. Est attendance: 40,000. For info: Jane Kirton, International Finals Rodeo, PO Box 83377, Oklahoma City, OK 73148. Phone: (405) 235-6540. Fax: (405) 235-6577.

LONGHORN WORLD CHAMPIONSHIP RODEO. Jan 15–18. Tulsa Convention Center, Tulsa, OK. More than 450 cowboys and cowgirls compete in seven professional contests ranging from bronco riding to bull riding for top prize money and world championship points. Featuring colorful opening pageantry and Big, Bad BONUS Bulls. Major final weekend Centennial event for Tulsa's year-long Centennial Celebration. 8th annual. Est attendance: 16,000. For info: W Bruce Lehrke, Pres, Longhorn World Chmpshp Rodeo Inc, PO Box 70159, Nashville, TN 37207. Phone: (615) 876-1016. Fax: (615) 876-4685. Email: lhrodeo@idt.net. WWW: http://longhornrodeo.com

RUCKER, JOHNNY: BIRTH ANNIVERSARY. Jan 15, 1917. John Joel (Johnny) Rucker, baseball player born at Crabapple, GA. Rucker was the nephew of pitcher Nap Rucker and once graced the cover of *Life* magazine. Died at Moultrie, GA, Aug 7, 1985.

SOLAITA, TONY: BIRTH ANNIVERSARY. Jan 15, 1947. Tolia (Tony) Solaita, baseball player born at Nuuyli, American Samoa. Solaita, the only native Samoan to play major league baseball, was shot to death in a dispute over land. Died at Tafuna, American Samoa, Feb 10, 1990.

SUPER BOWL I: ANNIVERSARY. Jan 15, 1967. The Green Bay Packers won the first NFL-AFL World Championship Game, defeating the Kansas City Chiefs, 35–10, at the Los Angeles Memorial Coliseum. Packers quarterback Bart Starr completed 16 of 23 passes for 250 yards and was named the game's Most Valuable Player. Pro football's title game later became known as the Super Bowl.

BIRTHDAYS TODAY

Delino Lamont DeShields, 29, baseball player, born Seaford, DE, Jan 15, 1969.
Robert Anthony (Bobby) Grich, 49, former baseball player, born Muskegon, MI, Jan 15, 1949.
Stephen Joseph (Steve) Gromek, 78, former baseball player, born Hamtramck, MI, Jan 15, 1920.
Michael Grant (Mike) Marshall, 55, former baseball player, born Adrian, MI, Jan 15, 1943.
Steven Rance Mulliniks, 42, former baseball player, born Tulare, CA, Jan 15, 1956.

Randy Lee White, 45, Pro Football Hall of Fame defensive tackle, born Wilmington, DE, Jan 15, 1953.

☆   ☆   ☆

JANUARY 16 — FRIDAY
Day 16 — 349 Remaining

SUPERBOWL CHAMPIONS THIS DATE
1972   Dallas Cowboys

COLLINS, JIMMY: BIRTH ANNIVERSARY. Jan 16, 1870. James Joseph (Jimmy) Collins, Baseball Hall of Fame third baseman born at Buffalo, NY. Collins was an innovative fielder who modernized third base play. He shifted in or back depending on the situation and challenged bunters by fielding their bunts barehanded and throwing them out. Collins played in the majors for 14 years and became the first manager to win a World Series (Boston, 1903). Inducted into the Hall of Fame in 1945. Died at Buffalo, NY, Mar 6, 1943.

DALLAS WINS SUPER BOWL VI: ANNIVERSARY. Jan 16, 1972. The Dallas Cowboys won the first Super Bowl in their history by defeating the Miami Dolphins, 24–3, in Super Bowl VI. Dallas was led by quarterback Roger Staubach, named the game's Most Valuable Player.

DEAN, DIZZY: BIRTH ANNIVERSARY. Jan 16, 1911. Jay Hanna ("Dizzy") Dean, Baseball Hall of Fame pitcher born at Lucas, AR. Following his baseball career, Dean established himself as a radio and TV sports announcer and commentator, becoming famous for his innovative delivery. "He slud into third," reported Dizzy, who on another occasion explained that "Me and Paul [baseball player brother Paul "Daffy" Dean] . . . didn't get much education." Died at Reno, NV, July 17, 1974.

FIRST FIVE-ON-FIVE BASKETBALL GAME: ANNIVERSARY. Jan 16, 1896. The University of Chicago men's basketball team defeated an Iowa YMCA team, 15–12, in the first game played with five players on each side. Previously, games had been played with nine on each side.

GREAT ST. LOUIS GOLF SHOW. Jan 16–18. Trans World Dome, St Louis, MO. A high-quality consumer trade show for the golf industry that showcases new products, purchasing opportunities, interactive entertainment and informative features. Est attendance: 25,000. For Info: David Sinykin, David Toushin & Assoc, 5775 Wayzata Blvd, Ste 850, Minneapolis, MN 55416. Phone: (612) 593-0353.

JIMMY THE GREEK FIRED: 10th ANNIVERSARY. Jan 16, 1988. Jimmy ("The Greek") Snider, a pro football gambling expert employed by CBS, was fired by the network because of racially insensitive remarks he made the previous day during an interview with WRC-TV in Washington, DC.

NEVADA STATE COWBOY ACTION SHOOTING CHAMPIONSHIPS. Jan 16–18. Pahrump, NV. Contestants dress in clothing from pre-1900 and use lever action or pump action guns also from pre-1900 or replicas. Western dramas are acted out using live ammunition. For local info: (702) 564-7762. For Nevada Tourism: Nevada Commission on Tourism, Capitol Complex, Carson City, NV 89710. Phone: (702) 687-4322 or (800) 227-0774. Fax: (702) 687-6779.

NO POINTS AFTER TOUCHDOWN?: ANNIVERSARY. Jan 16, 1952. The NFL Rules Committee voted 7–5 to eliminate points after touchdown and to make touchdowns worth an automatic seven points instead of six. Fortunately for traditionalists, a rules change required a vote of at least 10–2 for passage, so the proposal failed.

SEATTLE BOAT SHOW. Jan 16–25. The Kingdome, Seattle, WA. Huge display of new boats, accessories and services. A second show, Seattle Boats Afloat, is scheduled for Aug 1998. Large boats (35 ft or longer) on display in Puget Sound with over 70 accessories dealers on land. Call NW Marine Trade Assn for specific dates. Est attendance: 90,000. For info: NW Marine Trade Assn, 1900 N Northlake Way, #233, Seattle, WA 98103. Phone: (206) 634-0911. Fax: (206) 632-0078.

SEWARD POLAR BEAR JUMP FESTIVAL. Jan 16–18. Resurrection Bay, Seward, AK. Volunteers collect pledges to jump into bay in costumes. Festivities include goofy golf tournament, parade, dog weight pull, dog sled race, Polar Bear Arts and Crafts Fair, skijoring, ugly fish toss, Bachelor/Bachelorette Auction, ice bowling, talent show, Seafood Feed and much more. Benefits local nonprofit organizations and the American Cancer Society. The actual "Plunge" takes place on Saturday, Jan 17. Est attendance: 2,500. For info: Seward Polar Bear Jump Fest, PO Box 386, Seward, AK 99664. Phone: (907) 224-4049. Fax: (907) 224-4085.

WISCONSIN DELLS FLAKE OUT FESTIVAL. Jan 16–18. Tommy Bartlett Show Site, Wisconsin Dells, WI. Wisconsin sanctioned snow sculpting competition. Winners will compete in the National Snow Sculpting Competition. Other activities include ice-carving competition, snowmobile races, sleigh rides, ice skating and glowing hot-air balloons on Saturday evening and much more. Est attendance: 20,000. For info: Wisc Dells Visitor and Conv Bureau, PO Box 390, Wisconsin Dells, WI 53965. Phone: (800) 223-3557. WWW: http://www.wisdells.com

---

SPORTSCHASER OF THE DAY

"Dizzy" Dean was baptized "Jay Hanna" Dean? What was the given name of his brother "Daffy"?

BIRTHDAYS TODAY

Stephen Charles (Steve) Balboni, 41, former baseball player, born Brockton, MA, Jan 16, 1957.

		S	M	T	W	T	F	S
January						1	2	3
1998		4	5	6	7	8	9	10
		11	12	13	14	15	16	17
		18	19	20	21	22	23	24
		25	26	27	28	29	30	31

Mark Anthony Collins, 34, football player, born San Bernardino, CA, Jan 16, 1964.
Anthony Joseph (A.J.) Foyt, Jr, 63, former auto racer, born Houston, TX, Jan 16, 1935.
Ronald Samuel (Ron) Herbel, 60, former baseball player, born Denver, CO, Jan 16, 1938.
Donald James (Don) MacLean, 28, basketball player, born Palo Alto, CA, Jan 16, 1970.
Jack Burns McDowell, 32, baseball player, born Van Nuys, CA, Jan 16, 1966.

JANUARY 17 — SATURDAY
Day 17 — 348 Remaining

AFRMA RAT AND MOUSE SHOW. Jan 17 (or Jan 24). Wedgeworth Elementary School Auditorium, Hacienda Heights, CA. American Fancy Rat and Mouse Association show exhibits rats and mice of "fancy" species that make good pets. For info: AFRMA, 9230 64th St, Riverside, CA 92509-5924. Phone: (909) 685-2350. Fax: (818) 592-6319. Email: craigr@afrma.org. WWW: http://www.afrma.org/afrma

BRONCOS BEAT BROWNS: ANNIVERSARY. Jan 17, 1988. The Denver Broncos won their second consecutive AFC championship by defeating the Cleveland Browns, 38–33, at Denver's Mile High Stadium. Denver quarterback John Elway threw three touchdown passes, and Jeremiah Castille stripped the ball from Cleveland's Earnest Byner late in the game to preserve the victory.

CANADA: MINDEN SLED DOG DERBY. Jan 17–18. Minden, Ontario. World's largest limited-class speed sled-dog derby attracts top mushers from across North America. Est attendance: 7,000. For info: Minden Sled Dog Derby, Box 97, Minden, Ont, Canada K0M 2K0. Phone: (705) 286-1288. Fax: (705) 286-4768. Email: mindentimes@halhinet.on.ca.

CANADA: TORONTO INTERNATIONAL BOAT SHOW. Jan 17–25. Automotive and Coliseum Building, Exhibition Place, Toronto, Ontario. 40th annual show. More than 1,000 new boats make this Canada's largest boat shopping spree. Special deals on a wide selection including inflatables, personal watercraft, fishing boats, cruisers and sailboats. Informative boating and fishing seminars. For info: NMMA Canada, PO Box 38, 370 King St W, Ste 804, Toronto, Ont, Canada M5V 1J9. Phone: (416) 591-6772. Fax: (416) 591-3582.

CHICAGO'S WINDY CITY JITTERBUG CLUB DANCE. Jan 17 (also Jan 31) (tentative dates). Franklin Park, IL. Dance to the music of the '50s, '60s and more. Dances held twice a month at the Franklin Park American Legion Hall. Est attendance: 200. For info: CWCJC, PO Box 713, Franklin Park, IL 60131.

EARTHQUAKE DISRUPTS NBA: ANNIVERSARY. Jan 17, 1994. The Los Angeles earthquake forced postponement of a scheduled NBA game between the Lakers and the Sacramento Kings at the Great Western Forum. Earthquake damage forced the Clippers to move a pair of games from the Los Angeles Sports Arena. Their Jan 21 game against the Cleveland Cavaliers was played at the Forum, and their Jan 27 game against the New York Knicks was moved to The Pond in Anaheim.

FRANKLIN, BEN: BIRTH ANNIVERSARY. Jan 17, 1706. Benjamin (Ben) Franklin, swimmer, printer, diplomat and patriot born at Boston, MA. Franklin taught himself to swim at an early age and swam most of his life for exercise. He was often called upon to demonstrate his skills and usually did so willingly. In 1968, the International Swimming Hall of Fame recognized Franklin as an Outstanding Contributor to the sport. Died at Philadelphia, PA, Apr 17, 1790.

LEIBER, HANK: BIRTH ANNIVERSARY. Jan 17, 1911. Henry Edward (Hank) Leiber, baseball player born at Phoenix, AZ. Leiber played ten years as a major league outfielder for the New York Giants and Chicago Cubs. Died at Tucson, AZ, Nov 8, 1993.

PAUL BUNYAN SLED DOG RACES, WEIGHT PULL, SKIJORING AND MUTT RACES. Jan 17–18. Fair Grounds, Bemidji, MN. 26th annual competition. For info: Bemidji Area Chamber of Commerce, Carol Olson, Box 850, Bemidji, MN 56619-0850. Phone: (800) 458-2223.

PLANTE, JACQUES: BIRTH ANNIVERSARY. Jan 17, 1929. Jacques Plante, Hockey Hall of Fame goaltender, born at Mont-Carmel, Que, Canada. Plante won five consecutive Vezina Trophies and led the Montreal Canadiens to five consecutive Stanley Cups (1956–60). He was the first goalie to wear a face mask in a game. Inducted into the Hall of Fame in 1978. Died at Geneva, Switzerland, Feb 26, 1986.

PRO GOLFERS MEET TO FORM ASSOCIATION: ANNIVERSARY. Jan 17, 1916. A group of 35 New York area golf professionals met for lunch at the Taplow Club, hosted by department store magnate Rodman Wanamaker. They discussed forming a national organization to promote interest in the game and elevate the status of the professional golfer. The group appointed an organizing committee of seven to work on a constitution that was approved on Apr 16, forming the Professional Golfers' Association of America.

SENIOR BOWL FOOTBALL GAME. Jan 17. Ladd Memorial Stadium, Mobile, AL. All-star football game featuring the nation's top collegiate seniors on teams coached by NFL coaching staffs. Proceeds go to charities. Est attendance: 40,700. For info: Vic Knight, PR Dir, Senior Bowl, 63 S Royal St, Ste 406, Mobile, AL 36602. Phone: (334) 438-2276. Fax: (334) 432-0409. Email: srbowl@dibbs.net. WWW: http://www.dibbs.net/seniorbowl/

TIP-UP TOWN USA. Jan 17–18. (Also Jan 24–25.) Houghton Lake, MI. Winter festival featuring ice-fishing contests; softball on ice; tug-of-war games; Polar Bear Dip; a grand parade; Ferris wheel, helicopter, pony rides; concessions. Annually, the third and fourth weekends in January. Est attendance: 58,000. For info: Tim Romanowski, Info Mgr, Chamber of Commerce, 1625 W Houghton Lake Dr, Houghton Lake, MI 48629. Phone: (800) 248-5253.

USFTL NATIONAL FLAG AND TOUCH FOOTBALL CHAMPIONSHIPS. Jan 17–18. Orlando, FL. National championship for flag and touch football players in the USA. A double elimination tournament lasting two days. Adult men and women, youth, co-rec, and 35-and-over classifications. Annually, the weekend before the NFL Super Bowl. Est attendance: 5,000. For info: United States Flag/Touch Football League (USFTL), 7709 Ohio St, Mentor, OH 44060. Phone: (216) 974-8735. Fax: (216) 974-8441. Email: usftl@interax.com. WWW: http://www.e-sports.com/usftl

☆   ☆   ☆

BIRTHDAYS TODAY

Muhammad Ali (born Cassius Marcellus Clay, Jr), 56, former heavyweight champion boxer, born Louisville, KY, Jan 17, 1942.

Charles Theodore (Chili) Davis, 38, baseball player, born Kingston, Jamaica, Jan 17, 1960.

James Earl Jones, 67, actor (*The Great White Hope*, *Field of Dreams*), born Tate County, MS, Jan 17, 1931.

Kipchoge (Kip) Keino, 58, Olympic gold medal long distance runner, born Kipsamo, Kenya, Jan 17, 1940.

Darrell Ray Porter, 46, former baseball player, born Joplin, MO, Jan 17, 1952.

Jeremy Roenick, 28, hockey player, born Boston, MA, Jan 17, 1970.

Sylvain Turgeon, 33, former hockey player, born Noranda, Quebec, Canada, Jan 17, 1965.

Donald William (Don) Zimmer, 67, former baseball manager and player, born Cincinnati, OH, Jan 17, 1931.

JANUARY 18 — SUNDAY

Day 18 — 347 Remaining

SUPERBOWL CHAMPIONS THIS DATE
1976   Pittsburgh Steelers

CHAMPION RACE HORSE FOUND: ANNIVERSARY. Jan 18, 1941. The great thoroughbred racer Epinard was found by Paris police after being lost for several months during the Nazi occupation. Epinard was being used to make deliveries.

FIRST BLACK PLAYER IN NHL: 40th ANNIVERSARY. Jan 18, 1958. Willie O'Ree became the first black player in the National Hockey League when he played for the Boston Bruins in a game against the Montreal Canadiens. Boston won, 3–0.

FLOOD, CURT: BIRTH ANNIVERSARY. Jan 18, 1938. Curtis Charles (Curt) Flood, baseball player born at Houston, TX. Flood was one of baseball's best centerfielders in the 1960s, batting .293 over 15 seasons and playing spectacular defense. After the 1969 season, he refused to accept a trade from the St. Louis Cardinals to the Philadelphia Phillies. "I am not a piece of property to be bought and sold irrespective of my wishes," he said in a letter to Commissioner Bowie Kuhn. The resulting lawsuit went to the Supreme Court where Flood lost. But his stand, taken because he did not want to switch teams, paved the way for the end of baseball's reserve clause and the advent of free agency. Died at Los Angeles, CA, Jan 20, 1997.

McGOWAN, BILL: BIRTH ANNIVERSARY. Jan 18, 1896. William Aloysius (Bill) McGowan, Baseball Hall of Fame umpire born at Wilmington, DE. McGowan was arguably the best umpire in baseball history over his 30-year career, 1925 to 1954. He was selected to umpire the first All-Star game in 1933 and the first-ever American League playoff in 1948, plus eight World Series. Inducted into the Hall of Fame in 1992. Died at Silver Springs, MD, Dec 9, 1954.

METHODIST HEALTH CARE HOUSTON MARATHON. Jan 18. Houston, TX. 26th annual citywide race in conjunction with the Methodist Health Care Health & Fitness Exposition (Jan 16–17). Est attendance: 7,000. For info: Greg D. Goss, 720 N Post Oak Rd, #335, Houston, TX 77024. Phone: (713) 957-3453. Fax: (713) 957-3406. Email: marathon@ghgcorp.com.

PITTSBURGH WINS SUPER BOWL X: ANNIVERSARY. Jan 18, 1976. The Pittsburgh Steelers won their second consecutive Super Bowl, defeating the Dallas Cowboys, 21–17, in Super Bowl X. Pittsburgh wide receiver Lynn Swann was named the game's Most Valuable Player.

TEXAS STATE CHAMPIONSHIP DOMINO TOURNAMENT. Jan 18. Knights of Columbus Hall, Hallettsville, TX. Determines the "partner domino" champions in Texas. Est attendance: 1,700. For info: Knights of Columbus, Tommy Grahmann, Chair, Box 383, Hallettsville, TX 77964. Phone: (512) 798-2181.

BIRTHDAYS TODAY

Brady Kevin Anderson, 34, baseball player, born Silver Spring, MD, Jan 18, 1964.

Kevin Costner, 43, actor (*Field of Dreams, Bull Durham, Tin Cup*), born Compton, CA, Jan 18, 1955.

Mark Douglas Messier, 37, hockey player, born Edmonton, Alberta, Canada, Jan 18, 1961.

Joseph Paul (Joe) Schmidt, 66, former football coach and Pro Football Hall of Fame linebacker, born Mt. Oliver, PA, Jan 18, 1932.

JANUARY 19 — MONDAY

Day 19 — 346 Remaining

CHASE'S SPORTSQUOTE OF THE DAY

"Professional golfers of the Caucasian race, over the age of eighteen years, residing in North or South America, and who have served at least five years in the profession (either in the employ of a golf club in the capacity of a professional or in the employ of a professional as his assistant) shall be eligible for membership." — PGA Constitution (1943-1959)

ALL-CANADA SHOW. Jan 19–21. Indoor Sports Center, Rockford, IL. This consumer show allows individuals an opportunity to talk face-to-face with Canadian lodge representatives and outfitters to plan their hunting, fishing and adventure trips to Canada. For info: Rodney Schlafer, Show Dir, All-Canada Show, Bay-Lakes Mktg, Inc, 1889 Commerce Dr, Depere, WI 54115. Phone: (414) 983-9800 or (800) 325-6290. Fax: (414) 983-9985. WWW: http://www.allcanada.com

AUSTRALIA: AUSTRALIAN OPEN. Jan 19–Feb 1. National Tennis Centre, Flinders Park, Melbourne, Australia. The national tennis championships of Australia with competition in men's and women's singles and men's, women's and mixed doubles. One of the sport's Grand Slam events.

COLLEGE BASKETBALL TRIPLEHEADER: ANNIVERSARY. Jan 19, 1931. Six college basketball teams played a tripleheader at New York's Madison Square Garden, the first time the sport was played in a large arena instead of a small gym. In the tripleheader, Columbia University beat Fordham University, 26–18, Manhattan College defeated New York University, 16–14, and St. John's University beat City College of New York, 17–8.

FIRST COLLEGE HOCKEY GAME: 100th ANNIVERSARY. Jan 19, 1898. The first college ice hockey game ever played saw Brown University defeat Harvard University, 6–0. Fifty years later, the NCAA staged its first college hockey championship.

GANDIL, CHICK: BIRTH ANNIVERSARY. Jan 19, 1887. Arnold ("Chick") Gandil, baseball player born at St. Paul, MN. Gandil played first base for the infamous Black Sox and was one of the eight players banned for their involvement in the conspiracy to fix the 1919 World Series. Died at Calistoga, CA, Dec 13, 1970.

KING, MARTIN LUTHER, JR: BIRTHDAY OBSERVED. Jan 19. Public Law 98-144 designates the third Monday in January as an annual legal public holiday observing the birth of Martin Luther King, Jr. First observed in 1986.

	S	M	T	W	T	F	S
January 1998					1	2	3
	4	5	6	7	8	9	10
	11	12	13	14	15	16	17
	18	19	20	21	22	23	24
	25	26	27	28	29	30	31

PGA ADMITS BLACKS: ANNIVERSARY. Jan 19, 1952. The Professional Golfers Association of America amended its rules to allow black golfers to participate in tournaments.

UCLA STREAK SNAPPED: ANNIVERSARY. Jan 19, 1974. The longest winning streak in college basketball history came to an end as Notre Dame defeated UCLA, 71–70, to snap the Bruins's 88-game reign. Down by 11 points with less than four minutes to play, the Irish took the lead at 0:29 on Dwight Clay's jump shot from the corner.

WILKENS DOUBLE MILESTONE: ANNIVERSARY. Jan 19, 1985. Lenny Wilkens became the first person in NBA history to play and coach in 1,000 games as his Seattle Supersonics defeated the Cleveland Cavaliers, 106–105. Wilkens had played in 1,077 games in a career that ended in 1975.

BIRTHDAYS TODAY

Michael Adams, 35, basketball player, born Hartford, CT, Jan 19, 1963.

Ottis Jerome Anderson, 41, former football player, born West Palm Beach, FL, Jan 19, 1957.

Sylvain Cote, 32, hockey player, born Quebec City, Quebec, Canada, Jan 19, 1966.

Steven L. (Steve) DeBerg, 44, former football player, born Oakland, CA, Jan 19, 1954.

Stefan Edberg, 32, former tennis player, born Vastervik, Sweden, Jan 19, 1966.

Walter Jones, 24, football player, born Aliceville, AL, Jan 19, 1974.

Lucien James (Luc) Longley, 29, basketball player, born Melbourne, Australia, Jan 19, 1969.

Jonathan Trumpbour (Jon) Matlack, 48, former baseball player, born West Chester, PA, Jan 19, 1950.

Phillip Joseph (Phil) Nevin, 27, baseball player, born Fullerton, CA, Jan 19, 1971.

Daniel Edward (Dan) Reeves, 54, football coach and former player, born Rome, GA, Jan 19, 1944.

Christopher Andrew (Chris) Sabo, 36, former baseball player, born Detroit, MI, Jan 19, 1962.

Tiaina ("Junior") Seau, Jr, 29, football player, born San Diego, CA, Jan 19, 1969.

Jeff Van Gundy, 36, basketball coach, born Hemet, CA, Jan 19, 1962.

Tyrone Wheatley, 26, football player, born Inkster, MI, Jan 19, 1972.

JANUARY 20 — TUESDAY

Day 20 — 345 Remaining

SUPERBOWL CHAMPIONS THIS DATE

1980	Pittsburgh Steelers
1985	San Francisco 49ers

BILLS WIN AFC TITLE: ANNIVERSARY. Jan 20, 1991. The Buffalo Bills won the first of their record four consecutive AFC titles by overwhelming the Los Angeles Raiders, 51–3. Buffalo went on to lose Super Bowl XXV to the New York Giants, 20–19.

DITKA NAMED BEARS COACH: ANNIVERSARY. Jan 20, 1982. The Chicago Bears named former tight end Mike Ditka head coach. In 11 seasons, Ditka won 106 regular-season games and led the Bears to victory in Super Bowl XX.

ECKERT, SPIKE: BIRTH ANNIVERSARY. Jan 20, 1909. William Dole ("Spike") Eckert, baseball executive born at Freeport, IL. A retired Air Force general, Eckert was elected Commissioner of Baseball in 1965. He was completely ineffectual in that role and was removed from office on Feb 3, 1969. Died at Freeport, Grand Bahamas, Apr 16, 1971.

FIRST BASKETBALL GAME: ANNIVERSARY. Jan 20, 1891. Under the direction of Dr. James Naismith, the first basketball game was played at the International YMCA in Springfield, MA. Peach baskets with the bottoms still in them were used as the goals. It wasn't until 1905 that someone had the bright idea to remove the baskets' bottoms, thereby eliminating a climb up a ladder after every goal.

JAMES, BILL: BIRTH ANNIVERSARY. Jan 20, 1887. William Henry (Bill) James, baseball player born at Detroit, MI. James was known as "Big Bill" because he was 6 ft 4 in. He played for the 1919 Chicago White Sox, the team known as the Black Sox, but he was not involved in the scandal. Died at Venice, CA, May 24, 1942.

MOON PHASE: LAST QUARTER. Jan 20. Moon enters Last Quarter phase at 2:40 PM, EST.

MULLANE, TONY: BIRTH ANNIVERSARY. Jan 20, 1859. Anthony John (Tony) Mullane, baseball player born at Cork, Ireland. Mullane was a flashy, ambidextrous pitcher known as the "Apollo of the Box." He played without a glove and could pitch with either hand to the same batter. Died at Chicago, IL, Apr 25, 1944.

OLYMPIC BOYCOTT ANNOUNCED: ANNIVERSARY. Jan 20, 1980. President Jimmy Carter announced that the US Olympic team would not compete in the 1980 Summer Games in Moscow as a protest against the Soviet Union's military intervention in Afghanistan in December, 1979.

SOUTHWEST SENIOR INVITATIONAL GOLF CHAMPIONSHIP. Jan 20–22. Yuma Golf and Country Club, Yuma, AZ. A 36-hole medal play tournament, limited to 120 players 50 and older. For info: Caballeros de Yuma, Inc, Box 5987, Yuma, AZ 85366-5987. Phone: (520) 343-1715. Fax: (520) 783-1609.

BIRTHDAYS TODAY

Nelison ("Nick") Anderson, 30, basketball player, born Chicago, IL, Jan 20, 1968.
Rae Carruth, 24, football player, born Sacramento, CA, Jan 20, 1974.
Oswaldo Jose (Ozzie) Guillen, 34, baseball player, born Oculare del Tuy, Venezuela, Jan 20, 1964.
Ronald (Ron) Harper, 34, basketball player, born Dayton, OH, Jan 20, 1964.
Carol Elizabeth Heiss, 58, Olympic gold medal figure skater, born New York, NY, Jan 20, 1940.
Kevin Christian Maas, 33, former baseball player, born Castro Valley, CA, Jan 20, 1965.
Christopher Vernard (Chris) Morris, 32, basketball player, born Atlanta, GA, Jan 20, 1966.
John Phillips Naber, 42, broadcaster and Olympic gold medal swimmer, born Evanston, IL, Jan 20, 1956.
Camilo Alberto Pascual, 64, former baseball player, born Havana, Cuba, Jan 20, 1934.
Jalen Rose, 25, basketball player, born Detroit, MI, Jan 20, 1973.

JANUARY 21 — WEDNESDAY
Day 21 — 344 Remaining

SUPERBOWL CHAMPIONS THIS DATE
1979   Pittsburgh Steelers

BROWNING, JOHN: BIRTH ANNIVERSARY. Jan 21, 1855. John Moses Browning, gun maker and inventor born at Ogden, UT. Browning was taught gunsmithing by his Mormon pioneer father, Jonathan Browning. Starting the J.M. & M.S. Browning Arms Co with his brother at Morgan, UT, he designed guns for Winchester, Remington, Stevens and Colt as well as American and European armies. Browning had more gun patents than any other gunsmith in the world. He is best known worldwide for inventing the machine gun in 1890 and the automatic pistol in 1896. The Browning Arms Co is still located in Morgan, UT. Died in Belgium, Nov 26, 1926.

CHICAGO BOAT, SPORTS AND RV SHOW. Jan 21–25. McCormick Place, Chicago, IL. The Midwest's largest selection under one roof, the 68th annual Chicago Boat, Sports and RV Show offers more than 900 boats and 300 recreational vehicles. Informative boating and fishing seminars. For info: NMMA Boat Shows, 200 E Randolph Dr, Ste 500, Chicago, IL 60601. Phone: (312) 946-6262. Fax: (312) 946-0401.

FEMALE REPORTERS IN NHL LOCKER ROOM: ANNIVERSARY. Jan 21, 1975. Officials at the National Hockey League All-Star game made history by allowing female reporters in the players' locker rooms, a first for American professional sports. The coaches of the two squads arranged for reporters to interview players before they took their showers.

FONSECA, LEW: BIRTH ANNIVERSARY. Jan 21, 1899. Lewis Albert (Lew) Fonseca, baseball player and manager born at Oakland, CA. Fonseca played 12 years in the majors (1921–33) despite a tendency to get injured. He began taking movies of opposing players and turned this practice into the start of the annual All-Star game and World Series highlights films. Died at Ely, IA, Nov 26, 1989.

McENROE TEMPER TANTRUM: ANNIVERSARY. Jan 21, 1990. Tennis player John McEnroe's temper tantrum at the Australian Open got him disqualified from the tournament. McEnroe, leading his match against Mike Pernfors, became the first player ever tossed from this tournament.

PURDUE'S NUDE OLYMPICS: ANNIVERSARY. Jan 21, 1986. More than 100 students from Purdue University ran naked through the streets of West Lafayette, IN, in the school's quite unofficial Nude Olympics. The runners were undeterred by a temperature just a few degrees above freezing.

WINTER EQUESTRIAN FESTIVAL. Jan 21–Apr 2. Wellington and Tampa, FL. Largest hunter, jumper and dressage show in the country. For info: Stadium Jumping, Inc, 3104 Cherry Palm Dr, Tampa, FL 33619. Phone: (813) 623-5801.

BIRTHDAYS TODAY

Alan Paul Benes, 26, baseball player, born Evansville, IN, Jan 21, 1972.

Brian Walter Richard Bradley, 33, hockey player, born Kitchener, Ontario, Canada, Jan 21, 1965.

Geena Davis, 41, actress (*A League of Their Own*), born Ware, MA, Jan 21, 1957.

Christopher Andrew (Chris) Hammond, 32, baseball player, born Atlanta, GA, Jan 21, 1966.

Melton Andrew (Andy) Hawkins, 38, former baseball player, born Waco, TX, Jan 21, 1960.

Jack William Nicklaus, 58, golfer, born Columbus, OH, Jan 21, 1940.

Johnny Lane Oates, 52, baseball manager and former player, born Sylva, NC, Jan 21, 1946.

Hakeem Abdul Olajuwon (born Akeem Abdul Olajuwon), 35, basketball player, born Lagos, Nigeria, Jan 21, 1963.

Detlef Schrempf, 35, basketball player, born Leverkusen, West Germany, Jan 21, 1963.

Thomas James (Tom) Urbani, 30, baseball player, born Santa Cruz, CA, Jan 21, 1968.

JANUARY 22 — THURSDAY
Day 22 — 343 Remaining

SUPERBOWL CHAMPIONS THIS DATE
1984	Los Angeles Raiders
1989	San Francisco 49ers

ALL-CANADA SHOW. Jan 22–25. State Fair Park, West Allis, WI. This consumer show allows individuals an opportunity to talk face-to-face with Canadian lodge representatives and outfitters to plan their hunting, fishing and adventure trips to Canada. For info: Rodney Schlafer, Show Dir, All-Canada Show, Bay-Lakes Mktg, Inc, 1889 Commerce Drive, De Pere, WI 54115. Phone: (414) 983-9800 or (800) 325-6290. Fax: (414) 983-9985. WWW: http://www.allcanada.com

FOREMAN WINS HEAVYWEIGHT TITLE: 25th ANNIVERSARY. Jan 22, 1973. George Foreman won the heavyweight championship by knocking out Joe Frazier in the second round of a fight at Kingston, Jamaica. Foreman held the title until Oct 30, 1974, when he was knocked out by Muhammad Ali.

49ERS WIN SUPER BOWL XXIII: ANNIVERSARY. Jan 22, 1989. The San Francisco 49ers won their third Super Bowl by defeating the Cincinnati Bengals, 20–16, in Super Bowl XXIII. Down by three points with less than four minutes to play, San Francisco marched 92 yards in 11 plays and scored the winning touchdown on a pass from Joe Montana to John Taylor with 34 seconds remaining.

HOUSTON SHUT OUT IN OT: 15th ANNIVERSARY. Jan 22, 1983. The Houston Rockets became the first team in NBA history to be shut out in overtime as the Portland Trail Blazers defeated them, 113–96. Portland outscored the Rockets in OT, 17–0.

KNOXVILLE FISHING EXPO. Jan 22–25. Jacob Building at Chilhowee Park, Knoxville, TN. Annual event featuring the latest in fishing tackle, boats, boating equipment, guide services and other accessories. Top fishing pros will

January 1998
S	M	T	W	T	F	S
				1	2	3
4	5	6	7	8	9	10
11	12	13	14	15	16	17
18	19	20	21	22	23	24
25	26	27	28	29	30	31

demonstrate their techniques. Est attendance: 13,000. For info: Daryl Hobby, Esau, Inc, PO Box 50096, Knoxville, TN 37950. Phone: (423) 588-1233 or (800) 588-ESAU. Fax: (423) 588-6938.

NBA GRANTS FRANCHISES TO PHOENIX AND MILWAUKEE: 30TH ANNIVERSARY. Jan 22, 1968. The NBA Board of Governors awarded expansion franchises to Phoenix and Milwaukee. The Phoenix team adopted the nickname Suns, and the Milwaukee franchise became the Bucks.

SENIOR TOUR CREATED: ANNIVERSARY. Jan 22, 1980. The Tournament Policy Board of the PGA approved a plan to create a Senior Tour for golfers over the age of 50. The idea grew out of a single tournament phenomenon called the Legends of Golf, held in Austin, TX.

WIRTZ, ARTHUR: BIRTH ANNIVERSARY. Jan 22, 1901. Arthur Michael Wirtz, Sr, Hockey Hall of Fame executive and sports administrator born at Chicago, IL. Wirtz prospered in Depression Era real estate and got involved in indoor sports arena ownership. He brought ice skater Sonia Henie to the United States after the 1936 Olympics and launched the first ice show. He also owned the Chicago Blackhawks and was part-owner of the Chicago Bulls. Inducted into the Hockey Hall of Fame in 1971. Died at Chicago, July 21, 1983.

BIRTHDAYS TODAY

Michel (Mike) Bossy, 41, Hockey Hall of Fame right wing, born Montreal, Quebec, Canada, Jan 22, 1957.

Ralph Michael (Mike) Caldwell, 49, former baseball player, born Tarboro, NC, Jan 22, 1949.

George Edward Foreman, 49, boxer, born Marshall, TX, Jan 22, 1949.

Fletcher Joseph (Joe) Perry, 71, Pro Football Hall of Fame fullback, born Stevens, AR, Jan 22, 1927.

George Gerald Seifert, 58, former football coach, born San Francisco, CA, Jan 22, 1940.

Hugh Jeffery (Jeff) Treadway, 35, former baseball player, born Columbus, GA, Jan 22, 1963.

JANUARY 23 — FRIDAY
Day 23 — 342 Remaining

SPORTSCHASER OF THE DAY
Who was the first African American baseball player to be elected to the Baseball Hall of Fame?

AUGUSTA FUTURITY. Jan 23–31. Augusta, GA. Brings together the top cutting horses and riders in the world to compete for purse and awards of more than $600,000. Sponsors: Wrangler, John Deere, Budweiser, WRDW-TV12, Manna Pro Feed Co, Ariat Boots, Palmer & Cay Insurance, CellularOne, *Augusta Chronicle*, American Hat Co, USAir, Exiss Aluminum Trailers, Gist Silversmiths, and Montana Pride Feed. Est attendance: 42,000. For info: Skip Peterson, Dir of Mktg, PO Box 936, Augusta Futurity, Augusta, GA 30903. Phone: (706) 823-3370.

CARTER CAVES CRAWLATHON. Jan 23–25. Carter Caves State Resort Park, Olive Hill, KY. Weekend of caving for beginners and experienced. Est attendance: 500. For info: Carter Caves State Resort Pk, John Tierney, Naturalist, Olive Hill, KY 41164. Phone: (606) 286-4411. Fax: (606) 286-8165. Email: pp01175@ppp.kcc.edu.

GREAT KANSAS CITY GOLF SHOW. Jan 23–25. American Royal Center, Hale Arena, Kansas City, MO. A high-quality consumer trade show for the golf industry that showcases new products, purchasing opportunities, interactive entertainment and informative features. Est attendance: 15,000. For Info: David Sinykin, David Toushin &

Assoc, 5775 Wayzata Blvd, Ste 850, Minneapolis, MN 55416. Phone: (612) 593-0353.

KGBX SUPER BOWL FOOD FIGHT. Jan 23. KGBX studios, Springfield, MO. Station 105.9 KGBX celebrates the Super Bowl. Woody P. Snow and Janet Layne, the KGBX Morning Show, each pick their team in the Super Bowl and act as team captains in a foodfight. They invite listeners to the station to be involved in a food fight to support their favorite team. 40 participants and 100 on-lookers. Annually, the Friday before the Super Bowl. For info: Steve Kern, Promotions Dir, KGBX Radio, 840 S Glenstone, Springfield, MO 65802. Phone: (417) 869-1059. Fax: (417) 869-1000.

LONGHORN WORLD CHAMPIONSHIP RODEO. Jan 23–24 (tentative dates). Target Center, Minneapolis, MN. More than 150 cowboys and cowgirls compete in six professional contests ranging from bronc riding to bull riding for top prize money and world championship points. Featuring colorful opening pageantry and Big, Bad BONUS Bulls. 6th annual. Est attendance: 16,000. For info: W. Bruce Lehrke, Longhorn World Chmpshp Rodeo, Inc, PO Box 70159, Nashville, TN 37207. Phone: (615) 876-1016. Fax: (615) 876-4685. Email: lhrodeo@idt.net. WWW: http://www.longhornrodeo.com

MICRO BREW REVIEW & COOL DOG BALL. Jan 23. Helena Civic Center, Helena, MT. Sponsored by the Race to the Sky, this fourth annual kickoff party (race is 2 weeks later) features more than 30 micro brews from Montana and the northwest. Est attendance: 1,500. For info: Jim McHugh, Dir, Micro Brew Review, 2905 N Montana, Box 30-MUSH, Helena, MT 59601. Phone and fax: (406) 442-4008. WWW: http://www.race2sky.com

100-MILE SKATING RACE: 105th ANNIVERSARY. Jan 23, 1893. Joe Donahue won a 100-mile ice skating race at Stamford, CT. His winning time was seven hours, 11 minutes, 38.2 seconds.

PERFECT GAME ON TV: 10th ANNIVERSARY. Jan 23, 1988. For the first time ever, a bowler rolled a 300 game on television to win a professional tournament. Bob Benoit was the bowler. He won the Quaker State Open in Grand Prairie, TX, and earned a $100,000 bonus.

POLO: STERLING CUP. Jan 23–Feb 22. Wellington, FL. For info: Palm Beach Polo, Inc, 13420 South Shore Blvd, West Palm Beach, FL 33414. Phone: (561) 793-1440. Fax: (561) 790-3872.

RED WINGS SCORE 15: ANNIVERSARY. Jan 23, 1944. The Detroit Red Wings set an NHL record for consecutive goals scored when they defeated the New York Rangers, 15–0.

ROBINSON ELECTED TO HALL OF FAME: ANNIVERSARY. Jan 23, 1962. Jackie Robinson became the first black ballplayer to be elected to the Baseball Hall of Fame. Robinson broke baseball's color line in 1947 and played for the Brooklyn Dodgers through 1956.

SOUTHWESTERN EXPOSITION LIVESTOCK SHOW AND RODEO. Jan 23–Feb 8. Fort Worth, TX. Western-flavored extravaganza. Observed centennial in 1996. World's first indoor rodeo added in 1918 (45 acres under roof). Prize livestock displays, horse shows, midway, commercial exhibits and quality family-oriented entertainment. Est attendance: 800,000. For info: Delbert Bailey, PO Box 150, Fort Worth, TX 76101-0150. Phone: (817) 877-2400. Fax: (817) 877-2499. WWW: http://www.fwstockshowrodeo.com

---

BIRTHDAYS TODAY

John Joseph (Joey) Amalfitano, 64, former baseball manager and player, born San Pedro, CA, Jan 23, 1934.

Kurt Anthony Bevacqua, 51, former baseball player, born Miami Beach, FL, Jan 23, 1947.

Alfonso ("Chico") Carrasquel, 70, former baseball player, born Caracas, Venezuela, Jan 23, 1928.

Patrick Capper (Pat) Haden, 45, broadcaster and former football player, born Westbury, NY, Jan 23, 1953.

Gerald Louis (Jerry) Kramer, 62, author (*Instant Replay*) and former football player, born Jordan, MT, Jan 23, 1936.

Brendan Frederick Shanahan, 29, hockey player, born Mimico, Ontario, Canada, Jan 23, 1969.

Mark Edward Wohlers, 28, baseball player, born Holyoke, MA, Jan 23, 1970.

JANUARY 24 — SATURDAY
Day 24 — 341 Remaining

SUPERBOWL CHAMPIONS THIS DATE
1982   San Francisco 49ers

BOSSY NETS 50 IN 50: ANNIVERSARY. Jan 24, 1981. Right wing Mike Bossy of the New York Islanders scored his 50th goal in the season's 50th game as the Isles defeated the Quebec Nordiques, 7–3.

CANADA: CALGARY WINTER FESTIVAL. Jan 24–Feb 16. Calgary, Alberta. 10-day festival includes feature events that celebrate winter, sport and entertainment of all sorts. Something for everyone. Est attendance: 120,000. For info: Calgary Winter Festival, 634 6th Ave SW, Ste 100, Canada T2P 0S4. Phone: (403) 543-5480. Fax: (403) 543-5490. Email: winfest@telusplanet.net. WWW: http://www.discovercalgary.com/winterfest/events.html

COCHEMS, EDDIE: BIRTH ANNIVERSARY. Jan 24, 1877. Edward B. (Eddie) Cochems, football player and coach born at Sturgeon Bay, WI. Although others are sometimes given credit for introducing the forward pass, Cochems, in fact, was the one. He served on the committee to rewrite the football rules after President Theodore Roosevelt called for the game's abolition because of excessive violence. The new rules allowed for passing. That fall, Cochems's team, St. Louis University, used the pass to great effect, winning all 11 games and outscoring its opponents, 407 to 11. Died at Madison, WI, Apr 9, 1953.

"THE FIGHT OF THE WEEK" TV PREMIERE: 45th ANNIVERSARY. Jan 24, 1953. For 11 years, you could catch a boxing match every week on TV. Jack Drees announced the matches the first few seasons; Don Dunphy succeeded him.

49ERS WIN SUPER BOWL XVI: ANNIVERSARY. Jan 24, 1982. The San Francisco 49ers won Super Bowl XVI by defeating the Cincinnati Bengals, 26–21. The 49ers sprinted to a 20–0 lead and had to scramble to hold off the Bengals who rallied for 21 points in the second half.

FREEZE FOR FOOD 10K RACE AND 5K RUN/WALK. Jan 24. Vilas Park Shelter, Madison, WI. Fundraiser for Oxfam-America, sponsored by the Returned Peace Corps Volunteers of Wisconsin-Madison. $10 registration fee for each event. Times posted; prizes awarded for top pledge raisers and event finishers. We will never cancel the race due to weather! Est attendance: 150. For info: Dave or Deb Hamilton, Co-Dirs, RPCVs of Wisconsin, 1160 Washington Rd, Stoughton, WI 53589. Phone: (608) 751-6137 or (608) 246-6364.

GAINES WINS 800th GAME: ANNIVERSARY. Jan 24, 1990. Winston-Salem State defeated Livingstone, 79–70, to give coach Clarence "Big House" Gaines the 800th victory of his college basketball coaching career.

PITCH WITHIN 20 SECONDS: ANNIVERSARY. Jan 24, 1955. The Official Rules Committee of major league baseball announced a rules change to speed up the game. Pitchers will be required to deliver a pitch within 20 seconds after having taken a position on the pitching rubber. Prior to the new ruling, pitchers could wait as long as they wanted before throwing.

RHEM, FLINT: BIRTH ANNIVERSARY. Jan 24, 1901. Charles Flint Rhem, baseball player born at Rhems, SC. In 1930, Rhem, a heavy drinker, disappeared for two days during the season. He claimed to have been kidnapped by fans of the Brooklyn Dodgers. Died at Columbia, SC, July 30, 1969.

WINTER FEST. Jan 24–25 (tentative dates). Lake City, MN. Snowmobile events, winter golf classic, cross-country ski race, sleigh and cutter parade, taste fest, arts and crafts, snowmobile torchlight parade and fireworks. Est attendance: 5,000. For info: Winter Fest Chair, Lake City Area Chamber of Commerce, 212 S Washington St, Box 150, Lake City, MN 55041. Phone: (800) 369-4123.

BIRTHDAYS TODAY

Neil Patrick Allen, 40, former baseball player, born Kansas City, KS, Jan 24, 1958.

John Beasley (Jack) Brickhouse, 82, former broadcaster (Ford Frick Award winner), born Peoria, IL, Jan 24, 1916.

Robert Keith (Rob) Dibble, 34, former baseball player, born Bridgeport, CT, Jan 24, 1964.

Mary Lou Retton, 30, Olympic gold medal gymnast, born Fairmont, WV, Jan 24, 1968.

Timothy Paul (Tim) Stoddard, 45, former baseball player, born East Chicago, IN, Jan 24, 1953.

JANUARY 25 — SUNDAY

Day 25 — 340 Remaining

SUPERBOWL CHAMPIONS THIS DATE

1981	Oakland Raiders
1987	New York Giants

CHRIS STRATTON DART TOURNAMENT. Jan 25. Springbrook Golf Course, Battle Creek, MI. 6th annual

January *1998*	S	M	T	W	T	F	S
					1	2	3
	4	5	6	7	8	9	10
	11	12	13	14	15	16	17
	18	19	20	21	22	23	24
	25	26	27	28	29	30	31

benefit tournament dedicated to Chris Stratton, a great darter and well-liked person. Fifty percent of entry fees donated to American Cancer Society. Est attendance: 100. For info: Bill Buckner, Springbrook Golf Course, 1600 Ave A, Battle Creek, MI 49015. Phone: (616) 965-6512.

DAY, JOHN: DEATH ANNIVERSARY. Jan 25, 1925. John B. Day, baseball executive born at Cliffside, NJ, 1848. Day was the founding owner of the New York Giants, one of baseball's historic franchises. Financial reverses in the 1890s forced Day to sell the team in 1895, after which he became supervisor of National League umpires. Died at Cliffside.

FIRST WINTER OLYMPICS: ANNIVERSARY. Jan 25, 1924. The first Winter Olympic Games opened in Chamonix, France, with 281 male and 13 female athletes from 16 nations competing in five sports. US athletes won four medals. The Canadian hockey team overwhelmed its opponents, scoring 85 goals in three games.

GIANTS WIN SUPER BOWL XXI: ANNIVERSARY. Jan 25, 1987. The New York Giants defeated the Denver Broncos, 39–20, to win Super Bowl XXI. The victory gave New York its first NFL title in 30 years. Giants quarterback Phil Simms completed 22 of 25 passes for 268 yards and three touchdowns to win the game's Most Valuable Player award.

NATIONAL POPCORN DAY. Jan 25. A salute to popcorn. "What's more American than a super bowl of popcorn while watching the Super Bowl?" Annually, on Superbowl Sunday. For info: Polly Peterson, WROE-FM, 1724 W. Highland Ave, Appleton, WI 54914.

NBA'S 5,000,000th POINT: 10th ANNIVERSARY. Jan 25, 1988. Guard Rickey Green of the Utah Jazz scored the 5,000,000th point in NBA history in a game against the Cleveland Cavaliers. Green made a three-point shot at the buzzer ending the third quarter. The Jazz won, 119–96.

ONLY IHL DOUBLEHEADER: 45th ANNIVERSARY. Jan 25, 1953. The Cincinnati Mohawks and the Troy (OH) Bruins played the only doubleheader in the history of the International Hockey League, with one game being played in each team's home city. The Bruins won the first game in Troy, 3–0. The Mohawks won the nightcap in Cincinnati, 2–1.

PREFONTAINE, STEVE: BIRTH ANNIVERSARY. Jan 25, 1951. Steve Roland ("Pre") Prefontaine, long distance runner born at Coos Bay, OR. Prefontaine was an outstanding athlete whose grit, determination and activism personified Americans' growing interest in physical fitness, jogging and running. Although never an Olympic champion or world record holder, he set 14 US records during his career cut short by a fatal automobile accident on a road where he often trained. Died at Eugene, OR, May 30, 1975.

STUPOR BOWL SUNDAY. Jan 25. As millions of Americans settle in to watch testosterone-crazed jocks butt heads, football widows are encouraged to head out to shops, museums, theaters and restaurants–anywhere that is normally too crowded. No traffic, no parking hassles, no lines. It's the only day of the year when everything's open but nobody's there. He's made other plans and they don't include you so head out for some guilt-free fun and leave hubby home to wait on himself. As long as there's a Super Bowl, there'll be a Stupor Bowl Sunday. Remember, at kickoff time, it's time to kick up your heels! Sponsored by the National Football Widows League. For info: NFWL, PO Box 861001, St. Augustine, FL 32086. Phone: (904) 797-6797.

SUPER BOWL XXXIII. Jan 25. Jack Murphy Stadium, San Diego, CA. The championship game of the National Football League between the NFC and AFC champions. Annually, the last Sunday in January. Super Bowl XXXIII (Jan 31, 1999) is scheduled to be played in Miami, FL, and Super Bowl XXXIV (Jan 30, 2000) in Atlanta. GA. For info: PR Dept, Natl Football League, 410 Park Ave, New York, NY 10022. Phone: (212) 450-2000.

WINTER TRIATHLON. Jan 25. Muskegon Winter Sports Complex, Muskegon, MI. Contestants will compete in a 2.5K cross-country ski, two timed runs on the luge and four laps on the ice rink. Some instruction provided. For info: Muskegon Sports Council, PO Box 5085, North Muskegon, MI 49445. Phone: (616) 744-9629. Luge Club phone: (616) 759-2201.

BIRTHDAYS TODAY

Chris Chelios, 36, hockey player, born Chicago, IL, Jan 25, 1962.

Mark Super Duper (born Mark Kirby Dupas), 39, former football player, born Pineville, LA, Jan 25, 1959.

Lou Groza, 74, Pro Football Hall of Fame tackle and place-kicker, born Martins Ferry, OH, Jan 25, 1924.

William Earnest (Ernie) Harwell, 80, broadcaster (Ford Frick Award winner), born Washington, GA, Jan 25, 1918.

Donald (Don) Maynard, 63, Pro Football Hall of Fame wide receiver, born Crosbyton, TX, Jan 25, 1935.

Richard Joseph (Dick) McGuire, 72, former basketball coach and Basketball Hall of Fame guard, born Huntington, NY, Jan 25, 1926.

Christopher Lemonte (Chris) Mills, 28, basketball player, born Los Angeles, CA, Jan 25, 1970.

Esa Kalervo Tikkanen, 30, hockey player, born Helsinki, Finland, Jan 25, 1968.

JANUARY 26 — MONDAY
Day 26 — 339 Remaining

SUPERBOWL CHAMPIONS THIS DATE

1986	Chicago Bears
1992	Washington Redskins
1997	Green Bay Packers

ABRAMS, CAL: BIRTH ANNIVERSARY. Jan 26, 1924. Calvin Ross (Cal) Abrams, baseball player born at Philadelphia, PA. Abrams played eight years in the major leagues and hit .269. He is most famous for being thrown out at the plate by Richie Ashburn of the Philadelphia Phillies in the ninth inning of the final game of the 1950 season, thereby depriving his team, the Brooklyn Dodgers, of a shot at the pennant. Died at Ft Lauderdale, FL, Jan 26, 1997.

ALL-CANADA SHOW. Jan 26–28. Dane County Forum, Madison, WI. This consumer show allows individuals an opportunity to talk face-to-face with Canadian lodge representatives and outfitters to plan their hunting, fishing and adventure trips to Canada. For info: Rodney Schlafer, Show Dir, All-Canada Show, Bay-Lakes Mktg, Inc, 1889 Commerce Dr, De Pere, WI 54115. Phone: (414) 983-9800 or (800) 325-6290. Fax: (414) 983-9985. WWW: http://www.allcanada.com

BLAEHOLDER, GEORGE: BIRTH ANNIVERSARY. Jan 26, 1904. George Franklin Blaeholder, baseball player born at Orange, CA. Blaeholder pitched in the major leagues from 1925 through 1936. He is credited with inventing the slider. Died at Garden Grove, CA, Dec 29, 1947.

CHICAGO WINS SUPER BOWL XX: ANNIVERSARY. Jan 26, 1986. In their first Super Bowl outing the Chicago Bears romped over the New England Patriots to win Super Bowl XX, 46–10. Chicago spotted the Patriots a 3–0

lead but then scored the next 44 points while holding New England to seven yards rushing.

GRETZKY SCORES 50 IN 49: ANNIVERSARY. Jan 26, 1985. Center Wayne Gretzky of the Edmonton Oilers scored his 50th goal in the Oilers' 49th game, a 6–3 victory over the Pittsburgh Penguins.

HIGH SCHOOL SCORING RECORD: ANNIVERSARY. Jan 26, 1960. Danny Heater of Burnsville, WV, set a national high school basketball record by scoring 135 points in a single game. Heater went on to play college ball at the University of Richmond.

JORDAN, HENRY: BIRTH ANNIVERSARY. Jan 26, 1935. Henry Wendell Jordan, Pro Football Hall of Fame defensive tackle born at Emporia, VA. Jordan played college football at the University of Virginia and starred with the great Green Bay Packers teams of the 1960s. He compensated for lack of size with quickness and agility and was known for his witty, gracious manner. Inducted into the Pro Football Hall of Fame in 1995. Died at Milwaukee, WI, Feb 21, 1977.

CHASE'S SPORTSQUOTE OF THE DAY

"The way to catch a knuckleball is to wait until the ball stops rolling and then to pick it up." —Bob Uecker

---

BIRTHDAYS TODAY

Jeffery Glenn (Jeff) Branson, 31, baseball player, born Waynesboro, MS, Jan 26, 1967.

Wayne Douglas Gretzky, 37, hockey player, born Brantford, Ontario, Canada, Jan 26, 1961.

Paul Newman, 73, actor (Oscar for *The Color of Money*; *Slap Shot*), former auto racer, born Cleveland, OH, Jan 26, 1925.

Richard Spencer (Rick) Schu, 36, former baseball player, born Philadelphia, PA, Jan 26, 1962.

Robert George (Bob) Uecker, 63, broadcaster, actor (*Major League*) and former baseball player, born Milwaukee, WI, Jan 26, 1935.

Herbert Jackson (Jack) Youngblood, III, 48, former football player, born Monticello, FL, Jan 26, 1950.

JANUARY 27 — TUESDAY
Day 27 — 338 Remaining

SUPERBOWL CHAMPIONS THIS DATE
1991   New York Giants

BIRMINGHAM SPORT AND BOAT SHOW. Jan 27–Feb 1. Birmingham/Jefferson Civic Center, Birmingham, AL. For info: Double C Productions, Inc, Box 1678, Huntsville, TX 77342. Phone: (409) 295-9677. Fax: (409) 295-8859. Email: doublec@lcc.net. WWW: http://www.lcc.net/doublec

FALK, BIBB: BIRTH ANNIVERSARY. Jan 27, 1899. Bibb August Falk, baseball player, coach and manager born at Austin, TX. Falk played football and baseball in college and enjoyed a fine career as a major league outfielder. After retiring, he coached baseball at the University of Texas, winning the national championship in 1949 and 1950. Died at Austin, June 8, 1989.

GASTON, MILT: BIRTH ANNIVERSARY. Jan 27, 1896. Nathaniel Milton (Milt) Gaston, baseball player born at Ridgefield Park, NJ. Gaston pitched 11 seasons in the major leagues, once pitching a 14-hit shutout. Died at Hyannis, MA, Apr 26, 1996.

GIANTS WIN SUPER BOWL XXV: ANNIVERSARY. Jan 27, 1991. The New York Giants defeated the Buffalo Bills, 20–19, to win Super Bowl XXV. Buffalo kicker Scott Norwood saw his 47-yard field goal attempt sail wide with eight seconds to play.

GLOBETROTTERS BORN: ANNIVERSARY. Jan 27, 1927. The Harlem Globetrotters opened their first tour with a game in Hinckley, IL. Founded by Abe Saperstein as a spinoff from the great Harlem Renaissance team, the Globetrotters quickly became fan favorites around the world.

GRETZKY'S SCORING STREAK: ANNIVERSARY. Jan 27, 1984. Center Wayne Gretzky of the Edmonton Oilers scored a goal against the New Jersey Devils to extend his streak of scoring either a goal or an assist to 51 games, an NHL record. The Great One was stopped by the Los Angeles Kings, a team he later played for, the next night.

POLLARD, FRITZ: BIRTH ANNIVERSARY. Jan 27, 1894. Frederick Douglas (Fritz) Pollard, football player and coach, born at Chicago, IL. In 1915, while playing for Brown, Pollard became the second black football player to be named a consensus All-American. He turned pro in the infant days of the NFL, playing for and coaching several teams. From 1927 to 1933, he organized and coached the Chicago Brown Bombers, an independent team. Died at Silver Spring, MD, May 11, 1986.

January *1998*	S	M	T	W	T	F	S
					1	2	3
	4	5	6	7	8	9	10
	11	12	13	14	15	16	17
	18	19	20	21	22	23	24
	25	26	27	28	29	30	31

ROONEY, ART: BIRTH ANNIVERSARY. Jan 27, 1901. Art Rooney, Pro Football Hall of Fame executive born at Coulterville, PA. As founder of the Pittsburgh Steelers, Rooney endured decades of futility on the field before the Steelers won their first NFL championship, a victory over the Minnesota Vikings in Super Bowl IX (1975). Inducted into the Hall of Fame in 1964. Died at Pittsburgh, PA, Aug 25, 1988.

UCLA SETS RECORD: 25th ANNIVERSARY. Jan 27, 1973. The UCLA Bruins, led by center Bill Walton, beat Notre Dame, 82–63, to set an NCAA record with their 61st consecutive victory. The Bruins broke the record set by the University of San Francisco in 1956 when Bill Russell played center for the Dons.

BIRTHDAYS TODAY

Patrice Brisebois, 27, hockey player, born Montreal, Quebec, Canada, Jan 27, 1971.
Anthony Cris Collinsworth, 39, broadcaster and former football player, born Dayton, OH, Jan 27, 1959.
Michael Joseph (Mike) Hill, 59, golfer, born Jackson, MI, Jan 27, 1939.
John Lee Lowenstein, 51, former baseball player, born Wolf Point, MT, Jan 27, 1947.
Phillip Alan (Phil) Plantier, 29, baseball player, born Manchester, NH, Jan 27, 1969.

JANUARY 28 — WEDNESDAY
Day 28 — 337 Remaining

SUPERBOWL CHAMPIONS THIS DATE
1990   San Francisco 49ers
1996   Dallas Cowboys

DOAK, BILL: BIRTH ANNIVERSARY. Jan 28, 1891. William Leopold (Bill) Doak, baseball pitcher born at Pittsburgh, PA. Doak was a pitcher who relied on the spitball and was one of those allowed to continue throwing the pitch after it was banned in 1920. He designed the "Bill Doak glove" in 1918, his royalties from which often added up to $25,000 a year. Died at Bradenton, FL, Nov 26, 1954.

49ERS WIN SUPER BOWL XXIV: ANNIVERSARY. Jan 28, 1990. The San Francisco 49ers defeated the Denver Broncos, 55–10, to win Super Bowl XXIV. 49ers quarterback Joe Montana won the Super Bowl Most Valuable Player award for the third time. He completed 22 of 29 passes for 297 and five touchdowns, including three to wide receiver Jerry Rice.

LARY, LYN: BIRTH ANNIVERSARY. Jan 28, 1906. Lynford Hobart (Lyn) Lary, baseball player born at Armona, CA. Lary played shortstop in the major leagues for a dozen years. In 1931, he drove in 107 runs for the New York Yankees. Died at Downey, CA, Jan 9, 1973.

MESSENGER: DEATH ANNIVERSARY. Jan 28, 1808. Popularly known as "Imported Messenger," this horse was the "foundation" of the American Standardbred line of trotters that compete in harness racing. Bred in England in 1780 and raced there, he was brought to the US to stud and was purchased by Henry Astor. Messenger died on Long Island and was buried near Oyster Bay in ground that is now part of the Piping Rock Golf Course. The spirited trotter's burial drew a crowd of horse lovers and race fans, and he was saluted with several volleys of rifle fire. For info: Publicity Dept, United States Trotting Assn, 750 Michigan Ave, Columbus, OH 43215. Phone: (614) 224-2291.

MOON PHASE: NEW MOON. Jan 28. Moon enters New Moon phase at 1:01 AM, EST.

RUNNELS, PETE: 70TH BIRTH ANNIVERSARY. Jan 28, 1928. James Edward ("Pete") Runnels, baseball player born at Lufkin, TX. Runnels won the American League batting title in 1960 and 1962 while playing for the Boston Red Sox. Died at Pasadena, TX, May 20, 1991.

WRIGHT, GEORGE: BIRTH ANNIVERSARY. Jan 28, 1847. George Wright, Baseball Hall of Fame shortstop and sporting goods entrepreneur born at New York, NY. Wright and his brother Harry were two of baseball's earliest pioneers. He played for the 1869 Red Stockings, was the first player signed by the Boston Red Stockings in 1871 and joined with Henry A. Ditson in 1879 to form the Wright & Ditson sporting goods company. Inducted into the Hall of Fame in 1937. Died at Boston, MA, Aug 21, 1937.

YDE, EMIL: BIRTH ANNIVERSARY. Jan 28, 1900. Emil Ogden Yde, baseball player born at Great Lakes, IL. Yde was a submarine pitcher who helped the Pittsburgh Pirates win the 1925 National League pennant. He was a switch-hitter good enough to pinch hit. Died at Leesburg, FL, Dec 4, 1968.

BIRTHDAYS TODAY

Alan Alda (born Alphonso D'Abruzzo), 62, actor (*Paper Lion*), born New York, NY, Jan 28, 1936.
Michael Jerome Cage, 36, basketball player, born West Memphis, AR, Jan 28, 1962.
Colin John Campbell, 45, hockey coach and former player, born London, Ontario, Canada, Jan 28, 1953.
Tony Lorenzo Delk, 24, basketball player, born Covington, TN, Jan 28, 1974.
Michal Pivonka, 32, hockey player, born Kladno, Czechoslovakia, Jan 28, 1966.
Nicholas Raymond Leige (Nick) Price, 41, golfer, born Durban, South Africa, Jan 28, 1957.
William De Kova (Bill) White, 64, former baseball executive, broadcaster and player, born Lakewood, FL, Jan 28, 1934.

JANUARY 29 — THURSDAY
Day 29 — 336 Remaining

SUPERBOWL CHAMPIONS THIS DATE
1995   San Francisco 49ers

AT&T PEBBLE BEACH NATIONAL PRO-AM. Jan 29–Feb 1. Pebble Beach, CA. A PGA Tour tournament played at three courses on the Monterrey Peninsula. Formerly known as the Bing Crosby National Pro-Am. For info: PGA Tour, 112 TPC Blvd, Ponte Vedra Beach, FL 32082. Phone: (904) 285-3700.

CHATTANOOGA BOAT SHOW. Jan 29–Feb 1. Chattanooga Convention Center, Chattanooga, TN. 13th annual show featuring thousands of square feet of boats from the area's largest marine dealers and booths displaying everything from water skis and marine equipment to fishing tackle and floating docks. Est attendance: 12,000. For info: Cindy Crabtree, Esau, Inc, PO Box 50096, Knoxville, TN 37950. Phone: (423) 588-1233 or (800) 588-ESAU. Fax: (423) 588-6938.

DEMPSEY VOTED GREATEST: ANNIVERSARY. Jan 29, 1950. Heavyweight Jack Dempsey was voted the greatest boxer of the first half of the 20th century in a poll of sportswriters and broadcasters conducted by the Associated Press. Dempsey polled 251 votes to runnerup Joe Louis's 104.

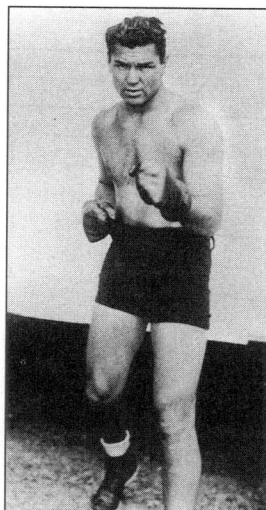
Jack Dempsey

49ERS WIN SUPER BOWL XXIX: ANNIVERSARY. Jan 29, 1995. The San Francisco 49ers defeated the San Diego Chargers, 49–26, to win Super Bowl XXIX. San Francisco scored on six of its eight first-half possessions to lead 28–10 at the half. 49ers quarterback Steve Young was the game's Most Valuable Player.

NATIONAL PUZZLE DAY. Jan 29. To recognize different puzzles and games and their creators. Call or write for free information on the origins and creators of puzzles and games. For info: Carol Handz, Coord, Jodi Jill Features, 1705 14th St, Ste 321, Boulder, CO 80301. Phone: (303) 786-9849. Fax: (303) 786-9849.

OLDFIELD, BARNEY: 120th BIRTH ANNIVERSARY. Jan 29, 1878. Berna Eli ("Barney") Oldfield, auto racer born at Wauseon, OH. Oldfield began racing bicycles in 1893 and switched to autos in 1902, almost immediately becoming a national hero for his exploits. On Memorial Day, 1903, he became the first American to drive one mile in one minute. He barnstormed across the country and in 1910 set a land speed record on the sand at Daytona Beach. He ran the first 100 mph lap at the Indianapolis Speedway and in his retirement was instrumental in forming a drivers' union. Died at Beverly Hills, CA, Oct 4, 1946.

PRO FOOTBALL HALL OF FAME ELECTS CHARTER MEMBERS: 35TH ANNIVERSARY. Jan 29, 1963. The Pro Football Hall of Fame in Canton, OH, announced the election of its charter members, 11 players and six executives. The players selected were Sammy Baugh, Dutch Clark, Red Grange, Mel Hein, Pete Henry, Cal Hubbard, Don Hutson, Johnny McNally, Bronko Nagurski, Ernie Nevers and Jim Thorpe. They were joined by Bert Bell, Joe Carr, George Halas, Curly Lambeau, Tim Mara and George Preston Marshall.

STRICTLY SAIL AT NAVY PIER. Jan 29–Feb 1. Navy Pier, Chicago, IL. 3rd annual show. The midwest's largest and most impressive sail-only show features the latest sailboats, equipment and services as well as seminars and attractions for all levels of sailing ability. For info: NMMA, 200 E Randolph Dr, Ste 500, Chicago, IL 60601. Phone: (312) 946-6262. Fax: (312) 946-0401.

BIRTHDAYS TODAY

Michael Peter (Mike) Aldrete, 37, baseball player, born Carmel, CA, Jan 29, 1961.

Sean Burke, 31, hockey player, born Windsor, Ontario, Canada, Jan 29, 1967.

Dominik Hasek, 33, hockey player, born Pardubice, Czechoslovakia, Jan 29, 1965.

Ronald Stacey King, 31, basketball player, born Lawton, OK, Jan 29, 1967.

David Alan LaFleur, 24, football player, born Lake Charles, LA, Jan 29, 1974.

Gregory Efthimios (Greg) Louganis, 38, Olympic gold medal diver, born San Diego, CA, Jan 29, 1960.

Andre Darnell Reed, 34, football player, born Allentown, PA, Jan 29, 1964.

William Joseph (Bill) Rigney, 80, former baseball manager and player, born Alameda, CA, Jan 29, 1918.

Kevin Lynn Roberson, 30, baseball player, born Decatur, IL, Jan 29, 1968.

Stephen Louis (Steve) Sax, 38, former baseball player, born Sacramento, CA, Jan 29, 1960.

Tom Selleck, 53, actor (*Mr. Baseball*), born Detroit, MI, Jan 29, 1945.

Aeneas Demetrius Williams, 30, football player, born New Orleans, LA, Jan 29, 1968.

JANUARY 30 — FRIDAY
Day 30 — 335 Remaining

SUPERBOWL CHAMPIONS THIS DATE

1983	Washington Redskins
1994	Dallas Cowboys

AMOROS, SANDY: BIRTH ANNIVERSARY. Jan 30, 1930. Edmundo ("Sandy") Amoros, baseball player born at Havana, Cuba. Amoros made a sensational catch in Game 7 of the 1955 World Series for the Brooklyn Dodgers against the New York Yankees, helping Brooklyn to win its only World Series. Died at Miami, FL, June 27, 1992.

CANADA: ONTARIO WINTER CARNIVAL BON SOO. Jan 30–Feb 8. Sault Ste. Marie, Ontario. One of Canada's largest winter carnivals features more than 125 festive indoor and hearty outdoor events for all ages during a 10-day winter extravaganza. Annually, the last weekend in January through the first weekend in February. Est attendance: 100,000. For info: Donna Gregg, Bon Soo Winter Carnival Inc, PO Box 781, Sault Ste. Marie, Ont, Canada P6A 5N3. Phone: (705) 759-3000. Fax: (705) 759-6950.

CELTICS RETIRE MCHALE'S NUMBER: ANNIVERSARY. Jan 30, 1994. The Boston Celtics retired No. 32, the jersey worn by forward Kevin McHale for 13 seasons, in a halftime ceremony. McHale scored 17,335 points, made seven All-Star teams and helped the Celtics win three NBA championships.

DAYTONA USA 2-HOUR ENDURANCE CHAMPIONSHIP. Jan 30. Daytona International Speedway, Daytona Beach, FL. 3rd annual showroom-stock endurance race. For info: John Story, Dir of Pub Rel, Daytona Intl Speedway, PO Box 2801, Daytona Beach, FL 32120-2801. Phone: (904) 947-6782. For tickets: (904) 253-RACE (7223). Fax: (904) 947-6791. WWW: http://daytonausa.com

January *1998*	S	M	T	W	T	F	S
					1	2	3
	4	5	6	7	8	9	10
	11	12	13	14	15	16	17
	18	19	20	21	22	23	24
	25	26	27	28	29	30	31

McCALL WINTER CARNIVAL. Jan 30–Feb 8. McCall, ID. Come beat the winter blahs at this celebration of winter that includes ice sculptures, dances, food, snowmobile races, sled dog races, beard contest, parade and a sculpting contest. Est attendance: 20,000. For info: McCall Chamber of Commerce, PO Box D, McCall, ID 83638. Phone: (208) 634-7631 or (800) 260-5130. Fax: (208) 634-7752. Email: mccallcc@cyberhighway.net. WWW: http://www.mccall-1achamber.org

NC RV AND CAMPING SHOW. Jan 30–Feb 1. Charlotte Merchandise Mart, Charlotte, NC. A display of the latest in recreation vehicles and accessories by various dealers. Est attendance: 14,000. For info: Apple Rock Advertising & Promotion, 1200 Eastchester Dr, High Point, NC 27265. Phone: (910) 881-7100. Fax: (910) 883-7198.

REDSKINS WIN SUPER BOWL XVII: 15th ANNIVERSARY. Jan 30, 1983. The Washington Redskins defeated the Miami Dolphins, 27–17, to win Super Bowl XVII. Washington, in winning its first NFL title in 40 years, was led by fullback John Riggins, who rushed for 166 yards on 38 carries and was named the game's Most Valuable Player.

SPORTSCHASER OF THE DAY

When the Washington Redskins defeated the Miami Dolphins, 27-17, in Super Bowl XVII, who was the game's Most Valuable Player?

BIRTHDAYS TODAY

Walter (Walt) Dropo, 75, former baseball player, born Moosup, CT, Jan 30, 1923.

Gene Hackman, 68, actor (*Hoosiers*), born San Bernardino, CA, Jan 30, 1930.

David Allen (Davey) Johnson, 55, baseball manager and former player, born Orlando, FL, Jan 30, 1943.

Boris Spassky, 61, former chess player, born Leningrad, USSR, Jan 30, 1937.

William Payne Stewart, 41, golfer, born Springfield, MO, Jan 30, 1957.

Curtis Northrop Strange, 43, golfer, born Norfolk, VA, Jan 30, 1955.

JANUARY 31 — SATURDAY
Day 31 — 334 Remaining

SUPERBOWL CHAMPIONS THIS DATE

1988	Washington Redskins
1993	Dallas Cowboys

BURNS, GEORGE: 105th BIRTH ANNIVERSARY. Jan 31, 1893. George Henry Burns, baseball player and manager born at Niles, OH. Burns was a first baseman and not related to his contemporary, outfielder George Joseph Burns. He had a 16-year career with five different American League teams and hit .307. Died at Kirkland, WA, Jan 7, 1978.

CHESAPEAKE BAY BOAT SHOW. Jan 31–Feb 8. Baltimore Convention Center, Baltimore, MD. The 44th annual Chesapeake Bay Boat Show presents the latest boats and accessories at the lowest prices, plus informative boating and fishing seminars. For info: NMMA Boat Shows, 600 Third Ave, 23rd Fl, New York, NY 10016. Phone: (212) 922-1212. Fax: (212) 922-9607.

DALLAS WINS SUPER BOWL XXVII: ANNIVERSARY. Jan 31, 1993. The Dallas Cowboys defeated the Buffalo Bills, 52–17, to win Super Bowl XXVII. The Cowboys' victory came three seasons after they won just one game and marked their return to elite status in the NFL under coach Jimmy Johnson.

FERGUSON, BOB: BIRTH ANNIVERSARY. Jan 31, 1845. Robert V. (Bob) Ferguson, baseball player, manager and umpire born at Brooklyn, NY. Ferguson was one of several early ballplayers to earn the nickname "Death to Flying Things" for his ability to catch fly balls. He played every position and was the game's first switch-hitter. Died at Brooklyn, May 3, 1894.

HUTSON, DON: 85th BIRTH ANNIVERSARY. Jan 31, 1913. Donald Montgomery (Don) Hutson, Pro Football Hall of Fame end born at Pine Bluff, AR. Hutson attended the University of Alabama where he starred on the team that won the 1935 Rose Bowl. He established himself as an outstanding pro with the Green Bay Packers, becoming the league's premier receiver. In 11 seasons, he led the league in receptions eight times and receiving yardage seven times. He caught 488 passes for 7,991 yards and 100 touchdowns. Most of his records lasted into the 1980s when each NFL season was much longer. Inducted as a charter member of the Hall of Fame in 1963. Died at Rancho Mirage, CA, June 26, 1997.

MACKINAW MUSH SLED DOG RACE. Jan 31–Feb 1. Old Railroad Depot, Mackinaw City, MI. Sanctioned ISDA event with purse and various classes. Races start at 9 each morning. Also children's events and weight pull. Annually, the first weekend in February. Est attendance: 1,000. For info: Mackinaw Area Tourist Bureau, 706 S Huron, Mackinaw City, MI 49701. Phone: (616) 436-5664. Fax: (616) 436-5991. Email: bjones@freeway.net. WWW: http://www.mackinawcity.com

ROBINSON, JACKIE: BIRTH ANNIVERSARY. Jan 31, 1919. Jack Roosevelt Robinson, Baseball Hall of Fame infielder born at Cairo, GA. Robinson was a star athlete at UCLA and an officer in the US Army during World War II. In Oct, 1945, Branch Rickey of the Brooklyn Dodgers signed Robinson to a contract to play professional baseball, thereby breaking the sport's unofficial, but firm, color line. Robinson proved to be an outstanding player who endured unimaginable racial taunts and still excelled. He won Rookie of the Year honors in 1947 and was the National League's Most Valuable Player in 1949. He led the Dodgers to six pennants and a World Series championship in 1955. Inducted into the Hall of Fame in 1962. Died at Stamford, CT, Oct 24, 1972.

ROLEX 24 AT DAYTONA. Jan 31–Feb 1. Daytona International Speedway, Daytona Beach, FL. 36th annual running of the most prestigious endurance race in North America (exotic purpose-built race cars). Sponsor: Rolex Watch. For info: John Story, Dir of Pub Rel, Daytona Intl Speedway, PO Box 2801, Daytona Beach, FL 32120-2801. Phone: (904) 947-6782. For tickets: (904) 253-RACE (7223). Fax: (904) 947-6791. WWW: http://www.daytona.com

SPEEDWEEKS. Jan 31–Feb 15. Daytona International Speedway, Daytona Beach, FL. The city becomes the "World Center of Racing" with three weekends of competition, including the Daytona 500. For info: Public Relations, Daytona Intl Speedway, Box 2801, Daytona Beach, FL 32120-2801.

WALCOTT, JERSEY JOE: BIRTH ANNIVERSARY. Jan 31, 1914. Jersey Joe Walcott, boxer born Arnold Raymond Cream at Merchantville, NJ. Walcott lost a heavyweight title fight to Joe Louis in 1947, but then defeated Ezzard Charles to win the title in 1951 after losing to him twice before. At 37 years of age, he was the oldest man to win the heavyweight crown. Died at Camden, NJ, Feb 27, 1994.

BIRTHDAYS TODAY

Robert John (Bob) Apodaca, 48, former baseball player, born Los Angeles, CA, Jan 31, 1950.

Ernest (Ernie) Banks, 67, Baseball Hall of Fame shortstop and first baseman, born Dallas, TX, Jan 31, 1931.

Bobby Dollas, 33, hockey player, born Montreal, Quebec, Canada, Jan 31, 1965.

Othella Harrington, 24, basketball player, born Jackson, MS, Jan 31, 1974.

Kenard Lang, 23, football player, born Orlando, FL, Jan 31, 1975.

Norman Mailer, 75, author and amateur boxer, born Long Branch, NJ, Jan 31, 1923.

Lynn Nolan Ryan, 51, former baseball player, born Refugio, TX, Jan 31, 1947.

Rafael Francisco Santana, 40, former baseball player, born La Romana, Dominican Republic, Jan 31, 1958.

FEBRUARY 1 — SUNDAY

Day 32 — 333 Remaining

BIRTH OF ABA: ANNIVERSARY. Feb 1, 1967. The American Basketball Association (ABA) was born with 10 teams and George Mikan as commissioner in its first season. The ABA lasted nine years before four teams, the Denver Nuggets, the Indiana Pacers, the New Jersey Nets and the San Antonio Spurs, were absorbed into the NBA.

BOOTH, ALBIE: 90th BIRTH ANNIVERSARY. Feb 1, 1908. Albert James (Albie) Booth, Jr, football player, coach and official born at New Haven, CT. Booth captained five athletic teams at Yale and won eight varsity letters, becoming one of the nation's most exciting halfbacks (1929–31) during college football's heyday. In his sophomore season, he scored all of Yale's points in an epic 21–13 victory over Army. After graduation, he entered business but stayed close to sports, coaching part-time and holding a variety of official positions. Died at New York, NY, Mar 1, 1959.

GREEN BAY COACHES RESIGN: 30th ANNIVERSARY. Feb 1, 1968. Green Bay Packers head coach Vince Lombardi resigned after nine seasons, five NFL titles and victories in the first two Super Bowls. Oddly enough, Green Bay's founding coach, Curly Lambeau, resigned on the same day in 1950 after 29 years on the job.

GROUNDHOG RUN. Feb 1. Kansas City, MO. 16th annual. The only 10K underground run in the world takes place on the Sunday closest to Groundhog Day at the Hunt Midwest Enterprises SubTropolis. More than 1,700 runners from all over the country participate in this event to benefit Children's TLC. Est attendance: 2,000. For info: Paula Yehle, Children's TLC, 2928 Main St, Kansas City, MO 64108. Phone: (816) 234-3392. Fax: (816) 234-3322.

JAWS INVITATIONAL TOW SURFING WORLD CHAMPIONSHIPS. Feb 1–Mar 31. Maui, HI. The first of what is scheduled to be an annual Tow Surfing championship. Competitors will be towed into the peaks of towering waves where they will be released to ride at speeds above 35 knots on footstrap-equipped tow boards–shorter, narrower and heavier than big wave boards. For media info: Adam Nagler, (808) 573-4018 (Email: ARNagler@aol.com) or Carol Hogan, (808) 325-7400 (Email: oceanpro@interpac.net). For contest info: Rodney Kilborn, (808) 575-9264.

LANE, FRANK: BIRTH ANNIVERSARY. Feb 1, 1896. Frank Charles Lane, baseball executive born at Cincinnati, OH. Lane served as general manager of four major league teams and earned the nickname "Trader Frank" for the more than 500 transactions he engineered. His teams never won a single pennant. Died at Richardson, TX, Mar 19, 1981.

NFL PRO BOWL. Feb 1. Aloha Stadium, Honolulu, HI. All-star football game involving the National and American Conferences of the National Football League. Est attendance: 50,000. For info: Aloha Stadium, PO Box 30666, Honolulu, HI 96820. Phone: (808) 486-9300.

THOMPSON, DANNY: BIRTH ANNIVERSARY. Feb 1, 1947. Danny Leon Thompson, baseball player born at Wichita, KS. Thompson became the regular shortstop for the Minnesota Twins in 1972, but he was diagnosed with leukemia less than a year later. He played four more seasons before dying at Rochester, MN, Dec 10, 1976.

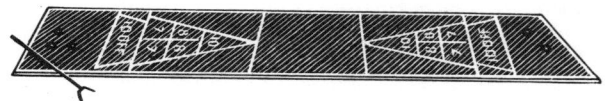

BIRTHDAYS TODAY

Paul L.D. Blair, 54, former baseball player, born Cushing, OK, Feb 1, 1944.

Theodore Roosevelt (T.R.) Dunn, 43, former basketball player, born Birmingham, AL, Feb 1, 1955.

Kent Franklin Mercker, 30, baseball player, born Dublin, OH, Feb 1, 1968.

Garrett Morris, 61, comedian ("Saturday Night Live"), born New Orleans, LA, Feb 1, 1937.

Timothy James (Tim) Naehring, 31, baseball player, born Cincinnati, OH, Feb 1, 1967.

Mark Recchi, 30, hockey player, born Kamloops, BC, Canada, Feb 1, 1968.

Geoff Sanderson, 26, hockey player, born Hay River, Northwest Territories, Canada, Feb 1, 1972.

Malik Sealy, 28, basketball player, born New York, NY, Feb 1, 1970.

February 1998	S	M	T	W	T	F	S
	1	2	3	4	5	6	7
	8	9	10	11	12	13	14
	15	16	17	18	19	20	21
	22	23	24	25	26	27	28

FEBRUARY 2 — MONDAY
Day 33 — 332 Remaining

CHASE'S SPORTSQUOTE OF THE DAY

"I knew it was time to quit when I was chewing out the referee and he walked off the penalty faster than I could keep up with him." —George Halas

ALL-CANADA SHOW. Feb 2–4. Aksarben, Omaha, NE. This consumer show allows individuals an opportunity to talk face-to-face with Canadian lodge representatives and outfitters to plan their hunting, fishing and adventure trips to Canada. For info: Rodney Schlafer, Show Dir, All-Canada Show, Bay-Lakes Mktg, Inc, 1889 Commerce Dr, Depere, WI 54115. Phone: (414) 983-9800 or (800) 325-6290. Fax: (414) 983-9985. WWW: http://www.allcanada.com

BABE VOTED INTO BASEBALL HALL OF FAME: ANNIVERSARY. Feb 2, 1936. The brand-new Baseball Hall of Fame in Cooperstown, NY, announced the election of its five charter members. With 226 ballots cast, 170 votes were required to gain election. Ty Cobb was named on 222 ballots, Babe Ruth on 215, Honus Wagner on 215, Christy Mathewson on 205 and Walter Johnson on 189.

BASKETBALL HALL OF FAME: CLASS OF 1998. Feb 2. Naismith Memorial Basketball Hall of Fame, Springfield, MA. The Hall of Fame announces its Class of '98, selected from a group of nominated in Oct, 1997. Enshrinement of the class will take place on Sept 28. For info: Robin Jonathan Deutsch, Dir Mktg/PR, Basketball Hall of Fame, 1150 W Columbus Ave, Box 179, Springfield, MA 01101-0179. Phone: (413) 781-6500.

BEN HOGAN'S ACCIDENT: ANNIVERSARY. Feb 2, 1949. Ben Hogan was involved in a near-fatal automobile accident when the car he was driving was hit head-on by a bus. Despite serious injuries, Hogan recovered to win the 1950 US Open, beating Lloyd Mangrum and George Fazio in a playoff.

BEVO SCORES 113: ANNIVERSARY. Feb 2, 1954. Bevo Francis of Rio Grande College scored a small-college record 113 points in a 134–91 victory over Hillsdale. Francis broke his own record of 84 points, set two weeks previously against Alliance College.

FORMATION OF NATIONAL LEAGUE: ANNIVERSARY. Feb 2, 1876. William Hulbert founded the National League of Professional Baseball Clubs at a meeting in Chicago. Original franchises were granted to Boston, Chicago, Cincinnati, Hartford, Louisville, New York, Philadelphia and St. Louis.

HALAS, GEORGE: BIRTH ANNIVERSARY. Feb 2, 1895. George ("Papa Bear") Halas, Pro Football Hall of Fame coach and owner born at Chicago, IL. After playing football at the University of Illinois and baseball with the New York Yankees, Halas helped found the National Football League and the Chicago Bears in 1920. As coach of the Bears for 40 years, he compiled a record of 324 wins, 151 losses and 31 ties. Inducted into the Hall of Fame as a charter member in 1963. Died at Chicago, Oct 31, 1983.

OVERALL, ORVAL: BIRTH ANNIVERSARY. Feb 2, 1881. Orval Overall, baseball player born at Farmersville, CA. Overall was one of three outstanding pitchers, along with Ed Reulbach and Mordecai Brown, for the great Chicago Cubs teams of 1907 to 1910. He won 23 games in 1907 and 20 in 1909, but hurt his arm in 1910. Died at Fresno, CA, July 14, 1947.

STUDENT BOWLS 900 SERIES: ANNIVERSARY. Feb 2, 1997. Jeremy Sonnenfeld, 20, from Sioux Falls, SD, bowled a 900 series, three consecutive perfect games, in a tournament in Omaha, NE. Sonnenfeld, a sophomore at the University of Nebraska majoring in business, had the series sanctioned by the American Bowling Congress two days later. Two other bowlers had bowled three consecutive perfect games, but neither met the exacting standards required to qualify as a 900 series. In December 1993 Tony Ockerman bowled his games over two sets of competition. In April 1996 Norm Duke bowled his games in the middle of an eight-game block.

UELSES VAULTS 16 FT: ANNIVERSARY. Feb 2, 1962. At the Millrose Games in Madison Square Garden, Marine Corps corporal John Uelses became the first man to pole vault higher than 16 feet, indoors or outdoors. Using a fiberglass pole, Uelses cleared 16 ft, ¼ in.

BIRTHDAYS TODAY

Roland Americo ("Buddy") Biancalana, 38, former baseball player, born Larkspur, CA, Feb 2, 1960.

Christie Brinkley, 45, former *Sports Illustrated* swimsuit issue model, born Monroe, MI, Feb 2, 1953.

Sean Michael Elliott, 30, basketball player, born Tucson, AZ, Feb 2, 1968.

Scott Gavin Erickson, 30, baseball player, born Long Beach, CA, Feb 2, 1968.

Dexter Manley, 39, former football player, born Houston, TX, Feb 2, 1959.

Albert Fred ("Red") Schoendienst, 75, former manager and Baseball Hall of Fame second baseman, born Germantown, IL, Feb 2, 1923.

FEBRUARY 3 — TUESDAY
Day 34 — 331 Remaining

BINGAMAN, LES: BIRTH ANNIVERSARY. Feb 3, 1926. Lester (Les) Bingaman, football player born at MacKenzie, TN. An enormous lineman, Bingaman starred at the University of Illinois and in the NFL with the Detroit Lions. Despite his size, 6'3" and 335 pounds, he was agile and quick as well as tough. After retirement, he was an assistant coach with the Lions and the Miami Dolphins. Died at Miami, FL, Nov 20, 1970.

ECKERT REMOVED FROM OFFICE: ANNIVERSARY. Feb 3, 1969. Baseball owners removed William D. ("Spike") Eckert from his position as Commissioner. Eckert had become a symbol of the game's blindness, and he had incurred the public's wrath for not cancelling games after the assassinations of Martin Luther King and Robert Kennedy in 1968. With the threat of a players' strike on the horizon, owners decided they needed a more forceful leader, and they eventually selected Bowie Kuhn.

MacPHAIL, LARRY: BIRTH ANNIVERSARY. Feb 3, 1890. Leland Stanford ("Larry") MacPhail, Sr, Baseball Hall of Fame executive born at Cass City, MI. MacPhail was one of baseball's most innovative general managers and owners. He introduced night baseball to the majors in Cincinnati and broke a boycott preventing radio broadcasts of games in New York City. Inducted into the Hall of Fame in 1978. Died at Miami, FL, Oct 1, 1975.

MOON PHASE: FIRST QUARTER. Feb 3. Moon enters First Quarter phase at 5:53 PM, EST.

PYLE, CASH AND CARRY: DEATH ANNIVERSARY. Feb 3, 1939. Charles C. ("Cash and Carry") Pyle, sports promoter born at Van Wert, OH, 1882. Pyle helped popularize the young sport of pro football in the 1920s by signing college star Red Grange to a contract that called for Grange to barnstorm in exhibition games and play for the Chicago Bears. Pyle put Grange in movies, worked a myriad of endorsement deals and even created a league to rival the NFL. Died at Los Angeles, CA.

SALLEE, SLIM: BIRTH ANNIVERSARY. Feb 3, 1885. Harry Franklin ("Slim") Sallee, baseball player born at Higginsport, OH. Sallee's best season as a major league pitcher was 1919 when he won 21 games for the Cincinnati Reds and one game against the Black Sox in the World Series. Died at Higginsport, Mar 22, 1950.

SHOEMAKER'S FINAL FINISH: ANNIVERSARY. Feb 3, 1990. Jockey Bill Shoemaker rode in the 40,350th and last race of his career, finishing fourth on a horse named Patchy Groundfog at Santa Anita. After 40 years of racing, Shoemaker's record stood at 8,833 wins, 6,136 places and 4,987 shows with $123,375,534 in earnings.

STEPHENS, HELEN: 80th BIRTH ANNIVERSARY. Feb 3, 1918. Helen Herring Stephens, Olympic gold medal sprinter, born at Fulton, MO. Known as the "Fulton Flash," Stephens earned the title "The World's Fastest Woman" by winning gold medals in the 100 meters and the 400-meter relay at the 1936 Olympics in Berlin. She held many scholastic and national records and also performed well in basketball, softball, bowling, fencing and swimming. Died at St. Louis, MO, Jan 17, 1994.

BIRTHDAYS TODAY

Jerome Austin (Jerry) Browne, 32, baseball player, born St. Croix, Virgin Islands, Feb 3, 1966.

Keith Edward Carney, 28, hockey player, born Pawtucket, RI, Feb 3, 1970.

Vlade Divac, 30, basketball player, born Prijepolje, Yugoslavia, Feb 3, 1968.

Robert Allen (Bob) Griese, 53, broadcaster and Pro Football Hall of Fame quarterback, born Evansville, IN, Feb 3, 1945.

Fredric Michael (Fred) Lynn, 46, former baseball player, born Chicago, IL, Feb 3, 1952.

Carol Mann, 57, LPGA Hall of Fame golfer, born Buffalo, NY, Feb 3, 1941.

Arnold Ray ("Bake") McBride, 49, former baseball player, born Fulton, MO, Feb 3, 1949.

Dwayne Rudd, 22, football player, born Batesville, MS, Feb 3, 1976.

Francis Asbury (Fran) Tarkenton, 58, Pro Football Hall of Fame quarterback, born Richmond, VA, Feb 3, 1940.

FEBRUARY 4 — WEDNESDAY
Day 35 — 330 Remaining

ARBITRATOR SEITZ'S DECISION UPHELD: ANNIVERSARY. Feb 4, 1976. US District Court Judge John W. Oliver upheld the ruling of baseball arbitrator Peter Seitz that had declared pitchers Andy Messersmith and Dave McNally to be free agents. The two had refused to sign contracts for 1974 as a test case and had argued that baseball's hallowed reserved clause bound them to their respective clubs not in perpetuity but for only one year beyond the expiration of their last signed contract.

BOWIE KUHN ELECTED COMMISSIONER: ANNIVERSARY. Feb 4, 1969. Owners of the 24 major league baseball clubs elected attorney Bowie Kuhn commissioner for a one-year term at a salary of $100,000. Kuhn, who succeeded William D. Eckert, became baseball's fifth commissioner. He served until 1984 when he replaced by Peter Ueberroth.

BROWN, JEROME: BIRTH ANNIVERSARY. Feb 4, 1965. Jerome Brown, football player born at Brooksville, FL. Brown was an All-American defensive tackle at the University of Miami and was drafted in 1987 by the Philadelphia Eagles. A two-time All-Pro, he was killed in a one-car accident. Died at Brooksville, FL, June 25, 1992.

CANADA: VANCOUVER SPORTSMEN'S SHOW. Feb 4–8. BC Place Stadium, Vancouver, British Columbia. Fishing, hunting, camping, outdoor equipment, boating, personal watercraft, 4-wheel drive vehicles and accessories, tourism, resorts, destinations, water sports, adventure sports, family entertainment and World of Dogs. Est attendance: 20,000. For info: Canadian Natl Sportsmen's Shows, 703 Evans Ave, Ste 202, Toronto, Ont, Canada M9C 5E9. Phone: (416) 695-0311. Fax: (416) 695-0381.

CANADA: VANCOUVER INTERNATIONAL BOAT SHOW. Feb 4–8. BC Place Stadium, Vancouver, British Columbia. Sail and powerboats, sailboards, inflatables, canoes, personal watercraft, marine electronics and accessories, marine services, charters, sailing schools, water skis, sporting goods, travel and resort destinations, fishing equipment and family entertainment. Est attendance: 45,000. For info: Canadian Natl Sportsmen's Shows, 703 Evans Ave, Ste 202, Toronto, Ont, Canada M9C 5E9. Phone: (416) 695-0311. Fax: (416) 695-0381.

HALFWAY POINT OF WINTER. Feb 4. At 3:01 AM, EST, on Feb 4, 44 days, 11 hours and 54 minutes of winter will have elapsed and the equivalent remain before 2:55 PM, EST, on Mar 20, 1998, which is the spring equinox and the beginning of spring.

JOHNSTON, NEIL: BIRTH ANNIVERSARY. Feb 4, 1929. Donald Neil Johnston, Basketball Hall of Fame center born at Chillicothe, OH. Johnston played basketball and baseball at Ohio State University and decided to forego finishing college to play pro baseball in the summer and pro basketball in the winter. After several seasons in the minor leagues, he quit baseball to concentrate on basketball where he became a standout with the Philadelphia Warriors. He led the NBA in scoring and field goal percentage three times and in rebounding once. He played in six All-Star games and coached the Warriors as well. Inducted into the Hall of Fame in 1990. Died at Bedford, TX, Sept 27, 1978.

LEMIEUX SCORES 600th GOAL: ANNIVERSARY. Feb 4, 1997. Mario Lemieux of the Pittsburgh Penguins scored into an empty net to become the seventh member of the NHL's 600-goal club. Pittsburgh beat the Vancouver Canucks, 6–4. Players who previously scored 600 goals are Gordie Howe, Bobby Hull, Marcel Dionne, Phil Esposito, Mike Gartner and Wayne Gretzky, who got his 600th goal in his 720th game, one more than Lemieux required.

NEW ORLEANS BOAT & SPORTFISHING SHOW. Feb 4–8. Louisiana Superdome, New Orleans, LA. 28th annual show of boat and marine products, fishing equipment and resort info. Informative boating and fishing seminars. For info: Natl Marine Manufacturers Assn, Sherron F. Smith, Show Mgr, 4051 Veterans Memorial Blvd, Ste 202, Metairie, LA 70002. Phone: (504) 885-9709. Fax: (504) 455-4966.

February 1998	S	M	T	W	T	F	S
	1	2	3	4	5	6	7
	8	9	10	11	12	13	14
	15	16	17	18	19	20	21
	22	23	24	25	26	27	28

1932 WINTER OLYMPICS OPEN: ANNIVERSARY. Feb 4, 1932. The third Winter Olympics opened at Lake Placid, NY, with 32 women and 274 men athletes representing 17 nations. This was the only edition of the Winter Games in which athletes from the US won more medals (six gold, four silver and two bronze) than athletes from any other country. The Games closed on Feb 15.

OCALA WINTER CIRCUIT. Feb 4–Mar 9 (various). Golden Hills International Show Grounds, Ocala, FL. Five weeks of hunter/jumper competition. Riders from beginning levels to world class can be seen in competition all week long, with the featured Grand Prix show jumping event each Sunday. The shows attract over 1,000 horses for each week of competition. Annually, February through early March. Est attendance: 15,000. For info and exact dates of circuit events: HITS, 13 Closs Dr, Rhinebeck, NY 12572. Phone: (914) 876-3666. Fax: (914) 876-5538. WWW: http://www.equisearch.com

SCHAEFER, GERMANY: BIRTH ANNIVERSARY. Feb 4, 1877. Herman A. ("Germany") Schaefer, baseball player born at Chicago, IL. One of baseball's zaniest characters, Schaefer once stole second, retreated to first on the next pitch and then stole second again. Died at Saranac Lake, NY, May 16, 1919.

SCOTLAND: OUTDOORS 98. Feb 4–8. Scottish Exhibition and Conference Centre, Glasgow, Strathclyde. Est attendance: 40,000. For info: Phone: (44) (141) 204-0123. Fax: (44) (141) 204-0077.

STARS & STRIPES WINS AMERICA'S CUP: 10th ANNIVERSARY. Feb 4, 1987. *Stars & Stripes*, skippered by Dennis Connor, defeated the Australian boat *Kookaburra III* for the fourth straight time to sweep the America's Cup challenge and return the prized trophy to the US. This was the last Cup defense to be contested by 12-meter yachts. It came four years after *Australia II* with John Bertrand as skipper wrested the Cup from the US for the first time ever.

BIRTHDAYS TODAY

Christopher Michael (Chris) Bando, 42, former baseball player, born Cleveland, OH, Feb 4, 1956.
Brandon Convery, 24, hockey player, born Kingston, Ontario, Canada, Feb 4, 1974.
Oscar de la Hoya, 25, boxer, born Los Angeles, CA, Feb 4, 1973.
Daniel Thomas (Dan) Plesac, 36, baseball player, born Gary, IN, Feb 4, 1962.
J. Danforth (Dan) Quayle, 51, 44th US Vice President, amateur golfer, born Indianapolis, IN, Feb 4, 1947.
Denis Joseph Savard, 37, former hockey player, born Pointe Gatineau, Quebec, Canada, Feb 4, 1961.
Lawrence Taylor, 39, former football player, born Williamsburg, VA, Feb 4, 1959.

☆ ☆ ☆

FEBRUARY 5 — THURSDAY
Day 36 — 329 Remaining

ALL-CANADA SHOW. Feb 5–8. Iowa State Fair Grounds, Des Moines, IA. This consumer show allows individuals an opportunity to talk face-to-face with Canadian lodge representatives and outfitters to plan their hunting, fishing and adventure trips to Canada. For info: Rodney Schlafer, Show Dir, All-Canada Show, Bay-Lakes Mktg, Inc, 1889 Commerce Dr, De Pere, WI 54115. Phone: (414) 983-9800 or (800) 325-6290. Fax: (414) 983-9985. WWW: http://www.allcanada.com

DICK BUTTON WINS GOLD MEDAL: 40th ANNIVERSARY. Feb 5, 1948. Dick Button became the first American to win a gold medal in figure skating when he triumphed at the Fifth Winter Olympics at St. Moritz, Switzerland. Button earned a second gold medal four years later at Oslo, Norway.

HENDERSON, CAM: BIRTH ANNIVERSARY. Feb 5, 1890. Eli Camden (Cam) Henderson, basketball player and coach born at Marion County, WV. Lack of financial resources caused Henderson to cut short his education at Glenville State College (WV) where he played three sports. He began coaching at Bristol High School and invented the zone defense in a local YMCA game. He coached at several colleges including Marshall College where he pioneered an innovative, fast-break offense. Died at Cedar Hill, KY, May 3, 1956.

HOAK, DON: BIRTH ANNIVERSARY. Feb 5, 1928. Donald Albert (Don) Hoak, baseball player born at Roulette, PA. Hoak was a tough third baseman who played with the Brooklyn Dodgers, the Chicago Cubs and the Pittsburgh Pirates. He was married to singer Jill Corey. Died at Pittsburgh, PA, Oct 9, 1969.

KLAMMER WINS DOWNHILL: ANNIVERSARY. Feb 5, 1976. Before a roaring crowd of fellow countrymen, Austrian Franz Klammer won the downhill ski race at the XIIth Winter Olympic Games at Innsbruck, Austria. Clad in bright yellow, Klammer electrified a worldwide television audience with his breathtaking run.

NOTRE DAME SIGNS WITH NBC: ANNIVERSARY. Feb 5, 1990. The University of Notre Dame broke with the College Football Association and became the first college to sell the rights to televise its home football games to a major network. The Irish and NBC signed a five-year contract to start in 1991.

PECKINPAUGH, ROGER: BIRTH ANNIVERSARY. Feb 5, 1891. Roger Thorpe Peckinpaugh, baseball player, manager and executive born at Wooster, OH. Peckinpaugh played shortstop for 17 years with four different clubs. He was player-manager of the New York Highlanders (later the Yankees) in 1914 at age 23. Playing for Washington in 1924, he made eight errors in the World Series. Died at Cleveland, OH, Nov 17, 1977.

BIRTHDAYS TODAY

Henry Louis (Hank) Aaron, 64, baseball executive and Baseball Hall of Fame outfielder, born Mobile, AL, Feb 5, 1934.
Roberto Alomar, 30, baseball player, born Ponce, Puerto Rico, Feb 5, 1968.
Michael Thomas (Mike) Heath, 43, former baseball player, born Tampa, FL, Feb 5, 1955.
Roger Thomas Staubach, 56, Pro Football Hall of Fame quarterback, born Cincinnati, OH, Feb 5, 1942.
James Leroy (Lee) Thomas, 62, baseball executive and former player, born Peoria, IL, Feb 5, 1936.
Darrell Waltrip, 51, auto racer, born Franklin, TN, Feb 5, 1947.

FEBRUARY 6 — FRIDAY
Day 37 — 328 Remaining

SPORTSCHASER OF THE DAY

Who are the only father and son to score 50 goals each in an NHL season?

BADGER STATE WINTER GAMES. Feb 6–8. Wausau, WI, and 10 other Central Wisconsin communities. 10th annual Olympic-style competition for Wisconsin residents of all ages and abilities attracts more than 5,000 participants in 9 sports: cross-country skiing, curling, downhill skiing, figure skating, ice hockey, ski jumping, snowshoe racing, snowboarding and speed skating. Annually, the first weekend of February. Major sponsors are: AT&T, Ameritech, GTE, Wisconsin Milk Marketing Board, WPS Health Insurance, Oscar Mayer Foods Corp and Tombstone Pizza. Presenting sponsor is Wausau Insurance Companies. Member of the National Congress of State Games. Est attendance: 21,000. For info: Otto Breitenbach, Exec Dir, or Jack Eich, PR Dir, Badger State Games, PO Box 1377, Madison, WI 53701-1377. Phone: (608) 251-3333.

BRETT HULL JOINS FATHER: ANNIVERSARY. Feb 6, 1990. Brett Hull of the St. Louis Blues scored his 50th goal of the season to join his father, Hall of Fame left wing Bobby Hull, as the only father-son combination in NHL history to score 50 goals in a season.

BULLNANZA. Feb 6–7. Lazy E Arena, Guthrie, OK. Present and past champions in exciting competition in bull riding. Annually, the first Friday and Saturday in February. Est attendance: 14,000. For info: Lazy E Arena, Rte 5, Box 393, Guthrie, OK 73044. Phone: (800) 595-RIDE. Fax: (405) 282-3785. Email: learena@ionet.net. WWW: http://www.lazye.com

BURGESS, SMOKY: BIRTH ANNIVERSARY. Feb 6, 1927. Forrest Harrill ("Smoky") Burgess, baseball player born at Caroleen, NC. Burgess was a four-time National League All-Star as a catcher. He played for the 1960 Pittsburgh Pirates, World Series champions, and in the later stages of his career was an outstanding pinch-hitter. Died at Asheville, NC, Sept 15, 1991.

February	S	M	T	W	T	F	S
1998	1	2	3	4	5	6	7
	8	9	10	11	12	13	14
	15	16	17	18	19	20	21
	22	23	24	25	26	27	28

CANADA: BRACEBRIDGE WINTER CARNIVAL. Feb 6–8. Gravenhurst, Ontario. Snowmobile activities and events, arts and crafts, children's ice and snow village, dances, winter baseball, broomball, helicopter rides, wreck 'm race, snow box derby, snow sculpture, turkey bowling, pancake breakfasts. More than 50 events–"The Best Family Winter Fun Under the Sun." Est attendance: 10,000. For info: Gravenhurst Chamber of Commerce, 295-1 Muskoka Rd S, Gravenhurst, Ont, Canada P1P 1J1. Phone: (705) 687-8432. Fax: (705) 687-4382. Email: chamber@muskoka.net.

CANADA: WINTERLUDE. Feb 6–8 (also Feb 13–15, 20–22). Ottawa, Ontario. 20th annual celebration of Canadian winter and traditions for the whole family. Skating on Rideau Canal, the world's longest skating rink, snow and ice sculptures, world-class figure skating, North America's largest snow playground and exciting Winter Triathlon. Warm-up at the Great Canadian Icebreaker, a winter spectacular featuring top Canadian artists and figure skaters. Est attendance: 650,000. For info: Natl Capital Commission, 40 Elgin St, Ste 202, Ottawa, Ont, Canada K1P 1C7. Phone: (613) 239-5000 or (800) 465-1867.

DOG SLED WEIGHT PULL CHAMPIONSHIPS AND WINTER CARNIVAL. Feb 6–7. Christmas Mountain Village, Wisconsin Dells, WI. Sled dog weight-pull contest. Sleigh rides, chili cook-off and winter golf. Craft fair, refreshments, skydiving, fireworks, children's activities, live entertainment and wood-splitting contests. Est attendance: 4,000. For info: Christmas Mountain Village, 5944 Christmas Mountain Rd, Wisconsin Dells, WI 53965. Phone: (608) 253-1000. Fax: (608) 254-3983.

JAPAN: WINTER OLYMPICS: OPENING CEREMONY AND DAY ONE OF COMPETITION. Feb 6. Nagano, Japan. See Japan: Winter Olympics: Opening Ceremony and Day One of Competition, Feb 7. Japan is 14 hours ahead of the Eastern Time zone in the US. The schedule of Olympic events will be listed in this book as they occur in the host city.

LAKE WINNEBAGO STURGEON SEASON. Feb 6–Mar 1 (tentative). Fond du Lac, WI, at the foot of the lake is the Sturgeon Capital of the World. The sturgeon species has remained unchanged for more than 50 million years and the Lake Winnebago region has one of the major populations of them. Shanty and equipment rental available; sturgeon fishing tag required. For info: Fond du Lac Conv Bureau, 19 W Scott St, Fond du Lac, WI 54935. Phone: (800) 937-9123 ext 95. Fax: (414) 929-6846. Email: fdlcvb@visitwisconsin.com. WWW: http://www.visitwisconsin.com/fdl

LONG, DALE: BIRTH ANNIVERSARY. Feb 6, 1926. Richard Dale Long, baseball player born at Springfield, MA. Long played ten years in the major leagues and once hit home runs in eight straight games. A lefthanded first baseman, he played catcher for two games in 1958. Died at Palm Coast, FL, Jan 27, 1991.

LONGHORN WORLD CHAMPIONSHIP RODEO. Feb 6–8. The Crown, Cincinnati, OH. More than 200 cowboys and cowgirls compete in six professional contests ranging from bronc riding to bull riding for top prize money and world championship points. Featuring colorful opening pageantry and Big, Bad BONUS Bulls. 24th annual. Est attendance: 24,000. For info: W. Bruce Lehrke, Pres, Longhorn World Chmpshp Rodeo, Inc, PO Box 70159, Nashville, TN 37207. Phone: (615) 876-1016. Fax: (615) 876-4685. Email: lhrodeo@idt.net. WWW: http://www.longhornrodeo.com

NATIONAL GIRLS AND WOMEN IN SPORTS DAY. Feb 6. Celebrates the passage of Title IX (in 1972), the law that guarantees gender equity in federally-funded school programs, including athletics. Sponsored by the Women's Sports Foundation and the National Association for Girls and Women in Sports. For info: Natl Assn for Girls and Women in Sports, 1900 Assn Dr, Reston, VA 20191. Phone: (703) 476-3450. Email: nagws@aahperd.org.

NRA RODEO FINALS. Feb 6–8. MetraPark Arena, Billings, MT. Rodeo action at its best–23rd annual finals. A fun-filled rodeo weekend in cowboy country! Est attendance: 16,000. For info: Northern Rodeo Assn, PO Box 1122, Billings, MT 59103. Phone: (406) 252-1122. Fax: (406) 252-0300.

PERCHVILLE USA. Feb 6–8. Tawas Bay, East Tawas, MI. A winter festival with ice-fishing contests, polar bear swims, go-kart races on the ice, IWPA dog weight pulls, softball tournaments and many children's activities. Annually, the first full weekend in February. Est attendance: 10,000. For info: Kimberly Lingo, Program Director, Tawas Area Chamber of Commerce, Box 608, Tawas City, MI 48764-0608. Phone: (517) 362-8643 or (800) 55-TAWAS.

ROFFE WINS ALPINE MEDAL: ANNIVERSARY. Feb 6, 1985. Skier Dianne Roffe, 17, took first place in a giant slalom race to become the first US woman to win a gold medal in a World Alpine Ski Championship race.

RUTH, BABE: BIRTH ANNIVERSARY. Feb 6, 1895. George Herman ("Babe") Ruth, Baseball Hall of Fame pitcher and outfielder born at Baltimore, MD. One of baseball's greatest heroes, George Herman "Babe" Ruth was raised at St. Mary's Industrial School for Boys. He was signed to a minor league baseball contract by Jack Dunn of the Baltimore Orioles and became known as "Dunn's Babe." An outstanding pitcher, Ruth began swatting home runs in record numbers and was converted to the outfield. He hit 714 home runs in 22 major league seasons of play (a record 60 in 1927) and played in 10 World Series. He was the game's greatest star and became an enduring legend. Inducted into the Hall of Fame in 1936. Died at New York, NY, on Aug 16, 1948.

SPORTSFEST '98. Feb 6–7. Held indoors at the Myriad Convention Center, Oklahoma City, OK. Oklahoma's amateur winter sports festival includes some 5,500 athletes competing in about 14 events, including gymnastics, basketball, tumbling, table tennis, volleyball and cheerleading plus a trade show and appearances by sports celebrities. Est attendance: 9,000. For info: Sooner State Games, 100 W Main, Ste 285, Oklahoma City, OK 73102. Phone: (405) 235-4222. Fax: (405) 232-7723. Email: snrstgms@aol.com.

WORLD SHOVEL RACE CHAMPIONSHIPS. Feb 6–8. Angel Fire, MN. This famous event highlights thrilling competition in production and modified divisions for several age groups. "Modified" competition reaches speeds of 75 mph. Spectator competition on stock grain scoop shovels. Est attendance: 3,000. For info: Angel Fire Resort, PO Drawer B, Angel Fire, NM 87710. Phone: (800) 633-7463 or (505) 377-4237. Fax: (505) 377-4395. Email: gmorton@angelfireresort.com. WWW: http://www.angelfireresort.com

WRIGHT, GLENN: BIRTH ANNIVERSARY. Feb 6, 1901. Forrest Glenn Wright, baseball player born at Archie, MO. Wright was one of the finest shortstops of the 1920s and 1930s. He was an outstanding fielder who could also hit with power. Died at Olathe, KS, Apr 6, 1984.

YUMA JAYCEES' SILVER SPUR RODEO. Feb 6–8. Yuma County Fairgrounds, Yuma, AZ. Three-day rodeo features professional rodeo cowboy action, preceded by a week of activities beginning with parade on Feb 1. Annually, in February. Sponsors: Budweiser, Dodge, Pepsi, Best Western Inn Suites and Jack-in-the-Box. Est attendance: 28,000. For info: Richard Metzler, Rodeo Chair, Silver Spur Rodeo, PO Box 2797, Yuma, AZ 85364. Phone: (520) 782-4955.

☆   ☆   ☆

BIRTHDAYS TODAY

William Chester (Bill) Dawley, 40, former baseball player, born Norwich, CT, Feb 6, 1958.
Ronald Wilson Reagan, 87, 40th US president, sportscaster and actor (*The Winning Team*), born Tampico, IL, Feb 6, 1911.
Michael Tucker, 54, actor (*Mighty Ducks II*), born Baltimore, MD, Feb 6, 1944.
Richard Walter (Richie) Zisk, 49, former baseball player, born New York, NY, Feb 6, 1949.

FEBRUARY 7 — SATURDAY
Day 38 — 327 Remaining

BASEBALL'S FIRST $2 MILLION MAN: ANNIVERSARY. Feb 7, 1982. Outfielder George Foster became baseball's highest-paid player and the first $2 million man when he signed a five-year contract with the New York Mets worth $10 million. Free agent Foster left the Cincinnati Reds' fabled "Big Red Machine," but his offensive production with the Mets never reached expectations. New York released him before the last year of his contract expired.

BUTTS, WALLY: BIRTH ANNIVERSARY. Feb 7, 1905. James Wallace (Wally) Butts, Jr, football player, coach and administrator born at Milledgeville, GA. Butts played football at Mercer College, coached at the prep level and became head coach and athletic director at the University of Georgia in 1939. His teams compiled a record of 140–86–9 over 21 seasons and played in eight bowl games. He retired from coaching in 1960 and as athletic director in 1964. Died at Athens, GA, Dec 17, 1973.

CRUMP FIRST WOMAN JOCKEY: ANNIVERSARY. Feb 7, 1969. Diana Crump became the first woman jockey to ride in a parimutuel race at a US track. Crump finished tenth in a field of 12 at Hialeah.

ENGLAND: BRISTOL CLASSIC CAR SHOW. Feb 7–8. Royal Bath and West Showground, Shepton Mallet, Somerset. Everything for the classic car enthusiast with club stands, trade stands and autojumble. Auction at 2 PM Sunday. Est attendance: 18,000. For info: Robert Ewin, Dir, Nationwide Exhibitions (UK) Ltd, PO Box 20, Fishponds, Bristol, England BS16 5QU. Phone: (44) (117) 970-1370. Fax: (44) (117) 970-1371. WWW: http://www.nationawideexhibitions.co.uk

FIRST SECURITY WINTER GAMES OF IDAHO. Feb 7–Mar 1. Idaho Falls, Sun Valley, Boise, McCall and Kellogg, ID. Idaho's official winter sports competition–15 days (three weekends) of competition in ice hockey, figure skating, alpine skiing, freestyle skiing, telemark skiing, snowboarding, cross-country skiing and snowmobiling with 3,000 participants. For info: Amy McDevitt, Exec Dir, Winter Games of Idaho, PO Box 15214, Boise, ID 83715. Phone: (208) 393-2255. Fax: (208) 393-2187.

FIRST SECURITY BOULDER MOUNTAIN TOUR. Feb 7. Galena Lodge, Sun Valley, ID. A 30K freestyle cross-country race from Galena Lodge to the Sawtooth National Recreation Area (SNRA) headquarters. For info: Sun Valley/Ketchum Chamber of Commerce, Box 2420, Sun Valley, ID 83353. Phone: (800) 634-3347 or (208) 726-3423. Fax: (208) 726-4533. Email: sunval@micron.net. WWW: http://www.visitsunvalley.com

JAPAN: WINTER OLYMPICS: OPENING CEREMONY AND DAY ONE OF COMPETITION. Feb 7. Nagano. The Opening Ceremony of the XVIIIth Winter Olympic Games will commence at 11 AM, local time. (Since Japan is 14 hours ahead of the Eastern Time zone in the US, the Opening Ceremony will begin at 9 PM, EST, Friday, Feb 6. Competition scheduled for Day One: men's ice hockey (preliminary games).

LESLIE SCORES 101: ANNIVERSARY. Feb 7, 1990. Lisa Leslie of Morningside HS, Inglewood, CA, scored 101 points in the first half of a game against South Torrance HS. The game ended at the half with the score at 102–24 as the South Torrance coach refused to let his team finish the game.

PERRY'S "BRR" (BIKE RIDE TO RIPPEY). Feb 7. Perry, IA. Winter bike riding. Twenty-two miles of frigid fun. Annually, the first Saturday in February. Est attendance: 2,000. For info: Chamber of Commerce, Kathy Hoskinson, 1226 Second St, Perry, IA 50220. Phone: (515) 465-4601. Fax: (515) 465-2256.

SITTLER SETS POINTS RECORD: ANNIVERSARY. Feb 7, 1979. The Toronto Maple Leafs' Darryl Sittler set an NHL record for most points in a game when he scored 6 goals and earned four assists in an 11–4 victory over the Boston Bruins.

SULLIVAN WINS HEAVYWEIGHT CROWN: ANNIVERSARY. Feb 7, 1882. John L. Sullivan won the bare-knuckle heavyweight championship of the world by defeating Paddy Ryan in a nine-round fight in Mississippi City, MS.

TOMS RIVER WILDFOWL ART AND DECOY SHOW. Feb 7–8. Toms River High School North, Toms River, NJ. 140 artists and carvers, decoy-carving competitions, decorative and gunning decoys, junior competition; free seminars on decoy carving, decoy painting and flat art painting; fine arts competition; decoy-painting competitions on Saturday (judging Sunday at 1 PM). Duck painting to entertain kids. Annually, the first weekend in February. Est attendance: 4,000. For info: Janet Sellitto, Mang Serv Coord, Ocean County YMCA, PO Box 130, Toms River, NJ 08754. Phone: (732) 341-9622, ext 214. Fax: (732) 341-1629. WWW: http://www.ocymca.org

USLA MICHIGAN STATE COMPETITION. Feb 7. Muskegon Luge Track, Muskegon Winter Sports Complex, Muskegon, MI. United States Luge Assn (USLA) competition. Open to the public. Competitors vary in skill; divisions by age group. Muskegon Luge is one of only two in country. For info: Muskegon Sports Council, PO Box 5085, North Muskegon, MI 49445. Phone: (616) 744-9629. Luge Club phone: (616) 759-2201.

BIRTHDAYS TODAY

Peter Bondra, 30, hockey player, born Luck, Ukraine, USSR, Feb 7, 1968.

Alexandre Daigle, 23, hockey player, born Montreal, Quebec, Canada, Feb 7, 1975.

Christopher Allen (Chris) Gardocki, 28, football player, born Stone Mountain, GA, Feb 7, 1970.

Juwan Antonio Howard, 25, basketball player, born Chicago, IL, Feb 7, 1973.

Carney Ray Lansford, 41, former baseball player, born San Jose, CA, Feb 7, 1957.

Stephen John (Steve) Nash, 24, basketball player, born Johannesburg, South Africa, Feb 7, 1974.

Daniel Raymond (Dan) Quisenberry, 45, former baseball player, born Santa Monica, CA, Feb 7, 1953.

FEBRUARY 8 — SUNDAY
Day 39 — 326 Remaining

ARCA 200 LATE MODEL STOCK CAR RACE. Feb 8. Daytona International Speedway, Daytona Beach, FL. 35th annual running. Season kickoff for the Bondo/Mar-Hyde Supercar Series. For info: John Story, Dir of Pub Rel, Daytona Intl Speedway, PO Box 2801, Daytona Beach, FL 32120-2801. Phone: (904) 947-6782. For tickets: (904) 253-RACE (7223). Fax: (904) 947-6791. WWW: http://www.daytonausa.com

BOWMAN EARNS 1,000th WIN: ANNIVERSARY. Feb 8, 1997. The Detroit Red Wings defeated the Pittsburgh Penguins, 6–5, in overtime, to make coach Scotty Bowman the first NHL coach to reach the 1,000-win plateau.

BUSCH CLASH OF '98. Feb 8. Daytona International Speedway, Daytona Beach, FL. Winners of Busch Pole Awards for the '97 NASCAR Winston Cup season. Sponsor: Busch Beer. For info: John Story, Dir of Pub Rel, Daytona Intl Speedway, PO Box 2801, Daytona Beach, FL 32120-2801. Phone: (904) 947-6782. For tickets: (904) 253-RACE (7223). Fax: (904) 947-6791. WWW: http://www.daytonausa.com

CANADA: YUKON QUEST 1,000-MILE SLED DOG RACE. Feb 8–20. Whitehorse, Yukon. The 15th annual "Challenge of the North" 1,000-mile dog sled race from Whitehorse, YT, to Fairbanks, AK. Top mushers from North America and around the world compete for the $125,000 purse. Est attendance: 10,000. For info: Yukon Quest Assn, Box 5555, Whitehorse, YT, Canada Y1A 5H4. Phone: (403) 668-4711. Info also from: Yukon Quest Intl, PO Box 75015, Fairbanks, AK 99707. Phone: (907) 452-7954. WWW: http://www.yukonquest.com

DALLAS TEXANS BECOME KANSAS CITY CHIEFS: 35th ANNIVERSARY. Feb 8, 1963. Less than two months after defeating the Houston Oilers in the second championship game of the American Football League, the Dallas Texans, owned by Lamar Hunt, moved to Kansas City and were renamed the Chiefs.

JAPAN: WINTER OLYMPICS: DAY TWO. Feb 8. Nagano. Competition: cross country skiing (women's 15 km classical); freestyle skiing (moguls preliminaries); snowboarding (men's giant slalom); alpine skiing (men's downhill); men's ice hockey (preliminary games); luge (men's singles); speed skating (men's 5,000 meters); women's ice hockey; and figure skating (pairs short program).

KIDD AND HEUGA WIN MEDALS: ANNIVERSARY. Feb 8, 1964. Billy Kidd and Jim Heuga became the first American men to win Olympic medals in Alpine skiing when they captured the silver and bronze medals, respectively, in the slalom at the IXth Winter Olympics at Innsbruck, Austria.

LOPEZ MAKES HALL OF FAME: ANNIVERSARY. Feb 8, 1987. Nancy Lopez won the 35th LPGA tournament of her career, the $200,000 Sarasota Classic, and earned induction into the LPGA Hall of Fame.

February 1998

	S	M	T	W	T	F	S
	1	2	3	4	5	6	7
	8	9	10	11	12	13	14
	15	16	17	18	19	20	21
	22	23	24	25	26	27	28

MAN O' WAR THE GREATEST: ANNIVERSARY. Feb 8, 1950. Man o' War was voted the greatest race horse of the first half of the 20th century in a poll conducted by the Associated Press. Man o' War raced as a 2- and 3-year old, winning 20 of 21 races and setting five track records.

PULLIAM, HARRY: BIRTH ANNIVERSARY. Feb 8, 1869. Harry Clay Pulliam, baseball executive born at Scottsville, KY. Pulliam was elected president of the National League in 1902 after being an official with the Pittsburgh Pirates. Intense controversies during his administration drove him to depression and suicide. Died at New York, NY, July 29, 1909.

BIRTHDAYS TODAY

Rod Earl Bernstine, 33, football player, born Fairfield, CA, Feb 8, 1965.

Joseph (Joe) Black, 74, former baseball player, born Plainfield, NJ, Feb 8, 1924.

Cletis Leroy (Clete) Boyer, 61, former baseball player, born Cassville, MO, Feb 8, 1937.

Dino Ciccarelli, 38, hockey player, born Sarnia, Ontario, Canada, Feb 8, 1960.

Alonzo Mourning, 28, basketball player, born Chesapeake, VA, Feb 8, 1970.

Kirk Muller, 32, hockey player, born Kingston, Ontario, Canada, Feb 8, 1966.

☆   ☆   ☆

FEBRUARY 9 — MONDAY
Day 40 — 325 Remaining

CHASE'S SPORTSQUOTE OF THE DAY

"It isn't the high price of stars that is expensive, it's the high price of mediocrity." —Bill Veeck

GTE CLASSIC. Feb 9–15. TPC of Tampa Bay, Tampa, FL. One of the premier stops on the Senior PGA Tour, attracting one of the strongest fields of top Senior Tour pros. The TPC of Tampa Bay affords outstanding "Stadium Golf"® viewing with amphitheater-style mounds along fairways and around greens. Pro-am event Wednesday and Thursday, followed by professional competitive rounds Fri–Sun. Est attendance: 165,000. For info: GTE Suncoast Classic, 16002 N Dale Mabry, Tampa, FL 33618. Phone: (813) 265-4653. Fax: (813) 265-4655. Email: damtram@gte.net. WWW: http://www.classic.gte.net

HUGHSON, TEX: BIRTH ANNIVERSARY. Feb 9, 1916. Cecil Carleton ("Tex") Hughson, baseball player born at Kyle, TX. Hughson played at the University of Texas and joined the Boston Red Sox in 1941. His career lasted a decade and was cut short by a sore arm. Died at San Marcos, TX, Aug 6, 1993.

JAPAN: WINTER OLYMPICS: DAY THREE. Feb 9. Nagano. Competition: curling (women's and men's preliminaries); snowboarding (women's giant slalom); alpine skiing (downhill portion of men's combined); cross country skiing (men's 30 km classical); women's ice hockey; biathlon (women's 15 km); men's ice hockey (preliminary games); luge (men's singles); and speed skating (men's 500 meters).

MAGIC'S ALL-STAR COMEBACK: ANNIVERSARY. Feb 9, 1992. Three months after announcing his retirement (on Nov 7, 1991) from the NBA because he had been infected with HIV, Magic Johnson led the West to a 153–113 victory over the East in the 42nd NBA All-Star Game. Magic was named All-Star Game MVP for the second time.

NATIONAL FIELD TRIAL CHAMPIONSHIP. Feb 9–20. (Monday–Friday only.) Ames Plantation, Grand Junction, TN. To select the national champion all-age bird dog. Est attendance: 8,000. For info: Natl Field Trial Champion Assn, Box 389, Grand Junction, TN 38039. Phone: (901) 878-1067. Fax: (901) 878-1068. Email: amesplan@aol.com.

PEDDLE PUSHERS' DAYS©98. Feb 9 (also May 9, Aug 9 and Nov 9). These quarterly celebrations honor those who ride bicycles, invented by Baron Karl von Drais of Karlsruhe, Germany, in 1816. Take a hike on a bike! For further info send $2 to cover cost of copying and postage to: 1437 W Rosemont, 1W, Chicago, IL 60660-1319. Phone: (773) 743-5341. Fax: (773) 743-5395. Email: kooper@interaccess.com.

TENNIS CHANGES THE RULES: ANNIVERSARY. Feb 9, 1912. The United States Lawn Tennis Association amended the playing rules for its men's singles championship. The defending champion lost his bye directly into the final and was required to play through the tournament.

VEECK, BILL: BIRTH ANNIVERSARY. Feb 9, 1914. William Louis (Bill) Veeck, Jr, Baseball Hall of Fame executive born at Chicago, IL. Veeck was baseball's premier promoter and showman as an owner of several teams. He integrated the American League, sent a midget to the plate to start a game and, in general, sought to provide fans with entertainment in addition to baseball. Inducted into the Hall of Fame in 1991. Died at Chicago, Jan 2, 1986.

WERTZ, VIC: BIRTH ANNIVERSARY. Feb 9, 1925. Victor Woodrow (Vic) Wertz, baseball player born at York, PA. A hard-hitting first baseman and outfielder, Wertz made one of the most famous outs in baseball history. In Game 1 of the 1954 World Series, he hit a long fly ball to dead centerfield at New York's Polo Grounds. The Giants' Willie Mays chased the ball down and made a spectacular catch over his shoulder. Died at Detroit, MI, July 7, 1983.

ZIMMERMAN, HEINIE: BIRTH ANNIVERSARY. Feb 9, 1887. Henry ("Heinie") Zimmerman, baseball player born at New York, NY. Zimmerman was an outstanding offensive infielder who let his penchant for zaniness get in the way. He was banned from baseball for life for attempting to bribe other players to fix games. He maintained connections with the New York underworld and co-owned a speakeasy with Dutch Schultz in 1929 and 1930. Died at New York, Mar 14, 1969.

BIRTHDAYS TODAY

Phil Jackson Ford, Jr, 42, former basketball player, born Rocky Mount, NC, Feb 9, 1956.

John Martin Kruk, 37, former baseball player, born Charleston, WV, Feb 9, 1961.

Todd William Lyght, 29, football player, born Kwajalein, Marshall Islands, Feb 9, 1969.

Peter Michael (Pete) O'Brien, 40, former baseball player, born Santa Monica, CA, Feb 9, 1958.

John Wallace, 24, basketball player, born Rochester, NY, Feb 9, 1974.

William Hayward ("Mookie") Wilson, 42, former baseball player, born Bamberg, SC, Feb 9, 1956.

FEBRUARY 10 — TUESDAY
Day 41 — 324 Remaining

BEATTY BREAKS FOUR-MINUTE MARK: ANNIVERSARY. Feb 10, 1962. Jim Beatty became the first American to break the four-minute barrier for the indoor mile run with a 3:58.9 clocking at a meet in Los Angeles.

BOWE JOINS/LEAVES MARINES: ANNIVERSARY. Feb 10, 1997. Heavyweight Riddock Bowe announced that he had retired from boxing in order to join the US Marines. He had enlisted on Jan 27 and reported to Parris Island on this date. On Feb 21, Bowe announced that he had changed his mind and that the Marines had agreed to release him. "He could not," said the Corps, "handle the regulated lifestyle." Bowe, 29, married and the father of five, had won the heavyweight championship in 1992 from Evander Holyfield only to surrender it to Holyfield in 1993. In his Marines stint, he endured 36 hours of actual training.

BROWN, WALTER: BIRTH ANNIVERSARY. Feb 10, 1905. Walter A. Brown, Basketball Hall of Fame executive born at Hopkinton, MA. Brown became president of Boston Garden in 1937 upon his father's death and held that position until 1964. He helped to found the National Basketball Association and was president and co-owner of the Boston Celtics. He maintained a high payroll to create the league's best franchise. Brown was also involved in international and Olympic hockey. Inducted into the Hall of Fame in 1965. Died at Hyannis, MA, Sept 7, 1964.

EVANS, BILLY: BIRTH ANNIVERSARY. Feb 10, 1884. William George (Billy) Evans, Baseball Hall of Fame umpire and executive born at Chicago, IL. Evans was an American League umpire from 1906 to 1927, arguing successfully for using four umpires in the World Series. He wrote *Knotty Problems of Baseball*, a casebook. After retiring, he became general manager of the Cleveland Indians and, later, the Detroit Tigers. Inducted into the Hall of Fame in 1973. Died at Miami, FL, Jan 23, 1956.

FULKS NETS 63: ANNIVERSARY. Feb 10, 1949. Joe Fulks of the Philadelphia Warriors set an NBA record by scoring 63 points in a game against the Indianapolis Jets. Fulks' total was the largest recorded by an NBA player before the introduction of the 24-second clock in 1954. His record stood until Nov 8, 1959, when Elgin Baylor of the Minneapolis Lakers scored 64 points.

GRAND CENTER BOAT SHOW. Feb 10–15. Grand Center, Grand Rapids, MI. This event brings together buyers and sellers of power and sail boats, boating accessories, docks, dockominiums and vacation properties. Est attendance: 32,000. For info: Henri Boucher, ShowSpan, Inc, 1400 28th St SW, Grand Rapids, MI 49509. Phone: (616) 530-1919. Fax: (616) 530-2122.

JAPAN: WINTER OLYMPICS: DAY FOUR. Feb 10. Nagano. Competition: curling (men's and women's preliminaries); alpine skiing (women's super-G); men's ice hockey (preliminary games); luge (women's singles); speed skating (men's 500 meters); and figure skating (pairs freestyle).

PENNOCK, HERB: BIRTH ANNIVERSARY. Feb 10, 1894. Herbert Jeffries ("Herb") Pennock, Baseball Hall of Fame pitcher and general manager born at Kennett Square, PA. Pennock was one of the best pitchers for the New York Yankees in the 1920s, a team that did not need a lot of good pitching but got it anyway. As general manager of the Philadelphia Phillies, he helped to build the "Whiz Kids," 1950 National League champions. Inducted into the Hall of Fame in 1948. Died at New York, NY, Jan 30, 1948.

SAINT LOUIS BOAT AND SPORTS SHOW. Feb 10–15. America's Center, St. Louis, MO. The 44th annual St. Louis Boat & Sports Show presents hundreds of boats, engines and marine accessories, with fishing gear and vacation resort displays, seminars, personal appearances and special attractions all under one roof. For info: NMMA Boat Shows, 1139 Olivette Executive Pkwy, St. Louis, MO 63132. Phone: (314) 567-0020. Fax: (314) 567-1810.

TILDEN, BILL: 105th BIRTH ANNIVERSARY. Feb 10, 1893. William Tatem (Bill) Tilden, Jr, tennis player born at Philadelphia, PA. Generally considered one of the greatest players of all time, Tilden won more tournaments than the record books can count. A nearly flawless player, he was also an egotistical showman on the court with an interest in show business. He turned pro in 1930 and continued to win regularly. Died at Hollywood, CA, June 5, 1953.

BIRTHDAYS TODAY

Ryan Eugene Bowen, 30, former baseball player, born Hanford, CA, Feb 10, 1968.

John Calipari, 39, basketball coach, born Moon, PA, Feb 10, 1959.

Leonard Kyle (Lenny) Dykstra, 35, baseball player, born Santa Ana, CA, Feb 10, 1963.

Dennis Louis Gentry, 39, former football player, born Lubbock, TX, Feb 10, 1959.

Robert Joseph (Bobby) Jones, 28, baseball player, born Fresno, CA, Feb 10, 1970.

Gregory John (Greg) Norman, 43, golfer, born Melbourne, Australia, Feb 10, 1955.

Claude Jayhawk Owens, II, 29, baseball player, born Cincinnati, OH, Feb 10, 1969.

Mark Andrew Spitz, 48, Olympic gold medal swimmer, born Modesto, CA, Feb 10, 1950.

Garry St. Jean, 48, former basketball coach, born Chicopee, MA, Feb 10, 1950.

FEBRUARY 11 — WEDNESDAY

Day 42 — 323 Remaining

BAER, MAX: BIRTH ANNIVERSARY. Feb 11, 1909. Maximillian Adalbert (Max) Baer, boxer born at Omaha, NE. Baer possessed awesome punching power and once knocked out a fighter who collapsed into a coma and died from his injuries. He won the heavyweight title from Primo Carnera on June 14, 1934, and lost it a year later to James J. Braddock, a severe underdog. Died at Hollywood, CA, Nov 21, 1959.

February 1998	S	M	T	W	T	F	S
	1	2	3	4	5	6	7
	8	9	10	11	12	13	14
	15	16	17	18	19	20	21
	22	23	24	25	26	27	28

BELIVEAU SCORES 500th GOAL: ANNIVERSARY. Feb 11, 1971. Center Jean Beliveau of the Montreal Canadiens scored the 500th goal of his career in his team's 6–2 win over the Minnesota North Stars. Beliveau finished his career with 507 goals and entered the Hockey Hall of Fame in 1972.

DOUGLAS BEATS TYSON: ANNIVERSARY. Feb 11, 1990. James ("Buster") Douglas scored a tremendous upset by knocking out Mike Tyson in the 10th round of a fight in Tokyo to win the heavyweight championship.

FRASER, GRETCHEN: BIRTH ANNIVERSARY. Feb 11, 1919. Gretchen Claudia Kunigk Fraser, Olympic gold medal skier born at Tacoma, WA. Fraser became the first American to win an Olympic gold medal in Alpine skiing when she captured first place in the special slalom (now known as the giant slalom) at the 1948 Winter Olympics at St. Moritz. She added a silver medal in the Alpine combined. Died at Sun Valley, ID, Feb 17, 1994.

HITCHCOCK, TOMMY: BIRTH ANNIVERSARY. Feb 11, 1900. Thomas Hitchcock, Jr, polo player born at Aiken, SC. Hitchcock was one of the nation's great polo players, winning junior and senior honors and international competitions as well. He was rated a ten-goal player, the highest ranking, and captained the US team at the 1924 Olympics. During World War II, Hitchcock served in the Army Air Corps and crashed his Mustang fighter. Died at Salisbury, England, Apr 19, 1944.

HULMAN, TONY: BIRTH ANNIVERSARY. Feb 11, 1901. Anton (Tony) Hulman, Jr, auto racing executive born at Terre Haute, IN. Hulman purchased the Indianapolis Motor Speedway from Captain Eddie Rickenbacker on Nov 14, 1945. He repaired and restored the facility and made the 500-mile race one of the premier events in sport. Hulman emphasized the human touch and became famous for his intonation before the beginning of each race, "Gentlemen, start your engines." Died at Indianapolis, IN, Oct 28, 1977.

JAPAN: WINTER OLYMPICS: DAY FIVE. Feb 11. Nagano. Competition: curling (women's and men's preliminaries); alpine skiing (slalom portion of men's combined); ski jumping (men's 90 meter); freestyle skiing (moguls finals); women's ice hockey; biathlon (men's 20 km); luge (women's singles); speed skating (women's 3,000 meters); and women's ice hockey.

MOON PHASE: FULL MOON. Feb 11. Moon enters Full Moon phase at 5:23 AM, EST.

NHL PLAYERS ASSOCIATION FORMED: ANNIVERSARY. Feb 11, 1957. The National Hockey League Players Association was organized with Ted Lindsay of the Detroit Red Wings elected president.

BIRTHDAYS TODAY

Todd Eric Benzinger, 35, former baseball player, born Dayton, KY, Feb 11, 1963.

Bernard Tyrone (Bernie) Bickerstaff, 54, basketball coach and executive, born Benham, KY, Feb 11, 1944.

Samuel Joseph (Sammy) Ellis, 57, former baseball player, born Youngstown, OH, Feb 11, 1941.

Benjamin Ambrosio (Ben) Oglivie, 49, former baseball player, born Colon, Panama, Feb 11, 1949.

Burt Reynolds, 62, actor (*Semi-Tough*), former football player, born Waycross, GA, Feb 11, 1936.

Thomas Martin (Tom) Veryzer, 45, former baseball player, born Port Jefferson, NY, Feb 11, 1953.

FEBRUARY 12 — THURSDAY
Day 43 — 322 Remaining

DANDRIDGE, RAY: DEATH ANNIVERSARY. Feb 12, 1994. Raymond (Ray) Dandridge, Baseball Hall of Fame third baseman born at Richmond, VA, 1913. Dandridge was a standout third baseman in the Negro Leagues. He was 35 years old when Organized Baseball called, but he never played a day in the major leagues. Inducted into the Hall of Fame in 1987. Died at Palm Beach, FL.

GATORADE 125-MILE QUALIFYING RACES (FOR DAYTONA 500). Feb 12. Daytona International Speedway, Daytona Beach, FL. 39th annual qualifying races for the Daytona 500, also determine starting positions 3–30. Sponsor: Gatorade. For info: John Story, Dir of Pub Rel, Daytona Intl Speedway, PO Box 2801, Daytona Beach, FL 32120-2801. Phone: (904) 947-6782. For tickets: (904) 253-RACE (7223). Fax: (904) 947-6791. WWW: http://daytonausa.com

HAFEY, CHICK: 95th BIRTH ANNIVERSARY. Feb 12, 1903. Charles James (Chick) Hafey, Baseball Hall of Fame outfielder born at Berkeley, CA. Hafey started as a pitcher but switched to the outfield in 1922. He was one of the first ballplayers to wear eyeglasses and compiled a .317 batting average. Inducted into the Hall of Fame in 1971. Died at Calistoga, CA, July 2, 1973.

JAPAN: WINTER OLYMPICS: DAY SIX. Feb 12. Nagano. Competition: curling (men's preliminaries); snowboarding (halfpipe preliminaries and finals); cross country skiing (men's 10 km classical and women's 10 km pursuit/freestyle); men's ice hockey (preliminary games); women's ice hockey; speed skating (men's 1,500 meters); women's ice hockey; and figure skating (men's short program).

MIAMI INTERNATIONAL BOAT SHOW AND SAILBOAT SHOW. Feb 12–18. Miami Beach Convention Center, Miami Beach, FL. (Watson Island and Biscayne Bay Mariott.) 57th annual boat show, the biggest in the US and considered the "main event" for product introductions. With more than 3,000 boats, this boat show offers an unparalleled opportunity to view the sport's latest products. For info: NMMA, 400 Arthur Godfrey Rd, Ste 310, Miami Beach, FL 33140. Phone: (305) 531-8410. Fax: (305) 534-3139.

NEW YORK-TO-PARIS AUTO RACE BEGINS: 90th ANNIVERSARY. Feb 12, 1908. Six automobiles left Times Square to begin a New York-to-Paris race that proved to be part sporting event and part expedition. The cars drove across the North American continent, took a boat across the Pacific and then raced across Siberia and Europe to the City of Lights. One car dropped out on the starting day; after a while, only two remained. A team of Americans reached Paris on July 31, four days after a German team, but the Americans were declared the winners because of a handicap imposed on the Germans. The Americans traveled 13,341 miles in 170 days.

RACE TO THE SKY–A GREAT MONTANA TRADITION SLED DOG RACE. Feb 12–20. 13th annual race starts near Helena, MT, ends at Missoula, MT. This 300-mile race along the Continental Divide is a beautiful and challenging trail. In what is known as the most beautiful dog sled race on earth, more than 30 teams compete from the US, Canada and Europe. Est attendance: 12,000. For info: Montana Sled Dog, Inc, 2905 Montana, Helena, MT 59601. Phone: (406) 442-4008.

ROWLAND, PANTS: BIRTH ANNIVERSARY. Feb 12, 1879. Clarence Henry ("Pants") Rowland, baseball player, manager and executive born at Platteville, WI. Rowland was a minor league catcher who managed the Chicago White Sox from 1915 through 1918. He became an umpire, a scout and president of the Pacific Coast League, 1944–54. Died at Chicago, IL, May 17, 1969.

STRICTLY SAIL–MIAMI. Feb 12–18. Miami Beach, FL. 13th annual show. Impressive sail-only show features the latest sailboats, equipment and services as well as seminars and attractions for all levels of sailing ability. For info: NMMA Boat Shows, 600 Third Ave, 23rd Fl, New York, NY 10016. Phone: (212) 922-1212. Fax: (212) 922-9607.

UNITED AIRLINES HAWAIIAN OPEN. Feb 12–15. Waialae CC, Honolulu, HI. A PGA Tour tournament. For info: PGA Tour, 112 TPC Blvd, Ponte Vedra Beach, FL 32082. Phone: (904) 285-3700.

WILSON, DON: BIRTH ANNIVERSARY. Feb 12, 1945. Donald Edward (Don) Wilson, baseball player born at Monroe, LA. Wilson pitched for the Houston Astros and had two no-hitters and an 18-strikeout performance to his credit. Died at Houston, TX, Jan 5, 1975.

BIRTHDAYS TODAY

Joe Don Baker, 62, actor (*The Natural*), born Groesbeck, TX, Feb 12, 1936.

Dominic Paul (Dom) DiMaggio, 81, former baseball player, born San Francisco, CA, Feb 12, 1917.

Joseph Henry (Joe) Garagiola, 72, broadcaster and former baseball player, born St. Louis, MO, Feb 12, 1926.

Owen Nolan, 26, hockey player, born Belfast, Northern Ireland, Feb 12, 1972.

Michel Petit, 34, hockey player, born St. Malo, Quebec, Canada, Feb 12, 1964.

William Felton (Bill) Russell, 64, former basketball coach and Basketball Hall of Fame center, born Monroe, LA, Feb 12, 1934.

FEBRUARY 13 — FRIDAY
Day 44 — 321 Remaining

SPORTSCHASER OF THE DAY

Who scored 100 points for Furman's basketball team in a 149-95 victory over Newberry in 1954?

ANCHORAGE FUR RENDEZVOUS. Feb 13–22. Anchorage, AK. "Alaska's largest celebration." Features four world championships in three sled dog races and dog weight-pulling contest. Carnival, native dances, Eskimo blanket toss, fur auction, snow sculpture, snow sports and much more–more than 120 events. 63rd annual rondy! Annually, beginning the second Friday in February and running for 10 days. Est attendance: 250,000. For info: Greater Anchorage, Inc, 327 Eagle St, Anchorage, AK 99501. Phone: (907) 277-8615 or (907) 274-1177. Fax: (907) 277-2199.

ATLANTIC CITY CLASSIC CAR AUCTION, FLEA MARKET AND ANTIQUE SHOW. Feb 13–15. The New Atlantic City Convention Center, Atlantic City, NJ. Hundreds of antique and classic cars on display and on sale.

February	S	M	T	W	T	F	S
1998	1	2	3	4	5	6	7
	8	9	10	11	12	13	14
	15	16	17	18	19	20	21
	22	23	24	25	26	27	28

Est attendance: 48,000. For info: Atlantic City Conv and Visitors Authority, 2314 Pacific Ave, Atlantic City, NJ 08401. Phone: (609) 449-7130.

CANADA: FESTIVAL DU VOYAGEUR. Feb 13–22. Winnipeg, Manitoba. More than 400 shows, food and "joie de vivre" of the fur-trade era. Sled dog races, snow sculptures, costumed interpreters in historic Fort Gibraltar, arts and crafts display and sale, French-Canadian cuisine and much more at Western Canada's largest winter festival. Est attendance: 150,000. For info: Festival du Voyageur, 768 Tache Ave, Winnipeg, Man, Canada R2H 2C4. Phone: (204) 237-7692. Fax: (204) 233-7576. Email: voyageur@festivalvoyageur.mb.ca. WWW: http://www.festivalvoyageur.mb.ca

CHASE, HAL: 115th BIRTH ANNIVERSARY. Feb 13, 1883. Harold Harris (Hal) Chase, baseball player born at Los Gatos, CA. Chase was a brilliant fielder as a first baseman whose reputation for dishonesty grew as his career lengthened. Accused more than once of throwing games, he was banned from several minor leagues but not the majors. Died at Colusa, CA, May 18, 1947.

COWBOY STATE GAMES WINTER SPORTS FESTIVAL. Feb 13–16. Casper, WY. The festival features a variety of winter sporting events for athletes of all ages. Est attendance: 1,600. For info: Eileen Ford, Cowboy State Games, PO Box 3485, Casper, WY 82602. Phone: (307) 577-1125. Fax: (307) 577-8111. Email: cwboygames@aol.com.

DISCOUNT AUTO PARTS 200. Feb 13. Daytona Beach, FL. 20th annual race is season kickoff for the NASCAR Goody's Dash Series. Sponsor: Discount Auto Parts. For info: John Story, Dir of Pub Rel, Daytona Intl Speedway, Po Box 2801, Daytona Beach, FL 32120-2801. Phone: (904) 947-6782. For tickets: (904) 253-RACE (7223). Fax: (904) 947-6791. WWW: http://www.daytonausa.com

ICESCAPE, NORTHEAST WISCONSIN'S WINTER FESTIVAL. Feb 13–15. Houdini Plaza, Appleton, WI. Winter festival featuring the Wisconsin State Ice Carving Championship, food, the "Avenue of Ice," family activities, cherries jubilee, the World's Largest Cup of Hot Chocolate, carriage rides and other winter fun. Est attendance: 35,000. For info: Brian Scharrer, Communications & Events Coordinator, Appleton Downtown Inc, PO Box 2272, Appleton, WI 54913-2272. Phone: (920) 954-9112. Fax: (920) 954-0219.

IROC XXII INTERNATIONAL RACE OF CHAMPIONS. Feb 13. Daytona International Speedway, Daytona Beach, FL. All-star race for the greatest drivers from different forms of racing in the US. Sponsor: True Value Hardware Stores. For info: John Story, Dir of Pub Rel, Daytona Intl Speedway, PO Box 2801, Daytona Beach, FL 32120-2801. Phone: (904) 947-6782. For tickets: (904) 253-RACE (7223). Fax: (904) 947-6791. WWW: http://www.daytonausa.com

JACKSON HOLE SHRINE CUTTER RACE. Feb 13–14. Melody Ranch, Jackson Hole, WY. Chariot racing Western-style as horse-drawn cutters vie in this 27th annual fundraiser. "The cutters run that a child may walk," spectators "bet" and the money goes to a hospital for crippled children in Salt Lake City. Annually, the Friday and Saturday before Presidents' Day. Est attendance: 7,000. For info: Jackson Hole Shrine Club, Box 2565, Jackson, WY 83001. Phone: (307) 733-1938.

JAPAN: WINTER OLYMPICS: DAY SEVEN. Feb 13. Nagano. Competition: curling (women's and men's preliminaries and tie-break); nordic combined (90 meter jumping); alpine skiing (men's super-G); luge (men's doubles); men's ice hockey (preliminary games); speed skating (women's 500 meters); figure skating (ice dancing compulsories).

LONGHORN WORLD CHAMPIONSHIP RODEO. Feb 13–15. The Show Me Center, Cape Girardeau, MO. More than 20 cowboys and cowgirls compete in six professional contests ranging from bronc riding to bull riding for top prize money and world championship points. Featuring colorful opening pageantry and Big, Bad BONUS Bulls. 11th annual. Est attendance: 14,000. For info: W. Bruce Lehrke, Pres, Longhorn World Chmpshp Rodeo, Inc, PO Box 70159, Nashville, TN 37207. Phone: (615) 876-1016. Fax: (615) 876-4685. Email: lhrodeo@idt.net. WWW: http://www.longhornrodeo.com

MOORE, DONNIE: BIRTH ANNIVERSARY. Feb 13, 1954. Donnie Ray Moore, baseball player born at Lubbock, TX. Moore became an outstanding relief pitcher after developing a forkball in the mid-1980s. He gave up a key home run in the 1986 American League Championship Series to Dave Henderson of the Boston Red Sox and gradually grew despondent. Died of a self-inflicted gunshot wound at Anaheim, CA, July 18, 1989.

NC RV AND CAMPING SHOW. Feb 13–15. Charlie Rose Expo Center, Fayetteville, NC. A display of the latest in recreation vehicles and accessories by various dealers. Est attendance: 5,000. For info: Apple Rock Advertising & Promotion, 1200 Eastchester Dr, High Point, NC 27265. Phone: (910) 881-7100. Fax: (910) 883-7198.

RECREATIONAL VEHICLE SHOW. Feb 13–15 (also Feb 20–22). Timonium State Fairgrounds, Timonium, MD. Mid-Atlantic's oldest, largest and best-attended RV show with exhibitors to display all the latest in motor homes, camping and RV accessories. Est attendance: 20,000. For info: Maryland Recreational Vehicle Assn, 8332 Pulaski Hwy, Baltimore, MD 21237. Phone: (410) 687-7200. Fax: (410) 686-1486.

SELVY SCORES 100: ANNIVERSARY. Feb 13, 1954. Frank Selvy of Furman University scored 100 points in a 149–95 victory over Newberry College. Selvy broke the record of 73 points set in 1951 by Temple's Bill Mlkvy. He made 41 field goals and 18 foul shots.

TROTTIER SCORES 500th GOAL: ANNIVERSARY. Feb 13, 1990. Bryan Trottier of the New York Islanders scored the 500th goal of his career in a 4–2 loss to the Calgary Flames. Trottier finished his career with 524 goals.

WHISKEY FLAT DAYS. Feb 13–16. Kernville, CA. Whiskey Flat Days commemorates the old Kernville that was called Whiskey Flat in 1860 before the name was changed to Kernville. We turn back the clock as the parade, stores and residents go back to the 1860s. Frog races, craft booths, rodeo, parade, games for small children, carnival, street dances, puppet shows, costume and whiskerino contests, melodrama and much more. Annually, the Friday–Monday of Presidents' Day weekend. Est attendance: 25,000. For info: Kernville Chamber of Commerce, PO Box 397, Kernville, CA 93238. Phone: (760) 376-2629. Fax: (760) 376-4371. Email: kcc@kernvalley.com. WWW: http://www.kernvalley.com/kerncofc/index.html

BIRTHDAYS TODAY

Salvatore Leonard (Sal) Bando, 54, baseball executive and former player, born Cleveland, OH, Feb 13, 1944.
Patricia Jane (Patty) Berg, 80, LPGA Hall of Fame golfer, born Minneapolis, MN, Feb 13, 1918.
Marc Joseph John Crawford, 37, hockey coach and former player, born Belleville, Ontario, Canada, Feb 13, 1961.
Matthew Todd (Matt) Mieske, 30, baseball player, born Midland, MI, Feb 13, 1968.
Edward Gay (Eddie) Robinson, 79, college football coach, born Jackson, LA, Feb 13, 1919.

Kevin Douglas Stocker, 28, baseball player, born Spokane, WA, Feb 13, 1970.
Mats Sundin, 27, hockey player, born Sollentuna, Sweden, Feb 13, 1971.

FEBRUARY 14 — SATURDAY
Day 45 — 320 Remaining

ACE BAILEY BENEFIT GAME: ANNIVERSARY. Feb 14, 1934. The Toronto Maple Leafs played a team of stars from the other National Hockey League teams in a special game to benefit Ace Bailey, a Toronto player who had suffered a fractured skull on Dec 2, 1933. The Maple Leafs won 7–3.

ALLEN, MEL: 85th BIRTH ANNIVERSARY. Feb 14, 1913. Mel Allen, sportscaster born Melvin Allen Israel at Birmingham, AL. Allen earned a law degree in 1936 from the University of Alabama, but his real love was sports. He left Alabama for the CBS radio network and was soon broadcasting New York Yankees and New York Giants baseball games and a host of other sporting events as well. He became the Yankees' lead announcer after World War II and became nationally famous for two phrases he used regularly: "How about that!" to describe a fine play and "Going, going, gone," his home run call. Years after being fired by the Yankees after the 1963 World Series, he attracted a new generation of listeners to his work on the weekly television show, "This Week in Baseball." Died at Greenwich, CT, June 16, 1996.

AMERICAN BOWLING CONGRESS CHAMPIONSHIPS TOURNAMENT. Feb 14–June 20. Reno, NV. 50,000 bowlers from around the country and several foreign locations compete for titles in singles, doubles, five-player team and all events in an arena setting. Lanes are specially built into the convention center each year. Est attendance: 100,000. For info: American Bowling Congress, 5301 S 76th St, Greendale, WI 53129-0500. Phone: (414) 421-6400. Fax: (414) 421-7977.

BARRETT, RED: BIRTH ANNIVERSARY. Feb 14, 1915. Charles Henry ("Red") Barrett, baseball player born at Santa Barbara, CA. Barrett led the National League in victories in 1945 with 23, but he is best known for having completed a 1944 game throwing only 58 pitches, believed to be a record. Died at Wilson, NC, July 28, 1990.

BOBBY ALLISON WINS DAYTONA: ANNIVERSARY. Feb 14, 1988. Bobby Allison became the first 50-year-old driver to win the Daytona 500 when he outdueled his 26-year-old son Davey.

ENGLAND: BRISTOL CLASSIC MOTORCYCLE SHOW. Feb 14–15. Royal Bath and West Showground, Shepton Mallet, Somerset, England. Everything for the motorcycle enthusiast with club stands, trade stands and autojumble. Est attendance: 17,000. For info: Robert Ewin, Dir, Nationwide Exhibitions (UK) Ltd, PO Box 20, Fishponds, Bristol, England BS16 5QU. Phone: (44) (117) 970-1370. Fax: (44) (117) 970-1371. WWW: http://www.nationwideexhibitions.co.uk

GARGOYLES 300 NASCAR BUSCH SERIES RACE. Feb 14. Daytona International Speedway, Daytona Beach, FL. 40th annual race is season kickoff for the NASCAR Busch series. Sponsor: Gargoyles. For info: John Story, Dir of Pub Rel, Daytona Intl Speedway, PO Box 2801, Daytona Beach, FL 32120-2801. Phone: (904) 947-6782. For tickets: (904) 253-RACE (7223). Fax: (904) 947-6791. WWW: http://www.daytonausa.com

GETZEIN, PRETZELS: BIRTH ANNIVERSARY. Feb 14, 1864. Charles H. ("Pretzels") Getzein, baseball player born in Germany. Getzein was a pitcher in the 1880s for the Detroit National League team and four others. He and catcher Charlie Ganzel were known as the "Pretzel Battery." Died at Chicago, IL, June 19, 1932.

HAYES, WOODY: 85th BIRTH ANNIVERSARY. Feb 14, 1913. Wayne Woodrow (Woody) Hayes, football coach born at Clifton, OH. Hayes became head coach at Ohio State in 1950 and remained there through the 1977 season. Known for an explosive temper and occasional sidelines antics, Hayes taught his teams ball-control offense epitomized by the phrase "three yards and a cloud of dust." During his tenure the Buckeyes won 205 games, lost 68 and tied 10. They won the national championship in 1968. Died at Upper Arlington, OH, Mar 12, 1987.

JAPAN: WINTER OLYMPICS: DAY EIGHT. Feb 14. Nagano. Competition: curling (men's and women's tie break and semifinals); alpine skiing (women's downhill); women's ice hockey; nordic combined (15 km): bobsled (two-man); men's ice hockey (preliminary games); speed skating (women's 500 meters); and figure skating (men's freestyle).

SEC MEN'S AND WOMEN'S SWIMMING AND DIVING CHAMPIONSHIPS. Feb 14–16 (diving); 18–21 (swimming). University of Florida, Gainesville, FL. For info: Southeastern Conference, 2201 Civic Center Blvd, Birmingham, AL 35203-1103. Phone: (205) 458-3010. Fax: (205) 458-3030. Email: cbloom@sec.org. WWW: http://www.secsports.com

SNOWFLAKE INTERNATIONAL SKI JUMP TOURNAMENT IN WESTBY. Feb 14–15. Westby, WI. More than 150 participants—young and old, novice as well as Olympic caliber–compete on five different hills in this international tournament at the US home of ski jumping. World-class champions from more than 11 countries soar 300 feet through the air as they jump Timber Coulee, a 90-meter hill–the same size hill used in the Winter Olympics. For info: Eddie Lundy, Mgr, Snowflake Ski Club, Rt 1, PO Box 103A, Westby, WI 54667-9739. Phone: (608) 634-3211.

SUGAR RAY WINS CROWN: ANNIVERSARY. Feb 14, 1951. Sugar Ray Robinson, often regarded as the greatest boxer of all time, won the world middleweight championship by knocking out Jake LaMotta in the 15th round of a fight in Chicago.

VALENTINE'S DAY. Feb 14. St. Valentine's Day celebrates the feasts of two Christian martyrs of this name. One, a priest and physician, was beaten and beheaded on the Flaminian Way at Rome, Italy, on Feb 14, AD 269, during the reign of Emperor Claudius II (who died of the plague less than a year later). Another Valentine, the Bishop of Terni, is said to have been beheaded, also on the Flaminian Way at Rome, on Feb 14 (possibly in a later year). Both history and legend are vague and contradictory about details of the Valentines and some say that Feb 14 was selected for the celebration of Christian martyrs as a diversion from the ancient pagan observance of Lupercalia. An old legend has it that birds choose their mates on Valentine's Day. Now it is one of the most widely observed unofficial holidays. It is an occasion for the exchange of gifts (usually books, flow-

ers or sweets) and greeting cards with affectionate or humorous messages.

WALKER LAKE FISH DERBY. Feb 14–16. Fishing contest for cutthroat trout, hobo dinner and liars contest. Tagged fish worth $25,000 and many more prizes. Est attendance: 1,250. For local info: Mineral County Chamber of Commerce, PO Box 1635, Hawthorne, NV 89415. Phone: (702) 945-5896. Fax: (702) 945-1257.

BIRTHDAYS TODAY

Drew Bledsoe, 26, football player, born Ellensburg, WA, Feb 14, 1972.

Jeffrey Alan (Jeff) Dellenbach, 35, football player, born Wausau, WI, Feb 14, 1963.

David Francis (Dave) Dravecky, 42, former baseball player, born Youngstown, OH, Feb 14, 1956.

Calle Johansson, 31, hockey player, born Goteborg, Sweden, Feb 14, 1967.

James Edward (Jim) Kelly, 38, former football player, born Pittsburgh, PA, Feb 14, 1960.

Steve McNair, 25, football player, born Mount Olive, MS, Feb 14, 1973.

Gheorghe Muresan, 27, basketball player, born Triteni, Romania, Feb 14, 1971.

Kelly Lee Stinnett, 28, baseball player, born Lawton, OK, Feb 14, 1970.

Petr Svoboda, 32, hockey player, born Most, Czechoslovakia, Feb 14, 1966.

Mary Kathryn ("Mickey") Wright, 63, LPGA Hall of Fame golfer, born San Diego, CA, Feb 14, 1935.

FEBRUARY 15 — SUNDAY
Day 46 — 319 Remaining

ALBRIGHT WINS WORLD TITLE: 45th ANNIVERSARY. Feb 15, 1953. Tenley Albright made figure skating history by becoming the first American woman to win the world's championship. She also skated her way to a silver medal at the 1952 Winter Olympics and a gold medal at the 1956 Winter Olympics.

BLAIK, RED: BIRTH ANNIVERSARY. Feb 15, 1897. Earl Henry ("Red") Blaik, football player and coach born at Detroit, MI. Blaik played three sports at Miami University (OH) and after graduation was appointed to the US Military Academy at West Point. In 1934 he was named head football coach at Dartmouth and moved to West Point in 1941. His teams won two national championships and seven Lambert Trophies, symbol of football supremacy in the East. He coached three Heisman Tro-

February 1998

S	M	T	W	T	F	S
1	2	3	4	5	6	7
8	9	10	11	12	13	14
15	16	17	18	19	20	21
22	23	24	25	26	27	28

phy winners and 35 All-Americans. Died at Colorado Springs, CO, May 6, 1989.

CANADA: SASK PROVINCIAL PRECISION ICE SKATING CHAMPIONSHIPS. Feb 15. Regina, Saskatchewan. For info: Sask Sport, 1870 Lorne St, Regina, Sask, Canada S4P 2L7. Phone: (306) 780-9300. Fax: (306) 781-6021.

DAYTONA 500. Feb 15. Daytona International Speedway, Daytona Beach, FL. 40th annual running of the "World's Greatest Race" is season kickoff for the NASCAR Winston Cup season. For info: John Story, Dir of Pub Rel, Daytona Intl Speedway, PO Box 2801, Daytona Beach, FL 32120-2801. Phone: (904) 947-6782. For tickets: (904) 253-RACE (7223). Fax: (904) 947-6791. WWW: http://www.daytonausa.com

DOUBLE GOLD MEDAL WINNER: ANNIVERSARY. Feb 15, 1932. The US four-man bobsled team won the gold medal at the Winter Olympics at Lake Placid, NY. On the team was Edward F. Eagan, who had won a gold medal in boxing at the 1920 Summer Olympics. Eagan thus became the first person to win gold medals in both winter and summer games.

EARNSHAW, GEORGE: BIRTH ANNIVERSARY. Feb 15, 1900. George Livingston Earnshaw, baseball player born at New York, NY. A large, genial pitcher known as "Moose," Earnshaw was a star pitcher for the Philadelphia Athletics, winning 67 games in 1929–31. He won a Bronze Star in World War II. Died at Little Rock, AR, Dec 1, 1976.

ESPO SCORES 1,000th POINT: ANNIVERSARY. Feb 15, 1974. Boston Bruins center Phil Esposito scored the 1,000th point of his career, an assist in Boston's 4–2 victory over the Vancouver Canucks. Esposito finished his career with 1590 points.

JAPAN: WINTER OLYMPICS: DAY NINE. Feb 15. Nagano. Competition: curling (men's and women's medal rounds); ski jumping (men's 120 meters); alpine skiing (downhill portion of women's combined); biathlon (women's 7.5 km); men's ice hockey (preliminary games); bobsled (two-man); speed skating (men's 1,000 meters); and figure skating (ice dancing original).

SPINKS DECISIONS ALI: 20th ANNIVERSARY. Feb 15, 1978. Leon Spinks won a 15-round split decision over Muhammad Ali to capture the heavyweight championship in a fight in Las Vegas.

BIRTHDAYS TODAY

Edgar Bennett, III, 29, football player, born Jacksonville, FL, Feb 15, 1969.

Ronald Charles (Ron) Cey, 50, former baseball player, born Tacoma, WA, Feb 15, 1948.

Timothy (Tim) Cheveldae, 30, hockey player, born Melville, Saskatchewan, Canada, Feb 15, 1968.

Charles Leonard (Chuck) Estrada, 60, former baseball player, born San Luis Obispo, CA, Feb 15, 1938.

Darrell Green, 38, football player, born Houston, TX, Feb 15, 1960.

Jaromir Jagr, 26, hockey player, born Kladno, Czechoslovakia, Feb 15, 1972.

Melido Perez, 32, former baseball player, born San Cristobal, Dominican Republic, Feb 15, 1966.

William Mark Price, 34, basketball player, born Bartlesville, OK, Feb 15, 1964.

☆   ☆   ☆

FEBRUARY 16 — MONDAY
Day 47 — 318 Remaining

CHASE'S SPORTSQUOTE OF THE DAY

"My greatest strength is that I have no weaknesses." — John McEnroe

CRESPI, CREEPY: 80th BIRTH ANNIVERSARY. Feb 16, 1918. Frank Angelo Joseph ("Creepy") Crespi, baseball player born at St. Louis, MO. Crespi played second base for five years with the St. Louis Cardinals. He earned his nickname for his habit of inching closer to the plate as the pitcher delivered the ball. Died at St. Louis, Mar 1, 1990.

HAMILTON, SLIDING BILLY: BIRTH ANNIVERSARY. Feb 16, 1866. William Robert ("Sliding Billy") Hamilton, Baseball Hall of Fame outfielder born at Newark, NJ. Hamilton was the leading base stealer of the 19th century though recordkeeping was not then what it is now. With Ed Delahanty and Sam Thompson, he formed one of baseball's greatest outfields. Inducted into the Hall of Fame in 1961. Died at Worcester, MA, Dec 15, 1940.

JAPAN: WINTER OLYMPICS: DAY TEN. Feb 16. Nagano. Competition: freestyle skiing (aerials preliminaries); cross country skiing (women's 4x5 km relay); men's ice hockey (preliminary games); speed skating (women's 1,500 meters); and figure skating (ice dancing freestyle).

JOHNSON WINS OLYMPIC DOWNHILL: ANNIVERSARY. Feb 16, 1984. Skier Bill Johnson became the first (and thus far, the only) American to win the Olympic downhill. Johnson's victory came at the 1984 Winter Olympics in Sarajevo, Yugoslavia.

LONGEST TENNIS MATCH: 30th ANNIVERSARY. Feb 16, 1968. At the US Indoor Championships at Salisbury, MD, the longest match in US Tennis Association history pitted Englishmen Mark Cox and Bob Wilson against Americans Charlie Pasarell and Ron Holmberg. After six hours and 23 minutes, Cox and Wilson emerged victorious, 26–24, 17–19, 30–28.

PRESIDENTS' DAY. Feb 16. The third Monday in February. Presidents' Day observes the birthdays of George Washington (Feb 22) and Abraham Lincoln (Feb 12). With the adoption of the Monday Holiday Law (which moved the observance of George Washington's birthday from Feb 22 each year to the third Monday in February), some of the specific significance of the event was lost, and added impetus was given to the popular description of that holiday as Presidents' Day. Present usage often regards Presidents' Day as a day to honor all former presidents of the US. Presidents' Day has statutory authority in Hawaii, Nebraska, Ohio and the Commonwealth of the Northern Mariana Islands, and popular recognition in most states.

BIRTHDAYS TODAY

Jerome Abraham Bettis, 26, football player, born Detroit, MI, Feb 16, 1972.

Terrence Michael (Terry) Crowley, 51, former baseball player, born New York, NY, Feb 16, 1947.

Jerry Wayne Hairston, 46, former baseball player, born Birmingham, AL, Feb 16, 1952.

John Patrick McEnroe, Jr, 39, former tennis player, born Wiesbaden, West Germany, Feb 16, 1959.

Peter Kelly Tripucka, 39, former basketball player, born Glen Ridge, NJ, Feb 16, 1959.

FEBRUARY 17 — TUESDAY
Day 48 — 317 Remaining

BARBER, RED: BIRTH ANNIVERSARY. Feb 17, 1908. Walter Lanier ("Red") Barber, broadcaster born at Columbus, MS. Barber's first professional play-by-play job was announcing the Cincinnati Reds starting with Opening Day, 1934, the first major league baseball game he had ever seen. Barber switched to the Brooklyn Dodgers and later the New York Yankees and became one of the game's premier announcers whose work was beloved by many. He broadcast the game in which Jackie Robinson broke baseball's color line and the game in which Roger Maris broke Babe Ruth's record for most home runs in a season. Well after he retired, he enjoyed a second career as a weekly commentator on National Public Radio, Died Oct 22, 1992, at Tallahassee, FL.

CRABBE, BUSTER: 90th BIRTH ANNIVERSARY. Feb 17, 1908. Clarence Lindon ("Buster") Crabbe, Olympic gold medal swimmer born at Oakland, CA. Crabbe's first-place finish in the 400-meter freestyle was the only swimming medal won by an American at the 1932 Olympic Games in Los Angeles. After his swimming career was over, he played Tarzan, Flash Gordon and Buck Rogers in the movies. Died at Scottsdale, AZ, Apr 23, 1983.

FIRST SIX-DAY BIKE RACE: ANNIVERSARY. Feb 17, 1899. The first six-day bicycle, featuring two-man teams, came to an end at New York's Madison Square Garden. The winning team of Charles Miller and Frank Waller rode a combined distance of 2,733 miles.

JAPAN: WINTER OLYMPICS: DAY ELEVEN. Feb 17. Nagano. Competition: alpine skiing (slalom portion of women's combined); ski jumping (men's 120 meter team); biathlon (men's 10 km); women's ice hockey (medal games); speed skating (men's 10,000 meters); and short track speed skating (men's 1,000 meters; women's 3,000 meters relay).

NEYLAND, ROBERT: BIRTH ANNIVERSARY. Feb 17, 1892. Robert Reese (Bob) Neyland, Jr, football player, coach and administrator born at Greenville, TN. Neyland played football at West Point and served in the American Expeditionary Forces in 1917. He moved to the University of Tennessee in 1925 to head the ROTC program and coach football. His Volunteers won 75 of 87 from 1926 to 1935. After a one-year hiatus, he returned to Tennessee where his teams won 33 straight games and held all opponents scoreless in 1939. After service in World War II, he returned to coaching again, with nearly equal success. His demeanor earned him the nickname, "The General." Died at New Orleans, LA, Mar 28, 1962.

PIPP, WALLY: 105th BIRTH ANNIVERSARY. Feb 17, 1893. Walter Clement (Wally) Pipp, baseball player born at Chicago, IL. Pipp was the New York Yankees starting first baseman who, on June 1, 1925, took a day off, allegedly for a headache. Lou Gehrig played in his place and did not come out of the lineup for 2,130 games. Died at Grand Rapids, MI, Jan 11, 1965.

WIGGINS, ALAN: 40th BIRTH ANNIVERSARY. Feb 17, 1958. Alan Anthony Wiggins, baseball player born at Los Angeles, CA. Wiggins played seven years in the major leagues but saw his career cut short by drug problems. Died at Los Angeles, Jan 9, 1991.

February 1998	S	M	T	W	T	F	S
	1	2	3	4	5	6	7
	8	9	10	11	12	13	14
	15	16	17	18	19	20	21
	22	23	24	25	26	27	28

BIRTHDAYS TODAY

James Nathaniel (Jim) Brown, 62, Pro Football Hall of Fame fullback, born St. Simon's Island, GA, Feb 17, 1936.
Bryan Keith Cox, 30, football player, born St. Louis, MO, Feb 17, 1968.
Roger Lee Craig, 68, former baseball manager and player, born Durham, NC, Feb 17, 1930.
Dennis Green, 49, football coach, born Harrisburg, PA, Feb 17, 1949.
Burt Carlton Hooton, 48, former baseball player, born Greenville, TX, Feb 17, 1950.
Michael Jeffrey Jordan, 35, basketball player and former minor league baseball player, born New York, NY, Feb 17, 1963.
David Klingler, 29, football player, born Stratford, TX, Feb 17, 1969.
Luc Robitaille, 32, hockey player, born Montreal, Quebec, Canada, Feb 17, 1966.

☆ ☆ ☆

FEBRUARY 18 — WEDNESDAY
Day 49 — 316 Remaining

ACC WOMEN'S SWIMMING AND DIVING CHAMPIONSHIPS. Feb 18–21. University of Virginia, Charlottesville, VA. For info: Atlantic Coast Conference, PO Drawer ACC, Greensboro, NC 27419-6999. Phone: (910) 854-8787. Fax: (910) 854-8797.

BIG EAST MEN'S AND WOMEN'S SWIMMING AND DIVING CHAMPIONSHIPS. Feb 18–21. University of Pittsburgh, Pittsburgh, PA. For info: Big East Conference, 56 Exchange Terrace, Providence, RI 02903. Phone: (401) 453-0660. Fax: (401) 751-8540.

COLLEGE BASKETBALL SCANDAL: ANNIVERSARY. Feb 18, 1951. New York County District Attorney Frank S. Hogan made the first arrests in a point-shaving scandal that rocked college basketball across the country. Hogan arrested players from the City College of New York, but before long the scandal spread to several other campuses, including Long Island University, New York University, Bradley and Kentucky.

GIPP, GEORGE: BIRTH ANNIVERSARY. Feb 18, 1895. George Gipp, college football player, born at Laurium, MI. Gipp was a legendary halfback for Notre Dame and the school's first All-American. His lifestyle, however, was sharply at odds with Ronald Reagan's portrayal of him in a movie about Knute Rockne. Gipp rarely went to class, opting instead for pool, gambling and chasing girls. He never uttered the famous words, "Win one for the Gipper." Still, he was a dominant player who epitomized Notre Dame's underdog fighting spirit. Died at South Bend, IN, Dec 14, 1920.

GORDON, JOE: BIRTH ANNIVERSARY. Feb 18, 1915. Joseph Lowell (Joe) Gordon, baseball player and manager born at Los Angeles, CA. Gordon played second base for the New York Yankees and the Cleveland Indians, including the 1948 Cleveland team that won the World Series. He managed several teams and was once traded to the Detroit Tigers, manager for manager. Died at Sacramento, CA, Apr 14, 1978.

JANSEN WINS GOLD: ANNIVERSARY. Feb 18, 1994. American speed skater Dan Jansen won a gold medal in the 1000-meter race at the Winter Olympics in Lillehammer, Norway. Favored to win at 500 meters in three straight Olympics but unsuccessful each time, Jansen overcame a slip to break the jinx. Speed skating fans who had watched Jansen struggle on the ice and deal with family tragedy rejoiced.

JAPAN: WINTER OLYMPICS: DAY TWELVE. Feb 18. Nagano. Competition: alpine skiing (men's giant slalom); cross country skiing (men's 4x10 km relay); freestyle skiing (aerials finals); men's ice hockey (quarterfinals); and figure skating (women's short program).

MILLER, BOB: BIRTH ANNIVERSARY. Feb 18, 1939. Robert Lane (Bob) Miller, baseball player born at St. Louis, MO. Miller was one of two Bob Millers, one left-handed and this one righthanded, who pitched for the New York Mets in their first year, 1962. He became a fine relief pitcher, playing with 11 clubs in all. Died at Rancho Bernardo, CA, Aug 6, 1993.

MILWAUKEE BOAT SHOW AT THE WISCONSIN CENTER. Feb 18–22. Wisconsin Center, Milwaukee, WI. This event brings together buyers and sellers of sail and power boats, including fishing boats, pontoons and boating accessories, as well as vacation property and travel destinations. Est attendance: 25,000. For info: Henri Boucher, ShowSpan, Inc, 1400 28th St SW, Grand Rapids, MI 49509. Phone: (616) 530-1919. Fax: (616) 530-2122.

PONTIAC SILVERDOME BOAT, SPORT AND FISHING SHOW. Feb 18–22. Pontiac Silverdome, Pontiac, MI. This event brings together buyers and sellers of boating, fishing and outdoor sporting products. US and Canadian hunting and fishing trips, as well as other vacation travel destinations, are featured. Est attendance: 30,000. For info: Henri Boucher, Show Span, Inc, 1400 28th St SW, Grand Rapids, MI 49509. Phone: (616) 530-1919. Fax: (616) 530-2122.

"THE KING" STRIKES OUT SIX: ANNIVERSARY. Feb 18, 1967. In a special exhibition of softball pitching versus baseball hitting, star softball hurler Eddie Feigner, known as "The King," struck out six of baseball's greatest hitters in a row: Willie Mays, Willie McCovey, Brooks Robinson, Roberto Clemente, Maury Wills and Harmon Killebrew.

BIRTHDAYS TODAY

Luis Enrique Arroyo, 71, former baseball player, born Penuelas, Puerto Rico, Feb 18, 1927.

Bruce Eugene Kison, 48, former baseball player, born Pasco, WA, Feb 18, 1950.

Charles Dallan (Dal) Maxvill, 59, former baseball executive and player, born Granite City, IL, Feb 18, 1939.

Alexander Mogilny, 29, hockey player, born Khabarovsk, USSR, Feb 18, 1969.

Bob St. Clair, 67, Pro Football Hall of Fame tackle, born San Francisco, CA, Feb 18, 1931.

John William Valentin, 31, baseball player, born Mineola, NY, Feb 18, 1967.

FEBRUARY 19 — THURSDAY
Day 50 — 315 Remaining

ACBL TOURNAMENT. Feb 19–22. Yuma, AZ. Bridge sectional. Annually, the second-to-last weekend in February. Est attendance: 600. For info: Marion Weatherwax, Yuma Inn Suites Hotel, Yuma, AZ 85365. Phone: (520) 343-0270.

ALL-CANADA SHOW. Feb 19–22. Brown County Expo, Green Bay, WI. This consumer show allows individuals an opportunity to talk face-to-face with Canadian lodge representatives and outfitters to plan their hunting, fishing and adventure trips to Canada. For info: Rodney Schlafer, Show Dir, All-Canada Show, Bay-Lakes Mktg, Inc, 1889 Commerce Drive, DePere, WI 54115. Phone: (414) 983-9800 or (800) 325-6290. Fax: (414) 983-9985. WWW: http://www.allcanada.com

BIG TEN WOMEN'S SWIMMING AND DIVING CHAMPIONSHIPS. Feb 19–21. University of Indiana, Bloomington, IN. Est attendance: 600. For info: Big Ten Conference, 1500 W Higgins Rd, Park Ridge, IL 60068-6300. Phone: (847) 696-1010. Fax: (847) 696-1150. WWW: http://www.bigten.org

BIG TWELVE WOMEN'S SWIMMING AND DIVING CHAMPIONSHIPS. Feb 19–21. University of Texas, Austin, TX. For info: Big Twelve Conference, 2201 Stemmons Freeway, 28th Floor, Dallas, TX 75207. Phone: (214) 742-1212. Fax: (214) 742-2046.

BLAIR WINS GOLD AGAIN: ANNIVERSARY. Feb 19, 1994. Olympian Bonnie Blair of Champaign, IL, became the first speed skater to win a gold medal in the same event in three consecutive Olympic Games when she won the 500 meters in Lillehammer, Norway. On Feb 23, she added a victory in the 1,000 meters to give her a total of five gold medals, more than any other American female athlete.

CANADA: INTERNATIONAL CURLING BONSPIEL. Feb 19–21. Dawson City, Yukon. 99th annual. Top of the World Curling Club hosts a 32-team bonspiel with prizes valued in excess of $6,000. For info: Yukon Tourism, Box 810, Dawson City, YT, Canada Y0B 1G0. Phone: (403) 993-5035. Fax: (403) 993-6477. Email: suzanne@dawson.net.

CANADA: TREK OVER THE TOP DESTINATION TOK. Feb 19–21. Dawson City, Yukon. A 400-mile round trip snowmobile run that departs Dawson City, Yukon, and follows the Top of the World/Taylor Highway into Tok, AK. The weekend involves a number of planned snowmobile events, banquets, live entertainment and a casino. Annually, usually the third weekend in February. Est attendance: 50. For info: Trek Over the Top, Box 100, Dawson City, YT, Canada Y0B 1G0. Phone: (403) 993-5873. Fax: (403) 993-7423. Email: ezalitis@dawsoncity.net or pcayen@dawsoncity.net. WWW: http://yukonweb.wis.net/special/trek

☆   ☆   ☆

CANADA: YUKON SOURDOUGH RENDEZVOUS. Feb 19–22. Whitehorse, Yukon. Mad trapper competitions, bike races, flour packing, beard-growing contests, Old Time Fiddle show, sourdough pancake breakfasts, can-can girls, talent shows, etc. Also, many family-oriented activities. Visitors welcome to participate. Est attendance: 15,000. For info: Yukon Sourdough Rendezvous, Box 5108, Canada Y1A 4S3. Phone: (403) 667-2148. Fax: (403) 668-6755. Email: ysr@hypertech.yk.ca. WWW: http://www.haylow.yk.net/rendez

GILBERT SCORES 1,000th POINT: ANNIVERSARY. Feb 19, 1977. Right wing Rod Gilbert of the New York Rangers scored the 1,000th point of his NHL career, a goal in the Rangers' 5–2 loss to the New York Islanders. Gilbert entered the Hockey Hall of Fame in 1982.

JAPAN: WINTER OLYMPICS: DAY THIRTEEN. Feb 19. Nagano. Competition: alpine skiing (women's slalom); nordic combined (90 meter team); biathlon (women's 4x7.5 km relay); speed skating (women's 1,000 meters); short track speed skating (women's 500 meters, men's 500 meters and men's 5,000 meter relay).

MAHRE BROTHERS WIN MEDALS: ANNIVERSARY. Feb 19, 1984. At the XIVth Winter Olympics in Sarajevo, Yugoslavia, skiers Phil and Steve Mahre of the US became the first brothers to finish first and second in the same Olympic event. Phil won the gold medal in the slalom, and Steve won the silver.

MOON PHASE: LAST QUARTER. Feb 19. Moon enters Last Quarter phase at 10:27 AM, EST.

PATERNO NAMED PENN STATE COACH: ANNIVERSARY. Feb 19, 1966. Penn State University named Joe Paterno its head football coach. Through the 1996 season, Paterno's teams had compiled a record of 289 wins, 74 losses and 3 ties. The Nittany Lions have won 17 bowl games and 2 national championships with Paterno at the helm.

SALOMON ELITE SPRINTS AND NORTHERN LAKES CO-OP 10K. Feb 19. Hayward, WI. These two ski events are part of the Birkebeiner Festival. In the Sprints top US and international skiers compete in short distance sprints along Hayward's Main St. The Co-Op 10K is a non-competitive event beginning on Main St and ends at the Hayward Civic Club Golf Course. For info: outside WI phone: (800) 872-2753; inside WI: (800) 722-3386.

SIMPLOT GAMES. Feb 19–21. Holt Arena, Idaho State University, Pocatello, ID. One of the nation's largest indoor high school track and field events, featuring 2,500 top high school athletes from the US and Canada. Free admission. Est attendance: 20,000. For info: Carol Lish, Exec Dir, Simplot Games, PO Box 912, Pocatello, ID 83204. Phone: (208) 238-2777 or (800) 635-9444. Fax: (208) 238-2760. Email: clish@simplot.com. WWW: http://www.simplot.com

SONS OF NORWAY BARNEBIRKIE. Feb 19. Hayward, WI. Largest children's cross-country ski event in America, with more than 1,700 participants, ages 3–13. The courses, designed specifically for children, are based on age and experience with distances of 1, 2.5 and 5 kilometers. For info outside WI Phone: (800) 872-2753; inside WI: (800) 722-3386.

YARBOROUGH WINS CONSECUTIVE DAYTONAS: ANNIVERSARY. Feb 19, 1984. Cale Yarborough became only the second driver to win consecutive Daytona 500 races by sweeping into the lead just two turns from the finish and taking the checkered flag. Yarborough joined Richard Petty in this select circle.

BIRTHDAYS TODAY

George Edward (Eddie) Arcaro, 82, former broadcaster and jockey, born Cincinnati, OH, Feb 19, 1916.

Timothy Philip (Tim) Burke, 39, former baseball player, born Omaha, NE, Feb 19, 1959.

James Michael (Mike) Cofer, 34, football player, born Columbia, SC, Feb 19, 1964.

Robert (Rob) DiMaio, 30, hockey player, born Calgary, Alberta, Canada, Feb 19, 1968.

Alvaro Alberto Espinoza, 36, baseball player, born Valencia, Carobobo, Venezuela, Feb 19, 1962.

June Sheldon Jones, III, 45, former football coach and player, born Portland, OR, Feb 19, 1953.

Hana Mandlikova, 35, tennis player, born Prague, Czechoslovakia, Feb 19, 1963.

Glyn Curt Milburn, 27, football player, born Santa Monica, CA, Feb 19, 1971.

David Keith (Dave) Stewart, 41, former baseball player, born Oakland, CA, Feb 19, 1957.

February	S	M	T	W	T	F	S
1998	1	2	3	4	5	6	7
	8	9	10	11	12	13	14
	15	16	17	18	19	20	21
	22	23	24	25	26	27	28

FEBRUARY 20 — FRIDAY
Day 51 — 314 Remaining

SPORTSCHASER OF THE DAY
When Brian Boitano won the figure skating gold medal in 1988, what other Brian won the silver medal?

ACC MEN'S AND WOMEN'S INDOOR TRACK AND FIELD CHAMPIONSHIPS. Feb 20–21. East Tennessee State University, Johnson City, TN. For info: Atlantic Coast Conference, PO Drawer ACC, Greensboro, NC 27419-6999. Phone: (910) 854-8787. Fax: (910) 854-8797.

APPLETON, SCOTT: BIRTH ANNIVERSARY. Feb 20, 1942. Gordon Scott Appleton, football player born at Brady, TX. Appleton was a star defensive tackle at the University of Texas, winning several individual honors and awards, including the 1963 Outland Trophy. Drafted by both the Houston Oilers (AFL) and the Dallas Cowboys (NFL), he played five seasons as a pro. In retirement, Appleton struggled with alcoholism and then became a minister. Died of heart disease at Austin, TX, Mar 2, 1992.

BOITANO WINS "BATTLE OF THE BRIANS": ANNIVERSARY. Feb 20, 1988. Brian Boitano of the US won the gold medal in men's figure skating at the XVth Winter Olympic Games at Calgary, Alberta, Canada. Boitano skated a nearly flawless free program to edge Brian Orser of Canada. The Soviet Union's Viktor Petrenko took the bronze.

BOSTON AFL TEAM NAMED PATRIOTS: ANNIVERSARY. Feb 20, 1960. One of eight charter members of the American Football League, the Boston franchise chose the nickname "Patriots" after a public contest. The team changed its name to the New England Patriots for the 1971 season.

BUSCH BUYS CARDINALS: 45th ANNIVERSARY. Feb 20, 1953. August A. Busch, president of Anheuser-Busch Brewery, purchased the St. Louis Cardinals Baseball Club from Fred Saigh, who was forced to sell the team by Commissioner Ford C. Frick after pleading no contest to tax evasion charges. Anheuser-Busch owned the Cardinals until 1995.

CANADA: BIG BROTHERS BOWL FOR MILLIONS. Feb 20–22. Bracebridge, Ont. Bowling fundraiser for Big Brothers of Muskoka. Annually, the third weekend in February. For info: Big Brothers of Muskoka, Bracebridge Chamber of Commerce, 1-1 Manitoba St, Bracebridge, Ont, Canada P1L 1S4. Phone: (705) 645-6259.

ESPOSITO SCORES 50th GOAL: ANNIVERSARY. Feb 20, 1971. Phil Esposito of the Boston Bruins became the

first NHL player to score his 50th goal in February when he tallied in a 5–4 loss to the Los Angeles Kings. Esposito finished the season with 76 goals.

GREAT MINNESOTA GOLF SHOW. Feb 20–22. HHH Metrodome, Minneapolis, MN. A high-quality consumer trade show for the golf industry that showcases new products, purchasing opportunities, interactive entertainment and informative features. Est attendance: 30,000. For info: David Sinykin, David Toushin & Assoc, 5775 Wayzata Blvd, Ste 850, Minneapolis, MN 55416. Phone: (612) 593-0353.

HOUSTON LIVESTOCK SHOW AND RODEO. Feb 20–Mar 8. Astrodome Complex, Houston, TX. Livestock show with more than 25,000 entries. "Wild rodeo action" and top-name musical entertainment. For info: Marketing Dept, Houston Livestock Show and Rodeo Assn, Box 20070, Houston, TX 77225-0070. Phone: (713) 791-9000. Fax: (713) 794-9528. WWW: http://www.hlsr.com and for pay-per-view info: http://www.rodeohouston.com

HOWE SIGNS WITH AEROS: ANNIVERSARY. Feb 20, 1974. Gordie Howe, the oldest player in NHL history, came out of retirement to play with his sons, Mark and Marty. He signed a four-year, $1 million contract with the Houston Aeros of the World Hockey Association.

INDIANAPOLIS BOAT, SPORT AND TRAVEL SHOW. Feb 20–Mar 1. Indiana State Fairgrounds, Indianapolis, IN. Est attendance: 200,000. For info: Kevin Renfro, VP, Ste E-2, Corporate Sq East, 2511 E 46th St, Indianapolis, IN 46205. Phone: (317) 546-4344. Fax: (317) 546-3002. Email: insportshow@iquest.net.

JAPAN: WINTER OLYMPICS: DAY FOURTEEN. Feb 20. Nagano. Competition: alpine skiing (women's giant slalom); cross country skiing (women's 30 km freestyle); nordic combined (4x5 km team); bobsled (four-man); men's ice hockey (semifinals); speed skating (women's 5,000 meters); and figure skating (women's freestyle).

LONGHORN WORLD CHAMPIONSHIP RODEO. Feb 20–22. The Palace of Auburn Hills, Auburn Hills, MI. More than 20 cowboys and cowgirls compete in six professional contests ranging from bronc riding to bull riding for top prize money and world championship points. Featuring colorful opening pageantry and Big, Bad BONUS Bulls. 20th annual. Est attendance: 35,000. For info: W. Bruce Lehrke, Pres, Longhorn World Chmpshp Rodeo, Inc, PO Box 70159, Nashville, TN 37207. Phone: (615) 876-1016. Fax: (615) 876-4685. Email: lhrodeo@idt.net. WWW: http://www.longhornrodeo.com

POLO: GOLD CUP/GOLD CUP OF THE AMERICAS. Feb 20–Mar 15 (tentative). Wellington, FL. For info: Palm Beach Polo, Inc, 13420 South Shore Blvd, West Palm Beach, FL 33414. Phone: (561) 793-1440. Fax: (561) 790-3872.

BIRTHDAYS TODAY

Charles Wade Barkley, 35, basketball player, born Leeds, AL, Feb 20, 1963.
Philip Anthony (Phil) Esposito, 1956, hockey executive, former coach and Hockey Hall of Fame center, born Sault Ste. Marie, Ontario, Canada, Feb 20, 1942.
Elroy Leon (Roy) Face, 70, former baseball player, born Stephentown, NY, Feb 20, 1928.
Thomas David (Tommy) Henrich, 85, former baseball player, born Masillon, OH, Feb 20, 1913.
Derek Jansen Lilliquist, 32, baseball player, born Winter Park, FL, Feb 20, 1966.
Stephon Marbury, 21, basketball player, born New York, NY, Feb 20, 1977.

Robert William (Bobby) Unser, 64, auto racer, born Albuquerque, NM, Feb 20, 1934.

FEBRUARY 21 — SATURDAY
Day 52 — 313 Remaining

AFL MERGES WITH NFL: ANNIVERSARY. Feb 21, 1970. After a protracted battle over players, fans and television ratings, the American Football League, founded in 1960, became part of the National Football League. Teams from the AFL were joined by the Cleveland Browns, the Pittsburgh Steelers and the Baltimore Colts to become the American Football Conference. Remaining NFL teams became the National Football Conference.

BIG EAST MEN'S AND WOMEN'S INDOOR TRACK AND FIELD CHAMPIONSHIPS. Feb 21–22. Carrier Dome, Syracuse University, Syracuse, NY. For info: Big East Conference, 56 Exchange Terrace, Providence, RI 02903. Phone: (401) 453-0660. Fax: (401) 751-8540.

BRIGHTON FIELD DAY AND RODEO. Feb 21–22. Brighton Indian Reservation, Okeechobee, FL. Arts and crafts, alligator wrestling, PRCA rodeo, animal show, parade and beautiful Native American clothing. Sponsor: Seminole Tribe of Florida. Annually, the third weekend in February. Est attendance: 5,500. For info: Ellen Click, Field Day Contact Person, Rte 6, Box 666, Okeechobee, FL 34974. Phone: (813) 763-4128. Fax: (941) 763-5077.

CANADA: SCOTT TOURNAMENT OF HEARTS PROVINCIAL CURLING CHAMPIONSHIP. Feb 21–Mar 1. Regina Exhibition Park and downtown hotels, Regina, Saskatchewan. The Canadian Women's Curling Championship is the premier women's sporting event in Canada showcasing the best female curlers from across the country. Weeklong activities include entertainment, Saskatchewan artisans show and sale, mini-spiels and tours. For info: (306) 522-1998 or Tourism Saskatchewan, 500–1900 Albert St, Regina, Sask, Canada S4P 2L7. Email: travel.info@toursask.sk.ca. WWW: http://www.toursask.com

CHILDREN'S WESTERN JAMBOREE. Feb 21–22. Guthrie, OK. This event brings the spirit of the old west into the lives of many with a fun-filled day of activities for children of all ages. For info: Lazy E Arena, Rte 5, Box 393, Guthrie, OK 73044-9205. Phone: (800) 595-RIDE or (405) 282-RIDE. Email: learena@ionet.net. WWW: http://www.lazye.com

DYNO AMERICAN BIRKEBEINER. Feb 21. Cable to Hayward, WI. The largest and most prestigious cross-country ski marathon in North America attracts more than 7,500 participants for the 52K trek from Mt Telemark in Cable to Hayward. Preceded by a nordic festival of related ski events and activities. Est attendance: 7,000. For info: American Birkebeiner Ski Foundation, Inc, Box 911, Hayward, WI 54843. Phone: (715) 634-5025 or in WI (800) 722-3386. Fax: (715) 634-5663. Email: birkie@win.bright.net. WWW: http://winona.com/birkie

ESA MID-WINTER SURFING CHAMPIONSHIP. Feb 21. Narragansett Town Beach, Narragansett, RI. Competition in all age categories and specialty events with prizes and trophies. Est attendance: 125. For info: Peter Pan, ESA Dir, 396 Main St, Wakefield, RI 02879. Phone: (401) 789-3399. Fax: (401) 782-0458.

FOY, JOE: 55th BIRTH ANNIVERSARY. Feb 21, 1943. Joseph Anthony (Joe) Foy, baseball player born at New York, NY. Foy was a third baseman who played with four teams between 1966 and 1971. He was Minor League Player of the Year in 1965. Died at New York, Oct 12, 1989.

HERITAGE BANK KORTELOPET. Feb 21. Hayward, WI. This 25K race is sister to the Dyno American Birkebeiner. Participants begin with Dyno American Birkebeiner racers, but the finish line is at the half-way point of the longer race. Open to skiers ages 13 and over. For info: Wisconsin Dept of Tourism, PO Box 7976, Madison, WI 53707. Fax: (414) 270-7170. Email: tourism@laughlin.com. WWW: http://tourism.state.wis.us Also, (715) 634-5025 or (800) 722-3386 in Wisconsin; (800) 872-2753 out of Wisconsin.

JAPAN: WINTER OLYMPICS: DAY FIFTEEN. Feb 21. Nagano. Competition: biathlon (men's 4x7.5 relay); bobsled (four-man); figure skating (exhibition); men's ice hockey (bronze medal game); short track speed skating (women's 1,000 meters, men's 500 meters and men's 5,000 meters relay).

KBCO/BUDWEISER CARDBOARD DOWNHILL DERBY. Feb 21. Arapahoe Basin Ski Area, CO. Teams design cardboard craft to take down a ski slope. Each team has a theme and designs the craft and costumes to correspond. Past entries have included a giant Bozo head, a pirate ship, a bi-plane–all made of cardboard, tape, glue and string. Est attendance: 5,000. For info: Julie Smith, Promotion Dir, KBCO 97.3 FM, 2500 Pearl St, Ste 315, Boulder, CO 80302. Phone: (303) 444-5600. Email: kbco@kbcoradio.com. WWW: http://www.kbcoradio.com Concert/info line: (303) 444-KBCO.

NBA'S MILKMAN SPECIAL: ANNIVERSARY. Feb 21, 1952. Following a performance by the Ice Follies, Boston Garden hosted an unusual NBA game between the Celtics and the Fort Wayne Pistons. The game began at midnight and was billed as a "Milkman's Special." Bob Cousy scored 24 points to lead Boston to an 88–67 victory before 2,368 fans.

OHIO WINTER SKI CARNIVAL. Feb 21–22. Mansfield, OH. Celebrate the season with racing both serious and fun including the famous bikini race on Saturday. Beer and bratwursts served outdoors. For info: Ohio Div of Trav & Tourism, 77 South High St, 29th Fl, Columbus, OH 43215-6108. Phone: (614) 466-8844. Fax: (614) 466-6744. WWW: http://www.travel.state.oh.us

WINTER GAMES. Feb 21. Flint Ridge State Memorial, Glenford, OH. Native American and pioneer games and programs for the entire family. For info: Ohio Div of Travel & Tourism, 77th South High St, 29th Fl, Columbus, OH 43215-6108. Phone: (614) 466-8844. Fax: (614) 466-6744. WWW: http://www.travel.state.oh.us

YAWKEY, TOM: 95th BIRTH ANNIVERSARY. Feb 21, 1903. Thomas Austin (Tom) Yawkey, Baseball Hall of Fame executive born at Detroit, MI. Yawkey purchased the Boston Red Sox in 1933 and held the club until his death. His reputation was that of a sporting gentleman who treated his team as a public trust and not as a business. Inducted into the Hall of Fame in 1980. Died at Boston, MA, July 9, 1976.

	S	M	T	W	T	F	S
February	1	2	3	4	5	6	7
1998	8	9	10	11	12	13	14
	15	16	17	18	19	20	21
	22	23	24	25	26	27	28

BIRTHDAYS TODAY

Oscar Gregorio Azocar, 33, former baseball player, born Soro, Venezuela, Feb 21, 1965.
John Eugene (Jack) Billingham, 55, former baseball player, born Orlando, FL, Feb 21, 1943.
John T. (Jack) Ramsay, 73, broadcaster and Basketball Hall of Fame coach, born Philadelphia, PA, Feb 21, 1925.
Joel Patrick Skinner, 37, former baseball player, born La Jolla, CA, Feb 21, 1961.
Alan Stuart Trammell, 40, former baseball player, born Garden Grove, CA, Feb 21, 1958.

FEBRUARY 22 — SUNDAY
Day 53 — 312 Remaining

ATTELL, ABE: BIRTH ANNIVERSARY. Feb 22, 1884. Abe Attell, boxer born Albert Knoehr at San Francisco, CA. Attell held the featherweight championship for 11 years in the early part of this century when boxing was not quite as organized as it could have been. A heavy gambler, he got involved in baseball's Black Sox scandal, actually delivering $10,000 to the player-conspirators. But he avoided prosecution, first by fleeing to Canada and then by convincing authorities that there were two Abe Attells and the other one was the guilty party. Died at Livingstone Manor, NY, Feb 6, 1970.

FINLEY, CHARLIE: 80th BIRTH ANNIVERSARY. Feb 22, 1918. Charles O. (Charlie) Finley, baseball executive born at Ensley, AL. Finley was the flamboyant and controversial owner who moved the Athletics from Kansas City to Oakland. He dressed his team in green and gold, had sheep grazing beyond the outfield wall, tangled often with Commissioner Bowie Kuhn, suggested that World Series games be played at night and put together a team that won three straight World Series (1972–74). Died at Chicago, IL, Feb 19, 1996.

FIRST RACE WON BY WOMAN JOCKEY: ANNIVERSARY. Feb 22, 1969. Barbara Jo Rubin became the first woman jockey to win a thoroughbred horse race in the United States. She rode Cohesion to victory by a neck over Reely Beeg in the ninth race at Charles Town Race Track in West Virginia.

JAPAN: WINTER OLYMPICS: DAY SIXTEEN OF COMPETITION AND CLOSING CEREMONY. Feb 22. Nagano. Competition: alpine skiing (men's slalom); cross country skiing (men's 50 km); and men's ice hockey (gold-medal game). The Closing Ceremony of the XVIIIth Winter Olympic Games will commence at 7:00 PM, local time. (Since Japan is 14 hours ahead of the Eastern Time zone in the US, the Closing Ceremony will begin at 5:00 AM, EST.)

KLEM, BILL: BIRTH ANNIVERSARY. Feb 22, 1874. William Joseph (Bill) Klem, Baseball Hall of Fame umpire born at Rochester, NY. Klem umpired in the National League from 1905 to 1941 and is generally considered

the greatest umpire ever. He worked 18 World Series and insisted that he never made a bad call. Inducted into the Hall of Fame in 1953. Died at Miami, FL, Sept 1, 1951.

LESNEVICH, GUS: BIRTH ANNIVERSARY. Feb 22, 1915. Gus Lesnevich, boxer born at Cliffside Park, NJ. Lesnevich rose from a Golden Gloves championship to the light heavyweight championship of the world. He won the title in 1941, had it "frozen" while he was in the Coast Guard during World War II and retained it after the war until being defeated in 1948. Died at Cliffside Park, Feb 28, 1964.

MIRACLE ON ICE: ANNIVERSARY. Feb 22, 1980. The US Olympic hockey team upset the team from the Soviet Union, 4–3, at the Lake Placid Winter Games to earn a victory often called the "Miracle on Ice." The Americans went on to defeat Finland two days later and win the gold medal.

MORAN, UNCLE CHARLIE: 120th BIRTH ANNIVERSARY. Feb 22, 1878. Charles Barthell ("Uncle Charlie") Moran, baseball and football player, baseball umpire and football coach born at Nashville, TN. Moran played college and professional football and professional baseball and umpired in the National League for 24 seasons, including four World Series. He is most remembered, however, for coaching tiny Centre College (KY) to a 6–0 upset of mighty Harvard in 1924. Died at Horse Cave, KY, June 13, 1949.

BIRTHDAYS TODAY

Amy Strum Alcott, 42, golfer, born Kansas City, MO, Feb 22, 1956.

George Lee ("Sparky") Anderson, 64, former baseball manager and player, born Bridgewater, SD, Feb 22, 1934.

Stephen David (Steve) Barber, 59, former baseball player, born Takoma Park, MD, Feb 22, 1939.

Julius Winfield ("Dr. J") Erving, II, 48, basketball executive, broadcaster and former basketball player, born Roosevelt, NY, Feb 22, 1950.

Pat LaFontaine, 33, hockey player, born St. Louis, MO, Feb 22, 1965.

Niki Lauda, 49, auto racer, author, born Vienna, Austria, Feb 22, 1949.

Dominic Roussel, 28, hockey player, born Hull, Quebec, Canada, Feb 22, 1970.

Jayson Williams, 30, basketball player, born Ritter, SC, Feb 22, 1968.

FEBRUARY 23 — MONDAY
Day 54 — 311 Remaining

CHASE'S SPORTSQUOTE OF THE DAY

"If the head slap were still legal in the NFL, Ed Jones would go down as the greatest defensive end of all time." —Dallas Cowboys assistant coach Ernie Stautner

DREYFUSS, BARNEY: BIRTH ANNIVERSARY. Feb 23, 1865. Barney Dreyfuss, baseball executive born at Freiburg, Germany. As owner of the Pittsburgh Pirates, Dreyfuss challenged the Boston Pilgrims to a post-season series in 1903, thereby creating the modern World Series. Died at New York, NY, Feb 5, 1932.

HEIDEN WINS FIFTH GOLD MEDAL: ANNIVERSARY. Feb 23, 1980. US speedskater Eric Heiden won the 10,000 meters race to capture his fifth gold medal at the Lake Placid Winter Olympics. Heiden also won at 500 meters, 1,000 meters, 1,500 meters and 5,000 meters.

HEISS WINS GOLD MEDAL: ANNIVERSARY. Feb 23, 1960. Carol Heiss won the gold medal in woman's figure skating at the VIIIth Winter Olympic Games in Squaw Valley, CA.

HOWARD, ELSTON: BIRTH ANNIVERSARY. Feb 23, 1929. Elston Gene Howard, baseball player born at St. Louis, MO. Howard was the first African-American to play for the New York Yankees. A catcher and an outfielder, he won the American League MVP award in 1963. Traded to the Boston Red Sox, he helped them win the 1967 AL pennant. Died at New York, NY, Dec 14, 1980.

KNIGHT THROWS CHAIR: ANNIVERSARY. Feb 23, 1985. Indiana University basketball coach Bobby Knight was ejected from a game against Purdue for throwing a chair onto the court. Knight received his first technical foul for protesting two fouls called by the officials against his team. As Purdue shot the technical, Knight hurled a chair from the bench area onto the court, earning his second technical and automatic ejection. Purdue won, 72–63.

BIRTHDAYS TODAY

Frederick (Fred) Biletnikoff, 55, Pro Football Hall of Fame wide receiver, born Erie, PA, Feb 23, 1943.

Roberto Martin Antonio (Bobby) Bonilla, 35, baseball player, born New York, NY, Feb 23, 1963.

Kenneth George (Ken) Boswell, 52, former baseball player, born Austin, TX, Feb 23, 1946.

John Druce, 32, hockey player, born Peterborough, Ontario, Canada, Feb 23, 1966.

Edward Lee ("Too Tall") Jones, 47, former football player, born Jackson, TN, Feb 23, 1951.

Dante Lavelli, 75, Pro Football Hall of Fame end, born Hudson, OH, Feb 23, 1923.

Philip D. ("Flip") Saunders, 43, basketball coach, born Cleveland, OH, Feb 23, 1955.

Jackie Larue Smith, 58, Pro Football Hall of Fame tight end, born Columbia, MS, Feb 23, 1940.

Rondell Bernard White, 26, baseball player, born Milledgeville, GA, Feb 23, 1972.

☆   ☆   ☆

FEBRUARY 24 — TUESDAY
Day 55 — 310 Remaining

GRETZKY BREAKS ESPO'S RECORD: ANNIVERSARY. Feb 24, 1982. Wayne Gretzky, 21-year-old center for the Edmonton Oilers, scored his 77th goal of the season against the Buffalo Sabres to break Phil Esposito's single-season goal-scoring record. With Esposito, who had scored 76 goals in the 1970–71 season, in attendance, Gretzky stole the puck and broke a 3–3 tie with seven minutes to play. He added two more goals in the game's final two minutes and finished the season with 92 goals.

HOCKEY TEAM WINS GOLD: ANNIVERSARY. Feb 24, 1980. Two days after defeating the Soviet Union 4–3, the US hockey team won the gold medal at the XIIIth Winter Olympic Games by beating Finland 4–2.

HOMER, WINSLOW: BIRTH ANNIVERSARY. Feb 24, 1836. Winslow Homer, artist born at Boston, MA. Homer was noted for the realism of his work from Civil War reportage to highly regarded rugged outdoor scenes of hunting and fishing. Died at Prout's Neck, ME, Sept 29, 1910.

JERRY JONES BUYS DALLAS COWBOYS: ANNIVERSARY. Feb 24, 1989. Jerry Jones announced that he had reached an agreement to buy the Dallas Cowboys from H.R. ("Bum") Bright and that he had replaced Tom Landry, the only head coach in Dallas history, with University of Miami coach Jimmy Johnson.

MATTI NYKANEN'S TRIPLE: ANNIVERSARY. Feb 24, 1988. Matti Nykanen of Finland, having already finished first in the 70- and 90-meter ski jumping events, won an unprecedented third gold medal in Nordic skiing when the Finnish team won the new 90-meter team jumping competition.

OOSTERBAAN, BENNIE: BIRTH ANNIVERSARY. Feb 24, 1906. Benjamin Gaylord (Bennie) Oosterbaan, football player, coach and administrator born at Muskegon, MI. Oosterbaan earned nine letters at the University of Michigan in baseball, basketball and football, winning All-American honors in 1925–27 at end. He remained at Michigan to be an assistant coach under Fielding Yost and became head coach in 1948. His Wolverines won one national championship. Died at Ann Arbor, MI, Oct 25, 1990.

SHROVETIDE PANCAKE RACE. Feb 24. Olney, Buckinghamshire, England and Liberal, Kansas. The pancake race at Olney has been run since 1445. Competitors must be women over 16 years of age, wearing traditional housewife's costume, including apron and headcovering. With a toss and flip of the pancake on the griddle that each must carry, the women dash from marketplace to the parish church, where the winner receives a kiss from the ringer of the Pancake Bell. Shriving service follows. Starting time for the race is usually 11:45 AM. Annually, on Shrove Tuesday.

WAGNER, HONUS: BIRTH ANNIVERSARY. Feb 24, 1874. John Peter ("Honus") Wagner, Baseball Hall of Fame shortstop born at Chartiers, PA. Wagner, who played 21 years in the majors (1897–1917), is generally considered the greatest shortstop in baseball history. His nickname, pronounced "HAN-us," is a corruption of Johannes, the German translation of his first name. Inducted into the Hall of Fame as a charter member in 1936. Died at Carnegie, PA, Dec 6, 1955.

BIRTHDAYS TODAY

Rene Arocha, 32, baseball player, born Havana, Cuba, Feb 24, 1966.
Nicholas Andrew (Nick) Esasky, 38, former baseball player, born Hialeah, FL, Feb 24, 1960.
Michael Robert (Mike) Fratello, 51, basketball coach, born Hackensack, NJ, Feb 24, 1947.

February 1998	S	M	T	W	T	F	S
	1	2	3	4	5	6	7
	8	9	10	11	12	13	14
	15	16	17	18	19	20	21
	22	23	24	25	26	27	28

Alexei Kovalev, 25, hockey player, born Togliatti, USSR, Feb 24, 1973.
Donald Vincent (Don) Majkowski, 34, football player, born Depew, NY, Feb 24, 1964.
Eddie Clarence Murray, 42, baseball player, born Los Angeles, CA, Feb 24, 1956.
Michael (Mike) Vernon, 35, hockey player, born Calgary, Alberta, Canada, Feb 24, 1963.

FEBRUARY 25 — WEDNESDAY
Day 56 — 309 Remaining

ACC MEN'S SWIMMING AND DIVING CHAMPIONSHIPS. Feb 25–28. University of Virginia, Charlottesville, VA. For info: Atlantic Coast Conference, PO Drawer ACC, Greensboro, NC 27419-6999. Phone: (910) 854-8787. Fax: (910) 854-8797.

BASCOM, "TEXAS ROSE": BIRTH ANNIVERSARY. Feb 25, 1922. Rose ("Texas Rose") Flynt Bascom, rodeo cowgirl born in Covington County, MS. A Cherokee-Choctaw Indian, Flynt married a rodeo cowboy and learned trick roping, becoming known as the greatest female trick roper in the world. She appeared on stage, in movies and on early TV. She toured with the USO during WWII, performing at every military base and military hospital in the US. After the war she toured the world, entertaining servicemen stationed overseas. In 1981 she was inducted into the National Cowgirl Hall of Fame (Hereford, TX). Died Sept 23, 1993.

CAMEL MOTORCYCLE WEEK. Feb 25–Mar 8. Daytona International Speedway, Daytona Beach, FL. Twelve days of action-packed motorcycle racing including the world's greatest motorcycle race (Daytona 200 by Arai on Mar 8) and the Daytona Supercross by Honda (Mar 7). Sponsor: Camel. For info: John Story, Dir of Pub Rel, Daytona Intl Speedway, PO Box 2801, Daytona Beach, FL 32120-2801. Phone: (904) 947-6782. For tickets: (904) 253-RACE (7223). Fax: (904) 947-6791. WWW: http://www.daytonausa.com

CARLTON TRADED TO PHILLIES: ANNIVERSARY. Feb 25, 1972. The St. Louis Cardinals, prodded by owner Gussie Busch, made one of the most one-sided trades in baseball history, sending pitcher Steve Carlton to the Philadelphia Phillies for pitcher Rick Wise. Carlton won 27 games for the Phillies and captured the Cy Young award and wound up in the Hall of Fame. Wise won 16 games and was traded to the Boston Red Sox in 1974.

CLAY BECOMES HEAVYWEIGHT CHAMP: ANNIVERSARY. Feb 25, 1964. Twenty-two-year-old Cassius Clay (later Muhammed Ali) became world heavyweight boxing champion by defeating Sonny Liston. At the height of his athletic career Ali was well known for both his fighting ability and personal style. His most famous saying was, "I am the greatest!" In 1967 he was convicted of violating the Selective Service Act and was stripped of his title for refusing to be inducted into the armed services during the Vietnam War. Ali cited religious convictions as his reason for refusal. In 1971 the Supreme Court reversed the conviction. Ali is the only fighter to win the heavyweight fighting title three separate times. He defended that title nine times.

GIRLS' HIGH SCHOOL SCORING RECORD: ANNIVERSARY. Feb 25, 1924. Marie Boyd of Lonaconing (MD) High School made an incredible 77 field goals and

a pair of foul shots in a game against Cumberland and Ursuline Academy. Her total points, 156, set a national girls' high school record that still stands. The final score: Lonaconing 162, Cumberland and Ursuline 3.

RIGGS, BOBBY: 80th BIRTH ANNIVERSARY. Feb 25, 1918. Robert Lorimer (Bobby) Riggs, tennis player born at Los Angeles, CA. The crafty Riggs won the US National Singles championship in 1939 and 1941 and won three titles at Wimbledon in 1939. After World War II, he turned pro successfully but won his greatest fame for a pair of "battle of the sexes" matches in 1973. He won the first of these against Margaret Court and lost the second to Billie Jean King. Died at Leucadia, CA, Oct 25, 1995.

SMU GETS "DEATH PENALTY": ANNIVERSARY. Feb 25, 1987. After a series of NCAA violations over a period of years, the football program at Southern Methodist University was suspended for one year. The investigation leading to the "death penalty" uncovered payments of $61,000 to players from a booster slush fund.

☆   ☆   ☆

BIRTHDAYS TODAY

Robert Earl (Bob) Brenly, 44, broadcaster and former baseball player, born Coshocton, OH, Feb 25, 1954.
Cesar Cedeno, 47, former baseball player, born Santo Domingo, Dominican Republic, Feb 25, 1951.
Tom Courtenay, 61, actor (*The Loneliness of the Long Distance Runner*), born Hull, England, Feb 25, 1937.
Byron Jaromir Dafoe, 27, hockey player, born Sussex, England, Feb 25, 1971.
Jeffrey Michael (Jeff) Fisher, 40, football coach and former player, born Culver City, CA, Feb 25, 1958.
Monford Merrill (Monte) Irvin, 79, Baseball Hall of Fame outfielder, born Columbia, AL, Feb 25, 1919.
Edward Francis (Ed) Lynch, 42, baseball executive and former player, born New York, NY, Feb 25, 1956.
Paul Andrew O'Neill, 35, baseball player, born Columbus, OH, Feb 25, 1963.
Darrell Kurt Rambis, 40, basketball player, born Cupertino, CA, Feb 25, 1958.
Ronald Edward (Ron) Santo, 58, former baseball player, born Seattle, WA, Feb 25, 1940.
Samaki Ijuma Walker, 22, basketball player, born Columbus, OH, Feb 25, 1976.

FEBRUARY 26 — THURSDAY
Day 57 — 308 Remaining

ACC WOMEN'S BASKETBALL TOURNAMENT. Feb 26–Mar 1. Independence Arena, Charlotte, NC. For info: Atlantic Coast Conference, PO Drawer ACC, Greensboro, NC 27419-6999. Phone: (910) 854-8787. Fax: (910) 854-8797.

ALEXANDER, GROVER CLEVELAND: BIRTH ANNIVERSARY. Feb 26, 1887. Grover Cleveland ("Pete") Alexander, Baseball Hall of Fame pitcher born at Elba, NE. Alexander won 373 games (tied for 3rd on the all-time list) pitching for 20 years with the Philadelphia Phillies, Chicago Cubs and St. Louis Cardinals. He won 30 or more games three times and won the National League earned run average title five times. In Game Seven of the 1926 World Series with St Louis ahead, 3–2, he staggered in from the bullpen to strike out the New York Yankees' Tony Lazzeri with the bases loaded and held New York at bay for the last two innings. Ronald Reagan played Alexander in the movie, *The Winning Team*. Inducted into the Hall of Fame in 1938. Died at St. Paul, NE, Nov 4, 1950.

ALL-CANADA SHOW. Feb 26–Mar 1. Canterbury Downs, Shakopee, MN. This consumer show allows individuals an opportunity to talk face-to-face with Canadian lodge representatives and outfitters to plan their hunting, fishing and adventure trips to Canada. For info: Rodney Schlafer, Show Dir, All-Canada Show, Bay-Lakes Mktg, Inc, 1889 Commerce Dr, De Pere, WI 54115. Phone: (414) 983-9800 or (800) 325-6290. Fax: (414) 983-9985. WWW: http://www.allcanada.com

BIG TEN MEN'S SWIMMING AND DIVING CHAMPIONSHIPS. Feb 26–28. University of Minnesota, Minneapolis, MN. Est attendance: 600. For info: Big Ten Conference, 1500 W Higgins Rd, Park Ridge, IL 60068-6300. Phone: (847) 696-1010. Fax: (847) 696-1110. WWW: http://www.bigten.org

BIG TWELVE MEN'S SWIMMING AND DIVING CHAMPIONSHIPS. Feb 26–28. Texas A&M University, College Station, TX. For info: Big Twelve Conference, 2201 Stemmons Freeway, 28th Floor, Dallas, TX 75207. Phone: (214) 742-1212. Fax: (214) 742-2046.

CHARRO DAYS. Feb 26–Mar 1. Brownsville, TX. Two Nations–Twin Cultures, a true example of international harmony and cooperation between Brownsville, Texas, and Matamoros, Mexico. Starts the last Thursday in February. Colorful celebration of the charro horseman of Mexico, a man of great riding skills. Dances, parades and carnival. Est attendance: 150,000. For info: Charro Days, Inc, PO Box 3247, Brownsville, TX 78523-3247. Phone: (956) 542-4245. Fax: (956) 542-6771.

CODY, BUFFALO BILL: BIRTH ANNIVERSARY. Feb 26, 1846. William Frederic ("Buffalo Bill") Cody, frontiersman born in Scott County, IA. Cody claimed to have killed more than 4,000 buffaloes. He was the subject of many heroic Wild West yarns, and he became successful as a showman and exhibitionist, taking his acts across the US and to Europe. Died at Denver, CO, Jan 10, 1917.

JANOWICZ, VIC: BIRTH ANNIVERSARY. Feb 26, 1930. Victor Felix (Vic) Janowicz, football and baseball player born at Elyria, OH. Janowicz played several sports in high school and decided against signing a baseball contract in order to play football at Ohio State. His junior year was his best, earning him the 1950 Heisman Trophy. After graduation and a year in the military, he played both pro football and major league baseball. Died at Columbus, OH, Feb 27, 1996.

JENKINS WINS GOLD MEDAL: ANNIVERSARY. Feb 26, 1960. David Jenkins of the US won the gold medal in men's figure skating at the VIIIth Winter Olympic Games at Squaw Valley, CA.

JOHN AND MABLE RINGLING MUSEUM OF ART MEDIEVAL FAIR. Feb 26–Mar 1. Sarasota, FL. A benefit for the Ringling Museum of Art featuring a 14th-century European village filled with food, arts and crafts, entertainment, armored jousting and a human chess match. Annually, the first weekend in March and the prior Thursday and Friday. Est attendance: 56,000. For info: (Apr to Nov) Medieval Fair, 1244 S Canterbury Rd, Ste 306, Shakopee, MN 55379. Phone: (800) 966-8215 or (612) 445-7361. Fax: (612) 445-7380. (Dec to Mar) Medieval Fair, Ringling Museum of Art, 5401 Bay Shore Rd, Sarasota, FL 34243. Phone: (941) 351-8497.

MOON PHASE: NEW MOON. Feb 26. Moon enters New Moon phase at 12:26 PM, EST.

PAC-10 WOMEN'S SWIMMING CHAMPIONSHIPS. Feb 26–28. Belmont Plaza, Los Angeles, CA. For info: PAC-10 Conference, 800 S Broadway, Ste 400, Walnut Creek, CA 94596. Phone: (510) 932-4411. Fax: (510) 932-4601.

PAC-10 MEN'S AND WOMEN'S DIVING CHAMPIONSHIPS. Feb 26–28. Arizona State University, Tempe, AZ.

For info: PAC-10 Conference, 800 S Broadway, Ste 400, Walnut Creek, CA 94596. Phone: (510) 932-4411. Fax: (510) 932-4601.

RUTH SIGNS WITH BRAVES: ANNIVERSARY. Feb 26, 1935. After being released by the New York Yankees, Babe Ruth signed a three-year contract with the Boston Braves. He played in only 28 games before retiring in May.

SOLAR ECLIPSE. Feb 26. Total eclipse of the sun. Central eclipse begins at 10:47 AM, EST, reaches greatest eclipse at 12:35 PM, EST, ends at 2:09 PM, EST. Visible in Pacific Ocean, extreme southwest and eastern parts of US, southeast Canada, Mexico, Central America, northern half of South America, West Indies, Atlantic Ocean, southern tip of Greenland, extreme western part of Iceland, Portugal and West Africa.

WERNER, BUDDY: BIRTH ANNIVERSARY. Feb 26, 1936. Wallace Jerold ("Buddy") Werner, skier born at Steamboat Springs, CO. Werner skied on three US Olympic teams and was the first American to break into the sport's top rank by winning important races in Europe. While filming a ski movie, he was overtaken by an avalanche that he attempted to outrace. Died at St. Moritz, Switzerland, Apr 12, 1964.

BIRTHDAYS TODAY

Rolando Antonio Blackman, 39, former basketball player, born Panama City, Panama, Feb 26, 1959.

John Edwin (Johnny) Blanchard, 65, former baseball player, born Minneapolis, MN, Feb 26, 1933.

Marshall William Faulk, 25, football player, born New Orleans, LA, Feb 26, 1973.

Elwin Charles ("Preacher") Roe, 83, former baseball player, born Ashflat, AR, Feb 26, 1915.

David Scott Service, 31, baseball player, born Cincinnati, OH, Feb 26, 1967.

Jack Thomas (J. T.) Snow, Jr, 30, baseball player, born Long Beach, CA, Feb 26, 1968.

FEBRUARY 27 — FRIDAY
Day 58 — 307 Remaining

SPORTSCHASER OF THE DAY
What baseball team did automobile tycoon Walter Briggs buy in 1935?

BIG TEN MEN'S INDOOR TRACK AND FIELD CHAMPIONSHIPS. Feb 27–28. Purdue University, West Lafayette, IN. Est attendance: 2,000. For info: Big Ten Conference, 1500 W Higgins Rd, Park Ridge, IL 60068-6300. Phone: (847) 696-1010. Fax: (847) 696-1150. WWW: http://www.bigten.org

BIG TEN WOMEN'S INDOOR TRACK AND FIELD CHAMPIONSHIPS. Feb 27–28. Michigan State University, East Lansing, MI. Est attendance: 3,000. For info: Big Ten Conference, 1500 W Higgins Rd, Park Ridge, IL 60068-6300. Phone: (847) 696-1010. Fax: (847) 696-1150. WWW: http://www.bigten.org

BIG TEN WOMEN'S BASKETBALL TOURNAMENT. Feb 27–Mar 2 (tentative dates). Indianapolis, IN. Big Ten Conference tournament for women's basketball. Winner of Big Ten Women's Basketball Tournament receives auto-

matic berth to NCAA Tournament. Est attendance: 25,000. For info: Big Ten Conference, 1500 W Higgins Rd, Park Ridge, IL 60068-6300. Phone: (847) 696-1010. Fax: (847) 696-1150. WWW: http://www.bigten.org

BIG TWELVE MEN'S AND WOMEN'S INDOOR TRACK CHAMPIONSHIPS. Feb 27–28. Iowa State University, Ames, IA. For info: Big Twelve Conference, 2201 Stemmons Freeway, 28th Floor, Dallas, TX 75207. Phone: (214) 774-2121. Fax: (214) 742-2046.

BISMARCK ALL-STATE INVITATIONAL VOLLEYBALL TOURNAMENT. Feb 27–Mar 2. Bismarck, ND. Watch more than 140 men's, women's and co-ed teams play from several states and Canadian Provinces. Or, recruit a team yourself! For info: Bismarck/Mandan Conv & Visitors Bureau, PO Box 2274, Bismarck, ND 58502. Phone: (800) 767-3555. Fax: (701) 222-0647.

BRIGGS, SPIKE: BIRTH ANNIVERSARY. Feb 27, 1877. Walter Owen ("Spike") Briggs, baseball executive born at Ypsilanti, MI. Briggs made a fortune in the automobile business and poured it into ownership of the Detroit Tigers. He bought the team in stages, securing the final piece in 1935. Died at Miami Beach, FL, Jan 17, 1952.

CARNAVAL MIAMI–1998. Feb 27–Mar 8. Little Havana, Miami, FL. Ten-day celebration includes 8K run (Feb 27), Carnaval Night (Feb 28), Carnaval in South Beach (Mar 1), Calle Ocho Cooking Contest (Mar 3), Carnaval Miami Golf Classic (Mar 5), Carnaval Miami Sports Festival and Carnaval Miami Internacional (Mar 7) and culminates with Callo Ocho: Open House (Mar 8). Endless entertainment in this 23-block party with musical stages, ethnic foods, dancing and plenty of events for the entire family. Billed as the largest block party in the world. Est attendance: 1,000,000. For info: Kiwanis Club of Little Havana, 1312 SW 27 Ave, 3rd Fl, Miami, FL 33145. Phone: (305) 644-8888. Fax: (305) 644-8693. WWW: http://www.carnavalmiami.org

DANZIG, ALLISON: 100th BIRTH ANNIVERSARY. Feb 27, 1898. Allison Danzig, sportswriter born at Waco, TX. Danzig graduated from Cornell University in 1921, worked for the *Brooklyn Eagle* for two years and moved to the *New York Times* in 1923. From that date until his retirement in 1968, he served as the *Times's* leading sportswriter. Danzig covered five Olympic Games, wrote about all sports and specialized in tennis and college football. Died at New York, NY, Jan 27, 1987.

GREAT MICHIGAN GOLF SHOW. Feb 27–Mar 1. Pontiac Silverdome, Pontiac, MI. A high-quality consumer trade show for the golf industry that showcases new products, purchasing oppotunities, interactive entertainment and informative features. For Info: David Sinykin, David Toushin & Assoc, 5775 Wayzata Blvd, Ste 850, Minneapolis, MN 55416. Phone: (612) 593-0353.

LONGHORN WORLD CHAMPIONSHIP RODEO. Feb 27–Mar 1. UTC Arena, Chattanooga, TN. More than 20 cowboys and cowgirls compete in six professional contests ranging from bronco riding to bull riding for top prize money and world championship points. Featuring colorful opening pageantry and Big, Bad BONUS Bulls. 16th annual. Est attendance: 1,500. For info: W. Bruce Lehrke, Pres, Longhorn World Championship Rodeo, Inc, PO Box 70159, Nashville, TN 37207. Phone: (615) 876-1016. Fax: (615) 876-4685. Email: lhrodeo@idt.net. WWW: http://www.longhornrodeo.com

MIKITA SCORES 500th GOAL: ANNIVERSARY. Feb 27, 1977. Center Stan Mikita of the Chicago Blackhawks scored the 500th goal of his career in Chicago's 4–3 loss to the Vancouver Canucks. Mikita finished his career with 541 goals and entered the Hockey Hall of Fame in 1983.

February
1998

S	M	T	W	T	F	S
1	2	3	4	5	6	7
8	9	10	11	12	13	14
15	16	17	18	19	20	21
22	23	24	25	26	27	28

POLO: GOVERNORS CHALLENGE CUP. Feb 27–Mar 28. Wellington, FL. For info: Palm Beach Polo, Inc, 13420 South Shore Blvd, West Palm Beach, FL 33414. Phone: (561) 793-1440. Fax: (561) 790-3872.

POLO: PALM BEACH POLO CUP. Feb 27–Mar 29. Wellington, FL. For info: Palm Beach Polo, Inc, 13420 South Shore Blvd, West Palm Beach, FL 33414. Phone: (561) 793-1440. Fax: (561) 790-3872.

RYAN, CONNIE: BIRTH ANNIVERSARY. Feb 27, 1920. Cornelius Joseph (Connie) Ryan, baseball player born at New Orleans, LA. Ryan was a solid second baseman in the 1940s and 1950s and briefly managed the Atlanta Braves and the Texas Rangers. Died at Metairie, LA, Jan 3, 1996.

SEC WOMEN'S BASKETBALL TOURNAMENT. Feb 27–Mar 1. Columbus, GA. For info: Southeastern Conference, 2201 Civic Center Blvd, Birmingham, AL 35203-1103. Phone: (205) 458-3010. Fax: (205) 458-3030. Email: cbloom@sec.org. WWW: http://www.secsports.org

SMITH, HILTON: BIRTH ANNIVERSARY. Feb 27, 1912. Hilton Lee Smith, baseball player born at Giddings, TX. Smith was a dominant pitcher in the Negro Leagues. He possessed a superb curve ball and was often considered the equal or better of Satchel Paige. Died at Kansas City, MO, Nov 18, 1983.

SNOWFEST. Feb 27–Mar 8. North Lake Tahoe, CA and NV, and Truckee, CA. Snowfest is a fantastic vacation opportunity, showcasing America's largest concentration of skiing and outdoor recreation combined with the fun, sparkle and excitement of 10 full days of over 100 special and unique events. Annually, beginning the Friday before the first Sunday in March. Est attendance: 130,000. For info: Festivals at Tahoe, PO Box 7590, Tahoe City, CA 96145. Phone: (916) 583-7625.

USA MOBIL INDOOR TRACK & FIELD CHAMPIONSHIPS. Feb 27–28. Georgia Dome, Atlanta, GA. The US National Championships and indoor Grand Prix Final. Est attendance: 25,000. For info: Pete Cava, Dir of Comm, USA Track & Field, PO Box 120, Indianapolis, IN 46225-0120. Phone: (317) 261-0500. WWW: http://www.usatf.org

BIRTHDAYS TODAY

Willie Anthony Banks, 29, baseball player, born Jersey City, NJ, Feb 27, 1969.

Raymond Emmett Berry, 65, former football coach and Pro Football Hall of Fame end, born Corpus Christi, TX, Feb 27, 1933.

Tony Gonzalez, 22, football player, born Torrance, CA, Feb 27, 1976.

Ronald William (Ron) Hassey, 45, former baseball player, born Tucson, AZ, Feb 27, 1953.

Loy Stephen Vaught, 31, basketball player, born Grand Rapids, MI, Feb 27, 1967.

Johnny Bilton Wockenfuss, 49, former baseball player, born Welch, WV, Feb 27, 1949.

James Ager Worthy, 37, broadcaster and former basketball player, born Gastonia, NC, Feb 27, 1961.

FEBRUARY 28 — SATURDAY
Day 59 — 306 Remaining

BASEBALL DRUG SUSPENSIONS: ANNIVERSARY. Feb 28, 1986. Baseball Commissioner Peter Ueberroth conditionally suspended seven players for their involvement with drugs. Disciplined were Joaquin Andujar, Dale Berra, Enos Cabell, Keith Hernandez, Jeffrey Leonard, Dave Parker and Lonnie Smith. The suspensions, set for one year, included a stipulation that the players could continue to play if they agreed to submit to random drug testing, contribute 100 hours of drug-related community service and 10% of their salaries to drug-prevention programs in their hometowns.

BASKETBALL ON TV: ANNIVERSARY. Feb 28, 1940. A basketball game between the University of Pittsburgh and Fordham University became the first game to be telecast live. Pitt won, 50–37, at Madison Square Garden.

BIG EAST WOMEN'S BASKETBALL TOURNAMENT. Feb 28–Mar 3. Louis Brown Athletic Center, Piscataway, NJ. For info: Big East Conference, 56 Exchange Terrace, Providence, RI 02903. Phone: (401) 453-0660. Fax: (401) 751-8540.

BLONDIN, CHARLES: BIRTH ANNIVERSARY. Feb 28, 1824. Charles Blondin, daring French acrobat and aerialist born Jean Francois Gravelet at St. Omer, France. He is especially remembered for walking across Niagara Falls on a tightrope, June 30, 1859, in front of a crowd estimated at more than 25,000. Died at London, England, Feb 19, 1897.

GIANTS RIDGE INTERNATIONAL CLASSIC MARATHON. Feb 28. Biwabik, MN. Top international men and women compete in 15K and 30K classic cross country ski races. Est attendance: 250. For info: John Filander, Events Program Dir, PO Box 190, Biwabik, MN 55708. Phone: (800) 688-7669. Fax: (218) 865-4733.

MARTIN, PEPPER: BIRTH ANNIVERSARY. Feb 29, 1904. John Leonard Roosevelt ("Pepper") Martin, baseball player born at Temple, OK. Known as the "Wild Horse of the Osage," he played third base for the Gashouse Gang, the St. Louis Cardinals of the 1930s. Died at McAlester, OK, Mar 5, 1965.

1960 HOCKEY TEAM WINS GOLD MEDAL: ANNIVERSARY. Feb 28, 1960. The US hockey team defeated Czechoslovakia, 9–4, to win the gold medal at the VIIIth Winter Olympic Games at Squaw Valley, CA.

PAC-10 WRESTLING CHAMPIONSHIPS. Feb 28–Mar 1. Cal State-Fullerton, Fullerton, CA. For info: PAC-10 Conference, 800 S Broadway, Ste 400, Walnut Creek, CA 94596. Phone: (510) 932-4411. Fax: (510) 932-4601.

PETTY'S FIRST GRAND NATIONAL VICTORY: ANNIVERSARY. Feb 28, 1960. Richard Petty won the first Grand National (later Winston Cup) stock car race of his career in Charlotte, NC. The victory earned him $800 and set him on the road toward 200 wins on the NASCAR circuit, including seven triumphs in the Daytona 500 and seven NASCAR driving titles.

SEC MEN'S AND WOMEN'S INDOOR TRACK AND FIELD CHAMPIONSHIPS. Feb 28–Mar 1. Louisiana State University, Baton Rouge, LA. For info: Southeastern Conference, 2201 Civic Center Blvd, Birmingham, AL 35203-1103. Phone: (205) 458-3010. Fax: (205) 458-3030. Email: cbloom@sec.org. WWW: http://www.secsports.org

BIRTHDAYS TODAY

Mario Gabrielle Andretti, 58, auto racer, born Montona, Trieste, Italy, Feb 28, 1940.

Vincent Jerome Askew, 32, basketball player, born Memphis, TN, Feb 28, 1966.

Adrian Delano Dantley, 42, former basketball player, born Washington, DC, Feb 28, 1956.

Eric Lindros, 25, hockey player, born London, Ontario, Canada, Feb 28, 1973.

Frank James Malzone, 68, former baseball player, born New York, NY, Feb 28, 1930.

Shawn McEachern, 29, hockey player, born Waltham, MA, Feb 28, 1969.

Charles Aaron ("Bubba") Smith, 53, former football player, born Orange, TX, Feb 28, 1945.

MARCH 1 — SUNDAY
Day 60 — 305 Remaining

CELTICS' 2,000th VICTORY: ANNIVERSARY. Mar 1, 1987. The Boston Celtics defeated the Detroit Pistons, 112–102, to become the first NBA franchise to win 2,000 games.

GRETZKY ALL-TIME ASSIST LEADER: 10th ANNIVERSARY. Mar 1, 1988. Center Wayne Gretzky of the Edmonton Oilers earned an assist in a game against the Los Angeles Kings to become the NHL's all-time career assist leader. It took Gretzky 681 games to garner 1,050 assists and surpass Gordie Howe who set the record in 1,767 games.

McKINNEY WINS WORLD CUP: 15th ANNIVERSARY. Mar 1, 1983. Skier Tamara McKinney became the first American woman skier to win the overall World Cup championship.

ROBYN SMITH WINS STAKES RACE: 25th ANNIVERSARY. Mar 1, 1973. Robyn Smith rode North Star to victory in the Paumanok Handicap at Aqueduct Racetrack to become the first woman jockey to win a stakes race.

ROZELLE, PETE: BIRTH ANNIVERSARY. Mar 1, 1926. Alvin Ray ("Pete") Rozelle, Commissioner of the National Football League born at South Gate, CA. Rozelle began his career in the public relations department of the Los Angeles Rams, became general manager and was elected commissioner in 1960. He built the NFL into a sporting power, uniting its development to television. He helped engineer the NFL's merger with the American Football League, created the Super Bowl as America's greatest sports extravaganza, conceived of the idea for Monday Night Football and persuaded NFL owners to accept revenue sharing. Died at Rancho Santa Fe, CA, Dec 6, 1996.

USCA MEN'S AND WOMEN'S NATIONAL CHAMPIONSHIPS (CURLING). Mar 1–7. Bismarck, ND. Curling national championship competition and USCA annual meeting. Est attendance: 4,000. For info: USA Curling, PO Box 866, Stevens Point, WI 54481. Phone: (715) 344-1199. Fax: (715) 344-6885. Email: usacurl@coredcs.com. WWW: http://www.usacurl.org

March 1998

	S	M	T	W	T	F	S
	1	2	3	4	5	6	7
	8	9	10	11	12	13	14
	15	16	17	18	19	20	21
	22	23	24	25	26	27	28
	29	30	31				

VAN CUYK, CHRIS: BIRTH ANNIVERSARY. Mar 1, 1927. Christian Gerald (Chris) Van Cuyk, baseball player born at Kimberly, WI. Van Cuyk pitched for the Brooklyn Dodgers from 1950 to 1952. His older brother Johnny also pitched for Brooklyn. Died at Hudson, FL, Nov 3, 1992.

BIRTHDAYS TODAY

Ronald (Ron) Francis, 35, hockey player, born Sault Ste. Marie, Ontario, Canada, Mar 1, 1963.

Johnny Cornelius Ray, 41, former baseball player, born Chouteau, OK, Mar 1, 1957.

Mayce Edward Christopher (Chris) Webber, III, 25, basketball player, born Detroit, MI, Mar 1, 1973.

Brian Joseph Winters, 46, former basketball coach and player, born New York, NY, Mar 1, 1952.

MARCH 2 — MONDAY
Day 61 — 304 Remaining

CHASE'S SPORTSQUOTE OF THE DAY

"He can speak ten languages, but he can't hit in any of them." —said of Moe Berg

BEE, CLAIR: BIRTH ANNIVERSARY. Mar 2, 1896. Clair Francis Bee, basketball player and Basketball Hall of Fame coach born at Grafton, WV. Bee played basketball at several colleges, but was much better known as one of the game's greatest innovators and promoters. He pioneered rules and strategy changes (including the three-second rule and the 1-3-1 zone defense) that helped make the sport a national attraction, and he also wrote the famous *Chip Hilton* stories for young people. Bee coached at Long Island University (1931–50), making the new school a power in the sport until the point-shaving scandals of the early 1950s. Many prominent coaches attended Bee's clinics and read his books. Inducted into the Hall of Fame in 1967. Died at Cleveland, OH, May 20, 1983.

BERG, MOE: BIRTH ANNIVERSARY. Mar 2, 1902. Morris (Moe) Berg, baseball player born at New York, NY. Berg was a weak-hitting catcher more renowned for his intellect and linguistic abilities. He lived a secretive life and was reputed to have been involved in espionage during the Second World War. Died at Belleville, NJ, May 29, 1972.

BOBBY HULL GETS SECOND 50: ANNIVERSARY. Mar 2, 1966. Left wing Bobby Hull of the Chicago Blackhawks became the first NHL player to score 50 goals in a season twice when he scored his 50th goal of the 1965–66 season in a 5–4 win over the Detroit Red Wings.

50

COOPER, MORT: BIRTH ANNIVERSARY. Mar 2, 1914. Morton Cecil (Mort) Cooper, baseball player born Atherton, MO. Pitcher Mort and his brother, catcher Walker, formed a brother-brother battery for the St. Louis Cardinals. Mort won 22 games in 1942 and 1944 to lead the Cards to a pair of National League pennants and World Series titles. Died at Little Rock, AR, Nov 17, 1958.

ESPO FIRST TO GET 100: ANNIVERSARY. Mar 2, 1969. Phil Esposito, center of the Boston Bruins, became the first player in National Hockey League history to score 100 points in a season when he scored a goal in Boston's 4–0 victory over the Pittsburgh Penguins.

KONSTANTY, JIM: BIRTH ANNIVERSARY. Mar 2, 1917. James Casimir (Jim) Konstanty, baseball player born at Strykersville, NY. Konstanty was the first relief pitcher ever given the MVP award, winning the National League honor in 1950 while pitching for the "Whiz Kids," the pennant-winning Philadelphia Phillies. Died at Oneonta, NY, June 11, 1976.

MILLER, DON: BIRTH ANNIVERSARY. Mar 2, 1902. Donald C. Miller, football player and coach born at Defiance, OH. Miller, a halfback, was the only member of the famed Four Horsemen of Notre Dame to start every game over a three-year varsity career. After graduation, he played pro football and coached for a few years, but devoted most of his life to a prominent legal career. Died at Cleveland, OH, July 28, 1979.

OTT, MEL: BIRTH ANNIVERSARY. Mar 2, 1909. Melvin Thomas (Mel) Ott, Baseball Hall of Fame outfielder born at Gretna, LA. Playing for the New York Giants, Ott hit 511 home runs, 3rd on the all-time list when he retired and a National League record until Willie Mays surpassed it in 1966. Ott's swing was characterized by an unusual, high leg kick that helped him reach the short fences of the Polo Grounds for two-thirds of his homers. Inducted into the Hall of Fame in 1951. Died at New Orleans, LA, Nov 21, 1958.

SANDBERG BECOMES HIGHEST PAID PLAYER: ANNIVERSARY. Mar 2, 1992. Second baseman Ryne Sandberg signed a four-year contract with the Chicago Cubs worth $28.4 million to become baseball's highest paid player, passing Bobby Bonilla of the New York Mets. The eight-time All-Star and nine-time Gold Glove winner retired in the middle of the 1994 season but returned to the game (at a far lower salary) in 1996.

WILT SCORES 100: ANNIVERSARY. Mar 2, 1962. Wilt Chamberlain poured in 100 points, an NBA record, as the Philadelphia Warriors defeated the New York Knicks, 169–147, in Hershey, PA. Chamberlain made 36 field goals and a record 28 foul shots and set yet another record by scoring 59 points in the second half.

BIRTHDAYS TODAY

Peter Sven (Pete) Broberg, 48, former baseball player, born West Palm Beach, FL, Mar 2, 1950.
Michael Brooks, 34, football player, born Ruston, LA, Mar 2, 1964.
Ronald Edwin (Ron) Gant, 33, baseball player, born Victoria, TX, Mar 2, 1965.
Donald Bernard (Don) Schwall, 62, former baseball player, born Wilkes-Barre, PA, Mar 2, 1936.
Terry Lee Steinbach, 36, baseball player, born New Ulm, MN, Mar 2, 1962.

MARCH 3 — TUESDAY
Day 62 — 303 Remaining

BIG TWELVE WOMEN'S BASKETBALL TOURNAMENT. Mar 3–7. Municipal Auditorium, Kansas City, MO. For info: Big Twelve Conference, 2201 Stemmons Freeway, 28th Floor, Dallas, TX 75207. Phone: (214) 742-1212. Fax: (214) 742-2046.

BILL MLKVY NETS 73: ANNIVERSARY. Mar 3, 1951. Bill Mlkvy of Temple University set an NCAA record by scoring 73 points in one game as Temple creamed Wilkes, 99–69.

BOROS, JULIUS: BIRTH ANNIVERSARY. Mar 3, 1920. Julius Nicholas Boros, golfer born at Fairfield, CT. Boros won the US Open in 1952 and 1963 and the PGA Championship in 1968. He had an easy, almost lazy swing that belied his ability to hit the ball hard and far. Died at Ft Lauderdale, FL, May 28, 1994.

KEELER, WEE WILLIE: BIRTH ANNIVERSARY. Mar 3, 1872. William Henry ("Wee Willie") Keeler, Baseball Hall of Fame outfielder born at Brooklyn, NY. Despite his small stature, Keeler was one of the best hitters of all time. His 44-game hitting streak in 1897 is still the National League mark although it was later tied by Pete Rose. His aphorism, "Hit 'em where they ain't," is solid advice for all batters. Inducted into the Hall of Fame in 1939. Died at New York, NY, Jan 1, 1923.

NCAA MEN'S DIVISION III BASKETBALL TOURNAMENT. Mar 3–5. First and second round sites TBA. For info: NCAA, 6201 College Blvd, Overland Park, KS 66211. Phone: (913) 339-1906.

SHOEMAKER WINS $100 MILLION: ANNIVERSARY. Mar 3, 1985. Willie Shoemaker became the first jockey to pass the $100 million mark in career earnings by riding Lord at War to victory in the Santa Anita Handicap.

UEBERROTH ELECTED COMMISSIONER: ANNIVERSARY. Mar 3, 1984. Major league baseball owners elected Peter V. Ueberroth, president of the Los Angeles Olympic Organizing Committee, to be Commissioner of Baseball to succeed Bowie Kuhn. Ueberroth assumed his duties after his responsibilities with the Olympics were finished, and he remained in office through Mar 31, 1989.

WARD, MONTE: BIRTH ANNIVERSARY. Mar 3, 1860. John Montgomery Ward, Baseball Hall of Fame infielder born at Bellefonte, PA. Ward helped to organize the Brotherhood of Professional Base Ball Players, the original players' union that led to the creation of the Players League, a third major league that played only one season, 1890. Inducted into the Hall of Fame in 1964. Died at Augusta, GA, Mar 4, 1925.

BIRTHDAYS TODAY

William Henry ("Skeeter") Barnes, 41, former baseball player, born Cincinnati, OH, Mar 3, 1957.
Neal Heaton, 38, former baseball player, born New York, NY, Mar 3, 1960.
Jacqueline (Jackie) Joyner-Kersee, 36, Olympic gold medal heptathlete, born East St. Louis, IL, Mar 3, 1962.
Brian Joseph Leetch, 30, hockey player, born Corpus Christi, TX, Mar 3, 1968.
Scott David Radinsky, 30, baseball player, born Glendale, CA, Mar 3, 1968.
Herschel Walker, 36, Heisman Trophy running back, born Wrightsville, GA, Mar 3, 1962.

☆   ☆   ☆

MARCH 4 — WEDNESDAY
Day 63 — 302 Remaining

BIG EAST MEN'S BASKETBALL TOURNAMENT. Mar 4–7. Madison Square Garden, New York, NY. For info: Big East Conference, 56 Exchange Terrace, Providence, RI 02903. Phone: (401) 453-0660. Fax: (401) 751-8540.

JOHNSON, BOB: BIRTH ANNIVERSARY. Mar 4, 1931. Robert (Bob) Johnson, hockey player, coach and executive born at Minneapolis, MN. Johnson played college hockey at the University of Minnesota and began coaching high school hockey in 1956. He moved to Colorado College in 1963 and to the University of Wisconsin in 1967. Johnson's Badgers won three NCAA titles. He coached four US National teams and the 1976 Olympic team. Johnson became head coach of the Calgary Flames in 1982 and led them to five straight Stanley Cup playoff appearances. He became executive director of the Amateur Hockey Association of the United States in 1987 and coach of the Pittsburgh Penguins in 1990. They won the Stanley Cup a year later. Johnson was named coach of the US team for the 1991 Canada Cup, but surgery for a brain tumor prevented his participation. He was known throughout the hockey world for his favorite saying, "It's a good day for hockey." Died at Colorado Springs, CO, Nov 26, 1991.

LAFLEUR GETS 1,000th POINT: ANNIVERSARY. Mar 4, 1981. Forward Guy Lafleur of the Montreal Canadiens scored the 1,000th point of his career, a goal in a 9–3 victory over the Winnipeg Jets. Lafleur finished with 1353 points and entered the Hockey Hall of Fame in 1988.

McCULLOUGH, CLYDE: BIRTH ANNIVERSARY. Mar 4, 1917. Clyde Edward McCullough, baseball player born at Nashville, TN. McCullough was a tough catcher who played from 1940 to 1956. He is reputed to be the last catcher not to use a chest protector. Died at San Francisco, CA, Sept 18, 1982.

NAIA MEN'S AND WOMEN'S SWIMMING AND DIVING NATIONAL CHAMPIONSHIPS. Mar 4–7. Federal Way, WA. Individuals compete for All-America honors while teams compete for the national championship. 18th annual competition for women and 42nd for men. Est attendance: 3,000. For info: Natl Assn of Intercollegiate Athletics, 6120 S Yale Ave, Ste 1450, Tulsa, OK 74136. Phone: (918) 494-8828. Fax: (918) 494-8841. Email: khenry@naia.org. WWW: http://www.naia.org

NCAA WOMEN'S DIVISION III BASKETBALL TOURNAMENT. Mar 4–7. First and second rounds at campus sites TBA. For info: NCAA, 6201 College Blvd, Overland Park, KS 66211. Phone: (913) 339-1906.

O'DOUL, LEFTY: BIRTH ANNIVERSARY. Mar 4, 1897. Frank Joseph ("Lefty") O'Doul, baseball player, manager and executive born at San Francisco, CA. O'Doul switching from pitching to the outfield and became one of the greatest players not in the Hall of Fame. His career batting average, .349, included hitting .398 in 1929 and .383 in 1930. After retiring, he helped to organize the major leagues in Japan. Died at San Francisco, Dec 7, 1969.

PFEFFER, JEFF: 110th BIRTH ANNIVERSARY. Mar 4, 1888. Edward Joseph ("Jeff") Pfeffer, baseball player born at Seymour, IL. Pfeffer pitched in the major leagues from 1911 through 1924. He appeared in the 1916 and 1920 World Series for the Brooklyn Dodgers. Died at Chicago, IL, Aug 15, 1972.

ROCKNE, KNUTE: 110th BIRTH ANNIVERSARY. Mar 4, 1888. Knute Rockne, football coach born at Voss, Norway. Rockne played end at the University of Notre Dame and then in 1918 was appointed head coach at his alma mater. Over 13 seasons, Rockne became a living legend, and Notre Dame football rose to a position of unprecedented prominence. His teams won 105 games (and three national championships) against only 12 losses and 5 ties. Rockne died in a plane crash at Bazaar, KS, Mar 31, 1931.

VANCE, DAZZY: BIRTH ANNIVERSARY. Mar 4, 1891. Arthur Charles ("Dazzy") Vance, Baseball Hall of Fame pitcher born at Orient, IA. Vance "dazzled" opposing teams with his pitching prowess. He won 197 games over 16 years, mostly with inept Brooklyn Dodgers teams. Inducted into the Hall of Fame in 1955. Died at Homosassa Springs, FL, Feb 16, 1961.

BIRTHDAYS TODAY

Brian Scott Barber, 25, baseball player, born Hamilton, OH, Mar 4, 1973.

Shane Patrick Conlan, 34, football player, born Frewsburg, NY, Mar 4, 1964.

Thomas Alan (Tom) Grieve, 50, baseball executive and former player, born Pittsfield, MA, Mar 4, 1948.

Brian Ronald Hunter, 30, baseball player, born Torrance, CA, Mar 4, 1968.

Peter Erling Jacobsen, 44, golfer, born Portland, OR, Mar 4, 1954.

Kevin Maurice Johnson, 32, basketball player, born Sacramento, CA, Mar 4, 1966.

☆ ☆ ☆

MARCH 5 — THURSDAY
Day 64 — 301 Remaining

ACC MEN'S BASKETBALL TOURNAMENT. Mar 5–8. Greensboro Coliseum Complex, Greensboro, NC. For info: Atlantic Coast Conference, PO Drawer ACC, Greensboro, NC 27419-6999. Phone: (910) 854-8787. Fax: (910) 854-8797.

BIG TEN MEN'S BASKETBALL TOURNAMENT. Mar 5–8. TBA. For info: Big Ten Conference, 1500 W Higgins Rd, Park Ridge, IL 60068-6300. Phone: (847) 696-1010. Fax: (847) 696-1150. WWW: http://www.bigten.org

BIG TWELVE MEN'S BASKETBALL TOURNAMENT. Mar 5–8. Kemper Arena, Kansas City, MO. For info: Big Twelve Conference, 2201 Stemmons Freeway, 28th Floor, Dallas, TX 75207. Phone: (214) 742-1212. Fax: (214) 742-2046.

BLUE, LU: BIRTH ANNIVERSARY. Mar 5, 1897. Luzerne Atwell (Lu) Blue, baseball player born at Washington, DC. Blue played for four major league teams from 1921 through 1933. He had a reputation as a difficult player to manage, but he hit very well and fielded with grace. Died at Alexandria, VA, July 28, 1958.

BOWLER ROLLS TWO PERFECT GAMES: ANNIVERSARY. Mar 5, 1924. Frank Carauna of Buffalo, NY, became the first bowler in history in roll two consecutive 300 games.

CHRISTMAN, PAUL: 80th BIRTH ANNIVERSARY. Mar 5, 1918. Paul Joseph Christman, football player and sportscaster born at St. Louis, MO. Christman played football at the University of Missouri under Coach Don Faurot. He excelled at quarterback and defensive halfback and led the Tigers to the 1939 Orange Bowl. Following military service during World War II, he played for the Chicago Cardinals, leading them to the NFL championship in 1947. In the 1960s, he was a color commentator on college football telecasts. Died at Lake Forest, IL, Mar 2, 1970.

March *1998*	S	M	T	W	T	F	S
	1	2	3	4	5	6	7
	8	9	10	11	12	13	14
	15	16	17	18	19	20	21
	22	23	24	25	26	27	28
	29	30	31				

DAYTONA INTERNATIONAL MOTORCYCLE SHOW. Mar 5–9. Daytona International Speedway, Daytona Beach, FL. Est attendance: 40,000. For info: Advanstar Expositions, 201 E Sandpointe Ave, Ste 600, Santa Ana, CA 92707-5761. Phone: (800) 854-3112 or (714) 513-8400.

DORAL-RYDER OPEN. Mar 5–8. Doral Resort & Spa, Miami, FL. A PGA Tour tournament with a full week of events, including a free outdoor pops concert, a skins game and three celebrity pro-ams. The Doral-Ryder Open is the nation's largest sports fund-raiser for the American Cancer Society. Est attendance: 150,000. For info: Walt Shuler, Mktg Dir, Doral-Ryder Open, PO Box 522927, Miami, FL 33152. Phone: (305) 477-4653. Fax: (305) 477-4914.

ENGLAND: CRUFTS DOG SHOW. Mar 5–8. National Exhibition Centre, Birmingham, West Midlands. The world's greatest dog show in which more than 18,000 top pedigree dogs compete for the Best in Show title, the most prestigious award in the world of dogs. Est attendance: 95,000. For info: Crufts Office, The Kennel Club, 1-5 Clarges St, London, England W1Y 8AB. Phone: (44) (171) 493-7838. Fax: (44) (171) 518-1028. For ticket info: (44) (171) 518-1012. WWW: http://www.crufts.org.uk

GIBBS RESIGNS AS REDSKINS COACH: ANNIVERSARY. Mar 5, 1993. Washington Redskins head coach Joe Gibbs resigned his position after 12 seasons. Gibbs' teams compiled a 140–65 record and won three Super Bowls.

IRSAY, ROBERT: 75th BIRTH ANNIVERSARY. Mar 5, 1923. Robert Irsay, football executive born at Chicago, IL. After making his fortune in heating and air conditioning, Irsay bought the Los Angeles Rams in 1972 and soon thereafter traded the entire franchise for the Baltimore Colts. In one of the most infamous moves in American sport, the Colts slipped out of town in the middle of the night in 1984 and relocated in Indianapolis. Died at Indianapolis, IN, Jan 14, 1997.

KNOXVILLE BOAT SHOW. Mar 5–8. Knoxville Convention Center, Knoxville, TN. 15th annual show featuring more than 50,000 sq feet of boats and 70 booths displaying scuba and marine equipment, water skis and much more. Est attendance: 14,000. For info: Cindy Crabtree, Event Coord, ESAU, Inc, PO Box 50096, Knoxville, TN 37950. Phone: (423) 588-1233 or (800) 588-ESAU. Fax: (423) 588-6938.

MOON PHASE: FIRST QUARTER. Mar 5. Moon enters First Quarter phase at 3:41 AM, EST.

NAIA MEN'S AND WOMEN'S INDOOR TRACK AND FIELD NATIONAL CHAMPIONSHIPS. Mar 5–7. Devaney Sports Center, Lincoln, NE. Individuals compete for All-America honors while teams compete for the national championship. 33rd men's and 18th women's annual competition. Est attendance: 2,500. For info: Natl Assn Intercollegiate Athletics, 6120 S Yale Ave, Ste 1450, Tulsa, OK 74136. Phone: (918) 494-8828. Fax: (918) 494-8841. Email: khenry@naia.org. WWW: http://www.naia.org

NCAA MEN'S DIVISION II BASKETBALL TOURNAMENT. Mar 5–8. Regionals at campus sites TBA. For info: NCAA, 6201 College Blvd, Overland Park, KS 66211. Phone: (913) 339-1906.

NCAA MEN'S AND WOMEN'S RIFLE CHAMPIONSHIPS. Mar 5–7 or 12–14. Site TBA. For info: NCAA, 6201 College Blvd, Overland Park, KS 66211. Phone: (913) 339-1906.

NCAA WOMEN'S DIVISION II BASKETBALL TOURNAMENT. Mar 5–8. Regionals at campus sites TBA. For info: NCAA, 6201 College Blvd, Overland Park, KS 66211. Phone: (913) 339-1906.

PAC-10 MEN'S SWIMMING CHAMPIONSHIPS. Mar 5–7. Belmont Plaza, Long Beach, CA. For info: PAC-10 Conference, 800 S Broadway, Ste 400, Walnut Creek, CA 94596. Phone: (510) 932-4411. Fax: (510) 932-4601.

SEC MEN'S BASKETBALL TOURNAMENT. Mar 5–8. Atlanta, GA. For info: Southeastern Conference, 2201 Civic Center Blvd, Birmingham, AL 35203-1103. Phone: (205) 458-3010. Fax: (205) 458-3030. Email: cbloom@sec.org. WWW: http://www.secsports.org

TESREAU, JEFF: BIRTH ANNIVERSARY. Mar 5, 1889. Charles Monroe ("Jeff") Tesreau, baseball player born at Ironton, MO. Tesreau pitched in the major leagues from 1912 throught 1918. He coached baseball at Dartmouth College for 27 years. Died at Hanover, NH, Sept 24, 1946.

THOMPSON, SAM: BIRTH ANNIVERSARY. Mar 5, 1860. Samuel (Sam) Thompson, baseball player born at Danville, IN. Thompson's size made him one of the most popular players of the 19th century. He hit 128 home runs and finished his career with the Detroit Tigers. Died at Detroit, MI, Nov 7, 1922.

BIRTHDAYS TODAY

Chad Everette Fonville, 27, baseball player, born Jacksonville, NC, Mar 5, 1971.
Jeffrey Bryan Hammonds, 27, baseball player, born Plainfield, NJ, Mar 5, 1971.
Michael Jerome Irvin, 32, football player, born Fort Lauderdale, FL, Mar 5, 1966.
Scott Allen Skiles, 34, basketball player, born LaPorte, IN, Mar 5, 1964.
Kenton Charles (Kent) Tekulve, 51, former baseball player, born Cincinnati, OH, Mar 5, 1947.
Laurence Tisch, 75, television executive, born New York, NY, Mar 5, 1923.
Michael Warren, 52, actor and former basketball player, born South Bend, IN, Mar 5, 1946.
Reggie Williams, 34, basketball player, born Baltimore, MD, Mar 5, 1964.
Frederick (Fred) Williamson, 60, former broadcaster and football player, born Gary, IN, Mar 5, 1938.

☆   ☆   ☆

MARCH 6 — FRIDAY
Day 65 — 300 Remaining

SPORTSCHASER OF THE DAY
Who coached the NFL's Chicago Cardinals to their only championship in 1947?

AMA NATIONAL HOT-SHOE DIRT TRACK. Mar 6. Daytona Beach Municipal Stadium, Daytona Beach, FL. For info: John Story, Dir of Pub Rel, Daytona Intl Speedway, PO Box 2801, Daytona Beach, FL 32120-2801. Phone: (904) 947-6782. For tickets: (904) 253-RACE (7223). Fax: (904) 947-6791. WWW: http://www.daytonausa.com

CLAY BECOMES ALI: ANNIVERSARY. Mar 6, 1964. Heavyweight champion Cassius Marcellus Clay announced that he had embraced the Nation of Islam and changed his name to Muhammad Ali. As Clay, he had won a gold medal in the 1960 Summer Olympic Games in Rome and captured the heavyweight crown with a stunning TKO of Sonny Liston at Miami Beach on Feb 25, 1964.

CONZELMAN, JIMMY: 100th BIRTH ANNIVERSARY. Mar 6, 1898. James G. (Jimmy) Conzelman, Pro Football Hall of Fame player and coach, born at St. Louis, MO. Conzelman played at Washington University, St. Louis, and at the Great Lakes Naval Training Station. He played for several pro teams in the 1920s and coached at his alma mater from 1934 to 1939. Returning to the pros in 1940 with the Chicago Cardinals, Conzelman coached them to the 1947 NFL title. Inducted into the Hall of Fame in 1964. Died at St. Louis, July 31, 1970.

FIRST WOMEN'S COLLEGIATE BASKETBALL GAME: ANNIVERSARY. Mar 6, 1892. The first women's collegiate basketball game was played at Smith College in Northampton, MA. Senda Berenson, then Smith's director of physical education and "mother of women's basketball," supervised the game, in which Smith's sophomore team beat the freshman team 5–4.

GROVE, LEFTY: BIRTH ANNIVERSARY. Mar 6, 1900. Robert Moses ("Lefty") Grove, Baseball Hall of Fame pitcher born at Lonaconing, MD. Grove is generally considered one of the best lefthanded pitchers of all time. He won 300 games even though he did not pitch in the major leagues until he was 25. Inducted into the Hall of Fame in 1947. Died at Norwalk, OH, May 22, 1975.

HAMILL WINS WORLD TITLE: ANNIVERSARY. Mar 6, 1976. Dorothy Hamill of the US completed women's figure skating celebrated double triumph by adding first place in the World's Championship, contested at Goteberg, Sweden, to the Olympic gold medal she won in February in Innsbruck, Austria.

KRONE SETS FEMALE JOCKEY RECORD: 10th ANNIVERSARY. Mar 6, 1988. Julie Krone won the 1,205th victory of her career, thereby becoming the all-time winningest female jockey in history. Krone rode Squawter, a filly, to victory in the ninth race at Aqueduct Racetrack.

LARDNER, RING: BIRTH ANNIVERSARY. Mar 6, 1885. Ringgold Wilmer (Ring) Lardner, sportswriter born at Niles, MI. Lardner wrote about sports for a variety of newspapers, mostly in Chicago. In both his columns and his short stories, he reproduced ballplayers' vernacular

	S	**M**	**T**	**W**	**T**	**F**	**S**
March	1	2	3	4	5	6	7
1998	8	9	10	11	12	13	14
	15	16	17	18	19	20	21
	22	23	24	25	26	27	28
	29	30	31				

speech patterns with great success, thereby laying the groundwork for generations of baseball fiction to come. Lardner abandoned baseball after the Black Sox scandal was exposed. He wrote songs, plays and magazine articles but never the novel that some of his friends thought he should. Taciturn and solemn with a biting sense of humor, Lardner drank and smoked to excess, even after contracting tuberculosis in 1926. Died at East Hampton, NY, Sept 25, 1933.

LONGHORN WORLD CHAMPIONSHIP RODEO. Mar 6–8. Von Braun Civic Center, Huntsville, AL. More than 200 cowboys and cowgirls compete in six professional contests ranging from bronco riding to bull riding for top prize money and world championship points. Featuring colorful opening pageantry and Big, Bad BONUS Bulls. 19th annual. Est attendance: 16,000. For info: W. Bruce Lehrke, Pres, Longhorn World Chmpshp Rodeo, Inc, PO Box 70159, Nashville, TN 37207. Phone: (615) 876-1016. Fax: (615) 876-4685. Email: lhrodeo@idt.net. WWW: http://www.longhornrodeo.com

NC RV AND CAMPING SHOW. Mar 6–8. NC State Fairgrounds, Raleigh, NC. A display of the latest in recreation vehicles and accessories by various dealers. Est attendance: 10,000. For info: Apple Rock Advertising & Promotions, 1200 Eastchester Dr, High Point, NC 27265. Phone: (910) 881-7100. Fax: (910) 883-7198.

NCAA DIVISION III WRESTLING CHAMPIONSHIPS. Mar 6–7. Finals. Upper Iowa University, Fayette, IA. For info: NCAA, 6201 College Blvd, Overland Park, KS 66211. Phone: (913) 339-1906.

SHAUGHNESSY, CLARK: BIRTH ANNIVERSARY. Mar 6, 1892. Clark Daniel Shaughnessy, football player and coach born at St. Cloud, MN. After playing football at the University of Minnesota, Shaughnessy strung together a coaching career at several institutions: Tulane, Loyola of the South, Chicago, Stanford, Maryland and Pittsburgh. He coached the Los Angeles Rams and assisted George Halas with the Chicago Bears. Shaughnessy is known as the father of the modern T formation and played a key role in developing modern pro defensive football. Died at Santa Monica, CA, May 15, 1970.

USFL OPENS FIRST SEASON: 15th ANNIVERSARY. Mar 6, 1983. The United States Football League opened its first season of play with five games. The USFL was designed to avoid competing with the NFL by playing in the spring, but it lasted only three years.

BIRTHDAYS TODAY

Theodore Wade (Ted) Abernathy, 65, former baseball player, born Stanley, NC, Mar 6, 1933.

Peter (Pete) Gray (born Peter J. Wyshner), 83, former baseball player, born Nanticoke, PA, Mar 6, 1915.

Shaquille Rashaun O'Neal, 26, basketball player, born Newark, NJ, Mar 6, 1972.

Octavio Victor ("Cookie") Rojas, 59, former baseball player, born Havana, Cuba, Mar 6, 1939.

Roger William Salkeld, 27, baseball player, born Burbank, CA, Mar 6, 1971.

Wilver Dornel (Willie) Stargell, 58, Baseball Hall of Fame outfielder and first baseman, born Earlsboro, OK, Mar 6, 1940.

MARCH 7 — SATURDAY

Day 66 — 299 Remaining

ACC WRESTLING CHAMPIONSHIPS. Mar 7. Duke University, Durham, NC. For info: Atlantic Coast Conference, PO Drawer ACC, Greensboro, NC 27419-6999. Phone: (910) 854-8787. Fax: (910) 854-8797.

AMA GRAND NATIONAL KICKOFF DIRT TRACK. Mar 7. Daytona Beach Municipal Stadium, Daytona Beach, FL. For info: John Story, Dir of Pub Rel, Daytona Intl Speedway, Box 2801, Daytona Beach, FL 32120-2801. Phone: (904) 254-6782. For tickets: (904) 253-RACE (7223). Fax: (904) 947-6791. WWW: http//www.daytonausa.com

BIG TEN WRESTLING CHAMPIONSHIPS. Mar 7–8. Penn State University, University Park, PA. For info: Big Ten Conference, 1500 W Higgins Rd, Park Ridge, IL 60068-6300. Phone: (847) 696-1010. Fax: (847) 696-1150. WWW: http://www.bigten.org

BIG TWELVE WRESTLING CHAMPIONSHIPS. Mar 7. University of Oklahoma, Norman, OK. For info: Big Twelve Conference, 2201 Stemmons Freeway, 28th Floor, Dallas, TX 75207. Phone: (214) 742-1212. Fax: (214) 742-2046.

DAYTONA SUPERCROSS BY HONDA. Mar 7. Daytona International Speedway, Daytona Beach, FL. One of the most famous and toughest Supercross races in the world. Sponsor: Honda. For info: John Story, Dir of Pub Rel, Daytona Intl Speedway, PO Box 2801, Daytona Beach, FL 32120-2801. Phone: (904) 947-6782. For tickets: (904) 253-RACE (7223). Fax: (904) 947-6791. WWW: http://www.daytonausa.com

HOLLOMAN, BOBO: BIRTH ANNIVERSARY. Mar 7, 1925. Alva Lee ("Bobo") Holloman, baseball player born at Thomaston, GA. Holloman was the third pitcher to throw a no-hitter in his first major league start. It occurred on May 6, 1953, but his career did not last out the year. Died at Athens, GA, May 1, 1987.

IDITAROD SLED DOG RACE. Mar 7. Anchorage to Nome, AK. The fabled 1,049-mile race with each sled drawn by 16 Northern Breed Dogs. For info: Iditarod Trail Committee, PO Box 870800, Wasilla, AK 99687. Phone: (907) 376-5155. Fax: (907) 373-6998. WWW: http://www.iditarod.com

MAHRE WINS THIRD WORLD CUP: 15th ANNIVERSARY. Mar 7, 1983. Skier Phil Mahre became the third man and the first American to win three overall Alpine World Cup championships in succession.

NAVIN, FRANK: BIRTH ANNIVERSARY. Mar 7, 1871. Frank Navin, baseball executive born at Adrian, MI. Navin rose from an accountant's position with the Detroit Tigers to club ownership. He sold out gradually to Walter Briggs during the Great Depression. Died at Detroit, MI, Nov 13, 1935.

NENANA TRIPOD RAISING FESTIVAL. Mar 7–8. Nenana, AK. Festival centers around the guessing of the exact time of the ice breakup on the Tanana River. Highlights include the raising of the tripod (Mar 8), Nenana Banana Eating, Weight Pull Contest (humans and dogs), sled-dog races, craft bazaar and much more. Est attendance: 4,000. For info: Nenana Ice Classic, Box 272, Nenana, AK 99760. Phone: (907) 832-5446. Fax: (907) 832-5888.

SAINT PATRICK'S DAY DOG FUN FAIR, PARADE AND CELEBRATION. Mar 7. Alexandria, VA. A celebration of Irish heritage and culture featuring a parade. Preceded by "dog fun fair." Parties in local restaurants with live entertainment immediately after parade. Free. Est attendance: 40,000. For info: Alexandria Conv and Visitors Assn, 221 King St, Alexandria, VA 22314-3209. Phone: (703) 838-4200. Fax: (703) 838-4683. Email: acva@erols.com. WWW: http://www.virginia.org

SOUTHEAST FLORIDA SCOTTISH FESTIVAL AND GAMES. Mar 7. Hialeah Park and Race Course, FL. Est attendance: 8,000. For info: Scottish-American Soc of Southeast Florida, 5901 NE 21 Rd, Fort Lauderdale, FL 33308. Phone: (954) 776-5675. Email: mfcampbell@juno.com.

SOVIETS WIN WORLD HOCKEY CHAMPIONSHIP: ANNIVERSARY. Mar 7, 1954. The Soviet Union entered international ice hockey competition for the first time and came away with the world championship. The Soviets defeated Canada in the gold medal game, 7–2, played at Stockholm, Sweden.

TRAIL'S END MARATHON. Mar 7. Oregon coast. Local and regional runners from across the nation are attracted to this officially sanctioned marathon run on Oregon's northern coast. One of the West Coast's oldest and finest runs. 26-mile, 385-yard marathon also includes an 8K run and walk. Est attendance: 1,000. For info: Oregon Road Runners Club, PO Box 549, Beaverton, OR 97075. Phone: (503) 646-7867. Fax: (503) 520-0242. Email: orrc@teleport.com. WWW: http://www.teleport.com/~orrc

12-FOOT BASKET EXPERIMENT: ANNIVERSARY. Mar 7, 1954. The Minneapolis Lakers defeated the Milwaukee Hawks, 65–63 in an NBA game for which the baskets were raised as an experiment from 10' to 12'.

WINTER GAMES OF OREGON. Mar 7–8. Portland and vicinity, OR. Alpine and Nordic competition to be held at Timberline and Ski Bowl. For info: Oregon Amateur Sports Foundation, 4840 SW Western Ave, Ste 900, Beaverton, OR 97005. Phone: (503) 520-1319.

BIRTHDAYS TODAY

Willie Lee ("Flipper") Anderson, Jr, 33, football player, born Philadelphia, PA, Mar 7, 1965.
Stephen Taylor (Steve) Beuerlein, 33, football player, born Hollywood, CA, Mar 7, 1965.
Jeffrey Alan (Jeff) Burroughs, 47, former baseball player, born Long Beach, CA, Mar 7, 1951.
Joseph (Joe) Carter, 38, baseball player, born Oklahoma City, OK, Mar 7, 1960.
Michael Eisner, 56, baseball and hockey executive, born Mt Kisco, NY, Mar 7, 1942.
Janet Guthrie, 60, former auto racer, born Iowa City, IA, Mar 7, 1938.
Franco Harris, 48, Pro Football Hall of Fame running back, born Ft Dix, NJ, Mar 7, 1950.
Jeffrey Franklin (Jeff) Kent, 30, baseball player, born Bellflower, CA, Mar 7, 1968.
Ivan Lendl, 38, tennis player, born Ostrava, Czechoslovakia, Mar 7, 1960.

MARCH 8 — SUNDAY
Day 67 — 298 Remaining

DAYTONA 200 BY ARAI. Mar 8. Daytona International Speedway, Daytona Beach, FL. Motorcycle road race for superbikes. Sponsor: Arai Helmets. For info: John Story, Dir of Pub Rel, Daytona Intl Speedway, PO Box 2801, Daytona Beach, FL 32120-2801. Phone: (904) 947-6782. For tickets: (904) 253-RACE (7223) Fax: (904) 947-6791. WWW: http://www.daytonausa.com

FRAZIER DECISIONS ALI: ANNIVERSARY. Mar 8, 1971. Joe Frazier won a 15-round, unanimous decision over Muhummad Ali at New York's Madison Square Garden to become the heavyweight champion of the world.

FURILLO, CARL: BIRTH ANNIVERSARY. Mar 8, 1922. Carl Anthony Furillo, baseball player born at Stony Creek Mills, PA. Furillo played right field for the Brooklyn Dodgers "Boys of Summer" teams of the late 1940s and 1950s. He compiled a .299 lifetime batting average and was known for his strong throwing arm, giving rise to the nickname, the "Reading Rifle." Died at Stony Creek Mills, Jan 21, 1989.

MARTINA PASSES $10 MILLION MARK: ANNIVERSARY. Mar 8, 1986. Martina Navratilova became the first woman tennis player to pass the $10 million mark in career earnings. She also set the single year record, $2,173,556, in 1984.

NBA DOUBLEHEADER: ANNIVERSARY. Mar 8, 1954. The Milwaukee Hawks and the Baltimore Bullets played the only two-team doubleheader in NBA history. The Hawks won both games, 64–54 and 65–54.

PAIR OF FOUR-POINT PLAYS: ANNIVERSARY. Mar 8, 1994. Scottie Pippen and Pete Myers of the Chicago Bulls became the first teammates in NBA history to make four-point plays in the same game. The Bulls beat the Atlanta Hawks, 116–95.

"SEZ WHO?" FOURPLAY! MARCH MADNESS. Mar 8–30. Hooters, Chicago, IL. 2-player man-and-woman teams compete against one another, trying to complete humorous, provocative and otherwise memorable quotes made by basketball personalities. Annually, from the Sunday in March when NCAA Tournament field is announced through Monday, 22 days later, when the championship game is played. Est attendance: 600. For info: Rich Bysina. Phone: (630) 682-3712.

BIRTHDAYS TODAY

Richard Anthony (Dick) Allen, 56, former baseball player, born Wampum, PA, Mar 8, 1942.
James Alan (Jim) Bouton, 59, author (*Ball Four*) and former baseball player, born Newark, NJ, Mar 8, 1939.
Susan Clark, 58, actress (*Babe*), born Sarnia, Ontario, Canada, Mar 8, 1940.
Brent Fedyk, 31, hockey player, born Yorkton, Saskatchewan, Canada, Mar 8, 1967.
Charley Pride, 60, singer and former minor league baseball player, born Sledge, MS, Mar 8, 1938.
James Edward (Jim) Rice, 45, former baseball player, born Anderson, SC, Mar 8, 1953.
Kenneth (Kenny) Smith, 33, basketball player, born New York, NY, Mar 8, 1965.
Charles Linwood ("Buck") Williams, 38, basketball player, born Rocky Mount, NC, Mar 8, 1960.

MARCH 9 — MONDAY
Day 68 — 297 Remaining

CHASE'S SPORTSQUOTE OF THE DAY

"I like the game, but I don't like the life." —Jackie Jensen on his fear of flying

AMERICAN BOWLING CONGRESS CONVENTION (WITH HALL OF FAME INDUCTION CEREMONIES). Mar 9–14. Reno, NV. Local, state and national bowling leaders gather to decide the rules of the game

March *1998*	S	M	T	W	T	F	S
	1	2	3	4	5	6	7
	8	9	10	11	12	13	14
	15	16	17	18	19	20	21
	22	23	24	25	26	27	28
	29	30	31				

in a democratic setting. The week features board of directors' meetings, special seminars, dinners honoring top leaders, Hall of Fame induction ceremonies and workshops. Est attendance: 5,000. For info: Mark Miller, American Bowling Congress Conv, 5301 S 76th St, Greendale, WI 53129-0500. Phone: (414) 423-3224. Fax: (414) 421-7977.

JENSEN, JACKIE: BIRTH ANNIVERSARY. Mar 9, 1927. Jack Eugene (Jackie) Jensen, baseball player born at San Francisco, CA. Jensen was an All-American at the University of California in both baseball and football. He starred in the outfield for the Boston Red Sox in the 1950s but retired prematurely, in part because of his fear of flying. Died at Charlottesville, VA, July 14, 1982.

SOUTHWORTH, BILLY: 105TH BIRTH ANNIVERSARY. Mar 9, 1893. William Harrison (Billy) Southworth, baseball player and manager born at Harvard, NE. Southworth played the outfield in the 1920s and hit a home run in 1926 that propelled the St. Louis Cardinals to the National League pennant. He managed the Cardinals to the pennant in 1942, 1943 and 1944. Died at Columbus, OH, Nov 15, 1969.

VAUGHAN, ARKY: BIRTH ANNIVERSARY. Mar 9, 1912. Joseph Floyd ("Arky") Vaughan, Baseball Hall of Fame shortstop born at Clifty, AR. Vaughan was the Pittsburgh Pirates' regular shortstop during the 1930s. He won the National League MVP award in 1935 and finished his career with the Brooklyn Dodgers. Inducted into the Hall of Fame in 1985. Died at Eagleville, CA, Aug 30, 1952.

WILLIAMS, LEFTY: 105th BIRTH ANNIVERSARY. Mar 9, 1893. Claude Preston ("Lefty") Williams, baseball player born at Aurora, MO. Williams was one of two Chicago White Sox pitchers accused of conspiring to throw the 1919 World Series. He and seven teammates were banned for life. Died at Laguna Beach, CA, Nov 4, 1959.

YARDLEY SCORES 2,000: 40th ANNIVERSARY. Mar 9, 1958. Forward George Yardley of the Detroit Pistons became the first NBA player to score 2,000 points in a season.

BIRTHDAYS TODAY

Mahmoud Abdul-Rauf (born Chris Wayne Jackson), 29, basketball player, born Gulfport, MS, Mar 9, 1969.
Brian Keith Bosworth, 33, former football player, born Oklahoma City, OK, Mar 9, 1965.

Dagoberto (Bert) Campaneris, 56, former baseball player, born Pueblo Nuevo, Cuba, Mar 9, 1942.

James Joseph (Jim) Colbert, 57, golfer, born Elizabeth, NJ, Mar 9, 1941.

Radek Dvorak, 21, hockey player, born Ceske Budejovice, Czechoslovakia, Mar 9, 1977.

Robert James (Bobby) Fischer, 55, former chess player, born Chicago, IL, Mar 9, 1943.

Phil Housley, 34, hockey player, born St. Paul, MN, Mar 9, 1964.

Terence John (Terry) Mulholland, 35, baseball player, born Uniontown, PA, Mar 9, 1963.

Benito Santiago, 33, baseball player, born Ponce, Puerto Rico, Mar 9, 1965.

Darrell Walker, 37, basketball coach and former player, born Chicago, IL, Mar 9, 1961.

MARCH 10 — TUESDAY
Day 69 — 296 Remaining

ABRAMSON, JESSE: BIRTH ANNIVERSARY. Mar 10, 1904. Jesse Peter Abramson, sportswriter born at Mountaindale, NY. One of the most knowledgeable reporters on track and field, Abramson covered every Summer Olympic Games from 1928 through 1976. His remarkable memory and concern for detail earned him the nickname, "The Book." Died at Mount Vernon, NY, June 11, 1979.

DRYDEN, CHARLIE: BIRTH ANNIVERSARY. Mar 10, 1860. Charles Dryden, sportswriter born at Monmouth, NH. Working for newspapers in Chicago and New York, Dryden wrote about sports with a sense of humor and gained fame for bestowing nicknames upon teams and players. He called the 1906 Chicago White Sox "The Hitless Wonders," White Sox owner Charles Comiskey "The Old Roman" and Chicago Cubs manager Frank Chance "The Peerless Leader." His most famous phrase captured the futility of the Washington Senators: "First in war, first in peace and last in the American League." Died at Biloxi, MS, Feb 11, 1931.

GIANTS HIRE WOMAN PA VOICE: ANNIVERSARY. Mar 10, 1993. The San Francisco Giants made baseball history by hiring Sherry Davis to be the team's public address announcer. Davis, a legal secretary, became the first woman PA voice in the major leagues after having done voice-over work since 1981.

GOLDENBERG, BUCKETS: BIRTH ANNIVERSARY. Mar 10, 1911. Charles R. ("Buckets") Goldenberg, football player, wrestler and restaurateur born at Odessa, Russia. Goldenberg's family came to Milwaukee when he was four. He played football at the University of Wisconsin and for the Green Bay Packers, excelling as an offensive and defensive lineman. He wrestled in the off-season and entered the restaurant business when he tired of travelling. Died at Greendale, WI, Apr 16, 1986.

JACOBS, MIKE: BIRTH ANNIVERSARY. Mar 10, 1880. Michael Strauss (Mike) Jacobs, sports promoter born at New York, NY. Jacobs promoted boxing matches at Madison Square Garden and other venues, eventually exerting nearly monopolistic control over the sport in New York City. He signed the young Joe Louis and promoted all his fights, thereby opening up boxing to full integration. Died at Miami Beach, FL, Jan 24, 1953.

McCORMICK, JIM: 80th DEATH ANNIVERSARY. Mar 10, 1918. James (Jim) McCormick, baseball player and manager born at Glasgow, Scotland, 1856. McCormick was one of early baseball's most durable pitchers, completing 466 games. He pitched in the 1870s and 1880s. Died at Paterson, NJ.

REEVES NAMED BRONCOS COACH: ANNIVERSARY. Mar 10, 1981. New Denver Broncos owner Edgar F. Kaiser, Jr, named Dallas Cowboys offensive coordinator Dan Reeves head coach. In 12 seasons, Reeves took the Broncos to three Super Bowls and compiled a 117–79–1 record.

BIRTHDAYS TODAY

Robert Michael (Bob) Bailor, 47, former baseball player, born Connellsville, PA, Mar 10, 1951.

Heywood Hale Broun, 80, broadcaster, born New York, NY, Mar 10, 1918.

John Anthony Cangelosi, 35, baseball player, born New York, NY, Mar 10, 1963.

Bob Greene, 51, journalist, born Columbus, OH, Mar 10, 1947.

Steven Roy (Steve) Howe, 40, former baseball player, born Pontiac, MI, Mar 10, 1958.

Ronald Jack (Ron) Mix, 60, Pro Football Hall of Fame offensive tackle, born Los Angeles, CA, Mar 10, 1938.

Roderick Kevin (Rod) Woodson, 33, football player, born Fort Wayne, IN, Mar 10, 1965.

MARCH 11 — WEDNESDAY
Day 70 — 295 Remaining

BIERMAN, BERNIE: BIRTH ANNIVERSARY. Mar 11, 1894. Bernard William (Bernie) Bierman, football coach born at Springfield, MN. Bierman ran track and played football at the University of Minnesota and then began coaching at the high school level. After World War I, he moved to the University of Montana and then, after several stops as an assistant, became head coach at his alma mater in 1932. His Golden Gophers won four national championships before his retirement in 1950. Died at Laguna Hills, CA, Mar 8, 1977.

NAIA MEN'S DIVISION II BASKETBALL NATIONAL CHAMPIONSHIP TOURNAMENT. Mar 11–17. Idaho Center, Nampa, ID. 32-team field competes for the national championship. 7th annual. Est attendance: 30,000. For info: Natl Assn of Intercollegiate Athletics, 6120 S Yale Ave, Ste 1450, Tulsa, OK 74136. Phone: (918) 494-8828. Fax: (918) 494-8841. Email: khenry@naia.org. WWW: http://www.naia.org

NAIA WOMEN'S DIVISION II BASKETBALL NATIONAL CHAMPIONSHIP TOURNAMENT. Mar 11–17. Sioux City Auditorium, Sioux City, IA. 32-team field competes for the national championship. 7th annual. Est attendance: 12,500. For info: Natl Assn of Intercollegiate Athletics, 6120 S Yale Ave, Ste 1450, Tulsa, OK 74136. Phone: (918) 494-8828. Fax: (918) 494-8841. Email: khenry@naia.org. WWW: http://www.naia.org

NATIONAL POWER BOAT SHOW. Mar 11–15. The New Atlantic City Convention Center, Atlantic City, NJ. A Miami-style boat show offers a vessel for virtually every taste and pocketbook, and boating browsers can board the boats and explore the interiors. Est attendance: 20,000. For info: Atlantic City Conv & Visitors Authority, 2314 Pacific Ave, Atlantic City, NJ 08401. Phone: (609) 449-7130.

NCAA MEN'S AND WOMEN'S DIVISION II SWIMMING AND DIVING CHAMPIONSHIPS. Mar 11–14. Finals at a site TBA. For info: NCAA, 6201 College Blvd, Overland Park, KS 66211. Phone: (913) 339-1906.

NCAA MEN'S AND WOMEN'S SKIING CHAMPIONSHIPS. Mar 11–14. Site TBA. For info: NCAA, 6201 College Blvd, Overland Park, KS 66211. Phone: (913) 339-1906.

NFL ADOPTS INSTANT REPLAY: ANNIVERSARY. Mar 11, 1986. After years of debate, NFL owners adopted a rules change allowing the limited use of televised replays to assist the officials on the field. This system was eliminated after the 1991 season.

OUTRIGGER HOTELS HAWAIIAN MOUNTAIN TOUR. Mar 11–15. Oahu, HI. Televised, preseason, 5-stage, international mountain bike race for professionals and amateurs. Includes Prologue, Time Trial, Cross Country, Downhill, Point-to-Point and Criterium. $50,000 pro purse awarded for men's and women's stages, overall individual GC and team GC. Automaximizer downhill stage race held in conjunction. Includes prologue, time trial, head to head, downhill duo, downhill and criterium. $20,000 pro purse. Est attendance: 10,000. For info: Event Marketing, Inc, Pauahi Tower, 1001 Bishop St, #880, Honolulu, HI 96813. Phone: (808) 521-4322. Fax: (808) 538-0314. Email: dey@emisport.net. WWW: http://emisport.com

WINTER EQUESTRIAN FESTIVAL. Mar 11–Apr 4. Bob Thomas Equestrian Center, Florida State Fairgrounds, Tampa, FL. Top riders compete in this festival known as the "world's richest hunter-jumper horse show circuit," with more than $1 million in prize money. Features 10 weeks of qualifying competition which begin at West Palm Beach and continue through the final three weeks at the FL Expo Park in Tampa. The tournament is divided as follows: Suncoast Internationale, Mar 11–15; Tampa Bay Classic, Mar 18–22; Tournament of Champions, Mar 25–29. Grand finale of the festival is the $100,000 Budweiser American Invitational Apr 4, 7 PM, in Tampa Stadium, an invitational world-class jumping competition (the first jewel in the Triple Crown of Show Jumping), also featuring band performances, parades and dressage demonstrations. For info: Stadium Jumping, Inc, 3104 Cherry Palm Dr, Ste 220, Tampa, FL 33619. Phone: (800) 237-8924 or (813) 623-5801. Fax: (813) 626-5369. WWW: http://www.stadiumjumping.com

BIRTHDAYS TODAY

Ken James Baumgartner, 32, hockey player, born Flin Flon, Manitoba, Canada, Mar 11, 1966.
Philip Poole (Phil) Bradley, 39, former baseball and football player, born Bloomington, IN, Mar 11, 1959.
Dock Phillip Ellis, 53, former baseball player, born Los Angeles, CA, Mar 11, 1945.
Cesar Francisco Geronimo, 50, former baseball player, born El Seibo, Dominican Republic, Mar 11, 1948.
Shawn Springs, 23, football player, born Silver Spring, MD, Mar 11, 1975.
Salomon Torres, 26, baseball player, born San Pedro de Macoris, Dominican Republic, Mar 11, 1972.

MARCH 12 — THURSDAY
Day 71 — 294 Remaining

DIDDLE, UNCLE ED: BIRTH ANNIVERSARY. Mar 12, 1895. Edgar Allen ("Uncle Ed") Diddle, Sr, basketball player and Basketball Hall of Fame coach born at Gradyville, KY. Diddle played several sports at Centre College and coached at Western Kentucky from 1923 through 1964. His teams won 759 games and 32 conference titles. The colorful coach chewed on a red towel along the side-

lines. Inducted into the Hall of Fame in 1971. Died at Bowling Green, KY, Jan 2, 1970.

FASTEST DISQUALIFICATION IN NBA HISTORY: ANNIVERSARY. Mar 12, 1956. Dick Farley of the Syracuse Nationals fouled out of an NBA game against the St. Louis Hawks after playing just five minutes, the fastest disqualification in league history.

HULL SCORES 51: ANNIVERSARY. Mar 12, 1966. Chicago Blackhawks left wing Bobby Hull became the first NHL player to score more than 50 goals in a season when he tallied his 51st goal of the year against the New York Rangers.

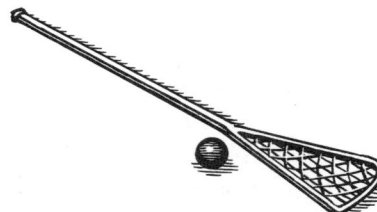

LUNAR ECLIPSE. Mar 12–13. Penumbral eclipse of the moon. Moon enters penumbra at approximately 9:14 PM, EST, reaches middle of eclipse at 11:20 PM, EST and leaves penumbra at 1:25 AM, EST. The beginning of the penumbral phase visible in North America except Alaska and northwestern Canada, Central America, South America, Europe, western Asia, Africa, Greenland, parts of Antarctica, the North polar region, the eastern South Pacific Ocean, the southeastern North Pacific Ocean, the Atlantic Ocean and western Indian Ocean; the end visible in North America, Central America, South America, Greenland, Iberian Peninsula, western France, British Isles, extreme western Africa, parts of Antarctica, extreme eastern Asia, the eastern half of the Pacific Ocean, the North Atlantic Ocean and the western South Atlantic Ocean.

MILLS, ABRAHAM: BIRTH ANNIVERSARY. Mar 12, 1844. Abraham Gilbert Mills, baseball executive born at New York, NY. Mills carried a bat and baseball with him during his service in the Civil War. He was president of the National League and, as chairman of the Mills Commission in 1905, helped to enshrine as fact the fanciful story that Abner Doubleday had invented baseball. Died at Falmouth, MA, Aug 26, 1929.

MOON PHASE: FULL MOON. Mar 12. Moon enters Full Moon phase at 11:34 AM, EST.

NCAA MEN'S DIVISION I BASKETBALL TOURNAMENT. Mar 12–15. First and second rounds at Hartford Civic Center, Hartford, CT; MCI Center, Washington, DC; Georgia Dome, Atlanta, GA; Rupp Arena, Lexington, KY; Myriad Convention Center, Oklahoma City, OK; United Center, Chicago, IL; Arco Arena, Sacramento, CA; and Boise State University, Boise, ID. For info: NCAA, 6201 College Blvd, Overland Park, KS 66211. Phone: (913) 339-1906.

NCAA WOMEN'S DIVISION III SWIMMING AND DIVING CHAMPIONSHIPS. Mar 12–14. Finals. St. Peter's RecPlex, St. Peter's, MO. For info: NCAA, 6201 College Blvd, Overland Park, KS 66211. Phone: (913) 339-1906.

SAINT PATRICK'S DAY DART TOURNAMENT. Mar 12–15. Battle Creek, MI. 14th annual tournament with seven separate contests to celebrate the luck of the Irish by encouraging the fast-growing interest in the US in the sport of darting. Annually, beginning the Thursday on or before St. Patrick's Day. Est attendance: 200. For info: Bill Buckner, Owner, Springbrook Golf Course, 1600 Ave A, Battle Creek, MI 49015. Phone: (616) 965-6512.

March 1998	S	M	T	W	T	F	S
		1	2	3	4	5	6	7
	8	9	10	11	12	13	14
	15	16	17	18	19	20	21
	22	23	24	25	26	27	28
	29	30	31				

TORVILL AND DEAN ACHIEVE PERFECTION: ANNIVERSARY. Mar 12, 1984. At the World Figure Skating Championships, Jayne Torvill and Christopher Dean of Great Britain became the first ice dancing team to earn nine perfect marks of 6.0.

BIRTHDAYS TODAY

John Andretti, 35, auto racer, born Indianapolis, IN, Mar 12, 1963.

John Wesley (Johnny) Callison, 59, former baseball player, born Qualls, OK, Mar 12, 1939.

Steven Allen (Steve) Finley, 33, baseball player, born Union City, TN, Mar 12, 1965.

Merton Edward Hanks, 30, football player, born Dallas, TX, Mar 12, 1968.

Vernon Sanders Law, 68, former baseball player, born Meridian, ID, Mar 12, 1930.

Raul Ramon Mondesi, 27, baseball player, born San Cristobal, Dominican Republic, Mar 12, 1971.

Dale Bryan Murphy, 42, former baseball player, born Portland, OR, Mar 12, 1956.

Isaiah ("J. R.") Rider, Jr, 27, basketball player, born Oakland, CA, Mar 12, 1971.

Darryl Eugene Strawberry, 36, baseball player, born Los Angeles, CA, Mar 12, 1962.

Rex Andrew Walters, 28, basketball player, born Omaha, NE, Mar 12, 1970.

MARCH 13 — FRIDAY
Day 72 — 293 Remaining

SPORTSCHASER OF THE DAY

Who hit two home runs in the 1911 World Series and earned the nickname "Home Run"?

AKC US CLASSIC CHAMPIONSHIP COON HUNT. Mar 13–14. County Fairgrounds, Orangeburg, SC. Coon hunters and sportsmen from the Southeast bring their dogs to compete. Est attendance: 5,000. For info: Carol P. Whisenhunt, Mktg, Orangeburg County C of C, PO Box 328, Orangeburg, SC 29116-0328. Phone: (803) 534-6821. Fax: (803) 531-9435.

BAKER, HOME RUN: BIRTH ANNIVERSARY. Mar 13, 1886. John Franklin ("Home Run") Baker, Baseball Hall of Fame third baseman born at Trappe, MD. Baker earned his nickname for leading the American League in home runs from 1911 through 1914 and for hitting a pair of homers in the 1911 World Series. Yet, in baseball's dead ball era, he never hit more than 12 in a single season. Inducted into the Hall of Fame in 1955. Died at Trappe, June 28, 1963.

CALLAGHAN, HELEN: BIRTH ANNIVERSARY. Mar 13, 1929. Helen Callaghan, baseball player born Helen St. Aubin at Vancouver, BC, Canada. St. Aubin and her sister, Margaret Maxwell, were recruited for the All-American Girls Professional Baseball League, which flourished in the 1940s when many major league players were off fighting World War II. She first played at age 15 for the Minneapolis Millerettes, an expansion team that moved to Indiana and became the Ft Wayne Daisies. The left-handed outfielder spent five years with the Daisies. For the 1945 season she led the league with a .299 average and 24 extra base hits. In 1946 she stole 114 bases in 111 games. She became known as the "Ted Williams of women's baseball." Her son Kelly Candaele's documentary on the women's 1940s baseball league inspired the film *A League of Their Own*. A second son, Casey Candaele, played major league baseball. Died at Santa Barbara, CA, Dec 8, 1992.

CHICAGO CARDINALS MOVE TO ST. LOUIS: ANNIVERSARY. Mar 13, 1960. National Football League owners voted to allow the Chicago Cardinals to move to St. Louis. The Cardinals are generally regarded as the oldest continuing operation in pro football, having been founded as the Morgan Athletic Club, a neighborhood team, in 1899. The Cardinals remained in St. Louis through the 1987 season after which owner Bill Bidwill transferred the team to Phoenix, AZ.

MILWAUKEE JOURNAL SENTINEL SPORTS SHOW. Mar 13–22. The Milwaukee Center, Milwaukee, WI. Travel and resort exhibits, hunting, fishing, boating and family travel and outdoor recreation. Largest outdoor show in Wisconsin. 59th annual show. Est attendance: 115,000. For info: Great Outdoors, 420 Lake Cook Rd, Deerfield, IL 60015. Phone: (847) 914-0630. Fax: (847) 914-0333.

NAIA WRESTLING NATIONAL CHAMPIONSHIPS. Mar 13–14. Jamestown Civic Center, Jamestown, ND. Individuals compete for All-America honors in 12 weight divisions, while teams compete for the national championship. 41st annual competition. Est attendance: 4,000. For info: Natl Assn of Intercollegiate Athletics, 6120 S Yale Ave, Ste 1450, Tulsa, OK 74136. Phone: (918) 494-8828. Fax: (918) 494-8841. Email: khenry@naia.org. WWW: http://www.naia.org

NBA CONSECUTIVE-GAME STREAK ENDS: ANNIVERSARY. Mar 13, 1983. Randy Smith's NBA consecutive-game streak came to an end as he played in his 906th straight game. Smith played for Buffalo, San Diego, Cleveland, New York and San Diego (again).

NCAA DIVISION II HOCKEY CHAMPIONSHIP. Mar 13–14. Finals. Site TBA. For info: NCAA, 6201 College Blvd, Overland Park, KS 66211. Phone: (913) 339-1906.

☆　☆　☆

NCAA DIVISION II WRESTLING CHAMPIONSHIPS. Mar 13–14. Finals. University of Southern Colorado, Pueblo, CO. For info: NCAA, 6201 College Blvd, Overland Park, KS 66211. Phone: (913) 339-1906.

NCAA MEN'S AND WOMEN'S DIVISION I INDOOR TRACK AND FIELD CHAMPIONSHIPS. Mar 13–14. Site TBA. For info: NCAA, 6201 College Blvd, Overland Park, KS 66211. Phone: (913) 339-1906.

NCAA MEN'S AND WOMEN'S DIVISION I DIVING CHAMPIONSHIPS. Mar 13–14. Regionals at US Naval Academy, Annapolis, MD; University of Georgia, Athens, GA; Miami University, Oxford, OH; University of Texas, Austin, TX; and US Air Force Academy, Colorado Springs, CO. For info: NCAA, 6201 College Blvd, Overland Park, KS 66211. Phone: (913) 339-1906.

NCAA MEN'S DIVISION III BASKETBALL TOURNAMENT. Mar 13–14. Sectionals at campus sites TBA. For info: NCAA, 6201 College Blvd, Overland Park, KS 66211. Phone: (913) 339-1906.

NCAA MEN'S AND WOMEN'S DIVISION II INDOOR TRACK AND FIELD CHAMPIONSHIPS. Mar 13–14. Finals at a site TBA. For info: NCAA, 6201 College Blvd, Overland Park, KS 66211. Phone: (913) 339-1906.

NCAA MEN'S AND WOMEN'S DIVISION III INDOOR TRACK AND FIELD CHAMPIONSHIPS. Mar 13–14. Finals. Brandeis University, Waltham, MA. For info: NCAA, 6201 College Blvd, Overland Park, KS 66211. Phone: (913) 339-1906.

NCAA WOMEN'S DIVISION III BASKETBALL TOURNAMENT. Mar 13–14. Sectionals at campus sites TBA. For info: NCAA, 6201 College Blvd, Overland Park, KS 66211. Phone: (913) 339-1906.

NCAA WOMEN'S DIVISION I BASKETBALL TOURNAMENT. Mar 13–16. First and Second Rounds: Campus sites TBA. For info: NCAA, 6201 College Blvd, Overland Park, KS 66211. Phone: (913) 339-1906.

NORTHWEST CRIBBAGE TOURNAMENT. Mar 13–15. Baker City, OR. Est attendance: 200. For info: Baker County VCB, 490 Campbell St, Baker City, OR 97814. Phone: (800) 523-1235.

POLO: US OPEN CHAMPIONSHIP & HANDICAP. Mar 13–Apr 12 (tentative). Wellington, FL. For info: Palm Beach Polo, Inc, 13420 South Shore Blvd, West Palm Beach, FL 33414. Phone: (561) 793-1440. Fax: (561) 790-3872.

STARTING GATE INVENTED: ANNIVERSARY. Mar 13, 1894. Englishman J. L. Johnstone invented the starting gate for horse racing.

TIMED EVENT CHAMPIONSHIP OF THE WORLD. Mar 13–15. Lazy E Arena, Guthrie, OK. The top all-around cowboys in the world compete for $140,000 in all five timed events. Est attendance: 17,000. For info: Lazy E Arena, Rte 5, Box 393, Guthrie, Ok 73044-9205. Phone: (800) 595-RIDE. Email: learena@ionet.net. WWW: http://www.lazye.com

BIRTHDAYS TODAY

Randy William Bass, 44, former baseball player, born Lawton, OK, Mar 13, 1954.
Thomas Andrew (Andy) Bean, 45, golfer, born Lafayette, GA, Mar 13, 1953.
William Nuschler (Will) Clark, Jr, 34, baseball player, born New Orleans, LA, Mar 13, 1964.
Trent Farris Dilfer, 26, football player, born Santa Cruz, CA, Mar 13, 1972.
Mariano Duncan, 35, baseball player, born San Pedro de Macoris, Dominican Republic, Mar 13, 1963.
Vance Edward Johnson, 35, football player, born Trenton, NJ, Mar 13, 1963.
Andre Previn Rison, 31, football player, born Flint, MI, Mar 13, 1967.

MARCH 14 — SATURDAY
Day 73 — 292 Remaining

BERING SEA ICE GOLF CLASSIC. Mar 14. Nome, AK. A six-hole course played on the frozen Bering Sea. The object is to land the bright-orange ricocheting golf ball into the sunken, flagged coffee cans before losing it among the built-up chunks of ice. Starts promptly at 10 AM at the Breakers Bar. Approximately 60 golfers. For info: Bering Sea Lions Club, Box 326, Nome, AK 99762. Phone: (907) 443-2226.

CANADIAN-AMERICAN DAYS FEST. Mar 14–22. Myrtle Beach, SC. Beach games and sporting events along with concerts, square dances and more. Est attendance: 100,000. For info: Wendy Cogan, Fest Mgr, Myrtle Beach Chamber of Commerce, PO Box 2115, Myrtle Beach, SC 29578. Phone: (803) 626-7444. WWW: http://www.myrtlebeach-info.com/

CHAMBERLAIN'S CONSECUTIVE COMPLETE GAME STREAK: ANNIVERSARY. Mar 14, 1962. Wilt Chamberlain of the Philadelphia Warriors completed a stretch of 47 consecutive games during which he played every minute. The streak, begun January 5 against the Syracuse Nationals and concluded against the Chicago Packers, stands as an NBA record.

DERBY. Mar 14. Biloxi, MS. Includes a 5K run and a 1K walk. Starts at 10:00 prior to the St. Patrick's Parade. For info: Hibernia Marching Soc of Mississippi, PO Box 707, Biloxi, MS 39533.

HOWE GETS 500TH GOAL: ANNIVERSARY. Mar 14, 1962. Right wing Gordie Howe of the Detroit Red Wings became the second player in NHL history to reach the 500-goal mark when he scored in a 3–2 loss to the New York Rangers. Howe wound up with 801 goals and entered the Hockey Hall of Fame in 1972.

McGUIRE'S 5K ST. PATRICK'S DAY PREDICTION RUN. Mar 14. Pensacola, FL. The largest, most popular 5K run in the history of Pensacola, "The Nation's Largest Prediction Run." 9 AM. Est attendance: 2,700. For info: Susi Lyon, McGuire's Irish Pub, 600 E Gregory St, Pensacola, FL 32501. Phone: (904) 433-6789. Fax: (904) 434-5400.

MULLEN GETS 500th GOAL: ANNIVERSARY. Mar 14, 1997. Joey Mullen of the Pittsburgh Penguins became the 25th player in National Hockey League history and the first American to score 500 regular-season goals. His tally came in a 6–3 loss to the Colorado Avalanche.

NEW ENGLAND SLED DOG RACES. Mar 14–15. Intown Trail, Rangeley, ME. Unlimited eight-dog, six-dog, four-dog pro and junior classes race, 1–9 miles, depending on the size of the team. Annually, the second weekend in March. Sponsor: New England Sled Dog Club. Est attendance: 500. For info: Gail Spaulding, Chamber of Commerce, PO Box 317, Rangeley, ME 04970. Phone: (207) 864-5364.

SHOEMAKER WINS 7,000th RACE: ANNIVERSARY. Mar 14, 1976. Jockey Bill Shoemaker won the 7,000th race of his career aboard Royal Derby II, a horse that hadn't won in three years. Shoemaker became the winningest jockey in history in 1970 when he surpassed Johnny Longden's total of 6,032. The Shoe retired in 1990 after having ridden 8,833 winners.

BIRTHDAYS TODAY

James Kevin Brown, 33, baseball player, born McIntyre, GA, Mar 14, 1965.
Billy Crystal, 51, actor (*City Slickers*), born Long Beach, NY, Mar 14, 1947.
Larry Demetric Johnson, 29, basketball player, born Tyler, TX, Mar 14, 1969.
Kirby Puckett, 37, former baseball player, born Chicago, IL, Mar 14, 1961.
Antowain Smith, 26, football player, born Montgomery, AL, Mar 14, 1972.
Wesley Sissel (Wes) Unseld, 52, basketball executive and Basketball Hall of Fame center and forward, born Louisville, KY, Mar 14, 1946.
Darcy Wakaluk, 32, hockey player, born Pincher Creek, Alberta, Canada, Mar 14, 1966.

MARCH 15 — SUNDAY
Day 74 — 291 Remaining

ANDREYCHUK SCORES 500TH GOAL: ANNIVERSARY. Mar 15, 1997. Dave Andreychuk of the New Jersey Devils became the 26th player in the National Hockey League and the second in two days to score 500 regular-season goals. Andreychuk's goal helped the Devils beat the Washington Capitals, 3–2.

March *1998*	S	M	T	W	T	F	S
	1	2	3	4	5	6	7
	8	9	10	11	12	13	14
	15	16	17	18	19	20	21
	22	23	24	25	26	27	28
	29	30	31				

ENGLAND: CHELTENHAM GOLD CUP MEETING. Mar 15–17. Cheltenham Racecourse, Prestbury, Cheltenham, Gloucestershire. Major national hunt meeting. Est attendance: 150,000. For info: Cheltenham Racecourse, Prestbury Park, Cheltenham, Gloucestershire, England. Phone: (44) (124) 251-3014. Fax: (44) (124) 222-4227.

LATHAM, ARLIE: BIRTH ANNIVERSARY. Mar 15, 1860. Walter Arlington (Arlie) Latham, baseball player born at West Lebanon, NH. Latham enjoyed a baseball career that spanned 76 years, starting as a professional player at age 15 in 1875 and concluding as custodian of the Yankee Stadium press box at age 92. Died at Garden City, NY, Nov 29, 1952.

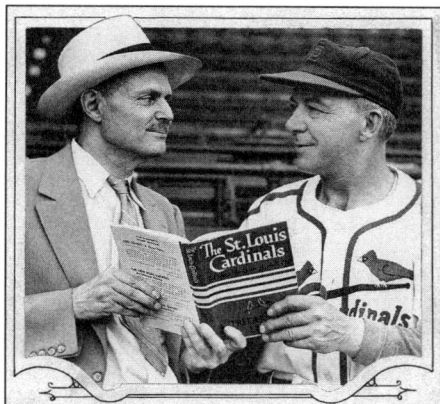

LIEB, FRED: 110th BIRTH ANNIVERSARY. Mar 15, 1888. Frederick George (Fred) Lieb, sportswriter born at Philadelphia, PA. Lieb wanted nothing more from life than the opportunity to write about baseball, and he virtually got his wish. He began a monthly column in *Baseball Magazine* in 1909 and was still writing a few months before his death. Lieb was a close friend of Babe Ruth, Kenesaw Mountain Landis and hundreds of other baseball figures. He is credited with calling Yankee Stadium the "House That Ruth Built" and with writing 18 books, including his autobiography, *Baseball As I Have Known It.* Died at Houston, TX, June 5, 1980.

SCHOLZ, JACKSON: BIRTH ANNIVERSARY. Mar 15, 1897. Jackson Volney Scholz, Olympic gold medal sprinter born at Buchanan, MI. Scholz won a gold medal on the 400-meter relay team at the 1920 Olympics and another gold in the 200 meters at the Paris Olympics of 1924, the Games depicted in the movie, *Chariots of Fire.* Scholz worked as a freelance journalist and wrote 31 sport novels for boys. Died at Del Ray Beach, FL, Oct 26, 1986.

SMITH WINS 877th GAME: ANNIVERSARY. Mar 15, 1997. The University of North Carolina men's basketball team defeated Colorado, 73–56, in the second round of the NCAA tournament to give coach Dean Smith the 877th victory of his career, one more than Adolph Rupp. Smith's win, his 63rd in NCAA play, came in his 36th season as a head coach.

STICKUM OUTLAWED: ANNIVERSARY. Mar 15, 1981. The National Football League prohibited the use of any sticky substances on the body, uniform or equipment of any player. The rules change was largely aimed at the defensive unit of the Los Angeles Raiders, winners of the 1981 Super Bowl, and in particular at LA defensive back Lester Hayes, who coated his arms and chest with Stickum and intercepted 13 passes during the 1980 season.

VAN BROCKLIN, NORM: BIRTH ANNIVERSARY. Mar 15, 1926. Norman (Norm) Van Brocklin, Pro Football Hall of Fame quarterback and coach born at Eagle Butte, SD. Van Brocklin played college football at Oregon and then signed with the Los Angeles Rams. He helped the Rams win their only NFL title in 1951. After finishing his playing career with the Philadelphia Eagles, he coached the Minnesota Vikings and the Atlanta Falcons. Inducted into the Hall of Fame in 1979. Died at Social Circle, GA, May 2, 1983.

BIRTHDAYS TODAY

Harold Douglas Baines, 39, baseball player, born St. Michael's, MD, Mar 15, 1959.
Bobby Lee Bonds, 52, former baseball player, born Riverside, CA, Mar 15, 1946.
Robert Terrell (Terry) Cummings, 37, basketball player, born Chicago, IL, Mar 15, 1961.
Michael Vaughn (Mickey) Hatcher, Jr, 43, former baseball player, born Cleveland, OH, Mar 15, 1955.
Nelson Joseph (Nellie) King, 70, broadcaster and former baseball player, born Shenandoah, PA, Mar 15, 1928.
Theodore Joseph (Ted) Marchibroda, 67, football coach and former player, born Franklin, PA, Mar 15, 1931.

☆ ☆ ☆

MARCH 16 — MONDAY
Day 75 — 290 Remaining

CHASE'S SPORTSQUOTE OF THE DAY

"My worst nightmare is that we'll get this new stadium built and Bidwill will want to move the team back to St. Louis. The thought keeps me awake at night." —St. Louis Mayor Vincent Schoemehl

---

FOWLER, BUD: 140th BIRTH ANNIVERSARY. Mar 16, 1858. John W. ("Bud") Fowler, baseball player born at Fort Plain, NY. Fowler was the first black professional baseball player. Excelling as a second baseman, he played for many teams in black and white leagues over a 30-year career. Died at Frankfort, NY, Feb 26, 1913.

HUTCHESON BECOMES LEADING COLLEGIATE SCORER: ANNIVERSARY. Mar 16, 1990. Phil Hutcheson of David Lipscomb University became the leading scorer in college basketball history when he reached 4,046 career points in an NAIA tournament game. Hutcheson, who scored in double figures in every college game he played, surpassed the mark set by Travis Grant of Kentucky State in 1969–72.

LONGEST SPGA PLAYOFF: ANNIVERSARY. Mar 16, 1997. Bob Murphy sank an 80-foot birdie putt on the 9th sudden-death hole to win the longest playoff in Senior PGA history. Murphy defeated Jay Sigel in an NAIA game at the Toshiba Senior Classic at Newport Beach, CA. Sigel's own 22-foot putt for birdie just missed. The previous record, 8 playoff holes, was set at the 1992 Showdown Classic with Orville Moody besting Bob Betley.

PHOENIX CARDINALS BECOME ARIZONA CARDINALS: ANNIVERSARY. Mar 16, 1994. Phoenix Cardinals owner Bill Bidwill announced that the team would henceforth be known as the Arizona Cardinals.

TEMPLE WINS FIRST NIT: 60th ANNIVERSARY. Mar 16, 1938. Temple University defeated Colorado, 60–36, to win the first National Invitation Tournament, played in New York's Madison Square Garden. The NIT was sponsored by the Metropolitan New York Basketball Writers Association and was the first postseason college basketball tournament. The NCAA tournament began one year later.

WANER, LLOYD: BIRTH ANNIVERSARY. Mar 16, 1906. Lloyd James Waner, Baseball Hall of Fame outfielder born at Harrah, OK. Waner was "Little Poison" to his brother Paul's "Big Poison." He played 18 years in the majors, mainly with the Pittsburgh Pirates. Inducted into the Hall of Fame in 1967. Died at Oklahoma City, OK, July 22, 1982.

BIRTHDAYS TODAY

Don Lee Blasingame, 66, former baseball player, born Corinth, MS, Mar 16, 1932.
Charles Lynn Hudson, 39, former baseball player, born Ennis, TX, Mar 16, 1959.
Hobert Neal (Hobie) Landrith, 68, former baseball player, born Decatur, IL, Mar 16, 1930.
Ozzie Newsome, 42, former football player, born Muscle Shoals, AL, Mar 16, 1956.
Rodney Peete, 32, football player, born Mesa, AZ, Mar 16, 1966.
Frederic Carl (Rick) Reichardt, 55, former baseball player, born Madison, WI, Mar 16, 1943.

MARCH 17 — TUESDAY
Day 76 — 289 Remaining

FIRST ISSUE OF *THE SPORTING NEWS*: ANNIVERSARY. Mar 17, 1886. The first issue of *The Sporting News* was published in St. Louis at a price of two cents per copy. *The Sporting News*, long known as "The Bible of Baseball" and a multi-sport magazine since 1942, is the oldest continuously published sports publication in the country.

JONES, BOBBY: BIRTH ANNIVERSARY. Mar 17, 1902. Robert Tyre (Bobby) Jones, Jr, golfer born at Atlanta, GA. Jones was an outstanding amateur champion during the 1920s. He is the only golfer to win the sport's Grand Slam, a quartet of tournaments then consisting of the US Amateur, the US Open, the British Amateur and the British Open, doing so in 1930, after which he retired. Along with Alister Mackenzie, he designed the Augusta National Golf Club and created the tournament that soon became known as the Masters. Died at Atlanta Dec 18, 1971.

NAIA MEN'S DIVISION I NATIONAL BASKETBALL CHAMPIONSHIP. Mar 17–23. Mabee Center, Tulsa, OK. 61st annual tournament. Est attendance: 35,000. For info: Natl Assn of Intercollegiate Athletics, 6120 S Yale Ave, Ste 1450, Tulsa, OK 74136. Phone: (918) 494-8828. Fax: (918) 494-8841. Email: khenry@naia.org. WWW: http://www.naia.org

PFEFFER, FRED: BIRTH ANNIVERSARY. Mar 17, 1860. Nathaniel Frederick (Fred) Pfeffer, baseball player, coach and manager born at Louisville, KY. Pfeffer played second base in the major leagues from 1882 through 1897. He published one of the first books on baseball, *Scientific Ball*, in 1889. Died at Chicago, IL, Apr 10, 1932.

March 1998	S	M	T	W	T	F	S
	1	2	3	4	5	6	7
	8	9	10	11	12	13	14
	15	16	17	18	19	20	21
	22	23	24	25	26	27	28
	29	30	31				

REISER, PETE: BIRTH ANNIVERSARY. Mar 17, 1919. Harold Patrick ("Pete") Reiser, baseball player, coach and manager born at St. Louis, MO. Reiser saw an extremely promising career come up short after he fractured his skull crashing into an outfield wall in 1942. In all, he was carried off the field nine separate times. Died at Palm Springs, CA, Oct 25, 1981.

ROOT, CHARLIE: BIRTH ANNIVERSARY. Mar 17, 1899. Charles Henry (Charlie) Root, baseball pitcher born at Middletown, OH. Root was the pitcher for the Chicago Cubs in the 1932 World Series when Babe Ruth hit his alleged "called shot" home run. Root denied that Ruth had indicated he would hit a home run before doing so. Died at Hollister, CA, Nov 5, 1970.

SAINT PATRICK'S DAY. Mar 17. Commemorates the patron saint of Ireland, Bishop Patrick (AD 389–461) who, about AD 432, left his home in the Severn Valley, England, and introduced Christianity into Ireland. Feast Day in the Roman Catholic Church. A national holiday in Ireland and Northern Ireland.

SCURRY, ROD: BIRTH ANNIVERSARY. Mar 17, 1956. Rodney Grant (Rod) Scurry, baseball player born at Sacramento, CA. Scurry pitched primarily in relief for the Pittsburgh Pirates and the Seattle Mariners (1980–88). Died at Reno, NV, Nov 5, 1992.

WERBLIN, SONNY: BIRTH ANNIVERSARY. Mar 17, 1910. David Abraham ("Sonny") Werblin, sports executive born at New York, NY. Werblin had several successful careers in radio, television and sports. After making a fortune in entertainment, he and several partners bought the New York Jets in 1963. He signed draft choice Joe Namath to a record contract for a football player and negotiated a large contract with NBC to televise AFL games. After selling his share of the Jets, he ran the New Jersey Sports and Exposition Authority and then became CEO of Madison Square Garden Corporation. Died at New York, Nov 21, 1991.

BIRTHDAYS TODAY

Daniel Rae (Danny) Ainge, 39, basketball coach, former basketball and baseball player, born Eugene, OR, Mar 17, 1959.
Samuel Adrain (Sammy) Baugh, 84, Pro Football Hall of Fame quarterback, born Temple, TX, Mar 17, 1914.
Samuel Paul (Sam) Bowie, 37, former basketball player, born Lebanon, PA, Mar 17, 1961.
Clarence Edwin (Cito) Gaston, 54, baseball manager and former player, born San Antonio, TX, Mar 17, 1944.
Henry John (Hank) Sauer, 81, former baseball player, born Pittsburgh, PA, Mar 17, 1917.
John Patrick Smiley, 33, baseball player, born Phoenixville, PA, Mar 17, 1965.

MARCH 18 — WEDNESDAY
Day 77 — 288 Remaining

NCAA BASKETBALL CHAMPIONS THIS DATE
1953   Indiana

ACIT CATHOLIC BASKETBALL TOURNAMENT. Mar 18–21. Frostburg State Univ, Frostburg, MD. Invitational tournament features eight teams from the US and Canada. Four games nightly. For info: ACIT, Joe Divico, PO Box 432, Cumberland, MD 21501-0432. Phone: (301) 724-5911. Fax: (301) 724-4001.

BRAVES ANNOUNCE SHIFT TO MILWAUKEE: 45th ANNIVERSARY. Mar 18, 1953. In baseball's first franchise shift in half a century, the Boston Braves announced that they would become the Milwaukee Braves. The team remained in Milwaukee through the 1965 season after which it moved to Atlanta.

COONEY, JOHNNY: BIRTH ANNIVERSARY. Mar 18, 1901. John Walter (Johnny) Cooney, baseball player and manager born at Cranston, RI. Cooney played in the major leagues from 1921 through 1944. His father and brother also played in the majors. Died at Sarasota, FL, July 8, 1986.

DODGE NATIONAL CIRCUIT FINALS RODEO. Mar 18–21. Holt Arena, Pocatello, ID. The top 2 winners of the 12 PRCA Rodeo Circuits compete in bull riding, bareback riding, saddle bronco riding, steer wrestling, calf roping, team roping, barrel racing and wrangler bullfights. Est attendance: 50,000. For info: PR Dir, Dodge Natl Circuit Finals Rodeo, PO Box 4541, Pocatello, ID 83205. Phone: (208) 233-1546.

DONOHUE, MARK: BIRTH ANNIVERSARY. Mar 18, 1937. Mark Donohue, auto racing driver, born at Summit, NJ. Donohue became a professional race driver in 1966 and, after success in a variety of different kinds of racing, gravitated toward Indy cars. He finished seventh in his first Indianapolis 500 and won the race in 1972. He came out of retirement in 1974 and was killed in a crash practicing for the Austrian Grand Prix. Died near Graz, Austria, Aug 19, 1975.

FRIEDMAN, BENNY: BIRTH ANNIVERSARY. Mar 18, 1905. Benjamin (Benny) Friedman, football player, coach and administrator born at Cleveland, OH. Friedman excelled at the University of Michigan, playing quarterback (1924–26) and earning All-American honors. As a pro, he played with the Cleveland Bulldogs, the Detroit Wolverines, the New York Giants and the Brooklyn Dodgers. He coached at CCNY and served as athletic director at Brandeis. Died at New York, NY, Nov 24, 1982.

JORDAN'S BACK: ANNIVERSARY. Mar 18, 1995. Michael Jordan, easily considered one of the National Basketball Assn's greatest all-time players, made history again when he announced that he was returning to professional play after a 17-month break. The 32-year-old star had retired just before the start of the 1993–94 season, following the murder of his beloved father, James Jordan. Jordan, who averaged 32.3 points a game during regular season play, had led the Chicago Bulls to three successive NBA titles. While retired, he tried a baseball career, playing for a Chicago White Sox minor league team, the Birmingham Barons. After Jordan's return, the Bulls added a fourth NBA World Championship in the '95–'96 season and a fifth in '96–'97.

NAIA WOMEN'S DIVISION I NATIONAL BASKETBALL CHAMPIONSHIP. Mar 18–24. Oman Arena, Jackson, TN. 32-team field competes for the national championship. 18th annual competition. Est attendance: 38,000. For info: Natl Assn of Intercollegiate Athletics, 6120 S Yale Ave, Ste 1450, Tulsa, OK 74136. Phone: (918) 494-8828. Fax: (918) 494-8841. Email: khenry@naia.org. WWW: http://www.naia.org

NCAA MEN'S DIVISION II BASKETBALL TOURNAMENT. Mar 18–21. Finals. Commonwealth Convention Center, Louisville, KY. For info: NCAA, 6201 College Blvd, Overland Park, KS 66211. Phone: (913) 339-1906.

NCAA WOMEN'S DIVISION II BASKETBALL TOURNAMENT. Mar 18–21. Finals at campus site TBA. For info: NCAA, 6201 College Blvd, Overland Park, KS 66211. Phone: (913) 339-1906.

NJCAA DIVISION II MEN'S BASKETBALL NATIONAL FINALS. Mar 18–21. Danville, IL. Junior College Division II national men's basketball finals tournament. Est attendance: 8,000. For info: Jeanie Cooke, Exec Dir, Danville Area Conv/Visitors Bureau, PO Box 992, Danville, IL 61834. Phone: (800) 383-4386.

THE ROCKET SCORES 50: ANNIVERSARY. Mar 18, 1945. Right wing Maurice ("The Rocket") Richard of the Montreal Canadiens became the first player in the NHL to score 50 goals in a season when he tallied in a 4–2 win over the Boston Bruins.

BIRTHDAYS TODAY

Geronimo Emiliano Berroa, 33, baseball player, born Santo Domingo, Dominican Republic, Mar 18, 1965.

Bonnie Blair, 34, Olympic gold medal speed skater, born Cornwall, NY, Mar 18, 1964.

Guy Carbonneau, 38, hockey player, born Sept-Iles, Quebec, Canada, Mar 18, 1960.

Dwayne Keith Murphy, 43, former baseball player, born Merced, CA, Mar 18, 1955.

George Plimpton, 71, author (*Paper Lion, Out of My League, The Bogey Man*), born New York, NY, Mar 18, 1927.

MARCH 19 — THURSDAY
Day 78 — 287 Remaining

NCAA BASKETBALL CHAMPIONS THIS DATE
1955	San Francisco
1960	Ohio State
1966	Texas Western

BAY HILL INVITATIONAL PRESENTED BY OFFICE DEPOT. Mar 19–22. Bay Hill Club, Orlando, FL. A PGA Tour tournament, formerly known as the Nestle Invitational. For info: PGA Tour, 112 TPC Blvd, Ponte Vedra Beach, FL 32082. Phone: (904) 285-3700.

BERENSON, SENDA: 130th BIRTH ANNIVERSARY. Mar 19, 1868. Senda Berenson Abbott, Basketball Hall of Fame physical educator and basketball innovator born at Biturmansk, Lithuania. Berenson and her family came to Boston in 1875. She studied physical education at the Boston Normal School of Gymnastics and taught physical training at Smith College. After reading about James Naismith's new game of basketball, she introduced it to her students in 1892, adapting the rules for girls: no snatching the ball away from opponents, no holding the ball for more than three seconds and no more than three dribbles. She also divided the court into three areas and forbade players from crossing the lines. These rules, incorporated into a rule book that Berenson edited for 18 years, remained substantially in force until the 1960s. Inducted into the Hall of Fame in 1985. Died at Santa Barbara, CA, Feb 16, 1954.

CANADA: PERCY DE WOLFE MEMORIAL RACE AND MAIL RUN. Mar 19–21. Dawson City, Yukon to Eagle, AK. A 210-mile race retracing the mail route. Fun for recreational and competitive mushers. Est attendance: 550. For info: Percy De Wolfe Memorial Race and Mail Run, PO Box 133, Dawson City, YT, Canada Y0B 1G0. Phone and Fax: (403) 993-6851.

FLORIDA STATE BOAT AND SPORTS SHOW. Mar 19–22. Florida Expo Park, Tampa, FL. Est attendance: 15,000. For info: Carolyn Luis, 400 Arthur Godfrey Rd, Ste 310, Miami Beach, FL 33140. Phone: (305) 531-8410. Fax: (305) 534-3139.

GRAND CENTER SPORT, FISHING AND TRAVEL SHOW. Mar 19–22. Grand Center, Grand Rapids, MI. This event brings together buyers and sellers of fishing boats and equipment, RVs, campers and their accessories, as well as other outdoor sporting goods. US and Canadian hunting and fishing trips and other vacation travel destinations are featured. All aspects of fishing, including tackle boats, seminars, demonstrations and displays are emphasized. Est attendance: 45,000. For info: Henri Boucher, ShowSpan, Inc, 1400 28th St SW, Grand Rapids, MI 49509. Phone: (616) 530-1919. Fax: (616) 530-2122.

IMMACULATA WINS FIRST AIAW CROWN: ANNIVERSARY. Mar 19, 1972. Immaculata College defeated West Chester State, 52–48, to win the first Association of Intercollegiate Athletics for Women national basketball tournament. The AIAW crowned a champion for 11 years, but most Division I teams entered the new NCAA tournament starting in 1982.

March *1998*	S	M	T	W	T	F	S
	1	2	3	4	5	6	7
	8	9	10	11	12	13	14
	15	16	17	18	19	20	21
	22	23	24	25	26	27	28
	29	30	31				

McGINNITY, IRON JOE: BIRTH ANNIVERSARY. Mar 19, 1871. Joseph Jerome ("Iron Joe") McGinnity, Baseball Hall of Fame pitcher born at Rock Island, IL. McGinnity pitched 10 years in the major leagues at the turn of the 20th century and never had a losing season. He earned his nickname for his durability, such as pitching both ends of a doubleheader, which he did five times in 1903. Inducted into the Hall of Fame in 1946. Died at New York, NY, Nov 14, 1929.

NCAA DIVISION I WRESTLING CHAMPIONSHIPS. Mar 19–21. Finals. Cleveland State University, Cleveland, OH. For info: NCAA, 6201 College Blvd, Overland Park, KS 66211. Phone: (913) 339-1906.

NCAA MEN'S DIVISION III SWIMMING AND DIVING CHAMPIONSHIPS. Mar 19–21. Finals. St. Peter's Rec-Plex, St. Peter's, MO. For info: NCAA, 6201 College Blvd, Overland Park, KS 66211. Phone: (913) 339-1906.

NCAA MEN'S AND WOMEN'S FENCING CHAMPIONSHIPS. Mar 19–22. Site TBA. For info: NCAA, 6201 College Blvd, Overland Park, KS 66211. Phone: (913) 339-1906.

NCAA MEN'S DIVISION I BASKETBALL TOURNAMENT. Mar 19–22. Regionals at Greensboro Coliseum, Greensboro, NC; Tropicana Field, St. Petersburg, FL; Kiel Center, St. Louis, MO; and Arrowhead Pond of Anaheim, Anaheim, CA. For info: NCAA, 6201 College Blvd, Overland Park, KS 66211. Phone: (913) 339-1906.

NHRA SLICK 50 NATIONALS. Mar 19–22. Houston Raceway Park, Baytown, TX. National Hot Rod Association's Nationals brings exciting racing action. For local info: Phone: (281) 383-2666. For other info: Clear Lake-NASA Area CVB, 1201 NASA Rd 1, Houston, TX 77058. Phone: (713) 488-7676 or (800) 844-LAKE. Fax: (713) 383-2666.

STRICTLY SAIL - NEW ENGLAND. Mar 19–22. East Hartford, CT. Impressive sail-only show features the latest sailboats, equipment and services as well as seminars and attractions for all levels of sailing ability. For info: NMMA Boat Shows, 600 Third Ave, 23rd Fl, New York, NY 10016. Phone: (212) 922-1212. Fax: (212) 922-9607.

TEXAS WESTERN WINS NCAA CROWN: ANNIVERSARY. Mar 19, 1966. Texas Western University (later the University of Texas at El Paso) won the NCAA Men's Basketball Tournament by upsetting the University of Kentucky, 72–65. The game took on national significance as Texas Western, coached by Don Haskins, started five black players against Kentucky's all-white team at a time when race relations in the US was a major political and social issue.

BIRTHDAYS TODAY

Don Richard (Richie) Ashburn, 71, Baseball Hall of Fame outfielder, born Tilden, NE, Mar 19, 1927.
Ivan Calderon, 36, former baseball player, born Fajardo, Puerto Rico, Mar 19, 1962.
Vladimir Konstantinov, 31, hockey player, born Murmansk, USSR, Mar 19, 1967.
Rick Mirer, 28, football player, born Goshen, IN, Mar 19, 1970.
Michael Kelvin (Mike) Norris, 43, former baseball player, born San Francisco, CA, Mar 19, 1955.
Philip Roth, 65, author (*The Great American Novel*), born Newark, NJ, Mar 19, 1933.

MARCH 20 — FRIDAY
Day 79 — 286 Remaining

NCAA BASKETBALL CHAMPIONS THIS DATE
1954	LaSalle
1965	UCLA

DIANE CRUMP WINS FIRST RACE: ANNIVERSARY. Mar 20, 1969. Jockey Diane Crump won the first race of her career less than two months after becoming the first woman to ride in a parimutuel race in the US. Her victory came at Gulfstream Park, FL.

FIRST COLLEGE BASKETBALL GAME: ANNIVERSARY. Mar 20, 1897. Yale beat Pennsylvania, 32–10, in the first men's intercollegiate basketball game, played in New Haven.

FIRST FIGURE SKATING CHAMPIONSHIPS: ANNIVERSARY. Mar 20, 1914. The first world's figure skating championships opened in New Haven, CT. Events included men's singles, women's singles, pairs and waltzing, later known as ice dancing.

FIRST NCAA HOCKEY CHAMPIONSHIP: 90th ANNIVERSARY. Mar 20, 1948. The first NCAA ice hockey championship concluded in Colorado Springs, CO. The University of Michigan defeated Dartmouth College, 8–4, to win the title.

LONGHORN WORLD CHAMPIONSHIP RODEO. Mar 20–22. Celeste Center, Columbus, OH. Held in conjunction with the Ohio Beef Expo and Ohio Deer & Turkey Expo. More than 300 cowboys and cowgirls compete in six professional contests ranging from bronc riding to bull riding for top prize money and world championship points. Featuring colorful opening pageantry and Big, Bad BONUS Bulls. 24th annual. Est attendance: 50,000. For info: W. Bruce Lehrke, Pres, Longhorn World Championship Rodeo, Inc, PO Box 70159, Nashville, TN 37207. Phone: (615) 876-1016. Fax: (615) 876-4685. Email: lhrodeo@idt.net. WWW: http://www.longhornrodeo.com

NCAA DIVISION III HOCKEY CHAMPIONSHIP. Mar 20–21 or 21–22. Finals. Site TBA. For info: NCAA, 6201 College Blvd, Overland Park, KS 66211. Phone: (913) 339-1906.

NCAA MEN'S DIVISION III BASKETBALL TOURNAMENT. Mar 20–21. Finals. Salem Civic Center, Salem, VA. For info: NCAA, 6201 College Blvd, Overland Park, KS 66211. Phone: (913) 339-1906.

NCAA WOMEN'S DIVISION III BASKETBALL TOURNAMENT. Mar 20–21. Finals at campus site TBA. For info: NCAA, 6201 College Blvd, Overland Park, KS 66211. Phone: (913) 339-1906.

NORTHEAST GREAT OUTDOORS SHOW. Mar 20–22. Empire State Plaza, Albany, NY. 12th annual expo with seminars by professional sportsmen, archery range, duck-calling contest, casting pool and lots more. Annually, the third full weekend in March. Est attendance: 30,000. For info: Heather Mabee, Exec Dir, Ed Lewi Assoc, 6 Chelsea Pl, Clifton Park, NY 12065. Phone: (518) 383-6183. Fax: (518) 383-6755.

OPEN NORTH AMERICAN CHAMPIONSHIP SLED DOG RACE. Mar 20–22. Fairbanks, AK. World-famous test of skill as mushers from around the world gather in Fairbanks to compete. Oldest, continuously held run, sprint, sled dog race in the world. No limit to the number of dogs in each team–there have been as many as 24 dogs run in one team. Times from three heats of 20, 20 and 27.6 miles each are combined to determine the winner. Est attendance: 5,000. For info: Alaska Dog Mushers Assn, Box 662, Fairbanks, AK 99707. Phone: (907) 479-8166.

SHAMROCK SPORTSFEST MARATHON. Mar 20–21. Pavilion Convention Center, Virginia Beach, VA. 8K, Masters 8K, 5K walk, sports and fitness expo, runner's clinic and children's marathon. Friday night pasta party. Sat night party. Est attendance: 25,000. For info: Shamrock Sportsfest, 2308 Maple St, Virginia Beach, VA 23451-1310. Phone: (757) 481-5090. Fax: (757) 481-2942. Email: sportsfest@juno.com.

SPRING. Mar 20–June 21. In the Northern Hemisphere spring begins today with the vernal equinox, at 2:55 PM, EST. Note that in the Southern Hemisphere today is the beginning of autumn. Sun rises due east and sets due west everywhere on Earth (except near poles) and the daylight length (interval between sunrise and sunset) is virtually the same everywhere: 12 hours, 8 minutes.

TAYLOR, FREDERICK: BIRTH ANNIVERSARY. Mar 20, 1856. Frederick Winslow Taylor, tennis player born at Philadelphia, PA. Otherwise known as the "Father of Scientific Management," Taylor was an innovative athlete who played sports precisely and absolutely by the rules. He was a baseball pitcher when the ball was still pitched underhand, a tennis player who invented sturdier nets and a golfer who devised an irrigation method for greens and several unique golf clubs. Died at Philadelphia, Mar 21, 1915.

WHOOPERS AND HOOPERS INVITATIONAL BASKETBALL TOURNAMENT. Mar 20–22. Hastings, NE. 17th annual tournament in which more than 140 teams and 1,400 invited basketball participants–former professional, collegiate and high school–compete five-on-five. Divided into six divisions including A (semi-pro or AAU caliber), B (upper intermediate), C (intermediate), D1 & D2 (small-town teams) and women's A (AAU caliber) and B (all others). Trophies awarded for top 4 places in each division. Est attendance: 3,000. For info: Whoopers and Hoopers, PO Box 1104, Hastings, NE 68902-1104. Phone: (402) 462-4159. Fax: (402) 461-4400. Email: dreynolds@tcgs.com.

SPORTSCHASER OF THE DAY
Who beat whom in the first men's intercollegiate basketball game?

BIRTHDAYS TODAY

George Lee Altman, 65, former baseball player, born Goldsboro, NC, Mar 20, 1933.

Daron Oshay ("Mookie") Blaylock, 31, basketball player, born Garland, TX, Mar 20, 1967.

Patrick (Pat) Corrales, 57, former baseball manager and player, born Los Angeles, CA, Mar 20, 1941.

Christopher Allen (Chris) Hoiles, 33, baseball player, born Bowling Green, OH, Mar 20, 1965.

Robert Gordon (Bobby) Orr, 50, Hockey Hall of Fame defenseman, born Parry Sound, Ontario, Canada, Mar 20, 1948.

Patrick James (Pat) Riley, 53, basketball coach and former player, born Schenectady, NY, Mar 20, 1945.

MARCH 21 — SATURDAY
Day 80 — 285 Remaining

NCAA BASKETBALL CHAMPIONS THIS DATE
1959	California
1964	UCLA
1970	UCLA

BABE DIDRIKSEN PITCHES FOR ATHLETICS: ANNIVERSARY. Mar 21, 1934. Babe Didriksen, perhaps the greatest women athlete of all time, pitched one inning of baseball for the Philadelphia Athletics in an exhibition game against the Brooklyn Dodgers. Babe hit the first batter she faced and walked the next. The third hit into a triple play.

BIG TEN WOMEN'S GYMNASTICS CHAMPIONSHIPS. Mar 21. University of Iowa, Iowa City, IA. For info: Big Ten Conference, 1500 W Higgins Rd, Park Ridge, IL 60068-6300. Phone: (847) 696-1010. Fax: (847) 696-1150. WWW: http://www.bigten.org

BIG TEN MEN'S GYMNASTICS CHAMPIONSHIPS. Mar 21–22. University of Michigan, Ann Arbor, MI. For info: Big Ten Conference, 1500 W Higgins Rd, Park Ridge, IL 60068-6300. Phone: (847) 696-1010. Fax: (847) 696-1150. WWW: http://www.bigten.org

BIG TWELVE WOMEN'S GYMNASTICS CHAMPIONSHIPS. Mar 21. University of Nebraska, Lincoln, NE. For info: Big Twelve Conference, 2201 Stemmons Freeway, 28th Floor, Dallas, TX 75207. Phone: (214) 742-1212. Fax: (214) 742-2046.

ENGLAND: HEAD OF THE RIVER RACE. Mar 21. Mortlake to Putney, River Thames, London. At 10 AM. Processional race for 420 eight-oared crews, starting at 10-second intervals. Est attendance: 7,000. For info: Mr A. P. Ruddle, 59 Berkeley Court, Oatlands Drive, Weybridge, Surrey, England KT13 9HY. Phone: (44) (193) 222-0401.

HOGAN, SHANTY: BIRTH ANNIVERSARY. Mar 21, 1906. James Francis ("Shanty") Hogan, baseball player born at Somerville, MA. Hogan earned his nickname for his size, 6'1" and 240 pounds. He was a catcher who played 13 years in the majors (1925–37) and hit .300 six times. Died at Boston, MA, Apr 7, 1967.

MAHOVLICH SCORES 500th GOAL: 25th ANNIVERSARY. Mar 21, 1973. Frank Mahovlich of the Montreal Canadiens scored the 500th goal of his career in a 3–2 victory over the Vancouver Canucks. Mahovlich finished his career with 533 goals and entered the Hockey Hall of Fame in 1981.

NCAA WOMEN'S DIVISION I BASKETBALL TOURNAMENT. Mar 21–23. Regionals at University of Dayton, Dayton, OH; Vanderbilt University, Nashville, TN; Lubbock Memorial Coliseum, Lubbock, TX; and Oakland Coliseum, Oakland, CA. For info: NCAA, 6201 College Blvd, Overland Park, KS 66211. Phone: (913) 339-1906.

PAC-10 GYMNASTICS CHAMPIONSHIPS. Mar 21. UCLA, Los Angeles, CA. For info: PAC-10 Conference, 800 S Broadway, Ste 400, Walnut Creek, CA 94596. Phone: (510) 932-4411. Fax: (510) 932-4601.

RAMS SIGN KENNY WASHINGTON: ANNIVERSARY. Mar 21, 1946. One year before Jackie Robinson began playing major league baseball, Kenny Washington broke the NFL's color line. Washington signed a contract to play for the Los Angeles Rams.

SEC GYMNASTICS CHAMPIONSHIPS. Mar 21. Louisiana State University, Baton Rough, LA. For info: Southeastern Conference, 2201 Civic Center Blvd, Bir-

mingham, AL 35203-1103. Phone: (205) 458-3010. Fax: (205) 458-3030. Email: cbloom@sec.org. WWW: http://www.secsports.com

SUTHERLAND, JOCK: BIRTH ANNIVERSARY. Mar 21, 1889. John Bain ("Jock") Sutherland, football player and coach born at Coupar-Angus, Scotland. Sutherland came to the US at age 18, entering the University of Pittsburgh when he was 25. Despite never having played football, he became an All-American guard and studied dentistry. He coached at Lafayette and Pittsburgh. After World War II, his coaching success with the Pittsburgh Steelers was cut short by a fatal brain tumor. Died at Pittsburgh, PA, April 11, 1948.

BIRTHDAYS TODAY

Herman Thomas (Tommy) Davis, 59, former baseball player, born New York, NY, Mar 21, 1939.
Michael Joseph (Mike) Dunleavy, 44, basketball coach and former player, born New York, NY, Mar 21, 1954.
Shawon Donnell Dunston, 35, baseball player, born New York, NY, Mar 21, 1963.
Johan Garpenlov, 30, hockey player, born Stockholm, Sweden, Mar 21, 1968.
Jay Walter Hilgenberg, 38, former football player, born Iowa City, IA, Mar 21, 1960.
Al Anthony Iafrate, 32, hockey player, born Dearborn, MI, Mar 21, 1966.
Vitaly Nikolaevich Potapenko, 23, basketball player, born Kiev, Ukraine, USSR, Mar 21, 1975.
Scott Christopher Williams, 30, basketball player, born Hacienda Heights, CA, Mar 21, 1968.

MARCH 22 — SUNDAY
Day 81 — 284 Remaining

NCAA BASKETBALL CHAMPIONS THIS DATE
1958	Kentucky
1969	UCLA

BOATING ACCIDENT KILLS BALLPLAYERS: ANNIVERSARY. Mar 22, 1993. Two members of the Cleveland Indians, Tim Crews and Steve Olin, were killed, and teammate Bob Ojeda was injured in a boating accident on Little Lake Nellie, FL. The trio, in Florida for spring training, hit a dock.

GOODMAN, BILLY: BIRTH ANNIVERSARY. Mar 22, 1926. William Dale (Billy) Goodman, baseball player born at Concord, NC. Goodman was a versatile player who compiled fine statistics but never achieved stardom. He won the American League batting title in 1950. Died at Sarasota, FL, Oct 1, 1984.

INTERNATIONAL PING PONG DAY©98. Mar 22. This day is designed to help meet the needs of avid fans and addicts who really enjoy playing the game. For further info send $2 to cover cost of copying and postage to: 1437 W Rosemont, 1W, Chicago, IL 60660-1319. Phone: 773743541. Fax: (773) 743-5395. Email: kooper@interaccess.com.

OWEN, MARV: BIRTH ANNIVERSARY. Mar 22, 1906. Marvin James (Marv) Owen, baseball player born at Agnew, CA. Owen was the stalwart third baseman for the Detroit Tigers in the 1930s. He hit .275 over nine seasons. Died at Mountain View, CA, June 22, 1991.

STOVEY, GEORGE: DEATH ANNIVERSARY. Mar 22, 1936. George Washington Stovey, baseball player born at Williamsport, PA, 1866. Of mixed racial parentage, Stovey was one of the players to whose presence in the lineup Cap Anson objected. Stovey's exclusion from an

March 1998	S	M	T	W	T	F	S
	1	2	3	4	5	6	7
	8	9	10	11	12	13	14
	15	16	17	18	19	20	21
	22	23	24	25	26	27	28
	29	30	31				

1887 exhibition game helped create baseball's color line. Died at Williamsport.

BIRTHDAYS TODAY

Sean Robert Berry, 32, baseball player, born Santa Monica, CA, Mar 22, 1966.

Shawn Paul Bradley, 26, basketball player, born Landstuhl, West Germany, Mar 22, 1972.

Marcus D. Camby, 24, basketball player, born Hartford, CT, Mar 22, 1974.

Robert Quinlan (Bob) Costas, 46, sportscaster, born New York, NY, Mar 22, 1952.

Glenallen Hill, 33, baseball player, born Santa Cruz, CA, Mar 22, 1965.

Charles Edward ("Easy Ed") Macauley, Jr, 70, Basketball Hall of Fame center and forward, born St. Louis, MO, Mar 22, 1928.

Ramon Jaime Martinez, 30, baseball player, born Santo Domingo, Dominican Republic, Mar 22, 1968.

Russell Maryland, 29, football player, born Chicago, IL, Mar 22, 1969.

Brian K. Shaw, 32, basketball player, born Oakland, CA, Mar 22, 1966.

MARCH 23 — MONDAY
Day 82 — 283 Remaining

NCAA BASKETBALL CHAMPIONS THIS DATE

1948	Kentucky
1957	North Carolina
1963	Loyola (IL)
1968	UCLA

CRAVATH, GAVVY: BIRTH ANNIVERSARY. Mar 23, 1881. Clifford Clarence ("Gavvy") Cravath, baseball player born at Escondido, CA. Cravath hit 24 home runs in 1915, the major league record until Babe Ruth came along. He led the National League in homers five times and tied for the league lead once. Died at Laguna Beach, CA, May 23, 1963.

MOORE, DAVEY: 35th DEATH ANNIVERSARY. Mar 23, 1963. Davey Moore, boxer born at Lexington, KY, Nov 1, 1933. Moore won the world featherweight championship in 1959. He defended the title successfully several times, but on Mar 21, 1963, he was knocked out by Ultiminio ("Sugar") Ramos. An hour after the fight, he went into a coma and died two days later at Los Angeles, CA.

QUICKEST THREE GOALS: ANNIVERSARY. Mar 23, 1952. Bill Mosienko of the Chicago Blackhawks set an NHL record by scoring three goals in 21 seconds in a game against the New York Rangers. Mosienko scored at 6:09, 6:20 and 6:30 of the third period against goalie Lorne Anderson. Chicago won, 7–6.

SPRING FEVER GOLF TOURNAMENT. Mar 23 (tentative). Houston, TX. Annual fundraiser sponsored by the Clear Lake Area Chamber of Commerce. For info: Clear Lake-NASA Area CVB, 1201 NASA Rd 1, Houston, TX 77058. Phone: (713) 488-7676 or (800) 844-LAKE. Fax: (713) 488-8981.

WLAF MAKES ITS DEBUT: ANNIVERSARY. Mar 23, 1991. The World League of American Football, part of a marketing attempt by the National Football League to extend the game's popularity in Europe, made its debut as the London Monarchs defeated the Frankfurt Galaxy, 24–11.

BIRTHDAYS TODAY

Roger Bannister, 69, physician, former track athlete, born Harrow, England, Mar 23, 1929.

Jason Frederick Kidd, 25, basketball player, born San Francisco, CA, Mar 23, 1973.

Moses Eugene Malone, 43, former basketball player, born Petersburg, VA, Mar 23, 1955.

Daren James Puppa, 33, hockey player, born Kirkland Lake, Ontario, Canada, Mar 23, 1965.

George Charles Scott, Jr, 54, former baseball player, born Greenville, MS, Mar 23, 1944.

MARCH 24 — TUESDAY
Day 83 — 282 Remaining

NCAA BASKETBALL CHAMPIONS THIS DATE

1956	San Francisco
1962	Cincinnati
1980	Louisville

DUGAS, GUS: BIRTH ANNIVERSARY. Mar 24, 1907. Augustin Joseph (Gus) Dugas, baseball player born at St-Jean-de-Matha, PQ, Canada. Dugas, an outfielder and first baseman, was the first Canadian-born player to appear in the major leagues. He played four seasons in the early 1930s and threw out the ceremonial first pitch at the first game in Montreal's Olympic Stadium in 1977. Died at Norwich, CT, Apr 14, 1997.

LONGEST NHL GAME: ANNIVERSARY. Mar 24, 1936. Mud Bruneteau of the Detroit Red Wings scored at 16:30 of the sixth overtime period to end the longest game in National Hockey League history. The goal gave the Red Wings a 1–0 victory over the Montreal Maroons in a Stanley Cup semifinal game. Detroit won the series, three games to none, and went on to defeat the Toronto Maple Leafs in the finals.

SHORE, ERNIE: BIRTH ANNIVERSARY. Mar 24, 1891. Ernest Grady (Ernie) Shore, baseball player born at East Bend, NC. On June 23, 1917, Boston Red Sox pitcher Babe Ruth was ejected from the game after protesting a walk to the leadoff batter. Shore replaced Ruth, the runner was caught stealing and Shore retired the next 26 men he faced. Died at Winston-Salem, NC, Sept 24, 1980.

SISLER, GEORGE: 105th BIRTH ANNIVERSARY. Mar 24, 1893. George Harold Sisler, Baseball Hall of Fame first baseman born at Manchester, OH. Sisler started out as a pitcher but was converted to a first baseman by Branch Rickey. He hit .407 in 1920 and .420 in 1922 and was a superb fielder. Inducted into the Hall of Fame in 1939. Died at St. Louis, MO, Mar 26, 1973.

BIRTHDAYS TODAY

Jesus Maria (Jay) Alou, 56, former baseball player, born Haina, Dominican Republic, Mar 24, 1942.
Wilson Eduardo Alvarez, 28, baseball player, born Maracaibo, Venezuela, Mar 24, 1970.
Pat Bradley, 47, LPGA Hall of Fame golfer, born Westford, MA, Mar 24, 1951.
Dennis Erickson, 51, football coach, born Everett, WA, Mar 24, 1947.
Patrick (Pat) Verbeek, 34, hockey player, born Sarnia, Ontario, Canada, Mar 24, 1964.
Lawrence Frank (Larry) Wilson, 60, former football executive and Pro Football Hall of Fame defensive back, born Rigby, ID, Mar 24, 1938.

MARCH 25 — WEDNESDAY
Day 84 — 281 Remaining

NCAA BASKETBALL CHAMPIONS THIS DATE

1947	Holy Cross
1961	Cincinnati
1967	UCLA
1972	UCLA
1974	North Carolina State

COSELL, HOWARD: 80th BIRTH ANNIVERSARY. Mar 25, 1918. Howard Cosell, sportscaster born at New York, NY. After earning a law degree, Cosell began his broadcasting career as the host of "Howard Cosell Speaking of Sports." He achieved national prominence and a great deal of notoriety for his support of Muhammad Ali's stand against the Vietnam War and then as co-host of ABC's Monday Night Football. Died at New York, Apr 23, 1994.

March *1998*	S	M	T	W	T	F	S
	1	2	3	4	5	6	7
	8	9	10	11	12	13	14
	15	16	17	18	19	20	21
	22	23	24	25	26	27	28
	29	30	31				

CRUTCHFIELD, JIMMIE: BIRTH ANNIVERSARY. Mar 25, 1910. John William ("Jimmie") Crutchfield, baseball player born at Ardmore, MO. Crutchfield was an all-star outfielder for the Pittsburgh Crawfords, a Negro Leagues team in the 1930s. He was fast and hit .325 in his career. Died at Chicago, IL, Mar 31, 1993.

FIRST THREE-POINTER: ANNIVERSARY. Mar 25, 1979. Chris Ford of the Boston Celtics made the first three-point field goal in NBA history in a game against the Houston Rockets.

HORTON SMITH WINS FIRST MASTERS: ANNIVERSARY. Mar 25, 1934. Horton Smith shot four-under-par 284 to capture the first Masters golf tournament by one stroke over Craig Wood. Smith won again in 1936. Wood lost a playoff to Gene Sarazen in 1935 and won his own green jacket in 1941.

HOWARD, FRANK: BIRTH ANNIVERSARY. Mar 25, 1909. Frank James Howard, football player and coach born at Barlow Bend, AL. Howard played guard at the University of Alabama where he was also named Phi Beta Kappa. He served as an assistant coach under Jess Neely at Clemson University and was named head coach in 1940. A noted southern rural raconteur, Howard's Tigers won eight conference crowns before his retirement in 1969. Died at Clemson, SC, Jan 26, 1996.

LEONARD, DUTCH: BIRTH ANNIVERSARY. Mar 25, 1909. Emil John ("Dutch") Leonard, baseball player born at Auburn, IL. A knuckleballer, Leonard pitched 20 years in the major leagues with four different teams. He pitched the game in 1944 that gave the St. Louis Browns their only American League pennant. Died at Springfield, IL, Apr 17, 1983.

BIRTHDAYS TODAY

Jeffrey Allen (Jeff) Cross, 32, football player, born Riverside, CA, Mar 25, 1966.
David Travis Fryman, 29, baseball player, born Lexington, KY, Mar 25, 1969.
Thomas Michael (Tom) Glavine, 32, baseball player, born Concord, MA, Mar 25, 1966.
Avery Johnson, 33, basketball player, born New Orleans, LA, Mar 25, 1965.
Lee Louis Mazzilli, 43, former baseball player, born New York, NY, Mar 25, 1955.
Thomas S. (Tom) Monaghan, 61, former baseball executive, born Ann Arbor, MI, Mar 25, 1937.
Debi Janine Thomas, 31, figure skater, born Poughkeepsie, NY, Mar 25, 1967.
Daniel Allen (Dan) Wilson, 29, baseball player, born Arlington Heights, IL, Mar 25, 1969.
Kenneth (Ken) Wregget, 34, hockey player, born Brandon, Manitoba, Canada, Mar 25, 1964.

MARCH 26 — THURSDAY
Day 85 — 280 Remaining

NCAA BASKETBALL CHAMPIONS THIS DATE

1946	Oklahoma A&M
1949	Kentucky
1952	Kansas
1973	UCLA
1979	Michigan State

ENGLE, RIP: BIRTH ANNIVERSARY. Mar 26, 1906. Charles Albert ("Rip") Engle, football player and coach born at Elk Lick (now Salisbury), PA. Engle played college sports, including football, at Western Maryland and then began coaching at the high school level. He became head coach at Brown in 1944 and moved to Penn State in 1950. He coached the Nittany Lions to a 104–48–4 record and retired in 1966. Died at Bellefonte, PA, Mar 7, 1983.

LOS ANGELES MARATHON QUALITY OF LIFE EXPO. Mar 26–28. Los Angeles Convention Center, Los Angeles, CA. Massive consumer show features health and fitness products and services, food and beverage sampling, financial institutions, travel, electronics, women's products and services, seminars and demonstrations. A bike section will also be featured. Est attendance: 68,000. For info: Mike Gerlowski, Dir Sales and Mktg, City of Los Angeles Marathon, Inc, 11110 W Ohio Ave, Ste 100, Los Angeles, CA 90025. Phone: (310) 444-5544 ext 45 or 56. Fax: (310) 473-8105. Email: lamarathon@aol.com.

NCAA MEN'S DIVISION I SWIMMING AND DIVING CHAMPIONSHIPS. Mar 26–28. Auburn University, Auburn, AL. For info: NCAA, 6201 College Blvd, Overland Park, KS 66211. Phone: (913) 339-1906.

SECOND-LARGEST TRADE IN NFL HISTORY: 45th ANNIVERSARY. Mar 26, 1953. The Cleveland Browns and the Baltimore Colts complete the second-largest trade in National Football League history involving 15 players. The Browns sent Tom Catlin, Don Colo, Hershel Forester, Mike McCormack and John Petibon to Baltimore in exchange for Harry Agganis, Dick Batten, Gern Nagler, Bert Rechichar, Ed Sharkey, Don Shula, Art Spinney, Stu Sheets, Carl Taseff and Elmer Willhoite.

THE PLAYERS CHAMPIONSHIP. Mar 26–29. TPC at Sawgrass, Ponte Vedra Beach, FL. A PGA Tour tournament, formerly known as the Tournament Players Championship. For info: PGA Tour, 112 TPC Blvd, Ponte Vedra Beach, FL 32082. Phone: (904) 285-3700.

WORLD CHAMPIONSHIP SNOWMOBILE HILL-CLIMB. Mar 26–28. Jackson, WY. Snowmobiles attempt to climb Snow King Mountain, 1,500 vertical feet. Sponsor: Jackson Hole Snow Devils. Est attendance: 7,000. For info: Visitor Services Mgr, Jackson Hole Snow Devils, Jackson Hole Chamber of Commerce, PO Box 3440, Jackson, WY 83001. Phone: (307) 733-3316. Fax: (307) 734-0370.

BIRTHDAYS TODAY

Marcus Allen, 38, Heisman Trophy running back, born San Diego, CA, Mar 26, 1960.

Uwe Konstantine Blab, 36, former basketball player, born Munich, West Germany, Mar 26, 1962.

James Caan, 58, actor (*Brian's Song*), born New York, NY, Mar 26, 1940.

Christopher Allen (Chris) Codiroli, 40, former baseball player, born Oxnard, CA, Mar 26, 1958.

Ann Elizabeth Meyers, 43, broadcaster and Basketball Hall of Fame forward, born San Diego, CA, Mar 26, 1955.

Richard Shane Reynolds, 30, baseball player, born Bastrop, LA, Mar 26, 1968.

Ulf Samuelsson, 34, hockey player, born Fagersta, Sweden, Mar 26, 1964.

Kevin Lee Seitzer, 36, baseball player, born Springfield, IL, Mar 26, 1962.

John Houston Stockton, 36, basketball player, born Spokane, WA, Mar 26, 1962.

Jose Luis Vizcaino, 30, baseball player, born San Cristobal, Dominican Republic, Mar 26, 1968.

MARCH 27 — FRIDAY
Day 86 — 279 Remaining

NCAA BASKETBALL CHAMPIONS THIS DATE

1939	Oregon
1945	Oklahoma A&M
1951	Kentucky
1971	UCLA
1978	Kentucky

CUBS NICKNAME COINED: ANNIVERSARY. Mar 27, 1902. The *Chicago Daily News* began calling the city's National League team the Cubs. Formed as the Chicago White Stockings, the team had also been known as the Colts and the Orphans.

FIRST NCAA TOURNAMENT: ANNIVERSARY. Mar 27, 1939. The Oregon Ducks defeated the Ohio State Buckeyes, 46–33, to win the first NCAA men's basketball tournament. Oregon beat Texas and Oklahoma to reach the final, held at Northwestern's Patten Gymnasium; Ohio State defeated Wake Forest and Villanova.

FUNKY WINKERBEAN: ANNIVERSARY. Mar 27, 1974. Anniversary of the nationally syndicated comic strip. For info: Tom Batiuk, Creator, 2750 Substation Rd, Medina, OH 44256. Phone: (330) 722-8755.

HUGGINS, MILLER: BIRTH ANNIVERSARY. Mar 27, 1879. Miller James Huggins, Baseball Hall of Fame manager born at Cincinnati, OH. Huggins played major league baseball, but he made his mark as manager of the New York Yankees from 1918 to his death. It was his job to ride herd on Babe Ruth. Inducted into the Hall of Fame in 1964. Died at New York, NY, Sept 25, 1929.

MOON PHASE: NEW MOON. Mar 27. Moon enters New Moon phase at 10:14 PM, EST.

NCAA DIVISION I HOCKEY CHAMPIONSHIP. Mar 27–29. Regionals at Pepsi Arena, Albany, NY (Mar 28–29) and University of Michigan, Ann Arbor, MI (Mar 27–28). For info: NCAA, 6201 College Blvd, Overland Park, KS 66211. Phone: (913) 339-1906.

NCAA WOMEN'S DIVISION I BASKETBALL TOURNAMENT. Mar 27–29. Final Four. Kemper Arena, Kansas City, MO. For info: NCAA, 6201 College Blvd, Overland Park, KS 66211. Phone: (913) 339-1906.

PERIGEAN SPRING TIDES. Mar 27–28. Spring tides, the highest possible tides, occur when New Moon or Full Moon falls within 24 hours of the moment the Moon is nearest Earth (perigee) in its monthly orbit on Mar 28, at 2 AM, EST.

POLO: INTERNATIONAL CHALLENGE CUP. Mar 27–Apr 19 (tentative). Wellington, FL. For info: Palm Beach Polo, Inc, 13420 South Shore Blvd, West Palm Beach, FL 33414. Phone: (561) 793-1440. Fax: (561) 790-3872.

POLO: SPRING CLASSIC CUP. Mar 27–Apr 12. Wellington, FL. For info: Palm Beach Polo, Inc, 13420 South Shore Rd, West Palm Beach, FL 33414. Phone: (561) 793-1440. Fax: (561) 790-3872.

POLO: WORLD CUP. Mar 27–Apr 19. Wellington, FL. For info: Palm Beach Polo, Inc, 13420 South Shore Blvd, West Palm Beach, FL 33414. Phone: (561) 793-1440. Fax: (561) 790-3872.

SPORTSCHASER OF THE DAY

The National League baseball team once known as the White Stockings is now known by what nickname?

BIRTHDAYS TODAY

John Wesley (Wes) Covington, 66, former baseball player, born Laurinburg, NC, Mar 27, 1932.
Randall Cunningham, 35, football player, born Santa Barbara, CA, Mar 27, 1963.
Jaime Navarro, 30, baseball player, born Bayamon, Puerto Rico, Mar 27, 1968.
Edward Lewis (Ed) Pinckney, 35, basketball player, born New York, NY, Mar 27, 1963.
Richard David (Dick) Ruthven, 47, former baseball player, born Sacramento, CA, Mar 27, 1951.
William Caleb (Cale) Yarborough, 58, former auto racer, born Timmonsville, SC, Mar 27, 1940.

MARCH 28 — SATURDAY
Day 87 — 278 Remaining

NCAA BASKETBALL CHAMPIONS THIS DATE

1942	Stanford
1944	Utah
1950	CCNY
1977	Marquette

BACK-TO-BACK PERFECT GAMES: ANNIVERSARY. Mar 28, 1989. Softball pitchers Cathy McAllister and Stefni Whitton of Southwestern Louisiana performed a feat unprecedented in NCAA history by throwing back-to-back perfect games against Southeastern Louisiana. McAllister won, 5–0, and Whitten struck out 14 in winning 7–0.

BUSCH, GUSSIE: BIRTH ANNIVERSARY. Mar 28, 1899. August Adolphus (Gussie) Busch, Jr, baseball executive born at St. Louis, MO. Busch bought the St. Louis Cardinals in 1953 and became one of the most influential team owners. He tied the success of the sport to the growth of his brewery's sales and took great pleasure in both. Died at St. Louis, Sept 29, 1989.

CCNY'S DOUBLE TITLES: ANNIVERSARY. Mar 28, 1950. The City College of New York (CCNY) defeated Bradley, 71–68, in the title game of the NCAA basketball tournament, thereby becoming the only team to win both that championship and the NIT title in the same year. Ten days before, CCNY had beaten Bradley, 69–61, to win the NIT.

COLTS SNEAK OUT OF BALTIMORE: ANNIVERSARY. Mar 28, 1984. With little or no warning, the Baltimore Colts loaded moving vans in the dead of night and left for Indianapolis. Baltimore was left without an NFL team until 1996 when the Cleveland Browns moved there and were renamed the Ravens.

DAYTONA BEACH SPRING '98 SPEEDWAY SPECTACULAR. Mar 28–29. Daytona International Speedway, Daytona Beach, FL. 9th annual car show of all makes and models of collector vehicles. Many car clubs make this their largest annual event. Show includes display of antiques, classics, sports cars, muscle cars, race cars, custom and special interest vehicles on the speedway infield both days, with a large swap meet of auto parts and accessories. Collector car sales corral, crafts sale. Annually, the last or next to the last weekend in March. Est

attendance: 25,000. For info: Rick D'Louhy, Exec Dir, Daytona Beach Racing and Recreational Facilities District, PO Box 1958, Daytona Beach, FL 32115-1958. Phone: (904) 255-7355.

NCAA MEN'S DIVISION I BASKETBALL TOURNAMENT. Mar 28–30. Final Four. Alamodome, San Antonio, TX. For info: NCAA, 6201 College Blvd, Overland Park, KS 66211. Phone: (913) 339-1906.

POSSUM PEDAL 100 BICYCLE RIDE/RACE. Mar 28. Courthouse Square, Graham, TX. Bicycle fun ride with 1,000 participants through the rolling hills and around Graham. Sponsor: Rotary Club of Graham Scholarship Fund. Annually, the "Taste of Graham." Est attendance: 3,000. For info: Possum Pedal 100, PO Box 1240, Graham, TX 76450. Phone: (800) 256-4844 or (940) 549-0780. Fax: (940) 549-7405. Email: bbsinc@wf.net.

RASCHI, VIC: BIRTH ANNIVERSARY. Mar 28, 1919. Victor John Angelo (Vic) Raschi, baseball player born at West Springfield, MA. Along with Allie Reynolds, Raschi helped form the nucleus of the pitching staff of the New York Yankees' five consecutive World Series winners, 1949–53. Raschi was known as the "Springfield Rifle." Died at Groveland, NJ, Oct 14, 1988.

SMITHSONIAN KITE FESTIVAL. Mar 28. National Mall, Washington, DC. 32nd annual. Rain date is Mar 29. For info: Smithsonian Institution, 900 Jefferson Dr SW, Washington, DC 20560. Phone: (202) 357-2700.

WILT RETIRES WITHOUT FOULING OUT: 25th ANNIVERSARY. Mar 28, 1973. Wilt Chamberlain retired from the NBA after playing in 1,045 games. During his entire 14-season career, Chamberlain never fouled out.

BIRTHDAYS TODAY

Richard Francis Dennis (Rick) Barry, III, 54, broadcaster and Basketball Hall of Fame forward, born Elizabeth, NJ, Mar 28, 1944.
Jeff Beukeboom, 33, hockey player, born Ajax, Ontario, Canada, Mar 28, 1965.
Shawn Kealoha Boskie, 31, baseball player, born Hawthorne, NV, Mar 28, 1967.
Glenn Earle Davis, 37, former baseball player, born Jacksonville, FL, Mar 28, 1961.
Ken Howard, 54, actor (*The White Shadow*), born El Centro, CA, Mar 28, 1944.
Craig Howard Paquette, 29, baseball player, born Long Beach, CA, Mar 28, 1969.
Byron Antom Scott, 37, basketball player, born Ogden, UT, Mar 28, 1961.
Gerald Eugene (Jerry) Sloan, 56, basketball coach and former player, born McLeansboro, IL, Mar 28, 1942.
Keith Matthew Tkachuk, 26, hockey player, born Melrose, MA, Mar 28, 1972.
Paul Anthony Wilson, 25, baseball player, born Orlando, FL, Mar 28, 1973.

March 1998	S	M	T	W	T	F	S
				1	2	3	4	5	6	7
	8	9	10	11	12	13	14
	15	16	17	18	19	20	21
	22	23	24	25	26	27	28
	29	30	31				

MARCH 29 — SUNDAY
Day 88 — 277 Remaining

NCAA BASKETBALL CHAMPIONS THIS DATE
1941	Wisconsin
1976	Indiana
1982	North Carolina

LOS ANGELES MARATHON. Mar 29. Los Angeles, CA. A multicultural athletic competition designed to foster community spirit as well as pride in one's physical well-being. Family Reunion Festival held in conjunction with marathon. Est attendance: 35,000. For info: Mike Gerlowski or John Wilson, Los Angeles Marathon, 11110 W Ohio Ave, Ste 100, Los Angeles, CA 90025. Phone: (310) 444-5544.

TUNNELL, EMLEN: BIRTH ANNIVERSARY. Mar 29, 1925. Emlen Tunnell, Pro Football Hall of Fame defensive back born at Bryn Mawr, PA. After playing college football at Iowa, Tunnell played for the New York Giants from 1948 through 1958 and finished his career with three seasons in Green Bay. Inducted into the Hall of Fame in 1967. Died at Pleasantville, NY, July 22, 1975.

YOUNG, CY: BIRTH ANNIVERSARY. Mar 29, 1867. Denton True ("Cy") Young, Baseball Hall of Fame pitcher born at Gilmore, OH. Young is baseball's all-time winningest pitcher, having accumulated 511 victories in his 22-year career. The Cy Young award is given each year in his honor to each major league's best pitcher. Inducted into the Hall of Fame in 1937. Died at Peoli, OH, Nov 4, 1955.

STANLEY CUP CHAMPIONS THIS DATE
1929	Boston Bruins

BIRTHDAYS TODAY

Earl Christian Campbell, 43, Heisman Trophy and Pro Football Hall of Fame running back, born Tyler, TX, Mar 29, 1955.

Walter ("Clyde") Frazier, Jr, 53, Basketball Hall of Fame guard, born Atlanta, GA, Mar 29, 1945.

Ronnie Henderson, 24, basketball player, born Gulfport, MS, Mar 29, 1974.

Thomas Francis (Tommy) Holmes, 81, former baseball player, born New York, NY, Mar 29, 1917.

Brian O'Neal Jordan, 31, baseball player, born Baltimore, MD, Mar 29, 1967.

Trevor Kidd, 26, hockey player, born Dugald, Manitoba, Canada, Mar 29, 1972.

Dennis Dale (Denny) McLain, 54, former baseball player, born Chicago, IL, Mar 29, 1944.

Geronimo Pena, 31, baseball player, born Distrito Nacional, Dominican Republic, Mar 29, 1967.

Kurt Thomas, 42, former gymnast, born Miami, FL, Mar 29, 1956.

MARCH 30 — MONDAY
Day 89 — 276 Remaining

NCAA BASKETBALL CHAMPIONS THIS DATE
1940	Indiana
1943	Wyoming
1981	Indiana
1987	Indiana

COLLINS, RIPPER: BIRTH ANNIVERSARY. Mar 30, 1904. James Anthony ("Ripper") Collins, baseball player, manager and sportscaster born at Altoona, PA. Collins got his nickname as a boy when he hit a ball that hit a fence nail, ripping the cover off. He played first base for the St. Louis Cardinals' Gas House Gang of the 1930s. Died at New Haven, CT, Apr 16, 1970.

DEBARTOLO BUYS 49ERS: ANNIVERSARY. Mar 30, 1977. A new era began in San Francisco football as Edward J. DeBartolo, Jr, bought the 49ers from the original owners. The 49ers never reached the NFL championship game while the Morabito family owned them, but they won five Super Bowls during the first 18 years of DeBartolo's tenure.

GALIMORE, WILLIE: BIRTH ANNIVERSARY. Mar 30, 1935. Willie Lee Galimore, football player born at St. Augustine, FL. Galimore was a star running back at Florida A&M and with the Chicago Bears from 1957 through 1963. He and teammate John Farrington died in an automobile accident at Rensselaer, IN, July 26, 1964.

KOUFAX AND DRYSDALE END HOLDOUT: ANNIVERSARY. Mar 30, 1966. Los Angeles Dodgers pitchers Sandy Koufax and Don Drysdale ended their joint month-long holdout by signing contracts for $130,000 and $105,000, respectively. Koufax (26–8 in 1965) and Drysdale (23–12) had shaken up the baseball establishment by joining forces and hiring lawyers to negotiate for them. Still, their contracts fell short of the three-year, $1.05 million deal they had sought.

VAN HALTREN, GEORGE: BIRTH ANNIVERSARY. Mar 30, 1866. George Edward Martin Van Haltren, baseball player born at St. Louis, MO. Van Haltren was a fan favorite while playing for the New York Giants in the 1890s. He was a graceful outfielder who could hit effectively and steal bases. Died at Oakland, CA, Sept 29, 1945.

CHASE'S SPORTSQUOTE OF THE DAY
"The only time I really try for a strikeout is when I'm in a jam. Most of the time I try to throw to spots. I try to get them to pop up or ground out." —Sandy Koufax

BIRTHDAYS TODAY

Chris Canty, 22, football player, born Voorhees, NJ, Mar 30, 1976.

David (Dave) Ellett, 34, hockey player, born Cleveland, OH, Mar 30, 1964.

Jack Thomas Lazorko, 42, former baseball player, born Hoboken, NJ, Mar 30, 1956.

Jerry Ray Lucas, 58, Basketball Hall of Fame forward and center, born Middletown, OH, Mar 30, 1940.

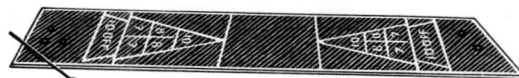

MARCH 31 — TUESDAY
Day 90 — 275 Remaining

NCAA BASKETBALL CHAMPIONS THIS DATE
1975	UCLA
1986	Louisville
1997	Arizona

ALM, JEFF: BIRTH ANNIVERSARY. Mar 31, 1968. Jeffrey Lawrence (Jeff) Alm, football player born at New York, NY, Mar 31, 1968. Alm played on Notre Dame's 1988 national championship team and was drafted by the Houston Oilers in 1990. Died of gunshot wounds in an apparent suicide after a friend riding in his car was killed in a crash at Houston, TX, Dec 14, 1993.

BIGBEE, CARSON: BIRTH ANNIVERSARY. Mar 31, 1895. Carson Lee Bigbee, baseball player born at Waterloo, OR. Bigbee played the outfield for the Pittsburgh Pirates from 1916 through 1926. He was a reliable hitter handicapped by injuries and poor eyesight. Died at Portland, OR, Oct 17, 1964.

DE PALMA, RALPH: DEATH ANNIVERSARY. Mar 31, 1956. Ralph De Palma, auto racer born at Troia, Italy, 1883. De Palma came to the US in the 1890s and began racing in his youth. The greatest driver of racing's early era, he drove in 2,889 races and won 2,557 of them, including the Indianapolis 500 in 1915. Died at South Pasadena, CA.

JOHNSON, JACK: 120th BIRTH ANNIVERSARY. Mar 31, 1878. Arthur John (Jack) Johnson, boxer born at Galveston, TX. Johnson entered pro boxing at a time when the leading white fighters ignored black contenders. The dearth of good competition, though, after the retirement of Jim Jeffries in 1905 gave Johnson a shot at the title, which he won on Dec 28, 1908, by defeating Tommy Burns. Johnson's flamboyant lifestyle and relationships with white women provoked the search for a "Great White Hope" to defeat him. A Mann Act conviction caused Johnson to flee to Europe. He eventually lost the title to Jess Willard in a 1915 fight in Havana, Cuba. Died at Raleigh, NC, June 10, 1946.

MAJOR LEAGUE BASEBALL REGULAR SEASON. Mar 31–Sept 27 (tentative). Major League Baseball opens a 26-week regular season leading to the playoffs and the World Series in October. The 15-team American League, established in 1901 and augmented this year by the Tampa Bay Devil Rays, begins its 98th season. The 15-team National League, established in 1876 and adding the Arizona Diamondbacks, begins its 123rd season. Each team plays a 162-game schedule. For info: American League, 350 Park Ave, New York, NY 10022. Phone: (212) 339-7600. Fax: (212) 593-7138. National League, 350 Park Ave, New York, NY 10022. Phone: (212) 339-7700. Fax: (212) 935-5069.
WWW: http://www.majorleaguebaseball.com/

VARIPAPA, ANDY: BIRTH ANNIVERSARY. Mar 31, 1891. Andrew (Andy) Varipapa, bowler born at Carfizzi, Italy. Varipapa came to the US in 1902 and began bowling in 1907. He gained national prominence with an important tournament victory in 1930 and remained active in the sport more than 70 years. He gave clinics, made films and invented trick shot bowling. At age 78,

unable to bowl righthanded because of wrist injuries, he began bowling lefthanded and carried a 180 average within 18 months. Died at Hempstead, NY, Aug 25, 1984.

WOODEN'S LAST TITLE: ANNIVERSARY. Mar 31, 1975. Two days after Coach John Wooden announced his intention to retire at season's end, the UCLA Bruins won their tenth NCAA title in 12 years, all under Wooden's tutelage. UCLA defeated Kentucky, 92–85, as Wooden closed his career with a 620–147 record.

BIRTHDAYS TODAY

Tom Barrasso, 33, hockey player, born Boston, MA, Mar 31, 1965.

Pavel Bure, 27, hockey player, born Moscow, USSR, Mar 31, 1971.

Gordon (Gordie) Howe, 70, Hockey Hall of Fame right wing, born Floral, Saskatchewan, Canada, Mar 31, 1928.

James Earl (Jimmy) Johnson, 60, Pro Football Hall of Fame defensive back, born Dallas, TX, Mar 31, 1938.

Edward Francis (Ed) Marinaro, 48, former football player, born New York, NY, Mar 31, 1950.

Rhea Perlman, 50, actress ("Cheers"), born New York, NY, Mar 31, 1948.

Herman ("J. R.") Reid, Jr, 30, basketball player, born Virginia Beach, VA, Mar 31, 1968.

Steven Delano (Steve) Smith, 29, basketball player, born Highland Park, MI, Mar 31, 1969.

APRIL 1 — WEDNESDAY
Day 91 — 274 Remaining

NCAA BASKETBALL CHAMPIONS THIS DATE

1985	Villanova
1991	Duke
1996	Kentucky

APRIL FOOLS' or ALL FOOLS' DAY. Apr 1. "The joke of the day is to deceive persons by sending them upon frivolous and nonsensical errands; to pretend they are wanted when they are not, or, in fact, any way to betray them into some supposed ludicrous situation, so as to enable you to call them 'An April Fool.'"–Brady's *Clavis Calendaria*, 1812. "The first of April, some do say,/Is set apart for All Fools' Day,/But why the people call it so,/Nor I nor they themselves do know."–*Poor Robin's Almanack* for 1760.

CHASE'S SPORTS CALENDAR DEADLINE APPROACHING. Apr 1. Time to plan ahead. Schedule 1999 celebrations and observances and submit information to *Chase's 1999 Sports Calendar of Events* by May 20, 1998. Sponsors/information suppliers of events in this book should have received confirmation/update ("Re-up") forms for the 1999 edition by this time. To submit new entries for consideration, use (or use a copy of) the form on the last page of this book. Send to: Editor, Chase's Sports Calendar, 2951 Dividend Park Dr, Florissant, MO 63031.

FIRST BASEBALL STRIKE BEGINS: ANNIVERSARY. Apr 1, 1972. The Major League Baseball Players Association went on strike for the first time, with the principal issue being contributions to the major league pension plan. The strike lasted 12 days and wiped out 86 regular season games.

GRAND STRAND FISHING RODEO. Apr 1–Oct 31. Myrtle Beach, SC. Awards for surf, inlet and deep-sea fish catches. For info: Chamber of Commerce, Box 2115, Myrtle Beach, SC 29578. Phone: (803) 626-7444. Fax: (803) 626-0009. WWW: http://www.myrtlebeach-info.com

HEATH, JEFF: BIRTH ANNIVERSARY. Apr 1, 1915. John Geoffrey (Jeff) Heath, baseball player and sportscaster born at Fort William, Ontario, Canada. Heath's family came to the US during the Great Depression. In 1941 he became the first player to hit a home run into the upper deck of Cleveland's Municipal Stadium. Died at Seattle, WA, Dec 9, 1975.

LAKERS' APRIL FOOL JOKE: ANNIVERSARY. Apr 1, 1990. Los Angeles Lakers Michael Cooper and Byron Scott appeared on an LA radio show and were informed during the broadcast that they had been traded to the Los Angeles Clippers for Benoit Benjamin and Jeff Martin. Lakers teammate Mychal Thompson called the show to say that the two wouldn't be missed. Host Joe McConnell then reminded his guests and his listeners that it was April Fools' Day.

McSHERRY, JOHN: DEATH ANNIVERSARY. Apr 1, 1996. John Patrick McSherry, umpire born at New York, NY, Sept 11, 1944. McSherry umpired his first National League game in 1971 and was, by the time of his death, a crew chief who was respected by players and colleagues alike. Severely overweight, McSherry suffered a fatal heart attack on the field at Cincinnati's Riverfront Stadium just prior to the start of the opening game of the season. Died at Cincinnati, OH.

NATIONAL KNUCKLES DOWN MONTH. Apr 1–30. To recognize and revive the American tradition of playing marbles and keep it rolling along. Please send SASE with inquiries. For info: Cathy C. Runyan, The Marble Lady, 7812 NW Hampton Rd, Kansas City, MO 64152. Phone: (816) 587-8687.

NATIONAL YOUTH SPORTS SAFETY MONTH. Apr 1–30. Bringing public attention to the prevalent problem of injuries in youth sports. This event promotes safety in sport activities and is supported by more than 60 national sports and medical organizations. For info: Michelle Glassman, Exec Dir, Natl Youth Sports Safety Fdtn, 333 Longwood Ave, Ste 202, Boston, MA 02115. Phone: (617) 277-1171. Fax: (617) 277-2278. Email: nyssf@aol.com.

NEW YORK LEGALIZES BETTING: ANNIVERSARY. Apr 1, 1940. New York governor Herbert Lehman signed a bill legalizing parimutuel wagering at the state's racetracks and outlawing bookmaking.

PATS GO PUBLIC: ANNIVERSARY. Apr 1, 1960. The Boston Patriots of the American Football League made Wall Street history by becoming the first professional sports team to issue public stock.

PRO-AM SNIPE EXCURSION AND HUNT. Apr 1. Moultrie, GA. Celebrating the time-honored custom of snipe hunting. The denim snipe has come back from the brink of extinction and will be honored at the 1998 event which will include a Snipe Parade, a Snipe Ball and festivities at the Denim Wing of the Snipe Museum at New Elm, GA. New Snipe-O-Rama racing oval open! Annually, Apr 1. For info: Beth Gay, PO Box 1110, Moultrie, GA 31776. Phone: (912) 985-6540.

SEATTLE PILOTS BECOME MILWAUKEE BREWERS: ANNIVERSARY. Apr 1, 1970. After one year as an American League expansion team, the Seattle Pilots moved to Milwaukee and became the Brewers. Car dealer Bud Selig purchased the team for $10.8 million.

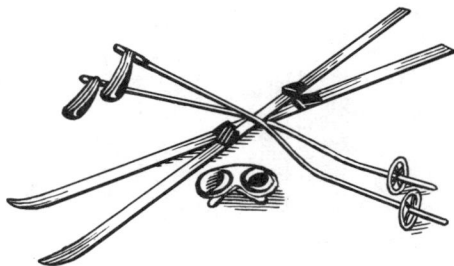

SPORTS EYE SAFETY MONTH. Apr 1–30. During this month's observance, Prevent Blindness America (formerly known as the National Society to Prevent Blindness) will encourage young athletes to wear eye/face protection when participating in sports. Materials that can easily be posted or distributed to the community will be provided. For info: Prevent Blindness America, 500 E Remington Rd, Schaumburg, IL 60173. Phone: (800) 331-2020. Fax: (847) 843-8458. WWW: http://www.prevent-blindness.org

TOUR de CURE. Apr 1–June 30. Thousands of cyclists participate in the American Diabetes Association's annual cycling event to raise money to help find a cure for diabetes and to provide information and resources to improve the lives of all people affected by diabetes. Tours are held in communities across America, combining fun and fitness with the chance to help people with diabetes. Contact your local affiliate. For info: American Diabetes Assn, Natl HQ, 1660 Duke St, Alexandria, VA 22314. Phone: (800) TOUR-888.

VILLANOVA UPSETS GEORGETOWN: ANNIVERSARY. Apr 1, 1985. In one of the greatest upsets in NCAA basketball tournament history, the Villanova University Wildcats upset the Hoyas of Georgetown University, 66–64, in the championship game. The Wildcats made 78% of their shots from the field and converted 22 of 27 free throws.

BIRTHDAYS TODAY

Richard Louis (Rich) Amaral, 36, baseball player, born Visalia, CA, Apr 1, 1962.
Frank Anthony Castillo, 29, baseball player, born El Paso, TX, Apr 1, 1969.
Kevin Jerome Duckworth, 34, basketball player, born Harvey, IL, Apr 1, 1964.
Mark A. Jackson, 33, basketball player, born New York, NY, Apr 1, 1965.
Philip Henry (Phil) Niekro, 59, Baseball Hall of Fame pitcher, born Blaine, OH, Apr 1, 1939.
Ronald Peter (Ron) Perranoski (born Ronald Peter Perzanowski), 62, former baseball player, born Paterson, NJ, Apr 1, 1936.
Libby Riddles, 42, dogsled racer, born Madison, WI, Apr 1, 1956.
Glenn Edward ("Bo") Schembechler, Jr, 69, former baseball executive and college football coach, born Barberton, OH, Apr 1, 1929.
Daniel Joseph ("Rusty") Staub, 54, former baseball player, born New Orleans, LA, Apr 1, 1944.
Scott Stevens, 34, hockey player, born Kitchener, Ontario, Canada, Apr 1, 1964.

April 1998

S	M	T	W	T	F	S
			1	2	3	4
5	6	7	8	9	10	11
12	13	14	15	16	17	18
19	20	21	22	23	24	25
26	27	28	29	30		

APRIL 2 — THURSDAY
Day 92 — 273 Remaining

NCAA BASKETBALL CHAMPIONS THIS DATE
1984   Georgetown
1990   UNLV

APPLING, LUKE: BIRTH ANNIVERSARY. Apr 2, 1909. Lucius Benjamin (Luke) Appling, Baseball Hall of Fame shortstop born at High Point, NC. Appling won two American League batting titles, hitting .310 over 20 years with the Chicago White Sox. Inducted into the Hall of Fame in 1964. Died at Cumming, GA, Jan 3, 1991.

ENGLAND: GRAND NATIONAL HORSERACING MEETING. Apr 2–4. Aintree Racecourse, Aintree, Liverpool. Britain's premier horse race and most famous steeplechase is run over 4.5 miles on this beautiful and legendary course. The Grand National race takes place on Apr 4, the culmination of the race meeting. Est attendance: 100,000. For info: Racecourse Mgr, Aintree Racecourse, Liverpool, Merseyside, England L9 5AS. Phone: (44) (151) 523-2600. Fax: (44) (151) 530-1512. WWW: http://www.demon.co.uk/racenews/aintree

JENNINGS, HUGH: BIRTH ANNIVERSARY. Apr 2, 1869. Hugh Ambrose Jennings, Baseball Hall of Fame player and manager born at Pittston, PA. Jennings played for the great Baltimore Orioles teams of the 1890s and went on to become a colorful manager, especially with the Detroit Tigers. Inducted into the Hall of Fame in 1945. Died at Scranton, PA, Feb 1, 1928.

MITCHELL STRIKES OUT RUTH AND GEHRIG: ANNIVERSARY. Apr 2, 1931. Jackie Mitchell, 17, became the first woman to pitch in a professional baseball game after she was signed to a contract by the Chattanooga Lookouts of the Southern Association. In an exhibition game against the New York Yankees, Mitchell struck out Babe Ruth (who took strike three) and Lou Gehrig (who gallantly missed three straight pitches) before Tony Lazzeri walked.

NCAA DIVISION I HOCKEY CHAMPIONSHIP. Apr 2–4. Finals. Fleet Center, Boston, MA. For info: NCAA, 6201 College Blvd, Overland Park, KS 66211. Phone: (913) 339-1906.

THREE-POINT FIELD GOAL: ANNIVERSARY. Apr 2, 1986. The NCAA basketball rules committee adopted the three-point field goal, setting the arc at a distance of 19 feet, 9 inches, from the basket.

☆   ☆   ☆

BIRTHDAYS TODAY

Roberto Francisco (Bobby) Avila, 74, former baseball player, born Veracruz, Mexico, Apr 2, 1924.
Peter Joseph (Pete) Incaviglia, 34, baseball player, born Pebble Beach, CA, Apr 2, 1964.
Albert Samuel (Al) Nipper, 39, former baseball player, born San Diego, CA, Apr 2, 1959.
Ayako Okamoto, 47, golfer, born Hiroshima, Japan, Apr 2, 1951.
Walter William (Billy) Pierce, 71, former baseball player, born Detroit, MI, Apr 2, 1927.
Richard Raymond (Dick) Radatz, 61, former baseball player, born Detroit, MI, Apr 2, 1937.
Carl Reginald (Reggie) Smith, 53, former baseball player, born Shreveport, LA, Apr 2, 1945.
Donald Howard (Don) Sutton, 53, broadcaster and former baseball player, born Clio, AL, Apr 2, 1945.

APRIL 3 — FRIDAY
Day 93 — 272 Remaining

NCAA BASKETBALL CHAMPIONS THIS DATE

1989	Michigan
1995	UCLA

ALZADO, LYLE: BIRTH ANNIVERSARY. Apr 3, 1949. Lyle Martin Alzado, football player born at New York, NY. Alzado grew up on Long Island and graduated from Yankton College in South Dakota with a bachelor's degree in special education. He played football, earning Little All-America honors, and was drafted in 1971 by the Denver Broncos. Alzado gained fame as part of Denver's "Orange Crush" defense and for his fierce demeanor. He was traded to the Cleveland Browns in 1979 and in 1982 to the Los Angeles Raiders. After retiring at the end of the 1985 season, Alzado acted in movies. He was diagnosed with brain cancer in 1991, which he attributed to a lifetime of steroid usage. He spent the last months of his life campaigning against steroids and human growth hormone. Died at Lake Oswego, OR, May 14, 1992.

AMERICAN CROSSWORD PUZZLE TOURNAMENT AND CONVENTION. Apr 3–5. Stamford Marriott Hotel, Stamford, CT. 300 solvers from the US and Canada compete on eight puzzles during this 21st annual event. Points are awarded for accuracy and speed. The final puzzle is played on giant white boards for everyone to watch. Prizes are awarded in 21 skill, age and geographical categories and the grand prize is $1,000. The weekend also includes group word games, guest speakers and appearances by celebrity crossword solvers. Solvers can compete at home for fun and receive a ranking in all their solving categories. Est attendance: 350. For info: Will Shortz, Dir, Amer Crossword Puzzle Tournament, 55 Great Oak Lane, Pleasantville, NY 10570. Phone: (914) 769-9128. Fax: (914) 769-9128.

CALICO HULLABALOO. Apr 3–5. Calico Ghost Town, Yermo, CA. Championship horseshoe-pitching and tobacco-spitting contests are two of the highlights at this festival located in an 1880s silver rush and mining town. Est attendance: 7,000. For info: Calico Ghost Town, PO Box 638, Yermo, CA 92398. Phone: (800) TO-CALICO. Fax: (760) 254-2047. Email: ruins@juno.com.

CREWS, TIM: BIRTH ANNIVERSARY. Apr 3, 1961. Stanley Timothy (Tim) Crews, baseball player born at Tampa, FL. Crews was a relief pitcher with the Dodgers and had signed as a free agent with the Cleveland Indians in January 1993. Died from injuries suffered in a boating accident at Orlando, FL, Mar 23, 1993.

DR. J'S NUMBER RETIRED: ANNIVERSARY. Apr 3, 1987. The New Jersey Nets honored former Net Julius ("Dr. J") Erving by retiring his number, 32. The ceremony occurred during a game against the Philadelphia 76ers, the team with whom Erving was finishing his 16-year career.

EAST TEXAS WALKING AND RACKING HORSE SHOW. Apr 3–4 (tentative). Central East Texas Fairgrounds, Marshall, TX. A charity horse show consisting of 50+ classes of walking horses, racking horses and spotted saddle horses. Three classes held for other breeds. Est attendance: 1,200. For info: Lenore Trachier, 101 Beth Ann Dr, Marshall, TX 75670. Phone: (903) 938-6754.

GREAT OUTDOOR SHOW. Apr 3–4. Northern State University's Barnett Center, Abeerdeen, SD. Displays, exposition of products and services for camping, hunting, fishing and more. For info: Mike Opp, Aberdeen Amer News, PO Box 4430, Aberdeen, SD 57402. Phone: (605) 225-4100.

MOON PHASE: FIRST QUARTER. Apr 3. Moon enters First Quarter phase at 3:18 PM, EST.

PERREAULT SCORES 1,000th POINT: ANNIVERSARY. Apr 3, 1982. Gilbert Perreault of the Buffalo Sabres scored the 1,000th point of his NHL career, an assist in the Sabres' 5–4 win over the Montreal Canadiens. Perreault finished his career with 1,326 points and was inducted into the Hockey Hall of Fame in 1990.

RATELLE SCORES 1,000th POINT: ANNIVERSARY. Apr 3, 1977. Center Jean Ratelle of the Boston Bruins scored the 1,000th point of his NHL career, an assist in the Bruins' 7–4 victory over the Toronto Maple Leafs. Ratelle finished his career with 1,267 points and entered the Hockey Hall of Fame in 1985.

STANLEY CUP CHAMPIONS THIS DATE

1930	Montreal Canadiens

BIRTHDAYS TODAY

Christopher Louis (Chris) Bosio, 35, baseball player, born Carmichael, CA, Apr 3, 1963.
Arthur John (Art) Ditmar, 69, former baseball player, born Winthrop, MA, Apr 3, 1929.
Pervis Ellison, 31, basketball player, born Savannah, GA, Apr 3, 1967.
Alexander Peter (Alex) Grammas, 72, former baseball manager and player, born Birmingham, AL, Apr 3, 1926.
Rodney Hampton, 29, football player, born Houston, TX, Apr 3, 1969.
Wallace Wade (Wally) Moon, 68, former baseball player, born Bay, AR, Apr 3, 1930.
James Thomas (Jim) Parker, 64, Pro Football Hall of Fame guard, born Macon, GA, Apr 3, 1934.

☆   ☆   ☆

APRIL 4 — SATURDAY
Day 94 — 271 Remaining

NCAA BASKETBALL CHAMPIONS THIS DATE

1983	North Carolina State
1988	Kansas
1994	Arkansas

BAY COUNTRY BOAT SHOW. Apr 4–5. Hollywood Volunteer Fire Department Grounds, Hollywood, MD. 10th annual Bay Country Boat Show includes more than 50 exhibitors of boats, trailers, accessories, nautical crafts, fishing tackle and refreshments. Both inside and outside exhibit areas. Est attendance: 3,000. For info: Bay Country Boat Show, Optimist Club of Hollywood, PO Box 369, Hollywood, MD 20636. Phone: (301) 373-5468. Fax: (301) 373-3501.

GIAMATTI, BART: 60th BIRTH ANNIVERSARY. Apr 4, 1938. Angelo Bartlett (Bart) Giamatti, Commissioner of Baseball and educator born at Boston, MA. Giamatti received his education at Yale, taught classics there and became Yale's youngest president at the age of 39 in 1978. Following his tenure at Yale, he became the president of baseball's National League in 1986, serving in that capacity until he was appointed Commissioner of Baseball on Apr 1, 1989. An accomplished author, he moved freely between the worlds of literature and baseball, often linking the two in the many articles he wrote. One week prior to his death, he signed an agreement placing Pete Rose on the permanently ineligible list. Died at Martha's Vineyard, MA, Sept 1, 1989.

HODGES, GIL: BIRTH ANNIVERSARY. Apr 4, 1924. Gilbert Ray (Gil) Hodges, baseball player and manager born at Princeton, IN. Hodges was the first baseman on the famous Brooklyn Dodgers "Boys of Summer" teams. He managed the New York Mets to the 1969 World Series title. Died at West Palm Beach, FL, Apr 2, 1972.

KITE FLITE. Apr 4. Space Center, Alamogordo, NM. Annual event with kite flight. Est attendance: 300. For info: Jack Moore, Public Affairs Officer, Space Center, PO Box 533, Alamogordo, NM 88311. Phone: (800) 545-4021. Fax: (505) 437-7722. Email: space-plan@nmsua.nmsu.edu. WWW: http://abcc.nmsu.edu/~bwood/

NORWAY: EASTER FESTIVAL (WITH WORLD CHAMPIONSHIP REINDEER RACES). Apr 4–13. Kautokeino and Karasjok. Colorful traditional Norwegian celebration with Sami (Lapp) weddings, traditional fair, concerts and the World Championship Reindeer Races. For info: Norwegian Tourist Board, 655 Third Ave, New York, NY 10017. Phone: (212) 949-2333. Fax: (212) 983-5260. Email: gonorway@interport.net. WWW: http://www.norway.org/web/norway/tourism.html

PEANUT-KIDS-BASEBALL DAY. Apr 4. Edwards-Freeman Nut Co, Conshohocken, PA. In a salute to the ingredients that relate to our national pastime, an annual observance is held at which MVP (Master Vendor, Peanuts) Cheryl Spielvogel throws out the first "ball" (bag of peanuts shaped like a baseball) to Philadelphia Phillies players, then to Little League players and others present. Annually, the Saturday prior to the Phillies' home opener. Sponsors: Conshohocken Little League, Edwards-Freeman Nut Co. Est attendance: 150. For info: Abe S. Rosen, Rosen-Coren Agency, Inc, 2381 Philmont Ave, Ste 117, Huntingdon Valley, PA 19006-6294. Phone: (215) 938-1017.

POTVIN SCORES 1,000th POINT: ANNIVERSARY. Apr 4, 1987. Denis Potvin of the New York Islanders, the highest-scoring defenseman in NHL history at the time, scored the 1,000th point of his career. Potvin entered the Hockey Hall of Fame in 1991.

SPEAKER, TRIS: 110th BIRTH ANNIVERSARY. Apr 4, 1888. Tristram E. (Tris) Speaker, Baseball Hall of Fame outfielder born at Hubbard City, TX. Known as the "Gray Eagle," Speaker was one of the greatest centerfielders of all time. He started his career with the Boston Red Sox,

where he was part of the Hooper-Speaker-Lewis outfield, and then achieved stardom in a second city, playing for the Cleveland Indians. Inducted into the Hall of Fame in 1937. Died at Lake Whitney, TX, Dec 8, 1958.

VOSMIK, JOE: BIRTH ANNIVERSARY. Apr 4, 1910. Joseph Franklin (Joe) Vosmik, baseball player born at Cleveland, OH. Vosmik was signed by the Indians upon the advice of the wife of the team's general manager. He hit .300 in six of his ten seasons as a regular. Died at Cleveland, Jan 2, 1962.

WOMEN'S INTERNATIONAL BOWLING CONGRESS CHAMPIONSHIP TOURNAMENT. Apr 4–May 24. Quad Cities, IA and IL. Est attendance: 150,000. For info: Ruth Williams, WIBC, 5301 S 76th St, Greendale, WI 53129. Phone: (414) 421-9000 or (414) 423-3224. Fax: (414) 421-7977.

BIRTHDAYS TODAY

William C. (Bill) Bridges, 59, former basketball player, born Hobbs, NM, Apr 4, 1939.

Pat Burns, 46, hockey coach, born St. Henri, Quebec, Canada, Apr 4, 1952.

JoAnne Gunderson Carner, 59, LPGA Hall of Fame golfer, born Kirkland, WA, Apr 4, 1939.

Jack Del Rio, Jr, 35, football player, born Castro Valley, CA, Apr 4, 1963.

Michael Peter (Mike) Epstein, 55, former baseball player, born New York, NY, Apr 4, 1943.

Raymond Earl (Ray) Fosse, 51, former baseball player, born Marion, IL, Apr 4, 1947.

James Louis (Jim) Fregosi, 56, former baseball manager and player, born San Francisco, CA, Apr 4, 1942.

John Allen Hannah, 47, Pro Football Hall of Fame guard, born Canton, GA, Apr 4, 1951.

Dale Hawerchuk, 35, hockey player, born Toronto, Ontario, Canada, Apr 4, 1963.

Thomas Mitchell (Tommy) Herr, 42, former baseball player, born Lancaster, PA, Apr 4, 1956.

Allan Wade Houston, 27, basketball player, born Louisville, KY, Apr 4, 1971.

Arnold Malcolm ("Mickey") Owen, 82, former baseball player, born Nixa, MO, Apr 4, 1916.

APRIL 5 — SUNDAY
Day 95 — 270 Remaining

NCAA BASKETBALL CHAMPIONS THIS DATE
1993   North Carolina

DEHNERT, DUTCH: 100th BIRTH ANNIVERSARY. Apr 5, 1898. Henry ("Dutch") Dehnert, Basketball Hall of Fame center, born at New York, NY. Dehnert did not play basketball in either high school or college, but he was signed to play with the Original Celtics because of his experience with early New York teams. He helped make the Celtics one of the game's greatest teams and was personally responsible for inventing the pivot play. He would back into his defender, take a pass from a guard, pick the guard's defender and either give the ball off or roll and shoot. The Original Celtics were inducted into the Hall of Fame as a team in 1959. Dehnert followed as an individual player in 1968. Died at Far Rockaway, NY, Apr 20, 1979.

DINNEEN, BILL: BIRTH ANNIVERSARY. Apr 5, 1876. William Henry (Bill) Dinneen, baseball player and umpire born at Syracuse, NY. Dinneen pitched in the major leagues for 12 years and won three games in the 1903 World Series. In 1909, he broke in as an American League umpire less than two weeks after retiring as a player and enjoyed a 29-year career. He was known as

	S	M	T	W	T	F	S
April				1	2	3	4
1998	5	6	7	8	9	10	11
	12	13	14	15	16	17	18
	19	20	21	22	23	24	25
	26	27	28	29	30		

Two ways to simplify your life with two different Chase's Calendars . . .

Chase's offers you two complete day-by-day calendars that let you find out quickly what's going on—today . . . tomorrow . . . every day of the year—and to plan ahead. Now it's easier than ever to make sure you receive the newest edition of *Chase's Calendar of Events* and of *Chase's Sports Calendar of Events* as soon as they are available.

☆ Simply return one of the Pre-Publication Order Forms below. Your copy of both *Chase's 1999 Calendar of Events* and *Chase's 1999 Sports Calendar of Events* will be reserved immediately and shipped just as soon as they are off the press.

☆ To receive *Chase's* calendars automatically every year, use the Standing Order Authorization. There's no chance of missing out on *Chase's Calendar* and *Chase's Sports Calendar*—each year's new edition will be shipped and billed automatically. You'll be notified in advance of shipment. You may change or cancel your Standing Order at any time.

Both convenient order options carry our unconditional guarantee—you may return *Chase's* calendars for any reason within 10 days of receipt for a full refund. Why not order today and be sure of starting 1999 with *Chase's Calendar of Events* and *Chase's Sports Calendar of Events* at your fingertips!

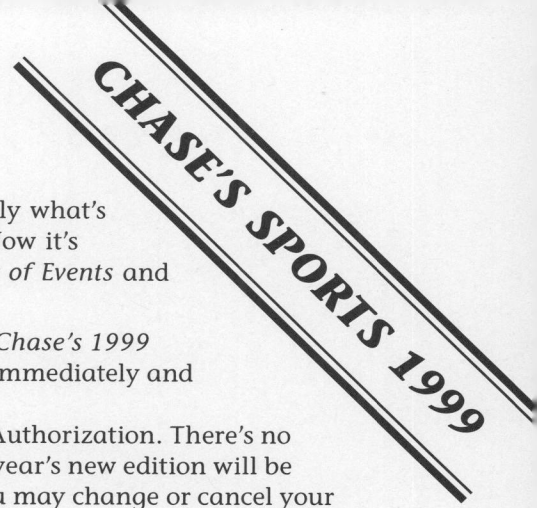

Mail to: NTC/Contemporary Publishing Co., Dept. C,
4255 W. Touhy Ave., Lincolnwood, IL 60646-1975

YES! Send me _____copies of
Chase's 1999 Calendar of Events at $59.95 each*
    Quantity Discounts:
    Deduct 10% per copy for 3–9 copies
    Deduct 20% per copy for 10 or more copies $ _____

YES! Send me _____copies of
Chase's 1999 Sports Calendar of Events at $29.95 each*
    Quantity Discounts:
    Deduct 10% per copy for 3–9 copies
    Deduct 20% per copy for 10 or more copies $ _____

Sales Tax:
    Add applicable tax in AL, CA, FL, IL, NC, NJ,
    NY, OH, PA, TX, WA $ _____
Shipping and Handling:
    Add $5.00 for first copy, $3.50 for each
    additional copy $ _____
☐ Check ☐ Money Order
    (payable to NTC/Contemporary Publishing Co.)   TOTAL $ _____
☐ VISA ☐ MasterCard ☐ AmEx ☐ Discover

Acct. _____ Exp. ____ /

X _____
Signature if charging to bank card

_____
Name (please print)

SHIP TO:

_____
Name

_____
Address

_____
Address

_____
City   State   Zip

STANDING ORDER/Authorization

To ensure that I receive each year's new annual edition(s) of ***Chase's*** calendars, please accept this Standing Order Authorization to ship me _____copies of each edition of ***Chase's Calendar of Events*** and _____ copies of each edition of ***Chase's Sports Calendar of Events***, beginning with the 1999 editions, and to bill me at the address shown above.

Signature _____
                            Date
Name _____
              (please print)
Phone (___) _____

*Prices subject to change without notice.   SP98

Mail to: NTC/Contemporary Publishing Co., Dept. C,
4255 W. Touhy Ave., Lincolnwood, IL 60646-1975

YES! Send me _____copies of
Chase's 1999 Calendar of Events at $59.95 each*
    Quantity Discounts:
    Deduct 10% per copy for 3–9 copies
    Deduct 20% per copy for 10 or more copies $ _____

YES! Send me _____copies of
Chase's 1999 Sports Calendar of Events at $29.95 each*
    Quantity Discounts:
    Deduct 10% per copy for 3–9 copies
    Deduct 20% per copy for 10 or more copies $ _____

Sales Tax:
    Add applicable tax in AL, CA, FL, IL, NC, NJ,
    NY, OH, PA, TX, WA $ _____
Shipping and Handling:
    Add $5.00 for first copy, $3.50 for each
    additional copy $ _____
☐ Check ☐ Money Order
    (payable to NTC/Contemporary Publishing Co.)   TOTAL $ _____
☐ VISA ☐ MasterCard ☐ AmEx ☐ Discover

Acct. _____ Exp. ____ /

X _____
Signature if charging to bank card

_____
Name (please print)

SHIP TO:

_____
Name

_____
Address

_____
Address

_____
City   State   Zip

STANDING ORDER/Authorization

To ensure that I receive each year's new annual edition(s) of ***Chase's*** calendars, please accept this Standing Order Authorization to ship me _____copies of each edition of ***Chase's Calendar of Events*** and _____ copies of each edition of ***Chase's Sports Calendar of Events***, beginning with the 1999 editions, and to bill me at the address shown above.

Signature _____
                            Date
Name _____
              (please print)
Phone (___) _____

*Prices subject to change without notice.   SP98

an excellent balls-and-strikes umpire with a short temper. Died at Syracuse, Jan 13, 1955.

GREAT WHITE HOPE: ANNIVERSARY. Apr 5, 1915. Towering Jess Willard beat Jack Johnson in the 26th round to win the heavyweight championship of the world in Havana, Cuba. Johnson, a black American who had held the title since defeating Tommy Burns in 1908, had been widely criticized for his flamboyant lifestyle. Willard, from Kansas, was touted as the "Great White Hope," whose goal it was to recapture the title for the "Caucasian race."

JULIAN, DOGGIE: BIRTH ANNIVERSARY. Apr 5, 1901. Alvin F. ("Doggie") Julian, Basketball Hall of Fame coach born at Reading, PA. Julian played several sports at Bucknell University and played minor league baseball before beginning his coaching career. He coached at Muhlenberg, Holy Cross and Dartmouth plus two years with the Boston Celtics. Inducted into the Hall of Fame in 1968. Died at Hanover, NH, July 28, 1967.

KAREEM BECOMES NBA'S LEADING SCORER: ANNIVERSARY. Apr 5, 1984. Los Angeles Lakers center Kareem Abdul-Jabbar hit a sky hook, his signature shot, with 8:53 left to play against the Utah Jazz to bring his regular-season career point total to 31,420, one more than record holder Wilt Chamberlain. Abdul-Jabbar retired after the 1988–89 season, having scored 38,387 points.

SENATORS OPEN LAST SEASON IN DC: ANNIVERSARY. Apr 5, 1971. The second incarnation of the Washington Senators opened their last season in the nation's capital, defeating the Oakland Athletics, 8–0. After the season, they moved to Arlington, TX, and became the Texas Rangers. The original Washington Senators became the Minnesota Twins in 1961.

US: DAYLIGHT SAVING TIME. Apr 5–Oct 25. Daylight Saving Time begins at 2 AM. The Uniform Time Act of 1966 (as amended in 1986 by Public Law 99–359), administered by the US Dept of Transportation, provides that Standard Time in each zone be advanced one hour from 2 AM on the first Sunday in April until 2 AM on the last Sunday in October (except where state legislatures provide exemption). Many use the popular rule "spring forward, fall back" to remember which way to turn their clocks. See also: "Standard Time" (Oct 25).

WARNER, POP: BIRTH ANNIVERSARY. Apr 5, 1871. Glenn Scobey ("Pop") Warner, football player and coach, born at Springville, NY. After playing several sports at Cornell, Warner began coaching football, most notably at the Carlisle Indian School where he coached Jim Thorpe. He coached three undefeated teams at the University of Pittsburgh and went to the Rose Bowl three times with Stanford. He ended a 44-year career at Temple. Died at Palo Alto, CA, Sept 7, 1954.

☆ ☆ ☆

BIRTHDAYS TODAY

Cris Howell Carpenter, 33, former baseball player, born St. Augustine, FL, Apr 5, 1965.
Ronald Lavern (Ron) Hansen, 60, former baseball player, born Oxford, NE, Apr 5, 1938.
Isaac Jason (Ike) Hilliard, 22, football player, born Patterson, LA, Apr 5, 1976.
Michael Moriarty, 56, actor (*Bang the Drum Slowly*), born Detroit, MI, Apr 5, 1942.
Renaldo Antonio (Rennie) Stennett, 47, former baseball player, born Colon, Panama, Apr 5, 1951.

APRIL 6 — MONDAY
Day 96 — 269 Remaining

NCAA BASKETBALL CHAMPIONS THIS DATE
1992   Duke

BIRTH OF MODERN OLYMPICS: ANNIVERSARY. Apr 6, 1896. The first modern Summer Olympic Games opened in Athens, Greece, with 311 competitors, all men, representing 13 nations. The very first race was the opening heat of the 100 meters, won by Francis Lane of the US. He finished fourth in the final won by another American, Thomas Burke. The first Olympics were funded by the sale of commemorative stamps and medals and by a gift of one million drachmas from George Averoff.

COCHRANE, MICKEY: 95th BIRTH ANNIVERSARY. Apr 6, 1903. Gordon Stanley ("Mickey") Cochrane, Baseball Hall of Fame catcher and manager born at Bridgewater, MA. Cochrane was an outstanding catcher for the Philadelphia Athletics, winning the American League MVP award in 1928, and the Detroit Tigers for whom he also managed. His skull was fractured in 1937, effectively ending his career. Inducted into the Hall of Fame in 1947. Died at Lake Forest, IL, June 28, 1962.

DESIGNATED HITTER INTRODUCED: 25th ANNIVERSARY. Apr 6, 1973. Following a rules change approved in January, Ron Blomberg of the New York Yankees became the first designated hitter in the American League in their Opening Day game against the Boston Red Sox. Blomberg came to bat for the first time with the bases loaded in the first inning and walked. The Red Sox won, 15–5. (See also Jan 11.)

FIRST KOREAN VICTORY: ANNIVERSARY. Apr 6, 1996. Pitching in relief, Chan Ho Park of the Los Angeles Dodgers became the first Korean to win a major league baseball game. Park pitched four scoreless innings against the Chicago Cubs, allowed three hits and struck out four. The Dodgers won, 3–1.

LOMBARDI, ERNIE: 90th BIRTH ANNIVERSARY. Apr 6, 1908. Ernest Natali (Ernie) Lombardi, Baseball Hall of Fame catcher born at Oakland, CA. Lombardi was extremely slow afoot, but he was a powerful hitter who caught for 17 years in the National League. He won the NL MVP award in 1938. Inducted into the Hall of Fame in 1986. Died at Santa Cruz, CA, Sept 26, 1977.

MAJOR LEAGUE SOCCER DEBUTS: ANNIVERSARY. Apr 6, 1996. Trying to capitalize on the momentum of the 1994 World Cup, held in the US, Major League Soccer, a new American professional league, made its debut. The San Jose Clash defeated DC United, 1–0, on a goal by Eric Wynalda. The game was played in San Jose before a capacity crowd of 31,683.

MARINERS DEBUT: ANNIVERSARY. Apr 6, 1977. The Seattle Mariners, an American League expansion team, made their regular season debut, losing to the California Angels, 7–0, at the Seattle Kingdome. Seattle's previous AL team, the Pilots, played only the 1969 season before moving to Milwaukee and becoming the Brewers. The Mariners won their first AL West division title in 1995.

CHASE'S SPORTSQUOTE OF THE DAY
"I've changed my mind about it. Instead of being bad, it stinks." —Sparky Anderson on the designated hitter

BIRTHDAYS TODAY

Rik Aalbert (Bert) Blyleven, 47, former baseball player, born Zeist, The Netherlands, Apr 6, 1951.

Bret Robert Boone, 29, baseball player, born El Cajon, CA, Apr 6, 1969.

Dave Cadigan, 33, former football player, born Needham, MA, Apr 6, 1965.

Gerald Diduck, 33, hockey player, born Edmonton, Alberta, Canada, Apr 6, 1965.

Ira Thomas (Tommy) Greene, 31, former baseball player, born Lumberton, NC, Apr 6, 1967.

Olaf Kolzig, 28, hockey player, born Johannesburg, South Africa, Apr 6, 1970.

John Ratzenberger, 51, actor ("Cheers"), born Bridgeport, CT, Apr 6, 1947.

Philip Raymond (Phil) Regan, 61, former baseball manager and player, born Ostego, MI, Apr 6, 1937.

Billy Dee Williams, 61, actor (*Brian's Song*), born New York, NY, Apr 6, 1937.

APRIL 7 — TUESDAY
Day 97 — 268 Remaining

NBA FINALS CHAMPIONS THIS DATE

1956   Philadelphia Warriors

BLUE JAYS DEBUT: ANNIVERSARY. Apr 7, 1977. The Toronto Blue Jays, an American League expansion team, played their first regular season game, beating the Chicago White Sox, 9–5, at Toronto's Exhibition Stadium. The Jays finished last in the AL East in 1977 with a record of 54–107. They won their first division title in 1985.

BREWERS DEBUT: ANNIVERSARY. Apr 7, 1970. Three weeks after moving hurriedly from Seattle, where they were called the Pilots, the Milwaukee Brewers made their American League debut, losing to the California Angels, 12–0, at Milwaukee County Stadium. The Brewers finished fourth in the AL West in 1970 with a record of 65–97. They won their first division pennant in 1982 but lost the World Series to the St. Louis Cardinals.

CAMP, WALTER: BIRTH ANNIVERSARY. Apr 7, 1859. Walter Chauncey Camp, college athlete, coach and administrator born at New Britain, CT. Camp played football and several other sports at Yale, but he gained prominence for helping to reshape the rules of rugby football into American football. Among his innovations were reducing the number of players on a side from 15 to 11, introducing the scrimmage, giving one team definite possession of the ball and proposing the downs system. He served as a volunteer coach at Yale and became a national figure as a promoter of football. He selected an All-American team from 1889 to 1925. Died at New York, NY, Mar 14, 1925.

LEONARD, BENNY: BIRTH ANNIVERSARY. Apr 7, 1896. Benny Leonard, boxer born at New York, NY. Leonard apprenticed as a printer but switched to fighting to survive in New York's rugged ethnic neighborhoods. He won the lightweight championship in 1917 and defended his title more than 80 times. He lost his wealth in the Great Crash. Died at New York, Apr 18, 1947.

MANAGER TED WILLIAMS: ANNIVERSARY. Apr 7, 1969. Ted Williams made his debut as a major league manager as the New York Yankees defeated his Washington Senators, 8–4, in Washington's RFK Stadium before 45,000. The Senators finished the year in fourth place in the AL West with a record of 86–76. Williams's managerial career lasted four seasons. His teams won 273 games and lost 364.

McGRAW, JOHN: 125th BIRTH ANNIVERSARY. Apr 7, 1873. John Joseph McGraw, Baseball Hall of Fame third baseman and manager born at Truxton, NY. Generally regarded as the best manager ever or close to it, McGraw ran the New York Giants with an iron hand from 1902 to 1932. A scrappy ballplayer with the Baltimore Orioles in the 1890s, McGraw demanded and got total effort from his players. Inducted into the Hall of Fame in 1937. Died at New Rochelle, NY, Feb 25, 1934.

SARAZEN'S DOUBLE EAGLE: ANNIVERSARY. Apr 7, 1935. In the final round of the second Masters Tournament, Gene Sarazen reached the par-5 15th hole four shots out of the lead. His drive left him 220 yards short of the cup. Sarazen hit his 4-wood and knocked the ball over the pond protecting the green, onto the fringe and into the hole for a double-eagle two. Sarazen tied Craig Wood at 282, six under par, and defeated him the next day in a playoff.

BIRTHDAYS TODAY

Ricardo (Ricky) Bones, 29, baseball player, born Salinas, Puerto Rico, Apr 7, 1969.

Robert George (Bobby) Del Greco, 65, former baseball player, born Pittsburgh, PA, Apr 7, 1933.

Robert Pershing (Bobby) Doerr, 80, Baseball Hall of Fame second baseman, born Los Angeles, CA, Apr 7, 1918.

Anthony Drew (Tony) Dorsett, 44, Heisman Trophy and Pro Football Hall of Fame running back, born Rochester, PA, Apr 7, 1954.

Theodore John (Ted) Nolan, 40, hockey coach and former player, born Sault Ste. Marie, Ontario, Canada, Apr 7, 1958.

Thomas Harold (Tom) Phoebus, 56, former baseball player, born Baltimore, MD, Apr 7, 1942.

Richard James (Ricky) Watters, 29, football player, born Harrisburg, PA, Apr 7, 1969.

APRIL 8 — WEDNESDAY
Day 98 — 267 Remaining

STANLEY CUP CHAMPIONS THIS DATE

1943   Detroit Red Wings

BELL, RICKY: BIRTH ANNIVERSARY. Apr 8, 1955. Ricky Lynn Bell, football player born at Houston, TX. Bell played football at the University of Southern California and then with the Tampa Bay Buccaneers and the San Diego Chargers. A running back, he excelled as a ball carrier and pass receiver until about 1980 when nagging injuries slowed him down considerably. He was eventually diagnosed with dermatomyositis, an inflammation of the skin and muscles, and cardiomyopathy, a muscular disease of the heart. Died at Inglewood, CA, Nov 28, 1994.

EXPOS DEBUT: ANNIVERSARY. Apr 8, 1969. The Montreal Expos, a National League expansion team, played their first regular season game, beating the New York Mets, 10–9, at NY's Shea Stadium. The Expos finished the year in sixth place in the NL East with a record of 52–110. They won their first division title in the strike-shortened 1994 season.

FIRST BLACK MANAGER: ANNIVERSARY. Apr 8, 1975. Frank Robinson made his debut as playing manager of the Cleveland Indians and the first black manager in the

April 1998	S	M	T	W	T	F	S
				1	2	3	4
	5	6	7	8	9	10	11
	12	13	14	15	16	17	18
	19	20	21	22	23	24	25
	26	27	28	29	30		

major leagues. Robinson hit a home run in his first at-bat as the Indians' designated hitter, and Cleveland beat the New York Yankees, 5–3.

FIRST INTERCOLLEGIATE RODEO: ANNIVERSARY.
Apr 8, 1939. The first Intercollegiate Rodeo was held at historic Godshall Ranch, Apple Valley, CA. The student cowboys and cowgirls, who hailed from California and Arizona colleges and universities, were assisted by world-champion professional cowboys including Harry Carey, Dick Foran, Curley Fletcher, Tex Ritter and Errol Flynn from Hollywood. Collegiate rodeos had been held since 1919 at Texas A&M University. College cowboys and cowgirls organized a national association in Texas in 1949 named the National Intercollegiate Rodeo Association, which continues today as the only national college rodeo organization. For info: Sylvia Mahoney, NIRA Alumni Natl Chair, Natl Intercollegiate Rodeo Assn, PO Box 1518, Vernon, TX 76385. Phone: (817) 552-5532.

HOME RUN RECORD SET BY HANK AARON: ANNIVERSARY.
Apr 8, 1974. Henry ("Hammerin' Hank") Aaron hit the 715th home run of his career, breaking the record set by Babe Ruth in 1935. Playing for the Atlanta Braves, Aaron broke the record in Atlanta in a game against the Los Angeles Dodgers. Al Downing was the pitcher who delivered the record-breaker. Aaron finished his career in 1976 with a total of 755 home runs. At the time of his retirement, Aaron also stood first in career RBIs, second in at-bats and runs scored and third in base hits.

JACOBS, HIRSCH: BIRTH ANNIVERSARY.
Apr 8, 1904. Hirsch Jacobs, thoroughbred trainer and owner born at New York, NY. Jacobs became a trainer in 1923 and was particularly adept at selecting horses in claiming races. He saddled 3,596 winners and earned $15,340,354. Died at Miami, FL, Feb 13, 1970.

KNIGHT, O. RAYMOND: BIRTH ANNIVERSARY.
Apr 8, 1872. O. Raymond Knight, rodeo promoter born at Payson, UT. In 1901, Knight's father, the Utah mining magnate Jesse Knight, founded the town of Raymond, Alberta, Canada. In 1902, young Raymond produced Canada's first rodeo, the "Raymond Stampede." He also built rodeo's first grandstand and first chute in 1903. He was known as the "Father of Canadian Rodeo." Died Feb 7, 1947. For info: John A. Bascom, Raymond Sports Hall of Fame, Max Court, Box 511, Raymond, Alberta, Canada T0K 2S0. Phone: (403) 752-3094.

OFF-TRACK BETTING BEGINS: ANNIVERSARY.
Apr 8, 1971. New York City changed the "Sport of Kings" irrevocably by opening the nation's first off-track betting system. Horseplayers were now able to patronize OTB parlors instead of going to the track to place their wagers.

TWO 300-GAME WINNERS: ANNIVERSARY.
Apr 8, 1987. For the first time in modern major league history, two 300-game winners pitched for the same team in the same game. Phil Niekro and Steve Carlton combined their pitching talents to lead the Cleveland Indians to a 14–3 victory over the Toronto Blue Jays. Niekro started for the Indians and earned his 312th career victory. Carlton pitched four shutout innings of relief.

☆   ☆   ☆

BIRTHDAYS TODAY

Gary Edmund Carter, 44, former baseball player, born Culver City, CA, Apr 8, 1954.
William D. Chase, 76, librarian and chronicler of contemporary civilization as cofounder and coeditor of *Chase's Annual Events*, born Lakeview, MI, Apr 8, 1922.
Mark Gregory Clayton, 37, former football player, born Indianapolis, IN, Apr 8, 1961.

John J. Havlicek, 58, Basketball Hall of Fame forward, born Lansing, OH, Apr 8, 1940.
James Augustus ("Catfish") Hunter, 52, Baseball Hall of Fame pitcher, born Hertford, NC, Apr 8, 1946.
Terry Porter, 35, basketball player, born Milwaukee, WI, Apr 8, 1963.

APRIL 9 — THURSDAY
Day 99 — 266 Remaining

STANLEY CUP CHAMPIONS THIS DATE

1932	Toronto Maple Leafs
1935	Montreal Maroons
1946	Montreal Canadiens

ASTRODOME OPENS: ANNIVERSARY.
Apr 9, 1965. Dubbed the "Eighth Wonder of the World," the Houston Astrodome opened with an exhibition game between the Houston Astros and the New York Yankees. President Lyndon Johnson attended the game, and Texas governor John Connally threw out the ceremonial first pitch. Mickey Mantle hit a home run, but the Astros prevailed, 2–1, in 12 innings.

CHANDLER SUSPENDS DUROCHER: ANNIVERSARY.
Apr 9, 1947. Baseball Commissioner A. B. ("Happy") Chandler suspended Brooklyn Dodgers manager Leo Durocher for one year because of Durocher's habit of consorting with unsavory characters, including gamblers. Burt Shotton took over for Durocher and managed the Dodgers to the National League pennant.

EBBETS FIELD OPENS: 85th ANNIVERSARY.
Apr 9, 1913. The Brooklyn Dodgers opened their new ballpark, Ebbets Field, but lost to the visiting Philadelphia Phillies, 1–0, before a crowd of 10,000. Ebbets Field was named for Charles Ebbets, the club's principal owner, and built at a cost of $750,000. It remained the Dodgers' home until they abandoned Brooklyn for Los Angeles after the 1957 season.

LAMBEAU, CURLY: 100th BIRTH ANNIVERSARY.
Apr 9, 1898. Earle Louis ("Curly") Lambeau, Pro Football Hall of Fame coach and executive born at Green Bay, WI. Lambeau played college football at Notre Dame and then founded the Green Bay Packers in 1919. He played for the Packers from their inception through 1927 and coached them from 1919 through 1949. Inducted as a charter member of the Hall of Fame in 1963. Died at Sturgeon Bay, WI, June 1, 1965.

ROBESON, PAUL: 100th BIRTH ANNIVERSARY. Apr 9, 1898. Paul Bustill Robeson, football player born at Princeton, NJ. Robeson excelled academically and athletically and was a singer and an actor besides. Only the third black man to attend Rutgers, he earned 12 athletic letters, was a two-time All-American and made Phi Beta Kappa. He played pro football to finance attendance at law school and then gave up the bar for a career in entertainment and political activism. Died at Philadelphia, PA, Jan 23, 1976.

ROCKIES DEBUT: ANNIVERSARY. Apr 9, 1993. The Colorado Rockies played their first official National League game, defeating the Montreal Expos, 11–4, behind first-inning home runs from leadoff hitter Eric Young and Charlie Hayes. 80,227 fans packed Denver's Mile High Stadium to set a major league Opening Day attendance record, surpassing the 78,672 who saw the San Francisco Giants and the Los Angeles Dodgers open the 1958 season at the Los Angeles Coliseum.

THE MASTERS. Apr 9–12. Augusta National G.C., Augusta, GA. The first of professional golf's four major championships. For info: Augusta Natl G.C., Augusta, GA 30904.

BIRTHDAYS TODAY

Helen Alfredsson, 33, golfer, born Goteborg, Sweden, Apr 9, 1965.

Paul Joseph Arizin, 70, Basketball Hall of Fame forward, born Philadelphia, PA, Apr 9, 1928.

Severiano (Seve) Ballesteros, 41, golfer, born Pedrena, Spain, Apr 9, 1957.

Anthony Michael (Mike) Brumley, 35, former baseball player, born Oklahoma City, OK, Apr 9, 1963.

Nathan (Nate) Colbert, 52, former baseball player, born St. Louis, MO, Apr 9, 1946.

Jose Alberto Guzman, 35, former baseball player, born Santa Isabel, Puerto Rico, Apr 9, 1963.

Graeme John Lloyd, 31, baseball player, born Geelong, Victoria, Australia, Apr 9, 1967.

William Harold (Hal) Morris, 33, baseball player, born Fort Rucker, AL, Apr 9, 1965.

Dennis Quaid, 44, actor (*Everybody's All-American*), born Houston, TX, Apr 9, 1954.

Rick Tocchet, 34, hockey player, born Scarborough, Ontario, Canada, Apr 9, 1964.

APRIL 10 — FRIDAY

Day 100 — 265 Remaining

NBA FINALS CHAMPIONS THIS DATE

| 1953 | Minneapolis Lakers |
| 1955 | Syracuse Nationals |

AFRMA RAT AND MOUSE DISPLAY. Apr 10–12 (or 17–19). America's Family Pet Expo, Fairplex, Pomona, CA. American Fancy Rat and Mouse Assn show exhibits rats and mice of "fancy" species that make good pets.

CANNON, JIMMY: BIRTH ANNIVERSARY. Apr 10, 1909. Jimmy Cannon, sportswriter born at New York, NY.

April *1998*	S	M	T	W	T	F	S
				1	2	3	4
	5	6	7	8	9	10	11
	12	13	14	15	16	17	18
	19	20	21	22	23	24	25
	26	27	28	29	30		

Cannon covered the Lindbergh kidnapping case and then switched to sports, eventually being ranked as New York City's leading sportswriter. He specialized in baseball, boxing and horse racing and was particularly critical of baseball and other sports for their racism. Died at New York, Dec 5, 1973.

COLT .45S DEBUT: ANNIVERSARY. Apr 10, 1962. The Houston Colt .45s, a National League expansion team, hosted the first major league game ever played in Texas, beating the Chicago Cubs, 11–2, before 25,000. The Colt .45s finished the year in eighth place with a record of 64–96. Renamed the Astros in 1965, they won their first division title in 1980.

CONNORS, CHUCK : BIRTH ANNIVERSARY. Apr 10, 1921. Kevin Joseph ("Chuck") Connors, actor and baseball player born at New York, NY. He played professional basketball and baseball before becoming an actor. "The Rifleman" of television fame, Chuck Connors played that role from 1958 to 1963. His portrayal of a slave owner in the miniseries *Roots* won him an Emmy nomination. Connors acted in more than 45 films and appeared on many TV series and specials. Died at Los Angeles, CA, Nov 10, 1992.

ENGLAND: DEVIZES TO WESTMINSTER INTERNATIONAL CANOE RACE. Apr 10–13. Starts from Wharf Car Park, Wharf St, Devizes, Wiltshire. Canoes race along 125 miles of the Kennet and Avon canals and the River Thames, ending at County Hall Steps, Westminster Bridge Rd, London. Est attendance: 6,000. For info: Paul Owen, 14 Milldown Ave, Goring on Thames, Reading, Berkshire, England RG8 0AS. Phone: (44) (149) 187-2042.

FIRST FOREIGNER TO WIN MASTERS: ANNIVERSARY. Apr 10, 1961. South African Gary Player shot an 8-under-par 280 to become the first foreign player to win the Masters. Player defeated Arnold Palmer and Charley Coe by one stroke. He won the tournament again in 1974 and 1978.

PGA FOUNDED: ANNIVERSARY. Apr 10, 1916. Following an organizational luncheon meeting in January, 82 charter members approved a constitution to create the Professional Golfers' Association of America. The members agreed to promote interest in the game of golf, elevate the standards of the golf professional's vocation, protect their mutual interests and establish a national professional championship.

YOUNGS, ROSS: BIRTH ANNIVERSARY. Apr 10, 1897. Ross Middlebrook Youngs, Baseball Hall of Fame outfielder born at Shiner, TX. Youngs played the outfield for the New York Giants in the years after World War I. He was exonerated of charges made in 1924 that he had taken money from gamblers to fix games. Inducted into the Hall of Fame in 1972. Died at San Antonio, TX, Oct 22, 1927.

STANLEY CUP CHAMPIONS THIS DATE

| 1934 | Chicago Black Hawks |
| 1956 | Montreal Canadiens |

BIRTHDAYS TODAY

Melvin Cornell (Mel) Blount, 50, Pro Football Hall of Fame cornerback, born Vidalia, GA, Apr 10, 1948.

Enrico Ciccone, 28, hockey player, born Montreal, Quebec, Canada, Apr 10, 1970.

Michael (Mike) Devereaux, 35, baseball player, born Casper, WY, Apr 10, 1963.

Marvin Freeman, 35, baseball player, born Chicago, IL, Apr 10, 1963.

George Kenneth (Ken) Griffey, Sr, 48, former baseball player, born Donora, PA, Apr 10, 1950.

David Halberstam, 64, author (*October 64, The Summer of '49, The Breaks of the Game, The Amateurs*), born New York, NY, Apr 10, 1934.

Frank Strong Lary, 68, former baseball player, born Northport, AL, Apr 10, 1930.

John Earl Madden, 62, broadcaster and former football coach, born Austin, MN, Apr 10, 1936.

Joe Don Meredith, 60, former broadcaster and football player, born Mt Vernon, TX, Apr 10, 1938.

Robert Jose (Bob) Watson, 52, baseball executive and former player, born Los Angeles, CA, Apr 10, 1946.

APRIL 11 — SATURDAY
Day 101 — 264 Remaining

NBA FINALS CHAMPIONS THIS DATE
1961   Boston Celtics

ANGELS DEBUT: ANNIVERSARY. Apr 11, 1961. The Los Angeles Angels, an American League expansion team, played their first regular season game, beating the Orioles in Baltimore, 7–2. The Angels finished the 1961 season in eighth place with a record of 70–91. Renamed the California Angels in 1966, they won their first division title in 1979.

EASTER BEACH RUN. Apr 11. Daytona Beach, FL. The 30th annual beach run on "the world's most famous beach" includes a 4-mile run for 28 age divisions and a 2-mile run for youth 11 years old and younger. Est attendance: 2,000. For info: Easter Beach Run, Daytona Beach Leisure Services Dept, PO Box 2451, Daytona Beach, FL 32115-2451. Phone: (904) 258-3169. Fax: (904) 239-6550.

GAITHER, JAKE: 95th BIRTH ANNIVERSARY. Apr 11, 1903. Alonzo Smith ("Jake") Gaither, athlete, football coach and athletic director born at Dayton, TN. Gaither was famed as the coach of Florida A&M's football team which he guided to a record of 203–36–4 from 1945 to 1960. He won six national black college championships and produced 36 All-Americans and 42 NFL players. Died at Tallahassee, FL, Feb 18, 1994.

GOALIE SCORES IN PLAY-OFFS: ANNIVERSARY. Apr 11, 1989. Goalie Ron Hextall of the Philadelphia Flyers scored an empty-net goal against the Washington Capitals as the Flyers won, 8–5. For Hextall it was the second goal of his career and the first scored by any goalie in a Stanley Cup play-off game.

METS DEBUT: ANNIVERSARY. Apr 11, 1962. The New York Mets, a National League expansion team, played their first regular season game, losing, 11–4, to the Cardinals in St. Louis. The Mets lost eight more games before winning one, and they finished the year in 10th place with a record of 40–120. The Mets won their first division title in 1969 and went on to stun the Baltimore Orioles in the World Series.

MOON PHASE: FULL MOON. Apr 11. Moon enters Full Moon phase at 6:23 PM, EDT.

NICKLAUS WINS FIRST MASTERS: 35th ANNIVERSARY. Apr 11, 1963. Jack Nicklaus, 23 years old, shot an even-par 72 in the final round to finish at 2-under-par 286 and win the Masters by one stroke over Tony Lema. Nicklaus's green jacket was his first of a record six, with his other victories coming in 1965, 1966, 1972, 1975 and 1986.

Jack Nicklaus

PILOTS DEBUT: ANNIVERSARY. Apr 11, 1969. The Seattle Pilots, an American League expansion team, played their first regular season game, defeating the Chicago White Sox, 7–0, at Seattle's Sick's Stadium. The Pilots finished the year in sixth place in the AL West and left Seattle in 1970 to become the Milwaukee Brewers.

76ERS END CELTICS' SKEIN: ANNIVERSARY. Apr 11, 1967. The Philadelphia 76ers defeated the Boston Celtics in Game 5 of the Eastern Conference Finals, 140–116, to advance to the NBA Finals. Philadelphia thus ended Boston's eight-year streak of NBA titles and went on to beat the San Francisco Warriors for the championship, four games to two. The 76ers had won 68 games in the regular season and in 1980 were voted the greatest team in NBA history.

STRAWBERRY HILL RACES. Apr 11. Fairgrounds on Strawberry Hill, Richmond, VA. Annual steeplechase featuring a week of festivities leading up to the event. Elegant prerace tent party and tailgate competition. $73,000 in purses. Sponsored by Atlantic Rural Exposition, Inc. Benefits the Richmond Symphony. Est attendance: 25,000. For info: Sue Mullins, Equine Dir, Strawberry Hill Races, PO Box 26805, Richmond, VA 23261. Phone: (804) 228-3238. Fax: (804) 228-3252. Email: equine@strawberryhill.com.

WHOOPING CRANE RUN. Apr 11. Fulton Navigation Park, Rockport, TX. 10th annual. 2-mile walk, 5K and 10K runs, plus ½K run for kids seven and under. Est attendance: 55. For info: Rockport Fulton YMCA, 104 N Church St, Rockport, TX 78382. Phone: (512) 790-9622. Fax: (512) 790-9696.

STANLEY CUP CHAMPIONS THIS DATE
1936   Detroit Red Wings

BIRTHDAYS TODAY

Shane William Collins, 29, former football player, born Roundup, MT, Apr 11, 1969.
James Tolbert (Jim) Hearn, 77, former baseball player, born Atlanta, GA, Apr 11, 1921.
Trevor Linden, 28, hockey player, born Medicine Hat, Alberta, Canada, Apr 11, 1970.
Isidro Pedroza (Sid) Monge, 47, former baseball player, born Agua Prieta, Mexico, Apr 11, 1951.
Bret William Saberhagen, 34, baseball player, born Chicago Heights, IL, Apr 11, 1964.
Walter Richard (Wally) Whitehurst, 34, baseball player, born Shreveport, LA, Apr 11, 1964.

APRIL 12 — SUNDAY

Day 102 — 263 Remaining

NBA FINALS CHAMPIONS THIS DATE
1954   Minneapolis Lakers
1958   St. Louis Hawks

BRAVES' FIRST GAME IN ATLANTA: ANNIVERSARY. Apr 12, 1966. The Atlanta Braves brought major league baseball to the South but lost their regular season opener, 3–2, to the Pittsburgh Pirates in 12 innings. The Braves finished the season in fifth place with a record of 85–77. They won their first division pennant in 1969.

EASTER SUNDAY. Apr 12. Commemorates the Resurrection of Christ. Most joyous festival of the Christian year. The date of Easter, a movable feast, is derived from the lunar calendar (as prescribed by the Council of Nicaea, AD 325): the first Sunday following the first full moon on or after the vernal equinox (Mar 20)–always between Mar 22 and Apr 25. Many other dates in the Christian year are derived from the date of Easter.

JOSS, ADDIE: BIRTH ANNIVERSARY. Apr 12, 1880. Adrian ("Addie") Joss, Baseball Hall of Fame pitcher born at Juneau, WI. Joss pitched a one-hitter in his major league debut and fashioned a spectacular career before being felled by tubercular meningitis. He threw two no-hitters and won 160 games in just nine years. Inducted into the Hall of Fame in 1978. Died at Toledo, OH, Apr 14, 1911.

April *1998*	S	M	T	W	T	F	S
				1	2	3	4
	5	6	7	8	9	10	11
	12	13	14	15	16	17	18
	19	20	21	22	23	24	25
	26	27	28	29	30		

KC ATHLETICS DEBUT: ANNIVERSARY. Apr 12, 1955. The Kansas City Athletics, transplanted from Philadelphia, opened their first season in their new home by defeating the Detroit Tigers, 6–2, at Municipal Stadium. The A's finished the year in sixth place with a record of 63–91. They never won a pennant in Kansas City and moved to Oakland after the 1967 season.

LAPCHICK, JOE: BIRTH ANNIVERSARY. Apr 12, 1900. Joseph Bohomiel (Joe) Lapchick, Basketball Hall of Fame player and coach born at Yonkers, NY. Lapchick played basketball for pay from an early age. In 1923 he joined the Original Celtics, one of the greatest pro teams of any era. The Celtics revolutionized the game with Lapchick as their great center. He began coaching at St. John's University in 1937, left for the New York Knicks in 1947 and returned to St. John's in 1957. The Celtics were inducted into the Hall of Fame in 1959, and Lapchick followed as an individual in 1966. Died at New York, Aug 10, 1970.

LAU, CHARLIE: 65th BIRTH ANNIVERSARY. Apr 12, 1933. Charles Richard (Charlie) Lau, baseball player and coach born at Romulus, MI. Lau was a major league catcher who gained fame as one of the game's most influential batting instructors. He taught his pupils, including George Brett, to hit line drives to the entire field. Died at Key Colony Beach, FL, Mar 18, 1984.

RED WINGS WIN RECORD GAME: ANNIVERSARY. Apr 12, 1996. The Detroit Red Wings set a National Hockey League record by winning their 61st regular season game, 5–3, over the Chicago Black Hawks. The previous record was held by the 1976–77 Montreal Canadiens. Detroit finished the season with 62 wins, 13 losses and 7 ties.

STANLEY CUP CHAMPIONS THIS DATE
1939   Chicago Black Hawks
1941   Boston Bruins

BIRTHDAYS TODAY

Donna Andrews, 31, golfer, born Lynchburg, VA, Apr 12, 1967.
John August (Johnny) Antonelli, 68, former baseball player, born Rochester, NY, Apr 12, 1930.
Adam Graves, 30, hockey player, born Toronto, Ontario, Canada, Apr 12, 1968.
Roman Hamrlik, 24, hockey player, born Gottwaldov, Czechoslovakia, Apr 12, 1974.
Michael Andrew (Mike) Macfarlane, 34, baseball player, born Stockton, CA, Apr 12, 1964.
Doug MacLean, 44, hockey coach, born Summerside, PEI, Canada, Apr 12, 1954.

APRIL 13 — MONDAY

Day 103 — 262 Remaining

NBA FINALS CHAMPIONS THIS DATE
1949   Minneapolis Lakers
1957   Boston Celtics

AARON'S FIRST GAME: ANNIVERSARY. Apr 13, 1954. Henry Aaron played left field for the Milwaukee Braves in his major league debut. The Braves lost to the Cincinnati Reds, 9–8, and Aaron went 0-for-5.

BUTTS, ALFRED: BIRTH ANNIVERSARY. Apr 13, 1899. Alfred M. Butts, inventor of Scrabble born at Poughkeepsie, NY. Butts was a jobless architect in the Depression when he invented the board game Scrabble. The game was just a fad for Butts's friends until a Macy's executive saw the game being played at a resort in 1952, and the world's largest store began carrying it. Manufacturing of the game was turned over to Selchow & Righter when 35 workers were producing 6,000 sets a week. Butts received three cents per set for years. He said, "One-third went to taxes. I gave one-third away, and the other third enabled me to have an enjoyable life." Died at Rhinebeck, NY, Apr 4, 1993.

DEVANEY, BOB: BIRTH ANNIVERSARY. Apr 13, 1915. Robert S. (Bob) Devaney, football coach and athletic administrator born at Saginaw, MI. Devaney was head coach at the University of Nebraska from 1962 through 1972, taking over a program that had enjoyed only three winning seasons in 21 years. He compiled a record of 101–20–2 and won national championships in 1970 and 1971. The latter team, with Heisman Trophy winner Johnny Rodgers and Outland Trophy winner Rich Glover on it, is often called the greatest college football team of all time. After the 1972 season, Devaney handed the coaching reins to Tom Osborne and concentrated on being Nebraska's athletic director, a position he held until January 1993. Died at Lincoln, NE, May 9, 1997.

ENGLAND: HALLATON BOTTLE KICKING. Apr 13. Hallaton, Leicestershire. Perhaps the origin of soccer in England could be found in this ancient custom of kicking bottles around. Annually, on Easter Monday.

FEDERAL LEAGUE OPENS: ANNIVERSARY. Apr 13, 1914. The Federal League opened its first season in Baltimore with the Terrapins defeating the Buffalo Buffeds, 3–2, before 27,140 fans. The Federal League accused the American and National Leagues of monopolistic practices and lasted only two seasons.

FIRST BASEBALL STRIKE ENDS: ANNIVERSARY. Apr 13, 1972. Major league baseball players and owners agreed on a settlement of the first strike by the Players Association in which owners added an additional $500,000 to the players' pension fund. The work stoppage had begun Apr 5 when the season opener was canceled.

LONG, GERMANY: BIRTH ANNIVERSARY. Apr 13, 1866. Herman C. ("Germany") Long, baseball player born at Chicago, IL. Long was rated one of the best shortstops of the 19th century. He was a superb fielder who hit consistently well and showed some power. Died at Denver, CO, Sept 17, 1909.

MILWAUKEE BRAVES DEBUT: 45th ANNIVERSARY. Apr 13, 1953. The Milwaukee Braves, having moved from Boston after playing there every year since 1871, opened the season by losing to the Reds in Cincinnati, 2–0. The Braves were the first major league team to shift cities since the 1902 Baltimore Orioles became the 1903 New York Highlanders (later the Yankees).

NICKLAUS WINS SIXTH MASTERS: ANNIVERSARY. Apr 13, 1986. Jack Nicklaus, at age 46, won his sixth Masters and became the oldest player to win the tournament. Nicklaus shot 279, nine under par, to defeat Greg Norman by one stroke.

ROSE GETS 4,000th HIT: ANNIVERSARY. Apr 13, 1984. Pete Rose of the Cincinnati Reds got the 4,000th hit of his major league career, a double off pitcher Jerry Koosman of the Philadelphia Phillies. Rose finished his career with 4,256 hits, the major league record.

TIGER WOODS WINS MASTERS: ANNIVERSARY. Apr 13, 1997. Tiger Woods, 21, became the youngest golfer to win the Masters and did so with a record score of 270, 18 under par and 12 shots better than Tom Kite, who finished second. Woods broke the record of 271 held by Jack Nicklaus (1965) and Raymond Floyd (1976). He broke the margin-of-victory record by three shots. He was almost two years younger than Seve Ballesteros, who won the 1980 Masters at 23 years, 14 days of age.

WHITE HOUSE EASTER EGG ROLL. Apr 13. Traditionally held at executive mansion's south lawn on Easter Monday. Custom said to have started at Capitol grounds about 1810. Transferred to White House lawn in 1870s.

STANLEY CUP CHAMPIONS THIS DATE	
1927	Ottawa Senators
1933	New York Rangers
1940	New York Rangers
1944	Montreal Canadiens

BIRTHDAYS TODAY

Dana Bruce Barros, 31, basketball player, born Boston, MA, Apr 13, 1967.
Wesley Polk (Wes) Chamberlain, 32, former baseball player, born Chicago, IL, Apr 13, 1966.
Mark Edward Leiter, 35, baseball player, born Joliet, IL, Apr 13, 1963.
Davis Milton Love, III, 34, golfer, born Charlotte, NC, Apr 13, 1964.
John Douglas (Doug) Strange, 34, baseball player, born Greenville, SC, Apr 13, 1964.

APRIL 14 — TUESDAY
Day 104 — 261 Remaining

CHASE'S SPORTSQUOTE OF THE DAY
"He plays a game with which I am not familiar." —Bobby Jones on Jack Nicklaus

BASEBALL OUTSIDE THE US: ANNIVERSARY. Apr 14, 1969. The first major league baseball game played outside the US occurred as the Montreal Expos hosted the St. Louis Cardinals at Jarry Park. The Expos, an expansion team, won, 8–7.

DE VICENZO SIGNS INCORRECT CARD: 30th ANNIVERSARY. Apr 14, 1968. After concluding the final round of the Masters with a magnificent 66, Argentinian Roberto de Vicenzo signed an incorrect scorecard that mistakenly recorded a par four on the 17th hole instead of a birdie three. Under the rules of golf, de Vicenzo was penalized one stroke, and Bob Goalby declared the winner. Said de Vicenzo, "What a stupid I am."

OPENING DAY BARRAGE: ANNIVERSARY. Apr 14, 1925. The Cleveland Indians defeated the St. Louis Browns, 21–14, in their season opener. Cleveland scored 12 runs in the eighth inning, thanks to five errors by the Browns.

RUTH PLAYS FIRST GAME FOR YANKEES: ANNIVERSARY. Apr 14, 1920. After being sold by the Boston Red Sox, Babe Ruth played his first game for the New York Yankees. He got two singles against the Philadelphia Athletics but made an error in the outfield, giving the A's two runs and a 3–1 victory.

STANLEY CUP CHAMPIONS THIS DATE	
1928	New York Rangers
1931	Montreal Canadiens
1948	Toronto Maple Leafs
1955	Detroit Red Wings
1960	Montreal Canadiens

BIRTHDAYS TODAY

Bradley David (Brad) Ausmus, 29, baseball player, born New Haven, CT, Apr 14, 1969.

Steven Thomas (Steve) Avery, 28, baseball player, born Trenton, MI, Apr 14, 1970.

William Stanley (Stan) Humphries, 33, football player, born Shreveport, LA, Apr 14, 1965.

David Christopher Justice, 32, baseball player, born Cincinnati, OH, Apr 14, 1966.

Gregory Alan (Greg) Maddux, 32, baseball player, born San Angelo, TX, Apr 14, 1966.

Meg Mallon, 35, golfer, born Natick, MA, Apr 14, 1963.

Brad Lee Pennington, 29, baseball player, born Salem, IN, Apr 14, 1969.

Peter Edward (Pete) Rose, 57, former baseball manager and player, born Cincinnati, OH, Apr 14, 1941.

APRIL 15 — WEDNESDAY

Day 105 — 260 Remaining

STANLEY CUP CHAMPIONS THIS DATE

| 1937 | Detroit Red Wings |
| 1952 | Detroit Red Wings |

BASEBALL COMES TO CALIFORNIA: 40th ANNIVERSARY. Apr 15, 1958. Major league baseball came to California as the San Francisco Giants, transplanted from New York, opened the season against the Los Angeles Dodgers, formerly of Brooklyn, at San Francisco's Seals Stadium. The Giants shut out their rivals, 8–0.

CREIGHTON, JIM: BIRTH ANNIVERSARY. Apr 15, 1841. James (Jim) Creighton, baseball player born at Brooklyn, NY. Baseball's first prominent pitcher, Creighton stretched the rules of the day, which called for underhand pitching with a straight arm and stiff wrist, and put a little snap in his deliveries. His aggressive style revolutionized what had been a recreational game. Died at Brooklyn, Oct 18, 1862.

DE PAOLO, PETER: 100th BIRTH ANNIVERSARY. Apr 15, 1898. Peter De Paolo, auto racer born at Roseland, NJ. De Paolo started his racing career as riding mechanic for his uncle, Ralph De Palma. He began driving in 1922 and won the Indianapolis 500 and the national championship three years later. After retirement, he became an unofficial ambassador for Indy, returning for the race every year and singing its theme song, "Back Home Again in Indiana," before the 1971 race. Died at Costa Mesa, CA, Nov 26, 1980.

INTERCOLLEGIATE BOWLING CHAMPIONSHIPS. Apr 15–19. Saginaw Valley State College, University Center, MI, (Men) and University of Nebraska-Lincoln, Lincoln, NE (Women). Top 16 men's and 16 women's teams qualify for the event through a variety of competitions throughout the year. Est attendance: 600. For info: Bowling, Inc, 5301 S 76th St, Greendale, WI 53129-1192. Phone: (414) 421-4700. Fax: (414) 421-9188.

JEFFRIES, JIM: BIRTH ANNIVERSARY. Apr 15, 1875. James Jackson (Jim) Jeffries, boxer born at Carroll, OH. Jeffries captured the world's heavyweight championship on June 9, 1899, defeating Bob Fitzsimmons in only his 13th professional fight. He defended the crown several

	S	M	T	W	T	F	S
April				1	2	3	4
1998	5	6	7	8	9	10	11
	12	13	14	15	16	17	18
	19	20	21	22	23	24	25
	26	27	28	29	30		

times and retired in 1905, coming out of retirement in 1910 in an unsuccessful attempt to wrest the title from Jack Johnson. Died at Burbank, CA, Mar 3, 1953.

ROBINSON'S NUMBER 42 RETIRED: ANNIVERSARY. Apr 15, 1997. In ceremonies marking the 50th anniversary of the debut of Jackie Robinson in the major leagues, Bud Selig, chairman of baseball's Executive Committee, announced that Robinson's uniform number 42 would be retired by all major league teams. Players then wearing 42 were allowed to continue to do so, but no team would ever assign 42 again.

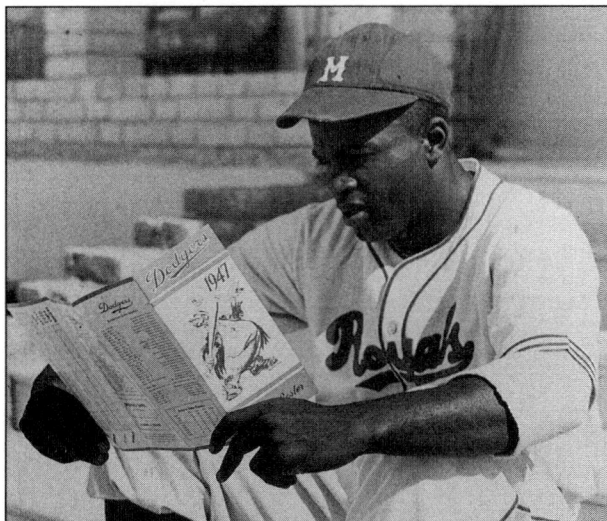

ROBINSON BREAKS THE COLOR LINE: ANNIVERSARY. Apr 15, 1947. Jackie Robinson became the first black American to play in the major leagues in the 20th century when he made his debut for the Brooklyn Dodgers against the Boston Braves. Robinson went 0-for-3 but scored the deciding run as the Dodgers prevailed, 5–3.

TAFT THROWS OUT FIRST BALL: ANNIVERSARY. Apr 15, 1910. William Howard Taft began the tradition of the president throwing out a ceremonial first pitch when he did the honors before the Washington Senators' opening game against the Philadelphia Athletics. Washington won the game, 3–0, as Walter Johnson pitched a one-hitter.

BIRTHDAYS TODAY

Evelyn Ashford, 41, Olympic gold medal track athlete, born Shreveport, LA, Apr 15, 1957.

Lonas Edgar (Ed) Bailey, 67, former baseball player, born Strawberry Plains, TX, Apr 15, 1931.

Jeromy Neal Burnitz, 29, baseball player, born Westminster, CA, Apr 15, 1969.

Michael Jerome Cooper, 42, former basketball player, born Los Angeles, CA, Apr 15, 1956.

William Henry (Willie) Davis, 58, former baseball player, born Mineral Springs, AR, Apr 15, 1940.

Todd Elik, 32, hockey player, born Brampton, Ontario, Canada, Apr 15, 1966.

APRIL 16 — THURSDAY

Day 106 — 259 Remaining

STANLEY CUP CHAMPIONS THIS DATE

| 1939 | Boston Bruins |
| 1949 | Toronto Maple Leafs |

1953	Montreal Canadiens
1954	Detroit Red Wings
1957	Montreal Canadiens
1961	Chicago Black Hawks

AVERILL'S DEBUT HOME RUN: ANNIVERSARY. Apr 16, 1929. Earl Averill of the Cleveland Indians became the first player in American League history to hit a home run in his first major league plate appearance. The Indians were playing the Detroit Tigers, and the homer came against pitcher Earl Whitehill. Cleveland won, 5–4, in 11 innings.

BULLS WIN 70 GAMES: ANNIVERSARY. Apr 16, 1996. The Chicago Bulls became the first NBA team to win 70 games in the regular season by defeating the Milwaukee Bucks, 86–80. After this game, Chicago's record stood at 70–9. The Bulls finished the year at 72–10 and won their fourth NBA title in six years.

FORT LAUDERDALE SPRING BOAT SHOW. April 16–19. Greater Fort Lauderdale/Broward County Convention Center. Everything from small boats to mega-yachts to boating equipment. For info: Greater Fort Lauderdale Conv/Visitors Bureau, 1850 Eller Dr, Ste 303, Fort Lauderdale, FL 33316. Phone: (954) 765-4466.

LEONARD, DUTCH: BIRTH ANNIVERSARY. Apr 16, 1892. Hubert Benjamin ("Dutch") Leonard, baseball player born at Birmingham, OH. Leonard pitched in the major leagues from 1913 through 1925. In 1926, he accused Ty Cobb and Tris Speaker of fixing a game in 1919, but Commissioner Kenesaw Landis exonerated the two. Died at Fresno, CA, July 11, 1952.

MCI CLASSIC. Apr 16–19. Harbor Town G.L., Hilton Head Island, SC. A PGA Tour tournament, formerly known as the Heritage Classic. Pretournament festivities include a parade enacting all the pomp and ceremony of ancient golfing traditions, a booming cannon and bagpipe music. Est attendance: 125,000. For info: PGA Tour, 112 TPC Blvd, Ponte Vedra Beach, FL 32082. Phone: (904) 285-3700.

MURPHY, ISAAC: BIRTH ANNIVERSARY. Apr 16, 1861. Isaac Murphy, jockey born at Frankfort, KY. Murphy enjoyed great success in the 1880s and won the Kentucky Derby in 1884, 1890 and 1891. He rode Salvator to victory in a famous match race against Tenny in 1890. His career was cut short by the arrival of racial segregation in racing and by alcoholism. Died at Lexington, KY, Feb 12, 1896.

NCAA MEN'S GYMNASTICS CHAMPIONSHIPS. Apr 16–18. Site TBA. For info: NCAA, 6201 College Blvd, Overland Park, KS 66211. Phone: (913) 339-1906.

NCAA WOMEN'S GYMNASTICS CHAMPIONSHIPS. Apr 16–18. University of California-Los Angeles, Los Angeles, CA. For info: NCAA, 6201 College Blvd, Overland Park, KS 66211. Phone: (913) 339-1906.

OPENING DAY NO-HITTER: ANNIVERSARY. Apr 16, 1940. Bob Feller of the Cleveland Indians pitched the only Opening Day no-hitter in major league history, beating the Chicago White Sox, 1–0. This was the first of three no-hitters for Feller, the others coming in 1946 and 1951.

PGA SENIORS' CHAMPIONSHIP. Apr 16–19. PGA National Golf Club, Palm Beach Gardens, FL. 59th competition for the oldest major championship in senior golf. Conducted by the Professional Golfers' Association of America. For info: Jamie Roggers, Admin Media Relations, PGA, Box 109601, Palm Beach Gardens, FL 33410-9601. Phone: (561) 624-8400. Fax: (561) 624-8448. WWW: http://www.pgaonline.com

SEC MEN'S TENNIS CHAMPIONSHIPS. Apr 16–19. Auburn University, Auburn, AL. For info: Southeastern Conference, 2201 Civic Center Blvd, Birmingham, AL 35203-1103. Phone: (205) 458-3010. Fax: (205) 458-3030. Email: cbloom@sec.org. WWW: http://www.secsports.org

SEC WOMEN'S TENNIS CHAMPIONSHIPS. Apr 16–19. University of Kentucky, Lexington, KY. For info: Southeastern Conference, 2201 Civic Center Blvd, Birmingham, AL 35203-1103. Phone: (205) 458-3010. Fax: (205) 458-3030. Email: cbloom@sec.org. WWW: http://www.secsports.org

WANER, PAUL: BIRTH ANNIVERSARY. Apr 16, 1903. Paul Glee Waner, Baseball Hall of Fame outfielder born at Harrah, OK. Waner was "Big Poison" to his brother Lloyd's "Little Poison." He played 20 years in the majors, mostly with the Pittsburgh Pirates, and won three National League batting titles. Inducted into the Hall of Fame in 1952. Died at Sarasota, FL, Aug 29, 1965.

WGN TELEVISES BASEBALL: ANNIVERSARY. Apr 16, 1940. WGN-TV in Chicago televised a baseball game for the first time. Jack Brickhouse did the play-by-play as the White Sox defeated the Cubs, 4–1, in an exhibition game at Wrigley Field.

BIRTHDAYS TODAY

Kareem Abdul-Jabbar (born Lewis Ferdinand Alcindor, Jr), 51, Basketball Hall of Fame center, born New York, NY, Apr 16, 1947.
Bruce Douglas Bochy, 43, baseball manager and former player, born Landes De Bussac, France, Apr 16, 1955.
Steven Charles (Steve) Emtman, 28, football player, born Spokane, WA, Apr 16, 1970.
Richard ("Night Train") Lane, 70, Pro Football Hall of Fame defensive back, born Austin, TX, Apr 16, 1928.
James Reynold (Jim) Lonborg, 56, former baseball player, born Santa Maria, CA, Apr 16, 1942.
Richard John (Rich) Rollins, 60, former baseball player, born Mt Pleasant, PA, Apr 16, 1938.

☆　☆　☆

APRIL 17 — FRIDAY

Day 107 — 258 Remaining

SPORTSCHASER OF THE DAY

Baseball innovator Alexander Cartwright was born in New York. Where did he die?

ACC MEN'S LACROSSE CHAMPIONSHIP. Apr 17–19. University of Virginia, Charlottesville, VA. For info: Atlantic Coast Conference, PO Drawer ACC, Greensboro, NC 27419-6999. Phone: (910) 854-8787. Fax: (910) 854-8797.

ACC MEN'S AND WOMEN'S OUTDOOR TRACK AND FIELD CHAMPIONSHIPS. Apr 17–18. Disney Complex, Orlando, FL. For info: Atlantic Coast Conference, PO Drawer ACC, Greensboro, NC 27419-6999. Phone: (910) 854-8787. Fax: (910) 854-8797.

ACC MEN'S GOLF CHAMPIONSHIPS. Apr 17–19. Old North State Club, Uwharrie Point, NC. For info: Atlantic Coast Conference, PO Drawer ACC, Greensboro, NC 27419-6999. Phone: (910) 854-8787. Fax: (910) 854-8797.

ACC WOMEN'S GOLF CHAMPIONSHIPS. Apr 17–19. Grandover East Course, Greensboro, NC. For info: Atlantic Coast Conference, PO Drawer ACC, Greensboro, NC 27419-6999. Phone: (910) 854-8787. Fax: (910) 854-8797.

ANSON, CAP: BIRTH ANNIVERSARY. Apr 17, 1852. Adrian Constantine ("Cap") Anson, Baseball Hall of Fame player and manager born at Marshalltown, IA. Anson played professional baseball from 1871 through 1897 and is considered one of the game's greatest first basemen. As a manager, he piloted the Chicago White Stockings (today's Cubs) to five National League pennants and a .575 winning percentage. Inducted into the Hall of Fame in 1939. Died at Chicago, IL, Apr 18, 1922.

CARTWRIGHT, ALEXANDER: BIRTH ANNIVERSARY. Apr 17, 1820. Alexander Joy Cartwright, Jr, baseball innovator born at New York, NY. Cartwright helped to organize the Knickerbocker Base Ball Club in 1845 and wrote the game's first rule book. He joined the California gold rush and eventually wound up in Hawaii, spreading the gospel of baseball all the way. Died at Honolulu, HI, July 12, 1892.

ERVING HITS 30,000-POINT MARK: ANNIVERSARY. Apr 17, 1987. Julius Erving of the Philadelphia 76ers scored 38 points to join Wilt Chamberlain and Kareem Abdul-Jabbar in the NBA's 30,000-point club.

FIESTA SAN ANTONIO. Apr 17–26. San Antonio, TX. Ten days of culture, heritage, beauty and remembrance. Parades, carnivals, sports, fireworks, music, ethnic feasts, art exhibits, dances–more than 150 events. This colorful fiesta originated in 1891 with the Battle of Flowers parade honoring the memory of Texas heroes who fought against Gen Santa Anna for Texan independence at the Alamo and San Jacinto. Est attendance: 3,500,000. For info: Mktg Coord, Fiesta San Antonio Commission, Inc, 122 Heiman, San Antonio, TX 78205. Phone: (210) 227-5191. Fax: (210) 227-1139. Email: fiesta@texas.net. WWW: http://texas.net/fiesta

	S	M	T	W	T	F	S
April				1	2	3	4
1998	5	6	7	8	9	10	11
	12	13	14	15	16	17	18
	19	20	21	22	23	24	25
	26	27	28	29	30		

HOOSIER HORSE FAIR EXPO. Apr 17–19. Indiana State Fairground Event Center, Indianapolis, IN. All-breed gathering and informative exposition. Est attendance: 55,000. For info: Deb Endres, Indiana Horse Council, 225 Southeast St, Ste 738, Indianapolis, IN 46202. Phone: (317) 692-7115.

KENTUCKY DERBY FESTIVAL. Apr 17–May 3. Louisville, KY. Civic celebration as Louisville warms up for the derby. About 70 events, two-thirds of which are free to the public. Est attendance: 1,500,000. For info: Kentucky Derby Festival, Inc, 1001 S Third St, Louisville, KY 40203. Phone: (502) 584-6383. Fax: (502) 589-4674. Email: kyderbyf@iglou.com. WWW: http://www.kdf.org

MANTLE'S FIRST GAME: ANNIVERSARY. Apr 17, 1951. Mickey Mantle of the New York Yankees made his major league debut and went 1-for-4 as the Yankees defeated the Boston Red Sox, 5–0.

MIKE SCHMIDT HITS FOUR HOME RUNS: ANNIVERSARY. Apr 17, 1976. Mike Schmidt of the Philadelphia Phillies became the first National League player since Bobby Lowe in 1894 to hit four home runs in consecutive at-bats in the same game. Schmidt's feat came against the Chicago Cubs in an 18–16, 10-inning Phillies win. Schmidt connected twice off Rick Reuschel, once off Rick's brother Phil and once off Darold Knowles. He added a single and totaled eight RBIs as Philadelphia came back from a 13–2 deficit.

NATIONAL LEAGUE PLAYS ON SUNDAY: ANNIVERSARY. Apr 17, 1892. The National League ended its ban on Sunday baseball as the Cincinnati Reds defeated the St. Louis Browns (later the Cardinals), 5–1. From its start in 1876, the NL had prohibited Sunday play. The rival American Association (1882–91) allowed games on Sunday, and when the two leagues merged, the ban was lifted.

POLO: CARIBBEAN CUP. Apr 17–26 (tentative). Wellington, FL. For info: Palm Beach Polo, Inc, 13420 South Shore Blvd, West Palm Beach, FL 33414. Phone: (561) 793-1440. Fax: (561) 790-3872.

SEC WOMEN'S GOLF CHAMPIONSHIPS. Apr 17–19. University of Alabama, Tuscaloosa, AL. For info: Southeastern Conference, 2201 Civic Center Blvd, Birmingham, AL 35203-1103. Phone: (205) 458-3010. Fax: (205) 458-3030. Email: cbloom@sec.org. WWW: http://www.secsports.org

BIRTHDAYS TODAY

Kenneth (Ken) Daneyko, 34, hockey player, born Windsor, Ontario, Canada, Apr 17, 1964.

Norman Julius ("Boomer") Esiason, 37, football player, born West Islip, NY, Apr 17, 1961.

Joseph (Joe) Foss, 83, first commissioner of the American Football League, born Sioux Falls, SD, Apr 17, 1915.

Marquis Deon Grissom, 31, baseball player, born Atlanta, GA, Apr 17, 1967.

Solomon Joseph (Solly) Hemus, 75, former baseball player and manager, born Phoenix, AZ, Apr 17, 1923.

Dennis Martin (Denny) Walling, 44, former baseball player, born Neptune, NJ, Apr 17, 1954.

APRIL 18 — SATURDAY

Day 108 — 257 Remaining

NBA FINALS CHAMPIONS THIS DATE
1962   Boston Celtics

ACC WOMEN'S LACROSSE CHAMPIONSHIP. Apr 18–19. University of Virginia, Charlottesville, VA. For info: Atlantic Coast Conference, PO Drawer ACC, Greensboro, NC 27419-6999. Phone: (910) 854-8787. Fax: (910) 854-8797.

BLOCK HOUSE STEEPLECHASE RACES. Apr 18. Foothills Equestrian Nature Center, Tryon, NC. 52nd annual running of the Block House Steeplechase. Est attendance: 15,000. For info: Mitzi Lindsey, Tryon Riding & Hunt Club, PO Box 1095, Tryon, NC 28782. Phone: (800) 438-3681. Fax: (704) 859-5598.

CANADA: JUNIOR HANDBALL PROVINCIALS. Apr 18–20. Regina, Saskatchewan. Junior provincial team handball. For info: Sask Sport, 1870 Lorne St, Regina, Sask, Canada S4P 2L7. Phone: (306) 780-9300. Fax: (306) 781-6021.

COMEBACK FROM 0–3: ANNIVERSARY. Apr 18, 1942. The Toronto Maple Leafs completed the greatest comeback in Stanley Cup playoff history by defeating the Detroit Red Wings, 3–1, in Game 7 of the finals. The Leafs were down three games to none before they evened the series with 4–3, 9–3 and 3–0 victories.

CRAWFORD, SAM: BIRTH ANNIVERSARY. Apr 18, 1880. Samuel Earl (Sam) Crawford, Baseball Hall of Fame outfielder born at Wahoo, NE. Crawford, known as "Wahoo Sam," played major league baseball for 19 years, mostly with the Detroit Tigers. He compiled a career batting average of .309 and hit 312 career triples, a record that still stands. Inducted into the Hall of Fame in 1957. Died at Hollywood, CA, June 15, 1968.

THE HOUSE THAT RUTH BUILT: 75th ANNIVERSARY. Apr 18, 1923. More than 74,000 fans attended opening day festivities as the New York Yankees inaugurated their new stadium in the Bronx. Babe Ruth christened the park with a game-winning three-run homer into the right-field bleachers. In his coverage of the game for the *New York Evening Telegram* sportswriter Fred Lieb described Yankee Stadium as "The House That Ruth Built," and the name stuck.

KENDUSKEAG STREAM CANOE RACE. Apr 18. Bangor, ME. 16.5-mile white-water open canoe race. Est attendance: 1,500. For info: Bangor Parks and Recreation Dept, 647 Main St, Bangor, ME 04401. Phone: (207) 947-1018. Fax: (207) 947-1605.

LEWIS, DUFFY: 110th BIRTH ANNIVERSARY. Apr 18, 1888. George Edward ("Duffy") Lewis, baseball player born at San Francisco, CA. Lewis formed one-third of one of baseball's best outfields, the other two members of which, Tris Speaker and Harry Hooper, were inducted into the Baseball Hall of Fame. Lewis hit .284 and played left field superbly. Died at Salem, NH, June 17, 1979.

McGRAW MANAGERIAL DEBUT: ANNIVERSARY. Apr 18, 1899. John McGraw, 26, made his debut as manager of the National League Baltimore Orioles as they played and beat the New York Giants, the team McGraw would later manage for 30 seasons.

NFL DRAFT. Apr 18–19. New York, NY. Teams in the National Football League engage in their annual selection of college players. The draft has been an NFL institution since 1936 when University of Chicago quarterback and Heisman Trophy winner Jay Berwanger, the first player ever chosen, declined to play for the Philadelphia Eagles and went into business instead.

ONE-ARMED OUTFIELDER: ANNIVERSARY. Apr 18, 1945. One-armed Pete Gray made his major league debut for the St. Louis Browns. Gray got one hit in four times at bat as the Browns beat the Detroit Tigers, 7–1. Gray hit .218 in 77 games.

SCHMIDT HITS 500th HOME RUN: ANNIVERSARY. Apr 18, 1987. The Philadelphia Phillies' Mike Schmidt hit the 500th home run of his career with two outs in the ninth inning of a game against the Pittsburgh Pirates. The Phillies rallied to win, 8–6. Schmidt finished his career with 548 homers, seventh on the all-time list.

SEC MEN'S GOLF CHAMPIONSHIP. Apr 18–20. University of Georgia, Athens, GA. For info: Southeastern Conference, 2201 Civic Center Blvd, Birmingham, AL 35203-1103. Phone: (205) 458-3010. Fax: (205) 458-3030. Email: cbloom@sec.org. WWW: http://www.secsports.org

WINE AND ROSES FESTIVAL. Apr 18. Bryan, TX. This event features the 15th annual Texas artists' competition. The winning painting becomes the focal point for next year's private-reserve wine label. Team grape-stomping competition, dozens of food and craft booths, a petting zoo, vineyard hayrides and tours, classic and antique cars plus a variety of live music performances. Est attendance: 6,000. For info: Steve Wiley, Mktg Dir, Messina Hof Wine Cellars, 4545 Old Reliance Rd, Bryan, TX 77808. Phone: (409) 778-1729. Fax: (409) 778-1729.

WORLD CHAMPIONSHIP GOLD PANNING COMPETITION. Apr 18–19. Consolidated Gold Mine, Dahlonega, GA. Competitions for the quickest gold panner. Annually, the third weekend in April. For info: Kate Brehe, Dahlonega-Lumpkin County Chamber of Commerce, 101 S Park St, Dahlonega, GA 30533. Phone: (706) 864-3711. Fax: (706) 864-7917. Email: dahlonegacoc@stc.net.

STANLEY CUP CHAMPIONS THIS DATE	
1942	Toronto Maple Leafs
1959	Montreal Canadiens
1963	Toronto Maple Leafs

BIRTHDAYS TODAY

Stephen Robert (Steve) Blass, 56, former baseball player, born Canaan, CT, Apr 18, 1942.

Geoff Bodine, 49, auto racer, born Chemung, NY, Apr 18, 1949.

Rico Joseph Brogna, 28, baseball player, born Turner Falls, MA, Apr 18, 1970.

James Michael (Jim) Eisenreich, 39, baseball player, born St. Cloud, MN, Apr 18, 1959.

Ed Garvey, 58, lawyer, union official, labor negotiator, born Burlington, WI, Apr 18, 1940.

Valeri Kamensky, 32, hockey player, born Voskresensk, USSR, Apr 18, 1966.

Wilber Buddyhia Marshall, 36, former football player, born Titusville, FL, Apr 18, 1962.

Dennis Lee Rasmussen, 39, former baseball player, born Los Angeles, CA, Apr 18, 1959.

William Layton (Willie) Roaf, 28, football player, born Pine Bluff, AR, Apr 18, 1970.

APRIL 19 — SUNDAY
Day 109 — 256 Remaining

STANLEY CUP CHAMPIONS THIS DATE

1947   Toronto Maple Leafs

BIG BROTHERS/BIG SISTERS APPRECIATION WEEK.
Apr 19–25. To honor the men and women who serve on a ONE-TO-ONE® basis as Big Brother and Big Sister volunteers who provide much-needed guidance and support to at-risk children, primarily from one-parent families, in need of an adult mentor and role model. For info: Mktg/Communications, Big Brothers/Big Sisters of America, 230 N 13th St, Philadelphia, PA 19107. Phone: (215) 567-7000. Fax: (215) 567-0394.

DODGERS PLAY IN NEW JERSEY: ANNIVERSARY. Apr 19, 1956. The Brooklyn Dodgers defeated the Philadelphia Phillies, 5–4, in 10 innings in a game played at Roosevelt Stadium in Jersey City. The game marked the first major league game played in NJ.

FIRST BOSTON MARATHON: ANNIVERSARY. Apr 19, 1897. John J. McDermott won the first running of the Boston Marathon with a time of 2:55:10.

JIMMY STEWART RELAY MARATHON. Apr 19. Griffith Park, Los Angeles, CA. Team relay with five people, each running 5.2 miles. Funds raised go to benefit the St. John's Child and Family Development Center, 16th annual marathon. Est attendance: 20,000. For info: Jimmy Stewart Relay Marathon, St. John's Health Ctr, 1328 22nd St, Santa Monica, CA 90404. Phone: (310) 829-8968. Fax: (310) 315-6167.

LONGEST GAME IN HISTORY: ANNIVERSARY. Apr 19, 1981. The Pawtucket Red Sox hosted the Rochester Red Wings in an International League game that turned into the longest contest in professional baseball history. It began on a cold Saturday night, Apr 18, and was suspended at 4:07 AM on Apr 19 with the teams tied, 2–2, after having played 32 innings. When the game resumed on June 23, Pawtucket pushed across the winning run in the bottom of the 33rd inning after only 18 minutes of play.

MOON PHASE: LAST QUARTER. Apr 19. Moon enters Last Quarter phase at 3:53 PM, EDT.

RODMAN THE REBOUNDER: ANNIVERSARY. Apr 19, 1992. Dennis Rodman of the Detroit Pistons won the first rebounding title of his NBA career. He snared 1,530 rebounds, 42.1% of Detroit's total, for an average of 18.7 per game.

WALTERS, BUCKY: BIRTH ANNIVERSARY. Apr 19, 1909. William Henry ("Bucky") Walters, baseball player and manager born at Philadelphia, PA. Walters won 20 games three times and led the Cincinnati Reds to the National League pennant in 1939 and 1940. In the 1940 World Series, he won two games. Died at Abington, PA, Apr 20, 1991.

WORLD COW CHIP–THROWING CHAMPIONSHIP® CONTEST. Apr 19. Beaver, OK. 28th annual. A highly specialized organic sporting event which draws dung flingers from around the world. A special division of this competition is held for politicians, who are known to be highly practiced in this area. Annually, the final day of

Cimarron Territory Celebration (Apr 11–19 in 1998). Est attendance: 1,500. For info: Rita Marshall, Secy, Beaver County Chamber of Commerce, PO Box 878, Beaver, OK 73932-0878. Phone and Fax: (405) 625-4726. Email: cowchipcapital@juno.com. WWW: http://nobleone@brightok.net/panhandle~beaver

---

BIRTHDAYS TODAY

Keith Jerome Jackson, 33, former football player, born Little Rock, AR, Apr 19, 1965.
Scott Andrew Kamieniecki, 34, baseball player, born Mt Clemens, MI, Apr 19, 1964.
George John ("Whitey") Kurowski, 80, former baseball player, born Reading, PA, Apr 19, 1918.
Brent Danem Mayne, 30, baseball player, born Loma Linda, CA, Apr 19, 1968.
Spike Dee Owen, 37, former baseball player, born Cleburne, TX, Apr 19, 1961.
Frank John Viola, Jr, 38, former baseball player, born Hempstead, NY, Apr 19, 1960.

APRIL 20 — MONDAY
Day 110 — 255 Remaining

STANLEY CUP CHAMPIONS THIS DATE

1958   Montreal Canadiens

AGGANIS, HARRY: BIRTH ANNIVERSARY. Apr 20, 1929. Harry Agganis, baseball player born at Lynn, MA. Agganis was a local favorite, playing football and baseball at Boston University and for the Red Sox before contracting leukemia. Died at Cambridge, MA, June 27, 1955.

BANCROFT, DAVE: BIRTH ANNIVERSARY. Apr 20, 1891. David James (Dave) Bancroft, Baseball Hall of Fame shortstop born at Sioux City, IA. Bancroft was a superior fielder for four National League teams (1915–29). He managed the Boston Braves and several minor league teams. Inducted into the Hall of Fame in 1971. Died at Superior, WI, Oct 9, 1972.

BOSTON MARATHON–102nd RUNNING. Apr 20. Boston, MA. The marathon begins in the rural New England town of Hopkinton, winds through eight cities and towns and finishes near downtown Boston. 1998 will be the 102nd year of this historic running event. 15,000 participants. Est attendance: 2,000,000. For info: Boston Athletic Assn, Boston Marathon, PO Box 1998, Hopkinton, MA 01748. Phone: (508) 435-6905. Email: mile27@star.net. WWW: http://www.bostonmarathon.org

CUBS OPEN IN WEEGHMAN PARK: ANNIVERSARY. Apr 20, 1916. The Chicago Cubs inherited Weeghman Park from the Chicago Whales of the defunct Federal League and used it as their home field starting with a game played on this date against the Cincinnati Reds. The Cubs won, 7–6, in 11 innings. Weeghman Park was renamed Wrigley Field in 1926.

FENWAY PARK OPENS: ANNIVERSARY. Apr 20, 1912. The Boston Red Sox opened their new ballpark, Fenway Park, with a 7–6 win over the New York Yankees in 11 innings.

NAVIN FIELD OPENS: ANNIVERSARY. Apr 20, 1912. The Detroit Tigers opened Navin Field (later Briggs Stadium and then Tiger Stadium) by defeating the Cleveland Naps (later the Indians), 6–5, in 11 innings.

PAC-10 WOMEN'S GOLF CHAMPIONSHIPS. Apr 20–22. University of Southern California, Los Angeles, CA. For

	S	M	T	W	T	F	S
April				1	2	3	4
1998	5	6	7	8	9	10	11
	12	13	14	15	16	17	18
	19	20	21	22	23	24	25
	26	27	28	29	30		

info: PAC-10 Conference, 800 S Broadway, Ste 400, Walnut Creek, CA 94596. Phone: (510) 932-4411. Fax: (510) 932-4601.

PATRIOT'S DAY IN MASSACHUSETTS AND MAINE. Apr 20. Commemorates Battles of Lexington and Concord, 1775. Annually, the third Monday in April. The Boston Marathon is held on this day each year.

TED WILLIAMS'S DEBUT: ANNIVERSARY. Apr 20, 1939. Ted Williams made his major league debut for the Boston Red Sox, getting one double in four at-bats, as the Sox lost to the New York Yankees, 2–0.

WORLD'S BIGGEST FISH FRY. Apr 20–25. Paris, TN. Huge festival with parades, arts and crafts, midway, antique car show, rodeo, catfish races and more than 13,000 lbs. of catfish with all the trimmings. 45th annual. Events held the last full week of April every year. Est attendance: 100,000. For info: World's Biggest Fish Fry, PO Box 444, Paris, TN 38242. Phone: (901) 644-1143. Fax: (901) 642-3431.

CHASE'S SPORTSQUOTE OF THE DAY

"A man has to have goals—for a day, for a lifetime—and that was mine, to have people say, 'There goes Ted Williams, the greatest hitter who ever lived.'"—Ted Williams

---

BIRTHDAYS TODAY

John Michael Carney, 34, football player, born Hartford, CT, Apr 20, 1964.
James Condia (Jimmy) Jones, 34, former baseball player, born Dallas, TX, Apr 20, 1964.
Donald Arthur (Don) Mattingly, 37, former baseball player, born Evansville, IN, Apr 20, 1961.
Ernest (Ernie) Stautner, 73, Pro Football Hall of Fame defensive tackle, born Prinzing-by-Cham, Bavaria, Germany, Apr 20, 1925.
Milton Edward (Milt) Wilcox, 48, former baseball player, born Honolulu, HI, Apr 20, 1950.

APRIL 21 — TUESDAY

Day 111 — 254 Remaining

NBA FINALS CHAMPIONS THIS DATE

1948	Baltimore Bullets
1951	Rochester Royals

FIRST RAINOUT IN LA: ANNIVERSARY. Apr 21, 1967. The scheduled game between the St. Louis Cardinals and the Dodgers in Los Angeles was rained out. This was the first Dodgers home game to be postponed since the team moved to Los Angeles in 1958.

LEAGUE PARK OPENS: ANNIVERSARY. Apr 21, 1915. The Cleveland Indians opened their new ballpark, League Park, and lost to the Detroit Tigers, 5–0, before a crowd of 19,867. League Park, with its short right field fence, remained the Indians' home until the 1940s when they moved their games to Municipal Stadium.

McCARTHY, JOE: BIRTH ANNIVERSARY. Apr 21, 1887. Joseph Vincent (Joe) McCarthy, Baseball Hall of Fame manager born at Philadelphia, PA. McCarthy managed the Chicago Cubs (1926–30), the New York Yankees (1931–46) and the Boston Red Sox (1948–50). He was a strict disciplinarian whose career winning percentage was .614, the highest in major league history. Inducted into the Hall of Fame in 1957. Died at Buffalo, NY, Jan 13, 1978.

OWEN, STEVE: 100th BIRTH ANNIVERSARY. Apr 21, 1898. Stephen Joseph (Steve) Owen, Pro Football Hall of Fame player, coach and executive born at Cleo Springs, OK. Owens played football at Phillip University and wrestled professionally under an assumed name to preserve his amateur standing. He played tackle for the New York Giants and is ranked as one of the game's greatest defensive players. He coached the Giants for 23 years (1931–53) and won two NFL titles. Regarded as an innovator, he devised the umbrella defense, forerunner of the 4–3, to stop the Cleveland Browns' passing attack. Inducted into the Pro Football Hall of Fame in 1966. Died at New York, NY, May 17, 1964.

ROSIE RUIZ FRAUD: ANNIVERSARY. Apr 21, 1980. Rosie Ruiz was the first woman to cross the finish line in the Boston Marathon, but she was soon disqualified after officials discovered that she had not run the entire course.

WILKINSON, J. L.: DEATH ANNIVERSARY. Apr 21, 1964. James L. Wilkinson, baseball executive born at Perry, IA, 1874. Wilkinson was a key owner in the Negro Leagues. He assembled the Kansas City Monarchs in 1920 and kept them going through 1948. Starting in 1930, the Monarchs traveled with their own portable lights to play night games. Died at Kansas City, MO.

STANLEY CUP CHAMPIONS THIS DATE

1951	Toronto Maple Leafs

BIRTHDAYS TODAY

Ed Belfour, 33, hockey player, born Carmen, Manitoba, Canada, Apr 21, 1965.
Alonza Benjamin (Al) Bumbry, 51, former baseball player, born Fredericksburg, VA, Apr 21, 1947.
Kenneth Gene (Ken) Caminiti, 35, baseball player, born Hanford, CA, Apr 21, 1963.
Richard Larry (Dick) Green, 57, former baseball player, born Sioux City, IA, Apr 21, 1941.
Brendan Malone, 56, former basketball coach, born New York, NY, Apr 21, 1942.
Jesse Russell Orosco, 41, baseball player, born Santa Barbara, CA, Apr 21, 1957.
Gary Charles Peters, 61, former baseball player, born Grove City, PA, Apr 21, 1937.

APRIL 22 — WEDNESDAY

Day 112 — 253 Remaining

NBA FINALS CHAMPIONS THIS DATE

1947	Philadelphia Warriors

BABE'S PITCHING DEBUT: ANNIVERSARY. Apr 22, 1914. Babe Ruth made his professional pitching debut, playing for the minor league Baltimore Orioles in his hometown. Allowing just six hits and contributing two singles himself, Ruth shut out the Buffalo Bisons, 6–0.

DOUTHIT, TAYLOR: BIRTH ANNIVERSARY. Apr 22, 1901. Taylor Lee Douthit, baseball player born at Little Rock, AR. Douthit was a solid outfielder in the 1920s, helping the St. Louis Cardinals to the National League pennant in 1926, 1928 and 1930. Died at Fremont, CA, May 28, 1986.

FIRST NATIONAL LEAGUE GAME: ANNIVERSARY.
Apr 22, 1876. In the first National League game ever played, the Boston Red Caps (later the Braves) defeated the hometown Philadelphia Athletics, 6–5. Jim O'Rourke got the first hit, and Joseph Borden, playing under the name of Josephs, was the winning pitcher.

KGBX TYPEWRITER TOSS. Apr 22. KGBX /FM Radio, Springfield, MO. Participating secretaries toss a typewriter from a lift truck nearly 50 feet in the air. The typewriter landing closest to the bull's-eye wins an array of prizes. Definitely a "smashing" success! Annually, Secretaries Day. 9th annual toss. Est attendance: 250. For info: Pamela Cooper, KGBX Radio, 1856 S Glenstone, Springfield, MO 65807. Phone: (417) 890-5555. Fax: (417) 890-5050. WWW: http://www.kgbx.com

NBA EXPANDS BY FOUR: ANNIVERSARY. Apr 22, 1987. The NBA awarded expansion franchises to Charlotte, Miami, Minnesota and Orlando at a cost of $32.5 million per team. The Charlotte Hornets and the Miami Heat began play in the 1988–89 season. The Minnesota Timberwolves and the Orlando Magic followed a year later.

RACKING HORSE SPRING CELEBRATION. Apr 22–25. Decatur, AL. Racking horses from throughout the country are shown each night, culminating with the selection of award winners. Est attendance: 25,000. For info: Jacklyn Bailey, Decatur Conv and Visitors Bureau, 719 Sixth Ave SE, PO Box 2349, Decatur, AL 35602. Phone: (205) 350-2028 or (800) 524-6181.

RUNNING OF THE RODENTS. Apr 22. Louisville, KY. 26th annual. To celebrate the prefinals "Rat Race" that occurs each year, to develop community spirit and to unoffically kick off the Kentucky Derby festivities. Est attendance: 250. For info: Emily Whalin, Spalding University, 851 S Fourth St, Louisville, KY 40203. Phone: (502) 585-7140 or (800) 896-8941. Fax: (502) 585-7158. Email: pr@spalding13.win.net. WWW: http://www.spalding.edu

STANLEY CUP CHAMPIONS THIS DATE
1945	Toronto Maple Leafs
1962	Toronto Maple Leafs

BIRTHDAYS TODAY

Deane Beman, 60, golfer and former golf executive, born Washington, DC, Apr 22, 1938.

Vernell Eufaye ("Bimbo") Coles, 30, basketball player, born Covington, VA, Apr 22, 1968.

Terry Jon Francona, 39, baseball manager and former player, born Aberdeen, SD, Apr 22, 1959.

Jeff Hostetler, 37, football player, born Hollsopple, PA, Apr 22, 1961.

James Edward (Jimmy) Key, 37, baseball player, born Huntsville, AL, Apr 22, 1961.

Michael Robert (Mickey) Morandini, 32, baseball player, born Kittanning, PA, Apr 22, 1966.

Peter Zezel, 33, hockey player, born Toronto, Ontario, Canada, Apr 22, 1965.

April 1998	S	M	T	W	T	F	S
				1	2	3	4
	5	6	7	8	9	10	11
	12	13	14	15	16	17	18
	19	20	21	22	23	24	25
	26	27	28	29	30		

APRIL 23 — THURSDAY
Day 113 — 252 Remaining

NBA FINALS CHAMPIONS THIS DATE
1950	Minneapolis Lakers

AARON'S FIRST HOMER: ANNIVERSARY. Apr 23, 1954. Henry Aaron of the Milwaukee Braves hit the first home run of his major league career. It came against Vic Raschi of the St. Louis Cardinals in the Braves' 7–5 victory. Aaron went on to hit 754 more homers, more than any other player.

ACC MEN'S AND WOMEN'S TENNIS CHAMPIONSHIPS. Apr 23–26. Site TBA. For info: Atlantic Coast Conference, PO Drawer ACC, Greensboro, NC 27419-6999. Phone: (910) 854-8787. Fax: (910) 854-8797.

ACC SOFTBALL TOURNAMENT. Apr 23–25. Florida State University, Tallahassee, FL. For info: Atlantic Coast Conference, PO Drawer ACC, Greensboro, NC 27419-6999. Phone: (910) 854-8787. Fax: (910) 854-8797.

BIG EAST MEN'S AND WOMEN'S TENNIS CHAMPIONSHIPS. Apr 23–26. University of Miami, Miami, FL. For info: Big East Conference, 56 Exchange Terrace, Providence, RI 02903. Phone: (401) 453-0660. Fax: (401) 751-8540.

BIG TWELVE MEN'S AND WOMEN'S TENNIS CHAMPIONSHIPS. Apr 23–26. University of Nebraska, Lincoln, NE. For info: Big Twelve Conference, 2201 Stemmons Freeway, 28th Floor, Dallas, TX 75207. Phone: (214) 742-1212. Fax: (214) 742-2046.

BOTTOMLEY, JIM: BIRTH ANNIVERSARY. Apr 23, 1900. James LeRoy (Jim) Bottomley, Baseball Hall of Fame first baseman born at Oglesby, IL. Bottomley played 16 seasons with the St. Louis Cardinals, Cincinnati Reds and St. Louis Browns. On Sept 16, 1924, he drove in 12 runs in one game to set a major league record. Inducted into the Hall of Fame in 1974. Died at St. Louis, MO, Dec 11, 1959.

PAC-10 MEN'S AND WOMEN'S TENNIS CHAMPIONSHIPS. Apr 23–26. Ojai, CA. For info: PAC-10 Conference, 800 S Broadway, Ste 400, Walnut Creek, CA 94596. Phone: (510) 932-4411. Fax: (510) 932-4601.

SODEN, ARTHUR: 155th BIRTH ANNIVERSARY. Apr 23, 1843. Arthur Henry Soden, baseball executive born at Framingham, MA. Soden was one of the original owners of the Boston Red Caps, the team that is now the Atlanta Braves. His legacy to the game includes the reserve clause that bound players to a team without their consent in perpetuity. Died at Lake Sunapee, NH, Aug 13, 1925.

24-SECOND CLOCK: ANNIVERSARY. Apr 23, 1954. The NBA approved a proposal by Syracuse Nationals owner Danny Biasone to adopt a 24-second clock. The rule stated that "a team in control of the ball must make an attempt to score within 24 seconds after gaining possession of the ball." Biasone promoted the rule to boost the league's offensive output. He decided on 24 seconds by dividing the total number of shots taken in an average game into 48 minutes, the time played in a regulation game.

US WRESTLING NATIONALS AND SE JUNIOR REGIONALS. April 23–26. Walt Disney World Sports Arena, Orlando, FL. More than 1,100 athletes in four divisions compete in the two international styles of wrestling–Freestyle and Greco-Roman. Competition for senior divisions (19 years and older) in men's Freestyle and Greco-Roman and in the women's division is part of the world team selection process for USA Wrestling's 1998 world teams. For info: USA Wrestling, 6155 Lehman Dr, Colorado Springs, CO 80918. Phone: (719) 598-8181. Fax: (719) 598-9440. Email: eventusaw@aol.com. WWW: http://www.usawrestling.org

WILHELM'S ONLY HOMER: ANNIVERSARY. Apr 23, 1952. Hoyt Wilhelm of the New York Giants won the first game of his major league career (in relief), and he also hit a home run in his first major league time at-bat. Although Wilhelm appeared in 1,070 games, he never hit another homer.

WILKINSON, BUD: BIRTH ANNIVERSARY. Apr 23, 1915. Charles ("Bud") Wilkinson, football player and coach and sportscaster born at Minneapolis, MN. Wilkinson played football at the University of Minnesota and entered coaching immediately after graduation. He succeeded Jim Tatum as head coach at Oklahoma in 1947 and remained through 1964. During his tenure, the Sooners compiled a record 47-game winning streak. He headed the President's Physical Fitness Council and, after retiring from coaching, analyzed football games on ABC television. Died at Oklahoma City, OK, Feb 9, 1994.

STANLEY CUP CHAMPIONS THIS DATE

1950	Detroit Red Wings

BIRTHDAYS TODAY

Adolf Louis (Dolf) Camilli, 91, former baseball player, born San Francisco, CA, Apr 23, 1907.
Leon James ("Duke") Carmel, 61, former baseball player, born New York, NY, Apr 23, 1937.
Rheal Paul Cormier, 31, baseball player, born Moncton, New Brunswick, Canada, Apr 23, 1967.
Gail Charles Goodrich, Jr, 55, Basketball Hall of Fame guard, born Los Angeles, CA, Apr 23, 1943.
Warren Edward Spahn, 77, Baseball Hall of Fame pitcher, born Buffalo, NY, Apr 23, 1921.

APRIL 24 — FRIDAY

Day 114 — 251 Remaining

NBA FINALS CHAMPIONS THIS DATE

1963	Boston Celtics
1967	Philadelphia 76ers

BIG TWELVE WOMEN'S GOLF CHAMPIONSHIP. Apr 24–26. University of Oklahoma, Norman, OK. For info: Big Twelve Conference, 2201 Stemmons Freeway, 28th Floor, Dallas, TX 75207. Phone: (214) 742-1212. Fax: (214) 742-2046.

CHANDLER ELECTED COMMISSIONER: ANNIVERSARY. Apr 24, 1945. Albert B. ("Happy") Chandler, US Senator from Kentucky, was elected Commissioner of Baseball by a unanimous vote of major league club owners. Chandler succeeded Kenesaw Mountain Landis who died in November 1944. He served one term and was replaced in 1951 by Ford C. Frick.

COUSY RETIRES: 35th ANNIVERSARY. Apr 24, 1963. Guard Bob Cousy of the Boston Celtics ended a 13-year career in the NBA by scoring 18 points against the Los Angeles Lakers and leading the Celtics to a fifth consecutive championship. Cousy made a brief comeback in the 1969–70 season but played only seven games.

EHMKE, HOWARD: BIRTH ANNIVERSARY. Apr 24, 1894. Howard Jonathan Ehmke, baseball player born at Silver Creek, NY. A pitcher with a career record of 166–166, Ehmke was a surprise starter in the first game of the 1929 World Series for the Philadelphia Athletics. He defeated the Chicago Cubs, 3–1. Died at Philadelphia, PA, Mar 17, 1959.

89er DAYS PRCA RODEO. Apr 24–25. Lazy E Arena, Guthrie, OK. Celebrate the land run of 1889 at Oklahoma's largest rodeo with more than 600 contestants competing. Est attendance: 17,000. For info: Lazy E Arena, Rte 5, Box 393, Guthrie, OK 73044. Phone: (405) 282-7433 or (800) 595-RIDE. Email: learena@ionet.net. WWW: http://www.lazye.com

FIRST AMERICAN LEAGUE GAMES: ANNIVERSARY. Apr 24, 1901. The American League made its debut as a major league with a schedule of four games. Three were rained out, but the Chicago White Stockings beat the Cleveland Blues, 8–2, to get the season under way. 14,000 saw the game played at the Chicago Cricket Club.

GREAT PLAINS ROWING CHAMPIONSHIPS. Apr 24–25. Lake Shawnee, Topeka, KS. 14th annual 60-event rowing regatta for high school, college, and master age oarspeople. Sponsors: US Rowing and many other groups. Est attendance: 12,000. For info: Don Craig, 4336 SE 25th St Terrace, Topeka, KS 66605. Phone: (913) 233-9951. Fax: (913) 233-9952. Email: 74452.410@compuserve.com. WWW: http://adamsnet.com/topekarowing

NATIONAL ATLANTIC CITY ARCHERY CLASSIC. Apr 24–26. The New Atlantic City Convention Center, Atlantic City, NJ. Est attendance: 6,000. For info: Atlantic City Conv and Visitors Authority, 2314 Pacific Ave, Atlantic City, NJ 08401. Phone: (609) 449-7142.

RATTLESNAKE DERBY. Apr 24–26. Mangum, OK. Hunters stalk these wily reptiles and attempt to bring in the most snakes and the longest snake. Snakeskins and meat will be sold, and entertainment will include live music, a carnival and flea market. A herpetologist will be on hand to educate festival goers. Est attendance: 40,000. For info: Chamber of Commerce, 222 W Jefferson, Mangum, OK 73554. Phone: (405) 782-2444.

RIVERFEST WEEKEND. Apr 24–26. Columbus, GA. Annually, the last weekend in April along the riverwalk in Columbus. Features the Salisbury Fair with games, olympics, pig races, rides, entertainment, arts and crafts, flea market, parades, corn bread cook-off and an orchid show and sale. Also featured are the Pig Jig with the Ham It Up parade and the South's most famous barbeque cook-off as well as live entertainment on four stages. Admission $4. Children under 6 $3. For info: Riverfest, PO Box 5128, Columbus, GA 31906. Phone: (706) 323-7979.

TAMPA AWARDED NFL FRANCHISE: ANNIVERSARY. Apr 24, 1974. The National Football League awarded a franchise for its 27th team to Tampa, FL. The team, called the Tampa Bay Buccaneers, began play in 1976.

SPORTSCHASER OF THE DAY

What surprise starting pitcher won the first game of the 1929 World Series for the Philadelphia Athletics?

BIRTHDAYS TODAY

Michael Roy (Mike) Blowers, 33, baseball player, born Wurzburg, West Germany, Apr 24, 1965.

Vince Ferragamo, 44, former football player, born Torrance, CA, Apr 24, 1954.

Larry Wayne ("Chipper") Jones, 26, baseball player, born De Land, FL, Apr 24, 1972.

Dino Radja, 31, basketball player, born Split, Croatia, Apr 24, 1967.

Omar Enrique Vizquel, 31, baseball player, born Caracas, Venezuela, Apr 24, 1967.

APRIL 25 — SATURDAY

Day 115 — 250 Remaining

NBA FINALS CHAMPIONS THIS DATE

1952	Minneapolis Lakers
1965	Boston Celtics

FOXFIELD RACES. Apr 25 (also Sept 27). Charlottesville, VA. Steeplechase horse racing. Est attendance: 20,000. For info: W. Patrick Butterfield, Racing Mgr, Foxfield Racing Assn, PO Box 5187, Charlottesville, VA 22905. Phone: (804) 293-9501. Fax: (804) 293-8169.

GREAT CARDBOARD BOAT REGATTA. Apr 25. SIUC Campus Lake, Carbondale, IL. Teams and individuals design, build, and race person-powered boats made of corrugated cardboard. "Titanic Award" for most spectacular sinking plus trophies for team spirit, most creative use of cardboard, best-dressed team, most spectacular-looking boat. Prizes for top finishers in three boat classes: Class I, propelled by oars or paddles; Class II, propelled by mechanical means such as paddle wheels, propellers; Class III, "Instant Boats" made from "Secret Kits" by spectators-turned-participants. Registration 10 AM; races begin at noon. 25th annual regatta. Additional competition at other locations across the country on various dates. Est attendance: 14,000. For info: Southern Illinois University, School of Art and Design, Carbondale, IL 62901. Phone: (618) 453-4315 or (618) 453-7548. Fax: (618) 453-7501. Email: arch@siu.edu or commodore@gcbr.com. WWW: http://www.gcbr.com

HANEY, FRED: 100th BIRTH ANNIVERSARY. Apr 25, 1898. Fred Girard Haney, baseball player, manager and executive born at Albuquerque, NM. Haney was a major league infielder for seven years. He managed the Milwaukee Braves to the National League pennant in 1957 and 1958. Died at Beverly Hills, CA, Nov 9, 1977.

KITEFEST. Apr 25–26. River Oaks Park, Kalamazoo, MI. Family-oriented kite-flying event includes sport kite competition, children's kite-making workshop, kite competitions and lots of kite flying, including indoors. Est attendance: 5,000. For info: John D. Cosby, Mktg Coord, Kalamazoo County Parks Dept, 2900 Lake St, Kalama-

April *1998*	S	M	T	W	T	F	S
				1	2	3	4
	5	6	7	8	9	10	11
	12	13	14	15	16	17	18
	19	20	21	22	23	24	25
	26	27	28	29	30		

zoo, MI 49001. Phone: (616) 383-8778. Fax: (616) 383-8724. WWW: http://www.kalcounty.com

LLOYD, POP: BIRTH ANNIVERSARY. Apr 25, 1884. John Henry ("Pop") Lloyd, Baseball Hall of Fame shortstop born at Palatka, FL. Lloyd was often compared to Honus Wagner and considered one of the best shortstops ever. He played and managed with black teams and made quite a career in Cuba where the fans nicknamed him "Cuchara" (scoop or shovel) for his big hands. Inducted into the Hall of Fame in 1977. Died at Atlantic City, NJ, Mar 19, 1965.

MARCH OF DIMES WALKAMERICA. Apr 25–26. The March of Dimes's largest fundraiser takes place in communities nationwide the last weekend in April with more than one million volunteers participating. Funds raised support research, education and community-based programs to prevent birth defects and to help lower the rate of premature births and infant mortality. Call your local chapter to learn how to participate. For info: March of Dimes Birth Defects Fdtn, Natl HQ, 1275 Mamaroneck Ave, White Plains, NY 10605. Phone: (914) 997-4574.

NBA DRAFTS FIRST BLACK PLAYER: ANNIVERSARY. Apr 25, 1950. The Boston Celtics made Chuck Cooper, an All-American from Duquesne University playing with the Harlem Globetrotters, the first black player drafted by any NBA team when they selected him in the second round.

NFL ADOPTS SUDDEN DEATH: ANNIVERSARY. Apr 25, 1974. The National Football League adopted a 15-minute, sudden death quarter in an effort to reduce the number of tie games. The league also moved the goal posts from the goal line to the back line of the end zone to make it more difficult to kick field goals.

MONDAY RESCUES FLAG: ANNIVERSARY. Apr 25, 1976. Center fielder Rick Monday of the Chicago Cubs rescued an American flag from several fans who ran onto the field and attempted to set it on fire. The incident occurred in Dodger Stadium in the fourth inning of a 5–4, 10-inning victory by the Dodgers.

PALMER WINS FIRST MASTERS: 40th ANNIVERSARY. Apr 25, 1958. Arnold Palmer struggled to a final round 73, one over par, but still won the first of his four Masters championships. Palmer finished at 284, one shot better than Doug Ford and Fred Hawkins. He would win the tournament again in 1960, 1962 (in a playoff) and 1964.

PERIGEAN SPRING TIDES. Apr 25–26. Spring tides, the highest possible tides, occur when New Moon or Full Moon falls within 24 hours of the moment the Moon is nearest Earth (perigee) in its monthly orbit, on Apr 25 at 2:00 PM, EDT.

SUGAR CREEK CANOE RACE AND TRI SPORT FESTIVAL. Apr 25–26. Crawfordsville, IN. More than 13 canoe races. 8K run, 30K bike race. Award presentations. Industrial Corporate Cup event (bike-run-canoe); also kayak race. Adult/child races. Food and craft booths. Hosted by the Jaycees. For info: Montgomery County Visitors and Conv Bureau, PO Box 305, Crawfordsville, IN 47933. Phone: (317) 362-5200.

STANLEY CUP CHAMPIONS THIS DATE
1964   Toronto Maple Leafs

BIRTHDAYS TODAY

David John (Dave) Corzine, 42, former basketball player, born Arlington Heights, IL, Apr 25, 1956.

Darren Lee Holmes, 32, baseball player, born Asheville, NC, Apr 25, 1966.

Meadow George ("Meadowlark") Lemon III, 66, former basketball player, born Lexington, SC, Apr 25, 1932.

Keith Anthony (Tony) Phillips, 39, baseball player, born Atlanta, GA, Apr 25, 1959.

Talia Shire, 52, actress (the Rocky movies), born New York, NY, Apr 25, 1946.

Darren Ray Woodson, 29, football player, born Phoenix, AZ, Apr 25, 1969.

APRIL 26 — SUNDAY
Day 116 — 249 Remaining

NBA FINALS CHAMPIONS THIS DATE
1964   Boston Celtics

ALEXANDER, DALE: 95th BIRTH ANNIVERSARY. Apr 26, 1903. David Dale Alexander, baseball player born at Greeneville, TN. Alexander was an outstanding hitter from his rookie year when he batted .343 to the end of his career. He won the American League batting title in 1932 with a .367 average despite being traded in June from the Detroit Tigers to the Boston Red Sox. Died at Greeneville, Mar 2, 1979.

BRUINS SNAP JINX: ANNIVERSARY. Apr 26, 1988. The Boston Bruins snapped a string of 18 straight Stanley Cup playoff series losses to the Montreal Canadiens, dating back to 1943, by ousting the Habs, four games to one. Boston used two goals each from Cam Neely and Steve Kasper and strong goaltending from Rejean Lemelin to defeat Montreal, 4–1.

ENGLAND: FLORA LONDON MARATHON. Apr 26. Starts Blackheath, finishes The Mall, London. Race held over a 26-mile course through the heart of London. For info: Debbie Sullivan, Flora London Marathon, PO Box 1234, London, England SE1 8RZ. Phone: (44) (171) 620-4117. Fax: (44) (171) 620-4208.

FIRST BALLPARK ORGAN: ANNIVERSARY. Apr 26, 1941. The Chicago Cubs became the first major league team to install an organ in their ballpark. Roy Nelson played a pregame program.

HOOPATHON. Apr 26. Rutgers Athletics Center, Piscataway, NJ. Annual free-throw contest with participants shooting against a 10-minute clock. Number of free throws supported by pledges by friends, family and coworkers with proceeds for the benefit of the Huntington's Disease Society of New Jersey. The Hoopathon Hall of Fame record is 209 hoops in 10 minutes. Hall of Fame also for the top fundraisers. For info: Bill Clancy, Club Basketball, USA, 215 North Ave W, Ste 205, Westfield, NJ 07090. Phone: (908) 756-4502. Fax: (908) 756-9698.

MARIS HITS NO. 1 OF 61: ANNIVERSARY. Apr 26, 1961. Roger Maris of the New York Yankees hit his first home run of the season against Paul Foytack of the Detroit Tigers. Maris went on to hit 60 more homers, breaking Babe Ruth's record for most home runs in a season.

MOON PHASE: NEW MOON. Apr 26. Moon enters New Moon phase at 7:41 AM, EDT.

TWINS DRAFTED: ANNIVERSARY. Apr 26, 1965. In the third round of the NBA draft, the New York Knicks selected Dick Van Arsdale. With the next pick, the Detroit Pistons drafted Dick's twin brother, Tom. Both went on to distinguished careers.

WILSON, HACK: BIRTH ANNIVERSARY. Apr 26, 1900. Lewis Robert ("Hack") Wilson, Baseball Hall of Fame outfielder born at Ellwood City, PA. Wilson set the National League record for home runs in a season when he hit 56 in 1930. Short and squat, he got his nickname from his resemblance to George Hackenschmidt, a Russian wrestler and strongman. Inducted into the Hall of Fame in 1979. Died at Baltimore, MD, Nov 23, 1948.

BIRTHDAYS TODAY

Fanny Blankers-Koen (born Francina Elsje Koen), 80, Olympic gold medal sprinter, born Amsterdam, Netherlands, Apr 26, 1918.

Donna de Varona, 51, women's sports executive, former broadcaster and Olympic gold medal swimmer, born San Diego, CA, Apr 26, 1947.

Stephen Paul (Steve) Lombardozzi, 38, former baseball player, born Malden, MA, Apr 26, 1960.

Natrone Jermaine Means, 26, football player, born Harrisburg, NC, Apr 26, 1972.

Amos Joseph Otis, 51, former baseball player, born Mobile, AL, Apr 26, 1947.

Michael Warren (Mike) Scott, 43, former baseball player, born Santa Monica, CA, Apr 26, 1955.

Virgil Oliver Trucks, 81, former baseball player, born Birmingham, AL, Apr 26, 1917.

Curtis Vernon Wilkerson, 37, former baseball player, born Petersburg, VA, Apr 26, 1961.

APRIL 27 — MONDAY
Day 117 — 248 Remaining

CHASE'S SPORTSQUOTE OF THE DAY
"Any ballplayer that don't sign autographs for little kids ain't an American. He's a Communist." —Rogers Hornsby

BABE RUTH DAY: ANNIVERSARY. Apr 27, 1947. Babe Ruth Day was celebrated in every ballpark in organized baseball in the US as well as Japan. Mortally ill with throat cancer, Ruth appeared at Yankee Stadium to thank his former club for the honor.

BIG TWELVE MEN'S GOLF CHAMPIONSHIP. Apr 27–28. Prairie Dunes C.C., Hutchinson, KS. For info: Big Twelve Conference, 2201 Stemmons Freeway, 28th Floor, Dallas, TX 75207. Phone: (214) 742-1212. Fax: (214) 742-2046.

ELLIS WINS HEAVYWEIGHT TITLE: 30th ANNIVERSARY. Apr 27, 1968. Jimmy Ellis won a 15-round decision over Jerry Quarry to capture the heavyweight championship. This fight at Oakland, CA, was the final in an eight-man elimination tournament to select a champion to replace Muhammad Ali, from whom the title was stripped.

HORNSBY, ROGERS: BIRTH ANNIVERSARY. Apr 27, 1896. Rogers Hornsby, Baseball Hall of Fame second baseman and manager born at Winters, TX. Hornsby was baseball's greatest right handed hitter, winning six batting titles in a row, hitting .424 in 1924 and leading the National League in home runs and runs batted in several times. As a manager, Hornsby was tough and uncompromising, showing little feeling for players not as good as he was. Inducted into the Hall of Fame in 1942. Died at Chicago, IL, Jan 5, 1963.

MARCIANO RETIRES: ANNIVERSARY. Apr 27, 1956. Rockey Marciano retired as the only undefeated heavyweight champion. He finished his career with a record of 49–0 with 43 knockouts and six title defenses.

PAC-10 MEN'S GOLF CHAMPIONSHIPS. Apr 27–29. Orinda C.C., CA. For info: PAC-10 Conference, 800 S Broadway, Ste 400, Walnut Creek, CA 94596. Phone: (510) 932-4411. Fax: (510) 932-4601.

VANCOUVER JOINS NBA: ANNIVERSARY. Apr 27, 1994. The NBA Board of Governors voted to grant an expansion franchise to the city of Vancouver, British Columbia. The Grizzlies, as the team was named, and the Toronto Raptors began play in the 1995–96 season.

WOMEN'S INTERNATIONAL BOWLING CONGRESS ANNUAL MEETING. Apr 27–29. Quad Cities, IL-IA. Est attendance: 3,500. For info: Mark Miller, WIBC, 5301 S 76th St, Greendale, WI 53129. Phone: (414) 423-3224. Fax: (414) 421-7977.

☆   ☆   ☆

BIRTHDAYS TODAY

Michael A. Booker, 23, football player, born Cincinnati, OH, Apr 27, 1975.
George Gervin, 46, Basketball Hall of Fame guard, born Detroit, MI, Apr 27, 1952.
John Eric Hillman, 32, former baseball player, born Gary, IN, Apr 27, 1966.
Enos Bradsher Slaughter, 82, Baseball Hall of Fame outfielder, born Roxboro, NC, Apr 27, 1916.
Willie Clay Upshaw, 41, former baseball player, born Blanco, TX, Apr 27, 1957.

	S	M	T	W	T	F	S
April 1998				1	2	3	4
	5	6	7	8	9	10	11
	12	13	14	15	16	17	18
	19	20	21	22	23	24	25
	26	27	28	29	30		

APRIL 28 — TUESDAY
Day 118 — 247 Remaining

NBA FINALS CHAMPIONS THIS DATE
1966   Boston Celtics

AARON HITS NO. 600: ANNIVERSARY. Apr 28, 1971. Henry Aaron of the Atlanta Braves hit the 600th home run of his career. It came against Gaylord Perry of the San Francisco Giants in a 6–5, 10-inning Giants victory.

CAVANAUGH, FRANK: BIRTH ANNIVERSARY. Apr 28, 1876. Francis W. (Frank) Cavanaugh, football coach born at Worcester, MA. Cavanaugh earned the nickname the "Iron Major" for heroism in World War I. After the armistice, he developed Boston College and Fordham into national football powers. Died at Marshfield, MA, Aug 29, 1933.

LUCAS, RED: BIRTH ANNIVERSARY. Apr 28, 1902. Charles Fred ("Red") Lucas, baseball player born at Columbia, TN. Lucas was a pitcher, who led the National League in complete games three times (1929, 1931 and 1932), and was a hitter good enough to pinch-hit regularly. Died at Englewood, TN, July 9, 1986.

WHITE SOX GET 23 SINGLES: ANNIVERSARY. Apr 28, 1901. The Chicago White Sox set a record by getting 23 hits, all singles, defeating the Cleveland Indians, 13–1. Pitcher Bock Baker gave up all the hits.

BIRTHDAYS TODAY

Thomas Leo (Tom) Browning, 38, former baseball player, born Casper, WY, Apr 28, 1960.
Mark Anthony Carrier, 30, football player, born Lake Charles, LA, Apr 28, 1968.
John Patrick Daly, 32, golfer, born Carmichael, CA, Apr 28, 1966.
Edward Paul (Ted) Donato, 30, hockey player, born Dedham, MA, Apr 28, 1968.
Barry Louis Larkin, 34, baseball player, born Cincinnati, OH, Apr 28, 1964.
Pedro Ramos, 63, former baseball player, born Pinar del Rio, Cuba, Apr 28, 1935.
Thomas Virgil (Tom) Sturdivant, 68, former baseball player, born Gordon, KS, Apr 28, 1930.

APRIL 29 — WEDNESDAY
Day 119 — 246 Remaining

CARLTON STRIKES OUT 3,000th: ANNIVERSARY. Apr 29, 1981. Steve Carlton of the Philadelphia Phillies struck out Tim Wallach of the Montreal Expos in the first inning of the Phillies' 6–2 victory. Wallach was the 3,000th strikeout victim of Carlton's career. He finished with 4,136.

CLEMENS STRIKES OUT 20: ANNIVERSARY. Apr 29, 1986. Roger Clemens of the Boston Red Sox set a new American League and major league record for most strikeouts in a nine-inning game when he struck out 20 Seattle Mariners in a 3–1 Red Sox victory. The previous American League record, 19 strikeouts, was set by Nolan Ryan on Aug 12, 1974.

FIRST NL EXTRA-INNING GAME: ANNIVERSARY. Apr 29, 1876. The Hartford and Boston clubs played the first extra-inning game in the National League. Hartford won, 3–2, in 10 innings.

HAWKS TRADE RUSSELL: ANNIVERSARY. Apr 29, 1956. The St. Louis Hawks traded their No. 1 draft choice, Bill Russell from the University of San Francisco, to the Boston Celtics for Cliff Hagan and Ed Macauley. Russell would lead the Celtics to 11 NBA titles in 13 seasons, but years later, Hawks owner Ben Kerner insisted he would make the trade again.

LAST HELMETLESS PLAYER RETIRES: ANNIVERSARY. Apr 29, 1997. Craig MacTavish, the last player to go without a helmet, retired from the National Hockey League. The NHL mandated helmets at the start of the 1979–80 season but allowed players then active to refrain by signing a waiver absolving the league of responsibility in case of head injury. MacTavish was the last remaining player of those who signed the waiver. He retired from the St. Louis Blues after a 16-year career during which he scored 213 goals. Despite his personal choice, he admitted, "Certainly, it's very dangerous out there without a helmet."

ONLY DERBY IN APRIL: ANNIVERSARY. Apr 29, 1901. For the first and only time, the Kentucky Derby was run in April instead of May. The winning colt was His Eminence, ridden by Jimmy Winkfield. Sannazarro finished second, a length-and-a-half back.

ORIOLES END LOSING STREAK: ANNIVERSARY. Apr 29, 1988. The 1988 Baltimore Orioles finally won a game after losing the first 21 games of the season. They beat the Chicago White Sox, 9–0, on a combined four-hitter by pitchers Mark Williamson and Dave Schmidt. The Orioles' streak, lasting from Apr 4 to 28, set an American League record but fell two losses short of the National League mark.

POLO: SOUTHERN SILVER CUP. Apr 29–May 10 (tentative). Wellington, FL. For info: Palm Beach Polo, Inc, 13420 South Shore Blvd, West Palm Beach, FL 33414. Phone: (561) 793-1440. Fax: (561) 790-3872.

BIRTHDAYS TODAY

Andre Kirk Agassi, 28, tennis player, born Las Vegas, NV, Apr 29, 1970.

George Herbert Allen, 76, former football coach, born Detroit, MI, Apr 29, 1922.

Luis Ernesto Aparicio, 64, Baseball Hall of Fame shortstop, born Maracaibo, Venezuela, Apr 29, 1934.

Bruce Douglas Driver, 36, hockey player, born Toronto, Ontario, Canada, Apr 29, 1962.

Dale Earnhardt, 46, auto racer, born Kannapolis, NC, Apr 29, 1952.

Sterling Alex Hitchcock, 27, baseball player, born Fayetteville, NC, Apr 29, 1971.

Curtis Shayne Joseph, 31, hockey player, born Keswick, Ontario, Canada, Apr 29, 1967.

John Laurence (Johnny) Miller, 51, broadcaster and golfer, born San Francisco, CA, Apr 29, 1947.

John Vander Wal, 32, baseball player, born Grand Rapids, MI, Apr 29, 1966.

APRIL 30 — THURSDAY

Day 120 — 245 Remaining

NBA FINALS CHAMPIONS THIS DATE

1971   Milwaukee Bucks

BIG TEN WOMEN'S TENNIS CHAMPIONSHIPS. Apr 30–May 3. University of Michigan, Ann Arbor, MI. For info: Big Ten Conference, 1500 W Higgins Rd, Park Ridge, IL 60068-6300. Phone: (847) 696-1010. Fax: (847) 696-1150. WWW: http://www.bigten.org

HIGHLANDERS WIN HOME OPENER: 95th ANNIVERSARY. Apr 30, 1903. The New York Highlanders won their home opener at Hilltop Park over the Washington Senators. The Highlanders had played the 1901 and 1902 American League seasons as the Baltimore Orioles. They changed their name to the New York Yankees in 1913.

JOSEY'S WORLD CHAMPION JUNIOR BARREL RACE. Apr 30–May 3. Josey's Ranch, Marshall, TX. Youth barrel-racing competition. Annually, the first weekend in May. Est attendance: 4,000. For info: Pam Whisenant, Dir of Conv and Visitor Development, Marshall Chamber of Commerce, PO Box 520, Marshall, TX 75671. Phone: (903) 935-7868. Fax: (903) 935-9982. Email: cvb@internetwork.net.

MAYS HITS FOUR HOME RUNS: ANNIVERSARY. Apr 30, 1961. Willie Mays of the San Francisco Giants became the eighth player in major league history to hit four home runs in a single game. Mays performed the feat at Milwaukee County Stadium as the Giants beat the Braves, 14–4.

MUHAMMAD ALI STRIPPED OF TITLE: ANNIVERSARY. Apr 30, 1967. Muhammad Ali was stripped of his world heavyweight boxing championship when he refused to be inducted into military service. Said Ali, "I have searched my conscience, and I find I cannot be true to my belief in my religion by accepting such a call." He had claimed exemption as a minister of the Black Muslim religion.

NCAA MEN'S VOLLEYBALL CHAMPIONSHIPS. Apr 30–May 2. University of Hawaii, Manoa, HI. For info: NCAA, 6201 College Blvd, Overland Park, KS 66211. Phone: (913) 339-1906.

ROBERTSON'S PERFECT GAME: ANNIVERSARY. Apr 30, 1922. Charlie Robertson of the Chicago White Sox pitched major league baseball's fifth regular-season perfect game, beating the Detroit Tigers in Detroit, 2–0. Robertson pitched in the majors for eight years and had a 49–80 record.

ROSE BUMPS PALLONE: 10TH ANNIVERSARY. Apr 30, 1988. During a game between the Cincinnati Reds and the New York Mets, Reds manager Pete Rose, objecting to a delayed call by umpire Dave Pallone, shoved Pallone twice after the ump accidentally poked Rose in the cheek. Rose was fined $10,000 and suspended for 30 days.

YOST, FIELDING: BIRTH ANNIVERSARY. Apr 30, 1871. Fielding Harris ("Hurry Up") Yost, football player, coach and administrator born at Fairview, WV. Yost developed the University of Michigan into one of college football's great early powers, winning a national championship in his first year, 1901, and the first Rose Bowl (1902) against Stanford. He remained at Michigan for 41 years as coach and/or athletic director. Died at Ann Arbor, MI, Aug 20, 1946.

BIRTHDAYS TODAY

Jeff Randall Brown, 32, hockey player, born Ottawa, Ontario, Canada, Apr 30, 1966.

Philip Mason (Phil) Garner, 50, baseball manager and former player, born Jefferson City, TN, Apr 30, 1948.

Charles Robert (Bob) Hendley, 59, former baseball player, born Macon, GA, Apr 20, 1939.

Pierre Page, 50, hockey coach, born St. Hermas, Quebec, Canada, Apr 30, 1948.

Isiah Lord Thomas, III, 37, basketball executive and former player, born Chicago, IL, Apr 30, 1961.

Al Lee Toon, Jr, 35, former football player, born Newport News, VA, Apr 30, 1963.

MAY 1 — FRIDAY

Day 121 — 244 Remaining

STANLEY CUP CHAMPIONS THIS DATE

1965   Montreal Canadiens

BATTLES, CLIFF: BIRTH ANNIVERSARY. May 1, 1910. Clifford Franklin (Cliff) Battles, Pro Football Hall of Fame halfback born at Akron, OH. Battles played football for West Virginia Wesleyan and then turned pro in 1932 with the Boston Redskins, soon to become the Washington Redskins. He helped Washington win the 1937 NFL title but retired at age 28 when owner George Preston Marshall would not offer him a raise. Inducted into the Pro Football Hall of Fame in 1968. Died at Akron, Apr 28, 1981.

BERARDINO, JOHNNY: BIRTH ANNIVERSARY. May 1, 1917. John (Johnny) Berardino, actor and baseball player born at Los Angeles, CA. Berardino played 11 seasons in the major leagues and was on the World Champion 1948 Cleveland Indians. After retiring, he became a successful soap-opera actor, spending more than three decades on "General Hospital." Died at Los Angeles, May 19, 1996.

BIG TEN WOMEN'S GOLF CHAMPIONSHIP. May 1–3. Penn State University, University Park, PA. For info: Big Ten Conference, 1500 W Higgins Rd, Park Ridge, IL 60068-6300. Phone: (847) 696-1010. Fax: (847) 696-1150. WWW: http://www.bigten.org

BIG TWELVE WOMEN'S SOFTBALL TOURNAMENT. May 1–3. ASA Hall of Fame Stadium, Oklahoma City, OK. For info: Big Twelve Conference, 2201 Stemmons Freeway, 28th Floor, Dallas, TX 75207. Phone: (214) 742-1212. Fax: (214) 742-2046.

CAGLE, CHRIS: BIRTH ANNIVERSARY. May 1, 1905. Christian Keener (Chris) Cagle, football player, coach and executive born at DeRidder, LA. Cagle was a three-time All-American at West Point in 1927, 1928 and 1929, but since he had played previously at Southwestern Louisiana Institute, a dispute over his eligibility resulted in a two-year cancellation of the Army-Navy game. He left West Point before graduating because he had violated academy rules by getting married. He played pro football for five years. Died after a fall down a stairway at New York, NY, Dec 23, 1942.

	S	M	T	W	T	F	S
May						1	2
	3	4	5	6	7	8	9
1998	10	11	12	13	14	15	16
	17	18	19	20	21	22	23
	24	25	26	27	28	29	30
	31						

KENNEDY NAMED NBA PRESIDENT: 35th ANNIVERSARY. May 1, 1963. J. Walter Kennedy was named the second president of the NBA, succeeding Maurice Podoloff, who retired after the 1962–63 season.

LOBSTER RACE AND OYSTER PARADE. May 1. Aiken, SC. The world's only thoroughbred lobster races and oyster party. The lobsters are raced in a unique sea-salt-water-filled track called "Lobster Downs." Beach music, gourmet seafood available. Oyster Parade at the "Mardi Claw" (our version of Mardi Gras) to highlight local land-locked maritime costumes will be held in Aiken's historical alley section. 14th annual Running of the Lobsters in Aiken. Est attendance: 6,000. For info: Greater Aiken Chamber of Commerce, Lobster Race/Oyster Parade, PO Box 892, Aiken, SC 29802. Phone: (803) 641-1111 or (803) 648-4981.

LONGEST MAJOR LEAGUE GAME: ANNIVERSARY. May 1, 1920. The Brooklyn Dodgers and the Boston Braves played the longest game in major league baseball history, but did not finish it. After 26 innings, the game was halted because of darkness with the score tied, 1–1. Each team used just one pitcher, Leon Cadore for the Dodgers and Joe Oeschger for the Braves, who gave up 12 and 9 hits, respectively. Despite its 26 innings, the game took just 3 hours, 50 minutes. The next day, the Dodgers lost to the Philadelphia Phillies in 13 innings. The day after that, they returned to Boston and lost again in 19 innings.

MAY DAY. May 1. The first day of May has been observed as a holiday since ancient times. Spring festivals, may-poles and maying still are common, but political content of May Day has grown since the 1880s, when it became a workers' day in the US. Now widely observed in socialist countries as a workers' holiday. More recently Loyalty Day and Law Day observances have been encouraged in the US (by presidential and other proclamations) on May 1, contrasting strongly with the workers' demonstrations abroad. In most European countries, when May Day falls on Saturday or Sunday, the Monday following is observed as a holiday, with bank and store closings, parades and other festivities.

NATIONAL BIKE MONTH. May 1–31. 41st annual celebration of bicycling for recreation and transportation. Local activities sponsored by bicycling organizations, environmental groups, PTAs, police departments, health organizations and civic groups. About five million participants nationwide. Annually, the month of May. For info: League of American Bicyclists, 190 W Ostend St, Ste 120, Baltimore, MD 21230-3755. Phone: (410) 539-3399.

NATIONAL PHYSICAL FITNESS AND SPORTS MONTH. May 1–31. Encourages individuals and organizations to promote fitness activities and programs. For info: President's Council on Physical Fitness and Sports, HHH Bldg, 200 Independence Ave, SW, Room 738H, Washington, DC 20201-0004. Phone: (202) 690-9000.

NATIONAL BARBECUE MONTH. May 1–31. To encourage people to start enjoying barbecuing early in the season when Daylight Saving Time lengthens the day. Annually, the month of May. Sponsor: Barbecue Industry Assn. For info: Donna H. Myers, DHM Group, Inc, PO Box 767, Holmdel, NJ 07733. Fax: (908) 946-3343.

NATIONAL FIBROMYALGIA MONTH. May 1–31. A monthlong campaign under the guidance of the Fibromyalgia Council of America to educate and alert the public about fibromyalgia (also known as fibrositis and the chronic muscle pain syndrome), an illness that is often associated with muscle pain, stiffness, fatigue, poor sleep, anxiety and depression. For info: Dr. Paul Davidson, Fibromyalgia Council of America, 200 Gate 5 Rd, PO Box 1336, Sausalito, CA 94966. Phone: (415) 332-4066. Fax: (415) 332-1832. Email: pssi@aol.com. WWW: http://www.nbn.com/people/healthrd

NATIONAL HAMBURGER MONTH. May 1–31. Sponsored by White Castle, the original fast-food hamburger chain, founded in 1921. To pay tribute to one of America's favorite foods. With or without condiments, on or off a bun or bread, hamburgers have grown in popularity since the early 1920s and are now an American meal mainstay. For info: White Castle System, Inc, Marketing Dept, 555 W Goodale St, Columbus, OH 43215-1171. Phone: (614) 228-5781. Fax: (614) 228-8841. WWW: http://www.whitecastle.com

NATIONAL TRAUMA AWARENESS MONTH. May 1–31. Each year no fewer than 150,000 Americans die as a result of traumatic injury. Annual campaign focusing on a different aspect of trauma (injury), providing a sober reminder that we must each work to create a healthier and safer society. For info: Ruth Pollack, PR Coord, American Trauma Soc, 8903 Presidential Pkwy, Ste 512, Upper Marlboro, MD 20772-2656. Phone: (301) 420-4189 or (800) 556-7890. Fax: (301) 420-0617.

NOLAN RYAN PITCHES SEVENTH NO-HITTER: ANNIVERSARY. May 1, 1991. Nolan Ryan of the Texas Rangers pitched the seventh no-hitter of his career, extending his own major league record. Ryan struck out 16 as the Rangers beat the Toronto Blue Jays, 3–0.

PRCA PRO RODEO. May 1–3 (tentative). Payson Rodeo Grounds, Payson, AZ. Some of the best veterans of professional rodeo. Benefits the Gary Hardt Athletic Scholarship fund and underprivileged and needy children of Gila County. Est attendance: 3,500. For info: Payson Chamber of Commerce, PO Box 1380, Payson, AZ 85547. Phone: (800) 672-9766. Fax: (520) 474-8812. Email: pcoc@netzone.com.

RICKEY HENDERSON STEALS BASE THEFT CROWN: ANNIVERSARY. May 1, 1991. Rickey Henderson of the Oakland Athletics stole third base, the 939th steal of his career, to set a new major league record, surpassing Lou Brock. The A's beat the New York Yankees, 7–4.

STRIKE OUT STROKES MONTH. May 1–31. Dedicated to the prevention of strokes. Factors resulting from heredity or natural processes can't be changed, but with proper medical treatment and healthful lifestyle adjustments some risk factors can be changed. Kit materials available for $15. For info: Frederick S. Mayer, Pres, Pharmacy Council on Stroke Prevention, PO Box 1336, Sausalito, CA 94966. Phone: (415) 332-4066. Fax: (415) 332-1832. Email: ppsi@aol.com.

TOAD SUCK DAZE. May 1–3. Downtown, Conway, AR. 17th annual event features toad jumping contests, concerts, parade, street dancing, tug-o-war, softball tourna-

ment, bike race, 5K and 10K runs, arts and crafts and more. Annually, the first weekend in May. Est attendance: 125,000. For info: Janiece Driscoll, c/o Conway Chamber of Commerce, PO Box 1492, Conway, AR 72033. Phone: (501) 327-7788. Fax: (501) 327-7790. WWW: http://www.conwayarkcc.org/daze

WILLIAMS, ARCHIE: BIRTH ANNIVERSARY. May 1, 1915. Archie Williams, Olympic gold medal sprinter born at Oakland, CA. Along with Jesse Owens and others, Williams helped debunk Adolf Hitler's theory of Aryan superiority at the 1936 Summer Olympics in Berlin. As a member of the US track team, Williams, an African American, won a gold medal by running the 400-meters in 46.5 seconds. He earned a degree in mechanical engineering from the University of California–Berkeley in 1939, but had to dig ditches for a time because he couldn't find an engineering job. He joined the Army Air Corps in 1942 and later trained pilots at Tuskegee Institute. When asked during a 1981 interview about his treatment by the Nazis during the Olympics, he replied, "Well, over there at least we didn't have to ride in the back of the bus." Died at Fairfax, CA, June 24, 1993.

WOMEN'S HEALTH CARE MONTH. May 1–31. To initiate a public education campaign devoted to increasing awareness of the many health concerns unique to women. Focus will be on the prevention of the major causes of death and poor health among women–heart disease, cancer, arthritis, osteoporosis and bone fractures, as well as on depression and alcoholism in women. There is a $15 charge for kit materials. Annually, the month of May. For info: Pharmacists Planning Service, Inc, 200 Gate Five Rd, Sausalito, CA 94966. Phone: (415) 332-4066. Fax: (415) 332-1832. Email: ppsi@aol.com.

WORLD CHAMPIONSHIP CRIBBAGE TOURNAMENT. May 1–3. Plumas County Fairgrounds, Quincy, CA. Founded in 1972, the country's oldest cribbage tournament now draws entrants from all over the country during the two-day event. Annually, the first weekend in May. Est attendance: 500. For info: Mike Taborski, Tournament Chair, PO Box B, Quincy, CA 95971. Phone: (916) 283-0800. Fax: (916) 283-3952. Email: featherpub@aol.com.

SPORTSCHASER OF THE DAY

What was the score of the longest major-league baseball game ever played?

☆   ☆   ☆

BIRTHDAYS TODAY

Charles (Chuck) Bednarik, 73, Pro Football Hall of Fame center and linebacker, born Bethlehem, PA, May 1, 1925.
Harry Caray (born Harry Christopher Carabini), 79, sportscaster, Ford Frick Award winner, born St. Louis, MO, May 1, 1919.
Steve Cauthen, 38, jockey, born Walton, KY, May 1, 1960.
Patrick John (Pat) Conacher, 39, hockey player, born Edmonton, Alberta, Canada, May 1, 1959.
Roy Lee Jackson, 44, former baseball player, born Opelika, AL, May 1, 1954.
Curtis Martin, 25, football player, born Pittsburgh, PA, May 1, 1973.
Oliver Genoa (Ollie) Matson, 68, Pro Football Hall of Fame halfback, born Trinity, TX, May 1, 1930.
Billy Eugene Owens, 29, basketball player, born Carlisle, PA, May 1, 1969.
Martin Armando Reynoso, 32, baseball player, born San Luis Potosi, Mexico, May 1, 1966.

MAY 2 — SATURDAY
Day 122 — 243 Remaining

NBA FINALS CHAMPIONS THIS DATE
1968   Boston Celtics

BARK IN THE PARK. May 2. Lincoln Park, Chicago, IL. In recognition of Be Kind to Animals Week, thousands of paws and feet will hit the ground running or walking for this 5K event. Entrance fee. Est attendance: 2,000. For info: The Anti-Cruelty Society, 157 W Grand Ave, Chicago, IL 60610.

BIG EAST SOFTBALL TOURNAMENT. May 2–3. University of Notre Dame, Notre Dame, IN. For info: Big East Conference, 56 Exchange Terrace, Providence, RI 02903. Phone: (401) 453-0660. Fax: (401) 751-8540.

BIG EAST MEN'S AND WOMEN'S OUTDOOR TRACK AND FIELD CHAMPIONSHIPS. May 2–3. Villanova University, Villanova, PA. For info: Big East Conference, 56 Exchange Terrace, Providence, RI 02903. Phone: (401) 453-0660. Fax: (401) 751-8540.

COLLINS, EDDIE: BIRTH ANNIVERSARY. May 2, 1887. Edward Trowbridge (Eddie) Collins, Sr, Baseball Hall of Fame second baseman and executive born at Millerton, NY. Collins moved from Columbia University to the Philadelphia Athletics, leading the A's to three World Series triumphs (1910, 1911, 1913). He was sold to the Chicago White Sox where he played 12 years and put in a stint as manager. After retiring, he was an executive with the Boston Red Sox. Inducted into the Hall of Fame in 1939. Died at Boston, MA, Mar 25, 1951.

CROSBY, BING: BIRTH ANNIVERSARY. May 2, 1904. Harry Lillis ("Bing") Crosby, singer, actor and amateur golfer born at Tacoma, WA. Crosby hosted an annual golf tournament that bore his name at Pebble Beach, CA, and also owned part of the Pittsburgh Pirates. Died while playing golf near Madrid, Spain, Oct 14, 1977.

DOUBLE NO-HITTER: ANNIVERSARY. May 2, 1917. Chicago Cubs lefthander James ("Hippo") Vaughn and Cincinnati Reds righthander Fred Toney combined for baseball's only double no-hitter. After both pitchers threw nine innings of no-hit ball, the Reds scored a run on two hits in the top of the 10th inning. Toney set the Reds down in order in the bottom of the 10th.

FIRST NL HOME RUN: ANNIVERSARY. May 2, 1876. Second baseman Ross Barnes of the Chicago White Stockings hit the first home run in National League history. It was an inside-the-park hit off William ("Cherokee") Fisher of the Cincinnati Red Stockings.

FLEMINGTON SPEEDWAY RACING SEASON. May 2–Oct 31 (Saturday nights). Flemington Fairgrounds, Flemington, NJ. Racing by various types of stock cars and other vehicles. 6 PM starting time. Est attendance: 5,000. For info: Paul Kuhl, Flemington Fairgrounds, PO Box 293, Rt 31, Flemington, NJ 08822. Phone: (908) 782-2413. Fax: (908) 806-8432.

GEHRIG'S STREAK ENDS: ANNIVERSARY. May 2, 1939. New York Yankees first baseman Lou Gehrig asked manager Joe McCarthy to take him out of the lineup for the game against the Detroit Tigers. By his sitting out, Gehrig's record streak of consecutive games played,

		S	M	T	W	T	F	S
May							1	2
		3	4	5	6	7	8	9
1998		10	11	12	13	14	15	16
		17	18	19	20	21	22	23
		24	25	26	27	28	29	30
		31						

begun May 25, 1925, stopped at 2,130. The slugger complained of fatigue, but he was really suffering from A.L.S., amyotrophic lateral sclerosis, a condition later known as Lou Gehrig's disease. Gehrig never played again.

Fred Toney

KBCO/BUDWEISER KINETIC SCULPTURE CHALLENGE. May 2. Boulder Reservoir, CO. Teams design kinetic sculptures that must be human-powered and able to travel over land and water. Each team has a theme and designs the sculpture and costumes to correspond. This all-day event includes a hot-air balloon classic, pancake breakfast to benefit a local charity, volleyball tournament and live music from world-class artists. Est attendance: 25,000. For info: KBCO 97.3 FM, 2500 Pearl St, Ste 315, Boulder, CO 80302. Phone: (803) 444-5600.

KENTUCKY DERBY. May 2. Churchill Downs, Louisville, KY. The running of "America's premier" thoroughbred horse race, inaugurated in 1875. First jewel in the "Triple Crown," traditionally followed by the Preakness (the second Saturday after Derby) and the Belmont Stakes (the fifth Saturday after Derby). Annually, the first Saturday in May. Est attendance: 135,000. For info: Churchill Downs, 700 Central Ave, Louisville, KY 40208. Phone: (502) 636-4400. WWW: http://kentuckyderby.com

LEE-JACKSON LACROSSE CLASSIC. May 2. Washington and Lee University, Lexington, VA. Communitywide event when the Washington and Lee University lacrosse team meets the Virginia Military Institute team. 2 PM. For info: Lexington Visitors Bureau, 106 E Washington St, Lexington, VA 24450. Phone: (540) 463-3777. Fax: (540) 463-1105. Email: lexington@rockbridge.net.

MUSIAL HITS FIVE HOMERS: ANNIVERSARY. May 2, 1954. Stan Musial of the St. Louis Cardinals hit five home runs in a doubleheader against the New York Giants in St. Louis, setting a major league record. The Cardinals won the first game, 10–6, but fell to the Giants in the nightcap, 9–7.

NATIONAL HOMEBREW DAY. May 2. A national celebration of more than 1.5 million amateur home brewers. Annually, the first Saturday in May. For info: American Homebrewers Assn, Box 1679, Boulder, CO 80306-1679. Phone: (303) 447-0816. Fax: (303) 447-2825. Email: info@aob.org. WWW: http://www.aob.org/aob

NEW ENGLAND VOLLEYBALL SERIES. May 2–3. (Every weekend through Sept 26–27). Various locations. Amateur volleyball tour. Travels to all six New England states. For info: Bradley J. Van Dussen, Shot Block Promotions, 83 Withington Rd, Newtonville, MA 02160-2037. Phone: (617) 965-SHOT (7468). Email: vball@shotblock.com. WWW: http://www.shotblock.com

USA RUGBY MEN'S COLLEGIATE NATIONAL CHAMPIONSHIP. May 2–3. University of California, Berkeley, CA. Top four men's collegiate teams come together to determine the bona fide collegiate champion in the US. For info: USA Rugby, 3595 E Fountain Blvd, Colorado Springs, CO 80910. Phone: (719) 637-1022. Fax: (719) 637-1315. Email: usarugby@rmii.com.

USA RUGBY MILITARY CHAMPIONSHIP. May 2–3. Site to be announced. Brings together military rugby players from throughout the US. The event allows other military players to play each other and play on the same team. For info: USA Rugby, 3595 E Fountain Blvd, Colorado Springs, CO 80910. Phone: (719) 637-1022. Fax: (719) 637-1315. Email: usarugby@rmii.com.

USA RUGBY WOMEN'S COLLEGIATE NATIONAL CHAMPIONSHIP. May 2–3. Penn State University, University Park, PA. Top four women's collegiate teams come together to determine the bona fide collegiate champion of the US. For info: USA Rugby, 3595 E Fountain Blvd, Colorado Springs, CO 80910. Phone: (719) 637-1022. Fax: (719) 637-1315. Email: usarugby@rmii.com.

VIRGINIA GOLD CUP. May 2. Great Meadow, The Plains, VA. Steeplechasing began in Ireland in 1762 when two horsemen held a cross-country match race to a faraway church steeple. Great Meadow is the largest steeplechase course in the country, with a spectacular hillside amphitheater. The Virginia Gold Cup race, sponsored by BMW and Land Rover, is run over a challenging 4-mile post and rail course of 23 fences. Advance tickets only. Benefits free year-round use of Great Meadow by non-profit community organizations activities. Annually, the first Saturday in May. Est attendance: 50,000. For info: Virginia Gold Cup Assn, Box 840, Warrenton, VA 22186. Phone: (540) 347-2612. Fax: (540) 349-1829. WWW: http://vagoldcup.com

STANLEY CUP CHAMPIONS THIS DATE
1967   Toronto Maple Leafs

BIRTHDAYS TODAY

Edward Francis (Eddie) Bressoud, 66, former baseball player, born Los Angeles, CA, May 2, 1932.

William James ("Gates") Brown, 59, former baseball player, born Crestline, OH, May 2, 1939.

Clay Palmer Carroll, 57, former baseball player, born Clanton, AL, May 2, 1941.

Larry Gatlin, 49, singer, songwriter, amateur golfer, born Odessa, TX, May 2, 1949.

Bobby Keith Moreland, 44, former baseball player, born Dallas, TX, May 2, 1954.

James (Jim) Walewander, 37, former baseball player, born Chicago, IL, May 2, 1961.

Jamaal Abdul-Lateef Wilkes (born Jackson Keith Wilkes), 45, former basketball player, born Berkeley, CA, May 2, 1953.

MAY 3 — SUNDAY
Day 123 — 242 Remaining

BILLYGOAT RUN. May 3. Amherst, MA. America's oldest long-distance orienteering event celebrates its 20th running. For info: Bill Jameson. Phone: (518) 877-8861. E-mail: jameson@albpig.cho.ge.com.

DIMAGGIO MAKES DEBUT: ANNIVERSARY. May 3, 1936. Joe DiMaggio made his major league debut for the New York Yankees and collected three hits in their 14–5 victory over the St. Louis Browns. For the year, DiMaggio hit .323 with 29 home runs and 125 runs batted in.

FIRST TELEVISED DERBY: ANNIVERSARY. May 3, 1952. CBS became the first network to televise the Kentucky Derby. Eddie Arcaro rode Hill Gail to a two-length victory over Sub Fleet. Blue Man was third. For Arcaro, it was a record fifth Derby win. Trainer Ben A. Jones won for the sixth time, also a record.

FRANKENMUTH SKYFEST. May 3. Frankenmuth, MI. To encourage participation in a healthy outdoor sport that adapts to all age groups. 1998 will be the 17th annual Skyfest. Annually, the first Sunday in May. Est attendance: 4,500. For info: Audrey Fischer, Kite Kraft, 576 S Main St, Frankenmuth, MI 48734. Phone: (517) 652-2961.

GENUINE RISK SECOND FILLY TO WIN DERBY: ANNIVERSARY. May 3, 1980. Genuine Risk, ridden by Jacinto Vasquez, became just the second filly to win the Kentucky Derby. She posted a one-length victory over Rumbo.

GOVERNOR'S BAY BRIDGE RUN. May 3. Sandy Point State Park, Annapolis, MD. "Maryland's Most Spectacular Run" 10K foot race across Chesapeake Bay Bridge, dramatic views of the bay and historic Annapolis; designer premium for all finishers; limited to 3,000 entries. Annually, the first Sunday in May. Since 1985. Est attendance: 3,000. For info: Annapolis Striders, Inc, PO Box 187, Annapolis, MD 21404-0187. Phone: (410) 268-1165.

MOON PHASE: FIRST QUARTER. May 3. Moon enters First Quarter phase at 6:04 AM, EDT.

NATIONAL GOLDEN GLOVES TOURNAMENT OF CHAMPIONS. May 3–9. Biloxi, MS. National Golden Gloves amateur boxing championship tournament. For info: Golden Gloves Assn of America Inc, 8801 Princess Jeanne NE, Albuquerque, NM 87112. Phone: (505) 298-8042. Fax: (505) 298-1191.

NBA HAWKS MOVE TO ATLANTA: 30th ANNIVERSARY. May 3, 1968. New owners Tom Cousins and Carl Sanders announced that the St. Louis Hawks of the NBA would move to Atlanta for the 1968–69 season. The team began as the Tri-Cities Blackhawks (1949–51), moved to Milwaukee and then to St. Louis in 1956.

QUEEN CITY ROAD RACE. May 3. Clarksville, TN. 5K and 1-mile races. 20th annual. For info: Clarksville Parks and Recreation, 1514 Golf Club Lane, Clarksville, TN 37040. Phone: (615) 645-7476.

RUSSELL, HONEY: 95th BIRTH ANNIVERSARY. May 3, 1903. John ("Honey") Russell, Basketball Hall of Fame player and coach born at New York, NY. Russell played in more than 3,200 pro basketball games in the sport's early years. In 1936, he became coach at Seton Hall University, remaining there for 11 seasons. He was also a baseball scout, a football scout and a promoter. Inducted into the Hall of Fame in 1964. Died at Livingston, NJ, Nov 15, 1973.

TATUM, GOOSE: BIRTH ANNIVERSARY. May 3, 1921. Reece ("Goose") Tatum, basketball player born at Calion, AR. Tatum played football and baseball and came into his own when Abe Saperstein asked him to play basketball with the Harlem Globetrotters. Tatum's best asset was his hands, big enough to allow him to hold the ball with one hand. He perfected the overhand hook shot later used by Wilt Chamberlain, Connie Hawkins and Kareem Abdul-Jabbar. Suspended by Saperstein in 1955, he formed his own team, the Harlem Magicians. Died at El Paso, TX, Jan 18, 1967.

TRADITIONAL PLOWING MATCH. May 3. Woodstock, VT. This 13th annual event features a horse- and oxen-drawn plowing competition as well as demonstrations of different plowing techniques. Est attendance: 1,050. For info: Deborah Bulissa, Exec Asst, Billings Farm and Museum, PO Box 489, Woodstock, VT 05091. Phone: (802) 457-2355. Fax: (802) 457-4663. Email: billings.farm@valley.net.

WINTERTHUR POINT-TO-POINT. May 3. Winterthur, DE. Steeplechase races, antique carriage parade, canine agility competition, kids' activities, tailgating plus much more! Call for pricing. Rain or shine event. Est attendance: 15,000. For info: Janet Davis, Dir, Point-to-Point, Winterthur, DE 19735. Phone: (302) 888-4600 or (800) 448-3883. Fax: (302) 888-1609.

BIRTHDAYS TODAY

Christopher John (Chris) Cannizzaro, 60, former baseball player, born Oakland, CA, May 3, 1938.
Ron Hextall, 34, hockey player, born Winnipeg, Manitoba, Canada, May 3, 1964.
Charles Edward (Chuck) Hinton, 64, former baseball player, born Rocky Mount, NC, May 3, 1934.
Jeffrey John Hornacek, 35, basketball player, born Elmhurst, IL, May 3, 1963.
Vyacheslav (Slava) Kozlov, 26, hockey player, born Voskresensk, USSR, May 3, 1972.
David Earl (Davey) Lopes, 53, former baseball player, born Providence, RI, May 3, 1945.

MAY 4 — MONDAY
Day 124 — 241 Remaining

STANLEY CUP CHAMPIONS THIS DATE
1969   Montreal Canadiens

AMERICAN BOWLING CONGRESS BUD LIGHT MASTERS TOURNAMENT. May 4-9. Reno, NV. Top pro-

	S	M	T	W	T	F	S
May						1	2
	3	4	5	6	7	8	9
1998	10	11	12	13	14	15	16
	17	18	19	20	21	22	23
	24	25	26	27	28	29	30
	31						

fessional and nonprofessional bowlers from across the country and several foreign nations compete for $235,000 in prize money and one of the sport's most prestigious titles. Each player rolls 10 qualifying games before a cut is made to the top 120 bowlers. Then another 5 qualifying games cut the field to 63, who join the defending champion in a unique 3-game, double-elimination match play format. Est attendance: 10,000. For info: Mark Miller, American Bowling Congress, 5301 S 76th St, Greendale, WI 53129-1127. Phone: (414) 423-3224. Fax: (414) 421-7977.

BASEBALL'S ONE MILLIONTH RUN: ANNIVERSARY. May 4, 1975. Bob Watson of the Houston Astros raced around the bases on Milt May's home run against the San Francisco Giants and crossed the plate with what was declared to be the one millionth run scored in major league baseball history. Watson's hustle paid off. Davey Concepcion of the Cincinnati Reds scored another run in a different game in a different city seconds later.

DANCER'S IMAGE VS. FORWARD PASS: 30th ANNIVERSARY. May 4, 1968. Jockey Bob Ussery rode Dancer's Image to a 1½-length victory over Forward Pass in the Kentucky Derby. Three days later, Dancer's Image was disqualified when tests revealed the presence of an illegal painkilling drug in his system, and Forward Pass was declared the winner. Peter Fuller, owner of Dancer's Image, subsequently challenged the disqualification, and the Kentucky Racing Commission split the difference, ruling that Dancer's Image won the race but Forward Pass could keep the purse.

FIRST PROFESSIONAL BASEBALL GAME: ANNIVERSARY. May 4, 1871. The first game in the new National Association, a full professional league, was played, pitting the Fort Wayne Kekiongas against the Forest City Club of Cleveland. Fort Wayne won, 2–0. James ("Deacon") White was the first man to bat; he got the first hit, a double, and was the first man erased in the first double play.

LAYDEN, ELMER: 95th BIRTH ANNIVERSARY. May 4, 1903. Elmer F. Layden, football player, coach and executive born at Davenport, IA. Layden was the fullback for Coach Knute Rockne's famous backfield, the Four Horsemen of Notre Dame. After graduating in 1925, he entered coaching and was appointed head coach at his alma mater in 1937. He left Notre Dame in 1941 to become NFL commissioner. Died at Chicago, IL, June 30, 1973.

SHOEMAKER STANDS UP IN THE SADDLE: ANNIVERSARY. May 4, 1957. Iron Liege, ridden by Bill Hartack, won the Kentucky Derby by a nose over Gallant Man, ridden by Bill Shoemaker. Gallant Man overtook Iron Liege in the stretch, but Shoemaker misjudged the finish line and stood up at the 1/16-pole, allowing Iron Liege to regain the lead and win the race.

TAFT SEES TWO BALL GAMES: ANNIVERSARY. May 4, 1910. President William Howard Taft watched the St. Louis Cardinals play the Cincinnati Reds at Robison Field, but he didn't stay for the end of the game, won by the Cards, 12–3. Instead, he left for Sportsman's Park to see the St. Louis Browns and the New York Yankees play a 3–3, 14-inning tie, a game called by darkness.

CHASE'S SPORTSQUOTE OF THE DAY
"Correct thinkers think that 'baseball trivia' is an oxymoron: nothing about baseball is trivial." —George Will

BIRTHDAYS TODAY
Alfred ("Butch") Beard, Jr, 51, former basketball coach and player, born Hardinsburg, KY, May 4, 1947.

Rene George Lachemann, 53, former baseball manager and player, born Los Angeles, CA, May 4, 1945.
Richard Max (Rick) Leach, 41, former baseball and football player, born Ann Arbor, MI, May 4, 1957.
Kenneth Ray (Ken) Oberkfell, 42, former baseball player, born Highland, IL, May 4, 1956.
Elizabeth Earle (Betsy) Rawls, 70, LPGA Hall of Fame golfer, born Spartanburg, SC, May 4, 1928.
George F. Will, 57, editor, columnist, baseball executive, born Champaign, IL, May 4, 1941.

MAY 5 — TUESDAY
Day 125 — 240 Remaining

NBA FINALS CHAMPIONS THIS DATE
1969   Boston Celtics

AMERICAN LEAGUE'S FIRST PERFECT GAME: ANNIVERSARY. May 5, 1904. Denton T. ("Cy") Young pitched the first perfect game in the American League, not allowing a single opposing player to reach first base. Young's outstanding performance led the Boston Americans in a 3–0 victory over Philadelphia in the American League. The Cy Young Award for pitching was named in his honor.

BENDER, CHIEF: 115th BIRTH ANNIVERSARY. May 5, 1883. Charles Albert ("Chief") Bender, Baseball Hall of Fame pitcher born at Crow Wing County, MN. Part Native American, Bender pitched for the Philadelphia Athletics from 1903 through 1914, winning 191 games. He played in the Federal League and then with the Philadelphia Phillies. Inducted into the Hall of Fame in 1953. Died at Philadelphia, PA, May 22, 1954.

NCAA WOMEN'S DIVISION III TENNIS CHAMPIONSHIPS. May 5–11. Finals at a site TBA. For info: NCAA, 6201 College Blvd, Overland Park, KS 66211. Phone: (913) 339-1906.

PETE ROSE GETS 3,000th HIT: 20th ANNIVERSARY. May 5, 1978. Pete Rose of the Cincinnati Reds got the 3,000th hit of his career, a single off Steve Rogers of the Montreal Expos. Rose played in the majors from 1963 through 1986 and wound up with 4,256 hits, more than any other player.

RICHMOND, LEE: BIRTH ANNIVERSARY. May 5, 1857. J. Lee Richmond, baseball player born at Sheffield, OH. A curve balling lefthander, he made his major league debut in 1879. He pitched baseball's first perfect game on June 12, 1880. Died at Toledo, OH, Sept 30, 1929.

SECRETARIAT WINS THE DERBY IN RECORD TIME: 25th ANNIVERSARY. May 5, 1973. Secretariat, ridden by Ron Turcotte, won the Kentucky Derby in the record time of 1:59.2. "Big Red," as he was known, beat Sham by 2 ½ lengths and went on to win the Triple Crown.

STANLEY CUP CHAMPIONS THIS DATE
1966   Montreal Canadiens

BIRTHDAYS TODAY

LaPhonso Darnell Ellis, 28, basketball player, born East St. Louis, IL, May 5, 1970.
Tommy Vann Helms, 57, former baseball manager and player, born Charlotte, NC, May 5, 1941.
Charles Harrison Nagy, 31, baseball player, born Fairfield, CT, May 5, 1967.
Ronald John (Ron) Oester, 42, former baseball player, born Cincinnati, OH, May 5, 1956.
Zigmund (Ziggy) Palffy, 26, hockey player, born Skalica, Czechoslovakia, May 5, 1972.

Mikael Renberg, 26, hockey player, born Pitea, Sweden, May 5, 1972.

☆   ☆   ☆

MAY 6 — WEDNESDAY
Day 126 — 239 Remaining

BABE RUTH'S FIRST MAJOR LEAGUE HOME RUN: ANNIVERSARY. May 6, 1915. George Herman ("Babe") Ruth of the Boston Red Sox hit his first major league home run in a game against the New York Yankees in New York.

BANNISTER SHATTERS FOUR-MINUTE MILE BARRIER: ANNIVERSARY. May 6, 1954. Running the mile for the British Amateur Athletic Association team in a meet at Oxford University, Roger Bannister broke the four-minute barrier with a time of 3:59.4. Bannister shattered the existing record, set by Gunder Haag of Sweden in 1945, by a full two seconds. Four minutes (or one minute per quarter-mile) was at the time considered not only a physical barrier but also a psychological one. In this epic race, Bannister relied on two teammates to pace him. Chris Brasher helped Bannister for the first two laps with times of 57.5 and 1:58.2. Chris Chataway sprang to the lead for the third quarter (3:00.5). Bannister followed Chataway around the curve and started his kick on the backstretch. He sprinted past Chataway and, as he broke the tape, into track history. But his record lasted little more than a month, until John Landy of Australia ran 3:58.0 on June 21.

BOBO'S ONE AND ONLY: 45th ANNIVERSARY. May 6, 1953. Alva ("Bobo") Holloman of the St. Louis Browns pitched a no-hitter in his first major league start, defeating the Philadelphia Athletics, 6–0. Holloman never pitched another complete game in his career which lasted just another 21 games.

BONNIE BLUE NATIONAL HORSE SHOW. May 6–9. Virginia Horse Center, Lexington, VA. Major all-breed event, "A"-rated show of the American Horse Show Association. For info: Lexington Visitors Bureau, 106 E Washington St, Lexington, VA 24450. Phone: (540) 463-3777. Fax: (540) 463-1105. Email: lexington@rockbridge.net.

HALFWAY POINT OF SPRING. May 6. At 12:59 AM, EDT, on May 6, 1998, 46 days, 9 hours and 4 minutes of spring will have elapsed, and the equivalent will remain before June 21, 9:03 AM, EDT, which is the summer solstice and the beginning of summer.

IRISH, NED: BIRTH ANNIVERSARY. May 6, 1905. Edward Simmons (Ned) Irish, Basketball Hall of Fame promoter born at Lake George, NY. Irish attended the University of Pennsylvania and covered its sports teams for six New York and ten Philadelphia newspapers. In 1928 he began working for the *New York World–Telegram* and specializing in college basketball. He persuaded Madison Square Garden to host the first college basketball doubleheader in 1934 and soon left journalism to become the Garden's basketball director. He regularly brought top college teams to New York and founded the National Invitation Tournament. He also helped found the NBA and the New York Knicks. Inducted into the Hall of Fame in 1964. Died at New York, NY, Jan 2, 1982.

LONGEST FOOTRACE BEGINS: ANNIVERSARY. May 6, 1929. The longest footrace in history began at City Hall in New York City. It concluded on July 24 in San Francisco, 3,415 miles later. 60-year-old Abraham Lincoln Monteverde, a veteran of more than 100 marathons, not only won the race but he was also the only competitor to finish.

PERRY WINS 300th GAME: ANNIVERSARY. May 6, 1982. Gaylord Perry of the Seattle Mariners defeated the New York Yankees, 7–3, to win the 300th game of his career. Long suspected of doctoring the baseball, Perry played for eight different teams over 22 years and won 314 games.

PROJECT ACES DAY. May 6. 10th annual celebration of fitness and unity worldwide when All Children Exercise Simultaneously. "The World's Largest Exercise Class" takes place the first Wednesday in May as schools in all 50 states and 50 different countries hold fitness classes, assemblies and other fitness education events involving millions of children, parents and teachers. Conducted in cooperation with the President's Council on Physical Fitness and Sports during National Physical Fitness and Sports Month. For info send SASE to: Youth Fitness Coalition, Inc, PO Box 6452, Jersey City, NJ 07306-0452. Phone: (201) 433-8993. Fax: (201) 332-3060.

SCOTT'S STREAK STOPPED: ANNIVERSARY. May 6, 1925. New York Yankees shortstop Everett Scott removed himself from the starting lineup and snapped his streak of 1,307 consecutive games played, started when he was a member of the Boston Red Sox. Scott gave way to Paul ("Pee Wee") Wanninger, whose major league career totaled 163 games. Scott's streak stood as the major league record until Lou Gehrig broke it.

WHALERS WIN FIRST WHA CROWN: 25th ANNIVERSARY. May 6, 1973. The New England Whalers won the first championship of the World Hockey Association. They defeated the Winnipeg Jets, 9–6, to win the final series, four games to one. Both teams later moved into the National Hockey League.

BIRTHDAYS TODAY

Larry Eugene Andersen, 45, former baseball player, born Portland, OR, May 6, 1953.
Bob Bassen, 33, hockey player, born Calgary, Alberta, Canada, May 6, 1965.
Thomas Edward (Tom) Bolton, 36, former baseball player, born Nashville, TN, May 6, 1962.
Martin Brodeur, 26, hockey player, born Montreal, Quebec, Canada, May 6, 1972.
William Alfred (Bill) Hands, 58, former baseball player, born Hackensack, NJ, May 6, 1940.
Willie Howard Mays, 67, Baseball Hall of Fame outfielder, born Westfield, AL, May 6, 1931.
Albert Hamilton (Al) Williams, 44, former baseball player, born Pearl Lagoon, Nicaragua, May 6, 1954.

MAY 7 — THURSDAY

Day 127 — 238 Remaining

NBA FINALS CHAMPIONS THIS DATE
1972   Los Angeles Lakers

BIG TEN MEN'S TENNIS CHAMPIONSHIPS. May 7–10. University of Minnesota, Minneapolis, MN. Est attendance: 400. For info: Big Ten Conference, 1500 W Higgins Rd, Park Ridge, IL 60068-6300. Phone: (847) 696-1010. Fax: (847) 696-1150. WWW: http://www.bigten.org

May 1998	S	M	T	W	T	F	S
						1	2
	3	4	5	6	7	8	9
	10	11	12	13	14	15	16
	17	18	19	20	21	22	23
	24	25	26	27	28	29	30
	31						

COOPER, GARY: BIRTH ANNIVERSARY. May 7, 1901. Frank James ("Gary") Cooper, actor born at Helena, MT. Cooper changed his name to Gary at the start of his movie career. His first major role was in *The Winning of Barbara Worth* in 1926. Many films followed, including *Pride of the Yankees*, the biography of Lou Gehrig. Died at Hollywood, CA, May 13, 1961.

ENGLAND: MITSUBISHI MOTORS BADMINTON HORSE TRIALS. May 7–10. Badminton, Avon. Famous international horse trials consisting of show jumping, cross-country and dressage. Est attendance: 200,000. For info: Box Office, Badminton Horse Trials, Badminton, Gloucester, England GL9 1DF. Phone: (44) (145) 421-8272. Fax: (44) (145) 421-8596. WWW: http://www.badminton-horse.co.uk

LA LAKERS WIN THEIR FIRST NBA TITLE: ANNIVERSARY. May 7, 1972. After trying and failing seven times since moving from Minneapolis in 1960, the Los Angeles Lakers won their first NBA championship, defeating the New York Knicks, 114–100, to win the series, four games to one. As the Minneapolis Lakers, the team had won five titles, the last one coming in 1954.

MARTIN Z. MOLLUSK DAY. May 7. Moorlyn Terrace Beach, Ocean City, NJ. If Martin Z. Mollusk, a hermit crab, sees his shadow at 11 AM, EST, summer comes a week early–if he doesn't, summer begins on time. 1998 will be the 24th annual observance. Est attendance: 300. For info: Mark Soifer, City Hall, Ocean City, NJ 08226. Phone: (609) 525-9300 or (609) 399-0272. Fax: (609) 399-0374.

NCAA WOMEN'S DIVISION I GOLF CHAMPIONSHIP. May 7–9. Regionals at sites TBA. For info: NCAA, 6201 College Blvd, Overland Park, KS 66211. Phone: (913) 339-1906.

RAIDERS WIN NFL SUIT: ANNIVERSARY. May 7, 1982. A federal jury decided that the National Football League was in violation of antitrust laws when it attempted to prohibit the Oakland Raiders from moving to Los Angeles. The Raiders, an original team in the American Football League, played in Oakland from 1960 through 1981 and in Los Angeles from 1982 through 1994 after which they returned to Oakland.

ROY CAMPANELLA NIGHT: ANNIVERSARY. May 7, 1959. 93,103 fans attended an exhibition game between the Los Angeles Dodgers and the New York Yankees at the Los Angeles Coliseum to show their support for injured Dodgers catcher Roy Campanella. A three-time Most Valuable Player in the National League, Campanella was permanently paralyzed in an automobile accident in December 1958. The evening's ceremonies, dubbed "Roy Campanella Night," preceded the game, won by the Yankees, 6–2.

SCORE GETS HIT IN EYE: ANNIVERSARY. May 7, 1957. In a game between the New York Yankees and the Cleveland Indians, Yankees infielder Gil McDougald rifled a line drive at pitcher Herb Score, hitting him on the right eye. The ball broke Score's nose and damaged his eye. He missed the rest of the season but returned to pitch in 1958.

WINNING COLORS THIRD FILLY TO WIN DERBY: ANNIVERSARY. May 7, 1988. Winning Colors, ridden by Gary Stevens, became the third filly and the first roan to win the Kentucky Derby. Forty Niner finished second, and Risen Star was third.

WRIGHT MAKES UNASSISTED TRIPLE PLAY: ANNIVERSARY. May 7, 1925. Shortstop Glenn Wright of the Pittsburgh Pirates completed the fourth unassisted triple play in major league baseball history in the ninth inning of a game against the St. Louis Cardinals. Wright caught a line drive hit by Jim Bottomley, stepped on second to double off Jimmy Cooney and then tagged Rogers Hornsby before he could retreat to first.

ZACHARY, TOM: BIRTH ANNIVERSARY. May 7, 1896. Jonathan Thompson Walton (Tom) Zachary, baseball player born at Graham, NC. Zachary is best known for surrendering Babe Ruth's 60th home run on Sept 30, 1927. He won two games in the 1924 World Series as the Washington Senators defeated the New York Giants. Died at Graham, Jan 24, 1969.

BIRTHDAYS TODAY

Anthony (Tony) Campbell, 36, former basketball player, born Teaneck, NJ, May 7, 1962.
Ronnie Keith Harmon, 34, football player, born New York, NY, May 7, 1964.
Jean Claude Mark Raymond, 61, broadcaster and former baseball player, born St. Jean, Quebec, Canada, May 7, 1937.
John Constantine (Johnny) Unitas, 65, Pro Football Hall of Fame quarterback, born Pittsburgh, PA, May 7, 1933.
Richard Hirschfeld (Dick) Williams, 69, former baseball manager and player, born St. Louis, MO, May 7, 1929.

MAY 8 — FRIDAY
Day 128 — 237 Remaining

NBA FINALS CHAMPIONS THIS DATE
1970   New York Knicks

ASSOCIATION OF COLLEGE UNIONS INTERNATIONAL BOWLING CHAMPIONSHIPS. May 8. Reno, NV. Top regional bowlers vie for doubles, singles and all-events titles, with the all-events champion earning a berth in the National Amateur Finals. Est attendance: 1,000. For info: American Bowling Congress, 5301 S 76th St, Greendale, WI 53129-1127. Phone: (414) 421-6400. Fax: (414) 421-7977.

BIG TEN SOFTBALL TOURNAMENT. May 8–9. Site of regular-season conference champion. For info: Big Ten Conference, 1500 W Higgins Rd, Park Ridge, IL 60068-6300. Phone: (847) 696-1010. Fax: (847) 696-1150. WWW: http://www.bigten.org

BIG TEN MEN'S GOLF CHAMPIONSHIP. May 8–10. University of Illinois, Urbana, IL. For info: Big Ten Conference, 1500 W Higgins Rd, Park Ridge, IL 60068-6300. Phone: (847) 696-1010. Fax: (847) 696-1150. WWW: http://www.bigten.org

BROUTHERS, DAN: 140th BIRTH ANNIVERSARY. May 8, 1858. Dennis Joseph ("Dan") Brouthers, baseball player born at Sylvan Lake, NY. Brouthers (pronounced BROO-thers) was a slugging first baseman in the 1880s and 1890s. Allegedly he was the first to urge batters to "keep your eye on the ball." Died at East Orange, NJ, Aug 2, 1932.

CARDINALS CLOSE OLD BUSCH STADIUM: ANNIVERSARY. May 8, 1966. The St. Louis Cardinals played their last game in old Busch Stadium, formerly known as Sportsman's Park, losing to the San Francisco Giants, 10–5. They opened new Busch Memorial Stadium on May 12.

FIRST 60-FOOT SHOT PUT: ANNIVERSARY. May 8, 1954. World-record holder William Parry O'Brien of the US became the first shot-putter to clear 60 feet with a throw of 60 feet, 5¼ inches, at a meet in Los Angeles. O'Brien won gold medals at the 1952 and 1956 Olympics and a silver medal at the 1960 games.

HUNTER PITCHES PERFECT GAME: 30th ANNIVERSARY. May 8, 1968. Jim ("Catfish") Hunter of the Oakland Athletics pitched a perfect game, defeating the Minnesota Twins, 4–0. This was the first regular-season perfect game in the American League since Charlie Robertson turned the trick in 1922.

KNICKS WIN FIRST NBA TITLE: ANNIVERSARY. May 8, 1970. The New York Knicks won their first NBA title, defeating the Los Angeles Lakers, 113–99, in Game 7 of the finals. The Knicks were led by injured center Willis Reed, who limped onto the court to score the game's first two baskets, and guard Walt Frazier, who scored 36 points.

LISTON, SONNY: BIRTH ANNIVERSARY. May 8, 1932. Charles ("Sonny") Liston, boxer born at St. Francis County, AR. Liston rose above a record of criminal activity to defeat Floyd Patterson for the heavyweight title on Sept 25, 1962. He defeated Patterson in a rematch but then lost the title to Cassius Clay, who later changed his name to Muhammad Ali. In a rematch Ali knocked out Liston with a punch few observers saw. Died at Las Vegas, NV, Dec 30, 1970.

MARIUCCI, JOHN: BIRTH ANNIVERSARY. May 8, 1916. John P. Mariucci, hockey player, coach and executive born at Eveleth, MN. Mariucci played hockey in high school and at the University of Minnesota where he earned All-American honors. He turned pro in 1940, played with the Chicago Black Hawks and became the first American-born player to captain an NHL team. After retiring, he coached at Minnesota and always sought out American players. Died at Minneapolis, MN, Mar 23, 1987.

OUIMET, FRANCIS: 105th BIRTH ANNIVERSARY. May 8, 1893. Francis DeSales Ouimet, golfer born at Brookline, MA. Ouimet is credited more than any other person with establishing the popularity of golf in the US. The son of a gardener, Ouimet began his golfing career as a caddy. In 1913, at age 20, he became a national hero and generated national enthusiasm for the game of golf when he became the first American and first amateur to win the US Open. He won the US Amateur in 1914 and 1931, and he was a member of the US Walker Cup team from its first tournament in 1922 until 1949, serving as its nonplaying captain for six of those years. In 1949, he established the Francis Ouimet Caddy Scholarship Fund, and in 1951, he became the first American to be elected captain of the Royal and Ancient Golf Club of St. Andrews, Scotland. Died at Wellesley, MA, Sept 2, 1967.

REGRET FIRST FILLY TO WIN DERBY: ANNIVERSARY. May 8, 1915. Regret, ridden by Joe Notter, became the first filly to win the Kentucky Derby. She led wire-to-wire and finished the 1¼-mile race in 2:05.2. Pebbles was second, two lengths behind, and Sharpshooter was third.

ROBINSON HITS HOME RUN OUT OF MEMORIAL STADIUM: ANNIVERSARY. May 8, 1966. Frank Robinson of the Orioles became the only player ever to hit a home run out of Baltimore's Memorial Stadium. His long drive over the left-field wall, against Luis Tiant of the Cleveland Indians, traveled an estimated 451 feet.

SEC SOFTBALL TOURNAMENT. May 8–10. Site TBA. For info: Southeastern Conference, 2201 Civic Center Blvd, Birmingham, AL 35203-1103. Phone: (205) 458-3010. Fax: (205) 458-3030. Email: cbloom@sec.org. WWW: http://www.secsports.org

SOVIETS BOYCOTT 1984 SUMMER OLYMPICS: ANNIVERSARY. May 8, 1984. The Soviet Union announced that it would not compete in the 1984 Summer Olympic Games, scheduled to open in Los Angeles on July 28. The Soviet National Olympic Committee's statement, issued on the day the Olympic torch relay began, declared that Soviet participation would be impossible because of "the gross flouting" of Olympic ideals by US authorities.

SPORTSCHASER OF THE DAY
Who was the first American golfer to win the US Open?

BIRTHDAYS TODAY

Douglas Leon (Doug) Atkins, 68, Pro Football Hall of Fame defensive end, born Humboldt, TN, May 8, 1930.
William Laird (Bill) Cowher, 41, football coach and former player, born Pittsburgh, PA, May 8, 1957.
Miguel Angel (Mike) Cuellar, 61, former baseball player, born Las Villas, Cuba, May 8, 1937.
Chester Cornelius ("Red") Hoff, 107, oldest living former major league baseball player, born Ossining, NY, May 8, 1891.
Dennis Patrick Leonard, 47, former baseball player, born New York, NY, May 8, 1951.
Ronald Mandel (Ronnie) Lott, 39, former football player, born Albuquerque, NM, May 8, 1959.

MAY 9 — SATURDAY
Day 129 — 236 Remaining

BRAILLE INSTITUTE-OPTIMIST TRACK AND FIELD OLYMPICS. May 9. Braille Institute Youth Center, Los Angeles, CA. To offer athletic competition to blind and visually impaired youths. Annually, the second Saturday in May. Co-sponsored by the Optimist Clubs of Southern California. Est attendance: 1,000. For info: Braille Institute, Communications Dept, 741 N Vermont Ave, Los Angeles, CA 90029. Phone: (213) 663-1111.

DELTA DEMOCRAT–TIMES GRAND PRIX CATFISH RACES. May 9. Greenville, MS. To recognize the noble racing heart of the thoroughbred pond-raised Mississippi catfish. 14th annual races. Annually, on the Saturday before Mother's Day. Est attendance: 10,000. For info: *Delta Democrat–Times*, Dan Way, Editor, Box 1618, Greenville, MS 38701. Phone: (601) 335-1155. Fax: (601) 335-2860.

EDDIE MURRAY'S DOUBLE DOUBLE: ANNIVERSARY. May 9, 1987. Switch-hitter Eddie Murray of the Baltimore Orioles became the first player in major league history to hit home runs from both sides of the plate in consecutive games.

ELECTRA GOAT BBQ COOK-OFF. May 9. Electra Goat Grounds, Electra, TX. Goat Cook-Off, Cow Patty Drop, live band, horseshoe tournament, tug-o-war, eating contest, children's games and crafts. Little Mr. and Miss Goat Competition. Dance 9 PM–1 AM after cook-off. Annually, the Saturday before Mother's Day. Est attendance: 1,500. For info: Dawn Dunsmore, Electra Chamber of Commerce, 112 W Cleveland, Electra, TX 76360. Phone: (817) 495-3577. Fax: (817) 495-3577.

GENTILE HITS CONSECUTIVE GRAND SLAMS: ANNIVERSARY. May 9, 1961. First baseman Jim Gentile of the Baltimore Orioles became the fourth player to hit grand slams in consecutive innings. Gentile hit his homers in the first and second innings of a game against the Minnesota Twins and added a sacrifice fly as the Orioles won, 13–5.

GONZALES, PANCHO: 70th BIRTH ANNIVERSARY. May 9, 1928. Richard Alonzo ("Pancho") Gonzales, tennis player born at Los Angeles, CA. A self-taught player, Gonzales won the 1948 US National Singles Championship and repeated in 1949. He turned pro and won the world's championship from 1954 through 1962. Gonzales was an aggressive, temperamental player who rarely trained. Died at Las Vegas, NV, July 3, 1994.

IROQUOIS STEEPLECHASE. May 9. Percy Warner Park, Nashville, TN. Nashville's original "Rite of Spring." This event is the oldest continuously run, weight-for-age steeplechase, held at Percy Warner Park. The steeplechase has a seven-race card with the featured Iroquois Memorial. Annually, the second Saturday in May. Est attendance: 30,000. For info: Linda Floyd, Steeplechase Office, 2424 Garland Ave, Nashville, TN 37212. Phone: (615) 332-7284. Fax: (615) 322-6453.

LONGEST EXTRA-INNING GAME: ANNIVERSARY. May 9, 1984. The Chicago White Sox defeated the Milwaukee Brewers, 7–6, on a Harold Baines home run in the 25th inning. The game, the first 17 innings of which were played the day before, was the longest extra-inning game by time, 8 hours, 6 minutes. The teams then played their regularly scheduled game of nine innings, making a total of 34 innings in two days.

ROCK-A-THON. May 9. Senior citizens and their friends, family and local businesses commit to rocking in rocking chairs to raise money for area children's hospitals. Money raised is often used by the neonatal and pediatrics units of these hospitals to purchase rocking chairs to be used to rock and comfort sick children. For info: Rock-a-thon/Mktg Dept, National Guest Homes, LLC, 8550 Katy Freeway, Ste 201, Houston, TX 77024. Phone: (713) 464-4884. Fax: (713) 464-4891.

SAVANNAH SCOTTISH GAMES AND HIGHLAND GATHERING. May 9. Old Fort Jackson, Savannah, GA. Clan tents, geological information, highland regimental pipe bands, Southeast Regional Scottish Highland Dancing Championship, single malt Scotch whiskey tasting, kilted golf, entertainment by Scotland's finest musicians and children's games. Est attendance: 5,000. For info: Savannah Scottish Games and Highland Gathering, PO Box 13435, Savannah, GA 31416.

BIRTHDAYS TODAY

David Benoit, 30, basketball player, born Lafayette, LA, May 9, 1968.
Anthony Keith (Tony) Gwynn, 38, baseball player, born Los Angeles, CA, May 9, 1960.
Calvin Jerome Murphy, 50, Basketball Hall of Fame guard, born Norwalk, CT, May 9, 1948.
John Anton Stuper, 41, former baseball player, born Butler, PA, May 9, 1957.
Mark Tinordi, 32, hockey player, born Red Deer, Alberta, Canada, May 9, 1966.
Steve Yzerman, 33, hockey player, born Cranbrook, BC, Canada, May 9, 1965.

May 1998	S	M	T	W	T	F	S
						1	2
	3	4	5	6	7	8	9
	10	11	12	13	14	15	16
	17	18	19	20	21	22	23
	24	25	26	27	28	29	30
	31						

MAY 10 — SUNDAY
Day 130 — 235 Remaining

NBA FINALS CHAMPIONS THIS DATE
1973   New York Knicks

AFL-NFL MERGER COMPLETE: ANNIVERSARY. May 10, 1969. The American Football League and the National Football League announced that plans for their merger and integration into one league with two conferences of 13 teams each were complete. Three NFL teams, the Baltimore Colts, the Cleveland Browns and the Pittsburgh Steelers, agreed to join the American Football Conference as part of the deal.

BARROW, ED: 130th BIRTH ANNIVERSARY. May 10, 1868. Edward Grant (Ed) Barrow, Baseball Hall of Fame manager and executive born at Springfield, IL. Barrow was a minor league executive when the Boston Red Sox named him field manager in 1918. In 1921 he became general manager of the New York Yankees and engineered their rise to decades of American League dominance. Inducted into the Hall of Fame in 1953. Died at Port Chester, NY, Dec 15, 1953.

BLANKENSHIP, TED: BIRTH ANNIVERSARY. May 10, 1901. Theodore (Ted) Blankenship, baseball player born at Bonham, TX. Blankenship was a workhorse pitcher for the woeful Chicago White Sox teams of the 1920s. His brother Homer also pitched in the majors. Died at Atoka, OK, Jan 14, 1945.

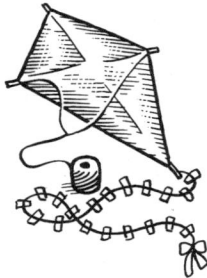

KITE DAY. May 10. Charlottesville, VA. Fly a kite at Ash Lawn-Highland, home of President James Monroe. Est attendance: 300. For info: Ash Lawn-Highland, Rt 6, Box 37, Charlottesville, VA 22902. Phone: (804) 293-9539. Fax: (804) 293-8000.

MOTHER'S DAY. May 10. Observed first in 1907 at the request of Anna Jarvis of Philadelphia, PA, who asked her church to hold service in memory of all mothers on the anniversary of her mother's death. Annually, the second Sunday in May.

MUDDER'S DAY OFF-ROAD CHALLENGE. May 10. Rhinelander, WI. 22K mountain bike race on the scenic Mudder's Day Trail at Holiday Acres Resort. Annually, on Mother's Day. Est attendance: 400. For info: Rhinelander Area Chamber of Commerce, PO Box 795, Rhinelander, WI 54501. Phone: (800) 236-4386.

SIR BARTON WINS DERBY: ANNIVERSARY. May 10, 1919. Sir Barton, ridden by Johnny Loftus, won the Kentucky Derby by five lengths. Leading wire-to-wire, he went on to become the first horse to win the Triple Crown (the Derby, the Preakness Stakes and the Belmont Stakes).

WILHELM PITCHES IN 1,000th GAME: ANNIVERSARY. May 10, 1970. Hoyt Wilhelm of the Atlanta Braves became the first major league pitcher to appear in 1,000 games when he was called in from the bullpen in a game against the St. Louis Cardinals. Wilhelm gave up three runs, and the Braves lost, 6–5.

STANLEY CUP CHAMPIONS THIS DATE
1970   Boston Bruins
1973   Montreal Canadiens

BIRTHDAYS TODAY
Randolph William (Randy) Cunneyworth, 37, hockey player, born Etobicoke, Ontario, Canada, May 10, 1961.
Daniel Leslie (Dan) Schayes, 39, basketball player, born Syracuse, NY, May 10, 1959.
Peter Alan (Pete) Schourek, 29, baseball player, born Austin, TX, May 10, 1969.
Ronald F. (Rony) Seikaly, 33, basketball player, born Beirut, Lebanon, May 10, 1965.
Robert Randall (Robby) Thompson, 36, baseball player, born West Palm Beach, FL, May 10, 1962.

☆   ☆   ☆

MAY 11 — MONDAY
Day 131 — 234 Remaining

STANLEY CUP CHAMPIONS THIS DATE
1968   Montreal Canadiens
1972   Boston Bruins

CHYLAK, NESTOR: BIRTH ANNIVERSARY. May 11, 1922. Nestor Chylak, baseball umpire born at Peckville, PA. Chylak umpired in the American League from 1954 to 1978, working six All-Star games and five World Series. Most observers considered him the finest AL umpire of his generation. Died at Dunmore, PA, Feb 17, 1982.

GEHRINGER, CHARLIE: 95th BIRTH ANNIVERSARY. May 11, 1903. Charles Leonard (Charlie) Gehringer, Baseball Hall of Fame second baseman born at Fowlerville, MI. Gehringer was known as the "Mechanical Man" for the methodical way he approached playing baseball. He hit .320 over 19 years with the Detroit Tigers. Inducted into the Hall of Fame in 1949. Died at Bloomfield Hills, MI, Jan 21, 1993.

MONTREAL WINS STANLEY CUP OVER EXPANSION BLUES: 30th ANNIVERSARY. May 11, 1968. The Montreal Canadiens completed a four-game sweep of the St. Louis Blues in the Stanley Cup finals, winning the fourth game, 3–2, in St. Louis. The 1967–68 season marked the debut of six expansion teams, the Los Angeles Kings, the Minnesota North Stars, the Oakland Seals, the Philadelphia Flyers, the Pittsburgh Penguins and the Blues. They were all grouped into the Western Conference, and one of them was guaranteed a spot in the finals.

MOON PHASE: FULL MOON. May 11. Moon enters Full Moon phase at 10:29 AM, EDT.

PITCHER DUNNING HITS LAST GRAND SLAM: ANNIVERSARY. May 11, 1971. Steve Dunning of the Cleveland Indians became the last pitcher in the American League to hit a grand slam prior to the inauguration of the designated-hitter rule in 1973. His homer, coming in a game against the Oakland A's pitcher Diego Segui, gave the Indians a 5–0 lead. They won the game, 7–5, but relief pitcher Phil Hennigan got the win.

SEWELL, RIP: BIRTH ANNIVERSARY. May 11, 1907. Truett Banks ("Rip") Sewell, baseball player born at Decatur, AL. Sewell pitched in the major leagues for 13 years. His famous pitch was the "eephus," a change of pace that arched 25 feet above the ground. Ted Williams hit an eephus for a three-run homer in the 1946 All-Star game. Died at Plant City, FL, Sept 3, 1989.

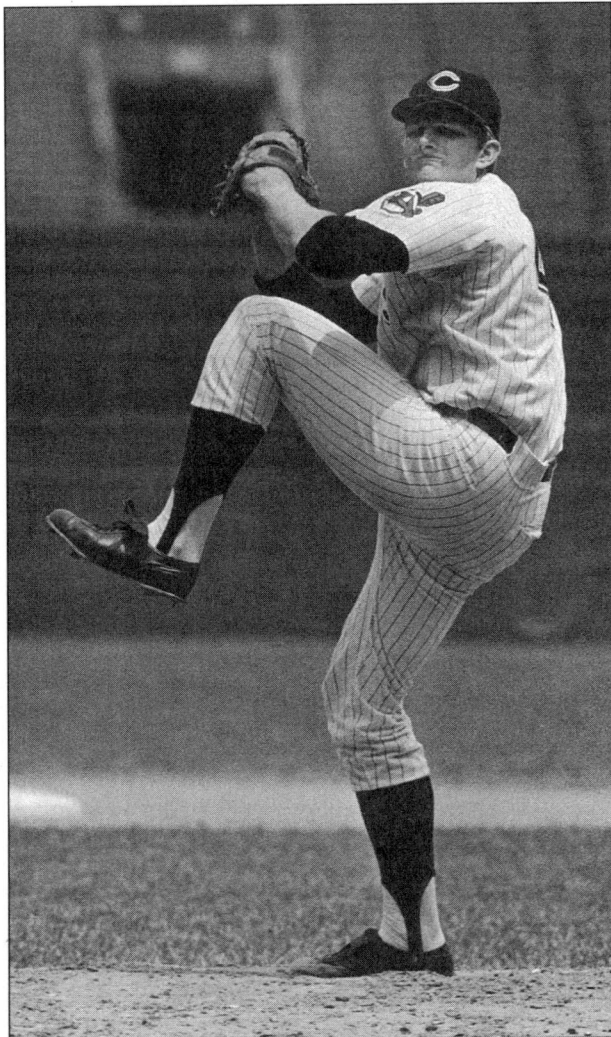

Pitcher Dunning Hits Last Grand Slam

CHASE'S SPORTSQUOTE OF THE DAY

"He's in a rut. Gehringer goes two for five on Opening Day and stays that way all season." —Lefty Gomez on Charlie Gehringer

BIRTHDAYS TODAY

Eugene Victor (Gene) Hermanski, 78, former baseball player, born Pittsfield, MA, May 11, 1920.

Milton Stephen (Milt) Pappas (born Miltiades Stergios Papastegios), 59, former baseball player, born Detroit, MI, May 11, 1939.

Francis Ralph (Frank) Quilici, 59, former baseball manager and player, born Chicago, IL, May 11, 1939.

Charles Walter (Walt) Terrell, 40, former baseball player, born Jeffersonville, IN, May 11, 1958.

	S	M	T	W	T	F	S
May						1	2
	3	4	5	6	7	8	9
1998	10	11	12	13	14	15	16
	17	18	19	20	21	22	23
	24	25	26	27	28	29	30
	31						

John Kennedy (Jack) Twyman, 64, Basketball Hall of Fame forward and guard, born Pittsburgh, PA, May 11, 1934.

Robert Andrew (Bobby) Witt, 34, baseball player, born Arlington, VA, May 11, 1964.

MAY 12 — TUESDAY
Day 132 — 233 Remaining

NBA FINALS CHAMPIONS THIS DATE
1974   Boston Celtics

ACC BASEBALL TOURNAMENT. May 12–17. Durham Bulls Park, Durham, NC. For info: Atlantic Coast Conference, PO Drawer ACC, Greensboro, NC 27419-6999. Phone: (910) 854-8787. Fax: (910) 854-8797.

BANKS HITS 500TH HOME RUN: ANNIVERSARY. May 12, 1970. Ernie Banks of the Chicago Cubs hit the 500th home run of his career off Pat Jarvis of the Atlanta Braves. The Cubs won the game, 4–3, at Wrigley Field. Banks played from 1953 through 1971 and wound up with 521 home runs.

CARDINALS OPEN NEW BUSCH STADIUM: ANNIVERSARY. May 12, 1966. The St. Louis Cardinals opened new Busch Memorial Stadium by defeating the Atlanta Braves, 4–3, in 12 innings. Felipe Alou hit a pair of homers for the Braves, but Lou Brock drove in the winning run with a single.

DUGAN, JUMPING JOE: BIRTH ANNIVERSARY. May 12, 1897. Joseph Anthony ("Jumping Joe") Dugan, baseball player born at Mahanoy City, PA. Dugan played third base for the Philadelphia Athletics and the New York Yankees in the Babe Ruth era. He earned his nickname for going AWOL early in his career. Died at Norwood, MA, July 7, 1982.

NCAA MEN'S DIVISION III GOLF CHAMPIONSHIPS. May 12–15. Jekyll Island, GA. For info: NCAA, 6201 College Blvd, Overland Park, KS 66211. Phone: (913) 339-1906.

NCAA WOMEN'S DIVISION II AND III GOLF CHAMPIONSHIPS. May 12–15 or 13–16. Site TBA. For info: NCAA, 6201 College Blvd, Overland Park, KS 66211. Phone: (913) 339-1906.

USFL FOUNDED: ANNIVERSARY. May 12, 1982. The United States Football League, a springtime alternative to the National Football League, was founded. The USFL played three seasons, 1983, 1984 and 1985, before going out of business.

WOLF, CHICKEN: BIRTH ANNIVERSARY. May 12, 1862. William Van Winkle ("Chicken") Wolf, baseball player born at Louisville, KY. Wolf played right field for the Louisville team in the American Association of the 1880s, at that time a major league. Died at Louisville, May 16, 1903.

WOMEN'S INTERNATIONAL BOWLING CONGRESS QUEEN'S TOURNAMENT. May 12–16. Quad Cities, IA and IL. For info: WIBC, 5301 S 76th St, Greendale, WI 53129. Phone: (414) 421-9000 or (414) 423-3224. Fax: (4144) 217-977.

BIRTHDAYS TODAY

Felipe Rojas Alou, 63, baseball manager and former player, born Santo Domingo, Dominican Republic, May 12, 1935.

Kevin Charles Bass, 39, former baseball player, born Redwood City, CA, May 12, 1959.

Lawrence Peter ("Yogi") Berra, 73, former baseball manager and Baseball Hall of Fame catcher, born St. Louis, MO, May 12, 1925.

Robert James Blackmon, 31, football player, born Bay City, TX, May 12, 1967.

Henry Ludwig (Hank) Borowy, 82, former baseball player, born Bloomfield, NJ, May 12, 1916.

Mark Willard Clark, 30, baseball player, born Bath, IL, May 12, 1968.

Emilio Estevez, 36, actor (*The Mighty Ducks, The Mighty Ducks II*), born New York, NY, May 12, 1962.

George Matthew Karl, 47, basketball coach and former player, born Penn Hills, PA, May 12, 1951.

Patricia Joan Keller (Patty) McCormick, 68, Olympic gold medal diver, born Seal Beach, CA, May 12, 1930.

Louis Rodman Whitaker, 41, former baseball player, born New York, NY, May 12, 1957.

MAY 13 — WEDNESDAY
Day 133 — 232 Remaining

BIG EAST BASEBALL TOURNAMENT. May 13–16. Thomas J. Dodd Memorial Stadium, Norwich, CT. For info: Big East Conference, 56 Exchange Terrace, Providence, RI 02903. Phone: (401) 453-0660. Fax: (401) 751-8540.

CUBS WIN 8,000th GAME: ANNIVERSARY. May 13, 1982. The Chicago Cubs, charter members of the National League, won the 8,000th game in their history, beating the Houston Astros in the Astrodome, 5–0. The Cubs began their existence as the Chicago White Stockings in the National Association (1871, 1874–5) and moved to the National League in 1876. The team changed its name to the Colts in 1890, to the Orphans in 1898 and the Cubs in 1902.

ENGLAND: ROYAL WINDSOR HORSE SHOW. May 13–17. Home Park, Windsor, Berkshire. Major annual show-jumping event with royal pageantry and color. For bookings: Royal Windsor Horse Show Box Office, (44) (175) 341-9341. Est attendance: 60,000. For info: Penelope Henderson, Sec'y, Royal Windsor Horse Show, The Royal Mews, England SL4 1NG. Phone: (44) (175) 386 0633. Fax: (44) (175) 383-1074.

GARDNER, LARRY: BIRTH ANNIVERSARY. May 13, 1886. William Lawrence (Larry) Gardner, baseball player born at Enosburg Falls, VT. Gardner was a dependable third baseman who moved right from the University of Vermont to the Boston Red Sox in 1908. He played in four World Series. Died at St. George, VT, Mar 11, 1976.

LOUIS, JOE: BIRTH ANNIVERSARY. May 13, 1914. Joseph Louis Barrow, heavyweight boxing champion born near Lafayette, AL. Louis, nicknamed the "Brown Bomber," is generally considered one of the greatest boxers of all time. He reigned as heavyweight champion from 1937 to 1949 and was immensely popular. Died at Las Vegas, NV, Apr 12, 1981. (Louis was buried in Arlington National Cemetery by presidential waiver, the 39th exception to the eligibility rules for burial there.)

MANTLE HITS 500th HOME RUN: ANNIVERSARY. May 13, 1967. Slugging outfielder Mickey Mantle of the New York Yankees hit the 500th home run of his career against Stu Miller of the Baltimore Orioles. The homer propelled the Yankees to a 6–5 victory. Mantle finished his career in 1968 with 536 home runs.

MUSIAL GETS 3,000th HIT: 40th ANNIVERSARY. May 13, 1958. Stan Musial of the St. Louis Cardinals got the 3,000th hit of his career, a pinch-hit double off Moe Drabowsky of the Chicago Cubs. Musial finished his career in 1963 with 3,630 hits, 1,815 at home and an equal number on the road.

RON NECCIAI STRIKES OUT THE SIDE: ANNIVERSARY. May 13, 1952. Pittsburgh Pirates farmhand Ron Necciai, pitching for the Bristol Twins in the Class D Appalachian League, threw a perfect game against the Welch Miners. Incredibly, Necciai struck out all 27 batters he faced in the Twins' 7–0 victory. He made the major leagues later that year, pitching in 12 games but winning only 1. In 54.2 innings, he struck out 31 batters and walked 32.

SEC BASEBALL TOURNAMENT. May 13–17. Site TBA. For info: Southeastern Conference, 2201 Civic Center Blvd, Birmingham, AL 35203-1103. Phone: (205) 458-3010. Fax: (205) 458-3030. Email: cbloom@sec.org. WWW: http://www.secsports.org

BIRTHDAYS TODAY

Juan Jose Beniquez, 48, former baseball player, born San Sebastian, Puerto Rico, May 13, 1950.

James Lamar ("Dusty") Rhodes, 71, former baseball player, born Mathews, AL, May 13, 1927.

Jose Antonio Rijo, 33, baseball player, born San Cristobal, Dominican Republic, May 13, 1965.

Dennis Keith Rodman, 37, basketball player, born Trenton, NJ, May 13, 1961.

John Junior Roseboro, 65, former baseball player, born Ashland, OH, May 13, 1933.

Robert John (Bobby) Valentine, 48, baseball manager and former player, born Stamford, CT, May 13, 1950.

Leon Lamar Wagner, 64, former baseball player, born Chattanooga, TN, May 13, 1934.

☆　☆　☆

MAY 14 — THURSDAY
Day 134 — 231 Remaining

NBA FINALS CHAMPIONS THIS DATE
1981　　Boston Celtics

BIG TWELVE BASEBALL TOURNAMENT. May 14–17. All Sports Stadium, Oklahoma City, OK (tentative site). For info: Big Twelve Conference, 2201 Stemmons Freeway, 28th Floor, Dallas, TX 75207. Phone: (214) 742-1212. Fax: (214) 742-2046.

COMBS, EARLE: BIRTH ANNIVERSARY. May 14, 1899. Earle Bryan Combs, Baseball Hall of Fame outfielder born at Pebworth, KY. Combs abandoned a career in education to play baseball. He played with the great New York Yankees teams of the 1920s and 1930s, scoring more than 100 runs eight consecutive years. Inducted into the Hall of Fame in 1970. Died at Richmond, KY, July 21, 1976.

DAUBERT, JAKE: BIRTH ANNIVERSARY. May 14, 1885. Jacob Ellsworth (Jake) Daubert, Jr, baseball player born at Shamokin, PA. Daubert was the best first baseman in the National League in the years just before World War I. He led the Brooklyn Dodgers to the pennant in 1916 and the Cincinnati Reds to a pennant in 1919. Died at Cincinnati, OH, Oct 9, 1924.

GTE BYRON NELSON CLASSIC. May 14–17. Irving, TX. A PGA Tour tournament played at two courses in Irving, TX. For info: PGA Tour, 112 TPC Blvd, Ponte Vedra Beach, FL 32082. Phone: (904) 285-3700.

LEFTHANDED CATCHER: ANNIVERSARY. May 14, 1989. Benny DiStefano of the Pittsburgh Pirates became the first lefthanded catcher in nine years when he played that position in the ninth inning of a 5–2 Pirates loss to the Atlanta Braves. The last lefthander to catch before DiStefano was Mike Squires of the Chicago White Sox in 1980.

MAGIC RETIRES AGAIN: ANNIVERSARY. May 14, 1996. Basketball player Earvin ("Magic") Johnson announced his retirement for the second time from the Los Angeles Lakers. Johnson had first retired before the start of the 1991–92 NBA season when he learned he was HIV-positive. Other players rebuffed his attempt to come back for the 1992–93 season, but he did play 32 games in 1995–96.

NCAA DIVISION III BASEBALL TOURNAMENT. May 14–17. Regionals at sites TBA. For info: NCAA, 6201 College Blvd, Overland Park, KS 66211. Phone: (913) 339-1906.

NCAA DIVISION II SOFTBALL TOURNAMENT. May 14–18. Finals. University of West Florida, Pensacola, FL. For info: NCAA, 6201 College Blvd, Overland Park, KS 66211. Phone: (913) 339-1906.

NCAA DIVISION III SOFTBALL TOURNAMENT. May 14–17. Finals. James I. Moyer Sports Complex, Salem, VA. For info: NCAA, 6201 College Blvd, Overland Park, KS 66211. Phone: (913) 339-1906.

NCAA MEN'S DIVISION I GOLF CHAMPIONSHIPS. May 14–16. Regionals at Oak Hills C.C., San Antonio, TX, and two other sites TBA. For info: NCAA, 6201 College Blvd, Overland Park, KS 66211. Phone: (913) 339-1906.

NCAA MEN'S DIVISION II TENNIS CHAMPIONSHIPS. May 14–17. Finals at a site TBA. For info: NCAA, 6201 College Blvd, Overland Park, KS 66211. Phone: (913) 339-1906.

NCAA WOMEN'S DIVISION II TENNIS CHAMPIONSHIPS. May 14–17. Finals at a site TBA. For info: NCAA, 6201 College Blvd, Overland Park, KS 66211. Phone: (913) 339-1906.

PAC-10 BASEBALL PLAYOFF. May 14-16. Site TBA. For info: PAC-10 Conference, 800 S Broadway, Ste 400, Wal-

nut Creek, CA 94596. Phone: (510) 932-4411. Fax: (510) 932-4601.

SIR BARTON WINS PREAKNESS: ANNIVERSARY. May 14, 1919. Just four days after winning the Kentucky Derby, Sir Barton, ridden by Johnny Loftus, won the Preakness Stakes. The colt went on to win the Belmont Stakes and became the first horse to win the Triple Crown.

WALSH, ED: BIRTH ANNIVERSARY. May 14, 1881. Edward Augustine (Ed) Walsh, Baseball Hall of Fame pitcher born at Plains, PA. Walsh used a fastball and a spitball to become one of the best pitchers of the early 20th century. He won 195 games and hurled 57 shutouts. Inducted into the Hall of Fame in 1946. Died at Pompano Beach, FL, May 26, 1959.

WALTER JOHNSON WINS 300th GAME: ANNIVERSARY. May 14, 1920. Pitcher Walter Johnson of the Washington Senators, considered by some to be the greatest pitcher of all time and the fastest, won the 300th game of his career, beating the Detroit Tigers, 9–8. Johnson played in the major leagues from 1907 through 1927. He compiled a record of 417 wins against 279 losses with an earned run average of 2.17.

STANLEY CUP CHAMPIONS THIS DATE

1977	Montreal Canadiens

BIRTHDAYS TODAY

Walter Berry, 34, former basketball player, born New York, NY, May 14, 1964.

Jose Manuel (Joey) Cora, 33, baseball player, born Caguas, Puerto Rico, May 14, 1965.

Jose Dennis Martinez, 43, former baseball player, born Granada, Nicaragua, May 14, 1955.

Atanasio ("Tony") Perez, 56, former baseball manager and player, born Camaguey, Cuba, May 14, 1942.

Michael Anthony (Mike) Quick, 39, former football player, born Hamlet, NC, May 14, 1959.

Jerome ("Pooh") Richardson, Jr, 32, basketball player, born Philadelphia, PA, May 14, 1966.

MAY 15 — FRIDAY
Day 135 — 230 Remaining

SPORTSCHASER OF THE DAY

What Cleveland Indians pitcher hurled a perfect game against the Toronto Blue Jays in 1981?

BIG TWELVE MEN'S AND WOMEN'S OUTDOOR TRACK CHAMPIONSHIPS. May 15–17. University of Missouri, Columbia, MO. For info: Big Twelve Conference, 2201 Stemmons Freeway, 28th Floor, Dallas, TX 75207. Phone: (214) 742-1212. Fax: (214) 742-2046.

FISHING HAS NO BOUNDARIES-YAKIMA. May 15–16 (tentative). Moses Lake, WA. A two-day fishing experience for disabled persons. Any disability, age, sex, race, etc, eligible. Fishing with experienced guides. For info: Ken Small, Fishing Has No Boundaries, 732 Summitview #523, Yakima, WA 98902. Phone: (509) 457-1366.

FISHING HAS NO BOUNDARIES-HAYWARD. May 15–17. Lake Chippewa Campgrounds, Hayward, WI. A three-day fishing experience for disabled persons. Any disability, age, sex, race, etc, eligible. Fishing with experienced guides on one of the best fishing waters in Wisconsin, attended by 200 participants and 500 volunteers. Advance registration before Feb 28 required. For info: Fishing Has No Boundaries, PO Box 375, Hayward, WI 54843. Phone: (715) 634-3185. Fax: (715) 634-1305.

May *1998*	S	M	T	W	T	F	S
						1	2
	3	4	5	6	7	8	9
	10	11	12	13	14	15	16
	17	18	19	20	21	22	23
	24	25	26	27	28	29	30
	31						

GATLINBURG SCOTTISH FESTIVAL AND HIGHLAND GAMES. May 15–17. Gatlinburg, TN. Celebration of Scotland, its people and traditions. Music, food and fun. Est attendance: 12,000. For info: Gatlinburg Chamber of Commerce, PO Box 527, Gatlinburg, TN 37738. Phone: (800) 568-4748 or (423) 436-2392. Fax: (423) 436-3704.

LEN BARKER PITCHES PERFECT GAME: ANNIVERSARY. May 15, 1981. Len Barker of the Cleveland Indians pitched a perfect game, the first in major league baseball in 13 years, defeating the Toronto Blue Jays, 3–0, in Cleveland. Barker finished the year at 8–7 and was traded to the Atlanta Braves during the 1983 season.

MILES CITY BUCKING HORSE SALE. May 15–17. Miles City, MT. Miles City is real "Lonesome Dove" country. Its annual bucking horse sale is where rodeo stock operators from around the West come to purchase their bucking horses for the coming rodeo season. As a festive event, the sale not only involves cowboys trying to ride some of the wildest horses in the country, but also western artists displaying and creating works in a weekend art show, an antique show featuring guns and coins, a western trade show featuring practical and gift items, a Saturday morning parade and Miles City's western attractions like the Range Riders Museum which chronicles the life of the cowboy on the northern Great Plains. (Miles City is the community featured in the novel and the two television miniseries about "Lonesome Dove.") Est attendance: 3,200. For info: Miles City Chamber of Commerce, 901 Main St, Miles City, MT 59301. Phone: (406) 232-2890.

MINT JULEP SCALE MEET. May 15–17. Rough River Dam State Resort Park, Falls of Rough, KY. A weekend for radio-controlled airplane enthusiasts. Est attendance: 400. For info: Tom DeHaven, Rec Supervisor, Rough River Dam State Resort Park, 450 Lodge Rd, Falls of Rough, KY 40119. Phone: (502) 257-2311.

NCAA MEN'S DIVISION III TENNIS CHAMPIONSHIPS. May 15–20. Finals. Williams College, Williamstown, MA. For info: NCAA, 6201 College Blvd, Overland Park, KS 66211. Phone: (913) 339-1906.

NCAA WOMEN'S LACROSSE CHAMPIONSHIPS. May 15–17. Finals for Divisions I, II and III. University of Maryland–Baltimore County, Baltimore, MD. For info: NCAA, 6201 College Blvd, Overland Park, KS 66211. Phone: (913) 339-1906.

SEASPACE. May 15–17. Hyatt Regency Downtown Hotel, Houston, TX. Scuba diving symposium featuring seminars, photo and video courses, photo contest and exhibit, film festival, environmental awareness area, free introduction to scuba and snorkeling, hall of exhibits and receptions. Sponsor: Houston Underwater Club. For more info send SASE. Est attendance: 8,000. For info: Seaspace, PO Box 3753, Houston, TX 77253-3753. Phone: (713) 721-8533. Fax: (713) 721-8533. WWW: http://www.seaspace.ycg.org

SEC MEN'S AND WOMEN'S OUTDOOR TRACK AND FIELD CHAMPIONSHIPS. May 15–17. University of Florida, Gainesville, FL. For info: Southeastern Conference, 2201 Civic Center Blvd, Birmingham, AL 35203-1103. Phone: (205) 458-3010. Fax: (205) 458-3030. Email: cbloom@sec.org. WWW: http://www.secsports.org

USA RUGBY NATIONAL HIGH SCHOOL CHAMPIONSHIP. May 15–16. Site to be announced. The top high school teams come together to determine the bona fide high school champion in the US. For info: USA Rugby, 3595 E Fountain Blvd, Colorado Springs, CO 80910. Phone: (719) 637-1022. Fax: (719) 637-1315. Email: usarugby@rmii.com. WWW: http://www.usarugby.com

BIRTHDAYS TODAY

George Howard Brett, 45, baseball executive and former player, born Glen Dale, WV, May 15, 1953.
Joey Matthew Browner, 38, former football player, born Warren, OH, May 15, 1960.
Desmond Kevin Howard, 28, football player, born Cleveland, OH, May 15, 1970.
Emmitt J. Smith, III, 29, football player, born Pensacola, FL, May 15, 1969.
John Andrew Smoltz, 31, baseball player, born Warren, MI, May 15, 1967.
Paul Robert Ysebaert, 32, hockey player, born Sarnia, Ontario, Canada, May 15, 1966.

MAY 16 — SATURDAY
Day 136 — 229 Remaining

NBA FINALS CHAMPIONS THIS DATE
1980   Los Angeles Lakers

AHPA FORMED: ANNIVERSARY. May 16, 1914. The Grand League of the American Horseshoe Pitchers Association was formed. The league set its first championship for Oct 23, 1915, at Kellerton, IA.

★ **ARMED FORCES DAY.** May 16. Presidential Proclamation 5983, of May 17, 1989, covers the third Saturday in May in all succeeding years. Originally proclaimed as "Army Day" for Apr 6, beginning in 1936 (S.Con.Res. 30 of Apr 2, 1936). S.Con.Res. 5 of Mar 16, 1937, requested annual Apr 6 issuance, which was done through 1949. Always the third Saturday in May since 1950. Traditionally issued once by each Administration.

ARMED FORCES DAY MILITARY VEHICLE RALLY AND SWAP MEET. May 16–17. Hawthorne, NV. Rally and swap meet of military vehicles from WW II to the present. For local info: Mineral County Chamber of Commerce, PO Box 1635, Hawthorne, NV 89415. Phone: (702) 945-5896. Fax: (702) 945-1257.

ATWOOD EARLY ROD RUN. May 16–17. Atwood, KS. Classic car show with several states represented. Includes downtown festival, remote-control car races, drag races, barbecue and '50s dance. Est attendance: 1,500. For info: Atwood Ambassadors, 410 N Fifth, PO Box 341, Atwood, KS 67730. Phone: (913) 626-3144. WWW: http://www.quality-pro.com/rodrun

AUTOMOTION. May 16–17. Wisconsin Dells, WI. 800 cars on display, including street machines, classics and antiques. Event includes swap meet, live entertainment, "Car Cruise" and other activities. Est attendance: 15,000. For info: Wisc Dells Visitor and Conv Bureau, Box 390, Wisconsin Dells, WI 53965. Phone: (800) 223-3557. WWW: http://www.wisdells.com

CUSTER STATE PARK SEASONAL VOLKSMARCH. May 16 (and various dates through Oct 31). Custer State Park, SD. Noncompetitive walks on a premarked trail. Walkers can earn awards or walk for free. Hike is 6.2 miles and begins at Peter Norbeck Visitors Center. SD state park license is required. For info: Craig Pugsley, Custer State Park, HC 83, Box 70, Custer, SD 57730-9506. Phone: (605) 255-4515.

FISHING HAS NO BOUNDARIES-MONTICELLO. May 16–17. Freeman Lake, Monticello, IN. A two-day event for disabled persons to experience fishing on the lake. Any disability, sex, age, race, etc, eligible. Est attendance: 50 participants and 130 volunteers. For info: FHNB, 7805 N Harrison, PO Box 325, Battleground, IN 47920. Phone: (765) 567-2567.

MARTIN, BILLY: 70th BIRTH ANNIVERSARY. May 16, 1928. Alfred Henry ("Billy") Martin, baseball manager and player born at Berkeley, CA. After a successful playing career mostly with the New York Yankees, the scrappy Martin managed five major league teams: the Yankees, Minnesota Twins, Detroit Tigers, Texas Rangers and Oakland Athletics. He compiled a record of 1,258 victories and 1,018 losses in his 16 seasons as a manager. His combative and fiery style both on and off the field kept him in the headlines, and he will long be remembered for his on-again/off-again relationship with Yankees owner George Steinbrenner, for whom he managed the Yankees five different times. Died in an auto accident at Johnson City, NY, Dec 25, 1989.

NATIONAL SAFE BOATING WEEK. May 16–22. Brings boating safety to the public's attention, decreases the number of boating fatalities and makes the waterways safer for all boaters. Sponsor: US Coast Guard. For info: Jo Calkin, Commandant (G-OPB-2), US Coast Guard, 2100 Second St SW, Washington, DC 20593. Phone: (800) 368-5647.

★ **NATIONAL SAFE BOATING WEEK.** May 16–22. Presidential Proclamation issued since 1995 for a week in May. From 1958 through 1977, issued for a week including July 4 (PL85–445 of June 4, 1958). From 1981 through 1994, issued for the first week in June (PL96–376 of Oct 3, 1980). Not issued from 1978 through 1980.

NEW YORK GOLDEN ARMS TOURNAMENT-MANHATTAN. May 16–17. 9th Avenue International Food Festival, Manhattan, NY. Arm-wrestling competition held at the festival determines borough winner who will compete in the Empire State Golden Arms Tournament of Champions on Oct 22. Twenty-block-long food fest. For info: New York Arm Wrestling Assn, Inc, 200-14 45th Dr, Bayside, NY 11361. Phone/fax: (718) 544-4592.

POLE, PEDAL, PADDLE. May 16. Jackson, WY. The original relay race of this kind. Alpine skiing, cross-country skiing, biking and boating from Teton Village to the Snake River. Sponsor: Jackson Hole Ski Club. For info: Jackson Hole Chamber of Commerce, Box E, Jackson, WY 83001. Phone: (307) 733-3316. Fax: (307) 733-5585.

POLE, PEDAL, PADDLE. May 16. Bend, OR. Five-stage iron-man-type race for singles, teams and couples; includes downhill skiing, nordic skiing, biking, canoeing and running. Annually, the third Saturday in May. Sponsors: US Bank, Pepsi, Bud Light, Teva, Cellular One, Z21TV. Est attendance: 12,000. For info: Mt Bachelor Ski Education Foundation, PO Box 388, Bend, OR 97709. Phone: (541) 388-0002. Fax: (541) 388-7848. Email: mbsef@bendnet.com. WWW: http://www.bendnet.com/ppp

PREAKNESS STAKES. May 16. Pimlico Race Course, Baltimore, MD. Running of the Preakness Stakes, middle jewel in the Triple Crown, inaugurated in 1873. Annually, the third Saturday in May–two Saturdays after the Kentucky Derby–and followed, three Saturdays later, by the Belmont Stakes. Est attendance: 100,000. For info: Maryland Jockey Club, Pimlico Race Course, Baltimore, MD 21215. Phone: (410) 542-9400. WWW: http://www.marylandracing.com

RIGLER, CY: BIRTH ANNIVERSARY. May 16, 1882. Charles ("Cy") Rigler, baseball umpire born at Massillon, OH. Rigler had a 30-year career as a National League umpire beginning in 1906. He worked in 10 World Series and invented the raised hand signal to indicate a strike. Died at Philadelphia, PA, Dec 21, 1936.

SNEAD CARDS A 59: ANNIVERSARY. May 16, 1959. Sam Snead shot an 11-under-par round of 59 at The Greenbrier in White Sulphur Springs, WV. Snead went out in 31, four under par, and came home in 28, seven under par.

24-HOUR RELAY FOR LIFE. May 16–17. Indian Field, Carlisle, PA. Teams of 8–12 runners or walkers take turns circling the track for an entire 24-hour period to raise money for the American Cancer Society. Est attendance: 200. For info: American Cancer Society-Cumberland Unit, 117 N Hanover, Carlisle, PA 17013. Phone: (717) 243-2140.

WALKER, RUBE: BIRTH ANNIVERSARY. May 16, 1926. Albert Bluford ("Rube") Walker, baseball player born at Lenoir, NC. Walker was a backup catcher for the Brooklyn Dodgers and an innovative pitching coach for the New York Mets. Died at Morganton, NC, Dec 12, 1992.

WEBSTER COUNTY WOODCHOPPING FESTIVAL (WITH WOODCHOPPING AND TURKEY-CALLING CHAMPIONSHIPS). May 16–24. Webster Springs, WV. South Eastern US World Championship Woodchopping Contest and State Championship Turkey-Calling Contest. Est attendance: 10,000. For info: Woodchopping Festival Committee, PO Box 227, Webster Springs, WV 26288. Phone: (304) 847-7666. Fax: (304) 847-5117.

May 1998	S	M	T	W	T	F	S
						1	2
	3	4	5	6	7	8	9
	10	11	12	13	14	15	16
	17	18	19	20	21	22	23
	24	25	26	27	28	29	30
	31						

STANLEY CUP CHAMPIONS THIS DATE
1976   Montreal Canadiens
1982   New York Islanders

BIRTHDAYS TODAY

Olga Korbut, 43, Olympic gold medal gymnast, born Grodno, USSR, May 16, 1955.

James John (Jim) Langer, 50, Pro Football Hall of Fame center, born Little Falls, MN, May 16, 1948.

John Scott (Jack) Morris, 43, former baseball player, born St. Paul, MN, May 16, 1955.

Rickey Eugene (Rick) Reuschel, 49, former baseball player, born Quincy, IL, May 16, 1949.

Gabriela Sabatini, 28, tennis player, born Buenos Aires, Argentina, May 16, 1970.

John Thomas Salley, 34, basketball player, born New York, NY, May 16, 1964.

Joan Benoit Samuelson, 41, Olympic gold medal marathoner, born Cape Elizabeth, ME, May 16, 1957.

Thurman Lee Thomas, 32, football player, born Houston, TX, May 16, 1966.

Alain Vigneault, 36, hockey coach and former player, born Quebec City, Quebec, Canada, May 16, 1962.

MAY 17 — SUNDAY
Day 137 — 228 Remaining

STANLEY CUP CHAMPIONS THIS DATE
1983   New York Islanders

AARON GETS 3,000th HIT: ANNIVERSARY. May 17, 1970. Henry Aaron of the Atlanta Braves, on his way to becoming baseball's all-time home run king, got the 3,000th hit of his career, a scratch single off Wayne Simpson of the Cincinnati Reds. Aaron finished his career in 1976 with a .305 batting average, 3,771 hits and 755 home runs.

BELL, COOL PAPA: 95th BIRTH ANNIVERSARY. May 17, 1903. James Thomas ("Cool Papa") Bell, Baseball Hall of Fame outfielder born at Starkville, MS. One of the preeminent stars of the Negro Leagues, Bell is generally considered one of the fastest players ever. Satchel Paige said Bell was so fast he could turn the light out at night and be in bed before the room got dark. Inducted into the Hall of Fame in 1974. Died at St. Louis, MO, Mar 7, 1991.

BETSY KING WINS LPGA CHAMPIONSHIP: ANNIVERSARY. May 17, 1992. Betsy King shot 267 to win the LPGA Championship by 11 strokes over Karen Noble. King recorded rounds of 68, 66, 67 and 66, the first time that any LPGA player finished four rounds under 70 in a major championship. Her 267 was the lowest score ever recorded by any golfer, man or woman, in a major championship.

BLUE JAYS' ATTENDANCE RECORD: ANNIVERSARY. May 17, 1992. The Toronto Blue Jays reached the one million mark in home attendance faster than any other team in baseball history. The Blue Jays drew 1,006,294 fans in just 21 dates, surpassing the record held jointly by the 1981 Los Angeles Dodgers and the 1991 Blue Jays.

D. C. BOOTH DAY (WITH FISH CULTURE HALL OF FAME). May 17. D. C. Booth Historic National Fish Hatchery, Spearfish, SD. Antique auto show, musical entertainment, refreshments, free tours of the historic Booth home, free fly-tying demonstration, installation of new members into the Fish Culture Hall of Fame. Est attendance: 1,200. For info: Molly Salcone, D.C. Booth Historic Natl Fish Hatchery, 423 Hatchery Circle, Spearfish, SD 57783. Phone: (605) 642-7730. Fax: (605) 642-2336.

EXAMINER BAY TO BREAKERS RACE. May 17. San Francisco, CA. Largest footrace in the world attracts 80,000 runners each year, from world-class athletes to fun runners; postrace festival, live concert, food and beverages. Annually, the third Sunday in May. Est attendance: 200,000. For info: *Examiner* Bay to Breakers, PO Box 429200, San Francisco, CA 94142. Phone: (415) 808-5000, ext 2222.

FIRST KENTUCKY DERBY: ANNIVERSARY. May 17, 1875. The first running of the Kentucky Derby took place at Churchill Downs, Louisville, KY. Jockey Oliver Lewis rode the horse Aristides in a winning time of 2:37.25.

NBA DRAFT LOTTERY. May 17. Teams that did not make the playoffs during the 1997–98 season pick their selection order for the 1998 draft. For info: Brian McIntyre, VP, PR, Natl Basketball Assn, Olympic Tower, 645 Fifth Ave, New York, NY 10022. Phone: (212) 407-8000.

NCAA DIVISION II BASEBALL TOURNAMENT. May 17 (tentative). Regionals at campus sites TBA. For info: NCAA, 6201 College Blvd, Overland Park, KS 66211. Phone: (913) 339-1906.

PAC-10 MEN'S AND WOMEN'S ROWING CHAMPIONSHIPS. May 17. Lake Natoma, CA. For info: PAC-10 Conference, 800 S Broadway, Ste 400, Walnut Creek, CA 94596. Phone: (510) 932-4411. Fax: (510) 932-4601.

POLE SITTER DIES AT INDY: ANNIVERSARY. May 17, 1996. Scott Brayton, pole sitter for the Indianapolis 500 in both 1995 and 1996, died when the car he was driving in practice crashed into the Turn 2 wall. The crash was caused by a deflated tire. Brayton became the 40th driver to die at Indy, either in practice, qualifying or during the race, and the first since Jovy Marcelo in 1992.

SPEAKER GETS 3,000th HIT: ANNIVERSARY. May 17, 1925. Cleveland Indians centerfielder Tris Speaker collected the 3,000th hit of his major league career off Tom Zachary of the Washington Senators. Speaker played from 1907 through 1928, got 3,515 hits and batted .344.

BIRTHDAYS TODAY

William H. (Bill) Blair, Jr, 56, former basketball coach, born Hazard, KY, May 17, 1942.

Hubert Ira Davis, Jr, 28, basketball player, born Winston-Salem, NC, May 17, 1970.

Craig Neil Erickson, 29, football player, born Boynton Beach, FL, May 17, 1969.

Jon Francis Koncak, 35, basketball player, born Cedar Rapids, IA, May 17, 1963.

Ray Charles ("Sugar Ray") Leonard, 42, former boxer, born Wilmington, NC, May 17, 1956.

Daniel Ricardo (Danny) Manning, 32, basketball player, born Hattiesburg, MS, May 17, 1966.

Norval Eugene (Norv) Turner, 46, football coach, born LeJeune, NC, May 17, 1952.

Osvaldo Jose (Ossie) Virgil, Sr, 65, former baseball player, born Montecristi, Dominican Republic, May 17, 1933.

MAY 18 — MONDAY
Day 138 — 227 Remaining

STANLEY CUP CHAMPIONS THIS DATE
1971   Montreal Canadiens

ADAMS, BABE: BIRTH ANNIVERSARY. May 18, 1882. Charles Benjamin ("Babe") Adams, baseball player and sportswriter born at Tipton, IN. Adams pitched for the Pittsburgh Pirates from 1909 through 1926. He won three complete games in the 1909 World Series against the Detroit Tigers. Died at Silver Spring, MD, July 27, 1968.

NAIA BASEBALL WORLD SERIES. May 18–23. Drillers Stadium, Tulsa, OK. 42nd annual competition. Est attendance: 20,000. For info: Natl Assn of Intercollegiate Athletics, 6120 S Yale Ave, Ste 1450, Tulsa, OK 74136. Phone: (918) 494-8828. Fax: (918) 494-8841. Email: khenry@naia.com. WWW: http://www.naia.org

NAIA MEN'S AND WOMEN'S OUTDOOR TRACK AND FIELD NATIONAL CHAMPIONSHIPS. May 18–20. Tulsa, OK. 47th annual men's and 18th annual women's competition. Est attendance: 2,500. For info: Natl Assn of Intercollegiate Athletics, 6120 S Yale Ave, Ste 1450, Tulsa, OK 74136. Phone: (918) 494-8828. Fax: (918) 494-8841. Email: khenry@naia.org. WWW: http://www.naia.org

NAIA MEN'S TENNIS NATIONAL CHAMPIONSHIPS. May 18–23. Shadow Mountain Tennis Club, Tulsa, OK. 47th annual competition. Est attendance: 1,500. For info: Natl Assn of Intercollegiate Athletics, 6120 S Yale Ave, Ste 1450, Tulsa, OK 74136. Phone: (918) 494-8828. Fax: (918) 494-8841. Email: khenry@naia.org. WWW: http://www.naia.org

NAIA SOFTBALL NATIONAL CHAMPIONSHIP. May 18–22. Arrowhead Softball Complex. 18th annual competition Est attendance: 2,000. For info: Natl Assn of Intercollegiate Athletics, 6120 S Yale Ave, Ste 1450, Tulsa, OK 74136. Phone: (918) 494-8828. Fax: (918) 494-8841. Email: khenry@naia.org. WWW: http://www.naia.org

NAIA WOMEN'S TENNIS NATIONAL CHAMPION-SHIPS. May 18–23. Tulsa Southern Tennis Club, Tulsa, OK. 18th annual tournament. Individuals compete for All-America honors, while teams compete for the national championship. Est attendance: 1,500. For info: Natl Assn of Intercollegiate Athletics, 6120 S Yale Ave, Ste 1450, Tulsa, OK 74136. Phone: (918) 494-8828. Fax: (918) 494-8841. Email: khenry@naia.org.

TIE GAME, TAKE TRAIN: ANNIVERSARY. May 18, 1957. The Chicago White Sox and the Baltimore Orioles played a 1–1 tie, a game called precisely at 10:20 PM so that the White Sox could catch a train out of Baltimore. The Orioles' Dick Williams hit a home run on the game's last pitch to tie the game and avoid defeat. The game was replayed from the beginning at a later date, and Baltimore won.

TIGERS ON STRIKE: ANNIVERSARY. May 18, 1912. Members of the Detroit Tigers protested a suspension to Ty Cobb, their star player, by refusing to play against the Philadelphia Athletics. Detroit manager Hugh Jennings recruited college players to avoid a forfeit, but his stopgap team lost 24–2. Al Travers gave up all 24 runs and

	May 1998	S	M	T	W	T	F	S
							1	2
		3	4	5	6	7	8	9
		10	11	12	13	14	15	16
		17	18	19	20	21	22	23
		24	25	26	27	28	29	30
		31						

never pitched in the major leagues again. Cobb persuaded his teammates to return to work the next day.

CHASE'S SPORTSQUOTE OF THE DAY
"There isn't enough mustard in the world to cover that hot dog." —Teammate Darold Knowles on Reggie Jackson

BIRTHDAYS TODAY
Erik Brian Hanson, 33, baseball player, born Kinnelon, NJ, May 18, 1965.
Reginald Martinez (Reggie) Jackson, 52, Baseball Hall of Fame outfielder, born Wyncote, PA, May 18, 1946.
Jari Kurri, 38, hockey player, born Helsinki, Finland, May 18, 1960.
Donyell Lamar Marshall, 25, basketball player, born Reading, PA, May 18, 1973.
Yannick Simone Camille Noah, 38, tennis player, born Sedan, France, May 18, 1960.
Brooks Calbert Robinson, 61, Baseball Hall of Fame third baseman, born Little Rock, AR, May 18, 1937.
Eric Orlando Young, 31, baseball player, born New Brunswick, NJ, May 18, 1967.

MAY 19 — TUESDAY
Day 139 — 226 Remaining

STANLEY CUP CHAMPIONS THIS DATE
1974   Philadelphia Flyers
1984   Edmonton Oilers

FERRELL BROTHERS HOMER: 65TH ANNIVERSARY. May 19, 1933. Brothers Rick and Wes Ferrell, catcher for the St. Louis Browns and pitcher for the Cleveland Indians, respectively, homered in the same game for the only time in their careers.

KATE SMITH WINS STANLEY CUP: ANNIVERSARY. May 19, 1974. Singer Kate Smith made a personal appearance at the Spectrum in Philadelphia to sing "God Bless America" before the seventh game of the Stanley Cup finals, pitting the Philadelphia Flyers against the Boston Bruins. The Flyers had enjoyed remarkable success when they played Smith's recording of the Irving Berlin song. For the decisive game, the personal touch worked. The Flyers won, 1–0.

MOON PHASE: LAST QUARTER. May 19. Moon enters Last Quarter phase at 12:35 AM, EDT.

NAIA MEN'S GOLF CHAMPIONSHIP. May 19–23. Southern Hills Country Club, Tulsa, OK. 47th annual. Est attendance: 500. For info: Natl Assn of Intercollegiate Athletics, 6120 S Yale Ave, Ste 1450, Tulsa, OK 74136. Phone: (918) 494-8828. Fax: (918) 494-8841. Email: khenry@naia.org. WWW: http://www.naia.org

NAIA WOMEN'S GOLF CHAMPIONSHIP. May 19–21. White Hawk Golf Club, Bixby, OK. 4th annual competition. Est attendance: 300. For info: Natl Assn of Intercollegiate Athletics, 6120 S Yale Ave, Ste 1450, Tulsa, OK 74136. Phone: (918) 494-8828. Fax: (918) 494-8841. Email: khenry@naia.org. WWW: http://www.naia.org

NATIONAL BIKE TO WORK DAY. May 19. At the state or local level, Bike to Work events are conducted by small and large businesses, city governments, bicycle clubs and environmental groups. About two million participants nationwide. Annually, the third Tuesday in May. For info: Bonnie McClun, Education Dir, League of American Bicyclists, 190 W Ostend St, Ste 120, Baltimore, MD 21230-3755. Phone: (410) 539-3399. Fax: (410) 539-3496. Email: labedu@aol.com. WWW: http://www.bikeleague.org

NCAA MEN'S DIVISION II GOLF CHAMPIONSHIPS. May 19–22. Finals. Mission Inn Golf and Tennis Resort, Howey-in-the-Hills, FL. For info: NCAA, 6201 College Blvd, Overland Park, KS 66211. Phone: (913) 339-1906.

SHOW, ERIC: BIRTH ANNIVERSARY. May 19, 1956. Eric Vaughn Show, baseball player born at Riverside, CA. Show pitched nine years with the San Diego Padres. His 94 victories made him the Padres' all-time leader. Died at Dulzura, CA, Mar 16, 1994.

WOMAN GETS TWO ACES: ANNIVERSARY. May 19, 1942. Mrs. W. Driver became the first golfer of either sex to get two holes-in-one in the same round. She aced the third hole and the eighth hole at Balgowlah Golf Club, Australia.

BIRTHDAYS TODAY

Luis Antonio Aquino, 33, former baseball player, born Rio Piedras, Puerto Rico, May 19, 1965.

Richard Aldo (Rick) Cerone, 44, former baseball player, born Newark, NJ, May 19, 1954.

William Charles (Bill) Fitch, 64, basketball coach, born Davenport, IA, May 19, 1934.

Kevin Garnett, 22, basketball player, born Mauldin, SC, May 19, 1976.

Elizabeth May (Betty) Jameson, 79, LPGA Hall of Fame golfer, born Norman, OK, May 19, 1919.

William (Bill) Laimbeer, Jr, 41, former basketball player, born Boston, MA, May 19, 1957.

Gilbert James (Gil) McDougald, 70, former baseball player, born San Francisco, CA, May 19, 1928.

Adolph (Dolph) Schayes, 70, former basketball coach and Basketball Hall of Fame forward and center, born New York, NY, May 19, 1928.

MAY 20 — WEDNESDAY

Day 140 — 225 Remaining

BOYER, KEN: BIRTH ANNIVERSARY. May 20, 1931. Kenton Lloyd (Ken) Boyer, baseball player and manager born at Liberty, MO. Boyer was an exceptional third baseman for the St. Louis Cardinals, winning the National League MVP award in 1964. He managed the Cards from 1978 through June 8, 1980. Died at Ballwin, MO, Sept 7, 1982.

CATSKILLS SUMMER SERIES. May 20–31 (also July 22–Aug 2 and Aug 26–30). Ellenville, NY, in the heart of the Catskill Mountains. Five weeks of hunter/jumper competition throughout the summer. Riders from beginning levels to world class can be seen in competition all week long with the featured Grand Prix show-jumping event each Sunday. Annually, spring and summer. Est attendance: 12,000. For info and exact dates of circuit events: HITS, 13 Closs Dr, Rhinebeck, NY 12572. Phone: (914) 876-3666. Fax: (914) 876-5538. WWW: http://www.equisearch.com

MILWAUKEE BRAVES SURPASS BOSTON ATTENDANCE: 45th ANNIVERSARY. May 20, 1953. In just their 13th game of the season, the Braves, in their first year in Milwaukee, surpassed their total 1952 attendance of 281,278, their last year in Boston.

MOORE, WILCY: BIRTH ANNIVERSARY. May 20, 1897. William Wilcy Moore, baseball player born at Bonita, TX. Moore pitched six years in the major leagues for the New York Yankees and the Boston Red Sox. He won 19 games for the 1927 Yankees in his rookie year. Died at Hollis, OK, Mar 29, 1963.

NATIONAL EMPLOYEE HEALTH AND FITNESS DAY. May 20. To focus on the importance of fitness and healthy lifestyles at the work site. For info: Natl Assn of Governor's Councils on Physical Fitness/Sports, 201 S Capitol Ave, Ste 560, Indianapolis, IN 46225-1072. Phone: (317) 237-5630. Fax: (317) 237-5632. Email: govcouncil@aol.com. WWW: http://fitnesslink.com/govcouncil/

NCAA MEN'S AND WOMEN'S DIVISION III OUTDOOR TRACK AND FIELD CHAMPIONSHIPS. May 20–23. Finals. Macalester College, St. Paul, MN. For info: NCAA, 6201 College Blvd, Overland Park, KS 66211. Phone: (913) 339-1906.

NCAA WOMEN'S DIVISION I GOLF CHAMPIONSHIPS. May 20–23. Finals. University of Wisconsin, Madison, WI. For info: NCAA, 6201 College Blvd, Overland Park, KS 66211. Phone: (913) 339-1906.

NO RAINOUT RECORD: ANNIVERSARY. May 20, 1985. The game between the Milwaukee Brewers and the Cleveland Indians in Cleveland was rained out. Remarkably, this was the first rainout of the season in either league after a major-league record 485 games had been played without a postponement.

☆   ☆   ☆

BIRTHDAYS TODAY

Bob Beers, 31, hockey player, born Pittsburgh, PA, May 20, 1967.

Thomas Terrell Brandon, 28, basketball player, born Portland, OR, May 20, 1970.

Vyacheslav (Slava) Fetisov, 40, hockey player, born Moscow, USSR, May 20, 1958.

Harold Peter ("Bud") Grant, 71, former basketball and football player and Pro Football Hall of Fame coach, born Superior, WI, May 20, 1927.

Stu Grimson, 33, hockey player, born Kamloops, BC, Canada, May 20, 1965.

Leroy Kelly, 56, Pro Football Hall of Fame running back, born Philadelphia, PA, May 20, 1942.

Bobby Ray Murcer, 52, former baseball player, born Oklahoma City, OK, May 20, 1946.

Liselotte Neumann, 32, golfer, born Finspang, Sweden, May 20, 1966.

Harold (Hal) Newhouser, 77, Baseball Hall of Fame pitcher, born Detroit, MI, May 20, 1921.

Todd Vernon Stottlemyre, 33, baseball player, born Yakima, WA, May 20, 1965.

David Lee Wells, 35, baseball player, born Torrance, CA, May 20, 1963.

MAY 21 — THURSDAY
Day 141 — 224 Remaining

STANLEY CUP CHAMPIONS THIS DATE
1979	Montreal Canadiens
1981	New York Islanders

AVERILL, EARL: BIRTH ANNIVERSARY. May 21, 1902. Howard Earl Averill, Baseball Hall of Fame outfielder born at Snohomish, WA. Averill was the first future Hall of Fame member to hit a home run in his first major league at-bat, doing so in 1929. He played for the Cleveland Indians, the Detroit Tigers and the Boston Braves and hit .318. Inducted into the Hall of Fame in 1975. Died at Everett, WA, Aug 16, 1983.

BIG TEN BASEBALL TOURNAMENT. May 21–24. Site of regular-season conference champion. For info: Big Ten Conference, 1500 W Higgins Rd, Park Ridge, IL 60068-6300. Phone: (847) 696-1010. Fax: (847) 696-1150. WWW: http://www.bigten.org

COLLEGE WORLD SERIES (NCAA DIVISION I BASE-BALL TOURNAMENT). May 21–24. Regionals at campus sites TBA. For info: NCAA, 6201 College Blvd, Overland Park, KS 66211. Phone: (913) 339-1906.

GRANT, EDDIE: 115th BIRTH ANNIVERSARY. May 21, 1883. Edward Leslie (Eddie) Grant, baseball player born at Franklin, MA. Grant played third base in the majors and retired in 1915 to practice law. In World War I, he led a mission to rescue the "Lost Battalion" and became the only major league ballplayer to be killed in action. Died at Argonne, France, Oct 5, 1918.

LUM PINCH-HITS FOR AARON: ANNIVERSARY. May 21, 1969. Henry Aaron of the Atlanta Braves was lifted for a pinch hitter for the first time in his career. Mike Lum batted for Aaron in the seventh inning of a game against the New York Mets after Aaron had come to the plate 9,015 times. Lum doubled, and the Braves won, 15–3.

NCAA MEN'S AND WOMEN'S DIVISION II OUTDOOR TRACK AND FIELD CHAMPIONSHIPS. May 21–23. Finals. Southern Illinois University, Edwardsville, IL. For info: NCAA, 6201 College Blvd, Overland Park, KS 66211. Phone: (913) 339-1906.

NCAA DIVISION I SOFTBALL WORLD SERIES. May 21–25. Finals. Amateur Softball Hall of Fame Stadium, Oklahoma City, OK. For info: NCAA, 6201 College Blvd, Overland Park, KS 66211. Phone: (913) 339-1906.

NCAA WOMEN'S DIVISION I TENNIS CHAMPIONSHIP. May 21–29. Finals. University of Notre Dame, Notre Dame, IN. For info: NCAA, 6201 College Blvd, Overland Park, KS 66211. Phone: (913) 339-1906.

SHORTEST NIGHT GAME: 55th ANNIVERSARY. May 21, 1943. In the shortest night game in major league history, the Chicago White Sox defeated the Washington Senators, 1–0, in one hour, 29 minutes.

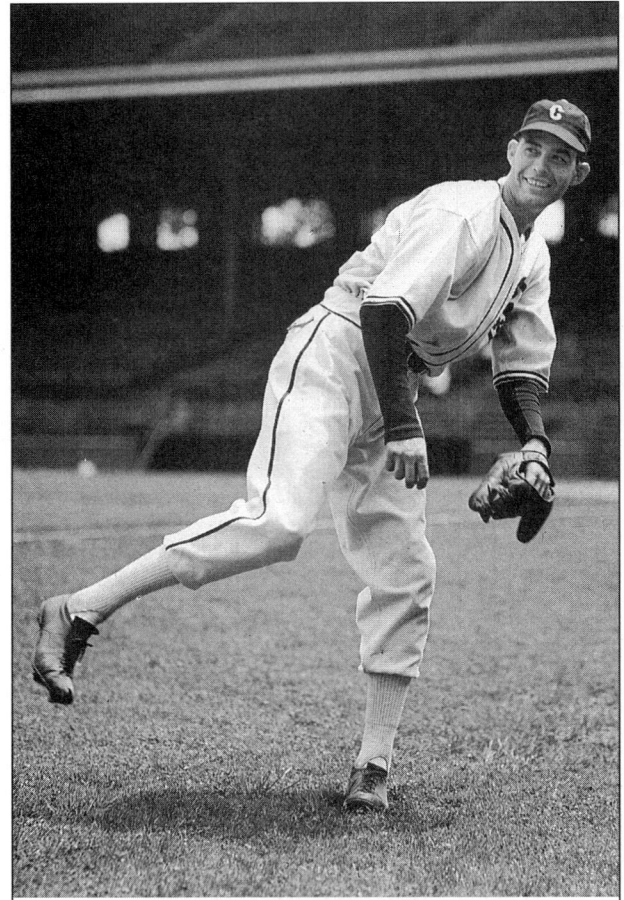

May 1998
S	M	T	W	T	F	S
					1	2
3	4	5	6	7	8	9
10	11	12	13	14	15	16
17	18	19	20	21	22	23
24	25	26	27	28	29	30
31						

STRATTON, MONTY: BIRTH ANNIVERSARY. May 21, 1912. Monty Franklin Pierce Stratton, baseball player born at Celeste, TX. Stratton's five-year career in the major leagues was ended when his leg was amputated after he accidentally shot himself in a hunting accident. Jimmy Stewart played Stratton in a very successful movie based roughly on his life. Died at Greenville, TX, Sept 29, 1982.

BIRTHDAYS TODAY

Tommy Albelin, 34, hockey player, born Stockholm, Sweden, May 21, 1964.

Robert Joe (Bobby) Cox, 57, baseball manager and former executive and player, born Tulsa, OK, May 21, 1941.

Kent Alan Hrbek, 38, former baseball player, born Minneapolis, MN, May 21, 1960.

Arnold Barry Latman, 62, former baseball player, born Los Angeles, CA, May 21, 1936.

Edward James (Eddie) Milner, 43, former baseball player, born Columbus, OH, May 21, 1955.

Ara Raoul Parseghian, 75, former broadcaster and college football coach, born Akron, OH, May 21, 1923.

David Raymond (Dave) Wannstedt, 46, football coach, born Pittsburgh, PA, May 21, 1952.

MAY 22 — FRIDAY
Day 142 — 223 Remaining

SPORTSCHASER OF THE DAY
Who was the first woman driver to qualify to race in the Indianapolis 500?

ALMA HIGHLAND FESTIVAL AND GAMES. May 22–24. Alma College, Alma, MI. Old-world pageantry honoring Scottish traditions–Highland dancing, piping, drumming, athletic competitions, clan tents and grand parade. 30th annual festival. Annually, Memorial Day weekend. Est attendance: 60,000. For info: Chamber of Commerce, 110 W Superior St, PO Box 516, Alma, MI 48801. Phone: (517) 463-8979.

BIG TEN MEN'S/WOMEN'S OUTDOOR TRACK AND FIELD CHAMPIONSHIPS. May 22–24. Ohio State University, Columbus, OH. For info: Big Ten Conference, 1500 W Higgins Rd, Park Ridge, IL 60068-6300. Phone: (847) 696-1010. Fax: (847) 696-1150. WWW: http://www.bigten.org

CANADA: KLONDIKE INTERNATIONAL DART TOURNAMENT. May 22–24. Dawson City, Yukon. Held at Gertie's. Singles, doubles and mixed. Cash prizes. Est attendance: 75. For info: Klondike Visitors Assn, Box 389, Dawson City, Yukon, Canada Y0B 1G0. Phone: (403) 668-4236. Fax: (403) 993-6415. Email: kva@hypertech.yk.ca.

DAWSON WALKED FIVE TIMES: ANNIVERSARY. May 22, 1990. The Cincinnati Reds intentionally walked outfielder Andre Dawson of the Chicago Cubs a record five times in a 16-inning game. Dawson's five free passes broke the record held by Roger Maris and Garry Templeton.

FIRST WOMAN TO QUALIFY FOR INDY: ANNIVERSARY. May 22, 1977. Janet Guthrie became the first woman driver to qualify for the Indianapolis 500 with an average speed of more than 188 miles per hour. She lasted only 27 laps in the race, dropping out when her car broke a valve seal.

GRUBSTAKE DAYS. May 22–25. Yucca Valley, CA. Includes parade, carnival, PCRA rodeo, dances, horseshoe tournament, food and community booths, arts and craft booths and breakfasts offered by local service organizations. Annually, Memorial Day weekend. Est attendance: 30,000. For info: Yucca Valley Chamber of Commerce, 56300 29 Palms Hwy, Ste D, Yucca Valley, CA 92284. Phone: (760) 365-6323. Fax: (760) 365-0763. Email: yvcc@desertgold.com.

MANTLE NEARLY LEAVES THE BUILDING: 35th ANNIVERSARY. May 22, 1963. Mickey Mantle of the New York Yankees hit a home run off Bill Fischer of the Kansas City Athletics as the Yankees beat the A's, 8–7. Mantle's blast caromed off the rooftop facade at Yankee Stadium and came within a few feet of becoming the only home run ever hit out of that park.

MEMORIAL DAY GOLF TOURNAMENT. May 22–24. Pinehurst Golf Course, Pinehurst, ID. Invitational tournament that brings in people from all over the Northwest. Also, long drive competition and horse race. Annually, Memorial Day weekend. For info: Stan Edwards, Pro, Pinehurst Golf Course, PO Box 908/Country Club Lane, Pinehurst, ID 83850. Phone: (208) 682-2013.

MEMORIAL WEEKEND SALMON DERBY. May 22–25. Petersburg, AK. Four days of fishing with more than $30,000 in prizes awarded! Est attendance: 400. For info: Petersburg Chamber of Commerce, PO Box 649, Petersburg, AK 99833. Phone: (907) 772-3646. Fax: (907) 772-3646. WWW: http://www.petersburg.org

★ **NATIONAL MARITIME DAY.** May 22. Presidential Proclamation always issued for May 22 since 1933. (Pub Res No. 7 of May 20, 1933.)

SIMMONS, AL: BIRTH ANNIVERSARY. May 22, 1902. Aloysius Harry (Al) Simmons, Baseball Hall of Fame outfielder born Aloysius Harry Syzmanski at Milwaukee, WI.

Simmons was a righthanded hitter known for pointing his left foot straight down the third-base line. This unorthodox style worked for him as he accumulated 2,926 hits in his career. Inducted into the Hall of Fame in 1953. Died at Milwaukee, May 26, 1956.

SMITH, HORTON: 90th BIRTH ANNIVERSARY. May 22, 1908. Horton Smith, golfer born at Springfield, MO. Smith won the first Masters in 1934 and then won it again in 1936. He played on seven Ryder Cup teams and was undefeated. After World War II, Smith played an active role in golf administration, serving as president of the PGA and the PGA Seniors. Died at Detroit, MI, Oct 15, 1963.

BIRTHDAYS TODAY

Mark Steven Brouhard, 42, former baseball player, born Burbank, CA, May 22, 1956.

Thomas Edward (Tommy) John, 55, former baseball player, born Terre Haute, IN, May 22, 1943.

Jose Ramon Mesa, 32, baseball player, born Azua, Dominican Republic, May 22, 1966.

Julian Tavarez, 25, baseball player, born Santiago, Dominican Republic, May 22, 1973.

MAY 23 — SATURDAY
Day 143 — 222 Remaining

ALABAMA JUBILEE. May 23–25. Point Mallard, Decatur, AL. Hot-air balloon races, arts, crafts, antique cars, water and air shows. Annually, Memorial Day weekend. Est attendance: 100,000. For info: Jacklyn Bailey, Decatur Conv and Visitors Bureau, Box 2349, 719 Sixth Ave SE, Decatur, AL 35602. Phone: (205) 350-2028 or (800) 524-6181. Email: dcvb@hiwaay.net.

FARMINGTON INVITATIONAL BALLOON FESTIVAL. May 23–24. Farmington, NM. Hot-air balloons launch off the banks of Farmington Lake. Famous Splash and Dash and Hare and Hound races included in the two-day event. Est attendance: 5,000. For info: Farmington Conv and Visitors Bureau, 203 W Main, Ste 401, Farmington, NM 87401. Phone: (800) 448-1240 or (505) 326-7602. Fax: (505) 327-0577. Email: fmncub@cyberport.com.

FIRST NIGHT GAME RAINED OUT: ANNIVERSARY. May 23, 1935. The first major league night game, scheduled to be played in Cincinnati, was rained out. History was made instead the following evening when the game was played.

HAGERMAN FOSSIL DAYS. May 23–24. Hagerman, ID. Old-fashioned, small-town family fun! Featuring a parade, mud races, mud volleyball, kids' fish scramble, bus tours of fossil beds, food galore, crafts and antiques and a variety of professional music from old-time fiddlers to blues, country, acoustic and rock 'n' roll. Est attendance: 4,000. For info: Chris Pothler, Hagerman Valley Chamber of Commerce. Phone: (208) 837-9131.

HEAD-OF-THE-MON-RIVER HORSESHOE TOURNAMENT. May 23–25. Fairmont, WV. Open to horseshoe pitchers with a 1998 State/National Horseshoe Pitchers Assn membership card. Est attendance: 300. For info: Tri-County Horseshoe Club Dir, Davis "Catfish" Woodward, 1133 Sunset Dr, Fairmont, WV 26554. Phone: (304) 366-3819.

HOY, DUMMY: BIRTH ANNIVERSARY. May 23, 1862. William Ellsworth ("Dummy") Hoy, baseball player born at Houcktown, OH. Despite losing his hearing from childhood meningitis, Hoy played major league baseball from 1888 to 1902. He was a fine defensive outfielder who once threw out three runners at home plate in one game. Died at Cincinnati, OH, Dec 15, 1961.

LITTLE 500. May 23. Anderson, IN. This 50th annual "Granddaddy of all sprint car races" concludes a week-long festival of events in Anderson and serves as an appetizer for the Indianapolis 500 held the next day. Drivers compete for more than $100,000 in prize money in this 500-lap sprint car race. Annually, the day before the Indy 500. Est attendance: 9,000. For info: Anderson Speedway, 1311 Pendleton Ave, Anderson, IN 46011. Phone: (765) 778-8168.

MEMORY DAYS. May 23–24. Grayson, KY. Parade, art show and horse show. Est attendance: 5,000. For info: Robert L. Caummisar, Chamber of Commerce, 301 W Main St, Grayson, KY 41143. Phone: (606) 474-9522.

NCAA DIVISION II BASEBALL TOURNAMENT. May 23–30. Finals. Paterson Field, Montgomery, AL. For info: NCAA, 6201 College Blvd, Overland Park, KS 66211. Phone: (913) 339-1906.

NCAA DIV III BASEBALL TOURNAMENT. May 23–27. Finals. Salem Baseball Stadium, Salem, VA. For info: NCAA, 6201 College Blvd, Overland Park, KS 66211. Phone: (913) 339-1906.

NCAA MEN'S DIVISION I LACROSSE CHAMPIONSHIP. May 23–25. Finals. Rutgers Stadium, New Brunswick, NJ. For info: NCAA, 6201 College Blvd, Overland Park, KS 66211. Phone: (913) 339-1906.

NCAA MEN'S DIVISION I TENNIS CHAMPIONSHIPS. May 23–31. Finals. University of Georgia, Athens, GA. For info: NCAA, 6201 College Blvd, Overland Park, KS 66211. Phone: (913) 339-1906.

PAC-10 MEN'S AND WOMEN'S OUTDOOR TRACK AND FIELD CHAMPIONSHIPS. May 23–24. Stanford University, Palo Alto, CA. For info: PAC-10 Conference, 800 S Broadway, Ste 400, Walnut Creek, CA 94596. Phone: (510) 932-4411. Fax: (510) 932-4601.

PHILLIPPE, DEACON: BIRTH ANNIVERSARY. May 23, 1872. Charles Louis ("Deacon") Phillippe, baseball pitcher born at Rural Retreat, VA. Phillippe led the Pittsburgh Pirates to National League dominance in the first decade of the 20th century. In the first modern World Series in 1903, he pitched five games and won three. Died at Avalon, PA, Mar 30, 1952.

TRADE AND TROPHY DAY. May 23. Caruthersville, MO. Antique car show in the courthouse parking lot with trophies awarded for Best of Show and Chamber of Commerce President's Choice. Nineteen classes with first, second and third place awards. There will also be a display of cars for sale. For autos 15 years or older. 36th annual. Est attendance: 2,000. For info: Tommy Clayton, Bootheel Antique Car Klub, 704 Cotton, Caruthersville, MO 63830. Phone: (573) 333-4445.

USA RUGBY WOMEN'S CLUB NATIONAL CHAMPIONSHIP. May 23–25. Minneapolis, MN. The top 12 women's club teams come together to compete and determine the top women's team in the US. For info: USA Rugby, 3595 E Fountain Blvd, Colorado Springs, CO 80910. Phone: (719) 637-1022. Fax: (719) 637-1315. Email: usarugby@rmii.com.

WHALERS CHANGE NAME: ANNIVERSARY. May 23, 1979. The New England Whalers of the National Hockey League changed their name to the Hartford Whalers. The team was an original member of the World Hockey Association and won the first WHA championship, the Avco World Cup in the, 1972–73 season. When the WHA folded following the 1978–79 season, the Whalers were one of four WHA teams taken into the National Hockey League.

WHEAT, ZACK: 110th BIRTH ANNIVERSARY. May 23, 1888. Zachariah David (Zack) Wheat, Baseball Hall of Fame outfielder born at Hamilton, OH. Wheat played left field for the Brooklyn Dodgers from 1909 to 1926. He hit .317, won one batting title and was never ejected from a game. Inducted into the Hall of Fame in 1959. Died at Sedalia, MO, Mar 11, 1972.

BIRTHDAYS TODAY

David Michael (Dave) Babych, 37, hockey player, born Edmonton, Alberta, Canada, May 23, 1961.
Reginald Leslie (Reggie) Cleveland, 50, former baseball player, born Swift Current, Saskatchewan, Canada, May 23, 1948.
Ricardo (Ricky) Gutierrez, 28, baseball player, born Miami, FL, May 23, 1970.
Marvelous Marvin Hagler (born Marvin Hagler), 44, former boxer, born at Newark, NJ, May 23, 1954.
John David Newcombe, 55, former tennis player, born Sydney, New South Wales, Australia, May 23, 1943.
Kevin Andrew Romine, 37, former baseball player, born Exeter, NH, May 23, 1961.

MAY 24 — SUNDAY
Day 144 — 221 Remaining

STANLEY CUP CHAMPIONS THIS DATE
1980	New York Islanders
1986	Montreal Canadiens
1990	Edmonton Oilers

BASEBALL FIRST PLAYED UNDER THE LIGHTS: ANNIVERSARY. May 24, 1935. The Cincinnati Reds defeated the Philadelphia Phillies by a score of 2–1, as more than 20,000 fans enjoyed the first night baseball game in the major leagues. The game was played at Crosley Field, Cincinnati, OH.

CANADIENS WIN 23rd STANLEY CUP: ANNIVERSARY. May 24, 1986. The Montreal Canadiens defeated the Calgary Flames, 4–3, to win the Stanley Cup, four games to one. For the Canadiens, it was their 23rd title, putting them one major-league championship ahead of the New York Yankees and their 22 World Series titles. Montreal won another Stanley Cup in 1993.

DEMARET, JIMMY: BIRTH ANNIVERSARY. May 24, 1910. James Newton (Jimmy) Demaret, golfer and sportscaster born at Houston, TX. Demaret won the Masters three times and teamed successfully with Ben Hogan in the 1947 and 1951 Ryder Cup matches. He wore flamboyant clothes and played to the crowd. He worked on golf telecasts and founded the Legends of Golf tournament that grew into the Senior Tour. Died at Houston, Dec 28, 1983.

DISPUTED WIN AT INDIANAPOLIS: ANNIVERSARY. May 24, 1981. Bobby Unser finished first in the Indianapolis 500, but after the race was over, the stewards penalized him one lap for passing cars illegally under the yellow caution flag. The penalty vaulted Mario Andretti into first place, but Unser and Roger Penske, owner of Unser's car, appealed the stewards' decision to the United States Auto Club. Four months later, USAC ruled that Unser was guilty but that the punishment was too severe. The lap penalty was replaced by a $40,000 fine, and Unser recovered the championship.

	S	M	T	W	T	F	S
May						1	2
	3	4	5	6	7	8	9
1998	10	11	12	13	14	15	16
	17	18	19	20	21	22	23
	24	25	26	27	28	29	30
	31						

INDIANAPOLIS 500. May 24. Indianapolis, IN. Recognized as the world's largest single-day sporting event. First race was in 1911. Annually, the Sunday of Memorial Day weekend. For info: Indianapolis Motor Speedway Corp, 4790 W 16th St, Indianapolis, IN 46222. Phone: (317) 481-8500. WWW: http://www.indyracingleague.com

MELON CITY CRITERIUM. May 24. Muscatine, IA. 20th annual daylong criterium at Weed Park has nine race categories for licensed US Cycling & Fitness members. Prize money of approximately $6,000. Est attendance: 3,000. For info: Greg Harper, c/o Harper's Cycling & Fitness, 1106 Grandview Ave, Muscatine, IA 52761. Phone: (319) 263-4043. Fax: (319) 263-9073.

NCAA MEN'S DIVISION II AND III LACROSSE CHAMPIONSHIP. May 24. Finals. Rutgers Stadium, New Brunswick, NJ. For info: NCAA, 6201 College Blvd, Overland Park, KS 66211. Phone: (913) 339-1906.

OESCHGER, JOE: BIRTH ANNIVERSARY. May 24, 1891. Joseph Carl (Joe) Oeschger, baseball player born at Chicago, IL. Oeschger and Leon Cadore were the two pitchers who went all the way in baseball's longest game, a 26-inning, 1–1 tie between the Brooklyn Dodgers and the Boston Braves on May 1, 1920. Died at Rohnert Park, CA, July 29, 1986.

ROC HILLCLIMB TIME TRAIL BIKE RACE. May 24. Roanoke, VA. 1.87 miles to top of scenic and historic Mill Mountain. Avg. gradient is 8% with 847ft elevation gain. Sanctioned by USCF. $2,500 cash and omnium. For info: Wendi Schultz, CFE Exec Dir, Roanoke Festival in the Park, PO Box 8276, Roanoke, VA 24014. Phone: (540) 342-2640.

THIRTEEN HALL OF FAMERS IN SAME GAME: 70th ANNIVERSARY. May 24, 1928. In a game between the Philadelphia Athletics and the New York Yankees, 13 future members of the Baseball Hall of Fame took the field. Ty Cobb, Tris Speaker, Mickey Cochrane, Al Simmons, Eddie Collins, Lefty Grove and Jimmie Foxx played for the Athletics. Earle Combs, Leo Durocher, Babe Ruth, Lou Gehrig, Tony Lazzeri and Waite Hoyt played for the Yankees. In addition, the two managers, Connie Mack and Miller Huggins, are also Hall of Famers.

BIRTHDAYS TODAY

Gregory (Greg) Briley, 33, former baseball player, born Greenville, NC, May 24, 1965.
Robert Thomas (Rob) Ducey, 33, former baseball player, born Toronto, Ontario, Canada, May 24, 1965.
Joe Dumars, III, 35, basketball player, born Shreveport, LA, May 24, 1963.
Mitchell (Mitch) Kupchak, 44, former basketball player, born Hicksville, NY, May 24, 1954.
James Ernest (Jim) Mora, 63, former football coach, born Los Angeles, CA, May 24, 1935.

MAY 25 — MONDAY
Day 145 — 220 Remaining

NBA FINALS CHAMPIONS THIS DATE
1975   Golden State Warriors

ALI BEATS LISTON IN REMATCH: ANNIVERSARY. May 25, 1965. Muhammad Ali knocked out Sonny Liston just one minute into the first round of a controversial rematch for the heavyweight championship in Lewiston, ME. Liston went down from a short right-hand punch that some swore never hit him.

BABE'S 714th BIG ONE: ANNIVERSARY. May 25, 1935. George Herman Ruth could barely run and could no longer hit like he used to, but occasionally the Babe could still put on a show with his bat. On May 25, Ruth, playing for the Boston Braves, hit three home runs before a crowd of only 10,000 at Pittsburgh's Forbes Field. His last home run of the day–his 714th in regular season play–proved to be Babe's last major league home run as well as his last big-league hit.

BOLDER BOULDER 10K. May 25. Boulder, CO. A 10K race of walkers, joggers and world-class runners through the streets of Boulder. Annually, on Memorial Day. Est attendance: 40,000. For info: Bill Reef, Bolder Boulder, PO Box 9125, Boulder, CO 80301-9125. Phone: (303) 444-7223. Fax: (303) 938-4863. Email: bolder10k@bolderboulder.com.

DIHIGO, MARTIN: BIRTH ANNIVERSARY. May 25, 1905. Martin Dihigo, Baseball Hall of Fame player and manager born at Matanzas, Cuba. Dihigo was the most versatile player in the Negro Leagues and one of the best. He excelled as a pitcher and as a hitter and played all positions except catcher. Inducted into the Hall of Fame in 1977. Died at Cienfuegos, Cuba, May 20, 1971.

FILION WINS 10,000TH RACE: ANNIVERSARY. May 25, 1987. Herve Filion drove Commander Bond to victory in the third race at Yonkers Raceway in New York to become the first harness racing driver to record 10,000 wins.

FRANCE: FRENCH OPEN. May 25–June 7. Stade Roland Garros, Paris, France. The national tennis championships of France with competition in men's and women's singles and men's, women's and mixed doubles. One of the sport's Grand Slam events.

GALAN, AUGIE: BIRTH ANNIVERSARY. May 25, 1912. August John (Augie) Galan, baseball player born at Berkeley, CA. Galan played outfield for five different teams over a 16-year career. A switch-hitter, he once hit home runs from both sides of the plate in the same game. Died at Fairfield, CA, Dec 28, 1993.

JENKINS STRIKES OUT 3,000th BATTER: ANNIVERSARY. May 25, 1982. Pitcher Ferguson Jenkins of the Chicago Cubs recorded the 3,000th strikeout in his major league career in a 2–1 loss to the San Diego Padres. Jenkins, the seventh pitcher to reach 3,000 strikeouts, wound up his career with 3,192 Ks, ninth on the all-time list.

MEMORIAL DAY. May 25. Legal public holiday. (PL90–363 sets Memorial Day on last Monday in May. Applicable to federal employees and District of Columbia.) Also known as Decoration Day. Most countries designate a day each year for decorating graves with flowers and for other memorial tributes to the dead. Especially an occasion for honoring those who have died in battle. (Observance dates from Civil War years in US: first documented observance at Waterloo, NY, May 5, 1865.)

MOON PHASE: NEW MOON. May 25. Moon enters New Moon phase at 3:32 PM, EDT.

NATIONAL TAP DANCE DAY. May 25. To celebrate this unique American art form that represents a fusion of African and European cultures and to transmit tap to succeeding generations through documentation and archival and performance support. Held on the anniversary of the birth of Bill "Bojangles" Robinson to honor his outstanding contribution to the art of tap dancing on stage and in films through the unification of diverse stylistic and racial elements.

NELSON, LINDSEY: BIRTH ANNIVERSARY. May 25, 1919. Lindsey Nelson, sportscaster born at Pulaski, TN. Nelson cut his broadcasting teeth in Knoxville, TN, and worked for the Liberty Radio Network in the early 1950s. For NBC television, he specialized in college football and gained an additional audience broadcasting Notre Dame games on a tape-delayed basis. In 1962 he joined Bob Murphy and Ralph Kiner as the original voices of the New York Mets. Died at Atlanta, GA, June 10, 1995.

SATURN FESTIVAL CUP BIKE RACE. May 25. Roanoke, VA. Sanctioned by USCF. $14,500 cash including prizes and omnium. Free race clinic available. Call for appli-

cation. For info: Roanoke Festival in the Park, PO Box 8276, Roanoke, VA 24014. Phone: (540) 342-2640.

TOUR OF SOMERVILLE. May 25. Somerville, NJ. The oldest continuously run major bicycle race in America. 1998 marks the 55th running. Attracts more than 600 top amateur cyclists for seven events. Annually, on Memorial Day. Est attendance: 40,000. For info: Dan Puntillo, Admin, PO Box 125, Somerville, NJ 08876. Phone: (908) 725-0461. Fax: (908) 722-5411.

TUNNEY, GENE: 100th BIRTH ANNIVERSARY. May 25, 1898. James Joseph ("Gene") Tunney, boxer and business executive born at New York, NY. Tunney won the light heavyweight championship in 1922 and defeated Jack Dempsey for the heavyweight title on Sept 23, 1926. Their rematch at Soldier Field in Chicago on Sept 22, 1927, was the famous "Long Count" fight in which Tunney remained on the canvas more than 10 seconds after Dempsey hovered over him, a subject of controversy ever since. Tunney died at New York, NY, Nov 7, 1978.

STANLEY CUP CHAMPIONS THIS DATE

1978	Montreal Canadiens
1989	Calgary Flames
1991	Pittsburgh Penguins

BIRTHDAYS TODAY

Shawn Antoski, 28, hockey player, born Brantford, Ontario, Canada, May 25, 1970.

Kendall Cedric Gill, 30, basketball player, born Chicago, IL, May 25, 1968.

Tarik Glenn, 22, football player, born Cleveland, OH, May 25, 1976.

David Michael (Dave) Hollins, 32, baseball player, born Buffalo, NY, May 25, 1966.

K.C. Jones, 66, former basketball coach and player, born Tyler, TX, May 25, 1932.

Robert Wesley (Bob) Knepper, 44, former baseball player, born Akron, OH, May 25, 1954.

William Walton (Bill) Sharman, 72, former basketball coach, executive and Basketball Hall of Fame guard, born Abilene, TX, May 25, 1926.

MAY 26 — TUESDAY
Day 146 — 219 Remaining

STANLEY CUP CHAMPIONS THIS DATE

1988	Edmonton Oilers

COAST-TO-COAST WALKING RACE: 70th ANNIVERSARY. May 26, 1928. Andrew Payne of Claremore, OK, arrived in New York, NY, on foot and was declared the winner of the first coast-to-coast walking race. Payne had left Los Angeles 573 hours before. He beat 273 other walkers over the 3,422-mile route.

GRANT, FRANK: DEATH ANNIVERSARY. May 26, 1937. Frank Grant, baseball player born at Pittsfield, MA, 1867. Grant was probably the best black ballplayer in the 19th century, but he never got to play in the major leagues. He played with teams in white minor leagues and with black teams and was an outstanding second baseman. Died at New York, NY.

HADDIX'S NEAR-PERFECT GAME: ANNIVERSARY. May 26, 1959. Lefthander Harvey Haddix of the Pittsburgh Pirates pitched a perfect game for 12 innings before losing to the Milwaukee Braves, 1–0, in the 13th. In the decisive frame, Braves second baseman Felix Man-

May
1998

	S	M	T	W	T	F	S
						1	2
	3	4	5	6	7	8	9
	10	11	12	13	14	15	16
	17	18	19	20	21	22	23
	24	25	26	27	28	29	30
	31						

118

tilla reached first on a throwing error by third baseman Don Hoak. Eddie Mathews sacrificed Mantilla to second, and Haddix walked Henry Aaron intentionally. Joe Adcock then hit a fly to deep right-center field that just cleared the fence for an apparent home run. Mantilla scored, but Aaron, who thought the ball landed on the field, touched second and headed for the dugout. Adcock kept running and was called out for passing Aaron, negating the home run. For the Braves, Lew Burdette pitched all 13 innings. He gave up 12 hits but got the victory.

ROSE, MAURI: BIRTH ANNIVERSARY. May 26, 1906. Mauri Rose, auto racer born at Columbus, OH. Rose ran in 15 straight Indianapolis 500s and won three times in 1941, 1947 and 1948. His success and consistency came despite the part-time nature of his career. His steady employment by a number of auto companies limited the time he could spend practicing and competing. Died at Detroit, MI, Jan 1, 1981.

SEWELL STRIKES OUT TWICE: ANNIVERSARY. May 26, 1930. Shortstop Joe Sewell of the Cleveland Indians, who struck out only three times in the entire season, fanned twice in the same game against Pat Carraway of the Chicago White Sox. Sewell played 14 years in the majors and struck out a total of 114 times.

BIRTHDAYS TODAY

Joseph Salvatore (Joe) Altobelli, 66, former baseball manager and player, born Detroit, MI, May 26, 1932.
Jason Phillip Bere, 27, baseball player, born Cambridge, MA, May 26, 1971.
Darrell Wayne Evans, 51, former baseball player, born Pasadena, CA, May 26, 1947.
Kevin Curtis Kennedy, 44, former baseball manager, born Los Angeles, CA, May 26, 1954.
Gregory Lenard (Greg) Lloyd, 33, football player, born Miami, FL, May 26, 1965.
Brent Woody Musburger, 59, broadcaster, born Portland, OR, May 26, 1939.
Wesley Darcel Walker, 43, former football player, born San Bernardino, CA, May 26, 1955.

MAY 27 — WEDNESDAY
Day 147 — 218 Remaining

STANLEY CUP CHAMPIONS THIS DATE
1975 Philadelphia Flyers

AERIAL GOLF: 70th ANNIVERSARY. May 27, 1928. A unique golfing event transpired at the Old Westbury Golf Club in New York. Two-person teams competed in an aerial golf tournament. One member of each team flew above the course in an airplane and dropped a ball as close to each hole as possible. The other team member, on the ground, then putted out. The winning team was William Hammond and M. M. Merrill.

BUCKS COUNTY SENIOR GAMES. May 27–June 5. Delaware Valley College, Doylestown, PA. Senior "Olympics" for ages 55 years and older. Winning competitors go to State Senior Games. Sponsored by the Bucks County Area Agency on Aging and the Bucks County Department of Parks and Recreation. Est attendance: 500. For info: Lisa Fraser, 901 E Bridgetown Pike, Langhorn, PA 19047. Phone: (215) 757-0571.

DEBUT OF OVERSIZED CATCHER'S MITT: ANNIVERSARY. May 27, 1960. Baltimore Orioles catcher Clint Courtney used an oversized mitt for the first time to catch knuckleballer Hoyt Wilhelm in a game against the New York Yankees. The mitt, designed by Orioles manager Paul Richards, was nearly 50% larger than a regular catcher's mitt. The Orioles won, 3–2.

FIRST RUNNING OF PREAKNESS: 125th ANNIVERSARY. May 27, 1873. The first running of the Preakness Stakes at Pimlico Race Track, MD, was won by Survivor with a time of 2:43. The winning jockey was G. Barbee, and the winning owner took one-year possession of the Woodlawn Vase, a trophy created in 1860 by Tiffany and Co. The Preakness was named for the colt that won the Dinner Party Stakes on the day the track opened in 1870. Preakness was shipped to Europe after being purchased by the Duke of Hamilton, who, some time later in a fit of pique, shot the horse dead.

HIGGINS, PINKY: BIRTH ANNIVERSARY. May 27, 1909. Michael Franklin ("Pinky") Higgins, Jr, baseball player and manager born at Red Oak, TX. Higgins was a major-league third baseman in the 1930s and 1940s and a manager of the Boston Red Sox in the 1950s. Died at Dallas, TX, Mar 21, 1969.

MONTREAL AND SAN DIEGO AWARDED FRANCHISES: 30th ANNIVERSARY. May 27, 1968. The National League voted to expand for the first time since 1962 and awarded franchises to Montreal (the first major league team outside the United States) and San Diego. The Montreal club was called the Expos. San Diego named its team the Padres.

MOORE, TERRY: BIRTH ANNIVERSARY. May 27, 1912. Terry Bluford Moore, baseball player born at Vernon, AL. Moore played center field for the St. Louis Cardinals in the late 1930s and 1940s. He hit .280 and was regarded as an outstanding defensive outfielder. Died at Collinsville, IL, Mar 29, 1995.

NATIONAL SENIOR HEALTH AND FITNESS DAY. May 27. Local sites in all 50 states. 5th annual event to promote the value of fitness and exercise for older adults. During this day–as part of Older Americans Month activities–seniors across the country are involved in organized health promotion activities. Annually, last Wednesday in May. For info: Tina Godin, Program Coord, Mature Market Resource Center, 621 E Park Ave, Libertyville, IL 60048. Phone: (800) 828-8225. Fax: (847) 816-8662. Email: maturemkt@aol.com. WWW: http://www.fitnessday.com

NCAA MEN'S DIVISION I GOLF CHAMPIONSHIPS. May 27–30. Finals. University of New Mexico, Albuquerque, NM. For info: NCAA, 6201 College Blvd, Overland Park, KS 66211. Phone: (913) 339-1906.

BIRTHDAYS TODAY

Jeffrey Robert (Jeff) Bagwell, 30, baseball player, born Boston, MA, May 27, 1968.
Jacob Donnell Brumfield, 33, baseball player, born Bogalusa, LA, May 27, 1965.
Pat Cash, 33, tennis player, born Melbourne, Australia, May 27, 1965.
Terry Lee Collins, 49, baseball manager, born Midland, MI, May 27, 1949.
Todd Randolph Hundley, 29, baseball player, born Martinsville, VA, May 27, 1969.
Darrell A. Russell, 22, football player, born Pensacola, FL, May 27, 1976.
Ray Sheppard, 32, hockey player, born Pembroke, Ontario, Canada, May 27, 1966.
Samuel Jackson (Sam) Snead, 86, golfer, born Hot Springs, VA, May 27, 1912.
Frank Edward Thomas, 30, baseball player, born Columbus, GA, May 27, 1968.
Jeffery Douglas (Doug) West, 31, basketball player, born Altoona, PA, May 27, 1967.

MAY 28 — THURSDAY
Day 148 — 217 Remaining

AMERICAN LEAGUE DIVIDES INTO TWO DIVISIONS: 30th ANNIVERSARY. May 28, 1968. The American League announced that it would split into two divisions for the 1969 season. Teams in the AL East included the Baltimore Orioles, the Boston Red Sox, the Cleveland Indians, the Detroit Tigers, the New York Yankees and the Washington Senators. The AL West was comprised of the California Angels, the Chicago White Sox, the Kansas City Royals, the Minnesota Twins, the Oakland Athletics and the Seattle Pilots.

CALIFORNIA SENIOR GAMES SACRAMENTO. May 28-31. Sacramento, CA. Athletic competition for men and women age 50 and older. Compete in five-year age divisions. Twenty-one sports. Est attendance: 1,000. For info: Pamela Rhodes, Coord, 6005 Folsom Blvd, Sacramento, CA 95819. Phone: (916) 277-6094. Fax: (916) 277-6074.

CANADA: ANNAPOLIS VALLEY APPLE BLOSSOM FESTIVAL. May 28–June 1. Windsor to Digby, Nova Scotia. Annual festival with barbecues, sports events, art show, Princess Tea, coronation ceremonies, dances, concerts, fireworks, craft fair, children's parade, Grand Street Parade, "Family Showcase '98" (family entertainment) and "Sunday in the Park" (family entertainment). Annually, since 1933. Est attendance: 125,000. For info: Festival Office, 37 Cornwallis St, Canada B4N 2E2. Phone: (902) 678-8322. Fax: (902) 678-3710. WWW: http://www.valleyweb.com

GILES, WARREN: BIRTH ANNIVERSARY. May 28, 1896. Warren Crandall Giles, Baseball Hall of Fame executive born at Tiskilwa, IL. Giles began his baseball career as a minor league team executive. He became general manager of the Cincinnati Reds and president of the National League. Inducted into the Hall of Fame in 1979. Died at Cincinnati, OH, Feb 7, 1979.

HERSHBERGER, WILLARD: BIRTH ANNIVERSARY. May 28, 1910. Willard McKee Hershberger, baseball player born at Lemon Cave, CA. Hershberger, a catcher, committed suicide during the 1940 season. Died at Boston, MA, Aug 3, 1940.

LICKING PRCA RODEO. May 28-30. Licking, MO. PRCA Rodeo. Annually, the weekend after Memorial Day. Est attendance: 9,000. For info: Vicki Peterson, Mktg, Licking Chamber of Commerce, PO Box 336, Licking, MO 65542. Phone: (573) 674-2510.

MAYS GETS FIRST HIT: ANNIVERSARY. May 28, 1951. After failing to get a hit in his first three major league games, Willie Mays of the New York Giants broke his 0-for-12 skein by hitting a home run off Warren Spahn of the Boston Braves.

MEMORIAL TOURNAMENT. May 28-31. Muirfield Village G.C., Dublin, OH. A PGA Tour tournament. For info: PGA Tour, 112 TPC Blvd, Ponte Vedra Beach, FL 32082. Phone: (904) 285-3700.

PORTLAND ROSE FESTIVAL. May 28–June 21. Portland, OR. Celebration includes more than 70 events featuring grand floral parade, hot-air balloons, band festivals, auto and ski races, carnival, air show and Navy ship visits. Est attendance: 2,000,000. For info: Clarence Moriwaki, Portland Rose Festival Assn, 220 NW Second Ave, Portland, OR 97209. Phone: (503) 227-2681. Fax: (503) 227-6603. Email: info@rosefestival.org. WWW: http://www.rosefestival.org

THORPE, JIM: 110th BIRTH ANNIVERSARY. May 28, 1888. James Francis (Jim) Thorpe, Olympic gold medal track athlete, baseball player and football player born at Prague, OK. Thorpe, a Native American, won the pentathlon and the decathlon at the 1912 Olympic games, but later lost his medals when Olympic officials declared a stint as a minor league baseball player besmirched his amateur standing. He later played professional baseball and football and was acclaimed the greatest male athlete of the first half of the 20th century. Died at Lomita, CA, Mar 28, 1953. (Thorpe's medals were returned to his family many years after his death when the earlier decision was reversed.)

BIRTHDAYS TODAY

Terrance Arthur (Terry) Crisp, 55, hockey coach and former player, born Parry Sound, Ontario, Canada, May 28, 1943.

William Donald (Bill) Doran, 40, former baseball player, born Cincinnati, OH, May 28, 1958.

Tory Epps, 31, football player, born Uniontown, PA, May 28, 1967.

Kirk Harold Gibson, 41, former baseball player, born Pontiac, MI, May 28, 1957.

Armon Louis Gilliam, 34, basketball player, born Pittsburgh, PA, May 28, 1964.

Mark Steven Howe, 43, former hockey player, born Detroit, MI, May 28, 1955.

Glen Anthony Rice, 31, basketball player, born Flint, MI, May 28, 1967.

David Donald Shula, 39, former football coach and player, born Lexington, KY, May 28, 1959.

Jerry Alan West, 60, basketball executive, former coach and Basketball Hall of Fame guard, born Cheylan, WV, May 28, 1938.

Ronald Lawrence (Ron) Wilson, 43, hockey coach, born Windsor, Ontario, Canada, May 28, 1955.

MAY 29 — FRIDAY
Day 149 — 216 Remaining

SPORTSCHASER OF THE DAY
Who broke Ty Cobb's American League record for most career stolen bases?

CENTRALIA ANCHOR FESTIVAL. May 29-31. Centralia City Square, Centralia, MO. This family festival has special events which include a fun run, 3-on-3 basketball, archery shoot, crafts, car show and free entertainment. Annually, the first weekend after Memorial Day. Est attendance: 25,000. For info: Centralia Chamber of Commerce, PO Box 235, Centralia, MO 65240. Phone: (573) 682-2272. Fax: (573) 682-1111.

COLLEGE WORLD SERIES (NCAA DIVISION I BASEBALL TOURNAMENT). May 29–June 6. Finals. Johnny Rosenblatt Stadium, Omaha, NE. For info: NCAA, 6201 College Blvd, Overland Park, KS 66211. Phone: (913) 339-1906.

COURT DECLARES BASEBALL A SPORT: ANNIVERSARY. May 29, 1922. The Supreme Court, in a decision written by Justice Oliver Wendell Holmes, declared that baseball "would not be called trade or commerce in the commonly accepted use of those words." The Court rejected the suit of the Baltimore Federal League club that wanted baseball made subject to federal antitrust legislation and interstate commerce regulation.

	S	M	T	W	T	F	S
May						1	2
1998	3	4	5	6	7	8	9
	10	11	12	13	14	15	16
	17	18	19	20	21	22	23
	24	25	26	27	28	29	30
	31						

FESTIVAL SOFTBALL TOURNAMENT. May 29–31. Roanoke and Salem, VA. 6th annual USSSA-sanctioned tournament includes double-elimination competition for men's teams and round robin for women's teams. Divisional/state berths awarded in all divisions. Call for registration and fees. For info: Roanoke Festival in the Park, PO Box 8276, Roanoke, VA 24014. Phone: (540) 342-2640.

FISHING HAS NO BOUNDARIES-EAGLE RIVER. May 29–31. "T" Docks, Dock Park, Eagle River, WI. A three-day fishing experience for disabled persons on the Eagle River Chain of 28 beautiful lakes. Any disability, age, sex, race, etc, eligible. Attended by 75 participants and 200 volunteers. For info: Wil Campbell, Fishing Has No Boundaries, PO Box 2200, Eagle River, WI 54521. Phone: (715) 479-9309. Fax: (715) 479-4782. Email: wbc1@newnorth.net.

FOYT WINS FOURTH INDY 500: ANNIVERSARY. May 29, 1977. A. J. Foyt became the first driver to win four Indianapolis 500s, but he had to share headlines with Janet Guthrie, the first woman to drive in the famous race. Foyt won his first Indy in 1961 and repeated in 1964 and 1967. Guthrie was forced out of the race after 27 laps because of mechanical problems.

HENDERSON BREAKS COBB'S RECORD: ANNIVERSARY. May 29, 1990. Rickey Henderson of the Oakland A's stole the 893rd base of his career, thereby breaking Ty Cobb's American League record, in a game against the Toronto Blue Jays.

HORSES FLY COAST TO COAST: ANNIVERSARY. May 29, 1946. Chakoora and Uleta, a pair of two-year-old fillies, became the first thoroughbreds to complete a transcontinental airplane trip. They flew from New York to California, a voyage that lasted 20 hours because of bad weather.

MOUNT EVEREST CONQUERED: 45th ANNIVERSARY. May 29, 1953. Mt Everest, the highest mountain in the world, was conquered for the first time by Edmund Hillary and Tensing Norgay.

NCAA ROWING CHAMPIONSHIPS. May 29–31. Site TBA. For info: NCAA, 6201 College Blvd, Overland Park, KS 66211. Phone: (913) 339-1906.

NORTHERN LEAGUE INDEPENDENT PROFESSIONAL BASEBALL SEASON. May 29–Aug 31. An 84-games-per-team schedule that will be played in St. Paul, MN; Duluth, MN; Fargo, ND; Sioux City, IA; Madison, WI; Sioux Falls, SD; Winnipeg, Manitoba and Thunder Bay, Ontario. Est attendance: 1,000,000. For info: Northern League, Inc, PO Box 1282, Durham, NC 27702. Phone: (919) 956-8150. Fax: (919) 683-2693. Email: northernlg@earthlink.net. WWW: http://fanlink.com/contents/leagues/nl.html

O.C.A. RANGE ROUND-UP. May 29–30. Lazy E Arena, Guthrie, OK. Working cowboys from 12 of Oklahoma's largest ranches compete in six events, including wild cow milking and the hilarious wild horse race. Est attendance: 14,000. For info: Lazy E Promotions, Rte 5, PO Box 393, Guthrie, OK 73044. Phone: (405) 282-7433 or (800) 595-RIDE. Email: learena@ionet.net. WWW: http://www.lazye.com

SOCCER TRAGEDY: ANNIVERSARY. May 29, 1985. A riot at Heysel soccer stadium in Brussels, Belgium, killed 39 people. Fans attending the European Cup Final, between Liverpool and Juventus of Turin, clashed before the match started. Some 400 persons were injured in the riot. The incident was televised and viewed by millions throughout Europe. More than two years later, Sept 2, 1987, the British government announced that 26 British soccer fans (identified from television tapes) would be extradited to Belgium for trial. Hooliganism at soccer matches became the target of increased security measures for most of England's more than 90 professional teams following the tragedy.

ZALE, TONY: 85th BIRTH ANNIVERSARY. May 29, 1913. Tony Zale, boxer born Anthony Florian Zaleski at Gary, IN. Zale, known as the Man of Steel, won the middleweight title in 1941 from George Abrams. After World War II, he engaged in three classic bouts with Rocky Graziano, winning the first and the third and losing the second. He lost the title to Marcel Cerdan and was inducted into the International Boxing Hall of Fame in 1991. Died at Portage, IN, Mar 20, 1997.

BIRTHDAYS TODAY

Eric Keith Davis, 36, baseball player, born Los Angeles, CA, May 29, 1962.

Ferris Roy Fain, 77, former baseball player, born San Antonio, TX, May 29, 1921.

Charles Dewayne (Charlie) Hayes, 33, baseball player, born Hattiesburg, MS, May 29, 1965.

Leslie Townes ("Bob") Hope, 95, golf tournament sponsor, born Eltham, England, May 29, 1903.

Mike Keane, 31, hockey player, born Winnipeg, Manitoba, Canada, May 29, 1967.

Johnny Lee ("Blue Moon") Odom, 53, former baseball player, born Macon, GA, May 29, 1945.

Wiliam Charles (Bill) Risley, 31, baseball player, born Chicago, IL, May 29, 1967.

Ken Schrader, 43, auto racer, born Fenton, MO, May 29, 1955.

Alfred (Al) Unser, Sr, 59, former auto racer, born Albuquerque, NM, May 29, 1939.

Francis Thomas (Fay) Vincent, Jr, 60, former commissioner of baseball, born Waterbury, CT, May 29, 1938.

MAY 30 — SATURDAY
Day 150 — 215 Remaining

STANLEY CUP CHAMPIONS THIS DATE
1985 Edmonton Oilers

AEP/FESTIVAL CLASSIC RUN. May 30. Roanoke, VA. 17th annual Festival 5K and 10K races. Call for registration fees and deadlines. Trophies and medals awarded at After Race celebration along with food, beverages and music. T-shirt included in fee. For info: Roanoke Festival in the Park, PO Box 8276, Roanoke, VA 24014. Phone: (540) 342-2640.

AMICALOLA FITNESS FESTIVAL. May 30. Dawsonville, GA. In the foothills of the North Georgia Mountains, runners from across the state come to participate in 2K, 5K and 10K runs; 15- and 30-mile bike courses; and a biathlon. Est attendance: 1,000. For info: Dawson County Chamber of Commerce, PO Box 299, Dawsonville, GA 30534. Phone: (706) 265-6278. Fax: (706) 265-6279.

DONLIN, TURKEY MIKE: 120th BIRTH ANNIVERSARY. May 30, 1878. Michael Joseph ("Turkey Mike") Donlin, baseball player born at Peoria, IL. Donlin enjoyed a 12-year career, checkered by injuries and controversies. He fancied himself a vaudeville star and made a few movies after his retirement. Died at Hollywood, CA, Sept 24, 1933.

JIMMY COONEY RECORDS TRIPLE PLAY: ANNIVERSARY. May 30, 1927. Shortstop Jimmy Cooney of the Chicago Cubs completed baseball's sixth unassisted triple play in a morning game against the Pittsburgh Pirates. In the fourth inning, Cooney caught Paul Waner's line drive, stepped on second to double off Lloyd Waner and tagged Clyde Barnhart, running from first to second.

KENNETT KIWANIS RODEO. May 30–31. Delta Fairgrounds, Kennett, MO. Largest cash-paying rodeo in the area. For info: Kennett Kiwanis Club, 1704 Allison, Kennett, MO 63857.

KOREA: TANO DAY. May 30. Fifth day of fifth lunar month. Summer food offered at the household shrine of the ancestors. Also known as Swing Day, since girls dressed in their prettiest clothes often compete in swinging matches. The Tano Festival usually lasts from the third through eighth day of the fifth lunar month: May 28–June 2.

METCALFE, RALPH: BIRTH ANNIVERSARY. May 30, 1910. Ralph Harold Metcalfe, Olympic gold medal sprinter born at Atlanta, GA. Metcalfe set world records in the 100 yards, 100 meters and 200 meters between 1932 and 1936. At the 1936 Berlin Olympics he finished second to Jesse Owens in the 100 meters and won a gold medal as a member of the 400-meter relay team. After World War II, Metcalfe was active in Chicago politics and served four terms in the US House of Representatives. Died at Chicago, IL, Oct 10, 1978.

PEACHTREE JUNIOR. May 30. Atlanta, GA. A 3K noncompetitive run for children ages 7–12. Entries limited to 2,500. Est attendance: 2,500. Send SASE for info: Atlanta

	S	**M**	**T**	**W**	**T**	**F**	**S**
May						1	2
	3	4	5	6	7	8	9
1998	10	11	12	13	14	15	16
	17	18	19	20	21	22	23
	24	25	26	27	28	29	30
	31						

Track Club, Peachtree Jr, 3097 E Shadowlawn Ave, Atlanta, GA 30305. WWW: http://www.atlantatrackclub.org

RAY HARROUN WINS FIRST INDIANAPOLIS 500: ANNIVERSARY. May 30, 1911. Ray Harroun won the first running of the Indianapolis 500 in 6 hours, 42 minutes and 8 seconds. Harroun started from the 28th position and averaged 74.602 miles per hour.

STOPPING FOR CHICKEN: ANNIVERSARY. May 30, 1912. During the second running of the Indianapolis 500, driver Ralph Mulford was told he would have to finish the race to collect 10th-place money. Mulford did so, but it took him eight hours, 53 minutes, more than 2½ hours longer than the winner. He stopped for fried chicken several times along the way, and the rule was changed the following year.

USA RUGBY DIVISIONS I AND II MEN'S CLUB CHAMPIONSHIP. May 30–31. San Diego, CA. The top four teams in Division I rugby compete to determine top men's club team. The top four Division II rugby teams come together to determine the top men's club team for Division II. For info: USA Rugby, 3595 E Fountain Blvd, Colorado Springs, CO 80910. Phone: (719) 637-1022. Fax: (719) 637-1315. Email: usarugby@rmii.com.

BIRTHDAYS TODAY

Allen Ray Aldridge, 26, football player, born Houston, TX, May 30, 1972.
Peter J. (P. J.) Carlesimo, 49, basketball coach and former player, born Scranton, PA, May 30, 1949.
Michael James (Mike) LaCoss, 42, former baseball player, born Glendale, CA, May 30, 1956.
Omar Joseph ("Turk") Lown, 74, former baseball player, born New York, NY, May 30, 1924.
Manuel Aristides (Manny) Ramirez, 26, baseball player, born Santo Domingo, Dominican Republic, May 30, 1972.
Gale Eugene Sayers, 55, Pro Football Hall of Fame running back, born Wichita, KS, May 30, 1943.

MAY 31 — SUNDAY
Day 151 — 214 Remaining

NBA FINALS CHAMPIONS THIS DATE
1983 Philadelphia 76ers

HUBBELL'S STREAK ENDS: ANNIVERSARY. May 31, 1937. The Brooklyn Dodgers defeated pitcher Carl Hubbell and the New York Giants, 10–3, snapping Hubbell's winning streak at 24 games, a major-league record. Hubbell's previous defeat had occurred on July 13, 1936. He finished that year with 16 straight wins and won 8 more in 1937 before losing to the Dodgers.

ITALY: PALIO DEI BALESTRIERI. May 31. Gubbio. The last Sunday in May is set aside for a medieval crossbow contest between Gubbio and Saensepolcro; medieval costumes, arms.

JOHNNY NEUN'S TRIPLE PLAY: ANNIVERSARY. May 31, 1927. One day after Jimmy Cooney made an unassisted triple play, Detroit Tigers first baseman Johnny Neun notched his own. In the ninth inning of a game against the Cleveland Indians, Neun caught a line drive hit by Homer Summa, tagged Charlie Jamieson between first and second and then ran to second base to triple off Glenn Myatt. The triple play ended the game with the Tigers ahead, 1–0.

LONGEST DOUBLEHEADER: ANNIVERSARY. May 31, 1964. The New York Mets and the San Francisco Giants played the longest doubleheader by time in major league history, the two games consuming nine hours, 52 minutes. The Giants won the first game in ordinary fashion, Juan Marichal beating the Mets, 5–3, in nine innings. But the second game went 23 innings and lasted 7:23 (a National League record) before the Giants emerged victorious, 8–6, on run-scoring hits by Del Crandall and Felipe Alou. 57,037 fans were on hand when the day began.

RUTH'S FINAL AT-BAT: ANNIVERSARY. May 31, 1935. Babe Ruth of the Boston Braves grounded out in his final major league at-bat against pitcher Jim Bivin of the Philadelphia Phillies.

STAR CITY GRAND PRIX–IN-LINE SKATING RACE. May 31. Roanoke, VA. 3rd annual 0.6 mile race. Awards, cash prizes and door prizes. Call for registration and fee. For info: Wendi Schultz, CFE Exec Dir, Roanoke Festival in the Park, PO Box 8276, Roanoke, VA 24014. Phone: (540) 342-2640.

WHITMAN, WALT: BIRTH ANNIVERSARY. May 31, 1819. Walter (Walt) Whitman, poet and journalist born at West Hills, NY. Following a short-lived and largely unsuccessful career in journalism, Whitman in 1855 published the collection of poetry for which he is now most famous, *Leaves of Grass*. Among his many interests was baseball, of which he said, "I see great things in baseball. It's our game, the American game." Died at Camden, NJ, Mar 26, 1892.

STANLEY CUP CHAMPIONS THIS DATE
1987   Edmonton Oilers

BIRTHDAYS TODAY

Tom Berenger, 48, actor (*Major League*), born Chicago, IL, May 31, 1950.

Jim Carey, 24, hockey player, born Dorchester, MA, May 31, 1974.

Kenneth (Kenny) Lofton, 31, baseball player, born East Chicago, IL, May 31, 1967.

Felix Anthony ("Tippy") Martinez, 48, former baseball player, born La Junta, CO, May 31, 1950.

Joseph William (Joe) Namath, 55, former broadcaster and Pro Football Hall of Fame quarterback, born Beaver Falls, PA, May 31, 1943.

Jeff Odgers, 29, hockey player, born Spy Hill, Saskatchewan, Canada, May 31, 1969.

Joseph Michael (Joe) Orsulak, 36, baseball player, born Glen Ridge, NJ, May 31, 1962.

Ray Clark Washburn, 60, former baseball player, born Pasco, WA, May 31, 1938.

JUNE 1 — MONDAY
Day 152 — 213 Remaining

NBA FINALS CHAMPIONS THIS DATE
1979   Seattle Supersonics

AMECHE, ALAN: 65th BIRTH ANNIVERSARY. June 1, 1933. Alan Dante ("The Horse") Ameche, football player born at Kenosha, WI. Ameche played fullback at the University of Wisconsin and won the 1954 Heisman Trophy. He turned pro with the Baltimore Colts and was named NFL Rookie of the Year. His most famous moment occurred in the 1958 NFL title game against the New York Giants. The game went into overtime, and Ameche scored the winning touchdown. Died at Houston, TX, Aug 8, 1988.

ASSAULT WINS TRIPLE CROWN: ANNIVERSARY. June 1, 1946. Assault, ridden by Warren Mehrtens, won the Belmont Stakes to become the seventh horse to win the Triple Crown. Owned by the King Ranch, Assault covered the 1½ miles in 2:30.4, defeating Natchez.

BAILEY OUTRACES JOHNSON: ANNIVERSARY. June 1, 1997. Canadian sprinter Donovan Bailey won a special 150-meter match race against American Michael Johnson to reassert his claim to the title of the "World's Fastest Human." After Bailey had won the 100 meters at the 1996 Summer Olympics and Johnson had won the 200 meters and the 400 meters, the two engaged in a nasty bragging-rights battle. This special race was supposed to put an end to their flap. But the race in Toronto proved inconclusive as Johnson, well behind at the halfway point, pulled up short, claiming that he had injured his left quadricep.

BRADLEY WINS ALL FOUR MAJORS: ANNIVERSARY. June 1, 1986. Pat Bradley won the LPGA Championship by one stroke over Patty Sheehan to become the first golfer to win all four women's major championships. Bradley won the du Maurier Classic in 1980 and 1986, the US Open in 1981 and the Dinah Shore in 1986. She was inducted into the LPGA Hall of Fame in 1991.

CANCER IN THE SUN MONTH. June 1–30. To promote education and awareness of the dangers of skin cancer from too much exposure to the sun. Kit of materials available for $15 from this nonprofit organization. For info: Frederick Mayer, Pres, Pharmacy Council on Dermatology (PCD), PO Box 1336, Sausalito, CA 94966. Phone: (415) 332-4066. Fax: (415) 332-1832. Email: ppsi@aol.com.

ENGLAND: DICING FOR BIBLES. June 1. An old Whitmonday ceremony at All Saints Church, St. Ives, Huntingdonshire. A bequest (in 1675) with the intent of providing Bibles for poor children of the parish required winning them at a dice game played in the church. In recent years the dicing has been moved from the altar to a "more suitable" place. Six Bibles are given on Whitmonday each year.

ENGLAND: INTERNATIONAL TT MOTORCYCLE RACES. June 1–12. Isle of Man. World-famous motorcycle road races held over a 38-mile course. Practice sessions will be held June 1-5. Est attendance: 40,000. For info: Road Race Dept, Auto Cycle Union, Wood St, Rugby, Warwickshire, England, CV21 2YX.

GEHRIG BEGINS STREAK: ANNIVERSARY. June 1, 1925. Lou Gehrig of the New York Yankees pinch-hit for Paul ("Pee Wee") Wanninger in the eighth inning to commence his streak of 2,130 consecutive games played. On the following day, Gehrig started at first base in place of Wally Pipp and remained in the lineup until May 2, 1939. Ironically, Wanninger had replaced Everett Scott as the Yankees regular shortstop on May 5, thereby ending Scott's string of 1,307 consecutive games played, the mark that Gehrig would surpass.

HOOSIER STATE GAMES. Various sites in Indiana during June and July. The Hoosier State Games is Indiana's only statewide amateur multisport festival. State champions will be crowned in more than a dozen sports throughout the spring and summer. For info: Indiana Sports Corp, 201 S Capitol Ave, Ste 1200, Indianapolis, IN 46225. Phone: (317) 237-5000 or (800) HI-FIVES. Fax: (317) 237-5041. Email: isc@indianasportscorp.com. WWW: http://www.indianasportscorp.com

INDIANA STATE SENIOR GAMES. June 1–6. Evansville, IN. Multisports events for people ages 55 and older. Hosted by the River City Senior Games. For info: Shelly Horton, River City Senior Games, PO Box 3938, Evansville, IN 47737-3938. Phone: (800) 253-2188.

MONROE, MARILYN: BIRTH ANNIVERSARY. June 1, 1926. Marilyn Monroe, actress and sex symbol born Norma Jean Mortensen or Baker in Los Angeles, CA. She had an unstable childhood in a series of orphanages and foster homes, but her remarkable film career came to epitomize Hollywood glamour. In 1954, she wed baseball legend Joe DiMaggio, but the marriage didn't last. Monroe remained fragile and insecure, tormented by the pressures of Hollywood life. Died at Los Angeles, Aug 5, 1962.

June 1998	S	M	T	W	T	F	S
		1	2	3	4	5	6
	7	8	9	10	11	12	13
	14	15	16	17	18	19	20
	21	22	23	24	25	26	27
	28	29	30				

MOON PHASE: FIRST QUARTER. June 1. Moon enters First Quarter phase at 9:45 PM, EDT.

MOSTIL, JOHNNY: BIRTH ANNIVERSARY. June 1, 1896. John Anthony (Johnny) Mostil, baseball player born at Chicago, IL. Mostil was an outfielder with the Chicago White Sox in the 1920s. In a bizarre incident in spring training, 1927, he slashed himself with a razor blade and pocketknife, trying to commit suicide. Died at Midlothian, IL, Dec 10, 1970.

NATIONAL FISHING WEEK. June 1–7. Annual celebration providing opportunities for youths to experience recreational fishing, learn about the environment firsthand and practice conservation ethics. We encourage all to take a friend fishing. Annually, the first full week in June beginning on Monday. For info: National Fishing Week Steering Committee, 1033 N Fairfax St, Ste 200, Alexandria, VA 22314-1540. Phone: (703) 684-3201. Fax: (703) 519-1872.

NIEKRO BROTHERS THE WINNINGEST: ANNIVERSARY. June 1, 1987. Phil Niekro pitched the Cleveland Indians to a 9–6 victory over the Detroit Tigers to put himself and his brother Joe into the lead as the winningest brothers in major-league pitching history. Their 530 combined victories surpassed Gaylord and Jim Perry. The Niekros ended their careers with 539 wins, 318 by Phil and 221 by Joe.

SCOTLAND: BRITISH AMATEUR GOLF CHAMPIONSHIP. June 1–6. Muirfield and Gullane #1, Edinburgh, Scotland. Est attendance: 180,000. For info: The Secretary, Royal and Ancient Golf Club, St. Andrews, Fife, Scotland KY16 9JD. Phone: (44) (133) 447-2112. Fax: (44) (133) 447-7580.

UPPERVILLE COLT AND HORSE SHOW. June 1–7. Warrenton, VA. 145th annual, the oldest show in the US. A weeklong "A-rated" horse show involving hundreds of horse and rider combinations from 8 to 10-year-old children in the pony divisions to leading Olympic and World Cup riders and horses in the Hunter, Jumper and Grand Prix divisions. Sunday's highlight is the prestigious $50,000 Budweiser/Upperville Jumper Classic sponsored by Budweiser. Est attendance: 5,500. For info: Tommy L. Jones, Upperville Colt and Horse Show, PO Box 1288, Warrenton, VA 20188. Phone: (540) 592-3858. Fax: (540) 253-576 or (540) 349-1829. WWW: http://www.upperville.com

STANLEY CUP CHAMPIONS THIS DATE
1992   Pittsburgh Penguins

Murray Baron, 31, hockey player, born Prince George, BC, Canada, June 1, 1967.
Wilmer Dean Chance, 57, former baseball player, born Wayne, OH, June 1, 1941.
Paul Douglas Coffey, 37, hockey player, born Weston, Ontario, Canada, June 1, 1961.
Jeff Hackett, 30, hockey player, born London, Ontario, Canada, June 1, 1968.
Cecil Randolph (Randy) Hundley, 56, former baseball player, born Martinsville, VA, June 1, 1942.
Alexi Lalas, 28, soccer player, born Birmingham, MI, June 1, 1970.
Kenneth Lee McMullen, 56, former baseball player, born Oxnard, CA, June 1, 1942.

JUNE 2 — TUESDAY
Day 153 — 212 Remaining

BRIDGES, MARSHALL: BIRTH ANNIVERSARY. June 2, 1931. Marshall Bridges, baseball player born at Jackson, MS. Bridges was a relief pitcher with four teams between 1959 and 1965. He played in the Negro Leagues before coming to the majors with the St. Louis Cardinals. Died at Jackson, Sept 3, 1990.

GAME DELAYED BY GNATS: ANNIVERSARY. June 2, 1959. The game between the Baltimore Orioles and the Chicago White Sox at Comiskey Park was delayed for nearly half an hour as swarms of gnats invaded the field. Bug spray and torches did not disperse the gnats, but a smoke bomb, set to be used as part of a postgame fireworks display, did. The Orioles won, 3–2.

GEHRIG, LOU: DEATH ANNIVERSARY. June 2, 1941. Henry Louis (Lou) Gehrig, Baseball Hall of Fame first baseman born Ludwig Heinrich Gehrig at New York, NY, June 19, 1903. Gehrig played baseball at Columbia and then signed with the New York Yankees, making his major league debut in 1923. Together with Babe Ruth, he personified the powerful Yankees lineup that came to be called "Murderers' Row." Gehrig played first base and hit .340 over 17 seasons with 493 home runs, 23 of them grand slams. He drove in 184 runs in 1931 and won the American League triple crown in 1934. He earned the nickname "the Iron Horse" for playing in a record 2,130 consecutive games, a streak stopped only by illness. Stricken with amyotrophic lateral sclerosis, a disease later called "Lou Gehrig's Disease," he retired abruptly in May 1939. Inducted into the Hall of Fame in 1939 by special election. Died at New York. (See also June 19.)

JACKSON, LARRY: BIRTH ANNIVERSARY. June 2, 1931. Lawrence Curtis (Larry) Jackson, baseball player born at Nampa, ID. Jackson was a workhorse pitcher who played 14 years in the majors with three teams without ever playing for a championship team. He became a politician after retiring from baseball. Died at Boise, ID, Aug 28, 1990.

ROBINSON, WILBERT: 135th BIRTH ANNIVERSARY. June 2, 1863. Wilbert Robinson, Baseball Hall of Fame manager and catcher born at Bolton, MA. Robinson was an outstanding catcher in the 19th century, especially for the great Baltimore Orioles teams of the 1890s. He managed the Brooklyn Dodgers during their inept 1920s. Inducted into the Hall of Fame in 1945. Died at Atlanta, GA, Aug 8, 1934.

RUTH RETIRES: ANNIVERSARY. June 2, 1935. Three days after he benched himself from his last game (May 30), George Herman ("Babe") Ruth announced his retirement from major league baseball.

WEISSMULLER, JOHNNY: BIRTH ANNIVERSARY. June 2, 1904. Peter John (Johnny) Weissmuller, actor and Olympic gold medal swimmer born at Windber, PA. Weissmuller won three gold medals at the 1924 Olympics and two more at the 1928 games. He set 24 world records and in 1950 was voted the best swimmer of the first half of the 20th century. After retiring from amateur competition, he appeared as Tarzan in a dozen movies and as "Jungle Jim" in the movies and on television. Died at Acapulco, Mexico, Jan 20, 1984.

BIRTHDAYS TODAY

Adam Creighton, 33, hockey player, born Burlington, Ontario, Canada, June 2, 1965.

Bryan Stanley Harvey, 35, baseball player, born Chattanooga, TN, June 2, 1963.

Dontae Antijuaine Jones, 23, basketball player, born Nashville, TN, June 2, 1975.

Michael Raymond (Mike) Kelly, 28, baseball player, born Los Angeles, CA, June 2, 1970.

Eugene Richard (Gene) Michael, 60, former baseball executive and player, born Kent, OH, June 2, 1938.

Kyle Petty, 38, auto racer, born Randleman, NC, June 2, 1960.

Larry Clark Robinson, 47, hockey coach and Hockey Hall of Fame defenseman, born Winchester, Ontario, Canada, June 2, 1951.

Craig Robert Stadler, 45, golfer, born San Diego, CA, June 2, 1953.

William Michael (Mike) Stanton, 31, baseball player, born Houston, TX, June 2, 1967.

June *1998*	S	M	T	W	T	F	S
		1	2	3	4	5	6
	7	8	9	10	11	12	13
	14	15	16	17	18	19	20
	21	22	23	24	25	26	27
	28	29	30				

JUNE 3 — WEDNESDAY
Day 154 — 211 Remaining

BASSLER, JOHNNY: BIRTH ANNIVERSARY. June 3, 1895. John Landis (Johnny) Bassler, baseball player born at Lancaster, PA. Bassler caught for the Detroit Tigers in the 1920s, but he liked the California lifestyle so much that he abandoned the major leagues to play in the Pacific Coast League. Died at Santa Monica, CA, June 29, 1979.

CANADA: THE NATIONAL TOURNAMENT. June 3–7. Spruce Meadows, Calgary, Alberta. The National Tournament features the Canadian Show Jumping Championship, including the Canadian Pacific World Cup and the Shell Cup. Enjoy country atmosphere in the Spruce Meadows Marketplace on the Plaza. Live entertainment and activities daily. Est attendance: 85,000. For info: Spruce Meadows, RR #9, Canada T2J 5G5. Phone: (403) 974-4200. Fax: (403) 947-4270. Email: smeadows@telusplanet.net. WWW: http://www.sprucemeadows.com

FIRST BASEBALL UNIFORMS: ANNIVERSARY. June 3, 1851. The Knickerbocker Base Ball Club of New York City donned the sport's first uniforms: straw hats, blue full-length trousers and white shirts.

GEHRIG HITS FOUR HOME RUNS: ANNIVERSARY. June 3, 1932. Lou Gehrig became the first American League player to hit four home runs in one game, doing so in a 20–13 New York Yankees victory over the Philadelphia Athletics. Gehrig hit his homers in four straight at-bats and narrowly missed a fifth. His teammate, Tony Lazzeri, hit for the cycle.

LONGEST NL NIGHT GAME: ANNIVERSARY. June 3, 1989. The Houston Astros defeated the Los Angeles Dodgers, 5–4, in 22 innings at the Astrodome. The longest night game by time in National League history, it lasted seven hours, 22 minutes.

MIGHTY CASEY HAS STRUCK OUT: 110th ANNIVERSARY. June 3, 1888. The famous comic baseball ballad "Casey at the Bat" was printed in the Sunday *San Francisco Examiner*. Appearing anonymously, it was written by Ernest L. Thayer. Recitation of "Casey at the Bat" became part of the repertoire of actor William DeWolf Hopper. The recitation took 5 minutes and 40 seconds. Hopper claimed to have recited it more than 10,000 times, the first being at Wallack's Theater in New York, NY, in 1888. (See also Thayer, Ernest Lawrence: Birth Anniversary, Aug 14.)

NCAA MEN'S AND WOMEN'S DIVISION I OUTDOOR TRACK AND FIELD CHAMPIONSHIPS. June 3–6. State University of New York at Buffalo, Buffalo, NY. For info: NCAA, 6201 College Blvd, Overland Park, KS 66211. Phone: (913) 339-1906.

☆   ☆   ☆

BIRTHDAYS TODAY

Russell (Russ) Courtnall, 33, hockey player, born Duncan, BC, Canada, June 3, 1965.

William John (Billy) Cunningham, 55, former basketball coach and Basketball Hall of Fame forward, born New York, NY, June 3, 1943.

Carl Edward Everett, 27, baseball player, born Tampa, FL, June 3, 1971.

James Edward (Jim) Gentile, 64, former baseball player, born San Francisco, CA, June 3, 1934.

Hale S. Irwin, 53, golfer, born Joplin, MO, June 3, 1945.

Stephen John (Steve) Lyons, 38, former baseball player, born Tacoma, WA, June 3, 1960.

JUNE 4 — THURSDAY
Day 155 — 210 Remaining

ASHMAN PLAYS 10 POSITIONS: 15th ANNIVER-SARY. June 4, 1983. Mike Ashman of the Albany-Colonie Athletics, a minor league team, became the first player in professional baseball history to play all 10 positions in a ball game. Ashman pitched, caught, played all infield and outfield positions and served as the team's designated hitter.

BEER NIGHT FORFEIT: ANNIVERSARY. June 4, 1974. The game between the Texas Rangers and the Indians at Cleveland's Municipal Stadium was forfeited to Texas when the Indians tied the score, 5–5, in the bottom of the ninth inning. Umpire Nestor Chylak awarded the game to Texas when carrousing fans, enlivened by an evening of ten cent beers, got out of hand.

EDWIN MOSES LOSES: ANNIVERSARY. June 4, 1987. The longest winning streak in track and field history came to an end as Danny Harris defeated Edwin Moses in the 400-meter hurdles at a meet in Madrid. Moses, who had won 122 races in a row dating back to Aug 26, 1977, finished .13 second behind.

EVERETT SALTY SEA DAYS. June 4–7. Everett, WA. Family events to celebrate Everett's beauty, carnival, food, novelty and commercial booths, arts and crafts, live entertainment, fireworks, classic car show, limited hydro races, Hawaiian outrigger races, various nautical events. Sponsor: City of Everett, Dwayne Lane, Cascade Savings Bank, Roy Robinson Chevy-GEO, Howard Johnson Plaza Hotel. Est attendance: 100,000. For info: Marion Pope, Exec Dir, Salty Sea Days Assn, PO Box 7050, Everett, WA 98201. Phone: (425) 339-1113. Fax: (425) 259-5143 or (425) 252-6630. Email: saltysea@aol.com. WWW: http://www.saltyseadays.org

FIRST RYDER CUP: ANNIVERSARY. June 4, 1927. A team of American professional golfers beat a team of British professional golfers to win the first Ryder Cup competition, 9½ to 2½. The Ryder Cup was presented by British businessman Samuel Ryder. The first biennial competition was held at Worcester Country Club (MA).

KEMPER OPEN. June 4–7. TPC at Avenel, Potomac, MD. A PGA Tour tournament. For info: PGA Tour, 112 TPC Blvd, Ponte Vedra Beach, FL 32082. Phone: (904) 285-3700.

MURNANE, TIM: BIRTH ANNIVERSARY. June 4, 1852. Timothy Hayes (Tim) Murnane, sportswriter and baseball player born at Naugatuck, CT. Murnane was a very popular player and a jovial, opinionated reporter. After his death, a charity game raised $10,000 for his family. Died at Boston, MA, Feb 7, 1917.

SCOTLAND: ROYAL SCOTTISH AUTOMOBILE CLUB INTERNATIONAL SCOTTISH RALLY. June 4–6. Throughout Scotland. Scotland's only international rally that attracts many of the world's leading drivers. Est attendance: 200,000. For info: Jonathan Lord, Royal Scottish Automobile Club (Motor Sport) Ltd, 11 Blythswood Sq, Glasglow, Scotland G2 4AG.

BIRTHDAYS TODAY

Derian Hatcher, 26, hockey player, born Sterling Heights, MI, June 4, 1972.
Sandra Jane Haynie, 55, LPGA Hall of Fame golfer, born Fort Worth, TX, June 4, 1943.
Andrea Jaeger, 33, former tennis player, born Chicago, IL, June 4, 1965.
Terrence Edward (Terry) Kennedy, 42, former baseball player, born Euclid, OH, June 4, 1956.

Xavier Maurice McDaniel, 35, former basketball player, born Columbia, SC, June 4, 1963.
Scott Daniel Servais, 31, baseball player, born LaCrosse, WI, June 4, 1967.

JUNE 5 — FRIDAY
Day 156 — 209 Remaining

NBA FINALS CHAMPIONS THIS DATE
1977 Portland Trail Blazers

ABL ADOPTS THREE-POINT FIELD GOAL: ANNIVERSARY. June 5, 1961. The American Basketball League, a short-lived challenger to the NBA, adopted a three-point field goal, an innovation that was later approved successively by the American Basketball Association, the NBA and the NCAA.

BLACK HILLS BICYCLE TREK CLASSIC. June 5–7. Spearfish, SD. Two-day organized ride in the Black Hills. Lodging and meals are provided, along with snacks and rest stops. Riders can pick options to meet their riding level. Est attendance: 250. For info: Kathleen A. Wiebers, American Lung Assn of South Dakota, 1212 W Elkhorn St, Ste 1, Sioux Falls, SD 57104. Phone: (800) 873-5864. Fax: (605) 336-7227. Email: amerlungsd@aol.com.

BULLNANZA-NASHVILLE. June 5–6. Municipal Auditorium, Nashville, TN. The Lazy E takes its most popular event on the road to the country music capital of the world. It's nothin' but bull ridin'! Est attendance: 17,000. For info: Lazy E Promotions, Rte 5, PO Box 393, Guthrie, OK 73044. Phone: (405) 282-7433 or (800) 595-RIDE. Email: learena@ionet.net. WWW:http://www.lazye.com For tickets: (615) 255-9600.

CHESBRO, JACK: BIRTH ANNIVERSARY. June 5, 1874. John Dwight (Jack) Chesbro, Baseball Hall of Fame pitcher born at North Adams, MA. Chesbro pitched in both major leagues and won 41 games for the New York Highlanders in 1904. Nevertheless, his wild pitch on the last day of the season allowed the winning run to score in a game that gave the pennant to Boston. Inducted into the Hall of Fame in 1946. Died at Conway, MA, Nov 6, 1931.

COUNT FLEET WINS TRIPLE CROWN: 55th ANNIVERSARY. June 5, 1943. Count Fleet, ridden by Johnny Longden, won the Belmont Stakes with a wire-to-wire performance. Fairy Manhurst was a distant second, 30 lengths behind. Count Fleet, the heavy favorite, thus became the sixth horse to win racing's Triple Crown, the Kentucky Derby, the Preakness and the Belmont.

FISHING HAS NO BOUNDARIES-THERMOPOLIS. June 5–7. Boysen Reservoir, Thermopolis, WY. A three-day fishing experience for disabled persons. Any disability, age, sex, race, etc, eligible. Fishing with experienced guides, attended by 80 participants and 100 volunteers. Annually, first full weekend in June. For info: Fishing Has No Boundaries, HSC C of C, Box 768, Thermopolis, WY 82443. Phone: (307) 864-3192 or (800) 786-6772. Fax: (307) 864-9463. Email: beutel@trib.com.

NELSON, BATTLING: BIRTH ANNIVERSARY. June 5, 1882. Battling Nelson, boxer born Oscar Nielson at Copenhagen, Denmark. Nelson fought three epic bouts against Joe Gans for the lightweight title. He was disqualified in the 42nd round on Sept 3, 1906; knocked Gans out in the 17th round on July 4, 1908; and knocked Gans out again in the 21st round two months later. Nelson was known for not bathing for weeks before a fight. Died at Chicago, IL, Feb 7, 1954.

OUTLAWS RODEO. June 5–6. Macon County Park, Macon, MO. Rodeo action with some of the best cowboys in the region. Exciting action, good food and lots of souvenirs. Est attendance: 4,500. For info: Crystal Lyda, Macon Area Chamber of Commerce, 218 N Rollins, Macon, MO 63552. Phone: (816) 385-5484. Fax: (816) 385-3972.

SKYDOME DEBUT: ANNIVERSARY. June 5, 1989. The Toronto Blue Jays made their debut at their new home, SkyDome, by losing to the Milwaukee Brewers, 5–3. The state-of-the-art facility cost $375 million to construct and featured a four-section retractable roof.

SOONER STATE SUMMER GAMES. June 5–6 (also June 13–14, 20–21 and 27–28). Oklahoma City, OK. Oklahoma amateur sports festival. More than 10,000 athletes of all ages from every county in the state. More than 34 sports competitions. Est attendance: 35,000. For info: Sooner State Games, 100 W Main, Ste 287, Oklahoma City, OK 73102. Phone: (405) 235-4222. Fax: (405) 232-7723. Email: snrstgms@aol.com.

WAR ADMIRAL WINS TRIPLE CROWN: ANNIVERSARY. June 5, 1937. War Admiral, a son of Man O'War, became the fourth horse to win the Triple Crown when he captured the Belmont Stakes by three lengths over Sceneshifter. Ridden by Charley Kurtsinger, War Admiral covered the 1½ miles in 2:28.3. Pompoon, second in the Kentucky Derby and the Preakness, finished out of the money.

SPORTSCHASER OF THE DAY

Which professional basketball league was the first to adopt the 3-point field goal?

BIRTHDAYS TODAY

Arthur (Art) Donovan, 73, Pro Football Hall of Fame defensive tackle, born New York, NY, June 5, 1925.
Martin Gelinas, 28, hockey player, born Shawinigan, Quebec, Canada, June 5, 1970.
Edwin David (Eddie) Joost, 82, former baseball manager and player, born San Francisco, CA, June 5, 1916.
Raymond Lewis (Ray) Lankford, 31, baseball player, born Los Angeles, CA, June 5, 1967.
Marion Motley, 78, Pro Football Hall of Fame fullback and linebacker, born Leesburg, GA, June 5, 1920.
Bob Probert, 33, hockey player, born Windsor, Ontario, Canada, June 5, 1965.

JUNE 6 — SATURDAY

Day 157 — 208 Remaining

NBA FINALS CHAMPIONS THIS DATE

1976   Boston Celtics

BELMONT STAKES. June 6. Belmont Park, Elmont, NY. Final race of the Triple Crown was inaugurated in 1867. Traditionally run on the fifth Saturday after the Kentucky Derby (third Saturday after Preakness). Est attendance: 60,000. For info: Press Office, New York Racing Assn, PO Box 90, Jamaica, NY 11417. Phone: (718) 641-4700. WWW: http://www.nyracing.com

June *1998*	S	M	T	W	T	F	S
		1	2	3	4	5	6
	7	8	9	10	11	12	13
	14	15	16	17	18	19	20
	21	22	23	24	25	26	27
	28	29	30				

BIRTH OF THE BAA: ANNIVERSARY. June 6, 1946. The Basketball Association of America was founded at a New York meeting of hockey team owners and arena managers interested in having their buildings used on open dates. The BAA played three seasons (1946–47, 1947–48 and 1948–49) after which it merged with the National Basketball League, founded in 1937, to form the National Basketball Association. Three original BAA teams remain: the Boston Celtics, the Golden State Warriors (originally the Philadelphia Warriors) and the New York Knicks.

☆   ☆   ☆

BUFFALO DAYS CELEBRATION (WITH BUFFALO CHIP THROWING). June 6–7. Luverne, MN. Parade, Arts in the Park, free barbecued buffalo burgers (while they last) and unique buffalo-chip throwing contest. Annually, the first weekend in June. Est attendance: 8,000. For info: Norma De Jongh, Exec Dir, Luverne Area Chamber of Commerce, 102 E Main, Luverne, MN 56156. Phone: (507) 283-4061. Fax: (507) 283-4061. Email: chamber@luverne.k12.mn.us.

CASEY FLIPS THE BIRD: 80th ANNIVERSARY. June 6, 1918. Casey Stengel returned to Ebbets Field for the first time since being traded from the Brooklyn Dodgers to the Pittsburgh Pirates over the winter. Stengel celebrated the occasion by striding to the plate for his first at-bat, calling time, doffing his cap and letting a live bird fly out. Fans broke into laughter.

DANIEL, DAN: BIRTH ANNIVERSARY. June 6, 1890. Daniel (Dan) Daniel, sportswriter born Daniel Markowitz at New York, NY. Daniel was regarded as one of the nation's finest and most authoritative baseball writers. He also helped Nat Fleischer found *The Ring*, boxing's most prestigious publication. Died at Pompano Beach, FL, July 1, 1981.

DENMARK: EEL FESTIVAL. June 6–7. Jyllinge (near Roskilde). Festival celebrated since 1968. Every restaurant and pub in town serves delicious fried eel. Other entertainments include theater, sports, tattoo bands, sailing competitions, flea markets and fireworks. Annually, the first weekend in June.

DICKEY, BILL: BIRTH ANNIVERSARY. June 6, 1907. William Malcolm (Bill) Dickey, Baseball Hall of Fame catcher born at Bastrop, LA. Dickey played 17 seasons with the New York Yankees and was a teammate of Babe Ruth, Lou Gehrig and Joe DiMaggio. He also helped improve the catching skills of Yogi Berra. Inducted into the Hall of Fame in 1954. Died at Little Rock, AR, Nov 12, 1993.

GOVERNOR'S CUP. June 6. Helena, MT. Montana's premier running event. Includes a marathon, marathon relay, 20K, 10K and 5K. Corporate entries. Approximately 7,000 runners. Annually, the first Saturday in June. Sponsor: Blue Cross/Blue Shield. Est attendance: 7,000. For info: Susan Frazee, Race Dir, Blue Cross & Blue Shield, Box 451, Helena, MT 59624. Phone: (406) 447-3414. Fax: (406) 442-6946. WWW: http://www.govcup.bcbsmt.com

GREAT CHUNKY RIVER RAFT RACE. June 6. Chunky, MS. Raft builders compete in four raft divisions in race held along the Chunky River. Cash prizes for most creative rafts. Live entertainment noon–4 PM. Raft divisions: flat-bottom boat, canoe, inflatable raft (store-bought), homemade raft. Est attendance: 2,500. For info: Lisa Cowart, Special Project/Market Coord, PO Box 4177, Meridian, MS 39304-4177. Phone: (601) 482-6161.

GREAT WISCONSIN DELLS BALLOON RALLY. June 6–7. Wisconsin Dells, WI. More than 90 vividly colored balloons compete in this annual event. Est attendance:

100,000. For info: Wisc Dells Visitor and Conv Bureau, PO Box 390, Wisconsin Dells, WI 53965. Phone: (800) 223-3557. WWW: http://www.wisdells.com

HETTINGER ANNUAL RODEO. June 6–7. Adams County Fairgrounds, Hettinger, ND. Annual event with two days of action-packed rodeo events. Two nights of live bands entertain the rodeo crowd in the evenings after the rodeos. An ice cream social and beef giveaway at the rodeos are some of the added features to this weekend of fun. Annually, the first weekend in June. Sponsored by the Hettinger Area Chamber of Commerce. Est attendance: 2,500. For info: Terri Thiel, Hettinger Chamber of Commerce, PO Box 1031, Hettinger, ND 58639. Phone: (701) 567-2531. Fax: (701) 567-2348. Email: adamsdv@hettinger.ctctel.com. WWW: http://www.hettinger.com

HONG KONG: INTERNATIONAL DRAGON BOAT RACES. June 6–7. A day recognizing the death of Qu Yuan, 4th-century BC poet and former minister of state who threw himself into the river in protest of the corruption of the court. Local dragon boat races are held on the fifth day of the fifth lunar month, preceding the international races by several days. For info: Hong Kong Tourist Assn, 590 Fifth Ave, 5th Floor, New York, NY 10036-4706. Phone: (212) 869-5008. Fax: (212) 730-2605. WWW: http://www.hkta.org

LADIES' DAY INITIATED IN BASEBALL: ANNIVERSARY. June 6, 1876. During a National League baseball game between the Cincinnati Red Stockings and the Louisville Grays, the Cincinnati owner noticed that a large number of women showed up in the park to watch handsome Tony Mullane pitch. Thereafter, he declared, Mullane would pitch every Tuesday, each occasion to be designated "Ladies' Day."

LET'S GO TO THE VIDEOTAPE: ANNIVERSARY. June 6, 1986. Manager Steve Boros of the San Diego Padres was ejected before the first pitch of a game with the Atlanta Braves when he attempted to give umpire Charlie Williams a videotape of a disputed play in the previous night's game, a 4–2 Braves victory.

MISSOURI STATE CHAMPIONSHIP RACKING HORSE SHOW. June 6. Stoddard County Fair Grounds, Dexter, MO. At this 21st annual event elegant showmanship by both horse and rider provides an afternoon and evening of spectator pleasure. Annually, the first Saturday in June. Est attendance: 500. For info: Missouri State Chmpshp Racking Horse Show, PO Box 21, Dexter, MO 63841. Phone: (573) 624-7458 or (800) 332-8857. Fax: (573) 624-7459.

MOKRAY, BILL: BIRTH ANNIVERSARY. June 6, 1907. William George (Bill) Mokray, Basketball Hall of Fame executive and historian born at Passaic, NJ. Mokray was a journalist, a publicist and the first director of basketball at Boston Garden. While working as the Boston Celtics public relations director, he also compiled statistics and edited the annual Converse *Basketball Yearbook*. He founded the *NBA Guide* and wrote the 900-page *Ronald Basketball Encyclopedia*. Inducted into the Hall of Fame in 1965. Died at Revere, MA, Mar 22, 1974.

SMALL CRAFT WEEKEND. June 6–7. Mystic Seaport, Mystic, CT. The 29th annual weekend when small-craft enthusiasts gather at the museum with their boats. Traditional small boats of every type sail from docks of Mystic Seaport on the Mystic River. Annually, first weekend in June. Est attendance: 4,000. For info: Mystic Seaport, 75 Greenmanville Ave, Mystic, CT 06355.

SOUTH JERSEY CANOE AND KAYAK CLASSIC. June 6. Ocean County Park, Rte 88, Lakewood, NJ. Canoe and kayak vendors from around the country set up on a beach to show the public the thrill of water sports. You may test-paddle the boats of your choice and attend a clinic about canoeing or kayaking throughout the day. Event is free. Annually, the first Saturday in June. Est attendance: 3,000. For info: Lillian Hoey, Recreation Leader, Wells Mills County Park, 905 Wells Mills Rd, Waretown, NJ 08758. Phone: (609) 971-3085. Fax: (609) 971-9540.

TAKE A KID FISHING WEEKEND. June 6–7. St. Paul, MN. Resident adults may fish without a license on these days when fishing with a child under age 16. For info: Jack Skrypek, Fisheries Chief, DNR, Box 12, 500 Lafayette Rd, St. Paul, MN 55155. Phone: (612) 296-0792. Fax: (612) 297-4916. WWW: http://www.dnr.state.mn.us/

TURQUOISE LAKE 20K ROAD/TRAIL RUN. June 6 (tentative). Leadville, CO. An accurate 20K race with elevations ranging from 9,870 to 10,200 feet. First 11K is on scenic, paved, hilly road and the last 9K is on rolling foot trail in trees next to a lake. Race is run no matter what the weather or snow conditions! Three-hour limit. This is one of many races held in the area. For info: Greater Leadville Area Chamber of Commerce, TL-20K, Leadville, CO 80461. Phone: (719) 486-8077 or (800) 933-3901. Email: leadville@sni.net.

TURTLE RACES. June 6. Eastern Illinois Fairgrounds, Danville, IL. More than 100 turtles compete in 33rd annual races throughout the day. Concessions available. Food and fun. Proceeds go to help people in the area with disabilities. Annually, the first Saturday in June. Est attendance: 3,500. For info: Nadine Schramm, Turtle Club, 2932 Batestown Rd, Oakwood, IL 61858. Phone: (217) 446-5327.

BIRTHDAYS TODAY

William Frederick (Bill) Bates, 37, football player, born Knoxville, TN, June 6, 1961.

Bjorn Rune Borg, 42, tennis player, born Sodertalje, Sweden, June 6, 1956.

Mike Croel, 29, football player, born Detroit, MI, June 6, 1969.

Derrel McKinley ("Bud") Harrelson, 54, former baseball manager and player, born Niles, CA, June 6, 1944.

Rueben Mayes, 35, former football player, born North Battleford, Saskatchewan, Canada, June 6, 1963.

Robert Cornelius (Bobby) Mitchell, 63, Pro Football Hall of Fame running back and receiver, born Hot Springs, AR, June 6, 1935.

Mervin Weldon (Merv) Rettenmund, 55, former baseball player, born Flint, MI, June 6, 1943.

JUNE 7 — SUNDAY
Day 158 — 207 Remaining

NBA FINALS CHAMPIONS THIS DATE
1978   Washington Bullets

AFL VOTES TO EXPAND: ANNIVERSARY. June 7, 1965. The executive committee of the American Football League met in New Jersey and voted to expand the league from eight teams to nine. Two months later, the league awarded the expansion franchise to Miami for $7.5 million. The ownership group headed by Joe Robbie and entertainer Danny Thomas named its team the Dolphins.

ALLEN STOMPS OFF: 60th ANNIVERSARY. June 7, 1938. Cleveland Indians pitcher Johnny Allen stomped off the mound and left the game when home plate umpire Bill McGowan ordered him to trim the dangling sleeve of his sweatshirt, saying it was a distraction. Cleveland manager Ossie Vitt fined Allen $250. The shirt ended up in the Hall of Fame.

BRADDOCK, JAMES: BIRTH ANNIVERSARY. June 7, 1906. James Walter Braddock, boxer born at New York, NY. Braddock rose from the ranks of undistinguished fighters to win three key bouts in 1934 and 1935 that propelled him to a match for the heavyweight title. He upset the defending champion, Max Baer, on June 13, 1935, remained inactive for two years and then lost his first title defense to Joe Louis. Died at North Bergen, NJ, Nov 29, 1974.

GALLANT FOX WINS TRIPLE CROWN: ANNIVERSARY. June 7, 1930. Gallant Fox, with jockey Earle Sande, became the second horse to win the Triple Crown. Trained by Sunny Jim Fitzsimmons, Gallant Fox won the Belmont Stakes by three lengths over Whichone in 2:31.3.

MAUI HARD ROCK CAFE ROCK'N'ROLL 10K RUN FOR THE HOMELESS. June 7. Lahaina, Maui, HI. Run over a certified measured course, starting and finishing at the Lahaina Hard Rock Cafe. Entertainment, awards and breakfast at the Hard Rock Cafe following the finish. Winners receive weekend travel packages to the Honolulu 10K. Open to all runners, walkers and race walkers. Est attendance: 500. For media info: Carol Hogan, (808) 325-7400 (Email: oceanpro@interpac.net). For race info: Maui Hard Rock Cafe, (808) 667-7400. WWW: http://www.holoholo.org/maui10k

MUNSON, THURMAN: BIRTH ANNIVERSARY. June 7, 1947. Thurman Lee Munson, baseball player born at Akron, OH. Munson played 11 years for the New York Yankees starting in 1970 and was regarded as one of the decade's top catchers. He won the Rookie of the Year award, three Gold Gloves and was named American League Most Valuable Player in 1976. His leadership helped the Yankees win pennants in 1976, 1977 and 1978. Died when a small plane he was flying crashed at Canton, OH, Aug 2, 1979.

OUTDOORS AND INDOORS: ANNIVERSARY. June 7, 1989. In the first game played both outdoors and indoors, the Toronto Blue Jays beat the Milwaukee Brewers, 4–2, at Toronto's SkyDome. The game began with the stadium's retractable roof open, but when thunder and dark clouds brought a threat of rain in the fifth inning, the roof was closed for the rest of the game.

June 1998	S	M	T	W	T	F	S
		1	2	3	4	5	6
	7	8	9	10	11	12	13
	14	15	16	17	18	19	20
	21	22	23	24	25	26	27
	28	29	30				

STEAMBOAT MARATHON. June 7. Steamboat Springs, CO. TAC-certified marathon, half-marathon, 10K run, 10K fitness walk plus ½K Fun Run, with cash prizes totaling $2,500 to be distributed for first through third places in the marathon, half-marathon and 10K races. Age-division awards will be presented in all races. Marathon and half-marathon courses follow a paved county road down the Elk River Valley. The race is a point-to-point race with free transportation to the start. The 10K is on a rolling paved road through Scenic Strawberry Park and Old Town Steamboat Springs. All races are organized by volunteer organizations. Pre-race events include the Pre-Race Pasta Dinner and guest speaker. Early entries must be postmarked by May 24, 1998; entry fee includes official race T-shirt. Est attendance: 2,000. For registration and entry fee info: Steamboat Springs Chamber Resort Assn, Inc, PO Box 774408, Steamboat Springs, CO 80477. Phone: (970) 879-0880. Fax: (970) 879-2543. Email: info@steamboat-chamber.com. WWW: http://www.steamboat-chamber.com

WALL REGIONAL HIGH SCHOOL RODEO. June 6–7. Rodeo Grounds, Wall, SD. All rodeo events featuring area high-school students. Admission. Est attendance: 800. For info: Paullyn Carey, Wall Chamber of Commerce, PO Box 527, Wall, SD 57790. Phone: (605) 279-2665.

WHIRLAWAY WINS TRIPLE CROWN: ANNIVERSARY. June 7, 1941. Whirlaway won the Belmont Stakes by 2½ lengths over Robert Morris to become the fifth horse to win the Triple Crown. Trained by Ben Jones for Calumet Farms and ridden by Eddie Arcaro, Whirlaway finished the Belmont in 2:31.

STANLEY CUP CHAMPIONS THIS DATE
1997   Detroit Red Wings

BIRTHDAYS TODAY

Douglas Terrell Buckley, 27, football player, born Pascagoula, MS, June 7, 1971.
Allen Iverson, 23, basketball player, born Hampton, VA, June 7, 1975.
Terance Mathis, 31, football player, born Detroit, MI, June 7, 1967.
Michael (Mike) Modano, 28, hockey player, born Livonia, MI, June 7, 1970.
Roberto Antonio Petagine, 27, baseball player, born Nueva Esparita, Venezuela, June 7, 1971.
Stephane Joseph Jean Richer, 32, hockey player, born Ripon, Quebec, Canada, June 7, 1966.
Herbert Jude (Herb) Score, 65, broadcaster and former baseball player, born Rosedale, NY, June 7, 1933.
Heathcliff Slocumb, 32, baseball player, born New York, NY, June 7, 1966.

JUNE 8 — MONDAY
Day 159 — 206 Remaining

NBA FINALS CHAMPIONS THIS DATE
1982   Los Angeles Lakers
1986   Boston Celtics

BELL SOUTH SENIOR CLASSIC AT OPRYLAND. June 8–13. Springhouse Golf Club, Nashville, TN. This Senior PGA tour event boasts the top players competing for $1.3 million. Also, Celebrity Shootout and Pro/Am tournament. Est attendance: 100,000. For info: John Subers, Tourn Dir, Bell South Senior Classic, 18 Springhouse Lane, Nashville, TN 37214. Phone: (615) 871-7888. Fax: (615) 871-5906. WWW: http://www.bellsouthsrclassic.com

BRUNET, GEORGE: BIRTH ANNIVERSARY. June 8, 1935. George Stuart Brunet, baseball player born at Houghton, MI. Brunet pitched in professional baseball for 33 years, including 15 years in the majors. He finished his career with 13 years in the Mexican League where he pitched 55 shutouts. Died at Poza Rica, Mexico, Oct 25, 1991.

ENNIS, DEL: BIRTH ANNIVERSARY. June 8, 1925. Delmer (Del) Ennis, baseball player born at Philadelphia, PA. Ennis played the outfield for the Whiz Kids, the 1950 Philadelphia Phillies who won the National League pennant. He knocked in 100 runs seven times in a 14-year career. Died at Huntingdon Valley, PA, Feb 8, 1996.

HOLY MOLEY MASCOT DAY©98. June 8. This day is dedicated to all the animals and other creatures that serve as team mascots and to the people who proudly wear the costumes that rile up the fans and garner team support and spirit. For more info send $2 to cover cost of copying and postage to: Adrienne Koopersmith, 1437 Rosemont, 1W, Chicago, IL 60660-1319. Phone: (773) 743-5341. Fax: (773) 743-5395. Email: koopersmith@interaccess.com.

KENNEDY, WALTER: BIRTH ANNIVERSARY. June 8, 1912. James Walter Kennedy, Basketball Hall of Fame executive born at Stamford, CT. Kennedy used a Notre Dame degree in journalism and business administration to create a multifaceted career in and around sports. His public relations firm represented the Harlem Globetrotters in the 1950s, and in 1959 he was elected mayor of Stamford. Four years later, he became commissioner of the NBA where he implemented an expansion program and developed the league's television package. He retired in 1975. Inducted into the Hall of Fame in 1980. Died at Stamford, CT, June 26, 1977.

McLENDON, GORDON: BIRTH ANNIVERSARY. June 8, 1921. Gordon Barton McLendon, sportscaster and executive born at Paris, TX. McLendon graduated from Yale University where he began broadcasting baseball and basketball games. After buying radio station KLIF in Dallas, TX, McLendon began to create a network of stations dedicated to daily sports programming, including both live and re-created events. The Liberty Radio Network grew to well over 200 stations, but collapsed rapidly in 1952 when major league owners, fearful of declining attendance, limited the number of games the network could broadcast. Died at Lake Dallas, TX, Sept 14, 1986.

MUNGO, VAN LINGLE: BIRTH ANNIVERSARY. June 8, 1911. Van Lingle Mungo, baseball player born at Pageland, SC. Mungo was a colorful pitcher in the 1930s with the Brooklyn Dodgers. His lilting name was the title of a popular baseball song in the 1970s. Died at Pageland, Feb 12, 1985.

★ **NATIONAL LITTLE LEAGUE BASEBALL WEEK.** June 8–14. Presidential Proclamation 3296, of June 4, 1959, covers all succeeding years. Always the week beginning with the second Monday in June. (H. Con. Res. 17 of June 1, 1959.)

OMAHA WINS TRIPLE CROWN: ANNIVERSARY. June 8, 1935. Omaha won the Belmont Stakes to become the third horse to win the Triple Crown. Ridden by Willie Saunders and trained by Sunny Jim Fitzsimmons, Omaha defeated Firethorn by 1½ lengths in a time of 2:30.3.

YANKEES RETIRE NO. 7: ANNIVERSARY. June 8, 1969. The New York Yankees honored Mickey Mantle by retiring his number 7 in a ceremony preceding a doubleheader against the Chicago White Sox. 60,096 fans came out to salute Mantle and to watch the Yankees sweep the Sox, 3–1 and 11–2. The Yankees have retired 12 numbers in all, more than any other baseball team.

CHASE'S SPORTSQUOTE OF THE DAY

"Mungo and I get along fine. I just tell him I won't stand for no nonsense—and then I duck." —Manager Casey Stengel on Van Lingle Mungo

Van Lingle Mungo

BIRTHDAYS TODAY

Herbert A. (Herb) Adderley, 59, Pro Football Hall of Fame cornerback, born Philadelphia, PA, June 8, 1939.

Mark Henry Belanger, 54, baseball union executive and former player, born Pittsfield, MA, June 8, 1944.

Phillippe Richard (Phil) Bourque, 36, hockey player, born Chelmsford, MA, June 8, 1962.

Lindsay Davenport, 22, tennis player, born Palos Verdes, CA, June 8, 1976.

Kevin Frank Gross, 37, baseball player, born Downey, CA, June 8, 1961.

David John (Dave) Mlicki, 30, baseball player, born Cleveland, OH, June 8, 1968.

Kevin D. Ritz, 33, baseball player, born Eatonstown, NJ, June 8, 1965.

Byron Raymond ("Whizzer") White, 81, former associate justice of the US Supreme Court and former football player, born Fort Collins, CO, June 8, 1917.

JUNE 9 — TUESDAY
Day 160 — 205 Remaining

NBA FINALS CHAMPIONS THIS DATE
1985   Los Angeles Lakers

FIRST WLAF CHAMPIONSHIP: ANNIVERSARY. June 9, 1991. The London Monarchs defeated the Barcelona Dragons, 21–0, at Wembley Stadium in London to win the first championship of the World League of American Football.

McCORMICK, FRANK: BIRTH ANNIVERSARY. June 9, 1911. Frank Andrew McCormick, baseball player born at New York, NY. McCormick was a slugging first baseman with the Cincinnati Reds from 1938 through 1945. He hit above .300 five times and led the National League in 1939 in runs batted in. Died at Manhasset, NY, Nov 21, 1982.

McCRACKEN, BRANCH: 90th BIRTH ANNIVERSARY. June 9, 1908. Emmett Branch McCracken, Basketball Hall of Fame player and coach born at Monrovia, IN. McCracken played at Indiana University where he was a consensus All-American and then coached at Ball State University and his alma mater. His "Hurrying Hoosiers," so called for their fast-break offense and tenacious defense, won national titles in 1940 and 1953. Inducted into the Hall of Fame in 1960. Died at Bloomington, IN, June 4, 1970.

OTT GETS EJECTED TWICE: ANNIVERSARY. June 9, 1946. Mel Ott of the New York Giants became the first manager to be ejected in both games of a doubleheader. The Pittsburgh Pirates beat the Giants twice, 2–1 and 5–1, but Ott was not around to see the end of either game.

SECRETARIAT WINS TRIPLE CROWN: 25th ANNIVERSARY. June 9, 1973. Secretariat, ridden by Ron Turcotte, won the Belmont Stakes in 2:24, a world-record time for 1½ miles. With his triumph, Secretariat became the ninth horse to win the Triple Crown. His margin of victory in the Belmont, an astounding 31 lengths, set a record for that race.

WAGNER GETS 3,000th HIT: ANNIVERSARY. June 9, 1914. Pittsburgh Pirates shortstop Honus Wagner, known as the "Flying Dutchman," became the first modern baseball player to get 3,000 hits in his career. Wagner played from 1897 through 1917 and finished with 3,418 hits.

STANLEY CUP CHAMPIONS THIS DATE
1993   Montreal Canadiens

BIRTHDAYS TODAY

Thomas Patrick (Tom) Edens, 37, former baseball player, born Ontario, Oregon, June 9, 1961.
Julio Enrique Gotay, 59, former baseball player, born Fajardo, Puerto Rico, June 9, 1939.

June *1998*	S	M	T	W	T	F	S
		1	2	3	4	5	6
	7	8	9	10	11	12	13
	14	15	16	17	18	19	20
	21	22	23	24	25	26	27
	28	29	30				

Jonathon Cecil (Jon) Harris, 24, football player, born Inwood, NY, June 9, 1974.
David Gene (Dave) Parker, 47, former baseball player, born Calhoun, MS, June 9, 1951.
Roy Frederick Smalley, Jr, 72, former baseball player, born Springfield, MO, June 9, 1926.
Wayman Lawrence Tisdale, 34, basketball player, born Tulsa, OK, June 9, 1964.
William Charles (Bill) Virdon, 67, former baseball manager and player, born Hazel Park, MI, June 9, 1931.

JUNE 10 — WEDNESDAY
Day 161 — 204 Remaining

STANLEY CUP CHAMPIONS THIS DATE
1996   Colorado Avalanche

AFFIRMED WINS TRIPLE CROWN: 20th ANNIVERSARY. June 10, 1978. Affirmed, ridden by Steve Cauthen, won the Belmont Stakes to become the 11th horse to win the Triple Crown. In one of racing's greatest two-horse competitions, Affirmed edged Alydar in all three Triple Crown races.

FRANCE: WORLD CUP. June 10–July 12. Various cities. Soccer's quadrennial international championship takes place in France for the first time since 1938. Thirty-two teams will commence round-robin play in 10 cities (Bordeaux, Lens, Lyons, Marseilles, Montpellier, Nantes, Paris, Saint-Denis, Saint-Etienne and Toulouse). Single-elimination play will culminate with the final game at Saint-Denis on July 12. For the 1998 World Cup, FIFA (Federation Internationale de Football Association), soccer's governing body, has increased the field from 24 to 32 teams, including automatic berths for defending champion Brazil and host France.

GEIBERGER SHOOTS 59: ANNIVERSARY. June 10, 1977. Pro golfer Al Geiberger shot a PGA-record score of 59 in the second round of the Memphis Classic at the Colonial Country Club. Geiberger made 11 birdies, six pars and an eagle on the par-72 course.

LAST AMATEUR TO WIN OPEN: 65th ANNIVERSARY. June 10, 1933. Golfer Johnny Goodman defeated Ralph Guldahl by one shot at North Shore Golf Club in Glenview, IL, to become the last amateur to win the US Open championship.

LEVINSKY, BATTLING: BIRTH ANNIVERSARY. June 10, 1891. Battling Levinsky, boxer born Barney Lebrowitz at Philadelphia, PA. Levinsky, light heavyweight champ from 1916 to 1920, holds the distinction of having fought three main events in three different places on the same day. On Jan 1, 1915, he fought in Brooklyn, New York City, and Waterbury, CT, a total of 32 rounds ending in three no-decisions. Died at Philadelphia, Feb 12, 1949.

LUCY HARRIS DRAFTED: ANNIVERSARY. June 10, 1977. Lucy Harris of Delta State became the first woman basketball player selected in the NBA draft. She was selected in the seventh round by the New Orleans Jazz but chose not to try out for the team.

MOON PHASE: FULL MOON. June 10. Moon enters Full Moon phase at 12:18 AM, EDT.

NUXHALL IS YOUNGEST PLAYER: ANNIVERSARY. June 10, 1944. With baseball's playing ranks depleted by World War II, Joe Nuxhall became the youngest person ever to play in a major league game. Nuxhall pitched ⅔ of an inning for the Cincinnati Reds in an 18–0 loss to the St. Louis Cardinals. Nuxhall was 15 years, 10 months and 11 days old.

RED RIVER RODEO. June 10–13. Wichita Falls, TX. Professional circuit rodeo held at the Wichita County Mounted Patrol Arena, this event features all of the traditional rodeo attractions. Est attendance: 20,000. For info: Kacey Gracy, Serv and Mktg Asst, Wichita Falls Conv & Visitors Bureau, 1000 Fifth St, Wichita Falls, TX 76301. Phone: (817) 716-5500 or (800) 799-6732. Fax: (800) 799-5509. WWW: http://www.viewscape.com

BIRTHDAYS TODAY

Floyd Franklin Bannister, 43, former baseball player, born Pierre, SD, June 10, 1955.

John Alban (Johnny) Edwards, 60, former baseball player, born Columbus, OH, June 10, 1938.

Daniel Francis (Dan) Fouts, 47, Pro Football Hall of Fame quarterback, born San Francisco, CA, June 10, 1951.

Kenneth Wayne (Ken) Singleton, 51, broadcaster and former baseball player, born New York, NY, June 10, 1947.

Brent Colin Sutter, 36, hockey player, born Viking, Alberta, Canada, June 10, 1962.

JUNE 11 — THURSDAY
Day 162 — 203 Remaining

BRESNAHAN, ROGER: BIRTH ANNIVERSARY. June 11, 1879. Roger Philip Bresnahan, Baseball Hall of Fame catcher born at Toledo, OH. Bresnahan caught for John McGraw's New York Giants in the first decade of the 20th century. He introduced shin guards in 1907. Inducted into the Hall of Fame in 1945. Died at Toledo, Dec 4, 1944.

FIRST HALF OF DOUBLE NO-HITTER: 60th ANNIVERSARY. June 11, 1938. Johnny Vander Meer of the Cincinnati Reds pitched a no-hitter against the Boston Braves, winning 2–0. Vander Meer returned to the mound four days later and no-hit the Brooklyn Dodgers, 6–0, to complete the only consecutive no-hitters in baseball history.

LOMBARDI, VINCE: 85th BIRTH ANNIVERSARY. June 11, 1913. Vincent Thomas (Vince) Lombardi, Pro Football Hall of Fame coach born at New York, NY. Lombardi played football for Fordham's famed "Seven Blocks of Granite" line in the mid-1930s, became a teacher and began to coach high school football. He became offensive line coach at West Point in 1949 and moved to the New York Giants in 1954. Five years later, he was named head coach of the Green Bay Packers, a position that lofted him to the peak of his profession. His Packers won five NFL titles and two Super Bowls in nine years, and Lombardi was generally regarded as the greatest coach and the finest motivator in pro football history. He retired in 1968 but was lured back into coaching the Washington Redskins a year later. He contracted cancer after coaching the Redskins only one season. Inducted into the Pro Football Hall of Fame in 1971. Died at Washington, DC, Sept 3, 1970.

NEVERS, ERNIE: 95th BIRTH ANNIVERSARY. June 11, 1903. Ernest Alonzo (Ernie) Nevers, Pro Football Hall of Fame player and coach born at Willow Ridge, MN. Nevers played three sports at Stanford, including football under coach Glenn ("Pop") Warner. He is generally regarded as one of the greatest college football players of all time and as one of America's genuine sports heroes. He pitched for the St. Louis Browns and played pro football with the Duluth Eskimos and the Chicago Cardinals. Inducted into the Hall of Fame as a charter member in 1963. Died at San Rafael, CA, May 3, 1976.

SEATTLE SLEW WINS TRIPLE CROWN: ANNIVERSARY. June 11, 1977. Seattle Slew, ridden by Jean Cruguet, became the 10th horse to win the Triple Crown by triumphing in the Belmont Stakes. Slew led wire-to-wire and defeated Run Dusty Run by four lengths.

SIR BARTON WINS TRIPLE CROWN: ANNIVERSARY. June 11, 1919. Sir Barton became the first horse to win racing's Triple Crown by winning the Belmont Stakes. With Johnny Loftus in the saddle, Sir Barton pulled away from the only two other horses in the race coming down the stretch and won the 1-3/8-mile race in 2:17.2, an American record.

BIRTHDAYS TODAY

David (Dave) Cash, Jr, 50, former baseball player, born Utica, NY, June 11, 1948.

John Gary Fencik, 44, former football player, born Chicago, IL, June 11, 1954.

Scott Edgar Mellanby, 32, hockey player, born Montreal, Quebec, Canada, June 11, 1966.

Joseph C. (Joe) Montana, Jr, 42, former football player, born New Eagle, PA, June 11, 1956.

Jackie Stewart, 59, former auto racer, born Dunbartonshire, Scotland, June 11, 1939.

Frank Joseph Thomas, 69, former baseball player, born Pittsburgh, PA, June 11, 1929.

JUNE 12 — FRIDAY
Day 163 — 202 Remaining

NBA FINALS CHAMPIONS THIS DATE

1984	Boston Celtics
1991	Chicago Bulls

BABE DIDRIKSON WINS BRITISH AMATEUR: 50th ANNIVERSARY. June 12, 1947. Mildred ("Babe") Didrikson Zaharias became the first American-born golfer to win the British Ladies' Amateur championship. Didrikson began her remarkable athletic career playing basketball and then switched to track and field. After the 1932 Olympics, she picked up golf. In 1948, she turned professional and joined the new Ladies' Professional Golf Association.

BADGER STATE SUMMER GAMES. June 12–14. (Finals June 25–28.) Regional competition in eight Wisconsin communities, finals in Madison. 14th annual Olympic-style competition for Wisconsin residents of all ages and abilities, featuring 26 sports and opening ceremonies. Major sponsors: AT&T, Ameritech, GTE, Wisconsin Milk Marketing Board, WPS Health Insurance Corp, Oscar Mayer Foods Corp and Tombstone Pizza. Member of the National Congress of State Games. 25,000 participants. Est attendance: 60,000. For info: Otto Breitenbach, Exec Dir, or Jack Eich, PR Dir, Badger State Games, PO Box 1377, Madison, WI 53701-1377. Phone: (608) 251-3333 or (608) 283-6407. Fax: (608) 283-6412.

CITATION WINS TRIPLE CROWN: 50th ANNIVERSARY. June 12, 1948. Eddie Arcaro rode Citation to victory in the Belmont Stakes, making the colt the eighth horse to win the Triple Crown and the last until 1973.

COWBOY STATE SUMMER GAMES. June 12–15. Casper, WY. The Summer Games feature more than 30 different events including everything from archery to wrestling, basketball to volleyball. Participation is open to Wyoming's amateur athletes of all ages. The Summer Games also feature a spectacular Opening Ceremony that will take place Friday evening, June 12. Est attendance: 4,000. For info: Eileen Ford, Cowboy State Games, PO Box 3485, Casper, WY 82602. Phone: (307) 577-1125. Fax: (307) 577-8111. Email: cwboygames@aol.com.

HOGAN WINS OPEN WITH RECORD SCORE: 50th ANNIVERSARY. June 12, 1948. Ben Hogan won the US Open at Riviera Country Club with a record score of 276, five strokes better than any previous Open score. For Hogan it was the first of four Open championships, the others coming in 1950, 1951 and 1953.

INTERLEAGUE PLAY BEGINS: ANNIVERSARY. June 12, 1997. Breaking with tradition, Major League Baseball inaugurated interleague play, regular season games between National League teams and American League teams. At 7:07 PM CDT, Mark Gar Darren Oliver of the Texas Rangers threw Ball One to Darryl Hamilton of the San Francisco Giants to start the first interleague game, won by the Giants, 4–3. In other interleague games on this date, the Anaheim Angels beat the San Diego Padres, 8–4, the Oakland A's defeated the Los Angeles Dodgers, 5–4, and the Seattle Mariners outslugged the Colorado Rockies, 12–11.

NATIONAL BASEBALL HALL OF FAME OPENS: ANNIVERSARY. June 12, 1939. The National Baseball Hall of Fame and Museum, Inc, was dedicated at Cooperstown, NY. More than 200 individuals have been honored for their contributions to the game of baseball by induction into the Baseball Hall of Fame. The first players chosen for membership (1936) were Ty Cobb, Honus Wagner, Babe Ruth, Christy Mathewson and Walter Johnson. Memorabilia from the history of baseball are housed at this shrine of America's national sport.

RICHMOND PITCHES PERFECT GAME: ANNIVERSARY. June 12, 1880. Lee Richmond of the Worcester Ruby Legs (National League) pitched baseball's first perfect game, 1–0, against the Cleveland Blues.

SCHMELING WINS HEAVYWEIGHT TITLE: ANNIVERSARY. June 12, 1930. German Max Schmeling won the vacant heavyweight title by defeating Jack Sharkey on a fourth-round foul. Schmeling held the title until 1932, when he lost a split decision to Sharkey.

STRAWBERRY FESTIVAL. June 12–14. Crawfordsville, IN. Festival at Lane Place includes 2½ days of arts and crafts, food, music and children's activities. All-day entertainment, car show (Sunday), softball and tennis tournaments, antique tractor exhibits and 10K run. All city museums open. Est attendance: 30,000. For info: Montgomery County Visitors & Conv Bureau, Inc, 412 E Main St, Crawfordsville, IN 47933. Phone: (800) 866-3973. Fax: (317) 362-5215. Email: mcvcb@tctc.com. WWW: http://www.tctc.com/~mcvcb

USA RUGBY MEN'S COLLEGIATE ALL-CONFERENCE CHAMPIONSHIP. June 12–14. Site TBA. The seven rugby territories bring their top collegiate rugby players together to form a collegiate squad. These seven squads meet to determine the top collegiate all-star team. For info: USA Rugby, 3595 E Fountain Blvd, Colorado Springs, CO 80910. Phone: (719) 637-1022. Fax: (719) 637-1315. Email: usarugby@rmii.com.

WHITE, SOL: 130th BIRTH ANNIVERSARY. June 12, 1868. King Solomon (Sol) White, baseball player and manager and sportswriter born at Bellaire, OH. White played five seasons in white organized baseball and the balance of his career as a player and manager in black baseball. He wrote *The History of Colored Baseball* in 1907. Died at New York, NY, August 1955.

SPORTSCHASER OF THE DAY

Who was the first American-born golfer to win the British Ladies' Amateur championship?

BIRTHDAYS TODAY

Marvin Philip (Marv) Albert (born Marvin Philip Aufrichtig), 55, sportscaster, born New York, NY, June 12, 1943.

Damon Jackson Buford, 28, baseball player, born Baltimore, MD, June 12, 1970.

George Herbert Walker Bush, 74, 41st US president, amateur golfer, former college baseball player, born Milton, MA, June 12, 1924.

Kerry Kittles, 24, basketball player, born Dayton, OH, June 12, 1974.

Ryan Anthony Klesko, 27, baseball player, born Westminster, CA, June 12, 1971.

Keith Alan Miller, 35, former baseball player, born Midland, MI, June 12, 1963.

Rory Darnell Sparrow, 40, former basketball player, born Suffolk, VA, June 12, 1958.

JUNE 13 — SATURDAY

Day 164 — 201 Remaining

NBA FINALS CHAMPIONS THIS DATE

1989	Detroit Pistons
1997	Chicago Bulls

"BIG MAC" SHORELINE SPRING SCENIC TOUR. June 13–14 (also Sept 12–13). Mackinaw City and Harbor Springs, MI. Bike tours of 25-, 50-, 75- and 100-mile

June 1998

S	M	T	W	T	F	S
	1	2	3	4	5	6
7	8	9	10	11	12	13
14	15	16	17	18	19	20
21	22	23	24	25	26	27
28	29	30				

routes between Mackinaw City and Harbor Springs. Each scenic tour will take you along the Lake Michigan shoreline past sparkling water and windswept dunes, through the renowned "Tunnel of Trees," over rolling hills and through quaint resort towns and old Native American villages steeped in legend and charm. Registration fee. Est attendance: 400. For info: Mackinaw Area Tourist Bureau, PO Box 160, Mackinaw City, MI 49701. Phone: (616) 436-5664 or (800) 666-0160. Fax: (616) 436-5991. Email: bjones@freeway.net. WWW: http://www.mackinawcity.com

BRADDOCK WINS HEAVYWEIGHT TITLE: ANNIVERSARY. June 13, 1935. James J. Braddock won a unanimous decision over Max Baer to win the heavyweight championship in a fight at Long Island City, NY. Braddock lost the title to Joe Louis in his next fight.

DODGERS INFIELD PUT TOGETHER: 25th ANNIVERSARY. June 13, 1973. The Los Angeles Dodgers started an infield of Steve Garvey at first base, Davey Lopes at second base, Bill Russell at shortstop and Ron Cey at third base for the first time. The quartet set a record by playing together for eight-and-a-half years.

FISHING HAS NO BOUNDARIES-PIERRE. June 13–14. Lake Oahe, Pierre, SD. A two-day fishing experience for disabled persons. Any disability, age, sex, race, etc, eligible. Fishing with experienced guides attended by 150 participants and 400 volunteers. For info: Fishing Has No Boundaries, Pierre Area Junior Chamber of Commerce, PO Box 548, Pierre, SD 57501. Phone: (800) 962-2034.

GRANGE, RED: 95th BIRTH ANNIVERSARY. June 13, 1903. Harold Edward ("Red") Grange, Pro Football Hall of Fame halfback and sportscaster born at Forskville, PA. Perhaps the most famous football player of all time, Grange had a spectacular college career at the University of Illinois, being named an All-American in 1923, 1924 and 1925. When Illinois dedicated its Memorial Stadium on Oct 18, 1924, against Michigan, Grange scored four touchdowns in the game's first 12 minutes. Known as the "Galloping Ghost," Grange joined the Chicago Bears in 1925 for what amounted to a barnstorming tour, the start of a professional career dictated by Grange and his manager, Charles C. ("Cash and Carry") Pyle. He retired in 1934 following a knee injury, having put pro football on the sports map. Grange entered business and did announcing work on radio and television. In retirement, he lived quietly and humbly. Inducted into the Hall of Fame as a charter member in 1963. Died at Lake Wales, FL, Jan 28, 1991.

GUS MACKER 3-ON-3 CHARITY BASKETBALL TOURNAMENT. June 13–14. Chillicothe, OH. To benefit Junior Achievement of Ross County, the one-and-only original in-the-streets, in-your-face, call-your-own-fouls, 3-on-3 outdoor backyard, the-way-it-was-meant-to-be-played Gus Macker Basketball Tournament. Annually, the second weekend in June. Est attendance: 30,000. For info: Junior Achievement, Conv and Visitor Bureau, PO Box 150, Chillicothe, OH 45601.

MATHEWSON WINS 300th GAME: ANNIVERSARY. June 13, 1912. Christy Mathewson of the New York Giants defeated the Chicago Cubs, 3–2, to win the 300th game of his career. Mathewson pitched in the majors from 1900 through 1916 and finished with 373 victories, tied for third on the all-time list with Grover Cleveland Alexander, behind only Cy Young and Walter Johnson.

MUTRIE, JIM: BIRTH ANNIVERSARY. June 13, 1851. James (Jim) Mutrie, cricket player and baseball manager born at Chelsea, MA. Mutrie made the transition from cricket to its American cousin, baseball. He managed the first incarnation of the New York Mets, a team in the American Association in 1883. As manager of the New York National League team in 1888, he lauded his big players as "my giants," giving the team its nickname. Died at New York, NY, Jan 24, 1938.

ROGUE RIVER JET BOAT MARATHON. June 13–14. Gold Beach, OR. Watch jet boats ply the twisted, rushing white water rapids of the mighty Rogue at speeds faster than your eyes can focus, starting from Jot's Resort at the mouth of the Rogue in Gold Beach, about 30 miles upriver to Agness, and back again. Other events include hydroplane racing and sprint-boat maneuvers. Est attendance: 4,000. For info: Gold Beach Chamber of Commerce, 29279 Ellensburg Ave, #3, Gold Beach, OR 97444. Phone: (800) 525-2334. Fax: (541) 247-0188. Email: goldbeach@harborside.com.

STURGIS REGIONAL HIGH-SCHOOL RODEO. June 13–14. Sturgis Fairgrounds, Sturgis, SD. A regional high-school rodeo. Admission. Est attendance: 1,000. For info: Bryce Sigman, Sturgis High School Rodeo Booster Club, HC 77, Box 56, Sturgis, SD 57785. Phone: (605) 347-4208.

YANKEE STADIUM SILVER JUBILEE: 50th ANNIVERSARY. June 13, 1948. The New York Yankees celebrated the 25th anniversary of the House That Ruth Built. Babe Ruth's famous uniform No. 3 became the first uniform number ever to be retired as Ruth made his final appearance at Yankee Stadium. He died just two months later.

YMCA ROCKY GAP TRIATHLON. June 13. Rocky Gap State Park, Cumberland, MD. The adult and team event includes a 1/4-mile swim, 10-mile bike and 2.8-mile run. Also youth event for kids 15 and under. Sponsored by Kelly-Springfield Tire Company, Memorial Hospital & Medical Center and Cycles N Things. Annually, the second weekend of June. Est attendance: 300. For info: Brian Mottern, Physical Dir, 205 Baltimore Ave, Cumberland, MD 21502. Phone: (301) 724-5445.

BIRTHDAYS TODAY

Sam Aaron Adams, 25, football player, born Houston, TX, June 13, 1973.

Bettina Bunge, 35, former tennis player, born Adliswick, Switzerland, June 13, 1963.

Valeri Bure, 24, hockey player, born Moscow, USSR, June 13, 1974.

Marcel Ernest Lachemann, 57, former baseball manager and player, born Los Angeles, CA, June 13, 1941.

Raimondas Sarunas Marciulionis, 34, basketball player, born Kaunas, USSR, June 13, 1964.

Melvin Lloyd (Mel) Parnell, 76, former baseball player, born New Orleans, LA, June 13, 1922.

JUNE 14 — SUNDAY

Day 165 — 200 Remaining

NBA FINALS CHAMPIONS THIS DATE

1987	Los Angeles Lakers
1990	Detroit Pistons
1992	Chicago Bulls
1995	Houston Rockets

ALL-CAR RALLY "DEMOLITION DERBY." June 14. Rodeo grounds, Belle Fourche, SD. This action-packed event is for the entire family. Open class and powder puff division. Admission. Est attendance: 2,500. For info: Denean Doyoe, All-Car Rally & Belle Fourche Chamber of Commerce, 415 Fifth Ave, Belle Fourche, SD 57717-1345. Phone: (605) 892-2676.

BAER WINS HEAVYWEIGHT TITLE: ANNIVERSARY.
June 14, 1934. Max Baer knocked out Primo Carnera in the 11th round of a fight at Long Island City, NY, to win the heavyweight title. Carnera had won the crown from Jack Sharkey. Baer lost it in his next fight to James J. Braddock.

ENGLAND: THE BRISTOL TO BOURNEMOUTH VINTAGE VEHICLE RUN.
June 14. Starts at Ashton Court Estate, Bristol, Avon; finishes at Undercliff Drive, Bournemouth, Dorset. More than 350 pre-1940 cars, motorcycles and light commercial vehicles will take part in this scenic 97-mile run. Est attendance: 7,000. For info: Alan Davidson, 63 Abbots Way, Yeovil, Somerset, England BA21 3HX.

HALL HITS FOR CYCLE: ANNIVERSARY.
June 14, 1876. Six years after playing centerfield for the Brooklyn Atlantics as they handed the famed Cincinnati Red Stockings their first loss ever, George Hall became the first major leaguer to hit for the cycle, that is, getting a single, a double, a triple and a home run in one game.

HARD ROCK CAFE 5K.
June 14. Hard Rock Cafe, 63 W Ontario, Chicago, IL. This 8th annual 5K (3.1 miles) is a family fun run with proceeds benefiting a to-be-designated charity. The race begins and ends at the cafe, and all runners are invited to join postrace festivities. Annually, in June. Sponsor: Hard Rock Cafe, Chicago, IL. Est attendance: 4,000. For info: c/o Chicago Event Mgmt, Inc, Hard Rock Cafe 5K, 900 W Jackson, Ste #8-W, Chicago, IL 60607. Phone: (312) 243-3274. Fax: (312) 243-5652.

RANGERS END STANLEY CUP JINX: ANNIVERSARY.
June 14, 1994. The New York Rangers defeated the Vancouver Canucks, 3–2, in Game 7 to win the Stanley Cup for the first time since 1940. The Rangers, led by Mark Messier, Brian Leetch and Mike Richter, ended a long drought that included defeats in the finals in 1950, 1972 and 1979.

RED STOCKINGS LOSE FIRST GAME: ANNIVERSARY.
June 14, 1870. The Cincinnati Red Stockings, baseball's first openly acknowledged professional team, lost to the Atlantics of Brooklyn, 8–7, in 11 innings. The Red Stockings were organized in 1869, toured the country and played the entire season without a loss. They began 1870 on the same note, winning 22 games straight before tasting defeat for the first time at the hands of the Atlantics. The team was disbanded at the end of the year, the owners claiming they had lost money.

STRAWBERRY 100 BIKE TOUR.
June 13. Crawfordsville, IN. A 25-to-50-miles-per-day event which covers the rural Crawfordsville community along scenic Sugar Creek. Registration includes lunch. Est attendance: 150. For registration info: Linda Daley, Montgomery County Visitors & Conv Bureau, Inc, PO Box 1186, Crawfordsville, IN 47933. Phone: (765) 866-1923. Fax: (765) 362-5215. Email: mcvcb@tctc.com. WWW: http://tctc.com/~mcvcb/

STANLEY CUP CHAMPIONS THIS DATE
1994   New York Rangers

June 1998	S	M	T	W	T	F	S
		1	2	3	4	5	6
	7	8	9	10	11	12	13
	14	15	16	17	18	19	20
	21	22	23	24	25	26	27
	28	29	30				

BIRTHDAYS TODAY
Gregory Allen (Greg) Brock, 41, former baseball player, born McMinnville, OR, June 14, 1957.
Eric Desjardins, 29, hockey player, born Rouyn, Quebec, Canada, June 14, 1969.
Stephanie Maria (Steffi) Graf, 29, tennis player, born Bruhl, West Germany, June 14, 1969.
Eric Arthur Heiden, 40, Olympic gold medal speed skater, born Madison, WI, June 14, 1958.
Eric Lloyd Murdock, 30, basketball player, born Somerville, NJ, June 14, 1968.
Donald (Don) Newcombe, 72, former baseball player, born Madison, NJ, June 14, 1926.
James Patrick, 35, hockey player, born Winnipeg, Manitoba, Canada, June 14, 1963.
Samuel Bruce (Sam) Perkins, 37, basketball player, born New York, NY, June 14, 1961.
Patricia Sue (Pat) Head Summitt, 46, college basketball coach and former player, born Clarksville, TN, June 14, 1952.

JUNE 15 — MONDAY
Day 166 — 199 Remaining

CHASE'S SPORTSQUOTE OF THE DAY
"It will revolutionize baseball; it will open a new area of alibis for the players." —Baseball executive Gabe Paul on the Astrodome

BASEBALL "RAIN IN" AT THE ASTRODOME: ANNIVERSARY.
June 15, 1976. A 10-in rainstorm caused the postponement of a regular season baseball game between the Pittsburgh Pirates and the Houston Astros at the Astrodome, a domed stadium. The rain caused flash floods that prevented everyone except members of both teams from getting to the ballpark.

BRUSH, JOHN: BIRTH ANNIVERSARY.
June 15, 1845. John Tomlinson Brush, Jr, baseball executive born at Clintonville, NY. Brush moved from the clothing business to baseball, owning in turn the Indianapolis team in the National League, the Cincinnati Reds and the New York Giants. He designed the rules governing the World Series. Died at Louisiana, MO, Nov 26, 1912.

CORSICANA 51, TEXARKANA 3: ANNIVERSARY.
June 15, 1902. A Texas League game between Corsicana and Texarkana was moved to a small ballpark in Ennis, TX, because of the restrictions of the state's Sunday blue laws. Corsicana adjusted to the intimate facility rather well, defeating Texarkana, 51–3. Corsicana's catcher, Jay Clarke, hit eight home runs.

DAHLGREN, BABE: BIRTH ANNIVERSARY.
June 15, 1912. Ellsworth Tenney ("Babe") Dahlgren, baseball player born at San Francisco, CA. Dahlgren played 12 seasons in the majors, but he is best known for playing first base for the New York Yankees on May 2, 1939, the day Lou Gehrig took himself out of the lineup after 2,130 consecutive games. Died at Arcadia, CA, Sept 4, 1996.

NEBRASKALAND DAYS AND BUFFALO BILL RODEO.
June 15–23. North Platte, NE. To relive the Old West. Parades, contests, shoot-outs, art shows, frontier revue, top country and western stars. Est attendance: 100,000. For info: Nebraskaland Days, Box 706, North Platte, NE 69103. Phone: (308) 532-7939. Fax: (308) 532-3789. Email: nld@nque.com. WWW: http://www.nque.com/nld

NICKLAUS SETS US OPEN RECORD: ANNIVERSARY.
June 15, 1980. Jack Nicklaus won his fourth US Open, shooting a record score of 272 at Baltusrol Golf Club. The previous record score for the Open was 275, held by Nicklaus (1967) and Lee Trevino (1968).

ROANOKE VALLEY HORSE SHOW. June 15–20. Salem Civic Center, Salem, VA. Multibreed horse show. Est attendance: 30,000. For info: Salem Civic Center, John Saunders, Box 886, Salem, VA 24153. Phone: (540) 375-3004.

SECOND HALF OF DOUBLE NO-HITTER: 60th ANNIVERSARY. June 15, 1938. Johnny Vander Meer of the Cincinnati Reds pitched his second consecutive no-hitter, whitewashing the Brooklyn Dodgers, 6–0, in the first night game played at Ebbets Field. On June 11, Vander Meer had no-hit the Boston Braves. His double no-hitters have yet to be duplicated. (See also June 11.)

WEAVER, MONTE: BIRTH ANNIVERSARY. June 15, 1906. Montgomery Morton (Monte) Weaver, baseball player born at Hilton, NC. Weaver won 22 games for the 1932 Washington Senators and lost an 11-inning duel with Carl Hubbell in Game 4 of the 1933 World Series. Died at Orlando, FL, June 14, 1994.

BIRTHDAYS TODAY

Johnnie B. ("Dusty") Baker, Jr, 49, baseball manager and former player, born Riverside, CA, June 15, 1949.
Jesse Belanger, 29, hockey player, born St. Georges de Beauce, Quebec, Canada, June 15, 1969.
Wade Anthony Boggs, 40, baseball player, born Omaha, NE, June 15, 1958.
Brett Morgan Butler, 41, baseball player, born Los Angeles, CA, June 15, 1957.
Mario M. Cuomo, 66, former governor of New York and former minor league baseball player, born New York, NY, June 15, 1932.
Michael George (Mike) Holmgren, 50, football coach, born San Francisco, CA, June 15, 1948.
Andrew Eugene (Andy) Pettitte, 26, baseball player, born Baton Rouge, LA, June 15, 1972.
Billy Leo Williams, 60, Baseball Hall of Fame outfielder, born Whistler, AL, June 15, 1938.

JUNE 16 — TUESDAY
Day 167 — 198 Remaining

NBA FINALS CHAMPIONS THIS DATE
1996   Chicago Bulls

CADDIE KICKS TOURNAMENT: ANNIVERSARY. June 16, 1946. Byron Nelson lost the US Open in a playoff and probably had his caddie to blame. In the third round of the tournament, with Nelson's ball in the rough, his caddie, Eddie Martin, stumbled and accidentally kicked the ball. Nelson incurred a one-stroke penalty and wound up tied after regulation play with Vic Ghezzi and Lloyd Mangrum, who won the playoff.

SQUEEZE PLAY FIRST USED: ANNIVERSARY. June 16, 1894. In a game against Princeton, two members of the Yale baseball team, George Case and Dutch Carter, executed baseball's first squeeze play. The squeeze play is executed with a runner on third with less than two outs. The batter bunts the ball, allowing the runner on third to score safely.

SURKONT, MAX: BIRTH ANNIVERSARY. June 16, 1922. Matthew Constantine (Max) Surkont, baseball player born at Central Falls, RI. Surkont was signed for a bonus of a franks-and-beans dinner and took 12 years to make the majors. He once struck out eight batters in a row. Died at Largo, FL, Oct 8, 1986.

BIRTHDAYS TODAY

Richard Leonard (Rick) Adelman, 52, former basketball coach and player, born Lynwood, CA, June 16, 1946.
LaJourdain J. ("J. J.") Birden, 33, football player, born Portland, OR, June 16, 1965.
Roberto Duran, 47, boxer, born Chorillo, Panama, June 16, 1951.
Ernest Thorwald (Ernie) Johnson, 74, former broadcaster and baseball player, born Brattleboro, VT, June 16, 1924.
Wallace Keith (Wally) Joyner, 36, baseball player, born Atlanta, GA, June 16, 1962.
Ronald LeFlore, 50, former baseball player, born Detroit, MI, June 16, 1948.
Philip Alfred (Phil) Mickelson, 28, golfer, born San Diego, CA, June 16, 1970.
Joyce Carol Oates, 60, author (*On Boxing*), born Lockport, NY, June 16, 1938.
Wayne Monte ("Tree") Rollins, 43, former basketball player, born Winter Haven, FL, June 16, 1955.

☆　　☆　　☆

JUNE 17 — WEDNESDAY
Day 168 — 197 Remaining

ABA TEAMS JOIN NBA: ANNIVERSARY. June 17, 1976. Four teams from the American Basketball Association joined the National Basketball Association as the ABA went out of business after nine years. The four teams, the Denver Nuggets, Indiana Pacers, New York Nets and San Antonio Spurs, brought the total number of teams in the NBA to 22.

BOWMAN, JOE: BIRTH ANNIVERSARY. June 17, 1910. Joseph Emil (Joe) Bowman, baseball player born at Argentine, KS. Bowman pitched for six teams between 1932 and 1945. He was the losing pitcher in the first major league night game, May 24, 1935. Died at Kansas City, MO, Nov 22, 1990.

BROWNING, PETE: BIRTH ANNIVERSARY. June 17, 1861. Louis R. ("Pete") Browning, baseball player born at Louisville, KY. Partially deaf, Browning was one of baseball's early great hitters who was victimized by alcohol. Insisting on custom-made bats, he accepted an offer from John Hillerich to make the first "Louisville Slugger" for him. Died at Louisville, Sept 10, 1905.

ECKERSALL, WALTER: BIRTH ANNIVERSARY. June 17, 1886. Walter Herbert Eckersall, football player and official born at Chicago, IL. Eckersall played quarterback at the University of Chicago and earned All-American honors in 1904, 1905 and 1906. He became a journalist and football referee, officiating many games involving Notre Dame. Died at Chicago, Mar 24, 1930.

MOON PHASE: LAST QUARTER. June 17. Moon enters Last Quarter phase at 6:38 AM, EDT.

O. J. SIMPSON'S CAR CHASE: ANNIVERSARY. June 17, 1994. Former football player and announcer O. J. Simpson was arrested in connection with the murder of his wife, Nicole Brown Simpson, and Ronald Goldman. Simpson had fled his home in the morning rather than be arrested. In the evening he and his friend Al Cowlings were in Simpson's white Ford Bronco. They led a horde of police cars on a long but slow car chase on Los Angeles's freeways and eventually wound up back at Simpson's home where he was apprehended. Television stations around the country followed these events live, and an estimated 90 million people watched. Simpson was later acquitted.

SOCCER'S WORLD CUP HELD IN US: ANNIVERSARY. June 17–July 17, 1994. The World Cup of soccer was played in the US for the first time. The international championship is held every four years. The 1994 games began in Chicago on June 17 with a match between Germany and Bolivia and ended in Los Angeles with a final between Brazil and Italy on July 17 with Brazil taking the Cup. Soccer, generally known as football outside the US, is the most popular spectator sport in the world, though it has never achieved great status in the US above the amateur level. The games were watched on television by billions of fans around the world.

STOKES, MAURICE: 65th BIRTH ANNIVERSARY. June 17, 1933. Maurice (Mo) Stokes, basketball player born at Pittsburgh, PA. Stokes played at St. Francis College (PA) and was drafted by the Rochester Royals of the NBA in 1955. He quickly became a top performer, winning the Rookie of the Year award in 1955–56 and making the All-Star team three years in a row. Following the 1957–58 season, Stokes collapsed and went into a coma. Encephalitis made him an invalid, but teammate Jack Twyman cared for him the rest of his life. Died at Cincinnati, OH, Apr 6, 1970.

	S	**M**	**T**	**W**	**T**	**F**	**S**
June		1	2	3	4	5	6
	7	8	9	10	11	12	13
1998	14	15	16	17	18	19	20
	21	22	23	24	25	26	27
	28	29	30				

USA MOBIL OUTDOOR TRACK AND FIELD CHAMPIONSHIPS. June 17–21. New Orleans, LA. The US national championships. For info: Pete Cava, Dir of Comm, USA Track and Field, PO Box 120, Indianapolis, IN 46206-0120. Phone: (317) 261-0500. WWW: http://www.usatf.org

BIRTHDAYS TODAY

Robert Lee (Bobby) Bell, 58, Pro Football Hall of Fame linebacker, born Shelby, NC, June 17, 1940.
David Ismael (Dave) Concepcion, 50, former baseball player, born Aragua, Venezuela, June 17, 1948.
Dermontti Farra Dawson, 33, football player, born Lexington, KY, June 17, 1965.
Stephane Fiset, 28, hockey player, born Montreal, Quebec, Canada, June 17, 1970.
Elroy Leon ("Crazylegs") Hirsch, 75, Pro Football Hall of Fame end and halfback, born Wausau, WI, June 17, 1923.
Ronald Jerome ("Popeye") Jones, 28, basketball player, born Dresden, TN, June 17, 1970.
Michael James (Mike) Milbury, 46, hockey executive, former coach and player, born Brighton, MA, June 17, 1952.
Venus Williams, 18, tennis player, born Lynwood, CA, June 17, 1980.

JUNE 18 — THURSDAY
Day 169 — 196 Remaining

BUTCH CASSIDY OUTLAW TRAIL RIDE. June 18–21. Diamond Mountain, Vernal, UT. Four days of historic trails, great food, programs around the campfire. Bring your own camper, tent, sleeping bag, horse and gear. Several rides of varying duration through beautiful scenery. What every horse lover wants to do on his horse. Sponsors: Dinosaur Travel Board, Uintah Arts Council, USU, IGA, McDonald's. Est attendance: 200. For info: Dinosaurland Travel Board, Exec Dir, 25 E Main, Vernal, UT 84078. Phone: (800) 477-5558 or (801) 789-6932. Fax: (801) 789-7465.

FIBA FOUNDED: ANNIVERSARY. June 18, 1932. The International Amateur Basketball Federation (FIBA), the body that governs Olympic basketball and other international competitions, was founded in Geneva, Switzerland.

GANZEL, CHARLIE: BIRTH ANNIVERSARY. June 18, 1862. Charles William (Charlie) Ganzel, baseball player born at Waterford, WI. One of five brothers to play professional baseball, Ganzel formed half of the "Pretzel Battery" with pitcher Charlie Getzein for the Detroit National League team in the 1880s. Ganzel's son also played in the majors. Died at Quincy, MA, Apr 7, 1914.

HODGES, RUSS: BIRTH ANNIVERSARY. June 18, 1910. Russell Patrick (Russ) Hodges, sportscaster born at Dayton, TN. Hodges was one of several Southerners (along with Mel Allen, Red Barber and Ernie Harwell) who prospered broadcasting baseball in New York City. His most famous call came on Oct 3, 1951, when Bobby Thomson of the New York Giants hit a home run to defeat the Brooklyn Dodgers in the third game of a National League playoff. Hodges yelled repeatedly, "The Giants win the pennant, the Giants win the pennant." Died at Mill Valley, CA, Apr 19, 1971.

MANISTEE COUNTY SPORT FISHING TOURNAMENT WEEK. June 18–28. Manistee County, MI. FMB Ladies Classic on June 19; Budweiser Pro-Am on June 20–21; MCSFA "10" Grand Open on June 27–28 ($20,000 guaranteed payout with 60-boat minimum). Est attendance: 2,500. For info: Capt Fred MacDonald, Tournament Coord, Manistee County Sport Fishing Assn, PO Box 98,

Manistee, MI 49660. Phone: (616) 398-FISH. Fax: (616) 723-2391.

OLDEST MANAGERIAL DEBUT: ANNIVERSARY. June 18, 1960. The San Francisco Giants fired manager Bill Rigney and replaced him with Tom Sheehan. At 66 years, two months and 18 days of age, Sheehan was the oldest man to debut as a major league manager.

SUTTON WINS 300th GAME: ANNIVERSARY. June 18, 1986. Don Sutton of the California Angels pitched a three-hitter against the Texas Rangers to win the 300th game of his career by the score of 5–1. Sutton pitched in the majors from 1966 to 1988 and finished with 324 victories.

US OPEN (GOLF) CHAMPIONSHIP. June 18–21. The Olympic Club at Lakeside, San Francisco, CA. The national golf championship of the US. For info: US Golf Assn, Golf House, Far Hills, NJ 07931. Phone: (908) 234-2300. Fax: (908) 234-9687. Email: usga@ix.netcom.com. WWW: http://www.usga.org

BIRTHDAYS TODAY

Santos (Sandy) Alomar, Jr, 32, baseball player, born Salinas, Puerto Rico, June 18, 1966.

Doug Bodger, 32, hockey player, born Chemainus, BC, Canada, June 18, 1966.

Louis Clark (Lou) Brock, 59, Baseball Hall of Fame outfielder, born El Dorado, AR, June 18, 1939.

Andres Jose Galarraga, 37, baseball player, born Caracas, Venezuela, June 18, 1961.

Delmer W. (Del) Harris, 61, basketball coach, born Plainfield, IN, June 18, 1937.

George Lawrence Mikan, Jr, 74, former basketball coach, executive and Basketball Hall of Fame center, born Joliet, IL, June 18, 1924.

Bruce Bernard Smith, 35, football player, born Norfolk, VA, June 18, 1963.

☆ ☆ ☆

JUNE 19 — FRIDAY

Day 170 — 195 Remaining

SPORTSCHASER OF THE DAY

Lloyd Waner was "Little Poison." Who was "Big Poison"?

AEROSPACE AMERICA. June 19–21. Will Rogers World Airport, Oklahoma City, OK. Considered one of the top five air shows in the world. More than 100 military aircraft, 85 warbirds, top aerobatic performers in the world, trade show. Annually, Father's Day weekend. Est attendance: 100,000. For info: Oklahoma City All Sports Assn, 100 W Main, Ste 285, Oklahoma City, OK 73102. Phone: (405) 236-5000. Fax: (405) 236-5008.

ANTIQUES ON THE BAY. June 19–20. St. Ignace, MI. Auto show. For info: Edward K. Reavie, Pres, Nostalgia Productions, Inc., 268 Hillcrest Blvd, St. Ignace, MI 49781. Phone: (906) 643-8087 or (906) 643-0313. Fax: (906) 643-9784. Email: edreavie@nostalgiaprod.com. WWW: http://www.nostalgia-prod.com

BIAS, LEN: DEATH ANNIVERSARY. June 19, 1986. Leonard Bias, basketball player born at Washington, DC, Nov 18, 1963. Bias played at the University of Maryland and was drafted in the first round by the Boston Celtics on June 17. Two days later, he suffered a heart attack induced by cocaine use. Died at Riverdale, MD.

CANADA: CANADIAN NORTH YELLOWKNIFE MIDNIGHT GOLF CLASSIC. June 19–20. Yellowknife, NWT. Thieving ravens stealing well-placed shots off the sand

fairways is one of the legendary hazards awaiting golfers at this all-night event. Nine new artificial greens await your best chip shot. Join local golf nuts and visiting celebrities in this rollicking social event that starts at 10 AM, Friday, and ends around noon, Saturday. Possible TSN coverage. Annually, the weekend closest to June 21. Est attendance: 300. For info: Yellowknife Golf Club, Box 388, Yellowknife, NWT, Canada X1A 2N3. Phone: (403) 873-4326. Fax: (403) 873-4129.

CANADA: MIDNIGHT MADNESS. June 19. Inuvik, NWT. Celebrates the summer solstice (24 hours of sunlight) with a variety of community events including the Midnight Sun Fun Run, walk or jog, music, midnight swim and dancing in Jim Koe Park, late-night sidewalk sales and other events. Annually, the Friday closest to summer solstice. For info: Corinne Yee-Creaghan, Box 1160, Inuvik, NWT, Canada X0E 0T0. Phone: (403) 979-2607. Fax: (403) 979-2071. Email: townrec1@inuvik.net. WWW: http://www.inuvik.net

CICOTTE, EDDIE: BIRTH ANNIVERSARY. June 19, 1884. Edward Victor (Eddie) Cicotte, baseball player born at Detroit, MI. Pitching for the Chicago White Sox, Cicotte won 28 games in 1917 and 29 in 1919, using his knuckleball to great effectiveness. He was implicated in the Black Sox scandal of 1919 and banned from baseball for life. Died at Detroit, May 5, 1969.

FIRST RUNNING OF THE BELMONT STAKES: 130th ANNIVERSARY. June 19, 1867. The first running of the Belmont Stakes took place at Jerome Park, NY. The team of jockey J. Gilpatrick and his horse Ruthless finished first in a time of 3:05. The Belmont Stakes continued at Jerome Park until 1889, then moved to Morris Park, NY, during 1890–1905, and in 1906 settled at Belmont Park, NY, where it has continued to the present day. The Belmont Stakes is the oldest event of horse racing's Triple Crown.

GEHRIG, LOU: BIRTH ANNIVERSARY. June 19, 1903. Henry Louis (Lou) Gehrig, Baseball Hall of Fame first baseman born Ludwig Heinrich Gehrig at New York, NY. Gehrig, known as the "Iron Horse," played in 2,130 consecutive games, a record not surpassed until Cal Ripken did so in 1995. He played 17 years with the Yankees, hit .340 and slugged 493 home runs, 23 of them grand slams. Gehrig retired abruptly in May 1939 and was diagnosed with the degenerative muscle disease amyotrophic lateral sclerosis, later known as Lou Gehrig's disease. Inducted into the Hall of Fame in 1939 by special election. Died at New York, June 2, 1941. (See also June 2.)

JACKALOPE DAYS. June 19–20 (tentative). Jackalope Square, Douglas, WY. In keeping with our "claim to fame" of being the "Home of the Jackalope," the Douglas Area Chamber of Commerce sponsors a "Jackalope Days" celebration. It is one of the many reasons why Douglas has been named one of 100 best small towns in America, twice! With events such as Bed Races, Jackalope Hunt, Poker Walk, volleyball, basketball, horseshoe tournaments, Jackalope Drink contest, Jackalope Bakeoff and kiddies games galore; Jackalope Days offers something for everyone! Annually, the third weekend in June. Est attendance: 2,500. For info: Douglas Area Chamber of Commerce, 121 Brownfield Rd, Douglas, WY 82633. Phone: (307) 358-2950. Fax: (307) 358-2950.

KNICKERBOCKERS PLAY NEW YORK CLUB: ANNIVERSARY. June 19, 1846. The Knickerbocker Club played a baseball game against the New York Club at the Elysian Fields in Hoboken, NJ. The New York Club, playing under rules devised by Alexander Cartwright of the Knickerbockers, won, 24–1. This game had been generally regarded as the first baseball match ever between two clubs, but recent research has unearthed earlier games in the fall of 1845.

MIDNIGHT SUN BASEBALL GAME. June 19. Fairbanks, AK. To celebrate the summer solstice. Game is played without artificial lights at 10:35 PM. Est attendance: 4,000. For info: Alaska Goldpanners, Box 71154, Fairbanks, AK 99707. Phone: (907) 451-0095.

MIGHTY MO 5K RUN/WALK. June 19–21. Riverfront, South Sioux City, NE. 7th annual run/walk with open, masters, age group, 1-mile run, and team competitions. More than $2,000 in prizes awarded. Annually, usually the third weekend in June, during the Waterfest celebration. Est attendance: 250. For info: South Sioux City Conv and Visitors Bureau, South Sioux City, NE 68776. Phone: (800) 793-6327. Fax: (402) 494-5010.

NATIONAL JUGGLING DAY. June 19. Juggling clubs affiliated with the International Jugglers Association in cities all over North America and the world hold local festivals to demonstrate, teach and celebrate their art. For info: Intl Jugglers Assn, PO Box 218, Montague, MA 01351. Phone: (413) 367-9398. Fax: (413) 367-0259. Email: ijugglersa@aol.com.

NORFOLK ANNUAL RODEO. June 19–21 (tentative). Sandy Rock Arena, Norfolk, NE. Three big days of rodeo, bareback riders, steer wrestling, calf roping, barrel racing, steer undecorating, break away roping and bull riding, clowns, mutton bustin'. Est attendance: 6,500. For info: Sonny Oestreich, Norfolk Annual Rodeo, 55726 851st Rd, Pierce, NE 68767. Phone: (402) 371-6908.

OLD SETTLERS' WEEKEND. June 19–21. Highmore, SD. Activities for the weekend include a road race, parade, demolition derby, rodeo and dances. A pedal pull takes place on Saturday. Admission for some events. Est attendance: 1,000. For info: Mary Ann Morford, Highmore Booster Club, PO Box 435, Highmore, SD 57345. Phone: (605) 852-2927.

PHILIP FESTIVAL DAYS. June 19–21. Philip, SD. Bed races, craft shows, bronc busting, 5K, 10K and kids' 1K runs, parade, quilt show and nightly dances all in the downtown area. Est attendance: 900. For info: Marion Matt, Philip Chamber of Commerce, PO Box 378, Philip, SD 57567. Phone: (605) 859-2525.

WANER GETS 3,000th HIT: ANNIVERSARY. June 19, 1942. The Boston Braves' Paul Waner, known as "Big Poison," got the 3,000th hit of his major league career, but the Pittsburgh Pirates defeated Boston, 7–6. Waner played in the majors from 1926 to 1945, mostly with the Pirates, and finished with 3,152 hits.

WONAGO WORLD CHAMPIONSHIP RODEO. June 19–21. State Fair Coliseum, Milwaukee, WI. More than 200 cowboys and cowgirls compete in six professional contests ranging from bronc riding to bull riding for top prize and world championship points. Featuring colorful opening pageantry and Big, Bad BONUS Bulls. Held in conjunction with West Allis Western Days and North America's Largest Horse Drawn Parade on June 18. 41st annual. Est attendance: 10,000. For info: W. Bruce Lehrke, Pres, Longhorn World Chmpshp Rodeo Inc, PO Box 70159, Nashville, TN 37207. Phone: (615) 876-1016. Fax: (615) 876-4685. Email: lhrodeo@idt.net. WWW: http://www.longhornrodeo.com

		S	M	T	W	T	F	S
June			1	2	3	4	5	6
1998		7	8	9	10	11	12	13
		14	15	16	17	18	19	20
		21	22	23	24	25	26	27
		28	29	30				

Waner Gets 3,000th Hit

BIRTHDAYS TODAY

Robert Thomas (Bob) Aspromonte, 60, former baseball player, born New York, NY, June 19, 1938.
Duane Eugene Kuiper, 48, broadcaster and former baseball player, born Racine, WI, June 19, 1950.
Johnnie Lee LeMaster, 44, former baseball player, born Portsmouth, OH, June 19, 1954.
Shirley Roques Muldowney, 58, former drag racer, born Schenectady, NY, June 19, 1940.
Leo Nomellini, 74, Pro Football Hall of Fame defensive tackle, born Lucca, Italy, June 19, 1924.
Jerry Reuss, 49, former baseball player, born St. Louis, MO, June 19, 1949.
James Michael (Jim) Slaton, 48, former baseball player, born Long Beach, CA, June 19, 1950.

JUNE 20 — SATURDAY

Day 171 — 194 Remaining

NBA FINALS CHAMPIONS THIS DATE

1993   Chicago Bulls

BROWNS IN TIGERS UNIFORMS: ANNIVERSARY. June 20, 1915. The St. Louis Browns arrived in Detroit for a game against the Tigers without their uniforms. The Tigers lent the Browns spare uniforms and then beat them, 1–0.

CANADA: FRIENDSHIP FESTIVAL. June 20–July 5. Fort Erie, Ontario, and Buffalo, NY. Stage entertainment, highland games, horse show, air show, sports tournaments, arts and crafts, custom cars, fireworks, midway, food court and children's festival. Est attendance: 300,000. For info: Tracy Leblanc, Gen Mgr, Friendship Festival, PO Box 1241, Fort Erie, Ont, Canada L2A 5Y2. Phone: (888) 333-1987 or (905) 871-6454. Fax: (905) 871-1266. Email: friendship@vaxxine.com. WWW: http://www.bridgeofpeace.org

GROTON TRIATHLON. June 20. Groton, SD. Combines the best of our recreational activities into one great event. Four-man teams start by shooting 50 clay pigeons each at Swisher's Sporting Clay facility, advance to Olive Grove Golf Course to play nine holes of golf and then finish at Jungle Lanes & Lounge and bowl three games. Prize money goes to the top teams and individuals. Annually, Father's Day weekend. For info: Rick Schelle, Groton Chamber of Commerce, 107 E Ninth Ave, Groton, SD 57445. Phone: (605) 397-2361.

LAKESTRIDE HALF-MARATHON. June 20. Ludington, MI. Half-marathon race that begins at Lakeshore Drive and Tinkham (by the beach) takes runners along a scenic course through the wooded trails and sand dunes of Lake Michigan at Ludington State Park. Annually, the third Saturday in June. Est attendance: 10,000. For info: Sue Brillhart, Exec VP, Ludington Area Conv and Visitors Bureau, 5827 W US 10, Ludington, MI 49431. Phone: (616) 845-0324. Fax: (616) 845-6857. Email: suelacub@aol.com. WWW: http://www.ludingtoncub.com

LONGEST DAM RUN. June 20 (tentative). Glasgow, MT. 4th annual run across the face of Fort Peck Dam (largest hydraulic earth-filled dam in the world). 10K, 5K run or walk and one-mile run. T-shirts for all entrants, prizes and lots of fun. Annually, the third weekend in June. Est attendance: 700. For info: Glasgow Area Chamber of Commerce & Agriculture, Inc, PO Box 832, Glasgow, MT 59230. Phone: (406) 228-2222. Fax: (406) 228-2244.

MACKINAW CITY FUDGE CLASSIC. June 20–21. Mackinaw City, MI. 8th annual fun run and jog. Saturday's 5K and 10K runs start at Mackinaw City High School and continue toward Wilderness Park. Sunday's jog is across the Mackinac Bridge. For info: Mackinaw City Chamber of Commerce, PO Box 856, Mackinaw City, MI 49701. Phone: (616) 436-5574.

MID-AMERICAN SPORT KITE CLASSIC. June 20–21. River Oaks Park, Kalamazoo, MI. A family-oriented sport kite competition, with events for Junior, Novice, Intermediate, Experienced and Master classes. Competitions for Individuals, Teams and Pairs in Precision and Ballet. Sponsors: Kazoo Stringfellows and Battle Creek Cloud Cutters Kite Clubs. Est attendance: 1,500. For info: John Cosby, Coord, PO Box 2241, Kalamazoo, MI 49003. Phone: (616) 345-5432. Fax: (616) 383-8778.

MIGHTY MUD MANIA III. June 20. Riverfront, South Sioux City, NE. 3rd annual mud obstacle course for children 7-13 years old. Mini-mud obstacle course for ages 3-6; puddle pool area for children two and under. Annually, during Waterfest Weekend Celebration. Est attendance: 150. For info: Tina Blackburn, Exec Dir, South Sioux City Conv & Visitors Bureau, 2700 Dakota Ave, South Sioux City, NE 68776. Phone: (800) 793-6327. Fax: (402) 494-5010.

NATIONAL HOLLERIN' CONTEST. June 20. Spivey's Corner, NC. 30th annual. To revive the almost lost art of hollerin' which was a means of communication in days gone by. Annually, the third Saturday in June. Est attendance: 3,000. For info: Ermon Godwin, Jr, Spivey's Corner Volunteer Fire Dept, PO Box 332, Spivey's Corner, NC 28335. Phone: (910) 567-2156.

NATIONAL JOUSTING HALL OF FAME JOUSTING TOURNAMENT. June 20. Natural Chimneys Regional Park, Mt Solon, VA. Ring jousting for novice, amateur, semiprofessional and professional jousters. Medieval jousting and Robin Hood skit. Annually, the third Saturday in June. Est attendance: 500. For info: Upper Valley Regional Park Authority, Box 478, Grottoes, VA 24441. Phone: (540) 350-2510. Fax: (540) 350-2140.

PATTERSON REGAINS HEAVYWEIGHT CROWN: ANNIVERSARY. June 20, 1960. Floyd Patterson became the first boxer to regain the heavyweight championship when he knocked out Ingemar Johansson of Sweden at 1:51 of the fifth round. Patterson won the crown for the first time on Nov 30, 1956, defeating Archie Moore. Johansson scored a TKO over the champion on June 26, 1959. Johansson also lost a third fight on Mar 13, 1961.

POSEY, CUM: BIRTH ANNIVERSARY. June 20, 1890. Cumberland Willis (Cum) Posey, Jr, baseball player, manager and executive born at Homestead, PA. Posey was an exceptional baseball and basketball player at Penn State. He owned and managed the Homestead Grays, perhaps the greatest black baseball team of the late 1920s. Died at Pittsburgh, PA, Mar 28, 1946.

RENO RODEO. June 20–28. Reno, NV. Top professional cowboys ride in the "Wildest, Richest Rodeo in the West." Includes parade, carnival and merchandise mart. 79th annual. Est attendance: 120,000. For info: Reno Rodeo Assn, Box 12335, Reno, NV 89510. Phone: (702) 329-3877 or for tickets: (800) 842-7633.

BIRTHDAYS TODAY

Leonard Ray (Len) Dawson, 63, Pro Football Hall of Fame quarterback, born Alliance, OH, June 20, 1935.

Andrew Auguste (Andy) Etchebarren, 55, former baseball player, born Whittier, CA, June 20, 1943.

John Goodman, 46, actor (*The Babe*), born Affton, MO, June 20, 1952.

Douglas Wayne (Doug) Gwosdz, 38, former baseball player, born Houston, TX, June 20, 1960.

David Earl (Dave) Nelson, 54, former baseball player, born Fort Sill, OK, June 20, 1944.

Richard William (Dickie) Thon, 40, former baseball player, born South Bend, IN, June 20, 1958.

Gary Andrew Varsho, 37, former baseball player, born Marshfield, WI, June 20, 1961.

☆   ☆   ☆

JUNE 21 — SUNDAY
Day 172 — 193 Remaining

BLOCK ISLAND RACE WEEK. June 21–26. Block Island, RI. Largest sailing event on the East Coast, drawing more than 150 boats and 2,000 sailors. Weeklong social events, competitions and family activities. For info: Peter Craig, Premiere Racing, 41 Elm St, Marblehead, MA 01945. Phone: (617) 639-9545. Fax: (617) 639-9171 or Rhode Island Tourism Division, 1 W Exchange St, Providence, RI 02903. Phone: (401) 227-2601.

BUNNING PITCHES PERFECT GAME: ANNIVERSARY. June 21, 1964. Jim Bunning of the Philadelphia Phillies pitched a perfect game against the New York Mets, winning, 6–0. Since Bunning had previously pitched a no-hitter for the Detroit Tigers, his effort against the Mets gave him a no-hitter in each league. Gus Triandos became the first catcher to handle a no-hitter in each league.

CASE, EVERETT: BIRTH ANNIVERSARY. June 21, 1900. Everett Norris Case, Basketball Hall of Fame coach born at Anderson, IN. Case coached high school basketball in Indiana and became head coach at North Carolina State University in 1946. His Wolfpack teams won 10 conference titles but had limited success in postseason play. He retired after the second game of the 1965–66 season, citing the pressures of coaching. Inducted into the Hall of Fame in 1981. Died at Raleigh, NC, Apr 30, 1966.

FATHER'S DAY. June 21. Recognition of the third Sunday in June as Father's Day occurred first at the request of Mrs John B. Dodd of Spokane, WA, on June 19, 1910. It was proclaimed for that date by the mayor of Spokane and recognized by the governor of Washington. The idea was publicly supported by President Calvin Coolidge in 1924 but not presidentially proclaimed until 1966. It was assured of annual recognition by Public Law 92–278 of April 1972.

HONOLULU HARD ROCK CAFE ROCK 'N' ROLL 10K RUN FOR THE HOMELESS and HAWAII STATE 10K CHAMPIONSHIPS. June 21. Honolulu, HI. 7th annual. Largest 10K run in Hawaii, named in 1996 the State 10K Championships by the Mid-Pacific Road Runners Club. Draws about 2,500 runners. Starts on Kapiolani Blvd near the Honolulu Hard Rock Cafe and finishes at Ala Moana Park. Busses take runners to awards presentation and breakfast at the Hard Rock Cafe following finish. Winners receive weekend travel packages to a neighboring island. A drawing is held for a trip for two to the Hard Rock Hotel & Casino in Las Vegas. Open to all runners, walkers, race walkers, wheelchair athletes and baby stroller divisions. Annually, on Father's Day. Starts at 6 AM. Est attendance: 3,000. For media info: Carol Hogan, (808) 325-7400. For race info: Hard Rock Cafe, (808) 955-7383 or John Clark, (808) 396-4227.

LOPAT, EDDIE: 80th BIRTH ANNIVERSARY. June 21, 1918. Edmund Walter (Eddie) Lopat, baseball player, coach and manager born Edmund Walter Lopatynski at New York, NY. Lopat was a successful lefthanded pitcher for the New York Yankees pennant winners of 1949 through 1953. He earned two nicknames, "Junk Man" for his array of off-speed pitches and "Steady Eddie," which belied his nervous disposition. Died at Darien, CT, June 15, 1992.

NOME RIVER RAFT RACE. June 21. Nome, AK. Homemade rafts paddle their way down the 1–2 mile course on the Nome River. The victorious team claims first-place recognition and the ownership of the fur-lined Honey-Bucket which is handed down from year to year. This event draws the entire town out for a fun afternoon at Nome's largest summer event. Annually, the Sunday closest to summer solstice. Est attendance: 300. For info: Bering Sea Lions Club, Box 326, Nome, AK 99762. Phone: (907) 443-5162. Fax: (907) 443-2012.

SHARKEY WINS HEAVYWEIGHT TITLE: ANNIVERSARY. June 21, 1932. Jack Sharkey won a 15-round split decision over Max Schmeling to capture the world heavyweight championship in a fight in New York. Schmeling had won the title two years before by defeating Sharkey on a foul. Sharkey kept the title for one year before being knocked out by Primo Carnera.

	S	**M**	**T**	**W**	**T**	**F**	**S**
June		1	2	3	4	5	6
1998	7	8	9	10	11	12	13
	14	15	16	17	18	19	20
	21	22	23	24	25	26	27
	28	29	30				

SUMMER. June 21–Sept 23. In the Northern Hemisphere summer begins today with the summer solstice, at 10:03 AM, EDT. Note that in the Southern Hemisphere today is the beginning of winter. Anywhere between the Equator and Arctic Circle, the sun rises and sets farthest north on the horizon for the year, and length of daylight is maximum (12 hours, 8 minutes at equator, increasing to 24 hours at Arctic Circle).

VAN ATTA, RUSS: BIRTH ANNIVERSARY. June 21, 1906. Russell Van Atta, baseball player born at Augusta, NJ. Van Atta pitched for seven years in the 1930s. He cut his hand in 1933 and switched from being a starting pitcher to a reliever. Died at Andover, NJ, Oct 10, 1986.

WHEEL TO WESTON. June 21. Downtown Weston, MO. Thirty-five- or fifty-mile bike ride from Kansas City, MO, to Weston, MO, to benefit American Diabetes Assn. Est attendance: 1,200. For info: Weston Development Co, 502 Main, Weston, MO 64098. Phone: (816) 640-2909. Fax: (816) 640-2909.

WNBA INAUGURAL SEASON: ANNIVERSARY. June 21, 1997. The Women's National Basketball Association opened its inaugural season with three games. The Houston Comets beat the Cleveland Rockers, 76–56, the New York Liberty defeated the Los Angeles Sparks, 67–57 and the Sacramento Monarchs beat the Utah Starzz, 70–60. Two teams, the Charlotte Sting and the Phoenix Mercury, began their season the following day with Phoenix defeating Charlotte, 76–59. Each team in the WNBA, a summer league operated by the NBA, played a 24-game schedule.

BIRTHDAYS TODAY

Thomas Doane (Tom) Chambers, 39, former basketball player, born Ogden, UT, June 21, 1959.

Derrick D. Coleman, 31, basketball player, born Mobile, AL, June 21, 1967.

Ron Albert Low, 48, hockey coach and former player, born Birtle, Manitoba, Canada, June 21, 1950.

Michael Joseph (Mike) McCormack, 68, former football coach and Pro Football Hall of Fame tackle, born Chicago, IL, June 21, 1930.

Donovan Alan Osborne, 29, baseball player, born Roseville, CA, June 21, 1969.

Richard Lee (Rick) Sutcliffe, 42, former baseball player, born Independence, MO, June 21, 1956.

JUNE 22 — MONDAY
Day 173 — 192 Remaining

NBA FINALS CHAMPIONS THIS DATE
1994   Houston Rockets

CHARLES WINS HEAVYWEIGHT TITLE: ANNIVERSARY. June 22, 1949. Ezzard Charles won a 15-round unanimous decision over Jersey Joe Walcott to win the heavyweight title, vacant by the retirement of Joe Louis on Mar 1. Charles held the title until July 18, 1951, when he was defeated by Walcott.

ENGLAND: ALL-ENGLAND LAWN TENNIS CHAMPIONSHIPS AT WIMBLEDON. June 22–July 5. Wimbledon, London, England. Men's and women's singles and men's, women's and mixed doubles championships for the most coveted titles in tennis. One of the sport's Grand Slam events. For info: All England Lawn Tennis and Croquet Club, Church Rd, Wimbledon, London, England SW19 5AE.

HUBBELL, CARL: 95th BIRTH ANNIVERSARY. June 22, 1903. Carl Owen Hubbell, Baseball Hall of Fame pitcher born at Carthage, MO. Known as the "Meal

Ticket," Hubbell was one of the best pitchers of the 1930s. In the 1934 All-Star game, he struck out five future Hall of Fame members consecutively. Inducted into the Hall of Fame in 1947. Died at Scottsdale, AZ, Nov 21, 1988.

JOE LOUIS WINS HEAVYWEIGHT TITLE: ANNIVERSARY.
June 22, 1937. Joe Louis, the "Brown Bomber," knocked out James J. Braddock in the eighth round of a fight at Chicago's Comiskey Park to win the heavyweight championship of the world, a title he held for 11 years.

LOUIS AVENGES DEFEAT BY SCHMELING: 60th ANNIVERSARY.
June 22, 1938. Heavyweight champion Joe Louis knocked out challenger and former champion Max Schmeling in the first round of a fight at Yankee Stadium. Louis's stunning beating avenged a 1936 defeat to Schmeling, the only fight Louis lost between 1934 and 1949. Because Schmeling was German and Louis was black, the fight was viewed by some as a triumph of American democracy over Nazi racism.

MARAVICH, PISTOL PETE: BIRTH ANNIVERSARY.
June 22, 1947. Peter Press ("Pistol Pete") Maravich, Basketball Hall of Fame guard born at Aliquippa, PA. Maravich was one of the greatest scorers and showmen in college basketball history, playing at Louisiana State University where his father, Press, was coach. As a pro with several teams, he was an all-star and led the NBA in scoring in 1976–77. Inducted into the Hall of Fame in 1987. He suffered a heart attack after a pickup game and died at Pasadena, CA, Jan 5, 1988.

O'BRIEN, DAVEY: BIRTH ANNIVERSARY.
June 22, 1917. Robert David (Davey) O'Brien, football player born at Dallas, TX. O'Brien backed up quarterback Sammy Baugh in his sophomore year at Texas Christian University and became a starter the next year. In 1937, his senior season, he led TCU to the national championship and won several awards, including the Heisman Trophy, as the nation's best player. He played pro football for two years and then retired to join the FBI. Each year, the Davey O'Brien Educational and Charitable Trust of Fort Worth presents the Davey O'Brien National Quarterback Award to the nation's top college quarterback. Died at Fort Worth, TX, Nov 18, 1977.

CHASE'S SPORTSQUOTE OF THE DAY

"The screwball's an unnatural pitch. Nature never intended a man to turn his hand like that throwing rocks at a bear."
—Carl Hubbell

BIRTHDAYS TODAY

Clyde Austin Drexler, 36, basketball player, born Houston, TX, June 22, 1962.
Maynard Faye Throneberry, 67, former baseball player, born Memphis, TN, June 22, 1931.
Jacob (Jake) Wood, 61, former baseball player, born Elizabeth, NJ, June 22, 1937.

JUNE 23 — TUESDAY
Day 174 — 191 Remaining

BASEBALL'S GREATEST RELIEF EFFORT: ANNIVERSARY.
June 23, 1917. Pitcher Ernie Shore of the Boston Red Sox retired all 26 men he faced in a game against the Washington Nationals. Babe Ruth, Boston's starting pitcher, walked the first batter and was ejected for arguing the call. Shore entered the game, the runner was caught stealing, and every other Washington batter was put out. The Red Sox won, 4–0.

FAUROT, DON: BIRTH ANNIVERSARY.
June 23, 1902. Donald Burrows (Don) Faurot, football player, coach and administrator born at Mountain Grove, MO. Faurot played at the University of Missouri, coached nine years at Northeast Missouri State Teachers College and then returned to his alma mater where he coached through 1956. He was an innovative and successful coach, introducing the split-T offense in 1941. After resigning as coach, he served as the Tigers' athletic director until 1967. Died at Columbia, MO, Oct 19, 1994.

JEWEL-OSCO NATIONAL AMATEUR ALL-STAR BASEBALL TOURNAMENT (NAABT).
June 23–29 (tentative). Chicago, IL. Features the nation's best 16–18-year-old amateur players representing: the American Amateur Baseball Congress, Babe Ruth League, Dixie Baseball, National Amateur Baseball Federation and PONY League. 100 all-stars are chosen from across the nation. Est attendance: 64,000. For info: Ron Berryman or Allan Cox, Amateur Baseball, Inc., 400 N Michigan Ave, Ste 1016, Chicago, IL 60611. Phone: (800) 622-2877 or (312) 245-8058.

KIVIAT, ABE: BIRTH ANNIVERSARY.
June 23, 1892. Abel Richard (Abe) Kiviat, track athlete and official born at New York, NY. Kiviat was the US's best middle-distance runner in the second decade of the 20th century. He won a silver medal in the 1500 meters in the 1912 Olympics. After injuries cut short his career, he served as press steward for numerous track meets. At the 1984 Summer Olympics, he was recognized as the nation's oldest medalist, and in 1984, he ran the Olympic flame across seven blocks of Manhattan. Died at Lakehurst, NJ, Aug 24, 1991.

MOON PHASE: NEW MOON.
June 23. Moon enters New Moon phase at 11:50 PM, EDT.

NATIONAL LEFT-HANDED TOURNAMENT.
June 23–26. 63rd annual golf tournament. Site TBA. Est attendance: 1,200. For info: Ed Martin, Exec Secy/Treas, NALG, 6448 Shawnee Ct, Independence, KY 41051. Phone: (800) 844-NALG. Email: nalgoffice@aol.com.

NIXON SIGNS TITLE IX: ANNIVERSARY.
June 23, 1972. President Richard Nixon signed the Higher Education Act of 1972, including Title IX which barred gender discrimination in athletics and all other activities at colleges and universities receiving federal assistance.

PIERSALL RUNS BACKWARDS: 35th ANNIVERSARY.
June 23, 1963. Outfielder Jimmy Piersall of the New York Mets hit the 100th home run of his career and celebrated by running the bases facing backwards. Philadelphia Phillies pitcher Dallas Green was not amused.

RUDOLPH, WILMA: BIRTH ANNIVERSARY.
June 23, 1940. Wilma Glodean Rudolph, Olympic gold medal sprinter born at Bethlehem, TN. Rudolph captured the hearts of America's Olympic fans when she won the 100 meters, the 200 meters and the 400-meter relay at the 1960 Rome games, thus becoming the first woman to win three gold medals at the same Olympics. She overcame polio as a child to star at Tennessee State University and won the Sullivan Award in 1961. Died at Brentwood, TN, Nov 12, 1994.

WORLD RECORD IN 200: ANNIVERSARY.
June 23, 1996. Michael Johnson set a world record of 19.66 seconds in the 200 meters at the US Olympic Trials in Atlanta. Johnson erased the previous record of 19.72 seconds, set by Pietro Mennea of Italy on Sept 12, 1979.

BIRTHDAYS TODAY

Martin Glenn (Marty) Barrett, 40, former baseball player, born Arcadia, CA, June 23, 1958.

James Joseph (Jim) Deshaies, 38, former baseball player, born Massena, NY, June 23, 1960.

Acie Boyd Earl, 28, basketball player, born Peoria, IL, June 23, 1970.

David Allan (Dave) Goltz, 49, former baseball player, born Pelican Rapids, MN, June 23, 1949.

Thomas Frank (Tom) Haller, 61, former baseball player, born Lockport, IL, June 23, 1937.

Hensley Filemon Acasio Meulens, 31, former baseball player, born Willemstad, Curacao, Netherlands Antilles, June 23, 1967.

Felix Potvin, 27, hockey player, born Anjou, Quebec, Canada, June 23, 1971.

JUNE 24 — WEDNESDAY
Day 175 — 190 Remaining

STANLEY CUP CHAMPIONS THIS DATE
1995   New Jersey Devils

APFA BECOMES THE NFL: ANNIVERSARY. June 24, 1922. The American Professional Football Association, founded at Canton, OH, in 1920, voted to change its name to the National Football League. In the 1922 season, the league fielded 18 teams, down from 22 the previous year.

DEMPSEY, JACK: BIRTH ANNIVERSARY. June 24, 1895. William Harrison ("Jack") Dempsey, boxer born at Manassa, CO. Dempsey boxed under several pseudonyms in western mining camps, came east and picked up Jack ("Doc") Kearns as his manager. After defeating all available heavyweights, Dempsey took on champion Jess Willard in Toledo, OH, on July 4, 1919. Dempsey won when Willard failed to answer the bell for the fourth round. He reigned as champ for seven years but defended his title only six times, losing to Gene Tunney in 1926. Following his boxing career, he became a successful New York restaurateur. Died at New York, NY, May 31, 1983.

LAKE PLACID HORSE SHOW. June 24–28. Lake Placid Show Grounds, Lake Placid, NY. Hunter/jumper competition. For info: Stadium Jumping, Inc, 3104 Cherry Palm Dr, Ste 220, Tampa, FL 33619. Phone: (800) 237-8924 or (813) 623-5801. Fax: (813) 626-5369.

MORGAN HITS 256th HOMER: ANNIVERSARY. June 24, 1984. Joe Morgan of the Oakland A's hit the 256th home run of his career to break the record held by Rogers Hornsby for most home runs by a second baseman.

NBA DRAFT. June 24. General Motors Place, Vancouver, BC, Canada. For info: Brian McIntyre, VP, PR, Natl Basketball Assn, Olympic Tower, 645 Fifth Ave, New York, NY 10022. Phone: (212) 407-8000.

SPOKANE BUS TRAGEDY: ANNIVERSARY. June 24, 1946. Nine members of the Spokane Indians baseball team in the Class B Western International League were killed when the team bus tumbled off a mountainside road on the way from Salem, OR, to Bremerton, WA.

June *1998*	S	M	T	W	T	F	S
		1	2	3	4	5	6
	7	8	9	10	11	12	13
	14	15	16	17	18	19	20
	21	22	23	24	25	26	27
	28	29	30				

SUTTON STRIKES OUT 3,000th BATTER: ANNIVERSARY. June 24, 1983. Pitcher Don Sutton of the Milwaukee Brewers struck out Alan Bannister of the Cleveland Indians, the 3,000th strikeout in his career. The Brewers won, 6–2. Sutton wound up his career with 3,574 strikeouts.

TAYLOR, CHUCK: BIRTH ANNIVERSARY. June 24, 1901. Charles B. (Chuck) Taylor, Basketball Hall of Fame contributor to the game born in Brown County, IN. Taylor played professional basketball for 11 seasons, but he is better known for organizing the first basketball clinic and for "Chuck Taylor All-Stars," the best-selling Converse sneaker that he designed in 1931. Inducted into the Hall of Fame in 1958. Died at Port Charlotte, FL, June 23, 1969.

US WOMEN'S AMATEUR PUBLIC LINKS (GOLF) CHAMPIONSHIP. June 24–28. Kapalua G.C., Kapalua, Maui, Hawaii. For info: US Golf Assn, Golf House, Far Hills, NJ 07931. Phone: (908) 234-2300. Fax: (908) 234-9687. Email: usga@ix.netcom.com. WWW: http://www.usga.org

BIRTHDAYS TODAY

Wayne John Cashman, 53, hockey coach and former player, born Kingston, Ontario, Canada, June 24, 1945.

Shane Churla, 33, hockey player, born Fernie, BC, Canada, June 24, 1965.

Phyllis George, 49, former sportscaster, former Miss America, born Denton, TX, June 24, 1949.

Samuel (Sam) Jones, 65, Basketball Hall of Fame guard, born Wilmington, NC, June 24, 1933.

Douglas Reid (Doug) Jones, 41, baseball player, born Covina, CA, June 24, 1957.

Bernard Irvine (Bernie) Nicholls, 37, hockey player, born Haliburton, Ontario, Canada, June 24, 1961.

Predrag ("Preki") Radosavljevic, 35, soccer player, born Belgrade, Yugoslavia, June 24, 1963.

Robert Reich, 52, US Secretary of Labor in first Clinton administration, born Scranton, PA, June 24, 1946.

Loren Lloyd Roberts, 43, golfer, born San Luis Obispo, CA, June 24, 1955.

JUNE 25 — THURSDAY
Day 176 — 189 Remaining

CANADA: THE NORTH AMERICAN. June 25–July 5. Spruce Meadows, Calgary, Alberta. Show jumping tournament. Enjoy country atmosphere in the Spruce Meadows Marketplace on the Plaza. For info: Spruce Meadows, RR #9, Calgary, AB, Canada T2J 5G5. Phone: (403) 974-4200. Fax: (403) 974-4270. Email: smeadows@telusplanet.net. WWW: http://www.sprucemeadows.com

FIRST AMERICAN TO WIN BRITISH OPEN: ANNIVERSARY. June 25, 1921. Golfer Jock Hutchinson became the first American to win the British Open by defeating Briton Roger Wethered by nine strokes in a 36–hole playoff. The Open Championship was played at St. Andrews, Scotland.

JOE LOUIS RETIRES: 50th ANNIVERSARY. June 25, 1948. Joe Louis defended his heavyweight championship by knocking out Jersey Joe Walcott in the 11th round of a fight at Yankee Stadium. This was Louis's last title defense after which he retired.

KIRBY, CLAY: 50th BIRTH ANNIVERSARY. June 25, 1948. Clayton Laws (Clay) Kirby, baseball player born at Washington, DC. Kirby lost 20 games for the San Diego Padres in 1969, their first season. In 1970, he was removed for a pinch-hitter in the eighth inning after

Joe Louis Retires

holding the New York Mets hitless. The Mets won, 3–0. Died at Arlington, VA, Oct 11, 1991.

KUHEL, JOE: BIRTH ANNIVERSARY. June 25, 1906. Joseph Anthony (Joe) Kuhel, baseball player born at Cleveland, OH. Kuhel's career started in 1930 and ended in 1947. He served two stints with the Washington Senators and two with the Chicago White Sox. Died at Kansas City, KS, Feb 26, 1984.

LONGEST WIMBLEDON MATCH: ANNIVERSARY. June 25, 1969. Pancho Gonzales and Charlie Pasarell played the longest match in Wimbledon history. After 112 games and 5 hours, 12 minutes, Gonzales emerged triumphant.

MOTOROLA WESTERN OPEN. June 25–28. Cog Hill G.&C.C. (Dubsdread), Lemont, IL. A PGA Tour tournament. Est attendance: 150,000. For info: Western Golf Assn, 1 Briar Rd, Golf, IL 60029. Phone: (847) 724-4600. Fax: (847) 724-7133.

NHL EXPANDS TO 30 TEAMS: ANNIVERSARY. June 25, 1997. The National Hockey League announced plans to grant franchises to four cities, thereby bringing the number of teams in the league to 30. Nashville will start

play in 1998–1999, Atlanta in 1999–2000 and Columbus and Minneapolis-St. Paul in 2000–2001.

STRAITS AREA ANTIQUE AUTO SHOW. June 25–27. St. Ignace, MI. For info: Edward K. Reavie, Pres, Nostalgia Productions, Inc., 268 Hillcrest Blvd, St. Ignace, MI 49781. Phone: (906) 643-8087 or (906) 643-0313. Fax: (906) 643-9784. Email: edreavie@nostalgiaprod.com. WWW: http://www.nostalgia-prod.com

VIRGINIA STATE HORSE SHOW ALL-BREED EVENT. June 25–28. Fairgrounds on Strawberry Hill, Richmond, VA. Competition for Arabians, Half-Arabians, Morgans, Miniatures, saddlebreds, jumpers, walking and driving horses. The most inclusive all-breed event in the state with the most divisions of competition. "A" rated by the American Horse Shows Assn. Highlights include "Championship Night" and "High Jump" competition. Est attendance: 5,000. For info: Sue Mullins, Equine Dir, PO Box 26805, Richmond, VA 23261. Phone: (804) 228-3238. Fax: (804) 228-3252. Email: equine@strawberryhill.com.

BIRTHDAYS TODAY

Wardell Stephen (Dell) Curry, 34, basketball player, born Harrisonburg, VA, June 25, 1964.

Douglas (Doug) Gilmour, 35, hockey player, born Kingston, Ontario, Canada, June 25, 1963.

Dikembe Mutombo Mpolondo Mukamba Jean Jacque Wamutombo, 32, basketball player, born Kinshasa, Zaire, June 25, 1966.

Willis Reed, Jr, 56, basketball executive, former coach and Basketball Hall of Fame center, born Hico, LA, June 25, 1942.

Aaron Helmer Sele, 28, baseball player, born Golden Valley, MN, June 25, 1970.

Robert Michael (Mike) Stanley, 35, baseball player, born Fort Lauderdale, FL, June 25, 1963.

JUNE 26 — FRIDAY

Day 177 — 188 Remaining

SPORTSCHASER OF THE DAY

What Civil War general was once credited with inventing baseball, but in reality had nothing to do with the game?

AUDI MOUNT WASHINGTON HILLCLIMB–THE CLIMB TO THE CLOUDS. June 26–28. Gorham, NH. The "Climb to the Clouds" hillclimb is America's oldest hillclimb, originating in 1904. An SCCA-sanctioned Sportscar Hillclimb, which benefits the DARE programs in northern New Hampshire. Est attendance: 7,000. For info: Paul Giblin, Dir, PO Box 278, Gorham, NH 03581. Phone: (603) 466-3988. Email: greatgln@mt-washington. WWW: http://www.mt-washington.com

BROWN, WILLARD: 85th BIRTH ANNIVERSARY. June 26, 1913. Willard Jessie Brown, baseball player born at Shreveport, LA. Brown played with the Kansas City Monarchs in the Negro National League and with the St. Louis Browns in 1947 when he was 34. He was the first African American to hit a home run in the American League. Died at Houston, TX, August 8, 1996.

CRYSTAL SPRINGS RANCH RODEO. June 26[-]28. Clear Lake, SD. PRCA rodeo featuring bareback, saddle bronc, steer wrestling, calf roping, barrel racing, team roping and bull riding. Other activities include trail rides, parade and ride show. Free camping. Admission to rodeo. Est attendance: 12,000.

DOUBLEDAY, ABNER: BIRTH ANNIVERSARY. June 26, 1819. Abner Doubleday, US Army officer born at Ballston Spa, NY. Doubleday attended school in Auburn, NY, and Cooperstown, NY, and graduated from West Point in 1842. After service in the Mexican War and the Seminole War, he commanded gunners who fired the first Union shots from Fort Sumter in April 1861, and fought in several major battles. In 1907, a commission investigating the origins of baseball decided that Doubleday had invented the game at Cooperstown in the summer of 1839. Subsequent research has debunked the commission's finding thoroughly. Died at Mendham, NJ, Jan 26, 1893.

FAMILY FUN DAYS. June 26–28. Pickerel Lake Recreational Area, Grenville, SD. Youth and adult games, including a casting contest, three-legged race, frisbee toss, water balloon toss, sack race and horseshoe toss. Evening awards presentation, nondenominational church service and rootbeer float festival. State park license required. Est attendance: 1,000. For info: Lori Skadsen, SD Game, Fish and Parks, Box 113, Grenville, SD 57239. Phone: (605) 486-4573.

INDIANS DON NUMBERS: ANNIVERSARY. June 26, 1916. When the Cleveland Indians walked onto the field for their game against the Chicago White Sox, their home uniforms were adorned with numbers on the left sleeve. This experiment was abandoned after a short while, and uniform numbers did not appear again until the New York Yankees adopted them in 1929, not on the sleeves but on the backs of their jerseys.

JOHANNSON WINS HEAVYWEIGHT TITLE: ANNIVERSARY. June 26, 1959. Ingemar Johannson of Sweden knocked out Floyd Patterson in the third round of a fight at Yankee Stadium to win the heavyweight championship. Patterson and Johannson fought twice more with Patterson regaining the title in June 1960 and defending it successfully in March 1961.

McQUADE BUDWEISER SOFTBALL TOURNAMENT. June 26–28. Bismarck & McQuade, ND. Challenge your team to the largest slow pitch softball tournament in the world, or watch one of the 400 teams from throughout the US compete. For info: Bismarck/Mandan Conv & Visitors Bureau, PO Box 2274, Bismarck, ND 58502. Phone: (800) 767-3555. Fax: (701) 222-0647.

POLLET, HOWIE: BIRTH ANNIVERSARY. June 26, 1921. Howard Joseph (Howie) Pollet, baseball player born at New Orleans, LA. Pollet joined the St. Louis Cardinals in 1941 and helped pitch them to pennants in 1942 and 1946. After retirement, he was a pitching coach and was in the insurance business. Died at Houston, TX, Aug 8, 1974.

WAR BOND FUND RAISER: ANNIVERSARY. June 26, 1944. The Brooklyn Dodgers, New York Yankees and New York Giants played a special exhibition game at the Polo Grounds before 50,000 fans. In the six-inning contest, each team played successive innings against the other two and then sat out a frame. The combined final score was Dodgers 5, Yankees 1, Giants 0. The proceeds of the game went to purchase war bonds.

WATER SKI DAYS. June 26–28. Lake City, MN. Gala water-ski shows, Grand Parade, Venetian sailboat parade, stage shows, arts and crafts show, classic car show and carni-

val. Est attendance: 20,000. For info: Water Ski Days Chair, Lake City Area Chamber of Commerce, 212 S Washington St, Box 150, Lake City, MN 55041. Phone: (800) 369-4123 or (612) 345-4123. Fax: (612) 345-4123.

ZAHARIAS, BABE DIDRIKSON: BIRTH ANNIVERSARY. June 26, 1914. Mildred Ella ("Babe") Didrikson, golfer and Olympic gold-medal track athlete born at Port Arthur, TX. An athletic prodigy with enormous talent, Didrikson was named an All-American in basketball when she was only 16. At the 1932 Olympic games, she won two gold medals and also set world records in the javelin throw and the 80-meter high hurdles. Only a judging technicality prevented her from obtaining a third gold medal in the high jump. Didrikson married professional wrestler George Zaharias in 1938, six years after she began playing golf casually. In 1946 Babe won the US Women's Amateur, and in 1947 she won 17 straight golf championships and became the first American winner of the British Ladies' Amateur. Turning professional in 1948, she won the US Women's Open in 1950 and 1954, the same year she won the All-American Open. Babe also excelled in softball, baseball, swimming, figure skating, billiards–even football. In a 1950 Associated Press poll she was named the top woman athlete of the first half of the 20th century. Died at Galveston, TX, Sept 27, 1956.

BIRTHDAYS TODAY

Harold Everett (Hal) Greer, 62, Basketball Hall of Fame guard, born Huntington, WV, June 26, 1936.

Ed Jovanovski, 22, hockey player, born Windsor, Ontario, Canada, June 26, 1976.

Jerome Kersey, 36, basketball player, born Clarksville, VA, June 26, 1962.

Greg LeMond, 37, cyclist, born Lakewood, CA, June 26, 1961.

Kirk McLean, 32, hockey player, born Willowdale, Ontario, Canada, June 26, 1966.

JUNE 27 — SATURDAY
Day 178 — 187 Remaining

AFL CONDUCTS SPECIAL DRAFT: ANNIVERSARY. June 27, 1962. The American Football League conducted a special draft of veteran players to assist its two weakest teams, the Oakland Raiders and the Denver Broncos. In the league's first two years, the Broncos had compiled a record of 7–20–1, and the Raiders were 8–20. The draft helped a bit. Denver finished 7–7 in 1962, but Oakland slipped to 1–13.

CLYDE MAKES DEBUT: 25th ANNIVERSARY. June 27, 1973. Eighteen-year-old David Clyde, recipient of a $125,000 bonus to sign with the Texas Rangers, made his major league debut against the Minnesota Twins. The Rangers won, 4–3, before 35,698 fans, the first sellout of the year at Arlington Stadium.

CORVETTE AND HIGH PERFORMANCE SUMMER MEET. June 27–28 (tentative). Puyallup, WA. Buy, sell and show cars and parts–new, used and reproductions. Est attendance: 3,250. For info: Larry W. Johnson, Show Organizer, PO Box 7753, Olympia, WA 98507. Phone: (360) 786-8844.

FIRST PLAYER TO GET SIX HITS: ANNIVERSARY. June 27, 1876. Davy Force, shortstop for the Philadelphia Athletics of the National League, became the first major league player to get six hits in one game. Force was nicknamed "Tom Thumb" because he stood only 5 ft, 4 in tall.

FISHING HAS NO BOUNDARIES-BEMIDJI. June 27–28. Lake Bemidji, MN. A two-day fishing experience for dis-

June 1998	S	M	T	W	T	F	S
		1	2	3	4	5	6
	7	8	9	10	11	12	13
	14	15	16	17	18	19	20
	21	22	23	24	25	26	27
	28	29	30				

abled persons. Any disability, age, sex, race, etc, eligible. Fishing with experienced guides attended by 75 participants and 130 volunteers. For info: Bemidji Chamber of Commerce, Fishing Has No Boundaries, 300 Bemidji Ave, PO Box 850, Bemidji, MN 56619-0850. Phone: (800) 458-2223, ext 100. Fax: (218) 759-0810.

GOWDY ENLISTS: ANNIVERSARY. June 27, 1917. Catcher Hank Gowdy of the Boston Braves became the first major league player to enlist in the military during World War I. He played 17 seasons in the majors and also served in the military during World War II.

MUSCLECAR MANIA. June 27. Cheboygan County Fairgrounds, Cheboygan, MI. Burnout contests, flame throwers, neon competition and muffler rapping. Program includes 18-mile muscle car cruise and contests. For info: Edward K. Reavie, Pres, Nostalgia Productions, Inc, 268 Hillcrest Blvd, St. Ignace, MI 49781. Phone: (906) 643-8087 or (906) 643-0313. Fax: (906) 643-9784. Email: edreavie@nostalgia-prod.com. WWW: http://www.nostalgia-prod.com

NBA DRAFT TELEVISED: ANNIVERSARY. June 27, 1989. The NBA draft was televised for the first time by WTBS. The Sacramento Kings selected center Pervis Ellison of Louisville with the first pick.

OLD MINER'S DAY. June 27. Chloride, AZ. Parade, live music, horseshoe pitching contest, street dance, swap meet, melodrama, vaudeville, burro/mule pack and obstacle event, games and shootouts. Annually, the last Saturday in June. Est attendance: 2,000. For info: Chloride Chamber of Commerce, PO Box 268, Chloride, AZ 86431. Phone: (520) 565-2204.

OLDEST PLAYER TO HIT HOME RUN: ANNIVERSARY. June 27, 1930. John Quinn, 46, Philadelphia Athletics pitcher, became the oldest player in major league history to hit a home run when he connected in a game against the St. Louis Browns. Quinn was also the winning pitcher.

BIRTHDAYS TODAY

Jeffrey Guy (Jeff) Conine, 32, baseball player, born Tacoma, WA, June 27, 1966.

James Patrick (Jim) Edmonds, 28, baseball player, born Fullerton, CA, June 27, 1970.

Craig Anthony Hodges, 38, former basketball player, born Park Forest, IL, June 27, 1960.

Tommy Tamio Kono, 68, Olympic gold medal weightlifter, born Sacramento, CA, June 27, 1930.

Chuck Connors Person, 34, basketball player, born Brantley, AL, June 27, 1964.

Americo Peter (Rico) Petrocelli, 55, former baseball player, born New York, NY, June 27, 1943.

JUNE 28 — SUNDAY
Day 179 — 186 Remaining

BRYAN, JIMMY: BIRTH ANNIVERSARY. June 28, 1926. James Ernest (Jimmy) Bryan, auto racer born at Phoenix, AZ. Bryan was known as "Cowboy Jim" for his penchant for Western attire and his swaying, bucking bronco style in the cockpit of his cars. He raced on dirt tracks, in Europe and at Indianapolis, winning the 500 in 1958. He won the USAC national championship in 1954, 1956 and 1957. Coming out of retirement, he returned to dirt track racing in 1960 but crashed in his first race. Died at Langhorne, PA, June 19, 1960.

NEW YORK GOLDEN ARMS TOURNAMENT–LONG ISLAND. June 28. Nassau Coliseum Fair, Uniondale, NY. Arm wrestling competition held at the fair determines borough winner who will compete in the Empire State

Golden Arms Tournament of Champions on Oct 22. For info: New York Arm Wrestling Assn, Inc, 200-14 45th Dr, Bayside, NY 11361. Phone/fax: (718) 544-4592.

RICKEY ALLOWS 13 STOLEN BASES: 85th ANNIVERSARY. June 28, 1913. Branch Rickey, catcher for the New York Yankees, allowed 13 stolen bases by the Washington Senators in a 16–5 Yankees loss.

SPECIAL RECREATION DAY. June 28. To focus attention on the recreation abilities, aspirations, needs and rights of people with disabilities. (See Special Recreation Week (June 28–July 4). For info: John A. Nesbitt, Pres, SRI, 362 Koser Ave, Iowa City, IA 52246-3038. Phone: (319) 337-7578. Fax: Available upon request. Email: john-nesbitt@uiowa.edu.

SPECIAL RECREATION WEEK. June 28–July 4. To focus attention on the recreation rights, needs, aspirations and abilities of people with disabilities–infants, children, youth, young adults, adults and seniors; living in the community, in residential services and in institutions; in 40 types of play, recreation and leisure pursuits. (Special Recreation Day: June 28.) For info: John A. Nesbitt, Pres, SRI, 362 Koser Ave, Iowa City, IA 52246-3038. Phone: (319) 337-7578. Fax: Available upon request. Email: john-nesbitt@uiowa.edu.

SUPREME COURT CLEARS ALI: ANNIVERSARY. June 28, 1971. The US Supreme Court voted 8–0 to overturn the 1967 conviction of Muhammad Ali for draft evasion.

TINKER STEALS HOME TWICE: ANNIVERSARY. June 28, 1910. Shortstop Joe Tinker of the Chicago Cubs became the first major leaguer to steal home twice in the same game as the Cubs beat the Cincinnati Reds, 11–1. Tinker was part of the famous double-play combination, Tinker to Evers to Chance.

TWO 300-GAME WINNERS: ANNIVERSARY. June 28, 1986. Don Sutton of the California Angels and Phil Niekro of the Cleveland Indians became the first pair of 300-game winners in the 20th century to start against each other. The Angels scored six runs in the bottom of the eighth inning to win the game, 9–3. Neither starter figured in the decision.

TYSON BITES HOLYFIELD'S EAR: ANNIVERSARY. June 28, 1997. In a fight for the WBA heavyweight championship in Las Vegas, challenger Mike Tyson was disqualified in the third round by referee Mills Lane for twice biting the ear of champion Evander Holyfield. After the fight, Tyson claimed that he had been upset that Holyfield head-butted him in the second round. The bites, which precipitated a near-riot in and about the ring, were an attempt at retaliation. On July 9, the Nevada Boxing Commission fined Tyson $3 million and revoked his boxing license.

WILLIAMS, KEN: BIRTH ANNIVERSARY. June 28, 1890. Kenneth Roy (Ken) Williams, baseball player born at Grants Pass, OR. Williams led the American League in 1922 in home runs and runs batted in when his team, the St. Louis Browns, lost a tight pennant race to the New York Yankees. Died at Grants Pass, Jan 22, 1959.

BIRTHDAYS TODAY

Don Edward Baylor, 49, baseball manager and former player, born Austin, TX, June 28, 1949.

Alphonso Erwin (Al) Downing, 57, former baseball player, born Trenton, NJ, June 28, 1941.

John Albert Elway, 38, football player, born Port Angeles, WA, June 28, 1960.

Mark Eugene Grace, 34, baseball player, born Winston-Salem, NC, June 28, 1964.

Robert Matthew (Bobby) Hurley, 27, basketball player, born Jersey City, NJ, June 28, 1971.

Kevin Michael Reimer, 34, former baseball player, born Macon, GA, June 28, 1964.

Joseph Charles (Joe) Sambito, 46, former baseball player, born New York, NY, June 28, 1952.

Chris Edward Speier, 48, former baseball player, born Alameda, CA, June 28, 1950.

JUNE 29 — MONDAY

Day 180 — 185 Remaining

CHASE'S SPORTSQUOTE OF THE DAY

"Ninety-five percent of me is very sad. But my knees—the other five percent—are very, very happy." —Dan Dierdorf, announcing his retirement

CARNERA WINS HEAVYWEIGHT TITLE: 65th ANNIVERSARY. June 29, 1933. Primo Carnera won the heavyweight championship of the world by knocking out Jack Sharkey in the sixth round of a fight at Long Island City, NY. Carnera held the title for only a year. He knocked out two contenders and then was defeated by Max Baer in June 1934.

FIRST SEVEN-FOOT HIGH JUMP: ANNIVERSARY. June 29, 1956. Charles Dumas of the US became the first high jumper to clear the seven-foot barrier when he reached seven ft, 5/8 in, at the US Olympic Trials meet in Los Angeles. He won the gold medal at the Melbourne Olympics later that year at a height of six ft, 11½ in.

McCREARY, CONN: DEATH ANNIVERSARY. June 29, 1979. Conn McCreary, jockey and thoroughbred trainer born at St. Louis, MO, 1921. To be a successful jockey, McCreary had to overcome very short legs that made staying on a horse difficult. He won the Kentucky Derby and Preakness aboard Pensive in 1944, the 1951 Derby aboard Count Turf and the 1952 Preakness on Blue Man. After retiring, he trained horses for 10 years. Died at Ocala, FL.

"MOONLIGHT" GRAHAM PLAYS ONLY GAME: ANNIVERSARY. June 29, 1905. Archibald Wright ("Moonlight") Graham, a real-life ballplayer made famous by his appearance in W. P. Kinsella's novel, *Shoeless Joe*, and the movie, *Field of Dreams*, played in his only major league game. A substitute outfielder for the New York Giants, Graham entered the game in the late innings, neither coming to bat nor making a fielding play. Poetic license in the book and film moved this game to 1922.

PORTSMOUTH SPARTANS MOVE TO DETROIT: ANNIVERSARY. June 29, 1934. After four years in the National Football League, the Portsmouth Spartans were sold to G. A. (Dick) Richards. He moved the team to Detroit and changed its nickname from the Spartans to the Lions.

TROUT, DIZZY: BIRTH ANNIVERSARY. June 29, 1915. Paul Howard ("Dizzy") Trout, baseball player and sportscaster born at Sandcut, IN. Trout was a star pitcher with the Detroit Tigers in the 1940s. He became a sportscaster and popular raconteur after retirement. His son Steve pitched in the majors from 1978 to 1989. Died at Harvey, IL, Feb 28, 1972.

TWIN NO-HITTERS: ANNIVERSARY. June 29, 1990. Dave Stewart of the Oakland Athletics pitched a 5–0 no-hitter against the Toronto Blue Jays at SkyDome. Later in the day Fernando Valenzuela of the Los Angeles Dodgers pitched a 6–0 no-hitter against the St. Louis Cardinals. This marked the first time in major league history that a no-hitter was recorded in each league on the same day and the first time in the 20th century that two pitchers hurled complete-game no-hitters on the same day.

BIRTHDAYS TODAY

Jeff Burton, 31, auto racer, born South Boston, VA, June 29, 1967.

Daniel Lee (Dan) Dierdorf, 49, broadcaster and Pro Football Hall of Fame offensive tackle, born Canton, OH, June 29, 1949.

Theoren (Theo) Fleury, 30, hockey player, born Oxbow, Saskatchewan, Canada, June 29, 1968.

Pedro Guerrero, 42, former baseball player, born San Pedro de Macoris, Dominican Republic, June 29, 1956.

Craig Hartsburg, 39, hockey coach and former player, born Stratford, Ontario, Canada, June 29, 1959.

Frederick Wayne (Rick) Honeycutt, 44, baseball player, born Chattanooga, TN, June 29, 1954.

Harmon Clayton Killebrew, 62, Baseball Hall of Fame third baseman, born Payette, ID, June 29, 1936.

Andrew Charles Lang, Jr, 32, basketball player, born Pine Bluff, AR, June 29, 1966.

JUNE 30 — TUESDAY

Day 181 — 184 Remaining

CANADA: RAYMOND STAMPEDE. June 30–July 1. Ray Knight Arena, Raymond, Alberta. Annual rodeo held at the home of Canada's first and oldest rodeo, started in 1902 by Ray Knight, founder of the town of Raymond. Est attendance: 3,500. For info: Al Heggie, Raymond Stampede Committee Chair, PO Box 335, Raymond, AB, Canada T0K 2S0. Phone: (403) 752-3661.

JONES, DAVY: BIRTH ANNIVERSARY. June 30, 1880. David Jefferson (Davy) Jones, baseball player born at Cambria, WI. Jones played in the outfield for the Detroit Tigers during the early years of the 20th century and was charged with being a settling influence on Ty Cobb. Died at Mankato, MN, Mar 30, 1972.

LEWIS, STRANGLER: BIRTH ANNIVERSARY. June 30, 1891. Ed ("Strangler") Lewis, professional wrestler born Robert Friedricks at Nekoosa, WI. Lewis wrestled when wrestling was a genuine sport, winning the world's championship in 1920 over Joe Stecher. He lost and regained the title several times over the next decade and retired after competing in more than 6,000 matches. Died at Muskogee, OK, Aug 7, 1966.

McCOVEY HITS 500th HOME RUN: 20th ANNIVERSARY. June 30, 1978. Willie McCovey of the San Francisco Giants became the 12th player in major league history to hit 500 home runs. His milestone blast came off pitcher Jamie Easterly of the Atlanta Braves, but the Giants lost, 10–5.

June *1998*	S	M	T	W	T	F	S
		1	2	3	4	5	6
	7	8	9	10	11	12	13
	14	15	16	17	18	19	20
	21	22	23	24	25	26	27
	28	29	30				

REEVES, DAN: BIRTH ANNIVERSARY. June 30, 1912. Daniel Farrell (Dan) Reeves, Pro Football Hall of Fame executive born at New York, NY. The heir to a chain of grocery stores, Reeves purchased the Cleveland Rams of the NFL in 1941. The team won the NFL title in 1945 but faltered financially. Reeves got the approval of his fellow owners to move the franchise to Los Angeles, the first major league team in any sport to play on the West Coast. The Rams survived a challenge from the AAFC while Reeves broke the league's color barrier and pioneered the use of television. Inducted into the Pro Football Hall of Fame in 1967. Died at New York, Apr 15, 1971.

RIVERFRONT STADIUM OPENS: ANNIVERSARY. June 30, 1970. The Cincinnati Reds opened their new home, Riverfront Stadium, with a game against the Atlanta Braves. 51,050 fans packed the new park, but Henry Aaron hit a home run for Atlanta in the first inning, and the Braves won, 8–2.

☆   ☆   ☆

BIRTHDAYS TODAY

Louis Raymond (Louie) Aguiar, 32, football player, born Livermore, CA, June 30, 1966.

Garret Joseph Anderson, 26, baseball player, born Los Angeles, CA, June 30, 1972.

Steve Duchesne, 33, hockey player, born Sept-Iles, Quebec, Canada, June 30, 1965.

Octavio Antonio (Tony) Fernandez, 36, baseball player, born San Pedro de Macoris, Dominican Republic, June 30, 1962.

Riverfront Stadium

Randy Ladouceur, 38, hockey player, born Brockville, Ontario, Canada, June 30, 1960.

Sterling Marlin, 41, auto racer, born Columbia, TN, June 30, 1957.

William Mervin (Billy) Mills, 60, Olympic gold medal long distance runner, born Pine Ridge, SD, June 30, 1938.

Chan Ho Park, 25, baseball player, born Kong Ju City, Korea, June 30, 1973.

Mitchell James (Mitch) Richmond, 33, basketball player, born Fort Lauderdale, FL, June 30, 1965.

Ronald Alan (Ron) Swoboda, 54, former baseball player, born Baltimore, MD, June 30, 1944.

Michael Gerald (Mike) Tyson, 32, former heavyweight champion boxer, born New York, NY, June 30, 1966.

JULY 1 — WEDNESDAY
Day 182 — 183 Remaining

CANADA: CANADA DAY. July 1. National holiday. Canada's national day, formerly known as Dominion Day. Observed on following day when July 1 is a Sunday. Commemorates the confederation of Upper and Lower Canada and some of the Maritime Provinces into the Dominion of Canada on July 1, 1867.

CANADA: CANADA DAY CELEBRATION. July 1. Lucky Lake Waterslide Park, Watson Lake, Yukon. Outdoor concert, triathlon, canoe jousting, stick gambling, helicopter peanut drop, water slide, races and games, birthday cake and lots more. Est attendance: 900. For info: Tracy Durocher, Recreation Programmer, Watson Lake Canada Day Celebration, Box 590, Watson Lake, YT, Canada Y0A 1C0. Phone: (403) 536-2246. Fax: (403) 536-2498. Email: towl@watson.net. WWW: http://www.yukon.net/northernlights

CANADA: HUG A COWBOY DAY. July 1. Raymond, Alta. Hug a cowboy to show your appreciation for their contributions to rodeos, country music, western dancing, cowboy movies and white-hatted heroes. Annually, on Canada Day, July 1. For info: Raymond Sports Hall of Fame, PO Box 511, Raymond, Alta, Canada T0K 2S0. Phone: (403) 752-3094.

CLARKSON, JOHN: BIRTH ANNIVERSARY. July 1, 1861. John Gibson Clarkson, Baseball Hall of Fame pitcher born at Cambridge, MA. Clarkson won 326 games in a 12-year career. He pitched mainly for the Chicago White Stockings and the Boston Beaneaters, National League teams in the late 19th century. Inducted into the Hall of Fame in 1963. Died at Cambridge, Feb 4, 1909.

CONNOR, ROGER: BIRTH ANNIVERSARY. July 1, 1857. Roger Connor, Baseball Hall of Fame outfielder born at Waterbury, CT. Connor was a powerful hitter in the 1880s and 1890s, compiling a .318 batting average over 18 seasons. He slugged more home runs (136) than any other 19th century player. Inducted into the Hall of Fame in 1976. Died at Waterbury, Jan 4, 1931.

ENGLAND: HENLEY ROYAL REGATTA. July 1–5. Henley-on-Thames, Oxfordshire. International rowing event that is one of the big social events of the year. Est attendance: 100,000. For info: The Secretary, Henley Royal Regatta, Regatta Headquarters, Henley-on-Thames, Oxfordshire, England RG9 2LY. Phone: (44) (149) 157-2153. Fax: (44) (149) 157-5509. WWW: http://www.henley-on-thames.org.uk

FIRST INTERCOLLEGIATE BASEBALL GAME: ANNIVERSARY. July 1, 1859. Amherst and Williams played the first intercollegiate baseball game, with Amherst winning, 73–32. The next day, Williams evened the score by defeating Amherst in a chess match.

FIRST TRIPLE CHAMP AT WIMBLEDON: ANNIVERSARY. July 1, 1920. Suzanne Lenglen of France became the first woman tennis player to win three Wimbledon championships in the same year. She won the singles title, the doubles and the mixed doubles.

I LOVE NEW YORK HORSE SHOW. July 1–5. Lake Placid Show Grounds, Lake Placid, NY. Hunter/Jumper competition. For info: Stadium Jumping, Inc, 3104 Cherry Palm Dr, Suite 220, Tampa, FL 33619. Phone: (800) 237-8924 or (813) 623-5801. Fax: (813) 626-5269.

MOON PHASE: FIRST QUARTER. July 1. Moon enters First Quarter phase at 2:43 PM, EDT.

NATIONAL HOT DOG MONTH. July 1–31. Celebrates one of America's favorite hand-held foods with fun facts and new topping ideas. More than 20 billion hot dogs per year are sold in the US. Sponsor: National Hot Dog & Sausage Council. For info: Natl Hot Dog & Sausage Council, 1700 N Moore St, Ste 1600, Arlington, VA 22209. Phone: (703) 841-2400. WWW: http://www.meatami@interramp.com

NATIONAL RECREATION AND PARK MONTH. July 1–31. To showcase and invite community participation in quality leisure activities for all segments of the population. For info: National Recreation and Park Assn, 2775 S Quincy St, Ste 300, Arlington, VA 22206. Phone: (703) 820-4940. WWW: http://www.nrpa.org/nrpa

OLD COMISKEY PARK OPENS: ANNIVERSARY. July 1, 1910. The Chicago White Sox opened their new home, originally called White Sox Park and later called Comiskey Park, losing to the St. Louis Browns, 2–0. Barney Pelty pitched the shutout for the Browns.

PLAY TACOMA DAYS. July 1–31. Tacoma, WA. A series of family events throughout the month of July celebrating Tacoma's recreation programs and opportunities, presented by Metro Parks Tacoma. These annual events include festivals, concerts, splash parties, salmon bakes, a golf tournament and much, much more. Est attendance: 280,000. For info: Metropolitan Park Dist, Rec Dept, 4702 S 19th St, Tacoma, WA 98405. Phone: (206) 305-1036. Fax: (206) 305-1014.

PRINCE, BOB: BIRTH ANNIVERSARY. July 1, 1916. Robert Ferris (Bob) Prince, sportscaster born at Los Angeles, CA. Prince began broadcasting Pittsburgh Pirates games in 1947 and soon became fully identified with the

		S	M	T	W	T	F	S
July					1	2	3	4
		5	6	7	8	9	10	11
1998		12	13	14	15	16	17	18
		19	20	21	22	23	24	25
		26	27	28	29	30	31	

fortunes of the team. Known as "the Gunner," Prince utilized a colorful style that endeared him to his listeners. His firing in 1975 occasioned protests by fans parading through downtown Pittsburgh. Died at Pittsburgh, PA, June 10, 1985.

STERN, BILL: BIRTH ANNIVERSARY. July 1, 1907. William (Bill) Stern, sportscaster born at Rochester, NY. Stern worked as the chief sports announcer on the NBC radio network from 1939 to 1952 and rivalled Ted Husing as the nation's leading sportscaster. Stern's critics complained that he owed his success to his voice only and that his knowledge of sports was often shallow and faulty, but he was enormously popular. He did not make the transition to television well and, in addition, battled an addiction to prescription drugs in the 1950s. Died at New York, NY, Nov 19, 1971.

BIRTHDAYS TODAY

Frank Matt Baumann, 65, former baseball player, born St. Louis, MO, July 1, 1933.

Shawn Burr, 32, hockey player, born Sarnia, Ontario, Canada, July 1, 1966.

Rodrigue Gabriel (Rod) Gilbert, 57, Hockey Hall of Fame right wing, born Montreal, Quebec, Canada, July 1, 1941.

Frederick Carlton (Carl) Lewis, 37, Olympic gold medal sprinter and long jumper, born Birmingham, AL, July 1, 1961.

Nancy Lieberman-Cline, 40, basketball player and broadcaster, born New York, NY, July 1, 1958.

JULY 2 — THURSDAY
Day 183 — 182 Remaining

BLACK HILLS ROUNDUP RODEO. July 2–4. Roundup Rodeo Grounds, Belle Fourche, SD. PRCA rodeo, carnival downtown, 4th of July parade, fireworks and the Miss South Dakota Rodeo pageant. Admission fee. Est attendance: 9,000. For info: David Pummel, Black Hills Roundup Committee, 1301 8th Ave, Belle Fourche, SD 57717. Phone: (605) 892-2076.

BOXING'S FIRST MILLION-DOLLAR GATE: ANNIVERSARY. July 2, 1921. Jack Dempsey successfully defended his heavyweight championship against French contender Georges Carpentier. The challenger staggered Dempsey in the second round, but the "Manassa Mauler" recovered and knocked out Carpentier in the fifth round. The fight grossed $1,789,238, boxing's first million-dollar gate, as 80,000 fans took their seats in a specially-built outdoor arena in Jersey City, NJ.

CANADA: NANISIVIK MIDNIGHT SUN MARATHON AND ROAD RACES. July 2–6. Nanisivik, Northwest Territories. Runners challenge the treeless pass that links the Inuit Village of Arctic Bay to the mining community of Nanisivik north of the Arctic Circle on the northern shore of Baffin Island. 10K, 32K, 42K and 100K races at heights from 2m to 535m and in temperatures ranging from −5°C to +10°C in what is considered the toughest road races in the world. The Ultra (to date conquered by only a handful of men and women) will be extended from 84K to 100K this year. Entrants stay with miners' families or in government houses in Nanisivik. Limited to 100 runners. For info: Midnight Sun Marathon, c/o Nanisivik Mine, PO Box 225, Canada X0A 0X0. Phone: (819) 436-8000. Fax: (819) 436-7435.

CANON GREATER HARTFORD OPEN. July 2–5. TPC at River Highlands, Cromwell, CT. A PGA Tour tournament, formerly known as the Insurance City Open and the Sammy Davis, Jr–Greater Hartford Open. Est attendance: 275,000. For info: Director, Canon Greater Hartford Open, One Financial Plaza, Hartford, CT 06103. Phone: (860) 522-4171. Fax: (860) 278-5574.

COLLIER, BLANTON: BIRTH ANNIVERSARY. July 2, 1906. Blanton Collier, football coach born at Millersburg, KY. A high school coach before World War II, Collier joined the staff of Coach Paul Brown at the Great Lakes Naval Training Center and then with the Cleveland Browns. He moved to Kentucky in 1954 and returned to the Browns as head coach in 1963. His Browns reached the NFL title game four times. Died at Houston, TX, Mar 22, 1983.

DEATH OF ESCOBAR: ANNIVERSARY. July 2, 1994. Andres Escobar, 27, a defender on Colombia's 1994 World Cup soccer team, was shot 12 times and killed by an unknown assailant in Medellin, Colombia. The shooting occurred ten days after Escobar had scored an "own goal," kicking the ball into his own net in a 2–1 opening round upset loss to the United States. Witnesses said the shooter shouted "Goal! Goal!" as he fired each shot.

DELAHANTY, ED: 95th DEATH ANNIVERSARY. July 2, 1903. Edward James (Ed) Delahanty, Baseball Hall of Fame outfielder born at Cleveland, OH, Oct 30, 1867. One of five brothers to play major league baseball, Delahanty starred with the Philadelphia team in the National League, compiling a .345 career batting average. His death was unusual. After being suspended in June, 1903, he left his team in Detroit and boarded a train for New York. Drunk, he was put off by the conductor for disorderly conduct near Niagara Falls. He started walking along the tracks, fell through a bridge and plunged over the falls. Inducted into the Hall of Fame in 1945. Died at Niagara Falls, NY.

DORAIS, GUS: BIRTH ANNIVERSARY. July 2, 1891. Charles Emile ("Gus") Dorais, football player, coach and administrator born at Chippewa Falls, WI. Dorais made headlines in 1913 when he quarterbacked Notre Dame to victory over Army, using forward passes to end Knute Rockne to engineer the upset. He coached at several colleges, most prominently the University of Detroit, and finished his career as coach of the Detroit Lions. Died at Birmingham, MI, Jan 4, 1954.

DOUBLE 1–0 GAMES: 65th ANNIVERSARY. July 2, 1933. The New York Giants beat the St. Louis Cardinals, 1–0, in both ends of a doubleheader. In the first game, an 18-inning affair, Carl Hubbell went all the way to defeat Tex Carlton, who pitched 16 innings. In the nightcap, Roy Parmelee bested Dizzy Dean.

HALFWAY POINT OF 1998. July 2. At noon on July 2, 1998, 182½ days of the year will have elapsed and 182½ will remain before Jan 1, 1999.

LACOSTE, RENE: BIRTH ANNIVERSARY. July 2, 1904. Jean Rene Lacoste, tennis player and clothier born at Paris, France. Lacoste, known as the Crocodile, was one of the quarter of great French tennis players in the 1920s known as the Four Musketeers. He won Wimbledon and the US championship twice each and the French Open three times and was ranked No. 1 in the world in 1926–27. He designed the first shirt specifically for tennis, a loose-fitting cotton polo shirt that soon became the standard. He adorned the Lacoste shirt with a small crocodile, the first apparel logo. Died at St. Jean-de-Luz, France, Oct 12, 1996.

MISSISSIPPI DEEP SEA FISHING RODEO. July 2–5. Gulfport, MS. 50th annual celebration, featuring fishing events, entertainment, rides, games and family fun. Sponsor: MS Deep Sea Rodeo, Inc. Est attendance: 100,000. For info: Ken Ernst, Treas, 2266 Sunkist Country Club Rd, Biloxi, MS 39532. Phone: (601) 863-2713.

OLDE GLORY DAYS '98. July 2–5. Downtown Square, Clinton, MO. Two nights of major entertainment, all free! Office olympics, 5K & fun run, 3-on-3 basketball, fine arts show, craft show, community picnic, grand parade, kids carnival, mega fireworks, "free acts" tent, food concessions, quilt show, pet show, log house tours and more old-fashioned fun for the family over the 4th! Est attendance: 50,000. For info: Olde Glory Days '98, 200 S Main St, The Depot, Clinton, MO 64735. Phone: (816) 885-8167 or (800) 222-5251. Fax: (816) 885-8166.

US WOMEN'S OPEN (GOLF) CHAMPIONSHIP. July 2–5. Blackwolf Run Golf Course at The American Club, Kohler, WI. One of the top golf courses in the US will host this year's Open, featuring 150 golfers from around the world. Television coverage on NBC. Practice rounds June 29–July 1. For info: US Golf Assn, Golf House, Far Hills, NJ 07931. Phone: (908) 234-2300. Fax: (908) 234-9687. Email: usga@ix.netcom.com. WWW: http://www.usga.org

"WORLD'S OLDEST RODEO." July 1–5 (tentative). Prescott, AZ. Dating back to 1888, this PRCA-approved rodeo features saddle and bareback bronc riding, bull riding, calf roping, steer wrestling, team roping and wild horse race. Est attendance: 30,000. For info: Prescott Frontier Days, Inc, Box 2037, Prescott, AZ 86302. Phone: (800) 358-1888. Email: pfdi@goodnet.com. WWW: http://www.goodnet.com/rodeo

ZUPPKE, BOB: BIRTH ANNIVERSARY. July 2, 1879. Robert Carl (Bob) Zuppke, football coach and administrator born at Berlin, Germany. After emigrating at age 2 to Milwaukee, Zuppke played basketball and studied art at the University of Wisconsin. He began coaching high school football and accepted the head job at the University of Illinois in 1913. His teams won four national championships, and Red Grange was the best player he coached. Zuppke retired after the 1941 season when the Illini went winless. Died at Champaign, IL, Dec 22, 1957.

BIRTHDAYS TODAY

Antonio Rafael (Tony) Armas, 45, former baseball player, born Anzoatequi, Venezuela, July 2, 1953.
Jose Canseco, Jr, 34, baseball player, born Havana, Cuba, July 2, 1964.
Eric Daze, 23, hockey player, born Montreal, Quebec, Canada, July 2, 1975.
Joseph David (Joe) Magrane, 34, broadcaster and former baseball player, born Des Moines, IA, July 2, 1964.
Harold Eugene (Hal) Reniff, 60, former baseball player, born Akron, OH, July 2, 1938.

JULY 3 — FRIDAY
Day 184 — 181 Remaining

SPORTSCHASER OF THE DAY

Who was the first African-American to play in the American League?

CANADA: CALGARY EXHIBITION AND STAMPEDE. July 3–12. Calgary, Alberta. Billed as the "Greatest Outdoor Show on Earth!" The world's top professional cowboys compete for supremacy during the Calgary Stampede Half Million Dollar Rodeo. Each evening, nine heart-stopping chuckwagon races explode in an all-out

		S	M	T	W	T	F	S
July					1	2	3	4
		5	6	7	8	9	10	11
1998		12	13	14	15	16	17	18
		19	20	21	22	23	24	25
		26	27	28	29	30	31	

dash to the finish. Outdoor stage spectaculars, International Stock Show, free pancake breakfasts, midway, casino and a city-wide celebration are what you can expect, jam-packed into 10 of the most varied and exciting days you'll ever experience. Est attendance: 1,200,000. For info: Calgary Stampede Assn, PO Box 1060 Stn M, Calgary, AB, Canada, T2P 2K8. Phone: (800) 661-1260.

EARTH AT APHELION. July 3. At approximately 8 PM, EDT, planet Earth will reach aphelion, that point in its orbit when it is farthest from the sun (about 94,510,000 miles). The Earth's mean distance from the sun (mean radius of its orbit) is reached early in the months of April and October. Note that Earth is farthest from the sun during Northern Hemisphere summer. See also: "Earth at Perihelion" (Jan 4).

HART WINS HEAVYWEIGHT TITLE: ANNIVERSARY. July 3, 1905. Marvin Hart won the vacant heavyweight title by knocking out Jack Root in the 12th round of a fight in Reno, NV. The referee for the fight was James Jeffries, whose retirement as champion in March had led to an elimination tournament.

INDIANS PURCHASE DOBY: ANNIVERSARY. July 3, 1947. The Cleveland Indians purchased the contract of outfielder Larry Doby from the Newark Eagles of the Negro National League. Doby thus became the first black player in the American League. He would make his debut as a player on July 5.

MARQUARD GOES TO 19–0: ANNIVERSARY. July 3, 1912. Rube Marquard of the New York Giants ran his season's record to 19–0 by defeating the Brooklyn Dodgers, 2–1. Marquard's 19 victories in a row in one season set a modern major league record. His streak came to an end on July 8 when he was beaten by the Chicago Cubs.

McDERMITT RANCH HAND RODEO. July 3–5. McDermitt, NV. Ranch hands from Nevada, Oregon and Idaho compete for prize money in a number of working events. Street contest and dances add to the festive weekend. Annually, first weekend in July. For local info: Phone: (800) WMCA-NEV. For Nevada Tourism: Nevada Commission on Tourism, Capitol Complex, Carson City, NV 89710. Phone: (702) 687-4322 or (800) 227-0774. Fax: (702) 687-6779.

PITCHER HITS TWO GRAND SLAMS: ANNIVERSARY. July 3, 1966. Tony Cloninger of the Atlanta Braves became the first player in National League history to hit two grand slams in the same game. He added a single to drive in 9 runs as the Braves beat the San Francisco Giants, 17–3.

ROSAR, BUDDY: BIRTH ANNIVERSARY. July 3, 1914. Warren Vincent ("Buddy") Rosar, baseball player born at Buffalo, NY. Rosar caught with four teams over a 13-year career. In 1946, he became the only catcher to play 100 or more games in a season without making an error. Died at Rochester, NY, Mar 13, 1994.

TOVAR, CESAR: BIRTH ANNIVERSARY. July 3, 1940. Cesar Leonardo Tovar, baseball player born at Caracas, Venezuela. Tovar hit .278 over 12 major-league seasons, mainly with the Minnesota Twins. On Sept 22, 1968, he became the second player to play all nine positions in a single game. Died at Caracas, June 14, 1994.

BIRTHDAYS TODAY

Moises Rojas Alou, 32, baseball player, born Atlanta, GA, July 3, 1966.
Tom Cruise, 36, actor (*The Color of Money*), born Syracuse, NY, July 3, 1962.
Daniel William (Danny) Heep, 41, former baseball player, born San Antonio, TX, July 3, 1957.

Neil Kennedy O'Donnell, 32, football player, born Morristown, NJ, July 3, 1966.

Edward Jack (Ed) Roebuck, 67, former baseball player, born East Millsboro, PA, July 3, 1931.

Teemu Selanne, 28, hockey player, born Helsinki, Finland, July 3, 1970.

Frank Daryl Tanana, 45, former baseball player, born Detroit, MI, July 3, 1953.

Gregory Lamont (Greg) Vaughn, 33, baseball player, born Sacramento, CA, July 3, 1965.

JULY 4 — SATURDAY
Day 185 — 180 Remaining

ANVIL MOUNTAIN RUN. July 4. Nome, AK. At 8 AM the day's activities start with the 17K run up 1,134-ft Anvil Mountain and back down to the city of Nome. Record time: 1 hr, 11 min, 23 sec. 20th running. Annually, July 4. Est attendance: 500. For info: Rasmussen's Music Mart, PO Box 2, Nome, AK 99762-0002. Phone: (907) 443-2798. Fax: (907) 443-5777.

CAPE FEAR 7s TOURNAMENT. July 4–5. UNCW, Wilmington, NC. 72-team Mid-Atlantic invitational rugby seven-men-a-side (and women) tournament. Annually, the weekend closest to the 4th of July. Est attendance: 1,200. For info: Bob Bogen, PO Box 5351, Wilmington, NC 28403. Phone: (910) 452-0543. Fax: (910) 452-9960. Email: bogen@wilmington.net.

DEMPSEY WINS HEAVYWEIGHT TITLE: ANNIVERSARY. July 4, 1919. Jack Dempsey, the "Manassa Mauler," won the heavyweight championship of the world when Jess Willard failed to answer the bell for the start of the fourth round. The fight, which drew fans from as far away as New York, was held outdoors in a specially-built arena outside Toledo, Ohio.

GREAT CARDBOARD BOAT REGATTA. July 4 (tentative). Rock Island, IL. Teams and individuals design, build and race person-powered boats made of corrugated cardboard. See following entry for full description. Registration 7:30; races begin 9 AM. Est attendance: 2,000. For info: Jerry Tutskey, Rock Island Parks and Recreation, 1320 24th St, Rock Island, IL 61201. Phone: (309) 788-7275. Fax: (309) 788-7278.

GREAT CARDBOARD BOAT REGATTA. July 4. Rotary Riverview Park, Sheboygan, WI. The most spectacular and hilarious races of somewhat seaworthy craft ever launched in Wisconsin. Person-powered cardboard boats compete in various classes for prizes. Awards for the most spirited team, the most beautiful boats, boats following a theme and the most spectacular sinking (Titanic Award). Prizes for top finishers in three boat classes: propelled by oars or paddles; propelled by mechanical means such as paddle wheels or propellers and "Instant Boats" made from "Secret Kits" by spectators-turned-participants. Est attendance: 16,000. For info: John Michael Kohler Arts Center, 608 New York Ave, PO Box 489, Sheboygan, WI 53082-0489. Phone: (414) 458-6144. Fax: (414) 458-4473.

HARVARD WINS HENLEY: ANNIVERSARY. July 4, 1914. The eight-oared crew with coxswain from Harvard University became the first American crew to win the Grand Challenge Cup, the top event at the Royal Henley Regatta in England.

INDEPENDENCE DAY CHALLENGE RUN. July 4. Boyne City, MI. A two-mile fun run and 10K through a residential district on blacktop. Both men's and women's races start at City Hall. Race director reserves right to add additonal age groups based on number of entries. Race will be postponed if temperature and relative humidity exceed 80° at starting time. Registration: $10 until July 1; $15 thereafter. Est attendance: 25,000. For info: Chamber of Commerce, 507 Spring St, Boyne City, MI 49712. Phone: (616) 582-6222.

INTERNATIONAL CHERRY PIT SPITTING CONTEST. July 4. Tree-Mendus Fruit Farm, Eau Claire, MI. A nutritious sport—is there a better way to dispose of the pits once you have eaten the cherry? Entrants eat a cherry and then spit the pit as far as possible on a blacktop surface. The entrant who spits the pit the farthest including the roll is the champ. Annually, the first Saturday in July. Est attendance: 1,000. For info: Tree-Mendus Fruit Farm, 9351 E Eureka Rd, Eau Claire, MI 49111. Phone: (616) 782-7101.

LENEXA FREEDOM RUN. July 4. Old Town, Lenexa, KS. 19th annual 10K and 5K runs. Est attendance: 1,500. For info: Lenexa Parks and Recreation, 13420 Oak, Lenexa, KS 66215-3652. Phone: (913) 541-8592. Fax: (913) 492-8118. WWW: http://www.ci.lenexa.ks.us

LOU GEHRIG DAY: ANNIVERSARY. July 4, 1939. Having left the Yankees lineup and retired from baseball in May, 1939, Lou Gehrig donned the New York uniform one more time for a special ceremony in his honor. His farewell speech of thanksgiving included the memorable words, "Today I consider myself the luckiest man on the face of the earth."

MACON COUNTY ANNUAL DEMOLITION DERBY. July 4. Macon County Park, Macon, MO. Enjoy the thrills and spills of north Missouri's #1 demolition derby. Lots of hard-hitting excitement. Est attendance: 3,000. For info: Crystal Lyda, Macon Area Chamber of Commerce, 218 N Rollins, Macon, MO 63552. Phone: (816) 385-5484. Fax: (816) 385-3972.

METS AND BRAVES WAKE UP THE NEIGHBORHOOD: ANNIVERSARY. July 4, 1984. The New York Mets defeated the Atlanta Braves, 16–13, in a 19-inning game at Atlanta-Fulton County Stadium. The game lasted until nearly 4 AM and was followed, as promised, by a fireworks show seen by approximately 10,000 fans who remained through the game. Residents of the neighborhood surrounding the stadium reportedly called the police when startled by the explosive noise.

MOUNT MARATHON RACE. July 4. Seward, AK. Grueling footrace begins in downtown Seward, then ascends and descends 3,022-ft Mt Marathon. Race began as a wager between two sourdoughs. 71st running. Est attendance: 20,000. For info: Seward Chamber of Commerce, PO Box 749, Seward, AK 99664. Phone: (907) 224-8051. Fax: (907) 224-5353. WWW: http://www.alaskaone.com/seward

NIEKRO STRIKES OUT 3,000: ANNIVERSARY. July 4, 1984. Knuckleballing pitcher Phil Niekro of the New York Yankees struck out Larry Parrish of the Texas Rangers for the 3,000th strikeout in Niekro's career. He pitched in the majors from 1964 to 1987 and wound up with 3,342 strikeouts.

PEACHTREE ROAD RACE. July 4. Atlanta, GA. 10K run. 50,000-runner limit; advance registration only. For those with access to Atlanta Journal-Constitution, application will appear on Mar 15. Others should send stamped envelope by Mar 1 to Peachtree '98, c/o Atlanta Track Club. 40,000 entrants on first-come basis and 10,000 selected by lottery from other entries postmarked in March 1998. Est attendance: 50,000. For info: Atlanta Track Club, 3097 E Shadowlawn Ave, Atlanta, GA 30305. WWW: http://www.atlantatrackclub.org

PEPSI 400. July 4. Daytona International Speedway, Daytona Beach, FL. 40th running of NASCAR Winston Cup's "Mid-Summer Classic." Sponsor: Pepsi. For info: John Story, Dir of Pub Rel, Daytona Intl Speedway, PO Box 28014, Daytona Beach, FL 32120-2801. Phone: (904) 254-2700. For tickets: (904) 253-RACE (7223). Fax: (904) 947-6791. WWW: http://www.daytonausa.com

PETWAY, BRUCE: DEATH ANNIVERSARY. July 4, 1941. Bruce Petway, baseball player and manager born at Nashville, TN, 1883. Petway was the first great catcher in black baseball. His best years predated the formation of the Negro Leagues, and his best season was 1910 when he hit .393 for the Chicago Leland Giants. Died at Chicago, IL.

SAPERSTEIN, ABE: BIRTH ANNIVERSARY. July 4, 1902. Abraham Michael (Abe) Saperstein, Basketball Hall of Fame executive born in London, England. Saperstein came to the US in 1905, played and coached basketball in Chicago and organized the Harlem Globetrotters in 1927. Originally an excellent and serious team, the Globetrotters evolved into the sport's premier entertainment, playing thousands of games around the world and almost never losing. Inducted into the Hall of Fame in 1970. Died at Chicago, IL, Mar 15, 1966.

WORLD'S GREATEST LIZARD RACE. July 4. Chaparral Park, Lovington, NM. Participants and observers cheer as their lizards and iguanas race down a 16-ft ramp; winners are awarded trophies. Many other lizard events will be held throughout the day. Entertainment and other games are also featured. Annually, July 4. For info: Lovington Chamber of Commerce, PO Box 1347, Lovington, NM 88260. Phone: (505) 396-5311. Fax: (505) 396-2823.

WROK/WZOK/WXXQ ANYTHING THAT FLOATS ROCK RIVER RAFT RACE. July 4. Rock River, Rockford, IL. More than 100 rafts compete for prizes in speed and creativity. Est attendance: 60,000. For info: Tom Garrett, WROK/WZOK/WXXQ Radios, 3901 Brendenwood Rd, Rockford, IL 61107. Phone: (815) 399-2233. Fax: (815) 399-8148.

BIRTHDAYS TODAY

Edison Rosanda (Ed) Armbrister, 50, former baseball player, born Nassau, Bahamas, July 4, 1948.
James Louis (Jim) Beattie, 44, baseball executive and former baseball player, born Hampton, VA, July 4, 1954.
Vinicio (Vinny) Castilla, 31, baseball player, born Oaxaca, Mexico, July 4, 1967.
Allen (Al) Davis, 69, football executive and former coach, born Brockton, MA, July 4, 1929.

July *1998*	S	M	T	W	T	F	S
				1	2	3	4
	5	6	7	8	9	10	11
	12	13	14	15	16	17	18
	19	20	21	22	23	24	25
	26	27	28	29	30	31	

Horace Grant, 33, basketball player, born Augusta, GA, July 4, 1965.
Harvey Grant, 33, basketball player, born Augusta, GA, July 4, 1965.
Harold Clifton (Hal) Lanier, 56, former baseball manager and player, born Denton, NC, July 4, 1942.
Jawann Oldham, 41, former basketball player, born Seattle, WA, July 4, 1957.
Pamela Howard (Pam) Shriver, 36, tennis player, born Baltimore, MD, July 4, 1962.
George Michael Steinbrenner III, 68, baseball executive, born Rocky River, OH, July 4, 1930.
Charles William (Chuck) Tanner, 69, former baseball manager and player, born New Castle, PA, July 4, 1929.

JULY 5 — SUNDAY
Day 186 — 179 Remaining

BROTHERS HIT HOME RUNS: ANNIVERSARY. July 5, 1935. Tony Cuccinello of the Brooklyn Dodgers and his brother, Al Cuccinello, of the New York Giants became the first brothers in major league history to hit home runs for opposing teams in the same game. The Dodgers won, 14–4.

COLUMBIA WINS AT HENLEY: ANNIVERSARY. July 5, 1887. A four-oar crew from Columbia University became the first American entry to win an event at the Henley Regatta in London. Columbia defeated a crew from Hertford College to win the Visitors Challenge Cup. An American crew did not win Henley's greatest prize, the Grand Challenge Cup, until 1914 when a Harvard crew did so.

DAVIS, DWIGHT: BIRTH ANNIVERSARY. July 5, 1879. Dwight Filley Davis, tennis player born at St. Louis, MO. Davis was a nationally prominent singles and doubles player, but his enduring contribution to his sport was his creation of the Davis Cup international competition. Davis purchased the cup from a Boston jeweler for $750 and helped win the first two competitions in 1900 and 1902. After retiring, he worked in government and was Secretary of War under President Calvin Coolidge. Died at Washington, DC, Nov 28, 1945.

DOBY BREAKS AL COLOR LINE: ANNIVERSARY. July 5, 1947. Larry Doby became the first African-American to play in the American League when he appeared as a pinch-hitter for the Cleveland Indians in a game against the Chicago White Sox. The Indians lost, 6–5.

QUINN, JACK: BIRTH ANNIVERSARY. July 5, 1884. John Picus (Jack) Quinn, baseball player born John Quinn Paykos at Jeanesville, PA. Quinn pitched regularly in the major leagues until he was 49 years old, making him the oldest regular roster player in major league history and the oldest to hit a home run and win a game. Died at Pottsville, PA, Apr 17, 1946.

76ERS TRADE WILT: 30th ANNIVERSARY. July 5, 1968. The Philadelphia 76ers traded center Wilt Chamberlain to the Los Angeles Lakers for three players, Darrell Imhoff, Archie Clark and Jerry Chambers and an unannounced amount of cash.

SPORTS DAY. July 5. Geddes, SD. Good old-fashioned family get-together at the Geddes Ball Park. Sports for the young and old. Family picnic. Admission fee. Est attendance: 3,000.

BIRTHDAYS TODAY

Curtis LeRoy (Curt) Blefary, 55, former baseball player, born New York, NY, July 5, 1943.
David William (Dave) Eiland, 32, former baseball player, born Dade City, FL, July 5, 1966.

Doby Breaks AL Color Line

Richard Michael ("Goose") Gossage, 47, former baseball player, born Colorado Springs, CO, July 5, 1951.

John Clark LeClair, 29, hockey player, born St. Albans, VT, July 5, 1969.

James David Lofton, 42, former football player, born Fort Ord, CA, July 5, 1956.

Gary Nathaniel Matthews, 48, former baseball player, born San Fernando, CA, July 5, 1950.

Timothy Howard (Tim) Worrell, 31, baseball player, born Pasadena, CA, July 5, 1967.

JULY 6 — MONDAY

Day 187 — 178 Remaining

CHASE'S SPORTSQUOTE OF THE DAY

"Arch [Ward] called me one day and asked me to have dinner with him. That was the year of the World's Fair in Chicago and Arch wanted to make an All-Star Game one of the highlights." —Will Harridge on the start of the All-Star Game

AL ENDS NL ALL-STAR GAME STREAK: 15th ANNIVERSARY. July 6, 1983. On the 50th anniversary of baseball's first All-Star game, the American League defeated the National League, 13–3, to snap the NL's 11-game winning streak. Fred Lynn hit the first grand slam in All-Star competition, off Attlee Hammaker in the third inning.

FIRST BLACK TITLE AT WIMBLEDON: ANNIVERSARY. July 6, 1957. Althea Gibson of the US became the first black person to win any Wimbledon title when she beat Darlene Hard, also of the US, 6–3, 6–2, to win the women's singles championship.

HARTZELL, ROY: BIRTH ANNIVERSARY. July 6, 1881. Roy Allen Hartzell, baseball player born at Golden, CO. Hartzell played shortstop for 13 years with the St. Louis Browns and the New York Yankees. His 91 RBIs for New York in 1911 were the most for any Yankees player during the team's first 13 years. Died at Golden, Nov 6, 1961.

MAJOR LEAGUE BASEBALL HOLDS FIRST ALL-STAR GAME: 65th ANNIVERSARY. July 6, 1933. Baseball's first official All-Star Game was held at Comiskey Park, Chicago, IL. Babe Ruth led the American League with a home run as they defeated the National League 4–2. Prior to the summer of 1933, All-Star contests consisted of pre- and post-season exhibitions that often found teams made up of a few stars playing beside journeymen and even minor leaguers.

NUDE RECREATION WEEK. July 6–12. To promote acceptance of the body and understanding of the nude recreation movement as a natural solution to many problems of modern living. Reviving the reality of the ancient Olympic Games which were also conducted in the nude. For info: The Naturist Soc, Box 132, Oshkosh, WI 54902. Phone: (414) 231-9950. Fax: (414) 231-9977. Email: naturist@naturist.com. WWW: http://www.naturist.com

O'NEILL, STEVE: BIRTH ANNIVERSARY. July 6, 1891. Stephen Francis (Steve) O'Neill, baseball player, coach and manager born at Minooka, PA. O'Neill caught in the majors in the 1920s and 1930s, after which he coached and managed for several teams, including the 1945 Detroit Tigers, who won the World Series. Died at Cleveland, OH, Jan 26, 1962.

RUFFIAN INJURED IN MATCH RACE: ANNIVERSARY. July 6, 1975. The filly Ruffian, undefeated in her career, met Kentucky Derby winner Foolish Pleasure in a special match race. On the backstretch, Ruffian sustained a severe leg injury and was pulled up by jockey Jacinto Vasquez. After a night of heroic medical and surgical efforts, she was humanely destroyed.

BIRTHDAYS TODAY

Matthew David (Matt) Bahr, 42, former football player, born Philadelphia, PA, July 6, 1956.

Kenneth Lance Johnson, 35, baseball player, born Lincoln Heights, IL, July 6, 1963.

Omar Olivares, 31, baseball player, born Mayaguez, Puerto Rico, July 6, 1967.

Douglas Bradford (Brad) Park, 50, Hockey Hall of Fame defenseman, born Toronto, Ontario, Canada, July 6, 1948.

Willie Larry Randolph, 44, former baseball player, born Holly Hill, SC, July 6, 1954.

Sylvester Stallone, 52, actor (Rocky films), born New York, NY, July 6, 1946.

Jason Dolph Thompson, 44, former baseball player, born Hollywood, CA, July 6, 1954.

JULY 7 — TUESDAY

Day 188 — 177 Remaining

BASEBALL ALL-STAR GAME. July 7 (tentative). Coors Field, Denver, CO. All-Stars from the American League oppose All-Stars from the National League in Major League Baseball's 69th All-Star Game. The first All-Star Game, played in 1933, proved so popular that it immediately became an annual affair. No game was played in 1945 because of World War II. Two games were played in 1959, 1960, 1961 and 1962.

CHARLES, EZZARD: BIRTH ANNIVERSARY. July 7, 1921. Ezzard Mack Charles, boxer born at Lawrenceville, GA. A precise boxer who liked to win on points, Charles lacked the killer instinct to be a truly great fighter. Nevertheless, he won the heavyweight championship on June 22, 1949, outpointing Jersey Joe Walcott after Joe Louis retired. Walcott took the crown from him in July, 1951. Died at Chicago, IL, May 28, 1975.

FERRIS, DAN: BIRTH ANNIVERSARY. July 7, 1889. Daniel Joseph (Dan) Ferris, amateur athletics administrator born at Pawling, NY. Ferris became secretary to James E. Sullivan, secretary-treasurer of the Amateur Athletic Union of the US (AAU) in 1907. He succeeded Sullivan in 1927 and did not relinquish this position until 1957. Ferris worked long days with a small staff in defense of pure amateurism. He engaged in many public controversies, including the dismissal of swimmer Eleanor Holm from the 1936 Olympic team for drinking champagne and the protracted conflict between the AAU and the NCAA for control of amateur athletics. Died at Amityville, NY, May 2, 1977.

HERMAN, BILLY: BIRTH ANNIVERSARY. July 7, 1909. William Jennings Bryan (Billy) Herman, Baseball Hall of Fame second baseman born at New Albany, IN. Herman played 15 seasons, participated in ten All-Star games and collected 2,345 hits. He later coached and managed. Inducted into the Hall of Fame in 1975. Died at West Palm Beach, FL, Sept 5, 1992.

PAIGE, SATCHEL: BIRTH ANNIVERSARY. July 7, 1906. Leroy Robert ("Satchel") Paige, Baseball Hall of Fame pitcher born at Mobile, AL. Paige was the greatest attraction in Negro Leagues baseball and one of black baseball's greatest players. He was also, at age 42, the first black pitcher in the American League. Inducted into the Hall of Fame in 1971. Died at Kansas City, MO, June 8, 1982.

SACRAMENTO LOSES FIRST AMERICAN CFL GAME: ANNIVERSARY. July 7, 1993. The Ottawa Rough Riders defeated the Sacramento Gold Miners, 32–23, to spoil the debut of the first US team in the Canadian Football League. Ottawa quarterback Tom Burgess passed for three touchdowns.

UNSEEDED BECKER WINS WIMBLEDON TITLE: ANNIVERSARY. July 7, 1985. 17-year-old Boris Becker of Germany became the youngest player and the first unseeded player to win the men's singles championship at Wimbledon. He defeated Kevin Curren, 6–3, 6–7, 7–6, 6–4.

BIRTHDAYS TODAY

Terry Paul Bevington, 42, baseball manager, born Akron, OH, July 7, 1956.
David Allen (Dave) Burba, 32, baseball player, born Dayton, OH, July 7, 1966.
Reginald John (Reggie) Cobb, 30, football player, born Knoxville, TN, July 7, 1968.
Edward Charles (Chuck) Knoblauch, 30, baseball player, born Houston, TX, July 7, 1968.
Joseph Steve (Joe) Sakic, 29, hockey player, born Burnaby, BC, Canada, July 7, 1969.
Ralph Lee Sampson, 38, former basketball player, born Harrisonburg, VA, July 7, 1960.
Matthew Jerome (Matt) Suhey, 40, former football player, born Bellefonte, PA, July 7, 1958.

JULY 8 — WEDNESDAY
Day 189 — 176 Remaining

BILLIE JEAN WINS THREE TITLES: ANNIVERSARY. July 8, 1967. Tennis player Billie Jean King of the United States won three titles at Wimbledon. She beat Ann Haydon Jones for the singles title, teamed with Rosie Casals for the women's doubles title and joined with Owen Davidson to capture the mixed doubles title.

BOCA GRANDE TARPON TOURNAMENT ("WORLD'S RICHEST"). July 8–9. Boca Grande Pass, Boca Grande, FL. Tarpon fishing; field limited to 60 boats; entry fee $3,500 per boat. With 60 entries, first place (largest tarpon) pays off $100,000. Annually, the week after the 4th of July. Est attendance: 800. For info: Boca Grande Chamber of Commerce, PO Box 704, Boca Grande, FL 33921. Phone: (941) 964-0568. Fax: (941) 964-0620. Email: bgcc@ewol.com. WWW: http://www.charlotte-online.com/bocagrande/

ELLIOT, JUMBO: BIRTH ANNIVERSARY. July 8, 1914. James Francis ("Jumbo") Elliot, track athlete and coach born at Philadelphia, PA. Elliot ran the quarter-mile at Villanova, but an injury prevented his qualifying for the 1936 Summer Olympic team. He stayed at Villanova to become one of the most successful track coaches, specializing in middle-distance runners. His athletes won eight NCAA team championships and 63 individual titles. Elliot coached as a volunteer; his income came from a construction equipment leasing firm he founded. Died at Juno Beach, FL, Mar 22, 1981.

GORBOUS, GLEN: BIRTH ANNIVERSARY. July 8, 1930. Glen Edward Gorbous, baseball player born at Drumheller, Alberta, Canada. Gorbous is one of only four Alberta natives to play major league baseball. He is best known for throwing a ball 445 ', 10 ", on the fly, a world record. Died at Calgary, Alberta, June 12, 1990.

July *1998*	S	M	T	W	T	F	S
				1	2	3	4
	5	6	7	8	9	10	11
	12	13	14	15	16	17	18
	19	20	21	22	23	24	25
	26	27	28	29	30	31	

MARQUARD'S STREAK ENDS: ANNIVERSARY. July 8, 1912. Pitcher Rube Marquard of the New York Giants was beaten by the Chicago Cubs, 7–2, ending his winning streak at 19 games, tying Tim Keefe's major league record for consecutive games won in a single season.

MONTANA GOVERNOR'S CUP WALLEYE TOURNAMENT. July 8–11. Fort Peck, MT. 11th annual. Two-person team event, limited to 200 teams. First place award of $10,000. There is an 80% payback of $260 entry fee. Kids' fishing event also. Annually, the second weekend in July. Est attendance: 1,000. For info: Glasgow Area Chamber of Commerce & Agriculture, Box 832, Glasgow, MT 59230. Phone: (406) 228-2222. Fax: (406) 228-2244.

O'DAY, HANK: BIRTH ANNIVERSARY. July 8, 1862. Henry Francis (Hank) O'Day, baseball player, manager and umpire born at Chicago, IL. O'Day pitched in the majors before the turn of the century and then worked as a National League umpire for 31 years. He handled the first World Series plus nine others, called the only unassisted triple play in World Series history and ruled Fred Merkle out at second base in baseball's greatest dispute, Sept 23, 1908. Died at Chicago, July 2, 1935.

SULLIVAN DEFEATS KILRAIN: ANNIVERSARY. July 8, 1889. John L. Sullivan, heavyweight champion of the world, defeated Jake Kilrain in the 75th round of a fight in Richburg, MS. This was the last bare-knuckles title fight after which boxing was governed by the Marquis of Queensbury rules.

TRIPLE-A BASEBALL ALL-STAR GAME. July 8 (tentative). Site TBA. All-Star game for players at the Triple-A minor league level. The format of this game is uncertain pursuant to Triple-A realignment approved in July, 1997. Annually, the day after the Major League All-Star game. Est attendance: 10,000. For info: American Assn, 6801 Miami Ave #3, Cincinnati, OH 45243. Phone: (513) 271-4800. Fax: (513) 271-7887.

BIRTHDAYS TODAY

Roone Pinckney Arledge, 67, television executive, born New York, NY, July 8, 1931.

Alan Dean Ashby, 47, former baseball player, born Long Beach, CA, July 8, 1951.

Robert Joseph (Bobby) Ayala, 29, baseball player, born Ventura, CA, July 8, 1969.

John David Crow, 63, Heisman Trophy halfback, born Marion, LA, July 8, 1935.

Karl Dykhuis, 26, hockey player, born Sept-Iles, Quebec, Canada, July 8, 1972.

John Harold (Jack) Lambert, 46, Pro Football Hall of Fame linebacker, born Mantua, OH, July 8, 1952.

Terry Stephen Puhl, 42, former baseball player, born Melville, Saskatchewan, Canada, July 8, 1956.

Albert Donald (Al) Spangler, 65, former baseball player, born Philadelphia, PA, July 8, 1933.

JULY 9 — THURSDAY
Day 190 — 175 Remaining

CANADA: BLUE JAYS CUP. July 9–14. Stonewall, Manitoba. 16–18-year-olds from each province in Canada participate in baseball tournament to select national champion. Top 30 players selected for National Youth Team Training Camp. Annually, the second weekend in July. Est attendance: 10,000. For info: Baseball Canada, 1600 James Naismith Dr, Ottawa, Ont, Canada K1B 5N4. Phone: (613) 748-5606. Fax: (613) 748-5767. Email: info@baseball.ca. WWW: http://www.baseball.ca

FIRST ALL-STAR GAME SHUTOUT: ANNIVERSARY. July 9, 1940. The National League recorded the first shutout in All-Star game history, defeating the American League, 4–0. Five National League pitchers held the Americans to three hits.

KINNICK, NILE: 80th BIRTH ANNIVERSARY. July 9, 1918. Nile Clarke Kinnick, Jr, college football player and war hero born at Adel, IA. Kinnick was the quintessential college football hero who excelled academically and athletically. He earned All-American honors as a sophomore and by his senior year was regarded as the nation's best back. After winning the Heisman Trophy and graduating Phi Beta Kappa, he entered law school. But World War II intervened, and he was killed in a plane crash at the Gulf of Paria, Venezuela, June 2, 1943.

MARSHALL GETS NFL FRANCHISE: ANNIVERSARY. July 9, 1932. The National Football League awarded its inactive Boston franchise to George Preston Marshall and a group of investors. The team used Braves Field in 1932 and was nicknamed the Braves. In 1933, the team played its home games at Fenway Park and changed its name to the Redskins. Four seasons later, the Redskins moved to Washington.

MOON PHASE: FULL MOON. July 9. Moon enters Full Moon phase at 12:01 PM, EDT.

NICKLAUS WINS FIRST BRITISH OPEN: ANNIVERSARY. July 9, 1966. Jack Nicklaus shot 282 at Muirfield to win his first British Open Championship. With this victory, Nicklaus joined Gene Sarazen, Ben Hogan and Gary Player as the only golfers to have won the four events comprising golf's modern Grand Slam: the Masters, the US Open, the British Open and the PGA Championship. Nicklaus won two other British Opens, in 1970 and 1978.

POST, WALLY: BIRTH ANNIVERSARY. July 9, 1929. Walter Charles (Wally) Post, baseball player born at St. Wendelin, OH. Post was a slugging outfielder who played in the major leagues from 1949 through 1964. He was considered one of the best home run hitters in the National League in the mid-1950s. Died at St. Henry, OH, Jan 6, 1982.

TRIPLE-A BASEBALL REALIGNS: ANNIVERSARY. July 9, 1997. Meeting in Des Moines, IA, for the annual Triple-A All-Star Game, owners of Triple-A minor league teams voted to realign from three leagues to two, effective with the start of the 1998 season. The vote kept teams of the International League and the Pacific Coast League together but split the American Association in two. One of the new leagues included the ten teams of the International League, Buffalo, Indianapolis and Louisville from the American Association and an expansion team in Durham, NC. The other new league included the ten teams of the Pacific Coast League, Iowa, Nashville, New Orleans, Oklahoma City and Omaha from the American Association and an expansion team in Memphis.

BIRTHDAYS TODAY

Michael Jay (Mike) Andrews, 55, former baseball player, born Los Angeles, CA, July 9, 1943.
Mark Steven Carreon, 35, baseball player, born Chicago, IL, July 9, 1963.
Tom Hanks, 42, actor (*A League of Their Own*), born Concord, CA, July 9, 1956.
Hector Headley Lopez, 69, former baseball player, born Colon, Panama, July 9, 1929.
Orenthal James (O.J.) Simpson, 51, former broadcaster, Heisman Trophy running back and Pro Football Hall of Fame running back, born San Francisco, CA, July 9, 1947.
Willie James Wilson, 43, former baseball player, born Birmingham, AL, July 9, 1955.

JULY 10 — FRIDAY

Day 191 — 174 Remaining

SPORTSCHASER OF THE DAY

What pitcher struck out five future Hall of Fame members consecutively in the 1934 All-Star Game?

AFRMA RAT AND MOUSE DISPLAY. July 10–26. Orange County Fair, Costa Mesa, CA. American Fancy Rat and Mice Association show exhibits rats and mice of "fancy" species that make good pets.

ASHE, ARTHUR: 55th BIRTH ANNIVERSARY. July 10, 1943. Arthur Robert Ashe, Jr, tennis player born at Richmond, VA. Ashe became a legend for his list of firsts as a black tennis player. He was chosen for the US Davis Cup team in 1963 and became captain in 1980. He won the US men's singles championship and US Open in 1968 and in 1975 the Men's Singles at Wimbledon. Ashe won a total of 33 career titles. In 1985 he was inducted into the International Tennis Hall of Fame. A social activist, Ashe worked to eliminate racism and stereotyping and was arrested numerous times while protesting. He helped create inner-city tennis programs for youths and wrote the three-volume *A Hard Road to Glory: A History of the African-American Athlete*. Aware that *USA Today* intended to publish an article revealing that he was infected with the AIDS virus, Ashe announced on Apr 8, 1992, that he probably contracted HIV through a transfusion during bypass surgery in 1983. In September of 1992 he began a $5 million fundraising effort on behalf of the Arthur Ashe Foundation for the Defeat of AIDS and during his last year campaigned for public awareness regarding the AIDS epidemic. Died at New York, NY, Feb 6, 1993.

DINOSAUR ROUNDUP RODEO. July 10–12. Vernal, UT. 46th annual presentation of one of the top PRCA rodeos, plus wrangler bull fights and fun for the entire family. Annually, the second weekend in July. Est attendance: 10,000. For info: Dinosaurland Travel Board, 25 E Main St, Vernal, UT 84078. Phone: (800) 421-9635 or (801) 789-1352.

HEYDLER, JOHN: BIRTH ANNIVERSARY. July 10, 1869. John Arnold Heydler, baseball executive born at Lafargeville, NY. Heydler was president of the National League from 1918 to 1934. He helped to found the Baseball Hall of Fame and, in 1929, suggested a rules change that became known as the designated hitter. Died at San Diego, CA, Apr 18, 1956.

HUBBELL STRIKES OUT FIVE HALL OF FAMERS: ANNIVERSARY. July 10, 1934. In baseball's second All-Star game, National League pitcher Carl Hubbell of the New York Giants struck out Babe Ruth, Lou Gehrig, Jimmie Foxx, Al Simmons and Joe Cronin in succession. All five were later inducted into the Hall of Fame. Hubbell gave up only two hits in three innings, but the American League won the game, 9–7.

ISUZU CELEBRITY GOLF CHAMPIONSHIP. July 10–12. Edgewood/Tahoe Golf Course, Lake Tahoe, NV. This three-day, 54-hole tournament features more than 70 current and former professional athletes and entertainment personalities who play to a USGA handicap of 10 or less. Past participants have included Johnny Bench, Michael Jordan, Dan Marino, Bryant Gumbel, Ivan Lendl, Mario Lemieux and many more. For info: NBC Sports, 30 Rockefeller Plaza, New York, NY 10112. Phone: (212) 664-5407.

KLEIN HITS FOUR HOME RUNS: ANNIVERSARY. July 10, 1936. Outfielder Chuck Klein of the Philadelphia Phillies became the fourth player in major league history to hit four home runs in one game. He completed the feat in a 10-inning game against the Pittsburgh Pirates in Forbes Field. The Phillies won, 9–6.

LOWE, BOBBY: 130th BIRTH ANNIVERSARY. July 10, 1868. Robert Lincoln (Bobby) Lowe, baseball player born at Pittsburgh, PA. Lowe was the first major league player to hit four home runs in a single game, accomplishing the feat in the second game of a Memorial Day doubleheader in 1894. He played for the great Boston teams of the 1890s. Died at Detroit, MI, Dec 8, 1951.

McNAMEE, GRAHAM: 110th BIRTH ANNIVERSARY. July 10, 1888. Graham McNamee, sportscaster born at Washington, DC. McNamee began his radio career in 1923 and made his reputation calling that year's World Series between the New York Giants and the New York Yankees. His breezy and informal style suited both the sporting events he covered and other news stories as well. His motto was, "I tell it as it looks to me." Died at New York, NY, May 9, 1942.

NFL TRAINING CAMPS—"THE CHEESE LEAGUE." July 10–Sept 1 (approximate). Football fans can enjoy football in summer in Wisconsin's "Cheese League" towns where training camps hold scrimmages and exhibition games. Four teams will train in Wisconsin starting in mid-July: the Chicago Bears at the University of Wisconsin-Platteville; the New Orleans Saints at the University of Wisconsin-La Crosse; the Kansas City Chiefs at the University of Wisconsin-River Falls; and the Green Bay Packers in De Pere. For schedule info: (414) 270-6200. WWW: http://tourism.state.wis.us

PROSPECT PARK FISHING CONTEST. July 10–18. Prospect Park, Brooklyn, NY. A contest for young anglers, 15

July 1998	S	M	T	W	T	F	S
				1	2	3	4
	5	6	7	8	9	10	11
	12	13	14	15	16	17	18
	19	20	21	22	23	24	25
	26	27	28	29	30	31	

and under, with prizes for the largest or most fish. At the Rustic Shelter lakeside, near the Kate Wollman Rink parking lot. Groups must register ahead of time. Est attendance: 700. For info: Public Info Mgr, Public Info Office—Hitchfield Villa, 95 Prospect Park W, Brooklyn, NY 11215. Phone: (718) 965-8954. Fax: (718) 965-8972. Email: prospect1@juno.com. WWW: http://www.prospectpark.com

SLOW-PITCH SOFTBALL TOURNAMENT. July 10–12. Elm Park, Williamsport, PA. 25th annual charitable tournament with 64 teams. Sponsor: Miller Lite. Est attendance: 8,500. For info: Don Phillips, Mid-State Beverage Co, Inc, 532 Sylvan Dr, South Williamsport, PA 17701. Phone: (717) 322-3331.

STATE GAMES OF OREGON. July 10–12. Portland, OR. Oregon's Olympic style amateur sports festival. Normally, the first weekend after July 4th. Est attendance: 16,000. For info: Kerry Duffy, Exec Dir, 4840 SW Western Ave, Ste 900, Beaverton, OR 97005. Phone: (503) 520-1319. Fax: (503) 520-9747.

WORLD CHAMPIONSHIP DOMINO TOURNAMENT. July 10–11. Kiwanis Community Bldg, Andalusia, AL. Prizes and trophies total $35,000. All profits from the tournament go to charity and to sponsor future tournaments. The primary charity is ASCCA, a camp for children and adults with disabilities. Annually, the second weekend in July. Sponsors: Andalusia Rotary Club, GTE, Columbia Andalusia Regional Hospital, Henderson Sewing Machine Co and Coca-Cola. For info: Charles G. Tomberlin, MD, Co-Chair, PO Box 276, Andalusia, AL 36420.

BIRTHDAYS TODAY

Eugene Leonard (Gene) Alley, 58, former baseball player, born Richmond, VA, July 10, 1940.

Martin Keevin (Marty) Cordova, 29, baseball player, born Las Vegas, NV, July 10, 1969.

Roger Timothy Craig, 38, former football player, born Davenport, IA, July 10, 1960.

Andre Nolan Dawson, 44, former baseball player, born Miami, FL, July 10, 1954.

Harold Abraham (Hal) McRae, 53, former baseball manager and player, born Avon Park, FL, July 10, 1945.

Sarah Virginia Wade, 53, former tennis player, born Bournemouth, England, July 10, 1945.

JULY 11 — SATURDAY

Day 192 — 173 Remaining

ALLISON, BOB: BIRTH ANNIVERSARY. July 11, 1934. William Robert (Bob) Allison, baseball player born at Raytown, MO. Allison played for the Washington Senators and the Minnesota Twins (1958–70) and formed half of a formidable slugging combination with Harmon Killebrew. He was Rookie of the Year in 1959 and hit a game-winning home run in Game 6 of the 1965 World Series. Died at Rio Verde, AZ, Apr 9, 1995.

BABE'S DEBUT IN MAJORS: ANNIVERSARY. July 11, 1914. Babe Ruth made his debut in major league baseball when he took the mound in Fenway Park for the Boston Red Sox against the Cleveland Indians. Ruth was relieved for the last two innings but was the winning pitcher in a 4–3 game.

BRAILLE RALLYE. July 11. Braille Institute Youth Center, Los Angeles, CA. Blind or visually impaired students from Braille Institute use braille or large-print instructions to navigate sighted drivers through more than 80 miles of LA streets. Celebrity drivers from television, radio and film help make this a special event. Annually, in July. For info: Braille Institute Communications Dept, 741 N

Vermont Ave, Los Angeles, CA 90029. Phone: (213) 663-1111, ext 276. Fax: (213) 663-0867.

CANADA: ANTIQUE AND CLASSIC BOAT SHOW. July 11. Sagamo Park, Lake Muskoka, Gravenhurst, Ontario. Largest in-water boat display (more than 100 boats) in Canada. Greatest variety of turn-of-the-century boats in North America. Antique Boat Flea Market, Field of Dreams and numerous boat-related land displays. Est attendance: 10,000. For info: The Antique & Classic Boat Society, Inc—Toronto Chapter, PO Box 305, Islington, Ontario, Canada M9A 4X3. Phone: (416) 299-3311. Fax: (416) 748-9767.

ELKHART GRAND PRIX AND MOTOR SPORTS WEEKEND. July 11–12. Elkhart, IN. The largest karting event race in the world follows a 4,900-ft course through downtown streets. More than 700 competitors from all over the world. Also features top-name race car drivers, antique and hot rod car show and swap meet, racing car displays, carnival and celebrity entertainment at the 9th annual race. Annually, the second weekend in July. Est attendance: 70,000. For info: Curt Paluzzi, Natl Kart News, 51535 Bittersweet Rd, Granger, IN 46530. Phone: (219) 277-0033. Fax: (219) 277-4279. Email: nkartnews@aol.com. WWW: http://www.nkn.com

FISHING HAS NO BOUNDARIES—MADISON. July 11–12. Lake Mendota, Madison, WI. A two-day fishing experience for persons with disabilities. Expected attendance of 100 participants and 300 volunteers. For info: FHNB, 4923 Hammersley Rd, Madison, WI 53711. Phone: (608) 271-0440.

GARDEN STATE GAMES. July 11–12. Rutgers University, New Brunswick, and Edison, NJ. Statewide Olympic-style multi-sport event featuring amateur athletes in 31 sports. Includes opening ceremonies, picnic, Health and Fitness Expo. Est attendance: 15,000. For info: Scott C. Bollwage, Exec Dir, Garden State Games, PO Box 6923, Edison, NJ 08818-6923. Phone: (908) 225-0303.

HAUGHTON, PERCY: BIRTH ANNIVERSARY. July 11, 1896. Percy Duncan Haughton, football player and coach and baseball executive born at New York, NY. Haughton played football and baseball at Harvard, coached at Cornell and returned to Harvard in 1908. Over nine years, his teams won 71 games, lost 7 and tied 5. He dominated the Eastern football scene, emphasizing quick execution and deception over brute strength. He was briefly president of the Boston Braves and served in the army during World War I. Died at New York, Oct 27, 1924.

HOLMES'S HITTING STREAK ENDS: ANNIVERSARY. July 11, 1945. Tommy Holmes of the Boston Braves went hitless, snapping his hitting streak at 37 games, then the National League record. Holmes's mark stood until 1978 when it was broken by Pete Rose.

RYAN STRIKES OUT 4,000th BATTER: ANNIVERSARY. July 11, 1985. Nolan Ryan of the Houston Astros became the first pitcher in baseball history to reach the 4,000 mark in career strikeouts when he made Danny Heep of the New York Mets his victim in the sixth inning. Ryan finished his career in 1993 with 5,714 strikeouts.

STOCK, MILT: 105th BIRTH ANNIVERSARY. July 11, 1893. Milton Joseph (Milt) Stock, baseball player and coach born at Chicago, IL. Stock was a major league infielder, but his most infamous moment came when he was the third base coach for the Brooklyn Dodgers in 1950. In the season's last game, he waved baserunner Cal Abrams home with the score tied in the ninth inning. Abrams was thrown out, and the Philadelphia Phillies won the game and the pennant in the tenth inning. Died at Fairhope, AL, July 16, 1977.

BIRTHDAYS TODAY

Andrew Jason (Andy) Ashby, 31, baseball player, born Kansas City, MO, July 11, 1967.

Billy Manual Ashley, 28, baseball player, born Taylor, MI, July 11, 1970.

Allan (Al) MacInnis, 35, hockey player, born Inverness, Nova Scotia, Canada, July 11, 1963.

Nathan Edward (Ed) Ott, 47, former baseball player, born Muncy, PA, July 11, 1951.

Leon Spinks, 45, former heavyweight champion boxer, born St. Louis, MO, July 11, 1953.

Rodney (Rod) Strickland, 32, basketball player, born New York, NY, July 11, 1966.

JULY 12 — SUNDAY

Day 193 — 172 Remaining

DISCO DEMOLITION NIGHT: ANNIVERSARY. July 12, 1979. The Chicago White Sox staged "Disco Demolition Night" as a promotion between games of a doubleheader against the Detroit Tigers. Fans, encouraged to bring disco records to the ballpark so that they could be destroyed, surged onto the field and caused such destruction that the second game had to be forfeited to the Tigers.

FIRST BLACKS IN ALL-STAR GAME: ANNIVERSARY. July 12, 1949. Jackie Robinson, Roy Campanella and Don Newcombe of the Brooklyn Dodgers and Larry Doby of the Cleveland Indians became the first black players to appear in baseball's All-Star game. The American League won the game, played in Ebbets Field, 11–7.

GARDEN STATE GAMES. July 12–13. Edison, NJ. Full-court, adult basketball tournament in three divisions: Open (over 20), Masters (over 30) and Seniors (over 50). Gold, silver and bronze medals. For info: Bill Clancy, Club Basketball, 215 North Ave W, Ste 205, Westfield, NJ 07090. Phone: (908) 756-4502. Fax: (908) 756-9698.

JONES WINS GRAND SLAM: ANNIVERSARY. July 12, 1930. Bobby Jones won the US Open golf championship by two strokes over Macdonald Smith at the Interlachen Country Club in Hopkins, MN. Having already won the British Open, the British Amateur and the US Amateur, Jones became the only golfer to win the Grand Slam.

NATIONAL THERAPEUTIC RECREATION WEEK. July 12–18. To increase awareness of therapeutic recreation programs and services, and to expand leisure opportunities for individuals with disabilities in their local communities. Annually, the second week in July. For info: Natl Therapeutic Recreation Soc, Ahren's NRPA Institute, 22377 Belmont Ridge Rd, Ashburn, VA 20148. Phone: (800) 626-NRPA. Email: ntrsnrpa@aol.com. WWW: http://www.nrpa.org

NEW YORK GOLDEN ARMS TOURNAMENT–QUEENS. July 12. Queens Festival, Flushing Meadows Park, Queens, NY. Arm wrestling competition held at the festival determines borough winner who will compete in the Empire State Golden Arms Tournament of Champions on Oct 22. For info: New York Arm Wrestling Assn, Inc, 200-14 45th Dr, Bayside, NY 11361. Phone and Fax: (718) 544-4592.

July *1998*	S	M	T	W	T	F	S
				1	2	3	4
	5	6	7	8	9	10	11
	12	13	14	15	16	17	18
	19	20	21	22	23	24	25
	26	27	28	29	30	31	

YOUNG WINS 300th GAME: ANNIVERSARY. July 12, 1901. Pitcher Denton True ("Cy") Young won the 300th game of his career, defeating the Philadelphia Athletics, 5–3. Young pitched in the major leagues from 1890 through 1911 and finished with 511 victories, more than anyone else.

YOUTH RODEO. July 12–13 (tentative). Dent County Fairgrounds, Salem, MO. Nationally approved youth rodeo, calf and goat roping, barrel racing, bull dogging and other events. Annually, the second weekend in July. Est attendance: 6,000. For info: Salem Chamber of Commerce, PO Box 385, Salem, MO 65560. Phone: (573) 729-6900. Fax: (573) 729-8780. Email: salcofc@fidnet.com. WWW: http://www.somo.com/salem

BIRTHDAYS TODAY

Ronald Ray (Ron) Fairly, 60, broadcaster and former baseball player, born Macon, GA, July 12, 1938.

Michael Anthony (Mike) Munoz, 33, baseball player, born Baldwin Park, CA, July 12, 1965.

Paul Theron Silas, 55, former basketball player and coach, born Prescott, AZ, July 12, 1943.

Richard Simmons, 50, TV personality, weight loss guru, author, born New Orleans, LA, July 12, 1948.

Mario Melvin Soto, 42, former baseball player, born Bani, Dominican Republic, July 12, 1956.

Kristi Tsuya Yamaguchi, 27, Olympic gold medal figure skater, born Hayward, CA, July 12, 1971.

JULY 13 — MONDAY

Day 194 — 171 Remaining

CHASE'S SPORTSQUOTE OF THE DAY

"Pro football gave me a good sense of perspective to enter politics. I'd already been booed, cheered, cut, sold, traded and hung in effigy." —Jack Kemp

COVALESKI, STANLEY: BIRTH ANNIVERSARY. July 13, 1889. Stanley Anthony Covaleski, Baseball Hall of Fame pitcher born Stanislaus Kowalewski at Shamokin, PA. Covaleski won 215 games in his career including three for the Cleveland Indians in the 1920 World Series. A spitballer, he was allowed to continue using that pitch after it was banned in 1920. Inducted into the Hall of Fame in 1969. Died at South Bend, IN, Mar 20, 1984.

HANKS, SAM: BIRTH ANNIVERSARY. July 13, 1914. Samuel (Sam) Hanks, Jr, auto racer born at Columbus, OH. Hanks enjoyed a successful career in midget cars, stock cars and Indy racing. He won the 1957 Indianapolis 500 at age 43, then the oldest driver to win that race. Died at Pacific Palisades, CA, June 27, 1994.

NATIONAL HIGH SCHOOL FINALS RODEO. July 13–19 (tentative). Gillette, WY. More than 1,500 teenage contestants from North America will compete in rodeo events patterned after official Pro-Rodeo Association guidelines. Annually, the third week in July. Est attendance: 95,000. For info: Natl High School Rodeo Assn, 11178 N Huron, Ste 7, Denver, CO 80234. Phone: (303) 452-0820 or (800) 46-NHSRA. Fax: (303) 452-0912.

NFL OWNERS TRADE TEAMS: ANNIVERSARY. July 13, 1972. Robert Irsay and Carroll Rosenbloom, NFL owners, swapped their teams in a professional sports first. Irsay paid $19 million to acquire the Los Angeles Rams from the estate of the late Dan Reeves. He then transferred ownership of the Rams to Carroll Rosenbloom in exchange for the Baltimore Colts.

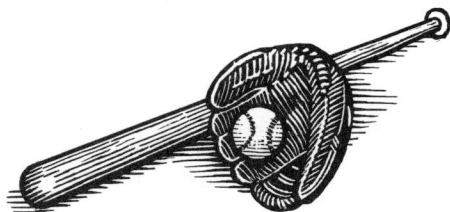

RUTH HITS 700th HOME RUN: ANNIVERSARY. July 13, 1934. Babe Ruth hit the 700th home run of his career against Tommy Bridges of the Detroit Tigers. The Yankees won the game, 4–2.

SHORTEST WIMBLEDON FINAL: ANNIVERSARY. July 13, 1881. William Renshaw won the first of his seven straight Wimbledon championships by defeating two-time defending champion John T. Hartley. Renshaw won, 6–0, 6–1, 6–1, in 37 minutes, the shortest Wimbledon men's final ever.

US AMATEUR PUBLIC LINKS (GOLF) CHAMPIONSHIP. July 13–18. Torrey Pines Golf Course, San Diego, CA. For info: US Golf Assn, Golf House, Championship Dept, Far Hills, NJ 07931. Phone: (908) 234-2300. Fax: (908) 234-9687.

WYNN WINS 300TH GAME: 35th ANNIVERSARY. July 13, 1963. Pitcher Early Wynn, 43 years old, won the 300th and last game of his career, pitching the first five innings of the Cleveland Indians' 7–4 victory over the Kansas City A's.

BIRTHDAYS TODAY

Jack Delane Aker, 58, former baseball player, born Tulare, CA, July 13, 1940.
Robert (Bob) Carpenter, 35, hockey player, born Beverly, MA, July 13, 1963.
Ruben Gomez, 71, former baseball player, born Arroyo, Puerto Rico, July 13, 1927.
John French (Jack) Kemp, 63, former US vice-presidential candidate (1996), former Secretary of Housing and Urban Development and former football player, born Los Angeles, CA, July 13, 1935.
Patrick Leland (Pat) Rapp, 31, baseball player, born Jennings, LA, July 13, 1967.
Erno Rubik, 54, inventor of the Rubik's Cube, born Budapest, Hungary, July 13, 1944.
Michael Spinks, 42, former heavyweight champion boxer, born St. Louis, MO, July 13, 1956.
David O'Neil Thompson, 44, Basketball Hall of Fame guard, born Shelby, NC, July 13, 1954.
Anthony Jerome ("Spud") Webb, 35, basketball player, born Dallas, TX, July 13, 1963.

JULY 14 — TUESDAY
Day 195 — 170 Remaining

AARON HITS 500TH HOME RUN: 30th ANNIVERSARY. July 14, 1968. Henry Aaron of the Atlanta Braves hit the 500th home run of his career, connecting off left-hander Mike McCormick of the San Francisco Giants. Aaron ended his career as baseball's all-time home run champ with 755 roundtrippers to his credit.

BASTILLE DAY MOONLIGHT GOLF TOURNAMENT. July 14. Greenleaf Point Golf Course, Fort McNair, Washington, DC. After a cookout, teams of four tee off wearing glow-in-the-dark necklaces and hitting glow-in-the-dark balls. Participants are given membership into the National Capital Moonlight Golf Association. Annually, July 14. For info: Ft McNair Sports Center, Bldg 17, 4th & P St SW, Washington, DC 20319-5050. Phone: (202) 685-3138.

CATCHER-UMP BROTHER DUO: ANNIVERSARY. July 14, 1972. In a first for major league baseball, Tom Haller was the catcher for the Detroit Tigers in a game for which his brother Bill was the home plate umpire.

CITATION PASSES $1 MILLION MARK: ANNIVERSARY. July 14, 1951. Citation, winner of the 1948 Triple Crown, became the first horse to pass the $1 million mark in career earnings by winning the Hollywood Gold Cup after which the colt was retired. Citation raced 45 times, won $1,085,760 and finished out of the money only once.

MATHEWS HITS 500th HOME RUN: ANNIVERSARY. July 14, 1967. Eddie Mathews of the Houston Astros hit the 500th home run of his career off Juan Marichal of the San Francisco Giants. Houston beat the Giants, 8–6. Mathews played in the majors from 1952 through 1968 and finished with 512 homers.

MURPHY, JOHNNY: 90th BIRTH ANNIVERSARY. July 14, 1908. John Joseph (Johnny) Murphy, baseball player and executive born at New York, NY. Murphy was a star relief pitcher for the New York Yankees from 1934 through 1946. He helped form the Major League Baseball Players Association and served as general manager of the New York Mets. Died at New York, Jan 14, 1970.

BIRTHDAYS TODAY

Lawrence Columbus ("Crash") Davis, 79, former baseball player, born Canon, GA, July 14, 1919.
Gerald Rudolph Ford (born Leslie King), 85, 38th US President, amateur golfer, born Omaha, NE, July 14, 1913.
Roosevelt (Rosey) Grier, 66, actor and former football player, born Cuthbert, GA, July 14, 1932.
Derrick Brant May, 30, baseball player, born Rochester, NY, July 14, 1968.
Steven Michael (Steve) Stone, 51, broadcaster and former baseball player, born Euclid, OH, July 14, 1947.
Robin Mark Ventura, 31, baseball player, born Santa Maria, CA, July 14, 1967.
Earl Craig Williams, Jr, 50, former baseball player, born Newark, NJ, July 14, 1948.

☆ ☆ ☆

JULY 15 — WEDNESDAY
Day 196 — 169 Remaining

ANTONELLI, JOHN: BIRTH ANNIVERSARY. July 15, 1915. John Lawrence Antonelli, baseball player born at Memphis, TN. Not the pitcher who played in the 1950s, this Antonelli was an infielder who played with the St. Louis Cardinals and the Philadelphia Phillies in the 1940s and then became a minor league manager. Died at Memphis, Apr 18, 1990.

DROPO GETS TWELVE STRAIGHT HITS: ANNIVERSARY. July 15, 1952. Walt Dropo of the Detroit Tigers tripled, singled and doubled in his first three at-bats in the second game of a doubleheader against the Washington Senators. The three hits gave him 12 in a row without making out, tying the major league record set by Mike ("Pinky") Higgins in 1938. Dropo went five-for-five the day before against the New York Yankees and four-for-four in the first game of the twin bill. His hit streak ended when he fouled out in his fourth at-bat, but he finished the day with another single.

FIRST NL NO-HITTER: ANNIVERSARY. July 15, 1876. Pitcher George Washington Bradley of St. Louis hurled the first no-hitter in the National League, defeating the Hartford Blues, 2–0.

POWELL, JAKE: 90th BIRTH ANNIVERSARY. July 15, 1908. Alvin Jacob (Jake) Powell, baseball player born at Silver Spring, MD. Powell was suspended in 1938 for making racially insensitive remarks during a radio interview. He committed suicide while being investigated on a bad-check charge. Died at Washington, DC, Nov 4, 1948.

<u>*BIRTHDAYS TODAY*</u>

Kim Alexis, 38, model, born Lockport, NY, July 15, 1960.

Donn Alvin Clendenon, 63, former baseball player, born Neosho, MO, July 15, 1935.

Lolita Davidovich, 37, actress (*Cobb*), born London, Ont, Canada, July 15, 1961.

Alexander George (Alex) Karras, 63, former broadcaster and football player, born Gary, IN, July 15, 1935.

Kirt Dean Manwaring, 33, baseball player, born Elmira, NY, July 15, 1965.

Khalid Reeves, 26, basketball player, born New York, NY, July 15, 1972.

Thomas Michael (Mike) Shannon, 59, broadcaster and former baseball player, born St. Louis, MO, July 15, 1939.

JULY 16 — THURSDAY
Day 197 — 168 Remaining

ADIOS BUTLER WINS CANE PACE: ANNIVERSARY. July 16, 1959. Adios Butler, driven by Clint Hodgins, won the Cane Pace, the first jewel in pacing's triple crown, at Yonkers Raceway. Adios Oregon finished second. Adios Butler went on to win the Messenger Stakes and the Little Brown Jug to become the first triple crown winner in pacing history.

CANADA: EXPLOITS VALLEY SALMON FESTIVAL. July 16–20. Grand Falls–Windsor, Newfoundland. The Exploits Valley Salmon Festival is the largest festival in Newfoundland and Labrador and consists of five days of nonstop activities. A slow-pitch softball tournament, horse show, a fishing derby, antique auto show, major rock concert, gospel concert, dances, a salmon dinner, craft show, a major children's entertainer, carnival rides, games and food booths. For the past five years this event has been named by the American Bus Association as one of the top 100 events in North America. Annually, the third weekend in July. Est attendance: 30,000. For info: Exploits Valley Salmon Fest, PO Box 439, Grand Falls-Windsor, Nfld, Canada A2A 2J8. Phone: (709) 489-0450. Fax: (709) 489-0454.

CAPITOL CURLING SUMMER BONSPIEL. July 16–18 (tentative). Bismarck, ND. Broaden your sport horizons by attending the 56-team open summer bonspiel at one of the finest curling facilities in the US. For info: Bismarck/Mandan Convention & Visitors Bureau, PO Box 2274, Bismarck, ND 58502. Phone: (800) 767-3555. Fax: (701) 222-0647.

DUROCHER JUMPS TO GIANTS: 50th ANNIVERSARY. July 16, 1948. After 8½ seasons as manager of the Brooklyn Dodgers, Leo Durocher resigned abruptly to accept the manager's job with the New York Giants. With Durocher at the helm, the Giants won two pennants, in 1951 by defeating the Dodgers in a playoff and in 1954 when they swept the Cleveland Indians in the World Series.

July *1998*	S	M	T	W	T	F	S
				1	2	3	4
	5	6	7	8	9	10	11
	12	13	14	15	16	17	18
	19	20	21	22	23	24	25
	26	27	28	29	30	31	

ENGLAND: OPEN (GOLF) CHAMPIONSHIP. July 16–19. Royal Birkdale Golf Course, Birkdale, England. One of professional golf's four major championships, known in the US as the British Open. Est attendance: 180,000. For info: The Secretary, St. Andrews, Royal and Ancient Golf Club, St. Andrews, Scotland KY16 9JD. Phone: (44) (133) 472-2112. Fax: (44) (133) 444-7580.

JACKSON, SHOELESS JOE: BIRTH ANNIVERSARY. July 16, 1889. Joseph Jefferson ("Shoeless Joe") Jackson, baseball player born at Brandon Mills, SC. Jackson's legendary excellence as one of the game's finest righthand hitters is besmirched by his alleged involvement in the Black Sox scandal of 1919. Jackson stood accused of participating in the conspiracy to throw the World Series, and he, along with seven teammates, was banned for life. Died at Greenville, SC, Dec 5, 1951.

McGRAW APPOINTED GIANTS MANAGER: 95th ANNIVERSARY. July 16, 1902. Midway through the season, John McGraw resigned as manager of the American League's Baltimore Orioles and was immediately named manager of the New York Giants of the National League, a position he held into the 1932 season. McGraw's teams won 10 pennants and three World Series.

MOON PHASE: LAST QUARTER. July 16. Moon enters Last Quarter phase at 11:13 AM, EDT.

RUTH BREAKS OWN RECORD: ANNIVERSARY. July 16, 1920. In his first season with the New York Yankees, Babe Ruth hit his 30th home run to break his own record, set in 1919 as a member of the Boston Red Sox. Ruth finished the year with 54 home runs. He hit 59 in 1921 and 60 in 1927.

SPORTS CLUB DAYS©98. July 16 (also Dec 16). These days celebrate sports clubs of all kinds: all the organizations that help active people engage in the sports and recreational activities they love. For further info send $2 to cover cost of copying and postage to: Adrienne Koopersmith, 1437 W Rosemont, 1W, Chicago, IL 60660-1437. Phone: (773) 743-5341. Fax: (773) 743-5395. Email: kooper@interaccess.com.

THREE RIVERS STADIUM OPENS: ANNIVERSARY. July 16, 1970. The Cincinnati Reds defeated the Pittsburgh Pirates, 3–2, to spoil the Pirates' debut in their new ballpark, Three Rivers Stadium.

<u>*BIRTHDAYS TODAY*</u>

Gary Allan Anderson, 39, football player, born Parys, Orange Free State, South Africa, July 16, 1959.

Margaret Smith Court, 56, former tennis player, born Albury, New South Wales, Australia, July 16, 1942.

Eddie Gene Fisher, 62, former baseball player, born Shreveport, LA, July 16, 1936.

Claude Lemieux, 33, hockey player, born Buckingham, Quebec, Canada, July 16, 1965.

Terry Lee Pendleton, 38, baseball player, born Los Angeles, CA, July 16, 1960.

Barry Sanders, 30, Heisman Trophy running back, born Wichita, KS, July 16, 1968.

Charles Daniel Smith, 33, basketball player, born Bridgeport, CT, July 16, 1965.

William Joseph VanLandingham, 28, baseball player, born Columbia, TN, July 16, 1970.

JULY 17 — FRIDAY
Day 198 — 167 Remaining

SPORTSCHASER OF THE DAY

What team stopped Joe DiMaggio's 56-game hitting streak in 1941?

BARNARD, ERNEST: BIRTH ANNIVERSARY. July 17, 1874. Ernest Sargent Barnard, baseball executive born at West Columbia, WV. Barnard, president of the Cleveland Indians, was named president of the American League after league owners ousted Ban Johnson in 1927. Reelected to a five-year term in 1930, he served only a few months. Died at Rochester, MN, Mar 27, 1931.

BIG SKY STATE GAMES. July 17–19. Billings, MT. An Olympic-styled festival for Montana citizens. This statewide multisport program is designed to inspire people of all ages and skill levels to develop their physical and competitive abilities to the height of their potential through participation in fitness activities. Est attendance: 12,000. For info: Big Sky State Games, Box 7136, Billings, MT 59103-7136. Phone: (406) 254-7426. Fax: (406) 254-7439. WWW: http://www.wtp.net/stgames

CANADA: SPORTSMAN RIVER ROAR POWERBOAT RACES. July 17–19. South Saskatchewan River, downtown Saskatoon, Saskatchewan, Canada. Formula 1 powerboats race in this internationally acclaimed Professional Outboard Performance Race Tour. Professional racers compete with boats capable of reaching speeds up to 130 mph. Held in conjunction with Saskatchewan Place's Taste of Saskatchewan where over 20 restaurants and organizations serve up their finest cuisine. Est attendance: 60,000. For info: (306) 665-2001 or Tourism Saskatchewan, 500—1900 Albert St, Canada S4P 4L9. Email: travel.info@sasktourism.sk.ca. WWW: http://www.sasktourism.com

DAYS OF '47 WORLD CHAMPION RODEO. July 17–24. Delta Center, Salt Lake City, UT. One of the largest rodeos in the world, this PRCA-approved rodeo attracts world-champion competitors for seven days of the roughest, toughest rodeos around. Includes the largest all-horse parade in the nation with more than 1,200 horses from across the US (July 17). Est attendance: 67,000. For info: Flip Harmon, Mktg, Days of '47 Rodeo Chair, PO Box 16507, Salt Lake City, UT 84116-0507. Phone: (801) 250-3890.

DIMAGGIO'S HITTING STREAK ENDS: ANNIVERSARY. July 17, 1941. Joe DiMaggio's 56-game hitting streak came to an end as the Yankees centerfielder was held hitless by pitchers Al Smith and Jim Bagby of the Cleveland Indians. The Yankees won, 4–3, but DiMaggio got no hits in four at-bats.

DOC MEDICH TO THE RESCUE: 20th ANNIVERSARY. July 17, 1978. Pitcher George ("Doc") Medich of the Texas Rangers saved the life of a fan suffering a heart attack before a game in Baltimore against the Orioles. Medich, a medical student, administered cardiac first aid until additional help arrived.

GIBSON STRIKES OUT 3,000: ANNIVERSARY. July 17, 1974. Bob Gibson of the St. Louis Cardinals struck out Cesar Geronimo of the Cincinnati Reds to become the second pitcher in baseball history, after Walter Johnson, to strike out 3,000 batters. Gibson pitched in the major leagues from 1959 through 1975 and finished with 3,117 strikeouts.

JOHNSON, DERON: 60th BIRTH ANNIVERSARY. July 17, 1938. Deron Roger Johnson, baseball player born at San Diego, CA. Johnson played 16 years in the majors for nine teams. He hit 245 home runs and led the National League in 1965 in runs batted in. Died at Poway, CA, Apr 23, 1992.

SHOW ME STATE GAMES. July 17–19. Columbia, MO. (Also July 24–26.) An Olympic-style athletic festival for Missouri citizens. This statewide multisport program is designed to inspire Missourians of every age and skill level to develop their physical and competitive abilities to the height of their potential through participation in fitness activities. Annually, the last two full weekends in July. Est attendance: 48,000. For info: Gary Filbert, Exec Dir, Show Me State Games, 404 Jesse Hall, Columbia, MO 65211. Phone: (573) 882-2101. Fax: (573) 884-4004. Email: show4games@aol.com. WWW: http://www.smsg.org

TWO TWINS TRIPLE PLAYS: ANNIVERSARY. July 17, 1990. The Minnesota Twins became the first team in major league history to record two triple plays in the same game when they turned the trick against the Boston Red Sox. But the Red Sox won, 1–0.

Doc Medich

BIRTHDAYS TODAY

Louis (Lou) Boudreau, 81, former broadcaster and Baseball Hall of Fame manager and shortstop, born Harvey, IL, July 17, 1917.

Calbert Nathaniel Cheaney, 27, basketball player, born Evansville, IN, July 17, 1971.

Donald Eulon (Don) Kessinger, 56, former baseball manager and player, born Forrest City, AR, July 17, 1942.

Roy David McMillan, 68, former baseball manager and player, born Bonham, TX, July 17, 1930.

Tommy Soderstrom, 29, hockey player, born Stockholm, Sweden, July 17, 1969.

Robert Thomas (Bobby) Thigpen, 35, former baseball player, born Tallahassee, FL, July 17, 1963.

☆   ☆   ☆

JULY 18 — SATURDAY
Day 199 — 166 Remaining

ANTIQUE AUTO SHOW. July 18. Wheaton Village, Millville, NJ. 15th annual show, held rain or shine. Est attendance: 1,500. For info: Wheaton Village, 1501 Glasstown Rd, Millville, NJ 08332. Phone: (609) 825-6800 or (800) 998-4552. Fax: (609) 825-2410. Email: mail@wheatonvillage.org. WWW: http://www.wheatonvillage.org

CHICAGO GOLF CLUB: 105th ANNIVERSARY. July 18, 1893. The first 18-hole golf course in America, laid out by Charles Blair MacDonald, was incorporated in Wheaton, IL. MacDonald was the architect of many of the early US courses which he attempted to model on the best in Scotland and England. It was his belief that at each tee a golfer should face a hazard at the average distance of his shot.

EVANS, CHICK: BIRTH ANNIVERSARY. July 18, 1890. Charles (Chick) Evans, Jr, golfer born at Indianapolis, IN. Evans competed as an amateur against the best professionals in the early 20th century, winning the US Open in 1916. In the 1920s he established the Chick Evans Caddie Foundation, later called the Evans Scholarship Fund, that has helped send over 4,000 people to college. Died at Chicago, IL, Nov 6, 1979.

FISHING HAS NO BOUNDARIES–SANDUSKY. July 18–19 (tentative). Lake Erie, Sandusky, OH. A two-day fishing experience for disabled persons. Any disability, age, sex, race, etc, eligible. Fishing with experienced guides attended by 75 participants and 200 volunteers. For info: Fishing Has No Boundaries, 3807 Deer Path Dr, Sandusky, OH 44870. Phone: (419) 626-6211.

FORBES TRIAL ENDS IN HUNG JURY: ANNIVERSARY. July 18, 1975. The trial of Boston Bruins hockey player Dave Forbes, indicted for excessive force during a game on Jan 4 when he hit Henry Boucha of the Detroit Red Wings with his stick, ended in a hung jury. The prosecution decided not to seek a retrial.

GOODWILL GAMES OPEN. July 18. New York, NY. The Fourth Goodwill Games stage their opening ceremonies with competition in 12 sports beginning on July 19. The Games are an international competition founded in 1986 by sports mogul Ted Turner. In 1998, 1,300 athletes from more than 60 countries will compete. For info: Media Relations, Goodwill Games, Turner Sports, Atlanta, GA 30343. Phone: (404) 827-4786.

LEADVILLE MOSQUITO MARATHON. July 18. Leadville, CO. Two races—a 26.6-mile marathon leaving from downtown Leadville and traveling east over North America's highest pass (Mosquito Pass) to within five miles of Fairplay, then back and a 15-mile run on the same course. 7th annual. For info: Greater Leadville Area Chamber of Commerce, PO Box 861, Leadville, CO 80461. Phone: (719) 486-3900 or (800) 933-3901. Fax: (719) 486-8478. Email: leadville@sni.net. WWW: http://www.colorado.com/leadville

MATTINGLY TIES LONG'S RECORD: ANNIVERSARY. July 18, 1987. First baseman Don Mattingly of the New York Yankees hit a home run in his eighth consecutive game, thereby tying the major league record set in 1956 by first baseman Dale Long of the Pittsburgh Pirates.

MAYS GETS 3,000 HITS: ANNIVERSARY. July 18, 1970. Willie Mays of the San Francisco Giants got the 3,000th hit of his career, a single off pitcher Mike Wegener of the Montreal Expos in a 10–1 Giants' victory. Mays played in the major leagues from 1951 through 1973 and finished with 3,283 hits.

NATIONAL SPORTING ASSOCIATION WORLD SPORTS EXPO '98. July 18–20. McCormick Place, Chicago, IL. The international kickoff of the exposition where sporting goods retailers will see 1999 products. Est atten-

July	S	M	T	W	T	F	S
1998				1	2	3	4
	5	6	7	8	9	10	11
	12	13	14	15	16	17	18
	19	20	21	22	23	24	25
	26	27	28	29	30	31	

dance: 90,000. For info: Larry Weindruch, Dir of Communications, Natl Sporting Goods Assn, 1699 Wall St, Mt Prospect, IL 60056-5780. Phone: (847) 439-4000. Fax: (847) 849-0111. Email: nsga1699@aol.com. WWW: http://www.nsgachicagoshow.com

WALCOTT WINS HEAVYWEIGHT TITLE: ANNIVERSARY. July 18, 1951. Jersey Joe Walcott won the heavyweight championship of the world when he knocked out Ezzard Charles in the seventh round of a fight at Forbes Field in Pittsburgh. Walcott, at 37 the oldest fighter to win the crown, kept the title until he was knocked out by Rocky Marciano on Sept 23, 1952.

WORLD CHAMPIONSHIP CARDBOARD BOAT RACE. July 18. Sandy Beach, Heber Springs, AR. Cardboard boats which defy natural laws float and race on Greers Ferry Lake; open to all comers; winner may compete in the Annual America's International Cardboard Cup Challenge; other activities scheduled all day. 11th annual race. Est attendance: 6,500. For info: Dianne Williams, Exec Dir, Chamber of Commerce, 1001 W Main, Heber Springs, AR 72543. Phone: (501) 362-2444 or (800) 77-HEBER. Fax: (501) 362-9953. Email: hebercoc@arkansas.net. WWW: http://www.heber-springs.com

BIRTHDAYS TODAY

Tenley Albright, 63, Olympic gold medal figure skater, born Newton Center, MA, July 18, 1935.

Richard Totten (Dick) Button, 69, broadcaster and Olympic gold medal figure skater, born Englewood, NJ, July 18, 1929.

Nicholas Alexander (Nick) Faldo, 41, golfer, born Welwyn Garden City, England, July 18, 1957.

Michael Lewis (Mike) Greenwell, 35, former baseball player, born Louisville, KY, July 18, 1963.

Anfernee Deon ("Penny") Hardaway, 26, basketball player, born Memphis, TN, July 18, 1972.

Calvin Peete, 55, golfer, born Detroit, MI, July 18, 1943.

Joseph Paul (Joe) Torre, 58, baseball manager and former player, born New York, NY, July 18, 1940.

JULY 19 — SUNDAY
Day 200 — 165 Remaining

APPLING HITS CRACKER JACK HOME RUN: 15th ANNIVERSARY. July 19, 1982. In the first Oldtimers' All-Star Classic, sponsored by Cracker Jack and played at RFK Stadium in Washington, DC, 75-year-old Luke Appling led off the game with a home run against pitcher Warren Spahn.

BARR, GEORGE: BIRTH ANNIVERSARY. July 19, 1892. George McKinley Barr, baseball umpire and executive born at Scammon, KS. Barr umpired in the National

League from 1931 through 1949, working two All-Star games and four World Series. In 1935, he opened the first professional umpires school in Hot Springs, AK. Died at Tulsa, OK, July 26,1974.

CY YOUNG WINS 500th GAME: ANNIVERSARY. July 19, 1910. Denton True ("Cy") Young of the Cleveland Naps of the American League won the 500th game of his pitching career, defeating the Washington Nationals, 5–4, in 11 innings. Young ended his career with 511 wins.

DAVIS, HARRY: 125th BIRTH ANNIVERSARY. July 19, 1873. Harry H. Davis, baseball player and manager born at Philadelphia, PA. Davis played for several teams around the turn of the century and once was traded between games of a doubleheader. As a member of the Philadelphia Athletics, he led the American League in home runs in 1904, 1905, 1906 and 1907. Died at Philadelphia, Aug 11, 1947.

FIRST UNASSISTED TRIPLE PLAY: ANNIVERSARY. July 19, 1909. Cleveland Blues shortstop Neal Ball recorded the first unassisted triple play in American League history in a game against the Boston Pilgrims. Ball caught a line drive hit by Amby McConnell, stepped on second base to double off Heine Wagner and tagged Jake Stahl before he could get back to first base. Ball also hit a home run as Cleveland won, 6–1.

KOENIG, MARK: BIRTH ANNIVERSARY. July 19, 1902. Mark Anthony Koenig, baseball player born at San Francisco, CA. Koenig was the last living member of the 1927 New York Yankees, considered by many to be baseball's greatest team. He also played for the Chicago Cubs and the New York Giants. Died at Willows, CA, Apr 22, 1993.

REGISTER'S ANNUAL GREAT BICYCLE RIDE ACROSS IOWA. July 19–25. A weeklong bicycle ride across Iowa with 7,500 riders from around the country. Annually, the last full week of July. After Nov 1 and before Mar 1 send a business-size self-addressed, stamped envelope to address below. Sponsor: *Des Moines Register*. Est attendance: 7,500. For info: Event Mktg Mgr, The *Des Moines Register*, 715 Locust, Des Moines, IA 50309. Phone: (515) 284-8282. Fax: (515) 284-8138. WWW: http://www.ragbrai.org

TY COBB GETS 4,000TH HIT: ANNIVERSARY. July 19, 1927. Tyrus Raymond (Ty) Cobb of the Philadelphia Athletics doubled off the glove of outfielder Harry Heilman of the Detroit Tigers, Cobb's old team, to record the 4,000th hit of his career.

WORLD CHAMPIONSHIP SNOWMOBILE WATER-CROSS. July 17–19. Grantsburg, WI. 22nd annual. Snowmobilers from around the world will compete on open water in oval, sprint and drag competitions. Rated one of the 10 best racing events in the US. For info: Wisconsin Dept of Tourism, PO Box 7976, Madison, WI 53707. Phone: (715) 463-5466. Fax: (414) 270-7170. Email: tourism@laughlin.com.

BIRTHDAYS TODAY

Philip Joseph (Phil) Cavaretta, 82, former baseball manager and player, born Chicago, IL, July 19, 1916.
Teresa Edwards, 34, basketball player, born Cairo, GA, July 19, 1964.
William Frederick (Billy) Gardner, 71, former manager and baseball player, born Waterford, CT, July 19, 1927.
Ilie Nastase, 52, former tennis player, born Bucharest, Romania, July 19, 1946.
Vincente Palacios, 35, former baseball player, born Veracruz, Mexico, July 19, 1963.
David Vincent Segui, 32, baseball player, born Kansas City, MO, July 19, 1966.

JULY 20 — MONDAY
Day 201 — 164 Remaining

CHASE'S SPORTSQUOTE OF THE DAY

"This particular game is a game of players. Your job is to try to direct them, try to teach them, try to get them to understand what it takes to go where they all want to go." —Chuck Daly

BASEBALL DECLARED NON-ESSENTIAL OCCUPATION: 80th ANNIVERSARY. July 20, 1918. Secretary of War Newton D. Baker ruled that baseball was a non-essential occupation during World War I. He stated that all players of draft age should seek "employment to aid successful prosecution of the war or shoulder guns and fight." On July 26, Baker allowed baseball to continue until Sept 1. Nearly 250 ballplayers entered the armed services.

FANS CHARGED TO SEE BASEBALL: 140th ANNIVERSARY. July 20, 1858. Approximately 1,500 baseball fans were charged 50 cents each to watch a baseball game between the New York All-Stars and a Brooklyn team at Fashion Race Course on Long Island. The All-Stars won this first game with an admission charge, 22–18.

FIRST PGA MEDAL PLAY CHAMPIONSHIP: 40th ANNIVERSARY. July 20, 1958. The PGA championship contested at match play since its inception in 1916 switched to medal or stroke play. Dow Finsterwald, runner-up in 1957 to Lionel Hebert, defeated Billy Casper by two strokes.

LAST PITCHER TO THROW BOTH ENDS OF DOUBLEHEADER: 15th ANNIVERSARY. July 20, 1973. Knuckleballer Wilbur Wood of the Chicago White Sox pitched both games of a doubleheader against the New York Yankees. No pitcher has done this since, but Wood lost both games.

MANUSH, HEINIE: BIRTH ANNIVERSARY. July 20, 1901. Henry Emmett ("Heinie") Manush, Baseball Hall of Fame outfielder born at Tuscumbia, AL. Manush played for the Detroit Tigers and several other teams in a 17-year career. In 1933, he became the first player to be ejected from a World Series game. Inducted into the Hall of Fame in 1964. Died in Sarasota, FL, May 12, 1971.

BIRTHDAYS TODAY

Walter Ray Allen, 23, basketball player, born Merced, CA, July 20, 1975.
Jimmy Carson, 30, hockey player, born Southfield, MI, July 20, 1968.
Charles Joseph (Chuck) Daly, 68, basketball coach and former broadcaster, born St. Mary's, PA, July 20, 1930.
Nelson Doubleday, 65, baseball executive, born Long Island, NY, July 20, 1933.
Peter Forsberg, 25, hockey player, born Ornskoldsvik, Sweden, July 20, 1973.
Sir Edmund Hillary, 79, explorer (first to climb Mt Everest), born Auckland, New Zealand, July 20, 1919.
Michael Ilitch, 69, sports executive and former minor league baseball player, born Detroit, MI, July 20, 1929.
Terrence Rodney (Terry) Murray, 48, former hockey coach and player, born Shawville, Ontario, Canada, July 20, 1950.
Pedro ("Tony") Oliva, 58, former baseball player, born Pinar del Rio, Cuba, July 20, 1940.

JULY 21 — TUESDAY
Day 202 — 163 Remaining

BATEMAN, JOHN: BIRTH ANNIVERSARY. July 21, 1942. John Alvin Bateman, baseball player born at Killeen, TX. Bateman was a catcher who played for three teams from 1963 through 1972. His best year was 1966 when he batted .279 for the Houston Astros and hit 17 home runs. Died at Sand Springs, OK, Dec 3, 1996.

EVERS, JOHNNY: BIRTH ANNIVERSARY. July 21, 1881. John Joseph (Johnny) Evers, Baseball Hall of Fame second baseman born at Troy, NY. Evers (pronounced EE-vers) was a member of the Tinker–to–Evers–to–Chance double play combination for the Chicago Cubs early in the 20th century. Evers was an aggressive player who never gave an inch. Inducted into the Hall of Fame in 1946. Died at Albany, NY, Mar 28, 1947.

FOUR HITS, FOUR DPS: ANNIVERSARY. July 21, 1975. Felix Millan of the New York Mets got four singles, but each time he was erased from the basepaths as teammate Joe Torre grounded into four double plays. The Mets lost to the Houston Astros, 6–2.

GRETZKY SIGNS WITH RANGERS: ANNIVERSARY. July 21, 1996. After playing less than half a season with the St. Louis Blues, the team to which he had been traded from the Los Angeles Kings, center Wayne Gretzky signed a 2-year contract with the New York Rangers estimated to be worth $4 million per year plus incentives. Gretzky earned his money and defied those who thought he was too old and fragile to play regularly any more. He played every one of the Rangers' games and finished fourth in the league in scoring.

JOHN HENRY RETIRES: ANNIVERSARY. July 21, 1985. John Henry, the greatest money winner in thoroughbred racing history, was retired after earning $6,597,947. John Henry started 83 races and won 39 times.

McSPADEN, JUG: 90th BIRTH ANNIVERSARY. July 21, 1908. Harold ("Jug") McSpaden, golfer born at Rosedale, KS. Known as one-half of the "Gold Dust Twins," McSpaden enjoyed success on the pro golf tour in the 1930s with his most prominent victory coming in the 1939 Canadian Open. In 1945, when Byron Nelson, the other "Gold Dust Twin," won 11 straight tournaments, McSpaden finished second 13 times. Found dead from carbon monoxide poisoning in his home at Kansas City, KS, Apr 22, 1996.

PALMER FIRST TO WIN $1 MILLION: 30th ANNIVERSARY. July 21, 1968. Arnold Palmer became the first golfer to surpass the $1 million mark in career earnings despite losing the PGA championship to Julius Boros by one stroke.

US JUNIOR AMATEUR (GOLF) CHAMPIONSHIP. July 21–25. Conway Farms Golf Course, Lake Forest, IL. For info: US Golf Assn, Golf House, Far Hills, NJ 07931. Phone: (908) 234-2300. Fax: (908) 234-9687. Email: usga@ix.netcom.com. WWW: http://www.usga.org

BIRTHDAYS TODAY

Michael Todd (Mike) Bordick, 33, baseball player, born Marquette, MI, July 21, 1965.

	S	M	T	W	T	F	S
July				1	2	3	4
1998	5	6	7	8	9	10	11
	12	13	14	15	16	17	18
	19	20	21	22	23	24	25
	26	27	28	29	30	31	

Arnold Palmer

Michael Lee (Mike) Cubbage, 48, former baseball manager and player, born Charlottesville, VA, July 21, 1950.
Henry Austin Ellard, 37, football player, born Fresno, CA, July 21, 1961.
Steven Philip (Steve) Gietschier, 50, archivist, historian, and compiler of *Chase's Sports Calendar of Events*, born New York, NY, July 21, 1948.
Alan Thomas (Al) Hrabosky, 49, broadcaster and former baseball player, born Oakland, CA, July 21, 1949.
Jon Lovitz, 41, actor (*A League of Their Own*), born Tarzana, CA, July 21, 1957.
Lyle Odelein, 30, hockey player, born Quill Lake, Saskatchewan, Canada, July 21, 1968.

JULY 22 — WEDNESDAY
Day 203 — 162 Remaining

CRAMER, DOC: BIRTH ANNIVERSARY. July 22, 1905. Roger Maxwell ("Doc") Cramer, baseball player born at Beach Haven, NJ. Cramer played 20 years in the majors and got 2,705 hits. He batted .300 or better eight times and rarely struck out. Died at Manahawkin, NJ, Sept 9, 1990.

GLASSCOCK, JACK: BIRTH ANNIVERSARY. July 22, 1859. John Wesley (Jack) Glasscock, baseball player born Wheeling, WV. One of the best shortstops of the 19th century, Glasscock was called "Pebbly Jack" for his habit of groundskeeping his position during play. Died at Wheeling, Feb 24, 1947.

HAINES, JESSE: 105th BIRTH ANNIVERSARY. July 22, 1893. Jesse Joseph Haines, Baseball Hall of Fame pitcher born at Clayton, OH. Between 1920 and 1937, Haines won 210 games for the St. Louis Cardinals. He pitched one no-hitter and won three World Series games. Inducted into the Hall of Fame in 1970. Died at Dayton, OH, Aug 5, 1978.

INTERNATIONAL CHALLENGE OF CHAMPIONS (BILLIARDS). July 22–23 (tentative). The Mohegan Sun, Uncasville, CT. The premier event in the sport of professional billiards. Champions of countries around the world qualify to compete in the tournament. The winner captures the most coveted title in the sport, "Champion of Champions," and winner-take-all purse of $50,000. Sanctioned by the World Pool-Billiard Association (worldwide governing body) and considered the supreme test of skill in the sport. Est attendance: 2,400. For info: Matt Braun, Billiards Intl, Ltd, 123 Highview Dr, Winsted, CT 06098. Phone: (203) 379-8414. Fax: (203) 738-4927.

PLAYER WINS PGA: ANNIVERSARY. July 22, 1962. Gary Player of South Africa became the first nonresident of the US to win the PGA championship. He defeated Bob Goalby by one stroke at Aronimink Golf Club in Newtown Square, PA.

WHITWORTH BECOMES ALL-TIME WINNER: ANNIVERSARY. July 22, 1984. Kathy Whitworth won the Rochester Open to become the all-time winningest professional golfer. Her 85th victory surpassed the 84 tournament wins of Sam Snead.

BIRTHDAYS TODAY

Timothy Donell (Tim) Brown, 32, Heisman Trophy wide receiver, born Dallas, TX, July 22, 1966.
Albert Walter ("Sparky") Lyle, 54, former baseball player, born DuBois, PA, July 22, 1944.
Manuel Joseph ("Jungle Jim") Rivera, 76, former baseball player, born New York, NY, July 22, 1922.
Scott Douglas Sanderson, 42, former baseball player, born Dearborn, MI, July 22, 1956.
David Andrew (Dave) Stieb, 41, former baseball player, born Santa Ana, CA, July 22, 1957.
Sergei Zubov, 28, hockey player, born Moscow, USSR, July 22, 1970.

JULY 23 — THURSDAY
Day 204 — 161 Remaining

BEAUMONT, GINGER: BIRTH ANNIVERSARY. July 23, 1876. Clarence Howeth ("Ginger") Beaumont, baseball player born at Rochester, WI. Beaumont won the National League batting title in 1902 and was the first player to bat in a World Series (1903). His nickname came from his red hair. Died at Burlington, WI, Apr 10, 1956.

CANADA: THE GREAT INTERNATIONAL WORLD CHAMPIONSHIP BATHTUB RACE & NANAIMO MARINE FESTIVAL. July 23–26. Nanaimo, British Columbia. The Great Race, which takes place on the last day of the Nanaimo Festival, involves 40–50 racing bathtubs from all over the world leaving Nanaimo harbor and traveling the Georgia Strait (approx 30 km) and arriving in Nanaimo at Departure Bay beach. The festival includes a variety of community and fun events, such as Sabor race, a parade, dances, Bavrain gardens, food fair, arts and crafts, outdoor concerts and a large fireworks display. Est attendance: 75,000. For info: Loyal Nanaimo Bathtub Society, 51A Commercial St, Nanaimo, BC, Canada V9R 5G3. Phone: (604) 753-7223. Fax: (604) 753-7244.

DRYSDALE, DON: BIRTH ANNIVERSARY. July 23, 1936. Donald Scott Drysdale, broadcaster and Baseball Hall of Fame pitcher born in Van Nuys, CA. Drysdale was an intimidating righthanded pitcher for the Brooklyn and Los Angeles Dodgers from 1956 to 1969, compiling a won-lost record of 209–166 with a career ERA of 2.95. Following his playing career he became a successful and popular broadcaster for the Chicago White Sox and then for the Dodgers. Inducted into the Hall of Fame in 1984. Died at Montreal, Quebec, Canada, July 3, 1993.

FIRST US SWIMMING SCHOOL OPENS: ANNIVERSARY. July 23, 1827. The first swimming school in the US opened in Boston, MA. Its pupils included John Quincy Adams and John James Audubon.

FITZSIMMONS, SUNNY JIM: BIRTH ANNIVERSARY. July 23, 1874. James Edward ("Sunny Jim") Fitzsimmons, thoroughbred trainer born at New York, NY. Fitzsimmons got his first job at a racetrack at age 11 and became a trainer in 1900. He saddled 2,428 winners in his 63-year career, including Triple Crown winners Gallant Fox and Omaha. "Mr. Fitz," as he was known, was particularly noted for his ability to bring horses to peak performance in big races. Died at Miami, FL, Mar 11, 1966.

GEHRIG HITS FIRST GRAND SLAM: ANNIVERSARY. July 23, 1925. Lou Gehrig of the New York Yankees hit the first grand slam of his career as the Yankees defeated the Washington Senators, 11–7. Gehrig hit 22 other grand slams and still holds the major league record.

MOON PHASE: NEW MOON. July 23. Moon enters New Moon phase at 9:44 AM, EDT.

NEBRASKA'S BIG RODEO. July 23–25. Fairgrounds, Burwell, NE. Professional rodeo. Contestants compete in four exciting performances in historic, outdoor rodeo arena. Added thrills—chuckwagon races, wild horse races, Dinnerbell Derby, bull fighting-Burwell style. Also, quilt and art shows, parade, flea market, llama and longhorn cattle show, country and western music and dancing and Miss Burwell Rodeo Pageant. Est attendance: 10,000. For info: Peggy Haskell, Garfield County Frontier Fair Assn, Box 747, Burwell, NE 68823. Phone: (308) 346-5210.

PONY GIRLS SOFTBALL SLOW-PITCH NATIONAL CHAMPIONSHIPS. July 23–26. Site TBA. Slow-Pitch National Championships for girls ages 9–18. Est attendance: 2,000. For info: PONY Baseball/Softball, PO Box 225, Washington, PA 15301. Phone: (412) 225-1060. Fax: (412) 225-9852. Email: pony@pulsenet.com. WWW: http://www.pony.org

RAWLS WINS FOURTH US OPEN: ANNIVERSARY. July 23, 1960. Betsy Rawls became the first golfer to win the US Women's Open four times, adding the 1960 title to those won in 1951, 1953 and 1957.

US SENIOR OPEN (GOLF) CHAMPIONSHIP. July 23–26. Riviera Country Club, Pacific Palisades, CA. For info: US Golf Assn, Golf House, Far Hills, NJ 07931. Phone: (908) 234-2300. Fax: (908) 234-9687. Email: usga@ix.netcom.com. WWW: http://www.usga.org

BIRTHDAYS TODAY

Elden Jerome Campbell, 30, basketball player, born Los Angeles, CA, July 23, 1968.
Charles Robert (Chuck) Crim, 37, former baseball player, born Van Nuys, CA, July 23, 1961.
Dimitri Khristich, 29, hockey player, born Kiev, USSR, July 23, 1969.
Gary Dwayne Payton, 30, basketball player, born Oakland, CA, July 23, 1968.
Harold Henry ("Pee Wee") Reese, 80, Baseball Hall of Fame shortstop, born Ekron, KY, July 23, 1918.

JULY 24 — FRIDAY
Day 205 — 160 Remaining

SPORTSCHASER OF THE DAY

Which American League team won the famous "Pine Tar" game in 1983?

ADDIE JOSS BENEFIT GAME: ANNIVERSARY. July 24, 1911. A group of American League all-stars played the Cleveland Indians in an exhibition game to benefit the widow of Addie Joss, Cleveland's star pitcher struck down by tubercular meningitis on Apr 14.

BRETT'S "PINE TAR" HOME RUN: 15th ANNIVERSARY. July 24, 1983. In a game against the New York Yankees, George Brett of the Kansas City Royals hit a two-run home run with two out in the top of the ninth inning to give the Royals an apparent 5–4 lead. Yankees manager Billy Martin protested the excessive amount of pine tar on Brett's bat, and the umpires declared him out. The Royals protested this decision, and American League Lee MacPhail overruled the umps. On August 18, the game was replayed from the point of the protest, and the Royals emerged triumphant.

BROCK, JIM: BIRTH ANNIVERSARY. July 24, 1936. James Lee (Jim) Brock, college baseball coach born at Phoenix, AZ. Brock was an outstanding coach at Arizona State University. His Sun Devils won the College World Series in 1977 and 1981, and his teams compiled a 977–378 record. Died at Mesa, AZ, June 12, 1994.

DAYS OF '76. July 24–26. Deadwood, SD. 75th anniversary of the Days of '76, with great events throughout the weekend. Three days of PRCA rodeo action and a Days of '76 parade featuring antique carriages and wagons. Admission. Est attendance: 13,000. For info: W.R. Davidson, Deadwood Visitors Bureau, 3 Siever St, Deadwood, SD 57732. Phone: (605) 578-1102.

DODGE CITY DAYS. July 24–Aug 2. Dodge City, KS. Western heritage celebration with concerts, arts and crafts, parades, PRCA rodeo, street dances, art show, antique car show. Est attendance: 75,000. For info: Dodge City Conv & Visitors Bureau, 3rd and W Wyatt Earp Blvd, PO Box 1474, Dodge City, KS 67801. Phone: (316) 225-8186. Fax: (316) 227-2957. Email: dcvb@pld.com. WWW: http://www.dodgecity.org

LUMBERJACK WORLD CHAMPIONSHIPS. July 24–26. Lumberjack Bowl, Hayward, WI. Professional male and female lumberjacks and logrollers from around the world compete in speed sawing, pole climbing, logrolling and chopping events in the Northwoods town of Hayward. Amateurs can also participate; there are logrolling events for kids and chopping and sawing competitions for adults. Visitors can also see saw carving demonstrations and displays. Annually, the last full weekend in July. Est attendance: 12,000. For info: Exec Dir, Lumberjack World Chmpshp, PO Box 666, Hayward, WI 54843. Phone: (715) 634-2484.

PRO FOOTBALL HALL OF FAME FESTIVAL. July 24–Aug 1. Canton, OH. To honor the 1998 Class of Enshrinees inducted into the Pro Football Hall of Fame. Est attendance: 500,000. For info: Pro Football Hall of Fame Fest, Dennis P. Saunier, Exec Dir, 229 Wells Ave NW, Canton, OH 44703. Phone: (800) 533-4302.

TENNESSEE SENIOR GAMES. July 24–30. Clarksville, TN. State finals for senior athletes ages 50 and older in 17 different "Olympic-style" sports. For info: Christine Dewbre, Tenn Sr Games, 3024 Delta Queen Dr, Nashville, TN 37214. Phone: (615) 902-9261. Fax: (615) 902-9261.

TENNIS ADOPTS TIE-BREAKER: ANNIVERSARY. July 24, 1970. The International Lawn Tennis Association changed tennis history by adopting a rule calling for sets tied 6–6 to be concluded by a nine-point tiebreaker.

	S	M	T	W	T	F	S
July				1	2	3	4
	5	6	7	8	9	10	11
1998	12	13	14	15	16	17	18
	19	20	21	22	23	24	25
	26	27	28	29	30	31	

UPPER OHIO VALLEY ITALIAN FESTIVAL. July 24–26. Wheeling, WV. An ethnic extravaganza in downtown Wheeling that includes bocca and morra games, food, entertainment, arts and crafts and much more. Est attendance: 200,000. For info: Wheeling Convention/Visitors Bureau, 1310 Market St, Wheeling, WV 26003. Phone: (800) 828-3097 or (304) 233-7709. WWW: http://wvweb.com/www/wheeling.html

WRONG WAY MARATHONER: 90th ANNIVERSARY. July 24, 1908. Dorando Pietri of Italy led the marathon at the 1908 Olympics as he entered the stadium for the race's conclusion. Dazed and confused, he began to run the wrong way. Officials tried to correct him, but he fell four times. When they helped him to his feet, he was disqualified, and John Hayes of the US came on to win the race.

BIRTHDAYS TODAY

Walter Jones Bellamy, 59, Basketball Hall of Fame center, born New Bern, NC, July 24, 1939.
Brian Keith Blades, 33, football player, born Fort Lauderdale, FL, July 24, 1965.
Barry Lamar Bonds, 34, baseball player, born Riverside, CA, July 24, 1964.
Kevin Gregory Butler, 36, football player, born Savannah, GA, July 24, 1962.
Joseph Barry (Joe Barry) Carroll, 40, former basketball player, born Pine Bluff, AR, July 24, 1958.
William Delford (Willie) Davis, 64, Pro Football Hall of Fame defensive end, born Lisbon, LA, July 24, 1934.
Julieanne Louise (Julie) Krone, 35, jockey, born Benton Harbor, MI, July 24, 1963.
Karl Malone, 35, basketball player, born Summerfield, LA, July 24, 1963.

JULY 25 — SATURDAY
Day 206 — 159 Remaining

AL DAVIS RESIGNS AS AFL COMMISSIONER: ANNIVERSARY. July 25, 1966. Al Davis, named commissioner of the American Football League just three and a half months earlier, resigned that post and returned to his previous position, president of the general partner of the Oakland Raiders. Davis resigned two weeks after NFL commissioner Pete Rozelle announced a merger between the two leagues.

ATLANTA HAWKS TOUR SOVIET UNION: ANNIVERSARY. July 25, 1988. The Atlanta Hawks began a 13-day trip through the Soviet Union by beating a Soviet team, 85–84. The Hawks won the second game but then lost the third to conclude the first such tour by an NBA team.

AU SABLE CANOE MARATHON AND RIVER FESTIVALS. July 25–26. Grayling and Oscoda, MI. Gather in Grayling for the 9 PM start of North America's longest, toughest nonstop canoe race. Some 50 teams, carrying canoes atop their heads, run through the downtown streets and launch them into the Au Sable River. During the pre-race action at this 50th annual event, you can frolic at a parade, county fair, arts and crafts show, ice cream social, antique car show, street dance and other festivities. While the hardy canoeists paddle for some 14 hours through the night, you can drive to Oscoda, stopping to cheer them on at bridges and dams along the 120-mile route. Be ready for the race's exciting finale! For info: Grayling Area Visitors Council, (800) 937-8837 or Oscoda-Au Sable Chamber of Commerce, (800) 235-4625.

GREAT TEXAS MOSQUITO FESTIVAL COMPETITIONS. July 25. Clute Municipal Park, Clute, TX. Co-ed volleyball tournament; doubles horseshoe pitching tournament; doubles washer pitching contest; Century Buzz bike tour with 12-, 30- and 60-mile routes; Mosquito Chase with one-mile and 5K runs, both of which are certified by USA Track and Field and a host of other great festival doings. Est attendance: 30,000. For info: Great Texas Mosquito Festival, PO Box 997, Clute, TX 77531. Phone: (800) 371-2971. Fax: (409) 265-8767.

LEFTY GROVE WINS 300th GAME: ANNIVERSARY. July 25, 1941. Robert ("Lefty") Grove of the Boston Red Sox won the 300th and last game of his major league career, defeating the Cleveland Indians, 10–6.

MID-SUMMER ANTIQUES AND COLLECTIBLES SHOW AND SALE. July 25–26. Millville, NJ. Rain or shine. Est attendance: 2,000. For info: Wheaton Village, 1501 Glasstown Rd, Millville, NJ. Phone: (609) 825-6800 or (800) 998-4552. Fax: (609) 825-2410. Email: mail@wheatonvillage.org. WWW: http://www.wheatonvillage.org

SILVER HOOPS 3-ON-3 BASKETBALL TOURNAMENT. July 25. Teaters Field, Kellogg, ID. This is the fifth year of this chamber event designed to have fun while raising funds to support the Kellogg Chamber of Commerce. Est attendance: 200. For info: Silver Hoops 3-on-3 Basketball Tournament, Kellogg Chamber of Commerce, 608 Bunker Ave, Kellogg, ID 83837. Phone: (208) 784-0821. Fax: (208) 783-4343. Email: kellogg@nidlink.com. WWW: http://www.nidlink.com/~kellogg

TENER, JOHN: 135th BIRTH ANNIVERSARY. July 25, 1863. John Kinley Tener, baseball player and executive born at County Tyrone, Ireland. Tener played amateur and professional baseball in the 19th century and retired to become a banker. He was president of the National League from 1913 to 1918. Died at Pittsburgh, PA, May 19, 1946.

TWO TRIPLE STEALS: ANNIVERSARY. July 25, 1930. The Philadelphia Athletics executed a triple steal in the first inning of a game against the Cleveland Indians and another one in the fourth inning. This is only game in which two triple steals have occurred.

VIRGINIA SCOTTISH GAMES. July 25–26. Alexandria, VA. Bagpipes, Highland dance, drumming, fiddling, Celtic harp competition, animal trials and Scottish athletic games competition and British antique car show. Scottish food and gifts are sold. Annually, the fourth weekend in July. Est attendance: 30,000. For info: Virginia Scottish Games Assoc, PO Box 1338, Alexandria, VA 22313. Phone: (703) 912-1943. WWW: http://www.alex.org/homepages/vsg/

Jose Joaquin Bautista, 34, baseball player, born Bani, Dominican Republic, July 25, 1964.
Dean Biasucci, 36, football player, born Niagara Falls, NY, July 25, 1962.
Stanley F. Dancer, 71, harness racer, born New Egypt, NY, July 25, 1927.
Douglas Dean (Doug) Drabek, 36, baseball player, born Victoria, TX, July 25, 1962.
Walter Jerry Payton, 44, Pro Football Hall of Fame running back, born Columbia, MS, July 25, 1954.
Edward Nelson (Ed) Sprague, Jr, 31, baseball player, born Castro Valley, CA, July 25, 1967.
Nathaniel (Nate) Thurmond, 57, Basketball Hall of Fame center, born Akron, OH, July 25, 1941.

JULY 26 — SUNDAY
Day 207 — 158 Remaining

BREADON, SAM: BIRTH ANNIVERSARY. July 26, 1876. Sam Breadon, baseball executive born at New York, NY. Breadon was principal owner of the St. Louis Cardinals from 1917 to 1947. He supplied the financial backing as Branch Rickey built the Cards into the National League's dominant team. Died at St. Louis, MO, May 10, 1949.

DOUBLE DECATHLON WINNER: ANNIVERSARY. July 26, 1952. Bob Mathias of the US won the decathlon at the 1952 Summer Olympics in Helsinki, Finland, to become the first athlete to win the Olympic decathlon twice. His first victory came in the 1948 London Games. Daley Thompson of Great Britain equalled Mathias's feat in 1980 and 1984.

GALLICO, PAUL: BIRTH ANNIVERSARY. July 26, 1897. Paul William Gallico, sportswriter born at New York, NY. Gallico put a twist on his career with the *New York Daily News* when he asked heavyweight champion Jack Dempsey to box a round with him in 1923. Thereafter, Gallico began to sample a wealth of other sports, competing against the very best. By 1936, Gallico was the highest-paid sportswriter in New York. He left the newspaper business to become a freelance writer and spent many years abroad attacking a variety of subjects. Died at Monte Carlo, Monaco, July 15, 1976.

KINDER, ELLIS: BIRTH ANNIVERSARY. July 26, 1914. Ellis Raymond Kinder, baseball player born at Atkins, AK. Kinder was a starting pitcher for the Boston Red Sox in the late 1940s and became a quality reliever in 1950. He pitched until he was 42 years old. Died at Jackson, TN, Oct 16, 1968.

WATERFIELD, BOB: BIRTH ANNIVERSARY. July 26, 1920. Robert (Bob) Waterfield, Pro Football Hall of Fame quarterback born at Elmira, NY. Waterfield competed in gymnastics and football at UCLA. After World War II, he joined the Cleveland Rams and became the first rookie quarterback to lead a team to the NFL title. Twice the league's MVP, Waterfield supplemented his passing skills with outstanding punting ability. Inducted into the Pro Football Hall of Fame in 1965. Died at Burbank, CA, Mar 25, 1983.

Martin Eugene (Marty) Bystrom, 40, former baseball player, born Coral Gables, FL, July 26, 1958.
Gregory Joseph (Greg) Colbrunn, 29, baseball player, born Fontana, CA, July 26, 1969.

Dorothy Hamill, 42, Olympic gold medal figure skater, born Riverside, CT, July 26, 1956.

Maxine ("Mickey") King, 54, Olympic gold medal diver, born Pontiac, MI, July 26, 1944.

Robert Lewis (Bob) Lilly, 59, Pro Football Hall of Fame defensive tackle, born Olney, TX, July 26, 1939.

Jody Eric Reed, 36, baseball player, born Tampa, FL, July 26, 1962.

Norman LeRoy (Norm) Siebern, 65, former baseball player, born St. Louis, MO, July 26, 1933.

James Hoyt Wilhelm, 75, Baseball Hall of Fame pitcher, born Huntersville, NC, July 26, 1923.

JULY 27 — MONDAY
Day 208 — 157 Remaining

CHASE'S SPORTSQUOTE OF THE DAY

"I never questioned the integrity of an umpire. Their eyesight, yes." —Leo Durocher

CONTINENTAL LEAGUE FORMED: ANNIVERSARY. July 27, 1959. New York City attorney William A. Shea announced plans to establish the Continental League, a third major baseball league, with Branch Rickey as president. Shea awarded franchises to New York, Houston, Toronto, Denver, and Minneapolis-St. Paul. The league never played a game, but all five cities eventually got major league teams: the New York Mets, the Houston Colt .45s, the Toronto Blue Jays, the Colorado Rockies and the Minnesota Twins.

DUROCHER, LEO: BIRTH ANNIVERSARY. July 27, 1905. Leo Ernest Durocher, baseball player and Baseball Hall of Fame manager born at West Springfield, MA. He began his major league baseball career with the New York Yankees in 1925 and also played for the St. Louis Cardinals and the Brooklyn Dodgers, where he first served as player-manager in 1939. His trademark phrase was, "Nice guys finish last." As a manager, he guided the New York Giants to two World Series, defeating the Cleveland Indians in 1954. He later coached for the Los Angeles Dodgers and managed the Chicago Cubs and the Houston Astros. Inducted into the Hall of Fame in 1994. Died at Palm Springs, CA, Oct 7, 1991.

FOUL BALL SUIT: ANNIVERSARY. July 27, 1921. Baseball fan Reuben Berman brought suit in New York County Supreme Court against the New York Giants, alleging that on May 16 the Giants had "wrongfully and unlawfully imprisoned and detained" him and threatened him with arrest. Berman further alleged that he was "greatly humiliated before a large crowd of people . . . and thereby was caused mental and bodily distress and was thereby greatly injured in his character and reputation and in his physical health." Berman's crime? He refused to return a foul ball he had caught to a stadium attendant. Allowing fans to keep foul balls was not yet a general practice, but the court awarded Berman $100.

LEMOND WINS TOUR DE FRANCE: ANNIVERSARY. July 27, 1986. Cyclist Greg Lemond became the first American to win the Tour de France, the most important bicycle race in the world.

MACKEY, BIZ: BIRTH ANNIVERSARY. July 27, 1897. Raleigh ("Biz") Mackey, baseball player and manager born at Eagle Pass, TX. Mackey was one of the best catchers in the Negro Leagues. He was particularly adept at handling pitchers and grooming younger players, including Roy Campanella, for top-flight competition. Died at Los Angeles, CA, date unknown.

SHORT MAJOR LEAGUE CAREER: 80th ANNIVERSARY. July 27, 1918. Harry Heitman of the Brooklyn Dodgers made his major league debut as the starting pitcher against the St. Louis Cardinals. He got the first man out, but then the next four batters got hits. Heitman left the game and never played professional baseball again.

TINKER, JOE: BIRTH ANNIVERSARY. July 27, 1880. Joseph Bert (Joe) Tinker, Baseball Hall of Fame shortstop born at Muscotah, KS. Tinker was part of the Chicago Cubs' famous Tinker–to–Evers–to–Chance double play combination. He played with the Reds after the Cubs, played and managed in the Federal League and then managed the Cubs. Inducted into the Hall of Fame in 1946. Died at Orlando, FL, July 27, 1948.

TRAPPERS STREAK SNAPPED: ANNIVERSARY. July 27, 1987. The Salt Lake City Trappers of the Pioneer League, an independent team without a major league affiliation or working agreement, lost to Billings, 7–5, thereby bringing their record 29-game winning streak to an end.

WORLD RECORD IN 100: ANNIVERSARY. July 27, 1996. Canadian sprinter Donovan Bailey won the 100 meters at the 1996 Summer Olympics in Atlanta in the world-record time of 9.84 seconds. The previous mark, set on July 6, 1994 by Leroy Burrell, was 9.85 seconds.

BIRTHDAYS TODAY

Leonard Harold (Len) Barker, 43, former baseball player, born Ft Knox, KY, July 27, 1955.

Raymond Otis (Ray) Boone, 75, former baseball player, born San Diego, CA, July 27, 1923.

Richard Fremont (Rich) Dauer, 46, former baseball player, born San Bernardino, CA, July 27, 1952.

Peggy Gale Fleming, 50, broadcaster and Olympic gold medal figure skater, born San Jose, CA, July 27, 1948.

Alexander Emmanuel (Alex) Rodriguez, 23, baseball player, born New York, NY, July 27, 1975.

Elliott Taylor ("Bump") Wills, 46, former baseball player, born Washington, DC, July 27, 1952.

JULY 28 — TUESDAY
Day 209 — 156 Remaining

FITZSIMMONS, FAT FREDDIE: BIRTH ANNIVERSARY. July 28, 1901. Frederick Landis ("Fat Freddie") Fitzsimmons, baseball player born at Mishawaka, IN. Fitzsimmons pitched for the New York Giants and the Brooklyn Dodgers (1925–43). He was a good hitter and coached with several teams after his retirement. Died at Yucca Valley, CA, Nov 18, 1979.

FOX, TERRY: 40th BIRTH ANNIVERSARY. July 28, 1958. Terrence Stanley (Terry) Fox, inspirational athlete born at Winnipeg, Manitoba, Canada. Fox captured the hearts and admiration of millions during his brief life. Stricken with cancer, requiring amputation of the athlete's right leg at age 18, Fox determined to devote his life to a fight against the disease. His "Marathon of Hope," a planned 5,200-mile run westward across Canada, started Apr 12, 1980, at St. John's, Newfoundland, and continued 3,328 miles to Thunder Bay, Ontario, Sept 1, 1980, when he was forced to stop by spread of the disease. During the run (on an artificial leg) he raised

	S	M	T	W	T	F	S
July				1	2	3	4
	5	6	7	8	9	10	11
1998	12	13	14	15	16	17	18
	19	20	21	22	23	24	25
	26	27	28	29	30	31	

$24 million for cancer research and inspired millions with his courage. Died at New Westminster, BC, Canada, June 28, 1981.

MARTINEZ PITCHES PERFECT GAME: ANNIVERSARY. July 28, 1991. Dennis Martinez of the Montreal Expos pitched a perfect game, defeating the Los Angeles Dodgers, 2–0, in Dodgers Stadium.

ROGIN, BULLET JOE: BIRTH ANNIVERSARY. July 28, 1889. Wilbur ("Bullet Joe") Rogin, baseball player born at Oklahoma City, OK. Rogin starred as both a pitcher and a hitter in the Negro Leagues and is generally considered one of the best pitchers in black baseball history. Died at Kansas City, MO, Mar 4, 1964.

BIRTHDAYS TODAY

David (Dave) Alexander, 34, football player, born Silver Spring, MD, July 28, 1964.
Vida Rochelle Blue, 49, former baseball player, born Mansfield, LA, July 28, 1949.
William Warren (Bill) Bradley, 55, former US senator and Basketball Hall of Fame forward, born Crystal City, MO, July 28, 1943.
Paul Douglas (Doug) Collins, 47, basketball coach and former player, born Christopher, IL, July 28, 1951.
Carmelo Martinez, 38, former baseball player, born Dorado, Puerto Rico, July 28, 1960.
Robert (Bob) Milacki, 34, baseball player, born Trenton, NJ, July 28, 1964.

JULY 29 — WEDNESDAY
Day 210 — 155 Remaining

CANADA: MUSKOKA DISTRICT KENNEL CLUB CHAMPIONSHIP SHOW. July 29–31. James D. Lang Activity Park, Bracebridge, Ontario. For info: Muskoka Dist Kennel Club, Bracebridge C of C, 1-1 Manitoba St, Bracebridge, Ont, Canada P1L-1S4. Phone: (705) 645-5801 or (705) 645-8121. Fax: (705) 645-7592. Email: bracecha@muskoka.com.

EXPERIMENTAL AIRCRAFT ASSOCIATION INTERNATIONAL FLY-IN. July 29–Aug 4. Wittman Regional Airport, Oshkosh, WI. The world's largest and most significant aviation event features more than 11,000 airplanes—home-built, antique, aerobatics planes, military and general aviation aircraft. International visitors can attend more than 500 educational forums, seminars and workshops and view the displays of more than 700 exhibitors, including the National Aeronautics and Space Administration (NASA), the National Transportation Safety Board (NTSB) and the Federal Aviation Administration (FAA). Daily air shows showcase the talents of the world's top aerobatics performers. 46th annual. Est attendance: 830,000. For info: Director, Intl Fly-in in Oshkosh, PO Box 3086, Oshkosh, WI 54903. Phone: (414) 426-4840. Fax: (414) 232-7772. Email: convention @eaa.org. WWW: http://www.fly-in.org

FESLER, WES: 90th BIRTH ANNIVERSARY. July 29, 1908. Wesley Eugene (Wes) Fesler, football player, coach and sportscaster born at Youngstown, OH. Fesler was a three-time All-American end at Ohio State University and played baseball and basketball, too. He coached several sports at several schools before being named head football coach at Ohio State in 1947. His Buckeyes did well, but he resigned after the 1950 season, citing the intense pressure of coaching in Columbus. Six weeks later, he agreed to coach at the University of Minnesota where he stayed three years. Died at Laguna Hills, CA, July 30, 1989.

FIRST EIGHT-FOOT HIGH JUMP. July 29, 1989. Javier Sotomayor of Cuba became the first man to high jump eight ft. He set the new world record at the Caribbean Championship meet in San Juan, Puerto Rico. Sotomayor held the previous record, seven ft, 11½ in, set in 1988 in Spain.

FIRST WORLD HEAVYWEIGHT TITLE FIGHT: ANNIVERSARY. July 29, 1751. Jack Slack of England, the acknowledged champion, defeated challenger M. Petit of France, in the first International World Title Prize Fight in Harlston, Norfolk, England.

GARVEY'S STREAK ENDS: 15th ANNIVERSARY. July 29, 1983. San Diego Padres first baseman Steve Garvey saw his consecutive game playing streak come to an end at 1,207 games, a National League record. He dislocated his left thumb in a collision at home plate with Atlanta Braves pitcher Pascual Perez and was unable to play in the second game of the doubleheader.

LASORDA RETIRES: ANNIVERSARY. July 29, 1996. Despite recovering successfully from a heart attack he suffered several weeks previously, Tommy Lasorda announced his retirement as manager of the Los Angeles Dodgers after 20 years at the helm. Lasorda finished his career in 12th place in total games managed. He had a record of 1599 wins, 13th best, and 1439 losses. His teams won the World Series in 1981 and 1988.

MARA, TIM: BIRTH ANNIVERSARY. July 29, 1887. Timothy James (Tim) Mara, Pro Football Hall of Fame executive born at New York, NY. Mara was a successful bookmaker who bought the New York franchise in the NFL in 1925 for $500. His team, the Giants, became one of the most successful in the league, withstanding challenges from two early American Football Leagues, the All-America Football Conference of the late 1940s and the New York Jets of the AFL of the 1960s. Inducted into the Pro Football Hall of Fame as a charter member in 1963. Died at New York, NY, Feb 16, 1959.

PONY GIRLS SOFTBALL FAST-PITCH NATIONAL CHAMPIONSHIPS. July 29–Aug 2. Site TBA. National girls fast-pitch softball championships for girls age 9–18. Est attendance: 5,000. For info: PONY Baseball/Softball, PO Box 225, Washington, PA 15301. Phone: (412) 225-1060. Fax: (412) 225-9852. Email: pony@pulsenet.com.

SARATOGA RACE COURSE OPENS. July 29–Sept 8. Saratoga Race Course, Saratoga Springs, NY. The finest thoroughbred racing at the oldest race track in the US. Closed Tues. Post time: 1 PM. Est attendance: 800,000. For info: Ed Lewi Assoc, 6 Chelsea Place, Clifton Park, NY 12065. Phone: (518) 383-6183. Fax: (518) 383-6755.

USFL WINS SUIT AGAINST NFL: ANNIVERSARY. July 29, 1986. The United States Football League won its antitrust suit against the National Football League, but the court awarded the upstart league only $1 (trebled to $3) instead of the $1.69 billion it sought. The jury deliberated five days before reaching its verdict.

BIRTHDAYS TODAY

Luis Rene Alicea, 33, former baseball player, born Santurce, Puerto Rico, July 29, 1965.
Daniel (Danny) Driessen, 47, former baseball player, born Hilton Head, SC, July 29, 1951.
William Thomas (Tommy) Gregg, Jr, 35, baseball player, born Boone, NC, July 29, 1963.
David Jeffrey (Dave) LaPoint, 39, former baseball player, born Glens Falls, NY, July 29, 1959.
Felix Mantilla, 64, former baseball player, born Isabela, Puerto Rico, July 29, 1934.

JULY 30 — THURSDAY
Day 211 — 154 Remaining

AFL'S FIRST PRESEASON GAME: ANNIVERSARY. July 30, 1960. The Boston Patriots defeated the Buffalo Bills, 28–7, at Buffalo's War Memorial Stadium in the first preseason game played in the new American Football League. Boston's defensive end Bob Dee scored the first touchdown by recovering a fumble.

BASEBALL ARTS FESTIVAL. July 30–Aug 2. Tarkio, MO. Displays of baseball artifacts and memorabilia, storytelling, photography workshop, baseball card show, games, contests and relays. Sponsored by the Missouri Arts Council and the Tarkio Cultural Development Committee. For info: Tarkio Chamber of Commerce, 222 Main, Tarkio, MO 64491. Phone: (816) 736-5772. Fax: (816) 736-5772.

CONTINENTAL AMATEUR BASEBALL ASSOCIATION TOURNAMENT. July 30–Aug 7. Tarkio, MO. This is the 13th year for the tournament for 11-year-olds. 24 teams from all over the US, including Hawaii, Puerto Rico and Guam, compete. As the oldest continuous site for the CABA, Tarkio has received the Tournament of Excellence Award since 1989. Teams and fans attend a KC Royals game on "break day" and parade on the field before the game. The tournament is combined with a festival "Exploring the Art of Baseball." Annually, beginning the last Thursday in July. For info: Tarkio Chamber of Commerce, 222 Main, Tarkio, MO 64491. Phone: (816) 736-5772. Fax: (816) 736-5772.

July 1998	S	M	T	W	T	F	S
				1	2	3	4
	5	6	7	8	9	10	11
	12	13	14	15	16	17	18
	19	20	21	22	23	24	25
	26	27	28	29	30	31	

FORD, HENRY: 135th BIRTH ANNIVERSARY. July 30, 1863. Henry Ford, automobile company executive born at Dearborn, MI. Besides his role as founder of the Ford Motor Company, Henry Ford was also a racing pioneer, using the sport to garner publicity for his main business. He won the only race he entered, a 25-mile contest in 1901. In 1902, he organized the company that made racing cars for Barney Oldfield. Ford's Model T won the New York-to-Seattle race in 1909. Died at Detroit, MI, Apr 17, 1947.

HANSEN'S UNASSISTED TRIPLE PLAY: 30th ANNIVERSARY. July 30, 1968. Washington Senators shortstop Ron Hansen completed the eighth regular-season unassisted triple play and the first one since 1927 in a game against the Cleveland Indians. In the first inning, Hansen snared a line drive hit by Jose Azcue, stepped on second base to double off Dave Nelson and then tagged Russ Snyder before he could get back to first. Hansen was traded to the Chicago White Sox three days later.

HIRSCH, MAX: BIRTH ANNIVERSARY. July 30, 1880. Maximilian Justice (Max) Hirsch, thoroughbred trainer born at Fredericksburg, TX. Hirsch was a jockey from age 14 to age 19 when he obtained his trainer's license. Closely associated with the King Ranch, he trained three winners of the Kentucky Derby, two of the Preakness Stakes and four of the Belmont Stakes. His most famous horse was Assault, winner of the 1946 Triple Crown. Died at New Hyde Park, NY, Apr 3, 1969.

RICHARD SUFFERS STROKE: ANNIVERSARY. July 30, 1980. After complaining for some time of a "dead arm," Houston Astros pitcher James Rodney Richard suffered a stroke during a workout. Doctors removed a blood clot from behind his right collarbone.

STENGEL, CASEY: BIRTH ANNIVERSARY. July 30, 1890. Charles Dillon ("Casey") Stengel, Baseball Hall of Fame outfielder and manager born at Kansas City, MO. Stengel played the outfield for several teams and earned a reputation for goofiness. He carried this over his career as a manager, but his success with the New York Yankees (ten pennants and seven World Series titles in 12 years) made him one of the game's enduring stars. Inducted into the Hall of Fame in 1966. Died at Glendale, CA, Sept 29, 1975.

BIRTHDAYS TODAY

James William (Bill) Cartwright, 41, former basketball player, born Lodi, CA, July 30, 1957.

Scott Brian Fletcher, 40, former baseball player, born Fort Walton Beach, FL, July 30, 1958.

Clinton Merrick (Clint) Hurdle, 41, former baseball player, born Big Rapids, MI, July 30, 1957.

Christopher Paul (Chris) Mullin, 35, basketball player, born New York, NY, July 30, 1963.

Joseph Henry (Joe) Nuxhall, 70, broadcaster and former baseball player, born Hamilton, OH, July 30, 1928.

Thomas Alan (Tom) Pagnozzi, 36, baseball player, born Tucson, AZ, July 30, 1962.

Douglas Lee (Doug) Rader, 54, former baseball manager and player, born Chicago, IL, July 30, 1944.

Arnold Schwarzenegger, 51, bodybuilder, actor, born Graz, Austria, July 30, 1947.

Ellis Clarence Valentine, 44, former baseball player, born Helena, AR, July 30, 1954.

JULY 31 — FRIDAY
Day 212 — 153 Remaining

SPORTSCHASER OF THE DAY

Against which team did Joe Adcock of the Milwaukee Braves hit four home runs in a single game in 1954?

ADCOCK HITS FOUR HOME RUNS: ANNIVERSARY. July 31, 1954. Joe Adcock of the Milwaukee Braves became the seventh player in major league history to hit four home runs in a single game. He added a double to lead the Braves to a 15–7 win over the Brooklyn Dodgers.

AMERICAN ROWING CHAMPIONSHIPS. July 31–Aug 2 (tentative). Syracuse, NY. Intermediate and seniors competition. Sponsor: US Rowing Association. Est attendance: 44,000. For info: US Rowing Association, 201 S Capitol Ave, Indianapolis, IN 46225. Phone: (317) 237-5656. Fax: (317) 237-5646.

AMERICAN LUMBERJACK CHAMPIONSHIPS AT LOG BOOM. July 31–Aug 2. Pettibone Park on the Mississippi River, La Crosse, WI. Historical family event featuring the best log rollers, axmen, sawyers, tree climbers in the world. Prairie La Crosse Rendezvous with more than 100 primitive camps of woodworkers, blacksmiths, spinners, weavers and more. Traditional music, food, art, children's games. Est attendance: 20,000. For info: Mississippi River Log Boom, PO Box 801, La Crosse, WI 54601. Phone: (608) 782-1003. Fax: (608) 782-4275.

DALEY, ARTHUR: BIRTH ANNIVERSARY. July 31, 1904. Arthur John Daley, sportswriter born at New York, NY. Daley played baseball at Fordham University but turned to sportswriting after injuring his thumb. He went to work for the *New York Times* in 1926 and became the first reporter to cover a sporting event overseas when he went to Berlin for the 1936 Summer Olympics. In 1942, he replaced John Kieran as writer of the "Sports of the Times" column, eventually producing over 10,000 columns. He won the Pulitzer Prize in 1956. Died at New York, Jan 3, 1974.

DOYLE, LARRY: BIRTH ANNIVERSARY. July 31, 1886. Lawrence Joseph (Larry) Doyle, baseball player born at Caseyville, IL. Doyle played infield for John McGraw's New York Giants for 12 years. He was named the National League's MVP in 1911 and was the Giants' captain. Died at Saranac Lake, NY, Mar 1, 1974.

FROG DAYS. July 31–Aug 2. Melvina, WI (Frogtown USA). True Americana served up family-style with men's 30-and-over 18-team softball tournament, frog racing for all ages and a Sunday chicken barbecue. Est attendance: 5,000. For info: Frog Days, Rte 1, Box 90, Cashton, WI 54619.

HOP, SKIP & JUMP DAY©98. July 31. This day celebrates the unbridled energy needed to hop, skip and jump, one of the best exercises ever and those who hop to it, skip to the opportunity and jump right on in! For further info, send $2 to cover cost of copying and postage to: Adrienne Koopersmith, 1437 W Rosemont, 1W, Chicago, IL 60660-1319. Phone: (773) 743-5341. Fax: (773) 743-5395. Email: kooper@interaccess.com.

MOON PHASE: FIRST QUARTER. July 31. Moon enters First Quarter phase at 8:05 AM, EDT.

MUNICIPAL STADIUM OPENS: ANNIVERSARY. July 31, 1932. The Cleveland Indians opened their new ballpark, Municipal Stadium, losing to the Philadelphia Athletics and pitcher Robert ("Lefty") Grove, 1–0, before 76,979. The Indians reserved their new home for Sunday and holiday games. They continued to play weekday games at League Park until the late 1940s.

ONLY ALL-STAR GAME TIE: ANNIVERSARY. July 31, 1961. The year's second All-Star game ended in a 1–1 tie at Fenway Park as heavy rain caused the game to be called after nine innings. Baseball inaugurated the custom of two All-Star games in 1959 and abandoned the practice after 1962. The 1961 tie was the only one in All-Star history.

RYAN WINS 300th GAME: ANNIVERSARY. July 31, 1990. Nolan Ryan of the Texas Rangers won the 300th game of his career, defeating the Milwaukee Brewers, 11–3. Ryan pitched in the major leagues from 1966 until 1993 and finished with 324 wins.

SHOW-ME SHOW-DOWN GRAND NATIONAL TRUCK & TRACTOR PULL. July 31–Aug 2. Macon County Park, Macon, MO. Heart-pounding, wheel-standing fun as the Macon Area Chamber of Commerce brings you awesome pulling power at this 11th annual event. Two-wheel drives, four-wheel drives and multi-engine super stock tractors. Lots of fun, food and souvenirs for all. Est attendance: 15,000. For info: Crystal Lyda, Macon Area Chamber of Commerce, 218 N Rollins, Macon, MO 63552. Phone: (816) 385-5484. Fax: (816) 385-3972.

"UNTIL THERE'S A CURE" DAY: ANNIVERSARY. July 31, 1994. The San Francisco Giants joined the battle against AIDS by staging "Until There's a Cure" Day at Candlestick Park. The Giants wore red ribbons sewn on their uniforms. Together with the visiting Colorado Rockies, they joined 700 AIDS volunteers to form a giant human red ribbon on the field. One dollar from the price of every ticket sold went to Bay Area AIDS organizations. The Giants won the game, 9–4, behind home runs by Barry Bonds, Darryl Strawberry and Matt Williams, who hit two.

BIRTHDAYS TODAY

Michael Scott Bankhead, 35, former baseball player, born Raleigh, NC, July 31, 1963.

Henry Albert (Hank) Bauer, 76, former baseball manager and player, born East St. Louis, IL, July 31, 1922.

Victor Jose (Vic) Davalillo, 62, former baseball player, born Cabimas, Venezuela, July 31, 1936.

Leon Durham, 41, former baseball player, born Cincinnati, OH, July 31, 1957.

Gustave Joseph (Gus) Frerotte, 27, football player, born Kittanning, PA, July 31, 1971.

Evonne Fay Goolagong, 47, former tennis player, born Griffith, New South Wales, Australia, July 31, 1951.

Curtis (Curt) Gowdy, 79, former broadcaster, born Green River, WY, July 31, 1919.

Kevin Darwin Greene, 36, football player, born Schenectady, NY, July 31, 1962.

Collie Antonio Langham, 26, football player, born Town Creek, AL, July 31, 1972.

Brian Skrudland, 35, hockey player, born Peace River, Alberta, Canada, July 31, 1963.

AUGUST 1 — SATURDAY
Day 213 — 152 Remaining

BLYLEVEN STRIKES OUT 3,000th BATTER: ANNIVERSARY. Aug 1, 1986. Pitcher Bert Blyleven of the Minnesota Twins became the tenth pitcher to pass the 3,000 mark in career strikeouts, beating the Oakland A's, 10–1.

CURTIS CUP. Aug 1–2. The Minikahda Club, Minneapolis, MN. Biennial competition between teams of amateur women golfers from the US and the British Isles. Named after British golfing sisters Harriot and Margaret Curtis. Contested in even-numbered years since 1932 (except during World War II). For info: US Golf Assn, Golf House, Far Hills, NJ 07931. Phone: (908) 234-2300. Fax: (908) 234-9687. Email: usga@ix.netcom.com. WWW: http://www.usga.org

ENGLAND: SKANDIA LIFE COWES WEEK. Aug 1–8. Cowes, Isle of Wight. Yachting festival covering all classes of yacht racing. Est attendance: 14,000. For info: Cowes Week Organizers, Cowes Combined Clubs, 18 Bath Rd, Cowes, Isle of Wight, England PO31 7QN. Phone: (44) (198) 329-5744. Fax: (44) (198) 329-5329.

FERRY SIGNS WITH IL MESSAGGERO ROMA: ANNIVERSARY. Aug 1, 1989. In an unprecedented move, Danny Ferry, formerly of Duke and the first-round draft choice of the Los Angeles Clippers, foresook the NBA to sign a contract with Il Messaggero Roma of the Italian League. Ferry played one season in Italy and then returned to the US to join the Cleveland Cavaliers, who had obtained his rights from the Clippers.

GORBOUS MAKES RECORD THROW: ANNIVERSARY. Aug 1, 1957. Minor league baseball player Glen Gorbous set a world record by throwing a baseball 445 feet, 10 inches, on the fly in a contest at Omaha Stadium, Omaha, NE. Gorbous used a six-step delivery to heave the ball from the right field corner to the left field corner. He retired from baseball two years later because of an arm injury.

McCOVEY HITS 18th GRAND SLAM: ANNIVERSARY. Aug 1, 1977. Willie McCovey of the San Francisco Giants hit the 18th and last grand slam of his career. His total still stands as the National League record. Lou Gehrig holds the major league record with 23.

McINTIRE'S ALMOST-NO-HITTER: ANNIVERSARY. Aug 1, 1906. Harry McIntire of the Brooklyn Superbas (later the Dodgers) pitched $10\frac{2}{3}$ innings of no-hit baseball before Claude Ritchey of the Pittsburgh Pirates singled. McIntire stayed in the game but lost it in the 13th inning, 1–0. His effort stands as the longest "almost-no-hitter" in major league history.

☆   ☆   ☆

NATIONAL BASEBALL CONGRESS WORLD SERIES. Aug 1–15 (tentative dates). Lawrence-Dumont Stadium, Wichita, KS. 64th annual National Baseball Congress World Series. Est attendance: 100,000. For info: National Baseball Congress, PO Box 1420, Wichita, KS 67201. Phone: (316) 267-3372 or x 204. Fax: (316) 267-3382. Email: nbc@wichitawranglers.com. WWW: http://www.wichitawranglers.com

NFL ADMITS FIVE FRANCHISES: ANNIVERSARY. Aug 1, 1925. The National Football League admitted five new franchises: a new Canton Bulldogs team, the Detroit Panthers, the New York Giants, the Pottsville Maroons and the Providence Steam Rollers. The Bulldogs and the Panthers lasted two seasons, the Maroons four and the Steam Rollers seven. The Giants still exist although they play in New Jersey.

OTT HITS 500TH HOME RUN: ANNIVERSARY. Aug 1, 1945. Outfielder Mel Ott of the New York Giants hit the 500th home run of his career in a 9–2 win over the Boston Braves at the Polo Grounds. At this point in baseball history, Ott stood third on the all-time home run list behind Babe Ruth with 714 and Jimmie Foxx with 531. Ott finished with 511 homers.

ROSE'S HITTING STREAK ENDS: 20th ANNIVERSARY. Aug 1, 1978. Pete Rose of the Cincinnati Reds saw his 44-game hitting streak come to an end as he went 0-for-4 against Larry McWilliams and Gene Garber of the Atlanta Braves in a 16–4 Braves win. Rose's streak tied Willie Keeler's mark, set in 1897, as the longest in National League history.

SAWYER TRIATHLON XVI. Aug 1. Tom Sawyer State Park, Louisville, KY. Participants swim ½ mile, bicycle 28 miles and run 5K cross country. Est attendance: 500. For info: Tim Curtis, Recreation Dir, E.P. Tom Sawyer Park, 3000 Freys Hill Rd, Louisville, KY 40241-2172. Phone: (502) 426-8950.

TALL TIMBER DAYS FESTIVAL. Aug 1–2. Grand Rapids, MN. Festival features the Sheer Brothers Lumberjack Show, chainsaw carvers, arts and crafts, Applecords Quartet, competitions, YMCA run, Native American dance & story-telling, in-line skating, canoeing and bed racing. Families welcome. Annually, the first full weekend in August. Est attendance: 30,000. For info: Tall Timber Days, PO Box 134, Grand Rapids, MN 55744. Phone: (218) 326-5618. Fax: (218) 326-5618. Email: mojo@uslink.net.

VIRGINIA STATE HORSE SHOW—QUARTER HORSE DIVISION. Aug 1–2. Fairgrounds on Strawberry Hill, Richmond, VA. Open, amateur, novice and youth competition for registered Quarter Horses. Est attendance: 1,000. For info: Sue Mullins, Equine Dir, PO Box 26805, Richmond, VA 23261. Phone: (804) 228-3238. Fax: (804) 228-3252. Email: equine@strawberryhill.com.

BIRTHDAYS TODAY

Greg Adams, 35, hockey player, born Nelson, BC, Canada, Aug 1, 1963.

Stacey Orlando Augmon, 30, basketball player, born Pasadena, CA, Aug 1, 1968.

George Irvin Bamberger, 73, former baseball manager and player, born New York, NY, Aug 1, 1925.

Gregory Eugene (Greg) Gross, 46, former baseball player, born York, PA, Aug 1, 1952.

Gregory Scott (Gregg) Jefferies, 31, baseball player, born Burlingame, CA, Aug 1, 1967.

Samuel (Sammy) Lee, 78, Olympic gold medal diver, born Fresno, CA, Aug 1, 1920.

Milton Scott (Milt) May, 48, former baseball player, born Gary, IN, Aug 1, 1950.

Anthony Joseph (Tony) Muser, 51, baseball manager and former player, born Van Nuys, CA, Aug 1, 1947.

AUGUST 2 — SUNDAY
Day 214 — 151 Remaining

AMES, RED: BIRTH ANNIVERSARY. Aug 2, 1882. Leon ("Red") Ames, baseball player born at Warren, OH. Ames pitched for the New York Giants and three other teams, winning 22 games in 1905 when the Giants won the World Series. In 1909 he pitched a no-hitter for nine innings, gave up a hit in the tenth and lost the game in the 13th. Died at Warren, Oct 8, 1936.

COLLEGE ALL-STARS UPSET PACKERS: 35th ANNIVERSARY. Aug 2, 1963. In the annual tilt between the defending NFL champions and a team of college all-stars on their way to their rookie pro seasons, the collegians upset the Green Bay Packers, 20–17. The College All-Star Game was contested from 1934 through 1977 with the collegians winning nine times and earning one tie (in the inaugural game).

HAMBLETONIAN STAKES. Aug 2. The Meadowlands, East Rutherford, NJ. The richest and most important race for trotting horses. First raced in 1926, this $1.2 million race, to be nationally televised, is the most coveted prize in trotting. For tickets call: (201) 935-8500. For info: Hambletonian Society, 1200 Tices Lane, East Brunswick, NJ 08816. Phone: (908) 249-8500. Fax: (908) 294-3170.

August 1998	S	M	T	W	T	F	S
							1
	2	3	4	5	6	7	8
	9	10	11	12	13	14	15
	16	17	18	19	20	21	22
	23	24	25	26	27	28	29
	30	31					

KIERAN, JOHN: BIRTH ANNIVERSARY. Aug 2, 1892. John Francis Kieran, sportswriter born at New York, NY. Kieran graduated from Fordham University and earned two advanced degrees. His wide knowledge made his writing for the *New York Times* different from other sportswriters and merited the first by-lined column in the *Times.* Kieran also served as a panelist for ten years on the radio quiz show, "Information Please." Died at Rockport, MA, Dec 10, 1981.

US WINS OLYMPIC BOXING TITLE: ANNIVERSARY. Aug 2, 1952. Five American boxers won gold medals at the Summer Olympics in Helsinki, Finland, giving the US the unofficial team championship for the first time. The gold medalists were flyweight Nate Brooks, light welterweight Charley Adkins, middleweight Floyd Patterson, light heavyweight Norvell Lee and heavyweight Eddie Sanders.

YELLOW BASEBALLS USED: 60th ANNIVERSARY. Aug 2, 1938. The Brooklyn Dodgers and the St. Louis Cardinals played a doubleheader in which they experimented with a yellow baseball in the first game. They went back to the traditional white ball for the second game, and the Dodgers won both contests, 6–2 and 9–3.

BIRTHDAYS TODAY

Anthony Lewis (Tony) Amonte, 28, hockey player, born Hingham, MA, Aug 2, 1970.

Cedric Z. Ceballos, 29, basketball player, born Maui, HI, Aug 2, 1969.

Linda Sue Fratianne, 38, figure skater, born Los Angeles, CA, Aug 2, 1960.

Lamar Hunt, 66, Pro Football Hall of Fame executive, born El Dorado, AR, Aug 2, 1932.

Jesus Manuel ("Bombo") Rivera, 46, former baseball player, born Ponce, Puerto Rico, Aug 2, 1952.

Timothy Stephen (Tim) Wakefield, 32, baseball player, born Melbourne, FL, Aug 2, 1966.

AUGUST 3 — MONDAY
Day 215 — 150 Remaining

CHASE'S SPORTSQUOTE OF THE DAY
"There's three parts to football: offense, defense and special teams. You'd no more ignore special teams than you would offense or defense." —Marv Levy

FIRST INTERCOLLEGIATE ROWING RACE: ANNIVERSARY. Aug 3, 1852. The first intercollegiate athletic competition, a rowing race between Harvard and Yale, took place on Lake Winnipesaukee, NH. Over a two-mile course, Harvard beat Yale by four lengths.

FORMATION OF NBA: ANNIVERSARY. Aug 3, 1949. The National Basketball Association (NBA) was established from the merger of the National Basketball League (NBL) and the Basketball Association of America (BAA).

GROVE SHUTS OUT YANKEES: 65th ANNIVERSARY. Aug 3, 1933. Lefty Grove and the Philadelphia Athletics shut out the New York Yankees, 7–0, the first time the Yankees had been blanked since Aug 2, 1931, a span of 309 games.

HEGAN, JIM: BIRTH ANNIVERSARY. Aug 3, 1920. James Edward (Jim) Hegan, baseball player and coach born at Lynn, MA. Hegan was the outstanding starting catcher for the Cleveland Indians' pennant winners in 1948 and 1954. After retiring, he coached for the Detroit Tigers and New York Yankees. Died at Swampscott, MA, June 17, 1984.

HEILMANN, HARRY: BIRTH ANNIVERSARY. Aug 3, 1894. Harry Edwin Heilmann, Baseball Hall of Fame outfielder born at San Francisco, CA. Heilmann hit .394 for the Detroit Tigers in 1921 and went on to win three American League batting titles. After retiring, he became a sportscaster for the Tigers. Inducted into the Hall of Fame in 1952. Died at Detroit, MI, July 9, 1951.

KENWOOD CUP: HAWAII INTERNATIONAL OCEAN RACING SERIES. Aug 3–14. Oahu, HI. 11th biennial. The Kenwood Cup is a series of 10 sailing races of varying distances and part of the Champagne Mumm World Cup international sailing series. 50 Grand Prix yachts, ranging in length from 35 to 82 feet, are expected from Australia, New Zealand, Canada, Europe and the US. There are four windward/leeward races (10-12 nautical miles each) and four ocean triangle races (22 nautical miles each) off Waikiki Beach, a 150-mile Honolulu-to-Maui race along Molokai's north shore, and a 390-mile race beginning and finishing off Oahu. Both long distance races finish off Diamond Head and can be viewed by spectators. Fun events include the Plymouth Cup team event with amateur boat construction to benefit charity. Est attendance: 2,000. For media info: Carol Hogan, (808) 325-7400. For race info: (808) 946-9061. Email: oceanpro@interpac.net. WWW: http://www.worldvoyager.com

STURGIS RALLY AND RACES. Aug 3–9. Sturgis, SD. The granddaddy of all motorcycle rallies and races. For 57 years the small community of Sturgis has welcomed motorcycle enthusiasts from around the world to a week of varied cycle racing, tours of the beautiful Black Hills, old and new cycles at the National Motorcycle Museum, trade shows and thousands of bikes on display. Annually, beginning the Monday after the first full weekend in August. Est attendance: 215,000. For info: Sturgis Rally & Races, Inc, PO Box 189, Sturgis, SD 57785. Phone: (605) 347-6570. Fax: (605) 347-3245. Email: srr@rally.sturgis.sd.us. WWW: http://www.rally.sturgis.sd.us

TRADE OF MANAGERS: ANNIVERSARY. Aug 3, 1960. In an unprecedented baseball transaction, two teams traded managers. The Cleveland Indians sent Joe Gordon to the Detroit Tigers for Jimmy Dykes.

WORLD FOOTBAG CHAMPIONSHIPS. Aug 3–9. Denver, CO. Seven-day sports event spotlights competition of footskills—the Super Bowl of footbag! Now in its 19th year, it attracts the world's top footbag competitors from the US and six other countries. Prize money exceeds $10,000. Sponsors: Mattel Sports, Adidas, Sipa Sipa Footbags and The World Footbag Association. Est attendance: 3,000. For info: Bruce Guettich, Dir, World Footbag Assn, PO Box 775208, Steamboat Springs, CO 80477. Phone: (800) 878-8787. Fax: (970) 870-2846. Email: wfa@worldfootbag.com. WWW: http://www.worldfootbag.com

BIRTHDAYS TODAY

Lance Dwight Alworth, 58, Pro Football Hall of Fame wide receiver, born Houston, TX, Aug 3, 1940.
Rodney Roy (Rod) Beck, 30, baseball player, born Burbank, CA, Aug 3, 1968.
Sidney Eugene (Sid) Bream, 38, former baseball player, born Carlisle, PA, Aug 3, 1960.
Kevin Daniel Elster, 34, baseball player, born San Pedro, CA, Aug 3, 1964.

James William (Jim) Gott, 39, former baseball player, born Hollywood, CA, Aug 3, 1959.
Marvin Daniel (Marv) Levy, 70, football coach, born Chicago, IL, Aug 3, 1928.
Trevor Price, 23, football player, born Winter Park, FL, Aug 3, 1975.

AUGUST 4 — TUESDAY
Day 216 — 149 Remaining

BECKLEY, JAKE: BIRTH ANNIVERSARY. Aug 4, 1867. Jacob Peter (Jake) Beckley, Baseball Hall of Fame first baseman born at Hannibal, MO. Beckley was a first baseman who played in the majors from 1888 to 1907. He is said to have invented the hidden ball trick. Inducted into the Hall of Fame in 1971. Died at Kansas City, MO, June 25, 1918.

CUNNINGHAM, GLENN: BIRTH ANNIVERSARY. Aug 4, 1909. Glenn V. Cunningham, track and field athlete born at Atlanta, KS. Cunningham overcame severe burns to his legs in a schoolhouse fire to become a great middle-distance runner. He won the Sullivan Award for 1933 and starred in the mile run as it became the premier track event. He set a world record, 4:06.7, in 1934 that lasted three years. After World War II, he and his wife opened a youth ranch and cared for more than 10,000 foster children plus ten of their own. Died at Menifee, AR, Mar 10, 1988.

LUQUE, ADOLFO: BIRTH ANNIVERSARY. Aug 4, 1890. Adolfo Luque, baseball player born at Havana, Cuba. Luque was the first Latin American player to appear in the World Series, with the 1919 Cincinnati Reds. Near the end of his career, he became a relief pitcher exclusively, a prototype for players to come. Died at Havana, July 3, 1957.

MOLYNEUX, TOM: 180th DEATH ANNIVERSARY. Aug 4, 1818. Tom Molyneux, boxer born in Virginia or Maryland, 1784. Molyneux was a slave who won his freedom by winning a fight on which his owner had wagered. He made his way to New York and then to England where he narrowly lost a fight against Tom Cribb on Dec 18, 1810, for the heavyweight title. Died at Dublin, Ireland.

SEAVER WINS 300th GAME: ANNIVERSARY. Aug 4, 1985. Tom Seaver, pitching for the Chicago White Sox against the Yankees in New York, won the 300th game of his career. He gave up seven hits, walked one and struck out seven as the Sox won, 4–1. Seaver pitched in the majors from 1967 through 1986, mostly for the New York Mets, and won 311 games.

US GIRLS' JUNIOR (GOLF) CHAMPIONSHIP. Aug 4–9. Merion Golf Course, Ardmore, PA. For info: US Golf Assn, Golf House, Far Hills, NJ 07931. Phone: (908) 234-2300. Fax: (908) 234-9687. Email: usga@ix.netcom.com. WWW: http://www.usga.org

YOUNGBLOOD HITS FOR TWO TEAMS: ANNIVERSARY. Aug 4, 1982. Joel Youngblood became the first major leaguer to play and get a hit for two different teams in two different cities in the same day. In an afternoon game, Youngblood drove in the winning run for the New York Mets as they beat the Cubs in Chicago, 7–4. After the game, he was traded to the Montreal Expos, who played in Philadelphia that night. Youngblood flew there, entered the game in the fourth inning and got a single.

BIRTHDAYS TODAY

William Roger Clemens, 36, baseball player, born Dayton, OH, Aug 4, 1962.
Jeff Gordon, 27, auto racer, born Pittsboro, IN, Aug 4, 1971.

George Dallas Green, 64, former baseball manager and player, born Newport, DE, Aug 4, 1934.

Cleon Joseph Jones, 56, former baseball player, born Plateau, AL, Aug 4, 1942.

Joseph Henri Maurice ("Rocket") Richard, 77, Hockey Hall of Fame right wing, born Montreal, Quebec, Canada, Aug 4, 1921.

John Riggins, 49, Pro Football Hall of Fame fullback, born Centralia, KS, Aug 4, 1949.

Mary Decker Slaney, 40, middle distance runner, born Bunnvale, NJ, Aug 4, 1958.

AUGUST 5 — WEDNESDAY
Day 217 — 148 Remaining

AARON, TOMMIE: BIRTH ANNIVERSARY. Aug 5, 1939. Tommie Lee Aaron, baseball player born at Mobile, AL. The brother of home run king Henry Aaron hit 13 homers in a seven-year major league career. Died at Atlanta, GA, Aug 16, 1984.

AMATEUR SOFTBALL ASSOCIATION GIRLS 14-AND-UNDER NATIONAL FAST-PITCH CHAMPIONSHIP. Aug 5–9. Sportscore, Rockford, IL. National Championship for Girls Fast-Pitch Softball teams, age 14 and under. Each team qualifies by winning its state or regional tournament. Always held during the week in August ending with the second Saturday and second Sunday of the month. Sponsor: Rockford Metropolitan Sports Authority, Rockford Area Convention & Visitors Bureau, Rockford Park District. Est attendance: 5,000. For info: Chuck Lockinger, 533 Burbank, Woodstock, IL 60098. Phone: (815) 338-8945. Fax: (815) 338-8945.

FIRST BASEBALL BROADCAST: ANNIVERSARY. Aug 5, 1921. Radio station KDKA in Pittsburgh broadcast a baseball game for the first time as the Pirates beat the Philadelphia Phillies, 8–5. Announcer Harold Arlin called the game.

FIRST HAMBLETONIAN DEAD HEAT: ANNIVERSARY. Aug 5, 1989. For the first time, the raceoff in the Hambletonian, harness racing's most prestigious race, ended in a dead heat with Park Avenue Joe being declared the winner over Probe. Park Avenue Joe finished second in the first heat and won the second heat. Probe won the first heat but broke stride and finished ninth in the second heat.

MUSTANG LEAGUE WORLD SERIES. Aug 5–8. Irving, TX. International youth baseball World Series for play-

August 1998	S	M	T	W	T	F	S
							1
	2	3	4	5	6	7	8
	9	10	11	12	13	14	15
	16	17	18	19	20	21	22
	23	24	25	26	27	28	29
	30	31					

ers league ages 9 and 10. Est attendance: 5,000. For info: Pony Baseball/Softball, Inc, PO Box 225, Washington, PA 15301. Phone: (412) 225-1060. Fax: (412) 225-9852. Email: pony@pulsenet.com. WWW: http://www.pony.org

PINCH-HIT HOME RUN RECORD: ANNIVERSARY. Aug 5, 1984. Cliff Johnson of the Toronto Blue Jays hit the 19th pinch-hit home run of his career to set the major league record as the Blue Jays beat the Baltimore Orioles, 4–3. Johnson hit an additional pinch-homer in 1986 to extend his record to 20.

RUPPERT, JACOB: BIRTH ANNIVERSARY. Aug 5, 1867. Jacob Ruppert, Jr, baseball executive born at New York, NY. Ruppert was the son of a brewery owner who purchased the New York Yankees in 1914 with Tillinghast Huston for $450,000. Ruppert bought Babe Ruth from the Boston Red Sox, built Yankee Stadium and made his team the best in baseball. Died at New York, Jan 13, 1939.

STARGELL HITS HOME RUN OUT OF DODGER STADIUM: ANNIVERSARY. Aug 5, 1969. Willie Stargell of the Pittsburgh Pirates hit the only home run ever out of Dodger Stadium. His blast off pitcher Alan Foster cleared the right-field pavilion and traveled an estimated 506 feet from home plate.

BIRTHDAYS TODAY

Nelson Kelley (Nellie) Briles, 55, broadcaster and former baseball player, born Dorris, CA, Aug 5, 1943.

Bernard (Bernie) Carbo, 51, former baseball player, born Detroit, MI, Aug 5, 1947.

Patrick Aloysius Ewing, 36, basketball player, born Kingston, Jamaica, Aug 5, 1962.

Gregory Fuller (Greg) Kite, 37, former basketball player, born Houston, TX, Aug 5, 1961.

John Garrett Olerud, 30, baseball player, born Seattle, WA, Aug 5, 1968.

Otis Henry Thorpe, 36, basketball player, born Boynton Beach, FL, Aug 5, 1962.

AUGUST 6 — THURSDAY
Day 218 — 147 Remaining

BLADES, RAY: BIRTH ANNIVERSARY. Aug 6, 1896. Francis Raymond (Ray) Blades, baseball player and manager born at Mt. Vernon, IL. Blades was a dependable outfielder who managed the St. Louis Cardinals in 1939. Died at Lincoln, IL, May 18, 1979.

FIRST WOMAN SWIMS THE ENGLISH CHANNEL: ANNIVERSARY. Aug 6, 1926. The first woman to swim the English Channel was 19-year-old Gertrude Ederle of New York, NY. Her swim was completed in 14 hours and 31 minutes.

MAGEE, SHERRY: BIRTH ANNIVERSARY. Aug 6, 1884. Sherwood Robert (Sherry) Magee, baseball player and umpire born at Clarendon, PA. Magee won the National League batting title in 1910, hitting .331 for the Philadelphia Phillies. After retiring, he became an NL umpire. Died at Philadelphia, PA, Mar 13, 1929.

PAIGE PITCHES COMPLETE GAME: ANNIVERSARY. Aug 6, 1952. Satchel Paige, at age 47, became the oldest pitcher to pitch a complete game, beating the Detroit Tigers, 1–0, in 12 innings.

SPLIT SEASON APPROVED: ANNIVERSARY. Aug 6, 1981. After a seven-week strike that cut the heart out of the regular baseball season, major league players approved a plan for a split season with the post-strike games to constitute the second half. The New York Yankees, Oakland Athletics, Philadelphia Phillies and Los

Angeles Dodgers were declared first-half champions, automatically qualifying for special divisional playoffs.

STRONG, KEN: BIRTH ANNIVERSARY. Aug 6, 1906. Elmer Kenneth (Ken) Strong, Jr, Pro Football Hall of Fame halfback and placekicker born at West Haven, CT. Strong played baseball and football at New York University and then played both sports professionally. His placekicking skills several times put him among the NFL's leading scorers. He coached kicking after he retired and wrote a book that incorporated motion picture studies. Inducted into the Pro Football Hall of Fame in 1967. Died at New York, NY, Oct 5, 1979.

BIRTHDAYS TODAY

Stanley Peter (Stan) Belinda, 32, baseball player, born Huntingdon, PA, Aug 6, 1966.
Ronald Gene (Ron) Davis, 43, former baseball player, born Houston, TX, Aug 6, 1955.
Dale Ellis, 38, basketball player, born Marietta, GA, Aug 6, 1960.
Clement Walter (Clem) Labine, 72, former baseball player, born Lincoln, RI, Aug 6, 1926.
John Alexander ("Andy") Messersmith, 53, former baseball player, born Toms River, NJ, Aug 6, 1945.
David Maurice Robinson, 33, basketball player, born Key West, FL, Aug 6, 1965.

AUGUST 7 — FRIDAY

Day 219 — 146 Remaining

SPORTSCHASER OF THE DAY

What golfer, known for his "grip it and rip it" approach, won the 1991 PGA championship?

ALABAMA PRO NATIONAL TRUCK AND TRACTOR PULL. Aug 7–8. Lexington, AL. Six different classes compete: Pro National 7500 Superstock, Pro National 6200 2-Wheel Drive Trucks, Pro National 7200 Modified Tractors (multiengine), State Level 6200 4-Wheel Drive Truck, Local Level 4x4 Street Class and Local Level 15,200 Farm Class. Est attendance: 20,000. For info: Debbie Wilson, Dir, Florence/Lauderdale Tourism, One Hightower Pl, Florence, AL 35630. Phone: (205) 740-4141 or (888) FLO-TOUR. Fax: (205) 740-4142.
WWW: http://www.flo-tour.org

BOOM DAYS. Aug 7–9. Leadville, CO. The city's oldest annual celebration features a large parade, street races, mining events, pack burro race and arts and crafts. Fun for the whole family. Est attendance: 25,000. For info: Gloria Cheshier, Chamber of Commerce, PO Box 861, Leadville, CO 80461. Phone: (719) 486-3900 or (800) 933-3901. Fax: (719) 486-8478. Email: leadville@sni.net WWW: http://www.colorado.com/leadville

CANADA: ABBOTSFORD INTERNATIONAL AIRSHOW. Aug 7–8. Abbotsford Airport, Abbotsford, British Columbia. Leading air show in North America attracts the world's top aeronautical performers. Thrill to the grace of the Canadian Snowbirds, the raw power of the international air demonstration squadrons, dramatic teams of daring performers and soloists. Static displays and food booths. Open daily 8–5; aerial show 11–5. Airshow camping facilities. Est attendance: 250,000. For info: Abbotsford Intl Airshow, 30470 Approach Dr, Abbotsford, BC, Canada V2T 6H5. Email: airshow@uniserve.com.

CANADA: CARDSTON STAMPEDE. Aug 7–8. Cardston, Alberta. Rodeo is part of Cardston's annual Heritage Days celebrations. Rodeo's first hornless bronc saddle is said to have debuted here in 1922. For info: Cardston

Heritage Days, PO Box 121, Cardston, Alberta, Canada, T0K 0K0. Phone: (403) 653-3943.

DALY WINS PGA: ANNIVERSARY. Aug 7, 1991. A last-minute entry who didn't have the opportunity to play a practice round, John Daly won the PGA Championship at Crooked Stick Golf Club in Indiana by three strokes over Bruce Lietzke. Daly endured a wealth of personal problems in the ensuing years, including marital difficulties and alcoholism. But he continued to thrill tournament crowds with his prodigious drives and his "grip it and rip it" approach to the game.

HALFWAY POINT OF SUMMER. Aug 7. At 5:20 AM, EDT, on Aug 7, 1998, 46 days, seven hours and 42 minutes will have elapsed and the equivalent will remain before 1:37 AM, EDT, Sept 22, 1998, the autumnal equinox and the beginning of autumn.

INTERNATIONAL AEROBATIC CHAMPIONSHIPS. Aug 7–10 (tentative). Fond du Lac County Airport, Fond du Lac, WI. Watch the best aerobatic pilots in the world compete! Forums, exhibits, pancake breakfast, plane rides. Est attendance: 10,000. For info: Fond du Lac Conv Bureau, 19 W Scott St, Fond du Lac, WI 54935. Phone: (800) 937-9123 ext 95. Fax: (920) 929-6846. Email: fdlcvb@visitwisconsin.com.
WWW: http://www.visitwisconsin.com/fdl

LARGEST MINOR LEAGUE CROWD: ANNIVERSARY. Aug 7, 1956. 57,000 people, the largest minor league baseball crowd in history, watched former Negro Leagues star and major leaguer Satchel Paige pitch for the Miami Marlins in an International League game against the Columbus Jets. The game was played at the Orange Bowl, and Miami won.

LUNAR ECLIPSE. Aug 7. Penumbral eclipse of the moon. Moon enters penumbra at 9:31 PM, EDT, reaches middle of eclipse at 10:24 PM, EDT and leaves penumbra at 11:18 PM, EDT. The beginning of the penumbral phase visible in eastern North America, Central America, South America, southern Greeland, Europe, extreme western Asia, Africa, most of Antarctica, western Indian Ocean, eastern South Pacific Ocean, southeastern North Pacific Ocean, Atlantic Ocean; the end of phase visible in North America except northern and western Canada and Alaska, Central America, South America, most of Europe, southern Greenland, Africa except the extreme east, most of Antarctica, the eastern South Pacific Ocean, southeastern North Pacific Ocean, Atlantic Ocean.

McKECHNIE, BILL: BIRTH ANNIVERSARY. Aug 7, 1886. William Boyd (Bill) McKechnie, Baseball Hall of Fame manager born at Wilkinsburg, PA. McKechnie is generally recognized as one of greatest strategic managers in history. He took three National League teams to the pennant, the Pittsburgh Pirates in 1925, the St. Louis Cardinals in 1928 and the Cincinnati Reds in 1939 and 1940. Inducted into the Hall of Fame in 1962. Died at Bradenton, FL, Oct 29, 1965.

MOON PHASE: FULL MOON. Aug 7. Moon enters Full Moon phase at 10:10 PM, EDT.

PALOMINO LEAGUE WORLD SERIES. Aug 7–11 (tentative dates). Greensboro, NC. International young adult baseball World Series for players of league ages 17 and 18. Est attendance: 6,650. For info: Pony Baseball/Softball, Inc, Box 225, Washington, PA 15301. Phone: (412) 225-1060. Fax: (412) 225-9852.
Email: pony@pulse.net.com. WWW: http://www.pony.org

TERRY, ADONIS: BIRTH ANNIVERSARY. Aug 7, 1864. William H. ("Adonis") Terry, baseball player born Westfield, MA. Terry was a 19th-century pitcher, but he played other positions, too. His nickname came from his good looks. Died at Milwaukee, WI, Feb 24, 1915.

THREE-ON-THREE CHAMPIONSHIP. Aug 7–9 (tentative). Fond du Lac, WI. Join the outdoor fun at this statewide three-on-three basketball competition, played on the lucky lottery portion of Main Street, known as the "Miracle Mile" in downtown Fond du Lac. Est attendance: 3,500. For info: Fond du Lac Conv Bureau, 19 W Scott St, Fond du Lac, WI 54935. Phone: (800) 937-9123 ext 95. Fax: (920) 929-6846. Email: fdlcvb@visitwisconsin.com. WWW: http://www.visitwisconsin.com/fdl

WAITZ WINS MARATHON: 15th ANNIVERSARY. Aug 7, 1983. At the first World Track and Field Championships at Helsinki, Finland, Grete Waitz of Norway won the women's marathon, an event for many years thought beyond the capability of women.

WAKE UP TO MISSOURI US NATIONAL HOT-AIR BALLOON CHAMPIONSHIPS. Aug 7–15. Columbia, MO. 200 hot-air balloons fill the skies of Columbia, as 100 pilots compete for $100,000 and the right to represent the US in the World Championships. Some 100 Fiesta balloons and special-shaped balloons are expected to fly during this event. Plus carnival, children's area, live music and crafts exhibits. Est attendance: 250,000. For info: Missouri Balloon Corp, 1400 Forum Blvd, Ste 20, Columbia, MO 65203. Phone: (573) 446-5566.

WORLD FREEFALL CONVENTION. Aug 7–16. Quincy, IL. Skydivers converge in Quincy and fill the skies with their brilliant colored parachutes. Spectators can enjoy the sights and take part in helicopter rides, biplane rides and hot-air balloon rides. Those wishing to skydive may purchase a tandem skydive or take lessons and skydive on their own. Est attendance: 20,000. For info: Rob Ebbing, World Freefall Convention, 1515 Kentucky, Quincy, IL 62301. Phone: (217) 222-5867. Fax: (217) 222-5867. Email: wffc@freefall.com. WWW: http://www.freefall.com

BIRTHDAYS TODAY

Everett Lamar ("Rocky") Bridges, 71, former baseball player, born Refugio, TX, Aug 7, 1927.
Dominic (Dom) Capers, 48, football coach, born Cambridge, OH, Aug 7, 1950.
Steven F. (Steve) Kemp, 44, former baseball player, born San Angelo, TX, Aug 7, 1954.
Don James Larsen, 69, former baseball player, born Michigan City, IN, Aug 7, 1929.
Alan Cedric Page, 53, Pro Football Hall of Fame defensive tackle, born Canton, OH, Aug 7, 1945.
Alberto Salazar, 41, marathon runner, born Havana, Cuba, Aug 7, 1957.

AUGUST 8 — SATURDAY

Day 220 — 145 Remaining

ALL-AMERICAN SOAP BOX DERBY. Aug 8. Derby Downs, Akron, OH. A weeklong festival culminating in world championship race by regional champs from US, Canada, Germany, Ireland, Australia and Philippines. 61st annual derby. Est attendance: 15,000. For info: Jeff Iula, Genl Mgr, Intl Soap Box Derby, Inc, PO Box 7233, Akron, OH 44306. Phone: (330) 733-8723. Fax: (330) 733-1370. Email: 2077607@mcimail.com. WWW: http://pages.prodigy.com/SOAPBOX

August *1998*	S	M	T	W	T	F	S
							1
	2	3	4	5	6	7	8
	9	10	11	12	13	14	15
	16	17	18	19	20	21	22
	23	24	25	26	27	28	29
	30	31					

CRATER LAKE RIM RUNS AND MARATHON. Aug 8. Crater Lake National Park, OR. One of the toughest and most spectacular races you'll ever run! Race routes are around Crater Lake, the deepest lake in the US. Included are 6.7-mile and 13-mile races and a full marathon. Est attendance: 500. For info: Crater Lake Rim Runs, 5830 Mack Ave, Klamath Falls, OR 97603. Phone: (541) 884-6939.

DREAM TEAM WINS GOLD MEDAL: ANNIVERSARY. Aug 8, 1992. The Dream Team, a specially-assembled team of NBA all-stars, defeated Croatia, 117–85, to win the gold medal at the 1992 Summer Olympics in Barcelona. The Dream Team, coached by Chuck Daly, included Charles Barkley, Larry Bird, Clyde Drexler, Patrick Ewing, Magic Johnson, Michael Jordan, Christian Laettner, Karl Malone, Chris Mullin, Scottie Pippen, David Robinson and John Stockton.

FIRST HAMBLETONIAN AT THE MEADOWLANDS: ANNIVERSARY. Aug 8, 1981. Shiaway St. Pat, driven by Ray Remmen, won the Hambletonian, the most important race for three-year-old trotters, contested for the first time at the Meadowlands in New Jersey.

FIRST WRIGLEY FIELD NIGHT GAME POSTPONED: 10th ANNIVERSARY. Aug 8, 1988. The first night game at Chicago's Wrigley Field was postponed by rain with the Cubs leading the Philadelphia Phillies, 3–1, in the bottom of the fourth inning. The Phillies' Phil Bradley led off the game with a home run, but in a postponed game all statistics are washed out.

INTER-STATE FAIR AND RODEO. Aug 8–16. Coffeyville, KS. "Largest outdoor fair and rodeo event in southeast Kansas and northeast Oklahoma." Est attendance: 60,000. For info: Montgomery County Fair Assn, Box 457, Coffeyville, KS 67337. Phone: (316) 251-2550. Fax: (316) 251-5448. Email: chamber@terraworld.net. WWW: http://www.coffeyville.com

JACOBS, HELEN: 90th BIRTH ANNIVERSARY. Aug 8, 1908. Helen Hull Jacobs, tennis player born at Globe, AZ. Jacobs won the US Women's singles championship at Forest Hills four times (1932–35) and finished second four other times. She was named Associated Press Female Athlete of the Year for 1933. Jacobs engaged in a storied rivalry with Helen Wills Moody, but she defeated Moody only once in their eleven meetings and that when Moody retired in the third set because of an injury. Died at Easthampton, NY, June 2, 1997.

MUD VOLLEYBALL TOURNAMENT. Aug 8. Rockford, IL. More than 300 teams from the Midwest participate in the world's largest one-day, one-site mud volleyball tournament. Benefit for Epilepsy Association. Est attendance: 5,000. For info: Epilepsy Assn, 321 W State St, Ste 208, Rockford, IL 61101.

PILOT PEN INTERNATIONAL TENNIS TOURNAMENT. Aug 8–16. Pilot Pen-Connecticut Tennis Center, Yale University, New Haven, CT. Championship level men's professional tennis tournament. 56 of the world's top singles players and 28 doubles teams compete for $1.04 million in prize money. Est attendance: 160,000. For info: Jewel Productions, Ltd, Pilot Pen Intl Tennis Tourn, 45 Yale Ave, New Haven, CT 06515-2253. Phone: (203) 776-7331 or (800) 548-6586. Fax: (203) 772-4647.

SEWARD SILVER SALMON DERBY. Aug 8–16. Seward, AK. Alaska's largest salmon derby. Fishermen vie for cash prizes, including tagged fish, daily top fish awards and sweepstakes drawing. 43rd annual. Est attendance: 10,000. For info: Seward Chamber of Commerce, PO Box 749, Seward, AK 99664. Phone: (907) 224-8051. Fax: (907) 224-5353. WWW: http://www.alaskaone.com/seward

SILVER VALLEY CLASSIC HORSESHOE TOURNAMENT. Aug 8–9. City Park, Kellogg, ID. Annually, the second weekend of August. Saturday, sanctioned National Horseshoe Assn singles tournament. Sunday, doubles fun tournament. For info: Don Heidt, 304 E Cameron Ave, Apt A, Kellogg, ID 83837. Phone: (208) 783-8211.

TEMPLE, JOHNNY: 70th BIRTH ANNIVERSARY. Aug 8, 1928. John Ellis Temple, baseball player born at Lexington, NC. Temple teamed with shortstop Roy McMillan to form a wonderful double play combination for the Cincinnati Reds in the 1950s. He was a six-time all-star, four times with the Reds and twice with the Cleveland Indians. Died at White Rock, SC, Jan 9, 1994.

TETONKAHA RENDEZVOUS. Aug 8–9. Oakwood Lakes State Park, Bruce, SD. Muzzle-loader contest, tomahawk and knife throw, log sawing, canoe races and more at this fair that presents the fur-trading atmosphere of the 1840s. Est attendance: 300. For info: Lee Kratochvil, Tetonkaha Rendezvous, 46109 202nd St, Bruse, SD 57220-5104. Phone: (605) 627-5441 or (605) 693-4589. Fax: (605) 627-5258.

WHITE SOX DON SHORTS: ANNIVERSARY. Aug 8, 1976. The Chicago White Sox made baseball sartorial history by donning shorts for a game against the Kansas City Royals. The Sox won, 5–2, but the shorts, a novelty thought up by owner Bill Veeck, lasted only a while.

BIRTHDAYS TODAY

Trev Alberts, 28, football player, born Cedar Falls, IA, Aug 8, 1970.

Elijah Alfred Alexander, III, 28, football player, born Fort Worth, TX, Aug 8, 1970.

Brad Dalgarno, 31, hockey player, born Vancouver, BC, Canada, Aug 8, 1967.

Frank Oliver Howard, 62, former baseball manager and player, born Columbus, OH, Aug 8, 1936.

Ronald Joseph (Ron) Karkovice, 35, baseball player, born Union, NJ, Aug 8, 1963.

Esther Williams, 75, swimmer and actress (*Take Me Out to the Ball Game*), born Los Angeles, CA, Aug 8, 1923.

AUGUST 9 — SUNDAY

Day 221 — 144 Remaining

CATALINA WATER SKI RACE. Aug 9. Long Beach, CA. International water-ski racing teams race 62 miles across open seas, round-trip from Long Beach to Catalina Island and back. Est attendance: 9,000. For info: Long Beach Boat and Ski Club, PO Box 2370, Long Beach, CA 90801. Phone: (714) 894-3498. Fax: (714) 893-2363.

COMPLETE GAMES STREAK: ANNIVERSARY. Aug 9, 1906. Jack Taylor of the St. Louis Cardinals pitched his 187th complete game in a row, not counting 15 relief appearances in which he needed no help. Taylor's incredible streak, begun June 13, 1901, was snapped in his next start, Aug 13, 1906.

EXETER ROAD RALLY. Aug 9. Exeter City Park, Exeter, NE. Participants decipher clues which take them throughout the countryside and into neighboring communities. Evening meal served. Registration 1 PM. 14th annual rally. Annually, the second Sunday in August. Est attendance: 150. For info: Norene Fitzgerald, Box 368, Exeter, NE 68351. Phone: (402) 759-4910. Fax: (402) 759-4455.

FIRST TENNIS ON TELEVISION: ANNIVERSARY. Aug 9, 1939. New York's experimental television station, W2XBS, broadcast tennis for the first time ever. Cameras were set up at the Eastern Grass Court championships at Rye, NY.

FIRST WRIGLEY FIELD NIGHT GAME: 10th ANNIVERSARY. Aug 9, 1988. After a postponement the night before, the first night game in Wrigley Field saw the Chicago Cubs defeat the New York Mets, 6–4.

ITALY: PALIO DEL GOLFO. Aug 9. La Spezia. A rowing contest over a 2,000-meter course. Annually, the second Sunday in August.

MARRIED AND DISQUALIFIED: ANNIVERSARY. Aug 9, 1957. The Amateur Athletic Union, governing body for amateur sports in the US, ruled that Lee Calhoun, gold medal winner in the 1956 Olympics in the 110-meter hurdles, had sacrificed his amateur standing. Calhoun had gotten married on the television show *Bride and Groom* and had accepted gifts from the show.

NATIONAL SCRABBLE CHAMPIONSHIP. Aug 9–13. Players compete for the national championship in the popular game invented by unemployed architect Alfred Butts in 1931. Est attendance: 500. For info: Kathy Hummel, Natl Scrabble Assn, Box 700, Front St Garden, Greenport, NY 11944. Phone: (516) 477-0033. Fax: (516) 477-0294. Email: info@scrabble.com. WWW: http://www.scrabble.com

PERSEID METEOR SHOWERS. Aug 9–13. Among the best known and most spectacular meteor showers are the Perseids, peaking about Aug 10–12. As many as 50–100 may be seen in a single night. Wish upon a "falling star"!

SEASON RESUMES WITH ALL-STAR GAME: ANNIVERSARY. Aug 9, 1981. The 1981 baseball season, interrupted by a players' strike, resumed with the All-Star game played in Cleveland's Municipal Stadium. 72,086 fans watched the National League defeat the American League, 5–4.

WALTON, IZAAK: BIRTH ANNIVERSARY. Aug 9, 1593. Izaak Walton, English author of classic treatise on fishing, *The Compleat Angler,* born at Stafford, England. He published his famous book in 1653. "Angling," Walton wrote, "may be said to be so like the mathematics, that it can never be fully learnt." Died at Wincester, England, Dec 15, 1683.

BIRTHDAYS TODAY

Tommie Lee Agee, 56, former baseball player, born Magnolia, AL, Aug 9, 1942.

Rod Jean Brind'Amour, 28, hockey player, born Ottawa, Ontario, Canada, Aug 9, 1970.

Robert Joseph (Bob) Cousy, 70, former soccer executive, former basketball coach and Basketball Hall of Fame guard, born New York, NY, Aug 9, 1928.

Vincent Joseph (Vinny) Del Negro, 32, basketball player, born Springfield, MA, Aug 9, 1966.

Ralph George Houk, 79, former baseball manager and player, born Lawrence, KS, Aug 9, 1919.

Brett Hull, 34, hockey player, born Belleville, Ontario, Canada, Aug 9, 1964.

Manuel Julian Javier, 62, former baseball player, born San Pedro de Macoris, Dominican Republic, Aug 9, 1936.

Rodney George (Rod) Laver, 60, former tennis player, born Rockhampton, Australia, Aug 9, 1938.

Kenneth Howard (Ken) Norton, Sr, 53, former boxer, born Jacksonville, IL, Aug 9, 1945.

Claude Wilson Osteen, 59, former baseball player, born Caney Springs, TN, Aug 9, 1939.

Deion Luwynn Sanders, 31, football and baseball player, born Fort Myers, FL, Aug 9, 1967.

Robert Guy (Bob) Scanlan, Jr, 32, baseball player, born Los Angeles, CA, Aug 9, 1966.

Ted Lyle Simmons, 49, former baseball executive and player, born Highland Park, MI, Aug 9, 1949.

John ("Hot Rod") Williams, 36, basketball player, born Sorrento, LA, Aug 9, 1962.

AUGUST 10 — MONDAY
Day 222 — 143 Remaining

CHASE'S SPORTSQUOTE OF THE DAY

"It is not how you hold your racket, it's how you hold your mind." —Perry Jones, US Davis Cup captain

BIRTH OF SABR: ANNIVERSARY. Aug 10, 1971. The Society for American Baseball Research, an organization of baseball historians, statisticians, researchers and fans, was founded at a meeting at Cooperstown, NY.

CLOSE BUT NO CIGAR: ANNIVERSARY. Aug 10, 1996. The attempt of the thoroughbred Cigar to set a modern North American record for consecutive races won at 17 came up one victory short as Dare and Go scored an upset in the Pacific Classic at Del Mar Race Track in San Diego, CA. Dare and Go, ridden by Alex Solis, came from off the pace to win by 3½ lengths. Cigar, tied with Citation at 16 straight wins, finished second. He had last lost on Oct 7, 1994, at Belmont Park, NY.

FEWEST PITCHES: ANNIVERSARY. Aug 10, 1944. Charles ("Red") Barrett of the Boston Braves pitched a 2–0 shutout against the Cincinnati Reds and threw only 58 pitches to complete the nine-inning game, a major league record for the fewest pitches in a complete game.

FIRST DAVIS CUP: ANNIVERSARY. Aug 10, 1900. The Davis Cup, an international team tennis competition established by American player Dwight Davis, was held for the first time with the United States defeating Great Britain, 3–0, in Boston.

KILLEBREW HITS 500th HOME RUN: ANNIVERSARY. Aug 10, 1971. Harmon Killebrew of the Minnesota Twins became the tenth player in major league history to reach the 500 mark in career home runs when he hit Nos. 500 and 501 off Mike Cuellar of the Baltimore Orioles in a 4–3 Orioles victory.

August 1998	S	M	T	W	T	F	S
							1
	2	3	4	5	6	7	8
	9	10	11	12	13	14	15
	16	17	18	19	20	21	22
	23	24	25	26	27	28	29
	30	31					

NAGY, STEVE: 85th BIRTH ANNIVERSARY. Aug 10, 1913. Steve Joseph Nagy, bowler born at Shoaf, Fayette County, PA. Nagy helped organize the Professional Bowlers Association and was elected Bowler of the Year in 1952 and 1955. Died at Cleveland, OH, Nov 10, 1966.

SLOAN, TOD: 125th BIRTH ANNIVERSARY. Aug 10, 1873. James Forman ("Tod") Sloan, jockey born at Kokomo, IN. Sloan invented the "monkey crouch" style of racing, tucking his knees under his chin and laying along the horse's neck. He won races in the United States and England and became one of the world's big spenders, going through a million dollars in two years. Died at Los Angeles, CA, Dec 21, 1933.

BIRTHDAYS TODAY

Charles Lee Glenn (Chuck) Carr, Jr, 30, baseball player, born San Bernardino, CA, Aug 10, 1968.
Rocco Domenico (Rocky) Colavito, 65, former baseball player, born New York, NY, Aug 10, 1933.
Bret Hedican, 28, hockey player, born St. Paul, MN, Aug 10, 1970.
William ("Red") Holzman, 78, former basketball player and Basketball Hall of Fame coach, born New York, NY, Aug 10, 1920.
Andrew Neal (Andy) Stankiewicz, 34, baseball player, born Inglewood, CA, Aug 10, 1964.
John Levell Starks, 33, basketball player, born Aug 10, 1965.

AUGUST 11 — TUESDAY
Day 223 — 142 Remaining

COLT LEAGUE WORLD SERIES. Aug 11–18. Lafayette, IN. International young adult baseball World Series for players of league ages 15 and 16. Est attendance: 10,000. For info: Pony Baseball/Softball, PO Box 225, Washington, PA 15301. Phone: (412) 225-1060. Fax: (412) 225-9852. Email: pony@pulsenet.com. WWW: http://www.pony.org

A HUNDRED WINS IN BOTH LEAGUES: ANNIVERSARY. Aug 11, 1970. Jim Bunning of the Philadelphia Phillies defeated the Houston Astros, 6–5, to become the first pitcher to win 100 games in each major league. Bunning, who started his career with the Detroit Tigers, became a Congressman from Kentucky after retiring from baseball and was inducted into the Baseball Hall of Fame in 1996.

NEWSOM, BOBO: BIRTH ANNIVERSARY. Aug 11, 1907. Louis Norman ("Bobo") Newsom, baseball player and sportscaster born at Hartsville, AL. Newsom was one of baseball's most traded players, rarely staying with one team more than a year and frequently only a month or so. He pitched a no-hitter for 9⅔ innings in 1938, but lost, 2–1. Died at Orlando, FL, Dec 7, 1962.

PADDOCK, CHARLIE: BIRTH ANNIVERSARY. Aug 11, 1900. Charles William (Charlie) Paddock, Olympic gold medal sprinter born at Gainesville, TX. Paddock set or tied world records in about 25 events, ranging from 50 yards to 250 meters, in a career that ran from 1913 to 1929. He won the 100 meters at the 1920 Olympics and gloried in his nickname, the "World's Fastest Human." Died in a military air crash at Sitka, AK, July 21, 1943.

PINSON, VADA: 60th BIRTH ANNIVERSARY. Aug 11, 1938. Vada Edward Pinson, baseball player and coach born at Memphis, TN. Pinson collected 2,757 hits in an 18-year career. He hit .343 for the Cincinnati Reds when they won the National League pennant in 1961. Died at Oakland, CA, Oct 21, 1995.

RUTH HITS 500th HOME RUN: ANNIVERSARY. Aug 11, 1929. Babe Ruth of the New York Yankees became the first player to hit 500 career home runs when he connected off Willis Hudlin as the Cleveland Indians defeated the Yankees, 6–5. The homer was also the 30th of the year for the Bambino.

SCHEFFING, BOB: 85th BIRTH ANNIVERSARY. Aug 11, 1913. Robert Boden (Bob) Scheffing, baseball player, manager and executive born at Overland, MO. Scheffing was a major league catcher, manager of the Detroit Tigers and general manager of the New York Mets. Died at Phoenix, AZ, Oct 26, 1985.

US WOMEN'S AMATEUR (GOLF) CHAMPIONSHIP. Aug 11–16. Barton Hills Country Club, Ann Arbor, MI. For info: US Golf Assn, Golf House, Far Hills, NJ 07931. Phone: (908) 234-2300. Fax: (908) 234-9687. Email: usga@ix.netcom.com. WWW: http://www.usga.org

BIRTHDAYS TODAY

Joel Craig Ehlo, 37, basketball player, born Lubbock, TX, Aug 11, 1961.

Hulk Hogan (born Terry Gene Bollea), 45, wrestler, actor, born Augusta, GA, Aug 11, 1953.

Carlos Alberto Martinez, 34, baseball player, born LaGuaira, Venezuela, Aug 11, 1964.

William Charles (Bill) Monbouquette, 62, former baseball player, born Medford, MA, Aug 11, 1936.

Bryn Nelson Smith, 43, former baseball player, born Marietta, GA, Aug 11, 1955.

AUGUST 12 — WEDNESDAY
Day 224 — 141 Remaining

CLIFT, HARLOND: BIRTH ANNIVERSARY. Aug 12, 1912. Harlond Benton Clift, baseball player born at El Reno, OK. Clift was one of baseball's best third baseman in the 1930s. He hit 34 home runs in 1938, a record for third basemen at the time, and was an outstanding fielder besides. Died at Yakima, WA, Apr 27, 1992.

DOWN WITH THE RATS: ANNIVERSARY. Aug 12, 1996. National Hockey League general managers agreed upon a rule change taking effect at the start of the 1996–97 season. If fans litter the ice during the game, the referee is empowered to give a warning and then, if the offense is repeated, to penalize the home team for delay of game. The rule was a response to fans of the Detroit Red Wings, whose tradition called for throwing octapi on the ice, and more particularly to fans of the Florida Panthers, who littered the ice with plastic rats after Panther goals during the 1995–96 season.

FIRST NFL TEAM TO PLAY OUTSIDE US: ANNIVERSARY. Aug 12, 1950. The New York Giants defeated the Ottawa Rough Riders of the Canadian Football League, 27–6, in an exhibition game played at Ottawa. The Giants thus became the first NFL team to play outside the US.

HUTCHINSON, FRED: BIRTH ANNIVERSARY. Aug 12, 1919. Frederick Charles (Fred) Hutchinson, baseball player and manager born at Seattle, WA. Hutchinson was a major league pitcher who started managing the Detroit Tigers before he stopped playing. Known as the "Big Bear" for his physique and his demeanor, Hutchinson struggled courageously against cancer. Died at Bradenton, FL, Nov 12, 1964.

MATHEWSON, CHRISTY: BIRTH ANNIVERSARY. Aug 12, 1880. Christopher (Christy) Mathewson, Baseball Hall of Fame pitcher born at Factoryville, PA. Mathewson, a college graduate, was one of baseball's first clean-cut stars. A pitcher, he hurled three shutouts in the 1905 World Series and ended his career with 373 wins. Inducted into the Hall of Fame in 1936. Died at Saranac Lake, NY, Oct 7, 1925.

SCHALK, RAY: BIRTH ANNIVERSARY. Aug 12, 1892. Raymond William (Ray) Schalk, Baseball Hall of Fame catcher born in Harvey, IL. Schalk played on the 1919 Chicago White Sox, but he did not participate in the conspiracy to fix the outcome. Inducted into the Hall of Fame in 1955. Died at Chicago, IL, May 19, 1970.

VIKINGS MOVE TO METRODOME: ANNIVERSARY. Aug 12, 1982. The Minnesota Vikings, who for years used the frozen tundra of Minneapolis's Metropolitan Stadium as a significant home-field advantage, made their debut in the Hubert H. Humphrey Metrodome. They beat the Seattle Seahawks in a preseason game.

WOJCIECHOWICZ, ALEX: BIRTH ANNIVERSARY. Aug 12, 1915. Alexander Francis (Alex) Wojciechowicz, Pro Football Hall of Fame center and linebacker born at South River, NJ. Wojciechowicz played for Fordham's legendary line, the "Seven Blocks of Granite," in the late 1930s. He was drafted by the Detroit Lions and later played for the Philadelphia Eagles, earning All-Pro honors four times. Inducted into the Pro Football Hall of Fame in 1968. Died at South River, July 13, 1992.

BIRTHDAYS TODAY

Robert Ray (Bob) Buhl, 70, former baseball player, born Saginaw, MI, Aug 12, 1928.

George F. McGinnis, 48, former basketball player, born Indianapolis, IN, Aug 12, 1950.

Pete Sampras, 27, tennis player, born Washington, DC, Aug 12, 1971.

Antoine Devon Walker, 22, basketball player, born Chicago, IL, Aug 12, 1976.

AUGUST 13 — THURSDAY
Day 225 — 140 Remaining

BROCK GET 3,000th HIT: ANNIVERSARY. Aug 13, 1979. Outfielder Lou Brock of the St. Louis Cardinals got the 3,000th hit of his career, an infield single against Dennis Lamp and the Chicago Cubs. St. Louis won the game, 3–2. Brock finished his career that season with 3,023 hits.

BRONCO LEAGUE WORLD SERIES. Aug 13–19. Monterey, CA. International youth baseball World Series for players of league ages 11 and 12. Est attendance: 10,000. For info: Pony Baseball/Softball, PO Box 225, Washington, PA 15301. Phone: (412) 225-1060. Fax: (412) 225-9852. Email: pony@pulsenet.com. WWW: http://www.pony.org

GORDON, SID: BIRTH ANNIVERSARY. Aug 13, 1917. Sidney (Sid) Gordon, baseball player born at New York, NY. Gordon played third base and the outfield for four National League teams. He was a fine defensive player known for his hustle. Died at New York, June 17, 1975.

HOGAN, WILLIAM BENJAMIN (BEN): BIRTH ANNIVERSARY. Aug 13, 1912. Golfer born at Dublin, TX. One of only four players to win all four major professional championships, his 63 career victories rank third behind Sam Snead and Jack Nicklaus. He was elected to the Golf Hall of Fame in 1974. Died at Fort Worth, TX, July 25, 1997.

JONES, FIELDER: BIRTH ANNIVERSARY. Aug 13, 1871. Fielder Allison Jones, baseball player and manager born at Shinglehouse, PA. Jones was player-manager of the 1906 Chicago White Sox, the famous "Hitless Wonders" who captured the American League pennant despite a .209 team batting average and beat the Chicago Cubs in the World Series. Died at Portland, OR, Mar 13, 1934.

PGA CHAMPIONSHIP. Aug 13–16. Sahale Country Club, Redmond, WA. The 80th national professional championship conducted by the Professional Golfers' Association of America. Est attendance: 150,000. For info: Kerry Haigh, Senior Dir of Tourn, PGA of America, Box 109601, Palm Beach Gardens, FL 33410-9601. Phone: (561) 624-8495. Fax: (561) 624-8429.

ROLLER DERBY BEGINS: ANNIVERSARY. Aug 13, 1935. The first roller derby competition, staged by promoter Leo Seltzer, took place in Chicago.

TIED AND TIED AGAIN: ANNIVERSARY. Aug 13, 1910. The Brooklyn Dodgers and the Pittsburgh Pirates played an unusual tie game, finishing at 8–8. Each team had 38 at-bats, 13 hits, 12 assists, two errors, five strikeouts, three walks, one hit batter and one passed ball.

UPSET DEFEATS MAN O'WAR: ANNIVERSARY. Aug 13, 1919. The aptly-named Upset defeated Man O'War to win the Sanford Memorial Stakes at Saratoga. The race marked Man O'War's only loss in 21 races.

WORLD'S OLDEST CONTINUOUS PRCA RODEO. Aug 13–16 (tentative). Payson, AZ. The Payson Rodeo has been held continuously since 1884. Named number one small outdoor rodeo in America! Est attendance: 20,000. For info: Payson Chamber of Commerce, Box 1380, Payson, AZ 85547. Phone: (800) 672-9766. Fax: (520) 474-8812. Email: pcoc@netzone.com.

BIRTHDAYS TODAY

Jay Campbell Buhner, 34, baseball player, born Louisville, KY, Aug 13, 1964.

Fidel Castro, 71, President of Cuba, former amateur baseball player, born Mayari, Oriente Province, Cuba, Aug 13, 1927.

Robert Earle (Bobby) Clarke, 49, hockey executive and Hockey Hall of Fame center, born Flin Flon, Manitoba, Canada, Aug 13, 1949.

Shayne Corson, 32, hockey player, born Barrie, Ontario, Canada, Aug 13, 1966.

Cris Edward Dishman, 33, football player, born Louisville, KY, Aug 13, 1965.

Alexander (Alex) Fernandez, 29, baseball player, born Miami Beach, FL, Aug 13, 1969.

James Timothy ("Mudcat") Grant, 63, former baseball player, born Lacoochee, FL, Aug 13, 1935.

Elvis Grbac, 28, football player, born Cleveland, OH, Aug 13, 1970.

Elizabeth (Betsy) King, 43, LPGA Hall of Fame golfer, born Reading, PA, Aug 13, 1955.

Mark Alan Lemke, 33, baseball player, born Utica, NY, Aug 13, 1965.

Thomas Albert (Tom) Prince, 34, baseball player, born Kankakee, IL, Aug 13, 1964.

August *1998*	S	M	T	W	T	F	S
							1
	2	3	4	5	6	7	8
	9	10	11	12	13	14	15
	16	17	18	19	20	21	22
	23	24	25	26	27	28	29
	30	31					

AUGUST 14 — FRIDAY
Day 226 — 139 Remaining

SPORTSCHASER OF THE DAY
Who wrote "Casey at the Bat"?

CANADA: SOURDOUGH RENDEZVOUS GOLD RUSH BATHTUB RACE. Aug 14–16. Beginning in Whitehorse, Yukon. 7th annual. 462-mile bathtub race from Whitehorse to Dawson. Est attendance: 2,000. For info: Derek Charlton, Mktg Dept, Yukon Sourdough Rendezvous Society, Box 5108, Canada Y1A 4S3. Phone: (403) 667-2148. Fax: (403) 668-6755. Email: ysr@hypertech.yk.ca. WWW: http://www.haylon.yk.net/rendez

DEAN, DAFFY: 85th BIRTH ANNIVERSARY. Aug 14, 1913. Paul Dee ("Daffy") Dean, baseball player born at Lucas, AR. Dizzy Dean's less-famous brother won 19 games in 1934 and 1935 for the St. Louis Cardinals before hurting his arm. Died at Springdale, AR, Mar 17, 1981.

FISHING HAS NO BOUNDARIES—WISCONSIN DELLS. Aug 14–16 (tentative). Wisconsin Dells, WI. A three-day fishing experience for disabled persons. Any disability, age, sex, race, etc, eligible. Fishing with experienced guides. For info: Frank Lucafo, Fishing Has No Boundaries, 3879 State Rd 13, Wisconsin Dells, WI 53965. Phone: (888) 667-8413.

FORMATION OF AFL: ANNIVERSARY. Aug 14, 1959. The formation of the American Football League was announced at a press conference in Chicago. Play was set to begin in 1960 with at least six and possibly eight franchises.

INTERNATIONAL SOFTBALL CONGRESS WORLD FAST-PITCH TOURNAMENT. Aug 14–23. Eddie C. Moore Complex, Clearwater, FL. Premier event in the sport features 48 of the top teams in the world competing for the coveted ISC World Championship in a double-elimination, 10-day tournament. Leading pitchers throw balls in excess of 100 mph from 46 feet, yet the best hitters consistently post averages well over .300. Annually, the second Friday in August. Est attendance: 100,000. For info: Intl Softball Congress, 6007 E Hillcrest Circle, Anaheim Hills, CA 92807. Phone: (714) 998-5694. Fax: (714) 282-7902.

LARGEST SOCCER CROWD: ANNIVERSARY. Aug 14, 1977. 77,691 fans, the largest crowd to that date to watch a soccer match in the US, saw the New York Cosmos, led by Pele, defeat the Fort Lauderdale Strikers, 8–3, in a National American Soccer League quarterfinal playoff game at the Meadowlands in East Rutherford, NJ.

MOON PHASE: LAST QUARTER. Aug 14. Moon enters Last Quarter phase at 3:48 PM, EDT.

OLDEST PITCHER TO WIN GAME: ANNIVERSARY. Aug 14, 1932. John Quinn, 49, became the oldest winning pitcher in baseball history as a member of the Brooklyn Dodgers. Quinn relieved Van Mungo in the ninth inning of a game against the New York Giants with the score tied, 1–1. The Dodgers won it in the 10th, and Quinn got credit for the victory.

TEXAS RANCH ROUNDUP. Aug 14–15. Wichita Falls, TX. Cowboys from prestigious ranches in Texas compete in the events that make up their daily work. Cattle roping and penning and other rodeo-type events plus ranch cooking contests, ranch talent contests. Est attendance: 17,000. For info: Kacey Gray, Mktg Asst, Wichita Falls Conv and Visitors Bureau, 1000 5th St, Wichita Falls, TX 76301. Phone: (800) 799-6732. Fax: (800) 799-5509. WWW: http://www.viewscape.com

THAYER, ERNEST LAWRENCE: 135th BIRTH ANNIVERSARY. Aug 14, 1863. Ernest Lawrence Thayer, poet and journalist born at Lawrence, MA. He wrote a series of comic ballads for the *San Francisco Examiner*, of which "Casey at the Bat" was the last. It was published on Sunday, June 3, 1888, and Thayer received $5 in payment for it. Recitations of the ballad by the actor William DeWolf Hopper greatly increased its popularity. It is said that by 1900 there were few Americans who had not heard of "Casey at the Bat." Died at Santa Barbara, CA, Aug 21, 1940. (See also Jun 3.)

365-INNING SOFTBALL GAME: ANNIVERSARY. Aug 14–15, 1976. The Gager's Diner softball team played the Bend'n Elbow Tavern in a 365-inning softball game in 1976. Starting at 10 AM Aug 14, the game was called because of rain and fog at 4 PM, Aug 15. The 70 players, including 20 women, raised $4,000 for construction of a new softball field and for the Monticello, NY, Community General Hospital. The Gagers beat the Elbows 491–467. To date, this remains the longest softball game on record.

BIRTHDAYS TODAY

Charles Neal Anderson, 34, former football player, born Graceville, FL, Aug 14, 1964.

Marty Glickman, 81, former broadcaster and track athlete, born New York, NY, Aug 14, 1917.

Joseph Milton (Joe) Grahe, 31, baseball player, born West Palm Beach, FL, Aug 14, 1967.

Mark Steven Gubicza, 36, baseball player, born Philadelphia, PA, Aug 14, 1962.

Earvin ("Magic") Johnson, Jr, 39, former basketball player, born Lansing, MI, Aug 14, 1959.

Edward Charles (Ed) O'Bannon, Jr, 26, basketball player, born Los Angeles, CA, Aug 14, 1972.

Robyn Smith, 54, jockey, born San Francisco, CA, Aug 14, 1944.

Rusty Wallace, 42, auto racer, born St. Louis, MO, Aug 14, 1956.

AUGUST 15 — SATURDAY

Day 227 — 138 Remaining

BIKE VAN BUREN XII. Aug 15–16. Van Buren County, IA. A laid-back bicycle tour of the villages, landmarks and landscape of this rural Iowa county. The "red carpet of hospitality" is rolled out for the bikers as they pass through. Est attendance: 550. For info: Mary E. Muir, Exec Dir, Villages of Van Buren, Inc, PO Box 9, Keosauqua, IA 52565. Phone: (800) 868-7822. Email: villages@netins.net. WWW: http://www.netins.net/showcase/Villages

COMISKEY, CHARLES: BIRTH ANNIVERSARY. Aug 15, 1859. Charles Albert Comiskey, Baseball Hall of Fame first baseman, manager and executive born at Chicago, IL. Comiskey's career spanned 50 years, 30 of them as founding owner of the Chicago White Sox. But before that, he was an outstanding and innovative player and a tough, successful manager. Inducted into the Hall of Fame in 1939. Died at Eagle River, WI, Oct 26, 1931.

CORVETTE SHOW. Aug 15–16. State Dock, Mackinaw City, MI. Parade of Corvettes on Friday at 7 PM. Show and visitor viewing, awards and Sunset Boat Cruise on Saturday. Est attendance: 3,000. For info: Corvette Show, 708 S Huron, Mackinaw City, MI 49701. Phone: (616) 436-5574 or (800) 666-0160. Fax: (616) 436-5991. Email: bjones@freeway.net. WWW: http://mackinawcity.com

FIRST WOMAN IN PRO FOOTBALL: ANNIVERSARY. Aug 15, 1970. Patricia Palinkas became the first woman to play in a professional football game when she held

Smoky Burgess

the ball for the point after touchdown kick by her husband, Steve, placekicker for the Orlando Panthers of the Atlantic Coast League. The snap was off-target, and Palinkas was tackled when she attempted to run with the errant ball.

FISHING HAS NO BOUNDARIES—CINCINNATI. Aug 15–16 (tentative). East Fork Lake, Fairfield, OH. A two-day fishing experience for disabled persons. Any disability, age, sex, race, etc, eligible. Fishing with experienced guides. For info: Mike Nesi, Fishing Has No Boundaries, 3449 Danbury Rd, Fairfield, OH 45014. Phone: (513) 874-0545.

FORFEIT BY GROUND CREW: ANNIVERSARY. Aug 15, 1941. The Washington Senators lost a game by forfeit when the umpires ruled that the ground crew at Griffith Stadium put the tarpaulin on the field too slowly during a rain storm. The Senators were beating the Boston Red Sox, 6–3, when the rain came in the eighth inning. The umpires decided that the ground crew deliberately moved much too slowly, hoping that the game would have to be called. It was—but because of the forfeit, the Red Sox won.

LEADVILLE TRAIL 100 BIKE RACE. Aug 15 (tentative). Leadville, CO. Some 400 cyclists compete in this 100-mile off-road bike race over Colorado's high peaks—out 50 miles to a peak above Twin Lakes and back to Leadville. Sponsor: Leadville Trail 100, Inc. Est attendance: 1,000. For info: Gloria Cheshier, Exec Dir, Greater Leadville Area Chamber of Commerce, PO Box 861, Leadville, CO 80461. Phone: (719) 486-3900 or (800) 933-3901. Fax: (719) 486-8478. Email: leadville@sni.net. WWW: http://www.colorado.com/leadville

MAINE HIGHLAND GAMES. Aug 15. Thomas Point Beach, Brunswick, ME. Presented by the Saint Andrew's Society of Maine. Adult athletics including tossing of the caber, wheat sheaf toss and putting of the stone; border collie herding demonstrations, Highland cattle and individual piping contests. Bagpipe bands, Highland and Scottish dancing, Scottish arts and crafts fair, folksingers, Scottish fiddling, children's games; American and Scottish foods galore. The only Scottish event of its kind held in Maine! Scots and non-Scots will enjoy the color, pageantry and friendly atmosphere. 20th annual games. Admission fees charge. Est attendance: 6,000. For info: Thomas Point Beach, 29 Meadow Rd, Brunswick, ME 04011. Phone: (207) 725-6009. WWW: http://www.thomaspointbeach.com

NATURAL CHIMNEYS JOUSTING TOURNAMENT. Aug 15. Natural Chimneys Regional Park, Mt Solon, VA. A modern version of a medieval contest, believed to be the oldest continuously held sporting event in America. Annually, the third Saturday in August. Est attendance: 500. For info: Upper Valley Regional Park Authority, Box 478, Grottoes, VA 24441. Phone: (540) 350-2510. Fax: (540) 350-2140.

PITCHER HITS HOMER IN EVERY PARK: ANNIVERSARY. Aug 15, 1955. Pitcher Warren Spahn of the Milwaukee Braves hit a home run off Mel Wright of the St. Louis Cardinals in Sportsman's Park, St. Louis, to give him at least one homer in every National League ballpark.

PONY LEAGUE WORLD SERIES. Aug 15-22. Washington, PA. International youth baseball World Series for teams of players ages 13 and 14. Est attendance: 16,700. For info: Pony Baseball/Softball, PO Box 225, Washington, PA 15301. Phone: (412) 225-1060. Fax: (412) 225-9852. Email: pony@pulsenet.com. WWW: http://www.pony.org

THREE MEN ON THIRD: ANNIVERSARY. Aug 15, 1926. Babe Herman of the Brooklyn Dodgers doubled with the bases loaded in a game against the Boston Braves. The hit drove in the winning run, but the runner on second, the runner on first and Herman all wound up on or near third base. Two of them were called out, so that Herman, in effect, doubled into a double play.

TWICE TOSSED: ANNIVERSARY. Aug 15, 1975. Manager Earl Weaver of the Baltimore Orioles, a frequent antagonist of umpires, was ejected during the first game of a doubleheader by Ron Luciano and then was ejected again by Luciano before the start of the second game.

BIRTHDAYS TODAY

Eric Bieniemy, 29, football player, born New Orleans, LA, Aug 15, 1969.
Scott David Brosius, 32, baseball player, born Hillsboro, OR, Aug 15, 1966.
Joseph Richard (Joey) Jay, 63, former baseball player, born Middletown, CT, Aug 15, 1935.
Jay Thomas (Tom) Kelly, 48, baseball manager and former player, born Graceville, MN, Aug 15, 1950.
George Warren ("Barney") Schultz, 71, former baseball player, born Beverly, NJ, Aug 15, 1927.
Eugene (Gene) Upshaw, 53, union executive and former football player, born Robstown, TX, Aug 15, 1945.

AUGUST 16 — SUNDAY
Day 228 — 137 Remaining

BASEBALL IN MEXICO: ANNIVERSARY. Aug 16, 1996. The San Diego Padres and the New York Mets made baseball history by playing the first major league game ever in Mexico. The two teams agreed to move their three-game series from San Diego to Monterrey in order to avoid a potential conflict with the Republican National Convention. The Padres won, 15–10, behind the starting pitching of Fernando Valenzuela, a native Mexican who also threw out the ceremonial first pitch.

EAGLES MOVE TO THE VET: ANNIVERSARY. Aug 16, 1971. The Philadelphia Eagles defeated the Buffalo Bills,

August 1998	S	M	T	W	T	F	S
							1
	2	3	4	5	6	7	8
	9	10	11	12	13	14	15
	16	17	18	19	20	21	22
	23	24	25	26	27	28	29
	30	31					

34–28, in a preseason game played at the Eagles' new home, Veterans Stadium. Since their first season in the NFL, 1933, the Eagles had played home games at Baker Bowl, Temple University Stadium, Franklin Field, Connie Mack Stadium and Municipal Stadium.

FIELD OF DREAMS FESTIVAL. Aug 16–18. Field of Dreams, Dyersville, IA. Included are a fantasy camp, celebrity baseball game and parade. Tickets go on sale in spring. Est attendance: 18,000. For info: Field of Dreams Festival, 108 2nd St SE, Dyersville, IA 52040. Phone: (319) 875-6012 or (800) 443-8981. Fax: (319) 875-8233.

FIRST ISSUE OF *SPORTS ILLUSTRATED*: ANNIVERSARY. Aug 16, 1954. The first issue of *Sports Illustrated* was published. The cover photograph showed Eddie Mathews of the Milwaukee Braves batting at Milwaukee County Stadium. The cover price was 25 cents.

JACOBSON, BABY DOLL: BIRTH ANNIVERSARY. Aug 16, 1890. William Chester ("Baby Doll") Jacobson, baseball player born at Cable, IL. Jacobson earned his nickname in the minor leagues from female fans who thought he was extremely handsome. He was a superior outfielder for six American League teams with a career batting average of .311. Died at Orion, IL, Jan 16, 1977.

JONES, WILLIE: BIRTH ANNIVERSARY. Aug 16, 1925. Willie Edward Jones, baseball player born at Dillon, SC. Jones, known as Puddin'head to his teammates, was the third baseman on the Whiz Kids, the 1950 Philadelphia Phillies team that won the National League pennant. Died at Cincinnati, OH, Oct 18, 1983.

LEADVILLE TRAIL 100—10K. Aug 16 (tentative). Leadville, CO. Out and back course using the first 3.1 miles and the last 3.1 miles of the famous Leadville Trail 100 Ultramarathon course. Starting elevation: 10,152 feet! Paved and dirt roads. Small entry fee. This is one of many races held in the area. For info: Gloria Cheshier, Greater Leadville Area Chamber of Commerce, PO Box 861, Leadville, CO 80461. Phone: (719) 486-3502 or (800) 933-3901. Email: leadville@sni.net.

NEW YORK GOLDEN ARMS TOURNAMENT–STATEN ISLAND. Aug 16. Staten Island, NY. Arm wrestling competition held at fair determines borough winner who will compete in Empire State Golden Arms Tournament of Champions on Oct 22. For info: New York Arm Wrestling Assn, Inc, 200-14 45th Dr, Bayside, NY 11361. Phone/fax: (718) 544-4592.

RAY CHAPMAN BEANED: ANNIVERSARY. Aug 16, 1920. Cleveland Indians shortstop Ray Chapman was hit in the head by a pitch thrown by Carl Mays of the New York Yankees. Chapman collapsed with a fractured skull and died the next day. His death stands as the only on-field fatality in major league history.

RUTH, BABE: 50th DEATH ANNIVERSARY. Aug 16, 1948. George Herman ("Babe") Ruth, Baseball Hall of Fame pitcher and outfielder born at Baltimore, MD, Feb 6, 1895. The left-handed pitcher and "Sultan of Swat" hit 714 home runs in 22 major league seasons of play and played in 10 World Series. Baseball fans mourned when he died of throat cancer. His body lay in state at the main entrance of Yankee Stadium where people waited in line for hours to march past the coffin. On Aug 19, countless numbers of people surrounded St. Patrick's Cathedral for the funeral mass and lined the streets along the route to the cemetery as America bade farewell to one of baseball's greatest legends. Died at New York, NY.

RUTH CLEARS COMISKEY ROOF: ANNIVERSARY. Aug 16, 1927. Babe Ruth of the New York Yankees became the first player to hit a home run over the roof of Chicago's Comiskey Park.

STAGG, AMOS ALONZO: BIRTH ANNIVERSARY. Aug 16, 1862. Amos Alonzo Stagg, football player and coach, born at West Orange, NJ. Stagg played baseball and football at Yale and then forsook the ministry for physical education. He built the football program at the University of Chicago as an integral part of William Rainey Harper's plan to build a great university. Over 40 years at Chicago, he became the game's greatest innovator and master strategist. When Chicago de-emphasized football, he moved to the College of the Pacific, finishing his career with a record of 314–181–15. Died at Stockton, CA, Mar 17, 1965.

BIRTHDAYS TODAY

Bret Edward Barberie, 31, baseball player, born Long Beach, CA, Aug 16, 1967.
Ben Terrence Coates, 29, football player, born Greenwood, SC, Aug 16, 1969.
Frank Newton Gifford, 68, broadcaster and Pro Football Hall of Fame halfback and end, born Santa Monica, CA, Aug 16, 1930.
Michael (Mike) Jorgensen, 50, former baseball manager and player, born Passaic, NJ, Aug 16, 1948.
Christian Emeka Okoye, 37, former football player, born Enugu, Nigeria, Aug 16, 1961.
Eric Jerrod Swann, 28, football player, born Pinehurst, NC, Aug 16, 1970.

AUGUST 17 — MONDAY
Day 229 — 136 Remaining

CHASE'S SPORTSQUOTE OF THE DAY

"If he held out his right arm, he'd be a railroad crossing."
—Joe Garagiola on Boog Powell

FISK HITS 328th HOME RUN: ANNIVERSARY. Aug 17, 1990. Carlton Fisk of the Chicago White Sox hit the 328th home run of his career as a catcher, surpassing the mark set by Johnny Bench. The White Sox beat the Texas Rangers, 4–2.

GEHRIG BREAKS SCOTT'S RECORD: 65th ANNIVERSARY. Aug 17, 1933. Lou Gehrig of the New York Yankees played in his 1,308th consecutive game to break the record held by Everett Scott. Gehrig went on to extend his streak to 2,130 games before leaving the Yankees lineup.

KEARNS, DOC: BIRTH ANNIVERSARY. Aug 17, 1882. Jack ("Doc") Kearns, born John Leo McKernan at Waterloo, MI. Kearns lived a wild life in the American West and finally settled on being a boxing promoter. His most famous fighter was Jack Dempsey, who won the heavyweight title in 1919, but he continued managing and promoting until his death. Died at Miami, FL, July 7, 1963.

TWO PITCHING RECORDS: ANNIVERSARY. Aug 17, 1894. Pitcher John Wadsworth of the Louisville club in the National League set two unfortunate records in the same game. He gave up 28 singles and 36 hits overall. Both marks still stand.

YORK, RUDY: 85th BIRTH ANNIVERSARY. Aug 17, 1913. Preston Rudolph (Rudy) York, baseball player born at Ragland, AL. York was an outstanding hitter for the Detroit Tigers but a woeful fielder at any position. He set a major league record, hitting 18 home runs in August, 1937. Died at Rome, GA, Feb 7, 1970.

BIRTHDAYS TODAY

Harrison V. Chase, 85, associate professor emeritus (Florida State University–Tallahassee), cofounder and coeditor of *Chase's Annual Events* (1957–70), born Big Rapids, MI, Aug 17, 1913.
Alexander (Alex) Cole, Jr, 33, baseball player, born Fayetteville, NC, Aug 17, 1965.
James Houston (Jim) Davenport, 65, former baseball manager and player, born Siluria, AL, Aug 17, 1933.
Robert DeNiro, 55, actor (*Bang the Drum Slowly, Raging Bull, The Fan*), born New York, NY, Aug 17, 1943.
Nelson Donald Emerson, 31, hockey player, born Hamilton, Ontario, Canada, Aug 17, 1967.
Christian Donald Laettner, 29, basketball player, born Angola, NY, Aug 17, 1969.
Jamie Macoun, 37, hockey player, born Newmarket, Ontario, Canada, Aug 17, 1961.
Nelson Piquet, 46, auto racer, born Brasilia, Brazil, Aug 17, 1952.
John Wesley ("Boog") Powell, 57, former baseball player, born Lakeland, FL, Aug 17, 1941.
Guillermo Vilas, 46, former tennis player, born Mar del Plata, Argentina, Aug 17, 1952.

AUGUST 18 — TUESDAY
Day 230 — 135 Remaining

AARON LOSES HOME RUN: ANNIVERSARY. Aug 18, 1965. Outfielder Henry Aaron of the Milwaukee Braves hit an apparent home run in St. Louis when he drove a ball over the right-field pavilion roof in right field. Home plate umpire Chris Pelekoudas nullified the homer, calling Aaron out for stepping out of the batter's box. The Braves still won, 6–2.

BRAVES FIELD OPENS: ANNIVERSARY. Aug 18, 1915. The Boston Braves opened their new ballpark, Braves Field, with a 3–1 victory over the St. Louis Cardinals. The Braves called this park home through the 1952 season after which they moved to Milwaukee.

CANADA: ROYAL RED ARABIAN HORSE SHOW. Aug 18–22. Regina Exhibition Park, Regina, Saskatchewan. Royal Red Canadian International Arabian Horse Show showcases some of the best Arabian and Half-Arabian horses in North America and beyond. Est attendance: 15,000. For info: (306) 781-9216 or Tourism Saskatchewan, 500-1900 Albert St, Regina, Sask, Canada S4P 4L9. Email: travel.info@toursask.sk.ca.

CLEMENTE, ROBERTO: BIRTH ANNIVERSARY. Aug 18, 1934. Roberto Walker Clemente, Baseball Hall of Fame outfielder born at Carolina, Puerto Rico. Clemente, one of the game's best and most exciting outfielders, played his entire career with the Pittsburgh Pirates, leading them to a World Series in 1971 and collecting 3,000 hits. While on a mission of mercy to deliver supplies to victims of a Nicaraguan earthquake, he perished in a plane crash. Inducted into the Hall of Fame in 1973 after the mandatory 5-year waiting period was waived. Died at San Juan, Puerto Rico, Dec 31, 1972.

GRIMES, BURLEIGH: 105th BIRTH ANNIVERSARY. Aug 18, 1893. Burleigh Arland Grimes, Baseball Hall of Fame pitcher and manager born at Emerald, WI. Grimes was the last legal spitball pitcher, a gritty performer who won 270 games in 19 years. He coached and managed after retiring as a player. Inducted into the Hall of Fame in 1964. Died at Clear Lake, WI, Dec 6, 1985.

JETS BEAT GIANTS: ANNIVERSARY. Aug 18, 1969. The New York Jets played their crosstown rivals, the Giants, for the first time and came away winners, 37–14, in this preseason game. Joe Namath threw three touchdown passes for the Jets.

MT WHITNEY SCALED: 125th ANNIVERSARY. Aug 18, 1873. Mt Whitney, the second highest peak in the US, was conquered for the first time by a trio of American climbers, Charles D. Begole, A.H. Johnson and John Lucas.

PODOLOFF, MAURICE: BIRTH ANNIVERSARY. Aug 18, 1890. Maurice Podoloff, Basketball Hall of Fame executive born at Elisabethgrad, Russia. Podoloff entered basketball through hockey and served as the first president of the Basketball Association of America, one of the NBA's two predecessor leagues. When the BAA merged with the National Basketball League in 1949, Podoloff was named the NBA's first president. He governed the league through its uneasy early years and secured its first national television contract. Inducted into the Hall of Fame in 1974. Died at New Haven, CT, Nov 24, 1985.

WEAVER, BUCK: BIRTH ANNIVERSARY. Aug 18, 1890. George Daniel ("Buck") Weaver, baseball player born at Pottstown, PA. Weaver was one of eight Chicago White Sox players suspended and later banned for life for conspiring to fix the 1919 World Series. He did not participate in the plot, but knew of it and declined to report it. Died at Chicago, IL, Jan 31, 1956.

BIRTHDAYS TODAY

Bruce Edwin Benedict, 43, former baseball player, born Birmingham, AL, Aug 18, 1955.
Geoff Courtnall, 36, hockey player, born Victoria, BC, Canada, Aug 18, 1962.
Rafer Lewis Johnson, 63, Olympic gold medal decathlete, born Hillsboro, TX, Aug 18, 1935.
Michael Eugene (Mike) LaValliere, 38, former baseball player, born Charlotte, NC, Aug 18, 1960.
Lafayette ("Fat") Lever, 38, former basketball player, born Pine Bluff, AR, Aug 18, 1960.
Brian Keith Mitchell, 30, football player, born Ft Polk, LA, Aug 18, 1968.

August 1998	S	M	T	W	T	F	S
							1
	2	3	4	5	6	7	8
	9	10	11	12	13	14	15
	16	17	18	19	20	21	22
	23	24	25	26	27	28	29
	30	31					

Robert Redford, 61, actor (*The Natural, Downhill Racer*), born Santa Monica, CA, Aug 18, 1937.
Robert (Bob) Zupcic, 32, former baseball player, born Pittsburgh, PA, Aug 18, 1966.

AUGUST 19 — WEDNESDAY
Day 231 — 134 Remaining

CARLETON, TEX: BIRTH ANNIVERSARY. Aug 19, 1906. James Otto ("Tex") Carleton, baseball player born at Comance, TX. Carleton won ten or more games in seven of his eight major league seasons and threw a no-hitter. Died at Fort Worth, TX, Jan 11, 1977.

COBB GETS 3,000th HIT: ANNIVERSARY. Aug 19, 1921. Outfielder Ty Cobb of the Detroit Tigers, at age 34, became the youngest player ever to get 3,000 hits in his career. Cobb played in the major leagues from 1905 to 1928 and was inducted into the Hall of Fame in 1936.

DONALD, ATLEY: BIRTH ANNIVERSARY. Aug 19, 1910. Richard Atley Donald, baseball player born at Morton, MS. Atley pitched eight years in the majors, all with the New York Yankees. In 1938, he set a rookie record by winning 12 straight decisions. Died at West Monroe, LA, Oct 19, 1992.

EDDIE GAEDEL AT BAT: ANNIVERSARY. Aug 19, 1951. In one of owner Bill Veeck's most outrageous promotions, the St. Louis Browns sent Eddie Gaedel, a midget, to the plate as the first batter in the second game of a doubleheader against the Detroit Tigers. Gaedel walked on four pitches and was lifted for a pinch-runner. Two days later, the American League banned Gaedel from further competition.

GIANTS TO MOVE TO SAN FRANCISCO: ANNIVERSARY. Aug 19, 1957. Horace Stoneham, principal owner of the New York Giants baseball team, announced that the board of directors had voted, 9–1, to move the franchise to San Francisco for the start of the 1958 season. The Giants were accompanied to the West Coast by the Dodgers who moved from Brooklyn to Los Angeles.

★ **NATIONAL AVIATION DAY.** Aug 19. Presidential Proclamation 2343, of July 25, 1939, covers all succeeding years. Always Aug 19 of each year since 1939. Observed annually on anniversary of birth of Orville Wright, who piloted "first self-powered flight in history," Dec 17, 1903. First proclaimed by President Franklin D. Roosevelt.

BIRTHDAYS TODAY

Morten Andersen, 38, football player, born Struer, Denmark, Aug 19, 1960.
William Jefferson (Bill) Clinton, 52, 42nd US president and amateur golfer, born Hope, AR, Aug 19, 1946.
Ronald Maurice (Ron) Darling, Jr, 38, former baseball player, born Honolulu, HI, Aug 19, 1960.
Gary Joseph Gaetti, 40, baseball player, born Centralia, IL, Aug 19, 1958.
Bobby Joseph Hebert, Jr, 38, football player, born Baton Rouge, LA, Aug 19, 1960.
Cindy Nelson, 43, former alpine skier, born Lutsen, MN, Aug 19, 1955.
Robert Clinton (Bobby) Richardson, 63, former baseball player, born Sumter, SC, Aug 19, 1935.
William Lee (Willie) Shoemaker, 67, former jockey, born Fabens, TX, Aug 19, 1931.
Darryl John Sutter, 40, hockey coach and former player, born Viking, Alberta, Canada, Aug 19, 1958.

AUGUST 20 — THURSDAY
Day 232 — 133 Remaining

COCKROACH DERBY. Aug 20. Rutgers University Cook Campus, New Brunswick, NJ. The 9th annual "Roach Derby" sponsored by the New Jersey Pest Control Association. Pits the fastest roaches in the Garden State against one another to determine the best. Est attendance: 500. For info: Alan Caruba, New Jersey Pest Control Assn, PO Box 40, Maplewood, NJ 07040. Phone: (973) 763-6392.

CRIM FESTIVAL OF RACES. Aug 20–22. Flint, MI. Festival includes 22nd-anniversary celebration, international 10-mile road race, 5K and 8K runs, 8K racewalk, 5K and 8K walks, one-mile run and teddy bear trot for children ages 4–12. Sports and fitness expo on Aug 20–22; Pasta Party on Aug 21 at University Pavilion Rink; and food festival on Aug 21–22. Est attendance: 30,000. For info: Crim Festival of Races, 503 S Sagarin St, Ste 110, Flint, MI 48502. Phone: (810) 235-3396. Fax: (810) 235-5311. WWW: http://www.doitsports.com/crim

FEATHERS, BEATTIE: 90th BIRTH ANNIVERSARY. Aug 20, 1908. William Beattie Feathers, football player and coach born at Bristol, VA. Feathers was an All-American back at the University of Tennessee in 1932. He starred in the first College All-Star game and, playing for the Chicago Bears, became the first NFL back to rush for more than 1,000 yards in one season. He coached at Appalachian State and North Carolina State. Died at Winston-Salem, NC, Mar 11, 1979.

FIRST 3-YEAR-OLD MILLIONAIRE: ANNIVERSARY. Aug 20, 1966. The thoroughbred Buckpasser, owned by Ogden Phipps, won the Travers Stakes at Saratoga to become the first 3-year-old to pass the $1 million mark in career earnings.

OHIO TOBACCO FESTIVAL WITH TOBACCO WORM RACE. Aug 20–23. Ripley, OH. Celebration in honor of southern Ohio's cash crop of white burley tobacco. 14th annual festival activities include tobacco worm race, five-mile run, arm wrestling, cow chip throw, pipe smoking, clogging competition, antique car show, continuous country music, queen contest, arts and crafts, quilt show and more. Est attendance: 50,000. For info: Ohio Tobacco Festival, Box 91, Ripley, OH 45167. Phone: (513) 392-4369. Fax: (513) 392-4299.

SOAP BOX DERBY WINNER DISQUALIFIED: 25th ANNIVERSARY. Aug 20, 1973. James Gronen was disqualified as champion, two days after winning the Soap Box Derby in Akron, OH. Officials discovered that Gronen's car was equipped with an illegal magnetic system that gave it an unfair advantage.

TENNESSEE WALKING HORSE NATIONAL CELEBRATION. Aug 20–29. Celebration Arena, Shelbyville, TN. More than 3,800 entries compete for more than $600,000 in prizes and awards and the World Grand Championship titles. Trade show also. A 10-day festival for the whole family. Est attendance: 250,000. For info: Barbara Simmons, Public Relations Dir, Tennessee Walking Horse Natl Celebration, Calhoun and Evans, Shelbyville, TN 37162. Phone: (615) 684-5915. Fax: (615) 684-5949.

YOUNGEST PLAYER TO HIT HOME RUN: ANNIVERSARY. Aug 20, 1945. Tommy Brown of the Brooklyn Dodgers became the youngest player in major league history to hit a home run when he connected against pitcher Preacher Roe of the Pittsburgh Pirates. Brown was 17 years, eight months and 14 days old.

BIRTHDAYS TODAY

Andrew Charles (Andy) Benes, 31, baseball player, born Evansville, IN, Aug 20, 1967.
Richard L. (Rich) Brooks, 57, former football coach, born Forest, CA, Aug 20, 1941.
Thomas Andrew (Tom) Brunansky, 38, former baseball player, born Covina, CA, Aug 20, 1960.
Donald (Don) King, 67, boxing promoter, born Cleveland, OH, Aug 20, 1931.
Mark Edward Langston, 38, baseball player, born San Diego, CA, Aug 20, 1960.
Alfonso Raymon (Al) Lopez, 90, Baseball Hall of Fame manager and catcher, born Tampa, FL, Aug 20, 1908.
Graig Nettles, 54, former baseball player, born San Diego, CA, Aug 20, 1944.
Kenneth Francis (Ken) Ruettgers, 36, former football player, born Bakersfield, CA, Aug 20, 1962.

AUGUST 21 — FRIDAY
Day 233 — 132 Remaining

SPORTSCHASER OF THE DAY

Which relief pitcher became the first to be credited with 300 saves in his career?

CANADA: CAVENDISH FARMS PEE WEE CHAMPIONSHIP. Aug 21–25. Summerside, Prince Edward Island. Baseball competition for 12–13-year-olds. Annually, the fourth weekend in August. Est attendance: 10,000. For info: Baseball Canada, 1600 James Naismith Dr, Ste 208, Gloucester, Ont, Canada K1B 5N4. Phone: (613) 748-5606. Fax: (613) 748-5767. Email: info@baseball.ca. WWW: http://www.baseball.ca

DICKSON, MURRY: BIRTH ANNIVERSARY. Aug 21, 1916. Murry Monroe Dickson, baseball player born at Tracy, MO. Dickson pitched mostly for noncompetitive teams but still won 172 games. He won 20 games in 1951 with the inept Pittsburgh Pirates and relieved twice in the 1958 World Series for the New York Yankees. Died at Kansas City, KS, Sept 21, 1989.

FINGERS RECORDS 300th SAVE: ANNIVERSARY. Aug 21, 1982. Relief pitcher Rollie Fingers of the Milwaukee Brewers became the first pitcher to record 300 saves in his career as the Brewers beat the Seattle Mariners, 3–2.

LARNED WINS USLTA TITLE: ANNIVERSARY. Aug 21, 1901. William Larned won the first of his seven men's singles titles at the US Lawn Tennis Association championships. Larned followed this victory with wins in 1902, 1907, 1908, 1909, 1910 and 1911.

MOON PHASE: NEW MOON. Aug 21. Moon enters New Moon phase at 10:03 PM, EDT.

SOLAR ECLIPSE. Aug 21. Annular eclipse of the sun. Central eclipse begins at 8:15 PM, EDT, reaches greatest eclipse at 10:14 PM, EDT and ends at 11:56 PM, EDT. Visible in North Indian Ocean, India, southeast Asia, southern China, Indonesia, Malaysia, Philippine Republic, southern Japan and Australia.

WILLIAMS, WOODY: BIRTH ANNIVERSARY. Aug 21, 1912. Woodrow Wilson (Woody) Williams, baseball player born at Pamplin, VA. In 1943, Williams collected only 26 hits for the Cincinnati Reds but 10 of them came in succession, tying the National League record. Died at Appomattox, VA, Feb 24, 1995.

BIRTHDAYS TODAY

James Eric (Jim) Bullinger, 33, baseball player, born New Orleans, LA, Aug 21, 1965.

Andujar Cedeno, 29, baseball player, born La Romana, Dominican Republic, Aug 21, 1969.

Wilton Norman (Wilt) Chamberlain, 62, former basketball coach and Basketball Hall of Fame center, born Philadelphia, PA, Aug 21, 1936.

Willie Edward Lanier, 53, Pro Football Hall of Fame linebacker, born Clover, VA, Aug 21, 1945.

James Robert (Jim) McMahon, 39, former football player, born Jersey City, NJ, Aug 21, 1959.

Karl Derrick ("Tuffy") Rhodes, 30, baseball player, born Cincinnati, OH, Aug 21, 1968.

John Karl Wetteland, 32, baseball player, born San Mateo, CA, Aug 21, 1966.

AUGUST 22 — SATURDAY

Day 234 — 131 Remaining

AMERICA'S CUP: ANNIVERSARY. Aug 22, 1851. A silver trophy (then known as the "Hundred Guinea Cup" and offered by the Royal Yacht Squadron) was won in a race around the Isle of Wight by the US yacht *America*. The trophy, later turned over to the New York Yacht Club, became known as the America's Cup.

DONATELLI, AUGIE: BIRTH ANNIVERSARY. Aug 22, 1914. August Joseph (Augie) Donatelli, baseball umpire born at Heilwood, PA. Donatelli advanced to the National League in 1950 after only four years as a minor league

August 1998	S	M	T	W	T	F	S
							1
	2	3	4	5	6	7	8
	9	10	11	12	13	14	15
	16	17	18	19	20	21	22
	23	24	25	26	27	28	29
	30	31					

umpire. He was the principal organizer of the umpires' union in 1964. Died at St. Petersburg, FL, May 24, 1990.

EAST COAST SURFING CHAMPIONSHIPS AND SPORTS FESTIVAL. Aug 22–30. Oceanfront to 12th St, Virginia Beach, VA. 36th annual championship. Pro and amateur surfing and volleyball, 5K run, skimboarding, outrigger canoe racing, team tug-of-war, bands, food. Est attendance: 100,000. For info: Virginia Beach Jaycees, PO Box 62041, Virginia Beach, VA 23466. Phone: (800) 861-7873. WWW: http://www.ecsc1.com

GREAT AMERICAN DUCK RACE. Aug 22–23. Deming, NM. "World's richest duck race." Also Duck Queen and Darling Duckling contests, Tortilla Toss, parade and other festivities. Est attendance: 24,000. For info: The Great American Duck Race of Deming, Inc, PO Box 1402, Deming, NM 88031. Phone: (800) 848-4955.

HEIN, MEL: BIRTH ANNIVERSARY. Aug 22, 1909. Melvin J. (Mel) Hein, Pro Football Hall of Fame center, born at Redding, CA. Hein played football at Washington State and captained the first Cougar team to go to the Rose Bowl (1931). He joined the New York Giants and garnered All-Pro honors eight years in a row. His 15-year career earned him the nickname "Old Indestructible." Inducted into the Hall of Fame as a charter member in 1963. Died at San Clemente, CA, Jan 31, 1992.

LEADVILLE TRAIL 100 ULTRAMARATHON. Aug 22–23. Leadville, CO. One of the toughest 100-mile foot races in the country, the course goes through the Rocky Mountains 50 miles to the ghost town of Winfield and back. Runners begin at 4 AM and must complete race in 30 hours. Sponsor: Leadville Trail 100, Inc. Est attendance: 2,000. For info: Gloria Cheshier, Exec Dir, Greater Leadville Chamber of Commerce, PO Box 861, Leadville, CO 80461. Phone: (719) 486-3900 or (800) 933-3901. Fax: (719) 486-8478. Email: leadville@sni.net. WWW: http://www.colorado.com/leadville

MARICHAL CLUBS ROSEBORO: ANNIVERSARY. Aug 22, 1965. While at bat against the Los Angeles Dodgers, pitcher Juan Marichal of the San Francisco Giants turned on catcher John Roseboro and clubbed him with his bat. Marichal took exception to a couple of return throws from Roseboro to the pitcher that he deemed too close to his head. Roseboro was cut on the head by the bat, and a brawl ensued. Marichal was later suspended eight playing days and fined a then-record $1,750.

RYAN STRIKES OUT 5,000: ANNIVERSARY. Aug 22, 1989. Nolan Ryan of the Texas Rangers became the first pitcher to strike out 5,000 batters when he fanned Rickey Henderson of the Oakland A's in the fifth inning of a 2–0 Oakland win. Henderson went down on a 3–2 count, swinging at a fastball. Ryan ended his career with 5,714 strikeouts.

SCHANG, WALLY: BIRTH ANNIVERSARY. Aug 22, 1889. Walter Henry (Wally) Schang, baseball player born at South Wales, NY. Schang, a catcher, played in six different World Series with three different teams. He is one of a few players to win the Series on three different teams. Died at St. Louis, MO, Mar 6, 1965.

SHOCKER, URBAN: BIRTH ANNIVERSARY. Aug 22, 1890. Urban James Shocker, baseball player born Urbain Jacques Shockcor at Cleveland, OH. Shocker was one of the last legal spitball pitchers. He had a 13-year major league career (1916–28) and never suffered a losing season. Died at Denver, CO, Sept 9, 1928.

TATUM, BIG JIM: 85th BIRTH ANNIVERSARY. Aug 22, 1913. James Moore ("Big Jim") Tatum, football player and coach born at McColl, SC. Tatum played baseball and football at the University of North Carolina before becoming one of the most successful football coaches in Atlantic Coast Conference history. After his 1946 Oklahoma team won the Gator Bowl, Tatum moved to the University of Maryland. In nine years, his Terps won one national championship and finished undefeated three times. Died at Chapel Hill, NC, July 12, 1959.

BIRTHDAYS TODAY

Charles Douglas (Doug) Bair, 49, former baseball player, born Defiance, OH, Aug 22, 1949.
Bertram Ray Burris, 48, former baseball player, born Idabel, OK, Aug 22, 1950.
Dean Evason, 34, hockey player, born Flin Flon, Manitoba, Canada, Aug 22, 1964.
Paul Leo Molitor, 42, baseball player, born St. Paul, MN, Aug 22, 1956.
Duane Charles ("Bill") Parcells, 57, football coach, born Englewood, NJ, Aug 22, 1941.
Hipolito Antonio Pichardo, 29, baseball player, born Jicome Esperanza, Dominican Republic, Aug 22, 1969.
Carl Michael Yastrzemski, 59, Baseball Hall of Fame outfielder, born Southampton, NY, Aug 22, 1939.

AUGUST 23 — SUNDAY
Day 235 — 130 Remaining

DAVIS, GEORGE: BIRTH ANNIVERSARY. Aug 23, 1870. George Stacey Davis, baseball player and manager born at Cohoes, NY. Davis played shortstop for the New York Giants in the 1890s and for the Chicago White Sox after the turn of the century. He was involved in the contract controversies surrounding the creation of the American League in 1901. Died at Philadelphia, PA, Oct 17, 1940.

FIRST BOXING MATCH TELEVISED: 65th ANNIVERSARY. Aug 23, 1933. Boxers Archie Sexton and Laurie Raiteri fought an exhibition at Broadcasting House in London. The fight was the first boxing match ever televised, if only on an experimental basis.

FIRST GAME BETWEEN AFL AND NFL: ANNIVERSARY. Aug 23, 1966. Following announcement of a planned merger between the American Football League and the National Football League, the Kansas City Chiefs of the AFL and the Chicago Bears of the NFL played the first exhibition game between teams from the rival leagues. The Chiefs won, 66–24.

LOLLAR, SHERMAN: BIRTH ANNIVERSARY. Aug 23, 1924. John Sherman Lollar, baseball player born at Durham, AR. Lollar was a slow-footed catcher who played 18 years in the majors with four teams. He was particularly adept at handling pitchers and hit 155 career home runs. Died at Springfield, MO, Sept 24, 1977.

MITCHELL, DALE: BIRTH ANNIVERSARY. Aug 23, 1921. Loren Dale Mitchell, baseball player born at Colony, OK. With two out in the top of the ninth inning in Game 5 of the 1956 World Series, Dale Mitchell of the Brooklyn Dodgers pinch-hit for pitcher Sal Maglie. New York Yankees pitcher Don Larsen struck Mitchell out, thereby completing the only perfect game in World Series history. Died at Tulsa, OK, Jan 5, 1987.

UMPIRE TOSSES TWO: ANNIVERSARY. Aug 23, 1952. In a game against the St. Louis Cardinals in New York, Giants infielder Bob Elliott objected to a called strike by kicking dirt and was ejected from the game by home plate umpire Augie Donatelli. Bobby Hofmann pinch-hit for Elliott and was called out on strikes. He objected and was also ejected.

BIRTHDAYS TODAY

Ronald Mark (Ron) Blomberg, 50, former baseball player, born Atlanta, GA, Aug 23, 1948.
Michael James (Mike) Boddicker, 41, former baseball player, born Cedar Rapids, IA, Aug 23, 1957.
Allan Mercer Bristow, Jr, 47, former basketball coach and player, born Richmond, VA, Aug 23, 1951.
Kobe B. Bryant, 20, basketball player, born Philadelphia, PA, Aug 23, 1978.
Ray Ferraro, 34, hockey player, born Trail, BC, Canada, Aug 23, 1964.
Julio Cesar Franco, 37, baseball player, born San Pedro de Macoris, Dominican Republic, Aug 23, 1961.
Glenn Healy, 36, hockey player, born Pickering, Ontario, Canada, Aug 23, 1962.
Christian Adolph ("Sonny") Jurgensen, III, 64, Pro Football Hall of Fame quarterback, born Wilmington, NC, Aug 23, 1934.
George Clyde Kell, 76, broadcaster and Baseball Hall of Fame third baseman, born Swifton, AR, Aug 23, 1922.
Cortez Kennedy, 30, football player, born Wilson, AR, Aug 23, 1968.
Shelley Long, 49, actress ("Cheers"), born Fort Wayne, IN, Aug 23, 1949.
Jeffrey Paul (Jeff) Manto, 34, former baseball player, born Bristol, PA, Aug 23, 1964.
Rik Smits, 32, basketball player, born Eindhoven, The Netherlands, Aug 23, 1966.

AUGUST 24 — MONDAY
Day 236 — 129 Remaining

CHASE'S SPORTSQUOTE OF THE DAY

"The truth is, breaking Lou Gehrig's record for consecutive games played was partly an unintended result of that early and then ongoing determination to keep as much of my destiny as possible in my own hands." —Cal Ripken

BROWNS FANS VOTE ON DECISIONS: ANNIVERSARY. Aug 24, 1951. St. Louis Browns owner Bill Veeck, one of baseball's greatest showmen, allowed fans attending a game against the Philadelphia Athletics to participate in the strategy decisions normally made by the team's manager. More than 1,000 fans were given placards reading "YES" and "NO" and were asked to vote on what the Browns should do at various points in the game. It worked; St. Louis won, 5–3.

CICCARELLI SENTENCED TO JAIL: ANNIVERSARY. Aug 24, 1988. Minnesota North Stars winger Dino Ciccarelli was sentenced to one day in jail and fined $1,000 for hitting Luke Richardson of the Toronto Maple Leafs during a game played Jan 8. The referee gave Ciccarelli a match penalty, and the league suspended him for 10 games. The fine and jail term were the first given to a hockey player for an on-ice incident.

HOOPER, HARRY: BIRTH ANNIVERSARY. Aug 24, 1887. Harry Bartholomew Hooper, Baseball Hall of Fame outfielder born at Elephant Head Homestead, CA. Hooper was one-third of the famous Boston Red Sox outfield that also included Tris Speaker and Duffy Lewis. He suggested to manager Ed Barrow that pitcher Babe Ruth should play every day in the outfield. Inducted into the Hall of Fame in 1971. Died at Santa Cruz, CA, Dec 18, 1974.

KAHANAMOKU, DUKE: BIRTH ANNIVERSARY. Aug 24, 1890. Duke Paoa Kahanamoku, Olympic gold medal swimmer born at Honolulu, HI. Kahanamoku won gold medals in the 100-meter freestyle at the 1912 Olympics and at the 1920 Olympics. He enjoyed a long career, not retiring from competition until age 42. Credited with inventing the flutter kick, Kahanamoku acted in movies and served as sheriff of Honolulu, running alternately on the Republican and Democratic tickets. Died at Honolulu, Jan 22, 1968.

LITTLE LEAGUE BASEBALL WORLD SERIES. Aug 24–29 (tentative). Williamsport, PA. Eight teams from the US and foreign countries compete for the World Championship. Est attendance: 100,000. For info: Little League Baseball HQ, Box 3485, Williamsport, PA 17701. Phone: (717) 326-1921. Fax: (717) 326-1074. WWW: http://www.littleleague.org

PENNEL VAULTS 17 FEET: 35th ANNIVERSARY. Aug 24, 1963. John Pennel of the US became the first pole vaulter to clear 17 feet when he vaulted 17 ', 3/4 ", at a meet in Miami.

ROSE MADE INELIGIBLE: ANNIVERSARY. Aug 24, 1989. Former baseball player and manager Pete Rose signed a five-page agreement with Major League Baseball placing his name on the permanently ineligible list. Rose did not admit to gambling on baseball although a report made to Commissioner Bart Giamatti concluded that he had. The agreement barred Rose from being considered for the Hall of Fame.

US AMATEUR (GOLF) CHAMPIONSHIP. Aug 24–30. Oak Hill Country Club, Rochester, NY. For info: US Golf Assn, Golf House, Far Hills, NJ 07931. Phone: (908) 234-2300. Fax: (908) 234-9687. Email: usga@ix.netcom.com. WWW: http://www.usga.org

BIRTHDAYS TODAY

Benoit Brunet, 30, hockey player, born Pointe-Claire, Quebec, Canada, Aug 24, 1968.

Gerry Cooney, 42, former boxer, born New York, NY, Aug 24, 1956.

Reginald Wayne (Reggie) Miller, 33, basketball player, born Riverside, CA, Aug 24, 1965.

Calvin Edwin (Cal) Ripken, Jr, 38, baseball player, born Havre de Grace, MD, Aug 24, 1960.

Timothy James (Tim) Salmon, 30, baseball player, born Long Beach, CA, Aug 24, 1968.

		S	M	T	W	T	F	S
August								1
1998		2	3	4	5	6	7	8
		9	10	11	12	13	14	15
		16	17	18	19	20	21	22
		23	24	25	26	27	28	29
		30	31					

Michael Edward (Mike) Shanahan, 46, football coach, born Oak Park, IL, Aug 24, 1952.

AUGUST 25 — TUESDAY
Day 237 — 128 Remaining

MANTLE MONUMENT DEDICATED: ANNIVERSARY. Aug 25, 1996. The New York Yankees dedicated a monument to the late Mickey Mantle at Monument Park in Yankee Stadium. The new monument joined three others honoring Babe Ruth, Lou Gehrig and Miller Huggins. Mantle died Aug 13, 1995.

POOL DAY©. Aug 25. This day, observed on the date of the first US Swimming Championships in 1888, celebrates two pools in the sports world: swimming holes and the ball-and-cue game. For further info send $2 to cover cost of copying and postage to: Adrienne Koopersmith, 1437 W Rosemont, 1W, Chicago, IL 60660-1347. Phone: (773) 743-5341. Fax: (773) 743-5395. Email: kooper@interaccess.com.

YOUNGEST 20-GAME WINNER: ANNIVERSARY. Aug 25, 1985. Dwight Gooden of the New York Mets became the youngest pitcher to win 20 games in a season. Gooden defeated the San Diego Padres, 9–3. He was 20 years, nine months and nine days old.

BIRTHDAYS TODAY

Albert Jojuan Belle, 32, baseball player, born Shreveport, LA, Aug 25, 1966.

Cornelius O'landa Bennett, 33, football player, born Birmingham, AL, Aug 25, 1965.

Roland Glen (Rollie) Fingers, 52, Baseball Hall of Fame pitcher, born Steubenville, OH, Aug 25, 1946.

Althea Gibson, 71, former tennis player, born Silver, SC, Aug 25, 1927.

Robert Keith Horry, 28, basketball player, born Andalusia, AL, Aug 25, 1970.

Darrell Dean Johnson, 70, former baseball manager and player, born Horace, NE, Aug 25, 1928.

Oddibe McDowell, Jr, 36, former baseball player, born Hollywood, FL, Aug 25, 1962.

AUGUST 26 — WEDNESDAY
Day 238 — 127 Remaining

ADAMS, SPARKY: BIRTH ANNIVERSARY. Aug 26, 1894. Earl John ("Sparky") Adams, baseball player born at Zerbe, PA. Adams was an infielder who batted .286 in 13 seasons with four teams. He led the National League in at-bats for three straight years, 1925–27. Died at Pottsville, PA, Feb 24, 1989.

FIRST BASEBALL GAMES TELEVISED: ANNIVERSARY. Aug 26, 1939. WXBS television in New York City broadcast major league baseball for the first time, a doubleheader between the Cincinnati Reds and the Brooklyn Dodgers at Ebbets Field. Announcer Red Barber interviewed Leo Durocher, manager of the Dodgers, and William McKechnie, manager of the Reds, between games.

BIRTHDAYS TODAY

Ricky Paul Bottalico, 29, baseball player, born New Britain, CT, Aug 26, 1969.

Myron Maynard Guyton, 31, football player, born Metcalf, GA, Aug 26, 1967.

Thomas William (Tommy) Heinsohn, 64, former coach and Basketball Hall of Fame forward, born Jersey City, NJ, Aug 26, 1934.

Chadden Michael (Chad) Kreuter, 34, baseball player, born Greenbrae, CA, Aug 26, 1964.

Jeffrey Dale (Jeff) Parrett, 37, baseball player, born Indianapolis, IN, Aug 26, 1961.

Alejandro (Alex) Trevino, 41, former baseball player, born Monterrey, Mexico, Aug 26, 1957.

AUGUST 27 — THURSDAY

Day 239 — 126 Remaining

HANLON, NED: BIRTH ANNIVERSARY. Aug 27, 1857. Edward Hugh (Ned) Hanlon, Baseball Hall of Fame player and manager born at Montville, CT. Hanlon managed the great Baltimore Orioles teams of the 1890s, the teams that devised an aggressive style of play called "inside baseball." Inducted into the Hall of Fame in 1996. Died at Baltimore, MD, Apr 14, 1937.

HENDERSON BREAKS BROCK'S SINGLE-SEASON RECORD: ANNIVERSARY. Aug 27, 1982. Oakland Athletics outfielder Rickey Henderson stole his 119th base of the season in a game against the Milwaukee Brewers, thereby breaking Lou Brock's major league record for most stolen bases in one season, set in 1974. Henderson added three more steals in the game, which Oakland lost, 5–4.

HOTTER-N-HELL HUNDRED. Aug 27–30. Wichita Falls, TX. Thousands of cyclists of all ages participate in the largest sanctioned century bicycle ride in the US. Aug 28-Criterium racing. Aug 29-Hotter-N-Hell ride. Aug 30-Criterium racing and time trials. Est attendance: 27,500. For info: Joe Schalling, Wichita Falls Conv & Vis Bureau, 1000 5th St, Wichita Falls, TX 76301. Phone: (817) 723-5800. Email: HH100@WF.net. WWW: http://www.wtr.com/hhh

LEAHY, FRANK: 90th BIRTH ANNIVERSARY. Aug 27, 1908. Francis William (Frank) Leahy, football player and coach born at O'Neill, NE. Leahy played at Notre Dame and then commenced an outstanding coaching career at Boston College and his alma mater. His career winning percentage stands second to Knute Rockne among coaches with ten years' service and was highlighted by the 37–0–2 mark achieved by Notre Dame from 1946 through 1949. Died at Portland, OR, June 21, 1973.

NEC WORLD SERIES OF GOLF. Aug 27–30. Firestone Country Club, Akron, OH. A PGA Tour tournament. For info: PGA Tour, 112 TPC Blvd, Ponte Vedra Beach, FL 32082. Phone: (904) 285-3700.

RICHARDS BARRED FROM US OPEN: ANNIVERSARY. Aug 27, 1976. Transexual tennis player Renee Richards, who had formerly competed as Dr. Richard Raskind, was barred from competing in the US Open Women's championship after refusing to submit to a chromosome qualification test.

BIRTHDAYS TODAY

David Gus ("Buddy") Bell, 47, baseball manager and former player, born Pittsburgh, PA, Aug 27, 1951.

Ernest Gilbert (Ernie) Broglio, 63, former baseball player, born Berkeley, CA, Aug 27, 1935.

Joseph Robert (Joe) Cunningham, 67, former baseball player, born Paterson, NJ, Aug 27, 1931.

Brian Wesley McRae, 31, baseball player, born Bradenton, FL, Aug 27, 1967.

Adam Oates, 36, hockey player, born Weston, Ontario, Canada, Aug 27, 1962.

Michael Dean Perry, 33, football player, born Aiken, SC, Aug 27, 1965.

James Howard (Jim) Thome, 28, baseball player, born Peoria, IL, Aug 27, 1970.

AUGUST 28 — FRIDAY

Day 240 — 125 Remaining

CANADA: CLASSIC BOAT FESTIVAL. Aug 28–30. Victoria, BC. Classic sail and power vessels from all over the west coast of the US, Canada and beyond gather in Victoria's Inner Harbour. View these lovingly restored and maintained boats with their polished brass fittings and rich teak and oak decks and hulls. Schooner races, sailpast, steamboat parade. Sponsored by Victoria Real Estate Board. For info: Victoria Real Estate Board, 3035 Nanaimo St, Victoria, BC, Canada V8T 4W2. Phone: (604) 385-7766. Fax: (604) 385-8773. Email: vreb@islandnet.com.

GRIMM, CHARLIE: 100th BIRTH ANNIVERSARY. Aug 28, 1898. Charles John (Charlie) Grimm, baseball player, manager, executive and sportscaster born at St. Louis, MO. Grimm had an extremely varied baseball career, starting with a job as a batboy at Sportsman's Park in St. Louis. He played for four teams over 20 years, managed and held several executive positions. Died at Scottsdale, AZ, Nov 15, 1983.

US WINS FIRST WALKER CUP: ANNIVERSARY. Aug 28, 1922. A team of amateur golfers from the United States defeated a team of amateur golfers from Great Britain, 8–4, to win the first Walker Cup competition. The Walker Cup was presented by American businessman George Walker and has generally been put in competition every two years.

BIRTHDAYS TODAY

Ronald Ames (Ron) Guidry, 48, former baseball player, born Lafayette, LA, Aug 28, 1950.

Scott Hamilton, 40, Olympic gold medal figure skater, born Toledo, OH, Aug 28, 1958.

Lee MacLeod Janzen, 34, golfer, born Austin, MN, Aug 28, 1964.

Darren Joel Lewis, 31, baseball player, born Berkeley, CA, Aug 28, 1967.

Louis Victor (Lou) Piniella, 55, baseball manager and former player, born Tampa, FL, Aug 28, 1943.

Michael Augustine (Mike) Torrez, 52, former baseball player, born Topeka, KS, Aug 28, 1946.

AUGUST 29 — SATURDAY

Day 241 — 124 Remaining

HOYLE, EDMOND: DEATH ANNIVERSARY ("ACCORDING TO HOYLE" DAY). Aug 29, 1769. Edmond Hoyle, games authority, born place unknown, ca. 1672. Today is a day to remember Hoyle and a day for fun and games *according to the rules*. Little is known about Hoyle. He is believed to have studied law. For many years he lived in London and gave instructions in the playing of games. His "Short Treatise" on the game of whist (published in 1742) became a model guide to the rules of the game. Hoyle's name became synonymous with the idea of correct play according to the rules, and the phrase "according to Hoyle" became a part of the English language. Died at London, Aug 29, 1769.

BROCK BREAKS COBB'S RECORD: ANNIVERSARY. Aug 29, 1977. Lou Brock stole the 893rd base of his career, surpassing Ty Cobb's modern record for career stolen bases.

CALVERT COUNTY JOUSTING TOURNAMENT. Aug 29. Christ Church grounds, Port Republic, MD. The 132nd annual tournament of Maryland's official state sport, steeped in colorful pageantry. Country supper, bazaar, organ recitals, children's activities, one-room schoolhouse, colonial church. Admission fee. Est attendance: 1,500. For info: Christ Church, 3100 Broomes Island Rd, Port Republic, MD 20676. Phone: (410) 586-0565.

CHAPTICO CLASSIC. Aug 29. Chaptico, MD. 15th annual Chaptico Classic for the benefit of Alternatives for Youth. 5K and 10K road race and walk. Annually, the last Saturday in August. For info: Michael J. Whitson, Race Dir, PO Box 746, Hugheville, MD 20637. Phone: (301) 475-2886. Fax: (301) 475-3157.

CHILI CHALLENGE OFF-ROAD BIKE RACE. Aug 29-30. Angel Fire, NM. Annual bike race held on the ski mountain in this beautiful alpine setting. All skill levels. Est attendance: 400. For info: Angel Fire Resort, PO Drawer B, Angel Fire, NM 87710. Phone: (800) 633-7463 or (505) 377-4207. Fax: (505) 377-4395. Email: gmorton@angelfireresort.com. WWW: http://www.angelfireresort.com

HYMAN, FLO: BIRTH ANNIVERSARY. Aug 29, 1954. Flora (Flo) Hyman, volleyball player born at Inglewood, CA. Hyman stood 6'5" and was regarded as the best player in the US, starring on the 1984 silver medal team. She suffered from Marfan's syndrome, a hidden congenital aorta disorder. Died at Matsue, Japan, Jan 24, 1986.

MOONLIGHT RAMBLE. Aug 29-30. Downtown St. Louis, MO. World's largest nighttime bicycle ride takes place through the streets of St. Louis. The event starts at Soldiers' Memorial in downtown St. Louis at midnight, Friday into Saturday. 34th annual. Est attendance: 12,500. For info: Exec Dir, Moonlight Ramble, 7187 Manchester, St. Louis, MO 63143. Phone: (314) 644-4660. Fax: (314) 644-6329. Email: ratz1@i1.net.

MOSES MALONE SKIPS COLLEGE: ANNIVERSARY. Aug 29, 1974. Moses Malone became the first basketball player to jump from high school to professional basketball, skipping college to sign a contract with the Utah Stars of the ABA.

STA-BIL NATIONALS CHAMPIONSHIP LAWN MOWER RACE. Aug 29. Rockford MetroCentre, Rockford, IL. Three classes of races for winners of regional races held across the US. Mowers will travel at speeds ranging from 10 mph to more than 50 mph. Held in conjunction with the On the Waterfront Festival. Est attendance: 2,000. For info: US Lawn Mower Racing Assn, 1812 Glenview Rd, Glenview, IL 60025. Phone: (847) 729-7363. Email: letsmow@aol.com. WWW: http://letsmow.com/us/mia

August *1998*	S	M	T	W	T	F	S
							1
	2	3	4	5	6	7	8
	9	10	11	12	13	14	15
	16	17	18	19	20	21	22
	23	24	25	26	27	28	29
	30	31					

Moses Malone

WICC GREATEST BLUEFISH TOURNAMENT ON EARTH. Aug 29-301. Long Island Sound, CT and NY. One of the nation's largest fishing tournaments of its kind. More than $50,000 in prizes for the biggest fish at this 16th annual tourney. Annually, the last weekend in August. Est attendance: 7,000. For info: Megan E. O'Connell, Tourn Dir, Bluefish Tournament, 2 Lafayette Sq, Bridgeport, CT 06604. Phone: (203) 366-2583.

BIRTHDAYS TODAY

Carl Banks, 36, football player, born Flint, MI, Aug 29, 1962.

Jon Casey, 36, hockey player, born Grand Rapids, MI, Aug 29, 1962.

Douglas Vernon (Doug) DeCinces, 48, former baseball player, born Burbank, CA, Aug 29, 1950.

Maurice Joseph ("Mickey") McDermott, 70, former baseball player, born Poughkeepsie, NY, Aug 29, 1928.

William Edward (Will) Perdue, III, 33, basketball player, born Melbourne, FL, Aug 29, 1965.

Pierre Turgeon, 29, hockey player, born Rouyn, Quebec, Canada, Aug 29, 1969.

Wyomia Tyus, 53, Olympic gold medal sprinter, born Griffin, GA, Aug 29, 1945.

AUGUST 30 — SUNDAY
Day 242 — 123 Remaining

ANNAPOLIS RUN. Aug 30. Navy-Marine Corps Memorial Stadium, Annapolis, MD. Maryland's premier 10-mile foot race, through historic Annapolis and along Naval Academy seawalls; designer premium for all finishers; entries limited to 4,000. Annually, the last Sunday of August since 1976. (Non-Labor Day weekend.) Est attendance: 4,000. For info: Annapolis Striders, Inc, PO Box 187, Annapolis, MD 21404-0187. Phone: (410) 268-1165.

COOPER, TARZAN: BIRTH ANNIVERSARY. Aug 30, 1907. Charles Theodore ("Tarzan") Cooper, Basketball Hall of Fame center born at Newark, DE. Four years after graduating from high school in Philadelphia in 1925, Cooper signed to play basketball with the New York Renaissance. He starred for the Rens for 11 years and helped make them one of the two greatest teams (along with the Original Celtics) of the era. The Rens were inducted into the Hall of Fame as a team in 1963. Cooper followed as an individual player in 1976. Died at Philadelphia, Dec 19, 1980.

CUYLER, KIKI: BIRTH ANNIVERSARY. Aug 30, 1899. Hazen Shirley ("Kiki") Cuyler, Baseball Hall of Fame outfielder born at Harrisville, MI. Cuyler was an outfielder in the 1920s and 1930s, primarily with the Pittsburgh Pirates. He was an outstanding hitter with good speed and fine defensive skills. Inducted into the Hall of Fame in 1968. Died at Ann Arbor, MI, Feb 11, 1950.

FIRST $1 MILLION RACE: ANNIVERSARY. Aug 30, 1981. Jockey Bill Shoemaker rode John Henry to a nose victory to win the inaugural running of the Arlington Million, the first $1 million horse race, at Arlington Park in Illinois.

MILLER, BING: BIRTH ANNIVERSARY. Aug 30, 1894. Edmund John ("Bing") Miller, baseball player born at Cheney, IA. Miller played 16 seasons in the outfield for four different teams. His best season was 1924 when he hit .324. Died at Philadelphia, PA, May 7, 1966.

MOON PHASE: FIRST QUARTER. Aug 30. Moon enters First Quarter phase at 1:06 AM, EDT.

NEW YORK GOLDEN ARMS TOURNAMENT–BRONX. Aug 30. Orchard Beach, Bronx, NY. Arm wrestling competition held at fair determines borough winner who will compete in the Empire State Golden Arms Tournament of Champions on Oct 22. For info: New York Arm Wrestling Assn, Inc, 200-14 45th Dr, Bayside, NY 11361. Phone/fax: (718) 544-4592.

BIRTHDAYS TODAY

Jean-Claude Killy, 55, Olympic gold medal alpine skier, born Saint Cloud, France, Aug 30, 1943.
Frank Edwin ("Tug") McGraw, 54, former baseball player, born Martinez, CA, Aug 30, 1944.
Robert Lee Parish, 45, basketball player, born Shreveport, LA, Aug 30, 1953.
Theodore Samuel (Ted) Williams, 80, Baseball Hall of Fame outfielder, born San Diego, CA, Aug 30, 1918.

AUGUST 31 — MONDAY
Day 243 — 122 Remaining

CHASE'S SPORTSQUOTE OF THE DAY

"It couldn't happen to a nicer guy—if you think managing is something nice to happen to you." —Walter Alston on Gil Hodges

BIRTH OF PROFESSIONAL FOOTBALL: ANNIVERSARY. Aug 31, 1895. A football team from Latrobe, PA, defeated a squad from Jeanette, PA, 12–0, in what could be regarded as the first professional football game. Latrobe quarterback John Brallier was paid $10 expense money.

FIRST COLLEGE ALL-STAR FOOTBALL GAME: ANNIVERSARY. Aug 31, 1934. The first College All-Star Football Game, matching the defending NFL champion against a team of college seniors from the previous season, was played at Chicago's Soldier Field. Organized by sportswriter Arch Ward, the game was an annual charity affair played through 1976. In the first game, the Chicago Bears and the All-Stars played to a 0–0 tie before a crowd of 79,432.

FIRST MAJOR COLLEGE FOOTBALL OVERTIME: ANNIVERSARY. Aug 31, 1996. Oklahoma State University defeated Southwest Missouri State University, 23–20, in the first Division I-A college football game to be decided in overtime. The game was tied, 17–17, at the end of regulation time. Under new rules effective this year, Southwest Missouri State got the ball first in overtime and kicked a 47-year field goal. Oklahoma State then got the ball and answered with a 13-yard touchdown run.

GRIFFEYS' FATHER-SON ACT: ANNIVERSARY. Aug 31, 1990. Ken Griffey, Jr, 20, and Ken Griffey, Sr, 40, made major league history by becoming the first father and son to play together in the same game. They played for the Seattle Mariners in a game against the Kansas City Royals.

HODGES HITS FOUR HOME RUNS: ANNIVERSARY. Aug 31, 1950. First baseman Gil Hodges of the Brooklyn Dodgers became the sixth player in major league history to hit four home runs in one game. He added a single as the Dodgers beat the Boston Braves, 19–3.

PLANK, EDDIE: BIRTH ANNIVERSARY. Aug 31, 1875. Edward Stewart (Eddie) Plank, Baseball Hall of Fame pitcher born at Gettysburg, PA. Plank won more games than any other left-handed pitcher in American League history during a 17-year career. His victory total, including those achieved in the Federal League, is 327. Inducted into the Hall of Fame in 1946. Died at Gettysburg, Feb 24, 1926.

POTATO BALL: ANNIVERSARY. Aug 31, 1987. Catcher Dave Bresnahan of Williamsport in the Class AA Eastern League introduced some humor into a game when he attempted to throw out a baserunner with a potato instead of the ball. He had concealed the potato in his shirt waiting for the proper moment. To punish his indiscretion, the team released Bresnahan but later retired his number, 59.

US OPEN (TENNIS). Aug 31–Sept 13. US National Tennis Center, Flushing Meadows, NY. The national tennis championships of the US with competitions in men's and women's singles and men's, women's and mixed doubles. One of the sport's Grand Slam events. For info: ATP Tour, 200 ATP Blvd, Ponte Vedra Beach, FL 32082. Phone: (904) 285-8000. Fax: (904) 285-5966.

WASHINGTON, KENNY: 80th BIRTH ANNIVERSARY. Aug 31, 1918. Kenneth S. (Kenny) Washington, football player born at Los Angeles, CA. After gaining All-American honors at UCLA, where he was a teammate of Jackie Robinson, Washington and Woody Strode became the first blacks to play in the NFL after World War II, breaking the league's color barrier with the Los Angeles Rams. He played three seasons and then retired to a career in business. Died at Los Angeles, June 24, 1971.

YOUNG, DICK: DEATH ANNIVERSARY. Aug 31, 1987. Dick Young, sportswriter born at New York, NY, 1917 or 1918. Young's career spanned nearly half a century. While covering the Brooklyn Dodgers, he pioneered an aggressive reporting style that saw him interview players before and after games to gather quotations he incorporated into his stories. His column, "Young Ideas," provided a forum for his increasingly acerbic and conservative views that he believed represented the viewpoint of the average fan. Died at New York.

BIRTHDAYS TODAY

Thomas Caesar (Tom) Candiotti, 41, baseball player, born Walnut Creek, CA, Aug 31, 1957.
Thomas (Tom) Coughlin, 52, football coach, born Waterloo, NY, Aug 31, 1946.
Von Francis Hayes, 40, former baseball player, born Stockton, CA, Aug 31, 1958.
Edwin Corley Moses, 43, Olympic gold medal hurdler, born Dayton, OH, Aug 31, 1955.
Scott Niedermayer, 25, hockey player, born Edmonton, Alberta, Canada, Aug 31, 1973.
Hideo Nomo, 30, baseball player, born Osaka, Japan, Aug 31, 1968.
Frank Robinson, 63, former baseball executive, manager and Baseball Hall of Fame outfielder, born Beaumont, TX, Aug 31, 1935.

SEPTEMBER 1 — TUESDAY
Day 244 — 121 Remaining

BROWN, JOHNNY MACK: BIRTH ANNIVERSARY. Sept 1, 1904. Johnny Mack Brown, football player and actor born at Dothan, AL. Brown played at the University of Alabama and starred on Coach Wallace Wade's undefeated 1925 team that defeated Washington in the 1926 Rose Bowl, 20–19. Brown took a screen test and acted in several dramatic films before appearing in the first of more than 300 westerns. Died at Woodland Hills, CA, Nov 14, 1974.

CORBETT, GENTLEMAN JIM: BIRTH ANNIVERSARY. Sept 1, 1866. James John ("Gentleman Jim") Corbett, boxer born at San Francisco, CA. Corbett boxed 61 rounds against Peter Jackson on May 21, 1891, to no decision, but the fight got him a match with heavyweight champion John L. Sullivan. This fight, on Sept 7, 1892, was the first governed by the Marquis of Queensbury Rules and the first in which the fighters used gloves. Corbett decisioned Sullivan in 21 rounds, using the jab, the punch he invented. Died at Bayside, NY, Feb 18, 1933.

EVERT WINS 100th MATCH: ANNIVERSARY. Sept 1, 1989. Chris Evert defeated Patricia Tarabini, 6–2, 6–4, in an early round of the US Open tennis tournament. The victory made Evert, playing in her final US Open, the first 100-match winner in the 108 years of US national tennis championship competition.

FREEDMAN, ANDREW: BIRTH ANNIVERSARY. Sept 1, 1860. Andrew Freedman, baseball executive born at New York, NY. Freedman purchased controlling interest of the New York Giants in 1895, but he was an extremely unpopular owner. He sold the team in 1902 because he was not making as much money as he had anticipated. Died at New York, Dec 4, 1915.

INTERNATIONAL GAY SQUARE DANCE MONTH. Sept 1–30. Emphasis on square-dancing as a healthy, fun recreational activity. For info: Intl Assn of Gay Square Dance Clubs (IAGSDC), PO Box 15428, Crystal City, VA 22215-0428. Phone: (800) 835-6462. Email: iagsdc@glyphic.com. WWW: http://www.glyphic.com/IAGSDC

MARCIANO, ROCKY: BIRTH ANNIVERSARY. Sept 1, 1923. Rocky Marciano, boxer born Rocco Francis Marchegiano at Brockton, MA. Marciano used superb conditioning to fashion an impressive record that propelled him to a fight against Jersey Joe Walcott for the heavyweight title on Sept 23, 1952. Marciano knocked Walcott out, and in 1956 he retired as the only undefeated heavyweight champion. Died in a plane crash at Newton, IA, Aug 31, 1969.

PIRATES LOSE THREE GAMES: ANNIVERSARY. Sept 1, 1890. The Pittsburgh Pirates lost three games in the same day to the Brooklyn Bridegrooms (later known as the Dodgers). In the morning, the Pirates scored nine runs in the ninth inning but lost, 10–9. In the afternoon, Pittsburgh dropped a doubleheader, 3–2 and 8–4.

SMOKY JOE BESTS THE BIG TRAIN: ANNIVERSARY. Sept 1, 1912. In a specially-arranged pitching matchup, Smoky Joe Wood of the Boston Red Sox outdueled Walter Johnson, the "Big Train," of the Washington Senators, 1–0. The victory was the 14th straight for Wood. Johnson had a 16-game winning streak earlier in the year.

BIRTHDAYS TODAY

Brian Bellows, 34, hockey player, born St. Catherines, Ontario, Canada, Sept 1, 1964.

Ricardo Adolfo (Rico) Carty, 59, former baseball player, born San Pedro de Macoris, Dominican Republic, Sept 1, 1939.

Timothy Duane (Tim) Hardaway, 32, basketball player, born Chicago, IL, Sept 1, 1966.

Vincent (Vinnie) Johnson, 42, former basketball player, born New York, NY, Sept 1, 1956.

Garry Lee Maddox, 49, former baseball player, born Cincinnati, OH, Sept 1, 1949.

David Lee West, 34, baseball player, born Memphis, TN, Sept 1, 1964.

SEPTEMBER 2 — WEDNESDAY
Day 245 — 120 Remaining

CANADA: GRAND FORKS INTERNATIONAL BASEBALL TOURNAMENT. Sept 2–7. James Donalson Park, Grand Forks, British Columbia. 12-team invitational tournament draws from the four corners of North America and from the Pacific Rim. Annually, Labor Day weekend, beginning Wednesday. Est attendance: 35,000. For info: Larry Seminoff, Box 1214, Grand Forks, BC, Canada V0H 1H0. Phone: (250) 442-2110. Fax: (250) 442-3788.

DAYS OF MARATHON: ANNIVERSARY. Sept 2–9, 490 BC. Anniversary of the events from which the marathon race is derived. Phidippides, "an Athenian and by profession and practice a trained runner," according to Herodotus, was dispatched from Marathon to Sparta (26 miles), Sept 2 (Metageitnion 28), to seek help in repelling the invading Persian army. Help being unavailable by religious law until after the next full moon, Phidippides

September 1998

	S	M	T	W	T	F	S
			1	2	3	4	5
	6	7	8	9	10	11	12
	13	14	15	16	17	18	19
	20	21	22	23	24	25	26
	27	28	29	30			

196

ran the 26 miles back to Marathon on Sept 4. Under the leadership of Miltiades, and without Spartan aid, the Athenians defeated the Persians at the Battle of Marathon on Sept 9. According to legend Phidippides carried the news of the battle to Athens and died as he spoke the words "Rejoice, we are victorious." The marathon race was revived at the 1896 Olympic Games in Athens to commemorate Phidippides' heroism. Course distance, since 1924, is 26 miles, 385 yards. Oldest in the US is the Boston Marathon, an annual event since 1897.

LIKE FATHER, LIKE SON: ANNIVERSARY. Sept 2, 1960. Nearing the end of his career, Ted Williams of the Boston Red Sox hit a home run against Don Lee, a pitcher for the Washington Senators. In 1939, Williams's rookie year, he had homered against Thornton Lee, Don's father.

NATIONAL STEARMAN FLY-IN. Sept 2–5. Galesburg, IL. The largest gathering of Stearman airplanes—the biplane trainers that gave wings to more military pilots than any other series of aircraft in the world. Annually, Wednesday through Saturday after Labor Day. Est attendance: 7,500. For info: Tourism Associate, Galesburg Area CVB, PO Box 749, Galesburg, IL 61402-0749. Phone: (309) 343-1194. Fax: (309) 343-1195. Email: gacvb@misslink.net. WWW: http://www.misslink.net/gacvb/

PINCH-RUNNER PINCHES BASES: ANNIVERSARY. Sept 2, 1909. Bill O'Hara of the New York Giants entered the game as a pinch-runner and promptly stole second base and third. He had done the same thing the day before, becoming the only pinch-runner to steal two bases two days in a row.

RUPP, ADOLPH: BIRTH ANNIVERSARY. Sept 2, 1901. Adolph Frederick Rupp, Basketball Hall of Fame coach born at Halstead, KS. Rupp played basketball in high school and at the University of Kansas where his coach was Forrest ("Phog") Allen. He became coach at the University of Kentucky in 1930 and remained there until he was forced to retire after the 1972 season. Rupp's teams won 874 games, ranking him first among college coaches, and four NCAA titles (1948, 1949, 1951 and 1958) and lost the final game twice. Inducted into the Hall of Fame in 1968. Died at Lexington, Dec 10, 1977.

SPALDING, ALBERT: BIRTH ANNIVERSARY. Sept 2, 1850. Albert Goodwill Spalding, Baseball Hall of Fame pitcher and executive born at Byron, IL. Spalding was a star pitcher in the 1870s and retired to run his sporting goods business, help administer the National League and attempt to popularize baseball throughout the world. Inducted into the Hall of Fame in 1939. Died at Point Loma, CA, Sept 9, 1915.

THRONEBERRY, MARV: 65th BIRTH ANNIVERSARY. Sept 2, 1933. Marvin Eugene (Marv) Throneberry, baseball player born at Collierville, TN. Throneberry parlayed modest talent into status as a fan favorite when he played for the New York Mets in 1962 and 1963. His fame was later reinforced when he appeared in a television beer commercial. Died at Fisherville, TN, June 23, 1994.

BIRTHDAYS TODAY

Nathaniel ("Tiny") Archibald, 50, Basketball Hall of Fame guard, born New York, NY, Sept 2, 1948.

Eldon LeRoy Auker, 88, former baseball player, born Norcatur, KS, Sept 2, 1910.

Terry Paxton Bradshaw, 50, broadcaster and Pro Football Hall of Fame quarterback, born Shreveport, LA, Sept 2, 1948.

James Scott (Jimmy) Connors, 46, former tennis player, born East St. Louis, IL, Sept 2, 1952.

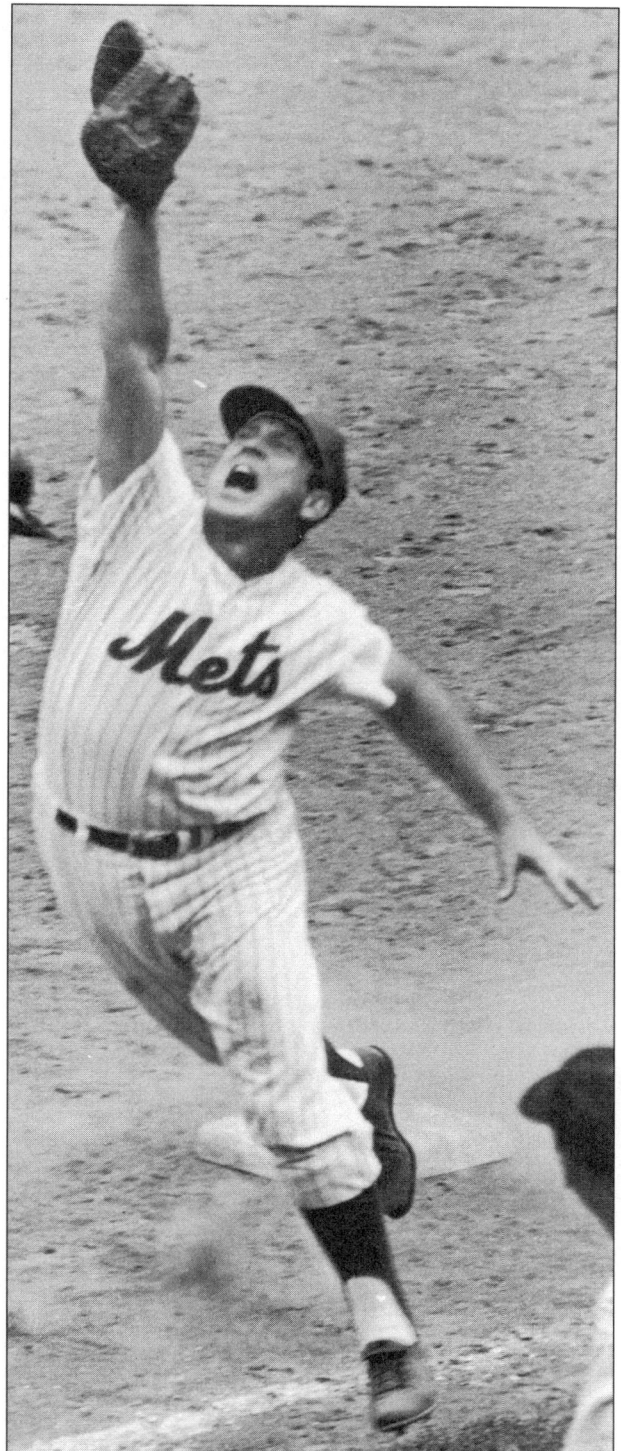

"Marvelous" Marv Throneberry

Eric Demetric Dickerson, 38, former football player, born Sealy, TX, Sept 2, 1960.

Mark Harmon, 47, actor, former football player, born Burbank, CA, Sept 2, 1951.

Rex Allen Hudler, 38, baseball player, born Tempe, AZ, Sept 2, 1960.

Richard Eugene (Rick) Manning, 44, former baseball player, born Niagara Falls, NY, Sept 2, 1954.

John Thompson, 57, college basketball coach, former player, born Washington, DC, Sept 2, 1941.

Peter Victor Ueberroth, 61, former commissioner of baseball and Olympics executive, born Evansville, IL, Sept 2, 1937.

SEPTEMBER 3 — THURSDAY
Day 246 — 119 Remaining

ALEXANDER PITCHES DOUBLEHEADER: ANNIVERSARY. Sept 3, 1917. Grover Cleveland Alexander of the Philadelphia Phillies pitched and won both ends of a doubleheader against the Brooklyn Dodgers. Alexander went the distance in both games, winning the opener, 5–0, and the nightcap, 9–3.

BILLY WILLIAMS'S STREAK ENDS: ANNIVERSARY. Sept 3, 1970. Outfielder Billy Williams of the Chicago Cubs asked to be taken out of the starting lineup, breaking his consecutive games played streak at 1,117, a National League record until Steve Garvey broke it in 1983.

GREAT PERSHING BALLOON DERBY. Sept 3–7. Brookfield, MO. Hot-air balloon flights, Balloon Glow, fly-in breakfast at Pershing Memorial Airport. Queen/Princess/Little Miss contest, craft fair in downtown Brookfield. All flights are subject to weather. Various admission fees and requirements for balloon flights. Annually, Labor Day weekend. Est attendance: 10,000. For info: Green Hills Ballooning, PO Box 451, Brookfield, MO 64628. Phone: (816) 376-3543 ext 3314 or (816) 258-5290.

KONETCHY, ED: BIRTH ANNIVERSARY. Sept 3, 1885. Edward Joseph (Ed) Konetchy, baseball player born at LaCrosse, WI. Konetchy played 15 years at first base and compiled 100 or more hits in 14 seasons. Four times he broke up potential no-hitters. Died at Fort Worth, TX, May 27, 1947.

ROCKFORD AREA SENIOR GAMES. Sept 3–6. Rockford, IL. Athletic and social events for adults ages 50 and up, including baseball hit, basketball three-on-three, basketball free throw, billiards, bowling, casting, croquet, cycling, darts, golf, horseshoes, miniature golf, shuffleboard, softball, swimming, table tennis, tennis, track and field and volleyball. Sponsored by the Rockford Park District. Annually, the first weekend after Labor Day. Est attendance: 800. For info: Rockford Park District, 1401 N Second St, Rockford, IL 61107-3086. Phone: (815) 987-8800 or TTY: (815) 963-DEAF. Fax: (815) 987-8877.

THIGPEN SETS SAVE RECORD: ANNIVERSARY. Sept 3, 1990. Relief pitcher Bobby Thigpen of the Chicago White Sox set a major league record for most saves in a season when he chalked up his 47th save in a 4–2 White Sox victory over the Kansas City Royals. Thigpen finished the season with 57 saves.

TWIN FALLS COUNTY FAIR AND RODEO. Sept 3–7. Filer, ID. County fair features PRCA rodeo, demolition derby, draft horse show, team sorting, livestock show, competitive exhibits (culinary arts, horticulture and fine arts), country music concerts and more. Annually since 1916, on Labor Day weekend beginning on Wednesday. Est attendance: 100,000. For info: Idaho Dept of Commerce, PO Box 83720, Boise, ID 83721-0093. Phone: (208) 326-4396. Fax: (208) 334-2631.

BIRTHDAYS TODAY

Alan Bannister, 47, former baseball player, born Montebello, CA, Sept 3, 1951.

Horatio Benedict (Bennie) Blades, 32, football player, born Fort Lauderdale, FL, Sept 3, 1966.

Luis Emilio Gonzalez, 31, baseball player, born Tampa, FL, Sept 3, 1967.

John Richard (Dick) Motta, 67, former basketball coach, born Midvale, UT, Sept 3, 1931.

Edward Raymond (Eddie) Stanky, 82, former baseball manager and player, born Philadelphia, PA, Sept 3, 1916.

Damon Lamon Stoudamire, 25, basketball player, born Portland, OR, Sept 3, 1973.

Renaldo Lavalle Wynn, 24, football player, born Chicago, IL, Sept 3, 1974.

SEPTEMBER 4 — FRIDAY
Day 247 — 118 Remaining

SPORTSCHASER OF THE DAY
What tennis player was known as "Little Mo"?

BRAVES PLAY TWO NINE TIMES: 70th ANNIVERSARY. Sept 4, 1928. The Boston Braves began an unprecedented and grueling string of nine doubleheaders played on nine straight days, a major league record.

BRITT DRAFT HORSE SHOW. Sept 4–6. Hancock County Fairgrounds, Britt, IA. Largest draft horse hitch show in North America, featuring 16 draft six-horse hitches from the US and Canada representing the very best of the Belgian, Percheron and Clydesdale and Shire performance horses. Annually, Labor Day weekend. Est attendance: 10,000. For info: Randel or Melodie Hiscocks, Britt Draft Horse Assn, PO Box 312, Britt, IA 50423. Phone: (515) 843-4181.

DODGE VINTAGE FESTIVAL. Sept 4–7. Lime Rock Park, Lakeville, CT. Vintage and historic car racing and car shows. Annually, Labor Day weekend. Est attendance: 15,000. For info: Lime Rock Park, PO Box 111, Lakeville, CT 06039.

DODGERS ATTENDANCE RECORD: ANNIVERSARY. Sept 4, 1966. The Los Angeles Dodgers became the first team in major league history to draw two million fans at home and two million on the road in the same season when they played the Reds in Cincinnati before a crowd of 18,670.

HOG CAPITAL OF THE WORLD FESTIVAL. Sept 4–7. Kewanee, IL. World's largest pork chop BBQ. Also features Model T races, four-mile run (Hog Stampede) and the Hogatta Regatta, plus professional entertainment, carnival, flea market, parade and more. Annually, Labor Day weekend. Est attendance: 60,000. For info: Mark Mikenas, Exec VP, Kewanee Chamber of Commerce, 113 East 2nd St, Kewanee, IL 61443. Phone: (309) 852-2175. Fax: (309) 852-2176. Email: kchamber@inw.net. WWW: http://www.kewanee-il.com

LITTLE MO WINS FIRST TITLE: ANNIVERSARY. Sept 4, 1951. Maureen Connolly, known as "Little Mo," won the first of her three straight US Lawn Tennis Association national championship at the age of 16. She defeated Shirley Fry, 6–3, 1–6, 6–4.

MATHEWSON VERSUS BROWN: ANNIVERSARY. Sept 4, 1916. In a specially arranged pitching matchup, Christy Mathewson of the Cincinnati Reds and Mordecai Brown of the Chicago Cubs hurled the final games of their careers against one another. The Reds won, 10–8.

September *1998*	S	M	T	W	T	F	S
			1	2	3	4	5
	6	7	8	9	10	11	12
	13	14	15	16	17	18	19
	20	21	22	23	24	25	26
	27	28	29	30			

MUSKIES INC INTERNATIONAL MUSKIE TOURNAMENT. Sept 4–6. North Central, MN. 31st annual fundraiser for nonprofit sportsman's organization. Proceeds go toward muskie stocking, rearing and research projects along with Dept of Natural Resources fisheries improvements. This tournament strongly encourages "catch and release." Annually, the Friday, Saturday and Sunday after Labor Day. The $40 entry fee entitles the contestant to participate in the Sunday banquet and compete for thousands of dollars in prizes. Grand Prize in the "Release Division" is a boat, motor and trailer with a retail value of approximately $18,000. We welcome corporate sponsorship inquiries. Est attendance: 600. For info: Dave Griffin, Twin Cities Chapter of Muskies, Inc, 4434 Dorchester Rd, Mound, MN 55364.

NATIONAL CHAMPIONSHIP CHUCKWAGON RACES. Sept 4–6. Clinton, AR. Five divisions of chuckwagon races; bronc fanning race; Snowy River race; live entertainment, barn dance, western show, western art, plus saddle, tack and clothing vendors. 13th annual races. Annually, Labor Day weekend. Est attendance: 20,000. For info: Dan Eoff, Rt 6, Box 187-1, Clinton, AR 72031. Phone: (501) 745-8407. Fax: (501) 745-4416.

OFFICE OLYMPICS. Sept 4. Downtown Shreveport, LA. A one-day event that spotlights the office employee! 100 teams of five (men and women) office workers compete in such zany events as The Water Break Relay, Beat the Clock, Carpool Chaos,The Office Chair Roll-off, Toss the Boss, Memo Mania, The Human Post-it-Note and Musical Office Chairs. Sponsor: KVKI Radio. Est attendance: 6,000. For info: Melinda R. Coyer, Office Olympics Founder, KVKI Radio, PO Box 31130, Shreveport, LA 71130-1130. Phone: (318) 688-1130. Fax: (318) 687-8574.

OKLAHOMA STATE PRISON RODEO. Sept 4–5. McAlester, OK. This PRCA rodeo held entirely behind the walls of the Oklahoma State Penitentiary features prison inmates who try their luck at such unusual contests as wild cow milking, bull and horse racing and "Money the Hard Way," as well as traditional rodeo contests. Est attendance: 15,000. For info: McAlester Chamber of Commerce, PO Box 759, McAlester, OK 74502. Phone: (918) 423-2550. Fax: (918) 423-1345.

SEDGMAN WINS USLTA CHAMPIONSHIP: ANNIVERSARY. Sept 4, 1951. Frank Sedgman became the first Australian to win the men's singles title at the US Lawn Tennis Association national championships at Forest Hills, NY. Sedgman defeated American Vic Seixas in straight sets.

VINTAGE AUTO RACE AND CONCOURS D'ELEGANCE. Sept 4–6. Steamboat Springs, CO. Street race and display of classic vintage automobiles. Annually, Labor Day weekend. Sponsors: Bridgestone, Sheraton, ITT. Est attendance: 15,000. For info: Janet Nichols, Special Events Coord, Steamboat Springs Chamber Resort Assn, PO Box 774408, Steamboat Springs, CO 80477. Phone: (970) 879-0880. Fax: (970) 879-2543. Email: info@steamboat-chamber.com. WWW: http://www.steamboat-chamber.com

WAITKUS, EDDIE: BIRTH ANNIVERSARY. Sept 4, 1919. Edward Stephen (Eddie) Waitkus, baseball player born at Cambridge, MA. A major league first baseman for 11 years, Waitkus was shot by a woman he did not know in a hotel room. The incident became the basis for the novel, *The Natural*, by Bernard Malamud. Died at Jamaica Plain, MA, Sept 15, 1972.

WISCONSIN STATE COW CHIP THROW. Sept 4–5. Prairie du Sac, WI. Cow Chip Throw. Anyone can participate; however, it takes a powerful toss to win. Also, chip chucking for children, a corporate throw, National Tug of War competition, 5K and 10K runs, an arts and crafts fair and bovine bingo (where a bet is placed on the location of a wandering cow's fresh pie). Est attendance: 40,000. For info: Wisconsin State Cow Chip Throw, PO Box 3, Prairie du Sac, WI 53578. Phone: (608) 643-4317. Fax: (608) 643-5421. Email: toolsmkt@bankpds.com.

YANKEES WIN FIFTH PENNANT IN A ROW: 45th ANNIVERSARY. Sept 4, 1953. The New York Yankees clinched their fifth consecutive American League pennant, a feat then unprecedented in baseball history. The Yankees went on to defeat the Brooklyn Dodgers in the World Series for their fifth Series crown in a row.

BIRTHDAYS TODAY

Doyle Lafayette Alexander, 48, former baseball player, born Cordova, AL, Sept 4, 1950.
Vaughn Allen Dunbar, 30, football player, born Fort Wayne, IN, Sept 4, 1968.
Raymond Loran Floyd, 56, golfer, born Fort Bragg, NC, Sept 4, 1942.
Dawn Fraser, 61, Olympic gold medal swimmer, born Balmain, Australia, Sept 4, 1937.
Kenneth Smith (Ken) Harrelson, 57, broadcaster, former baseball executive and player, born Woodruff, SC, Sept 4, 1941.
Michael Joseph (Mike) Piazza, 30, baseball player, born Norristown, PA, Sept 4, 1968.
Tomas Sandstrom, 34, hockey player, born Jakobstad, Finland, Sept 4, 1964.
James Grant (Jim) Schoenfeld, 46, hockey coach and former player, born Galt, Ontario, Canada, Sept 4, 1952.
John Vanbiesbrouck, 35, hockey player, born Detroit, MI, Sept 4, 1963.
Thomas Sturges (Tom) Watson, 49, golfer, born Kansas City, MO, Sept 4, 1949.
Frank White, Jr, 48, former baseball player, born Greenville, MS, Sept 4, 1950.

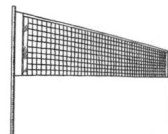

SEPTEMBER 5 — SATURDAY
Day 248 — 117 Remaining

ANNE MEYERS SIGNS WITH PACERS: ANNIVERSARY. Sept 5, 1979. Anne Meyers, All-American basketball player from UCLA, made history by signing a contract with the Indiana Pacers of the NBA, the first woman to do so. Meyers worked out with the team throughout training camp but was cut before the season began.

BABE RUTH'S FIRST PRO HOMER: ANNIVERSARY. Sept 5, 1914. Babe Ruth hit his first home run as a professional while playing for Providence in the International League. He pitched a one-hit shutout against Toronto.

BAUMAN HITS 72: ANNIVERSARY. Sept 5, 1954. Joe Bauman of the Roswell team in the Longhorn League hit three home runs to bring his season total to 72, a record for any level of professional play. Bauman was a poor defensive player and never made the major leagues.

BISHOP, MAX: BIRTH ANNIVERSARY. Sept 5, 1899. Max Frederick Bishop, baseball player born at Waynesboro, PA. Bishop was an infielder for 12 years in the American League. He played for the Philadelphia Athletics in the late 1920s and was part of one of owner Connie Mack's fire sales of players in 1933. Died at Waynesboro, Feb 24, 1962.

CAPITAL DISTRICT SCOTTISH GAMES. Sept 5–6. Altamont, NY. Celtic festival features the Northeastern US Pipe Band and Open Highland Dancing Championships, Highland athletics, Scottish dogs, country dancers, Celtic goods, Scottish and American food and beverages. Est attendance: 16,000. For info: Donald Martin, Capital District Scottish Games, 7 Lori Lane, Latham, NY 12110. Phone: (518) 785-5951.

CHARLESTON DISTANCE RUN. Sept 5. Charleston, WV. To provide an amateur 15-mile race of professional quality for residents and visitors to Charleston. A 5K (3.1 miles) race also will be held. Est attendance: 1,500. For info: Danny Wells, Race Dir, Charleston Festival Commission, Inc, PO Box 2749, Charleston, WV 25330. Phone: (304) 348-6419.

DENMARK: AARHUS FESTIVAL WEEK. Sept 5–14. Observed from the first Saturday in September and for nine days after, since 1965, with theater, ballet, opera, sports, exhibitions and special programs for children.

EVERT'S CAREER ENDS: ANNIVERSARY. Sept 5, 1989. Chris Evert's tennis career came to an end in the quarterfinals of the US Open when she was defeated, 7–6, 6–2, by Zina Garrison.

GIANTS RIDGE MOUNTAIN BIKE FESTIVAL. Sept 5. Biwabik, MN. Trail rides, uphill-downhill, cross-country. Est attendance: 400. For info: John Filander, Events Program Dir, PO Box 190, Biwabik, MN 55708. Phone: (800) 688-7669 or (218) 865-4143. Fax: (218) 865-4733.

ISRAELI OLYMPIC MASSACRE: ANNIVERSARY. Sept 5–6, 1972. Eleven members of the Israeli Olympic team were killed following an attack on the Olympic Village in Munich, Germany, by members of the Black September faction of the Palestinian Liberation Army. The Palestinians kidnapped athletes and coaches and made their way to the Munich airport where German forces, with the approval of the Israeli government, counterattacked. Four of the seven guerrillas were also killed. In retaliation, Israeli jets bombed Palestinian positions in Lebanon and Syria on Sept 8, 1972.

LAJOIE, NAP: BIRTH ANNIVERSARY. Sept 5, 1875. Napoleon (Nap) Lajoie, Baseball Hall of Fame second baseman born at Woonsocket, RI. Lajoie was a good enough player to have his team, the Cleveland Naps (later the Indians) named in his honor. He played 21 years in the major leagues and hit .338. Inducted into the Hall of Fame in 1937. Died at Daytona Beach, FL, Feb 7, 1959.

LUCAS, HENRY: BIRTH ANNIVERSARY. Sept 5, 1857. Henry Van Noye Lucas, baseball executive born at St.

Louis, MO. Lucas used his family fortune to organize the Union Association, a third major league that played only one year, 1884. He lost more than $250,000 in the venture. Died at St. Louis, Nov 15, 1910.

MAGIC CIRCLE BIKE CHALLENGE. Sept 5. Willcox, AZ. A 109-mile bicycle challenge with a 66-mile loop and 33-mile bike challenges. Annually, the Saturday before Labor Day. Sponsor: Rex Allen Days, Inc. Est attendance: 500. For info: Willcox Chamber of Commerce and Agriculture, 1500 N Circle I Rd, Willcox, AZ 85643. Phone: (520) 384-2272. Fax: (520) 384-0293.

OREGON TRAIL RODEO. Sept 5–7. Hastings, NE. PRCA-sanctioned rodeo. Annually, Saturday–Monday of Labor Day weekend. Est attendance: 5,500. For info: Sandy Himmelberg, Genl Mgr, Oregon Trail Rodeo, 947 S Baltimore, Hastings, NE 68901. Phone: (402) 462-3247. Fax: (402) 462-4731.

SHEPPARD, MEL: 115th BIRTH ANNIVERSARY. Sept 5, 1883. Melvin Winfield (Mel) Sheppard, Olympic gold medal middle distance runner born at Almenesson, NJ. Sheppard achieved fame for his frontrunning style of racing. He won three gold medals at the 1908 Olympics and one at the 1912 Stockholm Games. Died at New York, NY, Jan 4, 1942.

TUNA TOURNAMENT. Sept 5–7. Galilee, Narragansett, RI. More than 100 boats and up to 400 anglers registered. 39th annual tournament. For info: Rhode Island Economic Development Corporation, Marketing & Communications Division, 1 W Exchange St, Providence, RI 02903. Phone: (800) 556-2484 or (401) 277-2601. Fax: (401) 273-8270. Email: riedc@riedc.com. WWW: http://www.visitrhodeisland.com

WORLD AIR HOCKEY CHAMPIONSHIPS. Sept 5–6 (tentative dates). Dallas, TX. Event to determine US and international rankings. Est attendance: 100. For info: US Air Hockey Assn, PO Box 1024, Boulder, CO 80306. Phone: (303) 444-9164. Email: tweissm@compassnet.com. WWW: http://www.compassnet.com/tweissm/

BIRTHDAYS TODAY

Henry Eugene (Gene) Bearden, 78, former baseball player, born Lexa, AR, Sept 5, 1920.
Jeffrey Hoke (Jeff) Brantley, 35, baseball player, born Florence, AL, Sept 5, 1963.
Willie James Gault, 38, former football player, born Griffin, GA, Sept 5, 1960.
Candido (Candy) Maldonado, 38, former baseball player, born Humacao, Puerto Rico, Sept 5, 1960.
William Stanley (Bill) Mazeroski, 62, former baseball player, born Wheeling, WV, Sept 5, 1936.
Timothy Bernard (Tim) McKyer, 35, football player, born Orlando, FL, Sept 5, 1963.
Dennis Eugene Scott, 30, basketball player, born Hagerstown, MD, Sept 5, 1968.

SEPTEMBER 6 — SUNDAY
Day 249 — 116 Remaining

CANADA: GREAT KLONDIKE INTERNATIONAL OUTHOUSE RACE AND BATHROOM WALL LIMERICK CONTEST. Sept 6. Dawson City, Yukon. Crazy race of outhouses on wheels over a 1.5-mile course through the streets of downtown Dawson City. Awards presentation at Diamond Tooth Gertie's gambling hall following the race. Est attendance: 3,000. For info: Klondike Visitors Assn, Box 389, Dawson City, Yukon, Canada Y0B 1G0. Phone: (403) 993-5575. Fax: (403) 993-6415. Email: kva@hypertech.yk.ca.

September 1998	S	M	T	W	T	F	S
			1	2	3	4	5
	6	7	8	9	10	11	12
	13	14	15	16	17	18	19
	20	21	22	23	24	25	26
	27	28	29	30			

CHEETAH RUN. Sept 6. Throughout the Cincinnati Zoo in Ohio. The Cheetah Run is a 2.5-mile course throughout the beautiful zoo grounds. The race is followed by a Fun Run for children around Swan Lake. An awards ceremony follows the race. Est attendance: 1,500. For info: Events and Promotions Dept, Cincinnati Zoo and Botanical Garden, 3400 Vine St, Cincinnati, OH 45220. Phone: (513) 281-4701. Fax: (513) 559-7790. WWW: http://www.cincyzoo.org

DIMAGGIO, VINCE: BIRTH ANNIVERSARY. Sept 6, 1912. Vincent Paul DiMaggio, baseball player born at Martinez, CA. The oldest of the three major league DiMaggio brothers played ten years in the National League. Died at North Hollywood, CA, Oct 3, 1966.

EVERT WINS FIRST NATIONAL TITLE: ANNIVERSARY. Sept 6, 1975. Chris Evert won the first of her six US Open women's singles titles by defeating Evonne Goolagong, 5–7, 6–4, 6–2.

FABER, RED: 110th BIRTH ANNIVERSARY. Sept 6, 1888. Urban Clarence ("Red") Faber, Baseball Hall of Fame pitcher born at Cascade, IA. One of the last of the legal spitball pitchers, Faber starred for the Chicago White Sox from 1914 through 1933. He once threw only 67 pitches in a complete game. Inducted into the Hall of Fame in 1964. Died at Chicago, IL, Sept 25, 1976.

ITALY: HISTORICAL REGATTA. Sept 6. Venice. Traditional competition among two-oar racing gondolas, preceded by a procession of Venetian ceremonial boats of the epoch of the Venetian Republic. Annually, the first Sunday in September.

ITALY: JOUST OF THE SARACEN. Sept 6. Arezzo. The first Sunday in September is set aside for the Giostra del Saracino, a tilting contest of the 13th century, with knights in armor.

LUNAR ECLIPSE. Sept 6. Penumbral eclipse of the moon. Moon enters penumbra at 5:14 AM, EDT, reaches middle of eclipse at 7:10 AM, EDT, and leaves penumbra at 9:06 PM, EDT. Beginning of penumbral phase visible in North America except the extreme east, Central America, South America except the extreme east, Australia except the extreme west, New Zealand, most of Antarctica, extreme east Asia, most of the Pacific Ocean, extreme western Atlantic Ocean; end of phase visible in western North America, Australia, New Zealand, eastern half of Asia, most of Antarctica, Pacific Ocean except eastern South Pacific, eastern half of Indian Ocean.

MOON PHASE: FULL MOON. Sept 6. Moon enters Full Moon phase at 7:21 AM, EDT.

NATIONAL FOOTBALL LEAGUE REGULAR SEASON. Sept 6–Dec 27. The National Football League opens a 17-week regular season leading to Super Bowl XXXIII at Miami, FL, Jan 31, 1999. Each of the league's 30 teams plays a 16-game schedule with one bye week. Six teams from the American Football Conference and six from the National Football Conference will qualify for the playoffs commencing Jan 2–3. For info: Natl Football League, 410 Park Ave, 7th Fl, New York, NY 10022. Phone: (212) 450-2000. Fax: (212) 759-6367. WWW: http://www.nfl.com/

NATIONAL FRISBEE DISC FESTIVAL. Sept 6. Washington Monument grounds, Washington, DC. "Frisbee for the Family." Exhibitions of throwing and catching skills, frisbee-catching dogs, and clinics for the audience. Est attendance: 10,000. For info: Natl Frisbee Disc Festival, 6150 Bryantown Dr, Bryantown, MD 20617-2227. Phone: (301) 645-5043.

POTATO BOWL. Sept 6–12. Grand Forks, ND. Potato Bowl USA salutes the potato featuring football game, queen contest, concert, a parade and other events, including the 1998 North Central Regional Hot-Air Balloon Championship. For info: Grand Forks Conv and Visitors Bureau, 4251 Gateway Drive, Grand Forks, ND 58203. Phone: (800) 866-4566. Fax: (701) 746-0775. WWW: http://www.grandforks.cvb.org

ROSENBLOOM, SLAPSIE MAXIE: BIRTH ANNIVERSARY. Sept 6, 1904. Maxie ("Slapsie Maxie") Rosenbloom, boxer born at Leonard's Bridge, CT. Rosenbloom fought nearly 300 times and held the light heavyweight championship from 1930 to 1934. He used a defensive style and hit his opponents with open gloves, giving rise to his nickname. Died at South Pasadena, CA, Mar 6, 1976.

YEAGER INJURED: ANNIVERSARY. Sept 6, 1976. Los Angeles Dodgers catcher Steve Yeager, waiting in the on-deck circle, was seriously injured when he was struck in the neck by a shattered bat. The injury caused Yeager to introduce a new piece of baseball equipment, the neck protector, a flap attached to his catcher's mask.

YOUNGEST AMERICAN LEAGUE PLAYER: 55th ANNIVERSARY. Sept 6, 1943. The youngest player in American League history, Carl Scheib, made his major league debut at 16 years, eight months and five days of age in the second game of a doubleheader for the Philadelphia Athletics.

BIRTHDAYS TODAY

Ronald Bruce (Ron) Boone, 52, former basketball player, born Oklahoma City, OK, Sept 6, 1946.

Dow Finsterwald, 69, golfer, born Athens, OH, Sept 6, 1929.

Harold Bentley (Hal) Jeffcoat, 74, former baseball player, born West Columbia, SC, Sept 6, 1924.

Patrick James (Pat) Meares, 30, baseball player, born Salina, KS, Sept 6, 1968.

Gregory William (Greg) Olson, 38, former baseball player, born Marshall, MN, Sept 6, 1960.

Chad Scott, 24, football player, born Washington, DC, Sept 6, 1974.

Kevin Alvin Willis, 36, basketball player, born Los Angeles, CA, Sept 6, 1962.

☆   ☆   ☆

SEPTEMBER 7 — MONDAY
Day 250 — 115 Remaining

CHASE'S SPORTSQUOTE OF THE DAY
"I can lick any man in the house." —John L. Sullivan

BANGOR LABOR DAY ROAD RACE. Sept 7. Bass Park, Bangor, ME. Five-mile road race. Annually, on Labor Day. Est attendance: 200. For info: Bangor Parks and Rec Dept, Parks and Rec, 647 Main St, Bangor, ME 04401. Phone: (207) 947-1018. Fax: (207) 947-1605.

COLUMBIA RIVER CROSS CHANNEL SWIM. Sept 7. Hood River, OR. The annual swim across the mighty Columbia River draws 550 contestants each year to swim the approximately one mile distance for fun. Est attendance: 550. For info: Hood River County Chamber of Commerce, Columbia River Cross Channel Swim, 405 Portway, Hood River, OR 97031. Phone: (800) 366-3530. Fax: (541) 386-2057.

CORBETT–SULLIVAN PRIZE FIGHT: ANNIVERSARY. Sept 7, 1892. John L. Sullivan was knocked out by James J. Corbett in the 21st round of a prize fight at New Orleans, LA. It was the first major fight under the Marquess of Queensberry Rules.

FOUTZ, DAVE: BIRTH ANNIVERSARY. Sept 7, 1856. David Luther (Dave) Foutz, baseball player and manager born at Carroll County, MD. Foutz was an outstanding pitcher in the 19th century, especially with the St. Louis teams in the American Association. Sold to Brooklyn in 1887, he played outfield with distinction. Died at Waverly, MD, Mar 5, 1897.

GREAT BATHTUB RACE. Sept 7. Nome, AK. 21st annual. Lets people know that participants bathe at least once a year. Further, when politicians participate, they can let their constituents know that they clean up their act yearly. Bathtubs mounted on wheels are raced down Front Street. Each team has five members, one in the tub, with bubbles apparent in the bath water. Tub must be full of water at beginning and have at least 10 gallons at the finish line. The other four team members must wear large-brim hats and suspenders and carry either a bar of soap, washcloth, towel or bath mat for the entire race. Winning team claims trophy, a statue of Miss Piggy and Kermit taking a bath, which is handed down from year to year. Annually, at noon on Labor Day. Est attendance: 1,000. For info: Rasmussen's Music Mart, PO Box 2, Nome, AK 99762-0002. Phone: (907) 443-2798 or (907) 443-2219. Fax: (907) 443-5777.

LABOR DAY. Sept 7. Legal public holiday. Public Law 90–363 sets Labor Day on the first Monday in September. Observed on this day in all states and in Canada. First observance believed to have been a parade at 10 AM, on Tuesday, Sept 5, 1882, in New York, NY, probably organized by Peter J. McGuire, a Carpenters and Joiners Union secretary. In 1883, a union resolution declared "the first Monday in September of each year a Labor Day." By 1893, more than half of the states were observing Labor Day on one or another day, and a bill to establish Labor Day as a federal holiday was introduced in Congress. On June 28, 1894, President Grover Cleveland signed into law an act making the first Monday in September a legal holiday for federal employees and the District of Columbia.

MACKINAC BRIDGE WALK. Sept 7. St. Ignace, MI. Labor Day is the only day of the year pedestrians are permitted to walk across the five-mile-long span, one of the world's longest suspension bridges, connecting Michigan's two peninsulas. Walk is from St. Ignace to Mackinaw City. Est attendance: 55,000. For info: Mackinac Bridge Authority, 333 Interstate 75, St. Ignace, MI 49781. Phone: (906) 643-7600. Fax: (906) 643-7668. Email: i:rossj@state.mi.us.

ONLY SENATORS' HOME RUN AT HOME: ANNIVERSARY. Sept 7, 1945. The Washington Senators defeated the St. Louis Browns, 3–2, to stay a game-and-a-half behind the first-place Detroit Tigers. Roger Wolff pitched a 4-hitter, and Joe Kuhel hit an inside-the-park home run that was the only home run the Senators hit that year at their spacious home, Griffith Stadium.

RYAN'S EXPRESS: ANNIVERSARY. Sept 7, 1974. A pitch thrown by Nolan Ryan of the California Angels in a game against the Chicago White Sox was clocked at 100.8 miles per hour, the first time a pitched had ever been timed over 100 mph.

September 1998	S	M	T	W	T	F	S
			1	2	3	4	5
	6	7	8	9	10	11	12
	13	14	15	16	17	18	19
	20	21	22	23	24	25	26
	27	28	29	30			

SHOEMAKER BREAKS LONGDEN'S RECORD: ANNIVERSARY. Sept 7, 1970. Jockey Willie Shoemaker won the 6,033rd race of his career at Del Mar race track in California, surpassing the record for career wins previously held by Johnny Longden.

WAIKIKI ROUGHWATER SWIM. Sept 7. Waikiki Beach, Honolulu, HI. The 29th annual swim is 2.4 miles from Sans Souci Beach to Duke Kahanamoku Beach. "The World's Largest Open Water Swimming Event." Preregistration is required. Annually, Labor Day. Est attendance: 1,200. For info: Jim Anderson, One Keahole Place #1607, Honolulu, HI 96825-3414. Phone: (808) 396-8866. Fax: (808) 396-8868. Email: waikikijim@aol.com.

WILTSE, HOOKS: BIRTH ANNIVERSARY. Sept 7, 1880. George LeRoy ("Hooks") Wiltse, baseball player and manager born at Hamilton, NY. Wiltse pitched for John McGraw's New York Giants and jumped to the Federal League in 1915. In an emergency he played first base in Game 2 of the 1913 World Series. Using a fielder's glove, he snagged two ground balls in the bottom of the ninth inning and threw two runners out at the plate. Died at Long Beach, NY, Jan 21, 1959.

BIRTHDAYS TODAY

Corbin Bernsen, 44, actor (*Major League*), born North Hollywood, CA, Sept 7, 1954.
Willie Murphy Crawford, 52, former baseball player, born Los Angeles, CA, Sept 7, 1946.
Jason Derek Isringhausen, 26, baseball player, born Brighton, IL, Sept 7, 1972.
Jacques Gerard Lemaire, 53, hockey coach and Hockey Hall of Fame center, born Ville LaSalle, Quebec, Canada, Sept 7, 1945.
Antonio Keithflen McDyess, 24, basketball player, born Quitman, MS, Sept 7, 1974.
Gino Odjick, 28, hockey player, born Maniwaki, Quebec, Canada, Sept 7, 1970.
Joseph Oden (Joe) Rudi, 52, former baseball player, born Modesto, CA, Sept 7, 1946.
Mae Louise Suggs, 75, LPGA Hall of Fame golfer, born Atlanta, GA, Sept 7, 1923.
Sergio Sanchez Valdez, 33, baseball player, born Elias Pina, Dominican Republic, Sept 7, 1965.
Erik George Williams, 30, football player, born Philadelphia, PA, Sept 7, 1968.

SEPTEMBER 8 — TUESDAY
Day 251 — 114 Remaining

AUSTIN YOUNGEST OPEN CHAMPION: ANNIVERSARY. Sept 8, 1979. Tracy Austin, 16, became the youngest woman to win the US Open tennis championship when she upset Chris Evert Lloyd, 6–4, 6–3.

CAMPANERIS PLAYS ALL NINE POSITIONS: ANNIVERSARY. Sept 8, 1965. Bert Campaneris of the Oakland A's became the first player in major league history to play all nine positions in the same game. He performed the feat against the California Angels, but he had to leave the game after 8⅔ innings because of a collision with catcher Ed Kirkpatrick. The Angels won, 5–3, in 13 innings.

DAUGHERTY, DUFFY: BIRTH ANNIVERSARY. Sept 8, 1915. Hugh Duffy Daugherty, football player and coach born at Emeigh, PA. Daugherty played the line at Syracuse University and began coaching after World War II. He became head coach at Michigan State University in 1949 and retired 19 years later with his best teams playing in 1965 and 1966. He was a popular banquet speaker and, after retirement, a television commentator. Died at Santa Barbara, CA, Sept 25, 1987.

Campaneris Plays All Nine Positions

LAVER COMPLETES SECOND GRAND SLAM: ANNIVERSARY. Sept 8, 1969. Australian Rod Laver won the US Open by defeating fellow countryman Tony Roche in four sets to complete the second grand slam of his tennis career. Laver had previously won the Australian Open, the French Open and Wimbledon. His first grand slam occurred in 1962.

ROSE TIES COBB: ANNIVERSARY. Sept 8, 1985. Player-manager Pete Rose of the Cincinnati Reds singled in the first inning against the Chicago Cubs and again in the fifth inning to equal Ty Cobb's record for most hits in a career, 4,191.

BIRTHDAYS TODAY

Donald William (Don) Aase, 44, former baseball player, born Orange, CA, Sept 8, 1954.

Lemuel Jackson (Lem) Barney, 53, Pro Football Hall of Fame cornerback, born Gulfport, MS, Sept 8, 1945.

Maurice Edward (Mo) Cheeks, 42, former basketball player, born Chicago, IL, Sept 8, 1956.

Latrell Fontaine Sprewell, 28, basketball player, born Milwaukee, WI, Sept 8, 1970.

Rogatien Rosaire (Rogie) Vachon, 53, former hockey executive and player, born Palmarolle, Quebec, Canada, Sept 8, 1945.

Clarence Weatherspoon, 28, basketball player, born Crawford, MS, Sept 8, 1970.

SEPTEMBER 9 — WEDNESDAY

Day 252 — 113 Remaining

AMERICAN BOWLING CONGRESS FOUNDED: ANNIVERSARY. Sept 9, 1895. A group of bowling enthusiasts met in New York City's Beethoven Hall and founded the ABC. Since then the Congress has grown to become the world's largest sports membership organization with more than 2.4 million members. For info: American Bowling Congress, Bowling HQ, 5301 S 76th St, Greendale, WI 53129-1127. Phone: (414) 421-6400. Fax: (414) 421-1194.

CANADA: THE MASTERS. Sept 9–13. Spruce Meadows, Calgary, Alberta. World-class show jumping competition, along with Equi-Fair, Breeds for the World and Festival of Nations. Feature events are the Bank of Montreal Nations' Cup and the $725,000 du Maurier International, the world's most prestigious Grand Prix. Est attendance: 150,000. For info: Spruce Meadows, RR #9, Calgary, AB, Canada T2J 5G5. Phone: (403) 974-4200. Fax: (403) 974-4270. Email: smeadows@telusplanet.net. WWW: http://www.sprucemeadows.com

CHANCE, FRANK: BIRTH ANNIVERSARY. Sept 9, 1877. Frank Leroy Chance, Baseball Hall of Fame first baseman and manager born at Fresno, CA. Chance was part of the legendary "Tinker-to-Evers-to-Chance" double-play combination. As manager of the Chicago Cubs, his teams won four National League pennants and two World Series titles. Inducted into the Hall of Fame in 1946. Died at Los Angeles, CA, Sept 15, 1924.

FRISCH, FRANKIE: 100th BIRTH ANNIVERSARY. Sept 9, 1898. Frank Francis (Frankie) Frisch, Baseball Hall of Fame second baseman and manager born at New York, NY. In one of baseball's epic trades, the New York Giants sent Frisch to the St. Louis Cardinals for Rogers Hornsby in 1926 after the Cards, with Hornsby as manager, had won the World Series. Frisch led the Cards to pennants in 1928, 1930, 1931 and 1934. Inducted into the Hall of Fame in 1947. Died at Wilmington, DE, Mar 12, 1973.

HOYT, WAITE: BIRTH ANNIVERSARY. Sept 9, 1899. Waite Charles Hoyt, broadcaster and Baseball Hall of Fame pitcher born at New York, NY. Hoyt pitched excellent baseball for the New York Yankees from 1921 to 1929 and finished his career with several other teams. In retirement, he became a much beloved announcer in Cincinnati, OH. Inducted into the Hall of Fame in 1969. Died at Cincinnati, Aug 25, 1984.

KOUFAX PITCHES PERFECT GAME: ANNIVERSARY. Sept 9, 1965. Sandy Koufax pitched the fourth no-hitter of his career, a perfect game against the Chicago Cubs. Koufax struck out 14 batters, but the Dodgers won by only 1–0 as Cubs pitcher Bob Hendley gave up only one hit.

McCARTHY, CLEM: BIRTH ANNIVERSARY. Sept 9, 1882. Charles Louis ("Clem") McCarthy, sportscaster born at East Bloomfield, NY. McCarthy virtually invented calling horse races on the radio. His distinctive voice and staccato delivery endeared him to listeners. He called every Kentucky Derby from 1928 to 1950. Died at New York, NY, June 5, 1962.

OUTRIGGER HOTELS ANNUAL HAWAIIAN OCEAN-FEST. Sept 9–13. Oahu, HI. A variety of events celebrating Hawaii's ocean sports. The Hawaiian International Ocean Challenge Sept 5–6, competition between six-person teams of the world's best lifeguards in kayak, surf rescue, paddleboard, and outrigger canoe. Ocean Challenge includes a "World Team" selected from individual competition at the Walmea Open Ocean Challenge Sept 9; Outrigger's Waikiki Kings Race held Sept 13, an ocean ironman event with four continuous disciplines—run, kayak, swim, and paddleboard. Est attendance: 10,000. For info: Pauahi Tower, Event Marketing, 1001 Bishop St, Ste 880, Honolulu, HI 96813. Phone: (808) 521-4322. Fax: (808) 538-0314. Email: dey@emisport.com. WWW: http://www.emisport.com

SELIG NAMED ACTING COMMISSIONER: ANNIVER-SARY. Sept 9, 1992. Following the resignation of Commissioner Francis T. ("Fay") Vincent, Milwaukee Brewers owner Bud Selig assumed the commissioner's duties as chairman of the owners' executive committee. Insisting that a new labor agreement with the Major League Baseball Players' Association must precede the election of a new commissioner, the owners endured a players' strike in 1994 and the cancellation of that year's World Series with Selig in charge.

BIRTHDAYS TODAY

Benjamin Roy ("B. J.") Armstrong, 31, basketball player, born Detroit, MI, Sept 9, 1967.
Earl Douglas Averill, 67, former baseball player, born Cleveland, OH, Sept 9, 1931.
James Bernard (Jim) Corsi, 37, baseball player, born Newton, MA, Sept 9, 1961.
Alvin Glenn Davis, 38, former baseball player, born Riverside, CA, Sept 9, 1960.
Kevin John Hatcher, 32, hockey player, born Detroit, MI, Sept 9, 1966.
Daniel Lewis (Dan) Majerle, 33, basketball player, born Traverse City, MI, Sept 9, 1965.
Joseph Robert (Joe) Theismann, 49, broadcaster and Pro Football Hall of Fame quarterback, born New Brunswick, NJ, Sept 9, 1949.
Todd Edward Zeile, 33, baseball player, born Van Nuys, CA, Sept 9, 1965.

Roger Maris

SEPTEMBER 10 — THURSDAY
Day 253 — 112 Remaining

ANVIL MOUNTAIN 59-MINUTE, 37-SECOND CHALLENGE. Sept 10. Nome, AK. A running event that starts at the base of Anvil Mountain. Runners must run 834 feet up the face of the mountain and return in less than 59 minutes and 37 seconds or be disqualified from the competition. Trophies awarded for first–third finishers,

September *1998*	S	M	T	W	T	F	S
			1	2	3	4	5
	6	7	8	9	10	11	12
	13	14	15	16	17	18	19
	20	21	22	23	24	25	26
	27	28	29	30			

first woman finisher and first finisher 16 years of age or under. Annually, the second Thursday in September. Est attendance: 1,000. For info: Anvil Mountain Challenge, Rasmussen's Music Mart, PO Box 2, Nome, AK 99762-0002. Phone: (907) 443-2798 or (907) 443-2919. Fax: (907) 443-5777.

BUCHANAN, BUCK: BIRTH ANNIVERSARY. Sept 10, 1940. Junious ("Buck") Buchanan, Pro Football Hall of Fame defensive tackle born at Gainesville, AL. Buchanan played offensive and defensive tackle at Grambling and is rated one of the greatest small college athletes of all time. He signed with the Dallas Texans (later the Kansas City Chiefs) and played a key role on the team that lost Super Bowl I and won Super Bowl IV. A six-time All-Pro, he coached defensive linemen after retirement. Inducted into the Hall of Fame in 1990. Died at Kansas City, MO, July 16, 1992.

CROWLEY, JIM: BIRTH ANNIVERSARY. Sept 10, 1902. James H. (Jim) Crowley, football player and coach born at Chicago, IL. One of Notre Dame's famed Four Horsemen, Crowley played halfback for Knute Rockne's legendary backfield. He played pro football, coached at Michigan State and Fordham and served as commissioner of the All-America Football Conference. Died at Scranton, PA, Jan 15, 1986.

FULLERTON, HUGH: 125th BIRTH ANNIVERSARY. Sept 10, 1873. Hugh Stuart Fullerton, sportswriter born at Hillsboro, OH. Fullerton wrote mostly for Chicago newspapers and became famous for using statistics to predict the winner of each year's World Series. His accusations about the 1919 World Series, published in the New York *Evening World*, led to the investigation that uncovered the Black Sox Scandal. Died at Dunedin, FL, Dec 27, 1945.

GREAT PEANUT TOUR. Sept 10–13. Skippers, VA. Assorted bicycle rides from 13 to 125 miles. Special peanut tour ride to examine peanuts growing, method of harvesting and a sampling of more than 40 peanut goodies. Unique water stops, nature walks, music, campfires with marshmallow roast. Annually, the weekend following Labor Day. Est attendance: 1,500. For info: Robert C. Wrenn, Emporia Bicycle Club, PO Box 631, Emporia, VA 23847. Phone: (804) 348-4215. Fax: (804) 348-4020. Email: gpt@3rddoor.com.
WWW: http://www.3rddoor.com/~gpt/

KASS KOUNTY KING KORN KARNIVAL AND MUD DRAGS. Sept 10–13. Plattsmouth, NE. Krowning of a King and Queen of Kornland, three large parades. Free street entertainment, including fire department Wall of Water, flower show, Korn Palace, museum exhibits, Hauf Brau Garten, Ugly Pickup Contest, Cow Chip Bingo, fun run, scarecrow contest, flea market, go cart, two-wheel bicycle race, Mud Drag races and horseshoe tournament on Sunday and much more. Annually, the second weekend in September. Est attendance: 30,000. For info: Patricia Baburek, Coord, 141 S 3rd St, PO Box 40, Plattsmouth, NE 68048. Phone: (402) 296-4155. Fax: (402) 296-4082.

KELLY, HIGH POCKETS: BIRTH ANNIVERSARY. Sept 10, 1895. George Lange ("High Pockets") Kelly, Baseball Hall of Fame first baseman born at San Francisco, CA. Kelly played 16 years in the majors and anchored the infield for the New York Giants in the early 1920s. He was brilliant defensively and hit for power as well. Inducted into the Hall of Fame in 1973. Died at Burlingame, CA, Oct 13, 1984.

KLUSEWSKI, TED: BIRTH ANNIVERSARY. Sept 10, 1924. Theodore Bernard (Ted) Klusewski, baseball player and coach born at Argo, IL. A slugging first baseman, "Big Klu," as he was known, cut the sleeves off his uniform shirt to display his muscles. He played football in

Ted Klusewski

Casper N. (Cap) Boso, 35, former football player, born Kansas City, MO, Sept 10, 1963.

Matthew Allen (Matt) Geiger, 29, basketball player, born Salem, MA, Sept 10, 1969.

Randall David (Randy) Johnson, 35, baseball player, born Walnut Creek, CA, Sept 10, 1963.

Robert Jerry (Bob) Lanier, Jr, 50, Basketball Hall of Fame center, born Buffalo, NY, Sept 10, 1948.

Joe Nieuwendyk, 32, hockey player, born Oshawa, Ontario, Canada, Sept 10, 1966.

Arnold Daniel Palmer, 69, golfer, born Latrobe, PA, Sept 10, 1929.

Sedale Eugene Threatt, 37, basketball player, born Atlanta, GA, Sept 10, 1961.

SEPTEMBER 11 — FRIDAY
Day 254 — 111 Remaining

SPORTSCHASER OF THE DAY

How did legendary football coach Paul ("Bear") Bryant earn his nickname?

college and was a feared home run hitter for the Cincinnati Reds in the 1950s. Died at Cincinnati, OH, Mar 29, 1988.

LONGS PEAK SCOTTISH HIGHLAND FESTIVAL. Sept 10–13. Estes Park, CO. Scottish-Irish celebration with $5,000-purse athletic championships, pipe bands, highland and Irish dancing, and gathering of the clans. Annually, the first weekend after Labor Day. Est attendance: 30,000. For info: Longs Peak Scottish Highland Festival Inc, Box 1820, Estes Park, CO 80517. Phone: (970) 586-6308. Fax: (970) 586-6308.

MARIS, ROGER: BIRTH ANNIVERSARY. Sept 10, 1934. Roger Eugene Maris, baseball player born Roger Eugene Maras at Hibbing, MN. In 1961, Maris broke one of baseball's sacred records, hitting 61 home runs to surpass the mark of 60 set by Babe Ruth in 1927. He won the American League MVP award in 1960 and 1961 and finished his career with the St. Louis Cardinals. Died at Houston, TX, Dec 14, 1985.

US LOSES OLYMPIC BASKETBALL GAME: ANNIVERSARY. Sept 10, 1972. The United States lost its first basketball game in Olympic history, snapping a streak going back to 1936, when the Soviet Union won the gold medal game at the Munich Summer Games, 51–50. The game was quite controversial. After the clock expired with the US ahead, International Amateur Basketball Federation officials intervened and required the referees to replay the last three seconds. This time, the Soviets scored to eke out the victory. US officials protested in vain. The American team refused to accept the silver medals.

BRYANT, BEAR: 85th BIRTH ANNIVERSARY. Sept 11, 1913. Paul William ("Bear") Bryant, college football player and coach born at Moro Bottoms, AR. Bryant earned his nickname by wrestling a bear for money as a young man. He played football at the University of Alabama with All-Americans Don Hutson and Dixie Howell and began coaching in 1940. After World War II, he was named head coach at Maryland. He later coached at Kentucky, Texas A&M and Alabama (1958–82). His career was legendary. His Alabama teams appeared in bowl games 24 consecutive years and won six national championships. He won coach-of-the-year honors three times and finished his career with 325 wins, then a record. Died at Tuscaloosa, AL, Jan 26, 1983.

CANADA: TRAIL OF '98 INTERNATIONAL ROAD RELAY. Sept 11–12. Whitehorse, Yukon. Mixed, men, ladies and masters categories with teams consisting of 6–10 members, race the 176 km (110 mi) from tidewater in Skagway to Whitehorse. Est attendance: 1,500. For info: Sport Yukon, 4061 4th Ave, Whitehorse, YT, Canada Y1A 1H1. Phone: (403) 668-4236. Fax: (403) 667-4237. Email: sportyk@klondike.com.

FACE'S STREAK SNAPPED: ANNIVERSARY. Sept 11, 1959. The Los Angeles Dodgers beat the Pittsburgh Pirates, 5–4, by snapping the 22-game winning streak of the Pirates' ace reliever, Elroy Face. He finished the season with a record of 18–1.

HUFF 'N' PUFF HOT-AIR BALLOON RALLY. Sept 11–13. Topeka, KS. 24th annual hot-air balloon rally. Est attendance: 10,000. For info: Great Plains Balloon Club, Box 1093, Topeka, KS 66601. Phone: (913) 484-2289.

HUSBAND RACES AGAINST WIFE: ANNIVERSARY. Sept 11, 1976. In the third race at Latonia, jockeys John Oldham and Suzanne Picou became the first husband and wife to ride against each other in a US parimutuel race. Oldham finished second riding Harvey's Hope. Picou finished eleventh aboard My Girl Carla.

MONSTER MOPAR WEEKEND XII. Sept 11–13. Gateway International Raceway, Madison, IL. More than 500 restored Chrysler muscle cars and 400 race cars converge for a car show, race and swap meet. Est attendance: 9,000. For info: Scott Sieveking, Pres, S.S. Promotions, PO Box 686, Eureka, MO 63025. Phone: (314) 938-6629. Email: rbtrainman@aol.com.

MUNN, BIGGIE: 90th BIRTH ANNIVERSARY. Sept 11, 1908. Clarence L. ("Biggie") Munn, football player and coach and athletic administrator born at Grow Township, MN. Munn ran track and played football at the University of Minnesota. He coached at several institutions before being hired by Michigan State in 1947. His Spartans won 28 straight games over four seasons (1950–53) and one national championship. Died at Lansing, MI, Mar 18, 1975.

NATIONAL CHAMPIONSHIP AIR RACES. Sept 11–14. Reno/Stead Airport, Stead, NV. The world's largest-running air race, the only worldwide event featuring all four race classes: Unlimited, Formula One, AT-6 and Biplane. For local info: (800) FOR-RENO or (702) 972-6663. For Nevada Tourism: Nevada Commission on Tourism, Capitol Complex, Carson City, NV 89710. Phone: (702) 687-4322 or (800) 227-0774. Fax: (702) 687-6779.

ON THE WATERFRONT. Sept 11–13. St. Ignace. Auto show. For info: Edward K. Reavie, Nostalgia Productions, Inc, 268 Hillcrest Blvd, St. Ignace, MI 49781. Phone: (906) 643-8087 or (906) 643-0313. Fax: (906) 643-9784. Email: edreavie@nostalgiaprod.com. WWW: http://nostalgia-prod.com

PRO BULL RIDERS' TOUR CHALLENGE. Sept 11–12. Lazy E Arena, Guthrie, OK. Patterned after Bullnanza, the top bull riders in the world compete for $65,000. It's nothin' but bull ridin'! Est attendance: 14,000. For info: Lazy E Promotions, Rte 5, Box 393, Guthrie, OK 73044. Phone: (800) 595-RIDE or (405) 282-RIDE. WWW: http://www.lazye.com

September *1998*	S	M	T	W	T	F	S
			1	2	3	4	5
	6	7	8	9	10	11	12
	13	14	15	16	17	18	19
	20	21	22	23	24	25	26
	27	28	29	30			

ROSE BECOMES ALL-TIME HIT LEADER: ANNIVERSARY. Sept 11, 1985. Pete Rose of the Cincinnati Reds became baseball's all-time career hit leader when he singled in the first inning of a game against Eric Show of the San Diego Padres. The hit, coming on a 2–1 count, was Rose's 4,192nd, surpassing the mark previously held by Ty Cobb.

USA INTERNATIONAL DRAGON BOAT FESTIVAL. Sept 11–13. Dubuque, IA. Teams of 25 enthusiastic paddlers race ornately carved and painted dragon boats on the Mississippi River. Pageantry, competition, international fellowship. Held in conjunction with River Fest. Sponsor: Dubuque Chapter of the American Dragon Boat Association. Est attendance: 20,000. For info: Steven J. Rackis, 1480 Alta Pl, Dubuque, IA 52001. Phone: (319) 582-8050 or (319) 556-5800. Email: srackis@aol.com.

BIRTHDAYS TODAY

Lawrence Donald (Larry) Bearnarth, 57, former baseball player, born New York, NY, Sept 11, 1941.
Ellis Rena Burks, 34, baseball player, born Vicksburg, MS, Sept 11, 1964.
Thomas Wade (Tom) Landry, 74, Pro Football Hall of Fame coach and former player, born Mission, TX, Sept 11, 1924.
Jeffrey Lynn (Jeff) Newman, 50, former baseball manager and player, born Fort Worth, TX, Sept 11, 1948.
Donald Martin (Don) Slaught, 40, baseball player, born Long Beach, CA, Sept 11, 1958.

SEPTEMBER 12 — SATURDAY
Day 255 — 110 Remaining

AUTORAMA. Sept 12–13. Cincinnati Zoo and Botanical Garden, Cincinnati, OH. Antique, classic or custom-built hotrods compete for trophies in numerous categories. Registration fee includes family admission. Est attendance: 5,000. For info: Events/Promo Dept, Cincinnati Zoo and Botanical Garden, 3400 Vine St, Cincinnati, OH 45220. Phone: (513) 281-4701. Fax: (513) 559-7790. WWW: http://www.cincy.zoo.org

BETTENHAUSEN, TONY: BIRTH ANNIVERSARY. Sept 12, 1916. Melvin Eugene ("Tony") Bettenhausen, auto racer born at Tinley Park, IL. Bettenhausen began racing at 22 and competed in 14 Indianapolis 500s. He won the USAC national championship in 1951. Died in a crash at Indianapolis, IN, May 12, 1961.

BULLS SIGN JORDAN: ANNIVERSARY. Sept 12, 1984. The Chicago Bulls signed their No. 1 draft choice, Michael Jordan, a guard from the University of North Carolina. Jordan was the No. 3 choice overall behind Akeem (later Hakeem) Olajuwon, taken by Houston, and Sam Bowie, selected by Portland.

CHENEY STRIKES OUT 21: ANNIVERSARY. Sept 12, 1962. Tom Cheney of the Washington Senators set a major league record of most strikeouts in a game when he fanned 21 Baltimore Orioles in a 16-inning game that he won 2–1.

FISHING HAS NO BOUNDARIES—GRANTSBURG. Sept 12–13 (tentative). Grantsburg, IN. A two-day fishing experience for disabled persons. Any disability, age, sex, race, etc, eligible. Fishing with experienced guides. For info: Jaye and Bill Jones, Fishing Has No Boundaries, PO Box 14, Grantsburg, IN 47123. Phone: (812) 338-3907.

GOVERNOR'S CUP REGATTA. Sept 11–13. Connecticut River, Essex, CT. Three-day event includes Governor's Cup Race, Oar and Paddle Races, Cats and Gaffer's Race, Antique & Classic Power Boat Rendezvous, Classic Boat Parade (power and sail), Fife and Drum Corp Performance, Connecticut River Museum Open House, marine equipment auction and Blessing of the Fleet. Various dining and dancing events will be held throughout the three days. Est attendance: 750. For info: Connecticut River Museum, 67 Main St, Essec, CT 06426. Phone: (860) 767-8269 or (860) 767-2618. Fax: (860) 767-7028. Email: crm@connix.com.

HARVEST FESTIVAL PARADE AND PRCA RODEO. Sept 12–14. Pahrump Valley, NV. Rodeo, car races, carnival, deep-pit BBQ and dance. For local info: (800) 633-WEST or (702) 727-5800.

HORVATH, LES: BIRTH ANNIVERSARY. Sept 12, 1921. Leslie (Les) Horvath, football player born at South Bend, IN. Horvath played college football at Ohio State for coach Paul Brown and won the 1944 Heisman Trophy. After three years as a pro, he went to dental school, opening a practice in 1950. Died at Glendale, CA, Nov 15, 1995.

KELLER, KING KONG: BIRTH ANNIVERSARY. Sept 12, 1916. Charles Ernest ("King Kong") Keller, baseball player born at Middletown, MD. Keller played the outfield for 13 years with the New York Yankees and the Detroit Tigers (1939–52). A rugged complexion and a powerful swing gave rise to his nickname. Died at Frederick, MD, May 23, 1990.

LEAVENWORTH RIVER FEST. Sept 12–13. Leavenworth, KS. Outhouse races, antique car exhibits, parade, aircraft display and rides, Harley-Davidson motorcycle exhibit, arts and crafts and children's carnival. Plenty of entertainment, food, races and competitions and several feature attractions. Annually, the second weekend in September. Est attendance: 20,000. For info: Connie Hachenburg, Dir, Leavenworth-Lansing Conv/Visitors, 518 Shawnee, Box 44, Leavenworth, KS 66048. Phone: (913) 682-3924. Fax: (913) 682-8170.

LUDERUS, FRED: BIRTH ANNIVERSARY. Sept 12, 1885. Frederick William (Fred) Luderus, baseball player born at Milwaukee, WI. Luderus was a home-run hitting first baseman in the second decade of the 20th century. He helped the Philadelphia Phillies win the National League pennant in 1915. It was their first flag and their only one until 1950. Died at Three Lakes, WI, Jan 5, 1961.

MARYLAND RECREATIONAL VEHICLE SHOW. Sept 12–20. Timonium State Fairgrounds, Timonium, MD. 6th annual outdoor show of motorhomes, trailers, 5-wheel trailers and pickup campers, campground booths, accessories and related items. Annually, beginning the first Saturday after Labor Day. Est attendance: 8,000. For info: Richard T. Albright, Pres, Maryland Rec Vehicle Dealers Assn, Inc, 8332 Pulaski Hwy, Baltimore, MD 21237. Phone: (410) 687-7200. Fax: (410) 686-1486.

MOON PHASE: LAST QUARTER. Sept 12. Moon enters Last Quarter phase at 9:58 PM, EDT.

MORGAN HORSE VERSATILITY EVENT. Sept 12. McCulloch Farm, Old Lyme, CT. Demonstrations of all the different sports and activities that America's first breed of horse can perform. Est attendance: 450. For info: McCulloch Farm Whippoorwill Morgans, 100 Whippoorwill Rd, Old Lyme, CT 06371. Phone: (860) 434-7355. Fax: (860) 434-1638.

OWENS, JESSE: 85th BIRTH ANNIVERSARY. Sept 12, 1913. James Cleveland (Jesse) Owens, Olympic gold medal track athlete born at Oakville, AL. Owens won four gold medals at the 1936 Summer Olympic Games in Berlin, Germany, putting the lie to Hitler's theories of Aryan superiority. In his career, Owens set 11 world records. During a Big 10 meet at the University of Michigan in Ann Arbor on May 23, 1935, Owens, represent-

ing Ohio State University, broke five world records and tied a sixth in the space of 45 minutes. Died at Tucson, AZ, Mar 31, 1980.

WATERMELON SEED-SPITTING AND SPEED-EATING CHAMPIONSHIP IN PARDEEVILLE. Sept 12–13. Pardeeville, WI. 30th annual national competition with visitors from as far as New York and Australia. The current speed-eating record is 2.5 pounds of watermelon in 3.5 seconds. Included are a parade, entertainment and an evening band performance on Saturday. On Sunday the championships, free watermelon, pancake breakfast and much more. Annually, the first weekend after Labor Day. Est attendance: 6,000. For info: Pardeeville Area Business Assn (PABA), PO Box 337, Pardeeville, WI 53954. Phone: (608) 429-3121.

BIRTHDAYS TODAY

Kenneth Leonard ("Ki-Jana") Carter, 25, football player, born Westerville, OH, Sept 12, 1973.
Deron Leigh Cherry, 39, former football player, born Riverside, NJ, Sept 12, 1959.
Lennox Dominique ("Terry") Dehere, 27, basketball player, born New York, NY, Sept 12, 1971.
Patrick Alan (Pat) Listach, 31, baseball player, born Natchitoches, LA, Sept 12, 1967.
Michael Stephen (Mickey) Lolich, 58, former baseball player, born Portland, OR, Sept 12, 1940.
Vernon Maxwell, 33, basketball player, born Gainesville, FL, Sept 12, 1965.
Ricky Rudd, 42, auto racer, born Chesapeake, VA, Sept 12, 1956.

SEPTEMBER 13 — SUNDAY
Day 256 — 109 Remaining

CANADA: INTERNATIONAL TEXAS HOLDEM POKER TOURNAMENT. Sept 13. Dawson City, Yukon. Most northern Holdem Tournament hosted by White Ram Bed and Breakfast. Annually, the Sunday after Labor Day. For info: White Ram Manor B&B, Box 302, Dawson City, YT, Canada Y0B 1G0. Phone: (403) 993-5772. Fax: (403) 993-6509.

CORVETTE SHOW. Sept 13. (Rain date Sept 20.) Wheaton Village, Millville, NJ. Presented by Corvettes Unlimited Corvette Club. Est attendance: 1,500. For info: Wheaton Village, 1501 Glasstown Rd, Millville, NJ 08332. Phone: (609) 825-6800 or (800) 998-4552. Fax: (609) 825-2410. Email: mail@wheatonvillage.org. WWW: http://www.wheatonvillage.org

DAY RIDES EIGHT WINNERS: ANNIVERSARY. Sept 13, 1989. Jockey Pat Day rode eight winners in nine races at Arlington Park in Illinois, breaking the record for most winners in a single day of racing at one track. Day finished second in his sole loss.

ENCHANTED CIRCLE CENTURY BIKE TOUR. Sept 13. Red River, NM. 100-mile scenic ride and one of the longest and most difficult bicycle tours in the Southwest. Est attendance: 1,000. For info: Red River Chamber of Commerce, PO Box 870, Red River, NM 87558. Phone: (800) 348-6444. Fax: (505) 754-2944. Email: rrinfo@newmex.com. WWW: http://taoswebb.com/redriverinfo

FIRST NEW YORK CITY MARATHON: ANNIVERSARY. Sept 13, 1970. The first New York City marathon drew 126 runners, 55 of whom finished the course. Gary Muhrcke won the race with a time of 2:31:38.2.

FRANK, CLINT: BIRTH ANNIVERSARY. Sept 13, 1915. Clinton Edward (Clint) Frank, football player born at St. Louis, MO. Frank, an All-American tailback at Yale, won the 1937 Heisman Trophy. He declined to play pro football, opting instead for a career in advertising. Died at Evanston, IL, July 7, 1992.

ITALY: GIOSTRA DELLA QUINTANA. Sept 13. Foligno. A revival of a 17th-century joust of the Quintana, featuring 600 knights in full costume. Annually, the second Sunday in September.

MOLITOR GETS 3,000th HIT: ANNIVERSARY. Sept 13, 1996. Paul Molitor of the Minnesota Twins got the 3,000th hit of his career, a triple against Jose Rosado of the Kansas City Royals. The Twins lost, 6–5. Molitor became either the 20th or 21st player to reach the 3,000-hit plateau (depending on whether the list includes Adrian "Cap" Anson, whose statistics are in dispute). He was the first to triple for No. 3,000.

NORTHEAST MISSOURI TRIATHLON CHAMPI-ONSHIP. Sept 13. Thousand Hills State Park, Kirksville, MO. Swim 3/4 mile, bike 18 miles, run five miles. USA Triathlon Federation certified. Qualifier for International Course Nationals. Annually, the Sunday after Labor Day. Est attendance: 800. For info: KRXL Radio, Box 130, Kirksville, MO 63501. Phone: (816) 626-2213. Fax: (816) 626-2483.

PATRIOTS BROADCAST IN FRENCH: ANNIVERSARY. Sept 13, 1987. The New England Patriots became the first NFL team to broadcast its games on a regular basis on a French-Canadian radio network. Pierre Donais handled the play-by-play with radio station KCLM, a 50,000-watt station in Laval, Quebec, serving as the flagship.

ROMMEL, ED: BIRTH ANNIVERSARY. Sept 13, 1897. Edwin Aloysious (Ed) Rommel, baseball umpire and pitcher born at Baltimore, MD. Rommel is generally regarded as one of the first knuckleball pitchers. He won 170 games between 1920 and 1932 and was an American League umpire after retiring as a player. Died at Baltimore, Aug 26, 1970.

RUETHER, DUTCH: 105th BIRTH ANNIVERSARY. Sept 13, 1893. Walter Henry ("Dutch") Ruether, baseball player born at Alameda, CA. Ruether pitched for 11 seasons in the majors and won 19 games for the Cincinnati Reds as they won the World Series in 1919. He finished his career with the 1927 New York Yankees, winning 13 games against 6 losses. Died at Phoenix, AZ, May 16, 1970.

BIRTHDAYS TODAY

James Mitchell (Jim) Cleamons, 49, basketball coach and former player, born Lincolnton, NC, Sept 13, 1949.

John Rikard (Rick) Dempsey, 49, former baseball player, born Fayetteville, TN, Sept 13, 1949.

James Gregory (Greg) Hibbard, 34, former baseball player, born New Orleans, LA, Sept 13, 1964.

Travis James Knight, 24, basketball player, born Salt Lake City, UT, Sept 13, 1974.

Igor Kravchuk, 32, hockey player, born Ufa, USSR, Sept 13, 1966.

Dennis Edward (Denny) Neagle, Jr, 30, baseball player, born Gambrills, MD, Sept 13, 1968.

	S	**M**	**T**	**W**	**T**	**F**	**S**
September			1	2	3	4	5
1998	6	7	8	9	10	11	12
	13	14	15	16	17	18	19
	20	21	22	23	24	25	26
	27	28	29	30			

Bernabe Figueroa (Bernie) Williams, 30, baseball player, born San Juan, Puerto Rico, Sept 13, 1968.

Richard Charles (Rick) Wise, 53, former baseball player, born Jackson, MI, Sept 13, 1945.

SEPTEMBER 14 — MONDAY
Day 257 — 108 Remaining

CHASE'S SPORTSQUOTE OF THE DAY

"The off-the-field stuff can kill you. It can absolutely destroy you." —Denny McLain

---

BURNS MAKES UNASSISTED TRIPLE PLAY: 75th ANNIVERSARY. Sept 14, 1923. First baseman George Burns of the Boston Red Sox made the third unassisted triple play in major league history in the second inning of a game against Cleveland. Burns caught a line drive hit by Frank Brower, tagged Rube Lutzke before he could return to first and stepped on second before Riggs Stephenson could return.

GRIFFEYS HIT BACK-TO-BACK HOMERS: ANNIVERSARY. Sept 14, 1990. Ken Griffey, Sr, and Ken Griffey, Jr, father and son, hit unprecedented back-to-back home runs for the Seattle Mariners in a game against the California Angels. Kirk McCaskill was the pitcher. The Mariners lost, 7–5.

HUNDLEY SET HOMER MARK: ANNIVERSARY. Sept 14, 1996. Catcher Todd Hundley of the New York Mets hit his 41st home run of the year to set a major league record for most home runs in a season by a catcher. Roy Campanella hit 41 homers for the Brooklyn Dodgers in 1953, but one of these came when he pinch-hit on the last day of the season.

KETCHEL, STANLEY: BIRTH ANNIVERSARY. Sept 14, 1886. Stanley Ketchel, boxer born Stanislaus Kiecal at Grand Rapids, MI. Ketchel became a fighter after both his parents were murdered. He won the middleweight title in 1908 and proved to be one of the sport's most popular champions. In 1909 he took on heavyweight champ Jack Johnson and lasted 12 rounds despite giving away 35 pounds. Embroiled in a love triangle, he was fatally shot by Walter A. Dipley, a hired hand on the farm where Ketchel was training. Died at Conway, MO, Oct 15, 1910.

McLAIN WINS 30 GAMES: 30th ANNIVERSARY. Sept 14, 1968. Denny McLain of the Detroit Tigers defeated the Oakland A's, 5–4, to become the first pitcher since Dizzy Dean in 1934 to win 30 games in a season.

NICHOLS, KID: BIRTH ANNIVERSARY. Sept 14, 1869. Charles Augustus ("Kid") Nichols, Baseball Hall of Fame pitcher born at Madison, WI. Nichols was one of the greatest pitchers of the 19th century. In the 1890s, he led the Boston National League team to five championships in nine seasons, winning 30 or more games seven years in a row. Inducted into the Hall of Fame in 1949. Died at Kansas City, MO, Apr 11, 1953.

SOLO TRANSATLANTIC BALLOON CROSSING: ANNIVERSARY. Sept 14–18, 1984. Joe W. Kittinger, 56-year-old balloonist left Caribou, ME, in a ten-story-tall helium-filled balloon named *Rosie O'Grady's Balloon of Peace* on Sept 14, 1984, crossed the Atlantic Ocean and reached the French coast, above the town of Capbreton, in bad weather on Sept 17 at 4:29 PM, EDT. He crash-landed amid wind and rain near Savone, Italy, at 8:08 AM, EDT, Sept 18. Kittinger suffered a broken ankle when he was thrown from the balloon's gondola during the landing. His nearly 84-hour flight, covering about 3,535 miles, was the first solo balloon crossing of the Atlantic Ocean and a record distance for a solo balloon flight.

Denny McLain

ST LOUIS NATIONAL CHARITY HORSE SHOW: 20th ANNUAL. Sept 14–26 (tentative). Greensfelder Recreational Center (Queeny Park), Creve Coeur, MO. More than 4,000 owners and families, trainers and groomers from throughout the country will participate in this two-week event. Est attendance: 20,000. For info: President, St. Louis National Charity Horse Show, 1724 Clarkson Rd, Chesterfield, MO 63017. Phone: (314) 434-6622. Fax: (314) 434-6643.

TEAM USA WINS WORLD CUP: ANNIVERSARY. Sept 14, 1996. Team USA defeated Team Canada, 5–2, in Game 3 of the best-of-three final series to win hockey's World Cup. This competition matched teams of professionals from eight nations in a pair of round robins followed a single elimination bracket for the top four teams. Team Canada won the first game of the finals, 4–3, in overtime. Team USA won Game 2, 5–2, to even the series. Other teams represented Sweden, Finland, Russia, Germany, Slovakia and the Czech Republic.

US SENIOR WOMEN'S AMATEUR (GOLF) CHAMPIONSHIP. Sept 14–19. Golden Horseshoe Golf Course, Williamsburg, VA. For info: US Golf Assn, Golf House, Far Hills, NJ 07931. Phone: (908) 234-2300. Fax: (908) 234-9687. Email: usga@ix.netcom.com. WWW: http://www.usga.org

US SENIOR AMATEUR (GOLF) CHAMPIONSHIP. Sept 14–19. Skokie Country Club, Glencoe, IL. For info: US Golf Assn, Golf House, Far Hills, NJ 07931. Phone: (908) 234-2300. Fax: (908) 234-9687. Email: usga@ix.netcom.com. WWW: http://www.usga.org

BIRTHDAYS TODAY

David Michael Bell, 26, baseball player, born Cincinnati, OH, Sept 14, 1972.
Lawrence Harvey (Larry) Brown, 58, basketball coach and former player, born New York, NY, Sept 14, 1940.

Gerald Francis (Jerry) Coleman, 74, broadcaster and former baseball manager and player, born San Jose, CA, Sept 14, 1924.
Jerry Don Gleaton, 41, former baseball player, born Brownwood, TX, Sept 14, 1957.
Kurt Keola Gouveia, 34, football player, born Honolulu, HI, Sept 14, 1964.
Stanley Wilson (Stan) Williams, 62, former baseball player, born Enfield, NH, Sept 14, 1936.

☆   ☆   ☆

SEPTEMBER 15 — TUESDAY
Day 258 — 107 Remaining

ALI WINS TITLE FOR THIRD TIME: 20th ANNIVERSARY. Sept 15, 1978. Muhammad Ali became the only fighter to win the heavyweight championship for a third time when he scored a unanimous 15-round decision over Leon Spinks at the Louisiana Superdome. Ali, then known at Cassius Clay, won the title for the first time on Feb 25, 1964, over Sonny Liston. He regained the crown the first time on Oct 30, 1974, by knocking out George Foreman.

DODGERS PASS 3-MILLION MARK: 20th ANNIVERSARY. Sept 15, 1978. The Los Angeles Dodgers became the first major league baseball team to pass the 3-million mark in home attendance in a 5–0 victory over the Atlanta Braves.

GOTTLIEB, EDDIE: 100th BIRTH ANNIVERSARY. Sept 15, 1898. Edward (Eddie) Gottlieb, Basketball Hall of Fame executive born at Kiev, Russia. Barely 20 years old, Gottlieb organized the Philadelphia SPHAS, one of the best early professional basketball teams. He also promoted Negro Leagues baseball and wrestling. Gottlieb owned and coached the Philadelphia Warriors and helped to engineer the merger of the BAA and NBL in 1949. His innovative ideas to improve the game included doubleheaders involving four teams, outlawing zone defenses and awarding bonus foul shots. He also arranged the NBA's schedule for years. Inducted into the Hall of Fame in 1971. Died at Philadelphia, PA, Dec 7, 1979.

HARLEY, CHIC: BIRTH ANNIVERSARY. Sept 15, 1895. Charles Wesley ("Chic") Harley, football player born at Chicago, IL. Harley was a three-time All-American at Ohio State (1916–17, 1919) where he set a career scoring record that lasted 36 years. The Buckeyes won every game but one while Harley played. Ohio State constructed massive Ohio Stadium in 1922, nicknaming the structure the "House That Chic Built." Died at Danville, IL, Apr 21, 1974.

JAFFEE, IRVING: BIRTH ANNIVERSARY. Sept 15, 1906. Irving W. Jaffee, Olympic gold medal speed skater born at New York, NY. Jaffee began skating at the famous Roseland Ballroom and soon developed Olympic aspirations. At the 1928 Games in St. Moritz, he finished fourth in the 5,000 meters and had the best time in the 10,000 when the race was voided because of high temperatures. After retiring for a while to care for his mother, he began competing again and won both races at the 1932 Games in Lake Placid. Died at San Diego, CA, Mar 20, 1981.

ORIOLES SET NEW HOME RUN MARK: ANNIVERSARY. Sept 15, 1996. The Baltimore Orioles hit 5 home runs as they beat the Detroit Tigers, 16–6, to set a new major league record for most home runs in a season by a team. Mark Parent's 3-run homer in the 3rd inning was the record-breaker, the teams's 241st home run of the year, breaking the mark set by the 1961 New York Yankees. The Orioles ended the year with 257 homers.

SMITH, CHARLEY: BIRTH ANNIVERSARY. Sept 15, 1937. Charles William (Charley) Smith, baseball player born at Charleston, SC. Smith played third base with seven different teams. He was once traded for Ken Boyer and once for Roger Maris. Died at Reno, NV, Nov 29, 1994.

BIRTHDAYS TODAY

Earnest Alexander Byner, 36, football player, born Milledgeville, GA, Sept 15, 1962.
Sherman Douglas, 32, basketball player, born Washington, DC, Sept 15, 1966.
Tommy Lee Jones, 52, actor (*Cobb*), born San Saba, TX, Sept 15, 1946.
James Francis (Jim) Lynam, 57, former basketball coach, born Philadelphia, PA, Sept 15, 1941.
Daniel Constantine (Dan) Marino, Jr, 37, football player, born Pittsburgh, PA, Sept 15, 1961.
Joseph (Joe) Morris, 38, former football player, born Fort Bragg, NC, Sept 15, 1960.
Merlin Jay Olsen, 58, former broadcaster and Pro Football Hall of Fame defensive tackle, born Logan, UT, Sept 15, 1940.
Gaylord Jackson Perry, 60, Baseball Hall of Fame pitcher, born Williamston, NC, Sept 15, 1938.

SEPTEMBER 16 — WEDNESDAY
Day 259 — 106 Remaining

BIDWILL, CHARLES: BIRTH ANNIVERSARY. Sept 16, 1895. Charles W. Bidwill, Sr, Pro Football Hall of Fame executive born at Chicago, IL. A lawyer, Bidwill purchased the Chicago Cardinals of the NFL in 1933 and served as president of the team until his death. He loaned money to George Halas to buy the Chicago Bears. Bidwill kept a low profile as an owner but helped build the team that won the 1947 NFL championship several months after his death. Inducted into the Hall of Fame in 1967. Died at Chicago, Apr 19, 1947.

BIRTH OF USAC: ANNIVERSARY. Sept 16, 1955. The United States Auto Club (USAC) was formed to supervise four major categories of auto racing.

BOTTOMLEY DRIVES IN 12 RUNS: ANNIVERSARY. Sept 16, 1924. First baseman Jim Bottomley of the St. Louis Cardinals set a major league record by driving in 12 runs in a single game against the Brooklyn Dodgers. Bottomley got three singles, a double and a pair of home runs as the Cardinals won, 17–3.

BROWNING PITCHES PERFECT GAME: 10th ANNIVERSARY. Sept 16, 1988. Tom Browning of the Cincinnati Reds pitched the 11th perfect game in regular season major league play, defeating the Los Angeles Dodgers, 1–0.

BROWNS UPSET EAGLES: ANNIVERSARY. Sept 16, 1950. Playing in their first National Football League game, the Cleveland Browns defeated the NFL's defending champs, the Philadelphia Eagles, 35–10. The Browns had joined the NFL after four sterling years in the All-America Football Conference during which they won 52 games, lost four, tied one and captured all four championships. Cleveland carried its success into the NFL, fin-

ishing first in the American Conference and winning the league title, 30–28, over the Los Angeles Rams.

GOLDEN ASPEN MOTORCYCLE RALLY. Sept 16–20. Ruidoso, NM. Trade show, bike shows, riding tours, skill events, parade, awards banquet, stunt shows and thousands in prizes. Est attendance: 15,000. For info: Golden Aspen Rally Assn, PO Box 1458, Ruidoso, NM 88345. Phone: (800) 452-8045. Email: gara@usa.net. WWW: http://www.motorcyclerally.com

BIRTHDAYS TODAY

Elgin Gay Baylor, 64, former coach and Basketball Hall of Fame forward, born Washington, DC, Sept 16, 1934.
Orel Leonard Quinton Hershiser, IV, 40, baseball player, born Buffalo, NY, Sept 16, 1958.
Mark Alan Parent, 37, baseball player, born Ashland, OR, Sept 16, 1961.
Timothy (Tim) Raines, 39, baseball player, born Sanford, FL, Sept 16, 1959.
Mickey Lee Tettleton, 38, baseball player, born Oklahoma City, OK, Sept 16, 1960.
Amos Tom Wargo, 56, golfer, born Marlette, MI, Sept 16, 1942.
Robin R. Yount, 43, former baseball player, born Danville, IL, Sept 16, 1955.

SEPTEMBER 17 — THURSDAY
Day 260 — 105 Remaining

CONNOLLY, MAUREEN: BIRTH ANNIVERSARY. Sept 17, 1934. Maureen Catherine ("Little Mo") Connolly Brinker, tennis player born at San Diego, CA. Connolly became the second-youngest woman to win the US National championship at Forest Hills, NY, when she captured that title in 1951. She repeated in 1952 and won Wimbledon, too. In 1953, she became the first woman to win the Grand Slam, taking the US, French, Australian and Wimbledon championships. After winning a second straight French title and a third straight Wimbledon, she suffered a crushed leg in a horseback riding accident and never competed again. Died at Dallas, TX, June 21, 1969.

FIRST BLACK WOMAN IN USGA EVENT: ANNIVERSARY. Sept 17, 1956. Ann Gregory became the first black woman golfer to play in a USGA national championship when she participated in the Women's Amateur. Marlene Stewart won the championship, contested at Meridian Hills Country Club at Indianapolis, IN, by defeating JoAnne Gunderson, 2 and 1.

FOSTER, RUBE: BIRTH ANNIVERSARY. Sept 17, 1879. Andrew ("Rube") Foster, baseball player and Baseball Hall of Fame executive born at Calvert, TX. The son of a minister, Foster is known as the "Father of Negro Baseball." He was a manager and star pitcher, earning 51 victories in one year. After playing for the Chicago Lelands in 1907 and leading that team to a record of 110 wins and 10 losses, in 1908 he formed the Chicago American Giants who won 129 games and lost only 6 in their first season. In 1919, he called a meeting of black baseball owners and organized the first black baseball league, the Negro National League. He served as its president until his death. Inducted into the Hall of Fame in 1981. Died at Kankakee, IL, Dec 9, 1930.

HORSE RACING AT FAIRPLEX PARK. Sept 17–Oct 5. Fairplex Park, Pomona, CA. Thoroughbred, quarter horse, Arabian and Appaloosa horse racing during the Los Angeles County Fair. The Fairplex Park racing season ranks only behind the other major Southern California racetracks for average daily handle among all tracks in North America. Annually, beginning on the second Thursday after Labor Day, traditionally held between the

	September 1998	S	M	T	W	T	F	S
				1	2	3	4	5
		6	7	8	9	10	11	12
		13	14	15	16	17	18	19
		20	21	22	23	24	25	26
		27	28	29	30			

Del Mar and Oak Tree seasons. Presented by the Los Angeles County Fair Association. Est attendance: 100,000. For info: Communications Mgr, Fairplex, PO Box 2250, Pomona, CA 91769. Phone: (909) 623-3111. Fax: (909) 629-2067. Email: Robinson@fairplex.com. WWW: http://www.fairplex.com

KELLY, DAN: BIRTH ANNIVERSARY. Sept 17, 1936. Daniel (Dan) Kelly, sportscaster born at Ottawa, Ontario, Canada. Kelly began his broadcasting career at several small radio stations and eventually graduated to covering the Canadian Football League and the Montreal Canadiens. In 1968, he began a 21-year association with the St. Louis Blues and KMOX. His trademark slogan, "He shoots, he scores," made him famous in two countries. Died at Chesterfield, MO, Feb 10, 1989.

LITTLE BROWN JUG. Sept 17. Delaware County Fairgrounds, Delaware, OH. The Little Brown Jug brings together the best pacing horses in the world to race for more than $500,000. The contest will draw racing fans from three continents, swelling the small but picturesque town's population from 16,000 to 60,000 in a single day! Est attendance: 55,000. For info: US Trotting Assn, 750 Michigan Ave, Columbus, OH 43215. Phone: (614) 224-2291. Fax: (614) 224-4575. Email: jpawlak@ustrotting.com. WWW: http://www.ustrotting.com

NATIONAL FOOTBALL LEAGUE FORMED: ANNIVERSARY. Sept 17, 1920. The National Football League was formed in Canton, OH.

REGGIE JACKSON HITS 500th HOME RUN: ANNIVERSARY. Sept 17, 1984. Reggie Jackson of the New York Yankees became the 13th player to hit 500 home runs in his career when he connected off Bud Black of the Kansas City Royals.

SCHULTE, FRANK: BIRTH ANNIVERSARY. Sept 17, 1882. Frank Schulte, baseball player born at Cohocton, NY. Schulte began a 15-year career in the majors with the Chicago Cubs in 1904. He led the league in home runs in 1910 and won the Chalmers award in 1911, emblematic of the most valuable player. He also stole home 23 times in his career, tied for fifth on the all-time list. Died at Oakland, CA, Oct 2, 1949.

BIRTHDAYS TODAY

George Frederick Blanda, 71, Pro Football Hall of Fame quarterback and placekicker, born Youngwood, PA, Sept 17, 1927.

Anthony Carter, 38, former football player, born Riviera Beach, FL, Sept 17, 1960.

Orlando Manuel Cepeda, 61, former baseball player, born Ponce, Puerto Rico, Sept 17, 1937.

John Anthony Franco, 38, baseball player, born New York, NY, Sept 17, 1960.

Philip D. (Phil) Jackson, 53, basketball coach and former player, born Deer Lodge, MT, Sept 17, 1945.

Scott William Simpson, 43, golfer, born San Diego, CA, Sept 17, 1955.

Douglas (Doug) Smith, 29, basketball player, born Detroit, MI, Sept 17, 1969.

Rasheed Abdul Wallace, 24, basketball player, born Philadelphia, PA, Sept 17, 1974.

Robert Paul (Bobby) Wine, Sr, 60, former baseball manager and player, born New York, NY, Sept 17, 1938.

SEPTEMBER 18 — FRIDAY
Day 261 — 104 Remaining

SPORTSCHASER OF THE DAY
Who pitched a perfect game for 12 innings in 1959 only to lose in the 13th?

ANTIQUE AND CLASSIC CAR SHOW. Sept 18–20. Willow Park, Bennington, VT. Brass cars, Woodies, costume judging and events of skill and dexterity in handling these wonderful machines of yesteryear are all part of this car show. A flea market with auto-related parts and memorabilia entices collectors seeking that elusive fender or gas running lamp. A display and demonstration of antique motorcycles, tractor and farm machinery are also featured. Est attendance: 10,000. For info: Michael Williams, Bennington Area Chamber of Commerce, Veterans Memorial Dr, Bennington, VT 05201. Phone: (802) 447-3311. Fax: (802) 447-1163. Email: benncham@sover.net. WWW: http://www.bennington.com

BANKHEAD, SAM: BIRTH ANNIVERSARY. Sept 18, 1910. Samuel (Sam) Bankhead, baseball player and manager born at Empire, AL. Bankhead starred for several teams in the Negro Leagues from 1930 to 1950. In 1951 he became organized baseball's first black manager, handling the Farnham team in the Provincial League. Died at Pittsburgh, PA, July 24, 1976.

BLACK HILLS JEEP JAMBOREE. Sept 18–20. Deadwood, SD. Annual jamboree for 4-wheel drive enthusiasts, who try their luck on some of the roughest terrain in the Black Hills. For info: Sturgis Chamber of Commerce, PO Box 504, Sturgis, SD 57785. Phone: (605) 584-2940.

CLEMENS STRIKES OUT 20 AGAIN: ANNIVERSARY. Sept 18, 1996. Pitcher Roger Clemens of the Boston Red Sox tied his own record for most strikeouts in a 9-inning game when he struck out 20 Detroit Tigers in a 4–0 Red Sox victory. Clemens set the record on Apr 29, 1986, against the Seattle Mariners.

CROSLEY, POWEL: BIRTH ANNIVERSARY. Sept 18, 1886. Powel Crosley, Jr, baseball executive born at Cincinnati, OH. Crosley took a fortune made in the radio and appliance businesses and bought the Cincinnati Reds. He introduced night baseball to the majors in 1935 and generally let baseball men run his club. Died at Cincinnati, Mar 28, 1961.

GROH, HEINIE: BIRTH ANNIVERSARY. Sept 18, 1889. Henry Knight ("Heinie") Groh, baseball player born at Rochester, NY. Groh played 16 years in the major leagues and was the second baseman on the 1919 Cincinnati Reds, the team that beat the Black Sox. He used an unusually shaped bat called a "bottle bat." Died at Cincinnati, OH, Aug 22, 1968.

HADDIX, HARVEY: BIRTH ANNIVERSARY. Sept 18, 1925. Harvey Haddix, baseball player and coach born at Medway, OH. Haddix, a diminutive lefthander known as the "Kitten," pitched one of the most extraordinary games in baseball history. On May 26, 1959, while a member of the Pittsburgh Pirates, he threw a perfect game for 12 innings against the Milwaukee Braves. The game was scoreless, however, and the Braves got a hit in the 13th and won, 1–0. Died at Springfield, OH, Jan 9, 1994.

HALL OF FAME CATCH AND RELEASE. Sept 18–20. Lake Chippewa Flowage, Hayward, WI. 4th annual Catch & Release Walleye Tournament, held on the famous Chippewa Flowage. Fund raiser for Hall's building fund. Entry fee. Cash prizes based on number of entries. Annually, the second weekend after Labor Day. For info: Natl Fresh Water Fishing Hall of Fame, PO Box 33, Hayward, WI 54843. Phone: (715) 634-4440. Fax: (715) 634-4440.

IRON HORSE OUTRACED BY HORSE: ANNIVERSARY. Sept 18, 1830. In a widely celebrated race, the first locomotive built in America, the Tom Thumb, lost to a horse. Mechanical difficulties plagued the steam engine over the nine-mile course between Riley's Tavern and Baltimore, MD, and a boiler leak prevented the locomotive from finishing the race. In the early days of trains, engines were nicknamed "Iron Horses."

NEW HAMPSHIRE HIGHLAND GAMES. Sept 18–20. Loon Mountain, Lincoln, NH. From the tossing of the caber to the lilting melodies of the clarsach plus massed pipe bands on parade, there's something for everyone at New Hampshire's Highland Games: a three-day Scottish festival crammed with music, dance, crafts, athletic events, Scottish food and more. For those of Scottish heritage, there's also a chance to look up one's clan connection, as more than 60 Scottish clans and societies have tents with displays. Admission charged. Est attendance: 30,000. For info: New Hampshire Highland Games, PO Box 495, Dublin, NH 03444-0495. Phone: (603) 563-8801. Fax: (603) 563-8549. Email: nhscot@top.monad.net. WWW: http://newww.com/org/nhhg

☆   ☆   ☆

RACKING WORLD CELEBRATION. Sept 18–26. Decatur, AL. Week-long event featuring racking horses from across the nation. The highlight of the 75-class event is the crowning of the World Grand Racking Horse Champion on the last night. Annually, the last full week in September. Est attendance: 25,000. For info: Jacklyn Bailey, Decatur Conv and Visitors Bureau, 719 6th Ave SE, Decatur, AL 35602. Phone: (205) 350-2028 or (800) 524-6181. Email: dcvb@hiwaay.net.

SAN DIEGO BAYFAIR PRESENTS THE WORLD SERIES OF POWER BOAT RACING ON MISSION BAY. Sept 18–20. Mission Bay, San Diego, CA. Featured are the Bill Muncey Cup on Mission Bay, Thunderboats (Unlimited Hydroplanes), Formula One PROP Series, Intl Hot Boat Association Drag Boats, NASBOAT (Unlimited Lights) and more! Only event in the world with all the top motor sport and boating competitions all on the same body of water, all in the same week! Indy on water! Family festival, vendors, displays, interactive rides, concert and fireworks show. Coverage and advertising on ESPN TV and live radio. Annually, the third weekend of September. Est attendance: 160,000. For info: Thunderboats Unlimited, Inc, 4355 Ruffin Rd, Ste 315, San Diego, CA 92123. Phone: (619) 268-1250. Fax: (619) 268-3301. Email: buff@bayfair.com. WWW: http://www.bayfair.com

TWO DAYS, TWO NO-HITTERS: 30th ANNIVERSARY. Sept 18, 1968. Ray Washburn of the St. Louis Cardinals pitched a no-hitter against the San Francisco Giants one day after the Giants' Gaylord Perry no-hit the Cardinals.

September 1998	S	M	T	W	T	F	S
			1	2	3	4	5
	6	7	8	9	10	11	12
	13	14	15	16	17	18	19
	20	21	22	23	24	25	26
	27	28	29	30			

William Scott (Scotty) Bowman, 65, Hockey Hall of Fame coach, born Montreal, Quebec, Canada, Sept 18, 1933.

Kenneth Alven (Ken) Brett, 50, former baseball player, born New York, NY, Sept 18, 1948.

Tom Chorske, 32, hockey player, born Minneapolis, MN, Sept 18, 1966.

Richard Allen (Dick) Dietz, 57, former baseball player, born Crawfordsville, IN, Sept 18, 1941.

Toni Kukoc, 30, basketball player, born Split, Croatia, Sept 18, 1968.

Ryne Dee Sandberg, 39, baseball player, born Spokane, WA, Sept 18, 1959.

SEPTEMBER 19 — SATURDAY
Day 262 — 103 Remaining

BUD LIGHT 2-DAY OPEN BUDDY BASS TOURNAMENT. Sept 19–20. Mark Twain Lake, Blackjack Marina, Perry, MO. This 13th annual event is the largest bass tournament in the state of Missouri. With 500 entries first place is $10,000. Sponsored by the Golden Eagle Dist of Hannibal, MO, and the Mark Twain Lake Chamber of Commerce. Annually, the third weekend in September. For info: Mark Twain Lake Chamber of Commerce, PO Box 59, Perry, MO 63462. Phone: (573) 565-2228. Fax: (573) 565-3241.

CONERLY, CHARLIE: BIRTH ANNIVERSARY. Sept 19, 1921. Charles Albert (Charlie) Conerly, Jr, football player born at Clarksdale, MS. Conerly played halfback at the University of Mississipi for two years before entering the Marine Corps during World War II. He returned to Ole Miss in 1946 and switched to quarterback and became an All-American a year later. He played 14 years with the New York Giants, won the Rookie of the Year award in 1948 and was named MVP in 1959. He is often considered one of the greatest players not to be in the Pro Football Hall of Fame. Died at Memphis, TN, Feb 13, 1996.

ETTEN, NICK: 85th BIRTH ANNIVERSARY. Sept 19, 1913. Nicholas Raymond Thomas (Nick) Etten, baseball player born at Spring Grove, IL. Etten led the American League in home runs in 1944 and in runs batted in a year later. He played with both Philadelphia teams and the New York Yankees. Died at Hinsdale, IL, Oct 18, 1990.

FISHING HAS NO BOUNDARIES—CHICAGO. Sept 19–20 (tentative). Chain of Lakes near Antioch, IL. A two-day fishing experience for disabled persons. Any age, disability, sex, race, etc, are eligible. Attended by 100 participants and 300 volunteers. For info: FHNB, 157 Hillcrest Ave, Wood Dale, IL 60191. Phone: (312) 481-0000.

FLY-IN/DRIVE-IN. Sept 19–20. Arapahoe Airport, Arapahoe, NE. Nebraska Antique Airplane Association members and Antique and Classic Car owners fly or drive their craft/vehicles to the airport to display. Open to public. Breakfast on Saturday morning, banquet Saturday night. Annually, the third weekend in September. Est attendance: 500. For info: Araphoe Chamber of Commerce, Fly-In/Drive-In, PO Box 624, Arapahoe, NE 68922. Phone: (308) 962-7872.

FRICK ELECTED COMMISSIONER: ANNIVERSARY. Sept 19, 1951. National League President Ford C. Frick was elected the third Commissioner of Baseball to replace Albert B. ("Happy") Chandler. Frick, a former sportswriter, served until 1965.

HODAG MUSKIE CHALLENGE. Sept 19–20. Rhinelander, WI. $20,000 catch and release Muskie Tournament. Annually, the third weekend in September. Est attendance: 200 Teams. For info: Rhinelander Area Chamber of Commerce, PO Box 795, Rhinelander, WI 54501. Phone: (800) 236-4386. Fax: (715) 365-7467.

KINER HITS 50 FOR THE SECOND TIME: ANNIVERSARY. Sept 19, 1949. Ralph Kiner of the Pittsburgh Pirates hit his 50th home run of the season to become the first player in National League history to reach the 50 mark twice. After hitting 51 homers in 1947, Kiner finished the year with 54.

McINNIS, STUFFY: BIRTH ANNIVERSARY. Sept 19, 1890. John Phalen ("Stuffy") McInnis, baseball player born at Gloucester, MA. McInnis played in the major leagues 19 years (1909–27) and set the fielding standard for first basemen. He had a career fielding average of .991 and once went 163 games without committing an error. Died at Ipswich, MA, Feb 16, 1960.

MR TROUT FISHERMAN TOURNAMENT. Sept 19–20. Bennett Springs State Park, Lebanon, MO. 7th annual. Attendees (by invitation only) compete for the coveted Mr Trout trophy presented to the sportsman catching the longest trout. No shavin', no showerin' and lots of guy things. For info on setting up your own Mr Trout competition: PO Box 217, Madison, IL 62060.

OZARK HAM AND TURKEY FESTIVAL. Sept 19. California, MO. Held each year in appreciation of the two largest industries in the county. The festival includes sand volleyball tournament, car races, R/C vehicle races, parade, craft and food booths, BBQ contest, car show, folk art, live entertainment on four stages, twins contest and much more. Annually, the third Saturday in September. Est attendance: 18,000. For info: Ozark Ham & Turkey Festival, PO Box 85, California, MO 65018. Phone: (573) 796-3040. Fax: (573) 796-8309.

SHORT, CHRIS: BIRTH ANNIVERSARY. Sept 19, 1937. Christopher Joseph (Chris) Short, baseball player born at Milford, DE. Short was a lefthanded starting pitcher for the Philadelphia Phillies in the 1960s. He won 20 games in 1966. Died at Wilmington, DE, Aug 1, 1991.

SOUTHWEST IOWA PROFESSIONAL HOT-AIR BALLOON RACES. Sept 19–20. Creston, IA. Hare and hound races held at sunrise and sunset; night glow, art and book fairs, parade and marching band contest, craft show, flea market and much more. Annually, the third weekend in September. Est attendance: 7,000. For info: Chamber of Commerce, Box 471, Creston, IA 50801. Phone: (515) 782-7021. Fax: (515) 782-9927.

300 OAKS RACE. Sept 19. Bankston School campus, Greenwood, MS. 16th year of 10K run, 5K walk, 1-mile fun run. Trophies and medallions given to winners in age groups of five-year increments in 10K and 5K. Pre-race party on Sept 18 and post-race party including food and drink, after which prizes are awarded. This is a Grand Prix event

of the Mississippi Track Club. Outstanding hospitality from the organizers, great race course over flat territory in historic residential area. Annually, the third Saturday in September. Est attendance: 1,000. For info: Janice H. Moor, Exec VP, Greenwood-Leflore County Chamber of Commerce, PO Box 848, Greenwood, MS 38935-0848. Phone: (601) 453-4152. Fax: (601) 453-8003.

BIRTHDAYS TODAY

James Anthony (Jim) Abbott, 31, former baseball player, born Flint, MI, Sept 19, 1967.
Roger Angell, 78, sportswriter, born New York, NY, Sept 19, 1920.
Donald William (Don) Beaupre, 37, hockey player, born Waterloo, Ontario, Canada, Sept 19, 1961.
Gilbert Dionne, 28, hockey player, born Drummondville, Quebec, Canada, Sept 19, 1970.
Jim Druckenmiller, 26, football player, born Allentown, PA, Sept 19, 1972.
Joseph Vance (Joe) Ferguson, 52, former baseball player, born San Francisco, CA, Sept 19, 1946.
Brian Alfred Hill, 51, basketball coach, born East Orange, NJ, Sept 19, 1947.
Katrina McClain, 33, basketball player, born Washington, DC, Sept 19, 1965.
Joe Leonard Morgan, 55, broadcaster and Baseball Hall of Fame second baseman, born Bonham, TX, Sept 19, 1943.
Randall Kirk (Randy) Myers, 36, baseball player, born Vancouver, WA, Sept 19, 1962.
Alfred Adolph (Al) Oerter, Jr, 62, Olympic gold medal discus thrower, born New York, NY, Sept 19, 1936.
Edwin Donald ("Duke") Snider, 72, Baseball Hall of Fame outfielder, born Los Angeles, CA, Sept 19, 1926.

SEPTEMBER 20 — SUNDAY

Day 263 — 102 Remaining

ALEXANDER WINS 300th GAME: ANNIVERSARY. Sept 20, 1924. Pitcher Grover Cleveland Alexander of the Chicago Cubs won the 300th game of his career, defeating the New York Giants, 7–3, in 12 innings. Alexander finished his career with 373 wins.

BILLIE JEAN KING WINS THE "BATTLE OF THE SEXES": 25th ANNIVERSARY. Sept 20, 1973. Billie Jean King defeated Bobby Riggs in the nationally televised "Battle of the Sexes" tennis match in three straight sets.

BONURA, ZEKE: 90th BIRTH ANNIVERSARY. Sept 20, 1908. Henry John ("Zeke") Bonura, baseball player born at New Orleans, LA. Bonura played first base in the 1930s for the Chicago White Sox and three other teams. He was a fine hitter but a famously indifferent fielder. Died at New Orleans, Mar 9, 1987.

DRESSEN, CHARLIE: 100th BIRTH ANNIVERSARY. Sept 20, 1898. Charles Walter (Charlie) Dressen, baseball player and manager born at Decatur, IL. Dressen played infield in the major leagues with several teams, but made his mark as manager of the Brooklyn Dodgers from 1951 through 1953 and three other teams. He was at the Dodgers' helm when they lost the 1951 National League playoff to the New York Giants. Died at Detroit, MI, Aug 10, 1966.

"HEY RUBE GET A TUBE." Sept 20. Ocean Ave and Atlantic Ocean, Pt Pleasant Beach, NJ. A parade featuring zany floats, bands, clowns and more, followed by an Ocean Inner Tube Race. Contestants dash into the ocean and paddle backwards from one beach to another. Annually, the third Sunday in September. Est attendance: 20,000. For info: Lions Club, PO Box 444, Pt Pleasant, NJ 08742. Phone: (908) 899-3306 or (908) 892-5200. Fax: (908) 892-5505.

JERSEY SHORE SEA KAYAK AND BAY CANOEING SHOW. Sept 20. Berkeley Island County Park, Bayville, NJ. Canoe and sea kayak vendors from around the country set up on the beach and share the joys of watersport with the public. Test paddling is allowed all day and there are clinics to teach about canoeing and kayaking. At this show you may sign up for a trip for the following day. There is no fee. Annually, the third Saturday in September. Est attendance: 1,000. For info: Lillian Hoey, Rec Leader, Wells Mills County Park, 905 Wells Mills Rd, Waretown, NJ 08758. Phone: (609) 971-3085. Fax: (609) 971-9540.

MANTLE'S LAST HOMER: 30th ANNIVERSARY. Sept 20, 1968. Mickey Mantle of the New York Yankees hit the final home run of his career against Jim Lonborg of the Boston Red Sox. Mantle finished with 536 homers.

MOON PHASE: NEW MOON. Sept 20. Moon enters New Moon phase at 1:01 PM, EDT.

BIRTHDAYS TODAY

Arnold Jacob ("Red") Auerbach, 81, basketball executive and Basketball Hall of Fame coach, born New York, NY, Sept 20, 1917.
David Thomas (Dave) Gallagher, 38, former baseball player, born Trenton, NJ, Sept 20, 1960.
Donald A. Hall, 70, author (*Fathers Playing Catch with Sons*), born New Haven, CT, Sept 20, 1928.
Guy Damien Lafleur, 47, Hockey Hall of Fame right wing, born Thurso, Quebec, Canada, Sept 20, 1951.
James Charles (Jim) Taylor, 63, Pro Football Hall of Fame fullback, born Baton Rouge, LA, Sept 20, 1935.
Thomas Michael (Tom) Tresh, 61, former baseball player, born Detroit, MI, Sept 20, 1937.

SEPTEMBER 21 — MONDAY
Day 264 — 101 Remaining

CHASE'S SPORTSQUOTE OF THE DAY

"There's got to be more to life than what's going on down there." —Don Meredith, Monday Night Football announcer

BIRTH OF MONDAY NIGHT FOOTBALL: ANNIVERSARY. Sept 21, 1970. Following the complete merger of the American Football League and the National Football League, ABC joined CBS and NBC in televising weekly games with the debut of "Monday Night Football." The show began as an experiment but soon became an institution. Announcers Howard Cosell, Keith Jackson and Don Meredith called the first game, a 31–21 victory by the Cleveland Browns over the New York Jets.

September 1998	S	M	T	W	T	F	S
			1	2	3	4	5
	6	7	8	9	10	11	12
	13	14	15	16	17	18	19
	20	21	22	23	24	25	26
	27	28	29	30			

HULA HOOP DAY©. Sept 21. This day celebrates the famous plastic ring that went on sale for $1.98 in 1958. Within six months 30 million hoops had been sold. For further info send $2 to cover cost of copying and postage to: Adrienne Koopersmith, 1437 W Rosemont, 1W, Chicago, IL 60660-1319. Phone: (773) 743-5341. Fax: (773) 743-5395. Email: kooper@interaccess.com.

LOPEZ, AURELIO: 50th BIRTH ANNIVERSARY. Sept 21, 1948. Aurelio Alejandro Lopez, baseball player born at Tecamachalco, Mexico. Lopez was the star reliever for the 1984 World Series champion Detroit Tigers. He won ten games, picked up 14 saves and won a game in the ALCS and in the Series. Died in an auto accident in central Mexico, Sept 22, 1992.

MICHAEL SPINKS WINS HEAVYWEIGHT TITLE: ANNIVERSARY. Sept 21, 1985. Michael Spinks won the heavyweight championship by taking a unanimous 15-round decision over Larry Holmes in Las Vegas. Spinks held the title until June 27, 1988, when he was knocked out by Mike Tyson in the first round.

RAY, SHORTY: BIRTH ANNIVERSARY. Sept 21, 1884. Hugh L. ("Shorty") Ray, Pro Football Hall of Fame official born at Highland Park, IL. Ray was the NFL Supervisor of Officials from 1938 through 1952. He wrote the high school rule book that became the basis for all football rule books. He raised the quality of officiating by conducting seminars and requiring officials to take written exams. Inducted into the Hall of Fame in 1966. Died Sept 16, 1956.

SMITH, ELMER: BIRTH ANNIVERSARY. Sept 21, 1892. Elmer John Smith, baseball player born at Sandusky, OH. Smith hit the first World Series grand slam while playing for the Cleveland Indians. It came in the first inning of Game five of the 1920 Series off Burleigh Grimes of the Brooklyn Dodgers. Died at Columbia, KY, Aug 3, 1954.

BIRTHDAYS TODAY

Danny Bradford Cox, 39, former baseball player, born Northampton, England, Sept 21, 1959.
Bob Errey, 34, hockey player, born Montreal, Quebec, Canada, Sept 21, 1964.
Cecil Grant Fielder, 35, baseball player, born Los Angeles, CA, Sept 21, 1963.
Artis Gilmore, 49, former basketball player, born Chipley, FL, Sept 21, 1949.
Sidney A. Moncrief, 41, former basketball player, born Little Rock, AR, Sept 21, 1957.
Bill Murray, 48, actor (*Caddy Shack*), amateur golfer, born Evanston, IL, Sept 21, 1950.

SEPTEMBER 22 — TUESDAY
Day 265 — 100 Remaining

ANDERSON, HUNK: 100th BIRTH ANNIVERSARY. Sept 22, 1898. Heartley William ("Hunk") Anderson, football player and coach born at Tamarack, MI. Anderson played at Notre Dame under Knute Rockne and then with the Chicago Bears. In 1926, he became Rockne's fulltime assistant and was named head coach after Rockne was killed in a 1931 plane crash. After three seasons he moved to North Carolina State University and then served as line coach for several college and pro teams. Died at West Palm Beach, FL, Apr 24, 1978.

BOXING'S LONG COUNT: ANNIVERSARY. Sept 22, 1927. In a heavyweight title fight between champion Gene Tunney and former champ Jack Dempsey, Tunney was knocked down in the 7th round. Following the rules, referee Dave Barry refused to begin the count until Dempsey moved to a neutral corner. The extra few seconds allowed Tunney to recover and get up at the count of nine. He won the fight and retained the title. The fight, held at Soldier Field in Chicago, grossed $990,446, the largest fight purse to that time. Nearly half the population of the US is believed to have listened to the radio broadcast. Dempsey's appeal of the decision was denied, and he never fought again. Tunney retired the following year after one more (successful) fight.

DAUSS, HOOKS: BIRTH ANNIVERSARY. Sept 22, 1889. George August ("Hooks") Dauss, baseball player born at Indianapolis, IN. Dauss spent his entire 15-year career with the Detroit Tigers, winning 221 games. He got his nickname because of his tantalizing curve ball. Died at St. Louis, MO, July 27, 1963.

TOVAR PLAYS ALL NINE POSITIONS: 30th ANNIVERSARY. Sept 22, 1968. Cesar Tovar of the Minnesota Twins played all nine positions in a single game, one inning at each position. Tovar became the second player to perform this feat. Bert Campaneris did it on Sept 8, 1965.

YOUNG'S FINAL WIN: ANNIVERSARY. Sept 22, 1911. Cy Young won the 511th and last game of his career, a 1–0 shutout against the Pittsburgh Pirates.

BIRTHDAYS TODAY

Kenneth Joseph (Ken) Aspromonte, 67, former baseball manager and player, born New York, NY, Sept 22, 1931.
Walter Wayne (Wally) Backman, 39, former baseball player, born Hillsboro, OR, Sept 22, 1959.
Douglas Joseph (Doug) Camilli, 62, former baseball player, born Philadelphia, PA, Sept 22, 1936.
Vincent Maurice (Vince) Coleman, 37, former baseball player, born Jacksonville, FL, Sept 22, 1961.
Lawrence Edward (Larry) Dierker, 52, baseball manager, former broadcaster and player, born Hollywood, CA, Sept 22, 1946.
Pat Falloon, 26, hockey player, born Foxwarren, Manitoba, Canada, Sept 22, 1972.
Thomas Charles (Tommy) Lasorda, 71, Baseball Hall of Fame manager and former player, born Norristown, PA, Sept 22, 1927.
Robert Granville (Bob) Lemon, 78, former baseball manager and Baseball Hall of Fame pitcher, born San Bernardino, CA, Sept 22, 1920.
Jeffrey N. Leonard, 43, former baseball player, born Philadelphia, PA, Sept 22, 1955.
Michael Thomas (Mike) Richter, 32, hockey player, born Philadelphia, PA, Sept 22, 1966.

SEPTEMBER 23 — WEDNESDAY
Day 266 — 99 Remaining

ALOU TRIFECTA: ANNIVERSARY. Sept 23, 1996. Montreal Expos outfielder Moises Alou flied out to right field against the Atlanta Braves to make the final out in the final regular season game ever played at Atlanta-Fulton County Stadium. The Braves won, 3–1. Alou's out completed an unusual family coincidence. In the first game played at the same park on Apr 12, 1966, Moises's uncle, Matty Alou, was the first batter for the visiting Pittsburgh Pirates. His father, Felipe Alou, was the Braves's first batter. Pittsburgh won that game, 3–2, in 13 innings.

BASEBALL'S GREATEST DISPUTE: 90th ANNIVERSARY. Sept 23, 1908. In an important game between the Chicago Cubs and the New York Giants, the National League pennant race erupted in controversy during the bottom of the ninth with the score tied, 1–1, at the Polo Grounds, New York, NY. New York was at bat with two men on. The batter hit safely to center field, apparently scoring the winning run. But Chicago claimed that the

runner on first, Fred Merkle, seeing the run score, headed toward the clubhouse without touching second base. Chicago second baseman Johnny Evers attempted to get the ball and force Merkle at second, but he was prevented from doing so by the fans streaming onto the field. Harry C. Pulliam, NL president, upheld Evers's position and called the game a tie. When the game was replayed, the Cubs won 4–2. Fairly or not, the disputed play quickly became known as "Merkle's Boner."

CANSECO REACHES 40-40 CLUB: ANNIVERSARY. Sept 23, 1988. Jose Canseco of the Oakland A's became the first player ever to hit 40 home runs and steal 40 bases in the same season. In a game against the Milwaukee Brewers, he hit his 41st homer of the season and stole two bases, Nos. 39 and 40. The A's won, 9–8, in 14 innings.

FIRST FRONTIER DAYS: ANNIVERSARY. Sept 23, 1897. The city of Cheyenne, WY, held its first Frontier Days celebration, a one-day rodeo featuring a competition roping horses that had never been roped before. Frontier Days has grown to be the largest rodeo in the world.

QUICKEST BOXING MATCH: ANNIVERSARY. Sept 23, 1946. Al Couture recorded the quickest knockout in boxing history, flooring Ralph Walton with only half a second gone in the first round. Couture threw the knockout punch while Walton was still sitting in his corner adjusting his mouthpiece.

RHEAUME FIRST FEMALE IN NHL: ANNIVERSARY. Sept 23, 1992. 20-year-old Manon Rheaume became the first woman to play in an NHL game when the Tampa Bay Lightning took on the St. Louis Blues in an exhibition. Rheaume led the Lightning onto the ice, made seven saves in one period of action and left with the game tied, 2–2.

RIVER CITY ROUNDUP AND RODEO. Sept 23–28. Omaha, NE. Take a moment to reflect on the Midwest's proud past. A celebration of Omaha's agricultural and western heritage, including PRCA rodeo, hot-air balloon races, barbecue and chili contests, trail rides, the world's largest 4-H Livestock Expo and a down-town parade. Est attendance: 300,000. For info: Sherman Berg, Exec Dir, River City Roundup and Rodeo, 6800 Mercy Rd, Ste 206, Omaha, NE 68106. Phone: (402) 554-9610. Fax: (402) 554-9609. Email: knights@adnet.net.

TRIPLE PICKOFF: ANNIVERSARY. Sept 23, 1886. Pittsburgh pitcher Pud Galvin walked the bases loaded in a game against Brooklyn. He then picked George Smith off first, Bill McClellan off second and Jim McTamany off third.

BIRTHDAYS TODAY

Donald Audette, 29, hockey player, born Laval, Quebec, Canada, Sept 23, 1969.
Emilion Antonio (Tony) Fossas, 41, baseball player, born Havana, Cuba, Sept 23, 1957.
Peter Thomas (Pete) Harnisch, 32, baseball player, born Commack, NY, Sept 23, 1966.
Tony Joseph Mandarich (born Ante Josip Mandarich), 32, football player, born Oakville, Ontario, Canada, Sept 23, 1966.
Larry Hogan Mize, 40, golfer, born Augusta, GA, Sept 23, 1958.
Eric Scott Montross, 27, basketball player, born Indianapolis, IN, Sept 23, 1971.
Martin Edward (Marty) Schottenheimer, 55, football coach and former player, born Canonsburg, PA, Sept 23, 1943.

SEPTEMBER 24 — THURSDAY
Day 267 — 98 Remaining

ARMOUR, TOMMY: BIRTH ANNIVERSARY. Sept 24, 1895. Thomas Dickson (Tommy) Armour, golfer born at Edinburgh, Scotland. Blinded in one eye during World War I, Armour nevertheless became one of the great golfers of the 1920s. He won every important tournament and, after retiring, became a prominent teaching pro. He worked on the games of the likes of Bobby Jones and Babe Didrikson Zaharias. Died at Larchmont, NY, Sept 11, 1968.

BABE RUTH'S FAREWELL TO THE YANKEES: ANNIVERSARY. Sept 24, 1934. On this date Babe Ruth played his last game with the New York Yankees at Yankee Stadium.

FOXX HITS 500th HOME RUN: ANNIVERSARY. Sept 24, 1940. Jimmie Foxx of the Boston Red Sox hit the 500th home run of his career against pitcher George Caster of the Philadelphia Athletics, Foxx's former team. Ted Williams hit three homers in the same game, the first half of a doubleheader. Foxx played in the majors from 1925 through 1945 and hit a total of 534 homers.

KALINE GETS 3,000th HIT: ANNIVERSARY. Sept 24, 1974. Al Kaline of the Detroit Tigers doubled off Dave McNally of the Baltimore Orioles in the fourth inning of a 5–4 Orioles win. The hit was the 3,000th of Kaline's career which began in 1953 and ended in 1974.

NATIONAL MINIATURE GOLF CHAMPIONSHIP. Sept 24–27. Hawaiian Rumble miniature golf complex, Myrtle Beach, SC. Miniature golf players from around the world compete in four age groups: grade school, high school and college, adults, and seniors (50 and up) for the best in each division. National championship is televised on ESPN. Est attendance: 1,000. For info: Skip Laun, Exec Dir, Miniature Golf Assn of Amer, PO Box 32353, Jacksonville, FL 32237. Phone: (904) 781-4653 or (800) 688-1685. Fax: (904) 781-4843.

September	S	M	T	W	T	F	S
1998			1	2	3	4	5
	6	7	8	9	10	11	12
	13	14	15	16	17	18	19
	20	21	22	23	24	25	26
	27	28	29	30			

WORLD HOCKEY ASSOCIATION FORMED: ANNIVERSARY. Sept 24, 1971. The World Hockey Association announced its formation with 12 teams scheduled to begin play in 1972. The WHA lasted seven seasons after which four surviving teams entered the National Hockey League.

BIRTHDAYS TODAY

Hubert (Hubie) Brooks, Jr, 42, former baseball player, born Los Angeles, CA, Sept 24, 1956.
Otis Bernard Gilkey, 32, baseball player, born St. Louis, MO, Sept 24, 1966.
Charles Edward ("Mean Joe") Greene, 52, Pro Football Hall of Fame defensive tackle, born Temple, TX, Sept 24, 1946.
John Mackey, 57, Pro Football Hall of Fame tight end, born New York, NY, Sept 24, 1941.
James Kenneth (Jim) McKay (born James Kenneth McManus), 77, broadcaster, born at Philadelphia, PA, Sept 24, 1921.
Rafael Palmeiro, 34, baseball player, born Havana, Cuba, Sept 24, 1964.

SEPTEMBER 25 — FRIDAY
Day 268 — 97 Remaining

SPORTSCHASER OF THE DAY
How old was Satchel Paige estimated to be when he pitched in his last major league game?

BULLNANZA–RENO. Sept 25–26. Reno Livestock Events Ctr, Reno, NV. The Lazy E takes its most popular event on the road to Reno. It's nothin' but bull ridin'! Est attendance: 15,000. For info: Lazy E Arena, Rte 5, Box 393, Guthrie, OK 73044. Phone: (405) 282-7433 or (800) 595-RIDE(7433). Fax: (405) 282-3785. Email: learena@ionet.net.

FLATLANDERS FALL CLASSIC; FLATLANDERS FALL FESTIVAL; NORTHWEST KANSAS BIKE CLUB MOTORCYCLE SHOW; EARLY IRON CAR CLUB ROD RUN. Sept 25–27. Goodland, KS. Classic on Friday and Saturday features mini-sprint stock car races; Fall Festival on Saturday on Main Street is a street festival featuring crafts, food, entertainment; also on Saturday, the Motorcycle Show features Harleys, Hondas, Kawasakis, all brands, all accessories; Saturday and Sunday, the Early Iron Car Club Rod Run on Highways 24 and 27. Est attendance: 5,000. For other info: Goodland Chamber of Commerce, 104 W 11th, Goodland, KS 67735. Phone: (913) 899-7130. Fax: (913) 899-3061.

GLADSTONE DRIVING EVENT. Sept 25–28. Hamilton Farm, Gladstone, NJ. Equestrian combined driving competition in singles, pairs and four-in-hands. For info: Gladstone Equestrian Assn, PO Box 119, Gladstone, NJ 07934. Phone: (908) 234-0515.

JORDAN, SHUG: BIRTH ANNIVERSARY. Sept 25, 1910. James Ralph ("Shug") Jordan, football coach born at Selma, AL. Jordan played several sports at Auburn (then Alabama Polytechnic Institute) and after graduation became an assistant football coach and head basketball coach. He served in the army during World War II and then coached briefly at the University of Georgia. He returned to Auburn as football coach in 1951, won the national championship in 1957 and retired after the 1975 season with a record of 175–83–7. The football stadium at Auburn is named Jordan-Hare Stadium. Died at Auburn, July 17, 1980.

LISTON WINS HEAVYWEIGHT TITLE: ANNIVERSARY. Sept 25, 1962. Charles ("Sonny") Liston won the heavyweight championship by knocking out Floyd Patterson at 2:06 of the first round at Comiskey Park, Chicago. Liston defeated Patterson in a rematch and then lost to Cassius Clay in Feb, 1964.

MAJOR LEAGUE BASEBALL'S FIRST DOUBLEHEADER: ANNIVERSARY. Sept 25, 1882. On this date the first major league baseball doubleheader was played between the Providence and Worcester teams.

SATCHEL PAIGE'S LAST GAME: ANNIVERSARY. Sept 25, 1965. Satchel Paige, the oldest player in major league history at an estimated 59 years, 8 months, 5 days, pitched the last game of his career. He hurled three scoreless innings for the Kansas City Athletics against the Boston Red Sox. Paige gave up only one hit to Carl Yastrzemski.

SMITH, RED: BIRTH ANNIVERSARY. Sept 25, 1905. Walter Wellesley ("Red") Smith, sportswriter born at Green Bay, WI. Following the death of Grantland Rice in 1954, Smith became the most widely syndicated sports columnist in the country. He wrote for the *New York Herald Tribune* and later the *New York Times* and won the Pulitzer Prize in 1976. Smith shunned cliches and overblown prose and was generally considered one of the most literate sportswriters. Died at Stamford, CT, Jan 15, 1982.

BIRTHDAYS TODAY

Stephen Ralph (Steve) Arlin, 53, former baseball player, born Seattle, WA, Sept 25, 1945.

Glenn Dee Hubbard, 41, former baseball player, born Hahn, West Germany, Sept 25, 1957.

Eugene James (Geno) Petralli, 39, former baseball player, born Sacramento, CA, Sept 25, 1959.

Scottie Pippen, 33, basketball player, born Hamburg, AR, Sept 25, 1965.

Philip Francis (Phil) Rizzuto (born Fiero Francis Rizzuto), 81, broadcaster and Baseball Hall of Fame shortstop, born New York, NY, Sept 25, 1917.

John Franklin (Johnny) Sain, 81, former baseball player, born Havana, AR, Sept 25, 1917.

SEPTEMBER 26 — SATURDAY

Day 269 — 96 Remaining

BASKETBALL HALL OF FAME AWARDS DINNER. Sept 26. Springfield Marriott, Springfield, MA. National awards dinner hosted by the Basketball Hall of Fame. Annually, the Saturday before Hall of Fame enshrinement. Est attendance: 500. For info: Robin Jonathan Deutsch, Dir Mktg/PR, Basketball Hall of Fame, 1150 W Columbus Ave, Box 179, Springfield, MA 01101-0179. Phone: (413) 781-6500.

BIG EAST GOLF CHAMPIONSHIP. Sept 26–27. TPC Avenel, Potomac, MD. For info: Big East Conference, 56 Exchange Terrace, Providence, RI 02903. Phone: (401) 453-0660. Fax: (401) 751-8540.

BRIGGS AND STRATTON/AL'S RUN AND WALK FOR CHILDREN'S HOSPITAL OF WISCONSIN. Sept 26. Milwaukee, WI. Choose from an 8K run, 4.4-mile walk or two-mile walk along the lake and through the streets. Benefit fundraiser named after Al McGuire, network basketball announcer. Finish line party on Summerfest grounds with free entertainment and fitness expo. Est attendance: 20,000. For info: Children's Hospital Foundation, Briggs & Stratton/Al's Run & Walk, PO Box 1997 MS#3060, Milwaukee, WI 53201. Fax: (414) 266-6139. Email: alsrun@execpc.com. WWW: http://www.alsrun.execpc.com

BUFFALO ROUND-UP BICYCLE RALLY. Sept 26–27. Custer State Park, Custer, SD. Bicycle races. For info: Custer Co Chamber of Commerce, 615 Washington St, Custer, SD 57730. Phone: (605) 673-2244.

CALIFORNIA FREE-FISHING DAY. Sept 26. (Also June 6.) As proclaimed by the governor, fishing is free today in all California public waters. Observed in conjunction with National Hunting and Fishing Day (see below). For info: License and Revenue Branch, Dept of Fish and Game, 3211 S St, Sacramento, CA 93816. Phone: (916) 227-2244.

FRANCE, BILL: BIRTH ANNIVERSARY. Sept 26, 1909. William Henry Getty (Bill) France, Sr, stock car racing executive born at Washington, DC. While running a service station in Daytona Beach, FL, France took an interest in the auto races contested on the beach. He got involved in race promotion and organization and founded NASCAR in 1948. He remained at the helm long enough to see the once-primitive sport evolve into a series of fantastic spectator events. Died at Ormond Beach, FL, June 7, 1992.

GREAT RIVER GRAND PRIX. Sept 26–27 (tentative). Quincy, IL. Professional Go-Karters come from everywhere. Est attendance: 5,000. For info: Professional Karting Assn, PO Box 716, Quincy, IL 62306-0716. Phone: (217) 228-0925.

MARIS TIES RUTH: ANNIVERSARY. Sept 26, 1961. Roger Maris hit his 60th home run of the season to tie Babe Ruth's record. Maris's homer came off pitcher Jack Fisher of the Baltimore Orioles in the Yankees' 159th game.

★ **NATIONAL HUNTING AND FISHING DAY.** Sept 26. Presidential Proclamation 4682, of Sept 11, 1979, covers all succeeding years. Annually, the fourth Saturday of September.

OLD-TIME BARNEGAT BAY DECOY AND GUNNING SHOW. Sept 27–28. Pinelands High & Middle Schools and Tip Seaman County Park, Tuckerton, NJ. Gathering to celebrate the local waterfowling heritage. Emphasizes traditional skills such as decoy carving, working decoy rigs, sneakbox building, gunning, retrieving and goose calling contests. More than 500 vendors. Est attendance: 40,000. For info: Michael T. Mangum, Chief Naturalist, Wells Mills County Park, 905 Wells Mills Rd, Waretown, NJ 08758. Phone: (609) 971-3085. Fax: (609) 971-9540.

RYAN PITCHES FIFTH NO-HITTER: ANNIVERSARY. Sept 26, 1981. Nolan Ryan of the Houston Astros became the first pitcher to throw five career no-hitters. He blanked the Los Angeles Dodgers, 5–0, at the Astrodome. Ryan ended his career with seven no-hitters.

STEWART, BILL: BIRTH ANNIVERSARY. Sept 26, 1894. William J. (Bill) Stewart, hockey coach and referee and baseball umpire born at Fitchburg, MA. Stewart was an NHL referee from 1928 to 1941 except for a short period when he coached the Chicago Black Hawks. In that position for the 1937–38 season and part of the 1938–39 season, he became the first American to coach a team to the Stanley Cup. He also served as a National League umpire from 1933 to 1954. Died at Boston, MA, Feb 14, 1964.

TUNNEY WINS HEAVYWEIGHT TITLE: ANNIVERSARY. Sept 26, 1926. Gene Tunney won the heavyweight championship by taking a unanimous 15-round decision from Jack Dempsey, the champion since 1919. Tunney defeated Dempsey in a rematch, won one more fight and then retired.

BIRTHDAYS TODAY

Steven Bernard (Steve) Buechele, 37, former baseball player, born Lancaster, CA, Sept 26, 1961.
David Edwin (Dave) Duncan, 53, former baseball player, born Dallas, TX, Sept 26, 1945.
Craig William ("Ironhead") Heyward, 32, football player, born Passaic, NJ, Sept 26, 1966.
Craig Harlan Janney, 31, hockey player, born Hartford, CT, Sept 26, 1967.
David (Dave) Martinez, 34, baseball player, born New York, NY, Sept 26, 1964.

SEPTEMBER 27 — SUNDAY
Day 270 — 95 Remaining

ALSTON'S ONLY GAME: ANNIVERSARY. Sept 27, 1936. Walter Alston played in the only major league game of his career as a member of the St. Louis Cardinals. He entered the game as a substitute for first baseman Johnny Mize, made one error in two chances and struck out in his only plate appearance. Alston was inducted into the Hall of Fame in 1983, but as a manager, not a player.

BANKOH NA WAHINE O KE KAI. Sept 27. Molokai to Oahu, HI. Women's 40.8-mile, six-person championship outrigger canoe race. More than 65 teams of the best female outrigger canoe paddlers in the world compete for the championship title. Competitors come from Australia, New Zealand, mainland US, Canada, Tahiti and other countries. Traditionally, the Aloha Festivals Court is waiting to formally welcome the finishers when they arrive on the beach. Est attendance: 3,000. For media info: Carol Hogan, Ocean Promotion, (808) 325-7400 or Linda Chinn, Bank of Hawaii, (808) 537-8658. For race info: Hannie Anderson, (808) 262-7567. WWW: http://www.holoholo.org/canunews/index.html

	S	M	T	W	T	F	S
September			1	2	3	4	5
1998	6	7	8	9	10	11	12
	13	14	15	16	17	18	19
	20	21	22	23	24	25	26
	27	28	29	30			

BONDS JOINS 40–40 CLUB: ANNIVERSARY. Sept 27, 1996. Barry Bonds of the San Francisco Giants stole his 40th base of the year in a game against the Colorado Rockies to become only the second player in major league history to hit 40 home runs and steal 40 bases in the same season. Jose Canseco, the original member of the 40–40 club, achieved the feat in 1988. Bonds finished the year with 42 home runs and 40 steals.

FAMILY HEALTH AND FITNESS DAY—USA. Sept 27. 2nd annual event promoting the value of health and fitness for families. During this day families across the country will be involved in locally organized health promotion activities. For info: Pat Henze, Exec Dir, Health Information Resource Center, 621 E Park Ave, Libertyville, IL 60048. Phone: (800) 828-8225. Fax: (847) 816-8662. Email: hlthinfo@aol.com. WWW: http://www.fitnessday.com

FIRST $100G WINNER-TAKE-ALL RACE: ANNIVERSARY. Sept 27, 1947. Belmont Park hosted the first $100,000 winner-take-all thoroughbred race between Armed, then the leading money winner, and Assault, the 1946 Triple Crown winner. Armed won an easy victory.

GEHRIG'S FIRST AND LAST HOME RUNS: 65th ANNIVERSARY. Sept 27, 1923. Lou Gehrig of the New York Yankees hit the first home run of his career against pitcher Bill Piercy of the Boston Red Sox. On the same date fifteen years later, he hit his 493rd and last home run against Dutch Leonard of the Washington Senators.

NEW YORK GOLDEN ARMS TOURNAMENT–BROOKLYN. Sept 27. Atlantic Antic Festival, Atlantic Ave, Brooklyn, NY. Arm wrestling competition held at the festival detemines borough winner who will compete in the Empire State Golden Arms Tournament of Champions on Oct 22. Est attendance: 500,000. For info: New York Arm Wrestling Assn, Inc, 200-14 45th Dr, Bayside, NY 11361. Phone and Fax: (718) 544-4592.

WILSON HITS 56th HOME RUN: ANNIVERSARY. Sept 27, 1930. Hack Wilson of the Chicago Cubs hit two home runs, giving him 56 for the year. No one in the National League has ever hit more.

BIRTHDAYS TODAY

Richard Wallace (Dick) Hall, 68, former baseball player, born St. Louis, MO, Sept 27, 1930.
Stephen Douglas (Steve) Kerr, 33, basketball player, born Beirut, Lebanon, Sept 27, 1965.
Leonard James (Len) Matuszek, 44, former baseball player, born Toledo, OH, Sept 27, 1954.
John Michael (Johnny) Pesky (born John Michael Paveskovich), 79, former baseball manager and player, born Portland, OR, Sept 27, 1919.
Michael Jack (Mike) Schmidt, 49, Baseball Hall of Fame third baseman, born Dayton, OH, Sept 27, 1949.
Kathrynne Ann (Kathy) Whitworth, 59, LPGA Hall of Fame golfer, born Monahans, TX, Sept 27, 1939.

SEPTEMBER 28 — MONDAY
Day 271 — 94 Remaining

CHASE'S SPORTSQUOTE OF THE DAY

"The biggest problem today is that the Olympic Games have become so important that political people want to take control of them. Our only salvation is to keep free from politics." —Avery Brundage, 1964

BASKETBALL HALL OF FAME ENSHRINEMENT CEREMONIES. Sept 28. Springfield, MA. The Class of '98, announced in February, is inducted into the Naismith Memorial Basketball Hall of Fame. Est attendance: 1,500.

For info: Robin Jonathan Deutsch, Dir Mktg/PR, Basketball Hall of Fame, 1150 W Columbus Ave, PO Box 179, Springfield, MA 01101-0179. Phone: (413) 781-6500.

BLACK SOX INDICTED: ANNIVERSARY. Sept 28, 1920. Eight members of the 1919 Chicago White Sox were indicted by a grand jury in Chicago on charges that they conspired to fix the 1919 World Series and allowed the Cincinnati Reds to win. The eight players were Eddie Cicotte, Oscar ("Hap") Felsch, Charles ("Chick") Gandil, ("Shoeless") Joe Jackson, Fred McMullin, Charles ("Swede") Risberg, George ("Buck") Weaver and Claude ("Lefty") Williams. White Sox owner Charles Comiskey immediately suspended the eight. They were acquitted but were nevertheless banned from baseball for life.

BRUNDAGE, AVERY: BIRTH ANNIVERSARY. Sept 28, 1887. Avery Brundage, sports administrator born at Detroit, MI. Brundage was a track and field athlete in high school and at the University of Illinois. He made a fortune in the construction of buildings in Chicago and dedicated his life to the administration of amateur sports. He was elected to the International Olympic Committee in 1936 and served as president from 1952 to 1972. It was his controversial decision to continue the 1972 Munich Summer Games after the murder of 11 Israeli athletes by Palestinian terrorists. Died at Garmisch-Partenkirchen, West Germany, May 5, 1975.

FIRST NIGHT FOOTBALL GAME: ANNIVERSARY. Sept 28, 1892. The first night football game in America was played between Mansfield State Normal School (now Mansfield University) and Wyoming Seminary.

HARMON, TOM: BIRTH ANNIVERSARY. Sept 28, 1919. Thomas D. (Tom) Harmon, football player and sportscaster born at Gary, IN. Harmon became a national figure by his exploits in the backfield for the University of Michigan. Known as "Old 98," his uniform number, he won many awards, including the 1940 Heisman Trophy. After service in World War II, during which he bailed out twice from destroyed planes, Harmon played two years with the Los Angeles Rams. After retiring, he worked as a sportscaster. Died at Los Angeles, CA, Mar 15, 1990.

"HOMER IN THE GLOAMIN'": 60th ANNIVERSARY. Sept 28, 1938. Chicago Cubs catcher Gabby Hartnett hit his famous ninth-inning "homer in the gloamin" to give the Cubs a 6–5 victory over the Pittsburgh Pirates. The win was the ninth in a row for the Cubs and a key triumph on their way to the National League pennant.

MOON PHASE: FIRST QUARTER. Sept 28. Moon enters First Quarter phase at 5:11 PM, EDT.

SHORTEST GAME IN HISTORY: ANNIVERSARY. Sept 28, 1919. The shortest game in major league history saw the New York Giants defeat the Philadelphia Phillies, 6–1, in only 51 minutes. The game was the first half of a doubleheader.

TED WILLIAMS FINISHES AT .406: ANNIVERSARY. Sept 28, 1941. Ted Williams of the Boston Red Sox, starting the day with a batting average of .3995, went six-for-eight in a doubleheader against the Philadelphia Athletics to finish the season with a batting average of .406. Williams rejected manager Joe Cronin's suggestion to sit out the day and have his average rounded up to .400. He went four-for-five in the first game to raise his average to .404 and got two hits in three at-bats in the nightcap.

BIRTHDAYS TODAY

Johnny Earl Dawkins, Jr, 35, basketball player, born Washington, DC, Sept 28, 1963.

Grant Fuhr, 36, hockey player, born Spruce Grove, Alberta, Canada, Sept 28, 1962.

Grant Dwight Jackson, 56, former baseball player, born Fostoria, OH, Sept 28, 1942.

Stephen Neil (Steve) Kasper, 37, former hockey coach and player, born Montreal, Quebec, Canada, Sept 28, 1961.

Steve M. Largent, 44, Pro Football Hall of Fame wide receiver, born at Tulsa, OK, Sept 28, 1954.

Charles Robert (Charley) Taylor, 57, Pro Football Hall of Fame wide receiver, born Grand Prairie, TX, Sept 28, 1941.

Todd Roland Worrell, 39, baseball player, born Arcadia, CA, Sept 28, 1959.

SEPTEMBER 29 — TUESDAY
Day 272 — 93 Remaining

ASTROS RETIRE RYAN'S NUMBER: ANNIVERSARY. Sept 29, 1996. The Houston Astros retired uniform number 34 in honor of their former pitcher, Nolan Ryan, who played for Houston for nine seasons, (1980–88). The ceremony made Ryan the only player to have his number retired by three teams, the California Angels and the Texas Rangers having previously accorded him the honor.

DIVISION SERIES BEGIN. Sept 29 (tentative). Sites TBA. Major league baseball opens postseason play with the start of four Division Series. The National League and the American League each qualify four teams for the playoffs, the winners of the East, Central and West Divisions and the wild-card, the second-place team with the best record. The Division Series match these four teams in a best three-of-five format with the winners moving on to the League Championship Series.

PACIOREK GOES 3-FOR-3: 35th ANNIVERSARY. Sept 29, 1963. John Paciorek of the Houston Colt .45s played the only major league game of his career and got three hits in three times at bat with two walks, three RBIs and four runs scored. A back injury prevented his playing ever again. He is the only player to finish his career with a 1.000 batting average and as many as three hits.

PATTON, JIMMY: 65th BIRTH ANNIVERSARY. Sept 29, 1933. James Russel Patton, Jr, football player born at Greenville, MS. Despite his slight stature (5'11", 175 pounds), Patton played quarterback in high school, offensive and defensive halfback at the University of Mississippi and safety for the New York Giants. In his eight pro seasons, the Giants reached the NFL title game six times, and he made five Pro Bowls. Died in an automobile accident at Villa Rica, GA, Dec 26, 1972.

STAN MUSIAL'S LAST GAME: 35th ANNIVERSARY. Sept 29, 1963. Stan Musial played the last game of his career, going 2-for-3 as the St. Louis Cardinals defeated the Cincinnati Reds, 3–2.

TOLAN, EDDIE: 90th BIRTH ANNIVERSARY. Sept 29, 1908. Thomas Edward (Eddie) Tolan, Olympic gold medal sprinter born at Denver, CO. Tolan was the first black American athlete to win two gold medals, triumphing in the 100 meters and the 200 meters at the 1932 Olympics in Los Angeles. At his death, he still held the Michigan high school record of 9.8 seconds in the 100-yard dash. Died at Detroit, MI, Jan 31, 1967.

WILLIE MAKES "THE CATCH": ANNIVERSARY. Sept 29, 1954. Willie Mays made a fabulous over-the-shoulder catch that many regard as the most famous in baseball history. It came in the first game of the World Series as the New York Giants were playing the Cleveland Indians. Vic Wertz of the Indians hit a long drive to deep center field in the Polo Grounds. Mays turned on the ball, caught it running full stride about 475 feet from home plate, wheeled and threw. The Giants won the game, 3–0, in 10 innings on Dusty Rhodes's pinch-hit home run and swept the Indians in the Series.

☆　　☆　　☆

BIRTHDAYS TODAY

David (Dave) Andreychuk, 35, hockey player, born Hamilton, Ontario, Canada, Sept 29, 1963.

Orvon Gene Autry, 91, baseball executive, born Tioga, TX, Sept 29, 1907.

Steven Lee (Steve) Busby, 49, former baseball player, born Burbank, CA, Sept 29, 1949.

Butler By'not'e, III, 26, football player, born St. Louis, MO, Sept 29, 1972.

Warren Livingston Cromartie, 45, former baseball player, born Miami Beach, FL, Sept 29, 1953.

Bryant Gumbel, 50, broadcaster, born New Orleans, LA, Sept 29, 1948.

Hersey R. Hawkins, Jr, 32, basketball player, born Chicago, IL, Sept 29, 1966.

Brad Allen Lohaus, 34, basketball player, born New Ulm, MN, Sept 29, 1964.

Kenneth Howard (Ken) Norton, Jr, 32, football player, born Jacksonville, IL, Sept 29, 1966.

John MacBeth Paxson, 38, former basketball player, born Dayton, OH, Sept 29, 1960.

SEPTEMBER 30 — WEDNESDAY

Day 273 — 92 Remaining

BABE SETS HOME RUN RECORD: ANNIVERSARY. Sept 30, 1927. George Herman ("Babe") Ruth hit his 60th home run of the season off Tom Zachary of the Washington Senators. Ruth's record for the most homers in a single season stood for 34 years, until Roger Maris hit 61 in 1961.

BABE'S LAST GAME AS YANKEE: ANNIVERSARY. Sept 30, 1934. On this date Babe played his last game for the New York Yankees. Soon after, while watching the fifth game of the World Series (between the St. Louis Cardinals and Detroit Tigers) and angry that he was not to be named Yankees manager, Ruth told Joe Williams, sports editor of the Scripp-Howard newspapers, that after 15 seasons he would no longer be playing for the Yankees.

CLEMENTE'S LAST HIT: ANNIVERSARY. Sept 30, 1972. Roberto Clemente of the Pittsburgh Pirates doubled against New York Mets pitcher Jon Matlack as the Pirates defeated the Mets, 5–0. It was Clemente's 3,000th career hit and his last one as he was killed in a plane crash on Dec 31 delivering relief supplies to earthquake victims in Nicaragua.

FIRST TELEVISED WORLD SERIES: ANNIVERSARY. Sept 30, 1947. The first World Series to be televised opened with the New York Yankees beating the Brooklyn Dodgers, 5–3. The Yankees won the Series, four games to three.

HERSHISER'S SCORELESS STREAK: ANNIVERSARY. Sept 30, 1988. Pitcher Orel Hershiser of the Los Angeles Dodgers extended his streak of consecutive scoreless innings to 59, thereby breaking Don Drysdale's mark by one inning. Hershiser shut out the San Diego Padres for 10 innings, but the Padres won the game, 2–1, in 16 innings.

OUIMET WINS OPEN: 85th ANNIVERSARY. Sept 30, 1913. 20-year-old amateur Francis Ouimet shocked the golf world by winning the US Open, contested at The Country Club in Brookline, MA. Ouimet defeated seasoned professionals Harry Vardon and Ted Ray in a play-off, shooting 72 to Vardon's 77 and Ray's 78.

RUCKER, NAP: BIRTH ANNIVERSARY. Sept 30, 1894. George Napoleon (Nap) Rucker, baseball player born at Crabtree, GA. Rucker pitched for Brooklyn for a decade, 1907–16. His career record, 134–134, does not reflect his ability owing to the poor teams that surrounded him. Died at Alpharetta, GA, Dec 19, 1970.

BIRTHDAYS TODAY

Martina Hingis, 18, tennis player, born Kosice, Slovakia, Sept 30, 1980.

Scott Edward Lusader, 34, former baseball player, born Chicago, IL, Sept 30, 1964.

David Joseph (Dave) Magadan, 36, baseball player, born Tampa, FL, Sept 30, 1962.

John Joseph (Johnny) Podres, 66, former baseball player, born Witherbee, NY, Sept 30, 1932.

Robin Evan Roberts, 72, Baseball Hall of Fame pitcher, born Springfield, IL, Sept 30, 1926.

OCTOBER 1 — THURSDAY
Day 274 — 91 Remaining

BABE CALLS HIS SHOT: ANNIVERSARY. Oct 1, 1932. In the fifth inning of Game 3 of the World Series, with a count of two balls and two strikes and with hostile Cubs fans shouting epithets at him, Babe Ruth gestured and then hit a home run. The Yankees won the game and went on to sweep the Series. For more than half a century, baseball fans have debated whether Ruth pointed toward the bleachers and then, in effect, called his shot. Even eyewitnesses disagreed. Joe Williams of *The New York Times* wrote, "In no mistaken motions, the Babe notified the crowd that the nature of his retaliation would be a wallop right out of the confines of the park." But Cubs pitcher Charlie Root said, "Ruth did *not* point at the fence before he swung. If he'd made a gesture like that, I'd have put one in his ear and knocked him on his ass." Ruth's daughter has said that he denied it. But the Babe himself also claimed he had. Fact or folklore? Either way, legend!

BABE'S LAST PITCHING: ANNIVERSARY. Oct 1, 1933. Babe Ruth had pitched only once in 12 years when he took the mound for the New York Yankees in their final game of the season. Ruth hurled all nine innings, hit a home run in the fifth and beat his original team, the Boston Red Sox, 6–5. It was a fitting finish to his 20th season in the majors: because this turned out to be his last pitching appearance, his 1–0 record in 1933 meant that Ruth never had a losing season as a pitcher.

BROWNS WIN ONLY PENNANT: ANNIVERSARY. Oct 1, 1944. Emil ("Dutch") Leonard defeated the Detroit Tigers, 4–1, to pitch the St. Louis Browns to the only American League pennant in their history. The Browns went on to lose the World Series to the St. Louis Cardinals, four games to two.

BUICK CHALLENGE. Oct 1–4. Callaway Gardens Resort, Pine Mountain, GA. A PGA Tour tournament, formerly known as the Southern Open. For info: Roger Childers, VP, Callaway Gardens Resort, Inc, Pine Mountain, GA 31822. Phone: (800) 282-8181.

ENGLAND: NOTTINGHAM GOOSE FAIR. Oct 1–3. Forest Recreation Ground, Nottingham. Held annually since 1284 (except during the Great Plague in 1665 and the two World Wars), the fair formerly lasted three weeks and boasted as many as 20,000 geese on display. Now lasting three days, the Nottingham Goose Fair always begins on the first Thursday in October. A traditional fair with modern amusements.

FIRST MODERN WORLD SERIES GAME: 95th ANNIVERSARY. Oct 1, 1903. The Pittsburgh Pirates defeated the Boston Pilgrims (later the Red Sox), 7–3, in the first game of the 1903 World Series, the first postseason series matching the champions of the National League and the American League. Jimmy Sebring of Pittsburgh hit the first World Series home run. Deacon Phillippe was the winning pitcher, Cy Young the loser.

FIRST NL PLAY-OFF GAME: ANNIVERSARY. Oct 1, 1946. For the first time in National League history, two teams wound up tied for first place at the end of the regular season. The St. Louis Cardinals and the Brooklyn Dodgers compiled a record of 96–58, necessitating a three-game playoff. The Cards took the first game, 4–2, and won the second on Oct 3, 8–4.

HICKMAN, HERMAN: BIRTH ANNIVERSARY. Oct 1, 1911. Herman Michael Hickman, Jr, football player and coach, wrestler and sportscaster born at Johnson City, TN. Hickman played college football at the University of Tennessee under Coach Bob Neyland and three seasons of pro football with the Brooklyn Dodgers. He wrestled under the nickname "The Tennessee Terror" and coached at several colleges, including Yale. In 1952, he resigned to concentrate on television and radio. Died at Washington, DC, Apr 25, 1958.

MARIS HITS 61st HOME RUN: ANNIVERSARY. Oct 1, 1961. Roger Maris of the New York Yankees hit his 61st home run, breaking Babe Ruth's record for most home runs in a season. Maris hit his homer against pitcher Tracy Stallard of the Boston Red Sox as the Yankees won, 1–0. Controversy over the record arose because the American League had adopted a 162-game schedule in 1961. The Yankees actually played 163 games, with one tie, and Maris played in 161. In 1927, when Ruth set his record, the schedule called for 154 games. The Yankees played 155 games (again, a tie), and Ruth played in 151.

NATIONAL PHYSICAL THERAPY MONTH. Oct 1–31. To increase awareness of the role of physical therapy in health care, physical therapists celebrate by hosting special activities such as fitness clinics, open houses, hot lines, athletic events, health seminars and exhibits. Annually, the month of October. For info: American Physical Therapy Assn, 1111 N Fairfax St, Alexandria, VA 22314. Phone: (800) 999-2782 or (703) 706-3248.

NATIONAL ROLLER SKATING MONTH. Oct 1–31. A monthlong celebration recognizing the health benefits and recreational pleasure of this long-loved pastime. Also includes an emphasis on safe skating. For info: Roller Skating Assn, 6905 Corporate Dr, Indianapolis, IN 46278. Phone: (317) 875-3390. Fax: (317) 875-3394.

PELE PLAYS FINAL GAME: ANNIVERSARY. Oct 1, 1977. Pele, generally considered the greatest soccer player ever, played the last game of his career before 75,646 fans at Giants Stadium. Pele played the first half for the New York Cosmos and the second for Santos of Brazil, his original team.

THRILLER IN MANILA: ANNIVERSARY. Oct 1, 1975. Muhammad Ali scored a 15th-round TKO against Joe Frazier to retain the heavyweight championship in a fight billed as the "Thriller in Manila."

BIRTHDAYS TODAY

Rodney Cline (Rod) Carew, 53, Baseball Hall of Fame infielder, born Gatun, Canal Zone, Oct 1, 1945.
James Earl (Jimmy) Carter, Jr, 74, 39th US President and amateur softball player, born Plains, GA, Oct 1, 1924.
Roberto Conrado Kelly, 34, baseball player, born Panama City, Panama, Oct 1, 1964.
Anthonia Wayne ("Amp") Lee, 27, football player, born Chipley, FL, Oct 1, 1971.
Alton Lavelle Lister, 40, basketball player, born Dallas, TX, Oct 1, 1958.
Charles Dwayne (Chuck) McElroy, 31, baseball player, born Port Arthur, TX, Oct 1, 1967.
Mark David McGwire, 35, baseball player, born Pomona, CA, Oct 1, 1963.
Randy Quaid, 48, actor (*Dead Solid Perfect*), born Houston, TX, Oct 1, 1950.
Jeffrey James (Jeff) Reardon, 43, former baseball player, born Pittsfield, MA, Oct 1, 1955.
Grete Andersen Waitz, 45, marathoner, born Oslo, Norway, Oct 1, 1953.
Alexei Zhamnov, 28, hockey player, born Moscow, USSR, Oct 1, 1970.

OCTOBER 2 — FRIDAY

Day 275 — 90 Remaining

WORLD SERIES CHAMPIONS THIS DATE

1932	New York Yankees
1954	New York Giants

DENT'S HOMER WINS PLAYOFF: 20th ANNIVERSARY. Oct 2, 1978. Bucky Dent hit a three-run home run in the seventh inning to propel the New York Yankees to a 5–4 victory over the Boston Red Sox in a one-game playoff to decide the pennant in the American League

October 1998	S	M	T	W	T	F	S
					1	2	3
	4	5	6	7	8	9	10
	11	12	13	14	15	16	17
	18	19	20	21	22	23	24
	25	26	27	28	29	30	31

East. The Yankees went on to defeat the Kansas City Royals for the AL pennant and the Los Angeles Dodgers in the World Series.

GIBSON STRIKES OUT 17: 30th ANNIVERSARY. Oct 2, 1968. Bob Gibson of the St. Louis Cardinals struck out 17 Detroit Tigers, a record, in the first game of the World Series. The Tigers recovered to win the Series in seven games.

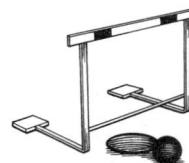

JOSS PITCHES PERFECT GAME: 90th ANNIVERSARY. Oct 2, 1908. Addie Joss of the Cleveland Naps (later the Indians) pitched the fourth perfect game in major league history. He defeated the Chicago White Sox, 1–0. Joss pitched a second no-hitter in 1910, also against Chicago.

NATIONAL HOCKEY LEAGUE REGULAR SEASON. Oct 2–Apr 18, 1999 (tentative). The National Hockey League opens its 82nd regular season leading to the playoffs and the Stanley Cup Finals. Each of the league's 27 teams (including the new Nashville franchise) plays an 82-game schedule. Eight teams from each of the two conferences qualify for the postseason. For info: Natl Hockey League, 1251 Avenue of the Americas, 47th Floor, New York, NY 10020. Phone: (212) 789-2000. Fax: (212) 789-2020. WWW: http://www.nhl.com/

ONLY 20TH-CENTURY TRIPLEHEADER: ANNIVERSARY. Oct 2, 1920. In the only major league tripleheader played in the 20th century, the Cincinnati Reds took two games from the Pittsburgh Pirates before the Pirates won the nightcap, called by darkness after six innings.

SOUTH DAKOTA RODEO ASSOCIATION CHAMPIONSHIP RODEO FINALS. Oct 2–4. Sioux Falls, SD. The best of the best. Top 12 cowboys and cowgirls in the state compete for $50,000 in prize money and year-end championship awards. Standard rodeo events plus rodeo dance at the Ramkota on Friday and Saturday nights. For info: Renee Sutton, SD Rodeo Assn, RR 2, Box 98, Burke, SD 57523. Phone: (605) 775-2158.

US OPEN STOCK DOG CHAMPIONSHIP. Oct 2–4. Hubert Bailey Farm, Dawsonville, GA. In the foothills of the Appalachian mountains, handlers from across the country will work both sheep and cattle. Also a petting zoo for children. Annually, in October. Est attendance: 3,000. For info: Dawson County Chamber of Commerce, PO Box 299, Dawsonville, GA 30534. Phone: (706) 265-6278. Fax: (706) 265-6279.

WICHITA STATE PLANE CRASH: ANNIVERSARY. Oct 2, 1970. Fourteen members of the football team at Wichita State University were killed when their plane crashed in the Rocky Mountains.

SPORTSCHASER OF THE DAY

What college football team had fourteen players perish in a 1970 plane crash?

BIRTHDAYS TODAY

Glenn Chris Anderson, 38, former hockey player, born Vancouver, BC, Canada, Oct 2, 1960.
Richard (Dick) Barnett, 62, former basketball player, born Gary, IN, Oct 2, 1936.
John Neuman Cook, 41, golfer, born Toledo, OH, Oct 2, 1957.

Thomas Muster, 31, tennis player, born Leibnitz, Austria, Oct 2, 1967.

Mark Robert Rypien, 36, football player, born Calgary, Alberta, Canada, Oct 2, 1962.

Maurice Morning (Maury) Wills, 66, former baseball manager and player, born Washington, DC, Oct 2, 1932.

OCTOBER 3 — SATURDAY
Day 276 — 89 Remaining

BEVENS'S NEAR NO-HITTER: ANNIVERSARY. Oct 3, 1947. New York Yankees pitcher Floyd ("Bill") Bevens carried a no-hitter into the ninth inning of Game 4 of the World Series against the Brooklyn Dodgers. With two out and runners on first and second as the result of walks, pinch-hitter Harry ("Cookie") Lavagetto doubled off the right-field wall in Ebbets Field. Two runs scored, the no-hitter evaporated and the Yankees lost the game.

BILLIE JEAN KING HAS $100,000 YEAR: ANNIVERSARY. Oct 3, 1971. Billie Jean King won the Virginia Slims Thunderbird tournament in Phoenix to become the first woman tennis player to win more than $100,000 in prize money in a single year.

BRETT WINS BATTING TITLES IN THREE DECADES: ANNIVERSARY. Oct 3, 1990. George Brett of the Kansas City Royals went 1-for-1 to finish the season with a .329 average, good enough to win his third American League batting title. Brett also won in 1976 and 1980, one title in three different decades.

CAP ANSON RETIRES: ANNIVERSARY. Oct 3, 1897. Adrian ("Cap") Anson played his last game of major league baseball and hit two home runs against the St. Louis Cardinals at age 46. Anson's career began in 1871 in the National Association.

CIRCLE CITY CLASSIC. Oct 3. RCA Dome, Indianapolis, IN. Bowl-style football game between two predominantly black universities is preceded by several days of related activities, including concerts, Coronation, College Fair and parade. Est attendance: 62,000. For info: Indiana Sports Corp, 201 S Capitol Ave, Ste 1200, Indianapolis, IN 46225. Phone: (317) 237-5000. Fax: (317) 237-5041. E-mail: isc@indianasportscorp.com. WWW: http://www.indianasportscorp.com

CLARKE, FRED: BIRTH ANNIVERSARY. Oct 3, 1872. Fred Clifford Clarke, Baseball Hall of Fame outfielder and manager born at Winterset, IA. Clarke batted .315 for the Louisville Colonels and Pittsburgh Pirates (1894–1915). He managed the Pirates to four National League pennants, five second-place finishes and the World Series title in 1909. Inducted into the Hall of Fame in 1951. Died at Winfield, KS, Aug 14, 1960.

COUNTRY FAIR ON THE SQUARE AND "ALL CAR SHOW." Oct 3–4. Downtown Square, Gainesville, TX. More than 100 vintage cars, classic cars, street rods and pickups, all makes and models on display. Entertainment, quilt show, food, arts display, children's activities and more. Annually, the first Saturday and Sunday in October. Est attendance: 5,000. For info: Gainesville Area Chamber of Commerce, PO Box 518, 101 S Culberson, Gainesville, TX 76240. Phone: (817) 665-2831. Fax: (817) 665-2833.

FIRST NFL GAME: ANNIVERSARY. Oct 3, 1920. The Dayton Triangles defeated the Columbus Panhandles, 14–0, in the first game played in the American Professional Football Association. The APFA became the National Football League in 1922, but this game is considered the NFL's first game. Lou Partlow of Dayton scored what is regarded as the NFL's first touchdown.

GIANTS BEAT DODGERS IN PLAY-OFF: ANNIVERSARY. Oct 3, 1962. The San Francisco Giants came from behind to defeat the Los Angeles Dodgers, 5–4, in the deciding game of their three-game National League play-off. The Giants scored four runs in the ninth inning to advance to the World Series where they lost to the New York Yankees, four games to three.

ROBINSON NAMED BASEBALL'S FIRST BLACK MAJOR LEAGUE MANAGER: ANNIVERSARY. Oct 3, 1974. The only major league player selected Most Valuable Player in both the American and National Leagues, Frank Robinson was hired by the Cleveland Indians as baseball's first black major league manager. During his playing career Robinson represented the American League in four World Series playing for the Baltimore Orioles, led the Cincinnati Reds to a National League pennant and hit 586 home runs in 21 years of play.

RUN TO READ. Oct 3. Central Library, Tulsa, OK. Annual 8K road race and 1-mile fun run benefiting Tulsa City–County Library's Ruth G. Hardman Adult Literacy Service. Entry fee includes a long-sleeved T-shirt. Annually, the first Saturday in October. Est attendance: 800. For info: Cathy Audley, Mgr, PR, Tulsa City–County Library System, 400 Civic Center, Tulsa, OK 74103. Phone: (918) 596-7897. Fax: (918) 596-7990.

RUNYON, DAMON: BIRTH ANNIVERSARY. Oct 3, 1880. Alfred Damon Runyon, sportswriter and author born at Manhattan, KS. Runyon began his newspaper career in the West and made his way to New York in 1911. He covered baseball and other sports, emphasizing the human interest details that went beyond traditional straight reporting. Runyon's syndicated work in sports and other topics made him one of the best-known writers in the country. He also wrote short stories, some of which formed the basis for the musical *Guys and Dolls*. Died at New York, NY, Dec 10, 1946.

SCOTTISH FESTIVAL AND HIGHLAND GAMES. Oct 3. Fairgrounds, Goshen, CT. Competition and demonstrations in Scottish athletic games such as caber toss, etc. Also clan tents, pipe bands, dancing, Scottish food and imports; continuous entertainment. Annually, the first Saturday in October. Est attendance: 7,000. For info: St. Andrew's Society of CT, PO Box 1195, Litchfield, CT 06759. Phone: (203) 366-0777.

☆ ☆ ☆

"THE SHOT HEARD ROUND THE WORLD": ANNIVERSARY. Oct 3, 1951. Bobby Thomson hit a three-run home run with one out in the bottom of the ninth inning off Ralph Branca to give the New York Giants a 5–4 victory over the Brooklyn Dodgers in the deciding game of the 1951 National League playoffs. The Giants entered the ninth trailing, 4–1. Whitey Lockman drove in one run, and then Thomson came to bat with runners on second and third. The home run has gone down in baseball legend as "The Shot Heard Round the World." The Giants' comeback in the pennant race to tie the Dodgers at the end of the regular season is known as "The Miracle of Coogan's Bluff."

SKAT-TRAK (JET SKI) WORLD FINALS (IJSBA). Oct 3–10. Nautical Inn Resort, Lake Havasu City, AZ. Est attendance: 50,000. For info: Tourism Bureau, 314 London Bridge Rd, Lake Havasu City, AZ 86403. Phone: (800) 242-8278.

US MID-AMATEUR (GOLF) CHAMPIONSHIP. Oct 3–8. NCR Country Club, Dayton, OH. For info: US Golf Assn, Golf House, Far Hills, NJ 07931. Phone: (908) 234-2300. Fax: (908) 234-9687. E-mail: usga@ix.netcom.com. WWW: http://www.usga.org

WALKTOBERFEST. Oct 3–4 (date may vary by location). Each October thousands of Americans participate in the American Diabetes Association's annual walk-a-thon to raise money to help find a cure for diabetes and to provide information and resources to improve the lives of all people affected by the disease. Walks are held in communities across America, combining fun and fitness with the chance to help people with diabetes. For info: Communications Dept, American Diabetes Assn, Natl HQ, 1660 Duke St, Alexandria, VA 22314. Phone: (800) 254-WALK.

WHIRLAWAY PASSES $500,000 MARK: ANNIVERSARY. Oct 3, 1942. Whirlaway, horse racing's Triple Crown winner in 1941, won the 1942 running of the Jockey Club Gold Cup and became the first horse to win more than $500,000 in career earnings.

WORLD FOOTBALL LEAGUE FORMED: 25th ANNIVERSARY. Oct 3, 1973. The World Football League was formed as a challenge to the National Football League, but it played less than two full seasons before folding.

WROK/WZOK/WXXQ CHILI SHOOT OUT. Oct 3. Rockford Speedway, Rockford, IL. More than 50 local chili-cooking teams compete for the honors of Rockford's Hottest & Best Tasting Chili. Bands perform all day long; patrons can participate in contests such as Cow Chip Throwing and Hot Pepper Eating. Money raised benefits Winnebago County D.A.R.E. program. Est attendance: 7,000. For info: Tom Garrett, WROK/WZOK/WXXQ Radios, 3901 Brendenwood Rd, Rockford, IL 61107. Phone: (815) 399-2233. Fax: (815) 299-8148.

BIRTHDAYS TODAY

Wilfredo Nieva (Wil) Cordero, 27, baseball player, born Mayaguez, Puerto Rico, Oct 3, 1971.

Frederick Steven (Fred) Couples, 39, golfer, born Seattle, WA, Oct 3, 1959.

Dennis Lee Eckersley, 44, baseball player, born Oakland, CA, Oct 3, 1954.

Patrick William (Pat) Flatley, 35, hockey player, born Toronto, Ontario, Canada, Oct 3, 1963.

Darrin Glen Fletcher, 32, baseball player, born Elmhurst, IL, Oct 3, 1966.

David Mark (Dave) Winfield, 47, former baseball player, born St. Paul, MN, Oct 3, 1951.

☆   ☆   ☆

OCTOBER 4 — SUNDAY
Day 277 — 88 Remaining

WORLD SERIES CHAMPIONS THIS DATE
1955   Brooklyn Dodgers

BROOKLYN WINS ONLY WORLD SERIES: ANNIVERSARY. Oct 4, 1955. Left-hander Johnny Podres pitched a 2–0 shutout against the New York Yankees to give the Brooklyn Dodgers their only World Series championship. Before this seven-game triumph, the Dodgers had lost the Series in 1920, 1941, 1947, 1949, 1952 and 1953. The Dodgers left Brooklyn for Los Angeles after the 1957 season.

October *1998*	S	M	T	W	T	F	S
					1	2	3
	4	5	6	7	8	9	10
	11	12	13	14	15	16	17
	18	19	20	21	22	23	24
	25	26	27	28	29	30	31

Brooklyn Wins Only World Series

FIRST US OPEN GOLF CHAMPIONSHIP: ANNIVERSARY. Oct 4, 1895. Horace Rawlins won the first US Open Golf Championship, contested at the Newport Golf Club in Newport, RI. Rawlins shot 173 over 36 holes to defeat Willie Dunn by 2 strokes.

INDIANS WIN PLAY-OFF: 40th ANNIVERSARY. Oct 4, 1948. The Cleveland Indians defeated the Boston Red Sox, 8–3, in a one-game play-off to decide the American League pennant. The Indians used the pitching of Gene Bearden and the hitting of player-manager Lou Boudreau to advance to the World Series against the Boston Braves.

KELLY, JOHNNY: BIRTH ANNIVERSARY. Oct 4, 1889. John Brendan (Johnny) Kelly, Olympic gold medal rower born at Philadelphia, PA. The son of working-class Irish immigrants, Kelly started his own construction company and became a millionaire. He began rowing in 1909 and compiled an impressive record, including three Olympic gold medals. His son, John, Jr, became a champion rower as well. His daughter Grace became Princess of Monaco. Died at Philadelphia, June 20, 1960.

LEAGUE CHAMPIONSHIP SERIES BEGIN: ANNIVERSARY. Oct 4, 1969. Following the inauguration of divisional play, teams from the National League and the American League opened competition in the first League Championship Series. The New York Mets beat the Atlanta Braves, 9–5, in the opening game of the NLCS. The Baltimore Orioles defeated the Minnesota Twins, 4–3, in 12 innings, in the first ALCS game.

OLIN, STEVE: BIRTH ANNIVERSARY. Oct 4, 1965. Steve Robert (Steve) Olin, baseball player born at Portland, OR. Olin pitched four seasons with the Cleveland Indians as a reliever. Died in a boating accident at Orlando, FL, Mar 22, 1993.

WORLD SERIES CHAMPIONS THIS DATE
1942	St. Louis Cardinals
1953	New York Yankees

BIRTHDAYS TODAY

Frank Peter Joseph Crosetti, 88, former baseball player, born San Francisco, CA, Oct 4, 1910.

A.C. Green, Jr, 35, basketball player, born Portland, OR, Oct 4, 1963.

Robert Lee (Sam) Huff, 64, Pro Football Hall of Fame linebacker, born Morgantown, WV, Oct 4, 1934.

Anthony (Tony) LaRussa, Jr, 54, baseball manager and former player, born Tampa, FL, Oct 4, 1944.

Charles Louis (Charlie) Leibrandt, Jr, 42, former baseball player, born Chicago, IL, Oct 4, 1956.

Roger Allen Pavlik, 31, baseball player, born Houston, TX, Oct 4, 1967.

Susan Sarandon (born Susan Tomaling), 52, actress (*Bull Durham*), born New York, NY, Oct 4, 1946.

James Francis (Jimy) Williams, 55, baseball manager and former player, born Santa Maria, CA, Oct 4, 1943.

OCTOBER 5 — MONDAY
Day 278 — 87 Remaining

CHASE'S SPORTSQUOTE OF THE DAY
"I like to see my players come to me as boys and leave as men." —Eddie Robinson

BAGBY, JIM: BIRTH ANNIVERSARY. Oct 5, 1889. James Charles Jacob Bagby, Sr, baseball player and umpire born at Barnett, GA. Bagby pitched the Cleveland Indians to the American League pennant in 1920, winning 31 games. He hit the first World Series home run by a pitcher in Game 5 of the 1920 Series against the Brooklyn Dodgers. Died at Marietta, GA, July 28, 1954.

CHADWICK, HENRY: BIRTH ANNIVERSARY. Oct 5, 1824. Henry Chadwick, Baseball Hall of Fame sportswriter and innovator born at Exeter, Devon, England. Known as the "Father of Baseball" and later as "Father Chadwick," he wrote voluminously about baseball, popularizing the game and protecting its integrity. He perfected the newspaper box score, served on the rules committee and devised the method of scoring games still in use. Inducted into the Hall of Fame in 1938. Died at New York, NY, Apr 20, 1908.

HARVEST MOON. Oct 5. So called because the full moon nearest the autumnal equinox extends the hours of light into the evening and helps harvesters with their long day's work. Moon enters Full Moon phase at 4:12 PM, EDT.

MICKEY OWEN'S DROPPED THIRD STRIKE: ANNIVERSARY. Oct 5, 1941. In the fourth game of the World Series between the Brooklyn Dodgers and the New York Yankees, Dodgers catcher Mickey Owen let a third strike get away from him in the ninth inning. The miscue allowed batter Tommy Henrich to reach first base safely after which the Yankees went on to score four runs and win the game, 7–4. The victory gave New York a lead of three games to one. They won the Series in five games.

MOON PHASE: FULL MOON. Oct 5. Moon enters Full Moon phase at 4:12 PM, EDT.

PERIGEAN SPRING TIDES. Oct 5–6. Spring tides, the highest possible tides, occur when New Moon or Full Moon takes place within 24 hours of the moment the Moon is nearest Earth (perigee) in its monthly orbit, on Oct 6, at 9 AM, EDT.

ROBINSON WINS 324th GAME: ANNIVERSARY. Oct 5, 1985. The Grambling Tigers defeated Prairie View A&M, 27–7, to give coach Eddie Robinson the 324th victory of his coaching career. With the win, Robinson became college football's all-time winningest coach, surpassing Paul ("Bear") Bryant.

WEST, SAMMY: BIRTH ANNIVERSARY. Oct 5, 1904. Samuel Filmore (Sammy) West, baseball player born at Gladewater, TX. West was a skilled outfielder for three major league teams (1927–42). He played in the first All-Star Game, substituting for Babe Ruth. Died at Lubbock, TX, Nov 23, 1985.

BIRTHDAYS TODAY
Raymond Lester ("Trace") Armstrong, 33, football player, born Bethesda, MD, Oct 5, 1965.
Rex Everett Chapman, 31, basketball player, born Bowling Green, KY, Oct 5, 1967.
Laura Davies, 35, golfer, born Coventry, England, Oct 5, 1963.
Grant Henry Hill, 26, basketball player, born Dallas, TX, Oct 5, 1972.
Mario Lemieux, 33, former hockey player, born Montreal, Quebec, Canada, Oct 5, 1965.
Patrick Roy, 33, hockey player, born Quebec City, Quebec, Canada, Oct 5, 1965.
Rey Francisco Sanchez, 31, baseball player, born Rio Pedras, Puerto Rico, Oct 5, 1967.
Barry Switzer, 61, football coach, born Crossett, AR, Oct 5, 1937.

OCTOBER 6 — TUESDAY
Day 279 — 86 Remaining

WORLD SERIES CHAMPIONS THIS DATE
1936	New York Yankees
1941	New York Yankees
1947	New York Yankees
1963	Los Angeles Dodgers

LEAGUE CHAMPIONSHIP SERIES BEGIN. Oct 6 (tentative). Sites TBA. Major League Baseball launches the second round of postseason play, the League Championship Series. The two winners of the National League's Division Series meet in the best four-of-seven NLCS. The two winners of the American League's Division Series meet in the best four-of-seven ALCS. Winners move on to the World Series.

NIEKRO WINS 300 GAMES: ANNIVERSARY. Oct 6, 1985. Pitcher Phil Niekro of the New York Yankees won the 300th game of his career, shutting out the Toronto Blue Jays, 8–0, on the last day of the regular season. Niekro finished his career in 1987 with 318 wins.

RUTH HITS THREE SERIES HOME RUNS: ANNIVERSARY. Oct 6, 1926. Babe Ruth hit three home runs in the fourth game of the World Series against the St. Louis Cardinals. The Yankees won the game, 10–5, but the Cardinals won the Series in seven games.

BIRTHDAYS TODAY

Dennis Ray ("Oil Can") Boyd, 39, former baseball player, born Meridian, MS, Oct 6, 1959.

Angelo Dominic ("Archi") Cianfrocco, 32, baseball player, born Rome, NY, Oct 6, 1966.

Gary Edward Gentry, 52, former baseball player, born Phoenix, AZ, Oct 6, 1946.

Gerald Wayne (Jerry) Grote, 56, former baseball player, born San Antonio, TX, Oct 6, 1942.

Rebecca Lobo, 25, basketball player, born Hartford, CT, Oct 6, 1973.

Ruben Angel Sierra, 33, baseball player, born Rio Piedras, Puerto Rico, Oct 6, 1965.

Gregory Lee (Greg) Walker, 39, former baseball player, born Douglas, GA, Oct 6, 1959.

OCTOBER 7 — WEDNESDAY

Day 280 — 85 Remaining

WORLD SERIES CHAMPIONS THIS DATE

1933	New York Giants
1935	Detroit Tigers
1950	New York Yankees
1952	New York Yankees

FIRST FEMALE GLOBETROTTER: ANNIVERSARY. Oct 7, 1985. Lynette Woodard, captain of the gold-medal-winning US basketball team at the 1984 Olympics, was selected to be the first woman to play for the Harlem Globetrotters.

GEORGIA TECH BEATS CUMBERLAND: ANNIVERSARY. Oct 7, 1916. Georgia Tech University defeated Cumberland, 222-0, in the most lopsided college football game of all time.

KLEIN, CHUCK: BIRTH ANNIVERSARY. Oct 7, 1904. Charles Herbert (Chuck) Klein, Baseball Hall of Fame outfielder born at Indianapolis, IN. Klein was the leading National League slugger around 1930 when hitting statistics were quite astronomical. He won the NL Triple Crown in 1933. Inducted into the Hall of Fame in 1980. Died at Indianapolis, Mar 28, 1958.

MEYER, LOUIS: DEATH ANNIVERSARY. Oct 7, 1994. Louis Meyer, auto racer born at New York, NY, July 1904. Meyer became the first three-time winner of the Indianapolis 500, capturing that race in 1928, 1933 and 1936. He also finished second once and fourth twice. After World War II, he was co-owner of the Offenhauser engine business, whose engines won every Indianapolis 500 from 1947 through 1964. Died at Las Vegas, NV.

PAYTON SETS TWO RECORDS: ANNIVERSARY. Oct 7, 1984. Running back Walter Payton of the Chicago Bears broke two records held by Jim Brown in the same game. He passed the mark of 12,312 career rushing yards and rushed for 100 yards or more for the 58th time in his career as the Bears beat the New Orleans Saints, 20-7.

VON DER AHE, CHRIS: BIRTH ANNIVERSARY. Oct 7, 1851. Christian Frederick Wilhelm (Chris) Von der Ahe, baseball executive born at Hille, Germany. A brewer and a flamboyant showman, Von der Ahe owned the champion St. Louis Browns of the American Association in the

	S	M	T	W	T	F	S
October					1	2	3
	4	5	6	7	8	9	10
1998	11	12	13	14	15	16	17
	18	19	20	21	22	23	24
	25	26	27	28	29	30	31

1880s. He conceived of the notion that beer should be sold in ballparks. Died at St. Louis, MO, June 7, 1913.

WALKER, FLEET: BIRTH ANNIVERSARY. Oct 7, 1856. Moses Fleetwood Walker, baseball player born at Mt Pleasant, OH. Walker played major league baseball for the 1884 Toledo team in the American Association. He was the last black American to play in the majors before baseball imposed its color line. Died at Cleveland, OH, May 11, 1924.

BIRTHDAYS TODAY

Frank Conrad (Frankie) Baumholtz, 80, former baseball player, born Midvale, OH, Oct 7, 1918.

Jose Rosario Cardenal, 55, former baseball player, born Matanzas, Cuba, Oct 7, 1943.

Richard Anthony (Rich) DeLucia, 34, baseball player, born Reading, PA, Oct 7, 1964.

Rudy Karl Law, 42, former baseball player, born Waco, TX, Oct 7, 1956.

Filomeno Coronado (Phil) Ortega, 59, former baseball player, born Gilbert, AZ, Oct 7, 1939.

Brian Louis Allen Sutter, 42, hockey coach and former player, born Viking, Alberta, Canada, Oct 7, 1956.

Blair Thomas, 31, football player, born Philadelphia, PA, Oct 7, 1967.

OCTOBER 8 — THURSDAY

Day 281 — 84 Remaining

WORLD SERIES CHAMPIONS THIS DATE

1919	Cincinnati Reds
1922	New York Giants
1927	New York Yankees
1930	Philadelphia Athletics
1939	New York Yankees
1940	Cincinnati Reds
1959	Los Angeles Dodgers

BUSH, DONIE: BIRTH ANNIVERSARY. Oct 8, 1887. Owen Joseph ("Donie") Bush, baseball player and manager born at Indianapolis, IN. Bush was an American League shortstop known for his hustle. He managed several clubs in the majors and the minors, spending 65 years in baseball. Died at Indianapolis, Mar 28, 1972.

CURTIS, MARGARET: 115th BIRTH ANNIVERSARY. Oct 8, 1883. Margaret Curtis, golfer and tennis player born at Boston, MA. Curtis won three women's amateur national golf championships in 1907, 1911 and 1912. She teamed with Evelyn Sears to win the 1908 women's tennis national doubles title. She played golf well into her 70s. The Curtis Cup, contested biennially between teams of amateur women golfers from the United States and Great Britain, was initiated by Curtis and her sister Harriott in 1932. Died at Boston, Dec 25, 1965.

DON LARSEN'S PERFECT GAME: ANNIVERSARY. Oct 8, 1956. Don Larsen of the New York Yankees pitched the only perfect game in World Series history. He defeated the Brooklyn Dodgers, 2–0, in Game 5. Pinch hitter Dale Mitchell, batting for Dodgers pitcher Sal Maglie, was called out on strikes for the last out.

FIRST BASKETBALL GAME AT SUPERDOME: ANNIVERSARY. Oct 8, 1975. In the first basketball game played at the Louisiana Superdome in New Orleans, the San Antonio Spurs of the American Basketball Association defeated the Atlanta Hawks of the National Basketball Association, 109–107, in an exhibition.

MERKLE'S BONER RESOLVED: 90th ANNIVERSARY. Oct 8, 1908. The Chicago Cubs defeated the New York Giants, 4–2, to win their third National League pennant in a row. The game was a replay of the Sept 23 game that ended in a disputed tie as umpire Hank O'Day called the Giants first baseman out for not touching second base on a hit by Al Bridwell that apparently scored the winning run. Cubs second baseman Johnny Evers called Merkle's mistake to the umpire's attention, and O'Day nullified the run. Both clubs protested, and league officials eventually ruled the game a tie.

MURTAUGH, DANNY: BIRTH ANNIVERSARY. Oct 8, 1917. Daniel Edward (Danny) Murtaugh, baseball player and manager born at Chester, PA. Murtaugh had a limited career as a major league infielder but enjoyed great success as manager of the Pittsburgh Pirates. His teams won the World Series in 1960 and 1971. Died at Chester, Dec 2, 1976.

RICKENBACKER, EDDIE: BIRTH ANNIVERSARY. Oct 8, 1890. Edward Vernon (Eddie) Rickenbacker, auto racing pioneer born at Columbus, OH. Besides his career in airplanes, "Captain Eddie" raced cars, once setting a land speed record at Daytona Beach, and founded the Rickenbacker Car Company in 1921. This racing enterprise developed four-wheel brakes, balloon tires and other improvements. He bought the Indianapolis Motor Speedway in 1927 and sold it to Tony Hulman in 1945. Died at Zurich, Switzerland, July 23, 1973.

BIRTHDAYS TODAY

Matthew Nicolas (Matt) Biondi, 33, Olympic gold medal swimmer, born Moraga, CA, Oct 8, 1965.

Enos Milton Cabell, 49, former baseball player, born Fort Riley, KS, Oct 8, 1949.

William David (Billy) Conn, Jr, 81, former boxer and referee, born Pittsburgh, PA, Oct 8, 1917.

Bill Elliott, 43, auto racer, born Dawsonville, GA, Oct 8, 1955.

Rashard Griffith, 24, basketball player, born Chicago, IL, Oct 8, 1974.

Michael Thomas (Mike) Morgan, 39, baseball player, born Tulare, CA, Oct 8, 1959.

Rashaan Iman Salaam, 24, Heisman Trophy running back, born San Diego, CA, Oct 8, 1974.

OCTOBER 9 — FRIDAY
Day 282 — 83 Remaining

WORLD SERIES CHAMPIONS THIS DATE

1928	New York Yankees
1934	St. Louis Cardinals
1938	New York Yankees
1944	St. Louis Cardinals
1949	New York Yankees
1958	New York Yankees
1961	New York Yankees
1966	Baltimore Orioles

FIRST PGA CHAMPIONSHIP: ANNIVERSARY. Oct 9, 1916. The recently formed Professional Golfer's Association of America held its first championship at Siwanoy Country Club in Bronxville, NY. The trophy and the lion's share of the $2,580 purse, both offered by department store magnate Rodman Wanamaker, were won by British golfer Jim Barnes. After the next two championships were canceled by World War I, Barnes won again in 1919.

LONGHORN WORLD CHAMPIONSHIP RODEO. Oct 9–10 (tentative). Charlotte Coliseum, Charlotte, NC. More than 200 cowboys and cowgirls compete in six professional contests ranging from bronc riding to bull riding for top prize money and world championship points. Featuring colorful opening pageantry and Big, Bad BONUS Bulls. 5th annual. Est attendance: 16,000. For info: W. Bruce Lehrke, Pres, Longhorn World Championship Rodeo, Inc, PO Box 70159, Nashville, TN 37207. Phone: (615) 876-1016. Fax: (615) 876-4685. E-mail: lhrodeo@idt.net. WWW: http://www.longhornrodeo.com

MARQUARD, RUBE: BIRTH ANNIVERSARY. Oct 9, 1889. Richard William ("Rube") Marquard, Baseball Hall of Fame pitcher born at Cleveland, OH. Marquard was an excellent pitcher, winning 204 games over 18 years. He was nicknamed after Rube Waddell, another pitcher whom he resembled. Inducted into the Hall of Fame in 1971. Died at Pikesville, MD, June 1, 1980.

MOOSE, BOB: BIRTH ANNIVERSARY. Oct 9, 1947. Robert Ralph (Bob) Moose, baseball player born at Export, PA. Moose pitched a no-hitter for the Pittsburgh Pirates, but his career was marred by injury. Died in an automobile accident at Martins Ferry, OH, Oct 9, 1976.

O'MALLEY, WALTER: 95th BIRTH ANNIVERSARY. Oct 9, 1903. Walter Francis O'Malley, baseball executive born at New York, NY. O'Malley, owner of the Brooklyn Dodgers when they left New York for Los Angeles for the 1958 season, is perhaps the most vilified man in baseball history. Nevertheless, he is responsible for expanding the sport to the West Coast. Died at Rochester, MN, Aug 9, 1979.

RED WING SHEEP DOG TRIAL. Oct 9–11. Red Wing, MN. Farmers' and ranchers' dogs compete. Est attendance: 700. For info: Charles O'Reilly, Course Dir, Red Wing Sheep Dog Trial Assn, 33933 200 Ave, Red Wing, MN 55066-7204. Phone: (800) 852-4422. E-mail: OReillyC@aol.com.

SEWELL, JOE: 100th BIRTH ANNIVERSARY. Oct 9, 1898. Joseph Wheeler (Joe) Sewell, Baseball Hall of Fame shortstop born at Titus, AL. Sewell joined the starting lineup of the Cleveland Indians on Aug 16, 1920, after Ray Chapman was fatally beaned. He struck out only 114 times in 7,132 at-bats. Inducted into the Hall of Fame in 1977. Died at Mobile, AL, Mar 6, 1990.

SPORTSCHASER OF THE DAY

Who owned the Dodgers when they left Brooklyn for Los Angeles after the 1957 season?

BIRTHDAYS TODAY

Kenneth (Kenny) Anderson, 28, basketball player, born New York, NY, Oct 9, 1970

Brian Jay Downing, 48, former baseball player, born Los Angeles, CA, Oct 9, 1950.

Felix Jose Fermin, 35, baseball player, born Mao, Valverde, Dominican Republic, Oct 9, 1963.

Joseph Anthony (Joe) Pepitone, 58, former baseball player, born New York, NY, Oct 9, 1940.

William Thomas (Bill) Pulsipher, 25, baseball player, born Fort Benning, GA, Oct 9, 1973.

Michael (Mike) Singletary, 40, former football player, born Houston, TX, Oct 9, 1958.

Annika Sorenstam, 28, golfer, born Stockholm, Sweden, Oct 9, 1970.

OCTOBER 10 — SATURDAY

Day 283 — 82 Remaining

WORLD SERIES CHAMPIONS THIS DATE

1924	Washington Senators
1926	St. Louis Cardinals
1931	St. Louis Cardinals
1937	New York Yankees
1945	Detroit Tigers
1951	New York Yankees
1956	New York Yankees
1957	Milwaukee Braves
1968	Detroit Tigers

ALEXANDER FANS LAZZERI: ANNIVERSARY. Oct 10, 1926. Veteran pitcher Grover Cleveland Alexander came out of the St. Louis Cardinals bullpen in the seventh inning of the seventh World Series game to strike out New York Yankees second baseman Tony Lazzeri with the bases loaded. The Cardinals held on to win the game, 3–2, as Babe Ruth was thrown out attempting to steal for the game's last out.

BILLUPS, LEWIS: 35th BIRTH ANNIVERSARY. Oct 10, 1963. Lewis Kenneth Billups, football player born at Tampa, FL. Billups played at North Alabama and was drafted by the Cincinnati Bengals. His career was marred by legal troubles including a year in jail for making threatening phone calls and allegations by a Seattle woman that Billups had sexually assaulted her. Died in a car crash at Orlando, FL, Apr 9, 1994.

JAPAN: HEALTH-SPORTS DAY. Oct 10. National holiday to encourage physical activity for building sound body and mind. Created in 1966 to commemorate the day of the opening of the XVIII Summer Olympic Games in Tokyo on Oct 10, 1964.

MOUNT RUSHMORE INTERNATIONAL MARATHON. Oct 10–11. Rapid City, SD. This marathon is a "nature" marathon, held in the scenic beauty of the Black Hills.

October *1998*	S	M	T	W	T	F	S
					1	2	3
	4	5	6	7	8	9	10
	11	12	13	14	15	16	17
	18	19	20	21	22	23	24
	25	26	27	28	29	30	31

2-mile and 5-mile run/walks, 26-mile marathon, and 26-mile marathon relay. Pasta feed at Mt Rushmore Oct 11. For info: Michelle Lintz, Rapid City Conv & Vis Bureau, 444 Mt Rushmore Rd N, PO Box 747, Rapid City, SD 57701. Phone: (605) 343-1744.

ROGOVIN, SAUL: 75th BIRTH ANNIVERSARY. Oct 10, 1923. Saul Walter Rogovin, baseball player born at New York, NY. Rogovin pitched eight seasons in the major leagues and won the American League ERA title in 1951. Died at New York, Jan 23, 1995.

WALKING WEEKEND. Oct 10–12. Northeastern CT. More than 50 guided historic, cultural and recreational walks through the Quinebaug-Shetucket Rivers Valley National Heritage Corridor. Est attendance: 3,000. For info: Northeast Connecticut Visitors District, PO Box 598, Putnam, CT 06260. Phone: (860) 928-1228. Fax: (860) 928-4720.

WASHINGTON SENATORS WIN ONLY WORLD SERIES: ANNIVERSARY. Oct 10, 1924. The Washington Senators defeated the New York Giants, 4–3, in 12 innings to win the seventh game of the only World Series championship in their history. The winning run scored when a ground ball bounced over Giants third baseman Fred Lindstrom's head. Walter Johnson was the winning pitcher in relief.

WELLS, WILLIE: BIRTH ANNIVERSARY. Oct 10, 1905. Willie ("The Devil") Wells, Baseball Hall of Fame shortstop born at Austin, TX. Wells is generally considered the greatest shortstop to play in the Negro Leagues. As manager of the Newark Eagles, he developed several players who became major leaguers. Inducted into the Hall of Fame in 1997. Died at Austin, Jan 21, 1989.

WORLD SERIES UNASSISTED TRIPLE PLAY: ANNIVERSARY. Oct 10, 1920. The Cleveland Indians defeated the Brooklyn Dodgers, 8–1, in the fifth game of the 1920 World Series. The Indians' Elmer Smith hit the first grand slam in World Series play in the first inning, and winning pitcher Jim Bagby hit the first World Series homer by a pitcher in the fourth inning. But the most famous play in the game was the unassisted triple play recorded by Cleveland's second baseman Bill Wambsganss in the fifth inning. Wamby caught a line drive hit by Clarence Mitchell, touched second to double off Pete Kilduff and tagged Otto Miller before he could return safely to first base.

WORLD WRISTWRESTLING CHAMPIONSHIPS. Oct 10. Petaluma, CA. Nationally recognized event with more than 500 entrants vying for the title of World Wristwrestling Champion. Est attendance: 1,000. For info: Bill Soberanes, c/o *Argus Courier*, 830 Petaluma Blvd N, Petaluma, CA 94952. Phone: (707) 778-1430.

BIRTHDAYS TODAY

Michael David (Mike) Adamle, 49, broadcaster and former football player, born Kent, OH, Oct 10, 1949.

Brett Lorenzo Favre, 29, football player, born Gulfport, MS, Oct 10, 1969.

Derrick Wayne McKey, 32, basketball player, born Meridian, MS, Oct 10, 1966.

Brett Perriman, 33, football player, born Miami, FL, Oct 10, 1965.

Chris Pronger, 24, hockey player, born Dryden, Ontario, Canada, Oct 10, 1974.

Fury Gene Tenace (born Fiore Gino Tennaci), 52, former baseball player, born Russelton, PA, Oct 10, 1946.

OCTOBER 11 — SUNDAY

Day 284 — 81 Remaining

WORLD SERIES CHAMPIONS THIS DATE

1913	Philadelphia Athletics
1918	Boston Red Sox
1943	New York Yankees
1948	Cleveland Indians

"AMERICAN WHEELS" CAR SHOW. Oct 11 (rain date Oct 25). Wheaton Village, Millville, NJ. Features cars from the '50s, '60s and '70s. Est attendance: 1,500. For info: Wheaton Village, 1501 Glasstown Rd, Millville, NJ 08332. Phone: (609) 825-6800 or (800) 998-4552. Fax: (609) 825-2410. Email: mail@wheatonvillage.org. WWW: http://www.wheatonvillage.org

BANKOH MOLOKAI HOE. Oct 11. Molokai to Oahu, HI. 47th annual men's 40.8-mile Molokai-to-Oahu championship six-person outrigger canoe race. Nearly 100 teams of the best outrigger canoe paddlers from around the world compete for the championship title. Spectators gather on the beach to watch the finish at Fort DeRussy Beach, Waikiki, when the teams are laden with leis. Est attendance: 4,000. For media info: Carol Hogan/Ocean Promotion, (808) 325-7400, or Linda Chinn, Bank of Hawaii, (808) 537-8658. For race info: Joan Malama, (808) 261-6615. E-mail: oceanpro@interpac.net. WWW: http://holoholo.org/canunews/index.html

CHIP BECK SHOOTS 59: ANNIVERSARY. Oct 11, 1991. Playing at Sunrise Golf Club, Chip Beck shot 59 in the third round of the Las Vegas Invitational to equal Al Geiberger's record for lowest score in a single round of a PGA tournament. But he did not win the tournament. Andrew Magee did, defeating D.A. Weibring on the second hole of a sudden-death playoff.

CLARK, DUTCH: BIRTH ANNIVERSARY. Oct 11, 1906. Earl Harry ("Dutch") Clark, Pro Football Hall of Fame player and coach, born at Fowler, CO. Clark attended Northwestern briefly and then Colorado College where he played football and became an All-American in 1929. He turned pro with the Portsmouth Spartans of the NFL and, after the team moved to Detroit and became the Lions, led the league in scoring three times. Clark later coached the Lions and the Cleveland Rams. Inducted into the Hall of Fame as a charter member in 1963. Died at Canon City, CO, Aug 5, 1978.

DYER, EDDIE: BIRTH ANNIVERSARY. Oct 11, 1900. Edwin Hawley (Eddie) Dyer, baseball player and manager born at Morgan City, LA. Dyer was a pitcher turned outfielder with a brief major league career. He became a manager and guided the St. Louis Cardinals to a World Series win in 1946. Died at Houston, TX, Apr 20, 1964.

FIRST 100-YARD DASH UNDER 10 SECONDS: ANNIVERSARY. Oct 11, 1890. John Owens ran the first 100-yard dash under 10 seconds at an AAU track meet in Washington. Owens's time was 9.8 seconds.

HEAD OF THE CONNECTICUT REGATTA. Oct 11. Connecticut River, Middletown, CT. Annual crew race regatta with 3,000 participants. Annually, the day before Columbus Day. Est attendance: 10,000. For info: Coordinator, Head of the Connecticut Regatta, PO Box 1, Middletown, CT 06422. Phone: (860) 346-1042 or (800) 486-3346. Fax: (860) 346-1043.

HOPPE, WILLIE: BIRTH ANNIVERSARY. Oct 11, 1887. William F. (Willie) Hoppe, billiards champion born at Cornwall on the Hudson, NY. He won tournaments from age 18 until age 64. Died at Miami, FL, Feb 1, 1959.

THE HUDSON HIGHLANDER. Oct 11. Fahnestock State Park, Putnam County, NY. America's internationally known ultra-distance orienteering race. For info: Paul Bennett. Phone: (201) 642-8427. E-mail: pdbennett@juno.com.

LASALLE BANKS CHICAGO MARATHON. Oct 11. Grant Park, Chicago, IL. Both the 21st annual marathon (26.2 miles) and the 8th annual 5K (3.1 miles) have reputations for attracting an international field of top athletes, and this marathon is ranked as one of the fastest in the world. Annually, a Sunday in October. Est attendance: 18,000. For info: Chicago Marathon, c/o Chicago Event Mgmt, Inc, 900 W Jackson, Ste 8-W, Chicago, IL 60607. Phone: (312) 243-3274. Fax: (312) 243-5652. WWW: http://www.chicagomarathon.com

MARSHALL, GEORGE PRESTON: BIRTH ANNIVERSARY. Oct 11, 1896. George Preston Marshall, Pro Football Hall of Fame executive born at Grafton, WV. Marshall made a fortune in the laundry business and became part-owner of the Boston Braves of the NFL in 1932. He bought the whole team, changed its name to the Redskins and moved it to Washington in 1937. The Redskins quickly became one of the league's most successful operations with Marshall leading the league in embracing television. He paid his players frugally, meddled in his coaches' decisions and promoted rules changes to encourage passing and field goals. Inducted into the Pro Football Hall of Fame as a charter member in 1963. Died at Washington, DC, Aug 9, 1969.

☆   ☆   ☆

BIRTHDAYS TODAY

Jason Arnott, 24, hockey player, born Collingwood, Ontario, Canada, Oct 11, 1974.

Maria Esther Andion Bueno, 59, former tennis player, born Sao Paulo, Brazil, Oct 11, 1939.

Curtis Glenn (Curt) Ford, 38, former baseball player, born Jackson, MS, Oct 11, 1960.

Greggory William (Gregg) Olson, 32, baseball player, born Scribner, NE, Oct 11, 1966.

Charles Christopher (Chris) Spielman, 33, football player, born Canton, OH, Oct 11, 1965.

Jon Steven (Steve) Young, 37, football player, born Salt Lake City, UT, Oct 11, 1961.

OCTOBER 12 — MONDAY

Day 285 — 80 Remaining

WORLD SERIES CHAMPIONS THIS DATE

1907	Chicago Cubs
1916	Boston Red Sox
1920	Cleveland Indians
1967	St. Louis Cardinals

BIRD MAKES NBA DEBUT: ANNIVERSARY. Oct 12, 1979. After an All-American career at Indiana State, forward Larry Bird made his professional debut with the Boston Celtics. He scored 14 points and had five assists in 28 minutes as the Celtics beat the Houston Rockets, 114–108. Bird soon proved his ability to shoot, pass and rebound. He led the Celtics to 32 more victories than they had the previous season and won the league's Rookie of the Year award.

CANADA: THANKSGIVING DAY. Oct 12. Annually, the second Monday in October.

COLUMBUS DAY OBSERVANCE. Oct 12. Public Law 90–363 sets observance of Columbus Day on the second Monday in October. Applicable to federal employees and to the District of Columbia, but observed also in most states on this day. Commemorates the landfall of Columbus in the New World, Oct 12, 1492.

CRONIN, JOE: BIRTH ANNIVERSARY. Oct 12, 1906. Joseph Edward (Joe) Cronin, Baseball Hall of Fame player, manager and executive born at San Francisco, CA. Cronin played shortstop for Pittsburgh, Washington and the Boston Red Sox. He was a manager and became the first former player to be elected league president. Inducted into the Hall of Fame in 1959. Died at Osterville, MA, Sept 7, 1984.

FERRELL, RICK: BIRTH ANNIVERSARY. Oct 12, 1905. Richard Benjamin (Rick) Ferrell, Baseball Hall of Fame catcher born at Durham, NC. Ferrell caught 1,806 games in the American League, a record at the time. He hit .281 over 18 years and formed a strong battery with his brother Wes. Inducted into the Hall of Fame in 1984. Died at Bloomfield Hills, MI, July 27, 1995.

MOON PHASE: LAST QUARTER. Oct 12. Moon enters Last Quarter phase at 7:11 AM, EDT.

TENNESSEE SCORELESS STREAK: ANNIVERSARY. Oct 12, 1940. The University of Tennessee football team defeated Tennessee-Chattanooga, 53–0, to extend its record streak of consecutive shutouts to 17 games. The streak started Nov 5, 1938, when the Vols beat the same team, and ended Oct 19, 1940, when Alabama scored 12 points but still lost, 27–12.

CHASE'S SPORTSQUOTE OF THE DAY

"I really don't like talking about money. All I can say is that the Good Lord must have wanted me to have it." —Larry Bird

BIRTHDAYS TODAY

Susan Anton, 48, actress (*Goldengirl*), born Yucaipa, CA, Oct 12, 1950.
Glenn Alfred Beckert, 58, former baseball player, born Pittsburgh, PA, Oct 12, 1940.
David (Dave) Brown, 36, hockey player, born Saskatoon, Saskatchewan, Canada, Oct 12, 1962.
Christopher Mark (Chris) Chandler, 33, football player, born Everett, WA, Oct 12, 1965.
Jean-Jacques (J.J.) Daigneault, 33, hockey player, born Montreal, Quebec, Canada, Oct 12, 1965.

October 1998

S	M	T	W	T	F	S
				1	2	3
4	5	6	7	8	9	10
11	12	13	14	15	16	17
18	19	20	21	22	23	24
25	26	27	28	29	30	31

Charles Sidney (Sid) Fernandez, 36, baseball player, born Honolulu, HI, Oct 12, 1962.
Todd Andrew Krygier, 33, hockey player, born Northville, MI, Oct 12, 1965.
Anthony Christopher (Tony) Kubek, 62, broadcaster and former baseball player, born Milwaukee, WI, Oct 12, 1936.
Jose Antonio Valentin, 29, baseball player, born Manati, Puerto Rico, Feb 12, 1969.

OCTOBER 13 — TUESDAY
Day 286 — 79 Remaining

WORLD SERIES CHAMPIONS THIS DATE

1903	**Boston Pilgrims**
1906	**Chicago White Sox**
1914	**Boston Braves**
1915	**Boston Red Sox**
1921	**New York Giants**
1960	**Pittsburgh Pirates**

BOSTON WINS FIRST WORLD SERIES: 95th ANNIVERSARY. Oct 13, 1903. The Boston Pilgrims (later the Red Sox) won the first modern World Series, defeating the Pittsburgh Pirates, five games to three. The Pilgrims won Game 8, 3–0.

FIRST WORLD SERIES NIGHT GAME: ANNIVERSARY. Oct 13, 1971. The first night game in World Series history matched the Pittsburgh Pirates and the Baltimore Orioles. Pittsburgh beat Baltimore, 4–3, behind three hits by Roberto Clemente, to tie the Series at two games apiece.

MAZEROSKI WINS SERIES: ANNIVERSARY. Oct 13, 1960. Second baseman Bill Mazeroski of the Pittsburgh Pirates led off the bottom of the ninth inning with a home run over the left-field wall to win Game 7 of the World Series against the New York Yankees, 10–9. Mazeroski hit the second pitch thrown to him by relief pitcher Ralph Terry. He was the first player to end a World Series with a homer in the bottom of the ninth.

SHAW, WILBUR: BIRTH ANNIVERSARY. Oct 13, 1902. Warren Wilbur Shaw, auto racer born at Shelbyville, IN. Shaw was racing cars by age 18. An early crash led him to invent the crash helmet. After several years of frustration, he won the Indianapolis 500 three times, in 1937, 1939 and 1940, the first consecutive victories by one driver. He served as Indy's president and general manager after Tony Hulman bought the Speedway in 1945. Died at Fort Wayne, IN, Oct 30, 1954.

SOMERS, CHARLES: 130th BIRTH ANNIVERSARY. Oct 13, 1868. Charles W. Somers, baseball executive born at Newark, OH. Somers was one of the founders of the American League. As the league's vice president, he held financial interests in four teams to help keep them solvent in their early years. Died at Put-in-Bay, OH, June 29, 1934.

WADDELL, RUBE: BIRTH ANNIVERSARY. Oct 13, 1876. George Edward ("Rube") Waddell, Baseball Hall of Fame pitcher born at Bradford, PA. Waddell is remembered as much for his carefree antics as for his excellent pitching. He won 191 games but never took the game too seriously. Inducted into the Hall of Fame in 1946. Died at San Antonio, TX, Apr 1, 1914.

BIRTHDAYS TODAY

Robert Sherwood (Bob) Bailey, 56, former baseball player, born Long Beach, CA, Oct 13, 1942.

George Allen Frazier, 44, former baseball player, born Oklahoma City, OK, Oct 13, 1954.

Derek Ricardo Harper, 37, basketball player, born Elberton, GA, Oct 13, 1961.

Richard Edward (Rich) Kotite, 56, former football coach and player, born New York, NY, Oct 13, 1942.

Edwin Lee (Eddie) Mathews, 67, Baseball Hall of Fame third baseman, born Texarkana, TX, Oct 13, 1931.

Jerry Lee Rice, 36, football player, born Starkville, MS, Oct 13, 1962.

Glenn Anton ("Doc") Rivers, 37, former basketball player, born Maywood, IL, Oct 13, 1961.

Reggie Wayne Theus, 41, former basketball player, born Inglewood, CA, Oct 13, 1957.

OCTOBER 14 — WEDNESDAY
Day 287 — 78 Remaining

WORLD SERIES CHAMPIONS THIS DATE

1905	New York Giants
1908	Chicago Cubs
1929	Philadelphia Athletics
1965	Los Angeles Dodgers
1984	Detroit Tigers

ALL-SHUTOUT WORLD SERIES: ANNIVERSARY. Oct 14, 1905. Christy Mathewson defeated the Philadelphia Athletics, 2–0, to win the World Series for the New York Giants in five games. All the games were shutouts, three by Mathewson and one each by New York's Joe McGinnity and Philadelphia's Chief Bender.

CHARLESTON, OSCAR: BIRTH ANNIVERSARY. Oct 14, 1896. Oscar McKinley Charleston, Baseball Hall of Fame outfielder and manager born in Indianapolis, IN. Charleston was perhaps the best overall ballplayer in the Negro Leagues, drawing comparisons to Ty Cobb. He played with the great Homestead Grays and Pittsburgh Crawfords teams of the 1930s and managed as well. Inducted into the Hall of Fame in 1976. Died at Philadelphia, PA, Oct 6, 1954.

END OF LONGEST NFL LOSING STREAK: ANNIVERSARY. Oct 14, 1945. The Chicago Cardinals (later the St. Louis, Phoenix and Arizona Cardinals) ended the longest losing streak in NFL history at 29 games by defeating the Chicago Bears, 16–7.

EWRY, RAY: 125th BIRTH ANNIVERSARY. Oct 14, 1873. Raymond Clarence (Ray) Ewry, Olympic gold medal track and field athlete born at Lafayette, IN. Ewry overcame polio as a child to win 10 Olympic gold medals, more than any other athlete. He won the standing broad jump and the standing high jump at the games of 1900, 1904, 1906 and 1908 and added gold medals in the standing triple jump in 1900 and 1904. None of these events is contested today. Died at New York, NY, Sept 29, 1937.

MACON, MAX: BIRTH ANNIVERSARY. Oct 14, 1915. Max Cullen Macon, baseball player born at Pensacola, FL. Macon was an unusual player who pitched and played first base and the outfield. He played for three teams from 1938 through 1947. Died at Jupiter, FL, Aug 5, 1989.

STUHLDREHER, HARRY: BIRTH ANNIVERSARY. Oct 14, 1901. Harry A. Stuhldreher, football player, coach and executive born at Massillon, OH. Stuhldreher called signals for Notre Dame's famed backfield, the Four Horsemen. After graduating in 1925, he played pro football and coached at Villanova and Wisconsin. Died at Pittsburgh, PA, Jan 26, 1965.

TAMPA BOAT SHOW. Oct 14–18. Tampa Convention Center and adjacent marina, Tampa, FL. 32nd annual show is Gulf Coast's premier nautical event, showcasing hundreds of new boats and accessories, plus informative boating and fishing seminars. Est attendance: 22,000. For info: Carolyn Luis, 400 Arthur Godfrey Rd, Ste 310, Miami Beach, FL 33140. Phone: (305) 531-8410. Fax: (305) 534-3139.

BIRTHDAYS TODAY

Willie Mays Aikens, 44, former baseball player, born Seneca, SC, Oct 14, 1954.

Harry David Brecheen, 84, former baseball player, born Broken Bow, OK, Oct 14, 1914.

Keith Alan Byars, 35, football player, born Dayton, OH, Oct 14, 1963.

Beth Daniel, 42, golfer, born Charleston, SC, Oct 14, 1956.

Joseph Elliott (Joe) Girardi, 34, baseball player, born Peoria, IL, Oct 14, 1964.

Tommy Harper, 58, former baseball player, born Oak Grove, LA, Oct 14, 1940.

James Arthur (Jim) Jackson, 28, basketball player, born Toledo, OH, Oct 14, 1970.

Charles (Charlie) Joiner, Jr, 51, Pro Football Hall of Fame wide receiver, born Many, LA, Oct 14, 1947.

Patrick Franklin (Pat) Kelly, 31, baseball player, born Philadelphia, PA, Oct 14, 1967.

Albert (Al) Oliver, 52, former baseball player, born Portsmouth, OH, Oct 14, 1946.

Dwayne Kenneth Schintzius, 30, basketball player, born Brandon, FL, Oct 14, 1968.

OCTOBER 15 — THURSDAY
Day 288 — 77 Remaining

WORLD SERIES CHAMPIONS THIS DATE

1917	Chicago White Sox
1923	New York Yankees
1925	Pittsburgh Pirates
1946	St. Louis Cardinals
1964	St. Louis Cardinals
1970	Baltimore Orioles

FIRST BLACK COACH IN NBA: ANNIVERSARY. Oct 15, 1966. Bill Russell made his debut as the first black coach in the NBA as his Boston Celtics defeated the San Francisco Warriors, 121–113, at Boston Garden. Russell served as the Celtics ' player-coach for three seasons and won two NBA titles.

GIBSON'S PINCH-HIT HOMER: ANNIVERSARY. Oct 15, 1988. Kirk Gibson hit a two-run, pinch-hit home run with two out in the bottom of the ninth inning to give the Los Angeles Dodgers a 5–4 win over the Oakland A's in the first game of the World Series. Gibson, hampered by a strained left knee, hobbled around the bases pumping his arm in jubilation. The Dodgers won the Series, four games to one.

LONGEST POSTSEASON GAME: ANNIVERSARY. Oct 15, 1986. Ray Knight of the New York Mets keyed a three-run rally in the ninth inning to tie the score in the sixth game of the National League Championship Series against the Houston Astros. The Mets won the game, 7–6, in 16 innings, to win the longest postseason game ever and the series as well.

NFL STRIKE ENDS: ANNIVERSARY. Oct 15, 1987. The National Football League Players Association ordered its members to return to work without a contract, effectively ending a 24-day strike against the NFL. The players reported after the owners' deadline and were told they would not play or be paid for the upcoming Sunday's games.

SLAUGHTER SCORES FROM FIRST: ANNIVERSARY. Oct 15, 1946. Enos Slaughter of the St. Louis Cardinals scored from first base on a short double by Harry Walker to defeat the Boston Red Sox, 4–3, in the seventh game of the World Series.

SULLIVAN, JOHN L.: 140th BIRTH ANNIVERSARY. Oct 15, 1858. John L. Sullivan, boxer born at Roxbury, MA. "The Great John L." was one of America's first sports heroes. He captured the world's bare-knuckle heavyweight championship on Feb 7, 1882, and went six years without defending the title. He won the last bare-knuckle fight in 1889 and then lost the title to James J. Corbett

in 1892. This was the first fight in which the boxers used gloves and were governed by the Marquis of Queensbury rules. Died at Abingdon, MA, Feb 2, 1918.

BIRTHDAYS TODAY

Penny Marshall, 56, director (*Big*, *A League of Their Own*), actress, born New York, NY, Oct 15, 1942.

James Alvin (Jim) Palmer, 53, broadcaster and Baseball Hall of Fame pitcher, born New York, NY, Oct 15, 1945.

Roscoe Tanner, 47, former tennis player, born Lookout Mountain, TN, Oct 15, 1951.

OCTOBER 16 — FRIDAY
Day 289 — 76 Remaining

WORLD SERIES CHAMPIONS THIS DATE

1909	Pittsburgh Pirates
1912	Boston Red Sox
1962	New York Yankees
1969	New York Mets
1983	Baltimore Orioles

CAIN, BOB: BIRTH ANNIVERSARY. Oct 16, 1924. Robert Max (Bob) Cain, baseball player born at Longford, KS. Cain pitched in 140 major league games over five years, but he will be remembered for the four balls he threw to midget Eddie Gaedel on Aug 19, 1951. In one of St. Louis Browns owner Bill Veeck's more outrageous promotions, Gaedel came to bat to open the second game of a doubleheader against the Detroit Tigers. He walked and was banned from baseball the next day. Died at Cleveland, OH, Apr 7, 1997.

DEVLIN, ART: BIRTH ANNIVERSARY. Oct 16, 1879. Arthur McArthur (Art) Devlin, baseball player and manager born at Washington, DC. Devlin was considered one of the finest third basemen of the early part of the 20th century. After playing 10 years in the majors, he managed a series of minor league teams. Died at Jersey City, NJ, Sept 18, 1948.

DODGE PRAIRIE CIRCUIT FINALS RODEO. Oct 16–17. Lazy E Arena, Guthrie, OK. The top 12 cowboys in each event from Oklahoma, Kansas and Nebraska compete for $60,000 and Circuit Championship titles. Est attendance: 15,000. For info: Lazy E Arena, Rt 5 Box 393, Guthrie, OK 73044. Phone: (405) 282-RIDE or (800) 595-RIDE. Fax: (405) 282-3785. E-mail: learena@ionet.net. WWW: http://www.lazye.com

GOSLIN, GOOSE: BIRTH ANNIVERSARY. Oct 16, 1900. Leon Allen ("Goose") Goslin, Baseball Hall of Fame outfielder born at Salem, NJ. Goslin was an American League outfielder for 18 years, and he ranks high in many all-time offensive categories. He once invented a zebra-striped bat to confuse pitchers, but it was ruled illegal. Inducted into the Hall of Fame in 1968. Died at Bridgetown, NJ, May 15, 1971.

HARRIDGE, WILL: 115th BIRTH ANNIVERSARY. Oct 16, 1883. William (Will) Harridge, Baseball Hall of Fame executive born at Chicago, IL. Harridge became president of the American League upon the death of Ernest Barnard in 1931. He had been private secretary to AL founder Ban Johnson. He resigned in 1958, having kept a fairly low profile. Inducted into the Hall of Fame in 1972. Died at Evanston, IL, Apr 9, 1971.

MIRACLE METS WIN SERIES: ANNIVERSARY. Oct 16, 1969. The "Miracle" New York Mets defeated the Baltimore Orioles, 5–3, to win the World Series, four games to one. Prior to the 1969 season, the Mets had never won more than 73 games. Their 100 regular season victories

October 1998

S	M	T	W	T	F	S
				1	2	3
4	5	6	7	8	9	10
11	12	13	14	15	16	17
18	19	20	21	22	23	24
25	26	27	28	29	30	31

and triumphs over the Atlanta Braves in the NLCS and the Orioles are regarded to be among recent baseball history's more improbable occurrences.

SMITH AND CARLOS GIVE BLACK POWER SALUTE: 30TH ANNIVERSARY. Oct 16, 1968. At the Mexico City Summer Olympics, American sprinters Tommie Smith and John Carlos, winners of the gold and bronze medals, respectively, in the 200-meter run, raised their black-gloved fists in a black power salute during the medal presentation to call attention to racism and poverty in the United States. Two days later, the pair was suspended by the US Olympic Committee and sent home.

SPORTSCHASER OF THE DAY

When the "Miracle Mets" won the 1969 World Series, which team did they defeat?

BIRTHDAYS TODAY

Melissa Louise Belote, 42, Olympic gold medal swimmer, born Washington, DC, Oct 16, 1956.

Manute Bol, 36, former basketball player, born Gogrial, Sudan, Oct 16, 1962.

David Albert (Dave) DeBusschere, 58, former baseball player, former basketball coach and executive, and Basketball Hall of Fame forward, born Detroit, MI, Oct 16, 1940.

Christopher John (Chris) Doleman, 37, football player, born Indianapolis, IN, Oct 16, 1961.

Juan Alberto Gonzalez, 29, baseball player, born Vega Baja, Puerto Rico, Oct 16, 1969.

Paul Kariya, 24, hockey player, born Vancouver, BC, Canada, Oct 16, 1974.

Darius Kasparaitis, 26, hockey player, born Elektrenai, USSR, Oct 16, 1972.

James Timothy (Tim) McCarver, 57, broadcaster and former baseball player, born Memphis, TN, Oct 16, 1941.

Walter Kevin McReynolds, 39, former baseball player, born Little Rock, AR, Oct 16, 1959.

Joseph Patrick (Joe) Murphy, 31, hockey player, born London, Ontario, Canada, Oct 16, 1967.

Kordell Stewart, 26, football player, born New Orleans, LA, Oct 16, 1972.

German Titov, 33, hockey player, born Moscow, USSR, Oct 16, 1965.

☆   ☆   ☆

OCTOBER 17 — SATURDAY

Day 290 — 75 Remaining

WORLD SERIES CHAMPIONS THIS DATE

1971	Pittsburgh Pirates
1974	Oakland A's
1978	New York Yankees
1979	Pittsburgh Pirates

ANDERSON, PAUL: BIRTH ANNIVERSARY. Oct 17, 1932. Paul Edward Anderson, Olympic gold medal weightlifter born at Toccoa, GA. Anderson won the heavyweight world championship in 1955 and a gold medal at the 1956 Melbourne Olympics. He was renowned as the "World's Strongest Man" for his feats of strength, including a backlift of 6,270 pounds. In 1962 he opened the Paul Anderson Youth Home. Died at Vidalia, GA, Aug 15, 1994.

CUMMINGS, CANDY: 150th BIRTH ANNIVERSARY. Oct 17, 1848. William Arthur ("Candy") Cummings, Baseball Hall of Fame pitcher born at Ware, MA. Cummings is generally regarded as the first pitcher to throw a curve ball. He learned the technique, he said, sailing oyster shells. He played in baseball's amateur era and as a professional. Inducted into the Hall of Fame in 1939. Died at Toledo, OH, May 16, 1924.

EWING, BUCK: BIRTH ANNIVERSARY. Oct 17, 1859. William Buckingham (Buck) Ewing, Baseball Hall of Fame catcher born at Hoagland, OH. Ewing was one of the best catchers of the 19th century and is credited by some with being the first to crouch immediately under the batter. Inducted into the Hall of Fame in 1939. Died at Cincinnati, OH, Oct 20, 1906.

FISHING HAS NO BOUNDARIES—TEMPE. Oct 17–18 (tentative). Tempe, AZ. A two-day fishing experience for disabled persons. Any disability, age, sex, race, etc, eligible. Fishing with experienced guides. For info: Don Price or David Helfand, Fishing Has No Boundaries, 2440 S. Mill, #103, Tempe, AZ 85282. Phone: (602) 784-4096.

GILLIAM, JIM: 70th BIRTH ANNIVERSARY. Oct 17, 1928. James William (Jim) Gilliam, baseball player at Nashville, TN. Gilliam, known as "Junior," was National League Rookie of the Year in 1953 after playing in the Negro Leagues. He was a steady infielder who became a respected coach after his retirement. Died at Inglewood, CA, Oct 8, 1978.

HEAD OF THE CHARLES REGATTA. Oct 17–18. Charles River, Cambridge and Boston, MA. The largest rowing event. More than 5,400 male and female athletes compete in 19 events. Races begin at about 7:50 AM and last until 4:30 PM. Est attendance: 250,000. For info: Head of the Charles, PO Box 52, Cambridge, MA 02238. Phone: (617) 864-8415. Fax: (617) 225-2391. E-mail: hotcharles@aol.com. WWW: http://www.hotc.org

INTERNATIONAL GOLD CUP. Oct 17. Great Meadow, The Plains, VA. A day of steeplechasing in the heart of Virginia's hunt country. Gates open at 10 AM for special events and activities. Corporate and chalet entertainment packages available. Conducted by the Virginia Gold Cup Assn for benefit of free year-round use of Great Meadow for nonprofit community activities. Est attendance: 45,000. For info: Virginia Gold Cup Assn, PO Box 840, Warrenton, VA 20188. Phone: (540) 347-2612. Fax: (540) 349-1829. WWW: http://www.vagoldcup.com

METS AND COLT .45S BORN: ANNIVERSARY. Oct 17, 1960. The National League announced that expansion franchises were being awarded to the New York Metropolitan Baseball Club, Inc, headed by Mrs. Joan Payson, and to a Houston group of investors led by Judge Roy Hofheinz. The two teams, later nicknamed the Mets and the Colt .45s, began play in the 1962 season.

ROLFE, RED: 90th BIRTH ANNIVERSARY. Oct 17, 1908. Robert Abial ("Red") Rolfe, baseball player and manager born at Penacook, NH. Rolfe played third base for the New York Yankees in the 1930s and 1940s. He coached baseball at Yale University, managed the Detroit Tigers and served as athletic director at Dartmouth College. Died at Guilford, NH, July 8, 1969.

WORLD SERIES BEGINS. Oct 17 (tentative). Sites TBA. Winners of the National League Championship Series and the American League Championship Series meet in the World Series. The best-four-of-seven Series opens with two games in the home park of the American League team followed by two games (and a third, if necessary) in the home park of the National League team. If needed, the Series returns to the American League park for Games Six and Seven.

WORLD SERIES EARTHQUAKE: ANNIVERSARY. Oct 17, 1989. Minutes before the start of Game 3 of the World Series between the Oakland A's and the San Francisco Giants, Candlestick Park and the Bay Area were rocked by an earthquake. The game was postponed and the Series delayed for 11 days.

BIRTHDAYS TODAY

Theodore Ernest (Ernie) Els, 29, golfer, born Johannesburg, South Africa, Oct 17, 1969.
Daniel John Willard (Danny) Ferry, 32, basketball player, born Hyattsville, MD, Oct 17, 1966.
Robert Craig ("Evel") Knievel, 60, motorcycle stunt performer, born Butte, MT, Oct 17, 1938.
John Steven Mabry, 28, baseball player, born Wilmington, DE, Oct 17, 1970.
Steve Douglas McMichael, 41, former football player, born Houston, TX, Oct 17, 1957.
Daniel Anthony (Dan) Pasqua, 37, former baseball player, born Yonkers, NY, Oct 17, 1961.
George Wendt, 50, actor ("Cheers"), born Chicago, IL, Oct 17, 1948.

OCTOBER 18 — SUNDAY

Day 291 — 74 Remaining

WORLD SERIES CHAMPIONS THIS DATE

1977   New York Yankees

ADAMS, CHARLES FRANCIS: BIRTH ANNIVERSARY. Oct 18, 1876. Charles Francis Adams, Hockey Hall of Fame executive born at Newport, VT. Adams secured a National Hockey League franchise for Boston in 1924 and named the team the Bruins. He used his substantial wealth, earned in the grocery business, to make the Bruins a success and to develop the league. His guarantee of $500,000 over four years for Bruins home games allowed construction of Boston Garden, opened in 1928. Adams also had an interest in horse racing, and he became a major stockholder in the Boston Braves. Inducted into the Hockey Hall of Fame in 1960. Died at Boston, MA, Oct 2, 1947.

AMERICAN BASKETBALL LEAGUE OPENS: ANNIVERSARY. Oct 18, 1996. The American Basketball League, a new professional league for women, opened its inaugural season with three games. The New England Blizzard defeated the Richmond Rage, 100–73, the Columbus Quest beat the Seattle Reign, 82–75, and the San Jose Lazers took the measure of the Atlanta Glory, 78–70. The Colorado Xplosion and the Portland Power were idle on the league's first night.

BERRY, CHARLIE: BIRTH ANNIVERSARY. Oct 18, 1902. Charles Francis (Charlie) Berry, baseball and football player, baseball umpire and football official born at Phillipsburg, NJ. Berry attended Lafayette College where he played baseball and was an All-American football player. After graduation he played pro football and major league baseball. After retiring, he became an NFL head linesman and an American League umpire, once calling a baseball doubleheader and an All-Star football game on the same day. Died at Evanston, IL, Sept 6, 1972.

	S	**M**	**T**	**W**	**T**	**F**	**S**
October					1	2	3
1998	4	5	6	7	8	9	10
	11	12	13	14	15	16	17
	18	19	20	21	22	23	24
	25	26	27	28	29	30	31

HAWKEYE MEDICAL SUPPLY HOSPICE ROAD RACES. Oct 18. Iowa City, IA. Annual road race attracts top runners from throughout the country. Est attendance: 8,000. For info: Iowa City Rd Races, Inc, PO Box 3148, Iowa City, IA 52244. Phone: (319) 338-8108 or (319) 337-6592. Fax: (319) 338-6822. E-mail: runicrr@aol.com. WWW: http://www.iowacity.net/runicrr

KIWANIS CLUB CAR SHOW. Oct 18 (tentative). Downtown Trenton, MO. 9th annual show features 15 classes of competition with trophies awarded in each class. Est attendance: 650. For info: Dave Woodson, Kiwanis Club Car Show, Rt 2, Trenton, MO 64683. Phone: (816) 359-5966 or (816) 359-4324. Fax: (816) 359-4325.

☆   ☆   ☆

MALARCHER, DAVE: BIRTH ANNIVERSARY. Oct 18, 1894. David Julius (Dave) Malarcher, baseball player and manager born at Whitehall, LA. Malarcher played and managed in the Negro Leagues from 1920 through 1934. After retiring, he became an accomplished poet. Died at Chicago, IL, May 11, 1982.

PINELLI, BABE: BIRTH ANNIVERSARY. Oct 18, 1895. Ralph Arthur ("Babe") Pinelli, baseball player and umpire born Rinaldo Angelo Paolinelli at San Francisco, CA. Pinelli was a major league infielder in the 1920s who became a National League umpire in 1935. He was behind the plate for Don Larsen's perfect game in the 1956 World Series. Died at Daly City, CA, Oct 2, 1984.

RED GRANGE'S EPIC DAY: ANNIVERSARY. Oct 18, 1924. Harold ("Red") Grange of the University of Illinois helped his team dedicate its new football stadium with a 39–14 victory over the University of Michigan. Grange scored four touchdowns in the game's first 12 minutes on runs of 95, 67, 56 and 44 yards. He returned to the field later to score a fifth rushing touchdown and to throw a pass for a sixth.

REGGIE'S THREE SERIES HOME RUNS: ANNIVERSARY. Oct 18, 1977. Reggie Jackson hit three home runs in three consecutive at-bats to lead the New York Yankees to a World Series championship over the Los Angeles Dodgers. Jackson's homers, all hit on the first pitch, came against Burt Hooton, Elias Sosa and Charlie Hough. They came in Game 6, won by New York, 8–4. Jackson hit two other home runs, in Games 4 and 5, to set a record for most homers in a six-game Series.

ROMP IN THE SWAMP FUN WALK. Oct 18. Gordon Bubolz Nature Preserve, Appleton, WI. Choose to hike ¼-, 1½-, 2½- or 4-mile distances on the Preserve's beautiful trail system. Rest stops along the way. Prizes for the most money raised. Est attendance: 800. For info: Elaine Meyer, Naturalist, 4815 N Lynndale Dr, Appleton, WI 54915. Phone: (414) 731-6041. Fax: (414) 731-9593. E-mail: bubolz@dataex.com. WWW: http://www.geocities.com/RainForest/4579

BIRTHDAYS TODAY

Michael Keller (Mike) Ditka, 59, football coach, former broadcaster and Pro Football Hall of Fame tight end, born Carnegie, PA, Oct 18, 1939.

Alvis Forrest Gregg, 65, former football coach and Pro Football Hall of Fame tackle, born Birthright, TX, Oct 18, 1933.

Thomas ("Hit Man") Hearns, 40, former boxer, born Detroit, MI, Oct 18, 1958.

George Andrew Hendrick, 49, former baseball player, born Los Angeles, CA, Oct 18, 1949.

Willie Watterson Horton, 56, former baseball player, born Arno, VA, Oct 18, 1942.

Martina Navratilova (born Martina Subertova), 42, former tennis player, born Prague, Czechoslovakia, Oct 18, 1956.

Kjell Samuelsson, 40, hockey player, born Tyngsryd, Sweden, Oct 18, 1958.

OCTOBER 19 — MONDAY
Day 292 — 73 Remaining

CHASE'S SPORTSQUOTE OF THE DAY

"What I remember most about the Rocket were his eyes. When he came flying toward you with the puck on his stick, his eyes were all lit up, flashing and gleaming like a pinball machine." —Glenn Hall on Maurice Richard

BROWN, THREE FINGER: BIRTH ANNIVERSARY. Oct 19, 1876. Mordecai Peter Centennial ("Three Finger") Brown, Baseball Hall of Fame pitcher born at Nyesville, IN. Brown won 239 games in his 14-year career and five World Series games. His nickname came from a childhood injury that cost him one finger and misshaped others. Inducted into the Hall of Fame in 1949. Died at Terre Haute, IN, Feb 14, 1948.

HOLMAN, NAT: BIRTH ANNIVERSARY. Oct 19, 1896. Nathan (Nat) Holman, Basketball Hall of Fame player and coach born at New York, NY. Holman coached at CCNY and simultaneously played for several pro teams including the Original Celtics. As a pivot man, he devised the pivot play, giving the ball off to a cutting player, and the man-to-man defensive switch. His 1950 CCNY team was the only team to win both the NCAA title and the NIT in the same year, but its players were later disgraced by a cheating scandal. Inducted into the Hall of Fame in 1964. Died at New York, NY, Feb 12, 1995.

RICHARD SCORES 500TH GOAL: ANNIVERSARY. Oct 19, 1957. Maurice ("Rocket") Richard of the Montreal Canadiens became the first player in the National Hockey League to score 500 goals when he tallied against the Chicago Blackhawks in a 3–1 Montreal victory. Richard finished his career with 544 goals and entered the Hockey Hall of Fame in 1961.

SNODGRASS, FRED: BIRTH ANNIVERSARY. Oct 19, 1887. Frederick Charles Snodgrass, baseball player born at Ventura, CA. Snodgrass was a fine outfielder, but in the 10th inning of the final game of the 1912 World Series, he dropped an easy fly ball, allowing the Boston Red Sox to score two runs and defeat the New York Giants. Died at Ventura, Apr 5, 1974.

BIRTHDAYS TODAY

Santos (Sandy) Alomar, Sr, 55, former baseball player, born Salinas, Puerto Rico, Oct 19, 1943.

Timothy Wayne (Tim) Belcher, 37, baseball player, born Sparta, OH, Oct 19, 1961.

Bradley Lee (Brad) Daugherty, 33, former basketball player, born Black Mountain, NC, Oct 19, 1965.

OCTOBER 20 — TUESDAY
Day 293 — 72 Remaining

WORLD SERIES CHAMPIONS THIS DATE

1982	St. Louis Cardinals
1988	Los Angeles Dodgers
1990	Cincinnati Reds

MANTLE, MICKEY: BIRTH ANNIVERSARY. Oct 20, 1931. Mickey Charles Mantle, Baseball Hall of Fame outfielder born at Spavinaw, OK. Mantle replaced Joe DiMaggio in center field for the New York Yankees and grew to become the most beloved player of his era. His battle with cancer raised awareness for organ donation and alcoholism. Inducted into the Hall of Fame in 1974. Died at Dallas, TX, Aug 13, 1995.

MOON PHASE: NEW MOON. Oct 20. Moon enters New Moon phase at 6:09 AM, EDT.

SINKWICH, FRANK: BIRTH ANNIVERSARY. Oct 20, 1920. Francis (Frank) Sinkwich, football player born at McKees Rocks, PA. Sinkwich played halfback at the University of Georgia and won the 1942 Heisman Trophy. He played professionally and won the NFL's 1944 MVP award, but his career was shortened by injury. Died at Athens, GA, Oct 22, 1990.

BIRTHDAYS TODAY

Reidel Clarence Anthony, 22, football player, born South Bay, FL, Oct 20, 1976.

Raymond Clay (Ray) Childress, Jr, 36, football player, born Memphis, TN, Oct 20, 1962.

David Scott (Dave) Collins, 46, former baseball player, born Rapid City, SD, Oct 20, 1952.

Keith Hernandez, 45, former baseball player, born San Francisco, CA, Oct 20, 1953.

Juan Antonio Marichal, 61, Baseball Hall of Fame pitcher, born Laguna Verde, Dominican Republic, Oct 20, 1937.

Robert James ("Rick") Monday, 53, former baseball player, born Batesville, AR, Oct 20, 1945.

Herman Joseph Moore, 29, football player, born Danville, VA, Oct 20, 1969.

Raymond Earl (Ray) Rhodes, 48, football coach and former player, born Mexia, TX, Oct 20, 1950.

Lee Roy Selmon, 44, Pro Football Hall of Fame defensive end, born Eufaula, OK, Oct 20, 1954.

OCTOBER 21 — WEDNESDAY
Day 294 — 71 Remaining

WORLD SERIES CHAMPIONS THIS DATE

1973	Oakland A's
1976	Cincinnati Reds
1980	Philadelphia Phillies

BEVENS, BILL: BIRTH ANNIVERSARY. Oct 21, 1916. Floyd Clifford ("Bill") Bevens, baseball player born at Hubbard, OR. Bevens nearly pitched the first no-hitter in World Series history, pitching for the New York Yankees against the Brooklyn Dodgers. In Game 4 of the 1947 Series, he carried his no-hitter into the ninth inning. With two out and two on, Cookie Lavagetto doubled home both runners, spoiling the no-hitter and winning the game, 3–2. Died at Salem, OR, Oct 26, 1991.

BLANDA'S STREAK ENDS: ANNIVERSARY. Oct 21, 1956. Quarterback and placekicker George Blanda of the Chicago Bears missed his first extra-point attempt after a record-setting 156 in a row. His kick sailed off to the left, but hardly mattered as the Bears defeated the Baltimore Colts, 58–27.

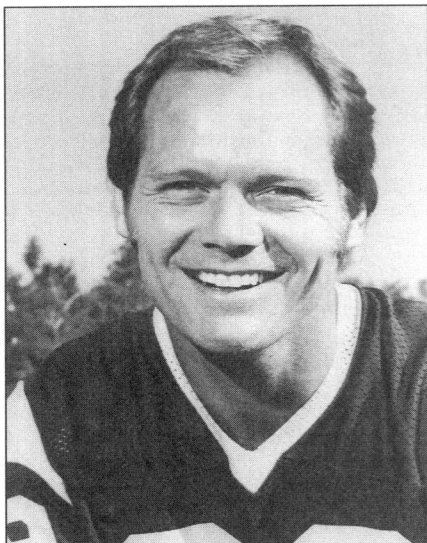

DRYER GETS TWO SAFETIES: 25th ANNIVERSARY. Oct 21, 1973. Fred Dryer, defensive end for the Los Angeles Rams, became the first player in NFL history to score two safeties in the same game in the Rams' 24–7 victory over the Green Bay Packers.

FISK'S 12TH-INNING HOME RUN: ANNIVERSARY. Oct 21, 1975. Catcher Carlton Fisk of the Boston Red Sox hit a home run in the 12th inning to defeat the Cincinnati Reds, 7–6, in the sixth game of the World Series. Fisk's dramatic homer forced a seventh game in what is generally considered one of the best World Series ever.

PHILLIES WIN FIRST WORLD SERIES: ANNIVERSARY. Oct 21, 1980. After falling short in 1915 and 1951, the Philadelphia Phillies won their first World Series, four games to two, over the Kansas City Royals. Philadelphia won Game 6, 4–1.

PICCOLO, BRIAN: 55th BIRTH ANNIVERSARY. Oct 21, 1943. Louis Brian Piccolo, football player born at Pittsfield, MA. He played running back at Wake Forest and with the Chicago Bears. His interracial friendship with Gale Sayers earned him a certain fame, but at age 26 he was stricken with embryonal cell carcinoma, a virulent form of cancer that took his life seven months later. Died at New York, NY, June 16, 1970. His life became the subject of a book, *Brian Piccolo: A Short Season*, and a made-for-television movie, *Brian's Song*.

BIRTHDAYS TODAY

George Antonio Bell, 39, former baseball player, born San Pedro de Macoris, Dominican Republic, Oct 21, 1959.
Bill Berg, 31, hockey player, born St. Catherines, Ontario, Canada, Oct 21, 1967.

October 1998

S	M	T	W	T	F	S
				1	2	3
4	5	6	7	8	9	10
11	12	13	14	15	16	17
18	19	20	21	22	23	24
25	26	27	28	29	30	31

Brian Piccolo

Edward Charles ("Whitey") Ford, 70, Baseball Hall of Fame pitcher, born New York, NY, Oct 21, 1928.
Michael Edward (Mike) Keenan, 49, former hockey coach and executive, born Whitby, Ontario, Canada, Oct 21, 1949.
William Ellis (Bill) Russell, 50, baseball manager and former player, born Pittsburg, KS, Oct 21, 1948.

OCTOBER 22 — THURSDAY
Day 295 — 70 Remaining

WORLD SERIES CHAMPIONS THIS DATE
1972	Oakland A's
1975	Cincinnati Reds

BECKMAN, JOHN: BIRTH ANNIVERSARY. Oct 22, 1895. John Beckman, Basketball Hall of Fame forward born at New York, NY. Beckman was one of the game's first great stars even though he did not attend college. He played in early professional leagues before World War I and joined the Original Celtics after the war. Beckman was an outstanding scorer, especially from the foul line. He played until age 46 when the Original Celtics disbanded in 1941. Inducted into the Hall of Fame in 1959. Died at Miami, FL, June 22, 1968.

CARR, JOE: BIRTH ANNIVERSARY. Oct 22, 1880. Joseph F. (Joe) Carr, Pro Football Hall of Fame executive born at Columbus, OH. Carr was a minor league baseball administrator, one of the founders of the 1925 American Basketball League and president of the American Professional Football Association (later the National Football League) from 1922 until his death. Carr stood for an honest game that could be embraced by a wide public. Inducted into the Pro Football Hall of Fame as a charter member in 1963. Died at Columbus, May 20, 1939.

EMPIRE STATE GOLDEN ARMS TOURNAMENT OF CHAMPIONS. Oct 22. Empire State Bldg, New York, NY.

Winners of the New York Golden Arms Tournaments from each of the boroughs and Long Island compete in this classic arm wrestling series finals. For info: New York Arm Wrestling Assn, Inc, 200-14 45th Dr, Bayside, NY 11361. Phone/fax: (718) 544-4592.

FALL CYCLE SCENE. Oct 22–25. Daytona International Speedway, Daytona Beach, FL. For info: Daytona Intl Speedway, John Story, PR, Box 2801, Daytona Beach, FL 32120-2801.

FIRST TELEVISED PRO FOOTBALL GAME: ANNIVERSARY. Oct 22, 1939. The Brooklyn Dodgers of the National Football League defeated the Philadelphia Eagles, 23–14, in the first televised pro football game, broadcast to about 1,000 homes in Brooklyn. The announcer was Allan ("Skip") Walz.

FOXX, JIMMIE: BIRTH ANNIVERSARY. Oct 22, 1907. James Emory (Jimmie) Foxx, Baseball Hall of Fame first baseman born at Sudlersville, MD. Foxx was a ferocious batter who hit 58 home runs in 1932, two short of Babe Ruth's record. He managed a team in the All-American Girls Professional Baseball League. Inducted into the Hall of Fame in 1951. Died at Miami, FL, July 21, 1967.

LONGEST NFL INTERCEPTION: ANNIVERSARY. Oct 22, 1961. Defensive back Erich Barnes of the New York Giants tied an NFL record by returning an intercepted pass 102 yards for a touchdown in the Giants' 17–16 loss to the Dallas Cowboys.

WORLD FOOTBALL LEAGUE DISBANDS: ANNIVERSARY. Oct 22, 1975. The World Football League, a 10-team enterprise struggling through its second season, suspended operations and disbanded prior to the 12th week of a 20-week schedule.

BIRTHDAYS TODAY

Brian Anthony Boitano, 35, Olympic gold medal figure skater, born Mountain View, CA, Oct 22, 1963.
Slater Nelson Martin, Jr, 73, Basketball Hall of Fame guard, born Houston, TX, Oct 22, 1925.
Harry William Walker, 82, former baseball manager and player, born Pascagoula, MS, Oct 22, 1916.
Wilbur Forrester Wood, 57, former baseball player, born Cambridge, MA, Oct 22, 1941.
Gerald Anthony Young, 34, former baseball player, born Tele, Honduras, Oct 22, 1964.

OCTOBER 23 — FRIDAY
Day 296 — 69 Remaining

WORLD SERIES CHAMPIONS THIS DATE

1910	Philadelphia Athletics
1993	Toronto Blue Jays

BLACKWELL, EWELL: BIRTH ANNIVERSARY. Oct 23, 1922. Ewell Blackwell, baseball player born at Fresno, CA. Known as "The Whip," Blackwell terrified right handed batters with his fearsome sidearm delivery. He pitched in the majors for 10 seasons, threw a no-hitter in 1947 and played in six straight All-Star Games. Died at Hendersonville, NC, Oct 29, 1996.

CARTER HOME RUN WINS WORLD SERIES: ANNIVERSARY. Oct 23, 1993. Joe Carter of the Toronto Blue Jays hit a three-run homer off relief pitcher Mitch Williams of the Philadelphia Phillies with one out in the bottom of the ninth inning to win the World Series for Toronto. Carter's homer, coming after a walk to Rickey Henderson and a single by Paul Molitor, gave the Blue Jays an 8–6 win and a four-games-to-two Series triumph. Only once before, in 1960, had the World Series been ended by a home run in the bottom of the ninth.

HEISMAN, JOHN: BIRTH ANNIVERSARY. Oct 23, 1869. John William Heisman, football player, coach and administrator born at Cleveland, OH. Heisman played football at Brown and Pennsylvania and began coaching at Oberlin. He moved to Akron, Oberlin again, Auburn, Clemson, Georgia Tech, Pennsylvania, Washington and Jefferson, and Rice. After his retirement, he became athletic director at the Downtown Athletic Club in New York. The club's award to the best college football player in the country was named in his honor posthumously. Died at New York, NY, Oct 3, 1936.

HULBERT, WILLIAM: BIRTH ANNIVERSARY. Oct 23, 1832. William Ambrose Hulbert, Baseball Hall of Fame executive born at Burlington Flats, NY. Hulbert founded the National League in 1876 and exercised strong leadership during his term as president. He expelled clubs and players for conduct he thought would jeopardize the game. Inducted into the Hall of Fame in 1995. Died at Chicago, IL, Apr 10, 1882.

KINARD, BRUISER: BIRTH ANNIVERSARY. Oct 23, 1914. Frank ("Bruiser") Kinard, Pro Football Hall of Fame lineman born at Pelahatchie, MS. Kinard was an outstanding two-way player who earned his nickname for his size and aggressiveness. He played at the University of Mississippi in the late 1930s and then professionally with the Brooklyn Dodgers (NFL) and the New York Yankees (AAFC). Inducted into the Hall of Fame as a charter member in 1963. Died at Jackson, MS, Sept 7, 1985.

LONGHORN WORLD CHAMPIONSHIP RODEO. Oct 23–24. Joel Coliseum, Winston-Salem, NC. More than 200 cowboys and cowgirls compete in six professional contests ranging from bronc riding to bull riding for top prize money and world championship points. Featuring colorful opening pageantry and Big, Bad BONUS Bulls. 29th annual. Est attendance: 18,000. For info: W. Bruce Lehrke, Pres, Longhorn World Chmpshp Rodeo, Inc, PO Box 70159, Nashville, TN 37207. Phone: (615) 876-1016. Fax: (615) 876-4685. E-mail: lhrodeo@idt.net. WWW: http://longhornrodeo.com

RICHMOND HIGHLAND GAMES AND CELTIC FESTIVAL. Oct 23–25. Fairgrounds, Strawberry Hill, Richmond, VA. Celebration of Scottish and Celtic heritage featuring athletic competition, clan tents, pipe bands, sheepdog demonstrations; dogs, livestock and horses of the British Isles; fiddle, harp and Highland dance competitions; food, pubs and whiskey tasting; kilted and clan miles; storytelling and more. Est attendance: 15,000. For info: Sue Mullins, Strawberry Hill, PO Box 26805, Richmond, VA 23261. Phone: (804) 228-3238. Fax: (804) 228-3252. E-mail: equine@strawberryhill.com.

STEPHENS, VERN: BIRTH ANNIVERSARY. Oct 23, 1920. Vernon Decatur (Vern) Stephens, baseball player born at McAlister, NM. Stephens was one of the leading shortstops of the 1940s and early 1950s. He played primarily with the St. Louis Browns and the Boston Red Sox. Died at Long Beach, CA, Nov 3, 1968.

SPORTSCHASER OF THE DAY
Which organization annually awards the Heisman Trophy?

BIRTHDAYS TODAY

James Paul David (Jim) Bunning, 67, US Congressman and Baseball Hall of Fame pitcher, born Southgate, KY, Oct 23, 1931.

Douglas Richard (Doug) Flutie, 36, Heisman Trophy quarterback, born Manchester, MD, Oct 23, 1962.

Alois Terry (Al) Leiter, 33, baseball player, born Toms River, NJ, Oct 23, 1965.

Pele (born Edson Arantes do Nascimento), 58, former soccer player, born Tres Coracoes, Brazil, Oct 23, 1940.

Juan ("Chi-Chi") Rodriguez, 64, golfer, born Rio Piedras, Puerto Rico, Oct 23, 1934.

Michael John (Mike) Tomczak, 36, football player, born Calumet City, IL, Oct 23, 1962.

OCTOBER 24 — SATURDAY

Day 297 — 68 Remaining

WORLD SERIES CHAMPIONS THIS DATE
1992   Toronto Blue Jays

BLUEGE, OSSIE: BIRTH ANNIVERSARY. Oct 24, 1900. Oswald Louis (Ossie) Bluege, baseball player, manager and executive born at Chicago, IL. Bluege is the only man to have played on all three of the Washington Senators' World Series teams. He played 18 years in the majors, primarily as a third baseman, and managed the Senators from 1943 through 1947. Died at Edina, MN, Oct 14, 1985.

SOCKALEXIS, LOUIS: BIRTH ANNIVERSARY. Oct 24, 1871. Louis M. Sockalexis, baseball player born at Old Town, ME. A Penobscot, Sockalexis is credited with being the first Native American to play major league baseball. He played for the Cleveland National League team in 1897–99, but his effect on that city was so strong that in 1914, its American League team was renamed the Indians in his honor. Died at Burlington, ME, Dec 24, 1913.

TORONTO TAKES SERIES TROPHY OUT OF US: ANNIVERSARY. Oct 24, 1992. The Toronto Blue Jays defeated the Atlanta Braves, 4–3, in 11 innings in Game 6 to become the first non-US-based team to win the World Series.

WILLIAMSON, NED: BIRTH ANNIVERSARY. Oct 24, 1857. Edward Nagle (Ned) Williamson, baseball player born at Philadelphia, PA. Williamson is regarded as the finest third baseman of the 1880s. He played for baseball's first real dynasty, the Chicago White Stockings, who won five early National League pennants. Died at Hot Springs, AR, Mar 3, 1894.

WORLD'S FIRST SOCCER CLUB: ANNIVERSARY. Oct 24, 1857. The world's first soccer club, the Sheffield Football Club in Sheffield, England, was founded. Six years later, the first soccer league, the Football Association of England, was founded.

BIRTHDAYS TODAY

Rafael Leonidas Belliard, 37, baseball player, born Puerto Nuevo Mao, Dominican Republic, Oct 24, 1961.

James Patrick (Jim) Brosnan, 69, author (*Pennant Race* and *The Long Season*) and former baseball player, born Cincinnati, OH, Oct 24, 1929.

October 1998	S	M	T	W	T	F	S
					1	2	3
	4	5	6	7	8	9	10
	11	12	13	14	15	16	17
	18	19	20	21	22	23	24
	25	26	27	28	29	30	31

Rawlins Jackson (Rawly) Eastwick, III, 48, former baseball player, born Camden, NJ, Oct 24, 1950.

Kenny Holmes, 25, football player, born Vero Beach, FL, Oct 24, 1973.

Jay McKinley Novacek, 36, football player, born Martin, SD, Oct 24, 1962.

Arthur Lee Rhodes, Jr, 29, baseball player, born Waco, TX, Oct 24, 1969.

Yelberton Abraham (Y.A.) Tittle, Jr, 72, Pro Football Hall of Fame quarterback, born Marshall, TX, Oct 24, 1926.

☆   ☆   ☆

OCTOBER 25 — SUNDAY

Day 298 — 67 Remaining

WORLD SERIES CHAMPIONS THIS DATE
1987   Minnesota Twins

COOKE, JACK KENT: BIRTH ANNIVERSARY. Oct 25, 1912. Jack Kent Cooke, sports entrepreneur born at Hamilton, Ontario, Canada. Cooke made his fortune, estimated at $825 million, in broadcasting, real estate and newspapers. He owned race horses, the Los Angeles Lakers, the Los Angeles Kings and the Washington Redskins. He also built the Fabulous Forum in Inglewood, CA, and was at the time of his death planning a new stadium for the Redskins in suburban Virginia. Crusty and flamboyant, he was married five times, once paying $49 million in a divorce settlement. Died at Washington, DC, Apr 6, 1997

HOLYFIELD WINS HEAVYWEIGHT TITLE: ANNIVERSARY. Oct 25, 1990. Evander Holyfield knocked out James ("Buster") Douglas in the third round of a fight in Las Vegas to win the heavyweight title. The fight was Douglas's first defense after his surprise victory over Mike Tyson Feb 10, 1990. Holyfield held the title until he was beaten by Riddick Bowe Nov 13, 1992.

MARSHALL'S WRONG-WAY RUN: ANNIVERSARY. Oct 25, 1964. In a game between the Minnesota Vikings and the San Francisco 49ers, Minnesota defensive end Jim Marshall picked up a fumble by 49ers quarterback Billy Kilmer and ran 66 yards into the wrong end zone. His gaffe resulted in a safety, 2 points for San Francisco, but the Vikings still prevailed, 27–22.

MOOKIE'S GROUNDER THROUGH BUCKNER'S LEGS: ANNIVERSARY. Oct 25, 1986. The New York Mets won Game 6 of the World Series, 6–5, in 10 innings, over the Boston Red Sox. The Mets made a dramatic comeback in the last inning, scoring three runs after two were out. Twice down to their last strike, they bunched three singles, a wild pitch and a ground ball by Mookie Wilson that went through the legs of first baseman Bill Buckner to eke out the victory.

US: DAYLIGHT SAVING TIME ENDS; STANDARD TIME RESUMES. Oct 25–Apr 4, 1999. Standard Time resumes at 2 AM on the last Sunday in October in each time zone, as provided by the Uniform Time Act of 1966 (as amended in 1986 by Public Law 99–359). Many use the popular rule "spring forward, fall back" to remember which way to turn their clocks. See also: "US: Daylight Saving Time" (Apr 5).

WOOD, SMOKY JOE: BIRTH ANNIVERSARY. Oct 25, 1889. Joe ("Smoky Joe") Wood, baseball player and coach born at Kansas City, MO. Wood is regarded as one of the fastest pitchers of all time even though his career was cut short by a sore arm. After becoming an outfielder and then retiring, he coached baseball at Yale. Died at West Haven, CT, July 27, 1985.

BIRTHDAYS TODAY

Robert William (Bobby) Brown, 74, former baseball executive and player, born Seattle, WA, Oct 25, 1924.

Kelly Wayne Chase, 31, hockey player, born Porcupine Plain, Saskatchewan, Canada, Oct 25, 1967.

Wendel Clark, 32, hockey player, born Kelvington, Saskatchewan, Canada, Oct 25, 1966.

David William (Dave) Cowens, 50, basketball coach and Basketball Hall of Fame center, born Newport, KY, Oct 25, 1948.

Daniel Wayne (Danny) Darwin, 43, former baseball player, born Bonham, TX, Oct 25, 1955.

Daniel Mack (Dan) Gable, 50, college wrestling coach and Olympic gold medal wrestler, born Waterloo, IA, Oct 25, 1948.

Robert Montgomery (Bobby) Knight, 58, college basketball coach and former player, born Orrville, OH, Oct 25, 1940.

Russell Charles (Russ) Meyer, 75, former baseball player, born Peru, IL, Oct 25, 1923.

Muffin Spencer-Devlin, 45, golfer, born Piqua, OH, Oct 25, 1953.

Patrick Travis (Pat) Swilling, 34, football player, born Toccoa, GA, Oct 25, 1964.

Robert Brown (Bobby) Thomson, 75, former baseball player, born Glasgow, Scotland, Oct 25, 1923.

☆　☆　☆

OCTOBER 26 — MONDAY
Day 299 — 66 Remaining

WORLD SERIES CHAMPIONS THIS DATE

1911	Philadelphia Athletics
1996	New York Yankees

DENKINGER'S CONTROVERSIAL CALL: ANNIVERSARY. Oct 26, 1985. The Kansas City Royals tied the World Series, three games to three, against the St. Louis Cardinals by winning Game 6, 2–1. A controversial call at first base by umpire Don Denkinger and a two-run single by Dane Iorg brought the Royals the win. Kansas City won the seventh game the next day, 11–0.

FULKS, JOE: BIRTH ANNIVERSARY. Oct 26, 1921. Joseph (Joe) Fulks, Basketball Hall of Fame forward born at Birmingham, KY. Fulks earned All-American honors at Murray State University in 1943 and developed the innovative jump shot, first using two hands and then gradually switching to one hand. After World War II, he was an outstanding scorer with the Philadelphia Warriors. On Feb 10, 1949, he scored 63 points in a game against the Indianapolis Jets, a league record at the time. Inducted into the Hall of Fame in 1977. Died at Eddyville, KY, Mar 21, 1976.

GLEASON, KID: BIRTH ANNIVERSARY. Oct 26, 1866. William J. ("Kid") Gleason, baseball player and manager born at Camden, NJ. Gleason was a major league pitcher around the turn of the century. His career spanned 23 years after which he coached and managed the Chicago White Sox, including the infamous 1919 "Black Sox." Died at Philadelphia, PA, Jan 2, 1933.

JOHNSON, JUDY: BIRTH ANNIVERSARY. Oct 26, 1899. William Julius (Judy) Johnson, Baseball Hall of Fame third baseman born at Snow Hill, MD. Johnson was a defensive specialist who hit for a high average with occasional power. After retiring, he scouted for several teams. Inducted into the Hall of Fame in 1975. Died at Wilmington, DE, June 14, 1989.

Jack Sharkey

MEN'S SENIOR BASEBALL LEAGUE WORLD SERIES.
Oct 26–Nov 7 (tentative). Various spring training facilities, Phoenix, AZ. The 11th annual National Amateur Hardball World Series for men 30 and over. 275 teams expected in 1998. Est attendance: 4,500. For info: MSBL, One Huntington Quadrangle, 3 No 7, Melville, NY 11797. Phone: (516) 753-6725. Fax: (516) 753-4031. WWW: http://www.msbl.com

SELEE, FRANK: BIRTH ANNIVERSARY. Oct 26, 1859. Frank Gibson Selee, baseball player, manager and executive born at Amherst, NH. Selee is probably the best baseball manager not in the Hall of Fame. He guided the Boston National League team of the 1890s to five pennants in nine years, and then, after moving to Chicago, built the team that won three straight pennants in 1906, 1907 and 1908. Died at Denver, CO, July 5, 1909.

SHARKEY, JACK: BIRTH ANNIVERSARY. Oct 26, 1902. Jack Sharkey, boxer born Joseph Paul Zukauskas at Binghamton, NY. Sharkey won the heavyweight championship on June 21, 1932, defeating Max Schmeling, and lost it a year later to Primo Carnera. After retirement, he became a referee and one of the world's top fly casters. Died at Beverly, MA, Aug 17, 1994.

CHASE'S SPORTSQUOTE OF THE DAY

"Children have been conceived and born during a Mike Hargrove at-bat." —Broadcaster Norm Hitzges

---

BIRTHDAYS TODAY

Walter Eugene ("Chuck") Foreman, 48, former football player, born Frederick, MO, Oct 26, 1950.
Dudley Michael (Mike) Hargrove, 49, baseball manager and former player, born Perryton, TX, Oct 26, 1949.
Colbert Dale ("Toby") Harrah, 50, former baseball player, born Sissonville, WV, Oct 26, 1948.
Stephen Douglas (Steve) Rogers, 49, former baseball player, born Jefferson City, MO, Oct 26, 1949.

OCTOBER 27 — TUESDAY

Day 300 — 65 Remaining

WORLD SERIES CHAMPIONS THIS DATE

1985	Kansas City Royals
1986	New York Mets
1991	Minnesota Twins

GEORGE, BILL: BIRTH ANNIVERSARY. Oct 27, 1930. William (Bill) George, Pro Football Hall of Fame linebacker, born at Waynesburg, PA. George played college football at Wake Forest and then was drafted by the Chicago Bears. Originally a middle guard, playing down on the line of scrimmage, George invented the position of middle linebacker, playing up and behind the line. Inducted into the Hall of Fame in 1974. Died in an automobile accident near Rockford, IL, Sept 30, 1982.

NFL AWARDS FRANCHISE TO CAROLINA: ANNIVERSARY. Oct 27, 1993. The NFL awarded its 29th franchise to the Carolina Panthers, who began play in the 1995 season.

October *1998*	S	M	T	W	T	F	S
					1	2	3
	4	5	6	7	8	9	10
	11	12	13	14	15	16	17
	18	19	20	21	22	23	24
	25	26	27	28	29	30	31

BIRTHDAYS TODAY

Paul Broten, 33, hockey player, born Roseau, MN, Oct 27, 1965.
Ruby Dee, 74, actress (*The Jackie Robinson Story*), born Cleveland, OH, Oct 27, 1924.
Elijah Jerry ("Pumpsie") Green, 65, former baseball player, born Oakland, CA, Oct 27, 1933.
Ralph McPherran Kiner, 76, broadcaster and Baseball Hall of Fame outfielder, born Santa Rita, NM, Oct 27, 1922.
Brad Lauer, 32, hockey player, born Humboldt, Saskatchewan, Canada, Oct 27, 1966.
Mary Terslegge Meagher, 34, Olympic gold medal swimmer, born Louisville, KY, Oct 27, 1964.
Leon Joseph ("Bip") Roberts, III, 35, baseball player, born Berkeley, CA, Oct 27, 1963.
Patty Sheehan, 42, LPGA Hall of Fame golfer, born Middlebury, VT, Oct 27, 1956.
William Charles (Bill) Swift, 37, baseball player, born South Portland, ME, Oct 27, 1961.
Dick Trickle, 57, auto racer, born Wisconsin Rapids, WI, Oct 27, 1941.

OCTOBER 28 — WEDNESDAY

Day 301 — 64 Remaining

WORLD SERIES CHAMPIONS THIS DATE

1981	Los Angeles Dodgers
1989	Oakland A's
1995	Atlanta Braves

FIRST MEN'S FIELD HOCKEY GAME: 70th ANNIVERSARY. Oct 28, 1928. The Westchester Field Hockey Club of Rye, NY, defeated the Germantown Cricket Club of Germantown, PA, 2–1, in the first organized men's field hockey game played in the US.

MOON PHASE: FIRST QUARTER. Oct 28. Moon enters First Quarter phase at 6:46 AM, EDT.

NATIONAL HORSE SHOW. Oct 28–31. Madison Square Garden, New York, NY. Hunters, Jumpers, Saddleseat, Rolex-Maclay Medal Finals. For info: Natl Horse Show, PO Box 2761, New York, NY 10116-2761. Phone: (516) 484-1865.

NEUN, JOHNNY: BIRTH ANNIVERSARY. Oct 28, 1900. John Henry (Johnny) Neun, baseball player and manager born at Baltimore, MD. Neun completed an unassisted triple play on May 31, 1927, while a member of the Detroit Tigers. He served as interim manager of the New York Yankees in 1946 and managed the Cincinnati Reds in 1947 and 1948. Died at Baltimore, Mar 28, 1990.

PAGE, JOE: BIRTH ANNIVERSARY. Oct 28, 1917. Joseph Francis (Joe) Page, baseball player born at Cherry Valley, PA. Page was a star relief pitcher for the New York Yankees in the late 1940s and helped develop the role now known as the "closer," the specialist whose job it is to finish games when his team has the lead. Died at Latrobe, PA, Apr 21, 1980.

SECRETARIAT'S CAREER ENDS: 25th ANNIVERSARY. Oct 28, 1973. Secretariat, the colt many considered the greatest thoroughbred racer of all time, concluded his career with a victory in the Canadian International Championship at Woodbine Race Course. His jockey on this occasion was Eddie Maple, substituting for the suspended Ron Turcotte.

BIRTHDAYS TODAY

Stephen Dennis (Steve) Atwater, 32, football player, born Chicago, IL, Oct 28, 1966.

Kevin Dineen, 35, hockey player, born Quebec City, Quebec, Canada, Oct 28, 1963.

Juan Andres Guzman, 32, baseball player, born Santo Domingo, Dominican Republic, Oct 28, 1966.

Benoit Hogue, 32, hockey player, born Repentigny, Quebec, Canada, Oct 28, 1966.

William Bruce Jenner, 49, broadcaster and Olympic gold medal decathlete, born Mount Kisco, NY, Oct 28, 1949.

Bowie Kent Kuhn, 72, former commissioner of baseball, born Takoma Park, MD, Oct 28, 1926.

Leonard Randolph (Lenny) Wilkens, 61, basketball coach and Basketball Hall of Fame guard, born New York, NY, Oct 28, 1937.

OCTOBER 29 — THURSDAY
Day 302 — 63 Remaining

BROWNS BECOME ORIOLES: 45th ANNIVERSARY. Oct 29, 1953. The sale of the St. Louis Browns from Bill Veeck to a group of Baltimore investors was completed, and the American League's most hapless team became the Orioles.

EBBETS, CHARLES: BIRTH ANNIVERSARY. Oct 29, 1859. Charles Hercules Ebbets, baseball executive born at New York, NY. Ebbets bought into the Brooklyn baseball club in 1890 and became controlling owner in 1898. He sold 50% of the team to build Ebbets Field, the park whose enduring reputation has been the model for the new, old-fashioned parks constructed in recent years. Died at New York, Apr 18, 1925.

FORT LAUDERDALE INTERNATIONAL BOAT SHOW. Oct 29–Nov 2. Greater Ft Lauderdale/Broward County Convention Center. Everything from small boats to megayachts to boating equipment. Visitors attend from all over the world. For info: Greater Ft Lauderdale Conv/Visitors Bureau, 1850 Eller Dr, Ste 303, Ft Lauderdale, FL 33316. Phone: (954) 765-4466.

NBA ANNOUNCES ITS 50 GREATEST PLAYERS: ANNIVERSARY. Oct 29, 1996. The National Basketball Association got set to launch its 50th anniversary season by announcing its 50 greatest players of all time. Ten of the 50 spent significant portions of their careers with the Boston Celtics.

THE TOUR CHAMPIONSHIP. Oct 29–Nov 1. East Lake Golf Course, Atlanta, GA. The PGA Tour tournament marking the end of the year's tour. For info: PGA Tour, 112 TPC Blvd, Ponte Vedra Beach, FL 32082. Phone: (904) 285-3700.

BIRTHDAYS TODAY

Jesse Lee Barfield, 39, former baseball player, born Joliet, IL, Oct 29, 1959.

James Blair (Jim) Bibby, 54, former baseball player, born Franklinton, NC, Oct 29, 1944.

Michael D'Andrea Carter, 38, former football player, born Dallas, TX, Oct 29, 1960.

Gustavo ("Karim") Garcia, 23, baseball player, born Ciudad Obregon, Mexico, Oct 29, 1975.

Michael Alfred (Mike) Gartner, 39, hockey player, born Ottawa, Ontario, Canada, Oct 29, 1959.

Joel Stuart Otto, 37, hockey player, born Elk River, MN, Oct 29, 1961.

John Thomas (J.T.) Smith, 43, former football player, born Leonard, TX, Oct 29, 1955.

OCTOBER 30 — FRIDAY
Day 303 — 62 Remaining

SPORTSCHASER OF THE DAY

Who knocked out Sonny Liston in 1964 to become heavyweight champion?

ALI REGAINS TITLE: ANNIVERSARY. Oct 30, 1974. Muhammad Ali regained the heavyweight title by knocking out defending champion George Foreman in the eighth round of a fight in Kinshasa, Zaire.

ATLAS, CHARLES: 105th BIRTH ANNIVERSARY. Oct 30, 1893. Charles Atlas, bodybuilder born Angelo Siciliano at Acri, Calabria, Italy. Atlas created a popular mail-order bodybuilding course, pegged to his own youthful troubles as a "97-lb weakling." The legendary sand-kicking episode used later in advertising for his course occurred at Coney Island when a lifeguard kicked sand in Atlas's face and stole his girlfriend. Three generations of comic book fans read his advertisements. Died at Long Beach, NY, Dec 24, 1972.

BIG EAST MEN'S AND WOMEN'S CROSS-COUNTRY CHAMPIONSHIPS. Oct 30. Franklin Park, Boston, MA. For info: Big East Conference, 56 Exchange Terrace, Providence, RI 02903. Phone: (401) 453-0660. Fax: (401) 751-8540.

BUCYK GETS 500th GOAL: ANNIVERSARY. Oct 30, 1975. Winger Johnny ("Chief") Bucyk of the Boston Bruins scored the 500th goal of his career in a 3–2 Bruins' victory over the St. Louis Blues. Bucyk finished his career with 556 goals and entered the Hockey Hall of Fame in 1981.

CASSIUS CLAY NAMED HEAVYWEIGHT CHAMP: ANNIVERSARY. Oct 30, 1964. Twenty-two-year-old Cassius Clay, who later changed his name to Muhammad Ali, became world heavyweight boxing champion by defeating Sonny Liston. Ali was well known for both his fighting ability and his personal style. His most famous saying was "I am the greatest!" Convicted of violating the Selective Service Act in 1967, he was stripped of his title; the Supreme Court reversed the decision, though, in 1971. Ali was the only fighter to win the heavyweight boxing title three separate times (and he defended that title nine times) until Evander Holyfield defeated Mike Tyson in 1996.

DAY, LEON: BIRTH ANNIVERSARY. Oct 30, 1916. Leon Day, Baseball Hall of Fame pitcher, outfielder and second baseman born at Alexandria, VA. Day was a star in the Negro Leagues in the 1930s and 1940s. Died at Baltimore, MD, Mar 13, 1995, one week after being elected to the Hall of Fame and four months before his induction.

NATIONAL BASKETBALL ASSOCIATION REGULAR SEASON. Oct 30–Apr 18, 1999 (tentative). The National Basketball Association opens its 53rd regular season leading to the playoffs and the NBA Finals. Each of the league's 29 teams plays an 82-game schedule. Eight teams from each of the two conferences qualify for the postseason. For info: Natl Basketball Assn, Olympic Tower, 645 Fifth Ave, New York, NY 10022. Phone: (212) 826-7000. WWW: http://www.nba.com/

TERRY, BILL: BIRTH ANNIVERSARY. Oct 30, 1898. William Harold (Bill) Terry, Baseball Hall of Fame first baseman and manager born at Atlanta, GA. Terry was the last National League player to hit .400, batting .401 in 1930. He succeed John McGraw as manager of the New York Giants in 1932. Inducted into the Hall of Fame in 1954. Died at Jacksonville, FL, Jan 9, 1989.

BIRTHDAYS TODAY

Joseph Wilbur (Joe) Adcock, 71, former baseball manager and player, born Coushatta, LA, Oct 30, 1927.
Robert Randall (Bobby) Bragan, 81, former baseball manager and player, born Birmingham, AL, Oct 30, 1917.
Ty Hubert Detmer, 31, football player, born San Marcos, TX, Oct 30, 1967.
Scott William Garrelts, 37, former baseball player, born Champaign, IL, Oct 30, 1961.
James Ray (Jim Ray) Hart, 57, former baseball player, born Hookerton, NC, Oct 30, 1941.
Diego Armando Maradona, 38, former soccer player, born Lanus, Argentina, Oct 30, 1960.
James Evan (Jim) Perry, 62, former baseball player, born Williamston, NC, Oct 30, 1936.
Mark Steven Portugal, 36, baseball player, born Los Angeles, CA, Oct 30, 1962.
Danilo Mora (Danny) Tartabull, 36, baseball player, born Miami, FL, Oct 30, 1962.

OCTOBER 31 — SATURDAY
Day 304 — 61 Remaining

ANTLEY WINS NINE RACES: ANNIVERSARY. Oct 31, 1987. Chris Antley became the first jockey to win nine races in a single day. He won four races in six tries at Aqueduct in the afternoon and five more in eight races at The Meadowlands at night.

CHAMPIONSHIP CAT SHOW. Oct 31–Nov 1. Indiana State Fairgrounds, Indianapolis, IN. Exhibition and judging of longhair and shorthair purebred cats and kittens and mixed-breed household pets. Est attendance: 2,500. For info: Indy Cat Club, Cat Fanciers Assn, Maribeth Echard, 8507 N Illinois, Indianapolis, IN 46260. Phone: (317) 251-4486. Fax: (317) 254-9688.

FIRST BLACK PLAYS IN NBA GAME: ANNIVERSARY. Oct 31, 1950. Earl Lloyd became the first black ever to play in an NBA game when he took the floor for the Washington Capitols in Rochester, NY. Lloyd was actually one of three blacks to become NBA players in the 1950 season, the others being Nat ("Sweetwater") Clifton, who was signed by the New York Knicks, and Chuck Cooper, who was drafted by the Boston Celtics (and debuted the night after Lloyd).

GIANT NFL TRADE COMPLETED: ANNIVERSARY. Oct 31, 1987. Running back Eric Dickerson signed a contract with the Indianapolis Colts to complete a complex, three-team NFL trade. The Colts got Dickerson from the Los Angeles Rams in exchange for one player and three draft choices. The Rams acquired an additional three draft picks and another player from the Buffalo Bills in exchange for the Colts' trading the rights to linebacker Cornelius Bennett to the Bills.

HALLOWE'EN or ALL HALLOW'S EVE. Oct 31. An ancient celebration combining Druid autumn festival and Christian customs. Hallowe'en (All Hallow's Eve) is the beginning of Hallowtide, a season that embraces the Feast of All Saints (Nov 1) and the Feast of All Souls (Nov 2). The observance, dating from the sixth or seventh centuries, has long been associated with thoughts of the dead, spirits, witches, ghosts and devils. In fact, the ancient Celtic Feast of Samhain, the festival that marked the beginning of winter and of the New Year, was observed on Nov 1.

HUBBARD, CAL: BIRTH ANNIVERSARY. Oct 31, 1900. Robert Cal Hubbard, Pro Football Hall of Fame tackle and Baseball Hall of Fame umpire born at Keytesville, MO. Hubbard played college and professional football and is regarded as one of the game's greatest linemen. After a short coaching career, he became an American League umpire and later supervisor of umpires. Inducted into the Pro Football Hall of Fame as a charter member in 1963 and into the Baseball Hall of Fame in 1976. Died at Milan, MO, Oct 19, 1977.

KELTNER, KEN: BIRTH ANNIVERSARY. Oct 31, 1916. Kenneth Frederick (Ken) Keltner, baseball player born at Milwaukee, WI. Keltner's two sterling plays at third base for the Cleveland Indians on July 17, 1941, helped end Joe DiMaggio's 56-game hitting streak. Died at Greenfield, WI, Dec 12, 1991.

BIRTHDAYS TODAY

Theodore ("Blue") Edwards, 33, basketball player, born Washington, DC, Oct 31, 1965.
Roger Kahn, 71, author (*The Boys of Summer, Good Enough to Dream, The Era* and *Memories of Summer*) and sportswriter, born New York, NY, Oct 31, 1927.
John Harding Lucas, Jr, 45, former basketball coach and player, born Durham, NC, Oct 31, 1953.
Frederick Stanley (Fred) McGriff, 35, baseball player, born Tampa, FL, Oct 31, 1963.
David Arthur (Dave) McNally, 56, former baseball player, born Billings, MT, Oct 31, 1942.
Matthew Dodge (Matt) Nokes, 35, former baseball player, born San Diego, CA, Oct 31, 1963.
Edward Kenneth (Eddie) Taubensee, 30, baseball player, born Beeville, TX, Oct 31, 1968.
Stephen Christopher (Steve) Trachsel, 28, baseball player, born Oxnard, CA, Oct 31, 1970.
Ross Verba, 25, football player, born West Des Moines, IA, Oct 31, 1973.

NOVEMBER 1 — SUNDAY
Day 305 — 60 Remaining

ENGLAND: RAC LONDON TO BRIGHTON VETERAN CAR RUN. Nov 1. London. A 57-mile run for a maximum of 400 veteran cars, along the A23 road from Serpentine Row, Hyde Park, London, to Madiera Drive, Brighton, England. Celebrates emancipation—the abolition in 1896 of English law requiring that a man carrying a red flag walk in front of motor vehicles. Annually, the first Sunday in November. Est attendance: 10,000,000. For info: RAC Motor Sports Assn Ltd, Events Department, Riverside Park, Colnbrook, England, SL3 OHG. Phone: (44) (175) 368-1736. Fax: (44) (175) 368-2938. E-mail: racmsa@compuserve.com.

FIRST BAA GAME: ANNIVERSARY. Nov 1, 1946. The New York Knickerbockers defeated the Toronto Huskies, 68–66, in the first regular season game ever played in the Basketball Association of America. (The BAA merged with the National Basketball League in 1949 to form the National Basketball Association.) For this inaugural contest, any fan taller than 6 ′ 8 ″ Huskies center George Nostrand was admitted free.

HOCKEY MASK INTRODUCED: ANNIVERSARY. Nov 1, 1959. Tired of stopping hockey pucks with his face, Montreal Canadiens goalie Jacques Plante, having received another wound, reemerged from the locker room with seven new stitches—and a plastic face mask he had made from fiberglass and resin. Although Cliff Benedict had tried a leather mask back in the '20s and the idea didn't catch on then, after Plante wore his, goalies throughout the NHL began wearing protective plastic face shields.

NATIONAL FOOTBALL WIDOWS MONTH. Nov 1–30. A time to recognize the sacrifices and contributions of the armchair quarterback's better half. The National Football Widows League (NFWL) wants sports-spurned spouses to know that they are not alone. There are ways of coping at this difficult time when husbands trade in their libidos for snack foods. It's time for football widows everywhere to stand up—and not just so hubby can find the remote. For info: NFWL, PO Box 861001, St. Augustine, FL 32086. Phone: (904) 797-6797.

NEW YORK CITY MARATHON. Nov 1. New York, NY. 29,000 runners from all over the world gather to compete in the largest spectator event with more than two million spectators watching from the sidelines. For info: NY Road Runners Club, 9 E 89th St, New York, NY 10128. Phone: (212) 423-3233. Fax: (212) 860-8421. E-mail: membership@nyrrc.org. WWW: http://www.nyrrc.org

NFL AWARDS FRANCHISE TO NEW ORLEANS: ANNIVERSARY. Nov 1, 1966. On All Saints Day, the National Football League awarded a franchise to New Orleans.

The team, nicknamed the Saints, began play in 1967 but did not finish a season at .500 until 1979.

NOTRE DAME USES FORWARD PASSES TO DEFEAT ARMY: 85TH ANNIVERSARY. Nov 1, 1913. In the first football game between two emerging gridiron powers, Notre Dame upset Army, 35–13, surprising the Cadets with an unprecedented barrage of forward passes. Quarterback Gus Dorais completed 14 of 17 passes for 243 yards. His frequent target was end Knute Rockne.

RICE, GRANTLAND: BIRTH ANNIVERSARY. Nov 1, 1880. Henry Grantland Rice, sportswriter born at Murfreesboro, TN. Rice played football and baseball at Vanderbilt, but after graduating in 1901, he quickly fell into sportswriting. He incorporated verse into his columns, the success of which got him to New York in 1911. Rice liked covering football best, but he also reveled in establishing nicknames, including the Four Horsemen, and promoting the careers of athletes. He wrote with great enthusiasm and helped create what many have called the Golden Age of Sports. Died at New York, NY, July 13, 1954.

SEABISCUIT DEFEATS WAR ADMIRAL: 60th ANNIVERSARY. Nov 1, 1938. In a special match race at Pimlico, Seabiscuit, ridden by George Wolff, defeated favored War Admiral before a crowd of 40,000. Seabiscuit captured the winner-take-all purse of $15,000.

Tahir ("Tie") Domi, 29, hockey player, born Windsor, Ontario, Canada, Nov 1, 1969.

Theodore Paul (Ted) Hendricks, 51, Pro Football Hall of Fame linebacker, born Guatemala City, Guatemala, Nov 1, 1947.

Gary Jim Player, 63, golfer, born Johannesburg, South Africa, Nov 1, 1935.

Victor Felipe (Vic) Power, 67, former baseball player, born Arecibo, Puerto Rico, Nov 1, 1931.

Gary Eugene Redus, 42, former baseball player, born Tanner, AL, Nov 1, 1956.

Fernando Anguamea Valenzuela, 38, baseball player, born Navojoa, Sonora, Mexico, Nov 1, 1960.

NOVEMBER 2 — MONDAY
Day 306 — 59 Remaining

CHASE'S SPORTSQUOTE OF THE DAY

"My greatest thrill? In 1921 I played for Little Rock in the Southern League and the first time I stepped on the field I was in awe. It held 4,500 people and I never saw a park that big. And there I was holding up my pants with a cotton rope." —Travis Jackson

AUSTRALIA: RECREATION DAY. Nov 2. Annually, the first Monday in November is observed as Recreation Day in Northern Tasmania, Australia.

BEACH TOWEL WINS $2 MILLION: ANNIVERSARY. Nov 2, 1990. Beach Towel, a three-year-old pacer, became the first harness horse to win $2 million in a single year by capturing the Breeders Crown three-year-old Colt and Gelding Pace. The victory pushed Beach Towel's earnings to $2,091,860.

HAUGHTON, BILLY: 75th BIRTH ANNIVERSARY. Nov 2, 1923. William Robert (Billy) Haughton, standardbred driver and trainer born at Gloversville, NY. Haughton won nearly 4,900 races in his career. Along with Stanley Dancer, he dominated the New York trotting scene in the 1950s and then moved on to a national career. He suffered severe head injuries in a three-horse accident at Yonkers Raceway and died at Valhalla, NY, July 15, 1986.

JACKSON, TRAVIS: 95th BIRTH ANNIVERSARY. Nov 2, 1903. Travis Calvin Jackson, Baseball Hall of Fame shortstop, born at Waldo, AR. Jackson played shortstop for the pennant-winning New York Giants teams of the 1920s and 1930s. Inducted into the Hall of Fame in 1982. Died at Waldo, July 27, 1987.

NFL ATTENDANCE RECORD: 40th ANNIVERSARY. Nov 2, 1958. The Chicago Bears and the Los Angeles Rams set an NFL single-game attendance record as 90,833 fans watched the Rams beat the Bears, 41–35, at the Los Angeles Coliseum.

SHERIDAN, JOHN: DEATH ANNIVERSARY. Nov 2, 1914. John F. Sheridan, baseball umpire born at Decatur, IL, 1852. Sheridan sported a walrus mustache and personified the transition from the contentious umpires of the 19th century to the professionalism of the 20th. He initiated crouching behind the catcher to see pitches better, but he wore neither shin guards nor chest protector. Died at San Jose, CA.

November 1998

S	M	T	W	T	F	S
1	2	3	4	5	6	7
8	9	10	11	12	13	14
15	16	17	18	19	20	21
22	23	24	25	26	27	28
29	30					

Larry Chatmon Little, 53, Pro Football Hall of Fame guard, born Groveland, GA, Nov 2, 1945.

Willie Dean McGee, 40, baseball player, born San Francisco, CA, Nov 2, 1958.

Orlando Luis Merced, 32, baseball player, born San Juan, Puerto Rico, Nov 2, 1966.

Thomas Marian (Tom) Paciorek, 52, broadcaster and former baseball player, born Detroit, MI, Nov 2, 1946.

David Knapp (Dave) Stockton, 57, golfer, born San Bernardino, CA, Nov 2, 1941.

John Samuel (Johnny) Vander Meer, 84, former baseball player, born Prospect Park, NJ, Nov 2, 1914.

NOVEMBER 3 — TUESDAY
Day 307 — 58 Remaining

FLEISCHER, NAT: BIRTH ANNIVERSARY. Nov 3, 1887. Nathaniel S. (Nat) Fleischer, sportswriter born at New York, NY. Fleischer founded *The Ring* magazine in 1922, a publication generally regarded worldwide as "The Bible of Boxing." He served as editor and publisher, produced a record book and wrote over 50 boxing biographies and histories. Died at New York, NY, June 25, 1972.

GENERAL ELECTION DAY. Nov 3. Many state and local government elections on this day, as well as presidential and congressional elections in the appropriate years. All US Congressional seats and one-third of US senatorial seats are up for election in even-numbered years. Presidential elections are held in even-numbered years that can be divided equally by four. Annually, the first Tuesday after the first Monday in November.

MIKITA SCORES 1,000TH POINT: 25th ANNIVERSARY. Nov 3, 1973. Center Stan Mikita of the Chicago Black Hawks scored the 1,000th point of his NHL career, gaining an assist in a 5–4 loss to the Minnesota North Stars. Mikita finished his career with 1,467 points and entered the Hockey Hall of Fame in 1983.

NAGURSKI, BRONKO: 90th BIRTH ANNIVERSARY. Nov 3, 1908. Bronislau ("Bronko") Nagurski, Pro Football Hall of Fame tackle and fullback born at Rainy River, Ontario, Canada. He played football at the University of Minnesota, earning All-American honors at both positions, and for the Chicago Bears. After retiring from football, Nagurski wrestled professionally and operated a gas station. Inducted into the Hall of Fame as a charter member in 1963. Died at International Falls, MN, Jan 7, 1990.

PERIGEAN SPRING TIDES. Nov 3–4. Spring tides, the highest possible tides, which occur when New Moon or

Full Moon takes place within 24 hours of the moment the Moon is nearest Earth (perigee) in its monthly orbit, on Nov 3, at 7 PM, EST.

SUMMA, HOMER: 100th BIRTH ANNIVERSARY. Nov 3, 1898. Homer Wayne Summa, baseball player born at Gentry, MO. Summa batted .302 over 10 major league seasons. In 1927, he lined into an unassisted triple play. Died at Los Angeles, CA, Jan 29, 1966.

BIRTHDAYS TODAY

Derrick Cope, 40, auto racer, born Spanaway, WA, Nov 3, 1958.

Dwight Michael ("Dewey") Evans, 47, former baseball player, born Santa Monica, CA, Nov 3, 1951.

Robert William Andrew (Bob) Feller, 80, Baseball Hall of Fame pitcher, born Van Meter, IA, Nov 3, 1918.

Kenneth Dale (Ken) Holtzman, 53, former baseball player, born St. Louis, MO, Nov 3, 1950.

Paul John Quantrill, 30, baseball player, born London, Ontario, Canada, Nov 3, 1968.

Philip (Phil) Simms, 42, sportscaster, former football player, born Lebanon, KY, Nov 3, 1956.

Robert Lynn (Bob) Welch, 42, former baseball player, born Detroit, MI, Nov 3, 1956.

NOVEMBER 4 — WEDNESDAY
Day 308 — 57 Remaining

CONSIDINE, BOB: BIRTH ANNIVERSARY. Nov 4, 1906. Robert Bernard (Bob) Considine, sportswriter and author born at Washington, DC. Considine parlayed some early success as a tennis player and a job as a federal government clerk into a career as a sportswriter. He covered baseball starting in 1933 and soon became a columnist for the Hearst newspapers. He branched out into politics and national affairs and served as a war correspondent during World War II. He wrote or coauthored more than 25 books, including the screenplay for *Pride of the Yankees*, the film biography of Lou Gehrig. Died at New York, NY, Sept 1, 1975.

DOUGLAS, BOB: BIRTH ANNIVERSARY. Nov 4, 1884. Robert L. (Bob) Douglas, Basketball Hall of Fame executive born at St. Kitts, British West Indies. Douglas came to the US in 1888 and played basketball before founding the New York Renaissance, one of the game's greatest teams, in 1922. The Rens got their name from the Harlem Renaissance ballroom where they played their home games, but they barnstormed extensively as well. Over 22 years, they won 2,381 games, including the 1931 World Professional Championship. The Rens were inducted into the Hall of Fame as a team in 1963. Douglas followed as an individual contributor in 1971. Died at New York, NY, July 16, 1979.

FIRST FREE AGENT DRAFT: ANNIVERSARY. Nov 4, 1976. Major league baseball held its first draft of players who had declared themselves free agents. 24 players from 13 clubs were available for selection. Reggie Jackson eventually signed the most lucrative contract in this group, $2.9 million over five years, to play with the New York Yankees.

HUNTER'S MOON. Nov 4. The full moon following Harvest Moon. So called because the moon's light in evening extends day's length for hunters. Moon enters Full Moon phase at 12:18 AM, EST.

LEACH, TOMMY: BIRTH ANNIVERSARY. Nov 4, 1877. Thomas William (Tommy) Leach, baseball player born at French Creek, NY. Leach was a swift third baseman and outfielder in the first two decades of the 20th century. In retirement, he helped found the Florida State League. Died at Haines City, FL, Sept 29, 1969.

MOON PHASE: FULL MOON. Nov 4. Moon enters Full Moon phase at 12:18 AM, EDT.

SAWATSKI, CARL: BIRTH ANNIVERSARY. Nov 4, 1927. Carl Ernest Sawatski, baseball player and executive born at Shickshinny, PA. Sawatski played 11 years in the majors as a catcher and served as president of the Texas League. Died at Little Rock, AR, Nov 24, 1991.

STARK, DOLLY: BIRTH ANNIVERSARY. Nov 4, 1897. Albert ("Dolly") Stark, baseball umpire and sportscaster born at New York, NY. Stark played in the minor leagues and then switched to umpiring. He began the practice of following runners around the bases to be close enough to a play to make the right call. Died at New York, Aug 24, 1968.

TORONTO GRANTED NBA FRANCHISE: ANNIVERSARY. Nov 4, 1993. The NBA Board of Governors accepted a recommendation from the Expansion Committee to award a franchise to a Toronto group headed by John Bitove, Jr. The team, later named the Raptors, began play in the 1995–96 season.

BIRTHDAYS TODAY

Carlos Obed Baerga, 30, baseball player, born San Juan, Puerto Rico, Nov 4, 1968.

Eric Fichaud, 23, hockey player, born Montreal, Quebec, Canada, Nov 4, 1975.

John Patsy ("Tito") Francona, 65, former baseball player, born Aliquippa, PA, Nov 4, 1933.

Richard Morrow (Dick) Groat, 68, former baseball player, born Wilkinsburg, PA, Nov 4, 1930.

Eric Peter Karros, 31, baseball player, born Hackensack, NJ, Nov 4, 1967.

Orlando Lamar Pace, 23, football player, born Sandusky, OH, Nov 4, 1975.

NOVEMBER 5 — THURSDAY
Day 309 — 56 Remaining

FIRST SHATTERED BACKBOARD: ANNIVERSARY. Nov 5, 1946. Chuck Connors of the Boston Celtics became the first NBA player to shatter a backboard, doing so during the pregame warm-up in Boston Garden. Connors also played major league baseball with the Brooklyn Dodgers and the Chicago Cubs and gained fame as star of the television series, "The Rifleman."

NEALE, GREASY: BIRTH ANNIVERSARY. Nov 5, 1891. Alfred Earle ("Greasy") Neale, baseball player and Pro Football Hall of Fame player and coach born at Parkersburg, WV. Neale, with his childhood nickname, played baseball and football at West Virginia Wesleyan. He spent eight seasons as a major league outfielder and coached at a variety of colleges. In 1941, he became head coach of the Philadelphia Eagles, winning two NFL titles. A football innovator, he is credited with devising an early version of the 4–3 defense. Inducted into the Hall of Fame in 1967. Died at Lake Worth, FL, Nov 1, 1973.

BIRTHDAYS TODAY

Robert Cary Blanchard, 30, football player, born Fort Worth, TX, Nov 5, 1968.

Ralph Joseph ("Putsy") Caballero, 71, former baseball player, born New Orleans, LA, Nov 5, 1927.

Todd Collins, 27, football player, born Walpole, MA, Nov 5, 1971.

Johnny David Damon, 25, baseball player, born Fort Riley, KS, Nov 5, 1973.

Javier Lopez, 28, baseball player, born Ponce, Puerto Rico, Nov 5, 1970.

Lloyd Anthony Moseby, 39, former baseball player, born Portland, AR, Nov 5, 1959.

Jerry Darnell Stackhouse, 24, basketball player, born Kinston, NC, Nov 5, 1974.

William Theodore (Bill) Walton, III, 46, broadcaster and Basketball Hall of Fame center and forward, born La Mesa, CA, Nov 5, 1952.

Kellen Boswell Winslow, 41, Pro Football Hall of Fame tight end, born St. Louis, MO, Nov 5, 1957.

Alexei Yashin, 25, hockey player, born Sverdlovsk, USSR, Nov 5, 1973.

NOVEMBER 6 — FRIDAY
Day 310 — 55 Remaining

SPORTSCHASER OF THE DAY
Who published The Sporting News from 1914 to 1962?

BIG EAST WOMEN'S SOCCER CHAMPIONSHIP. Nov 6–8. University of Connecticut, Storrs, CT. For info: Big East Conference, 56 Exchange Terrace, Providence, RI 02903. Phone: (401) 453-0660. Fax: (401) 751-8540.

CANZONERI, TONY: 90th BIRTH ANNIVERSARY. Nov 6, 1908. Tony Canzoneri, boxer born at Slidell, LA. At various times between 1928, when he was only 19, and 1936, Canzoneri held the featherweight, lightweight and junior welterweight titles. A popular fighter who dressed well and kept a cigar clutched between his teeth, Canzoneri later ran a restaurant, acted and led a dance band. Died at New York, NY, Dec 10, 1959.

HALFWAY POINT OF AUTUMN. Nov 6. At 10:16 PM, EST, on Nov 6, 1998, 44 days, 21 hours and 39 minutes of autumn will have elapsed and the equivalent will remain before 8:56 PM, EST, on Dec 21 which is the winter solstice and the beginning of winter.

JOHNSON, WALTER: BIRTH ANNIVERSARY. Nov 6, 1887. Walter Perry Johnson, Baseball Hall of Fame pitcher born at Humboldt, KS. Johnson may well have been the best and the fastest pitcher of all time. He won 417 games, more than anyone else except Cy Young, and his nickname, the "Big Train," indicates the respect with which other players regarded his fastball. Inducted into the Hall of Fame as a charter member in 1936. Died in Washington, DC, Dec 10, 1946.

	S	**M**	**T**	**W**	**T**	**F**	**S**
November	1	2	3	4	5	6	7
1998	8	9	10	11	12	13	14
	15	16	17	18	19	20	21
	22	23	24	25	26	27	28
	29	30					

MAYS, REX: DEATH ANNIVERSARY. Nov 6, 1949. Rex Mays, auto racer born at Glendale, CA, 1913. Mays won two national driving championships in his 18-year career, but his aggressive style often led to equipment failure. He held the pole position four times at the Indianapolis 500, finished second twice but never won the race. His deep concern for driver safety once led him to crash his car rather than hit another driver. Died in a crash at Del Mar, CA.

NAISMITH, JAMES: BIRTH ANNIVERSARY. Nov 6, 1861. James Naismith, inventor of basketball born at Almonte, Ontario, Canada. Naismith invented basketball at the Springfield, MA, YMCA, as an indoor game to be played during the winter for exercise. He moved to Denver and then to the University of Kansas, but he never received recognition as the "father of basketball." A minister and a physical educator, he shunned competitive athletics and had little to do with the development of the game he invented. Inducted into the Basketball Hall of Fame as a charter member in 1959. Died at Lawrence, KS, Nov 28, 1939.

SPINK, TAYLOR: 110th BIRTH ANNIVERSARY. Nov 6, 1888. John George Taylor Spink, sports publisher born at St. Louis, MO. Spink inherited management of *The Sporting News* upon the death of his father in 1914. He made the weekly newspaper into the "Bible of Baseball," a trade paper of indispensable value to all those connected with the game. Spink was a baseball insider; his publication not only reported on what had happened, but also advocated what should happen. Died at St. Louis, Dec 7, 1962.

WALSH INVITATIONAL RIFLE TOURNAMENT. Nov 6–8 (also Nov 13–15 and 20–22). Xavier University, Cincinnati, OH. To promote marksmanship and sportsmanship in the competitive spirit of collegiate athletics. International smallbore rifle and air rifle match open to all competitors. Recognized as "the largest indoor smallbore and air rifle match in the nation." Sponsor: Xavier University Athletic Department. Est attendance: 300. For info: Alan Joseph, O'Conner Sports Ctr, Dept of Athletics, Xavier Univ, 3800 Victory Pkwy, Cincinnati, OH 45207-6114. Phone: (513) 745-3413. Fax: (513) 745-4390.

BIRTHDAYS TODAY

Derrick Scott Alexander, 27, football player, born Detroit, MI, Nov 6, 1971.

John Robert Candelaria, 45, former baseball player, born New York, NY, Nov 6, 1953.

Chad David Curtis, 30, baseball player, born Marion, IN, Nov 6, 1968.
Mack Jones, 60, former baseball player, born Atlanta, GA, Nov 6, 1938.
William Erik Kramer, 34, football player, born Encino, CA, Nov 6, 1964.
Gerald Antonio Riggs, 38, former football player, born Tullos, LA, Nov 6, 1960.

NOVEMBER 7 — SATURDAY
Day 311 — 54 Remaining

BERENSON SCORES SIX GOALS: 30th ANNIVERSARY. Nov 7, 1968. Center Gordon ("Red") Berenson of the St. Louis Blues scored six goals in a game against the Philadelphia Flyers to tie the record for most goals in a game set by Syd Howe of the Detroit Red Wings in 1944.

BIG EAST FIELD HOCKEY CHAMPIONSHIP. Nov 7–8. Villanova University, Villanova, PA. For info: Big East Conference, 56 Exchange Terrace, Providence, RI 02903. Phone: (401) 453-0660. Fax: (401) 751-8540.

BREEDERS' CUP CHAMPIONSHIP. Nov 7. Churchill Downs, Louisville, KY. Join the excitement of the 15th annual Breeders' Cup, the Super Bowl of horse racing. Est attendance: 60,000. For info: Breeders Cup Ltd, PO Box 4230, Lexington, KY 40544. Phone: (606) 223-5444. Fax: (606) 223-3945.
E-mail: breederscup@breederscup.com.
WWW: http://www.breederscup.com/

CANADA: FARMFAIR INTERNATIONAL. Nov 7–15. Northlands Park, Edmonton, Alberta, Canada. The largest purebred livestock show and sale in Canada. Features traditional western-style family entertainment, best-of-breed shows, purebred cattle sales, draft horse pulling and team cattle penning competitions and Alberta's only western-themed trade and gift show. Est attendance: 50,000. For info: Cheryl Herchen, Northlands Park, PO Box 1480, Edmonton, Alta, Canada T5J 2N5. Phone: (403) 471-7210 or (888) 800-PARK. Fax: (403) 471-8176.
E-mail: npmarket@planet.eon.net.
WWW: http://www.northlands.com

CARTER RELEASED: ANNIVERSARY. Nov 7, 1985. Former middleweight boxer Rubin ("Hurricane") Carter was released from Rahway (New Jersey) State Prison after serving 19 years for a triple murder committed in a Paterson, NJ, bar in 1966. US District Court Judge J. Lee Sorokin ruled that prosecutors had violated the civil rights of Carter and a codefendant during their trials in 1967 and 1976.

MAGIC JOHNSON RETIRES: ANNIVERSARY. Nov 7, 1991. Earvin ("Magic") Johnson of the Los Angeles Lakers retired from basketball after announcing that he had tested positive for HIV. Despite his retirement, Johnson played in the 1992 NBA All-Star game and in the 1992 Olympics as a member of the first US Dream Team. He coached the Lakers for part of the 1993–94 season and played part of the 1995–96 season before retiring again.

STEEPLECHASE AT CALLAWAY GARDENS. Nov 7. Pine Mountain, GA. A seven-race steeplechase "meet" where riders match their horses for speed and split-second timing over bush jumps. Box seating and infield tailgating spaces available. Est attendance: 12,000. For info: The Steeplechase at Callaway Gardens, PO Box 2311, Columbus, GA 31902. Phone: (706) 324-6252. Fax: (706) 324-3651.

BIRTHDAYS TODAY

James Lee (Jim) Kaat, 60, broadcaster and former baseball player, born Zeeland, MI, Nov 7, 1938.

John Albert ("Buck") Martinez, 50, broadcaster and former baseball player, born Redding, CA, Nov 7, 1948.
Joseph Franklin (Joe) Niekro, 54, former baseball player, born Martin's Ferry, OH, Nov 7, 1944.
Richard Lee (Dick) Stuart, 66, former baseball player, born San Francisco, CA, Nov 7, 1932.

NOVEMBER 8 — SUNDAY
Day 312 — 53 Remaining

AMERICAN SPORTS TRIVIA WEEK. Nov 8–14. Celebrates Americans' fascination with trivial information about sports, including baseball, football, basketball, hockey, auto racing and many more. For info: Judy Colbert, Tuff Turtle Publishing, Box 3308, Crofton, MD 21114-0308. Phone: (301) 858-0196.
E-mail: tuffturtle@aol.com.

AMERICAN QUARTER HORSE ASSOCIATION WORLD CHAMPIONSHIP SHOW. Nov 8–21. Oklahoma City, OK. Largest invitational world championship show. For info: AQHA, PO Box 200, Amarillo, TX 79168. Phone: (806) 376-4811. Fax: (806) 349-6409.
E-mail: aqhamail@arn.net. WWW: http://www.aqha.com

CUCCINELLO, TONY: BIRTH ANNIVERSARY. Nov 8, 1907. Anthony Francis (Tony) Cuccinello, baseball player and coach born at New York, NY. Cuccinello played 15 years in the major leagues and lost the 1945 American League batting championship on the season's last day. Died at Tampa, FL, Sept 19, 1995.

HARRIS, BUCKY: BIRTH ANNIVERSARY. Nov 8, 1896. Stanley Raymond ("Bucky") Harris, Baseball Hall of Fame player and manager born at Port Jervis, NY. Harris became manager of the Washington Senators when he was only 28. He wound up managing more major league games than any one except Connie Mack and John McGraw. Inducted into the Hall of Fame in 1975. Died at Bethesda, MD, Nov 8, 1977.

Frank McGuire

McGUIRE, FRANK: BIRTH ANNIVERSARY. Nov 8, 1916. Frank Joseph McGuire, Basketball Hall of Fame coach born at New York, NY. McGuire coached successfully at both the college and pro levels. His 1952 St. John's team lost to Kansas in the NCAA title game. In 1957, his University of North Carolina team defeated Kansas and Wilt Chamberlain to win the NCAA title. He coached the Philadelphia Warriors in the NBA and then returned to the college ranks at the University of South Carolina. Inducted into the Hall of Fame in 1976. Died at Columbia, SC, Oct 11, 1994.

NCAA DIVISION II FIELD HOCKEY CHAMPIONSHIP. Nov 8. Finals at a campus site TBA. For info: NCAA, 6201 College Blvd, Overland Park, KS 66211. Phone: (913) 339-1906.

NFL RECORD FIELD GOAL: ANNIVERSARY. Nov 8, 1970. Tom Dempsey of the New Orleans Saints set an NFL record by kicking a 63-yard field goal to give the Saints a 19–17 victory over the Detroit Lions.

NOTRE DAME TIES ARMY: ANNIVERSARY. Nov 8, 1946. The University of Notre Dame football team tied Army, 0–0, to snap West Point's 26-game winning streak.

RICHARD BECOMES NHL'S LEADING SCORER: ANNIVERSARY. Nov 8, 1952. Maurice ("Rocket") Richard of the Montreal Canadiens became the leading career goal scorer in the National Hockey League with his 325th goal in a 6–4 win over the Chicago Black Hawks.

BIRTHDAYS TODAY

Eric Todd Anthony, 31, baseball player, born San Diego, CA, Nov 8, 1967.
Jeffrey Michael (Jeff) Blauser, 33, baseball player, born Los Gatos, CA, Nov 8, 1965.
John Allen Denny, 46, former baseball player, born Prescott, AZ, Nov 8, 1952.
Qadry Rahmadan Ismail, 28, football player, born Newark, NJ, Nov 8, 1970.
Edward Emil (Ed) Kranepool, 54, former baseball player, born New York, NY, Nov 8, 1944.
Jose Antonio Offerman, 30, baseball player, born San Pedro de Macoris, Dominican Republic, Nov 8, 1968.
Henry Anderson Rodriguez, 31, baseball player, born Santo Domingo, Dominican Republic, Nov 8, 1967.
John Dwight Smith, 35, baseball player, born Tallahassee, FL, Nov 8, 1963.

NOVEMBER 9 — MONDAY
Day 313 — 52 Remaining

CHASE'S SPORTSQUOTE OF THE DAY

"I'll never make the mistake of being seventy again." — Casey Stengel after being fired at age 70

CHADWICK, FLORENCE: 80th BIRTH ANNIVERSARY. Nov 9, 1918. Florence May Chadwick, swimmer born at San Diego, CA. Chadwick never won a national title and failed to qualify for the US Olympic team in 1936, but she won enduring fame by becoming the first woman to swim the English Channel in both directions. She swam from France to England on Aug 8, 1950, and from England to France a year later. She made other long-

November 1998

S	M	T	W	T	F	S
1	2	3	4	5	6	7
8	9	10	11	12	13	14
15	16	17	18	19	20	21
22	23	24	25	26	27	28
29	30					

distance swims as well, including the Bristol Channel, the Catalina Island-to-California swim and the Strait of Gilbraltar. Died at San Diego, Mar 15, 1995.

GRAHAM, MOONLIGHT: BIRTH ANNIVERSARY. Nov 9, 1876. Archibald Wright ("Moonlight") Graham, baseball player born at Fayetteville, NC. Graham's brief major league career (one game and no at-bats) was fictionalized in *Field of Dreams*. Died at Chisholm, MN, Aug 25, 1965.

IKE BREAKS KNEECAP: ANNIVERSARY. Nov 9, 1912. West Point cadet Dwight D. Eisenhower broke his kneecap in a football game against Tufts University and gave up the sport forever. He did go on to prominence in other fields.

LIPSCOMB, BIG DADDY: BIRTH ANNIVERSARY. Nov 9, 1931. Gene Allen ("Big Daddy") Lipscomb, football player and wrestler born at Detroit, MI. Lipscomb was known as "Big Daddy" because he could not remember his teammates' names and called everyone "Little Daddy." He made All-Pro three times with the Baltimore Colts (1957, 1958 and 1959) and was one of the first defensive linemen to develop a distinct on-field personality. He supplemented his football income by wrestling professionally. Died at Baltimore, MD, May 10, 1963.

YANKEES FIRE STENGEL: ANNIVERSARY. Nov 9, 1960. The New York Yankees fired their manager, Casey Stengel, despite his having won 10 pennants and seven World Series in 12 years. Stengel returned to baseball in 1962 as first manager of the New York Mets.

BIRTHDAYS TODAY

David Robert Duval, 27, golfer, born Jacksonville, FL, Nov 9, 1971.
Lou Ferrigno, 47, actor (*Pumping Iron*, "The Incredible Hulk"), former bodybuilder, born New York, NY, Nov 9, 1951.
Robert (Bob) Gibson, 63, Baseball Hall of Fame pitcher, born Omaha, NE, Nov 9, 1935.
William Robert (Bill) Guerin, 28, hockey player, born Wilbraham, MA, Nov 9, 1970.
Dorrel Norman Elvert ("Whitey") Herzog, 67, former baseball manager, executive and player, born New Athens, IL, Nov 9, 1931.
Thomas Daniel (Tom) Weiskopf, 56, broadcaster and golfer, born Massillon, OH, Nov 9, 1942.

ADAM DUNN

☆ ☆ ☆

NOVEMBER 10 — TUESDAY
Day 314 — 51 Remaining

CASH, NORM: BIRTH ANNIVERSARY. Nov 10, 1934. Norman Dalton Cash, baseball player born at Justiceburg, TX. Cash won the American League batting title in 1961 and led the league in home runs. He hit .385 in the 1968 World Series. Died in a boating accident at Charlevoix, MI, Oct 12, 1986.

DYKES, JIMMY: BIRTH ANNIVERSARY. Nov 10, 1896. James Joseph (Jimmy) Dykes, baseball player and manager born at Philadelphia, PA. Dykes played infield for the Philadelphia Athletics and Chicago White Sox. He managed several teams and was once traded, manager for manager, from the Detroit Tigers to the Cleveland Indians. Died at Philadelphia, June 15, 1976.

FIRST BREEDERS' CUP: ANNIVERSARY. Nov 10, 1984. The first Breeders' Cup day of thoroughbred racing was held at Hollywood Park in California. Wild Again won the feature race, the $3 million Breeders' Cup Classic, beating Slew O' Gold and Gate Dancer.

HOWE SETS GOAL RECORD: 35th ANNIVERSARY.
Nov 10, 1963. Gordie Howe of the Detroit Red Wings scored the 545th goal of his career to surpass the mark held by Maurice Richard of the Montreal Canadiens.

MOON PHASE: LAST QUARTER. Nov 10. Moon enters Last Quarter phase at 7:28 AM, EDT.

SUMMERS, BILL: BIRTH ANNIVERSARY. Nov 10, 1895. William Reed (Bill) Summers, baseball umpire born at Harrison, NJ. Summers moved into umpiring from a career as a professional boxer. He was a member of the committee that rewrote the baseball rule book in 1950. Died at Upton, MA, Sept 12, 1966.

BIRTHDAYS TODAY

Isaac Isidore Bruce, 26, football player, born Fort Lauderdale, FL, Nov 10, 1972.
Jack Anthony Clark, 43, former baseball player, born New Brighton, PA, Nov 10, 1955.
Donald Eugene (Gene) Conley, 68, former baseball and basketball player, born Muskogee, OK, Nov 10, 1930.
Robert Leon ("Butch") Huskey, 27, baseball player, born Anadarko, OK, Nov 10, 1971.
Larry Alton Parrish, 45, former baseball player, born Winter Haven, FL, Nov 10, 1953.
Kenneth Scott (Kenny) Rogers, 34, baseball player, born Savannah, GA, Nov 10, 1964.

NOVEMBER 11 — WEDNESDAY
Day 315 — 50 Remaining

CASE, GEORGE: BIRTH ANNIVERSARY. Nov 11, 1915. George Washington Case, baseball player born at Trenton, NJ. Case was an outfielder who led the American League in stolen bases six times in the late 1930s and early 1940s. He once got nine hits in a doubleheader. Died at Trenton, Jan 23, 1989.

DAY, NED: BIRTH ANNIVERSARY. Nov 11, 1911. Edward P. (Ned) Day, bowler born at Los Angeles, CA. Day was one of the first bowlers to tour, playing matches and giving exhibitions, including one at Harry Truman's White House. He was named Bowler of the Year in 1943 and 1944 and carried a 200 average over a 28-year career. Died at Milwaukee, WI, Nov 26, 1971.

DODD, BOBBY: 90th BIRTH ANNIVERSARY. Nov 11, 1908. Robert Lee (Bobby) Dodd, football player, coach and administrator born at Galax, VA. Dodd earned 16 letters in high school and played quarterback at the University of Tennessee. He coached at Georgia Tech from 1945 to 1967, and his teams won 9 of 13 bowl games. He developed the "belly series" offense and sought to motivate his players with lavish praise. Died at Atlanta, GA, June 21, 1988.

KNICKS' FIRST GAME AT MADISON SQUARE GARDEN: ANNIVERSARY. Nov 11, 1946. The New York Knickerbockers of the Basketball Association of America (predecessor of the NBA) played their first home game at Madison Square Garden. Before a crowd of 17,205, the Knicks lost in overtime to the Chicago Stags, 78–68. The halftime entertainment consisted of a fashion show and a brief exhibition basketball game between the New York Giants football team and members of the Original Celtics, basketball's legendary team from the 1920s.

MARANVILLE, RABBIT: BIRTH ANNIVERSARY. Nov 11, 1891. Walter James Vincent ("Rabbit") Maranville, Baseball Hall of Fame infielder born at Springfield, MA. Maranville was a slick-fielding infielder who played with the 1914 "Miracle" Braves and enjoyed a 23-year career. He was known for his antics, on the field and off.

Inducted into the Hall of Fame in 1954. Died at New York, NY, Jan 5, 1954.

TRAYNOR, PIE: BIRTH ANNIVERSARY. Nov 11, 1899. Harold Joseph ("Pie") Traynor, Baseball Hall of Fame third baseman born at Framingham, MA. Traynor is considered one of the greatest third basemen of all time. He was a superb hitter and an absolute genius with the glove. Inducted into the Hall of Fame in 1948. Died at Pittsburgh, PA, Mar 16, 1972.

BIRTHDAYS TODAY

Jacinto Damion Easley, 29, baseball player, born New York, NY, Nov 11, 1969.
Roberto Manuel Hernandez, 34, baseball player, born Santurce, Puerto Rico, Nov 11, 1964.
Reynaldo (Rey) Ordonez, 26, baseball player, born Havana, Cuba, Oct 11, 1972.
James Cory Snyder, 36, former baseball player, born Inglewood, CA, Nov 11, 1962.
Frank Urban ("Fuzzy") Zoeller, 47, golfer, born New Albany, IN, Nov 11, 1951.

NOVEMBER 12 — THURSDAY
Day 316 — 49 Remaining

FIRST PROFESSIONAL FOOTBALL PLAYER: 105th ANNIVERSARY. Nov 12, 1892. William "Pudge" Heffelfinger became the first professional football player when he was paid $25 for expenses and a cash bonus of $500. It was the cash bonus that made him professional. Scoring the winning touchdown for the Allegheny Athletic Association, he helped his team beat the Pittsburgh Athletic Club 4–0. For info: Joe Horrigan, Historian, Football Hall of Fame, 2121 George Halas Dr, Canton, OH 44708.

LANDIS NAMED COMMISSIONER: ANNIVERSARY. Nov 12, 1920. In the wake of the growing scandal surrounding accusations that members of the Chicago White Sox conspired to fix the 1919 World Series, baseball owners appointed Federal Judge Kenesaw Mountain Landis the game's first commissioner with extremely broad powers. Landis replaced the National Commission, a three-man governing board, and served until his death in 1944.

MAYS, CARL: 105th BIRTH ANNIVERSARY. Nov 12, 1893. Carl William Mays, baseball player born at Liberty, KY. Mays was a submarine pitcher who started his career with the Boston Red Sox and was traded to the New York Yankees. In 1920, he hit Ray Chapman of the Cleveland Indians in the head with a pitched ball. Chapman died the next day. Died at El Cajon, CA, Apr 4, 1971.

SHULA WINS 100 IN 10: ANNIVERSARY. Nov 12, 1972. Don Shula of the Miami Dolphins became the first NFL coach to win 100 regular season games in only 10 seasons as the Miami Dolphins defeated the New England Patriots, 52–0.

BIRTHDAYS TODAY

Ronald Raymond (Ron) Bryant, 51, former baseball player, born Redlands, CA, Nov 12, 1947.

Nadia Comaneci, 37, Olympic gold medal gymnast, born Onesti, Romania, Nov 12, 1961.

Jody Richard Davis, 42, former baseball player, born Gainesville, GA, Nov 12, 1956.

Gregory Carpenter (Greg) Gagne, 37, baseball player, born Fall River, MA, Nov 12, 1961.

Kenneth Roy (Ken) Houston, 54, Pro Football Hall of Fame defensive back, born Lufkin, TX, Nov 12, 1944.

Jeffrey Scott (Jeff) Reed, 36, baseball player, born Joliet, IL, Nov 12, 1962.

Samuel (Sammy) Sosa, 30, baseball player, born San Pedro de Macoris, Dominican Republic, Nov 12, 1968.

Gary Montez Thurman, Jr, 34, former baseball player, born Indianapolis, IN, Nov 12, 1964.

NOVEMBER 13 — FRIDAY
Day 317 — 48 Remaining

SPORTSCHASER OF THE DAY

Who was the first NBA player to score 20,000 points in his career?

BIG EAST MEN'S SOCCER CHAMPIONSHIP. Nov 13–15. Rutgers University, Piscataway, NJ. For info: Big East Conference, 56 Exchange Terrace, Providence, RI 02903. Phone: (401) 453-0660. Fax: (401) 751-8540.

BILKO, STEVE: 70th BIRTH ANNIVERSARY. Nov 13, 1928. Steven Thomas (Steve) Bilko, baseball player born at Nanticoke, PA. Bilko was a phenomenal minor league slugger who never quite made it in the majors. In 1955, 1956 and 1957, he hit 37, 55 and 56 homers in the Pacific Coast League. Died at Wilkes-Barre, PA, Mar 7, 1978.

LONGHORN WORLD CHAMPIONSHIP FINALS RODEO. Nov 13–14. Municipal Auditorium, Nashville, TN. Top 96 contestants from more than 1,200 who competed in 11 different 1998 Longhorn rodeos across the country. 1998 championships in seven professional contests ranging from bronc riding to bull riding. Featuring colorful opening pageantry and Big, Bad BONUS Bulls. 33rd annual. Est attendance: 30,000. For info: W. Bruce Lehke, Pres, Longhorn World Championship Rodeo, Inc, PO Box 70159, Nashville, TN 37207. Phone: (615) 876-1016. Fax: (615) 876-4685. E-mail: lhrodeo@idt.net. WWW: http://www.longhornrodeo.com

November *1998*	S	M	T	W	T	F	S
	1	2	3	4	5	6	7
	8	9	10	11	12	13	14
	15	16	17	18	19	20	21
	22	23	24	25	26	27	28
	29	30					

PETTIT SCORES 20,000 POINTS: ANNIVERSARY. Nov 13, 1964. Forward Bob Pettit of the St. Louis Hawks became the first player in NBA history to reach the 20,000-point mark when he scored 29 points in a 123–106 loss to the Cincinnati Royals.

SANDE, EARLE: 100th BIRTH ANNIVERSARY. Nov 13, 1898. Earle Sande, jockey born at Groton, SD. Sande began riding in the West and then moved east to become a professional jockey. Sande rode many of the best horses of his era, including Man O'War and Gallant Fox, a Triple Crown winner. He won the Kentucky Derby three times and the Belmont Stakes five times. Died at Jacksonville, OR, Aug 20, 1968.

SEYBOLD, SOCKS: BIRTH ANNIVERSARY. Nov 13, 1870. Ralph Orlando ("Socks") Seybold, baseball player born at Washingtonville, OH. Seybold hit 16 home runs in 1902, a mark that stood as the American League season record until Babe Ruth hit 29 in 1919. His career was ended in 1908 by a broken leg. Died at Greensburg, PA, Dec 22, 1921.

WATERFOWL FESTIVAL (WITH GOOSE- AND DUCK-CALLING CHAMPIONSHIPS). Nov 13–15. Easton, MD. The World Championship Goose- and Regional Duck-Calling Contests take place during this three-day festival. Also includes retriever demonstrations, sporting clays tournament and decoy auction as well as wildlife exhibitors presenting wildlife art, carvings sculpture, decoys, seminars and more. Annually, the second full weekend in November. Proceeds contributed to conservation. Est attendance: 18,000. For info: Waterfowl Festival, PO Box 929, Easton, MD 21601. Phone: (410) 822-4567. Fax: (410) 820-9286. WWW: http://www.waterfowlfest.org

BIRTHDAYS TODAY

Mark Fitzpatrick, 30, hockey player, born Toronto, Ontario, Canada, Nov 13, 1968.

Patrick George (Pat) Hentgen, 30, baseball player, born Detroit, MI, Nov 13, 1968.

Maurice Wesley (Wes) Parker, 59, former baseball player, born Evanston, IL, Nov 13, 1939.

Melvin Leon (Mel) Stottlemyre, Sr, 57, former baseball player, born Hazelton, MO, Nov 13, 1941.

Vincent Frank (Vinny) Testaverde, 35, football player, born New York, NY, Nov 13, 1963.

Charles (Charlie) Tickner, 45, former figure skater, born Oakland, CA, Nov 13, 1953.

NOVEMBER 14 — SATURDAY
Day 318 — 47 Remaining

BIRTH OF AMERICAN LEAGUE: ANNIVERSARY. Nov 14, 1900. Ban Johnson, president of the minor Western League, announced his intention to upgrade its status to a major league and to change its name to the American League.

FIRST NFL 400-YARD GAME: 55th ANNIVERSARY. Nov 14, 1943. Sid Luckman of the Chicago Bears became the first professional quarterback to pass for more than 400 yards in a single game, throwing for 433 yards and seven touchdowns as the Bears walloped the New York Giants, 56–7.

MARSHALL FOOTBALL TRAGEDY: ANNIVERSARY. Nov 14, 1970. Forty-three members of the football team from Marshall University in Huntington, WV, were killed when a plane in which they were flying crashed in Kenova, WV.

NCAA DIVISION III FIELD HOCKEY CHAMPIONSHIP. Nov 14–15. Finals at a campus site TBA. For info: NCAA, 6201 College Blvd, Overland Park, KS 66211. Phone: (913) 339-1906.

BIRTHDAYS TODAY

Guillermo (Willie) Hernandez, 44, former baseball player, born Aguada, Puerto Rico, Nov 14, 1954.

James Anthony (Jimmy) Piersall, 69, former baseball player, born Waterbury, CT, Nov 14, 1929.

Curtis Montague (Curt) Schilling, 32, baseball player, born Anchorage, AK, Nov 14, 1966.

Jack Wayne Sikma, 43, former basketball player, born Kankakee, IL, Nov 14, 1955.

NOVEMBER 15 — SUNDAY
Day 319 — 46 Remaining

ALLEN, PHOG: BIRTH ANNIVERSARY. Nov 15, 1885. Forrest Clare ("Phog") Allen, basketball player and Basketball Hall of Fame coach born at Jamesport, MO. Allen met Dr. James Naismith, inventor of basketball, while Allen was a student at the University of Kansas and Naismith was coaching there. Allen played for Naismith and then became a coach himself, primarily at his alma mater until 1956 when he was forced to retire. Over 46 years, his teams won 771 games and lost only 233. He wrote three books about the sport and was instrumental in having basketball added to the Olympic program in 1936. Inducted into the Hall of Fame in 1959. Died at Lawrence, KS, Sept 16, 1974.

BELL, GUS: 70th BIRTH ANNIVERSARY. Nov 15, 1928. David Russell ("Gus") Bell, baseball player born at Louisville, KY. Bell was nicknamed "Gus" by his parents in honor of former player Gus Mancuso. He played out-

field for the Cincinnati Reds and several other teams in the 1950s and 1960s. His son, Buddy Bell, and his grandson, David Bell, both reached the majors as well. Died at Cincinnati, OH, May 7, 1995.

FIRST BLACK PROFESSIONAL HOCKEY PLAYER: ANNIVERSARY. Nov 15, 1950. When Arthur Dorrington signed a contract to play hockey with the Atlantic City Seagulls of the Eastern Amateur League on Nov 15, 1950, he became the first black man to play organized hockey in the US. He played for the Seagulls during the 1950 and 1951 seasons.

NAVRATILOVA RETIRES: ANNIVERSARY. Nov 15, 1994. Ending her professional tennis career, Martina Navratilova played a losing first-round match against Gabriela Sabatini in the 1994 season-ending Virginia Slims tournament. Hardly a ripple was made in one of the most impressive records in tennis history. During 21 years of play Navratilova chalked up a career tally of 1,443–211 singles match record and 167 titles (the most ever for anyone, male or female). She recorded 18 Grand Slam singles titles, 31 Grand Slam women's doubles championships and six career Grand Slam mixed doubles championships.

STERN NAMED NBA COMMISSIONER: 15th ANNIVERSARY. Nov 15, 1983. David J. Stern was named the fourth commissioner of the NBA, effective Feb 1, 1984. He replaced Larry O'Brien, commissioner from 1975 to 1984.

13 PLAYERS FOUL OUT: ANNIVERSARY. Nov 15, 1952. In an NBA overtime game between the Baltimore Bullets and the Syracuse Nationals, a record 13 players, five Bullets and eight Nats, fouled out. The referees let some of the Syracuse players back into the game and called a technical foul every time one of them committed an additional personal foul. Baltimore won, 97–91.

BIRTHDAYS TODAY

Gregory C. (Greg) Anthony, 31, basketball player, born Las Vegas, NV, Nov 15, 1967.

Otis Armstrong, 48, former football player, born Chicago, IL, Nov 15, 1950.

NOVEMBER 16 — MONDAY
Day 320 — 45 Remaining

CHASE'S SPORTSQUOTE OF THE DAY
"At the end of the third quarter, I was willing to settle for a scoreless tie." —Oklahoma coach Bud Wilkinson before losing to Notre Dame

BURKE, GLENN: BIRTH ANNIVERSARY. Nov 16, 1952. Glenn Lawrence Burke, baseball player born at Oakland, CA. Burke spent four seasons in the majors (1976–79) with the Los Angeles Dodgers and the Oakland Athletics. He was the first former baseball player the cause of whose death was acknowledged as AIDS. Died at San Leandro, CA, May 30, 1995.

FIFTH DOWN: ANNIVERSARY. Nov 16, 1940. Cornell University played Dartmouth College in football and came away with a victory. But the winning touchdown was scored on a fifth-down play, given to Cornell by referee's error. After the game, Cornell did the honorable thing, surrendering the triumph.

NOTRE DAME SNAPS OKLAHOMA'S STREAK: ANNIVERSARY. Nov 16, 1957. Notre Dame upset Oklahoma, 7–0, to snap the Sooners' NCAA record 48-game winning streak. Dick Lynch scored the game's only touchdown.

TRIPLE CROWN OF SURFING SERIES: EVENT 1. Nov 16–25. Alii Beach Park, Haleiwa, North Shore Oahu, HI. 16th annual. The Triple Crown Series is professional, big-wave surfing on Oahu's north shore. Est attendance: 5,000. For media info: Carol Hogan, (808) 325-7400. E-mail: oceanpro@interpac.net. For contest info: Randy Rarick, (808) 638-7266, or Fred Williamson, (808) 377-5850. WWW: http://www.holoholo.org/triplecrown/

UNIVERSITY OF CHICAGO'S FIRST FOOTBALL VICTORY: ANNIVERSARY. Nov 16, 1892. The University of Chicago, which played to a 0–0 tie with Northwestern in its first-ever football game on the preceding Oct 22, won its first game for Coach Amos Alonzo Stagg, 10–4, against Illinois in Chicago. A founding member of the Big Ten, Chicago eliminated its football program for many years, but now competes in the University Athletic Association against the likes of New York University, Emory and Washington University in St. Louis.

BIRTHDAYS TODAY

Dwight Eugene ("Doc") Gooden, 34, baseball player, born Tampa, FL, Nov 16, 1964.
Christopher Deane (Chris) Haney, 30, baseball player, born Baltimore, MD, Nov 16, 1968.
Terry Labonte, 42, auto racer, born Corpus Christi, TX, Nov 16, 1956.
Harvey Banks Martin, 48, former football player, born Dallas, TX, Nov 16, 1950.
Corey Allen Pavin, 39, golfer, born Oxnard, CA, Nov 16, 1959.
Joseph Henry ("Jo Jo") White, 52, former basketball player, born St. Louis, MO, Nov 16, 1946.

NOVEMBER 17 — TUESDAY
Day 321 — 44 Remaining

ECKERT NAMED COMMISSIONER: ANNIVERSARY. Nov 17, 1965. Baseball owners elected William D. ("Spike") Eckert Commissioner of Baseball. Eckert, a retired Air Force general and comptroller of the Air Force, proved to be a poor choice. He was removed from office in 1969.

GARCIA, MIKE: 75th BIRTH ANNIVERSARY. Nov 17, 1923. Edward Miguel (Mike) Garcia, baseball player born at San Gabriel, CA. Garcia, known as the "Big Bear," was one of the Cleveland Indians' best starting pitchers in the early 1950s. He won 19 games in 1954 when the Indians won the American League pennant. Died at Fairview Park, OH, Jan 13, 1986.

	S	M	T	W	T	F	S
November	1	2	3	4	5	6	7
1998	8	9	10	11	12	13	14
	15	16	17	18	19	20	21
	22	23	24	25	26	27	28
	29	30					

HEIDI GAME: 30th ANNIVERSARY. Nov 17, 1968. NBC Television cut away from the broadcast of a football game between the Oakland Raiders and the New York Jets with several minutes remaining on the clock in order to begin a special production of *Heidi* on time. After the special began, the Raiders scored two touchdowns in the final minute to earn a 43–32 comeback victory. Football fans deluged NBC with telephone calls, and networks eventually decided to delay the start of regular programming if athletic events ran over their allotted time.

NFL STRIKE ENDS: ANNIVERSARY. Nov 17, 1982. NFL players, on strike for two months, ended their walkout, but the season, originally set for 16 games, had to be cut to nine games. The regular playoff arrangement was also scrapped, replaced by a special Super Bowl Tournament involving the 16 teams with the best records.

BIRTHDAYS TODAY

Gary Bell, 62, former baseball player, born San Antonio, TX, Nov 17, 1936.
Elvin Ernest Hayes, 53, Basketball Hall of Fame center, born Rayville, LA, Nov 17, 1945.
Robert Bruce (Bob) Mathias, 68, former congressman and Olympic gold medal decathlete, born Tulare, CA, Nov 17, 1930.
Martin Scorsese, 56, director (*The Color of Money, Raging Bull*), born New York, NY, Nov 17, 1942.
George Thomas (Tom) Seaver, 54, Baseball Hall of Fame pitcher, born Fresno, CA, Nov 17, 1944.
Paul Anthony Sorrento, 33, baseball player, born Somerville, MA, Nov 17, 1965.
Mitchell Steven (Mitch) Williams, 34, former baseball player, born Santa Ana, CA, Nov 17, 1964.

NOVEMBER 18 — WEDNESDAY
Day 322 — 43 Remaining

COOMBS, JACK: BIRTH ANNIVERSARY. Nov 18, 1882. John Wesley (Jack) Coombs, baseball player born at LeGrande, IA. Coombs was an outstanding pitcher for Connie Mack's Philadelphia Athletics, winning 31 games in 1910. He contracted typhoid fever in 1913 and pitched sparingly after that. Died at Palestine, TX, Apr 15, 1957.

KOONCE, CAL: BIRTH ANNIVERSARY. Nov 18, 1940. Calvin Lee (Cal) Koonce, baseball player born at Fayetteville, NC. Koonce pitched for three major league teams, including the 1969 World Champion New York Mets, for whom he made 40 relief appearances. Died at Hope Mills, NC, Oct 28, 1993.

McGUIRE, DEACON: 135th BIRTH ANNIVERSARY. Nov 18, 1863. James Thomas ("Deacon") McGuire, baseball player and manager born at Youngstown, OH. McGuire was a catcher who began a 26-year career in 1884. He played for 12 different teams and earned his nickname for his sense of fair play. Died at Albion, MI, Oct 31, 1936.

MOON PHASE: NEW MOON. Nov 18. Moon enters New Moon phase at 11:27 PM, EST.

PRESEASON NIT. Nov 18 (tentative). College basketball's premier preseason tournament begins with eight first-round games and four second-round games at campus locations. The semifinals and final are scheduled for Madison Square Garden in New York on Nov 25 and Nov 27. For info: Media Relations, Madison Square Garden, 2 Pennsylvania Plaza, New York, NY 10001. Phone: (212) 465-6000.

ST. JOHN, LYNN: BIRTH ANNIVERSARY. Nov 18, 1876. Lynn Wilbur St. John, Basketball Hall of Fame administrator born at Union City, PA. St. John served on basketball's Joint Rules Committee from 1912 to 1937 and helped to bring the game under one set of playing rules. He was coach and athletic director at Ohio State University where the basketball arena is named in his honor and helped organize the first Olympic basketball competition in 1936. Inducted into the Hall of Fame in 1962. Died at Columbus, OH, Sept 30, 1950.

SCOTLAND: SCOTTISH OPEN BADMINTON CHAMPIONSHIP. Nov 18–22. Kelvin Hall International Sports Arena, Glasgow. A European Badminton Union Grand Prix. Est attendance: 7,000. For info: Scottish Badminton Union, Cockburn Centre, 40 Bogmoor Pl, Scotland G51 4TQ. Phone: (44) (141) 445-1218. Fax: (44) (141) 425-1218.

SULLIVAN, JAMES: BIRTH ANNIVERSARY. Nov 18, 1860. James Edward Sullivan, amateur sports promoter born at New York, NY. Sullivan helped to establish the Amateur Athletic Union in 1888 to preserve pure amateurism. He also worked as president of the American Sports Publishing Company and edited Spalding's Athletic Library series. The Sullivan Memorial Trophy is presented annually in his honor to the best amateur athlete in the US. Died at New York, Sept 16, 1914.

WORLD TOUR BEGINS: 110th ANNIVERSARY. Nov 18, 1888. Albert G. Spalding's attempt to introduce baseball to the entire world began as he, the Chicago White Stockings and a group of all-star players set sail from San Francisco for Honolulu, the first stop on their round-the-world tour.

BIRTHDAYS TODAY

Alphonse Dante Bichette, 35, baseball player, born West Palm Beach, FL, Nov 18, 1963.
Kenneth William (Ken) Burkhart (born Kenneth William Burkhardt), 82, former baseball umpire and player, born Knoxville, TN, Nov 18, 1916.
Samuel James (Sam) Cassell, 29, basketball player, born Baltimore, MD, Nov 18, 1969.
Thomas (Tom) Gordon, 31, baseball player, born Sebring, FL, Nov 18, 1967.
Raghib Ramadian ("Rocket") Ismail, 29, football player, born Elizabeth, NJ, Nov 18, 1969.
Seth Joyner, 34, football player, born Spring Valley, NY, Nov 18, 1964.
Gene William Mauch, 73, former baseball manager and player, born Salina, KS, Nov 18, 1925.
Harold Warren Moon, 42, football player, born Los Angeles, CA, Nov 18, 1956.
Mark Joseph Petkovsek, 33, baseball player, born Beaumont, TX, Nov 18, 1965.
Gary Antonian Sheffield, 30, baseball player, born Tampa, FL, Nov 18, 1968.
Alan Shepherd, 75, former astronaut and lunar golfer, born East Derry, NH, Nov 18, 1923.
Allen Kenneth Watson, 28, baseball player, born New York, NY, Nov 18, 1970.

NOVEMBER 19 — THURSDAY
Day 323 — 42 Remaining

CAMPANELLA, ROY: BIRTH ANNIVERSARY. Nov 19, 1921. Roy Campanella, Baseball Hall of Fame catcher born at Philadelphia, PA. One of the first black major leaguers and a star of one of baseball's greatest teams, the Brooklyn Dodgers' "Boys of Summer," Campy, as he was often called, was named the National League MVP three times in his 10 years of play, in 1951, 1953 and 1955. Campanella had his highest batting average in 1951 (.325), and in 1953 he established three single-season records for a catcher—most putouts (807), most home runs (41) and most runs batted in (142)—as well as having a batting average of .312. His career was cut short on Jan 28, 1958, when an automobile accident left him paralyzed. Campy gained even more fame after his accident as an inspiration and spokesman for people with disabilities. Inducted into the Hall of Fame in 1969. Died at Woodland Hills, CA, June 26, 1993.

NOTRE DAME–MICHIGAN STATE TIE: ANNIVERSARY. Nov 19, 1966. In one of the more famous college football match-ups between teams ranked No. 1 and No. 2, top-ranked Notre Dame tied second-ranked Michigan State, 10–10.

RYAN FIRST MILLION-DOLLAR PLAYER: ANNIVERSARY. Nov 19, 1979. Pitcher Nolan Ryan became the first baseball free agent to sign a contract for a salary of one million dollars per year. Ryan moved from the California Angels to the Houston Astros.

SCOTT, EVERETT: BIRTH ANNIVERSARY. Nov 19, 1892. Lewis Everett Scott, baseball player born at Bluffton, IN. Shortstop Scott held baseball's record for consecutive games played before Lou Gehrig. His streak, 1,307 games long, ended in 1925. Died at Fort Wayne, IN, Nov 2, 1960.

SUNDAY, BILLY: BIRTH ANNIVERSARY. Nov 19, 1862. William Ashley Sunday, baseball player born at Ames, IA. Sunday was a major league outfielder in the 1880s before leaving the game to become an evangelist. Died at Chicago, IL, Nov 6, 1935.

ZAMBONI PROPOSAL: ANNIVERSARY. Nov 19, 1993. Alan Giarettino proposed marriage to Christy Stubblefield while she rode around the ice rink on the Zamboni during the intermission between the second and third periods of an East Coast Hockey League game in Huntington, WV. Stubblefield thought she had earned the ride by winning a contest. In truth, Giarettino had arranged the contest so that he could walk onto the ice during the ride, hand her a bouquet and drop to one knee. She said yes.

BIRTHDAYS TODAY

Robert Raymond (Bob) Boone, 51, former baseball manager and player, born San Diego, CA, Nov 19, 1947.
Gary Thomas DiSarcina, 31, baseball player, born Malden, MA, Nov 19, 1967.
Dickie Ray Noles, 42, former baseball player, born Charlotte, NC, Nov 19, 1956.
Ahmad Rashad (born Bobby Moore), 49, broadcaster and former football player, born Portland, OR, Nov 19, 1949.
Robert (Bobby) Tolan, 53, former baseball player, born Los Angeles, CA, Nov 19, 1945.
Robert Edward (Ted) Turner, 60, baseball, basketball and cable TV executive, born Cincinnati, OH, Nov 19, 1938.

NOVEMBER 20 — FRIDAY
Day 324 — 41 Remaining

SPORTSCHASER OF THE DAY

When the Stanford University band rushed onto the football field prematurely during a 1982 game, what team used the confusion to win the game?

CADORE, LEON: BIRTH ANNIVERSARY. Nov 20, 1890. Leon Joseph Cadore, baseball player born at Chicago, IL. Cadore is most famous for pitching all 26 innings for the Brooklyn Dodgers in baseball's longest game, a 1–1 tie with the Boston Braves on May 1, 1920. Died at Spokane, WA, Mar 16, 1958.

CAL VS THE STANFORD BAND: ANNIVERSARY. Nov 20, 1982. The University of California football team defeated Stanford University, 25–20, on a most unusual last play. Stanford was ahead, 20–19, and had to kick off with only a few seconds left. The Cal players knew that if any of them were tackled, the game would be over. They began an unscripted series of five laterals that landed them in the end zone after they dodged all the Stanford players and the Stanford band which had rushed onto the field prematurely.

GRIFFITH, CLARK: BIRTH ANNIVERSARY. Nov 20, 1869. Clark Calvin Griffith, Baseball Hall of Fame pitcher and executive born at Stringtown, MO. Griffith pitched and managed the New York Highlanders (later the Yankees) and the Cincinnati Reds. He became owner of the Washington Senators and held the team until his death. Inducted into the Hall of Fame in 1946. Died at Washington, DC, Oct 27, 1955.

LANDIS, KENESAW: BIRTH ANNIVERSARY. Nov 20, 1866. Kenesaw Mountain Landis, Baseball Hall of Fame executive born at Millville, OH. Landis, a federal judge, was named the first Commissioner of Baseball in 1920. He ruled with an absolutely firm hand and imposed his view of how baseball should operate upon owners and players alike. Inducted into the Hall of Fame in 1944. Died at Chicago, IL, Nov 25, 1944.

STARTER HALL OF FAME TIP-OFF CLASSIC. Nov 20 (tentative). Springfield Civic Center, Springfield, MA. Official opening game of intercollegiate basketball season. Est attendance: 9,000. For info: Robin Deutsch, Dir Mktg/PR, Basketball Hall of Fame, 1150 W Columbus Ave, Box 179, Springfield, MA 01101. Phone: (413) 781-6500.

BIRTHDAYS TODAY

Alejandro (Alex) Arias, 31, baseball player, born New York, NY, Nov 20, 1967.

Marcus D. (Mark) Gastineau, 42, former football player, born Ardmore, OK, Nov 20, 1956.

John William ("Jay") Johnstone, 53, former baseball player, born Manchester, CT, Nov 20, 1945.

NOVEMBER 21 — SATURDAY
Day 325 — 40 Remaining

BIG EAST VOLLEYBALL CHAMPIONSHIP. Nov 21–22. University of Pittsburgh, PA. For info: Big East Conference, 56 Exchange Terrace, Providence, RI 02903. Phone: (401) 453-0660. Fax: (401) 751-8540.

FRENCHMAN ROWS ACROSS PACIFIC: ANNIVERSARY. Nov 21, 1991. Gerard d'Aboville completed a four-month solo journey across the Pacific Ocean on Nov 21, 1991. D'Aboville began rowing across the Pacific on July 11 when he left Choshi, Japan. His journey ended at Ilwaco, WA.

November *1998*	S	M	T	W	T	F	S
	1	2	3	4	5	6	7
	8	9	10	11	12	13	14
	15	16	17	18	19	20	21
	22	23	24	25	26	27	28
	29	30					

HIGH, ANDY: BIRTH ANNIVERSARY. Nov 21, 1897. Andrew Aird (Andy) High, baseball player born at Ava, IL. High was one of three brothers to play major league baseball. He was a versatile player who spent 13 years in the majors with five National League teams. Died at Toledo, OH, Feb 22, 1981.

LINDSTROM, FREDDIE: BIRTH ANNIVERSARY. Nov 21, 1905. Frederick Charles (Freddie) Lindstrom, Baseball Hall of Fame third baseman and outfielder born at Chicago, IL. Lindstrom played for the New York Giants in the 1920s and 1930s. In the 1924 World Series, a ground ball hit a pebble and bounced over his head, allowing the run that gave the championship to the Washington Senators. Inducted into the Hall of Fame in 1976. Died at Chicago, Oct 4, 1981.

NAIA MEN'S AND WOMEN'S CROSS-COUNTRY NATIONAL CHAMPIONSHIP. Nov 21. Site TBA. Men compete on an 8K course and women compete on a 5K course with the top 25 individual finishers in each championship receiving All-America honors. 43rd annual men's, 19th annual women's. For info: Natl Assn of Intercollegiate Athletics, 6120 S Yale Ave, Tulsa, OK 74136-4223. Phone: (918) 494-8828. Fax: (918) 494-8841. E-mail: khenry@naia.org. WWW: http://www.naia.org

NCAA MEN'S AND WOMEN'S DIVISION III CROSS-COUNTRY CHAMPIONSHIPS. Nov 21. Finals at site TBA. For info: NCAA, 6201 College Blvd, Overland Park, KS 66211. Phone: (913) 339-1906.

NCAA WOMEN'S DIVISION III SOCCER CHAMPIONSHIP. Nov 21–22. Finals at a campus site TBA. For info: NCAA, 6201 College Blvd, Overland Park, KS 66211. Phone: (913) 339-1906.

NEWCOMBE WINS FIRST CY YOUNG AWARD: ANNIVERSARY. Nov 21, 1956. Don Newcombe of the Brooklyn Dodgers won the first Cy Young award, given to the

most outstanding pitcher in the major leagues. He added the National League Most Valuable Player Award to his trophy case as well.

NFL RESUMES AFTER STRIKE: ANNIVERSARY. Nov 21, 1982. After a strike that commenced on Sept 23, the NFL resumed play with the seven intervening weeks of the season having been canceled.

RICHARDS, PAUL: 90th BIRTH ANNIVERSARY. Nov 21, 1908. Paul Rapier Richards, baseball player, manager and executive born at Waxahachie, TX. Richards was a catcher with marginal ability, but an innovative manager and executive. He invented the oversized catcher's mitt to handle knuckleball pitchers and the "Iron Mike" pitching machine. Died at Waxahachie, May 4, 1986.

THAILAND: ELEPHANT ROUND-UP AT SURIN. Nov 21. Elephant demonstrations in morning, elephant races and tug-of-war between 100 men and one elephant. Annually, on the third Saturday in November since 1961. Special trains from Bangkok on previous day.

YANKEES BUY DIMAGGIO: ANNIVERSARY. Nov 21, 1934. The New York Yankees paid the San Francisco Seals $25,000 and four players for Joe DiMaggio. Despite DiMaggio's 61-game hitting streak in 1933 and his .341 batting average in 1934, the Yankees kept him with the Seals for 1935. He hit .398.

BIRTHDAYS TODAY

Troy Kenneth Aikman, 32, football player, born West Covina, CA, Nov 21, 1966.

George Kenneth (Ken) Griffey, Jr, 29, baseball player, born Donora, PA, Nov 21, 1969.

Vernon Earl ("The Pearl") Monroe, 54, Basketball Hall of Fame guard, born Philadelphia, PA, Nov 21, 1944.

Stanley Frank ("Stan the Man") Musial, 78, Baseball Hall of Fame outfielder and first baseman, born Donora, PA, Nov 21, 1920.

Olden Polynice, 34, basketball player, born Port-au-Prince, Haiti, Nov 21, 1964.

James Stephen (Jim) Ringo, 67, Pro Football Hall of Fame center, born Orange, NJ, Nov 21, 1931.

☆   ☆   ☆

NOVEMBER 22 — SUNDAY
Day 326 — 39 Remaining

BARTELL, DICK: BIRTH ANNIVERSARY. Nov 22, 1907. Richard William (Dick) Bartell, baseball player born at Chicago, IL. Bartell earned the nickname "Rowdy Richard" for his tough play as a shortstop with an 18-year career. He was the starting shortstop for the National League in the first All-Star Game in 1933. Died at Alameda, CA, Aug 4, 1995.

BOSTOCK, LYMAN: BIRTH ANNIVERSARY. Nov 22, 1950. Lyman Wesley Bostock, baseball player born at Boston, MA. Bostock played four years in the major leagues before being fatally shot. Died at Denver, CO, Sept 16, 1968.

CANADA: CANADIAN WESTERN AGRIBITION. Nov 22–29. Regina, Saskatchewan. Canada's premier agricultural event is the world's largest indoor livestock show and marketplace. More than 4,000 cattle, sheep, swine and horses are brought to Agribition, plus pedigreed seed show and agricultural trade and technology show. Also, a variety of entertainment. Est attendance: 150,000. For info: (306) 565-0565 or Tourism Saskatchewan, 500—1900 Albert St, Canada S4P 4L9. Email: travel.info@sasktourism.sk.ca. WWW: http://www.sasktourism.com

FIRST AFL DRAFT: ANNIVERSARY. Nov 22, 1959. The American Football League, set to begin play in 1960, held its first draft of college players. First-round choices of the eight teams included: Gerhard Schwedes (Boston), Richie Lucas (Buffalo), Don Meredith (Dallas), Roger LeClerc (Denver), Billy Cannon (Houston), Monty Stickles (Los Angeles), Dale Hackbart (Minneapolis) and George Izo (New York).

GRETZKY SCORES 500th GOAL: ANNIVERSARY. Nov 22, 1986. Center Wayne Gretzky of the Edmonton Oilers scored the 500th goal of his National Hockey League career in only his 575th game, a 5–2 victory over the Vancouver Canucks.

LOWEST-SCORING NBA GAME: ANNIVERSARY. Nov 22, 1950. The Fort Wayne Pistons used a stall tactic to defeat the Minneapolis Lakers, 19–18, in the lowest-scoring NBA game ever. The game drew a large crowd for 50 cent father-son night, but was so boring that people were reading newspapers in the stands during play. The game led to the adoption of the 24-second clock in 1954.

NATIONAL GAME AND PUZZLE WEEK. Nov 22–28. To increase appreciation of games and puzzles while conserving the tradition of investing time with family and friends. Annually, the last week in November. For info: Dana Heideman, Patch Products, Beloit, WI 53512-0268. Phone: (608) 362-6896. Fax: (608) 362-8178. E-mail: patch@patchproducts.com. WWW: http://www.patchproducts.com

NCAA MEN'S AND WOMEN'S DIVISION II CROSS COUNTRY CHAMPIONSHIPS. Nov 22. Finals. University of Kansas, Lawrence, KS. For info: NCAA, 6201 College Blvd, Overland Park, KS 66211. Phone: (913) 339-1906.

PINEY CREEK SNOWSHOE RUN. Nov 22 (tentative). Ski Cooper near Leadville, CO. The course consists of about four miles of unpacked, semi-packed and packed snow. Elevation: 10,500 feet. This is the first in a series of five races. This is one of many races held in the Leadville area. For info: Piney Creek Nordic Center, c/o Greater Leadville Area Chamber of Commerce, Leadville, CO 80461. Phone: (800) 933-3901. Fax: (719) 486-8478. E-mail: leadville@sni.net. WWW: http://www.colorado.com/leadville

TYSON WINS HEAVYWEIGHT TITLE: ANNIVERSARY. Nov 22, 1986. Mike Tyson won the WBC heavyweight championship by knocking out Trevor Berbick in the second round of a fight in Las Vegas. Tyson became the youngest heavyweight champion in history and added the WBA version of the title on Mar 7, 1987.

BIRTHDAYS TODAY

Mel Agee, 30, football player, born Chicago, IL, Nov 22, 1968.

Eric Andre Allen, 33, football player, born San Diego, CA, Nov 22, 1965.

Boris Franz Becker, 31, tennis player, born Leimen, Germany, Nov 22, 1967.

Selva Lewis (Lew) Burdette, 72, former baseball player, born Nitro, WV, Nov 22, 1926.

Steven Leonard (Steve) DeOssie, 36, football player, born Tacoma, WA, Nov 22, 1962.

Harry Edwards, 56, sports sociologist, born St. Louis, MO, Nov 22, 1942.

Lew Hays, 84, Cofounder of PONY League baseball, born Butler, PA, Nov 22, 1914.

Mariel Hemingway, 37, actress (*Personal Best*), born Ketchum, ID, Nov 22, 1961.

Byron Dwight Houston, 29, basketball player, born Watonga, KS, Nov 22, 1969.

Billie Jean Moffitt King, 55, former tennis player, born Long Beach, CA, Nov 22, 1943.
Gregory Michael (Greg) Luzinski, 48, former baseball player, born Chicago, IL, Nov 22, 1950.

NOVEMBER 23 — MONDAY
Day 327 — 38 Remaining

CHASE'S SPORTSQUOTE OF THE DAY

"Tiant is the Fred Astaire of baseball." —Roger Angell on Luis Tiant

ASHFORD, EMMETT : BIRTH ANNIVERSARY. Nov 23, 1914. Emmett Littleton Ashford, baseball umpire born at Los Angeles, CA. Ashford was the first black to umpire a major league baseball game. Ashford began his pro career calling games in the minors in 1951 and went to the majors in 1966. He was noted for his flamboyant style when calling strikes and outs as well as for his dapper dress which included cufflinks with his uniform. Died at Marina del Rey, CA, Mar 1, 1980.

FIRST PLAY-BY-PLAY FOOTBALL GAME BROAD-CAST: ANNIVERSARY. Nov 23, 1919. The first play-by-play football game broadcast in the US took place on this day. In the game that was broadcast Texas A&M blanked the University of Texas, 7–0.

FLUTIE'S HAIL MARY PASS: ANNIVERSARY. Nov 23, 1984. Quarterback Doug Flutie of Boston College passed for 472 yards and led the Eagles to a 47–45 upset of the Miami University Hurricanes. Flutie won the game with a desperation, "Hail Mary" touchdown pass that end Gerald Phelan caught in the end zone.

NAIA MEN'S SOCCER NATIONAL CHAMPIONSHIP. Nov 23–28. Site TBA. 12-team field competes for national championship. 40th annual. Est attendance: 3,000. For info: Natl Assn of Intercollegiate Athletics, 6120 S Yale Ave, Ste 1450, Tulsa, OK 74136-4223. Phone: (918) 494-8828. Fax: (918) 494-8841. E-mail: khenry@naia.org. WWW: http://www.naia.org

NAIA WOMEN'S SOCCER NATIONAL CHAMPI-ONSHIP. Nov 23–28. Site TBA. 8-team field competes for national championship. 15th annual. Est attendance: 3,000. For info: Natl Assn of Intercollegiate Athletics, 6120 S Yale Ave, Ste 1450, Tulsa, OK 74136-4223. Phone: (918) 494-8828. Fax: (918) 494-8841. E-mail: khenry@naia.org. WWW: http://www.naia.org

NCAA MEN'S AND WOMEN'S DIVISION I CROSS-COUNTRY CHAMPIONSHIPS. Nov 23. Finals. University of Kansas, Lawrence, KS. For info: NCAA, 6201 College Blvd, Overland Park, KS 66211. Phone: (913) 339-1906.

SCHUMACHER, HAL: BIRTH ANNIVERSARY. Nov 23, 1910. Harold Henry (Hal) Schumacher, baseball player born at Hinckley, NY. Schumacher pitched his entire 13-year career with the New York Giants (1931–46) and won 158 games. Died at Cooperstown, NY, Apr 21, 1993.

BIRTHDAYS TODAY

Vincent Lamont (Vin) Baker, 27, basketball player, born Lake Wales, FL, Nov 23, 1971.

November *1998*	S	M	T	W	T	F	S
	1	2	3	4	5	6	7
	8	9	10	11	12	13	14
	15	16	17	18	19	20	21
	22	23	24	25	26	27	28
	29	30					

Saku Koivu, 24, hockey player, born Turku, Finland, Nov 23, 1974.
Dale Curtis Sveum, 35, baseball player, born Richmond, CA, Nov 23, 1963.
Luis Clemente Tiant, 58, former baseball player, born Marinao, Cuba, Nov 23, 1940.
Andrew Toney, 41, former basketball player, born Birmingham, AL, Nov 23, 1957.
George Harry Yardley, III, 70, Basketball Hall of Fame forward, born Hollywood, CA, Nov 23, 1928.

NOVEMBER 24 — TUESDAY
Day 328 — 37 Remaining

BURNS, GEORGE: BIRTH ANNIVERSARY. Nov 24, 1889. George Joseph Burns, baseball player born at Utica, NY. Burns was an outfielder and not related to his contemporary, first baseman George Henry Burns. He wore a special cap and blue sunglasses to help him cope with the sun at the Polo Grounds. Died at Gloversville, NY, Aug 15, 1966.

McALLESTER THROWN FOR TOUCHDOWN: ANNI-VERSARY. Nov 24, 1904. University of Tennesse fullback Sam McAllester was thrown for a touchdown to give the Volunteers a 7–0 victory over the University of Alabama. McAllester wore a special leather belt with handgrips sewn on the sides. His team engineered a 50-yard touchdown drive by repeatedly throwing him over the line of scrimmage, including one toss for the game's only touchdown. Football's rules were later changed to prohibit abetting the ballcarrier.

MEDWICK, DUCKY: BIRTH ANNIVERSARY. Nov 24, 1911. Joseph Michael ("Ducky") Medwick, Baseball Hall of Fame outfielder born at Carteret, NJ. Medwick was a member of the St. Louis Cardinals' famous Gas House Gang and won the National League Triple Crown in 1937. His career batting average was .324. Inducted into the Hall of Fame in 1968. Died at St. Petersburg, FL, Mar 21, 1975.

BIRTHDAYS TODAY

David (Dave) Bing, 55, Basketball Hall of Fame guard, born Washington, DC, Nov 24, 1943.
Robert Bartmess (Bob) Friend, 68, former baseball player, born Lafayette, IN, Nov 24, 1930.
David Andrew (Dave) Hansen, 30, baseball player, born Long Beach, CA, Nov 24, 1968.
Robert W. (Bob) Hill, 50, former basketball coach, born Columbus, OH, Nov 24, 1948.
Edward Joseph (Eddie) Johnston, 63, former hockey coach and player, born Montreal, Quebec, Canada, Nov 24, 1935.
Albert Lee (Al) Martin, 31, baseball player, born West Covina, CA, Nov 24, 1967.
Larry Benard (Ben) McDonald, 31, baseball player, born Baton Rouge, LA, Nov 24, 1967.
James Thomas (Jim) Northrup, 59, former baseball player, born Breckenridge, MI, Nov 24, 1939.
Keith Primeau, 27, hockey player, born Toronto, Ontario, Canada, Nov 24, 1971.
Oscar Palmer Robertson, 60, Basketball Hall of Fame guard, born Charlotte, TN, Nov 24, 1938.
Rudolph (Rudy) Tomjanovich, 50, basketball coach and former player, born Hamtramck, MI, Nov 24, 1948.
Randy Lee Velarde, 36, baseball player, born Midland, TX, Nov 24, 1962.
Stephen Wayne (Steve) Yeager, 50, former baseball player, born Huntington, WV, Nov 24, 1948.

NOVEMBER 25 — WEDNESDAY
Day 329 — 36 Remaining

CARRS GREAT ALASKA SHOOTOUT. Nov 25–28. Sullivan Area, Anchorage, AK. Top NCAA basketball action as eight men's division I teams from around the country compete. Est attendance: 45,000. For info: Univ of Alaska-Anchorage, Athletic Dept, Anchorage, AK 99508. Phone: (907) 786-1307. Fax: (907) 563-4565.
Email: antlm@uaa.alaska.edu.
WWW: http://www.uaa.alaska.edu/athletic

MATHESON, BOB: BIRTH ANNIVERSARY. Nov 25, 1944. Robert Edward (Bob) Matheson, football player born at Boone, NC. Matheson played at Duke and was drafted in 1967 by the Cleveland Browns. After four seasons, he was traded to the Miami Dolphins where he became an integral part of the famous "No Name" defense that helped win two Super Bowls. The Dolphins' "53" defense, utilizing Matheson as a linebacker, was named after his uniform number. Died at Durham, NC, Sept 5, 1994.

NO MAS, NO MAS: ANNIVERSARY. Nov 25, 1980. Roberto Duran quit fighting with 16 seconds left in the eighth round, saying "No mas, no mas (No more, no more)," allowing ("Sugar") Ray Leonard to regain the WBC welterweight title.

BIRTHDAYS TODAY

Christopher D. (Cris) Carter, 33, football player, born Troy, OH, Nov 25, 1965.
Russell Earl ("Bucky") Dent (born Russell Earl O'Dey), 47, former baseball manager and player, born Savannah, GA, Nov 25, 1951.
Joseph Paul (Joe) DiMaggio, 84, Baseball Hall of Fame outfielder, born Martinez, CA, Nov 25, 1914.
Joe Jackson Gibbs, 58, auto racing executive, broadcaster and Pro Football Hall of Fame coach, born Mocksville, NC, Nov 25, 1940.
Yatil Green, 25, football player, born Lake City, FL, Nov 25, 1973.
Bernie Joseph Kosar, Jr, 35, former football player, born Boardman, OH, Nov 25, 1963.
Leonard Edward (Lenny) Moore, 65, Pro Football Hall of Fame halfback, born Reading, PA, Nov 25, 1933.
Anthony Eugene Peeler, 29, basketball player, born Kansas City, MO, Nov 25, 1969.
Mark Anthony Whiten, 32, baseball player, born Pensacola, FL, Nov 25, 1966.

NOVEMBER 26 — THURSDAY
Day 330 — 35 Remaining

AMERICAN BICYCLE ASSOCIATION GRAND NATIONALS. Nov 26–29. Myriad Convention Center, Oklahoma City, OK. This World Championship BMX (bike motocross) competition draws more than 10,000 contestants and out-of-state spectators, from at least 15 countries, making it the largest out-of-state visitor attraction in the nation to be held during the Thanksgiving holidays. Est attendance: 25,000. For info: OK City All Sports Assn, 100 W Main, Ste 285, Oklahoma City, OK 73102. Phone: (405) 236-5000. Fax: (405) 236-5008.

ATLANTA MARATHON AND ATLANTA HALF-MARATHON. Nov 26. Atlanta, GA. 26.2-mile and 13.1-mile races. Advance registration only; entry forms available in July. Send SASE. Est attendance: 8,000. For info: Atlanta Track Club, Atlanta Marathon, 3097 E Shadowlawn Ave, Atlanta, GA 30305. Race Hot line (Atlanta area) (404) 262-RACE.
WWW: http://www.atlantatrackclub.org

DUFFY, HUGH: BIRTH ANNIVERSARY. Nov 26, 1866. Hugh Duffy, Baseball Hall of Fame outfielder born at River Point, RI. Duffy had a 68-year career in baseball. He starred for the Boston teams of the 1890s and hit .438 in 1894, the all-time record. After his retirement, he was a manager, coach, executive and a scout until his death. Inducted into the Hall of Fame in 1945. Died at Allston, MA, Oct 19, 1954.

ELLIOTT, BOB: BIRTH ANNIVERSARY. Nov 26, 1916. Robert Irving (Bob) Elliott, baseball player and manager born at San Francisco, CA. Elliott played with the Pittsburgh Pirates from 1939 through 1945 and was an outstanding clutch hitter. Traded to the Boston Braves, he became the first third baseman to win the National League MVP award in 1947 and helped the Braves to the 1948 pennant. Died at San Diego, CA, May 4, 1966.

GOMEZ, LEFTY: 90th BIRTH ANNIVERSARY. Nov 26, 1908. Vernon Louis ("Lefty") Gomez, Baseball Hall of Fame pitcher born at Rodeo, CA. Gomez was a star pitcher with the New York Yankees from 1930 to 1942. He won six World Series games without a defeat and was the winning pitcher in the first All-Star Game. Inducted into the Hall of Fame in 1972. Died at Greenbrae, CA, Feb 17, 1989.

JOHNSON, BOB: BIRTH ANNIVERSARY. Nov 26, 1906. Robert Lee (Bob) Johnson, baseball player born at Pryor, OK. Part Cherokee, Johnson patrolled the outfield for the Philadelphia Athletics from 1933 through 1941, driving in 100 runs seven times. He hit 288 home runs in his career. Died at Tacoma, WA, July 6, 1982.

MOON PHASE: FIRST QUARTER. Nov 26. Moon enters First Quarter phase at 7:23 PM, EST.

RED GRANGE'S FIRST GAME AS A PROFESSIONAL: ANNIVERSARY. Nov 26, 1925. After finishing his college football career at the University of Illinois, Harold ("Red") Grange, perhaps the most famous player of all time, played his first game as a professional. Wearing the uniform of the Chicago Bears, Grange was held to 35 yards rushing in a 0–0 tie against the Chicago Cardinals.

TENNEY, FRED: BIRTH ANNIVERSARY. Nov 26, 1871. Frederick Clay (Fred) Tenney, baseball player and manager born at Georgetown, MA. Tenney was among the first college graduates to play major league baseball and was a left-handed catcher to boot. He switched to first base, playing for the Boston Beaneaters (later the Braves) and the New York Giants. Died at Boston, MA, July 3, 1952.

THANKSGIVING DAY. Nov 26. Legal public holiday. (Public Law 90–363 sets Thanksgiving Day on the fourth Thursday in November). Observed on this day in all states.

TRIPLE CROWN OF SURFING SERIES: EVENT 2. Nov 26–Dec 7. Sunset Beach, North Shore, Oahu, HI. 16th annual. The Triple Crown of Surfing series is professional, big-wave surfing for men and women. Est attendance: 7,500. For media info: Carol Hogan, (808) 325-7400. Fax: (808) 325-7400. E-mail: oceanpro@interpac.net. For contest info: Randy Rarick, (808) 638-7266, or Fred Williamson, (808) 377-5850.
WWW: http://www.holoholo.org/triplecrown/

TURKEY TROT. Nov 26. Parkersburg City Park Pavilion, Parkersburg, WV. Three-mile fun run/walk on Thanksgiving morning. Drawings held for frozen turkeys and each participant receives a long-sleeved T-shirt. Est attendance: 650. For info: Rehab Services Dept, St. Joseph's Hospital, PO Box 327, Parkersburg, WV 26102. Phone: (304) 424-4393. Fax: (304) 424-4430.

BIRTHDAYS TODAY

Mario Antoine Elie, 35, basketball player, born New York, NY, Nov 26, 1963.

Charles Edward (Chuck) Finley, 36, baseball player, born Monroe, LA, Nov 26, 1962.

Richard Joseph (Richie) Hebner, 51, former baseball player, born Boston, MA, Nov 26, 1947.

Johnny Lyndell Hector, 38, former football player, born Lafayette, LA, Nov 26, 1960.

Dale Jarrett, 42, auto racer, born Conover, NC, Nov 26, 1956.

Shawn T. Kemp, 29, basketball player, born Elkhart, IN, Nov 26, 1969.

Chris Osgood, 26, hockey player, born Peace River, Alberta, Canada, Nov 26, 1972.

Arthur (Art) Shell, 52, former football coach and Pro Football Hall of Fame tackle, born Charleston, SC, Nov 26, 1946.

Jan Stenerud, 56, Pro Football Hall of Fame placekicker, born Fetsund, Norway, Nov 26, 1942.

Jeffrey Allen (Jeff) Torborg, 57, broadcaster and former baseball manager and player, born Plainfield, NJ, Nov 26, 1941.

NOVEMBER 27 — FRIDAY

Day 331 — 34 Remaining

SPORTSCHASER OF THE DAY

What famous broadcaster began his career as a mascot at Columbia University?

BUSH, BULLET JOE: BIRTH ANNIVERSARY. Nov 27, 1892. Leslie Ambrose ("Bullet Joe") Bush, baseball player born at Brainerd, MN. Bush won 195 games as a pitcher in 17 major league seasons. He was a temperamental player who gave his managers difficulty, once screaming curses at Miller Huggins who had ordered him to issue an intentional walk. Died at Ft Lauderdale, FL, Nov 1, 1974.

DAYTONA TURKEY RUN. Nov 27–29. Daytona International Speedway, Daytona Beach, FL. 25th annual car show of all makes of 1972 and older collector vehicles. Show includes display of classics, sports cars, muscle cars, race cars, and custom and special-interest vehicles on the speedway infield all three days with a large swap meet of auto parts and accessories and car sales corral. Also crafts sale. Annually, Thanksgiving weekend. Est attendance: 60,000. For info: Rick D'Louhy, Exec Dir, Daytona Beach Racing and Recreational Facilities District, PO Box 1958, Daytona Beach, FL 32115-1958. Phone: (904) 255-7355.

FISH HOUSE PARADE. Nov 27. Aitkin, MN. 8th annual special parade of uniquely decorated fish houses used for ice fishing during the winter. Annually, the Friday after Thanksgiving. Est attendance: 2,000. For info: Carroll Kukowski, Exec Dir, Aitkin Area Chamber of Commerce, PO Box 127, Aitkin, MN 56431. Phone: (800) 526-8342. Fax: (218) 927-4494. E-mail: upnorth@aitkin.com WWW: http://aitkin.com

HOWE GETS 1,000TH POINT: ANNIVERSARY. Nov 27, 1960. Right wing Gordie Howe of the Detroit Red Wings scored the 1,000th point of his NHL career, tallying an assist in a Red Wings victory over the Toronto Maple Leafs. Howe finished his 26-year career with 1,850 points.

HUSING, TED: BIRTH ANNIVERSARY. Nov 27, 1901. Edward Britt (Ted) Husing, sportscaster born at New York, NY. Husing moved from a job as varsity sports mascot

Smoky Burgess

	S	M	T	W	T	F	S
November	1	2	3	4	5	6	7
1998	8	9	10	11	12	13	14
	15	16	17	18	19	20	21
	22	23	24	25	26	27	28
	29	30					

at Columbia University to a career as a radio announcer where he gradually focused on sports. He made his mark doing college football games for the CBS network, using careful preparation, wide knowledge and precise speech to develop a national reputation. Died at Pasadena, CA, Aug 10, 1962.

McNALLY, JOHNNY BLOOD: BIRTH ANNIVERSARY. Nov 27, 1904. John Victor ("Johnny Blood") McNally, Pro Football Hall of Fame halfback born at New Richmond, WI. McNally left Notre Dame over discipline code violations. Heading for a tryout with a semipro team, he adopted the name Johnny Blood, based on the Rudolf Valentino film *Blood and Sand*. He played 15 years in the NFL and led the Green Bay Packers to four titles. A flamboyant player who ignored team rules with abandon, he proved a disaster as a coach. Inducted into the Hall of Fame as a charter member in 1963. Died at Palm Springs, CA, Nov 28, 1965.

NATIONAL FINALS STEER ROPING. Nov 27–28. Lazy E Arena, Guthrie, OK. The World Championship and $90,000 are at stake as the top 15 steer ropers in the world compete. Est attendance: 12,000. For info: Lazy E Arena, Rt 5, Box 393, Guthrie, OK 73044. Phone: (405) 282-7433 or (800) 595-RIDE(7433). Fax: (405) 282-3785. E-mail: learena@ionet.net. WWW: http://www.lazye.com

NCAA MEN'S DIVISION III SOCCER CHAMPIONSHIP. Nov 27–28 or 28–29. Finals at a campus site TBA. For info: NCAA, 6201 College Blvd, Overland Park, KS 66211. Phone: (913) 339-1906.

WORLD'S CHAMPIONSHIP DUCK-CALLING CONTEST AND WINGS OVER THE PRAIRIE FESTIVAL. Nov 27–28. Stuttgart, AR. Besides the championship competition this festival also offers a fun shoot, 10K race, sporting collectibles, commercial exhibitors, Sportsman's Dinner and Dance, duck gumbo cook-off, carnival, arts and crafts booths and more. Annually, Thanksgiving weekend. Est attendance: 65,000. For info: Stuttgart Chamber of Commerce, 507 S Main, Stuttgart, AR 72160. Phone: (870) 673-1602. Fax: (870) 673-1604.

BIRTHDAYS TODAY

Larry Christopher Allen, 27, football player, born Los Angeles, CA, Nov 27, 1971.
David John (Dave) Giusti, 59, former baseball player, born Seneca Falls, NY, Nov 27, 1939.
Randy Andre Milligan, 37, former baseball player, born San Diego, CA, Nov 27, 1961.
Michael Lorri (Mike) Scioscia, 40, former baseball player, born Upper Darby, PA, Nov 27, 1958.
Jose Milages Tartabull, 60, former baseball player, born Cienfuegos, Cuba, Nov 27, 1938.
Nickey Maxwell (Nick) Van Exel, 27, basketball player, born Kenosha, WI, Nov 27, 1971.

NOVEMBER 28 — SATURDAY
Day 332 — 33 Remaining

BILLIKENS WIN FIRST NCAA SOCCER TITLE: ANNIVERSARY. Nov 28, 1959. The St. Louis University Billikens won the first NCAA soccer championship, defeating the University of Bridgeport, 5–2.

NCAA DIVISION I-AA FOOTBALL CHAMPIONSHIP. Nov 28. First round at campus sites TBA. For info: NCAA, 6201 College Blvd, Overland Park, KS 66211. Phone: (913) 339-1906.

PEITZ, HEINIE: BIRTH ANNIVERSARY. Nov 28, 1870. Henry Clement ("Heinie") Peitz, baseball player born at St. Louis, MO. Peitz was one of baseball's best catchers

around the turn of the century. He hit .271 over 16 seasons. Died at Cincinnati, OH, Oct 23, 1943.

PICARD, HENRY: BIRTH ANNIVERSARY. Nov 28, 1907. Henry B. Picard, golfer born at Plymouth, MA. Picard won 30 tournaments, including the 1938 Masters and the 1939 PGA Championship. He was golf's leading money winner in 1941. Early in his career, he became the only golfer to defeat Walter Hagen in a playoff, doing so in the 1932 Carolina Open. Died at Charleston, SC, Apr 30, 1997.

THE SKINS GAME. Nov 28–29. Site TBA. A special PGA-sponsored tournament matching four outstanding golfers. In the skins format, each hole is worth a certain amount of money called a skin. Players attempt to win the skin by winning the hole. If two or more players tie on a given hole, the skin and the prize money carry over to the next hole. For info: PGA Tour, 112 TPC Blvd, Ponte Vedra Beach, FL 32082. Phone: (904) 285-3700.

TWO TDS ON RECOVERED FUMBLES: 50th ANNIVERSARY. Nov 28, 1948. Dippy Evans of the Chicago Bears became the first player in NFL history to score two touchdowns on recovered fumbles in the same game as the Bears defeated the Washington Redskins, 48–13.

BIRTHDAYS TODAY

Pedro Julio Astacio, 29, baseball player, born Hato Mayor, Dominican Republic, Nov 28, 1969.
John David Burkett, 34, baseball player, born New Brighton, PA, Nov 28, 1964.
Sixto Joaquin Lezcano, 45, former baseball player, born Arecibo, Puerto Rico, Nov 28, 1953.
John Sylvester (Johnny) Newman, Jr, 35, basketball player, born Danville, PA, Nov 28, 1963.
Randy Newman, 55, singer/songwriter, composer (score *The Natural*), born New Orleans, LA, Nov 28, 1943.
David Allen (Dave) Righetti, 40, former baseball player, born San Jose, CA, Nov 28, 1958.
Roy James Tarpley, Jr, 34, former basketball player, born New York, NY, Nov 28, 1964.
Paul D. Warfield, 56, Pro Football Hall of Fame receiver, born Warren, OH, Nov 28, 1942.
Walter William (Walt) Weiss, Jr, 35, baseball player, born Tuxedo, NY, Nov 28, 1963.
Matthew Derrick (Matt) Williams, 33, baseball player, born Bishop, CA, Nov 28, 1965.

NOVEMBER 29 — SUNDAY
Day 333 — 32 Remaining

BOARDWALK KENNEL CLUB DOG SHOW. Nov 29. The New Atlantic City Convention Center, Atlantic City, NJ. One of the largest all-breed dog shows in the country with more than 2,200 entrants from across the US and Canada. Est attendance: 5,000. For info: Atlantic City Conv & Visitors Authority, 2314 Pacific Ave, Atlantic City, NJ 08401. Phone: (609) 449-7142.

DETROIT'S FIRST THANKSGIVING GAME: ANNIVERSARY. Nov 29, 1934. The Detroit Lions played their first Thanksgiving Day game, the start of an NFL tradition, and lost to the Chicago Bears, 19–16.

FIRST ARMY-NAVY GAME: ANNIVERSARY. Nov 29, 1904. Army played Navy for the first time in football, but Navy won, 24–0.

BIRTHDAYS TODAY

Neal LaMoy Broten, 39, hockey player, born Roseau, MN, Nov 29, 1959.
DeCovan Kadell (Dee) Brown, 30, basketball player, born Jacksonville, FL, Nov 29, 1968.

Michael Anthony (Mike) Easler, 48, former baseball player, born Cleveland, OH, Nov 29, 1950.
William Ashley (Bill) Freehan, 57, former baseball player, born Detroit, MI, Nov 29, 1941.
Howard Michael Johnson, 38, former baseball player, born Clearwater, FL, Nov 29, 1960.
Jamal Mashburn, 26, basketball player, born New York, NY, Nov 29, 1972.
Richard John (Dick) McAuliffe, 59, former baseball player, born Hartford, CT, Nov 29, 1939.
Saturnino Orestes Armas ("Minnie") Minoso, 76, former baseball player, born Havana, Cuba, Nov 29, 1922.
Vincent Edward (Vin) Scully, 71, broadcaster (Ford Frick award winner), born New York, NY, Nov 29, 1927.

☆ ☆ ☆

NOVEMBER 30 — MONDAY
Day 334 — 31 Remaining

CHASE'S SPORTSQUOTE OF THE DAY

"If I lose, then I still will have the most thrilling thing of all—the money." —Floyd Patterson

MARBERRY, FIRPO: BIRTH ANNIVERSARY. Nov 30, 1899. Frederick ("Firpo") Marberry, baseball player and umpire born at Streetman, TX. Marberry became a relief pitcher early in his career, helping to establish relieving as a distinct job description. He was an American League umpire in 1935 but returned to the mound the following year. Died at Mexia, TX, June 30, 1976.

PATTERSON WINS HEAVYWEIGHT TITLE: ANNIVERSARY. Nov 30, 1956. Floyd Patterson won the heavyweight title by knocking out Archie Moore in the fifth round of a fight in Chicago. Patterson claimed the title made vacant by the retirement of Rocky Marciano on Apr 27.

Patterson Wins Heavyweight Title

BIRTHDAYS TODAY

Vincent Edward ("Bo") Jackson, 36, former baseball player and Heisman Trophy running back, born Bessemer, AL, Nov 30, 1962.
Ivan ("Pudge") Rodriguez, 27, baseball player, born Vega Baja, Puerto Rico, Nov 30, 1971.
Craig Steven Swan, 48, former baseball player, born Van Nuys, CA, Nov 30, 1950.
Robert Alan (Bob) Tewksbury, 38, baseball player, born Concord, NH, Nov 30, 1960.
William Ernest (Bill) Walsh, 67, football executive and Pro Football Hall of Fame coach, born Los Angeles, CA, Nov 30, 1931.
Paul Douglas Westphal, 48, former basketball coach and former player, born Torrance, CA, Nov 30, 1950.

DECEMBER 1 — TUESDAY
Day 335 — 30 Remaining

ALSTON, WALTER: BIRTH ANNIVERSARY. Dec 1, 1911. Walter Emmons Alston, baseball player and Baseball Hall of Fame manager born at Venice, OH. Alston struck out in his only major league at-bat, but he became one of the game's most successful managers. Working under a series of one-year contracts with the Brooklyn and Los Angeles Dodgers from 1954 through 1976, Alston won seven National League pennants and four World Series. Inducted into the Hall of Fame in 1983. Died at Oxford, OH, Oct 1, 1984.

BINGO'S BIRTHDAY MONTH. Dec 1–31. To celebrate the innovation and manufacture of the game of Bingo in 1929 by Edwin S. Lowe. Today Bingo played as a charitable fundraiser brings in five billion dollars. For info: Roger Snowden, Pres, Bingo Bugle, Inc, Box 527, Vashon, WA 98070. Phone: (800) 327-6437.

LAVAGETTO, COOKIE: BIRTH ANNIVERSARY. Dec 1, 1912. Harry Arthur ("Cookie") Lavagetto, baseball player and manager born at Oakland, CA. Lavagetto was the first manager of the Minnesota Twins, but he is best remembered for breaking up Floyd Bevans's bid for a no-hitter in Game 4 of the 1947 World Series. Lavagetto doubled with two out in the bottom of the ninth inning, spoiling Bevans's effort and winning the game for the Brooklyn Dodgers. Died at Orinda, CA, Aug 10, 1990.

NICKLAUS PASSES $2 MILLION MARK: 25th ANNIVERSARY. Dec 1, 1973. Jack Nicklaus won the Disney World Open to become the first golfer to earn more than $2 million in career winnings.

REULBACH, ED: BIRTH ANNIVERSARY. Dec 1, 1882. Edward Marvin (Ed) Reulbach, baseball pitcher born at Detroit, MI. Reulbach pitched from 1905 to 1917 and won 181 games. He starred for the great Chicago Cubs teams of 1906, 1907 and 1908. Died at Glens Falls, NY, July 17, 1961.

ZAMBONI MEDICAL ALERT: ANNIVERSARY. Dec 1, 1989. The Centers for Disease Control revealed in the *Journal of the American Medical Association* that fumes from a Zamboni ice machine could make fans at a hockey game sick if the rink is not properly ventilated.

BIRTHDAYS TODAY

Carol Alt, 38, model, born New York, NY, Dec 1, 1960.
George Arthur Foster, 50, former baseball player, born Tuscaloosa, AL, Dec 1, 1948.
Martin Whitford (Marty) Marion, 81, former baseball manager and player, born Richburg, SC, Dec 1, 1917.

Harry Arthur ("Cookie") Lavagetto

Calvin Coolidge Julius Caesar Tuskahoma (Cal) McLish, 73, former baseball player, born Anadarko, OK, Dec 1, 1925.
Gregory Winston (Greg) McMichael, 32, baseball player, born Knoxville, TN, Dec 1, 1966.
Kirk Wesley Rueter, 28, baseball player, born Centralia, IL, Dec 1, 1970.
Reginald Laverne (Reggie) Sanders, 31, baseball player, born Florence, SC, Dec 1, 1967.
Lee Buck Trevino, 59, golfer, born Dallas, TX, Dec 1, 1939.
Larry Kenneth Walker, 32, baseball player, born Maple Ridge, BC, Canada, Dec 1, 1966.
Stephen John (Steve) Walsh, 32, football player, born St. Paul, MN, Dec 1, 1966.

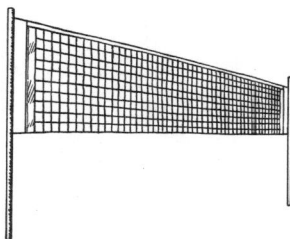

DECEMBER 2 — WEDNESDAY
Day 336 — 29 Remaining

NAIA WOMEN'S NATIONAL VOLLEYBALL CHAMPI-ONSHIP. Dec 2–5. Site to be determined. 20 teams compete in a pool play tournament to determine the national champion. 18th annual championship. Est attendance: 3,000. For info: Natl Assn of Intercollegiate Athletics, 6120 S Yale Ave, Ste 1450, Tulsa, OK 74136-4223. Phone: (918) 494-8828. Fax: (918) 494-8841. Email: khenry@naia.org. WWW: http://www.naia.org

WHITE, DEACON: BIRTH ANNIVERSARY. Dec 2, 1847. James Laurie ("Deacon") White, baseball player born at Caton, NY. White was a catcher in the earliest days of professional baseball and was the first man to bat in the first game in baseball's first professional league. Died at Aurora, IL, July 7, 1939.

BIRTHDAYS TODAY

Pedro Borbon, 52, former baseball player, born Valverde De Mao, Dominican Republic, Dec 2, 1946.
William Ferdie (Willie) Brown, 58, Pro Football Hall of Fame defensive back, born Yazoo City, MS, Dec 2, 1940.
Randy Gardner, 40, figure skater, born Marina del Rey, CA, Dec 2, 1958.
Darryl Andrew Kile, 30, baseball player, born Garden Grove, CA, Dec 2, 1968.
Monica Seles, 25, tennis player, born Novi Sad, Yugoslavia, Dec 2, 1973.
Ronald (Ron) Sutter, 35, hockey player, born Viking, Alberta, Canada, Dec 2, 1963.

DECEMBER 3 — THURSDAY
Day 337 — 28 Remaining

COLLINS, JOE: BIRTH ANNIVERSARY. Dec 3, 1922. Joseph Edward (Joe) Collins, baseball player born at Scranton, PA. As a first baseman for the New York Yankees, Collins played in seven World Series. He hit two home runs off Don Newcombe in Game 1 of the 1955 Series. Died at Union, NJ, Aug 30, 1989.

MOON PHASE: FULL MOON. Dec 3. Moon enters Full Moon phase at 10:19 PM, EST.

NCAA MEN'S DIVISION II SOCCER CHAMPIONSHIP. Dec 3–5 or 4–6. Finals at a campus site TBA. For info: NCAA, 6201 College Blvd, Overland Park, KS 66211. Phone: (913) 339-1906.

SIMPSON, HARRY: BIRTH ANNIVERSARY. Dec 3, 1925. Harry Leon Simpson, baseball player born at Atlanta, GA. Simpson started his major league career in 1951 with the Cleveland Indians, and then, over seven more seasons, he played with the Kansas City Athletics, the New York Yankees, the Athletics again, the Chicago White Sox and the Pittsburgh Pirates. His nickname was "Suitcase." Died at Akron, OH, Apr 3, 1979.

BIRTHDAYS TODAY

Damon Scott Berryhill, 35, former baseball player, born South Laguna, CA, Dec 3, 1963.
Toi Fitzgerald Cook, 34, football player, born Chicago, IL, Dec 3, 1964.
Darryl Quinn Hamilton, 35, baseball player, born Baton Rouge, LA, Dec 3, 1963.
Igor Larionov, 38, hockey player, born Voskresensk, USSR, Dec 3, 1960.
Rick Ravon Mears, 47, auto racer, born Wichita, KS, Dec 3, 1951.
Ruthford Eduardo ("Chico") Salmon, 58, former baseball player, born Colon, Panama, Dec 3, 1940.

DECEMBER 4 — FRIDAY
Day 338 — 27 Remaining

SPORTSCHASER OF THE DAY

Glenn Davis was Army's "Mr. Outside." Who was "Mr. Inside"?

BLANCHARD FIRST JUNIOR TO WIN HEISMAN TROPHY: ANNIVERSARY. Dec 4, 1945. Fullback Felix ("Doc") Blanchard of Army became the first junior to win the Heisman Trophy, emblematic of college football's best player. "Mr. Inside" to teammate Glenn Davis's "Mr. Out-

December 1998	S	M	T	W	T	F	S
			1	2	3	4	5
	6	7	8	9	10	11	12
	13	14	15	16	17	18	19
	20	21	22	23	24	25	26
	27	28	29	30	31		

side," Blanchard also won the Sullivan Award, given to the country's best overall athlete.

BURKETT, JESSE: 130th BIRTH ANNIVERSARY. Dec 4, 1868. Jesse Cail Burkett, Baseball Hall of Fame outfielder born at Wheeling, WV. Burkett could pitch, but he was a superior hitter, compiling batting averages in excess of .400 in 1895 and 1896. His nickname, "the Crab," came from his disposition on the field. Inducted into the Hall of Fame in 1946. Died at Worcester, MA, May 27, 1953.

ENGLAND: WINMAU WORLD DARTS CHAMPIONSHIPS. Dec 4–5. London. Major event in the darts calendar with top players from all over the world competing. Est attendance: 1,500. For info: Mr Olly Croft, Dir, British Darts Organisation, 2 Pages Lane, London, England N10 1PS.

FIRST BLACK NO. 1 NFL DRAFT CHOICE: ANNIVERSARY. Dec 4, 1961. Syracuse University halfback and Heisman Trophy winner Ernie Davis became the first African American to be selected first in the NFL draft when he was picked by the Washington Redskins.

GULICK, LUTHER: BIRTH ANNIVERSARY. Dec 4, 1865. Luther Hasley Gulick, sports administrator born at Honolulu, HI. A pioneer in the YMCA, Gulick designed the triangular logo symbolizing the physical, emotional and intellectual development that is still the Y's goal. While working in Springfield, MA, in 1891, Gulick persuaded Dr. James Naismith to devise an indoor game for use during the winter at the School for Christian Workers. The result was basketball. Inducted into the Basketball Hall of Fame in 1959. Died at South Casco, ME, Aug 13, 1918.

JAYHAWK SHOOTOUT. Dec 4–6. Coffeyville, KS. Kansas Jayhawk Community College Conference men's and women's basketball showcase. Est attendance: 10,000. For info: Athletic Dir, Coffeyville Community College, 400 W 11th St, Coffeyville, KS 67337. Phone: (316) 252-7070. Fax: (316) 252-7098. E-mail: terryb@raven.ccc.cc.ks.us WWW: http://www.ccc.ccks.us

KUENN, HARVEY: BIRTH ANNIVERSARY. Dec 4, 1930. Harvey Edward Kuenn, Jr, baseball player and manager born at Milwaukee, WI. Kuenn was a fine-hitting shortstop and outfielder in both leagues. He managed the 1982 Milwaukee Brewers, known as "Harvey's Wallbangers," to the American League pennant. Died at Peoria, IL, Feb 28, 1988.

NATIONAL FINALS RODEO. Dec 4–13. Thomas and Mack Center, Las Vegas, NV. The National Finals Rodeo is the premier event in professional rodeo. Reserved for the top 15 contestants in seven events—bareback riding, steer wrestling, team roping, saddle bronc riding, calf roping, women's barrel racing and bull riding—the NFR brings together the best contestants, best livestock and best contract personnel in the industry. Est attendance: 170,000. For info: Attn: Steve Fleming, Professional Rodeo Cowboys Assn, 101 Pro Rodeo Dr, Colorado Springs, CO 80919. Phone: (719) 593-8840, (702) 739-3900 or for ticket info (800) 848-4615.

NCAA WATER POLO CHAMPIONSHIP. Dec 4–6. Finals at a site TBA. For info: NCAA, 6201 College Blvd, Overland Park, KS 66211. Phone: (913) 339-1906.

NCAA WOMEN'S DIVISION III VOLLEYBALL CHAMPIONSHIP. Dec 4–5. Finals at a site TBA. For info: NCAA, 6201 College Blvd, Overland Park, KS 66211. Phone: (913) 339-1906.

NCAA WOMEN'S DIVISION II VOLLEYBALL CHAMPIONSHIP. Dec 4–6. Finals at a site TBA. For info: NCAA, 6201 College Blvd, Overland Park, KS 66211. Phone: (913) 339-1906.

NCAA WOMEN'S DIVISION II SOCCER CHAMPIONSHIP. Dec 4–6. Finals at a campus site TBA. For info: NCAA, 6201 College Blvd, Overland Park, KS 66211. Phone: (913) 339-1906.

NCAA WOMEN'S DIVISION I SOCCER CHAMPIONSHIP. Dec 4–6. Finals. University of North Carolina–Greensboro, Greensboro, NC. For info: NCAA, 6201 College Blvd, Overland Park, KS 66211. Phone: (913) 339-1906.

SHAWKEY, BOB: BIRTH ANNIVERSARY. Dec 4, 1890. James Robert (Bob) Shawkey, baseball player and manager born in Sigel, PA. Shawkey pitched for the New York Yankees in the 1920s, including the game that opened Yankee Stadium. He managed the Yankees to a third-place finish in 1930. Died at Syracuse, NY, Dec 31, 1980.

BIRTHDAYS TODAY

Jeff Blake, 28, football player, born Daytona Beach, FL, Dec 4, 1970.
Helen M. Chase, 74, homemaker and now-retired chronicler of contemporary civilization as coeditor of *Chase's Annual Events*, born Whitehall, MI, Dec 4, 1924.
Alex Peter Delvecchio, 67, Hockey Hall of Fame center, born Fort William, Ontario, Canada, Dec 4, 1931.
Barbaro Garbey, 42, former baseball player, born Santiago, Cuba, Dec 4, 1956.
Bernard King, 42, former basketball player, born New York, NY, Dec 4, 1956.
Stanley Roger (Stan) Smith, 52, former tennis player, born Pasadena, CA, Dec 4, 1946.
Lee Arthur Smith, 41, baseball player, born Jamestown, LA, Dec 4, 1957.
Corliss Mondari Williamson, 25, basketball player, born Russellville, AR, Dec 4, 1973.

☆   ☆   ☆

DECEMBER 5 — SATURDAY
Day 339 — 26 Remaining

ARMY-NAVY FOOTBALL GAME. Dec 5. Veterans Stadium, Philadelphia, PA. The 99th game in one of college football's oldest traditional rivalries. Est attendance: 67,000.

INTERNATIONAL HOCKEY LEAGUE FOUNDED: ANNIVERSARY. Dec 5, 1945. The IHL, founded in Windsor, Ontario, Canada, was designed to provide playing opportunities for Detroit–Windsor-area players returning home from service in World War II. Four teams played a 15-game schedule in 1945–46. Since that time, the IHL has become one of hockey's established minor leagues, with its franchises often serving as "farm teams" for National Hockey League teams. For info: Intl Hockey League, 1577 N Woodward Ave, Bloomfield Hills, MI 48304. Phone: (810) 258-0580. Fax: (810) 258-0940. WWW: http://www.theihl.com

MANCUSO, GUS: BIRTH ANNIVERSARY. Dec 5, 1905. August Rodney (Gus) Mancuso, baseball player born at Galveston, TX. Mancuso was one of the top catchers of the 1930s, especially for the pennant-winning New York Giants. Died at Houston, TX, Oct 26, 1984.

PICKETT, BILL: BIRTH ANNIVERSARY. Dec 5, 1870. Bill Pickett, rodeo cowboy born at Williamson County, TX. Inventor of bulldogging, the modern rodeo event that involves wrestling a running steer to the ground. Died at Tulsa, OK, Apr 21, 1932.

TEBEAU, PATSY: BIRTH ANNIVERSARY. Dec 5, 1864. Oliver Wendell ("Patsy") Tebeau, baseball player and manager born at St. Louis, MO. Tebeau was an infielder in the 1890s and managed the St. Louis Cardinals in 1899 but resigned during the following season, charging that management was grooming John McGraw to replace him. Died at St. Louis, May 15, 1918.

WRIGLEY, PHILIP: BIRTH ANNIVERSARY. Dec 5, 1894. Philip Knight Wrigley, baseball executive born at Chicago, IL. Wrigley inherited the Chicago Cubs upon his father's death in 1932. His family actually owned the team for 60 years until selling it to the Tribune Company in 1981. Died at Elkhart, WI, Apr 12, 1977.

BIRTHDAYS TODAY

Cornelius Clifford (Cliff) Floyd, 26, baseball player, born Chicago, IL, Dec 5, 1972.
Tyrone Eugene (Gene) Harris, 34, baseball player, born Sebring, FL, Dec 5, 1964.
Art Monk, 41, former football player, born White Plains, NY, Dec 5, 1957.
James William (Jim) Plunkett, Jr, 51, Heisman Trophy quarterback, born San Jose, CA, Dec 5, 1947.
Gary Steven Roenicke, 44, former baseball player, born Covina, CA, Dec 5, 1954.
Jerry Lanston (Lanny) Wadkins, 49, golfer, born Richmond, VA, Dec 5, 1949.

DECEMBER 6 — SUNDAY
Day 340 — 25 Remaining

BILL LOCKYER CHRISTMAS REGATTA. Dec 6. Marine Stadium, Lone Beach, CA. Rowing sprint regatta for junior, elite and master rowers, all boat categories. Annually, the first weekend in December. Est attendance: 1,000. For info: Long Beach Rowing Assn, 5750 Boathouse Lane, PO Box 3879, Long Beach, CA 90803. Phone: (562) 438-3352. Fax: (562) 438-3352.

CONLAN, JOCKO: BIRTH ANNIVERSARY. Dec 6, 1899. John Bertrand ("Jocko") Conlan, baseball player and Baseball Hall of Fame umpire born at Chicago, IL. Conlan played in the majors but made his reputation as one of the National League's most colorful umpires. He was particularly remembered for his run-ins with Leo Durocher. Inducted into the Hall of Fame in 1974. Died at Scottsdale, AZ, Apr 16, 1989.

HACK, STAN: BIRTH ANNIVERSARY. Dec 6, 1909. Stanley Camfield (Stan) Hack, baseball player and manager born at Sacramento, CA. Hack was a fixture at third base for the Chicago Cubs for 16 years (1932–47). He hit .348 in four World Series. Died at Dixon, IL, Dec 15, 1979.

LAZZERI, TONY: 95th BIRTH ANNIVERSARY. Dec 6, 1903. Anthony Michael (Tony) Lazzeri, Baseball Hall of Fame second baseman born at San Francisco, CA. Lazzeri was the New York Yankees' regular second baseman from 1926 to 1937. He was a powerful clutch hitter who attracted many new Italian American fans to the game. Inducted into the Hall of Fame in 1991. Died at Millbrae, CA, Aug 6, 1946.

LITTLE, LOU: 105th BIRTH ANNIVERSARY. Dec 6, 1893. Louis Lawrence (Lou) Little, football player and coach born at Boston, MA. Little played football at the University of Pennsylvania and professionally, but he made his reputation as a college coach at Georgetown and Columbia. His 1933 Columbia team defeated highly favored Stanford in the 1934 Rose Bowl. He retired in 1957. Died at Delray Beach, FL, May 28, 1979.

NAVRATILOVA STREAK ENDS: ANNIVERSARY. Dec 6, 1984. The longest winning streak in the history of women's tennis came to an end when Helena Sukova defeated Martina Navratilova, who had won 74 matches in a row, starting Jan 15, 1974.

NCAA DIVISION I-AA FOOTBALL CHAMPIONSHIP. Dec 6. Quarterfinals at campus sites TBA. For info: NCAA, 6201 College Blvd, Overland Park, KS 66211. Phone: (913) 339-1906.

BIRTHDAYS TODAY

Robert Kevin Appier, 31, baseball player, born Lancaster, CA, Dec 6, 1967.
Stephen Wayne (Steve) Bedrosian, 41, former baseball player, born Methuen, MA, Dec 6, 1957.
Lawrence Robert (Larry) Bowa, 53, former baseball manager and player, born Sacramento, CA, Dec 6, 1945.
Otto Graham, 77, former football coach and Pro Football Hall of Fame quarterback, born Waukegan, IL, Dec 6, 1921.
Walter Ray Perkins, 57, former football coach, born Mount Olive, MS, Dec 6, 1941.
Andy Robustelli, 73, former football executive and Pro Football Hall of Fame defensive end, born Stamford, CT, Dec 6, 1925.

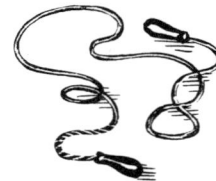

DECEMBER 7 — MONDAY
Day 341 — 24 Remaining

CHASE'S SPORTSQUOTE OF THE DAY
"That isn't an arm, it's a rifle." —Gene Tenace on Johnny Bench

BROUN, HEYWOOD: BIRTH ANNIVERSARY. Dec 7, 1886. Heywood Broun, sportswriter born at New York, NY. Broun dropped out of Harvard University to become a sportswriter and was highly regarded for his wit and his way with words. He covered politics, wrote theater reviews, published fiction and became a widely read columnist. His son, Heywood Hale Broun, became a sportscaster. Died at New York, Dec 18, 1939.

FISH, HAMILTON: 110th BIRTH ANNIVERSARY. Dec 7, 1888. Hamilton Fish, football player born at Garrison, NY. He played football at Harvard and was named to Walter Camp's 1908 and 1909 All-America teams. He also played basketball and soccer and graduated cum laude in 1910. After serving in the Army during World War I, he entered politics and sat in the House of Representatives from 1919 to 1945. Died at age 102 at Cold Spring, NY, Jan 18, 1991.

MOST BORING CELEBRITIES OF THE YEAR. Dec 7. The 15th annual announcement of this list, which annually includes leading sports figures. For info: Alan Caruba, founder, The Boring Institute, PO Box 40, Maplewood, NJ 07040. Phone: (973) 763-6392. Fax: (973) 763-4287.

	S	M	T	W	T	F	S
December			1	2	3	4	5
1998	6	7	8	9	10	11	12
	13	14	15	16	17	18	19
	20	21	22	23	24	25	26
	27	28	29	30	31		

ZASLOFSKY, MAX: BIRTH ANNIVERSARY. Dec 7, 1925. Max Zaslofsky, basketball player and coach born at New York, NY. Zaslofsky played for coach Joe Lapchick at St. John's University but joined the Chicago Stags of the BAA after one year. He made the All-Star team four years running and was a leading scorer. After the formation of the NBA, he played with the New York Knicks, the Baltimore Bullets, the Milwaukee Hawks and the Fort Wayne Pistons. He favored the two-hand set shot over the jump shot and scored many of his baskets from beyond 30 feet. Died at New York, NY, Oct 15, 1985.

BIRTHDAYS TODAY

Robert ("Bo") Belinsky, 62, former baseball player, born New York, NY, Dec 7, 1936.

Johnny Lee Bench, 51, broadcaster and Baseball Hall of Fame catcher, born Oklahoma City, OK, Dec 7, 1947.

Larry Joe Bird, 42, basketball coach and former player, born West Baden, IN, Dec 7, 1956.

Alexander (Alex) Johnson, 56, former baseball player, born Helena, AR, Dec 7, 1942.

Victor Kermit Kiam II, 72, former sports executive, born New Orleans, LA, Dec 7, 1926.

Constantino (Tino) Martinez, 31, baseball player, born Tampa, FL, Dec 7, 1967.

Osvaldo Jose (Ossie) Virgil, Jr, 42, former baseball player, born Mayaguez, Puerto Rico, Dec 7, 1956.

DECEMBER 8 — TUESDAY
Day 342 — 23 Remaining

AUSTIN, JIMMY: BIRTH ANNIVERSARY. Dec 8, 1879. James Philip (Jimmy) Austin, baseball player and manager born at Swansea, Wales. Austin, third baseman for the St. Louis Browns, was part of the greatest baseball action photograph ever taken. The picture, shot in 1910 by Charles Martin Conlon, shows Ty Cobb, gritting his

teeth and flashing his spikes, sliding into Austin on a steal of third. Died at Laguna Beach, CA, Mar 6, 1965.

BELMONT, AUGUST: BIRTH ANNIVERSARY. Dec 8, 1816. August Belmont, thoroughbred owner born at Alzey, Rhenish Palatinate, Germany. Belmont was an agent for the Rothschilds when he came to the US in 1837. He organized August Belmont and Company, a financial institution, and amassed a large fortune. After the Civil War, he helped to revive horse racing, organized the American Jockey Club and founded the Belmont Stakes. Died at New York, NY, Nov 24, 1890.

HEXTALL SCORES GOAL: ANNIVERSARY. Dec 8, 1987. Ron Hextall of the Philadelphia Flyers became the first goalie in NHL history to shoot the puck into the opposing team's net in a 5–2 victory over the Boston Bruins.

NFL'S MOST LOPSIDED VICTORY: ANNIVERSARY. Dec 8, 1940. The Chicago Bears won the NFL championship by defeating the Washington Redskins, 73–0, the most one-sided victory in the league's title game.

THOMPSON, HANK: BIRTH ANNIVERSARY. Dec 8, 1925. Henry Curtis (Hank) Thompson, baseball player born at Oklahoma City, OK. Thompson was the first black to play for both the St. Louis Browns and the New York Giants. Died at Fresno, CA, Sept 30, 1969.

BIRTHDAYS TODAY

Gordon Arthur ("Red") Berenson, 57, college hockey coach and former player, born Regina, Saskatchewan, Canada, Dec 8, 1939.

Stephen John (Steve) Elkington, 36, golfer, born Inverell, Australia, Dec 8, 1962.

Timothy John (Tim) Foli, 48, former baseball player, born Culver City, CA, Dec 8, 1950.

Barry Foster, 30, former football player, born Hurst, TX, Dec 8, 1968.

Jeffrey Scott (Jeff) George, 31, football player, born Indianapolis, IN, Dec 8, 1967.

Michael Cole (Mike) Mussina, 30, baseball player, born Williamsport, PA, Dec 8, 1968.

DECEMBER 9 — WEDNESDAY
Day 343 — 22 Remaining

HAZLE, HURRICANE: BIRTH ANNIVERSARY. Dec 9, 1930. Robert Sidney ("Hurricane") Hazle, baseball player born at Laurens, SC. Hazle joined the Milwaukee Braves from the minors in late July 1957. He hit .403 over 41 games to help the Braves win the National League pennant. Died at Columbia, SC, Apr 25, 1992.

KELLEY, JOE: BIRTH ANNIVERSARY. Dec 9, 1871. Joseph James (Joe) Kelley, Baseball Hall of Fame outfielder born at Cambridge, MA. Kelley played for the great Baltimore Orioles teams of the 1890s. In 17 years, he hit .319. Inducted into the Hall of Fame in 1971. Died at Baltimore, MD, Aug 14, 1943.

NFL'S SNEAKERS GAME: ANNIVERSARY. Dec 9, 1934. The New York Giants defeated the Chicago Bears, 30–13, to win the NFL championship in a game that became known as the "Sneakers Game." With the field at the Polo Grounds covered by ice and the temperature at 9 degrees, the Giants donned sneakers in the second half to gain better traction. They scored 27 points in the fourth quarter to overcome a 13–3 deficit.

TRIPLE CROWN OF SURFING SERIES: EVENT 3. Dec 9–20. Ehukai Beach Park, North Shore, Oahu, HI. 16th annual. The Triple Crown of Surfing series is professional, big-wave surfing for men and women. After this event, champions are crowned. Est attendance: 12,500. For media info: Carol Hogan, (808) 325-7400. E-mail: oceanpro@interpac.net. For contest info: Randy Rarick (808) 638-7266 or Fred Williamson (808) 377-5850. WWW: http://www.holoholo.org/triplecrown/

BIRTHDAYS TODAY

Raymond Mitchell (Ray) Agnew, 31, football player, born Winston-Salem, NC, Dec 9, 1967.

Otis Lee Birdsong, 43, former basketball player, born Winter Haven, FL, Dec 9, 1955.

Chris Boniol, 27, football player, born Alexandria, LA, Dec 9, 1971.

Richard Marvin (Dick) Butkus, 56, former broadcaster and Pro Football Hall of Fame linebacker, born Chicago, IL, Dec 9, 1942.

David ("Deacon") Jones, 60, Pro Football Hall of Fame defensive end, born Eatonville, FL, Dec 9, 1938.

Thomas Oliver (Tom) Kite, Jr, 49, golfer, born Austin, TX, Dec 9, 1949.

Petr Nedved, 27, hockey player, born Liberec, Czechoslovakia, Dec 9, 1971.

James David (Jim) Riggleman, 46, baseball manager, born Fort Dix, NJ, Dec 9, 1952.

December 1998

S	M	T	W	T	F	S
		1	2	3	4	5
6	7	8	9	10	11	12
13	14	15	16	17	18	19
20	21	22	23	24	25	26
27	28	29	30	31		

Anthony Giacinto (Tony) Tarasco, 28, baseball player, born New York, NY, Dec 9, 1970.

Delbert Bernard (Del) Unser, 54, former baseball player, born Decatur, IL, Dec 9, 1944.

Todd Matthew Van Poppel, 27, baseball player, born Hinsdale, IL, Dec 9, 1971.

DECEMBER 10 — THURSDAY
Day 344 — 21 Remaining

FIRST US HEAVYWEIGHT CHAMP DEFEATED IN ENGLAND: ANNIVERSARY. Dec 10, 1810. Tom Molyneaux, the first unofficial heavyweight champion of the US, had been a freed slave from Virginia. He was beaten in the 40th round by Tom Cribb, the English champion, in a boxing match at Copthall Common in London.

HARPER, JESSE: 115th BIRTH ANNIVERSARY. Dec 10, 1883. Jesse C. Harper, football player, coach and administrator born at Pawpaw, IL. Harper played football at the University of Chicago under the legendary Amos Alonzo Stagg. He became head coach and athletic director at Notre Dame in 1913 and plotted the famed upset of Army utilizing the forward pass. At age 33, he retired to operate a cattle ranch, returning to Notre Dame for two years after Knute Rockne died in 1931. Died at Sitka, KS, July 31, 1961.

MOON PHASE: LAST QUARTER. Dec 10. Moon enters Last Quarter phase at 12:53 PM, EST.

NORRIS, JIM: BIRTH ANNIVERSARY. Dec 10, 1879. James D. (Jim) Norris, Sr, Hockey Hall of Fame executive and sports promoter born at St. Catherines, Ontario, Canada. Norris made an enormous fortune in a variety of businesses and invested heavily in indoor sports arenas, including Detroit's Olympia (and its team, renamed the Red Wings) and New York's Madison Square Garden. He built the Red Wings into an NHL power. Inducted into the Hockey Hall of Fame in 1958. Died at Chicago, IL, Dec 4, 1952.

BIRTHDAYS TODAY

Mark Anthony Aguirre, 39, former basketball player, born Chicago, IL, Dec 10, 1959.

Paul Andre Assenmacher, 38, baseball player, born Allen Park, MI, Dec 10, 1960.

Robert Bowlby (Rob) Blake, 29, hockey player, born Simcoe, Ontario, Canada, Dec 10, 1969.

Richard Douglas (Doug) Henry, 35, baseball player, born Sacramento, CA, Dec 10, 1963.

Steven (Steve) Renko, 54, former baseball player, born Kansas City, KS, Dec 10, 1944.

Melquiades (Mel) Rojas, 32, baseball player, born Haina, Dominican Republic, Dec 10, 1966.

DECEMBER 11 — FRIDAY
Day 345 — 20 Remaining

SPORTSCHASER OF THE DAY
What football team won all four All-America Football Conference championship games?

AUSTRALIA: PRESIDENTS CUP. Dec 11–13. Royal Melbourne Golf Course, Melbourne. A biennial golf competition matching a team of US professionals against a team of professionals from the rest of the world, excluding Europe. The Presidents Cup was first contested in 1994. For info: PGA Tour, 12 TPC Blvd, Ponte Vedra Beach, FL 32082. Phone: (904) 285-3700.

JOHN HENRY PASSES $4 MILLION MARK: 15th ANNIVERSARY. Dec 11, 1983. Thoroughbred John Henry became the first race horse to earn more than $4 million when he won the Hollywood Turf Cup under jockey Chris McCarron.

LAST AAFC GAME: ANNIVERSARY. Dec 11, 1949. The Cleveland Browns defeated the San Francisco 49ers, 21–7, to win the fourth and last championship game in the All-America Football Conference. The Browns thereby completed a four-season sweep of AAFC titles. Two days before the final game, NFL Commissioner Bert Bell announced that three AAFC teams, the Browns, the 49ers and the Baltimore Colts, would be admitted into the senior league.

NCAA MEN'S DIVISION I SOCCER CHAMPIONSHIP. Dec 11–13. Finals. University of Richmond, Richmond, VA. For info: NCAA, 6201 College Blvd, Overland Park, KS 66211. Phone: (913) 339-1906.

RADBOURNE, HOSS: BIRTH ANNIVERSARY. Dec 11, 1854. Charles Gardner ("Hoss") Radbourne, Baseball Hall of Fame pitcher born at Rochester, NY. Radbourne was one of the most durable and successful pitchers of the 1880s. In 1884, he was credited with 59 complete-game victories. Inducted into the Hall of Fame in 1939. Died at Bloomington, IL, Feb 5, 1897.

TONEY, FRED: BIRTH ANNIVERSARY. Dec 11, 1887. Frederick Arthur (Fred) Toney, baseball player born at Nashville, TN. On May 10, 1909, Toney pitched a 17-inning no-hitter in the minor leagues. On May 2, 1917, while a member of the Cincinnati Reds, he hooked up with Chicago Cubs pitcher Hippo Vaughn to fashion a double no-hitter. The Reds got a run in the 10th inning, and Toney retired the Cubs to preserve his no-hitter and garner the win. Died at Nashville, Mar 11, 1953.

BIRTHDAYS TODAY

Shareef Abdur-Rahim, 22, basketball player, born Marietta, GA, Dec 11, 1976.

Daniel Alfredsson, 26, hockey player, born Grums, Sweden, Dec 11, 1972.

Derek Nathaniel Bell, 30, baseball player, born Tampa, FL, Dec 11, 1968.

Jay Stuart Bell, 33, baseball player, born Pensacola, FL, Dec 11, 1965.

Dave Gagner, 34, hockey player, born Chatham, Ontario, Canada, Dec 11, 1964.

Michael Alan (Mike) Henneman, 37, baseball player, born St. Charles, MO, Dec 11, 1961.

Thomas Sylvester Howard, 34, baseball player, born Middletown, OH, Dec 11, 1964.

DECEMBER 12 — SATURDAY
Day 346 — 19 Remaining

AMOS ALONZO STAGG BOWL (NCAA DIVISION III FOOTBALL CHAMPIONSHIP). Dec 12. Salem Stadium, Salem, VA. Est attendance: 8,000. For info: NCAA, 6201 College Blvd, Overland Park, KS 66211. Phone: (913) 339-1906.

ARMSTRONG, HENRY: BIRTH ANNIVERSARY. Dec 12, 1912. Henry Armstrong, boxer born Henry Jackson, Jr, at Columbus, MS. Armstrong was the first boxer to hold three world titles simultaneously. He won the featherweight title on Oct 29, 1937, the welterweight title on May 31, 1938, and the lightweight title three months later. Died at Los Angeles, CA, Oct 22, 1988.

GREAT SNOWPLOW PLAY: ANNIVERSARY. Dec 12, 1982. The New England Patriots defeated the Miami Dolphins, 3–0, in a driving snowstorm at Foxboro Stadium. The winning points came on a late field goal by John Smith, kicked after a snowplow came onto the field and cleared a spot for Smith and his holder.

HULL GETS 1,000th POINT: ANNIVERSARY. Dec 12, 1971. Left wing Bobby Hull of the Chicago Black Hawks got the 1,000th point of his NHL career, an assist in the first period of a 5–3 victory over the Minnesota North Stars. Hull finished his career with 1,170 points and entered the Hockey Hall of Fame in 1983.

NCAA DIVISION II FOOTBALL CHAMPIONSHIP. Dec 12. Final at site TBA. For info: NCAA, 6201 College Blvd, Overland Park, KS 66211. Phone: (913) 339-1906.

NCAA DIVISION I-AA FOOTBALL CHAMPIONSHIP. Dec 12. Semifinals at campus sites TBA. For info: NCAA, 6201 College Blvd, Overland Park, KS 66211. Phone: (913) 339-1906.

OFF-TRACK, OFF-BEAT SNOWSHOE RACE. Dec 12 (tentative). Sugar Loafin' Campground near Leadville, CO. This classic snowshoe experience promises to live up to its reputation as one of the wildest, most fun and unique events anywhere. Participants will cover over six miles of unknown terrain, all through deep snow. Registration starts at the campground at 8:30 AM on race day. There is a small fee. This is one of many showshoe races held in the area. For info: Greater Leadville Area Chamber of Commerce, PO Box 861, Leadville, CO 80461. Phone: (719) 486-3900 or (800) 933-3901. Fax: (719) 486-8478. E-mail: leadville@sni.net. WWW: http://www.colorado.com/leadville

SMITH, PHENOMENAL: BIRTH ANNIVERSARY. Dec 12, 1864. John Francis ("Phenomenal") Smith, baseball player born John Francis Gammon at Philadelphia, PA. Smith's pitching record belied his nickname. He won 57 games in his career and lost 77. Died at Manchester, NH, Apr 3, 1952.

BIRTHDAYS TODAY

Tracy Ann Austin, 36, former tennis player, born Rolling Hills Estates, CA, Dec 12, 1962.

Kelly Michael Buchberger, 32, hockey player, born Langenburg, Saskatchewan, Canada, Dec 12, 1966.

Steven Michael (Steve) Farr, 42, former baseball player, born Cheverly, MD, Dec 12, 1956.

Ralph Allen Garr, 53, former baseball player, born Monroe, LA, Dec 12, 1945.

Robert Lee (Bob) Pettit, Jr, 66, Basketball Hall of Fame forward and center, born Baton Rouge, LA, Dec 12, 1932.

John Randle, 31, football player, born Hearne, TX, Dec 12, 1967.

Cathy Rigby, 46, former gymnast, born Long Beach, CA, Dec 12, 1952.

James Gorman Thomas, 48, former baseball player, born Charleston, SC, Dec 12, 1950.

Reinard Wilson, 25, football player, born Lake City, FL, Dec 12, 1973.

DECEMBER 13 — SUNDAY
Day 347 — 18 Remaining

JOHNSON, GUS: 60th BIRTH ANNIVERSARY. Dec 13, 1938. Gus Johnson, Jr, basketball player born at Akron, OH. Johnson played at the University of Akron, Boise (ID) Junior College and the University of Idaho. He was drafted by the Washington Bullets and helped make them a perennial contender for playoff honors. Johnson was the prototype of the power forward. He could score from the corner and was one of the first players to use the slam dunk. He finished his career with the Phoenix Suns. Died at Akron, OH, Apr 28, 1987.

VUKOVICH, BILL: 80th BIRTH ANNIVERSARY. Dec 13, 1918. William Vukovich, Sr, born William Vucerovich at Fresno, CA. Vukovich began racing midget cars in 1938 and picked up his career after World War II. Known as the "Mad Russian" for his hell-bent style, he won the 1953 Indianapolis 500 from the pole and the 1954 race as well. Ahead again in the 1955 race, he crashed on the 57th lap. Died at Indianapolis, IN, May 30, 1955.

BIRTHDAYS TODAY

Dale Anthony Berra, 42, former baseball player, born Ridgewood, NJ, Dec 13, 1956.

December 1998	S	M	T	W	T	F	S
			1	2	3	4	5
	6	7	8	9	10	11	12
	13	14	15	16	17	18	19
	20	21	22	23	24	25	26
	27	28	29	30	31		

Richard Lamar Dent, 38, former football player, born Atlanta, GA, Dec 13, 1960.

Lawrence Eugene (Larry) Doby, 74, former baseball manager and player, born Camden, SC, Dec 13, 1924.

Carl Daniel Erskine, 72, former baseball player, born Anderson, IN, Dec 13, 1926.

Sergei Fedorov, 29, hockey player, born Pskov, USSR, Dec 13, 1969.

Robert Michael (Bob) Gainey, 45, hockey executive, former coach and Hockey Hall of Fame forward, born Peterborough, Ontario, Canada, Dec 13, 1953.

Ferguson Arthur Jenkins, 55, Baseball Hall of Fame pitcher, born Chatham, Ontario, Canada, Dec 13, 1943.

Jermaine O'Neal, 20, basketball player, born Columbia, SC, Dec 13, 1978.

George Thomas Shuba, 74, former baseball player, born Youngstown, OH, Dec 13, 1924.

DECEMBER 14 — MONDAY
Day 348 — 17 Remaining

CHASE'S SPORTSQUOTE OF THE DAY

"Bill Buckner had a nineteen-game hitting streak going and always wore the same underwear. Of course, he had no friends." —Lenny Randle

DAVIS, ERNIE: BIRTH ANNIVERSARY. Dec 14, 1939. Ernest (Ernie) Davis, Heisman Trophy running back born at New Salem, PA. Davis played football at Syracuse and won the Heisman Trophy in 1961. Drafted by the Washington Redskins and then traded to the Cleveland Browns, Davis never played pro football because he was stricken by leukemia. Died at Cleveland, OH, May 18, 1963.

DIONNE GETS 500th GOAL: ANNIVERSARY. Dec 14, 1982. Marcel Dionne of the Los Angeles Kings scored the 500th goal of his career in a 7–2 loss to the Washington Capitals. Dionne played from 1971–72 through 1988–89 and finished his career with 731 goals.

HALCYON DAYS. Dec 14–28. Traditionally, the seven days before and the seven days after the winter solstice. To the ancients a time when a fabled bird (called the halcyon) calmed the wind and waves, a time of calm and tranquility.

HEAT FINALLY WINS: ANNIVERSARY. Dec 14, 1988. The Miami Heat defeated the Los Angeles Clippers in Los Angeles to earn the first victory in the franchise's history. The Heat, in their first season, had gone 17 games without a win, an NBA record for most consecutive defeats at the start of a season.

LONGEST US SOCCER GAME: ANNIVERSARY. Dec 14, 1985. UCLA defeated American University, 1–0, with a goal in the eighth overtime period to win the NCAA soccer championship in the longest game in US college soccer history.

BIRTHDAYS TODAY

Craig Alan Biggio, 33, baseball player, born Smithtown, NY, Dec 14, 1965.

William Joseph (Bill) Buckner, 49, former baseball player, born Vallejo, CA, Dec 14, 1949.

Kenneth Wade (Ken) Hill, 33, baseball player, born Lynn, MA, Dec 14, 1965.

Anthony George Douglas Mason, 32, basketball player, born Miami, FL, Dec 14, 1966.

Bill Ranford, 32, hockey player, born Brandon, Manitoba, Canada, Dec 14, 1966.

DECEMBER 15 — TUESDAY
Day 349 — 16 Remaining

BASEBALL'S MOST LOPSIDED TRADE: ANNIVER-SARY. Dec 15, 1900. In the most lopsided trade in baseball history, the New York Giants shipped pitcher Amos Rusie to the Cincinnati Reds for pitcher Christy Mathewson. Rusie won 245 games, all with the Giants and all before the trade; Mathewson won 373 games, all with the Giants and all after the trade.

DEMPSEY, JACK: BIRTH ANNIVERSARY. Dec 15, 1862. Jack ("Nonpareil") Dempsey, boxer born at County Kildare, Ireland. Not the 20th-century heavyweight champ, this earlier Dempsey was the first fighter recognized as world middleweight champion. He won the newly created title on July 30, 1884, defeating George Fulljames. Died at Portland, OR, Nov 2, 1895.

HAWLEY RIDES 500th WINNER: 25th ANNIVER-SARY. Dec 15, 1973. Jockey Sandy Hawley became the first to win 500 races in a single year when he rode Charlie Jr to victory in the third race at Laurel Race Course in Maryland.

HUNTER RULED A FREE AGENT: ANNIVERSARY. Dec 15, 1974. Pitcher Jim ("Catfish") Hunter was ruled a free agent by arbitrator Peter Seitz who decided that Oakland A's owner Charley Finley had not fulfilled the terms set forth in Hunter's contract. Hunter later signed to play with the New York Yankees.

THIRD MADISON SQUARE GARDEN OPENS: ANNI-VERSARY. Dec 15, 1925. The Montreal Canadiens defeated the New York Americans, 3–1, as the third version of Madison Square Garden opened in New York. The game attracted more than 17,000 fans, including Mayor John F. Hylan, to what was then the world's largest ice hockey arena.

BIRTHDAYS TODAY

Stanley Raymond (Stan) Bahnsen, 54, former baseball player, born Council Bluffs, IA, Dec 15, 1944.

Nicholas (Nick) Buoniconti, 58, former football player, born Springfield, MA, Dec 15, 1940.

Arthur Henry (Art) Howe, Jr, 52, baseball manager and former player, born Pittsburgh, PA, Dec 15, 1946.

James Richard (Jim) Leyland, 54, baseball manager, born Toledo, OH, Dec 15, 1944.

Daryl Turner, 37, former football player, born Wadley, GA, Dec 15, 1961.

Maurice Samuel (Mo) Vaughn, 31, baseball player, born Norwalk, CT, Dec 15, 1967.

DECEMBER 16 — WEDNESDAY
Day 350 — 15 Remaining

JONES WINS FIRST SULLIVAN AWARD: ANNIVER-SARY. Dec 16, 1930. Golfer Bobby Jones won the first James E. Sullivan Award as the nation's best amateur athlete. The award was established by the Amateur Athletic Union to honor its former president and is presented annually to the athlete who, "by his or her performance, example and influence as an amateur, has done the most during the year to advance the cause of sportsmanship."

O. J. RUSHES FOR 2,000 YARDS: 25th ANNIVERSARY. Dec 16, 1973. O. J. Simpson of the Buffalo Bills became the first running back to rush for more than 2,000 yards in a season, passing the milestone in a game against the New York Jets. Simpson ended the season with 2,003 yards, surpassing the previous record of 1,863 yards set by Jim Brown.

PARKER, BUDDY: 85th BIRTH ANNIVERSARY. Dec 16, 1913. Raymond Klein ("Buddy") Parker, football player and coach born at Kemp, TX. Parker played halfback at Centenary College and in 1934 kicked a field goal to upset Texas. He played with the Detroit Lions and the Cardinals for whom he was a player-coach. Named head coach of the Lions in 1951, he built a strong squad that won the NFL championship in 1952 and 1953. He resigned in 1957 and moved to the Pittsburgh Steelers with whom he enjoyed less success. He is generally credited with inventing the "two-minute offense." Died at Kaufman, TX, Mar 22, 1982.

SHELLENBACK, FRANK: 100th BIRTH ANNIVER-SARY. Dec 16, 1898. Frank Victor Shellenback, baseball player and manager born at Joplin, MO. Shellenback was an outstanding pitcher in the Pacific Coast League, his best pitch being the spitball, banned in the majors. As manager of the San Diego PCL team, he converted Ted Williams from a pitcher to an outfielder. Died at Newton, MA, Aug 17, 1969.

BIRTHDAYS TODAY

Michael Kendall (Mike) Flanagan, 47, former baseball player, born Manchester, NH, Dec 16, 1951.

Christopher Carlos (Chris) Jones, 33, baseball player, born Utica, NY, Dec 16, 1965.

William ("The Refrigerator") Perry, 36, former football player, born Aiken, SC, Dec 16, 1962.

Adolfo Emilio Phillips, 57, former baseball player, born Bethania, Panama, Dec 16, 1941.

William Oliver (Billy) Ripken, 34, baseball player, born Havre de Grace, MD, Dec 16, 1964.

Clifford Ralph Robinson, 32, basketball player, born Buffalo, NY, Dec 16, 1966.

DECEMBER 17 — THURSDAY
Day 351 — 14 Remaining

FIRST FLIGHT TRADITIONAL ANNIVERSARY CELE-BRATION. Dec 17. Kill Devil Hills, NC. Each year since 1928, on the anniversary of the Wright Brothers' first successful heavier-than-air flight at Kitty Hawk, NC, on Dec 17, 1903, a celebration has been held at the Wright Brothers National Memorial with wreaths, flyover and other observances, regardless of the weather.

FIRST NFL CHAMPIONSHIP GAME: 65th ANNIVER-SARY. Dec 17, 1933. The Chicago Bears won the National Football League's first championship game, defeating the New York Giants, 23–21. The Bears scored the winning touchdown on a pass-and-lateral play begun by Bronko Nagurski.

NCAA WOMEN'S DIVISION I VOLLEYBALL CHAM-PIONSHIP. Dec 17–19. Finals. University of Wisconsin, Madison, WI. For info: NCAA, 6201 College Blvd, Overland Park, KS 66211. Phone: (913) 339-1906.

WRIGHT BROTHERS FIRST POWERED FLIGHT: 95th ANNIVERSARY. Dec 17, 1903. Orville and Wilbur Wright, brothers, bicycle shop operators, inventors and aviation pioneers, after three years of experimentation with kites and gliders, achieved the first documented successful powered and controlled flights of an airplane. The flights, near Kitty Hawk, NC, piloted first by Orville and then by Wilbur Wright, were sustained for less than one minute but represented man's first powered airplane flight and the beginning of a new form of transportation.

★ **WRIGHT BROTHERS DAY.** Dec 17. Presidential Proclamation always issued for Dec 17 since 1963 (PL88–209 of Dec 17, 1963). Issued twice earlier at Congressional request in 1959 and 1961.

BIRTHDAYS TODAY

Craig Berube, 33, hockey player, born Calihoo, Alberta, Canada, Dec 17, 1965.
Tyrone Scott Braxton, 34, football player, born Madison, WI, Dec 17, 1964.
Vincent Damphousse, 31, hockey player, born Montreal, Quebec, Canada, Dec 17, 1967.
Albert King, 39, former basketball player, born New York, NY, Dec 17, 1959.
Robert Michael (Bob) Ojeda, 41, former baseball player, born Los Angeles, CA, Dec 17, 1957.
Curtis John Pride, 30, baseball player, born Washington, DC, Dec 17, 1968.

DECEMBER 18 — FRIDAY
Day 352 — 13 Remaining

SPORTSCHASER OF THE DAY

Where did the NFL stage its first indoor postseason play-off game?

COBB, TY : BIRTH ANNIVERSARY. Dec 18, 1886. Tyrus Raymond (Ty) Cobb, Baseball Hall of Fame outfielder born at Narrows, GA. Perhaps baseball's greatest player and perhaps its meanest, Cobb compiled a career batting average of .367, the best ever. He played 24 years and got more hits than any other player, until Pete Rose. Inducted into the Hall of Fame in 1936. Died at Atlanta, GA, July 17, 1961.

MOON PHASE: NEW MOON. Dec 18. Moon enters New Moon phase at 5:42 PM, EST.

NFL'S INDOOR PLAY OFF: ANNIVERSARY. Dec 18, 1932. The NFL held a postseason play off game with the Chicago Bears defeating the Portsmouth (OH) Spartans, 9–0. The intended site of the game, Wrigley Field, was so frozen that officials moved the game indoors to Chicago Stadium. The field was 80 yards long, and the goal posts were set on the goal lines instead of at the back of the end zones.

TRIPLETT, COAKER: BIRTH ANNIVERSARY. Dec 18, 1911. Herman Coaker Triplett, baseball player born at Boone, NC. Triplett played the outfield for the Chicago Cubs, the St. Louis Cardinals and the Philadelphia Phillies from 1938 through 1945. Died at Boone, Jan 30, 1992.

December 1998

S	M	T	W	T	F	S
		1	2	3	4	5
6	7	8	9	10	11	12
13	14	15	16	17	18	19
20	21	22	23	24	25	26
27	28	29	30	31		

UNDERDOG DAY. Dec 18. To salute, before the year's end, all of the underdogs and unsung heroes—the Number Two people who contribute so much to the Number One people we read about. [In the world of sports, today is the day to salute assistant coaches and trainers and cut men and outriders and ball boys and girls and all those who believe that winning is not everything.] For info: P. Moeller, Chief Underdog, Box 71, Clio, MI 48420-1042.

VERSALLES, ZOILO: BIRTH ANNIVERSARY. Dec 18, 1939. Zoilo Casanova Versalles, baseball player born at Havana, Cuba. Versalles played 12 seasons in the major leagues and won the American League Most Valuable Player award in 1965. Died at Bloomington, MN, June 9, 1995.

BIRTHDAYS TODAY

Don Lee Beebe, 34, football player, born Aurora, IL, Dec 18, 1964.
William Allen (Willie) Blair, 33, baseball player, born Paintsville, KY, Dec 18, 1965.
Peter Boulware, 24, football player, born Columbia, SC, Dec 18, 1974.
Gino Nicholas Cimoli, 69, former baseball player, born San Francisco, CA, Dec 18, 1929.
James (Jim) Clancy, 43, former baseball player, born Chicago, IL, Dec 18, 1955.
Charles Oakley, 35, basketball player, born Cleveland, OH, Dec 18, 1963.
William Joseph (Bill) Skowron, 68, former baseball player, born Chicago, IL, Dec 18, 1930.

DECEMBER 19 — SATURDAY
Day 353 — 12 Remaining

FRICK, FORD: BIRTH ANNIVERSARY. Dec 19, 1894. Ford Christopher Frick, sportswriter and Baseball Hall of Fame executive born at Wawaka, IN. Frick was a newspaperman who became Babe Ruth's ghostwriter, president of the National League and Commissioner of Baseball. He ruled in 1961 that Roger Maris's home run record would have to be categorized separately from Ruth's because the American League had lengthened its schedule from 154 to 162 games. Inducted into the Hall of Fame in 1970. Died at Bronxville, NY, Apr 8, 1978.

GRETZKY GETS 1,000th POINT: ANNIVERSARY. Dec 19, 1984. Wayne Gretzky of the Edmonton Oilers got the 1,000th point of his career, an assist in a 7–3 victory over the Los Angeles Kings.

HINKLE, TONY: BIRTH ANNIVERSARY. Dec 19, 1899. Paul D. ("Tony") Hinkle, football coach and Basketball Hall of Fame coach born at Logansport, IN. Hinkle was one of the giants of the coaching profession, spending all five decades of his career at Butler University. His teams won over 600 games, and over 50 of his former players became coaches. Inducted into the Hall of Fame in 1965. Died at Indianapolis, IN, Sept 21, 1992.

LAYNE, BOBBY: BIRTH ANNIVERSARY. Dec 19, 1926. Robert Lawrence (Bobby) Layne, Pro Football Hall of Fame quarterback born at Santa Ana, TX. Layne starred at the University of Texas before and after serving in the Merchant Marines during World War II. As a pro, he led the Detroit Lions to the NFL title in 1952, 1953 and 1957. His flamboyant leadership on the field was matched by a boisterous off-the-field lifestyle. Inducted into the Pro Football Hall of Fame in 1967. Died at Lubbock, TX, Dec 1, 1986.

NAIA FOOTBALL NATIONAL CHAMPIONSHIP GAME. Dec 19. Savannah, TN. 16-team field competes, ending with the final two teams vying for the national championship. 43rd annual. Est attendance: 7,000. For info: Natl

Robert Lawrence (Bobby) Layne

Assn of Intercollegiate Athletics, 6120 S Yale Ave, Ste 1450, Tulsa, OK 74136-4223. Phone: (918) 494-8828. Fax: (918) 494-8841. Email: khenry@naia.org. WWW: http://www.naia.org

NCAA DIVISION I-AA FOOTBALL CHAMPIONSHIP. Dec 19. Final. Tennessee Bicentennial Stadium, Chattanooga, TN. For info: NCAA, 6201 College Blvd, Overland Park, KS 66211. Phone: (913) 339-1906.

ORANGE BOWL INTERNATIONAL TENNIS CHAMPIONSHIPS. Dec 19–27 (tentative). Miami, FL. One of the top junior tournaments in the world. Past performers include Chris Evert, John McEnroe, Ivan Lendl, Bjorn Borg, Gabriela Sabatini, Mary Joe Fernandez, Boris Becker, Stefan Edberg and Jennifer Capriati. Est attendance: 10,000. For info: Orange Bowl Committee, 601 Brickell Key Dr, Ste 206, Miami, FL 33131. Phone: (305) 371-4600.

WOOLPERT, PHIL: BIRTH ANNIVERSARY. Dec 19, 1915. Philipp D. (Phil) Woolpert, Basketball Hall of Fame coach born at Danville, KY. Woolpert played at Loyola University of Los Angeles, graduating in 1940, and began coaching at St. Ignatius High School in San Francisco. In 1950 he moved to the University of San Francisco where he put together one of the greatest college teams ever. Led by Bill Russell and KC Jones, the Dons won their last 26 games in 1954–55 and all 29 games in 1955–56. They won consecutive NCAA titles, too. Woolpert resigned in 1958–59 but later coached in the American Basketball League and at the University of San Diego. Inducted into the Hall of Fame in 1992. Died at Sequim, WA, May 5, 1987.

BIRTHDAYS TODAY

Rex Edward Barney, 74, baseball public address announcer and former baseball player, born Omaha, NE, Dec 19, 1924. Found dead Aug 12, 1997.

Santana N. Dotson, 29, football player, born New Orleans, LA, Dec 19, 1969.

Kristin Folkl, 23, basketball and volleyball player, born St. Louis, MO, Dec 19, 1975.

Thomas James (Tom) Gugliotta, 29, basketball player, born Huntington Station, NY, Dec 19, 1969.

Albert William (Al) Kaline, 64, Baseball Hall of Fame outfielder, born Baltimore, MD, Dec 19, 1934.

Kevin Edward McHale, 41, basketball executive and former player, born Hibbing, MN, Dec 19, 1957.

Arvydas Sabonis, 34, basketball player, born Kaunas, Lithuania, USSR, Dec 19, 1964.

Bryant Antoine Westbrook, 24, football player, born Charlotte, NC, Dec 19, 1974.

Reginald Howard (Reggie) White, 37, football player, born Chattanooga, TN, Dec 19, 1961.

DECEMBER 20 — SUNDAY
Day 354 — 11 Remaining

HARTNETT, GABBY: BIRTH ANNIVERSARY. Dec 20, 1900. Charles Leo ("Gabby") Hartnett, Baseball Hall of Fame catcher born at Woonsocket, RI. Hartnett was one of the game's outstanding catchers. His most famous moment was the "Homer in the Gloamin'," a late-season, late-inning home run that helped the Chicago Cubs win the 1938 National League pennant. Inducted into the Hall of Fame in 1955. Died at Park Ridge, IL, Dec 20, 1972.

HAWAIIAN CHRISTMAS LOOONG DISTANCE INVITATIONAL ROUGH-H2O SWIM. Dec 20. Waikiki Beach, Honolulu, HI. 18th annual 7K (4.33 mile) swim across Waikiki Bay and return. Preregistration is required. Hawaii's longest open-ocean race. Annually, the week following Honolulu Marathon. Est attendance: 90. For info: Jim Anderson, One Keahole Place #1607, Honolulu, HI 96825-3414. Phone: (808) 396-8866. Fax: (808) 396-8868. E-mail: waikikijim@aol.com.

HICKEY, EDDIE: BIRTH ANNIVERSARY. Dec 20, 1902. Edgar S. (Eddie) Hickey, basketball player and Basketball Hall of Fame coach born at Reynolds, NE. Hickey played several sports at Creighton University and began coaching at Creighton Prep High School while still an undergraduate. He moved to the university in 1935· and became one of the country's most successful coaches. After nine years, he moved to St. Louis University, where his Billikens won the 1948 NIT, and in 1958 to Marquette University. Over 37 years of coaching, he won 570 games against only 268 losses. Inducted into the Hall of Fame in 1978. Died at Mesa, AZ, Dec 5, 1980.

LAFLEUR GETS 500th GOAL: 15th ANNIVERSARY. Dec 20, 1983. Guy Lafleur of the Montreal Canadiens scored the 500th goal of his career in a 6–0 victory over the New York Rangers. Lafleur played 17 years in the NHL and finished his career with 560 regular-season goals.

MERKLE, FRED: 110th BIRTH ANNIVERSARY. Dec 20, 1888. Frederick Charles (Fred) Merkle, baseball player born at Watertown, WI. Merkle will forever occupy a place in baseball history for his part in the events of Sept 23, 1908, when his team, the New York Giants, played the Chicago Cubs in a crucial game. Merkle was on first in the bottom of the ninth when the winning run apparently scored on a single. As was customary, he did not touch second base. Cubs second baseman Johnny Evers set off baseball's greatest dispute by demanding that Merkle be called out. Died at Daytona Beach, FL, Mar 2, 1956.

NBA GRANTS FRANCHISE TO SEATTLE: ANNIVERSARY. Dec 20, 1966. The NBA granted a franchise to Seattle for the 1967–68 season. The SuperSonics, as the team was nicknamed, were joined by the San Diego Clippers, to become the league's 11th and 12th teams.

PIPGRAS, GEORGE: BIRTH ANNIVERSARY. Dec 20, 1899. George William Pipgras, baseball player and umpire born at Ida Grove, IA. Pipgras pitched for the New York Yankees and then became an umpire. He once ejected 17 players from a game between the Chicago White Sox and the St. Louis Browns. Died at Gainesville, FL, Oct 19, 1986.

POTVIN PASSES ORR: ANNIVERSARY. Dec 20, 1985. Denis Potvin of the New York Islanders assisted on Mike Bossy's goal against the New York Rangers to earn the 916th point of his career, breaking Bobby Orr's NHL record for most career points by a defenseman.

RAMADAN: THE ISLAMIC MONTH OF FASTING. Dec 20–Jan 17, 1999. Begins on Islamic lunar calendar date Ramadan 1, 1419. (Gregorian [Western] calendar date may vary since each new month of the Islamic calendar begins only when Allah reveals the first sliver of the new moon.) Ramadan, the ninth month of the Islamic calendar, is holy because it was during this month that the Holy Qur'an (Koran) was revealed. All adults of sound body and mind fast from dawn (before sunrise) until sunset to achieve spiritual and physical purification and self-discipline, abstaining from food, drink and intimate relations. It is a time for feeling a common bond with the poor and needy, a time for piety and prayer. Different methods for "anticipating" the visibility of the new moon crescent at Mecca are used by different Muslim sects or groups. *Chase's* uses anticipated dates furnished by the American Muslim Council. US EST date may vary.

RICHARD GETS 1,000th POINT: 25th ANNIVERSARY. Dec 20, 1973. Henri Richard, the "Pocket Rocket," of the Montreal Canadiens, scored the 1,000th point of his NHL career, an assist in a 2–2 tie with the Buffalo Sabres. Richard finished his career with 1,046 points and entered the Hockey Hall of Fame in 1979.

RICKEY, BRANCH: BIRTH ANNIVERSARY. Dec 20, 1881. Wesley Branch Rickey, Baseball Hall of Fame player, manager and executive born at Lucasville, OH. Rickey was baseball's greatest and most innovative general manager. He invented the farm system, instituted unique training and teaching methods and, most prominently, signed Jackie Robinson to play major league baseball with the Brooklyn Dodgers. Inducted into the Hall of Fame in 1967. He died from a heart attack suffered Nov 13, 1965, while being inducted into the Missouri Sports Hall of Fame. Died at Columbia, MO, Dec 9, 1965.

WIGHTMAN, HAZEL: BIRTH ANNIVERSARY. Dec 20, 1886. Hazel Virginia Hotchkiss Wightman, tennis player born at Healdsburg, CA. Known as the "Queen Mother of Tennis," Wightman was a championship player, an

	S	**M**	**T**	**W**	**T**	**F**	**S**
December			1	2	3	4	5
1998	6	7	8	9	10	11	12
	13	14	15	16	17	18	19
	20	21	22	23	24	25	26
	27	28	29	30	31		

instructor, a benefactor and the donor of the Wightman Cup, a trophy offered for competition between teams of women players from the US and England. Died at Chestnut Hill, MA, Dec 5, 1974.

BIRTHDAYS TODAY

Cecil Celester Cooper, 49, former baseball player, born Brenham, TX, Dec 20, 1949.

Jose DeLeon, 38, former baseball player, born Rancjo Viejo, LaVega, Dominican Republic, Dec 20, 1960.

Oscar Charles Gamble, 49, former baseball player, born Ramer, AL, Dec 20, 1949.

Nathaniel (Nate) Newton, 37, football player, born Orlando, FL, Dec 20, 1961.

DECEMBER 21 — MONDAY

Day 355 — 10 Remaining

CHASE'S SPORTSQUOTE OF THE DAY

"Make the hard ones look easy and the easy ones look hard." —Walter Hagen

GIBSON, JOSH: BIRTH ANNIVERSARY. Dec 21, 1912. Joshua (Josh) Gibson, Baseball Hall of Fame catcher born at Buena Vista, GA. Gibson is regarded as the greatest slugger to play in the Negro Leagues and perhaps the greatest ballplayer ever. Gibson starred with the Pittsburgh Crawfords. His long home runs are the stuff of legend. Inducted into the Hall of Fame in 1972. Died at Pittsburgh, PA, Jan 20, 1947.

HAGEN, WALTER: BIRTH ANNIVERSARY. Dec 21, 1892. Walter Charles B. Hagen, golfer born at Rochester, NY. Hagen won two US Opens, four British Opens and five PGA Championships. He was extraordinary in match play, including the Ryder Cup, because he was a master scrambler and absolutely unflappable. He was also a colorful showman who brought the game to the masses and helped to increase prize money. Died at Traverse City, MI, Oct 5, 1969.

ROSS, BARNEY: BIRTH ANNIVERSARY. Dec 21, 1909. Barney Ross, boxer born Barnet David Rosofsky at New York, NY. Ross was the first boxer to hold two titles simulataneously. He won the lightweight crown in 1932 and the welterweight crown in 1934. He also won a Silver Star during World War II as a Marine. Died at Chicago, IL, Jan 18, 1967.

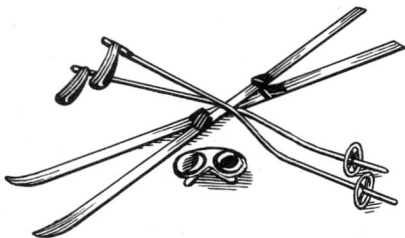

WINTER. Dec 21–Mar 20, 1999. In the Northern Hemisphere winter begins today with the winter solstice, at 8:56 PM, EST. Note that in the Southern Hemisphere today is the beginning of summer. Between Equator and Arctic Circle the sunrise and sunset points on the horizon are farthest south for the year, and daylight length is minimum (ranging from 12 hours, 8 minutes, at the equator to zero at the Arctic Circle).

BIRTHDAYS TODAY

Joaquin Andujar, 46, former baseball player, born San Pedro de Macoris, Dominican Republic, Dec 21, 1952.

Christine Marie (Chris) Evert, 44, broadcaster and former tennis player, born Fort Lauderdale, FL, Dec 21, 1954.

Delorez Florence Griffith-Joyner, 39, Olympic gold medal track athlete, born Los Angeles, CA, Dec 21, 1959.

Thomas Anthony (Tom) Henke, 41, former baseball player, born Kansas City, MO, Dec 21, 1957.

David Arthur (Dave) Kingman, 50, former baseball player, born Pendleton, OR, Dec 21, 1948.

Roger Alan McDowell, 38, baseball player, born Cincinnati, OH, Dec 21, 1960.

Terry Richard Mills, 31, basketball player, born Romulus, MI, Dec 21, 1967.

Andrew James (Andy) Van Slyke, 38, former baseball player, born Utica, NY, Dec 21, 1960.

Karrie Webb, 24, golfer, born Ayr, Queensland, Australia, Dec 21, 1974.

DECEMBER 22 — TUESDAY

Day 356 — 9 Remaining

BIRTH OF USGA: ANNIVERSARY. Dec 22, 1894. The United States Golf Association, the governing body for golf in the US, was founded at a meeting of representatives from five golf clubs.

BRUTON, BILLY: BIRTH ANNIVERSARY. Dec 22, 1925. William Haron (Billy) Bruton, baseball player born at Panola, AL. Bruton hit the first-ever home run for the Milwaukee Braves in their debut game on Apr 14, 1953. He led the National League in stolen bases in 1953, 1954 and 1955. Died at Marshallton, DE, Dec 5, 1995.

ESPOSITO SCORES 500th GOAL: ANNIVERSARY. Dec 22, 1974. Center Phil Esposito of the Boston Bruins scored the 500th goal of his career in a 5–4 win over the Detroit Red Wings. Esposito played from 1963–64 through 1980–81 and finished with 717 regular season goals.

HULL SCORES 500th GOAL: ANNIVERSARY. Dec 22, 1996. Right wing Brett Hull of the St. Louis Blues became the 24th player in NHL history to score 500 regular-season goals. He tallied goals Nos. 498, 499 and 500 in a 7–4 victory over the Los Angeles Kings. Another goal, originally thought to be No. 500, was later credited to teammate Stephane Matteau. Hull and his father Bobby thus became the first father-and-son duo in NHL history to score 500 goals each.

MACK, CONNIE: BIRTH ANNIVERSARY. Dec 22, 1862. Cornelius Alexander McGillicuddy (Connie Mack), Baseball Hall of Fame manager and executive born at East Brookfield, MA. Mack was a major league catcher who became the original manager and co-owner of the Philadelphia Athletics in 1901. He managed the team, always wearing street clothes and signaling to his players with a scorecard, through the 1950 season and retired after the 1953 season. The Mackmen often finished as also-rans, but his teams did win nine pennants and five World Series. Inducted into the Hall of Fame in 1937. Died at Germantown, PA, Feb 8, 1956.

☆   ☆   ☆

BIRTHDAYS TODAY

Mateo (Matty) Alou, 60, former baseball player, born Haina, Dominican Republic, Dec 22, 1938.

Steven Norman (Steve) Carlton, 54, Baseball Hall of Fame pitcher, born Miami, FL, Dec 22, 1944.

Steven Patrick (Steve) Garvey, 50, former baseball player, born Tampa, FL, Dec 22, 1948.

David Glen Nied, 30, former baseball player, born Dallas, TX, Dec 22, 1968.

Jan Stephenson, 47, golfer, born Sydney, Australia, Dec 22, 1951.

Glenn Dwight Wilson, 40, former baseball player, born Baytown, TX, Dec 22, 1958.

DECEMBER 23 — WEDNESDAY
Day 357 — 8 Remaining

FIRST JUDO DEMONSTRATION IN US: ANNIVERSARY. Dec 23, 1921. Jigoro Kano, a Japanese, gave the first demonstration of judo in the US at the New York Athletic Club. The crowd watched politely.

HUBBS, KEN: BIRTH ANNIVERSARY. Dec 23, 1941. Kenneth Douglass (Ken) Hubbs, baseball player born at Riverside, CA. Hubbs was a fine defensive second base-man who won the National League Rookie of the Year award and a Gold Glove award in 1962. Died in a plane crash at Provo, UT, Feb 15, 1964.

IMMACULATE RECEPTION: ANNIVERSARY. Dec 23, 1972. The Pittsburgh Steelers defeated the Oakland Raiders, 13–7, in an AFC first-round playoff game. The Raiders were ahead, 7–6, with 22 seconds to play, and Pittsburgh had the ball on its own 40-yard line. Steelers quarterback Terry Bradshaw threw a desperation pass intended for John ("Frenchy") Fuqua. The ball deflected off an Oakland defender into the waiting arms of Franco Harris, who rumbled into the end zone for the winning score. The play has since been known as the "Immaculate Reception."

TROTTING ASSOCIATION FOUNDED: 60th ANNIVERSARY. Dec 23, 1938. Several regional organizations came together in Indianapolis, IN, to found the United States Trotting Association, the governing body for harness racing. The association set uniform rules and regulations and spurred the growth of a sport now followed by nearly 25 million fans.

BIRTHDAYS TODAY

Jack Raphael Ham, 50, Pro Football Hall of Fame line-backer, born Johnstown, PA, Dec 23, 1948.

James Joseph (Jim) Harbaugh, 35, football player, born Toledo, OH, Dec 23, 1963.

Paul Hornung, 63, broadcaster and Pro Football Hall of Fame running back, born Louisville, KY, Dec 23, 1935.

Petr Klima, 34, hockey player, born Chaomutov, Czecho-slovakia, Dec 23, 1964.

Jerome Martin (Jerry) Koosman, 56, former baseball player, born Appleton, MN, Dec 23, 1942.

Robert Joseph (Bobby) Ross, 62, football coach, born Richmond, VA, Dec 23, 1936.

William Vernell (Willie) Wood, 62, Pro Football Hall of Fame safety, born Washington, DC, Dec 23, 1936.

DECEMBER 24 — THURSDAY
Day 358 — 7 Remaining

BROWNS WIN NFL CHAMPIONSHIP: ANNIVERSARY. Dec 24, 1950. The Cleveland Browns defeated the Los Angeles Rams, 30–28, to win the NFL championship. The Browns claimed the title in their first year in the league after the demise of the All-America Football Conference. The Rams, incidentally, had been the Cleveland Rams before they left for the West Coast after the 1945 season.

CHRISTMAS EVE. Dec 24. Family gift-giving occasion in many Christian countries.

OTIS, BILL: BIRTH ANNIVERSARY. Dec 24, 1889. Paul Franklin (Bill) Otis, baseball player born at Scituate, MA. At the time of his death, Otis was the oldest former major leaguer even though his career with the New York Yankees lasted only four games. Died at Duluth, MN, Dec 15, 1990.

UNGER STARTS STREAK: 30th ANNIVERSARY. Dec 24, 1968. Center Garry Unger played his first NHL game and thereby began a streak of 914 consecutive games played. Unger's feat stood as the NHL record until it was broken by Doug Jarvis in 1987.

BIRTHDAYS TODAY

John Francis D'Acquisto, 47, former baseball player, born San Diego, CA, Dec 24, 1951.

Franklin Crisostomo (Frank) Taveras, 49, former baseball player, born Las Matas de Santa Cruz, Dominican Republic, Dec 24, 1949.

December 1998	S	M	T	W	T	F	S
			1	2	3	4	5
	6	7	8	9	10	11	12
	13	14	15	16	17	18	19
	20	21	22	23	24	25	26
	27	28	29	30	31		

☆ ☆ ☆

DECEMBER 25 — FRIDAY
Day 359 — 6 Remaining

SPORTSCHASER OF THE DAY
What Chicago White Sox second baseman was inducted into the Hall of Fame in 1997?

CHAPMAN, BEN: 90th BIRTH ANNIVERSARY. Dec 25, 1908. William Benjamin (Ben) Chapman, baseball player and manager born at Nashville, TN. Chapman hit .302 over 15 seasons and was the first American League batter in the first All-Star Game (1933). He was a vocal opponent of Jackie Robinson's presence in the major leagues. Died at Hoover, AL, July 7, 1993.

CHEVROLET, LOUIS: 120th BIRTH ANNIVERSARY. Dec 25, 1878. Louis Joseph Chevrolet, auto racing driver and engineer born at LaChaux-de-Fonds, Switzerland. Chevrolet emigrated to Montreal in 1900 and moved to New York in 1902. He worked on early automobiles, drove in races and designed cars for the company that bore his name but which he did not own. His career was marked by a series of business failures and personal and family tragedies. Died at Detroit, MI, June 6, 1941.

CHRISTMAS. Dec 25. Christian festival commemorating the birth of Jesus of Nazareth. Most popular of Christian observances, Christmas as a Feast of the Nativity dates from the 4th century. Although Jesus's birth date is not known, the Western church selected Dec 25 for the feast, possibly to counteract the non-Christian festivals of that approximate date. Many customs from non-Christian festivals (Roman Saturnalia, Mithraic sun's birthday, Teutonic yule, Druidic and other winter solstice rites) have been adopted as part of the Christmas celebration (lights, mistletoe, holly and ivy, holiday tree, wassailing and gift giving, for example). Some Orthodox Churches celebrate Christmas on Jan 7 based on the "old calendar" (Julian). Theophany (recognition of the divinity of Jesus) is observed on this date and also on Jan 6, especially by the Eastern Orthodox Church.

FOX, NELLIE: BIRTH ANNIVERSARY. Dec 25, 1927. Jacob Nelson (Nellie) Fox, Baseball Hall of Fame second baseman born at St. Thomas, PA. Fox is generally rated one of the greatest defensive second basemen of all time. He starred with the Chicago White Sox American League pennant winners in 1959 and was renowned as an exceptional fielder and a timely hitter. Inducted into the Hall of Fame in 1997. Died at Baltimore, MD, Dec 1, 1975.

GALVIN, PUD: BIRTH ANNIVERSARY. Dec 25, 1855. James Francis ("Pud") Galvin, Baseball Hall of Fame pitcher born at St. Louis, MO. Galvin was one of the outstanding pitchers of the 19th century. He won 361 games and pitched professional baseball's first perfect game in 1876. Inducted into the Hall of Fame in 1965. Died at Pittsburgh, PA, Mar 7, 1902.

KELLY TIRES BLUE-GRAY ALL-STAR FOOTBALL CLASSIC. Dec 25. Cramton Bowl, Montgomery, AL. College seniors from northern schools compete against their southern counterparts. Sponsors: Montgomery Lion's Club and Kelly Tires. Est attendance: 22,000. For info: Charles W. Jones, Exec Dir, Box 94, Montgomery, AL 36101-0094. Phone: (334) 265-1266. Fax: (334) 265-5944.

TROUPPE, QUINCY: BIRTH ANNIVERSARY. Dec 25, 1912. Quincy Thomas Trouppe, baseball player and manager born at Dublin, GA. Trouppe played and managed in the Negro Leagues for nearly a quarter-century. He was a catcher and a switch-hitter. Died at St. Louis, MO, Aug 10, 1993.

BIRTHDAYS TODAY
Stu Barnes, 28, hockey player, born Edmonton, Alberta, Canada, Dec 25, 1970.
Lawrence Richard (Larry) Csonka, 52, Pro Football Hall of Fame running back, born Stow, OH, Dec 25, 1946.
Ned Franklin Garver, 73, former baseball player, born Ney, OH, Dec 25, 1925.
Rickey Henley Henderson, 40, baseball player, born Chicago, IL, Dec 25, 1958.
Alvin Neil (Al) Jackson, 63, former baseball player, born Waco, TX, Dec 25, 1935.
Gene William Lamont, 52, baseball manager and former player, born Rockford, IL, Dec 25, 1946.
Naeole, Chris, 24, football player, born Kailua, HI, Dec 25, 1974.
Jesus Manuel (Manny) Trillo, 48, former baseball player, born Carapito, Venezuela, Dec 25, 1950.

DECEMBER 26 — SATURDAY
Day 360 — 5 Remaining

BOXING DAY. Dec 26. Ordinarily observed on the first day after Christmas. Now a legal holiday in Canada, the United Kingdom and many other countries. Formerly (according to Robert Chambers) a day when Christmas gift boxes were "regularly expected by a postman, the lamplighter, the dustman, and generally by all those functionaries who render services to the public at large, without receiving payment therefore from any individual." When Boxing Day falls on a Saturday or Sunday, the Monday or Tuesday immediately following may be proclaimed or observed as a bank or public holiday.

BULKELEY, MORGAN: BIRTH ANNIVERSARY. Dec 26, 1837. Morgan Gardner Bulkeley, Baseball Hall of Fame executive born at East Haddam, CT. Bulkeley served as president of the National League for its first year, 1876. He was a figurehead faced with several troubling administrative problems. Inducted into the Hall of Fame in 1937. Died at Hartford, CT, Nov 6, 1922.

FIRST BLACK HEAVYWEIGHT CHAMPION: 90TH ANNIVERSARY. Dec 26, 1908. Jack Johnson became the first black man to win the heavyweight championship when he knocked out Tommy Burns in the 14th round of a fight in Sydney, Australia.

JESSE OWENS RACES A HORSE: ANNIVERSARY. Dec 26, 1936. Sprinter Jesse Owens, hero of the 1936 Berlin Olympics, raced against a horse at Havana, Cuba. Owens took on Julio McGraw in a 100-yard dash and won.

KWANZAA. Dec 26–Jan 1, 1999. American black family observance (since 1966) in recognition of traditional African harvest festivals. Stresses unity of the black family, with communitywide harvest feast (karamu) on seventh day. Kwanzaa means "first fruit" in Swahili. An optional observance to avoid commercialization of Christmas traditions.

MOON PHASE: FIRST QUARTER. Dec 26. Moon enters First Quarter phase at 5:46 AM, EST.

WKA DAYTONA CLASSIC DIRT KARTING RACES. Dec 26–30. Daytona Beach Municipal Stadium, Daytona Beach, FL. For info: John Story, Dir of Pub Rel, Daytona Intl Speedway, Box 2801, Daytona Beach, FL 32120-2801. Phone: (904) 254-6782. For tickets: (904) 253-RACE (7223). Fax: (904) 947-6791. WWW: http://www.daytonausa.com

First Black Heavyweight Champion

WORLD ENDURO CHAMPIONSHIP KART RACES. Dec 26–30. Daytona International Speedway, Daytona Beach, FL. For info: John Story, Dir of Pub Rel, Daytona Intl Speedway, Box 2801, Daytona Beach, FL 32120-2801. Phone: (904) 253-6782. For tickets: (904) 253-RACE (7223). Fax: (904) 947-6791. WWW: http://www.daytonausa.com

BIRTHDAYS TODAY

Esteban Beltre, 31, baseball player, born Ingenio Quisfuella, Dominican Republic, Dec 26, 1967.

Susan Butcher, 44, sled dog racer, born Cambridge, MA, Dec 26, 1954.

Carroll Christopher (Chris) Chambliss, 50, former baseball player, born Dayton, OH, Dec 26, 1948.

George Earl ("Storm") Davis, 37, former baseball player, born Dallas, TX, Dec 26, 1961.

Carlton Ernest Fisk, 51, former baseball player, born Bellows Falls, VT, Dec 26, 1947.

Jeffrey Wayne (Jeff) King, 34, baseball player, born Marion, IN, Dec 26, 1964.

December 1998	S	M	T	W	T	F	S
			1	2	3	4	5
	6	7	8	9	10	11	12
	13	14	15	16	17	18	19
	20	21	22	23	24	25	26
	27	28	29	30	31		

Mario Mendoza, 48, former baseball player, born Chihuahua, Mexico, Dec 26, 1950.

Osborne Earl (Ozzie) Smith, 44, broadcaster and former baseball player, born Mobile, AL, Dec 26, 1954.

DECEMBER 27 — SUNDAY
Day 361 — 4 Remaining

CAYLEY, GEORGE: 225TH BIRTH ANNIVERSARY. Dec 27, 1773. Sir George Cayley, aviation pioneer, scientist and inventor born at Scarborough, Yorkshire, England. Cayley was a theoretician who designed airplanes, helicopters and gliders. He is credited as the father of aerodynamics, and he was the pilot of the world's first manned glider flight. Died at Brompton Hall, Yorkshire, Dec 15, 1857.

WARD, ARCH: BIRTH ANNIVERSARY. Dec 27, 1896. Arch Ward, sportswriter and promoter born at Irwin, IL. As sports editor of the *Chicago Tribune*, Ward conceived of both the baseball All-Star Game and the College Football All-Star Game. He did not pretend in his writing and editing to any sort of objectivity, believing it his duty to promote the sports he was covering and to sell newspapers. Died at Chicago, IL, July 9, 1955.

BIRTHDAYS TODAY

Kevin Lars Constantine, 40, hockey coach, born International Falls, MN, Dec 27, 1958.

Philip Joseph (Phil) Gagliano, 57, former baseball player, born Memphis, TN, Dec 27, 1941.

James Joseph (Jim) Leyritz, 35, baseball player, born Lakewood, OH, Dec 27, 1963.

Dean William Palmer, 30, baseball player, born Tallahassee, FL, Dec 27, 1968.

Roy Hilton White, 55, former baseball player, born Los Angeles, CA, Dec 27, 1943.

DECEMBER 28 — MONDAY
Day 362 — 3 Remaining

CHASE'S SPORTSQUOTE OF THE DAY

"Some coaches are fortunate in that they inherit teams that are instant winners. I was fortunate enough to have a team that had the potential to grow into a winner." — Weeb Ewbank on taking over the Colts

ALL-COLLEGE BASKETBALL TOURNAMENT. Dec 28–30. Myriad Convention Center, Oklahoma City, OK. The oldest college basketball tournament in the country, outdating the NCAA, NAIA and the NIT. Host school is Oklahoma University. Rest of field to be announced; 156 universities have competed. Annually, between Christmas and New Year's. Est attendance: 25,000. For info: Stanley Draper, Jr, OK City All Sports Assn, 100 W Main, Ste 285, Oklahoma City, OK 73102. Phone: (405) 236-5000. Fax: (405) 236-5008.

BRIDGES, TOMMY: BIRTH ANNIVERSARY. Dec 28, 1906. Thomas Jefferson Davis (Tommy) Bridges, baseball player born at Gordonsville, TN. Bridges won 194 games during 16 seasons with the Detroit Tigers (1930–46). He pitched three one-hitters and 33 shutouts. Died at Nashville, TN, Apr 19, 1968.

GREATEST NFL GAME: 40th ANNIVERSARY. Dec 28, 1958. In what is generally considered the greatest game in NFL history, the Baltimore Colts defeated the New York Giants, 23–17, in overtime, to win the NFL championship. The Colts had the ball, third-down-and-goal, on the Giants' one-yard line when quarterback Johnny Unitas handed the ball to fullback Alan Ameche. The Wisconsin graduate and Heisman Trophy winner bulled into the end zone to conclude the first sudden-death NFL game.

LYONS, TED: BIRTH ANNIVERSARY. Dec 28, 1900. Theodore Amar (Ted) Lyons, Baseball Hall of Fame pitcher born at Lake Charles, LA. Lyons started for the Chicago White Sox from 1924 through 1942. He pitched well, much better than the rest of his team played, and developed a knuckleball after he hurt his arm in 1931. Inducted into the Hall of Fame in 1955. Died at Sulphur, LA, July 25, 1986.

BIRTHDAYS TODAY

Raymond Jean (Ray) Bourque, 38, hockey player, born Montreal, Quebec, Canada, Dec 28, 1960.
Carlos A. Carson, 40, former football player, born Lake Worth, FL, Dec 28, 1958.
Hubert Myatt (Hubie) Green, III, 52, golfer, born Birmingham, AL, Dec 28, 1946.
Charles Ray Knight, 46, baseball manager and former player, born Albany, GA, Dec 28, 1952.
William Francis (Bill) Lee, 52, former baseball player, born Burbank, CA, Dec 28, 1946.
Rob Niedermayer, 24, hockey player, born Cassiar, BC, Canada, Dec 28, 1974.
Zane William Smith, 38, baseball player, born Madison, WI, Dec 28, 1960.

DECEMBER 29 — TUESDAY
Day 363 — 2 Remaining

HAYES PUNCHES CLEMSON PLAYER: 20th ANNIVERSARY. Dec 29, 1978. Ohio State University football coach Woody Hayes punched a player from Clemson University during Clemson's 19–15 victory in the Gator Bowl. Hayes was upset that the Buckeyes were losing, but OSU officials were upset, too. They fired Hayes for the incident.

OSMANSKI, BILL: BIRTH ANNIVERSARY. Dec 29, 1915. William (Bill) Osmanski, football player born at Providence, RI. A graduate of Holy Cross, Osmanski was first-round draft choice of the Chicago Bears in 1939. He led the league in rushing as a rookie and scored the first touchdown in the Bears' legendary 73–0 defeat of the Washington Redskins in the 1940 NFL championship game. Died at Chicago, IL, Jan 1, 1997.

WILLARD, JESS: BIRTH ANNIVERSARY. Dec 29, 1881. Jess Willard, boxer born at Pottawatomie County, KS. The towering Willard, 6'6¼" tall, took the heavyweight title from Jack Johnson in a fight at Havana, Cuba, on Apr 5, 1915. He defended his title only once in four years and then lost it to Jack Dempsey on July 4, 1919. Died at Los Angeles, CA, Dec 15, 1968.

BIRTHDAYS TODAY

Ted Danson, 51, actor ("Cheers"), born San Diego, CA, Dec 29, 1947.
Mervyn Fernandez, 39, former football player, born Merced, CA, Dec 29, 1959.
Thomas Lorenzo (Tom) Knight, 24, football player, born Summit, NJ, Dec 29, 1974.
James Raleigh Mouton, 30, baseball player, born Denver, CO, Dec 29, 1968.
Raymon Ernest (Ray) Nitschke, 62, Pro Football Hall of Fame linebacker, born Elmwood Park, IL, Dec 29, 1936.
Scott Patrick Ruffcorn, 29, baseball player, born New Braunfels, TX, Dec 29, 1969.
Devon Markes White, 36, baseball player, born Kingston, Jamaica, Dec 29, 1962.

DECEMBER 30 — WEDNESDAY
Day 364 — 1 Remaining

GRETZKY GETS 50 IN 39: ANNIVERSARY. Dec 30, 1981. Center Wayne Gretzky of the Edmonton Oilers scored five goals to lead his team to a 7–5 win over the Philadelphia Flyers. His fifth goal, into an empty net, was his 50th of the year, scored in only 39 games.

NANCE, JIM: BIRTH ANNIVERSARY. Dec 30, 1942. James Solomon (Jim) Nance, football player born at Indiana, PA. Nance played fullback at Syracuse University (1962–64) and for the Boston (later New England) Patriots, setting several AFL records. He finished his career with the New York Jets and the Memphis team in the short-lived World Football League. Died at Quincy, MA, June 16, 1992.

PLYMOUTH HOLIDAY BOWL PARADE AND GAME. Dec 30 (tentative). Along Harbor Drive, San Diego, CA. The morning of the Plymouth Holiday Bowl football game (teams picked from Pac 10, Big 12 and Western Athletic conferences). This televised parade features floats, marching bands, giant balloons and unique specialty units. Parade at 10 AM, game in evening. Est attendance: 100,000. For info: Mark Neville, Holiday Bowl, PO Box 601400, San Diego, CA 92160-1400. Phone: (619) 283-5808. Fax: (619) 281-7947.

BIRTHDAYS TODAY

Kerry Michael Collins, 26, football player, born West Lawn, PA, Dec 30, 1972.
Sean Marielle Higgins, 30, basketball player, born Los Angeles, CA, Dec 30, 1968.
Ben Johnson, 37, former track athlete, born Falmouth, Jamaica, Dec 30, 1961.
Sanford (Sandy) Koufax, 63, former broadcaster and Baseball Hall of Fame pitcher, born Brooklyn, NY, Dec 30, 1935.
Michelle McGann, 29, golfer, born West Palm Beach, FL, Dec 30, 1969.
Frank Joseph Torre, 67, former baseball player, born New York, NY, Dec 30, 1931.
Eldrick ("Tiger") Woods, 23, golfer, born Cypress, CA, Dec 30, 1975.

DECEMBER 31 — THURSDAY
Day 365 — 0 Remaining

CLEMENTE, ROBERTO: DEATH ANNIVERSARY. Dec 31, 1972. Roberto Clemente y Walker, Baseball Hall of Fame outfielder born at Carolina, Puerto Rico, Aug 18, 1934. Clemente was one of the game's all-time best outfielders, excelling at bat, on the bases and in the field. He won four National League batting titles and led the Pittsburgh Pirates to a World Series championship in 1971. While organizing relief efforts for the victims of a Nicaraguan earthquake, he perished in a plane crash. Inducted as the first Latin American player into the Hall of Fame in 1973, without the usual five-year waiting period. Died near Carolina.

CONNOLLY, TOM: BIRTH ANNIVERSARY. Dec 31, 1870. Thomas Henry (Tom) Connolly, Sr, Baseball Hall of Fame umpire born at Manchester, England. Connolly is regarded as the dean of American League umpires, working from 1901 to 1931 when he was named umpire-in-chief. He once went 10 seasons without ejecting anyone from a game. Inducted as the first umpire in the Hall of Fame in 1953. Died at Natick, MA, Apr 28, 1961.

JONES, BEN: BIRTH ANNIVERSARY. Dec 31, 1882. Benjamin Allyn (Ben) Jones, thoroughbred trainer born at Parnell, MO. Jones saddled six Kentucky Derby winners, two of whom, Whirlaway and Citation, won the Triple Crown. He trained for Calumet Farms from 1939 until 1947 when he became the stable's general manager. Died at Lexington, KY, June 13, 1961.

KELLY, KING: BIRTH ANNIVERSARY. Dec 31, 1857. Michael Joseph ("King") Kelly, Baseball Hall of Fame catcher and outfielder born at Troy, NY. Kelly was baseball's first superstar, his personality and behavior outdistancing his talents, which were themselves considerable. Kelly was an innovative player who took advantage of every situation. Inducted into the Hall of Fame in 1945. Died at Boston, MA, Nov 8, 1894.

NEW YEAR'S EVE. Dec 31. The last evening of the Gregorian calendar year, traditionally a night for merrymaking to welcome in the new year.

NFL'S COLDEST TITLE GAME: ANNIVERSARY. Dec 31, 1967. The Green Bay Packers defeated the Dallas Cowboys, 21–17, to win the NFL championship. The game was played in Green Bay with the temperature at −14. Packers quarterback Bart Starr scored the winning touchdown on a quarterback sneak with 13 seconds left to play.

YOU'RE ALL DONE DAY. Dec 31. Acknowledge all that you have accomplished in the past year and savor the satisfaction of every time you crossed home plate, every touchdown you scored, every three-pointer you made, every time you put the puck in the net, every finish line you crossed or every time you gave your very best effort.

BIRTHDAYS TODAY

Richard Warren (Rick) Aguilera, 37, baseball player, born San Gabriel, CA, Dec 31, 1961.

Thomas Joseph (Tommy) Byrne, 79, former baseball player, born Baltimore, MD, Dec 31, 1919.

Tyrone Kennedy Corbin, 36, basketball player, born Columbia, SC, Dec 31, 1962.

Hugh Edward McElhenny, 70, Pro Football Hall of Fame halfback, born Los Angeles, CA, Dec 31, 1928.

Joseph Heath Shuler, 27, football player, born Bryson City, NC, Dec 31, 1971.

LEAGUE AND TEAM ADDRESSES

Major League Baseball

Commissioner's Office
350 Park Ave
New York, NY 10022
(212) 339-7800

American League
350 Park Ave
New York, NY 10022
(212) 339-7600

National League
350 Park Ave
New York, NY 10022
(212) 339-7700

AMERICAN LEAGUE
East Division
Baltimore Orioles
333 W Camden St
Baltimore, MD 21201
(410) 685-9800
Ticket info:
Oriole Park at Camden
   Yards (RS)
(410) 481-SEAT
Ft. Lauderdale Stadium (ST)
Ft. Lauderdale, FL
(954) 776-1921
(800) 236-8908

Boston Red Sox
4 Yawkey Way
Boston, MA 02215
(617) 267-9440
Ticket info:
Fenway Park (RS)
(617) 267-8661
City of Palms Park (ST)
Ft. Myers, FL
(941) 334-4700

Detroit Tigers
Tiger Stadium
Detroit, MI 48216
(313) 962-4000
Ticket info:
Tiger Stadium (RS)
(313) 963-2050
Joker Marchant
   Stadium (ST)
Lakeland, FL
(941) 499-8229

New York Yankees
Yankee Stadium
E 161 St and River Ave
Bronx, NY 10451
(718) 293-4300
Ticket info:
Yankee Stadium (RS)
(718) 293-6000
Legends Field (ST)
Tampa, FL
(305) 776-1921

Toronto Blue Jays
One Blue Jays Way
Ste 3200
Toronto, ON M5V 1J1
(416) 341-1000
Ticket info:
Sky Dome (RS)
(416) 341-1111
Dunedin Stadium at Grant
   Field (ST)
Dunedin, FL
(813) 733-0429
(800) 707-8269

Central Division
Chicago White Sox
333 W 35th St
Chicago, IL 60616
(312) 674-1000
Ticket info:
Comiskey Park (RS)
(312) 674-1000
Ed Smith Stadium (ST)
Sarasota, FL
(813) 287-8844

Cleveland Indians
2401 Ontario St
Cleveland, OH 44115
(216) 420-4200
Ticket info:
Jacobs Field (RS)
(216) 241-8888
Chain O'Lakes (ST)
Winter Haven, FL
(813) 293-3900

Kansas City Royals
PO Box 419969
Kansas City, MO 64141-
   6969
(816) 921-2200
Ticket info:
Kauffman Stadium (RS)
(816) 921-8000
Baseball City Stadium (ST)
Haines City, FL
(941) 424-2500

Milwaukee Brewers
County Stadium
PO Box 3099
Milwaukee, WI 53201-3099
(414) 933-4114
Ticket info:
County Stadium (RS)
(414) 933-9000
Compadre Stadium (ST)
Chandler, AZ
(602) 895-1200

Minnesota Twins
34 Kirby Puckett Place
Minneapolis, MN 55415
(800) 33-TWINS
Ticket info:
Metrodome (RS)
(800) 33-TWINS
Lee County Sports
   Complex (ST)
Ft. Myers, FL
(800) 338-9467

West Division
Anaheim Angels
2000 Gene Autry Way
Anaheim, CA 92806
(714) 937-7200
(213) 625-1123
Ticket info:
Anaheim Stadium (RS)
(714) 634-2000
Diablo Stadium (ST)
Tempe, AZ
(602) 678-4444
(714) 634-2000

Oakland Athletics
7677 Oakport St, Ste 200
Oakland, CA 94621
(510) 638-4900
Ticket info:
Oakland-Alameda County
   Coliseum (RS)
(510) 638-4627
Phoenix Stadium (ST)
Phoenix, AZ
(602) 392-0074

Seattle Mariners
PO Box 4100
83 King St
Seattle, WA 98104
(206) 628-3555
Ticket info:
The Kingdome (RS)
(206) 628-3555
Peoria Stadium (ST)
Peoria, AZ
(602) 784-4444

Tampa Bay Devil Rays
Tropicana Field
One Tropicana Dr
St. Petersburg, FL 33705
(813) 825-3137
Ticket info:
The Thunderdome (RS)
(813) 825-3250
Al Lang Stadium (ST)
St. Petersburg, FL 33705
(813) 822-3384

Texas Rangers
1000 Ballpark Way
Arlington, TX 76011
(817) 273-5222
Ticket info:
The Ballpark in Arlington
   (RS)
(817) 273-5100
Charlotte County Stadium
   (ST)
Port Charlotte, FL
(941) 625-9500

NATIONAL LEAGUE
East Division
Atlanta Braves
PO Box 4064
Atlanta, GA 30302
(404) 522-7630
Ticket info:
Turner Field (RS)
(404) 522-7630
Municipal Stadium (ST)
West Palm Beach, FL
(407) 683-6100

Florida Marlins
2267 NW 199th St
Miami, FL 33056
(305) 626-7400
Ticket info:
Pro Player Stadium (RS)
(305) 930-HITS
Space Coast Stadium (ST)
Melbourne, FL
(407) 633-9200

Montreal Expos
4549 Pierre-de-Coubertin
   Ave
Montreal, QC H1V 3N7
(514) 253-3434
Ticket info:
Olympic Stadium (RS)
(800) GO-EXPOS
Municipal Stadium (ST)
West Palm Beach, FL
(407) 684-6801

(RS) = Regular Season
(ST) = Spring Training

New York Mets
123-10 Roosevelt Ave
Flushing, NY 11368
(718) 507-6387
Ticket info:
Shea Stadium (RS)
(718) 507-8499
St. Lucie County Stadium
(ST)
Port St. Lucie, FL
(561) 871-2115

Philadelphia Phillies
PO Box 7575
Philadelphia, PA 19101
(215) 463-6000
Ticket info:
Veterans Stadium (RS)
(215) 463-1000
Jack Russell Stadium (ST)
Clearwater, FL
(813) 442-8496
(215) 463-1000

Central Division
Chicago Cubs
1060 W Addison St
Chicago, IL 60613-4397
(312) 404-2827
Ticket info:
Wrigley Field (RS)
(312) 404-2827
HoHoKam Park (ST)
Mesa, AZ
(800) 638-4253

Cincinnati Reds
100 Cinergy Field
Cincinnati, OH 45202
(513) 421-4510
Ticket info:
Cinergy Field (RS)
(513) 421-7337
(800) 829-5353
Plant City Stadium (ST)
Plant City, FL
(813) 752-7337

Houston Astros
PO Box 288
Houston, TX 77001-0288
(713) 799-9500
Ticket info:
The Astrodome (RS)
(713) 799-9555
Osceola County Stadium
(ST)
Kissimmee, FL
(407) 933-2520

Pittsburgh Pirates
600 Stadium Circle
Pittsburgh, PA 15212
(412) 323-5000
Ticket info:
Three Rivers Stadium (RS)
(800) BUY-BUCS
McKechnie Field (ST)
Bradenton, FL
(941) 748-4610

St. Louis Cardinals
250 Stadium Plaza
St. Louis, MO 63102
(314) 421-3060
Ticket info:
Busch Stadium (RS)
(314) 421-2400
Roger Dean Stadium (ST)
Jupiter, FL
TBA

West Division
Arizona Diamondbacks
PO Box 2095
Phoenix, AZ 85004
(602) 514-8500
Ticket info:
Bank One Ballpark (RS)
(602) 514-8400
TBA (ST)
Tucson, AZ
TBA

Colorado Rockies
2001 Blake St
Denver, CO 80205-2000
(303) 292-2000
Ticket info:
Coors Field (RS)
(303) 762-5437
Hi Corbett Field (ST)
Tucson, AZ
(800) 388-ROCK

Los Angeles Dodgers
1000 Elysian Park Ave
Los Angeles, CA 90012
(213) 224-1500
Ticket info:
Dodger Stadium (RS)
(213) 224-1400
Holman Stadium (ST)
Vero Beach, FL
(561) 569-6858

San Diego Padres
PO Box 2000
San Diego, CA 92112-2000
(619) 283-4494
Ticket info:
Jack Murphy Stadium (RS)
(619) 283-4494
(888) 723-7379
Peoria Stadium (ST)
Peoria, AZ
(602) 878-4337

San Francisco Giants
3 Com Park at Candlestick
Point
San Francisco, CA 94124
(415) 468-3700
Ticket info:
3 Com Park (RS)
(414) 467-8000
Scottsdale Stadium (ST)
Scottsdale, AZ
(602) 990-7972

National Football League

National Football League
410 Park Ave
New York, NY 10022
(212) 758-1500

**AMERICAN FOOTBALL
CONFERENCE**
Eastern Division
Buffalo Bills
One Bills Dr
Orchard Park, NY 14127
(716) 648-1800
Ticket info:
Rich Stadium
(716) 649-0015

Indianapolis Colts
PO Box 535000
Indianapolis, IN 46253
(317) 297-2658
Ticket info:
RCA Dome
(317) 297-7000

Miami Dolphins
7500 SW 30th St
Davie, FL 33314
(305) 452-7000
Ticket info:
Joe Robbie Stadium
(305) 620-2578

New England Patriots
60 Washington St
Foxboro, MA 02035
(508) 543-8200
Ticket info:
Foxboro Stadium
(508) 543-1776

New York Jets
1000 Fulton Ave
Hempstead, NY 11550
(516) 538-6600
Ticket info:
Giants Stadium
(516) 538-7200

Central Division
Baltimore Ravens
11001 Owings Mills Blvd
Owings Mills, MD 21117
(410) 654-6200
Ticket info:
Memorial Stadium
(888) 972-8367

Cincinnati Bengals
200 Riverfront Stadium
Cincinnati, OH 45202
(513) 621-3550
Ticket info:
Riverfront Stadium
(513) 621-3550

Jacksonville Jaguars
One Stadium Pl
Jacksonville, FL 32202
(904) 633-6000
Ticket info:
Jacksonville Municipal
Stadium
(904) 633-2000

Pittsburgh Steelers
300 Stadium Circle
Pittsburgh, PA 15212
(412) 323-1200
Ticket info:
Three Rivers Stadium
(412) 323-1200

Tennessee Oilers
TBA
TBA
Ticket info:
TBA
Ticket info:
The Astrodome

Western Division
Denver Broncos
13655 Broncos Pkwy
Englewood, CO 80112
(303) 649-9000
Ticket info:
Mile High Stadium
(303) 433-7466

Kansas City Chiefs
One Arrowhead Dr
Kansas City, MO 64129
(816) 924-9300
Ticket info:
Arrowhead Stadium
(816) 924-9400

Oakland Raiders
1 Hegenberger Road
Oakland, CA 94621
(310) 322-3451
Ticket info:
Oakland-Alameda County
    Coliseum
(800) 949-2626

San Diego Chargers
PO Box 609609
San Diego, CA 92160-9609
(619) 280-2111
Ticket info:
San Diego Jack Murphy
    Stadium
(619) 280-2121

Seattle Seahawks
11220 NE 53rd St
Kirkland, WA 98033
(206) 827-9777
Ticket info:
Kingdome
(206) 827-9766

**NATIONAL FOOTBALL
CONFERENCE**
Eastern Division
Arizona Cardinals
PO Box 888
Phoenix, AZ 85001-0888
(602) 379-0101
Ticket info:
Sun Devil Stadium
(602) 379-0102

Dallas Cowboys
One Cowboys Pkwy
Irving, TX 75063
(214) 556-9900
Ticket info:
Texas Stadium
(214) 579-5000

New York Giants
East Rutherford, NJ 07073
(201) 935-8111
Ticket info:
Giants Stadium
(201) 935-8222

Philadelphia Eagles
3501 S Broad St
Philadelphia, PA 19148
(215) 463-2500
Ticket info:
Veterans Stadium
(215) 463-5500

Washington Redskins
PO Box 17247
Dulles International
    Airport
Washington, DC 20041
(703) 478-8900
Ticket info:
Robert F. Kennedy Stadium
(202) 546-2222

Central Division
Chicago Bears
Halas Hall
250 N Washington Rd
Lake Forest, IL 60045
(847) 295-6600
Ticket info:
Soldier Field
(847) 615-2327

Detroit Lions
1200 Featherstone Rd
Pontiac, MI 48342
(810) 335-4131
Ticket info:
Pontiac Silverdome
(810) 335-4151

Green Bay Packers
PO Box 10628
Green Bay, WI 54307-0628
(414) 496-5700
Ticket info:
Lambeau Field
(414) 496-5719

Minnesota Vikings
9520 Viking Dr
Eden Prairie, MN 55344
(612) 828-6500
Ticket info:
Metrodome
(612) 333-8828

Tampa Bay Buccaneers
One Buccaneer Pl
Tampa, FL 33607
(813) 870-2700
Ticket info:
Tampa Stadium
(813) 870-2700

Western Division
Atlanta Falcons
Atlanta Falcons Complex
One Falcon Place
Suwanee, GA 30174
(404) 945-1111
Ticket info:
Georgia Dome
(404) 223-8000

Carolina Panthers
800 S Mint St
Charlotte, NC 28202-1502
(704) 358-7000
Ticket info:
Carolinas Stadium
(704) 358-7800

New Orleans Saints
7800 Airline Highway
Metairie, LA 70003
(504) 733-0255
Ticket info:
Louisiana Superdome
(504) 731-1700

St. Louis Rams
1 Rams Way
St. Louis, MO 63045
(314) 982-7267
Ticket info:
Trans World Dome
(314) 425-8830

San Francisco 49ers
4949 Centennial Blvd
Santa Clara, CA 95054-
    1229
(408) 562-4949
Ticket info:
3 Com Park at Candlestick
    Point
(415) 468-2249

National Basketball Association

National Basketball
    Association
Olympic Tower
645 Fifth Ave
New York, NY 10022
(212) 407-8000

New Jersey Office
450 Harmon Meadow Blvd
Secaucus, NJ 07094
(201) 865-1500

EASTERN CONFERENCE
Atlantic Division
Boston Celtics
151 Merrimac St
Boston, MA 02114
(617) 523-6050
Ticket info:
Fleet Center
(617) 523-3030

Miami Heat
SunTrust International
    Center
One SE 3rd Ave, Ste 2300
Miami, FL 33131
(305) 577-4328
Ticket info:
Miami Arena
(305) 577-4328

New Jersey Nets
405 Murray Hill Pkwy
East Rutherford, NJ 07073
(201) 935-8888
Ticket info:
Continental Arena
(201) 935-8888

New York Knicks
Two Pennsylvania Plaza
New York, NY 10121-0091
(212) 465-6000
Ticket info:
Madison Square Garden
(212) 465-JUMP

Orlando Magic
One Magic Place
Orlando Arena
Orlando, FL 32801
(407) 649-3200
Ticket info:
Orlando Arena
(800) 338-0005

Philadelphia 76ers
1 CoreStates Complex
PO Box 25040
Philadelphia, PA 19148
(215) 339-7600
Ticket info:
CoreStates Center
(215) 339-7676

Washington Wizards
USAir Arena
Landover, MD
(301) 773-2255
Ticket info:
USAir Arena
(301) 622-3865

Central Division
Atlanta Hawks
One CNN Center
Ste 405, South Tower
Atlanta, GA 30303
(404) 827-3800
Ticket info:
The Omni
(800) 326-4000

Charlotte Hornets
100 Hive Dr
Charlotte, NC 28217
(704) 357-0252
Ticket info:
Charlotte Coliseum
(704) 522-6500

Chicago Bulls
1901 W Madison St
Chicago, IL 60612
(312) 455-4000
Ticket info:
United Center
(312) 559-1212

Cleveland Cavaliers
1 Center Court
Cleveland, OH 44115-4001
(216) 420-2000
Ticket info:
Gund Arena
(216) 420-2000

Detroit Pistons
Two Championship Dr
Auburn Hills, MI 48362
(810) 377-0100
Ticket info:
The Palace of Auburn Hills
(810) 377-0100

Indiana Pacers
300 E Market St
Indianapolis, IN 46204
(317) 263-2100
Ticket info:
Market Square Arena
(317) 239-5151

Milwaukee Bucks
1001 N Fourth St
Milwaukee, WI 53203-1312
(414) 227-0500
Ticket info:
Bradley Center
(414) 276-4545

Toronto Raptors
20 Bay St, Ste 1702
Toronto, ON M5J 2N8
(416) 214-2255
Ticket info:
SkyDome
(416) 366-3865

WESTERN CONFERENCE
Midwest Division
Dallas Mavericks
777 Sports St
Dallas, TX 75207
(214) 748-1808
Ticket info:
Reunion Arena
(214) 939-2800

Denver Nuggets
1635 Clay St
Denver, CO 80204
(303) 893-6700
Ticket info:
McNichols Sports Arena
(303) 893-6700

Houston Rockets
Ten Greenway Plaza,
    Ste 400
Houston, TX 77046
(713) 627-3865
Ticket info:
The Summit
(713) 627-3865

Minnesota Timberwolves
600 First Ave N
Minneapolis, MN 55403
(612) 673-1600
Ticket info:
Target Center
(612) 673-1600

San Antonio Spurs
100 Montana St
San Antonio, TX 78203-
    1031
(210) 554-7700
Ticket info:
Alamodome
(210) 554-7787

Utah Jazz
301 West South Temple
Salt Lake City, UT 84101
(801) 325-2500
Ticket info:
Delta Center
(801) 325-2500

Vancouver Grizzlies
800 Griffiths Way
Vancouver, BC V6B 6G1
(604) 899-4666
Ticket info:
Bear Country at General
    Motors Place
(604) 899-4666

Pacific Division
Golden State Warriors
1221 Broadway, 20th Floor
Oakland, CA 94621-1918
(510) 986-2200
Ticket info:
San Jose Arena
(510) 986-2222

Los Angeles Clippers
3939 S Figueroa St
Los Angeles, CA 90037
(213) 745-0400
Ticket info:
LA Memorial Sports Arena
Arrowhead Pond of
    Anaheim
(213) 745-0500

Los Angeles Lakers
3900 W Manchester Blvd
PO Box 10
Inglewood, CA 90306
(310) 419-3100
Ticket info:
The Great Western Forum
(310) 419-3100

Phoenix Suns
201 E Jefferson
Phoenix, AZ 85004
(602) 379-7900
Ticket info:
America West Arena
(602) 379-7867

Portland Trail Blazers
One Center Court, Ste 200
Portland, OR 97227
(503) 234-9291
Ticket info:
The Rose Garden
(503) 234-9291

Sacramento Kings
One Sports Pkwy
Sacramento, CA 95834
(916) 928-0000
Ticket info:
ARCO Arena
(916) 928-6900

Seattle Supersonics
190 Queen Anne Ave N,
    Ste 200
Seattle, WA 98109-9711
(206) 281-5800
Ticket info:
Key Arena
(206) 283-3865

☆ *Chase's 1998 SPORTS Calendar of Events* ☆

National Hockey League

National Hockey League
1251 Ave of the Americas
47th Fl
New York, NY 10020
(212) 789-2000

Toronto Office
75 International Blvd
Ste 300
Rexdale, ON M9W 6L9
(416) 798-0809

Montreal Office
1800 McGill College Ave
Ste 2600
Montreal, QC H3A 3J6
(514) 288-9220

EASTERN CONFERENCE
Atlantic Division
Florida Panthers
100 North East Third Ave
10th Fl
Fort Lauderdale, FL 33301
(305) 768-1900

New Jersey Devils
PO Box 504
East Rutherford, NJ 07073
(201) 935-6050

New York Islanders
Nassau Veterans Memorial
    Coliseum
Uniondale, NY 11553
(516) 794-4100

New York Rangers
4 Pennsylvania Plaza
New York, NY 10001
(212) 465-6000

Philadelphia Flyers
CoreStates Center
3601 S Broad St
Philadelphia, PA 19148
(215) 465-4500

Tampa Bay Lightning
501 E Kennedy Blvd
Tampa, FL 33602
(813) 229-2658

Washington Capitals
1 Harry S Truman Dr
Landover, MD 20785
(301) 386-7000

Northeast Division
Boston Bruins
1 Fleet Center, Ste 250
Boston, MA 02114-1313
(617) 624-1900

Buffalo Sabres
Marine Midland Arena
One Main St
Buffalo, NY 14203
(716) 856-7300
Ticket info:
(716) 888-4000

Carolina Hurricanes
5000 Aerial Center, Ste 100
Morrisville, NC 27560
(919) 967-PUCK

Montreal Canadiens
1260 rue de la Gauchetiere
    Ouest
Montreal, QC H3B 5E8
(514) 932-2582

Ottawa Senators
301 Moodie Dr, Ste 200
Nepean, ON K2H 9C4
(613) 721-0115

Pittsburgh Penguins
Gate No 9
Civic Arena
Pittsburgh, PA 15219
(412) 642-1300

WESTERN CONFERENCE
Central Division
Chicago Black Hawks
1901 W Madison St
Chicago, IL 60612
(312) 455-7000

Dallas Stars
211 Cowboys Pkwy
Irving, TX 75063
(214) 868-2890

Detroit Red Wings
600 Civic Center Dr
Detroit, MI 48226
(313) 296-7544

Phoenix Coyotes
One Renaissance Square
2 North Central, Ste 1930
Phoenix, AZ 85004
(602) 379-2800

St. Louis Blues
1401 Clark St
St. Louis, MO 63103
(314) 622-2500

Toronto Maple Leafs
60 Carlton St
Toronto, ON M5B 1L1
(416) 977-1641

Pacific Division
Mighty Ducks of Anaheim
2695 E Katella Ave
PO Box 61077
Anaheim, CA 92803-6177
(714) 704-2700

Calgary Flames
PO Box 1540
Station M
Calgary, AB T2P 3B9
(403) 777-2177

Colorado Avalanche
1635 Clay St
Denver, CO 80204
(303) 893-6700

Edmonton Oilers
Edmonton Coliseum
Edmonton, AB T5B 4M9
(403) 474-8561
Ticket info:
(403) 471-2191

Los Angeles Kings
3900 W Manchester Blvd
Inglewood, CA 90305
(310) 419-3160

San Jose Sharks
525 W Santa Clara St
San Jose, CA 95113
(408) 287-7070

Vancouver Canucks
800 Griffiths Way
Vancouver, BC V6B 6G1
(604) 899-4600

Most teams do not have a separate phone number for ticket information.

SPORTS HALLS OF FAME

Baseball Hall of Fame

PLAYERS

Aaron, Henry, 1982
Alexander, Grover Cleveland, 1938
Anson, Cap, 1939
Aparicio, Luis, 1984
Appling, Luke, 1964
Ashburn, Richie, 1995
Averill, Earl, 1975
Baker, Home Run, 1955
Bancroft, Dave, 1971
Banks, Ernie, 1977
Beckley, Jake, 1971
Bell, Cool Papa, 1974
Bench, Johnny, 1989
Bender, Chief, 1953
Berra, Yogi, 1972
Bottomley, Jim, 1974
Boudreau, Lou, 1970
Bresnahan, Roger, 1945
Brock, Lou, 1985
Brouthers, Dan, 1945
Brown, Mordecai, 1949
Bunning, Jim, 1996
Burkett, Jesse, 1946
Campanella, Roy, 1969
Carew, Rod, 1991
Carey, Max, 1961
Carlton, Steve, 1994
Chance, Frank, 1946
Charleston, Oscar, 1976
Chesbro, Jack, 1946
Clarke, Fred, 1945
Clarkson, John, 1963
Clemente, Roberto, 1973
Cobb, Ty, 1936
Cochrane, Mickey, 1947
Collins, Eddie, 1939
Collins, Jimmy, 1945
Combs, Earle, 1970
Comiskey, Charley, 1939 (also a founder)
Connor, Roger, 1976
Coveleski, Stanley, 1969
Crawford, Sam, 1957
Cronin, Joe, 1956
Cummings, Candy, 1939
Cuyler, Kiki, 1968
Dandridge, Ray, 1987
Day, Leon, 1995
Dean, Dizzy, 1953
Delahanty, Ed, 1945
Dickey, Bill, 1954
Dihigo, Martin, 1977
DiMaggio, Joe, 1955
Doerr, Bobby, 1986
Drysdale, Don 1984
Duffy, Hugh, 1945
Evers, Johnny, 1946
Ewing, Buck, 1939
Faber, Red, 1964
Feller, Bob, 1962
Ferrell, Rick, 1984

Fingers, Rollie, 1992
Flick, Elmer, 1963
Ford, Whitey, 1974
Foster, Bill, 1996
Foster, Rube, 1981
Fox, Nellie, 1997
Foxx, Jimmie, 1951
Frisch, Frankie, 1947
Galvin, Pud, 1965
Gehrig, Lou, 1939
Gehringer, Charley, 1949
Gibson, Bob, 1981
Gibson, Josh, 1972
Gomez, Lefty, 1972
Goslin, Goose, 1968
Greenberg, Hank, 1956
Grimes, Burleigh, 1964
Grove, Lefty, 1947
Hafey, Chick, 1971
Haines, Jesse, 1970
Hamilton, Billy, 1961
Hartnett, Gabby, 1955
Heilmann, Harry, 1952
Herman, Billy, 1975
Hooper, Harry, 1971
Hornsby, Rogers, 1942
Hoyt, Waite, 1969
Hubbell, Carl, 1947
Hunter, Catfish, 1987
Irvin, Monte, 1973
Jackson, Reggie, 1993
Jackson, Travis, 1982
Jenkins, Ferguson, 1991
Jennings, Hugh, 1945
Johnson, Judy, 1975
Johnson, Walter, 1936
Joss, Addie, 1978
Kaline, Al, 1980
Keefe, Tim, 1964
Keeler, Willie, 1939
Kell, George, 1983
Kelley, Joe, 1971
Kelly, George, 1973
Kelly, Mike, 1945
Killebrew, Harmon, 1984
Kiner, Ralph, 1975
Klein, Chuck, 1980
Koufax, Sandy, 1972
Lajoie, Nap, 1937
Lazzeri, Tony, 1991
Lemon, Bob, 1976
Leonard, Buck, 1972
Lindstrom, Fred, 1976
Lloyd, John Henry, 1977
Lombardi, Ernie, 1986
Lyons, Ted, 1955
Mantle, Mickey, 1974
Manush, Heinie, 1964
Maranville, Rabbit, 1954
Marichal, Juan, 1983
Marquard, Rube, 1971
Mathews, Eddie, 1978

Mathewson, Christy, 1936
Mays, Willie, 1979
McCarthy, Tommy, 1946
McCovey, Willie, 1986
McGinnity, Joe, 1946
Medwick, Joe, 1968
Mize, Johnny, 1981
Morgan, Joe, 1990
Musial, Stan, 1969
Newhouser, Hal, 1992
Nichols, Kid, 1949
Niekro, Phil, 1997
O'Rourke Jim, 1945
Ott, Mel, 1951
Paige, Satchel, 1971
Palmer, Jim, 1990
Pennock, Herb, 1948
Perry, Gaylord, 1991
Plank, Eddie, 1946
Radbourn, Hoss, 1939
Reese, Pee Wee, 1984
Rice, Sam, 1963
Rixey, Eppa, 1963
Rizzuto, Phil, 1994
Roberts, Robin, 1976
Robinson, Brooks, 1983
Robinson, Frank, 1982
Robinson, Jackie, 1962
Roush, Edd, 1962
Ruffing, Red, 1967
Rusie, Amos, 1977
Ruth, Babe, 1936
Schalk, Ray, 1955
Schmidt, Mike, 1995
Schoendienst, Red, 1989
Seaver, Tom, 1992
Sewell, Joe, 1977
Simmons, Al, 1953
Sisler, George, 1939
Slaughter, Enos, 1985
Snider, Duke, 1980
Spahn, Warren, 1973
Spalding, Al, 1939
Speaker, Tris, 1937
Stargell, Willie, 1988
Terry, Bill, 1954
Thompson, Sam, 1974
Tinker, Joe, 1946
Vance, Dazzy, 1955
Vaughan, Arky, 1985
Waddell, Rube, 1946
Wagner, Honus, 1936
Wallace, Bobby, 1953
Walsh, Ed, 1946
Waner, Lloyd, 1967
Waner, Paul, 1952
Ward, John Montgomery, 1964
Welch, Mickey, 1973
Wells, Willie, 1997
Wheat, Zack, 1959
Wilhelm, Hoyt, 1985

Williams, Billy, 1987
Williams, Ted, 1966
Willis, Vic, 1995
Wilson, Hack, 1979
Wynn, Early, 1972
Yastrzemski, Carl, 1989
Young, Cy, 1937
Youngs, Ross, 1972

MANAGERS

Alston, Walter, 1983
Durocher, Leo, 1994
Griffith, Clark, 1946
Hanlon, Ned, 1996
Harris, Bucky, 1975
Huggins, Miller, 1964
Lasorda, Tommy, 1997
Lopez, Al, 1977
Mack, Connie, 1937
McCarthy, Joe, 1957
McGraw, John, 1937
McKechnie, Bill, 1962
Robinson, Wilbert, 1945
Stengel, Casey, 1966
Weaver, Earl, 1996
Wright, George, 1937
Wright, Harry, 1953

UMPIRES

Barlick, Al, 1989
Conlan, Jocko, 1974
Connolly, Tommy, 1953
Evans, Billy, 1973
Hubbard, Cal, 1976
Klem, Bill, 1953
McGowan, Bill, 1992

EXECUTIVES

Barrow, Ed, 1953
Bulkeley, Morgan, 1937
Chandler, Happy, 1982
Frick, Ford, 1970
Giles, Warren, 1979
Harridge, Will, 1972
Johnson, Ban, 1937
Landis, Kenesaw, 1944
MacPhail, Larry, 1978
Rickey, Branch, 1967
Veeck, Bill, 1991
Weiss, George, 1971
Yawkey, Tom, 1980

ORGANIZERS

Cartwright, Alexander, 1938
Chadwick, Henry, 1938

FOUNDERS

Comiskey, Charley, 1939 (also a player)
Hulbert, William, 1995

☆ Chase's 1998 SPORTS Calendar of Events ☆

Pro Football Hall of Fame

Adderley, Herb, 1980
Alworth, Lance, 1978
Atkins, Doug, 1982
Badgro, Morris (Red), 1981
Barney, Lem, 1992
Battles, Cliff, 1968
Baugh, Sammy, 1963
Bednarik, Chuck, 1967
Bell, Bert, 1963
Bell, Bobby, 1983
Berry, Raymond, 1973
Bidwill, Charles W., 1967
Biletnikoff, Fred, 1988
Blanda, George, 1981
Blount, Mel, 1989
Bradshaw, Terry, 1989
Brown, Jim, 1971
Brown, Paul, 1967
Brown, Roosevelt, 1975
Brown, Willie, 1984
Buchanan, Buck, 1990
Butkus, Dick, 1979
Campbell, Earl, 1991
Canadeo, Tony, 1974
Carr, Joe, 1963
Chamberlin, Guy, 1965
Christiansen, Jack, 1970
Clark, Dutch, 1963
Connor, George, 1975
Conzelman, Jimmy, 1964
Creekmur, Lou, 1996
Csonka, Larry, 1987
Davis, Al, 1992
Davis, Willie, 1981
Dawson, Len, 1987
Dierdorf, Dan, 1996
Ditka, Mike, 1988
Donovan, Art, 1968
Dorsett, Tony, 1994
Driscoll, Paddy, 1965
Dudley, Bill, 1966
Edwards, Turk, 1969
Ewbank, Weeb, 1978
Fears, Tom, 1970
Finks, Jim, 1995
Flaherty, Ray, 1976
Ford, Len, 1976
Fortmann, Danny, 1965
Fouts, Dan, 1993
Gatski, Frank, 1985

George, Bill, 1974
Gibbs, Joe, 1996
Gifford, Frank, 1977
Gillman, Sid, 1983
Graham, Otto, 1965
Grange, Red, 1963
Grant, Bud, 1994
Greene, Joe, 1987
Gregg, Forrest, 1977
Griese, Bob, 1990
Groza, Lou, 1974
Guyon, Joe, 1966
Halas, George, 1963
Ham, Jack, 1988
Hannah, John, 1991
Harris, Franco, 1990
Haynes, Mike, 1997
Healey, Ed, 1964
Hein, Mel, 1963
Hendricks, Ted, 1990
Henry, Wilbur, 1963
Herber, Arnie, 1966
Hewitt, Bill, 1971
Hinkle, Clarke, 1964
Hirsch, Elroy (Crazy Legs), 1968
Hornung, Paul, 1986
Houston, Ken, 1986
Hubbard, Cal, 1963
Huff, Sam, 1982
Hunt, Lamar, 1972
Hutson, Don, 1963
Johnson, Jimmy, 1994
Johnson, John Henry, 1987
Joiner, Charlie, 1996
Jones, Deacon, 1980
Jones, Stan, 1991
Jordan, Henry, 1995
Jurgensen, Sonny, 1983
Kelly, Leroy, 1994
Kiesling, Walter, 1966
Kinard, Frank (Bruiser), 1971
Lambeau, Curly, 1963
Lambert, Jack, 1990
Landry, Tom, 1990
Lane, Dick (Night Train), 1974
Langer, Jim, 1987
Lanier, Willie, 1986

Largent, Steve, 1995
Lary, Yale, 1979
Lavelli, Dante, 1975
Layne, Bobby, 1967
Leemans, Tuffy, 1978
Lilly, Bob, 1980
Little, Larry, 1993
Lombardi, Vince, 1971
Luckman, Sid, 1965
Lyman, Roy (Link), 1964
Mackey, John, 1992
Mara, Tim, 1963
Mara, Wellington, 1997
Marchetti, Gino, 1972
Marshall, George Preston, 1963
Matson, Ollie, 1972
Maynard, Don, 1987
McAfee, George, 1966
McCormack, Mike, 1984
McElhenny, Hugh, 1970
McNally, Johnny (Blood), 1963
Michalske, August (Mike), 1964
Millner, Wayne, 1968
Mitchell, Bobby, 1983
Mix, Ron, 1979
Moore, Lenny, 1975
Motley, Marion, 1968
Musso, George, 1982
Nagurski, Bronko, 1963
Namath, Joe, 1985
Neale, Earle (Greasy), 1969
Nevers, Ernie, 1963
Nitschke, Ray, 1978
Noll, Chuck, 1993
Nomellini, Leo, 1969
Olsen, Merlin, 1982
Otto, Jim, 1980
Owen, Steve, 1966
Page, Alan, 1988
Parker, Clarence (Ace), 1972
Parker, Jim, 1973
Payton, Walton, 1993
Perry, Joe, 1969
Pihos, Pete, 1970
Ray, Hugh (Shorty), 1966
Reeves, Daniel F., 1967

Renfro, Mel, 1996
Riggins, John, 1992
Ringo, Jim, 1981
Robustelli, Andy, 1971
Rooney, Arthur J., 1964
Rozelle, Pete, 1985
Sayers, Gale, 1977
Schmidt, Joe, 1973
Schramm, Tex, 1991
Selmon, Lee Roy, 1995
Shell, Art, 1989
Shula, Don, 1997
Simpson, O.J., 1985
Smith, Jackie, 1994
St. Clair, Bob, 1990
Starr, Bart, 1977
Staubach, Roger, 1985
Stautner, Ernie, 1969
Stenerud, Jan, 1991
Strong, Ken, 1967
Stydahar, Joe, 1967
Tarkenton, Fran, 1986
Taylor, Charley, 1984
Taylor, Jim, 1976
Thorpe, Jim, 1963
Tittle, Y.A., 1971
Trafton, George, 1964
Trippi, Charlie, 1968
Tunnell, Emlen, 1967
Turner, Clyde (Bulldog), 1966
Unitas, John, 1979
Upshaw, Gene, 1987
Van Brocklin, Norm, 1971
Van Buren, Steve, 1965
Walker, Doak, 1986
Walsh, Bill, 1993
Warfield, Paul, 1983
Waterfield, Bob, 1965
Webster, Mike, 1997
Weinmeister, Arnie, 1984
White, Randy, 1994
Willis, Bill, 1977
Wilson, Larry, 1978
Winslow, Kellen, 1995
Wojciechowicz, Alex, 1968
Wood, Willie, 1989

Naismith Memorial Basketball Hall of Fame

PLAYERS
Abdul-Jabbar, Kareem, 1995
Archibald, Tiny, 1991
Arizin, Paul, 1977
Barlow, Tom, 1980
Barry, Rick, 1987
Baylor, Elgin, 1976
Beckman, John, 1972
Bellamy, Walt, 1993
Belov, Sergei, 1992

Bing, Dave, 1990
Blazejowski, Carol, 1994
Borgmann, Bennie, 1961
Bradley, Bill, 1982
Brennan, Joseph, 1974
Cervi, Al, 1984
Chamberlain, Wilt, 1978
Cooper, Chuck, 1976
Cosic, Kresimir, 1996
Cousy, Bob, 1970
Cowens, Dave, 1991

Crawford, Joan, 1997
Cunningham, Billy, 1986
Curry, Denise, 1997
Davies, Bob, 1969
DeBernardi, Forrest, 1961
DeBusschere, Dave, 1982
Dehnert, Dutch, 1968
Donovan, Anne, 1995
Endacott, Paul, 1971
English, Alex, 1997
Erving, Julius, 1993

Foster, Bud, 1964
Frazier, Walt, 1987
Friedman, Marty, 1971
Fulks, Joe, 1977
Gale, Laddie, 1976
Gallatin, Harry, 1991
Gates, William, 1989
Gervin, George, 1996
Gola, Tom, 1975
Goodrich, Gail, 1996
Greer, Hal, 1981

Gruenig, Ace, 1963
Hagan, Cliff, 1977
Hanson, Victor, 1960
Harris, Lusia, 1992
Havlicek, John, 1983
Hawkins, Connie, 1992
Hayes, Elvin, 1990
Heinsohn, Tommy, 1986
Holman, Nat, 1964
Houbregs, Bob, 1987
Howell, Bailey, 1997
Hyatt, Chuck, 1959
Issel, Dan, 1993
Jeannette, Buddy, 1994
Johnson, William, 1976
Johnston, Neil, 1990
Jones, K.C., 1989
Jones, Sam, 1983
Krause, Moose, 1975
Kurland, Bob, 1961
Lanier, Bob, 1992
Lapchick, Joe, 1966
Lieberman-Cline, Nancy, 1996
Lovellette, Clyde, 1988
Lucas, Jerry, 1979
Luisetti, Hank, 1959
McCracken, Branch, 1960
McCracken, Jack, 1962
McDermott, Bobby, 1988
Macauley, Ed, 1960
Maravich, Pete, 1987
Martin, Slater, 1981
McGuire, Dick, 1993
Meyers, Ann, 1993
Mikan, George, 1959
Mikkelsen, Vern, 1995
Miller, Cheryl, 1995
Monroe, Earl, 1990
Murphy, Calvin, 1993
Murphy, Stretch, 1960
Page, Pat, 1962
Pettit, Bob, 1970
Phillip, Andy, 1961
Pollard, Jim, 1977
Ramsey, Frank, 1981
Reed, Willis, 1981
Robertson, Oscar, 1979
Roosma, John, 1961

Russell, Honey, 1964
Russell, Bill, 1974
Schayes, Dolph, 1972
Schmidt, Ernest, 1973
Schommer, John, 1959
Sedran, Barney, 1962
Semenova, Juliana, 1993
Sharman, Bill, 1975
Steinmetz, Christian, 1961
Thompson, Cat, 1962
Thompson, David, 1996
Thurmond, Nate, 1984
Twyman, Jack, 1982
Unseld, Wes, 1988
Vandivier, Fuzzy, 1974
Wachter, Ed, 1961
Walton, Bill, 1993
Wanzer, Bobby, 1987
West, Jerry, 1979
White, Nera, 1992
Wilkens, Lenny, 1989
Wooden, John, 1960
Yardley, George, 1996

COACHES
Anderson, Harold, 1984
Auerbach, Red, 1968
Barry, Sam, 1978
Blood, Ernest, 1960
Cann, Howard, 1967
Carlson, Clifford, 1959
Carnesecca, Lou, 1992
Carnevale, Ben, 1969
Carril, Pete, 1997
Case, Everett, 1981
Crum, Denny, 1994
Daly, Chuck, 1994
Dean, Everett, 1966
Diaz-Miguel, Antonio, 1997
Diddle, Ed, 1971
Drake, Bruce, 1972
Gaines, Clarence, 1981
Gardner, Jack, 1983
Gill, Slats, 1967
Gomelsky, Alexandr, 1967
Harshman, Marv, 1984
Haskins, Don, 1997

Hickey, Eddie, 1978
Hobson, Howard, 1965
Holzman, Red, 1986
Iba, Henry, 1968
Julian, Doggie, 1967
Keaney, Frank, 1960
Keogan, George, 1961
Knight, Bob, 1991
Kundla, John, 1995
Lambert, Ward, 1960
Litwack, Harry, 1975
Loeffler, Kenny, 1964
Lonborg, Dutch, 1972
McCutchan, Arad, 1980
McGuire, Al, 1992
McGuire, Frank, 1976
Meanwell, Walter, 1959
Meyer, Ray, 1978
Miller, Ralph, 1988
Ramsay, Jack, 1992
Rubini, Cesare, 1994
Rupp, Adolph, 1968
Sachs, Leonard, 1961
Shelton, Everett, 1979
Smith, Dean, 1982
Taylor, Fred, 1985
Teague, Bertha, 1984
Wade, Margaret, 1984
Watts, Stanley, 1985
Wooden, John, 1972
Woolpert, Phil, 1992

CONTRIBUTORS
Abbott, Senda, 1984
Allen, Phog, 1959
Bee, Clair, 1967
Brown, Walter, 1965
Bunn, John, 1964
Douglas, Bob, 1971
Duer, Al, 1981
Fagan, Clifford, 1983
Fisher, Harry, 1973
Fleisher, Larry, 1991
Gottlieb, Eddie, 1971
Gulick, Luther, 1959
Harrison, Luther, 1979
Hepp, Ferenc, 1980
Hickox, Ed, 1959
Hinkle, Tony, 1965
Irish, Ned, 1964

Jones, William, 1964
Kennedy, Walter, 1980
Liston, Emil, 1974
McLendon, John, 1978
Mokray, Bill, 1965
Morgan, Ralph, 1959
Morgenweck, Frank, 1962
Naismith, James, 1959
Newell, Pete, 1978
O'Brien, John, 1961
O'Brien, Larry, 1991
Olsen, Harold, 1959
Podoloff, Maurice, 1973
Porter, H.V., 1960
Reid, William, 1963
Ripley, Elmer, 1972
St. John, Lynn, 1962
Saperstein, Abe, 1970
Schabinger, Arthur, 1961
Stagg, Amos Alonzo, 1959
Stankovich, Boris, 1991
Steitz, Ed, 1983
Taylor, Chuck, 1968
Tower, Oswald, 1959
Trester, Arthur, 1961
Wells, Clifford, 1971
Wilke, Lou, 1982

REFEREES
Enright, Jim, 1978
Hepbron, George, 1960
Hoyt, George, 1961
Kennedy, Matthew, 1959
Leith, Lloyd, 1982
Mihalik, Zigmund, 1986
Nucatola, John, 1977
Quigley, Ernest, 1961
Shirley, Dallas, 1979
Strom, Earl, 1995
Tobey, David, 1961
Walsh, David, 1961

TEAMS
First Team, 1959
Original Celtics, 1959
Buffalo Germans, 1961
Renaissance, 1963

Hockey Hall of Fame

PLAYERS
Abel, Sid, 1969
Adams, Jack, 1959
Apps, Syl, 1961
Armstrong, George, 1975
Bailey, Ace, 1975
Bain, Dan, 1945
Baker, Hobey, 1945
Barber, Bill, 1990
Barry, Marty, 1965
Bathgate, Andy, 1978
Bauer, Bobby, 1996
Beliveau, Jean, 1972
Benedict, Clint, 1965

Bentley, Doug, 1964
Bentley, Max, 1966
Blake, Toe, 1966
Boivin, Leo, 1986
Boon, Dickie, 1952
Bossy, Mike, 1991
Bouchard, Butch, 1966
Boucher, Frank, 1958
Boucher, George, 1960
Bower, Johnny, 1976
Bowie, Russell, 1945
Brimsek, Frank, 1966
Broadbent, Punch, 1962
Broda, Turk, 1967

Bucyk, John, 1981
Burch, Billy, 1974
Cameron, Harry, 1962
Cheevers, Gerry, 1985
Clancy, King, 1958
Clapper, Dit, 1947
Clarke, Bobby, 1987
Cleghorn, Sprague, 1958
Colville, Neil, 1967
Conacher, Charlie, 1961
Conacher, Lionel, 1994
Connell, Alex, 1958
Cook, Bill, 1952
Cook, Bun, 1995

Coulter, Art, 1974
Cournoyer, Yvan, 1982
Cowley, Bill, 1968
Crawford, Rusty, 1962
Darragh, Jack, 1962
Davidson, Scotty, 1950
Day, Hap, 1961
Delvecchio, Alex, 1977
Denneny, Cy, 1959
Dionne, Marcel, 1992
Drillon, Gord, 1975
Drinkwater, Graham, 1950
Dryden, Ken, 1983

Dumart, Woody, 1992
Dunderdale, Tommy, 1974
Durnan, Bill, 1964
Dutton, Red, 1958
Dye, Babe, 1970
Esposito, Phil, 1984
Esposito, Tony, 1988
Farrell, Arthur, 1965
Flaman, Fern, 1990
Foyston, Frank, 1958
Fredrickson, Frank, 1958
Gadsby, Bill, 1970
Gainey, Bob, 1992
Gardiner, Chuck, 1945
Gardiner, Herb, 1958
Gardner, Jimmy, 1962
Geoffrion, Bernie, 1972
Gerard, Eddie, 1945
Giacomin, Eddie, 1987
Gilbert, Rod, 1982
Gilmour, Billy, 1962
Goheen, Moose, 1952
Goodfellow, Ebbie, 1963
Grant, Mike, 1950
Green, Shorty, 1962
Griffis, Si, 1950
Hainsworth, George, 1961
Hall, Glenn, 1975
Hall, Joe, 1961
Harvey, Doug, 1973
Hay, George, 1958
Hern, Riley, 1962
Hextall, Bryan, 1969
Holmes, Hap, 1972
Hooper, Tom, 1962
Horner, Red, 1965
Horton, Tim, 1977
Howe, Gordie, 1972
Howe, Syd, 1965
Howell, Harry, 1979
Hull, Bobby, 1983
Hutton, Bouse, 1962
Hyland, Harry, 1962
Irvin, Dick, 1958
Jackson, Busher, 1971
Johnson, Ching, 1958
Johnson, Moose, 1952
Johnson, Tom, 1970
Joliat, Aurel, 1947
Keats, Duke, 1958
Kelly, Red, 1969
Kennedy, Ted, 1966
Keon, Dave, 1986
Lach, Elmer, 1966
Lafleur, Guy, 1988
Lalonde, Newsy, 1950
Laperriere, Jacques, 1987
Lapointe, Guy, 1993
Laprade, Edgar, 1993
Laviolette, Jack, 1962
Lehman, Hughie, 1958
Lemaire, Jacques, 1984
LeSueur, Percy, 1961
Lewis, Herbie, 1989
Lindsay, Ted, 1966
Lumley, Harry, 1980
MacKay, Mickey, 1952

Mahovlich, Frank, 1981
Malone, Joe, 1950
Mantha, Sylvio, 1960
Marshall, Jack, 1965
Maxwell, Fred, 1962
McDonald, Lanny, 1992
McGee, Frank, 1945
McGimsie, Billy, 1962
McNamara, George, 1958
Mikita, Stan, 1983
Moore, Dickie, 1974
Moran, Paddy, 1958
Morenz, Howie, 1945
Mosienko, Bill, 1965
Nighbor, Frank, 1947
Noble, Reg, 1962
O'Connor, Buddy, 1988
Oliver, Harry, 1967
Olmstead, Bert, 1985
Orr, Bobby, 1979
Parent, Bernie, 1984
Park, Brad, 1988
Patrick, Lester, 1947
Patrick, Lynn, 1980
Perreault, Gilbert, 1990
Phillips, Tommy, 1945
Pilote, Pierre, 1975
Pitre, Didier, 1962
Plante, Jacques, 1978
Potvin, Denis, 1991
Pratt, Babe, 1966
Primeau, Joe, 1963
Pronovost, Marcel, 1978
Pulford, Bob, 1991
Pulford, Harvey, 1945
Quackenbush, Bill, 1976
Rankin, Frank, 1961
Ratelle, Jean, 1985
Rayner, Chuck, 1973
Reardon, Ken, 1966
Richard, Henri, 1979
Richard, Maurice, 1961
Richardson, George, 1950
Roberts, Gordon, 1971
Robinson, Larry, 1995
Ross, Art, 1945
Russell, Blair, 1965
Russell, Ernie, 1965
Ruttan, Jack, 1962
Salming, Borje, 1996
Savard, Serge, 1986
Sawchuk, Terry, 1971
Scanlan, Fred, 1965
Schmidt, Milt, 1961
Schriner, Sweeney, 1962
Seibert, Earl, 1963
Seibert, Oliver, 1961
Shore, Eddie, 1947
Shutt, Steve, 1993
Siebert, Babe, 1964
Simpson, Joe, 1962
Sittler, Darryl, 1989
Smith, Alf, 1962
Smith, Billy, 1993
Smith, Clint, 1991
Smith, Hooley, 1972
Smith, Tommy, 1973
Stanley, Allan, 1981

Stanley, Barney, 1962
Stewart, Jack, 1964
Stewart, Nels, 1962
Stuart, Bruce, 1961
Stuart, Hod, 1945
Taylor, Cyclone, 1947
Thompson, Tiny, 1959
Tretiak, Vladislav, 1989
Trihey, Harry, 1950
Ullman, Norm, 1982
Vezina, Georges, 1945
Walker, Jack, 1960
Walsh, Marty, 1962
Watson, Harry E., 1962
Watson, Harry P., 1994
Weiland, Cooney, 1971
Westwick, Harry, 1962
Whitcroft, Frederick, 1962
Wilson, Gord, 1962
Worsley, Gump, 1980
Worters, Roy, 1969

BUILDERS
Adams, Charles F., 1960
Adams, Weston W., 1972
Ahearn, Frank, 1962
Ahearne, Bunny, 1977
Allan, Sir Montagu, 1945
Allen, Keith, 1992
Arbour, Al, 1996
Ballard, Harold, 1977
Bauer, Father David, 1989
Bickell, J.P., 1978
Bowman, Scottie, 1991
Brown, George V., 1961
Brown, Walter A., 1962
Buckland, Frank, 1975
Butterfield, Jack, 1980
Calder, Frank, 1947
Campbell, Angus, 1964
Campbell, Clarence, 1966
Cattarinich, Joseph, 1977
Dandurand, Leo, 1963
Dilio, Frank, 1964
Dudley, George, 1958
Dunn, Jimmy, 1968
Eagleson, Alan, 1982
Francis, Emile, 1982
Gibson, Jack, 1976
Gorman, Tommy, 1963
Griffiths, Frank, 1993
Hanley, Bill, 1986
Hay, Charles, 1974
Hendy, Jim, 1968
Hewitt, Foster, 1965
Hewitt, William, 1947
Hume, Fred, 1962
Imlach, Punch, 1984
Ivan, Tommy, 1974
Jennings, Bill, 1975
Johnson, Bob, 1992
Juckes, Gordon, 1979
Kilpatrick, General J.R., 1960
Knox, Seymour III, 1993
Leader, Al, 1969

LeBel, Bob, 1970
Lockhart, Tommy, 1965
Loicq, Paul, 1961
Mariucci, John, 1985
Mathers, Frank, 1992
McLaughlin, Major Frederic, 1963
Milford, Jake, 1984
Molson, Senator Hartland De Montarville, 1973
Nelson, Francis, 1947
Norris, Bruce, 1969
Norris, James, 1958
Norris, James D., 1962
Northey, William, 1947
O'Brien, J. Ambrose, 1962
O'Neil, Brian, 1994
Page, Fred, 1993
Patrick, Frank, 1958
Pickard, Allan, 1958
Pilous, Rudy, 1985
Poile, Bud, 1990
Pollock, Sam, 1978
Raymond, Senator Donat, 1958
Robertson, John Ross, 1947
Robinson, Claude, 1947
Ross, Philip, 1976
Sabetzki, Gunther, 1995
Selke, Frank, 1960
Sinden, Harry, 1983
Smith, Frank, 1962
Smyth, Conn, 1958
Snider, Ed, 1988
Stanley of Preston, Lord, 1945
Sutherland, Captain James, 1947
Tarasov, Anatoli, 1974
Torrey, Bill, 1995
Turner, Lloyd, 1958
Tutt, Thayer, 1978
Voss, Carl, 1974
Waghorne, Fred, 1961
Wirtz, Arthur, 1971
Wirtz, Bill, 1976
Ziegler, John, 1987

REFEREES/LINESMEN
Armstrong, Neil, 1991
Ashley, John, 1981
Chadwick, Bill, 1964
D'Amico, John, 1993
Elliott, Chaucer, 1961
Hayes, George, 1988
Hewitson, Bobby, 1963
Ion, Mickey, 1961
Pavelich, Marty, 1987
Rodden, Mike, 1962
Smeaton, Cooper, 1961
Storey, Red, 1967
Udvari, Frank, 1973

PGA/World Golf Hall of Fame

MEN
Anderson, Willie, 1975
Armour, Tommy, 1976
Ball, John Jr, 1977
Barnes, Jim, 1989
Boros, Julius, 1982
Braid, James, 1976
Casper, Billy, 1978
Cooper, Lighthouse
  Harry, 1992
Cotton, Thomas, 1980
Demaret, Jimmy, 1983
DeVincenzo, Roberto,
  1989
Evans, Chick, 1975
Floyd, Ray, 1989
Guldahl, Ralph, 1981
Hagen, Walter, 1974

Hilton, Harold, 1978
Hogan, Ben, 1974
Irwin, Hale, 1992
Jones, Bobby, 1974
Little, Lawson, 1980
Littler, Gene, 1990
Locke, Bobby, 1977
Middlecoff, Cary, 1986
Morris, Tom Jr, 1975
Morris, Tom Sr, 1976
Nelson, Byron, 1974
Nicklaus, Jack, 1974
Ouimet, Francis, 1974
Palmer, Arnold, 1974
Player, Gary, 1974
Runyan, Paul, 1990
Sarazen, Gene, 1974
Smith, Horton, 1990

Snead, Sam, 1974
Taylor, John H, 1975
Thomson, Peter, 1988
Travers, Jerry, 1976
Travis, Walter, 1979
Trevino, Lee, 1981
Vardon, Harry, 1974
Watson, Tom, 1988

WOMEN
Berg, Patty, 1974
Carner, JoAnne, 1985
Howe, Dorothy C.H., 1978
Lopez, Nancy, 1989
Rawls, Betsy, 1987
Suggs, Louise, 1979
Vare, Glenna Collett,
  1975

Wethered, Joyce, 1975
Whitworth, Kathy, 1982
Wright, Mickey, 1976
Zaharias, Babe
  Didrikson, 1974

CONTRIBUTORS
Campbell, William, 1990
Corcoran, Fred, 1975
Crosby, Bing, 1978
Dey, Joe, 1975
Graffis, Herb, 1977
Harlow, Robert, 1988
Hope, Bob, 1983
Jones, Robert Trent, 1987
Rodriguez, Chi Chi, 1992
Ross, Donald, 1977
Tufts, Richard, 1992

LPGA Hall of Fame

PLAYERS
Berg, Patty, 1951
Bradley, Pat, 1991
Carner, JoAnne, 1982
Haynie, Sandra, 1977

Jameson, Betty, 1951
King, Betsy, 1995
Lopez, Nancy, 1987
Mann, Carol, 1977
Rawls, Betsy, 1960

Sheehan, Patty, 1993
Suggs, Louise, 1951
Whitworth, Kathy, 1975
Wright, Mickey, 1964

Zaharias, Babe
  Didrikson, 1951

CONTRIBUTOR
Shore, Dinah, 1994

ANNUAL SPORTS AWARD WINNERS

Associated Press Athlete of the Year

YEAR	MALE
1931	Pepper Martin, baseball
1932	Gene Sarazen, golf
1933	Carl Hubbell, baseball
1934	Dizzy Dean, baseball
1935	Joe Louis, boxing
1936	Jesse Owens, track
1937	Don Budge, tennis
1938	Don Budge, tennis
1939	Nile Kinnick, football
1940	Tom Harmon, football
1941	Joe DiMaggio, baseball
1942	Frank Sinkwich, football
1943	Gunder Haegg, track
1944	Byron Nelson, golf
1945	Byron Nelson, golf
1946	Glenn Davis, football
1947	Johnny Lujack, football
1948	Lou Boudreau, baseball
1949	Leon Hart, football
1950	Jim Konstanty, baseball
1951	Dick Kazmaier, football
1952	Bob Mathias, track
1953	Ben Hogan, golf
1954	Willie Mays, baseball
1955	Hopalong Cassady, football
1956	Mickey Mantle, baseball
1957	Ted Williams, baseball
1958	Herb Elliot, track
1959	Ingemar Johansson, boxing
1960	Rafer Johnson, track
1961	Roger Maris, baseball
1962	Maury Wills, baseball
1963	Sandy Koufax, baseball
1964	Don Schollander, swimming
1965	Sandy Koufax, baseball
1966	Frank Robinson, baseball
1967	Carl Yastrzemski, baseball
1968	Denny McLain, baseball
1969	Tom Seaver, baseball
1970	George Blanda, football
1971	Lee Trevino, golf
1972	Mark Spitz, swimming
1973	O.J. Simpson, football
1974	Muhammad Ali, boxing
1975	Fred Lynn, baseball
1976	Bruce Jenner, track
1977	Steve Cauthen, horse racing
1978	Ron Guidry, baseball
1979	Willie Stargell, baseball
1980	US Olympic hockey team
1981	John McEnroe, tennis
1982	Wayne Gretzky, hockey
1983	Carl Lewis, track
1984	Carl Lewis, track
1985	Dwight Gooden, baseball
1986	Larry Bird, basketball
1987	Ben Johnson, track
1988	Orel Hershiser, baseball
1989	Joe Montana, football
1990	Joe Montana, football
1991	Michael Jordan, basketball
1992	Michael Jordan, basketball
1993	Michael Jordan, basketball
1994	George Foreman, boxing
1995	Cal Ripken, baseball
1996	Michael Johnson, track

YEAR	FEMALE
1931	Helene Madison, swimming
1932	Babe Didrikson, track
1933	Helen Jacobs, tennis
1934	Virginia Van Wie, golf
1935	Helen Wills Moody, tennis
1936	Helen Stephens, track
1937	Katherine Rawls, swimming
1937	Patty Berg, golf
1939	Alice Marble, tennis
1940	Alice Marble, tennis
1941	Betty Hicks Newell, golf
1942	Gloria Callen, swimming
1943	Patty Berg, golf
1944	Ann Curtis, swimming
1945	Babe Didrikson Zaharias, golf
1946	Babe Didrikson Zaharias, golf
1947	Babe Didrikson Zaharias, golf
1948	Fanny Blankers-Koen, track
1949	Marlene Bauer, golf
1950	Babe Didrikson Zaharias, golf
1951	Maureen Connolly, tennis
1952	Maureen Connolly, tennis
1953	Maureen Connolly, tennis
1954	Babe Didrikson Zaharias, golf
1955	Patty Berg, golf
1956	Pat McCormick, diving
1957	Althea Gibson, tennis
1958	Althea Gibson, tennis
1959	Maria Bueno, tennis
1960	Wilma Rudolph, track
1961	Wilma Rudolph, track
1962	Dawn Fraser, swimming
1963	Mickey Wright, golf
1964	Mickey Wright, golf
1965	Kathy Whitworth, golf
1966	Kathy Whitworth, golf
1967	Billie Jean King, tennis
1968	Peggy Fleming, skating
1969	Debbie Meyer, swimming
1970	Chi Cheng, track
1971	Evonne Goolagong, tennis
1972	Olga Korbut, gymnastics
1973	Billie Jean King, tennis
1974	Chris Evert, tennis
1975	Chris Evert, tennis
1976	Nadia Comaneci, gymnastics
1977	Chris Evert, tennis
1978	Nancy Lopez, golf
1979	Tracy Austin, tennis
1980	Chris Evert Lloyd, tennis
1981	Tracy Austin, tennis
1982	Mary Decker Tabb, track
1983	Martina Navratilova, tennis
1984	Mary Lou Retton, gymnastics
1985	Nancy Lopez, golf
1986	Martina Navratilova, tennis
1987	Jackie Joyner-Kersee, track
1988	Florence Griffith Joyner, track
1989	Steffi Graf, tennis
1990	Beth Daniel, golf
1991	Monica Seles, tennis
1992	Monica Seles, tennis
1993	Sheryl Swoopes, basketball
1994	Bonnie Blair, speed skating
1995	Rebecca Lobo, basketball
1996	Amy Van Dyken, swimming

James E. Sullivan Memorial Award

YEAR	WINNER
1930	Bobby Jones, golf
1931	Barney Berlinger, track
1932	Jim Bausch, track
1933	Glenn Cunningham, track
1934	Bill Bonthron, track
1935	Lawson Little, golf
1936	Glenn Morris, track
1937	Don Budge, tennis
1938	Don Lash, track
1939	Joe Burk, rowing
1940	Greg Rice, track
1941	Leslie MacMitchell, track
1942	Cornelius Warmerdam, track
1943	Gilbert Dodds, track
1944	Ann Curtis, swimming
1945	Doc Blanchard, football
1946	Arnold Tucker, football
1947	John B. Kelly, Jr, rowing
1948	Bob Mathias, track
1949	Dick Button, skating
1950	Fred Wilt, track
1951	Bob Richards, track
1952	Horace Ashenfelter, track
1953	Sammy Lee, diving
1954	Mal Whitfield, track
1955	Harrison Dillard, track
1956	Pat McCormick, diving
1957	Bobby Morrow, track
1958	Glenn Davis, track
1959	Parry O'Brien, track
1960	Rafer Johnson, track
1961	Wilma Rudolph, track

☆ *Chase's 1998 SPORTS Calendar of Events* ☆

YEAR	WINNER
1962	James Beatty, track
1963	John Pennel, track
1964	Don Schollander, swimming
1965	Bill Bradley, basketball
1966	Jim Ryun, track
1967	Randy Matson, track
1968	Debbie Meyer, swimming
1969	Bill Toomey, track
1970	John Kinsella, swimming
1971	Mark Spitz, swimming
1972	Frank Shorter, track
1973	Bill Walton, basketball
1974	Rick Wohlhuter, track
1975	Tim Shaw, swimming
1976	Bruce Jenner, track
1977	John Naber, swimming
1978	Tracy Caulkins, swimming
1979	Kurt Thomas, gymnastics
1980	Eric Heiden, speed skating
1981	Carl Lewis, track
1982	Mary Decker, track
1983	Edwin Moses, track
1984	Greg Louganis, diving
1985	Joan Benoit Samuelson, track
1986	Jackie Joyner-Kersee, track
1987	Jim Abbott, baseball
1988	Florence Griffith Joyner, track
1989	Janet Evans, swimming
1990	John Smith, wrestling
1991	Mike Powell, track
1992	Bonnie Blair, speed skating
1993	Charlie Ward, football
1994	Dan Jansen, speed skating
1995	Bruce Baumgartner, wrestling
1996	Michael Johnson, track

The Sporting News Sportsman of the Year

YEAR	WINNER
1968	Denny McLain, baseball
1969	Tom Seaver, baseball
1970	John Wooden, basketball
1971	Lee Trevino, golf
1972	Charles O. Finley, baseball
1973	O.J. Simpson, football
1974	Lou Brock, baseball
1975	Archie Griffin, football
1976	Larry O'Brien, basketball
1977	Steve Cauthen, horse racing
1978	Ron Guidry, baseball
1979	Willie Stargell, baseball
1980	George Brett, baseball
1981	Wayne Gretzky, hockey
1982	Whitey Herzog, baseball
1983	Bowie Kuhn, baseball
1984	Peter Ueberroth, Los Angeles Oympics
1985	Pete Rose, baseball
1986	Larry Bird, basketball
1987	no award
1988	Jackie Joyner-Kersee, track
1989	Joe Montana, football
1990	Nolan Ryan, baseball
1991	Michael Jordan, basketball
1992	Mike Krzyzewski, basketball
1993	Cito Gaston and Pat Gillick, baseball
1994	Emmitt Smith, football
1995	Cal Ripken, baseball
1996	Joe Torre, baseball

Sports Illustrated Sportsman of the Year

YEAR	WINNER
1954	Roger Bannister, track
1955	Johnny Podres, baseball
1956	Bobby Morrow, track
1957	Stan Musial, baseball
1958	Rafer Johnson, track
1959	Ingemar Johansson, boxing
1960	Arnold Palmer, golf
1961	Jerry Lucas, basketball
1962	Terry Baker, football
1963	Pete Rozelle, football
1964	Ken Venturi, golf
1965	Sandy Koufax, baseball
1966	Jim Ryun, track
1967	Carl Yastrzemski, baseball
1968	Bill Russell, basketball
1969	Tom Seaver, baseball
1970	Bobby Orr, hockey
1971	Lee Trevino, golf
1972	Billie Jean King, tennis
1973	John Wooden, basketball / Jackie Stewart, auto racing
1974	Muhammad Ali, boxing
1975	Pete Rose, baseball
1976	Chris Evert, tennis
1977	Steve Cauthen, horse racing
1978	Jack Nicklaus, golf
1979	Terry Bradshaw, football / Willie Stargell, baseball
1980	US Olympic hockey team
1981	Sugar Ray Leonard, boxing
1982	Wayne Gretzky, hockey
1983	Mary Decker, track
1984	Mary Lou Retton, gymnastics / Edwin Moses, track
1985	Kareem Abdul-Jabbar, basketball
1986	Joe Paterno, football
1987	"8 Athletes Who Care": Bob Bourne, hockey / Kip Keino, track / Judi Brown King, track / Dale Murphy, baseball / Chip Rives, football / Patty Sheehan, golf / Rory Sparrow, basketball / Reggie Williams, football
1988	Orel Hershiser, baseball
1989	Greg LeMond, cycling
1990	Joe Montana, football
1991	Michael Jordan, basketball
1992	Arthur Ashe, tennis
1993	Don Shula, football
1994	Bonnie Blair, speed skating / Johan Olav Koss, speed skating
1995	Cal Ripken, baseball
1996	Tiger Woods, golf

Heisman Trophy

YEAR	WINNER
1935	Jay Berwanger, Chicago, QB
1936	Larry Kelley, Yale, E
1937	Clint Frank, Yale, HB
1938	Davey O'Brien, TCU, QB
1939	Nile Kinnick, Iowa, HB
1940	Tom Harmon, Michigan, HB
1941	Bruce Smith, Minnesota, HB
1942	Frank Sinkwich, Georgia, TB
1943	Angelo Bertelli, Notre Dame, QB
1944	Les Horvath, Ohio State, TB-QB
1945	Doc Blanchard, Army, FB
1946	Glenn Davis, Army, HB
1947	Johnny Lujack, Notre Dame, QB
1948	Doak Walker, SMU, HB
1949	Leon Hart, Notre Dame, E
1950	Vic Janowicz, Ohio State, HB
1951	Dick Kazmaier, Princeton, TB

☆ *Chase's 1998 SPORTS Calendar of Events* ☆

YEAR	WINNER
1952	Billy Vessels, Oklahoma, HB
1953	Johnny Lattner, Notre Dame, HB
1954	Alan Ameche, Wisconsin, FB
1955	Howard Cassady, Ohio State, HB
1956	Paul Hornung, Notre Dame, QB
1957	John David Crow, Texas A&M, HB
1958	Pete Dawkins, Army, HB
1959	Billy Cannon, LSU, HB
1960	Joe Bellino, Navy, QB
1961	Ernie Davis, Syracuse, HB
1962	Terry Baker, Oregon State, QB
1963	Roger Staubach, Navy, QB
1964	John Huarte, Notre Dame, QB
1965	Mike Garrett, USC, HB
1966	Steve Spurrier, Florida, QB
1967	Gary Beban, UCLA, QB
1968	O.J. Simpson, USC, HB
1969	Steve Owens, Oklahoma, HB
1970	Jim Plunkett, Stanford, QB
1971	Pat Sullivan, Auburn, QB
1972	Johnny Rodgers, Nebraska, FL
1973	John Cappelletti, Penn State, RB
1974	Archie Griffin, Ohio State, RB
1975	Archie Griffin, Ohio State, RB
1976	Tony Dorsett, Pittsburgh, RB
1977	Earl Campbell, Texas, RB
1978	Billy Sims, Oklahoma, RB
1979	Charles White, USC, RB
1980	George Rogers, South Carolina, RB
1981	Marcus Allen, USC, RB
1982	Herschel Walker, Georgia, RB
1983	Mike Rozier, Nebraska, RB
1984	Doug Flutie, Boston College, QB
1985	Bo Jackson, Auburn, RB
1986	Vinny Testaverde, Miami (FL), QB
1987	Tim Brown, Notre Dame, WR
1988	Barry Sanders, Oklahoma State, RB
1989	Andre Ware, Houston, QB
1990	Ty Detmer, BYU, QB
1991	Desmond Howard, Michigan, WR
1992	Gino Torretta, Miami (FL), QB
1993	Charlie Ward, Florida State, QB
1994	Rashaan Salaam, Colorado, RB
1995	Eddie George, Ohio State, RB
1996	Danny Wuerffel, Florida, QB

CHAMPIONSHIPS: TEAM AND INDIVIDUAL

World Series

YEAR	WINNER	LOSER	GAMES	YEAR	WINNER	LOSER	GAMES
1903	Boston AL	Pittsburgh NL	5–3	1950	New York AL	Philadelphia NL	4–0
1904	No series played			1951	New York AL	New York NL	4–2
1905	New York NL	Philadelphia AL	4–1	1952	New York AL	Brooklyn NL	4–3
1906	Chicago AL	Chicago NL	4–2	1953	New York AL	Brooklyn NL	4–2
1907	Chicago NL	Detroit AL	4–0*	1954	New York NL	Cleveland AL	4–0
1908	Chicago NL	Detroit AL	4–1	1955	Brooklyn NL	New York AL	4–3
1909	Pittsburgh NL	Detroit AL	4–3	1956	New York AL	Brooklyn NL	4–3
1910	Philadelphia AL	Chicago NL	4–1	1957	Milwaukee NL	New York AL	4–3
1911	Philadelphia AL	New York NL	4–2	1958	New York AL	Milwaukee NL	4–3
1912	Boston AL	New York NL	4–3*	1959	Los Angeles NL	Chicago AL	4–2
1913	Philadelphia AL	New York NL	4–1	1960	Pittsburgh NL	New York AL	4–3
1914	Boston NL	Philadelphia AL	4–0	1961	New York AL	Cincinnati NL	4–1
1915	Boston AL	Philadelphia NL	4–1	1962	New York AL	San Francisco NL	4–3
1916	Boston AL	Brooklyn NL	4–1	1963	Los Angeles NL	New York AL	4–0
1917	Chicago AL	New York NL	4–2	1964	St. Louis NL	New York AL	4–3
1918	Boston AL	Chicago NL	4–2	1965	Los Angeles NL	Minnesota AL	4–3
1919	Cincinnati NL	Chicago AL	5–3	1966	Baltimore AL	Los Angeles NL	4–0
1920	Cleveland AL	Brooklyn NL	5–2	1967	St. Louis NL	Boston AL	4–3
1921	New York NL	New York AL	5–3	1968	Detroit AL	St. Louis NL	4–3
1922	New York NL	New York AL	4–0*	1969	New York NL	Baltimore AL	4–1
1923	New York AL	New York NL	4–2	1970	Baltimore AL	Cincinnati NL	4–1
1924	Washington AL	New York NL	4–3	1971	Pittsburgh NL	Baltimore AL	4–3
1925	Pittsburgh NL	Washington AL	4–3	1972	Oakland AL	Cincinnati NL	4–3
1926	St. Louis NL	New York AL	4–3	1973	Oakland AL	New York NL	4–3
1927	New York AL	Pittsburgh NL	4–0	1974	Oakland AL	Los Angeles NL	4–1
1928	New York AL	St. Louis NL	4–0	1975	Cincinnati NL	Boston AL	4–3
1929	Philadelphia AL	Chicago NL	4–1	1976	Cincinnati NL	New York AL	4–0
1930	Philadelphia AL	St. Louis NL	4–2	1977	New York AL	Los Angeles NL	4–2
1931	St. Louis NL	Philadelphia AL	4–3	1978	New York AL	Los Angeles NL	4–2
1932	New York AL	Chicago NL	4–0	1979	Pittsburgh NL	Baltimore AL	4–3
1933	New York NL	Washington AL	4–1	1980	Philadelphia NL	Kansas City AL	4–2
1934	St. Louis NL	Detroit AL	4–3	1981	Los Angeles NL	New York AL	4–2
1935	Detroit AL	Chicago NL	4–2	1982	St. Louis NL	Milwaukee AL	4–3
1936	New York AL	New York NL	4–2	1983	Baltimore AL	Philadelphia NL	4–1
1937	New York AL	New York NL	4–1	1984	Detroit AL	San Diego NL	4–1
1938	New York AL	Chicago NL	4–0	1985	Kansas City AL	St. Louis NL	4–3
1939	New York AL	Cincinnati NL	4–0	1986	New York NL	Boston AL	4–3
1940	Cincinnati NL	Detroit AL	4–3	1987	Minnesota AL	St. Louis NL	4–3
1941	New York AL	Brooklyn NL	4–1	1988	Los Angeles NL	Oakland AL	4–1
1942	St. Louis NL	New York AL	4–1	1989	Oakland AL	San Francisco NL	4–0
1943	New York AL	St. Louis NL	4–1	1990	Cincinnati NL	Oakland AL	4–0
1944	St. Louis NL	St. Louis AL	4–2	1991	Minnesota AL	Atlanta NL	4–3
1945	Detroit AL	Chicago NL	4–3	1992	Toronto AL	Atlanta NL	4–2
1946	St. Louis NL	Boston AL	4–3	1993	Toronto AL	Philadelphia NL	4–2
1947	New York AL	Brooklyn NL	4–3	1994	Series canceled		
1948	Cleveland AL	Boston NL	4–2	1995	Atlanta NL	Cleveland AL	4–2
1949	New York AL	Brooklyn NL	4–1	1996	New York AL	Atlanta NL	4–2

* One tie

Super Bowl

GAME	DATE	PLACE	WINNER	LOSER	SCORE
I	January 15, 1967	Los Angeles	Green Bay NFL	Kansas City AFL	35–10
II	January 14, 1968	Miami	Green Bay NFL	Oakland AFL	33–14
III	January 12, 1969	Miami	New York AFL	Baltimore NFL	16–7
IV	January 11, 1970	New Orleans	Kansas City AFL	Minnesota NFL	23–7
V	January 17, 1971	Miami	Baltimore AFC	Dallas NFC	16–13
VI	January 16, 1972	New Orleans	Dallas NFC	Miami AFC	24–3
VII	January 14, 1973	Los Angeles	Miami AFC	Washington NFC	14–7
VIII	January 13, 1974	Houston	Miami AFC	Minnesota NFC	24–7
IX	January 12, 1975	New Orleans	Pittsburgh AFC	Minnesota NFC	16–6
X	January 18, 1976	Miami	Pittsburgh AFC	Dallas NFC	21–17
XI	January 9, 1977	Pasadena	Oakland AFC	Minnesota NFC	32–14
XII	January 15, 1978	New Orleans	Dallas NFC	Denver AFC	27–10
XIII	January 21, 1979	Miami	Pittsburgh AFC	Dallas NFC	35–31
XIV	January 20, 1980	Pasadena	Pittsburgh AFC	Los Angeles NFC	31–19
XV	January 25, 1981	New Orleans	Oakland AFC	Philadelphia NFC	27–10
XVI	January 24, 1982	Pontiac, MI	San Francisco NFC	Cincinnati AFC	26–21
XVII	January 30, 1983	Pasadena	Washington NFC	Miami AFC	27–17
XVIII	January 22, 1984	Tampa	Los Angeles AFC	Washington NFC	38–9
XIX	January 20, 1985	Stanford, CA	San Francisco NFC	Miami AFC	38–16
XX	January 26, 1986	New Orleans	Chicago NFC	New England AFC	46–10
XXI	January 25, 1987	Pasadena	New York NFC	Denver AFC	39–20
XXII	January 31, 1988	San Diego	Washington NFC	Denver AFC	42–10
XXIII	January 22, 1989	Miami	San Francisco NFC	Cincinnati AFC	20–16
XXIV	January 28, 1990	New Orleans	San Francisco NFC	Denver AFC	55–10
XXV	January 27, 1991	Tampa	New York NFC	Buffalo AFC	20–19
XXVI	January 26, 1992	Minneapolis	Washington NFC	Buffalo AFC	37–24
XXVII	January 31, 1993	Pasadena	Dallas NFC	Buffalo AFC	52–17
XXVIII	January 30, 1994	Atlanta	Dallas NFC	Buffalo AFC	30–13
XXIX	January 29, 1995	Miami	San Francisco NFC	San Diego AFC	49–26
XXX	January 28, 1996	Tempe, AZ	Dallas NFC	Pittsburgh AFC	27–17
XXXI	January 26, 1997	New Orleans, LA	Green Bay NFC	New England AFC	35–21

College Football National Championship

Selected by: the Helms Athletic Foundation (1883–1935); the Dickinson System (1924–40); the Associated Press (1936–   ); United Press (1950–57); International News Service (1952–57); United Press International (1958–90), the Football Writers Association of America (1954–   ); the National Football Foundation and Hall of Fame (1959–   ); and *USA Today*/CNN (1991–   ). In 1991, the UPI poll merged with the NFF–Hall of Fame poll, and the American Football Coaches Association switched its poll from UPI to *USA Today*/CNN.

YEAR	TEAM				
1883	Yale	1899	Harvard	1916	Pittsburgh
1884	Yale	1900	Yale	1917	Georgia Tech
1885	Princeton	1901	Michigan	1918	Pittsburgh
1886	Yale	1902	Michigan	1919	Harvard
1887	Yale	1903	Princeton	1920	California
1888	Yale	1904	Penn	1921	Cornell
1889	Princeton	1905	Chicago	1922	Cornell
1890	Harvard	1906	Princeton	1923	Illinois
1891	Yale	1907	Yale	1924	Notre Dame
1892	Yale	1908	Penn	1925	Alabama (H)
1893	Princeton	1909	Yale		Dartmouth (D)
1894	Yale	1910	Harvard	1926	Alabama (H)
1895	Penn	1911	Princeton		Stanford (D)
1896	Princeton	1912	Harvard	1927	Illinois
1897	Penn	1913	Harvard	1928	Georgia Tech (H)
1898	Harvard	1914	Army		USC (D)
		1915	Cornell	1929	Notre Dame

☆ Chase's 1998 SPORTS Calendar of Events ☆

YEAR	TEAM
1930	Notre Dame
1931	USC
1932	USC (H)
	Michigan (D)
1933	Michigan
1934	Minnesota
1935	Minnesota (H)
	SMU (D)
1936	Minnesota
1937	Pittsburgh
1938	TCU
1939	Texas A&M
1940	Minnesota
1941	Minnesota
1942	Ohio State
1943	Notre Dame
1944	Army
1945	Army
1946	Notre Dame
1947	Notre Dame
1948	Michigan
1949	Notre Dame
1950	Oklahoma
1951	Tennessee
1952	Michigan State (AP, UP)
	Georgia Tech (INS)
1953	Maryland
1954	Ohio State (AP, INS)
	UCLA (UP, FW)

1955	Oklahoma
1956	Oklahoma
1957	Auburn (AP)
	Ohio State (UP, FW, INS)
1958	LSU (AP, UPI)
	Iowa (FW)
1959	Syracuse
1960	Minnesota (AP, UPI, NFF)
	Mississippi (FW)
1961	Alabama (AP, UPI, NFF)
	Ohio State (FW)
1962	USC
1963	Texas
1964	Alabama (AP, UPI)
	Arkansas (FW)
	Notre Dame (NFF)
1965	Alabama (AP, FW—tie)
	Michigan State (UPI, NFF, FW—tie)
1966	Notre Dame (AP, UPI, FW, NFF—tie)
	Michigan State (NFF—tie)
1967	USC
1968	Ohio State
1969	Texas
1970	Nebraska (AP, FW)
	Texas (UPI, NFF—tie)
	Ohio State (NFF—tie)
1971	Nebraska
1972	USC

1973	Notre Dame (AP, FW, NFF)
	Alabama (UPI)
1974	Oklahoma (AP)
	USC (UPI, FW, NFF)
1975	Oklahoma
1976	Pittsburgh
1977	Notre Dame
1978	Alabama (AP, FW, NFF)
	USC (UPI)
1979	Alabama
1980	Georgia
1981	Clemson
1982	Penn State
1983	Miami, FL
1984	Brigham Young
1985	Oklahoma
1986	Penn State
1987	Miami, FL
1988	Notre Dame
1989	Miami, FL
1990	Colorado (AP, FW, NFF)
	Georgia Tech (UPI)
1991	Miami, FL (AP)
	Washington (USA, FW, NFF)
1992	Alabama
1993	Florida State
1994	Nebraska
1995	Nebraska
1996	Florida

(H) = Helms Athletic Foundation
(D) = Dickinson System
(AP) = Associated Press
(UP) = United Press International
(INS) = International News Service

(UPI) = United Press International
(FW) = Football Writers Association of America
(NFF) = National Football Foundation

NBA Championship

SEASON	WINNER	LOSER	GAMES
1946–1947	Philadelphia Warriors	Chicago Stags	4–1
1947–1948	Baltimore Bullets	Philadelphia Warriors	4–2
1948–1949	Minneapolis Lakers	Washington Capitols	4–2
1949–1950	Minneapolis Lakers	Syracuse Nationals	4–2
1950–1951	Rochester Royals	New York Knicks	4–3
1951–1952	Minneapolis Lakers	New York Knicks	4–3
1952–1953	Minneapolis Lakers	New York Knicks	4–1
1953–1954	Minneapolis Lakers	Syracuse Nationals	4–3
1954–1955	Syracuse Nationals	Ft. Wayne Pistons	4–3
1955–1956	Philadelphia Warriors	Ft. Wayne Pistons	4–1
1956–1957	Boston Celtics	St. Louis Hawks	4–3
1957–1958	St. Louis Hawks	Boston Celtics	4–2
1958–1959	Boston Celtics	Minneapolis Lakers	4–0
1959–1960	Boston Celtics	St. Louis Hawks	4–3
1960–1961	Boston Celtics	St. Louis Hawks	4–1
1961–1962	Boston Celtics	Los Angeles Lakers	4–3
1962–1963	Boston Celtics	Los Angeles Lakers	4–2
1963–1964	Boston Celtics	San Francisco Warriors	4–1
1964–1965	Boston Celtics	Los Angeles Lakers	4–1
1965–1966	Boston Celtics	Los Angeles Lakers	4–3
1966–1967	Philadelphia 76ers	San Francisco Warriors	4–2

☆ Chase's 1998 SPORTS Calendar of Events ☆

SEASON	WINNER	LOSER	GAMES
1967–1968	Boston Celtics	Los Angeles Lakers	4–2
1968–1969	Boston Celtics	Los Angeles Lakers	4–3
1969–1970	New York Knicks	Los Angeles Lakers	4–3
1970–1971	Milwaukee Bucks	Baltimore Bullets	4–0
1971–1972	Los Angeles Lakers	New York Knicks	4–1
1972–1973	New York Knicks	Los Angeles Lakers	4–1
1973–1974	Boston Celtics	Milwaukee Bucks	4–3
1974–1975	Golden State Warriors	Washington Bullets	4–0
1975–1976	Boston Celtics	Phoenix Suns	4–2
1976–1977	Portland Trail Blazers	Philadelphia 76ers	4–2
1977–1978	Washington Bullets	Seattle SuperSonics	4–3
1978–1979	Seattle SuperSonics	Washington Bullets	4–1
1979–1980	Los Angeles Lakers	Philadelphia 76ers	4–2
1980–1981	Boston Celtics	Houston Rockets	4–2
1981–1982	Los Angeles Lakers	Philadelphia 76ers	4–2
1982–1983	Philadelphia 76ers	Los Angeles Lakers	4–0
1983–1984	Boston Celtics	Los Angeles Lakers	4–3
1984–1985	Los Angeles Lakers	Boston Celtics	4–2
1985–1986	Boston Celtics	Houston Rockets	4–2
1986–1987	Los Angeles Lakers	Boston Celtics	4–2
1987–1988	Los Angeles Lakers	Detroit Pistons	4–3
1988–1989	Detroit Pistons	Los Angeles Lakers	4–0
1989–1990	Detroit Pistons	Portland Trail Blazers	4–1
1990–1991	Chicago Bulls	Los Angeles Lakers	4–1
1991–1992	Chicago Bulls	Portland Trail Blazers	4–2
1992–1993	Chicago Bulls	Phoenix Suns	4–2
1993–1994	Houston Rockets	New York Knicks	4–3
1994–1995	Houston Rockets	Orlando Magic	4–0
1995–1996	Chicago Bulls	Seattle SuperSonics	4–2
1996–1997	Chicago Bulls	Utah Jazz	4–2

NCAA Men's Basketball National Tournament

YEAR	WINNER	RUNNER-UP	SCORE	THIRD PLACE*	
1939	Oregon	Ohio State	46–33	Oklahoma	Villanova
1940	Indiana	Kansas	60–42	Duquesne	USC
1941	Wisconsin	Washington State	39–34	Arkansas	Pittsburgh
1942	Stanford	Dartmouth	53–38	Colorado	Kentucky
1943	Wyoming	Georgetown	46–34	DePaul	Texas
1944	Utah	Dartmouth	42–40 (OT)	Iowa State	Ohio State
1945	Oklahoma A&M	NYU	49–45	Arkansas	Ohio State
				THIRD PLACE*	**FOURTH PLACE***
1946	Oklahoma A&M	North Carolina	43–40	Ohio State	California
1947	Holy Cross	Oklahoma	58–47	Texas	CCNY
1948	Kentucky	Baylor	58–42	Holy Cross	Kansas State
1949	Kentucky	Oklahoma A&M	46–36	Illinois	Oregon State
1950	CCNY	Bradley	71–68	NC State	Baylor
1951	Kentucky	Kansas State	68–58	Illinois	Oklahoma A&M
1952	Kansas	St. John's	80–63	Illinois	Santa Clara
1953	Indiana	Kansas	69–68	Washington	LSU
1954	La Salle	Bradley	92–76	Penn State	USC
1955	San Francisco	La Salle	77–63	Colorado	Iowa
1956	San Francisco	Iowa	83–71	Temple	SMU
1957	North Carolina	Kansas	54–53 (3OT)	San Francisco	Michigan State
1958	Kentucky	Seattle	84–72	Temple	Kansas State

☆ *Chase's 1998 SPORTS Calendar of Events* ☆

YEAR	WINNER	RUNNER-UP	SCORE	THIRD PLACE*	FOURTH PLACE*
1959	California	West Virginia	71–70	Cincinnati	Louisville
1960	Ohio State	California	75–55	Cincinnati	NYU
1961	Cincinnati	Ohio State	70–65 (OT)	St. Joseph's (PA)	Utah
1962	Cincinnati	Ohio State	71–59	Wake Forest	UCLA
1963	Loyola (IL)	Cincinnati	60–58 (OT)	Duke	Oregon State
1964	UCLA	Duke	98–83	Michigan	Kansas State
1965	UCLA	Michigan	91–80	Princeton	Wichita State
1966	Texas Western	Kentucky	72–65	Duke	Utah
1967	UCLA	Dayton	79–64	Houston	North Carolina
1968	UCLA	North Carolina	78–55	Ohio State	Houston
1969	UCLA	Purdue	92–72	Drake	North Carolina
1970	UCLA	Jacksonville	80–69	New Mexico State	St. Bonaventure
1971	UCLA	Villanova	68–62	Western Kentucky	Kansas
1972	UCLA	Florida State	81–76	North Carolina	Louisville
1973	UCLA	Memphis State	87–66	Indiana	Providence
1974	NC State	Marquette	76–64	UCLA	Kansas
1975	UCLA	Kentucky	92–85	Louisville	Syracuse
1976	Indiana	Michigan	86–68	UCLA	Rutgers
1977	Marquette	North Carolina	67–59	UNLV	NC-Charlotte
1978	Kentucky	Duke	94–88	Arkansas	Notre Dame
1979	Michigan State	Indiana State	75–64	DePaul	Penn
1980	Louisville	UCLA	59–54	Purdue	Iowa
1981	Indiana	North Carolina	63–50	Virginia	LSU

				THIRD PLACE*	
1982	North Carolina	Georgetown	63–62	Houston	Louisville
1983	NC State	Houston	54–52	Georgia	Louisville
1984	Georgetown	Houston	84–75	Kentucky	Virginia
1985	Villanova	Georgetown	66–64	Memphis State	St. John's
1986	Louisville	Duke	72–69	Kansas	LSU
1987	Indiana	Syracuse	74–73	Providence	UNLV
1988	Kansas	Oklahoma	83–79	Arizona	Duke
1989	Michigan	Seton Hall	80–79 (OT)	Duke	Illinois
1990	UNLV	Duke	103–73	Arkansas	Georgia Tech
1991	Duke	Kansas	72–65	North Carolina	UNLV
1992	Duke	Michigan	71–51	Cincinnati	Indiana
1993	North Carolina	Michigan	77–71	Kansas	Kentucky
1994	Arkansas	Duke	77–72	Arizona	Florida
1995	UCLA	Arkansas	89–78	North Carolina	Oklahoma State
1996	Kentucky	Syracuse	76–67	Massachusetts	Mississippi State
1997	Arizona	Kentucky	84–79 (OT)	Minnesota	North Carolina

*In the years 1939–1945 and 1982 through the present, no competition was held between the two teams eliminated in the national semifinals. In the intervening years, 1946–1981, such a game was played.

NCAA Women's Basketball National Tournament

YEAR	WINNER	RUNNER-UP	SCORE	THIRD PLACE*	
1982	Louisiana Tech	Cheyney State	76–62	Maryland	Tennessee
1983	USC	Louisiana Tech	69–67	Georgia	Old Dominion
1984	USC	Tennessee	72–61	Cheyney State	Louisiana Tech
1985	Old Dominion	Georgia	70–65	NE Louisiana	Western Kentucky
1986	Texas	USC	97–81	Tennessee	Western Kentucky
1987	Tennessee	Louisiana Tech	67–44	Long Beach State	Texas
1988	Louisiana Tech	Auburn	56–54	Long Beach State	Tennessee
1989	Tennessee	Auburn	76–60	Louisiana Tech	Maryland
1990	Stanford	Tennessee	88–81	Louisiana Tech	Virginia
1991	Tennessee	Virginia	70–67 (OT)	Connecticut	Stanford
1992	Stanford	Western Kentucky	78–62	SW Missouri State	Virginia
1993	Texas Tech	Ohio State	84–82	Iowa	Vanderbilt
1994	North Carolina	Louisiana Tech	60–59	Alabama	Purdue
1995	Connecticut	Tennessee	70–64	Georgia	Stanford
1996	Tennessee	Georgia	83–65	Connecticut	Stanford
1997	Tennessee	Old Dominion	68–59	Stanford	Notre Dame

*There is no consolation game between losers in the semifinals.

College Basketball National Invitation Tournament

YEAR	WINNER	RUNNER-UP	SCORE
1938	Temple	Colorado	60–36
1939	Long Island U (Brooklyn)	Loyola (IL)	44–32
1940	Colorado	Duquesne	51–40
1941	Long Island U (Brooklyn)	Ohio	56–42
1942	West Virginia	Western Kentucky	47–45
1943	St. John's	Toledo	48–27
1944	St. John's	DePaul	47–39
1945	DePaul	Bowling Green	71–54
1946	Kentucky	Rhode Island	46–45
1947	Utah	Kentucky	49–45
1948	Saint Louis	New York University	65–52
1949	San Francisco	Loyola (IL)	48–47
1950	CCNY	Bradley	69–61
1951	Brigham Young	Dayton	62–43
1952	La Salle	Dayton	75–64
1953	Seton Hall	St. John's	58–46
1954	Holy Cross	Duquesne	71–62
1955	Duquesne	Dayton	70–58
1956	Louisville	Dayton	93–80
1957	Bradley	Memphis State	84–83
1958	Xavier	Dayton	78–74 (OT)
1959	St. John's	Bradley	76–71 (OT)
1960	Bradley	Providence	88–72
1961	Providence	Saint Louis	62–59
1962	Dayton	St. John's	73–67
1963	Providence	Canisius	81–66
1964	Bradley	New Mexico	86–54
1965	St. John's	Villanova	55–51
1966	Brigham Young	New York University	97–84

* Overtime

☆ *Chase's 1998 SPORTS Calendar of Events* ☆

YEAR	WINNER	RUNNER-UP	SCORE
1967	Southern Illinois	Marquette	71–56
1968	Dayton	Kansas	61–48
1969	Temple	Boston College	89–76
1970	Marquette	St. John's	65–53
1971	North Carolina	Georgia Tech	84–66
1972	Maryland	Niagara	100–69
1973	Virginia Tech	Notre Dame	92–91 (OT)
1974	Purdue	Utah	97–81
1975	Princeton	Providence	80–69
1976	Kentucky	North Carolina-Charlotte	71–67
1977	St. Bonaventure	Houston	94–91
1978	Texas	North Carolina State	101–93
1979	Indiana	Purdue	53–52
1980	Virginia	Minnesota	58–55
1981	Tulsa	Syracuse	86–84 (OT)
1982	Bradley	Purdue	67–58
1983	Fresno State	DePaul	69–60
1984	Michigan	Notre Dame	83–63
1985	UCLA	Indiana	65–62
1986	Ohio State	Wyoming	73–63
1987	Southern Mississippi	La Salle	84–80
1988	Connecticut	Ohio State	72–67
1989	St. John's	Saint Louis	73–65
1990	Vanderbilt	Saint Louis	74–72
1991	Stanford	Oklahoma	78–72
1992	Virginia	Notre Dame	81–76 (OT)
1993	Minnesota	Georgetown	62–61
1994	Villanova	Vanderbilt	80–73
1995	Virginia Tech	Marquette	65–64 (OT)
1996	Nebraska	St. Joseph's	60–54
1997	Michigan	Florida State	82–73

Stanley Cup

SEASON	WINNER		
1892–1893	Montreal Amateur Athletic Assn	1912–1913	Quebec Bulldogs
1893–1894	Montreal Amateur Athletic Assn	1913–1914	Toronto Blueshirts
1894–1895	Montreal Victorias	1914–1915	Vancouver Millionaires
1895–1896	(Feb 1896) Winnipeg Victorias	1915–1916	Montreal Canadiens
1895–1896	(Dec 1896) Montreal Victorias	1916–1917	Seattle Metropolitans
1896–1897	Montreal Victorias	1917–1918	Toronto Arenas
1897–1898	Montreal Victorias	1918–1919	canceled*
1898–1899	Montreal Shamrocks	1919–1920	Ottawa Senators
1899–1900	Montreal Shamrocks	1920–1921	Ottawa Senators
1900–1901	Winnipeg Victorias	1921–1922	Toronto St. Patricks
1901–1902	Montreal Amateur Athletic Assn	1922–1923	Ottawa Senators
1902–1903	Ottawa Silver Seven	1923–1924	Montreal Canadiens
1903–1904	Ottawa Silver Seven	1924–1925	Victoria Cougars
1904–1905	Ottawa Silver Seven	1925–1926	Montreal Maroons
1905–1906	Montreal Wanderers	1926–1927	Ottawa Senators
1906–1907	(Jan 1907) Kenora Thistles	1927–1928	New York Rangers
1906–1907	(Mar 1907) Montreal Wanderers	1928–1929	Boston Bruins
1907–1908	Montreal Wanderers	1929–1930	Montreal Canadiens
1908–1909	Ottawa Senators	1930–1931	Montreal Canadiens
1909–1910	Montreal Wanderers	1931–1932	Toronto Maple Leafs
1910–1911	Ottawa Senators	1932–1933	New York Rangers
1911–1912	Quebec Bulldogs	1933–1934	Chicago Black Hawks
		1934–1935	Montreal Maroons

*Competition was canceled after five games because of a flu epidemic.

☆ *Chase's 1998 SPORTS Calendar of Events* ☆

SEASON	WINNER		
1935–1936	Detroit Red Wings	1966–1967	Toronto Maple Leafs
1936–1937	Detroit Red Wings	1967–1968	Montreal Canadiens
1937–1938	Chicago Black Hawks	1968–1969	Montreal Canadiens
1938–1939	Boston Bruins	1969–1970	Boston Bruins
1939–1940	New York Rangers	1970–1971	Montreal Canadiens
1940–1941	Boston Bruins	1971–1972	Boston Bruins
1941–1942	Toronto Maple Leafs	1972–1973	Montreal Canadiens
1942–1943	Detroit Red Wings	1973–1974	Philadelphia Flyers
1943–1944	Montreal Canadiens	1974–1975	Philadelphia Flyers
1944–1945	Toronto Maple Leafs	1975–1976	Montreal Canadiens
1945–1946	Montreal Canadiens	1976–1977	Montreal Canadiens
1946–1947	Toronto Maple Leafs	1977–1978	Montreal Canadiens
1947–1948	Toronto Maple Leafs	1978–1979	Montreal Canadiens
1948–1949	Toronto Maple Leafs	1979–1980	New York Islanders
1949–1950	Detroit Red Wings	1980–1981	New York Islanders
1950–1951	Toronto Maple Leafs	1981–1982	New York Islanders
1951–1952	Detroit Red Wings	1982–1983	New York Islanders
1952–1953	Montreal Canadiens	1983–1984	Edmonton Oilers
1953–1954	Detroit Red Wings	1984–1985	Edmonton Oilers
1954–1955	Detroit Red Wings	1985–1986	Montreal Canadiens
1955–1956	Montreal Canadiens	1986–1987	Edmonton Oilers
1956–1957	Montreal Canadiens	1987–1988	Edmonton Oilers
1957–1958	Montreal Canadiens	1988–1989	Calgary Flames
1958–1959	Montreal Canadiens	1989–1990	Edmonton Oilers
1959–1960	Montreal Canadiens	1990–1991	Pittsburgh Penguins
1960–1961	Chicago Black Hawks	1991–1992	Pittsburgh Penguins
1961–1962	Toronto Maple Leafs	1992–1993	Montreal Canadiens
1962–1963	Toronto Maple Leafs	1993–1994	New York Rangers
1963–1964	Toronto Maple Leafs	1994–1995	New Jersey Devils
1964–1965	Montreal Canadiens	1995–1996	Colorado Avalanche
1965–1966	Montreal Canadiens	1996–1997	Detroit Red Wings

The Masters

YEAR	WINNER	SCORE	YEAR	WINNER	SCORE	YEAR	WINNER	SCORE
1934	Horton Smith	284	1956	Jack Burke, Jr	289	1978	Gary Player	277
1935	Gene Sarazen	282*	1957	Doug Ford	283	1979	Fuzzy Zoeller	280*
1936	Horton Smith	285	1958	Arnold Palmer	284	1980	Seve Ballesteros	275
1937	Byron Nelson	283	1959	Art Wall, Jr	284	1981	Tom Watson	280
1938	Henry Picard	285	1960	Arnold Palmer	282	1982	Craig Stadler	284*
1939	Ralph Guldahl	279	1961	Gary Player	280	1983	Seve Ballesteros	280
1940	Jimmy Demaret	280	1962	Arnold Palmer	280*	1984	Ben Crenshaw	277
1941	Craig Wood	280	1963	Jack Nicklaus	286	1985	Bernhard Langer	282
1942	Byron Nelson	280*	1964	Arnold Palmer	276	1986	Jack Nicklaus	279
1943	not held		1965	Jack Nicklaus	271	1987	Larry Mize	285*
1944	not held		1966	Jack Nicklaus	288*	1988	Sandy Lyle	281
1945	not held		1967	Gay Brewer, Jr	280	1989	Nick Faldo	283*
1946	Herman Keiser	282	1968	Bob Goalby	277	1990	Nick Faldo	278*
1947	Jimmy Demaret	281	1969	George Archer	281	1991	Ian Woosnam	277
1948	Claude Harmon	279	1970	Billy Casper	279*	1992	Fred Couples	275
1949	Sam Snead	282	1971	Charles Coody	279	1993	Bernhard Langer	277
1950	Jimmy Demaret	283	1972	Jack Nicklaus	286	1994	Jose Maria Olazabal	279
1951	Ben Hogan	280	1973	Tommy Aaron	283	1995	Ben Crenshaw	274
1952	Sam Snead	286	1974	Gary Player	278	1996	Nick Faldo	276
1953	Ben Hogan	274	1975	Jack Nicklaus	276	1997	Tiger Woods	270
1954	Sam Snead	289*	1976	Ray Floyd	271			
1955	Cary Middlecoff	279	1977	Tom Watson	276			

*Won playoff

US Open (Golf)

YEAR	MEN'S CHAMPION
1895	Horace Rawlins
1896	James Foulis
1897	Joe Lloyd
1898	Fred Herd
1899	Willie Smith
1900	Harry Vardon
1901	Willie Anderson
1902	Laurie Auchterlonie
1903	Willie Anderson
1904	Willie Anderson
1905	Willie Anderson
1906	Alex Smith
1907	Alec Ross
1908	Fred McLeod
1909	George Sargent
1910	Alex Smith
1911	John McDermott
1912	John McDermott
1913	Francis Ouimet*
1914	Walter Hagen
1915	John Travers*
1916	Chick Evans*
1917	not held
1918	not held
1919	Walter Hagen
1920	Ted Ray
1921	Jim Barnes
1922	Gene Sarazen
1923	Bobby Jones*
1924	Cyril Walker
1925	Willie Macfarlane
1926	Bobby Jones*
1927	Tommy Armour
1928	Johnny Farrell
1929	Bobby Jones*
1930	Bobby Jones*
1931	Billy Burke
1932	Gene Sarazen
1933	Johnny Goodman*
1934	Olin Dutra
1935	Sam Parks, Jr
1936	Tony Manero
1937	Ralph Guldahl
1938	Ralph Guldahl
1939	Byron Nelson
1940	Lawson Little
1941	Craig Wood
1942	not held
1943	not held
1944	not held
1945	not held

1946	Lloyd Mangrum
1947	Lew Worsham
1948	Ben Hogan
1949	Cary Middlecoff
1950	Ben Hogan
1951	Ben Hogan
1952	Julius Boros
1953	Ben Hogan
1954	Ed Furgol
1955	Jack Fleck
1956	Cary Middlecoff
1957	Dick Mayer
1958	Tommy Bolt
1959	Billy Casper
1960	Arnold Palmer
1961	Gene Littler
1962	Jack Nicklaus
1963	Julius Boros
1964	Ken Venturi
1965	Gary Player
1966	Billy Casper
1967	Jack Nicklaus
1968	Lee Trevino
1969	Orville Moody
1970	Tony Jacklin
1971	Lee Trevino
1972	Jack Nicklaus
1973	Johnny Miller
1974	Hale Irwin
1975	Lou Graham
1976	Jerry Pate
1977	Hubert Green
1978	Andy North
1979	Hale Irwin
1980	Jack Nicklaus
1981	David Graham
1982	Tom Watson
1983	Larry Nelson
1984	Fuzzy Zoeller
1985	Andy North
1986	Ray Floyd
1987	Scott Simpson
1988	Curtis Strange
1989	Curtis Strange
1990	Hale Irwin
1991	Payne Stewart
1992	Tom Kite
1993	Lee Janzen
1994	Ernie Els
1995	Corey Pavin
1996	Steve Jones
1997	Ernie Els

YEAR	WOMEN'S CHAMPION
1946	Patty Berg
1947	Betty Jameson
1948	Babe Zaharias
1949	Louise Suggs
1950	Babe Zaharias
1951	Betsy Rawls
1952	Louise Suggs
1953	Betsy Rawls
1954	Babe Zaharias
1955	Fay Crocker
1956	Kathy Cornelius
1957	Betsy Rawls
1958	Mickey Wright
1959	Mickey Wright
1960	Betsy Rawls
1961	Mickey Wright
1962	Murle Lindstrom
1963	Mary Mills
1964	Mickey Wright
1965	Carol Mann
1966	Sandra Spuzich
1967	Catherine Lacoste*
1968	Susie M. Berning
1969	Donna Caponi
1970	Donna Caponi
1971	JoAnne Carner
1972	Susie M. Berning
1973	Susie M. Berning
1974	Sandra Haynie
1975	Sandra Palmer
1976	JoAnne Carner
1977	Hollis Stacy
1978	Hollis Stacy
1979	Jerilyn Britz
1980	Amy Alcott
1981	Pat Bradley
1982	Janet Anderson
1983	Jan Stephenson
1984	Hollis Stacy
1985	Kathy Baker
1986	Jane Geddes
1987	Laura Davies
1988	Liselotte Neumann
1989	Betsy King
1990	Betsy King
1991	Meg Mallon
1992	Patty Sheehan
1993	Lauri Merten
1994	Patty Sheehan
1995	Annika Sorenstam
1996	Annika Sorenstam

* Amateur

US Open (Tennis)

YEAR	MEN'S CHAMPION
1881	Richard Sears
1882	Richard Sears
1883	Richard Sears
1884	Richard Sears
1885	Richard Sears
1886	Richard Sears
1887	Richard Sears
1888	Henry Slocum, Jr
1889	Henry Slocum, Jr
1890	Oliver Campbell
1891	Oliver Campbell
1892	Oliver Campbell
1893	Robert Wrenn
1894	Robert Wrenn
1895	Fred Hovey
1896	Robert Wrenn
1897	Robert Wrenn
1898	Malcolm Whitman
1899	Malcolm Whitman
1900	Malcolm Whitman
1901	Bill Larned
1902	Bill Larned
1903	Laurie Doherty
1904	Holcombe Ward
1905	Beals Wright
1906	Bill Clothier
1907	Bill Larned
1908	Bill Larned
1909	Bill Larned
1910	Bill Larned
1911	Bill Larned
1912	Maurice McLoughlin
1913	Maurice McLoughlin
1914	Dick Williams
1915	Bill Johnston
1916	Dick Williams
1917	Lindley Murray
1918	Lindley Murray
1919	Bill Johnston
1920	Bill Tilden
1921	Bill Tilden
1922	Bill Tilden
1923	Bill Tilden
1924	Bill Tilden
1925	Bill Tilden
1926	Rene Lacoste
1927	Rene Lacoste
1928	Henri Cochet
1929	Bill Tilden
1930	John Doeg
1931	Ellsworth Vines
1932	Ellsworth Vines
1933	Fred Perry
1934	Fred Perry
1935	Wilmer Allison
1936	Fred Perry
1937	Don Budge
1938	Don Budge

*This was an amateur-only tournament from its inception through 1967. In 1968 and 1969, there were both amateur and open competitions. Since 1970 it has been an open tournament.

1939	Bobby Riggs
1940	Don McNeill
1941	Bobby Riggs
1942	Fred Schroeder
1943	Joe Hunt
1944	Frank Parker
1945	Frank Parker
1946	Jack Kramer
1947	Jack Kramer
1948	Pancho Gonzales
1949	Pancho Gonzales
1950	Arthur Larsen
1951	Frank Sedgman
1952	Frank Sedgman
1953	Tony Trabert
1954	Vic Seixas
1955	Tony Trabert
1956	Ken Rosewall
1957	Mal Anderson
1958	Ashley Cooper
1959	Neale Fraser
1960	Neale Fraser
1961	Roy Emerson
1962	Rod Laver
1963	Rafael Osuna
1964	Roy Emerson
1965	Manuel Santana
1966	Fred Stolle
1967	John Newcombe
1968	Arthur Ashe (Amateur)*
	Arthur Ashe (Open)*
1969	Stan Smith (Amateur)*
	Rod Laver (Open)*
1970	Ken Rosewall
1971	Stan Smith
1972	Ilie Nastase
1973	John Newcombe
1974	Jimmy Connors
1975	Manuel Orantes
1976	Jimmy Connors
1977	Guillermo Vilas
1978	Jimmy Connors
1979	John McEnroe
1980	John McEnroe
1981	John McEnroe
1982	Jimmy Connors
1983	Jimmy Connors
1984	John McEnroe
1985	Ivan Lendl
1986	Ivan Lendl
1987	Ivan Lendl
1988	Mats Wilander
1989	Boris Becker
1990	Pete Sampras
1991	Stefan Edberg
1992	Stefan Edberg
1993	Pete Sampras
1994	Andre Agassi
1995	Pete Sampras
1996	Pete Sampras

YEAR	WOMEN'S CHAMPION
1887	Ellen Hansell
1888	Bertha Townsend
1889	Bertha Townsend
1890	Ellen Roosevelt
1891	Mabel Cahill
1892	Mabel Cahill
1893	Aline Terry
1894	Helen Hellwig

1895	Juliette Atkinson
1896	Elizabeth Moore
1897	Juliette Atkinson
1898	Juliette Atkinson
1899	Marion Jones
1900	Myrtle McAteer
1901	Elizabeth Moore
1902	Marion Jones
1903	Elizabeth Moore
1904	May Sutton
1905	Elizabeth Moore
1906	Helen Homans
1907	Evelyn Sears
1908	Maud B. Wallach
1909	Hazel Hotchkiss
1910	Hazel Hotchkiss
1911	Hazel Hotchkiss
1912	Mary Browne
1913	Mary Browne
1914	Mary Browne
1915	Molla Bjurstedt
1916	Molla Bjurstedt
1917	Molla Bjurstedt
1918	Molla Bjurstedt
1919	Hazel Wightman
1920	Molla Mallory
1921	Molla Mallory
1922	Molla Mallory
1923	Helen Wills
1924	Helen Wills
1925	Helen Wills
1926	Molla Mallory
1927	Helen Wills
1928	Helen Wills
1929	Helen Wills
1930	Betty Nuthall
1931	Helen Moody
1932	Helen Jacobs
1933	Helen Jacobs
1934	Helen Jacobs
1935	Helen Jacobs
1936	Alice Marble
1937	Anita Lizana
1938	Alice Marble
1939	Alice Marble
1940	Alice Marble
1941	Sarah Cooke
1942	Pauline Betz
1943	Pauline Betz
1944	Pauline Betz
1945	Sarah Cooke
1946	Pauline Betz
1947	Louise Brough
1948	Margaret duPont
1949	Margaret duPont
1950	Margaret duPont
1951	Maureen Connolly
1952	Maureen Connolly
1953	Maureen Connolly
1954	Doris Hart
1955	Doris Hart
1956	Shirley Fry
1957	Althea Gibson
1958	Althea Gibson
1959	Maria Bueno
1960	Darlene Hard
1961	Darlene Hard
1962	Margaret Smith
1963	Maria Bueno
1964	Maria Bueno

☆ Chase's 1998 SPORTS Calendar of Events ☆

YEAR	WOMEN'S CHAMPION
1965	Margaret Smith
1966	Maria Bueno
1967	Billie Jean King
1968	Margaret Court (Amateur)*
	Virginia Wade (Open)*
1969	Margaret Court (Amateur)*
	Margaret Court (Open)*
1970	Margaret Court
1971	Billie Jean King
1972	Billie Jean King
1973	Margaret Court
1974	Billie Jean King
1975	Chris Evert
1976	Chris Evert
1977	Chris Evert
1978	Chris Evert
1979	Tracy Austin
1980	Chris Evert Lloyd
1981	Tracy Austin
1982	Chris Evert Lloyd
1983	Martina Navratilova
1984	Martina Navratilova
1985	Hana Mandlikova
1986	Martina Navratilova
1987	Martina Navratilova
1988	Steffi Graf
1989	Steffi Graf
1990	Gabriela Sabatini
1991	Monica Seles
1992	Monica Seles
1993	Steffi Graf
1994	Arantxa Sanchez Vicario
1995	Steffi Graf
1996	Steffi Graf

Soccer's World Cup

YEAR	WINNER	RUNNER-UP	SCORE	HOST COUNTRY
1930	Uruguay	Argentina	4–2	Uruguay
1934	Italy	Czechoslovakia	2–1 (OT)	Italy
1938	Italy	Hungary	4–2	France
1942	canceled			
1946	canceled			
1950	Uruguay	Brazil	2–1	Brazil
1954	West Germany	Hungary	3–2	Switzerland
1958	Brazil	Sweden	5–2	Sweden
1962	Brazil	Czechoslovakia	3–1	Chile
1966	England	West Germany	4–2 (OT)	England
1970	Brazil	Italy	4–1	Mexico
1974	West Germany	Holland	2–1	West Germany
1978	Argentina	Holland	3–1 (OT)	Argentina
1982	Italy	West Germany	3–1	Spain
1986	Argentina	West Germany	3–2	Mexico
1990	West Germany	Argentina	1–0	Italy
1994	Brazil	Italy	0–0*	United States
1998				France

*Tied 0–0 after 30 minutes of overtime; Brazil won on penalty kicks, 3–2.

Heavyweight Boxing Champions

BOXER	YEAR		
John L. Sullivan	1885–1892		
James J. Corbett	1892–1897		
Bob Fitzsimmons	1897–1899		
James J. Jeffries	1899–1905		
Marvin Hart	1905–1906		
Tommy Burns	1906–1908		
Jack Johnson	1908–1915		
Jess Willard	1915–1919		
Jack Dempsey	1919–1926		
Gene Tunney	1926–1928		
Max Schmeling	1930–1932		
Jack Sharkey	1932–1933		
Primo Carnera	1933–1934		
Max Baer	1934–1935		
James J. Braddock	1935–1937		
Joe Louis	1937–1949		
Ezzard Charles	1949–1951		
Jersey Joe Walcott	1951–1952		
Rocky Marciano	1952–1956		
Floyd Patterson	1960–1962		
Sonny Liston	1962–1964		
Cassius Clay (Muhammad Ali)	1964–1970		
Ernie Terrell	1965–1967	(WBA)	
Joe Frazier	1968–1970	(NYSAC)	
Jimmy Ellis	1968–1970	(WBA)	
Joe Frazier	1970–1973		
George Foreman	1973–1974		
Muhammad Ali	1974–1978		
Leon Spinks	1978		
Ken Norton	1978	(WBC)	
Larry Holmes	1978–1980	(WBC)	
Muhammad Ali	1978–1979		
John Tate	1979–1980	(WBA)	
Mike Weaver	1980–1982	(WBA)	

☆ *Chase's 1998 SPORTS Calendar of Events* ☆

BOXER	YEAR	
Larry Holmes	1980–1985	
Michael Dokes	1982–1983	(WBA)
Gerrie Coetzee	1983–1984	(WBA)
Tim Witherspoon	1984	(WBC)
Pinklon Thomas	1984–1986	(WBC)
Greg Page	1984–1985	(WBA)
Michael Spinks	1985–1987	
Tim Witherspoon	1986	(WBA)
Trevor Berbick	1986	(WBC)
Mike Tyson	1986–1987	(WBC)

James Smith	1986–1987	(WBA)
Tony Tucker	1987	(IBF)
Mike Tyson	1987–1990	
Buster Douglas	1990	
Evander Holyfield	1990–1992	
Riddock Bowe	1992–1993	(WBA, IBF)
Lennox Lewis	1992–1994	(WBC)
Evander Holyfield	1993–1994	(WBA, IBF)
Michael Moorer	1994	(WBA, IBF)
Oliver McCall	1994–1995	(WBC)
George Foreman	1994–1995	(WBA, IBF)
Bruce Seldon	1995–1996	(WBA)
George Foreman	1995	(IBF)
Frank Bruno	1995–1996	(WBC)
Mike Tyson	1996	(WBC)
Michael Moorer	1996–	(IBF)
Mike Tyson	1996	(WBA)
Evander Holyfield	1996–	(WBA)
Lennox Lewis	1997–	(WBC)

WBA = World Boxing Association
NYSAC = New York State Athletic Commission
WBC = World Boxing Council
IBF = International Boxing Federation

Kentucky Derby

YEAR	WINNER							
1875	Aristides	1905	Agile	1936	Bold Venture	1967	Proud Clarion
1876	Vagrant	1906	Sir Huon	1937	War Admiral	1968	Forward Pass
1877	Baden-Baden	1907	Pink Star	1938	Lawrin	1969	Majestic Prince
1878	Day Star	1908	Stone Street	1939	Johnstown	1970	Dust Commander
1879	Lord Murphy	1909	Wintergreen	1940	Gallahadion	1971	Canonero II
1880	Fonso	1910	Donau	1941	Whirlaway	1972	Riva Ridge
1881	Hindoo	1911	Meridian	1942	Shut Out	1973	Secretariat
1882	Apollo	1912	Worth	1943	Count Fleet	1974	Cannonade
1883	Leonatus	1913	Donerail	1944	Pensive	1975	Foolish Pleasure
1884	Buchanan	1914	Old Rosebud	1945	Hoop, Jr	1976	Bold Forbes
1885	Joe Cotton	1915	Regret	1946	Assault	1977	Seattle Slew
1886	Ben Ali	1916	George Smith	1947	Jet Pilot	1978	Affirmed
1887	Montrose	1917	Omar Khayyam	1948	Citation	1979	Spectacular Bid
1888	MacBeth II	1918	Exterminator	1949	Ponder	1980	Genuine Risk
1889	Spokane	1919	Sir Barton	1950	Middleground	1981	Pleasant Colony
1890	Riley	1920	Paul Jones	1951	Count Turf	1982	Gato Del Sol
1891	Kingman	1921	Behave Yourself	1952	Hill Gail	1983	Sunny's Halo
1892	Azra	1922	Morvich	1953	Dark Star	1984	Swale
1893	Lookout	1923	Zev	1954	Determine	1985	Spend A Buck
1894	Chant	1924	Black Gold	1955	Swaps	1986	Ferdinand
1895	Halma	1925	Flying Ebony	1956	Needles	1987	Alysheba
1896	Ben Brush	1926	Bubbling Over	1957	Iron Liege	1988	Winning Colors
1897	Typhoon II	1927	Whiskery	1958	Tim Tam	1989	Sunday Silence
1898	Plaudit	1928	Reigh Count	1959	Tomy Lee	1990	Unbridled
1899	Manuel	1929	Clyde Van Dusen	1960	Venetian Way	1991	Strike the Gold
1900	Lieutenant Gibson	1930	Gallant Fox	1961	Carry Back	1992	Lil E. Tee
1901	His Eminence	1931	Twenty Grand	1962	Decidedly	1993	Sea Hero
1902	Alan-a-Dale	1932	Burgoo King	1963	Chateaugay	1994	Go For Gin
1903	Judge Himes	1933	Brokers Tip	1964	Northern Dancer	1995	Thunder Gulch
1904	Elwood	1934	Cavalcade	1965	Lucky Debonair	1996	Grindstone
		1935	Omaha	1966	Kauai King	1997	Silver Charm

Triple Crown Winners

YEAR	HORSE	JOCKEY			
1919	Sir Barton	Johnny Loftus	1943	Count Fleet	Johnny Longden
1930	Gallant Fox	Earl Sande	1946	Assault	Warren Mehrtens
1935	Omaha	Willie Saunders	1948	Citation	Eddie Arcaro
1937	War Admiral	Charley Kurtsinger	1973	Secretariat	Ron Turcotte
1941	Whirlaway	Eddie Arcaro	1977	Seattle Slew	Jean Cruguet
			1978	Affirmed	Steve Cauthen

Indianapolis 500

YEAR	WINNER	MPH	NOTES	YEAR	WINNER	MPH	NOTES
1911	Ray Harroun	74.602		1955	Bob Sweikert	128.213	
1912	Joe Dawson	78.719		1956	Pat Flaherty	128.490	
1913	Jules Goux	75.933		1957	Sam Hanks	135.601	
1914	Rene Thomas	82.474		1958	Jimmy Bryan	133.791	
1915	Ralph DePalma	89.840		1959	Rodger Ward	135.857	
1916	Dario Resta	84.001	(scheduled for 300 miles)	1960	Jim Rathmann	138.767	
1917	not held			1961	A.J. Foyt	139.130	
1918	not held			1962	Rodger Ward	140.293	
1919	Howdy Wilcox	88.050		1963	Parnelli Jones	143.137	
1920	Gaston Chevrolet	88.618		1964	A.J. Foyt	147.350	
1921	Tommy Milton	89.621		1965	Jim Clark	150.686	
1922	Jimmy Murphy	94.484		1966	Graham Hill	144.317	
1923	Tommy Milton	90.954		1967	A.J. Foyt	151.207	
1924	L.L. Corum & Joe Boyer	98.234		1968	Bobby Unser	152.882	
1925	Peter DePaolo	101.127		1969	Mario Andretti	156.867	
1926	Frank Lockhart	95.904	(400 miles; rain)	1970	Al Unser	155.749	
1927	George Souders	97.545		1971	Al Unser	157.735	
1928	Louie Meyer	99.482		1972	Mark Donohue	162.962	
1929	Ray Keech	97.585		1973	Gordon Johncock	159.036	(332.5 miles; rain)
1930	Billy Arnold	100.448		1974	Johnny Rutherford	158.589	
1931	Louis Schneider	96.629		1975	Bobby Unser	149.213	(435 miles; rain)
1932	Fred Frame	104.144		1976	Johnny Rutherford	148.725	
1933	Louie Meyer	104.162		1977	A.J. Foyt	161.331	
1934	Bill Cummings	104.863		1978	Al Unser	161.363	
1935	Kelly Petillo	106.240		1979	Rick Mears	158.899	
1936	Louie Meyer	109.069		1980	Johnny Rutherford	142.862	
1937	Wilbur Shaw	113.580		1981	Bobby Unser	139.084	(penalty placing him second overruled by USAC)
1938	Floyd Roberts	117.200					
1939	Wilbur Shaw	115.035					
1940	Wilbur Shaw	114.277					
1941	Floyd Davis & Mauri Rose	115.117		1982	Gordon Johncock	162.029	
1942	not held			1983	Tom Sneva	162.117	
1943	not held			1984	Rick Mears	163.612	
1944	not held			1985	Danny Sullivan	152.982	
1945	not held			1986	Bobby Rahal	170.722	
1946	George Robson	114.820		1987	Al Unser	162.175	
1947	Mauri Rose	116.338		1988	Rick Mears	149.809	
1948	Mauri Rose	119.814		1989	Emerson Fittipaldi	167.581	
1949	Bill Holland	121.327		1990	Arie Luyendyk	185.981	
1950	Johnnie Parsons	124.002	(345 miles; rain)	1991	Rick Mears	176.457	
1951	Lee Wallard	126.244		1992	Al Unser, Jr	134.477	
1952	Troy Ruttman	128.922		1993	Emerson Fittipaldi	157.207	
1953	Bill Vukovich	128.740		1994	Al Unser, Jr	160.872	
1954	Bill Vukovich	130.840		1995	Jacques Villeneuve	153.616	
				1996	Buddy Lazier	147.956	
				1997	Arie Luyendyk	145.827	

☆ Chase's 1998 SPORTS Calendar of Events ☆

Winston Cup

YEAR	WINNER						
1949	Red Byron	1961	Ned Jarrett	1974	Richard Petty	1987	Dale Earnhardt
1950	Bill Rexford	1962	Joe Weatherly	1975	Richard Petty	1988	Bill Elliott
1951	Herb Thomas	1963	Joe Weatherly	1976	Cale Yarborough	1989	Rusty Wallace
1952	Tim Flock	1964	Richard Petty	1977	Cale Yarborough	1990	Dale Earnhardt
1953	Herb Thomas	1965	Ned Jarrett	1978	Cale Yarborough	1991	Dale Earnhardt
1954	Lee Petty	1966	David Pearson	1979	Richard Petty	1992	Alan Kulwicki
1955	Tim Flock	1967	Richard Petty	1980	Dale Earnhardt	1993	Dale Earnhardt
1956	Buck Baker	1968	David Pearson	1981	Darrell Waltrip	1994	Dale Earnhardt
1957	Buck Baker	1969	David Pearson	1982	Darrell Waltrip	1995	Jeff Gordon
1958	Lee Petty	1970	Bobby Isaac	1983	Bobby Allison	1996	Terry Labonte
1959	Lee Petty	1971	Richard Petty	1984	Terry Labonte		
1960	Rex White	1972	Richard Petty	1985	Darrell Waltrip		
		1973	Benny Parsons	1986	Dale Earnhardt		

The America's Cup

YEAR	WINNER	COUNTRY		YEAR	WINNER	COUNTRY
Schooners and J-Class Boats				**12-Meter Boats**		
1851	America	USA		1958	Columbia	USA
1870	Magic	USA		1962	Weatherly	USA
1871	Columbia and Sappho	USA		1964	Constellation	USA
1876	Madeleine	USA		1967	Intrepid	USA
1881	Mischief	USA		1970	Intrepid	USA
1885	Puritan	USA		1974	Courageous	USA
1886	Mayflower	USA		1977	Courageous	USA
1887	Volunteer	USA		1980	Freedom	USA
1893	Vigilant	USA		1983	Australia II	Australia
1895	Defender	USA		1987	Stars & Stripes	USA
1899	Columbia	USA				
1901	Columbia	USA		**60-ft Catamaran vs 133-ft Monohull**		
1903	Reliance	USA		1988	Stars & Stripes	USA
1920	Resolute	USA				
1930	Enterprise	USA		**75-ft International America's Cup Class**		
1934	Rainbow	USA		1992	America3	USA
1937	Ranger	USA		1995	Black Magic I	New Zealand

ODDS AND ENDS

Commissioners and Presidents

BASEBALL

Commissioner	Year
Kenesaw Mountain Landis	1920–1944
Albert (Happy) Chandler	1945–1951
Ford C. Frick	1951–1965
William Eckert	1965–1968
Bowie Kuhn	1969–1984
Peter Ueberroth	1984–1989
A. Bartlett Giamatti	1989
Fay Vincent	1989–1992
Allan H. (Bud) Selig*	1992–

President, National League	Year
Morgan G. Bulkeley	1876
William A. Hulbert	1877–1882
A.G. Mills	1883–1884
Nicholas Young	1885–1902
Henry Pulliam	1903–1909
Thomas J. Lynch	1910–1913
John K. Tener	1914–1918
John A. Heydler	1918–1934
Ford C. Frick	1935–1951
Warren Giles	1951–1969
Charles (Chub) Feeney	1970–1986
A. Bartlett Giamatti	1987–1989
William White	1989–1994
Leonard Coleman	1994–

President, American League	Year
Byron Bancroft (Ban) Johnson	1901–1927
Ernest Barnard	1927–1931
William Harridge	1931–1959
Joe Cronin	1959–1973
Lee McPhail	1974–1983
Dr. Robert Brown	1984–1994
Gene Budig	1994–

NATIONAL FOOTBALL LEAGUE

President	Year
Jim Thorpe	1920
Joe Carr	1921–1939
Carl Storck	1939–1941

Commissioner	Year
Elmer Layden	1941–1946
Bert Bell	1946–1959
Austin Gunsel (acting)	1959–1960
Alvin (Pete) Rozelle	1960–1989
Paul Tagliabue	1989–

NATIONAL BASKETBALL COMMISSIONER

Commissioner	Year
Maurice Podoloff	1949–1963
Walter Kennedy	1963–1975
Lawrence O'Brien	1975–1984
David Stern	1984–

NATIONAL HOCKEY LEAGUE

President	Year
Frank Calder	1917–1943
Mervyn (Red) Dutton	1943–1946
Clarence Campbell	1946–1977
John A. Ziegler, Jr	1977–1992
Gil Stein	1992–1993

Commissioner	Year
Gary B. Bettman	1993–

NCAA

Executive Director	Year
Walter Byers	1951–1988
Richard Schultz	1988–1993
Cedric Dempsey	1993–

*Chairman of the Executive Committee

Baseball's Work Stoppages

YEAR	WORK STOPPAGE	LENGTH	DATES	BASIC ISSUE
1972	Strike	13 days	Apr 1–13	pensions
1973	Lockout	17 days	Feb 8–25	salary arbitration
1976	Lockout	17 days	Mar 1–17	free agency
1980	Strike	8 days	Apr 1–8	free agent compensation
1981	Strike	50 days	June 12–July 31	free agent compensation
1985	Strike	2 days	Aug 6–7	salary arbitration
1990	Lockout	32 days	Feb 15–Mar 18	salary arbitration and salary cap
1994–1995	Strike	234 days	Aug 12, 1994–Apr 2, 1995	salary cap and revenue sharing

Sites of the Modern Olympic Games

YEAR	SUMMER GAMES	WINTER GAMES
1896	Athens, Greece	
1900	Paris, France	
1904	St. Louis, MO, USA	
1906	Athens, Greece (unofficial)	
1908	London, England	
1912	Stockholm, Sweden	
1916	Berlin, Germany (canceled)	
1920	Antwerp, Belgium	
1924	Paris, France	Chamonix, France
1928	Amsterdam, Holland	St. Moritz, Switzerland
1932	Los Angeles, CA, USA	Lake Placid, NY, USA
1936	Berlin, Germany	Garmisch-Partenkirchen, Germany
1940	Tokyo, Japan (canceled)	Sapporo, Japan (canceled)
1944	London, England (canceled)	Cortina d'Ampezzo, Italy (canceled)
1948	London, England	St. Moritz, Switzerland
1952	Helsinki, Finland	Oslo, Norway
1956	Melbourne, Australia	Cortina d'Ampezzo, Italy
1960	Rome, Italy	Squaw Valley, CA, USA
1964	Tokyo, Japan	Innsbruck, Austria
1968	Mexico City, Mexico	Grenoble, France
1972	Munich, West Germany	Sapporo, Japan
1976	Montreal, Quebec, Canada	Innsbruck, Austria
1980	Moscow, USSR	Lake Placid, NY, USA
1984	Los Angeles, CA, USA	Sarajevo, Yugoslavia
1988	Seoul, South Korea	Calgary, Alberta, Canada
1992	Barcelona, Spain	Albertville, France
1994	————————	Lillehammer, Norway
1996	Atlanta, GA, USA	————————
1998	————————	Nagano, Japan
2000	Sydney, Australia	————————
2002	————————	Salt Lake City, UT, USA

DIRECTORY OF SPORTS ORGANIZATIONS

AIR HOCKEY
US Air Hockey Assn
PO Box 1024
Boulder, CO 80306
(303) 444-9164

AIR SPORTS
Balloon Federation of
America
112 E Salem
Indianola, IA 50125
(515) 961-8809
(515) 961-3537 FAX

Parachutists Over Phorty Soc
3350 St Francis Pl
Long Beach, CA 90805
(310) 633-1226
(310) 630-2389

Soaring Society of America,
Inc
PO Box E
Hobbs, NM 88241-1308
(505) 392-1177
(505) 392-8154 FAX

US Parachute Assn
1440 Duke St
Alexandria, VA 22314
(703) 836-3495
(703) 836-2843 FAX

USA Pro Sky Diving Team
PO Box 57
Huntington Beach, CA 92648
(714) 536-4900
(714) 323-4026

ARCHERY
Natl Archery Assn of the US
One Olympic Plaza
Colorado Springs, CO 80909
(719) 578-4576
(719) 632-4733 FAX

Natl Field Archery Assn
31407 Outer I-10
Redlands, CA 92373
(909) 794-2133
(909) 794-8512 FAX

ARM WRESTLING
American Arm Wrestling
Assn
PO Box 79
Scranton, PA 18504
(717) 342-4984
(717) 342-1368 FAX

Intl Federation of Arm
Wrestling/IFAW
4219 Burbank Blvd
Burbank, CA 91505
(818) 953-2222
(818) 953-2220 FAX

New York Arm Wrestling
Assn/IFAW
PO Box 770-323
Woodside, NY 11377
(718) 544-4592
(718) 544-4592 FAX

AUTO SPORTS
All-American Soap Box Derby
PO Box 7233
Akron, OH 44306
(330) 733-8723
(330) 733-1370 FAX

American Canadian
Tour/ACT
9 Stowe St
Waterbury, VT 05676
(802) 244-6963
(802) 244-1616 FAX

American City Racing
League, Inc
1864 Lake Dr
Cardiff, CA 92007
(619) 753-3127
(619) 942-6406 FAX

American Mini-Sprint Assn
336 S Green St
Brownsburg, IN 46112
(317) 852-6802
(317) 852-6802 FAX

American Speed Assn/ASA
202 S Main St
Pendleton, IN 46064
(317) 778-8088
(317) 778-4006

American Three Quarter
Midget Racing Assn, Inc
48 Mechanics St
Reinholds, PA 17569
(717) 336-4800

Automobile Racing Club of
America/ARCA
PO Box 5217
Toledo, OH 43611
(313) 847-6726
(313) 847-3137 FAX

Championship Auto Racing
Teams/Indycar
755 W Big Beaver Rd, Ste 800
Troy, MI 48084
(810) 362-8800
(810) 362-8810 FAX
Schedule available in August

Indianapolis Motor Speedway
Corp
4790 W 16th St
Indianapolis, IN 46222
(317) 481-8500
(317) 248-6759 FAX

Indy Racing League
4790 W 16th St
Indianapolis, IN 46224
(317) 481-8500
(317) 484-6525 FAX
Schedule available in January

Intl Hot Rod Assn/IHRA
Hwy 11E
Bristol, TN 37620
(423) 764-1164
(423) 764-4460 FAX

Intl Kart Federation
4650 Arrow Hwy, Ste B4
Montclair, CA 91763
(909) 625-5497
(909) 621-6019 FAX

Intl Motor Contest Assn/IMCA
1800 W D St
Vinton, IA 52349
(319) 472-2201
(319) 472-2218 FAX

Intl Motor Sports Assn,
Inc/IMSA
3502 Henderson Blvd
Tampa, FL 33609
(813) 877-4672
(813) 876-4604 FAX

Intl Race of Champions,
Inc/IROC
45 Park Rd
Tinton Falls, NJ 07724
(908) 542-4762
(908) 542-2122 FAX

Mickey Thompson
Entertainment Group/
MTEG
2000 Gene Autry Way,
Ste 305
Anaheim, CA 92806
(714) 254-3001
(714) 254-3002 FAX

Natl Assn for Stock Car Auto
Racing/NASCAR
1801 W Intl Speedway Blvd
Daytona Beach, FL 32114
(904) 253-0611
(904) 252-2875 FAX
Schedule available in
December

Natl Championship Racing
Assn/NCRA
10835 E Admiral Pl
Tulsa, OK 74116
(918) 234-4958
(918) 437-1460 FAX

Natl Hot Rod Assn/NHRA
PO Box 5555
Glendora, CA 91741-0750
(818) 914-4761
(818) 963-5360 FAX

Natl St Rod Assn/NSRA
4030 Park Ave
Memphis, TN 38111
(901) 452-4030

Race Car Club of
America/RCCA
166 Elm St
New Rochelle, NY 10805
(914) 576-RCCA

SCCA Pro Racing, Ltd.
9033 E Easter Pl
Englewood, CO 80112
(303) 694-7223
(303) 694-7391 FAX

Short Course Off-Rd Drivers
Assn/SODA
7839 W North Ave
Wauwatosa, WI 53213
(414) 452-SODA

Southern United Professional
Racing/SUPR
12561 S Choctaw
Baton Rouge, LA 70815
(504) 275-5040
(504) 273-3166 FAX

Sports Car Club of
America/SCCA
PO Box 3278
Englewood, CO 80112
(303) 694-7222
(303) 694-791 FAX

Sportscar Vintage Racing
Assn
8 N Atlantic Wharf
Charleston, SC 29401
(803) 723-7872
(803) 723-7372 FAX

Sprint Car Racing Assn
9723 Washburn Rd
Downey, CA 90241
(310) 862-9122
(310) 862-9902 FAX

Sprint 100 Racing Assn
10306 Wise Rd, #B
Auburn, CA 95603
(916) 888-7221

United Drag Racers Assn
7601 Hamilton Ave
Burr Ridge, IL 60521
(708) 887-0442
(708) 887-0443 FAX

United Midget Auto Racing
Assn/UMARA
PO Box 264
Braidwood, Il 60408-0264
(815) 458-2627

☆ *Chase's 1998 SPORTS Calendar of Events* ☆

United Racing Club/URC
PO Box 4318
Wayne, NJ 07474-4318
(201) 628-1693
(201) 628-1693 FAX

US Auto Club
4910 W 16th St
Indianapolis Speedway, IN
    46224
(317) 247-5151
(317) 247-0123 FAX

Western Racing Assn
4385 Mentone Ave
Culver City, CA 90232
(310) 839-5023

World of Outlaws/WoO
624 Krona Dr, Ste 115
Plano, TX 75074
(214) 424-2202
(214) 423-3930 FAX

World Pulling Intl, Inc/WPI
6969 Worthington-Galena Rd
Worthington, OH 43085
(614) 436-1761
(614) 436-0964 FAX

BADMINTON
US Badminton Assn
One Olympic Plaza
Colorado Springs, CO 80909
(719) 578-4808
(719) 578-4507 FAX

BASEBALL
(NL and AL
are on page 279)
Professional
American Assn/AAA
6801 Miami Ave, Ste 3
Cincinnati, OH 45243
(513) 271-4800
(513) 271-7887 FAX
Schedule available in January

Appalachian League
283 Deerchase Circle
Statesville, NC 28677
(704) 873-5300
(704) 873-4333 FAX
Schedule available in October

Arizona League
PO Box 4941
Scottsdale, AZ 85261-4941
(602) 483-8224
(602) 443-3450
Schedule available in June

California League/A
2380 S Bascom Ave, Ste 200
Campbell, CA 95008
(408) 379-8038
(408) 369-1409 FAX
Schedule available in
    December

Carolina League/A
PO Box 9503
Greensboro, NC 27429
(910) 691-9030
(910) 691-9070 FAX
Schedule available in
    November

Eastern League/AA
PO Box 60687
Harrisburg, PA 17106
(717) 233-4909
(717) 236-6672 FAX
Schedule available in
    December

Florida State League/A
103 E Orange Ave
Daytona Beach, FL 32114
(904) 252-7479
(904) 252-7495 FAX
Schedule available in
    December

Frontier Professional Baseball,
    Inc
PO Box 2662
Zanesville, OH 43702
(614) 452-7400
(614) 452-2999 FAX
Schedule available in
    December

Gulf Coast League
1503 Clower Creek Dr, H-262
Sarasota, FL 34231
(813) 966-6407
(813) 966-6872 FAX

Hawaii Winter Baseball, Inc
905 Makahiki Way, Unit C
Honolulu, HI 96826
(808) 973-7247
(808) 973-7117 FAX
Schedule available in June

Intl League/AAA
55 S High St, Ste 202
Dublin, OH 43017
(614) 791-9300
(614) 791-9009 FAX
Schedule available in January
    or February

Mexican League
Angel Pola No. 16
Col. Periodista
C.P. 11220
Mexico
(905) 557-10-07
(905) 557-14-08 FAX

Midwest League/A
PO Box 936
Beloit, WI 53512-0936
(608) 364-1188
(608) 364-1913 FAX
Schedule available between
    November and February

New York–Pennsylvania
    League/A
1629 Oneida St
Utica, NY 13501
(315) 733-8036
(315) 797-7403 FAX
Schedule available in March

Northern League of Pro-
    fessional Baseball Clubs
524 S Duke St
Durham, NC 27701
(919) 956-8150
(919) 683-2693 FAX
Schedule available in
    December

Northwest League/A
PO Box 4941
Scottsdale, AZ 85261
(602) 483-8224
(602) 493-3450 FAX
Schedule available in October

Pacific Coast League/AAA
2345 S Alma School Rd,
    Ste 110
Mesa, AZ 85210
(602) 838-2171
(602) 838-2741 FAX
Schedule available in January

Pioneer Baseball League/A
PO Box 2564
Spokane, WA 99220
(509) 456-7615
(509) 456-0136 FAX
Schedule available in
    December

South Atlantic League/A
PO Box 38
Kings Mountain, NC 28066
(704) 739-3466
(704) 739-1974
Schedule available in
    December

Southern League/AA
1 Depot St, Ste 300
Marietta, GA 30060
(404) 428-4749
(404) 428-4849 FAX
Schedule available in
    December

Texas Baseball League/AA
2442 Facet Oak
San Antonio, TX 78232
(210) 545-5297
(210) 545-5298 FAX
Schedule available in October

Texas-Louisiana Professional
    Baseball League
401 Cypress, Ste 300
Abilene, TX 79601
(915) 677-4501
(915) 677-4215 FAX
Schedule available in
    February

Other Baseball
Organizations
Adray Collegiate Baseball
    League
c/o Bob Atkins, Dir
30432 Glenmuer
Farmington Hills, MI 48018
(810) 626-1479

Alaska Central Baseball
    League
PO Box 318
Kenai, AK 99611
(907) 283-7133
(907) 283-3390 FAX

All-American Amateur
    Baseball Assn
c/o Tom Checkush, Secretary
340 Walker Dr
Zanesville, OH 43701
(614) 453-1444
(614) 453-7349 FAX

All-American Women's
    Baseball League
80 Fifth Ave, Ste 1506
New York, NY 10011
(212) 741-4668
(212) 741-5285 FAX

American Amateur Baseball
    Congress
118-119 Redfield Plaza
Marshall, MI 49068
(616) 781-2002
(616) 781-2060 FAX

American Legion Baseball
PO Box 1055
Indianapolis, IN 46206
(317) 630-1213
(317) 630-1280 FAX

American Women's Baseball
    Assn, Inc/AWBA
PO Box 1639
Chicago, IL 60690-1639
(312) 404-0932

Atlantic Collegiate Baseball
    League
2365 E 13th St
Brooklyn, NY 11229
(718) 648-2468

Babe Ruth Baseball &
    Softball
PO Box 5000
1770 Brunswick Pike
Trenton, NJ 08638
(609) 695-1434
(609) 695-2505 FAX

Baseball Canada/Canadian
    Federation of Amateur
    Baseball
1600 James Naismith Dr
Gloucester, ON
Canada K1B 5N4
(613) 748-5606
(613) 748-5767 FAX

☆ *Chase's 1998 SPORTS Calendar of Events* ☆

Cape Cod Baseball League
PO Box 164
S Harwich, MA 02661
(508) 432-1774
(508) 432-9766 FAX

Central Illinois Collegiate
League
RR 13, Box 369
Bloomington, IL 61704
(309) 828-4429

Collegiate Summer Baseball
Assn
3723 Hermes Dr
Cincinnati, OH 45247
(513) 385-8831

Continental Amateur
Baseball Assn
82 University St
Westerville, OH 43081-2023
(614) 882-1361
(614) 899-2103 FAX

Dixie Baseball, Inc
215 Watauga Lane
PO Box 193
Montgomery, AL 33610-0193
(615) 821-6811

Great Lakes Summer
Collegiate League
PO Box 1121
Bowling Green, OH 43402
(419) 354-5556

Jayhawk League
5 Adams Pl
Halstead, KS 67056
(316) 835-2589
(316) 755-1285 FAX

Korean Amateur Baseball
Assn
18031 Rocky Ridge Lane
Olney, MD 20832
(301) 924-5521

Little League Baseball Inc
PO Box 3485
Williamsport, PA 17701
(717) 326-1921
(717) 326-1074 FAX

Men's Senior Baseball League
One Huntington Quadrangle,
3N07
Melville, NY 11797
(516) 753-6725
(516) 753-4031 FAX

Metropolitan Baseball
League, Inc
289 McBride Ave
Paterson, NJ 07501
(201) 523-6479

Natl Amateur Baseball
Federation
PO Box 705
Bowie, MD 20718
(301) 262-5005
(301) 262-5005 FAX

Natl Baseball Congress
300 S Sycamore
Wichita, KS 67213
(316) 267-3372
(316) 267-3382 FAX

Northeastern Collegiate
Baseball League
905 Ontario St
Schenectady, NY 12306
(518) 372-5296
(800) 836-0610
(518) 482-0935 FAX

Pony Baseball and Softball
PO Box 225
Washington, PA 15301
(412) 225-1060
(412) 225-9852 FAX

San Diego Collegiate League
948 Jasmine Ct
Carlsbad, CA 92009
(619) 438-0347

Stars of Tomorrow, Inc
Baseball Tournaments
3466 Lasey Blvd S
La Crosse, WI 54602
(608) 788-0700
(608) 788-8391 FAX

USA Baseball
2160 Greenwood Ave
Trenton, NJ 08609
(609) 586-2381
(609) 587-1818 FAX

Valley Baseball League
PO Box 2246
Staunton, VA 24402-2246
(703) 885-8901
(703) 885-7612 FAX

BASKETBALL
(NBA is on page 281)
American Basketball League
1900 Embarcadero Rd, Ste
100
Palo Alto, CA 94303
(415) 856-3200
(415) 856-3280 FAX

Atlantic Basketball Assn
PO Box 12727
Wilmington, DE 19850-2727
(302) 426-9344
(302) 426-9335 FAX

Continental Basketball Assn
701 Market St, Ste 140
St Louis, MO 63101
(314) 621-7222
(314) 621-1202 FAX
Schedule available in June

Biddy Basketball
4711 Bancroft Dr
New Orleans, LA 70122
(504) 288-5128

Club Basketball USA/NJ Corp
Sports League
215 N Ave, Ste 205
Westfield, NJ 07090
(908) 756-4502
(908) 756-9698

Harlem Globetrotters
400 E Van Buren, Ste 300
Phoenix, AZ 85004
(602) 258-0000
(602) 253-5612 FAX
Schedule for top 50 major
cities available in August;
schedule for smaller cities
available in November

Harlem Wizards Entertain-
ment Basketball, Inc
PO Box 7267
North Bergen, NJ 07047
(201) 854-6365
(800) 367-7213
(201) 854-6381 FAX

Sonny Hill Basketball League,
Inc
429 S 50th St
Philadelphia, PA 19143
(215) 474-2801
(215) 474-2931 FAX

Natl Wheelchair Basketball
Assn
1100 Blythe Blvd
Charlotte, NC 28217
(704) 355-1064

Rucker Professional Basketball
League
2340 Third Ave
New York, NY 10037
(212) 410-3240

US Basketball League
46 Quirk Rd
Milford, CT 06460
(203) 877-9508
(800) THE-USBL
(203) 878-8109 FAX

Youth Basketball of America,
Inc
PO Box 3067
Orlando, FL 32821
(407) 363-YBOA
(407) 363-0599 FAX

BIATHLON
US Biathlon Assn
421 Old Military Rd
Lake Placid, NY 12946
(518) 523-3836

BILLIARDS
Billiard Congress of America
910 23rd Ave
Coralville, IA 52241-1221
(319) 351-2112
(319) 351-7767 FAX

Billiards Intl, Ltd.
123 Highview Dr
Winsted, CT 06098
(203) 379-8414
(203) 738-4927 FAX

Professional Billiards Tour
Assn
4311 Lee Rd
Spring Hill, FL 34608-3853
(352) 688-5837
(352) 686-5515 FAX

Women's Professional Billiard
Assn
214 E Jefferson St
Grand Ledge, MI 48837
(517) 627-WPBA
(517) 627-3811 FAX

BOATING
Intl Hot Boat Assn/IHBA
619 N Poplar St
Orange, CA 92668
(714) 634-4422
(714) 634-3602 FAX

Intl Jet Sports Boating Assn
1239 E Warner Ave
Santa Ana, CA 92705
(714) 751-4277
(714) 751-8418 FAX

Intl Outboard Grand
Prix/IOGP
4545 S Mingo Rd
Tulsa, OK 74146
(918) 663-7776
(918) 663-5343

Prosail
301 E Blvd
Charlotte, NC 28203
(704) 376-0736
(704) 376-2003 FAX

Super Boat Racing
1323 20th Terrace
Key West, FL 33040
(305) 296-8963
(305) 296-9770 FAX

Thunderboats UnLtd
4355 Ruffin Rd, Ste 315
San Diego, CA 92123-4309
(619) 268-1250
(619) 268-3301

Unlimited Racing
Commission
414 Pontius Ave N, Ste C
Seattle, WA 98109
(206) 467-1368
(206) 467-0235 FAX

US Offshore Racing Assn
18 N Franklin Blvd
Pleasantville, NJ 08232
(609) 383-3700
(609) 383-9501 FAX

US Sailing Assn
PO Box 1260
Portsmouth, RI 02871
(410) 683-0800
(410) 683-0840 FAX

BOBSLEDDING
US Bobsled & Skeleton
    Federation, Inc
PO Box 828
Lake Placid, NY 12946
(518) 523-1842
(518) 523-9491 FAX

BOCCE
Intl Bocce Assn
400 Rutger St
PO Box 170
Utica, NY 13503-0170
(315) 733-9611

BOWLING
American Blind Bowling Assn
411 Sheriff St
Mercer, PA 16137
(412) 662-5748

American Bowling Congress
5201 S 76th St
Greendale, WI 53129
(414) 421-6400
(414) 421-1194 FAX

Ladies Pro Bowlers Tour
7171 Cherryvale Blvd
Rockford, IL 61112
(815) 332-5756
(815) 332-9636

Natl Amateur Bowlers Inc
PO Box 17-1610
Kansas City, KS 66117
(913) 621-7337
(913) 342-7218 FAX

Natl Deaf Bowling Assn
9244 E Mansfield Ave
Denver, CO 80237
(303) 771-9018 TDD only

Natl Duckpin Bowling
    Congress
4991 Fairview Ave
Linthicum Heights, MD
    21090-1466
(410) 521-3276
(800) 221-3564
(410) 636-3256 FAX

Professional Bowlers Assn of
    America/PBA
PO Box 5118
Akron, OH 44334-0118
(216) 836-5568
(216) 836-2107 FAX

USA Bowling
5201 S 76th St
Greendale, WI 52129
(414) 421-9008

Women's Intl Bowling
    Congress, Inc/WIBC
5301 S 76th St
Greendale, WI 52129
(414) 421-9000
(414) 421-4420 FAX

Young American Bowling
    Alliance/YABA
5201 S 76th St
Greendale, WI 52129-1192
(414) 421-4700
(414) 421-1301 FAX

BOXING
Golden Gloves Assn of
    America, Inc
8801 Princess Jeanne NE
Albuquerque, NM 87112
(505) 298-8042
(595) 298-1191 FAX

Intl Veteran Boxer's Assn
35 Brady Ave
New Rochelle, NY 10805
(914) 235-6820

US Amateur Boxing, Inc/USA
    Boxing
One Olympic Plaza
Colorado Springs, CO 80909
(719) 579-4506
(719) 632-3426 FAX

CANOEING/KAYAKING
American Canoe Assn
7432 Alban Station Blvd,
    Ste B-226
Springfield, VA 22150
(703) 451-0141
(703) 451-2245 FAX

US Canoe & Kayak Team
Pan American Plaza
201 S Capitol Ave, Ste 610
Indianapolis, IN 46225
(317) 237-5690
(317) 237-5694 FAX

CLIMBING
American Alpine Club
710 10th St, Ste 100
Golden, CO 80401
(303) 384-0110
(303) 384-0111 FAX

American Sport Climbers
    Federation
35 Greenfield Dr
Moraga, CA 94556
(510) 376-1640
(510) 376-1640 FAX

CROQUET
Croquet Fdtn of America
11588-B Polo Club Road
Wellington, FL 33414
(407) 753-9080
(407) 753-8801 FAX

US Croquet Assn
11588-B Polo Club Road
Wellington, FL 33414
(407) 753-9080
(407) 753-8801 FAX

CURLING
US Curling Assn
1100 Centerpoint Dr
Stevens Point, WI 54481
(715) 344-1199
(715) 344-6885 FAX

US Women's Curling Assn
PO Box 244
Hartland, WI 53029

CYCLING
American Bicycle Assn/ABA
9831 S 51st St, Ste D135
Phoenix, AZ 85044
(602) 961-1903
(602) 961-1842 FAX

American Motorcyclist Assn
PO Box 6114
Westerville, OH 43081-6114
(614) 891-2425
(800) AMA-JOIN
(614) 891-5012 FAX

Intl Drag Bike Assn
3936 Raceway Park Rd
Mt Olive, AL 35117
(205) 849-7886
(800) 553-IDBA
(205) 841-0553 FAX

League of American Bicyclists
190 W Ostend St, Ste 120
Baltimore, MD 21230-3755
(410) 539-3399
(410) 539-3496 FAX

Natl Bicycle League, Inc
3958 Brown Park Dr, Ste D
Hilliard, OH 43026
(614) 777-1625
(614) 777-1680 FAX

Natl Cycling League
532 La Guardia Pl, Ste 162
New York, NY 10012
(212) 777-3611
(212) 260-7424 FAX

Ultra Marathon Cycling Assn
2761 N Marengo Ave
Altadena, CA 91001
(818) 794-3119
(818) 794-3119 FAX

US Cycling
One Olympic Plaza
Colorado Springs, CO 80909
(719) 578-4581
(719) 578-4628 FAX

Western Eastern Roadracer's
    Assn
PO Box 440549
Kennesaw, GA 30144
(770) 924-8404
(770) 924-1277 FAX

Women On Wheels, Inc
    Motorcycle Assn
PO Box 081454
Racine, WI 53408-1454
(414) 637-6943
(800) 322-1969

World Professional Motorcycle
    Jumping Assn
655 Deep Valley Dr, Ste 110
Rolling Hills Estates, CA
    90274
(310) 541-1206
(310) 541-4446 FAX

Youth Bike League
201 McKnight Park Dr
Pittsburgh, PA 15237
(412) 367-4034
(412) 367-4559 FAX

DARTS
American Darts Organization
652 S Brookhurst Ave, Ste 543
Anaheim, CA 92804
(714) 254-0212
(714) 254-0214 FAX

EQUESTRIAN
Amateur Riders Club of The
    Americas
716 Kingston Rd
Princeton, NJ 08540
(609) 924-6446
(609) 683-8313 FAX

American Grandprix Assn
840 Natl City Bank Bldg
Cleveland, OH 44114
(216) 781-2050
(216) 781-5333 FAX

American Horse Council, Inc
1700 K St, NW, Ste 300
Washington, DC 20006-3805
(202) 296-4031
(202) 296-1970 FAX

American Horse Shows Assn,
    Inc
220 E 42nd St
New York, NY 10017-5876
(212) 972-2472
(212) 983-7286 FAX

☆ *Chase's 1998 SPORTS Calendar of Events* ☆

American Miniature Horse
  Assn
5601 S Interstate Hwy 35W
Alvarado, TX 76009
(817) 783-5600
(817) 783-6403 FAX

American Morgan Horse Assn
PO Box 960
Shelburne, VT 05482-0960
(802) 985-4944
(802) 985-8897 FAX

American Paint Horse Assn
PO Box 961023
Ft. Worth, TX 76161
(817) 439-3400
(817) 439-3484 FAX

American Quarter Horse Assn
PO Box 200
Amarillo, TX 79168
(806) 376-4811
(806) 376-8304 FAX

American Saddlebred Horse
  Assn
Kentucky Horse Park
4093 Iron Works Pike
Lexington, KY 40511
(606) 259-2742
(606) 259-1628 FAX

American Vaulting Assn
642 Alford Pl
Bainbridge Island, WA 98110-
  4608
(206) 780-9353
(206) 780-9355 FAX

Breeders' Cup Ltd
PO Box 4230
Lexington, KY 40544
(606) 223-5444
(606) 223-3945 FAX

Desert Circuit
13 Closs Dr
Rhinebeck, NY 12572
(914) 876-2833
(914) 876-5538 FAX

Gladstone Equestrian Assn
PO Box 119
Gladstone, NJ 07934
(908) 234-0151
(908) 234-0863 FAX

Hambletonian Soc
1200 Tices Lane
East Brunswick, NJ 08816
(908) 249-8500
(908) 249-3170 FAX

Hampton Classic Horse Show,
  Inc
PO Box 3013
Bridgehampton, NY 11932
(516) 537-3177
(516) 537-7028 FAX

Intl Arabian Horse Assn
10805 E Betthany Dr
Aurora, CO 80014
(303) 696-4500
(303) 696-4599 FAX

Natl Cutting Horse Assn
4704 Hwy 377 S
Fort Worth, TX 76116-8805
(817) 244-6188
(817) 244-2015 FAX

Natl Jousting Assn
PO Box 14
Mt. Solon, VA 22843
(301) 223-9468

Natl Steeplechase Assn
400 Fair Hill Dr
Elkton, MD 21921
(410) 392-0700
(410) 392-0706

US Combined Training Assn
PO Box 2247
Leesburg, VA 22075
(703) 779-0440
(703) 779-0550 FAX

US Dressage Federation, Inc
PO Box 6669
Lincoln, NE 68506-0669
(402) 434-8550
(402) 434-8570 FAX

US Equestrian Team
Pottersville Rd
Gladstone, NJ 07934
(908) 234-1251
(908) 234-9417 FAX

US Polo Assn
4059 Iron Works Pike
Lexington, KY 40511
(606) 255-0593
(606) 231-9738 FAX

US Trotting Assn
750 Michigan Ave
Columbus, OH 43215-1191
(614) 224-2291
(614) 224-4575 FAX

EXERCISE/FITNESS
Amateur Bodybuilding Assn
Gold's Gym
1307 W 6th St
Corona, CA 91720
(909) 734-3900

Intl Aerobic Federation
PO Box 9337
San Jose, CA 95157
(408) 255-5531

Intl Competitive Aerobics
  Federation
9000 Sunset Blvd, Ste 1408
Los Angeles, CA 90069
(310) 278-9700
(310) 278-2148 FAX

Intl Federation of Body
  Builders
2875 Bates Rd
Montreal, QC
Canada H3S 1B7
(514) 731-3783
(514) 731-7982 FAX

Intl Fitness Sanctioning Body
PO Box 2378
Corona, CA 91718-2378
(909) 371-0606
(909) 371-0608 FAX

US Powerlifting Federation,
  Inc
PO Box 650
Roy, UT 84067
(801) 776-3628

US Weightlifting Federation
One Olympic Plaza
Colorado Springs, CO 80909
(719) 578-4508
(719) 578-4741 FAX

World Natural Bodybuilding
  Federation
350 Fifth Ave, Ste 8216
New York, NY 10118
(212) 947-4322
(212) 947-2384 FAX

FENCING
Natl Intercollegiate Women's
  Fencing Assn
3 Derby Lane
Dumont, NJ 07628
(201) 384-1722

US Fencing Assn
One Olympic Plaza
Colorado Springs, CO 80909
(719) 578-4511
(719) 632-5737 FAX

FIELD HOCKEY
US Field Hockey Assn
One Olympic Plaza
Colorado Springs, CO 80909
(719) 578-4567
(719) 632-0979 FAX

FISHING
Bassing America Corp.
PO Box 796908
Dallas, TX 75379-6908
(214) 380-2656
(800) 972-3369
(214) 380-2621 FAX

Bass'N Gal
PO Box 13925
Arlington, TX 76094
(817) 265-6214
(817) 265-6290 FAX

US Fishing Assn, Inc
4398 Sunbelt Dr
Dallas, TX 75248
(214) 713-6207
(214) 380-2621 FAX

FOOTBALL
(NFL is on page 280)
American Football Assn
PO Box 43885
Las Vegas, NV 89116
(702) 431-2100
(702) 641-3432 FAX

Arena Football
2200 W Commercial Blvd, Ste
  101
Ft. Lauderdale, FL 33309
(954) 777-2700
(954) 777-0045 FAX

Canadian Football League
110 Eglinton Ave W
Toronto, ON
Canada M4R 1A3
(416) 322-9650
(416) 322-9651 FAX
Schedule available in March

US Flag & Touch Football
  League
7709 Ohio St
Mentor, OH 44060
(216) 974-8735
(216) 974-8735 FAX

World League of American
  Football
410 Park Ave
New York, NY 10022
(212) 758-1500
(212) 872-7464 FAX

FRISBEE
US Disc Sports Assn
855 Tunjunga Valley Rd
Sunland, CA 91040
(818) 353-6339

World Flying Disc Federation
200 Linden
Ft. Collins, CO 80524
(303) 484-6932
(303) 490-2714 FAX

GOLF
American Junior Golf Assn
2415 Steeplechase Lane
Roswell, GA 30076
(404) 998-4653
(404) 992-9783 FAX

Celebrity Golf Assn/CGA
205 D Center Ave, Ste 630
Ft. Lee, NJ 07024
(201) 944-4471
(201) 944-3193 FAX

Futures Golf Tour
909 W Main St
Avon Park, FL 33825
(941) 453-4455
(941) 453-4466 FAX

Gold Coast Pro Golf Tour
4483 Luxembourg Ct, #105
Lake Worth, FL 33467
(407) 967-6883
(800) 345-5066
(407) 969-3329 FAX

Group Fore–Women's
    Professional Golf Tour
1259 El Camino Real, Ste 153
Menlo Park, CA 94025
(415) 327-5207
(415) 327-5208 FAX

Hooters Professional Golf Tour
202 Commerce Dr
Peachtree City, GA 30269
(770) 486-8687
(800) 992-8748
(770) 486-1055 FAX

Ladies' Professional Golf
    Assn/LPGA
2570 W Intl Speedway Blvd,
    Ste B
Daytona Beach, FL 32114
(904) 254-8800
(904) 254-4755 FAX

Miniature Golf Assn of
    America
PO Box 32353
Jacksonville, FL 32237
(904) 781-GOLF
(904) 781-4843 FAX

Natl Assn of Left-Handed
    Golfers
6488 Shawnee Ct
Independence, KY 41051
(800) 844-NALG

PGA Tour
112 TPC Blvd, Sawgrass
Ponte Vedra Beach, FL 32082
(904) 285-3700
(904) 285-7913 FAX
Schedule available in October

Professional Golfers' Assn of
    America/PGA of America
100 Ave of the Champions
PO Box 109601
Palm Beach Gardens, FL
    33410
(407) 624-8400
(407) 624-8452 FAX

US Blind Golfers Assn
160 Lago Vista Blvd
Casselberry, FL 32707
(407) 332-0700

US Golf Assn/USGA
PO Box 708
Far Hills, NJ 07931-0708
(908) 234-2300
(908) 234-9687 FAX

Western Golf Assn
1 Briar Rd
Golf, IL 60029
(847) 724-4600
(847) 724-7133 FAX

GREYHOUND RACING
American Greyhound Council
1065 NE 125th St, Ste 219
N Miami, FL 33161-5832
(305) 893-2101
(305) 893-5633 FAX

GYMNASTICS
US Sports Acrobatics
    Federation/USSAF
PO Box 8158
Riverside, CA 92515-8158
(909) 785-2293
(909) 785-2291 FAX

USA Gymnastics
Pan American Plaza
201 S Capitol Ave, Ste 300
Indianapolis, IN 46225
(317) 237-5050
(317) 237-5069 FAX

HANDBALL
US Handball Assn
2333 N Tucson Blvd
Tucson, AZ 85716-2726
(520) 795-0434
(520) 795-0465

HORSESHOES
Natl Horseshoe Pitchers Assn
PO Box 7927
Columbus, OH 43207
(614) 444-8510
(614) 444-8510 FAX

ICE HOCKEY
(NHL is on page 283)
American Hockey League
425 Union St
W Springfield, MA 01089
(413) 781-2030
(413) 733-4767 FAX
Schedule available in
    September

Central Hockey League
5840 S Memorial Dr, Ste 302
Tulsa, OK 74145
(918) 664-8881
(918) 664-2215 FAX
Schedule available in August

Colonial Hockey League
34400 Utica Rd
Fraser, MI 48026
(810) 296-5510
(810) 296-5515 FAX
Schedule available in August

East Coast Hockey League
125 Village Blvd
Princeton, NJ 08450
(609) 452-0770
(609) 452-7147 FAX
Schedule available in August

Intl Hockey League
1577 N Woodward Ave,
    Ste 212
Bloomfield Hills, MI 48304
(810) 258-0580
(810) 258-0940 FAX

Hockey North America/Natl
    Novice Hockey Assn
11501 Sunset Hills Rd,
    4th Floor
Reston, VA 22090-4704
(703) 471-0400
(800) 446-2539
(703) 904-7160 FAX

US Hockey League
300 N 5th St, Ste 2
Grand Forks, ND 58203
(701) 775-6839
(701) 775-2684 FAX

USA Hockey
4965 N 30th St
Colorado Springs, CO 80919
(719) 599-5500
(719) 599-5994 FAX

ICE RACING
Intl Ice Racing Assn
PO Box 8105
St Paul, MN 55108
(612) 538-8012

ICE SKATING
Amateur Speedskating Union
    of the US
1033 Shady Lane
Glen Ellyn, IL 60137
(630) 790-3230

US Figure Skating Assn
20 First St
Colorado Springs, CO 80906
(719) 635-5200
(719) 635-9548 FAX

US Intl Speedskating Assn
PO Box 16157
Rocky River, OH 44116
(216) 899-0128
(216) 899-0109 FAX

IN-LINE SKATING
Intl In-Line Skating Assn
3720 Farragut Ave, Ste 400
Kensington, MD 20895
(301) 942-9770
(301) 942-9771 FAX

Natl In-Line Basketball
    League/NIBBL
Pier 62, Ste 301
New York, NY 10012
(212) 336-6450
(212) 336-6122 FAX

Natl In-Line Hockey
    Assn/NIHA
999 Brickell Ave, 9th Floor
Miami, FL 33131
(305) 358-8988
(305) 358-0046 FAX

KITING
American Kitefliers Assn
1559 Rockville Pike
Rockville, MD 20852-1651
(800) AKA-2550

KORFBALL
US Korfball Federation
1636 S Florence Pl
Tulsa, OK 74104
(918) 742-0354

LACROSSE
Lacrosse Foundation, Inc
113 W University Pkwy
Baltimore, MD 21210
(410) 235-6882
(410) 366-6735 FAX

Lacrosse USA, Inc
PO Box 1116
Basalt, CO 81621
(303) 927-9338
(303) 927-9751 FAX

Major Indoor Lacrosse League
2310 W 75th St
Prairie Village, KS 66208
(913) 384-8960
(913) 384-8961 FAX

US Club Lacrosse Assn, Inc
2600 Whitney Ave
Baltimore, MD 21215
(410) 235-8532

US Intercollegiate Lacrosse
    Assn
Washington & Lee Univ
Drawer 928
Lexington, VA 24450
(703) 463-8684
(703) 463-8669 FAX

US Women's Lacrosse Assn
48 Boulder Brick Rd
Wellesley, MA 02181
(617) 235-7903

LUGE
Rd Racing Assn Intl for
    Luge/RAIL
18734 Kenya St
Northridge, CA 91326
(818) 368-6826

US Luge Assn
PO Box 651
Lake Placid, NY 12946
(518) 523-2071
(518) 523-4106 FAX

☆ *Chase's 1998 SPORTS Calendar of Events* ☆

MARTIAL ARTS

American Amateur Karate
Federation
1930 Wilshire Blvd, Ste 1208
Los Angeles, CA 90057
(213) 483-8261

Intl Martial Arts Games
Committee/IMAGC
291 Springfield Ave,
Ste 104-204
Berkeley Heights, NJ 07922
(908) 665-4205
(908) 771-5524 FAX

US Judo, Inc
PO Box 10013
El Paso, TX 79991
(915) 565-8754

US Taekwondo Union
One Olympic Plaza
Colorado Springs, CO 80909
(719) 578-4632
(719) 578-4642 FAX

US Tang Soo Do Moo Duk
Kwan
PO Box 154
Springfield, NJ 07081
(201) 467-3971
(201) 467-5716 FAX

USA Karate Federation
1300 Kenmore Blvd
Akron, OH 44314
(216) 753-3114
(216) 753-6967 FAX

ORIENTEERING

US Orienteering Federation
PO Box 1444
Forest Park, GA 30051
(404) 363-2110
(404) 363-2110 FAX

PADDLE TENNIS

US Paddle Tennis Assn
PO Box 14962
Santa Rosa, CA 95402
(707) 585-7995
(707) 586-3763 FAX

PENTATHLON

US Modern Pentathlon Assn
530 McCullough Ave, Ste 619
San Antonio, TX 78215
(210) 246-3000
(210) 246-3096 FAX

PETANQUE

Federation of Petanque USA
Inc
208 N Royal St
Alexandria, VA 22314
(800) 296-2961

PLATFORM TENNIS

American Platform Tennis
Assn
PO Box 43336
Upper Montclair, NJ 07043
(201) 744-1190
(201) 783-4407 FAX

RACQUETBALL

American Amateur
Racquetball Assn
185 W Uintah St
Colorado Springs, CO 80904-
2921
(719) 635-5396
(719) 635-0685 FAX

Women's Professional
Racquetball Assn
PO Box 17633
Anaheim, CA 92817-7633
(714) 281-0241
(714) 281-2410 FAX

RODEO

Intl Pro Rodeo Assn, Inc
PO Box 83377
Oklahoma City, OK 73148
(405) 235-6540
(405) 235-6577 FAX

Longhorn World
Championship Rodeo, Inc
3679 Knight Rd
Whites Creek, TN 37189
(615) 876-1016
(615) 876-4685 FAX

Natl High School Rodeo Assn,
Inc
11178 N Huron, #7
Denver, CO 80234
(303) 452-0820
(303) 452-0912 FAX

Natl Intercollegiate Rodeo
Assn
2316 Eastgate N, Ste 160
Walla Walla, WA 99362
(509) 529-4402
(509) 525-1090 FAX

Natl Little Britches Rodeo
Assn
1045 W Rio Grande
Colorado Springs, CO 80906
(719) 389-0333
(800) RODEO-94
(719) 578-1367 FAX

ROLLER HOCKEY

Roller Hockey International
13070 Fog Hill Dr
Grass Valley, CA 95945
(916) 272-7825
(916) 272-7858 FAX

ROLLER SKATING

US Amateur Confederation of
Roller Skating
PO Box 6579
Lincoln, NE 68506
(402) 483-7551
(402) 483-1465 FAX

ROWING/CREW

Head of the Charles Regatta
PO Box 52
Cambridge, MA 02238
(617) 864-8415
(617) 236-5955

Scholastic Rowing Assn of
America
120 US Ave
Gibbsboro, NJ 08026
(609) 784-3878

US Rowing Assn
201 S Capitol Ave, Ste 400
Indianapolis, IN 46225
(317) 237-5656
(317) 237-5646 FAX

RUGBY

Cape Fear Rugby Sevens
Tournament
Box 5351, Station 1
Wilmington, NC 28403
(910) 256-4658

USA Rugby
3595 E Fountain Blvd
Colorado Springs, CO 80910
(719) 637-1022
(719) 637-1315 FAX

USA Rugby-East, Inc
2312 Hillbeck
Columbia, SC 29210
(803) 254-4561
(803) 798-2137 FAX

Western Rugby Football
Union of the US
1405 E Meadow
Kirksville, MO 63501
(816) 626-2324
(816) 626-2728 FAX

RUNNING

Assn of Rd Racing Athletes
PO Box 21021
Spokane, WA 99201-7197
(509) 838-8784

Rd Runners Club of America
1150 S Washington St,
Ste 250
Alexandria, VA 22314
(703) 836-0558
(703) 836-4430 FAX

SHOOTING

Amateur Trapshooting Assn
601 W Natl Rd
Vandalia, OH 45377
(513) 898-4638
(513) 898-5472 FAX

Intl Handgun Metallic
Silhouette Assn
PO Box 5038
Meriden, CT 06450
(230) 237-5244
(230) 237-5244 FAX

USA Shooting
One Olympic Plaza
Colorado Springs, CO 80909
(719) 578-4670
(719) 635-7989 FAX

Natl Rifle Assn
11250 Waples Mill Rd
Fairfax, VA 22030-7400
(703) 267-1000
(703) 267-3971 FAX

Natl Skeet Shooting Assn
5931 Roft Rd
San Antonio, TX 78253
(210) 688-3371
(210) 688-3014 FAX

Natl Sporting Clays
Assn/NSCA
5931 Roft Rd
San Antonio, TX 78253
(210) 688-3371

SHUFFLEBOARD

Intl Shuffleboard Assn, Inc
(Oct–Mar)
Box 102
Bradenton, FL 34209
(941) 792-7286
(941) 792-5963 FAX

Intl Shuffleboard Assn, Inc
(Apr–Sept)
1743 Macedonia Rd
Midland, OH 45148
(937) 685-4915
(937) 685-2063

SKATEBOARDING

Natl Skateboard Assn
7555 Redbud Rd
Granite Bay, CA 95661
(916) 791-3720
(916) 791-3722 FAX

SKIING/SNOWBOARDING

American Birkebeiner Ski
Fdtn/Worldloppet
PO Box 911
Hayward, WI 54843
(715) 634-5025

Intl Snowboard Federation
Box 477
Vail, CO 81658
(303) 949-5473
(303) 949-4949 FAX

North American Pro Ski Corp.
PO Box 680
Bath, ME 04530
(207) 443-2743
(207) 443-3847 FAX

☆ *Chase's 1998 SPORTS Calendar of Events* ☆

Professional Snowboarders
  Assn of North America
0213 Meile Ln
Edwards, CO 81632
(970) 926-SNOW
(970) 926-9696 FAX

Ski for Light, Inc
1455 W Lake St
Minneapolis, MN 55408
(612) 827-3232
(612) 633-4452 FAX

US Deaf Skiers Assn
130 Rosewood Pl
Bridgeport, CT 06610
(203) 372-7248

US Skiing
PO Box 100
Park City, UT 84060
(801) 649-9090
(801) 649-3613 FAX

SLED DOG RACING
Iditarod Trail Committee Sled
  Dog Race
PO Box 870800
Wasilla, AK 99687
(907) 376-5155
(907) 373-6998 FAX

US Sled Dog Sports Federation
1848 A Commercenter E
San Bernardino, CA 92408
(714) 889-1000
(909) 884-0015 FAX

SOCCER
American Professional Soccer
  League/APSL
2 Village Rd
Horsham, PA 19044

Continental Indoor Soccer
  League
16027 Ventura Blvd, Ste 605
Encino, CA 91436
(818) 906-7627
(818) 906-7693 FAX

Lone Star Soccer Alliance
538 Wentworth
Richardson, TX 75081
(214) 234-5454

Major Soccer League/MLS
2049 Century Park E,
  Ste 4390
Los Angeles, CA 90067
(310) 772-2600
(310) 843-4837 FAX

Natl Professional Soccer
  League/NPSL
115 Dewalt Ave, NW
Canton, OH 44702
(330) 455-4625
(330) 455-3885 FAX

US Amateur Soccer Assn,
  Inc/USASA
7800 River Rd
North Bergen, NJ 07047
(201) 861-6277
(201) 861-6341 FAX

US Interregional Soccer
  League/USISL
14947 N Dale
Mabry Hwy, Ste 211
North Bldg, Grand Plaza
Tampa, FL 33618
(813) 963-3909
(813) 963-3807 FAX

US Soccer Federation
1801-181 S Prairie Ave
Chicago, IL 60616
(312) 808-1300
(312) 808-1301 FAX

US Youth Soccer Assn
899 Presidential Dr, Ste 117
Richardson, TX 75081
(214) 235-4499
(800) 4SO-CCER
(214) 235-4480 FAX

SOFTBALL
Intl Softball Congress, Inc
6007 E Hillcrest Circle
Anaheim Hills, CA 92807
(714) 998-5694
(714) 282-7902 FAX

Natl Softball Assn
PO Box 23403
Lexington, KY 40523
(606) 887-4114
(606) 887-4874 FAX

Natl Wheelchair Softball Assn
1616 Todd Ct
Hastings, MN 55033
(612) 437-1792

Over-the-Line Players Assn
PO Box 8964
San Diego, CA 92138

Pro Beach Softball Assn
821 Ensenada Ct
San Diego, CA 92109
(619) 294-4685

Senior Softball–USA, Inc
9 Fleet Ct
Sacramento, CA 95831-2542
(916) 393-8566
(916) 393-8350 FAX

US Slo-Pitch Softball Assn
PO Box 2047
Petersburg, VA 23804
(804) 732-4099
(804) 732-1704 FAX

USA Softball
2801 NE 50th St
Oklahoma City, OK 73111
(405) 424-5266
(405) 424-3855 FAX

Women's Professional
  Fastpitch
90 Madison St, Ste 200
Denver, CO 80202
(303) 316-7800
(303) 316-2779 FAX

SQUASH
Natl Squash Tennis Assn
c/o Yale Club
50 Vanderbilt Ave
New York, NY 10017
(212) 661-2070

US Squash Racquets Assn
PO Box 1216
Bala-Cynwyd, PA 19004-1216
(610) 667-4006
(610) 667-6539 FAX

STICKBALL
Natl Stickball League
19 Hampton Rd
Rockville Center, NY 11570
(516) 887-5339

SURFING
Assn of Surfing Professionals
17942 Sky Park Circle
4401/HJ
Irvine, CA 92714
(714) 851-2774
(714) 851-2773 FAX

Professional Surfing Assn of
  America
530 Sixth St
Hermosa Beach, CA 90254
(310) 372-0414
(310) 372-7457 FAX

Triple Crown, Inc
5563 Haleola St
Honolulu, HI 96821
(808) 377-5850
(808) 377-5850 FAX

US Surfing Federation
350 Jericho Turnpike
Jericho, NY 11753
(516) 935-0400
(516) 942-4705 FAX

SWIMMING/DIVING
US Diving, Inc
201 S Capitol Ave, Ste 430
Indianapolis, IN 46225
(317) 237-5252
(317) 237-5257 FAX

US Swimming, Inc
One Olympic Plaza
Colorado Springs, CO 80909
(719) 578-4578
(719) 578-4669 FAX

US Synchronized Swimming
Pan American Plaza
201 S Capitol Ave, Ste 510
Indianapolis, IN 46225
(317) 237-5700
(317) 237-5705 FAX

TABLE TENNIS
USA Table Tennis
One Olympic Plaza
Colorado Springs, CO 80909
(719) 578-4583
(719) 632-6971 FAX

TEAM HANDBALL
US Team Handball Federation
One Olympic Plaza
Colorado Springs, CO 80909
(719) 578-4582
(719) 475-1240 FAX

TENNIS
ATP Tour
200 ATP Tour Blvd
Ponte Vedra Beach, FL 32082
(904) 285-8000
(904) 285-5966 FAX

American Tennis Assn
16th & Kennedy Sts NW
Washington, DC 20011
(202) 291-9893
(202) 291-9887 FAX

Les Grandes Dames
1152 New York Ave
Winter Park, FL 32789
(407) 628-1682

Natl Fdtn of Wheelchair
  Tennis
940 Calle Amanecer, Ste B
San Clemente, CA 92672
(714) 361-6811

US Recreational Tennis Assn
3112 Adderley Ct
Silver Spring, MD 20906
(301) 598-4820

US Tennis Assn/USTA
70 W Red Oak Lane
White Plains, NY 10604
(914) 696-7000
(914) 696-7167 FAX

World Team Tennis Inc
445 N Wells, Ste 404
Chicago, IL 60610
(312) 245-5300
(312) 245-5321 FAX

WTA Tour
1266 E Main St, 4th Pl
Stamford, CT 06902-3546
(203) 978-1740
(203) 978-1702 FAX

☆ *Chase's 1998 SPORTS Calendar of Events* ☆

TRACK & FIELD
Intercollegiate Assn of
  Amateur Athletes of
  America/IC4A
PO Box 3
Centerville, MA 02632
(508) 771-5060
(508) 771-9481 FAX

USA Track & Field
PO Box 120
Indianapolis, IN 46206-0120
(317) 261-0500
(317) 261-0481 FAX

TRIATHLON
Triathlon Federation/USA
PO Box 15820
Colorado Springs, CO 80935
(719) 597-9090
(800) TRI-1USA
(719) 597-2121 FAX

World Triathlon Corp.
PO Box 1608
Tarpon Springs, FL 34688-
  1608
(813) 942-4767
(813) 942-1987 FAX

TUG-OF-WAR
Tug-of-War Intl Federation
3742 Hwy 213 S, Box 77
Orfordville, WI 53576-0077
(608) 879-2869
(608) 879-2103 FAX

VOLLEYBALL
Assn of Midwest Volleyball
  Professionals, Inc
1229 N North Branch St,
  #212E
Chicago, IL 60622-2411
(312) 266-8580

Assn of Volleyball
  Professionals/AVP
330 Washington Blvd, Ste 600
Marina del Rey, CA 90292
(310) 577-0775
(310) 577-0777 FAX

Natl Volleyball League/NVA
1001 Mission St
S Pasadena, CA 91030
(800) 682-6820
(800) 5-SPIKER FAX

US Volleyball Assn
3595 E Fountain Blvd, Ste I-2
Colorado Springs, CO 80910-
  1740
(719) 637-8300
(719) 597-6307 FAX

Women's Professional
  Volleyball Assn/WPVA
840 Apollo St, Ste 205
El Segunda, CA 90245
(310) 726-0700
(310) 726-0719 FAX

WATER POLO
US Water Polo, Inc
201 S Capitol Ave, Ste 520
Indianapolis, IN 46225
(317) 237-5599
(317) 237-5590 FAX

WATER SKIING
American Water Ski Assn
799 Overlook Dr
Winter Haven, FL 33884
(813) 324-4341
(800) 533-AWSA
(813) 325-8259 FAX

WINDSURFING
Intl Women's Boardsailing
  Assn
PO Box 116
Hood River, OR 97031
(541) 427-8566

US Professional Windsurfing
  Assn
Bayview Business Park #10
Gilford, NH 03246
(603) 293-2727
(603) 293-2723 FAX

US Windsurfing Assn
PO Box 978
Hood River, OR 97031
(541) 386-8708
(541) 386-2108 FAX

WRESTLING
USA Wrestling
6155 Lehman Dr
Colorado Springs, CO 80918
(719) 598-8181
(719) 598-9440 FAX

USA Wrestling–Women's
  Wrestling Committee
6155 Lehman Dr
Colorado Springs, CO 80918
(719) 598-8181
(719) 598-9440 FAX

MULTI-SPORT
ORGANIZATIONS
Amateur Athletic Union of
  the US
The Walt Disney World Resort
PO Box 1000
Lake Buena Vista, FL 32800-
  1000
(407) 363-6170
(407) 363-6171 FAX

American Sportscasters Assn
5 Beekman St, Ste 814
New York, NY 10038
(212) 227-8080
(212) 571-0556 FAX

Athletes in Action
5778 State Route 350
Oregonia, OH 45054
(573) 933-2421
(573) 933-2422 FAX

Black Coaches Assn
PO Box J
Des Moines, IA 50311
(515) 327-1248

Fellowship of Christian
  Athletes
8701 Leeds Rd
Kansas City, MO 64129
(816) 921-0909

Natl Assn of Sports Officials
2017 Lathrop Ave
Racine, WI 53405
(414) 632-5448
(414) 632-5460 FAX

Natl Fed of State High School
  Assns
11724 NW Plaza Circle
Kansas City, MO 64195-0626
(816) 464-5400
(816) 464-5571 FAX

Special Olympics Intl
1325 G St NW, Ste 500
Washington, DC 20005-4709
(202) 628-3630
(202) 824-0200 FAX

US Olympic Committee
One Olympic Plaza
Colorado Springs, CO 80909
(719) 632-5551
(719) 578-4654 FAX

ALPHABETICAL INDEX

Events are generally listed under key words; many broad categories have been created, including African-American, Agriculture, Animals, Archery, Automobiles, Aviation, Badminton, Baseball, Basketball, Bicycle, Boats, Bodybuilding and Weightlifting, Bowling, Boxing, Children, Curling, Dance, Darts, Fishing, Football, Games, Golf, Gun Shows and Shooting Events, Health and Welfare, Hockey (Air), Hockey (Ice), Horses, Horseshoes, Hunting, Kites, Logger/Lumberjack Sports, Motorcycle, Olympics, Parades, Polo, Rodeo, Running, Super Bowl, Surfing, Swimming and Diving, Television, Tennis, Track and Field, Triathlon, Volleyball, Walking and many more. Events that can be attended are also listed under the states or countries where they are to be held. This index indicates only the initial date for each event; see the chronology for inclusive dates of events lasting more than one day.

Mitchell Strikes Out Ruth and Gehrig: Anniv, **Apr 2**
Mitchell, Dale: Birth Anniv, **Aug 23**
Mize, Johnny: Birth Anniv, **Jan 7**
Molitor Gets 3,000th Hit: Anniv, **Sept 13**
Monday Rescues Flag: Anniv, **Apr 25**
Monroe, Marilyn: Birth Anniv, **June 1**
Montreal and San Diego Awarded Franchises: Anniv, **May 27**
Mookie's Grounder Through Buckner's Legs: Anniv, **Oct 25**
Moonlight Graham Plays Only Game: Anniv, **June 29**
Moore, Donnie: Birth Anniv, **Feb 13**
Moore, Terry: Birth Anniv, **May 27**
Moore, Wilcy: Birth Anniv, **May 20**
Moose, Bob: Anniv, **Oct 9**
Moran, Uncle Charlie: Birth Anniv, **Feb 22**
Morgan Hits 256th Homer: Anniv, **June 24**
Mostil, Johnny: Birth Anniv, **June 1**
Mullane, Tony: Birth Anniv, **Jan 20**
Mungo, Van Lingle: Birth Anniv, **June 8**
Municipal Stadium Opens: Anniv, **July 31**
Munson, Thurman: Birth Anniv, **June 7**
Murnane, Tim: Birth Anniv, **June 4**
Murphy, Johnny: Birth Anniv, **July 14**
Murtaugh, Danny: Birth Anniv, **Oct 8**
Musial Gets 3,000th Hit: Anniv, **May 13**
Musial Hits Five Homers: Anniv, **May 2**
Mustang League World Series (Irving, TX), **Aug 5**
Mutrie, Jim: Birth Anniv, **June 13**
NAIA Softball Chmpshp (Broken Arrow, OK), **May 18**
NAIA World Series (Sioux City, IA), **May 18**
Natl Little League Base Week, **June 8**
Navin Field Opens: Anniv, **Apr 20**
Navin, Frank: Birth Anniv, **Mar 7**
NCAA Div I Tourn (Finals) (Omaha, NE), **May 29**
NCAA Div I Tourn (Regionals), **May 21**
NCAA Div II Tourn (Finals) (Montgomery, AL), **May 23**
NCAA Div II Tourn (Regionals), **May 17**
NCAA Div III Tourn (Finals) (Salem, VA), **May 23**
NCAA Div III Tourn (Regionals), **May 14**
Neun, Johnny: Birth Anniv, **Oct 28**
Newcombe Wins First Cy Young Award: Anniv, **Nov 21**
Newsom, Bobo: Birth Anniv, **Aug 11**
Nichols, Kid: Birth Anniv, **Sept 14**
Niekro Brothers the Winningest: Anniv, **June 1**
Niekro Strikes Out 3,000: Anniv, **July 4**
Niekro Wins 300 Games: Anniv, **Oct 6**
No Rainout Record: Anniv, **May 20**
Nolan Ryan Pitches Seventh No-Hitter: Anniv, **May 1**
Northern League Independent Pro Baseball Season (various), **May 29**
Nuxhall Is Youngest Player: Anniv, **June 10**
O'Day, Hank: Birth Anniv, **July 8**
O'Doul, Lefty: Birth Anniv, **Mar 4**
O'Malley, Walter: Birth Anniv, **Oct 9**
O'Neill, Steve: Birth Anniv, **July 6**
Oeschger, Joe: Birth Anniv, **May 24**
Old Comiskey Park Opens: Anniv, **July 1**
Oldest Managerial Debut: Anniv, **June 18**
Oldest Pitcher to Win Game: Anniv, **Aug 14**
Oldest Player to Hit Home Run: Anniv, **June 27**
Olin, Steve: Birth Anniv, **Oct 4**
One-Armed Outfielder: Anniv, **Apr 18**
Only 20th-Century Tripleheader: Anniv, **Oct 2**
Only All-Star Game Tie: Anniv, **July 31**
Only Senators' Home Run at Home: Anniv, **Sept 7**
Opening Day Barrage: Anniv, **Apr 14**
Opening Day No-Hitter: Anniv, **Apr 16**
Orioles End Losing Streak: Anniv, **Apr 29**
Orioles Set New Home Run Mark: Anniv, **Sept 15**
Otis, Bill: Birth Anniv, **Dec 24**
Ott Gets Ejected Twice: Anniv, **June 9**
Ott Hits 500th Home Run: Anniv, **Aug 1**
Ott, Mel: Birth Anniv, **Mar 2**
Outdoors and Indoors: Anniv, **June 7**
Overall, Orval: Birth Anniv, **Feb 2**
Owen, Marv: Birth Anniv, **Mar 22**
PAC-10 Playoff, **May 14**

Paciorek Goes 3-for-3: Anniv, **Sept 29**
Page, Joe: Birth Anniv, **Oct 28**
Paige Pitches Complete Game: Anniv, **Aug 6**
Paige, Satchel: Birth Anniv, **July 7**
Palomino League World Series (Greensboro, NC), **Aug 7**
Peanut-Kids-Baseball Day (Conshohocken, PA), **Apr 4**
Peckinpaugh, Roger: Birth Anniv, **Feb 5**
Peitz, Heinie: Birth Anniv, **Nov 28**
Pennock, Herb: Birth Anniv, **Feb 10**
Perry Wins 300th Game: Anniv, **May 6**
Pete Rose Gets 3,000th Hit: Anniv, **May 5**
Petway, Bruce: Death Anniv, **July 4**
Pfeffer, Fred: Birth Anniv, **Mar 17**
Pfeffer, Jeff: Birth Anniv, **Mar 4**
Phillies Win First World Series: Anniv, **Oct 21**
Phillippe, Deacon: Birth Anniv, **May 23**
Piersall Runs Backwards: Anniv, **June 23**
Pilots Debut: Anniv, **Apr 11**
Pinch-Hit Home Run Record: Anniv, **Aug 5**
Pinch-Runner Pinches Bases: Anniv, **Sept 2**
Pinelli, Babe: Birth Anniv, **Oct 18**
Pinson, Vada: Birth Anniv, **Aug 11**
Pipgras, George: Birth Anniv, **Dec 20**
Pipp, Wally: Birth Anniv, **Feb 17**
Pirates Lose Three Games: Anniv, **Sept 1**
Pitch Within 20 Seconds: Anniv, **Jan 24**
Pitcher Dunning Hits Last Grand Slam: Anniv, **May 11**
Pitcher Hits Homer in Every Park: Anniv, **Aug 15**
Pitcher Hits Two Grand Slams: Anniv, **July 3**
Plank, Eddie: Birth Anniv, **Aug 31**
Pollet, Howie: Birth Anniv, **June 26**
Pony League World Series (Washington, PA), **Aug 15**
Posey, Cum: Birth Anniv, **June 20**
Post, Wally: Birth Anniv, **July 9**
Potato Ball: Anniv, **Aug 31**
Powell, Jake: Birth Anniv, **July 15**
Pratt, Del: Birth Anniv, **Jan 10**
Prince, Bob: Birth Anniv, **July 1**
Pulliam, Harry: Birth Anniv, **Feb 8**
Quinn, Jack: Birth Anniv, **July 5**
Radbourne, Hoss: Birth Anniv, **Dec 11**
Raschi, Vic: Birth Anniv, **Mar 28**
Ray Chapman Beaned: Anniv, **Aug 16**
Red Stockings Lose First Game: Anniv, **June 14**
Reggie Jackson Hits 500th Home Run: Anniv, **Sept 17**
Reggie's Three Series Home Runs: Anniv, **Oct 18**
Reiser, Pete: Birth Anniv, **Mar 17**
Reulbach, Ed: Birth Anniv, **Dec 1**
Rhem, Flint: Birth Anniv, **Jan 24**
Richard Suffers Stroke: Anniv, **July 30**
Richards, Paul: Birth Anniv, **Nov 21**
Richmond Pitches Perfect Game: Anniv, **June 12**
Richmond, Lee: Birth Anniv, **May 5**
Rickert, Marv: Birth Anniv, **Jan 8**
Rickey Allows 13 Stolen Bases: Anniv, **June 28**
Rickey Henderson Steals Base Theft Crown: Anniv, **May 1**
Rickey, Branch: Birth Anniv, **Dec 20**
Rigler, Cy: Birth Anniv, **May 16**
Riverfront Stadium Opens: Anniv, **June 30**
Robertson's Perfect Game: Anniv, **Apr 30**
Robinson Breaks the Color Line: Anniv, **Apr 15**
Robinson Elected to Hall of Fame: Anniv, **Jan 23**
Robinson Hits Home Run Out of Memorial Stadium: Anniv, **May 8**
Robinson Named First Black Manager: Anniv, **Oct 3**
Robinson's Number 42 Retired: Anniv, **Apr 15**
Robinson, Jackie: Birth Anniv, **Jan 31**
Robinson, Wilbert: Birth Anniv, **June 2**
Rockies Debut: Anniv, **Apr 9**
Rogin, Bullet Joe: Birth Anniv, **July 28**
Rogovin, Saul: Birth Anniv, **Oct 10**
Rolfe, Red: Birth Anniv, **Oct 17**
Rommel, Ed: Birth Anniv, **Sept 13**
Ron Necciai Strikes Out the Side: Anniv, **May 13**
Root, Charlie: Birth Anniv, **Mar 17**
Rosar, Buddy: Birth Anniv, **July 3**
Rose Becomes All-Time Hit Leader: Anniv, **Sept 11**
Rose Bumps Pallone: Anniv, **Apr 30**

Rose Gets 4,000th Hit: Anniv, **Apr 13**
Rose Made Ineligible: Anniv, **Aug 24**
Rose Ties Cobb: Anniv, **Sept 8**
Rose's Hitting Streak Ends: Anniv, **Aug 1**
Rowe, Schoolboy: Birth Anniv, **Jan 11**
Rowland, Pants: Birth Anniv, **Feb 12**
Roy Campanella Night: Anniv, **May 7**
Rucker, Johnny: Birth Anniv, **Jan 15**
Rucker, Nap: Birth Anniv, **Sept 30**
Ruether, Dutch: Birth Anniv, **Sept 13**
Runnels, Pete: Birth Anniv, **Jan 28**
Ruppert, Jacob: Birth Anniv, **Aug 5**
Ruth Breaks Own Record: Anniv, **July 16**
Ruth Clears Comiskey Roof: Anniv, **Aug 16**
Ruth Hits 500th Home Run: Anniv, **Aug 11**
Ruth Hits 700th Home Run: Anniv, **July 13**
Ruth Hits Three Series Home Runs: Anniv, **Oct 6**
Ruth Plays First Game for Yankees: Anniv, **Apr 14**
Ruth Retires: Anniv, **June 2**
Ruth Signs with Braves: Anniv, **Feb 26**
Ruth Sold to Yankees: Anniv, **Jan 3**
Ruth's Final At-Bat: Anniv, **May 31**
Ruth, Babe: Birth Anniv, **Feb 6**
Ruth, Babe: Death Anniv, **Aug 16**
Ryan First Million-Dollar Player: Anniv, **Nov 19**
Ryan Pitches Fifth No-Hitter: Anniv, **Sept 26**
Ryan Strikes Out 4,000th Batter: Anniv, **July 11**
Ryan Strikes Out 5,000: Anniv, **Aug 22**
Ryan Wins 300th Game: Anniv, **July 31**
Ryan's Express: Anniv, **Sept 7**
Ryan, Connie: Birth Anniv, **Feb 27**
Sallee, Slim: Birth Anniv, **Feb 3**
Sandberg Becomes Highest Paid Player: Anniv, **Mar 2**
Satchel Paige's Last Game: Anniv, **Sept 25**
Sawatski, Carl: Birth Anniv, **Nov 4**
Schaefer, Germany: Birth Anniv, **Feb 4**
Schalk, Ray: Birth Anniv, **Aug 12**
Schang, Wally: Birth Anniv, **Aug 22**
Scheffing, Bob: Birth Anniv, **Aug 11**
Schmidt Hits 500th Home Run: Anniv, **Apr 18**
Schulte, Frank: Birth Anniv, **Sept 17**
Schulte, Fred: Birth Anniv, **Jan 13**
Schumacher, Hal: Birth Anniv, **Nov 23**
Score Gets Hit in Eye: Anniv, **May 7**
Scott's Streak Stopped: Anniv, **May 6**
Scott, Everett: Birth Anniv, **Nov 19**
Scurry, Rod: Birth Anniv, **Mar 17**
Season Resumes with All-Star Game: Anniv, **Aug 9**
Seattle Pilots Become Milwaukee Brewers: Anniv, **Apr 1**
Seaver Wins 300th Game: Anniv, **Aug 4**
SEC Tourn, **May 13**
Second Half of Double No-Hitter: Anniv, **June 15**
Selee, Frank: Birth Anniv, **Oct 26**
Selig Named Acting Commissioner: Anniv, **Sept 9**
Senators Open Last Season in DC: Anniv, **Apr 5**
Sewell Strikes Out Twice: Anniv, **May 26**
Sewell, Joe: Birth Anniv, **Oct 9**
Sewell, Luke: Birth Anniv, **Jan 5**
Sewell, Rip: Birth Anniv, **May 11**
Seybold, Socks: Birth Anniv, **Nov 13**
Shawkey, Bob: Birth Anniv, **Dec 4**
Shellenback, Frank: Birth Anniv, **Dec 16**
Sheridan, John: Death Anniv, **Nov 2**
Shibe, Ben: Death Anniv, **Jan 14**
Shocker, Urban: Birth Anniv, **Aug 22**
Shore, Ernie: Birth Anniv, **Mar 24**
Short Major League Career: Anniv, **July 27**
Short, Chris: Birth Anniv, **Sept 19**
Shortest Game in History: Anniv, **Sept 28**
Shortest Night Game: Anniv, **May 21**
Show, Eric: Birth Anniv, **May 19**
Simmons, Al: Birth Anniv, **May 22**
Simpson, Harry: Birth Anniv, **Dec 3**
Sisler, George: Birth Anniv, **Mar 24**
SkyDome Debut: Anniv, **June 5**
Slaughter Scores from First: Anniv, **Oct 15**
Smith, Charlie: Birth Anniv, **Sept 15**
Smith, Elmer: Birth Anniv, **Sept 21**
Smith, Hilton: Birth Anniv, **Feb 27**
Smith, Phenomenal: Birth Anniv, **Dec 12**
Smoky Joe Bests the Big Train: Anniv, **Sept 1**

☆ *Chase's 1998 SPORTS Calendar of Events* ☆   Index

Howe, Art: Birth, Dec 15
Howe, Gordie: Birth, Mar 31
Howe, Mark: Birth, May 28
Howe, Steve: Birth, Mar 10
Hoy, Dummy: Birth Anniv, May 23
Hoyle, Edmund: Death Anniv, Aug 29
Hoyt, Dewey LaMarr: Birth, Jan 1
Hoyt, Waite: Birth Anniv, Sept 9
Hrabosky, Al: Birth, July 21
Hrbek, Kent: Birth, May 21
Hrudey, Kelly Stephen: Birth, Jan 13
Hubbard, Cal: Birth Anniv, Oct 31
Hubbard, Glenn: Birth, Sept 25
Hubbell, Carl: Birth Anniv, June 22
Hubbs, Ken: Birth Anniv, Dec 23
Hudler, Rex: Birth, Sept 2
Hudson Highlander (Putnam County, NY),
    Oct 11
Hudson, Charles: Birth, Mar 16
Huff n Puff Hot Air Balloon Rally (Topeka, KS),
    Sept 11
Huff, Sam: Birth, Oct 4
Hug a Cowboy Day (Raymond, Alta), July 1
Huggins, Miller: Birth Anniv, Mar 27
Hughson, Tex: Birth Anniv, Feb 9
Hula Hoop Day©, Sept 21
Hulbert, William: Birth Anniv, Oct 23
Hull, Bobby: Hull Gets 1,000th Point: Anniv,
    Dec 12
Hull, Brett: Birth, Aug 9
Hull, James Kent: Birth, Jan 13
Hull, Robert Marvin (Bobby): Birth, Jan 3
Hulman, Tony: Birth Anniv, Feb 11
Humphries, Stan: Birth, Apr 14
Hundley, Randy: Birth, June 1
Hundley, Todd: Birth, May 27
Hunt, Lamar: Birth, Aug 2
Hunter's Moon, Nov 4
Hunter, Brian Ronald: Birth, Mar 4
Hunter, Catfish: Birth, Apr 8
Hunting
    Cheltenham Gold Cup Mtg (Prestbury, England),
        Mar 15
    Great Outdoor Show (Aberdeen, SD), Apr 3
    Hunting and Fish Day, Natl (Pres Proc), Sept 26
    Milwaukee Journal Sentinel Sports Show
        (Milwaukee, WI), Mar 13
    Northeast Great Outdoors Show (Albany, NY),
        Mar 20
    Waterfowl Festival (Easton, MD), Nov 13
    World's Chmpshp Duck-Calling Contest and
        Wings over the Prairie Fest (Stuttgart, AR),
        Nov 27
Hurdle, Clint: Birth, July 30
Hurley, Bobby: Birth, June 28
Husing, Ted: Birth Anniv, Nov 27
Huskey, Butch: Birth, Nov 10
Hutchinson, Fred: Birth Anniv, Aug 12
Hutson, Don: Birth Anniv, Jan 31
Hyman, Flo: Birth Anniv, Aug 29
I Love New York Horse Show (Lake Placid, NY),
    July 1
Iafrate, Al: Birth, Mar 21
Ice Skating
    Boitano Wins "Battle of the Brians": Anniv,
        Feb 20
    Dick Button Wins Gold Medal: Anniv, Feb 5
    Hamill Wins World Title: Anniv, Mar 6
    Heiss Wins Gold Medal: Anniv, Feb 23
    Jenkins Wins Gold Medal: Anniv, Feb 26
    Torvill and Dean Achieve Perfection: Anniv,
        Mar 12
Icescape (Appleton, WI), Feb 13
Idaho
    Dodge Natl Circuit Finals Rodeo (Pocatello),
        Mar 18
    First Security Boulder Mountain Tour (Sun
        Valley), Feb 7
    First Security Winter Games of Idaho (5 cities),
        Feb 7
    Hagerman Fossil Days (Hagerman), May 23
    McCall Winter Carnival (McCall), Jan 30
    Memorial Day Golf Tourn (Pinehurst), May 22
    NAIA Men's Division II Basketball Chmpshp
        (Nampa), Mar 11
    NCAA Men's Div I Bask Tourn (1st/2nd rounds)
        (Boise), Mar 12

Silver Hoops 3-on-3 Tourn (Kellogg), July 25
Silver Valley Horseshoe Tourn (Kellogg), Aug 8
Simplot Games (Pocatello), Feb 19
Twin Falls County Fair and Rodeo (Filer), Sept 3
Iditarod Sled Dog Race (Anchorage, AK), Mar 7
Ilitch, Mike: Birth, July 20
Illinois
    All-Canada Show (Rockford), Jan 19
    All-Canada Show (St. Charles), Jan 15
    Amateur Soft Assn Girls 14-and-Under Natl Fast-
        Pitch Chmpshp (Rockford), Aug 5
    Bark in the Park (Chicago), May 2
    Big Ten Men's Golf Chmpshp (Urbana), May 8
    Chicago Boat, Sports and RV Show (Chicago),
        Jan 21
    Chicago Marathon (Chicago), Oct 11
    Chicago's Windy City Jitterbug Dance (Franklin
        Pk), Jan 17
    Fishing Has No Boundaries (Chicago), Sept 19
    Great Cardboard Boat Regatta (Carbondale),
        Apr 25
    Great Cardboard Boat Regatta (Rock Island),
        July 4
    Great River Grand Prix (Quincy), Sept 26
    Hard Rock Cafe 5K (Chicago), June 14
    Hog Capital of the World Festival (Kewanee),
        Sept 4
    Jewel-Osco Natl Amateur All-Star Base Tourn
        (Chicago), June 23
    Lawn Mower Race, Sta-Bil Natl Chmpshp
        (Rockford), Aug 29
    Monster Mopar Weekend (Madison), Sept 11
    Motorola Western Open (Lemont), June 25
    Mud Volleyball Tourn (Rockford), Aug 8
    NCAA Men's Div I Bask Tourn (1st/2nd rounds)
        (Chicago), Mar 12
    NCAA Men's/Women's Div II Outdoor Track/Field
        Chmpshp (Finals) (Edwardsville), May 21
    NJCAA Div II Men's Natl Basketball Finals
        (Danville), Mar 18
    Rockford Area Senior Games (Rockford), Sept 3
    Sez Who? Fourplay March Madness (Chicago),
        Mar 8
    Sporting Assn World Sports Expo, Natl
        (Chicago), July 18
    Stearman Fly-In, Natl (Galesburg), Sept 2
    Strictly Sail at Navy Pier (Chicago), Jan 29
    Turtle Races (Danville), June 6
    US Junior Amateur (Golf) Chmpshp (Lake
        Forest), July 21
    US Senior Amateur (Golf) Chmpshp (Glencoe),
        Sept 14
    WIBC Chmpshp Tourn (Quad Cities), Apr 4
    WIBC Queen's Tourn (Quad Cities), May 12
    Women's Intl Bowling Congress Annual Mtg
        (Quad Cities), Apr 27
    World Freefall Convention (Quincy), Aug 7
    WROK/WZOK/WXXQ Anything that Floats Raft
        Race (Rockford), July 4
    WROK/WZOK/WXXQ Chili Shoot Out (Rockford),
        Oct 3
Incaviglia, Pete: Birth, Apr 2
Independence Day Challenge Run (Boyne City,
    MI), July 4
Independence Day, US (Fourth of July)
    Independence Day Challenge Run (Boyne City,
        MI), July 4
    Lizard Race, World's Greatest (Lovington, NM),
        July 4
Indiana
    All-Canada Show (Indianapolis), Jan 12
    Big East Soft Tourn (Notre Dame), May 2
    Big Ten Men's Indoor Track and Field Chmpshp
        (West Lafayette), Feb 27
    Big Ten Women's Bask Tourn (Indianapolis),
        Feb 27
    Big Ten Women's Swimming and Diving
        Chmpshp (Bloomington), Feb 19
    Chmpshp Cat Show (Indianapolis), Oct 31
    Circle City Classic (Indianapolis), Oct 3
    Colt League Pony Baseball World Series
        (Lafayette), Aug 11
    Elkhart Grand Prix/Motor Sports Weekend
        (Elkhart), July 11
    Fishing Has No Boundaries (Grantsburg),
        Sept 12
    Fishing Has No Boundaries (Monticello), May 16

Hoosier Horse Fair Expo (Indianapolis), Apr 17
Hoosier State Games, June 1
Indiana State Senior Games (Evansville), June 1
Little 500 (Anderson), May 23
NCAA Women's Div I Tennis Chmpshp (Finals)
    (Notre Dame), May 21
Strawberry 100 Bike Tour (Crawfordsville),
    June 14
Strawberry Fest (Crawfordsville), June 12
Sugar Creek Canoe Race and Tri Sport Fest
    (Crawfordsville), Apr 25
Inner Tube Race: "Hey Rube Get a Tube" (Pt
    Pleasant, NJ), Sept 20
Inter-State Fair and Rodeo (Coffeyville, KS),
    Aug 8
Intercollegiate Bowl Chmpshp (University
    Center, MI, and Lincoln, NE), Apr 15
Intl Dragon Boat Races (Hong Kong), June 6
Intl Texas Holdem Poker Tourn (Dawson City,
    YT, Canada), Sept 13
Iowa
    All-Canada Show (Des Moines), Feb 5
    Big Ten Women's Gymnastics Chmpshp (Iowa
        City), Mar 21
    Big Twelve Men's/Women's Indoor Track
        Chmpshp (Ames), Feb 27
    Bike Van Buren (Van Buren County), Aug 15
    Britt Draft Horse Show (Britt), Sept 4
    Field of Dreams Fest (Dyersville), Aug 16
    Hawkeye Medical Supply Hospice Road Races
        (Iowa City), Oct 18
    Melon City Criterium (Muscatine), May 24
    NAIA Baseball World Series (Sioux City),
        May 18
    NAIA Wom Div II Basketball Chmpshp (Sioux
        City), Mar 11
    NCAA Div III Wrest Chmpshp (Finals) (Fayette),
        Mar 6
    Perry's "BRR" (Bike Ride to Rippey) (Perry),
        Feb 7
    Register's Bicycle Ride Across Iowa (Des
        Moines), July 19
    Southwest Iowa Prof Hot-Air Balloon Races
        (Creston), Sept 19
    USA Intl Dragon Boat Fest (Dubuque), Sept 11
    WIBC Chmpshp Tourn (Quad Cities), Apr 4
    WIBC Queen's Tourn (Quad Cities), May 12
    Women's Intl Bowling Congress Annual Mtg
        (Quad Cities), Apr 27
Irish, Ned: Birth Anniv, May 6
IROC XXII Intl Race of Champions (Daytona,
    FL), Feb 13
Iroquois Steeplechase (Nashville, TN), May 9
Irsay, Robert: Birth Anniv, Mar 5
Irvin, Michael: Birth, Mar 5
Irvin, Monte: Birth, Feb 25
Irwin, Hale: Birth, June 3
Ismail, Qadry Rahmadan: Birth, Nov 8
Ismail, Rocket: Birth, Nov 18
Israel
    Israeli Olympic Massacre: Anniv, Sept 5
Isringhausen, Jason Derek: Birth, Sept 7
Isuzu Celebrity Golf Chmpshp (Lake Tahoe,
    NV), July 10
Italian Fest, Upper Ohio Valley (Wheeling, WV),
    July 24
Italy
    Giostra della Quintana (Joust), Sept 13
    Historical Regatta, Sept 6
    Joust of the Saracen, Sept 6
    Palio Dei Balestrieri (crossbow), May 31
    Palio del Golfo, Aug 9
Iverson, Allen: Birth, June 7
Jackalope Days (Douglas, WY), June 19
Jackson Hole Shrine Cutter Race (Jackson
    Hole, WY), Feb 13
Jackson, Al: Birth, Dec 25
Jackson, Bo: Birth, Nov 30
Jackson, Danny Lynn: Birth, Jan 5
Jackson, Grant: Birth, Sept 28
Jackson, Jim: Birth, Oct 14
Jackson, Keith: Birth, Apr 19
Jackson, Larry: Birth Anniv, June 2
Jackson, Mark: Birth, Apr 1
Jackson, Phil: Birth, Sept 17
Jackson, Reggie: Birth, May 18
Jackson, Roy Lee: Birth, May 1

NCAA Men's Div I Bask Tourn (1st/2nd rounds) (Lexington), **Mar 12**
NCAA Men's Div II Bask Tourn (Finals) (Louisville), **Mar 18**
Running of the Rodents (Louisville), **Apr 22**
Sawyer Triathlon (Louisville), **Aug 1**
SEC Women's Tennis Chmpshp (Lexington), **Apr 16**
Kentucky Derby
Dancer's Image vs. Forward Pass: Anniv, **May 4**
First Televised Derby: Anniv, **May 3**
Genuine Risk Second Filly to Win Derby: Anniv, **May 3**
Kentucky Derby (Louisville), **May 2**
Kentucky Derby Fest (Louisville), **Apr 17**
Kentucky Derby, First: Anniv, **May 17**
Only Derby in April: Anniv, **Apr 29**
Regret First Filly to Win: Anniv, **May 8**
Secretariat Wins in Record Time: Anniv, **May 5**
Shoemaker Stands Up in the Saddle: Anniv, **May 4**
Sir Barton Wins: Anniv, **May 10**
Winning Colors Third Filly to Win: Anniv, **May 7**
Kenwood Cup, Hawaii Intl Ocean Racing Series (Oahu, HI), Aug 3
Kerr, Steve: Birth, Sept 27
Kersey, Jerome: Birth, June 26
Kessinger, Don: Birth, July 17
Ketchel, Stanley: Birth Anniv, Sept 14
Key, Jimmy: Birth, Apr 22
KGBX Super Bowl Food Fight (Springfield, MO), Jan 23
KGBX Typewriter Toss (Springfield, MO), Apr 22
Khabibulin, Nikolai: Birth, Jan 13
Khristich, Dimitri: Birth, July 23
Kiam, Victor Kermit, II: Birth, Dec 7
Kidd, Jason: Birth, Mar 23
Kidd, Trevor: Birth, Mar 29
Kieran, John: Birth Anniv, Aug 2
Kile, Darryl: Birth, Dec 2
Killebrew, Harmon: Birth, June 29
Killy, Jean-Claude: Birth, Aug 30
Kinard, Bruiser: Birth Anniv, Oct 23
Kinder, Ellis: Birth Anniv, July 26
Kiner, Ralph: Birth, Oct 27
King, Albert: Birth, Dec 17
King, Bernard: Birth, Dec 4
King, Betsy: Birth, Aug 13
King, Billie Jean: Birth, Nov 22
King, Don: Birth, Aug 20
King, Jeff: Birth, Dec 26
King, Martin Luther, Jr, Birthday Observed, Jan 19
King, Mickey: Birth, July 26
King, Nellie: Birth, Mar 15
King, Stacey: Birth, Jan 29
Kingman, Dave: Birth, Dec 21
Kinnick, Nile: Birth Anniv, July 9
Kirby, Clay: Birth Anniv, June 25
Kison, Bruce: Birth, Feb 18
Kite Flite (Alamagordo, NM), Apr 4
Kite, Greg: Birth, Aug 5
Kite, Tom: Birth, Dec 9
Kiteday (Charlottesville, VA), May 10
Kitefest (Kalamazoo, MI), Apr 25
Kites
Frankenmuth Skyfest (Frankenmuth, MI), **May 3**
Kite Flite (Alamogordo, NM), **Apr 4**
Kiteday (Charlottesville, VA), **May 10**
Kitefest (Kalamazoo, MI), **Apr 25**
Mid-American Sport Kite Classic (Kalamazoo, MI), **June 20**
Smithsonian Kite Festival (Washington, DC), **Mar 28**
Sno'Fly (Kalamazoo, MI), **Jan 1**
Kittle, Ronald Dale (Ron): Birth, Jan 5
Kittles, Kerry: Birth, June 12
Kiviat, Abe: Birth Anniv, June 23
Kiwanis Club Car Show (Trenton, MO), Oct 18
Klein, Chuck: Birth Anniv, Oct 7
Kleine, Joseph William (Joe): Birth, Jan 4
Klem, Bill: Birth Anniv, Feb 22
Klesko, Ryan: Birth, June 12
Klima, Petr: Birth, Dec 23
Klingler, David: Birth, Feb 17
Klondike Intl Dart Festival (Dawson City, Yukon, Canada), May 22

Klusewski, Ted: Birth Anniv, Sept 10
Kneivel, Evel: Birth, Oct 17
Knepper, Bob: Birth, May 25
Knight, Bobby: Birth, Oct 25
Knight, O. Raymond: Birth Anniv, Apr 8
Knight, Ray: Birth, Dec 28
Knight, Tom: Birth, Dec 29
Knight, Travis: Birth, Sept 13
Knoblauch, Chuck: Birth, July 7
Knoxville Boat Show (Knoxville, TN), Mar 5
Knoxville Fishing Expo (Knoxville, TN), Jan 22
Knuckles Down Month, Natl, Apr 1
Koenig, Mark: Birth Anniv, July 19
Koivu, Saku: Birth, Nov 23
Kolzig, Olaf: Birth, Apr 6
Koncak, Jon: Birth, May 17
Konetchy, Ed: Birth Anniv, Sept 3
Kono, Tommy: Birth, June 27
Konstantinov, Vladimir: Birth, Mar 19
Konstanty, Jim: Birth Anniv, Mar 2
Koonce, Cal: Birth Anniv, Nov 18
Koosman, Jerry: Birth, Dec 23
Korbut, Olga: Birth, May 16
Korea: Tano Day, May 30
Kosar, Bernie: Birth, Nov 25
Kotite, Rich: Birth, Oct 13
Koufax, Sandy: Birth, Dec 30
Kovalev, Alexei: Birth, Feb 24
Kozlov, Slava: Birth, May 3
Kramer, Erik: Birth, Nov 6
Kramer, Jerry: Birth, Jan 23
Kranepool, Ed: Birth, Nov 8
Kravchuk, Igor: Birth, Sept 13
Kress, Red: Birth Anniv, Jan 2
Kreuter, Chad: Birth, Aug 26
Krone, Julie: Birth, July 24
Kruk, John: Birth, Feb 9
Krygier, Todd: Birth, Oct 12
Kubek, Tony: Birth, Oct 12
Kuczynski, Bert: Birth Anniv, Jan 8
Kuenn, Harvey: Birth Anniv, Dec 4
Kuhel, Joe: Birth Anniv, June 25
Kuhn, Bowie: Birth, Oct 28
Kuiper, Duane: Birth, June 19
Kukoc, Toni: Birth, Sept 18
Kupchak, Mitch: Birth, May 24
Kurowski, Whitey: Birth, Apr 19
Kurri, Jari: Birth, May 18
Kwanzaa, Dec 26
Labine, Clem: Birth, Aug 6
Labonte, Terry: Birth, Nov 16
Labor Day, Sept 7
Lachemann, Marcel: Birth, June 13
Lachemann, Rene: Birth, May 4
LaCoss, Mike: Birth, May 30
Lacoste, Rene: Birth Anniv, July 2
Lacrosse
ACC Men's Chmpshp (Charlottesville, VA), **Apr 17**
ACC Women's Chmpshp (Charlottesville, VA), **Apr 18**
Lacrosse Classic, Lee-Jackson (Lexington, VA), **May 2**
NCAA Men's Div I Chmpshp (Finals) (New Brunswick, NJ), **May 23**
NCAA Men's Div II/III Chmpshp (Finals) (News Brunswick, NJ), **May 24**
NCAA Women's Chmpshp (Baltimore, MD), **May 15**
Ladies' Day Initiated in Baseball: Anniv, June 6
Ladouceur, Randy: Birth, June 30
Laettner, Christian: Birth, Aug 17
LaFleur, David: Birth, Jan 29
Lafleur, Guy: Birth, Sept 20
Lafontaine, Pat: Birth, Feb 22
Laimbeer, Bill: Birth, May 19
Lajoie, Nap: Birth Anniv, Sept 5
Lake Placid Horse Show (Lake Placid, NY), June 24
Lake Winnebago Sturgeon Season (Fond du Lac, WI), Feb 6
Lakestride Half-Marathon (Ludington, MI), June 20
Lalas, Alexi: Birth, June 1
Lambeau, Curly: Birth Anniv, Apr 9
Lambert, John Harold (Jack): Birth, July 8
Lamont, Gene: Birth, Dec 25

Land, Andrew: Birth, June 29
Landis, Kenesaw: Birth Anniv, Nov 20
Landrith, Hobie: Birth, Mar 16
Landry, Tom: Birth, Sept 11
Lane, Frank: Birth Anniv, Feb 1
Lane, Night Train: Birth, Apr 16
Lang, Kenard: Birth, Jan 31
Langer, Jim: Birth, May 16
Langham, Antonio: Birth, July 31
Langston, Mark: Birth, Aug 20
Lanier, Bob: Birth, Sept 10
Lanier, Hal: Birth, July 4
Lanier, Willie: Birth, Aug 21
Lankford, Ray: Birth, June 5
Lansford, Carney: Birth, Feb 7
Lapchick, Joe: Birth Anniv, Apr 12
LaPoint, Dave: Birth, July 29
Lardner, Ring: Birth Anniv, Mar 6
Largent, Steve: Birth, Sept 28
Larionov, Igor: Birth, Dec 3
Larkin, Barry: Birth, Apr 28
Larsen, Don: Birth, Aug 7
Larsen, Don: Don Larsen's Perfect Game: Anniv, Oct 8
LaRussa, Tony: Birth, Oct 4
Lary, Frank: Birth, Apr 10
Lary, Lyn: Birth Anniv, Jan 28
LaSalle Banks Chicago Marathon (Chicago, IL), Oct 11
Lasorda, Tommy: Birth, Sept 22
Latham, Arlie: Birth Anniv, Mar 15
Latman, Barry: Birth, May 21
Lau, Charlie: Birth Anniv, Apr 12
Lauda, Niki: Birth, Feb 22
Lauer, Brad: Birth, Oct 27
Lavagetto, Cookie: Birth Anniv, Dec 1
LaValliere, Mike: Birth, Aug 18
Lavelli, Dante: Birth, Feb 23
Laver, Rod: Birth, Aug 9
Law, Rudy: Birth, Oct 7
Law, Vernon: Birth, Mar 12
Lawn Mower Race, Sta-Bil Natl Chmpshp (Rockford, IL), Aug 29
Layden, Elmer: Birth Anniv, May 4
Layne, Bobby: Birth Anniv, Dec 19
Lazorko, Jack: Birth, Mar 30
Lazzeri, Tony: Birth Anniv, Dec 6
Leach, Rick: Birth, May 4
Leach, Tommy: Birth Anniv, Nov 4
Leadville Mosquito Marathon (Leadville, CO), July 18
Leadville Trail 100 Bike Race (Leadville, CO), Aug 15
Leadville Trail 100 Ultramarathon (Leadville, CO), Aug 22
Leadville Trail 100—10K (Leadville, CO), Aug 16
Leahy, Frank: Birth Anniv, Aug 27
Leavenworth River Fest (Leavenworth, KS), Sept 12
LeClair, John: Birth, July 5
Lee, Amp: Birth, Oct 1
Lee, Bill: Birth, Dec 28
Lee, Sammy: Birth, Aug 1
Lee-Jackson Lacrosse Classic (Lexington, VA), May 2
Leetch, Brian: Birth, Mar 3
Lefevbre, James Kenneth (Jim): Birth, Jan 7
LeFlore, Ron: Birth, June 16
Left-Handed (Golf) Tourn, Natl, June 23
Leiber, Hank: Birth Anniv, Jan 17
Leibrandt, Charlie: Birth, Oct 4
Leiter, Al: Birth, Oct 23
Leiter, Mark: Birth, Apr 13
Lemaire, Jacques: Birth, Sept 7
LeMaster, Johnnie: Birth, June 19
Lemieux, Claude: Birth, July 16
Lemieux, Mario: Birth, Oct 5
Lemke, Mark: Birth, Aug 13
Lemon, Bob: Birth, Sept 22
Lemon, Meadowlark: Birth, Apr 25
Lemond Wins Tour de France: Anniv, July 27
LeMond, Greg: Birth, June 26
Lendl, Ivan: Birth, Mar 7
Lenexa Freedom Run (Lenexa, KS), July 4
Leonard, Benny: Birth Anniv, Apr 7
Leonard, Dennis: Birth, May 8
Leonard, Dutch: Birth Anniv, Apr 16

NAIA Chmpshp (Broken Arrow, OK), **May 18**
NCAA Div I World Series (Finals) (Oklahoma City, OK), **May 21**
NCAA Div II Tourn (Finals) (Pensacola, FL), **May 14**
NCAA Div III Tourn (Finals) (Salem, VA), **May 14**
Pony Girls Fast-Pitch Natl Chmpshps, **July 29**
Pony Girls Slow-Pitch Natl Chmpshps, **July 23**
SEC Tourn, **May 8**
Slow Pitch Softball Tourn (Williamsport, PA), **July 10**
Softball Congress World Fast-Pitch Tourn, Intl (Clearwater, FL), **Aug 14**
The King Strikes Out Six: Anniv, **Feb 18**
365-Inning Softball Game: Anniv, **Aug 14**
Softball Congress World Fast-Pitch Tourn, Intl (Clearwater, FL), Aug 14
Sojo, Luis Beltran: Birth, **Jan 3**
Solaita, Tony: Birth Anniv, **Jan 15**
Solomon, Freddie: Birth, **Jan 11**
Solstice, Summer, **June 21**
Solstice, Winter, **Dec 21**
Somers, Charles: Birth Anniv, **Oct 13**
Sons of Norway Barnebirkie (Hayward, WI), **Feb 19**
Sooner State Summer Games (Oklahoma City, OK), **June 5**
Sorenstam, Annika: Birth, **Oct 9**
Sorrento, Paul: Birth, **Nov 17**
Sosa, Sammy: Birth, **Nov 12**
Soto, Mario: Birth, **July 12**
Sourdough Rendezvous Bathtub Race (Whitehorse, YT, Canada), **Aug 14**
South Carolina
 Canadian-American Days Fest (Myrtle Beach), **Mar 14**
 Coon Hunt, AKC US Classic (Orangeburg), **Mar 13**
 Grand American Coon Hunt (Orangeburg), **Jan 2**
 Grand Strand Fishing Rodeo (Myrtle Beach), **Apr 1**
 Lobster Race and Oyster Parade (Aiken), **May 1**
 MCI Classic (Hilton Head Island), **Apr 16**
 Miniature Golf Chmpshp, Natl (Myrtle Beach), **Sept 24**
South Dakota
 All-Car Rally "Demolition Derby" (Belle Fourche), **June 14**
 Black Hills Bicycle Trek (Spearfish), **June 5**
 Black Hills Jeep Jamboree (Deadwood), **Sept 18**
 Black Hills Rouncup Rodeo (Belle Fourche), **July 2**
 Buffalo Round-Up Bicycle Rally (Custer), **Sept 26**
 Crystal Springs Ranch Rodeo (Clear Lake), **June 26**
 Custer State Park Seasonal Volksmarch (Custer), **May 16**
 D. C. Booth Day (Spearfish), **May 17**
 Days of '76 (Deadwood), **July 24**
 Family Fun Days (Grenville), **June 26**
 Fishing Has No Boundaries (Pierre), **June 13**
 Great Outdoor Show (Aberdeen), **Apr 3**
 Groton Triathlon (Groton), **June 20**
 Mount Rushmore Intl Marathon (Rapid City), **Oct 10**
 Old Settlers' Weekend (Highmore), **June 19**
 Philip Fest Days (Philip), **June 19**
 South Dakota Rodeo Association Chmpshp Rodeo Finals (Sioux Falls), **Oct 2**
 Sports Day (Geddes), **July 5**
 Sturgis Rally & Races (Sturgis), **Aug 3**
 Sturgis Regional High School Rodeo (Sturgis), **June 13**
 Tetonkaha Rendezvous (Bruce), **Aug 8**
 Wall Regional High School Rodeo (Wall), **June 7**
South Jersey Canoe/Kayak Classic (Lakewood, NJ), June 6
Southeast Florida Scottish Fest & Games (Hialeah, FL), Mar 7
Southwest Iowa Prof Hot-Air Balloon Races (Creston, IA), Sept 19
Southwest Senior Invitational Golf Chmpshp (Yuma, AZ), Jan 20
Southwestern Bell Cotton Bowl Classic (Dallas, TX), Jan 1

Southwestern Expo Livestock Show/Rodeo (Ft Worth, TX), **Jan 23**
Southworth, Billy: Birth Anniv, **Mar 9**
Spahn, Warren: Birth, **Apr 23**
Spalding, Albert: Birth Anniv, **Sept 2**
Spangler, Al: Birth, **July 8**
Sparrow, Rory: Birth, **June 12**
Spassky, Boris: Birth, **Jan 30**
Speaker, Tris: Birth Anniv, **Apr 4**
Special Recreation Day, **June 28**
Special Recreation Week, **June 28**
Speed Skating
 Blair Wins Gold Again: Anniv, **Feb 19**
 Heiden Wins Fifth Gold Medal: Anniv, **Feb 23**
 Jaffee, Irving: Birth Anniv, **Sept 15**
 Jansen Wins Gold: Anniv, **Feb 18**
Speedweeks (Daytona Beach, FL), **Jan 31**
Speier, Chris: Birth, **June 28**
Spencer, Felton LaFrance: Birth, **Jan 5**
Spencer-Devlin, Muffin: Birth, **Oct 25**
Spielman, Chris: Birth, **Oct 11**
Spink, Taylor: Birth Anniv, **Nov 6**
Spinks, Leon: Birth, **July 11**
Spinks, Michael: Birth, **July 13**
Spitz, Mark: Birth, **Feb 10**
Sport, Boat and RV Show, San Antonio (San Antonio, TX), **Jan 7**
Sporting Assn World Sports Expo, Natl (Chicago, IL), **July 18**
Sports Club Days©98, **July 16**
Sports Day (Geddes, SD), **July 5**
Sports Eye Safety Month, **Apr 1**
Sports, Physical Fitness and, Month, Natl, **May 1**
Sportsfest (Oklahoma City, OK), **Feb 6**
Sportsman River Road Powerboat Races (Saskatoon, Sask, Canada), **July 17**
Sprague, Ed: Birth, **July 25**
Sprewell, Latrell: Birth, **Sept 8**
Spring Begins, **Mar 20**
Spring, Halfway Point, **May 6**
Spring, Shawn: Birth, **Mar 11**
St. Louis Natl Charity Horse Show Creve Coeur, MO), **Sept 14**
St. Clair, Bob: Birth, **Feb 18**
St. Jean, Garry: Birth, **Feb 10**
St. John, Lynn: Birth Anniv, **Nov 18**
Sta-bil Natl Chmpshp Lawn Mower Race (Rockford, IL), **Aug 29**
Stackhouse, Jerry: Birth, **Nov 5**
Stadler, Craig: Birth, **June 2**
Stagg, Amos Alonzo: Birth Anniv, **Aug 16**
Stahl, Chick: Birth Anniv, **Jan 10**
Stallcup, Virgil: Birth Anniv, **Jan 3**
Stallone, Sylvester: Birth, **July 6**
Stankiewicz, Andy: Birth, **Aug 10**
Stanky, Eddie: Birth, **Sept 3**
Stanley, Mike: Birth, **June 25**
Stanton, Mike: Birth, **June 2**
Star City Grand Prix In-Line Skating Race (Roanoke, VA), **May 31**
Stargell, Willie: Birth, **Mar 6**
Stark, Dolly: Birth Anniv, **Nov 4**
Starks, John: Birth, **Aug 10**
Starr, Bryan Bartlett (Bart): Birth, **Jan 9**
Starter Hall of Fame Tip-Off Classic (Springfield, MA), **Nov 20**
State Games of Oregon (Portland, OR), **July 10**
Staub, Rusty: Birth, **Apr 1**
Staubach, Roger: Birth, **Feb 5**
Stautner, Ernie: Birth, **Apr 20**
Steamboat Marathon (Steamboat Springs, CO), **June 7**
Stearman Fly-In, Natl (Galesburg, IL), **Sept 2**
Steeplechase at Callaway Gardens (Pine Mountain, GA), **Nov 7**
Steer Roping, Natl Finals (Guthrie, OK), **Nov 27**
Steinbach, Terry: Birth, **Mar 2**
Steinbrenner, George: Birth, **July 4**
Stenerud, Jan: Birth, **Nov 26**
Stengel, Casey: Birth Anniv, **July 30**
Stengel, Casey: Yankees Fire Stengel: Anniv, **Nov 9**
Stennett, Rennie: Birth, **Apr 5**
Stephens, Helen: Birth Anniv, **Feb 3**
Stephens, Vern: Birth Anniv, **Oct 23**
Stephenson, Jan: Birth, **Dec 22**

Stern, Bill: Birth Anniv, **July 1**
Stevens, Scott: Birth, **Apr 1**
Stewart, Bill: Birth Anniv, **Sept 26**
Stewart, Dave: Birth, **Feb 19**
Stewart, Jackie: Birth, **June 11**
Stewart, Jimmy, Relay Marathon (Los Angeles, CA), **Apr 19**
Stewart, Kordell: Birth, **Oct 16**
Stewart, Payne: Birth, **Jan 30**
Stieb, Dave: Birth, **July 22**
Stinnett, Kelly: Birth, **Feb 14**
Stock Dog Chmpshp, US Open (Dawsonville, GA), **Oct 2**
Stock, Milt: Birth Anniv, **July 11**
Stocker, Kevin: Birth, **Feb 13**
Stockton, Dave: Birth, **Nov 2**
Stockton, John: Birth, **Mar 26**
Stoddard, Tim: Birth, **Jan 24**
Stokes, Maurice: Birth Anniv, **June 17**
Stone, Steve: Birth, **July 14**
Stottlemyre, Mel: Birth, **Nov 13**
Stottlemyre, Todd: Birth, **May 20**
Stoudamire, Damon: Birth, **Sept 3**
Stovey, George: Death Anniv, **Mar 22**
Straits Area Antique Auto Show (St. Ignace, MI), **June 25**
Strange, Curtis: Birth, **Jan 30**
Strange, Doug: Birth, **Apr 13**
Stratton, Monty: Birth Anniv, **May 21**
Strawberry 100 Bike Tour (Crawfordsville, IN), **June 14**
Strawberry Fest (Crawfordsville, IN), **June 12**
Strawberry Hill Races (Richmond, VA), **Apr 11**
Strawberry, Darryl: Birth, **Mar 12**
Strickland, Rod: Birth, **July 11**
Strictly Sail - Miami (Miami Beach, FL), **Feb 12**
Strictly Sail - New England (East Hartford, CT), **Mar 19**
Strictly Sail at Navy Pier (Chicago, IL), **Jan 29**
Strike Out Strokes Month, **May 1**
Strokes Month, Strike Out, **May 1**
Strong, Ken: Birth Anniv, **Aug 6**
Stuart, Dick: Birth, **Nov 7**
Stuhldreher, Harry: Birth Anniv, **Oct 14**
Stuper, John: Birth, **May 9**
Stupor Bowl Sunday, **Jan 25**
Sturdivant, Tom: Birth, **Apr 28**
Sturgis Rally & Races (Sturgis, SD), **Aug 3**
Sturgis Regional High School Rodeo (Sturgis, SD), **June 13**
Sugar Bowl (New Orleans, LA), **Jan 1**
Sugar Bowl: Anniv, **Jan 1**
Sugar Creek Canoe Race and Tri Sport Fest (Crawfordsville, IN), **Apr 25**
Suggs, Louise: Birth, **Sept 7**
Suhey, Matt: Birth, **July 7**
Sullivan, James: Birth Anniv, **Nov 18**
Sullivan, John L.: Birth Anniv, **Oct 15**
Summa, Homer: Birth Anniv, **Nov 3**
Summer Arrival: Martin Z. Mollusk Day (Ocean City, NJ), **May 7**
Summer Begins, **June 21**
Summer, Halfway Point, **Aug 7**
Summers, Bill: Birth Anniv, **Nov 10**
Summitt, Pat Head: Birth, **June 14**
Sunday, Billy: Birth Anniv, **Nov 19**
Sundin, Mats: Birth, **Feb 13**
Super Bowl
 Cowboys Advance to Fifth: Anniv, **Jan 7**
 XI (1977): Raiders Win Their First Super Bowl: Anniv, **Jan 9**
 IV (1970): Kansas City Wins Super Bowl IV: Anniv, **Jan 11**
 KGBX Food Fight (Springfield, MO), **Jan 23**
 IX (1975): Pittsburgh Wins Super Bowl IX: Anniv, **Jan 12**
 I (1967): Anniv, **Jan 15**
 Popcorn Day, Natl, **Jan 25**
 VII (1973): Miami Completes Undefeated Season: Anniv, **Jan 11**
 XVII (1983): Redskins Win Super Bowl XVII: Anniv, **Jan 30**
 VI (1972): Dallas Wins Super Bowl VI: Anniv, **Jan 16**
 XVI (1982): 49ers Win Super Bowl XVI: Anniv, **Jan 24**
 Stupor Bowl Sunday, **Jan 25**

Wake Up to Missouri US Natl Hot Air Balloon Chmpshp (Columbia, MO), **Aug 7**
Wakefield, Tim: Birth, Aug 2
Walcott, Jersey Joe: Birth Anniv, Jan 31
Walewander, Jim: Birth, May 2
Walker Lake Fish Derby (Walker Lake, NV), **Feb 14**
Walker, Antoine: Birth, Aug 12
Walker, Darrell: Birth, Mar 9
Walker, Ewell Doak, Jr: Birth, Jan 1
Walker, Fleet: Birth Anniv, Oct 7
Walker, Greg: Birth, Oct 6
Walker, Harry: Birth, Oct 22
Walker, Herschel: Birth, Mar 3
Walker, Larry: Birth, Dec 1
Walker, Rube: Birth Anniv, May 16
Walker, Samaki: Birth, Feb 25
Walker, Wesley: Birth, May 26
Walking
  Chaptico Classic (Chaptico, MD), **Aug 29**
  Custer State Park Seasonal Volksmarch (Custer, SD), **May 16**
  Mackinac Bridge Walk (St. Ignace to Mackinaw City, MI), **Sept 7**
  Mighty Mo 5K Run/Walk (South Sioux City, NE), **June 19**
  300 Oaks Race (Greenwood, MS), **Sept 19**
  WalkAmerica, March of Dimes, **Apr 25**
  Walking Weekend (Quinebaug-Shetucket Natl Heritage Corridor of CT), **Oct 10**
  Walktoberfest (Amer Diabetes Assn), **Oct 3**
Wall Regional High School Rodeo (Wall, SD), **June 7**
Wallace, John: Birth, Feb 9
Wallace, Rasheed: Birth, Sept 17
Wallace, Rusty: Birth, Aug 14
Walling, Denny: Birth, Apr 17
Walls, Lee: Birth Anniv, Jan 6
Walsh Invitational Rifle Tourn (Cincinnati, OH), **Nov 6**
Walsh, Bill: Birth, Nov 30
Walsh, Ed: Birth Anniv, May 14
Walsh, Steve: Birth, Dec 1
Walters, Bucky: Birth Anniv, Apr 19
Walters, Rex: Birth, Mar 12
Walton, Bill: Birth, Nov 5
Walton, Izaak: Birth Anniv, Aug 9
Waltrip, Darrell: Birth, Feb 5
Waner, Lloyd: Birth Anniv, Mar 16
Waner, Paul: Birth Anniv, Apr 16
Wannstedt, Dave: Birth, May 21
Ward, Arch: Birth Anniv, Dec 27
Ward, Monte: Birth Anniv, Mar 3
Warfield, Paul: Birth, Nov 28
Wargo, Tom: Birth, Sept 16
Warner, Pop: Birth Anniv, Apr 5
Warren, Michael: Birth, Mar 5
Washburn, Ray: Birth, May 31
Washington
  Corvette and High Performance Summer Meet (Puyallup), **June 27**
  Everett Salty Sea Days (Everett), **June 4**
  Fishing Has No Boundaries (Yakima), **May 15**
  NAIA Swimming and Diving Chmpshps (Federal Way), **Mar 4**
  PGA Golf Chmpshp (Redmond), **Aug 13**
  Play Tacoma Days (Tacoma), **July 1**
  Seattle Boat Show (Seattle), **Jan 16**
Washington, District of Columbia
  Bastille Day Moonlight Golf Tourn, **July 14**
  Frisbee Disc Fest, Natl (Washington), **Sept 6**
  NCAA Men's Div I Bask Tourn (1st/2nd rounds) (Washington), **Mar 12**
  Smithsonian Kite Festival (Washington), **Mar 28**
  White House Easter Egg Roll, **Apr 13**
Washington, Gene Alden: Birth, Jan 14
Washington, Kenny: Birth Anniv, Aug 31
Water Ski Days (Lake City, MN), June 26
Waterfield, Bob: Birth Anniv, July 26
Waterfowl Festival (Easton, MD), Nov 13
Watermelon Seed-Spitting and Speed-Eating Chmpshp (Pardeeville, WI), **Sept 12**
Watson, Allen: Birth, Nov 18
Watson, Bob: Birth, Apr 10
Watson, Tom: Birth, Sept 4
Watters, Ricky: Birth, Apr 7
Weatherspoon, Clarence: Birth, Sept 8

Weaver, Buck: Birth Anniv, Aug 18
Weaver, Monte: Birth Anniv, June 15
Webb, Karrie: Birth, Dec 21
Webb, Spud: Birth, July 13
Webber, Chris: Birth, Mar 1
Webster County Woodchopping Fest (Webster Springs, WV), **May 16**
Weiskopf, Tom: Birth, Nov 9
Weiss, Walt: Birth, Nov 28
Welch, Bob: Birth, Nov 3
Wells, David: Birth, May 20
Wells, Willie: Birth Anniv, Oct 10
Wendt, George: Birth, Oct 17
Werblin, Sonny: Birth Anniv, Mar 17
Werner, Buddy: Birth Anniv, Feb 26
Wertz, Vic: Birth Anniv, Feb 9
West Virginia
  Charleston Distance Run (Charleston), **Sept 5**
  Head-of-the-Mon-River Horseshoe Tourn (Fairmont), **May 23**
  Turkey Trot (Parkersburg), **Nov 26**
  Webster County Woodchopping Fest (Webster Springs), **May 16**
West, David Lee: Birth, Sept 1
West, Doug: Birth, May 27
West, Jerry: Birth, May 28
West, Sammy: Birth Anniv, Oct 5
Westbrook, Bryant: Birth, Dec 19
Western Stock Show and Rodeo, Natl (Denver, CO), **Jan 10**
Westphal, Paul: Birth, Nov 30
Weteland, John: Birth, Aug 31
Wheat, Zack: Birth Anniv, May 23
Wheatley, Tyrone: Birth, Jan 19
Wheel to Weston (Kansas City and Weston, MO), **June 21**
Whiskey Flat Days (Kernville, CA), Feb 13
Whitaker, Lou: Birth, May 12
Whitaker, Pernell: Birth, Jan 2
White House Easter Egg Roll (Washington, DC), **Apr 13**
White, Bill: Birth, Jan 28
White, Deacon: Birth Anniv, Dec 2
White, Devon: Birth, Dec 29
White, Frank: Birth, Sept 4
White, Jo Jo: Birth, Nov 16
White, Michael (Mike): Birth, Jan 4
White, Randy Lee: Birth, Jan 15
White, Reggie: Birth, Dec 19
White, Rondell: Birth, Feb 23
White, Roy: Birth, Dec 27
White, Sol: Birth Anniv, June 12
White, Whizzer: Birth, June 8
Whitehurst, Wally: Birth, Apr 11
Whiten, Mark: Birth, Nov 25
Whitman, Walt: Birth Anniv, May 31
Whitney, Pinky: Birth Anniv, Jan 2
Whitworth, Kathy: Birth, Sept 27
Whoopers and Hoopers Invitational Bask Tourn (Hastings, NE), **Mar 20**
Whooping Crane Run (Rockport, TX), Apr 11
WICC Greatest Bluefish Tourn (Long Island Sound, CT and NY), **Aug 29**
Widow: Natl Football Widows Month, Nov 1
Wiggins, Alan: Birth Anniv, Feb 17
Wightman, Hazel: Birth Anniv, Dec 20
Wilcox, Milt: Birth, Apr 20
Wildfowl Art & Decoy Show, Toms River (Toms River, NJ), **Feb 7**
Wilhelm, Hoyt: Birth, July 26
Wilkens, Lenny: Birth, Oct 28
Wilkerson, Curtis: Birth, Apr 26
Wilkes, Jamaal: Birth, May 2
Wilkins, Jacques Dominique: Birth, Jan 12
Wilkinson, Bud: Birth Anniv, Apr 23
Wilkinson, J. L.: Death Anniv, Apr 21
Will, George F.: Birth, May 4
Willard, Jess: Birth Anniv, Dec 29
Williams, Aeneas: Birth, Jan 29
Williams, Al: Birth, May 6
Williams, Archie: Birth Anniv, May 1
Williams, Bernie: Birth, Sept 13
Williams, Billy Dee: Birth, Apr 6
Williams, Billy: Birth, June 15
Williams, Buck: Birth, Mar 8
Williams, Dick: Birth, May 7
Williams, Earl: Birth, July 14

Williams, Erik: Birth, Sept 7
Williams, Esther: Birth, Aug 8
Williams, Jayson: Birth, Feb 22
Williams, Jimy: Birth, Oct 4
Williams, John ("Hot Rod"): Birth, Aug 9
Williams, Ken: Birth Anniv, June 28
Williams, Lefty: Birth Anniv, Mar 9
Williams, Matt: Birth, Nov 28
Williams, Mitch: Birth, Nov 17
Williams, Reggie: Birth, May 5
Williams, Scott: Birth, Mar 21
Williams, Stan: Birth, Sept 14
Williams, Ted: Birth, Aug 30
Williams, Woody: Birth Anniv, Aug 21
Williamson, Corliss: Birth, Dec 4
Williamson, Fred: Birth, Mar 5
Williamson, Ned: Birth Anniv, Oct 24
Willis, Kevin: Birth, Sept 6
Wills, Bump: Birth, July 27
Wills, Maury: Birth, Oct 2
Wilson, Dan: Birth, Mar 25
Wilson, Don: Birth Anniv, Feb 12
Wilson, Glenn: Birth, Dec 22
Wilson, Hack: Birth Anniv, Apr 26
Wilson, Larry: Birth, Mar 24
Wilson, Mookie: Birth, Feb 9
Wilson, Paul: Birth, Mar 28
Wilson, Reinard: Birth, Dec 12
Wilson, Ron: Birth, May 28
Wilson, Willie James: Birth, July 9
Wiltse, Hooks: Birth Anniv, Sept 7
Wimbledon (London, England), June 22
Wine, Bobby: Birth, Sept 17
Winfield, Dave: Birth, Oct 3
Winkerbean, Funky: Anniv, Mar 27
Winslow, Kellen: Birth, Nov 5
Winter Begins, Dec 21
Winter Equestrian Fest (Tampa, FL), Mar 11
Winter Equestrian Fest (Wellington & Tampa, FL), **Jan 21**
Winter Festivals and Celebrations
  Aspen/Snowmass Winterskol (Snowmass Village, CO), **Jan 14**
  Badger State Winter Games (Wausau, WI), **Feb 6**
  Calgary Winter Fest (Calgary, AB, Canada), **Jan 24**
  Dog Sled Chmpshp/Winter Carnival (Wisconsin Dells, WI), **Feb 6**
  Icescape (Appleton, WI), **Feb 13**
  McCall Winter Carnival (McCall, ID), **Jan 30**
  Ohio Winter Ski Carnival (Mansfield, OH), **Feb 21**
  Snowfest (Tahoe City, CA), **Feb 27**
  Tip-Up Town USA (Houghton Lake, MI), **Jan 17**
  Winter Carnival Bon Soo (Sault Ste Marie, Ont, Canada), **Jan 30**
  Winter Fest (Lake City, MN), **Jan 24**
  Winter Games (Glenford, CH), **Feb 21**
  Winter Games of Oregon (various), **Mar 7**
  Winter Triathlon (Muskegon, MI), **Jan 25**
  Winterfest (Chesterland, OH), **Jan 10**
  Winterlude (Ottawa, Ont, Canada), **Feb 6**
  Wisconsin Dells Flake Out Fest (Wisconsin Dells, WI), **Jan 16**
Winter, Halfway Point, Feb 4
Winters, Brian: Birth, Mar 1
Winterthur Point-to-Point (Winterthur, DE), **May 3**
Wirtz, Arthur: Birth Anniv, Jan 22
Wisconsin
  Aerobatic Chmpshps, Intl (Fond du Lac), **Aug 7**
  All-Canada Show (Green Bay), **Feb 19**
  All-Canada Show (Madison), **Jan 26**
  All-Canada Show (Milwaukee), **Jan 22**
  American Lumberjack Chmpshps at Log Boom (LaCrosse), **July 31**
  Automotion (Wisconsin Dells), **May 16**
  Badger State Summer Games, **June 12**
  Badger State Winter Games (Wausau), **Feb 6**
  Briggs & Stratton/Al's Run & Walk (Milwaukee), **Sept 26**
  Chmpshp Snowmobile Derby (Eagle River), **Jan 15**
  Dog Sled Chmpshp/Winter Carnival (Wisconsin Dells), **Feb 6**

☆ NOTES ☆

JANUARY	JULY
FEBRUARY	**AUGUST**
MARCH	**SEPTEMBER**
APRIL	**OCTOBER**
MAY	**NOVEMBER**
JUNE	**DECEMBER**

☆ NOTES ☆

JANUARY	JULY
FEBRUARY	AUGUST
MARCH	SEPTEMBER
APRIL	OCTOBER
MAY	NOVEMBER
JUNE	DECEMBER

Yes! Please send me additional copies of *Chase's 1998 Calendar of Events* and *1998 Chase's Sports Calendar of Events*.

Ship to _____

Address _____

_____

City, State, Zip _____

Phone (_____) _____

Please send me _____ copies of the 1998 edition of
CHASE'S CALENDAR OF EVENTS at $59.95 each $_____

and _____ copies of the 1998 edition of

CHASE'S SPORTS CALENDAR OF EVENTS at $29.95 each $_____

Add applicable sales tax in AL, CA, FL, IL, NC, NJ, NY, OH, PA, TX, WA $_____

Shipping & Handling: Add $5.00 for the first copy,
$3.50 for each additional copy $_____

Total $_____

☐ Check or money order enclosed payable to: NTC/Contemporary Publishing Co.

Charge my   ☐ Visa   ☐ MasterCard   ☐ American Express   ☐ Discover Card

Acct. # _____   Exp. Date _____/_____

X _____
Signature (if charging to bankcard)

Name (please print) _____

STANDING ORDER AUTHORIZATION

To make sure that I receive each year's new edition, please accept this Standing Order Authorization to ship me _____ copies of *Chase's Calendar of Events* and _____ copies of *Chase's Sports Calendar of Events*, beginning with the 1999 edition. Bill me at the address shown at the top of this order form. I understand that I may cancel my Standing Order at any time.

X _____
Signature   Date

(_____) _____
Name (please print)   Phone

GUARANTEE: Any book you order is unconditionally guaranteed and may be returned within 10 days of receipt for full refund.

Mail to: **NTC/Contemporary Publishing Company, Dept. C**
4255 W Touhy Ave
Lincolnwood, IL 60646-1975

There is no charge for being listed in **Chase's Sports Calendar of Events**. Use the form below to submit new entries for forthcoming editions. Background information about your entry is also appreciated. Please be sure your dates are confirmed for 1999, or clearly indicate if dates are tentative. Use a separate sheet for each entry submitted. Information selected by the editors may be used and publicized through their books, electronic formats, syndicated services and/or other related products and services. The editors reserve the right to select and edit information received. Mail all information to: Sports Calendar Editor, *Chase's Sports Calendar of Events*, NTC/Contemporary Publishing Co, 4255 W Touhy Ave, Lincolnwood, IL 60646-1975.

☞DEADLINE FOR 1999 EDITION: MAY 25, 1998.   PLEASE TYPE OR PRINT VERY CLEARLY.

1. Exact name of entry:
2. Exact INCLUSIVE DATES for 1999:
3. If applicable, estimated attendance (one figure—grand total all days):
4. Location (site [not address], city and state):
5. Brief description:

6. Formula—ONLY if used to set date(s) each year (Example: Annually, the third Monday in May):

7. For public use, complete contact info to be printed in book—name, address, phone, fax, e-mail, web.

8. For Chase's staff use, complete address info we can use to mail our update form to you next year—name, title or department, organization name, address:

9. For Chase's staff use, name, dept and phone and fax numbers of person we can call with questions about your entry:

10. Person furnishing information: (print) _____ (sign) _____
11. PLEASE CIRCLE THE EXACT INCLUSIVE DATES FOR YOUR 1999 EVENT ON THE CALENDAR BELOW.

1999
Key dates

M. L. King Birthday Jan 18	Passover Apr 1–8	Summer June 21	Columbus Day Oct 11
Chinese New Year Feb 16	Easter Apr 4 (Apr 11EO)	Labor Day Sept 6	Thanksgiving Nov 25
Presidents' Day Feb 15	Mother's Day May 9	Rosh Hashanah Sept 11–12	Chanukah Dec 4–11
Lent begins Feb 17 (Feb 22EO)	Memorial Day May 31	Autumn Sept 23	Ramadan Dec 9
Spring Mar 20	Father's Day June 20	Yom Kippur Sept 20	Winter Dec 22

1999

JAN
S	M	T	W	T	F	S
					1	2
3	4	5	6	7	8	9
10	11	12	13	14	15	16
17	18	19	20	21	22	23
24	25	26	27	28	29	30
31						

APR
S	M	T	W	T	F	S
				1	2	3
4	5	6	7	8	9	10
11	12	13	14	15	16	17
18	19	20	21	22	23	24
25	26	27	28	29	30	

JULY
S	M	T	W	T	F	S
				1	2	3
4	5	6	7	8	9	10
11	12	13	14	15	16	17
18	19	20	21	22	23	24
25	26	27	28	29	30	31

OCT
S	M	T	W	T	F	S
					1	2
3	4	5	6	7	8	9
10	11	12	13	14	15	16
17	18	19	20	21	22	23
24	25	26	27	28	29	30
31						

FEB
S	M	T	W	T	F	S
	1	2	3	4	5	6
7	8	9	10	11	12	13
14	15	16	17	18	19	20
21	22	23	24	25	26	27
28						

MAY
S	M	T	W	T	F	S
						1
2	3	4	5	6	7	8
9	10	11	12	13	14	15
16	17	18	19	20	21	22
23	24	25	26	27	28	29
30	31					

AUG
S	M	T	W	T	F	S
1	2	3	4	5	6	7
8	9	10	11	12	13	14
15	16	17	18	19	20	21
22	23	24	25	26	27	28
29	30	31				

NOV
S	M	T	W	T	F	S
	1	2	3	4	5	6
7	8	9	10	11	12	13
14	15	16	17	18	19	20
21	22	23	24	25	26	27
28	29	30				

MAR
S	M	T	W	T	F	S
	1	2	3	4	5	6
7	8	9	10	11	12	13
14	15	16	17	18	19	20
21	22	23	24	25	26	27
28	29	30	31			

JUNE
S	M	T	W	T	F	S
		1	2	3	4	5
6	7	8	9	10	11	12
13	14	15	16	17	18	19
20	21	22	23	24	25	26
27	28	29	30			

SEPT
S	M	T	W	T	F	S
			1	2	3	4
5	6	7	8	9	10	11
12	13	14	15	16	17	18
19	20	21	22	23	24	25
26	27	28	29	30		

DEC
S	M	T	W	T	F	S
			1	2	3	4
5	6	7	8	9	10	11
12	13	14	15	16	17	18
19	20	21	22	23	24	25
26	27	28	29	30	31	

Note: This page may be photocopied to submit additional event entries to **Chase's 1999 Sports Calendar of Events**.

4255 W Touhy Ave, Lincolnwood, IL 60646-1975 • Phone (847) 679-5500 • Fax (847) 679-6388